ENCYCLOPEDIA OF WORLD BIOGRAPHY

6

ENCYCLOPEDIA OF WORLD BIOGRAPHY

SECOND EDITION

$$\frac{\text{Ford}}{\text{Grilliparzer}} \quad \textbf{6}$$

GALE

DETROIT · NEW YORK · TORONTO · LONDON

Staff

Senior Editor: Paula K. Byers
Project Editor: Suzanne M. Bourgoin
Managing Editor: Neil E. Walker

Editorial Staff: Luann Brennan, Frank V. Castronova, Laura S. Hightower, Karen E. Lemerand, Stacy A. McConnell, Jennifer Mossman, Maria L. Munoz, Katherine H. Nemeh, Terrie M. Rooney, Geri Speace

Permissions Manager: Susan M. Tosky
Permissions Specialist: Maria L. Franklin
Permissions Associate: Michele M. Lonoconus
Image Cataloger: Mary K. Grimes

Production Director: Mary Beth Trimper
Production Manager: Evi Seoud
Production Associate: Shanna Heilveil
Product Design Manager: Cynthia Baldwin
Senior Art Director: Mary Claire Krzewinski

Research Manager: Victoria B. Cariappa
Research Specialists: Michele P. LaMeau, Andrew Guy Malonis, Barbara McNeil, Gary J. Oudersluys
Research Associates: Julia C. Daniel, Tamara C. Nott, Norma Sawaya, Cheryl L. Warnock
Research Assistant: Talitha A. Jean

Graphic Services Supervisor: Barbara Yarrow
Image Database Supervisor: Randy Bassett
Imaging Specialist: Mike Lugosz

Manager of Data Entry Services: Eleanor M. Allison
Data Entry Coordinator: Kenneth D. Benson

Manager of Technology Support Services: Theresa A. Rocklin
Programmers/Analysts: Mira Bossowska, Jeffrey Muhr, Christopher Ward

Copyright © 1998
Gale Research
835 Penobscot Bldg.
Detroit, MI 48226-4094

ISBN 0-7876-2221-4 (Set)
ISBN 0-7876-2546-9 (Volume 6)

Library of Congress Cataloging-in-Publication Data

Encyclopedia of world biography / [edited by Suzanne Michele Bourgoin and Paula Kay Byers].
    p. cm.
    Includes bibliographical references and index.
    Summary: Presents brief biographical sketches which provide vital statistics as well as information on the importance of the person listed.
    ISBN 0-7876-2221-4 (set : alk. paper)
    1. Biography—Dictionaries—Juvenile literature. [1. Biography.]
I. Bourgoin, Suzanne Michele, 1968- . II. Byers, Paula K. (Paula Kay), 1954- .
CT 103.E56 1997
920′ .003—dc21   97-42327
                      CIP
                      AC

Printed in the United States of America
10 9 8 7 6 5 4 3

ENCYCLOPEDIA OF WORLD BIOGRAPHY

6

F

Ford Madox Ford

The English author Ford Madox Ford (1873-1939) is best known for his novels *The Good Soldier* and *Parade's End*. An outstanding editor, he published works by many significant writers of his era.

Ford Madox Ford was born Ford Madox Hueffer in Merton, England, on Dec. 17, 1873, the son of Dr. Francis Hueffer, a German, who was once music editor of the *Times*. His maternal grandfather, Ford Madox Brown, the painter, had been one of the founders of the Pre-Raphaelite movement, and an aunt was the wife of William Rossetti. In 1919 he changed his name from Hueffer to Ford, for reasons that were probably connected with his complicated marital affairs. He was educated in England, Germany, and especially France, and it is said that he first thought out his novels in French.

By the age of 22 Ford had written four books, including a fairy tale, *The Brown Owl*, written when he was 17 and published when he was 19. In 1898 Joseph Conrad, on the recommendation of William Ernest Henley, suggested that Ford become his collaborator, and the result was collaboration on *The Inheritors* (1901), *Romance* (1903), parts of *Nostromo*, and *The Nature of a Crime*. Ford's *Joseph Conrad* (1924) discusses the techniques they used.

In 1908 Ford began the periodical *English Review* in order to publish Thomas Hardy's ''The Sunday Morning Tragedy,'' which had been rejected everywhere else. Other contributors included Conrad, William James, W. H. Hudson, John Galsworthy, T. S. Eliot, Robert Frost, Norman Douglas, Wyndham Lewis, H. G. Wells, D. H. Lawrence, and Anatole France. After World War I Ford founded the *Transatlantic Review*, which numbered among its contributors James Joyce and Ernest Hemingway.

In 1914 Ford published what he intended to be his last novel, *The Good Soldier*. Out of his experiences in wartime England and service in a Welsh regiment, he then wrote the series of novels that is chiefly responsible for his high reputation: *Some Do Not, No More Parades,* and *A Man Could Stand Up,* published in 1924-1926, and the final volume, *The Last Post,* published in 1928. The view of war in these has been described as detached and disenchanted, and the novels are innovative as well as traditional. His novels were not widely read, but a revival of interest in his work began with *New Directions 1942,* a symposium by distinguished writers, dedicated to his memory. His war tetralogy was republished in 1950-1951 as *Parade's End,* along with *The Good Soldier*.

In his later years Ford preferred life in Provence and the United States, spending his last years as a teacher at Olivet College in Michigan with the professed aim of restoring the lost art of reading. Ford wrote more than 60 books. Among these works were volumes of poetry, critical studies (*The English Novel: From the Earliest Days to the Death of Joseph Conrad,* 1929; *Return to Yesterday,* 1932), and memoirs (*It Was the Nightingale,* 1933; *Mightier Than the Sword,* 1938). Ford Madox Ford died at Beauville, France, on July 26, 1939.

Further Reading

An excellent critical study of Ford's career is R. W. Lid, *Ford Madox Ford: The Essence of His Art* (1964). Arthur Mizener, *The Saddest Story: A Biography of FordMadox Ford* (1971), is a thorough study. See also Douglas Goldring, *The Last Pre-Raphaelite: A Record of the Life and Writings of Ford Madox Ford* (1948; published as *Trained for Genius,* 1949); John A. Meixner, *Ford Madox Ford's Novels: A Critical Study* (1962);

Paul L. Wiley, *Novelist of Three Worlds: Ford Madox Ford* (1962); and H. Robert Huntley, *The Alien Protagonist of Ford Madox Ford* (1970). For discussions of particular novels see Robie Macaulay's introduction to *Parade's End* (1950) and Mark Schorer's introduction to *The Good Soldier* (1951).

Additional Sources

Ford, Ford Madox, *It was the nightingale,* New York: Octagon Books, 1975, 1933.
Judd, Alan, *Ford Madox Ford,* Cambridge, Mass.: Harvard University Press, 1991.
Saunders, Max, *Ford Maddox Ford: a dual life,* New York: Oxford University Press, 1996. □

Gerald Ford

Gerald Ford (born 1913) served as Republican leader in the House of Representatives before being selected by President Nixon to replace Spiro Agnew as vice president in 1973. A year later he replaced Nixon himself, who resigned due to the Watergate crisis. In the 1976 presidential election Ford lost to Jimmy Carter.

Gerald Ford was born Leslie Lynch King, Jr., in Omaha, Nebraska, on July 14, 1913. Shortly afterward, his mother divorced and moved to Grand Rapids, Michigan. After she remarried, he was adopted by and legally renamed for his stepfather, becoming Gerald Rudolph Ford, Jr.

Ford's personality and career were clearly shaped by his family and community. Though not wealthy, the family was by Ford's later account "secure, orderly, and happy." His early years were rather ideal: handsome and popular, Gerald worked hard and graduated in the top five percent of his high school class. He also excelled in football, winning a full athletic scholarship to the University of Michigan, where he played center and, in his final year, was selected to participate in the Shrine College All-Star game. His football experiences, Ford later contended, helped instill in him a sense of fair play and obedience to rules.

Ford had a good formal education. After graduation from the University of Michigan, where he developed a strong interest in economics, he was admitted to Yale Law School. Here he graduated in the top quarter percent of the class (1941), which included such future luminaries as Potter Stewart and Cyrus Vance. Immediately after graduation, Ford joined with his college friend Philip Buchen in a law partnership in Grand Rapids; in early 1942 he enlisted in the Navy, serving throughout World War II and receiving his discharge as a lieutenant commander in February 1946.

Early Political Career

Ford was now ideally positioned to begin the political career which had always interested him. His stepfather was the Republican county chairman in 1944, which was certainly an advantage for Ford. A staunch admirer of Grand Rapids' conservative-but-internationalist senator Arthur Vandenberg, young Ford re-established himself in law practice and took on the Fifth District's isolationist congressman, Bartel Jonkman, in the 1948 primary for a seat in the House of Representatives. He won with 62 percent of the primary vote and repeated that generous margin of victory against his Democratic foe in the general election.

From the outset of his House career Gerald Ford displayed the qualities—and enjoyed the kind of help from others—which led to his rise to power in the lower house. His loyal adherence to the party line and cultivation of good will in his personal relations was soon rewarded with a seat on the prestigious Appropriations Committee. When Dwight Eisenhower gained the White House in 1952, Ford again found himself in an advantageous position since he had been one of 18 Republican congressmen who had initially written Eisenhower to urge him to seek the nomination.

Rise to House Leadership

During the 1950s Ford epitomized the so-called "Eisenhower wing" of the GOP ("Grand Old Party") in both his active support for internationalism in foreign policy (coupled with a nationalistic and patriotic tone) and his basic conservatism on domestic issues. He also developed close associations with other young GOP congressmen such as Robert Griffin of Michigan and Melvin Laird of Wisconsin who were rising to positions of influence in the House. Meanwhile, he continued to build his reputation as a solid party man with expertise on defense matters.

In 1963 he reaped the first tangible rewards of his party regularity, hard work, and good fellowship as he was elevated to the chairmanship of the House Republican Conference. Two years later, at the outset of the 89th Congress, a revolt led by his young, image-conscious party colleagues (prominent among them Griffin, Laird, Charles Goodell of New York, and Donald Rumsfeld of Illinois) propelled Ford into the post of minority leader.

Minority Leader

In a sense, Ford was fortunate to be in the minority party throughout his tenure as floor leader, for those years (1965-1973)—dominated by the Vietnam War and Watergate—presented nearly insurmountable obstacles to constructive policymaking. He tried to maintain a "positive" image for the GOP, initially supporting President Johnson's policies in Vietnam while attempting to pose responsible alternatives to Great Society measures. Gradually he broke from Johnson's Vietnam policy, calling for more aggressive pursuit of victory there.

During the Nixon years, Ford gained increasing visibility as symbol and spokesman for GOP policies. His party loyalty as minority leader made him a valuable asset to the Nixon administration. He was instrumental in securing passage of revenue-sharing, helped push the ill-fated Family Assistance (welfare reform) Plan, and took a pragmatic, essentially unsympathetic stance on civil rights issues—especially school bussing. He made perhaps his greatest public impact in these years when in 1970—seemingly in retaliation for the Senate's rejection of two conservative Southerners nominated by Nixon for seats on the Supreme Court—he called for the impeachment of the liberal Justice William O. Douglas, claiming Douglas was guilty of corruption and inappropriate behavior. The impeachment effort was unsuccessful, and when the ailing Douglas eventually retired from the Court in 1975 Ford issued a laudatory public statement.

Ford also enhanced his reputation as a "hawk" on defense matters during these years. He was one of the few members of Congress who was kept informed by Nixon of the bombings of Cambodia before the controversial invasion of that country in the spring of 1970. Even after the Watergate scandal broke in 1973, Ford remained doggedly loyal long after many of his party colleagues had begun to distance themselves from President Nixon.

Ford retained his personal popularity with all elements of the GOP even while involving himself deeply in these controversial areas. His reputation for non-ideological practicality ("a Congressman's Congressman," he was sometimes labeled), coupled with personal qualities of openness, geniality, and candor, made him the most popular (and uncontroversial) of all possible choices for nomination by Nixon to the vice presidency in late 1973, under the terms of the 25th Amendment, to succeed the disgraced Spiro T. Agnew.

Loyal Vice President

The appropriate congressional committees conducted thorough hearings on even the well-liked Ford, but discovered no evidence linking him to Watergate. He was confirmed by votes of 92 to three in the Senate and 387 to 35 in the House, becoming the nation's first unelected vice president on December 6, 1973. At his swearing-in, Ford charmed a public sorely in need of discovering a lovable politician, stating with humility, "I am a Ford, not a Lincoln." He promised "to uphold the Constitution, to do what is right . . . , and . . . to do the very best that I can do for America."

Nixon and Ford were never personally close, but the latter proved to be a perfect choice for the job. His characteristic loyalty determined his course: during the eight-plus months he served as vice president, Ford made approximately 500 public appearances in 40 states, traveling over 100,000 miles to defend the president. He was faithful to Nixon to the end; even in early August of 1974, after the House Judiciary Committee had voted a first article of impeachment against the president, Ford continued to defend Nixon and condemned the committee action as "partisan."

Always a realist, however, Ford allowed aides to lay the groundwork for his possible transition to the White House. When Nixon resigned on August 9, 1974, the unelected vice president was prepared to become the nation's first unelected president.

The White House Years

Once in the White House, Ford displayed a more consistently conservative ideology than ever before. While holding generally to the policies of the Nixon administration, he proved more unshakably committed than his predecessor to both a conservative, free market economic approach and strongly nationalistic defense and foreign policies. In attempting to translate his objectives into policy, however, President Ford was frequently blocked by a Democratic Congress intent on flexing its muscles in the wake of Watergate and Nixon's fall. The result was a running battle of vetoes and attempted overrides throughout the brief Ford presidency.

Ford made two quick tactical errors, whatever the merits of the two decisions. On September 8, 1974 he granted a full pardon to Richard Nixon, in advance, for any crimes he may have committed while in office, and a week later he announced a limited amnesty program for Vietnam-era deserters and draft evaders which angered the nationalistic right even while, in stark contrast to the pardon of Nixon, it seemed to many others not to go far enough in attempting to heal the wounds of the Vietnam War.

Gerald Ford governed the nation in a difficult period. Though president for only 895 days (the fifth shortest tenure in American history), he faced tremendous problems. After the furor surrounding the pardon subsided, the most important issues faced by Ford were inflation and unemployment, the continuing energy crisis, and the repercussions—both actual and psychological—from the final "loss" of South Vietnam in April 1975. Ford consistently championed legislative proposals to effect economic recovery by reducing taxes, spending, and the federal role in the national economy, but he got little from Congress except a temporary tax reduction. Federal spending continued to rise despite his call for a lowered spending ceiling. By late 1976 inflation, at least, had been checked somewhat; on the other hand, unemployment remained a major problem, and the 1976 election occurred in the midst of a recession. In energy matters, congressional Democrats consistently opposed Ford's proposals to tax imported oil and to deregulate domestic oil and natural gas. Eventually Congress approved only a very gradual decontrol measure.

Ford believed he was particularly hampered by Congress in foreign affairs. Having passed the War Powers Resolution in late 1973, the legislative branch first investigated, and then tried to impose restrictions on, the actions of the Central Intelligence Agency (CIA). In the area of war powers, Ford clearly bested his congressional adversaries. In the *Mayaquez* incident of May 1975 (involving the seizure of a U.S.-registered ship of that name by Cambodia), Ford retaliated with aerial attacks and a 175-marine assault without engaging the formal mechanisms required by the 1973 resolution. Although the actual success of this commando operation was debatable (39 crew members and the ship rescued, at a total cost of 41 other American lives), American honor had been vindicated and Ford's approval ratings rose sharply. Having succeeded in defying its provisions, Ford continued to speak out against the War Powers Resolution as unconstitutional even after he left the White House.

Ford basically continued Nixon's foreign policies, and Secretary of State Henry Kissinger was a dominant force in his administration as he had been under Nixon. Under increasing pressure from the nationalist right, Ford stopped using the word "detente," but he continued Nixon's efforts to negotiate a second SALT (Strategic Arms Limitation Treaty), and in 1975 he signed the Helsinki Accords, which recognized political arrangements in Eastern Europe which had been disputed for more than a generation.

The 1976 Election

Ford had originally stated he would not be a candidate on the national ticket in 1976, but he changed his mind. He faced a stiff challenge for the nomination, however; former Governor Ronald Reagan of California, champion of the Republican right, battled him through the 1976 primary season before succumbing narrowly at the convention. Running against Democrat Jimmy Carter of Georgia in November, Ford could not quite close the large gap by which he had trailed initially. He fell just short of victory. He received over 39 million popular votes to Carter's 40.8 million, winning 240 electoral votes to his opponent's 297. At the age of 63 he left public office—at the exact time he had earlier decided that he would retire.

Gerald Ford prospered as much after leaving the White House as any president had ever done. Moving their primary residence to near Palm Springs, California, he and his popular wife Betty (the former Elizabeth Warren, whom he married in 1948) also maintained homes in Vail, Colorado, and Los Angeles. Besides serving as a consultant to various businesses, by the mid-1980s Ford was on the boards of directors of several major companies, including Shearson/ American Express, Beneficial Corporation of New Jersey, and Twentieth Century-Fox Film Corporation. Estimated to be earning $1 million per year, Ford shared a number of investments with millionaire Leonard Firestone and busied himself with numerous speaking engagements. Some criticized him for trading on his prestige for self-interest, but Ford remained clear of charges of wrongdoing and saw no reason to apologize for his success. Long a spokesman for free enterprise and individual initiative, it is somehow fitting that he became a millionaire in his post-presidential years.

In December, 1996 *Business Week* said that the former President had amassed a fortune of close to $300 million over the past two decades, largely from buying and selling U.S. banks and thrifts. Still, his fiscal success didn't diminish his concern over Congress's decision to cut off funds for all living former Presidents as of 1998. In July 1996 Ford paid a visit to several Congressmen, in the hope of urging a Congressional change of heart. Unfortunately for Presidents Carter, Reagan, and Ford, it appears that the Congressional decision is firm, especially in this era of scrutinizing every item in the Federal budget.

In 1997 Ford participated in "The Presidents' Summit on America's Future," along with former presidents Bush and Carter, and President Clinton, as well as General Colin

Powell, and former first ladies Nancy Reagan and Lady Bird Johnson. The purpose of the gathering was to discuss volunteerism and community service, and marked the first occasion when living former presidents convened on a domestic policy.

Further Reading

Richard Reeves's *A Ford Not a Lincoln* (1975) and Jerald F. ter Horst's *Gerald Ford and the Future of the Presidency* (1974) provide interesting coverage of his pre-presidential years; the former is more critical than the latter. Ford's autobiography, *A Time to Heal* (1979), is the best source available on his early life, while Robert Hartmann's *Palace Politics: An Inside Account of the Ford Years* (1980) and Ron Nessen's *It Sure Looks Different from the Inside* (1978) give interesting glimpses of Ford as president. The most systematic treatment of Ford's presidency is in A. James Reichley, *Conservatives in an Age of Change: The Nixon and Ford Administrations* (1981). Also see Robert Hartman's *Palace Politics: An Inside Account of the Ford Years* (1990). □

Henry Ford

After founding the Ford Motor Company, the American industrialist Henry Ford (1863-1947) developed a system of mass production based on the assembly line and the conveyor belt which produced a low-priced car within reach of middle-class Americans.

The oldest of six children, Henry Ford was born on July 30, 1863, on a prosperous farm near Dearborn, Mich. He attended school until the age of 15, meanwhile developing a dislike of farm life and a fascination for machinery. In 1879 Ford left for Detroit. He became an apprentice in a machine shop and then moved to the Detroit Drydock Company. During his apprenticeship he received $2.50 a week, but room and board cost $3.50 so he labored nights repairing clocks and watches. He later worked for Westinghouse, locating and repairing road engines.

His father wanted Henry to be a farmer and offered him 40 acres of timberland, provided he give up machinery. Henry accepted the proposition, then built a first-class machinist's workshop on the property. His father was disappointed, but Henry did use the 2 years on the farm to win a bride, Clara Bryant.

Ford's First Car

Ford began to spend more and more time in Detroit working for the Edison Illuminating Company, which later became the Detroit Edison Company. By 1891 he had left the farm permanently. Four years later he became chief engineer; he met Thomas A. Edison, who eventually became one of his closest friends.

Ford devoted his spare time to building an automobile with an internal combustion engine. His first car, finished in 1896, followed the attempts, some successful, of many other innovators. His was a small car driven by a two-cylinder, four-cycle motor and by far the lightest (500 pounds) of the early American vehicles. The car was mounted on bicycle wheels and had no reverse gear.

In 1899 the Detroit Edison Company forced Ford to choose between automobiles and his job. Ford chose cars and that year formed the Detroit Automobile Company, which collapsed after he disagreed with his financial backers. His next venture was the unsuccessful Henry Ford Automobile Company. Ford did gain some status through the building of racing cars, which culminated in the "999," driven by the famous Barney Oldfield.

Ford Motor Company

By this time Ford had conceived the idea of a low-priced car for the masses, but this notion flew in the face of popular thought, which considered cars as only for the rich. After the "999" victories Alex Y. Malcomson, a Detroit coal dealer, offered to aid Ford in a new company. The result was the Ford Motor Company, founded in 1903, its small, $28,000 capitalization supplied mostly by Malcomson. However, exchanges of stock were made to obtain a small plant, motors, and transmissions. Ford's stock was in return for his services. Much of the firm's success can be credited to Ford's assistants—James S. Couzens, C. H. Wills, and John and Horace Dodge.

By 1903 over 1,500 firms had attempted to enter the fledgling automobile industry, but only a few, such as Ransom Olds, had become firmly established. Ford began production of a Model A, which imitated the Oldsmobile, and followed with other models, to the letter S. The public responded, and the company flourished. By 1907 profits exceeded $1,100,000, and the net worth of the company stood at $1,038,822.

Ford also defeated the Selden patent, which had been granted on a "road engine" in 1895. Rather than challenge the patent's validity, manufacturers secured a license to produce engines. When Ford was denied such a license, he fought back; after 8 years of litigation, the courts decided the patent was valid but not infringed. The case gave the Ford Company valuable publicity, with Ford cast as the underdog, but by the time the issue was settled, the situations had been reversed.

New Principles

In 1909 Ford made the momentous decision to manufacture only one type of car—the Model T, or the "Tin Lizzie." By now he firmly controlled the company, having bought out Malcomson. The Model T was durable, easy to operate, and economical; it sold for $850 and came in one color—black. Within 4 years Ford was producing over 40,000 cars per year.

During this rapid expansion Ford adhered to two principles: cutting costs by increasing efficiency and paying high wages to his employees. In production methods Ford believed the work should be brought by conveyor belt to the worker at waist-high level. This assembly-line technique required 7 years to perfect. In 1914 he startled the industrial world by raising the minimum wage to $5 a day, almost double the company's average wage. In addition, the "Tin Lizzie" had dropped in price to $600; it later went down to $360.

World War I

Ford was now an internationally known figure, but his public activities were less successful than his industrial ones. In 1915 his peace ship, the *Oskar II,* sailed to Europe to seek an end to World War I. His suit against the *Chicago Tribune* for calling him an anarchist received unfortunate publicity. In 1918 his race for the U.S. Senate as a Democrat met a narrow defeat. Ford's saddest mistake was his approval of an anti-Semitic campaign waged by the Ford-owned newspaper, the *Dearborn Independent.*

When the United States entered World War I, Ford's output of military equipment and his promise to rebate all profits on war production (he never did) silenced critics. By the end of the conflict his giant River Rouge plant, the world's largest industrial facility, was nearing completion. Ford gained total control of the company by buying the outstanding stock.

In the early 1920s the company continued its rapid growth, at one point producing 60 percent of the total United States output. But clouds stirred on the horizon. Ford was an inflexible man and continued to rely on the Model T, even as public tastes shifted. By the middle of the decade Ford had lost his dominant position to the General Motors Company. He finally saw his error and in 1927 stopped production of the Model T. However, since the new Model A was not produced for 18 months, there was a good deal of unemployment among Ford workers. The new car still did not permanently overtake the GM competition, Chevrolet; and Ford remained second.

Final Years

Ford's last years were frustrating. He never accepted the changes brought about by the Depression and the 1930s New Deal. He fell under the spell of Harry Bennett, a notorious figure with underworld connections, who, as head of Ford's security department, influenced every phase of company operations and created friction between Ford and his son Edsel. For various reasons Ford alone in his industry refused to cooperate with the National Recovery Administration. He did not like labor unions, refused to recognize the United Automobile Workers, and brutally repressed their attempts to organize the workers of his company.

Ford engaged in some philanthropic activity, such as the Henry Ford Hospital in Detroit. The original purpose of the Ford Foundation, established in 1936 and now one of the world's largest foundations, was to avoid estate taxes. Ford's greatest philanthropic accomplishment was the Ford Museum and Greenfield Village in Dearborn, Mich.

A stroke in 1938 slowed Ford, but he did not trust Edsel and so continued to exercise control of his company. During World War II Ford at first made pacifist statements but did retool and contribute greatly to the war effort. Ford's grandson Henry Ford II took over the company after the war. Henry Ford died on April 7, 1947.

Further Reading

Ford's own books, written in collaboration with Samuel Crowther, provide useful information: *My Life and Work* (1922), *Today and Tomorrow* (1926), and *Moving Forward* (1930). The writings on Ford are voluminous. The most authoritative on the man and the company are by Allan Nevins and Frank E. Hill, *Ford: The Times, the Man, the Company* (1954), *Ford: Expansion and Challenge, 1915-1933* (1957), and *Ford: Decline and Rebirth, 1933-1962* (1963). The best short studies are Keith Theodore Sward, *The Legend of Henry Ford* (1948), and Roger Burlingame, *Henry Ford: A Great Life in Brief* (1955). More recent works are Booton Herndon, *Ford: An Unconventional Biography of the Men and Their Times* (1969), and John B. Rae, *Henry Ford* (1969). Of the books by men who worked with Ford, Charles E. Sorensen, *My Forty Years with Ford* (1956), is worth reading. See also William Adams Simonds, *Henry Ford: His Life, His Work, His Genius* (1943), and William C. Richards, *The Last Billionaire: Henry Ford* (1948). □

Henry Ford II

Henry Ford II (1917-1987) was an American industrialist. He turned his grandfather's faltering automobile company into the second largest industrial corporation in the world.

Henry Ford II was born in Detroit, Michigan on September 4, 1917, the grandson of the automobile pioneer Henry Ford. After graduation from the Hotchkiss School in Lakeville, Connecticut, in 1936, Henry entered Yale University, where he specialized in sociology, a study that evidently influenced him a great deal. He lacked sufficient credits to graduate but left college anyway in 1940 to marry and begin work at the family firm, the Ford Motor Company.

In 1941 Ford was drafted and became an ensign at the Great Lakes Naval Training School. Meanwhile, conditions at the family firm—which had been losing money under the autocratic control of his grandfather—deteriorated further. A crisis was reached with the death of Ford's father in 1943. President Franklin D. Roosevelt's Cabinet deactivated Ford from the Navy so that he could aid in operating the company in its war work. Thus, at the age of 25 Ford was thrown into a situation for which he had little preparation. However, he was able to win his grandfather's confidence and grasp control of the chaotic, nebulous organization.

In September 1945 Henry Ford II became president of the Ford Motor Company and began recruiting an expert management team. By 1949 the company had been revitalized and restructured, and it had produced a new car comparable to the Model T and Model A. During the 1950s the firm moved into second place in automobile sales and became the industry's leader in product innovation. By 1960 Ford was so confident that he began to assume a one-man control reminiscent of that of his grandfather.

However, the younger Ford's individualism was tempered by a strong sense of social responsibility, which he had expressed publicly since his earliest days in business. He served as an alternate delegate to the United Nations under President Dwight D. Eisenhower in 1953 and as chairman of the National Alliance for Businessmen (which sought jobs for the unemployed) under President Lyndon B. Johnson in 1968. The 1970s saw Ford add the problems of pollution and environmental control to his earlier concerns for labor relations, business ethics, international trade, and civil rights.

Ford retired from his presidency in 1960, although he remained active in the business. He was named chairman of the board and chief executive officer, until he retired from Ford Motor Company in 1979. He died in 1987.

Further Reading

There is no biography of Ford. The best account of his life and early business career is found in Allan Nevins and Frank E. Hill, *Ford: Decline and Rebirth, 1933-1962* (1963). Less scholarly but more recent is Booton Herndon, *Ford: An Unconventional Biography of the Men and Their Times* (1969), which offers many revealing insights into Ford's personality and character. □

John Ford

The English author John Ford (1586-1639?) was the last great tragic dramatist of the English Renaissance. His work is noted for its stylistically simple and pure expression of powerful, shocking themes.

John Ford, the second son of Thomas Ford, was baptized at Ilsington, Devonshire, on April 17, 1586. The Devonshire Fords were a well-established family, and John's father appears to have been a fairly well-to-do member of the landed gentry.

In 1602 Ford entered the Middle Temple, one of the London Inns of Court. Although designed primarily to provide training in the law, the Inns of Court at this time also attracted young men who had no intention of entering the legal profession. Ford probably acquired his knowledge of Plato, Aristotle, and the Latin classics while in residence at the Middle Temple, where he remained for about 15 years.

During his early years in London, Ford wrote a few undistinguished nondramatic works. Not until 1621 did he turn to writing for the stage. From 1621 to 1625 he collaborated on at least five plays with Thomas Dekker, John Webster, and Samuel Rowley—all experienced and successful dramatists. From 1625 until the end of his literary career Ford worked alone, writing about a dozen plays (some of which are lost). Ford's reputation as a major dramatist rests on two of these unaided efforts: *'Tis Pity She's a Whore* and *The Broken Heart.*

Ford has been called a decadent playwright because of his frank treatment of lurid and sensational themes. In *'Tis*

Pity She's a Whore (1629?-1633) the central character, Giovanni, having become involved in an incestuous and adulterous affair with his sister, is finally led to kill her. With his sister's heart on the point of his dagger, Giovanni triumphantly proclaims his misdeeds, whereupon he is himself killed.

The Broken Heart (ca. 1627-1631?), while less obviously sensational, also treats of abnormal characters caught in highly unusual situations. The action of the play is set in Sparta, and its principal characters illustrate the typically Spartan virtues of rigorous self-discipline and overriding concern for personal honor. In the final act, when Princess Calantha is told of the deaths of her father, her friend, and her betrothed, she suppresses all signs of emotion. Only when she has set the affairs of the kingdom in order does she reveal the unbearable psychological strain put upon her; with ceremonious dignity she weds her dead lover and successfully commands her heart to break.

Nothing is known of Ford's activities after 1639, when his last known play was printed. No record of his death or burial has been found.

Further Reading

The standard life of Ford is M. Joan Sargeaunt, *John Ford* (1935). For the dating of Ford's plays (an extremely difficult task) see Gerald Eades Bentley, *The Jacobean and Caroline Stage,* vol. 3 (1956). Ford's intellectual makeup and his moral views are treated at length in G.F. Sensabaugh, *The Tragic Muse of John Ford* (1944), and Mark Stavig, *John Ford and the Traditional Moral Order* (1968). □

John Sean O'Feeney Ford

John Sean O'Feeney Ford (ca. 1895-1973) was an American film director who, with other pioneers in the movie industry, transformed a rudimentary entertainment medium into a highly personalized and expressive art form.

John Sean O'Feeney Ford was born around February 1, 1895, the youngest child of Irish immigrant parents. Ford graduated from high school in 1913 and attended the University of Maine. He entered the film industry in 1914 as a property man, directed his first film, *Tornado,* in 1917, and continued to produce silent films at the rate of five to ten each year. He established his reputation as a leading silent-film maker with *The Iron Horse* (1924), one of the first epic westerns, and *Four Sons* (1928), his initial attempt at a personal cinematic statement. Both films are now part of the silent-screen museum repertory.

But Ford was to make his great contribution as a director of talking motion pictures and in 1935 produced *The Informer,* often described as the first creative sound film. Dealing with a tragic incident in the Irish Rebellion of 1922, Ford and his scriptwriter transformed a melodramatic novel into a compassionate, intensely dramatic, visually expres-

sive film. It received the Academy Award and the New York Film Critics Award for best direction. That same year Ford directed *Steamboat 'Round the Bend* and *The Whole Town's Talking,* which though neglected at the time are now considered on a par with *The Informer.*

With *Stagecoach* (1939) Ford established the American western as mythic archetype. His sculptured landscapes and pictorial compositions immediately impressed critics and audiences. With this film Ford formally renounced the realistic montage film theories of D.W. Griffith and the Russian director Sergei Eisenstein to develop a film esthetic that substituted camera movement and precise framing of spatial relationships for dramatic cutting and visual contrast. Ford utilized auditory effects to increase a scene's psychological tension.

In 1940 Ford began work on the film version of John Steinbeck's Depression novel, *The Grapes of Wrath.* Ignoring Steinbeck's propagandistic intentions and philosophizing, Ford concentrated on the human elements in the story and unified the episodic structure of the novel with a controlled use of visual symbolism. The film remains remarkable in several respects, most notably in Ford's ability to achieve an appropriately harsh and naturalistic style without sacrificing his poetic sensibility. This success brought the director his second Oscar and New York Film Critics Award. The following year Ford's most romantic film, *How Green Was My Valley,* a lyrical and nostalgic evocation of life in a Welsh mining town, earned him his third series of awards.

In addition to his work for the American Office of Strategic Services during World War II, Ford produced two excellent naval documentaries in 1945, a sex hygiene film for soldiers, and a commercial war movie, *They Were Expendable* (1945). After the war Ford released his second great western, *My Darling Clementine* (1946), which combined epic realism with poetic luminosity to create the most beautiful western to date. This was Ford's finest film. Only slightly less successful were *Fort Apache* (1948) and *She Wore a Yellow Ribbon* (1949). His best film of the early 1950s was *The Quiet Man* (1952), a delightfully energetic comedy about exotic domestic rituals in a small Irish province, for which he received his fourth Oscar. *The Searchers* (1957) was an intense, psychological western about a group of pioneers seeking a young girl captured by the Indians. Ford next turned to the conflicts of ward politics in the Irish section of Boston in *The Last Hurrah* (1958).

With the exception of *Sergeant Rutledge* (1961) and *The Man Who Shot Liberty Valance* (1963), Ford's films of the 1960s were not on the same level as his earlier work. *Cheyenne Autumn* (1964), treating the tragedy of the American Indian, lacked his characteristic personal involvement and visual freshness. *Young Cassidy,* a biography of writer Sean O'Casey, was abandoned by the ailing Ford and completed by a lesser British director. Partially deaf and afflicted with poor vision (he wore a patch over one eye), Ford lived with his wife in Los Angeles during the early 1970s and died in 1973.

Over the years Ford evolved a concise cinematic vocabulary, consisting of subtle camera movement, graduated long shots, and unobtrusive editing. Notable for their realistic detail, pictorial beauty, and dynamic action sequences, his films have exerted a pronounced influence on the work of other directors. Winner of numerous awards and international citations, Ford is unique among American directors in having won the admiration of the middlebrow, establishment critics for his early social dramas (*The Informer, The Grapes of Wrath*) and the respect of the intellectual European and avant-garde critics for the more stylized films (*My Darling Clementine, The Searchers*) of his later years. As film historian Andrew Sarris recorded, "Ford developed his craft in the twenties, achieved dramatic force in the thirties, epic sweep in the forties, and symbolic evocation in the fifties."

Further Reading

The outstanding critical and biographical studies of Ford are in French. The only full-length work in English is Peter Bogdanovich, *John Ford* (1968). Of particular interest are sections in Roger Manvell, *Film* (1946); George Bluestone, *Novels into Film* (1957); and Andrew Sarris, *The American Cinema, 1929-1968* (1968). Jean Mitry's *Cahiers du cinema* interview with the director can be found in Andrew Sarris, ed., *Interviews with Film Directors* (1968). ☐

Paul Leicester Ford

Paul Leicester Ford (1865-1902) was an American bibliographer, editor, biographer, and novelist.

Paul Leicester Ford was born in Brooklyn, N.Y., the son of a bibliophile whose superb collection of Americana was valued at $100,000. An injury to his spine hindered Paul's growth; he had to be educated by tutors. In time his omnivorous reading in his father's library (encouraged by a scholarly brother, Worthington), his life in a select social environment, and his extensive travels in North and South America and in Europe extended his cultural interests.

Ford's first publication, at the age of 11, *The Webster Geneology* (sic), accompanied by learned notes, was privately printed. He went on to publish several bibliographies—of books by and about Alexander Hamilton (1886) and Benjamin Franklin (1889), the *Check-List of American Magazines Published in the Eighteenth Century* (1889), and of literature relating to the adoption of the U.S. Constitution (1896). He reprinted in facsimile early books on colonial America by Thomas Hariot and John Brereton, John Milton's *Comus,* and Francis Bacon's *Essayes.* His major achievements were the editing of *The Works of Thomas Jefferson* in 10 volumes (1892-1899), *The Political Writings of John Dickinson, 1764-1774* (1895), and *The Federalist* (1898).

Ford turned from bibliography to literary endeavors. His two popular biographical studies were *The True George Washington* (1896) and *The Many-sided Franklin* (1899). Less idolatrous than previous studies of the same men, Ford's biographies still made their subjects humanly attractive.

Ford also wrote a number of novels, two of which were very popular. *The Honorable Peter Stirling* (1894) was based upon Ford's brief foray into politics. Partly because the protagonist was thought to be modeled on Grover Cleveland, and partly because the book—almost uniquely in its time—pictured a "good" boss sympathetically, it became a best seller. In a corrupt world of city and state politics, Stirling stands out as "a practical idealist" who, at a time when he takes a stand that threatens to lose him votes, says, "Votes be damned!" *Janice Meredith: A Story of the American Revolution* (1899) made use of Ford's historical knowledge. In a period when historical novels were flourishing, it sold 200,000 copies and was put on the stage in 1901-1902. Three other novels published between 1897 and 1902, though moderately successful, attracted less attention.

Despite his physical handicaps, Ford was very active socially. At the age of 37, at the height of his powers, having edited and written more than 70 books, he died tragically when a disinherited brother shot him.

Further Reading

Gordon Milne, *The American Political Novel* (1966), discusses *The Honorable Peter Stirling* in its literary context.

Additional Sources

Dubois, Paul Z., *Paul Leicester Ford: an American man of letters 1865-1902*, New York: B. Franklin, 1977. □

James Forman

James Forman (born 1928), a writer, journalist, political philosopher, human rights activist, and revolutionary socialist, was a leader of the Student Non-violent Coordinating Committee (SNCC) during most of its active period.

James Forman was born in Chicago, Illinois, on October 4, 1928. He spent his early life on a farm in Marshall County, Mississippi. Upon graduating from Englewood High School in Chicago, he attended junior college for a semester. He then joined the U.S. Air Force as a personnel classification specialist. Having completed a four-year tour-of-duty, he enrolled at the University of Southern California; however, his studies were interrupted when a false arrest charge kept him from taking his final examinations. This also gave a new meaning to the racism he had observed in the armed services and elsewhere.

Returning from Chicago, Forman excelled in the intellectually-charged environment of Roosevelt University.

There he served as president of the student body and chief delegate to the 1956 National Student Association. In the fall of 1957 he began graduate studies at Boston University in African affairs, yet could not reconcile himself to studying Africa when children in Little Rock, Arkansas, were trying to integrate a school. He left Boston and went to the South as a reporter for the *Chicago Defender*. During this period he also wrote a novel about the ideal interracial civil rights group whose philosophy of non-violence would produce massive social change.

Forman returned to Chicago to teach, and became involved with the Emergency Relief Committee, a group affiliated with the Congress of Racial Equality (CORE) and dedicated to providing food and clothing to black sharecroppers evicted from their homes for registering to vote in Fayette County, Tennessee. In 1960 he formally joined the civil rights movement by going to Monroe, North Carolina, to assist Robert F. Williams, head of the local chapter of the National Association for the Advancement of Colored People (NAACP). In his confrontation with local white people, Williams had been censured by the NAACP for his call of armed self-defense. Though still teaching in Chicago, Forman maintained his ties with the southern student activists and from them heard about a newly formed group called SNCC (Student Non-violent Coordinating Committee), which was structured much like the organization his novel suggested. After some debate, Forman left teaching and went to SNCC's national headquarters in Atlanta. Within a week he was appointed executive secretary, in 1961.

Forman's greatest contribution to SNCC in eight years of involvement was his ability to provide the administrative skills and political sophistication the organization needed. He hired an efficient staff, brought professionalism to the research and fund-raising activities as well as discipline and direction to SNCC's various factions. He realized the need for specialized skills and made office-work, research, and fund-raising all part of SNCC's revolutionary activities.

As executive secretary of SNCC, Forman was involved in every major civil rights controversy in the nation. He coordinated the famous "Freedom Rides" and advocated the use of white civil rights workers in white communities. He started the Albany Movement, which paved the way for Martin Luther King's campaign there. He criticized the 1963 March on Washington as a "sell-out" by black leaders to the Kennedy administration and the liberal-labor vote. In 1964 Forman and Fannie Lou Hamer opposed the compromise worked out by the Democratic Party and the Mississippi Freedom Democratic Party at the Democratic National Convention. In addition, he questioned the capitalistic orientation of mainstream black leaders and castigated them for not understanding the correlations among capitalism, racism, and imperialism. Forman also noted that most civil rights groups were not effective or enduring because they were "leader-centered" rather than being "group or people-centered." Some of those other civil rights leaders saw Forman as something of a hothead. As James Farmer noted in his autobiography, *Lay Bare the Heart,* "Forman was volatile and uncompromising, an angry young man. His head had been clubbed many times on the front lines in Dixie. He was impatient with Urban League and NAACP types; he was nervous and perhaps a trifle battle-fatigued."

As director of the International Affairs Commission of SNCC, Forman and ten other staff members went to Africa in 1964 as guests of the government of Guinea. This trip began to alter his views, and he developed a global analysis of racism. His understanding was shaped by reading the works of Frantz Fanon, Che Guevara, Kwame Nkrhumah, Fidel Castro, and Malcolm X. In 1967 he delivered a paper in Zambia entitled: "The Invisible Struggle Against Racism, Colonialism and Apartheid." His internationalist orientation lead him to accept an appointment in the Black Panther Party (BPP) as minister of foreign affairs and director of political education in 1968. (Early in 1967 SNCC and the BPP had coordinated a number of ventures and activities.)

This alliance soon ended, and Forman even left SNCC in 1969 when he was essentially deposed by H. Rap Brown, then chairman of the committee. Before Forman left, he delivered one of the most provocative challenges to come out of the 1960s. In a speech given in April of 1969 at the Black Economic Development Conference, Forman called for "a revolutionary black vanguard" to seize the government and redirect its resources. In addition, in his now famous "Black Manifesto" he demanded that "white Christian Churches and Jewish Synagogues, which are part and parcel of the system of capitalism," pay half-a-billion dollars to blacks for reparations for slavery and racial exploitation. He wanted the money to create new black institutions. Specifically, he demanded a Southern Land Bank, four

major publishing and printing enterprises, four television networks, a Black Labor Strike and Defense Fund Training Center, and a new black university. Interesting enough, some funds did come in; however, most were given to the traditional black churches and organizations.

In some ways, "The Black Manifesto" was Forman's greatest moment. He had linked contemporary wealth with historic exploitation; thus, he presented the ultimate challenge to American society. In the early 1970s Forman spent most of his time writing his mammoth work on black revolutionaries. In 1977 he enrolled as a graduate student at Cornell University. He received a Masters of Professional Studies (M.P.S.) in African and Afro-American history in 1980.

In 1983 Forman served a one-year term as legislative assistant to the president of the Metropolitan Washington Central Labor Council (AFL-CIO). He was chairman of the Unemployed and Poverty Council (UPAC), a civil and human rights group in Washington, D.C. As one of the major leaders of the civil rights era, James Forman continued to represent a dimension of black activism which sought to develop a revolutionary organization in America. He also received a Ph.D. in 1985 from the Union of Experimental Colleges and Universities in cooperation with the Institute of Policy Studies. In April 1990, Forman was honored by the National Conference of Black Mayors, who awarded him their Fannie Lou Hamer Freedom Award.

Further Reading

Forman was a prolific writer. He was most noted for: *1967: High Tide of Black Resistance* (1967); *Sammy Younge, Jr.: The First Black College Student to Die in the Black Liberation Movement* (1968); *Liberation: Viendra d'une Chose Noir* (1968); "The Black Manifesto" (1969); *The Political Thought of James Forman* (1970); *The Making of Black Revolutionaries* (1972, 1985); and *Self-Detertion: An Examination of the Question and its Applications to the African-American People* (1980, 1984). He also wrote for newspapers, journals, and magazines. Books in which Forman is discussed in detail include *Black Awakening in Capitalist America: An Analytical History* by Robert L. Allen (1969); *In Struggle: SNCC and the Black Awakening of the 1960s* by Claybourne Carson (1981); *Power on the Left: American Radical Movements Since 1946* by Lawrence Lader (1979); and *The River of No Return: The Autobiography of a Black Militant and the Life and Death of SNCC* by Cleveland Sellers and Robert Terrell (1973). A Web site containing information on SNCC's formation in the 1960s, and an article entitled *SNCC: Basis of Black Power* can be found at http://jefferson.village.virginia.edu/sixties/ HTML_docs/Primary/manifestos/SNCC_bla. □

Edwin Forrest

The actor Edwin Forrest (1806-1872) was the first great American-born tragedian. Heroic in technique, he was acclaimed by the popular audience but often scorned by the cultured. His career had important social and political implications.

dwin Forrest, the fifth child of a destitute Philadelphia family, left school when he was 10. At 14 he gained his first professional role. Though his talent was immediately apparent, there was no place for him on eastern stages, so he joined companies that played in the West and South. Returning to the prestigious theaters of the East in 1825, he was inspired and praised by Edmund Kean, the English actor, and made a great success acting Othello. At the age of 21 Forrest was a star, playing all the important Shakespearean roles. He was the only American actor who could challenge the English domination of the stage.

Forrest offered prizes for original American plays, especially with parts he might play. *Metamora* (1828), *The Gladiator* (1831), and *The Broker of Bogota* (1834) were the most successful. Forrest became wealthy, partly from these roles, but he paid the authors no royalties beyond the original prize.

While touring England in 1837, Forrest met and married Catherine Sinclair. He also met William Macready, the English actor who competed with Forrest for preeminence.

Forrest's technique, like his temperament, was heroic and physical rather than subtle. As an actor, he embodied all the robust, uninhibited majesty that Americans saw in themselves as a nation. His voice could make the pits tremble; his eloquence was marvelous for the large theaters of the time; and his furious realism, especially in scenes of combat, terrified his stage opponents. William Winter later said he was a "vast animal bewildered by a grain of genius." Forrest's heroic pose and strong nationalism were not lost upon the popular audience, which felt a traditional cultural inferiority to England.

In 1849 the long-standing competition between Forrest and Macready exploded into riot. Forrest insisted that Macready had insulted him; Forrest's followers insisted that the Englishman had insulted America. Macready versus Forrest became a struggle of England against America, rich against poor, the elite against the common. A mob stormed the Astor Place Theater in New York City, where Macready was playing; and the militia in quelling the riot killed at least 22 persons. Forrest's reputation was tarnished by the tragedy.

That same year Forrest accused his wife of adultery; the long and sordid litigation came to the divorce court in 1851. Though Catherine was vindicated, America had its first actor's divorce scandal, and Forrest's Othello was more popular than ever.

Forrest soon retired. Though he returned to the stage in 1860, his grandiloquent, strenuous style of acting was passing from favor. Some critics still insist, however, that he was the greatest actor America has ever produced.

Further Reading

William R. Alger, *Life of Edwin Forrest, the American Tragedian* (1877), is the standard biography. Lawrence Barrett, *Edwin Forrest* (1881), is an account by an actor. For a negative view of Forrest as "always the slave of his ignorance" see William Winter, *The Wallet of Time*, vol. 1 (1913). Lloyd R. Morris, *Curtain Time* (1953), gives an excellent brief evaluation of Forrest. □

John Forrest

John Forrest, 1st Baron Forrest of Bunbury (1847-1918), was an Australian explorer, administrator, and political leader. He gained a reputation as a capable and resolute expedition leader, but his greatest achievement was the economic development of Western Australia.

ohn Forrest was born in Bunbury, a small town south of Perth, Western Australia, on Aug. 22, 1847. He was educated at Bishop's School, Perth, and joined the colonial Survey Department in 1865. Four years later, as leader of an expedition in search of a long-missing exploring party, he penetrated well beyond settled areas.

In 1870, with his brother Alexander, Forrest led an expedition from Perth to Adelaide (over 1,500 miles) along the Great Australian Bight, generally traversing desolate tracts that had been crossed only once, 30 years before. A second grueling expedition—again undertaken with his brother—was the crossing in 1874 from Champion Bay, on the west coast, to the Musgrave Ranges in central Australia, during which the economic value of this vast area was reviewed.

These expeditions gained for Forrest a variety of honors and established his reputation as a man of intrepidity and initiative in practical matters. He received a grant of 5,000 acres of land, the Royal Geographical Society awarded him its Gold Medal, and European institutions honored him with awards.

In Colonial Administration

In 1876 Forrest was appointed deputy surveyor general of Western Australia. He was commissioner of crown lands and surveyor general from 1883 and led an expedition to the Kimberley district in the far northwest of the colony in preparation for its occupation by cattlemen. As a respected member of the Executive Council and the Legislative Council, Forrest was the natural choice as premier and treasurer when responsible government was introduced in Western Australia in 1890. He was knighted the following year.

With the unearthing of large quantities of gold in the Coolgardie and Kalgoorlie areas, Western Australia's economy boomed in the mid-1890s. From 50,000 inhabitants in 1891, the colony's population increased to 150,000 in less than 7 years, and Forrest provided stable government and a steady hand. Railways were extended, farming methods were improved, and a water pipeline was built to the distant desert gold fields. Education was extended and fees abolished in public schools. In 1899 women were granted the franchise.

Forrest attended the 1891 convention called to discuss federation of the Australian colonies, and the follow-up convention of 1897-1898; generally his attitude to federation was cautious, with the emphasis on the need to protect the rights of less populous states, and it was only a wave of popular sentiment that carried Western Australia into the Commonwealth.

In Federal Government

With the setting up of the federal government, Forrest resigned from Western Australia's legislature to join the ministry of Edmund Barton, which was sworn in on Jan. 1, 1901. Forrest was elected to the House of Representatives in the March poll. At first postmaster general, he transferred later to the Ministry of Defence (1901-1903). He served in all non-Labour ministries until 1914 and was acting prime minister from March to June 1907. However, lacking political finesse, Forrest never gained a large personal following. His reputation was built on rugged honesty and able administration (even though he was not an active deviser of policies). His reputation as treasurer rested mainly on his conservative tendencies. Forrest strongly advocated a transcontinental rail link; work on this began under Labour—his political opponents—in 1910.

When William Morris Hughes broke with the Labour party in 1917 and formed a coalition ministry, Forrest was appointed treasurer. In February 1918 he became the first native-born Australian to be raised to the peerage. He resigned office with the intention of taking his seat in the House of Lords, but while en route to London he died at sea on Sept. 3, 1918. He was buried in Sierra Leone; later his remains were taken to Perth for reburial.

Further Reading

Forrest's reports on his explorations are *Journal of an Exploring Expedition to the Country Eastward to Port Eucla and Thence to Adelaide* (1870); *Journal of Proceedings of the Western Australian Exploring Expedition through the Centre of Australia* (1875); and *Explorations in Australia* (1875). Forrest's *Notes on Western Australia* (1884) provides background material. See also Geoffrey Rawson, *Desert Journeys* (1948). Forrest's premiership is covered in Sir Hal Colebatch, ed., *A Story of a Hundred Years: Western Australia, 1829-1929* (1929), and in Frank K. Crowley, *Australia's Western Third* (1960). The federal governments in which Forrest served are examined in H. G. Turner, *The First Decade of the Australian Commonwealth . . . 1901-1910* (1911), and in A. N. Smith, *Thirty Years: The Commonwealth of Australia, 1901-1931* (1933). □

Nathan Bedford Forrest

A Confederate general in the American Civil War, Nathan Bedford Forrest (1821-1877) ranks as a near genius of war. He was a daring and successful cavalry leader who had few peers.

Nathan Bedford Forrest, eldest son of his family, was born near Chapel Hill, Tenn., on July 13, 1821. The family moved to Mississippi in 1834, and Forrest's father died when the boy was 16. As head of the house, Forrest farmed, traded horses and cattle, and finally traded slaves. Slowly he accumulated the capital to buy Mississippi and Arkansas plantations. At length a wealthy man, he married Mary Ann Montgomery in 1845. Moving to Memphis in 1849, he was active in city affairs and served as alderman. Denied formal education, he taught himself to write and speak clearly and learned mathematics; yet he never learned to spell.

With the Civil War coming, Forrest enlisted as a private in the Confederate Army. Since he raised and equipped a cavalry battalion at his own expense, he was appointed lieutenant colonel in 1861. As a cavalry leader, Forrest displayed spectacular talent. His men were devoted to him, admiring his stature, commanding air, courtesy, even his ferociousness.

Forrest took part in the defense of Ft. Donelson, Tenn., in 1862. He persuaded his superiors to let his troops escape before the surrender, which endeared him to the troops. As a full colonel at Shiloh, he received a bad wound. In 1862, commissioned brigadier general, he began a long and lustrous association with the Confederate Army of Tennessee.

A succession of commanders realized Forrest's talent as a raider and used him to wreak havoc behind enemy lines. Forrest believed in surprise, audacity, and nerve. His men became splendid scouts as well as superb raiders. His philosophy of war is distilled in his maxim, "Get there first with the most."

Several of Forrest's battles were minor classics of cavalry tactics. Near Rome, Ga., in 1863, he outmaneuvered and captured a raiding Union column. In 1864 he defeated a much larger Union force at Brice's Cross Roads, Miss. In planning this action Forrest had taken account of weather, terrain, the condition of his own and of enemy troops, deployment of the enemy column, time, and distance in a deft blending of strategy, tactics, and logistics.

Not always affable, Forrest had troubles with some superiors, especially Gen. Braxton Bragg. Forrest thought Bragg unfair, jealous, and discriminatory regarding the Chickamauga campaign, and he took his grievance to President Jefferson Davis. Davis transferred Forrest and in 1863 commissioned him major general.

Although historians still argue over Forrest's responsibility for the Ft. Pillow massacre, in which Union African American troops were slaughtered, it appears that Forrest did not order the massacre. Lack of evidence prevents a definite conclusion. Toward the end of the war Forrest raided successfully in Mississippi, Tennessee, and Alabama.

Promoted to lieutenant general in 1865, Forrest fought increasing enemy forces with dwindling ranks. The long spring raid of Union general James H. Wilson pushed him back to the defense of the Confederate ordnance center at Selma, Ala., where he was finally defeated. He surrendered on May 9, 1865.

After the war Forrest lived in Memphis, Tenn. He was evidently active in organizing the Ku Klux Klan but abandoned it when its course turned violent. For several years he was president of the Selma, Marion and Memphis Railroad. He died in Memphis.

Further Reading

The best biography of Forrest is Robert S. Henry, *"First with the Most" Forrest* (1944), although Andrew N. Lytle, *Bedford Forrest and His Critter Company* (1931; rev. ed. 1960), and John A. Wyeth, *That Devil Forrest* (1959; originally published as *Life of Nathan Bedford Forrest,* 1899), are both good. □

James Vincent Forrestal

James Vincent Forrestal (1892-1949) was the first secretary of the U.S. Department of Defense. He was instrumental in building America's Navy during World War II and contributed to the unification of the armed forces.

James Forrestal was born on Feb. 15, 1892, in Matteawan (now part of Beacon), N.Y. His father owned a successful construction and contracting business and had married Mary A. Toohey; James was the youngest of their three sons.

Young Forrestal studied at St. Joachim's Parochial School and graduated from Matteawan High School. He began work as a cub reporter on the *Matteawan Journal.* When he became city editor for the *Poughkeepsie News Press,* he realized that he needed a college education to advance his career. He went to Dartmouth in 1911, the next year transferring to Princeton. As a senior he was on the student council and editor of the *Daily Princetonian;* his class voted him the "man most likely to succeed." However, about 6 weeks before graduation Forrestal left Princeton and never received a bachelor's degree. One of the reasons was that he had flunked an English course and did not make up the credits.

Forrestal worked briefly as a salesman. Then, as a reporter with the *New York World,* he came into contact with Wall Street society. In 1916 he joined the investment banking house of William Read and Company (soon Dillon, Read and Company). Except for service in the Navy during World War I, he remained with the company until 1940. Beginning as a bond salesman, Forrestal rapidly rose to partnership in the firm; in 1938 he became its president. As a result of several spectacular transactions, he was considered the "boy wonder" of Wall Street.

Secretary of the Navy

In 1940 at the peak of his career Forrestal accepted appointment as a $10,000-a-year administrative assistant to President Franklin D. Roosevelt. After 6 weeks in this position he was designated the first undersecretary of the Navy, a post newly created by Congress. During the next 4 years he transformed his post into a nerve center, coordinating the Navy Department's whole procurement and production war effort. His success in expanding the Navy was so great that by the end of World War II the American Navy was stronger than all other navies in the world combined.

On the death of Navy Secretary Frank Knox in April 1944, Roosevelt made Forrestal secretary. In this office for 4 years, he strongly opposed measures designed to make Germany and Japan completely impotent and strenuously objected to sharing atomic information. On the other hand, he supported America's continued effort to sustain the Chinese Nationalists against the Chinese Communists and urged the United States to retain formerly Japanese-held bases in the Pacific. He was an advocate of aid to free peoples and of containment of Soviet influence long before these policies were promulgated in the Truman Doctrine of 1947.

Secretary of Defense

Believing that the oil-producing states in the Middle East were of strategic importance to the United States, Forrestal opposed actions favorable to the creation of the state of Israel in 1947 and 1948. He was also enmeshed in the postwar dispute over unification of the armed services. The Army favored unification, but the Navy feared it. A battle ensued both in Congress and within the government. Forrestal supported greater unity but not complete integration. As a result of President Harry Truman's mediation, the National Security Act, adopted on July 26, 1947, effected among other things the reorganization that created a single Department of Defense, with the secretary of defense given Cabinet rank. Truman's appointment of Forrestal as the first secretary of defense in July 1948 was unanimously acclaimed by the nation's press.

Forrestal gave an impression of toughness and strength. His tight mouth, piercing eyes, and the way he carried himself made him seem more robust than he actually was. In the last months of his life he was mentally disturbed. In March 1949 he resigned as defense secretary, and shortly afterward he was placed under psychiatric care at the Bethesda Naval Hospital. On May 22, 1949, he committed suicide.

Further Reading

An indispensable book on Forrestal is *The Forrestal Diaries* (1951), edited by Walter Millis with the collaboration of E. S. Duffield (1951). Arnold A. Rogow, *James Forrestal: A Study of Personality, Politics, and Policy* (1963), attempts to probe Forrestal's life psychoanalytically. For details on Forrestal's role in the reorganization of the Navy Department and expansion of the Navy during World War II see Robert H. Connery, *The Navy and the Industrial Mobilization in World War II* (1951), and Robert Greenhalgh Albion and Robert Howe Connery, *Forrestal and the Navy* (1962). □

Edward Morgan Forster

The English novelist and essayist Edward Morgan Forster (1879-1970) was concerned with the conflict between the freedom of the spirit and the conventions of society.

Educated at Tonbridge School (which he disliked intensely), E. M. Forster went on to Cambridge. His father, an architect, had died when Forster was only 2 years old, but a legacy from an aunt afforded him his education and the opportunity to travel. It was his experience of Cambridge and of travel in Europe after taking his degree in 1901 which stimulated Forster's imagination and thought and led to the extraordinary burst of creative activity which produced a volume of short stories, *The Celestial Omnibus and Other Stories* (1911), and four novels in quick succession: *Where Angels Fear to Tread* (1905), *The Longest Journey* (1907), *A Room with a View* (1908), and *Howard's End* (1910).

Where Angels Fear To Tread presents a conflict between two worlds, represented by the English town of Sawston ("that hole," as one of the characters calls it) on the one hand and the Italian town of Monteriano on the other. Those two worlds are characterized by the English Herritons, seeking to buy (or, as eventually transpires, steal) the child of their dead sister, and Gino, the Italian father of the child. Linking the two is Caroline Abbott; loved by Philip Herriton and in love with Gino, she is the meeting point of one world with another. In the novel the child is killed and the Herritons leave Italy, which they had once thought beautiful. No happy resolution is afforded, unless it is that Philip Herriton does abandon his home in Sawston—and the values it represents—to make his living in London. Such endings of loss, death, and disappointment, redeemed only by the possibility of future change and the knowledge of the existence of beauty, are characteristic of Forster's fiction.

And characteristic, too, are the instruments Forster uses: the settled, conventional middle-class English brought into sudden and unnerving contact with a strange and more exotic people.

A Passage to India

In 1912 Forster first visited India, and after spending the war years from 1915 to 1918 in Alexandria with the Red Cross, he returned to India in 1922 as private secretary to the maharajah of the state of Dewas Senior. India is the location for Forster's only novel set entirely out of England, *A Passage to India,* which, begun in 1912, was not completed until after Forster's second visit and was finally published in 1924. The conflicting worlds which Forster treats in this novel are those of the colonial English and the native Indian.

On the title page of *Howard's End* Forster had placed the phrase "Only connect." It is Forster's instruction to people whose most significant failure, as he sees it, is their reluctance to destroy the barriers of prejudice that have risen to divide them. This thought is also evident in *A Passage to India*. At the center of the novel are two characters—the Indian, Aziz, and the Englishman, Fielding—each intellectual, each aware of the traditions of his country yet largely freed from them, and each desiring to be friends. Yet circumstances, forged by inexplicable and supernatural impulses and abetted by worldly prejudice, transpire to separate them and breed a reluctant mistrust. As the novel closes, they both desire friendship: "But the horses . . . the earth . . . the temples, the tank, the jail, the palace, the birds, the carrion, the guest house, . . . they didn't want it; they said in their hundred voices 'No, not yet,' and the sky said, 'No, not there.'" The division between the two men is confirmed. It is the division also between their two nations; and it is the division, Forster implies, which characterized the 20th century and stems from man's failure to overcome his individual and traditional differences.

A Passage To India is generally conceded to be Forster's finest novel. The novel is essentially dramatic, the characters completely realized; and people, theme, and plot fuse into a totally convincing action. Yet although this novel suggests that Forster had acquired a complete mastery of the genre, he subsequently published no more novels. His later work—written at his home in Abinger or at King's College, Cambridge (of which he was elected a fellow in 1927 and where he resided from the end of World War II until his death)—took the form of literary criticism, biography, and general essays.

Nonfiction Works

Alexandria: A History and a Guide (1922) and *Pharos and Pharillon* (1923) are superficially histories and guides, as the subtitle of the first suggests. But fundamentally they present the comments of a liberal, thoughtful, and Hellenistic mind on human manners and traditions. This characteristic bent of mind is evident in all of Forster's subsequent essays.

Perhaps the most noted and influential of these is the volume of criticism *Aspects of the Novel,* the text of the

Clark Lectures which Forster delivered in 1927. This work advances a theory of characterization and of "pattern and rhythm" in the novel. Forster asserts that characters are either flat—types or caricatures, particularly useful in comedy—or round—capable of surprising the reader, yet in a totally convincing fashion. He speculates that a sort of symphonic rhythm (the "three large blocks of sound" that make up Beethoven's Fifth Symphony, for example) may have its counterpart in fiction. These thoughts provide an illustration of Forster's own concern as a novelist. For his own characters do, in fact, range from the flattest of symbols to the complex and surprising cipher of human personality; and his own novels are sometimes built out of three recognizable parts and controlled by recurrent symbols.

Further literary essays are contained in *Abinger Harvest* (1936) and *Two Cheers for Democracy* (1951). In their impressionistic re-creation of their subjects' styles and preoccupations, and their idiosyncratic use of personal anecdote, these essays suggest the influence of Virginia Woolf and Lytton Strachey—reminding the reader that Forster was at the center of the Bloomsbury group. A constant awareness of the progress and possible destruction of human civilization is characteristic of the finest of these essays and reveals directly what perhaps is one of the driving intellectual forces of the novels. The epilogues to "The Pageant of Abinger" in *Abinger Harvest* and "The Last of Abinger" in *Two Cheers for Democracy* voice a detestation of the increasing dominance of material values.

Firm opposition to prejudice, racism, and totalitarianism has seldom been more finely expressed than in *Two Cheers for Democracy,* and the long essay "What I Believe" remains the moving credo of a man who in an age of increasing uniformity insists upon the rights and sanctity of the individual and the importance of the personal life. A balance between the right of every human individual to be uniquely himself and the right of every community to organize in order to preserve that individual uniqueness is finely maintained by Forster. Because the political system in which Forster was nurtured attempts to sustain this balance, he is prepared to give it two cheers: "Two cheers are quite enough: there is no occasion to give three. Only Love, the Beloved Republic, deserves that." The knowledge that the beloved republic can neither be founded by his race nor banished from its aspirations furnishes the despair and the hope which are inseparable in all of Forster's writing.

Further Reading

Rose Macauley provided an early personal appreciation of Forster's work in *The Writings of E. M. Forster* (1938), and a quite different though no less personal tribute is Natwahr-Singh, ed., *E. M. Forster: A Tribute* (1964). There are many good critical studies of Forster's work. J. K. Johnstone in *Bloomsbury Group* (1954) devotes a long section to an analysis of Forster's novels which has probably not been surpassed. Among the more recent serious critical studies are H. J. Oliver, *The Art of E. M. Forster* (1960); J. B. Beer, *The Achievement of E. M. Forster* (1962); and Frederick C. Crews, *E. M. Forster: The Perils of Humanism* (1962). □

Abe Fortas

A noted civil libertarian, Abe Fortas (1910-1982) served only four years on the Supreme Court before a series of charges led to his resignation.

Abe Fortas, who was nominated by his friend President Lyndon B. Johnson to the U.S. Supreme Court in 1965, was born on June 19, 1910, in Memphis, Tennessee. His parents were Orthodox Jews who had emigrated from England. At the age of 15 he was graduated second in his class from a Memphis public high school and earned a scholarship to Southwestern College (now Rhodes College) in his hometown.

He received his B.A. in 1930 and, based on his stellar performance as an undergraduate, both Harvard and Yale Law Schools offered him scholarships. (A $50 difference per month in the Yale stipend resulted in Fortas' choice of New Haven over Cambridge.) The future justice's consistency as a scholar continued in law school. By his senior year he was editor-in-chief of the *Yale Law Journal,* a position usually reserved for the student achieving the top academic rank in the class. He received his law degree in 1933.

An offer to join the Yale faculty capped Fortas' laudable law school career. Before he could begin his teaching duties, however, he left for Washington to plunge into the New Deal as a member of the legal staff of the Agricultural Adjustment Administration. William O. Douglas (also a future justice of the U.S. Supreme Court) called him from there to the Securities and Exchange Commission in 1934. During these years Fortas managed to hold his faculty position at Yale while participating in the whirlwind life of a New Dealer. In 1935 he married Carolyn Eugenia Agger, whom he had met while at Yale.

Fortas left academics in 1939, however, to work under the tutelage of Harold Ickes as general counsel of the Public Works Administration. The formidable Ickes was so impressed with Fortas' work that in 1942 he promoted him to be his undersecretary of the Department of the Interior. Fortas continued to serve in the Franklin Roosevelt administration throughout World War II. When the conflict ended, Fortas joined his former Yale law professor, Thurman Arnold, as a partner in the new firm of Arnold & Fortas, which was to become one of Washington, D.C.'s most successful and prominent law firms. Later his wife became one of the firm's partners. She and her husband had no children.

One of the many contacts Abe Fortas made during his New Deal years was with a young congressman from Texas, Lyndon Johnson. In 1948 he defended Johnson in a challenge to his Texas Democratic senatorial primary victory. This marked the beginning of Fortas' long friendship with Johnson. In 1964 LBJ won the presidency in his own right, after having completed the term of the assassinated John F. Kennedy. Fortas declined Johnson's offer to name him attorney general.

In 1965 President Johnson persuaded Justice Arthur J. Goldberg to accept an appointment to be the United States

criminal cases. Once on the Court, Fortas wrote the majority opinion for the 7:2 decision in *Tinker* v. *Des Moines Independent Community School District* (1969). The Court ruled that students have a right, under the First Amendment, to engage in peaceful, nondisruptive protest. The public school had banned the wearing of black armbands by students to protest the Vietnam War. The Court found that the armbands were not disruptive and that the school had violated the students' First Amendment rights, which protect the freedom of oral *and* symbolic speech.

In May of 1969 *LIFE* magazine charged Fortas with unethical behavior. The magazine revealed that in 1966 Fortas had received $20,000 from the family foundation of Louis Wolfson, an indicted stock manipulator. This was the first of what was to be a series of annual payments. Fortas had returned the money, however, and terminated the relationship. There was some talk of impeachment in Congress, and Fortas decided to resign from the Court on May 14, 1969. In his letter of resignation Fortas asserted his innocence and stated that he was leaving his position to allow the Court "to proceed with its work without the harassment of debate concerning one of its members." He returned to his private practice and died, at the age of 71, on April 5, 1982.

Further Reading

Kalman, Laura, *Abe Fortas: a biography,* New Haven: Yale University Press, 1990.
Murphy, Bruce Allen, *Fortas: the rise and ruin of a Supreme Court Justice,* New York: W. Morrow, 1988. □

Ambassador to the United Nations. On July 28, 1965, after two decades of private practice, Fortas was nominated by Johnson to replace Goldberg on the Supreme Court. LBJ's memoirs describe his reasons for nominating Fortas to be an associate justice: "I was confidant that the man [Fortas] would be a brilliant and able jurist. He had the experience and the liberalism to espouse the causes that both I and Arthur Goldberg believed in. He had the strength of character to stand up for his own convictions, and he was a humanitarian." Johnson was also interested in continuing the tradition of the Supreme Court's "Jewish seat." So, in all categories, Fortas was the perfect nominee. The Senate confirmed him by a voice vote on August 11, 1965.

In 1968 Chief Justice Earl Warren announced his decision to retire. Johnson had declared that he would not run in the November presidential election, but he sought to nominate Fortas to become chief justice before he left office. During the confirmation process, the U.S. Senate found that Fortas had counseled Johnson on national policy even after he had become a Supreme Court justice. It was also revealed that Fortas had received $15,000 to conduct a series of university seminars in the summer of 1968. In October of 1968 a filibuster in the Senate stalled Fortas' confirmation. Amid charges of cronyism from Democrats and Republicans, Johnson withdrew the nomination.

Even before his elevation to the Supreme Court Fortas had been a noted civil libertarian. In fact, the Supreme Court had appointed him as counsel for the indigent Clarence Earl Gideon, whose famous 1963 case of *Gideon* v. *Wainwright* set the precedent for the right to counsel in virtually all

James Forten

James Forten (1766-1842), one of America's most prominent black abolitionists, was also an inventor and entrepreneur and one of the wealthiest Americans of his day.

James Forten was born free in Philadelphia on Sept. 2, 1766. For a short time he attended a Quaker school, but at 14 he entered the Navy. During the American Revolution, Forten's patriotic zeal was illustrated when his ship was captured by a British frigate and he was taken prisoner. Because of his youth he was offered his freedom—in England. He replied: "I am here a prisoner for the liberties of my country. I never, *never* shall prove a traitor to her interests!"

After the Revolution, Forten was apprenticed to a sailmaker. He quickly mastered the trade, and by the time he was 20 he was a top sailmaker. Shortly thereafter he invented a device for the improved handling of sails and became the owner of his own sail loft. Soon he was the wealthiest black man in Philadelphia and one of the most affluent Americans of his time. His holdings were estimated at more than $100,000.

Forten used his money for humanitarian causes. He was a strong advocate of women's rights, temperance, and the freedom of African Americans who were still slaves. At first Forten thought the colonization of free blacks in Africa might be the best policy. He reasoned that they could "never become a people" until they were entirely free of the white majority. However, in 1817, when the issue was discussed in a public meeting in Philadelphia, Forten found the sentiments of the 3,000 free blacks who attended overwhelmingly against colonization. They were Americans, and they saw no reason why they should leave America, and Forten sensed that they were right. Subsequently he vigorously opposed the expatriation schemes of the Colonization Society, and he influenced William Lloyd Garrison and Theodore Weld to see that black people should be free—in America, their own homeland.

Forten is best known as an abolitionist, and he spent a good part of his fortune underwriting Garrison's fiery *Liberator*. But Forten was also a leading citizen of Philadelphia and highly respected by both races. He was president of the Moral Reform Society and was a leader in the "Convention movement," which was started in the 1830s to improve the circumstances of black Americans. He died on March 4, 1842.

Further Reading

The only full-length study of Forten is Esther M. Douty's book for young adults, *Forten, the Sailmaker: Pioneer Champion of Negro Rights* (1968), which leaves much to be desired. Forten is best seen in the context of his times in John Hope Franklin, *From Slavery to Freedom: A History of Negro Americans* (1947; 3d ed. rev. 1967). Wilhelmena S. Robinson, *Historical Negro Biographies* (1967; 2d ed. 1968), contains an account of Forten. See also William Loren Katz, *Eyewitness: The Negro in American History* (1967), and Ray Allen Billington, "James Forten: Forgotten Abolitionist," in August Meier and Elliott Rudwick, eds., *The Making of Black America: Essays in Negro Life and History* (2 vols., 1969). □

Timothy Thomas Fortune

Timothy Thomas Fortune (1856–1928) was one of the most prominent black journalists involved in the flourishing black press of the post-Civil War era.

Though not as well known today as many of his contemporaries, T. Thomas Fortune was the foremost African American journalist of the late nineteenth and early twentieth centuries. Using his editorial position at a series of black newspapers in New York City, Fortune established himself as a leading spokesman and defender of the rights of African Americans in both the South and the North.

Besides using his journalistic pulpit to demand equal economic opportunity for blacks and equal protection under the law, Fortune founded the Afro-American League, an equal rights organization that preceded the Niagara Move-

ment and the National Association for the Advancement of Colored People (NAACP), to extend this battle into the political arena. But his great hopes for the league never materialized, and he gradually began to abandon his militant position in favor of educator/activist Booker T. Washington's compromising, accommodationist stance. Fortune's later years, wracked by alcohol abuse, depression, and poverty, precipitated a decline in his once-prominent reputation as well.

Fortune was born a slave in Marianna, Florida, in 1856. Early in his boyhood he was exposed to the three factors that later dominated his life—journalism, white racism, and politics. After slavery was abolished in 1863, his father, Emanuel Fortune, went on to become a member of the 1868 Florida constitutional convention and the state's House of Representatives. Southern whites, resentful of black political participation, intimidated blacks through acts of violence; Jackson County, the Fortunes' hometown, witnessed some of the worst examples. Continued threats from the Ku Klux Klan forced the elder Fortune to move to Jacksonville, where he remained active in Florida politics until the 1890s.

Young Fortune became a page in the state Senate, observing firsthand some of the more sordid aspects of post-Civil War Reconstruction era politics, in particular white politicians who took advantage of black voters. He also preferred to spend his time hanging around the offices of various local newspapers rather than in school. As a result, when he left Florida in 1876 at the age of 19, his formal education consisted of only a few months spent in schools sponsored by the Freedmen's Bureau, but his informal education had trained him to be a printer's apprentice.

Fortune entered the preparatory department of Howard University in Washington, D.C. Lack of money limited his stay to one year, and he spent part of his time there working in the printshop of the *People's Advocate*, an early black newspaper. While in Washington he married his Florida sweetheart, Carrie Smiley. For the next two years he taught school and read voraciously on his own in literature, history, government, and law. Largely self-taught, he developed a distinctive writing and eloquent speaking style that few of his contemporaries could match.

Back in Florida, Fortune seethed under the South's racial intolerance, which seemed to increase after Reconstruction, the period of postwar transition during which the southern states were reintegrated into the Union. Leaving for good in 1881, he moved to New York City, working as a printer at the *New York Sun*. Soon he caught the attention of *Sun* editor Charles A. Dana, who promoted him to the editorial staff. But within the year Fortune left to follow in the footsteps of earlier black writers like John B. Russwurm and Frederick Douglass who had established their own newspapers to voice the black cause. Securing financial backing, he became editor and co-owner first of the weekly *New York Globe*, and then of the *New York Freeman*, which in 1887 was renamed the *New York Age*. It soon became the country's leading black newspaper.

Part of the reason for the papers' success was their high literary quality and Fortune's meticulous editing. More important, however, were their distinctive editorials written by his talented pen. Fortune's unabashed and indignant denunciations of American racism, as well as his reasoned arguments in favor of equal treatment and equality for blacks, made him the most influential black journalist in the United States.

Early on he summed up his viewpoint in an essay entitled "The Editor's Mission." Blacks must have a voice in deciding their own destiny, Fortune wrote, and not trust whites to define their "place." Since most of the northern and southern white press was opposed to equal rights, blacks needed their own newspapers to counter this influence. "The mark of color," he said, made the African American "a social pariah, to be robbed, beaten, and lynched," and one who "has got his own salvation to work out, of equality before the laws, with almost the entire population of the country arrayed against him." Leading this struggle was the special mission of the black editor.

Typical of his editorials was Fortune's scathing critique of the U.S. Supreme Court's 1883 decision, which declared the Civil Rights Act of 1875 unconstitutional. (The Civil Rights Act had guaranteed equal justice to all, regardless of race.) The ruling left blacks feeling as if they had been "baptized in ice water," he wrote. "We are declared to be created equal, and entitled to certain rights," but given the Court's interpretation "there is no law to protect us in the enjoyment of them. We are aliens in our own land."

The Militant Editor

Increasingly bitter over governmental failure to protect its black citizens, Fortune began to urge blacks not only to defend themselves with physical force, but also "to assert their manhood and citizenship" by striking back against white outrages. "We do not counsel violence," he wrote in a *Globe* editorial, "we counsel manly retaliation." Frequent similar remarks began to alarm both whites and cautious blacks, giving Fortune a growing reputation as a dangerous agitator.

Continuing his outspoken crusade against segregation and for equal rights, Fortune campaigned against racially separate schools in New York City. Occasionally he was arrested for protesting against racial discrimination in public accommodations. Typical of his denunciation of any form of racial distinction was his attack on antimiscegenation laws, which prohibited sexual relations between a man and a woman of different races, and his defense of the rights of persons of different racial backgrounds to marry. He also began popularizing the term "Afro-American" in contrast to the more popular use at the time of "colored" and "Negro."

The publication of *Black and White: Land, Labor and Politics in the South* in 1884 was the crowning effort of this radical phase of Fortune's career. Divided into two parts, the book first bitterly and eloquently rebuked American racism. Speaking firsthand, Fortune described the prejudices of white society, particularly in the current South where blacks "are more absolutely under the control of the southern whites; they are more systematically robbed of their labor; they are more poorly housed, clothed and fed, than under the slave regime."

In the book's second half, Fortune applied the theories of American economist Henry George and German political philosopher Karl Marx to southern society, portraying blacks as akin to peasant and laboring classes throughout the world. He predicted that the region's future battles would not be racial or political, but labor-based. Calling for organization and union between northern and southern laborers, black and white, he concluded that "the condition of the black and white laborer is the same, and . . . consequently their cause is common."

Redemption Through Politics

Though his primary roles remained those of editor and journalist, Fortune increasingly regarded political activity as indispensable to achieving his goal of equal rights for all. Black Americans would have to use their political rights to protect themselves and determine their own destiny. But his disillusionment with the existing political parties and skepticism of white politicians made this a tortuous path to chart or follow.

Unlike most African Americans of his era, Fortune held no special affinity for the Republican Party. While most black leaders and black newspapers felt a special allegiance to the party of Abraham Lincoln, Fortune denounced the Compromise of 1877, whereby the Republicans ended Reconstruction and sacrificed the constitutional rights of southern blacks to retain the presidency.

His 1885 pamphlet, *The Negro in Politics,* openly challenged Frederick Douglass's dictum that "the Republican Party is the ship, all else the open sea." Instead, Fortune decreed "Race first, then party!" Declaring that the Republicans had deserted their black supporters, he actively campaigned for Grover Cleveland, the Democratic presidential candidate, in 1888. But after Cleveland's defeat, he acknowledged that the southern-dominated Democratic party was hopelessly racist and grudgingly became a nominal Republican.

Afro-American League

Besides attempting to mobilize black Americans through the press and political action, Fortune proposed the creation of an Afro-American League. As set forth in an 1887 editorial, he envisioned a national all-black coalition of state and local chapters to assert equal rights and protest discrimination, disenfranchisement, lynching, and mob law.

In December of 1889, more than one hundred delegates from 23 states met in Chicago to organize the league. Their goal was attaining full citizenship and equality. Speaking as temporary chairman, Fortune declared, "We shall no longer accept in silence a condition which degrades manhood and makes a mockery of our citizenship."

Instead of the controversial Fortune, delegates elected a more conciliatory figure as league president: Joseph C. Price, president of Livingstone College. Fortune became the secretary. Despite his strenuous efforts to organize local chapters and raise funds, the league faltered. At its second convention in 1891, delegates came from only seven states. Hopes for a significant legal victory in a railroad discrimination case to publicize the organization and its mission were thwarted. Lack of funds and mass support caused the league to fold in 1893.

Five years later the idea was resurrected as the National Afro-American Council. Fortune now had doubts about such an organization and initially refused to accept its presidency. But he remained close to the group and became president in 1902. Like its predecessor, the council made few achievements. Fortune, discouraged over the seeming apathy of the black masses, resigned the presidency in 1904.

The Perils of Independent Thinking

After the death of Frederick Douglass in 1895, Fortune became the best known militant black spokesman in the North. But his crusading attitude and political independence exacted a toll. Most small newspapers of his era, white or black, depended upon political advertising and patronage as their main source of income. Black newspapers generally supported the Republican Party. When Fortune proudly trumpeted his independent political leanings, he effectively closed the door on Republican monetary support or advertising.

As a result, Fortune's papers faced recurring financial crises. Compelled to seek outside work, he frequently freelanced for his old paper, the *Sun,* and many other publications. Gradually he became dependent upon small sums from Booker T. Washington, the more pragmatic and conciliatory educator and black leader.

Alliance With Washington

Washington and Fortune seemingly made strange bedfellows. Apparent opposites—the former a soft-spoken accommodationist and the latter a militant agitator—in actuality, they were very good friends who corresponded almost daily throughout the 1890s. Their relationship was based on mutual affection, mutual self-interest, similar backgrounds, and the same ultimate goals for people of color. Born as slaves in the same year and growing up in the Reconstruction South, both men felt a deep obligation to their native region and a duty to improve the condition of southern blacks.

Like Washington, Fortune emphasized the importance of education and believed that practical vocational training was the immediate educational need for blacks as they emerged from slavery. He, too, counseled success through thrift, hard work, and the acquisition of land, believing that education and economic progress were necessary before blacks could attain full citizenship rights.

Although the two leaders played different roles and presented contrasting public images, their alliance was mutually useful. Fortune was editor of the leading black newspaper, and Washington needed the *Age* to present and defend his ideas and methods. Fortune also helped edit Washington's speeches and was the ghostwriter for books and articles appearing under his name, including *A New Negro for a New Century* and *The Negro in Business.*

Similarly, as Washington's reputation and influence grew, particularly in Republican circles, he could be a powerful friend. For years he secretly subsidized the *Age,* helping to keep it solvent. Fortune hoped for Washington's intercession with President Theodore Roosevelt for a permanent political appointment, but all he received was a temporary mission to the Philippines in 1903.

Fortune's dependency on Washington continued to grow. He bought an expensive house, Maple Hill, in Red Bank, New Jersey, in 1901. Its mortgage payments, added to the financial woes of the *Age,* compounded his monetary problems. As attacks mounted on Washington for his accommodationist methods, Fortune felt compelled to defend his friend. But Washington's more militant black critics, notably W. E. B. Du Bois and the leaders of the 1905 Niagara Movement, simply denounced Fortune as an untrustworthy, former "Afro-American agitator."

A new generation of black leaders was appearing, and Fortune's influence was beginning to wane. He broke with Washington and joined members of the Niagara Group in criticizing President Roosevelt's discharge of black troops following a riot in Brownsville, Texas, in 1906.

Declining Years

Needing Washington's support though ideologically drawn to his detractors, Fortune faced a crossroads: his life began to disintegrate. Disillusioned and discouraged after his long efforts on behalf of black America, he separated from his wife, increased his heavy drinking, and suffered what his contemporaries described as a nervous breakdown. Washington took control of the *Age* in 1907 by becoming one of the principal stockholders. Later that year Fortune sold his interest in the paper to Fred R. Moore, who became the new editor. This effectively ended Fortune's influence as a black leader.

Now a confirmed alcoholic, Fortune spent the next several years as a virtual derelict, unable to find steady employment. Desperate, he wrote a plaintive letter to Washington's secretary in 1913 asking: "What am I to do? The Negro papers are not able to pay for extra work and the daily papers do not care for Negro productions of any kind. Under such circumstances I face the future with $5 in hand and 57 years as handicap."

From time to time he found work as an editorial writer and correspondent for the *Age* and the *Amsterdam News.* He edited the *Washington Sun* for a few months before it folded. Slowly he recovered. In 1919 he joined the staff of the *Norfolk Journal and Guide,* continuing to write commentaries and editorials for the rest of his life. He became editor of *Negro World,* black nationalist leader Marcus Garvey's publication, in 1923, remaining there until his death in 1928.

In "The Quick and the Dead," an article published soon after Washington's death, Fortune attempted to evaluate his own role as a black leader. He praised his early crusading efforts for civil rights as editor and then organizer of the Afro-American League, attributing his failure to apathy and lack of support in the black community.

Many critics agree that it was all but impossible for anyone to achieve the ambitious goals Fortune had set given the climate of the times in which he lived. And when he abandoned his militant ideology to promote Washington's more accommodationist methods, Fortune destroyed his own credibility as a leader—and his personal integrity as well. This was something he could not live with, and it seemed to destroy him. As Emma Lou Thornbrough wrote in her biography *T. Thomas Fortune: Militant Journalist,* "Unable to bend as Washington had, he was broken."

Further Reading

Fortune, T. Thomas, *Black and White: Land, Labor and Politics in the South,* Arno Press, 1968.
Franklin, John Hope and August Meier, editors, *Black Leaders of the 20th Century,* University of Illinois Press, 1981.
Franklin, John Hope, *From Slavery to Freedom: A History of Negro Americans,* Alfred A. Knopf, 1947.
Thornbrough, Emma Lou, *T. Thomas Fortune: Militant Journalist,* University of Chicago Press, 1972. □

Ugo Foscolo

The Italian author Ugo Foscolo (1778-1827) was a poet, critic, and dramatist as well as a patriot. His romantic temperament and flamboyant life characterize his role as a key transitional figure in Italian literary history.

Born Niccolò Foscolo on the Greek island of Zante on Feb. 6, 1778, he soon adopted the pseudonym Ugo. Well educated in philosophy, classics, and Italian literature, in 1792 Foscolo moved to Venice, where he immediately became embroiled in the struggle for independence. After writing "Ode to Bonaparte the Liberator" (1797), Foscolo began a life of exile, during which he fought against Austria, first in Venice, then in Romagna, in Genoa, and even in France (1804-1806).

Concurrent with his military exploits, Foscolo gave literary expression to his ideological aspirations and to the numerous amorous experiences of these years in odes, sonnets, plays, the epistolary novel *The Last Letters of Jacopo Ortis* (1802), and the long poem *On Tombs* (1807). As professor of rhetoric at Padua (1809), Foscolo espoused in his lectures the view—new in Italy—that poetic beauty arose from the fusion of imitation with the genius of the individual creator.

Banished for his anti-French drama *Aiace* (1811), Foscolo went to Florence, where he completed his translation of Laurence Sterne's *Sentimental Journey* and wrote his third tragedy, *Ricciarda.* He also worked assiduously on *The Graces;* although never given final form, these fragmentary hymns, characterized by delicate musical and plastic sensibility, represent Foscolo's best lyric poetry. In 1815 Foscolo fled to Zurich, where he republished *Ortis* and composed several works against those Italians receptive to foreign occupation. The next year Foscolo went to London, where

he authored critical essays, reworked *Ortis* and *The Graces,* and participated actively in British literary society until his death at Turnham Green near London on Sept. 10, 1827. In 1871 the transfer of his remains to Sta Croce in Florence conferred upon Foscolo a well-deserved place among the other great Italians entombed there.

Ortis and *On Tombs* best exemplify the major themes of Foscolo's works: the search for glory, beauty which restores serenity to man's turbulent life, patriotic exile and its attendant loss of liberty, and the inspirational value of tombs of illustrious men. The later versions of *Ortis* portray the life of Jacopo, driven from his Venetian home by foreign occupation. Disappointed by unfulfilled love and comforted only by the sight of tombs dedicated to great Italians, Jacopo commits suicide, thus terminating his lonely struggle against tyranny and hypocrisy. *On Tombs,* written after Napoleon had prohibited funereal monuments, is also strongly autobiographical and didactic. Animated by rich imagery and lyrical language, it also stresses the inspirational value of tombs and the pain of exile.

Foscolo's vitality and unflagging quest for freedom account for his immense popularity during subsequent Italian struggles for unification and independence.

Further Reading

The only full-length studies of Foscolo in English concern his stay and activities in England: E.R. Vincent, *Byron, Hobhouse, and Foscolo: New Documents in the History of Collaboration* (1949) and *Ugo Foscolo: An Italian in Regency England* (1953). □

Harry Emerson Fosdick

Harry Emerson Fosdick (1878-1969), American preacher, was a popular exponent of liberal Protestantism and a key figure in the struggle to relate the Christian community to its contemporary technological and urbanized culture.

Harry Emerson Fosdick was born in Buffalo, N.Y., on May 24, 1878, the son of a high school teacher. Reared to traditional religious sympathies, Fosdick questioned his faith while in college. By the time he graduated from Colgate University in 1900, his new religious views rejected biblical literalism in favor of "modernist" theological attitudes that coincided with the emerging scientific world view currently sweeping America.

Fosdick entered Union Theological Seminary in New York City to prepare for the ministry. A center of theological liberalism even at this early date, the seminary further confirmed his new religious commitments. After graduation in 1903, his first pastorate was in a Baptist church in Montclair, N.J. During his 11 years there, Fosdick advocated liberal views, both in the pulpit and in published articles. He also perfected a pastoral and preaching technique that made him a model minister for a generation of churchmen.

Fosdick first attracted national attention for his role in the fundamentalist-modernist controversy of the 1920s. Politician William Jennings Bryan and conservative churchmen attacked him, especially after a sermon in 1922 entitled "Shall the Fundamentalists Win?" Efforts to remove Fosdick from the Presbyterian church in New York City where he was then minister were ultimately successful. The imbroglio led one of Fosdick's most famous parishioners, John D. Rockefeller, Jr., to initiate the proposals that led to the establishment of a large, nonsectarian church where Fosdick would be the principal minister. Here, at Riverside Church, Fosdick's congregation became one of the most famous Protestant groups in the nation. Dedicated in 1931, the church provided for Fosdick's preaching a weekly forum until his retirement in 1946. The church symbolized his belief in interracial unity and a nonsectarian, ecumenical approach to church life.

Fosdick sought to adapt Christianity to the increasingly sophisticated urban milieu, stressing the intellectual respectability possible in Christian teachings and repudiating the theological obscurantism that had served as the basis of much popular, evangelical Protestantism in the 19th century. Fosdick was a prolific publicist, publishing 40 volumes in all. He preached to a nationwide audience each week on radio, and he influenced a generation of fledgling ministers as professor of homiletics at Union Seminary. Relatively undoctrinaire, he was capable of seeing the flaws in his own

religious perspective, as evidenced in a sermon, "The Church Must Go beyond Modernism."

A supporter of America's intervention in World War I, Fosdick had become a thoroughgoing pacifist by the time of World War II. Above all, his sermons dealt with contemporary problems. He was perhaps the most widely known and respected preacher of his generation.

Further Reading

Fosdick's sprightly autobiography, *The Living of These Days* (1956), describes his career up to the mid-1950s.

Additional Sources

Miller, Robert Moats, *Harry Emerson Fosdick: preacher, pastor, prophet,* New York: Oxford University Press, 1985. ☐

Bob Fosse

Legendary director/choreographer Bob Fosse (1927–1987) is known for hits such as *Sweet Charity,* with its trademark jazzy number, "Hey Big Spender," and *Cabaret.*

Bob Fosse began his unusual career as a dancer in the late 1940s, touring with companies of *Call Me Mister* and *Make Mine Manhattan.* After playing the lead in a summer-stock production of *Pal Joey,* then choreographing a showcase called *Talent 52,* Fosse was given a screen test by M-G-M and went on to appear in the film *Kiss Me Kate* (1953). This appearance, in a highly original dance number, led to Fosse's first job as a choreographer, the Jerome Robbins-directed Broadway hit *The Pajama Game* (1954). Soon after, he met the talented dancer Gwen Verdon, and the two proceeded to collaborate on several hit shows, including *Damn Yankees* (1955, film 1958), *New Girl in Town* (1957), and *Redhead* (1959). (Fosse and Verdon married soon after.) He was also frequently sought out as the "doctor" on shows in trouble, especially *How to Succeed in Business Without Really Trying* and *Little Me* (both 1962).

Choreography Showcased Unique Style

Fosse's best collaboration with Verdon, *Sweet Charity* (1966, film 1969), demonstrated their perfect compatibility as a creative team and also flaunted his trademark style as a choreographer. Strongly influenced by choreographer Jack Cole, Fosse staged dance numbers that were highly stylized, using staccato movements and erotic suggestion. The "Steam Heat" number from *The Pajama Game* and "Hey Big Spender" from *Sweet Charity* were trademark Fosse numbers—jazzy, machinelike motion and cocky, angular, even grotesque poses. He favored style over substance (his patented knee slides and spread-finger hands), and minimalistic costuming (all black, accentuated by hats and gloves). A perfectionist, Fosse liked detail in his choreography and would position his dancers down to the

murderess Roxie Hart. *Chicago* was a cynical, stylized homage to 1920s-era burlesque and vaudeville. In the fascinating but disturbing film *All That Jazz* (1979), he used the heart attack (including a filmed bypass operation) to kill off the main character, an obsessive, womanizing, workaholic director clearly based on Fosse. His other 1970s stage musical was the innovative *Dancin'* (1978), which featured three acts constructed purely of dance numbers, eliminating story, song, and characters.

Fosse's work in the 1980s received mixed responses. His film *Star 80* (1983) explored the violent, obsessive relationship between Playboy-model-turned-actress Dorothy Stratten and Paul Snider, the husband who brutally murdered her in 1980. Audiences and critics did not respond to the tough, gruesome subject matter. Nor did they appear to enjoy the jazz ballet *Big Deal* (1986), Fosse's last Broadway show. A revival of *Sweet Charity* in 1986 was more successful, but just as the touring company was about to be launched, Fosse died of a heart attack on 23 September 1987.

Further Reading

Martin Gottfried, *All His Jazz: The Life and Death of Bob Fosse* (New York: Bantam Books, 1990).
Kevin Boyd Grubb, *Razzle Dazzle: The Life and Work of Bob Fosse* (New York: St. Martin's Press, 1989). □

Dian Fossey

Dian Fossey (1932-1985) was the world's leading authority on the mountain gorilla before her murder, probably at the hands of poachers, in December of 1985.

Dian Fossey's short life was characterized in equal parts by tragedy, controversy, and extraordinary courage and dedication to the animals she made her life work. That dedication drew her back to Africa over and over despite broken bones, failing health, and threats to her life. All and all, she spent 18 years studying the mountain gorillas and working for their survival as a species.

An unlikely chain of circumstances led Fossey to study the mountain gorilla and to her eventual demise high in the fog enshrouded mountains of eastern Africa. Born in San Francisco on January 16, 1932, Fossey was fascinated with animals from an early age. She entered the University of California at Davis to study pre-veterinary medicine but found it difficult to master courses in chemistry and physics. Instead she completed a B.A. in 1954 from San Jose State University in occupational therapy. In 1956 she took a job at Kosair Crippled Children's Hospital in Louisville, Kentucky, where she could pursue her interest in horses during her free time.

In 1963 Fossey obtained a bank loan for $8,000, took a leave from her job as a physical therapist, and went to Africa to seek out paleontologist Louis Leakey, who had mentored

angles of their feet or their little fingers. As his career progressed, Fosse became increasingly fascinated with expressing sexuality and decadence through dance.

Had Hit with *Cabaret*

Fosse's peak year was 1973. In addition to his *Cabaret* Oscar, he nabbed Tonys for his direction and choreography of the Broadway musical *Pippin*, the eerily magical and sexually decadent story of the son of King Charlemagne on a journey of self-discovery. Like *Cabaret* , *Pippin* featured exaggerated, grotesque makeup and costuming and erotic dance numbers. Fosse's experiment—to place the story and music at the service of choreography—paid off when *Pippin* (helped by a television advertising campaign) became Fosse's longest-running Broadway show. That same year he won an Emmy for directing and choreographing Minnelli's television special *Liza with a Z,* which garnered high ratings and featured groundbreaking production numbers. In 1973 Fosse seemed to be everywhere.

Heart Attack Led to Autobiographical Film

In *Lenny* (1974), an exploration of the life of controversial comic Lenny Bruce, Fosse experimented with a mock-documentary filmmaking style. He identified with Bruce's attempt to liberate inhibited audiences with shocking and challenging material. Fosse suffered a heart attack while editing *Lenny* and rehearsing the successful Broadway musical *Chicago* (1975), which starred Verdon as notorious

Jane Goodall in her pioneering work with chimpanzees. She hoped that Leakey could help her find a job studying gorillas. Later in her life Fossey explained this change in her life course by saying that she felt extraordinarily drawn to Africa and particularly to the mountain gorillas of Rwanda and Zaire (now Congo). This interest was fueled in part by reading the work of George Schaller, who had spent 1959 doing the first comprehensive study of these animals.

Fossey appeared at Leakey's dig site at Olduvai Gorge in Tanzania without an invitation. He mistook her for a tourist and charged a fee to view the excavation. Despite this inauspicious beginning, Fossey clearly made an impression. Nearly six feet tall, with long black hair and a husky voice—the result of chain smoking—she must have been a startling apparition. While walking through the site, she tripped and fell, breaking her ankle and a newly excavated fossil in the process. Leakey's wife Mary bound up her ankle and she proceeded onwards to the mountains of Zaire (now Congo), where she caught her first glimpse of the mountain gorilla.

Her funds exhausted, Fossey returned to Louisville and to her job. In 1966 it was Leakey who sought her out. He wanted her to study the gorillas on a long-term basis and had found a patron who would support the research. Leakey was interested in studies of primates because he believed their behavior would shed light on the behavior of the early hominids whose fossilized bones he was excavating at Olduvai Gorge. He believed that Fossey would be an ideal person to carry out the study because of her intense interest and because he thought that women were more patient and better observers than men and, therefore, made better naturalists.

Fossey accepted Leakey's invitation eagerly. Since she had no formal training she made a brief stop at Jane Goodall's research center at Gombe to learn Goodall's revolutionary methods of fieldwork and data collection. She then proceeded onward to Schaller's old camp in Congo.

The gorillas that Fossey was to study inhabit a narrow strip of forest that covers the sides of several extinct volcanoes on the borders between Rwanda, Congo, and Uganda. Much of their habitat is rain forest at an altitude of 10,000 feet or more. The mountain gorillas can be distinguished from other types of gorillas partly by their adaptions to the climate and altitude: thick coats, broad chests, and large hands and feet. Mature males stand between five and six feet when upright and far outweigh a human being of equivalent size.

Fossey's research in Congo was interrupted July 10, 1967, when she was held for two weeks by soldiers. After escaping from her captors, she relocated to the Rwanda side of the mountains in the Parc National des Vulcans. This would become the Karasoke Research Center where she would carry out her work for the next 17 years.

At Karasoke Fossey studied 51 gorillas in four relatively stable groups. Despite their menacing appearance, Fossey found the gorillas to be quite shy and retiring. She gained their trust through quiet and patient observation and by imitating the gorillas' behavior until she could sit amongst them and could move about or touch the animals without frightening them.

When Fossey first began her research, the number of these gorillas was less than 500 and rapidly diminishing due to the encroachment of farmers and predation from poachers. She was particularly distressed by the practice of killing an entire group of adult gorillas in order to obtain young gorillas to be sold to zoos. In 1978, after the death of Digit, one of her most beloved silverback males, she began taking up unconventional means to protect the gorillas from poachers and from encroaching cattle farmers. She held poachers prisoner, torturing them or frightening them or kidnapping their children, with the idea that this would give them a sense of what gorillas were experiencing at their hands.

On December 24, 1985, Fossey was killed in her cabin at Karasoke, her skull split by a *panga,* the type of large knife used by poachers. Her murderer has not been identified.

Further Reading

Fossey has described her own work in *Gorillas in the Mist* (1983). A film of the same name was released in 1988 starring Sigourney Weaver. Biographical information can be found in Farley Mowat's *Woman in the Mists* (1987), Sy Montgomery's *Walking with the Great Apes* (1991), and Donna Haraway's *Primate Visions* (1989). Fossey also wrote a number of articles for *National Geographic Magazine* . Additional information on gorillas can be found in Allan Goodall's *The Wandering Gorillas* (1979) and Michael Nichols' *Struggle for Survival in the Virungas* (1989). □

Abigail Kelley Foster

American reformer Abigail Kelley Foster (1810-1887) was a pioneer in the abolitionist movement and contributed to the developing suffragist principles of her time.

The daughter of Irish Quakers, Abby Kelley was born in Pelham, Mass., on Jan. 15, 1810. She was raised in Worcester and educated at the Friends' School in Providence, R.I. She became a schoolteacher and showed gifts of eloquence and public presence. Abolitionists William Lloyd Garrison and Theodore D. Weld urged her to join their cause. In 1837 she became an antislavery lecturer—the first woman to do so after the Grimké sisters, and the first woman to face mixed and often hostile audiences under the same conditions as men.

Though denounced and ridiculed, Kelley entered alien environments in Connecticut and Pennsylvania, meeting antagonism with oratorical power and a firm grasp of her subject. As a symbol of Garrisonian extremism, she roused criticism among moderate abolitionists who were outraged by Garrison's determination to involve women in decision making. At the 1840 annual meeting of the American Anti-Slavery Society in New York, Kelley was elected to the business committee. At this point the moderates withdrew to form the rival American and Foreign Anti-Slavery Society.

In 1845 Miss Kelley married Stephen Symonds Foster. He too had endured many mob actions, was noted for his denunciations of slavery, and had authored *The Brotherhood of Thieves: A True Picture of the American Church and Clergy* (1843). The couple was honored by James Russell Lowell in his "Letter from Boston" (1846). Lowell, like others, had noticed the contrast between their personal mildness and decorum and the violent language they employed in public address.

Such was Abby's reputation that as late as 1850 the managers of the Woman's Rights Convention doubted whether she should be allowed onto the platform. When she appeared, she began with the words, "Sisters, bloody feet have worn smooth the path by which you come here!"

The Fosters settled on a farm near Worcester and, though engaged in rural pursuits, maintained their war against social discriminations. They refused to pay taxes to a state which deprived Abby of her right to the vote, and twice they had their property sold at auction to satisfy that debt. The friends who purchased back the farm for them were ultimately reimbursed. Their last cause was in helping get passage of the 15th Amendment to the Constitution, which gave the vote to former slaves, though not to women. Abby, surviving her husband, died on Jan. 14, 1887.

Further Reading

Information on Abby Foster is in Inez H. Irwin, *Angels and Amazons: A Hundred Years of American Women* (1933); Lillian O'Connor, *Pioneer Women Orators: Rhetoric in the Ante-Bellum Reform Movement* (1954); and Alma Lutz, *Crusade for Freedom: Women of the Antislavery Movement* (1968). □

Stephen Collins Foster

The American composer Stephen Collins Foster (1826-1864) was one of the first professional songwriters in the country, and his minstrel tunes, particularly, were among the most successful songs of the era just before the Civil War.

Stephen Foster was born in Lawrenceville, Pa., near Pittsburgh, on July 4, 1826. His father had settled in Pittsburgh when it was still a frontier settlement; later he became a successful businessman. Stephen's mother was the daughter of an aristocratic family from Delaware. The youngest of the children, Stephen was loved by his family, who nevertheless failed to understand either his artistic temperament or his dreaming, indolent ways. The boy attended schools around Pittsburgh and Allegheny and later enrolled in the academies at Athens and Towanda. But he was interested neither in schooling nor in business. He tried a number of occupations, but none with much enthusiasm.

Young Composer

Stephen early displayed a musical talent, which his family persistently failed to take seriously. (In 19th-century America, music was viewed as an essential part of a young lady's upbringing but not a profession for middle-class boys.) About the age of 10 he began composing tunes, and at 17 he wrote his first published song, "Open Thy Lattice, Love," in several respects typical of the sentimental parlor songs he would produce over the next 20 years. Well suited to the genteel tastes of the time, this song is in the manner of an English air, with touches of Irish and Scottish songs.

Foster was sent to Cincinnati in 1846 to serve as bookkeeper for his brother's steamboat company. He disliked the work almost immediately, continued writing tunes, and soon met a music publisher. Four of Foster's songs, including "Old Uncle Ned" and "Oh! Susanna," which he sold for practically nothing, made so much profit for the publisher that Foster determined to make song writing his profession. He returned to Pittsburgh to enjoy his most productive years. As time went by and as his introspective disposition became more apparent, his songs became increasingly melancholic and lost much of the spontaneous fun and rollicking good humor of the earlier tunes.

Connection with Minstrelsy

While living along the Ohio River, Foster came in contact with the blackface minstrelsy so popular in pre-Civil War America. Many of the composer's best-known songs were written for the minstrel stage, although Foster actually preferred more polite, parlor ballads. For several years E. P. Christy, of the famous Christy Minstrels, had the official right to introduce Foster's songs, and at the composer's

suggestion Christy took credit for "Old Folks at Home." Since there was public prejudice against African American tunes of this type, Foster initially sought to keep his name in the background. By 1852, however, he wrote Christy, "I have concluded to reinstate my name on my songs and to pursue the Ethiopian business without fear or shame." The composer entered into a publishing agreement with Firth, Pond and Company in 1849 which granted him standard royalties. Over the next 11 years Foster's total earnings from his songs slightly exceeded $15,000, most of this from sheet music sales. Always a poor businessman, the musician never realized the full commercial potential of his best music.

Domestic Life

On July 22, 1850, Foster married Jane Denny Mc-Dowell, daughter of a Pittsburgh physician. The couple lived for several years with Foster's parents and had one daughter. The marriage was plagued with difficulties, mainly resulting from Foster's impractical nature. In 1853, for unknown reasons, Foster left his wife and went to New York City. A year later the family was reunited for a few months in Hoboken, N.J. In October 1854 Foster took his wife and child back to Pennsylvania, leaving them again in 1860, when publishing ventures returned him to New York. He remained in New York, part of the time with his wife and daughter, until his death in 1864. At the time of his death he was living alone at the American Hotel. Taken with fever, he arose after several days of illness and fell, cutting himself on the washbasin and lying unconscious until discovered by a

chambermaid. He was taken to a hospital, where he died on Jan. 13, 1864, weakened by fever and loss of blood.

His Nostalgia

Foster's tragic life was punctuated with financial and personal disasters. The gradual disintegration of his character almost literally ended him in the gutter. That he loved his home is indicated in his songs, for he probably reached his greatest heights as a poet of homesickness. Yet he was never able to achieve the domestic solidarity he longed for. His love songs are less plausible, mingling love with nostalgia, while the sweethearts of his lyrics are almost always unattainable, either dead or distant. The poet dwells on them only in memory. In "I Dream of Jeanie with the Light Brown Hair" (1854) Jeanie is gone, and in "Beautiful Dreamer," his last love song (copyrighted in 1864), the love object is asleep. A few of Foster's nonsense songs have obtained lasting popularity because of their vital melodies. "Oh! Susanna" became the theme song of the forty-niners on their trek to California, and "De Camptown Races" with its "doodah" chant remains a perennial favorite.

View of the South

Foster's primary fame rests on his songs of the antebellum South, and taken song for song, these remain his best. At the time "Old Folks at Home" was written, the composer had never been south of the Ohio River, except, possibly, on visits to Kentucky. The name "Swanee River" was found on a map; Foster thought it sounded better than the "Pedee River" he originally intended. The musician's concept of African American life was gained principally from childhood visits to black church services and from minstrel shows. Not until 1852 did Foster make a brief trip through the plantation South on a visit to New Orleans with his wife. Certainly the African American element in his songs is slight, essentially shaped by the white man's sentimentalized notions of African American character. While Foster was an avowed Democrat and an opponent of abolition, his song "My Old Kentucky Home" was originally entitled "Poor Uncle Tom, Good Night" and bears certain similarities to Harriet Beecher Stowe's book *Uncle Tom's Cabin.* The song pictures happy "darkies," who when "hard times comes a-knocking at the door" have to part, as they are sent "where the head must bow and the back will have to bend." "Old Black Joe" (1860) reflects this same unrealistic view of blacks before the Civil War—a view widely held among Northern whites. Aside from his own sentimentality, Foster was writing for a market, and he produced songs to appeal to blackface minstrels.

Worth as a Composer

Foster's strength as a composer lay in his gift for poignant melody; some of his simplest tunes are among his finest. Since he had little formal training as a musician, his compositions sprang far more from his heart than from his mind and even occasionally fell into amateurishness. Pressed by financial considerations, he was never able to cultivate a musicianship of subtlety or depth. He was nevertheless adept enough to harmonize his tunes instinctively in a manner consistent with their overall mood—that is, quite directly and simply, allowing the melody to predominate. In this regard he has been compared with the Austrian composer Franz Schubert. Yet, unlike many of the professional musicians of the seaboard cities of the early United States, Foster did not imitate foreign models. The influences shaping his music were predominantly American, and therefore his tunes are perhaps as native as any produced in the United States during the early 19th century. At the same time Foster's songs are fundamentally human and are of fairly universal appeal. One American writer of the day, reporting on his visit to the Orient in 1853, said that he had heard ''Oh! Susanna'' sung by a Hindu musician in Delhi.

Foster composed over 200 songs. Approximately 150 were parlor songs; about 30 were written for minstrel shows. Of far lesser quality were his religious hymns published in 1863. Foster also wrote occasional pieces such as ''Santa Anna's Retreat from Buena Vista,'' a quick-step for piano. Although his songs have often been spoken of loosely as folk music, in their sentimentality and nostalgia they reflect the temperament and character of their composer and fall more accurately into the category of popular art.

Further Reading

The standard biography of Foster is John Tasker Howard, *Stephen Foster, America's Troubador* (1934; rev. ed. 1953). The serious researcher will find Evelyn Foster Morneweck, *Chronicles of Stephen Foster's Family* (2 vols., 1944), indispensable. Foster's participation in politics is satisfactorily covered in Fletcher Hodges, *Stephen Foster, Democrat* (1946). Interesting sections on Foster may be found in Gilbert Chase, *America's Music: From the Pilgrims to the Present* (1955; 2d ed. 1966), and Wilfrid Mellers, *Music in a New Found Land* (1964). Recommended for general historical background are Carl F. Wittke, *Tambo and Bones: A History of the American Minstrel Stage* (1930), the classic study of minstrelsy, but with no particular reference to Foster's music; and E. Douglas Branch, *The Sentimental Years, 1836-1860* (1934).

Additional Sources

Milligan, Harold Vincent, *Stephen Collins Foster: a biography of America's folk-song composer,* New York: Gordon Press, 1977, 1920. □

William Zebulon Foster

William Zebulon Foster (1881-1961), a leading figure in the Communist Party of the United States for 4 decades, was the patriarch of American communism.

Born in Taunton, Mass., the son of a poor railroad worker, William Foster grew up in a Philadelphia slum. He started working at the age of 7; at 17 he was a migrant laborer. For 20 years he traveled America and much of the world, working at a variety of frequently brutal jobs. These experiences made him a thoroughgoing radical.

Expelled from the Socialist party because of his extreme views, in 1909 Foster joined the revolutionary Industrial Workers of the World, working as a pamphleteer and agitator. He also formed short-lived syndicalist and workers educational leagues and helped organize packing house workers during World War I.

Foster gained national prominence as the leading organizer in the steel strike of 1919, which crippled much of America's economy for months and further intensified the antiradical hysteria that swept the country in the aftermath of the war and the Bolshevik Revolution in Russia. For many Foster came to symbolize the ''Red menace.'' In 1921, after attending the Red International of Labor Unions in Moscow in behalf of his own newly formed Trade Union Educational League, Foster and his aide, Earl Browder, joined the underground American Communist party. In 1922 the U.S. government charged Foster with criminal syndicalism in connection with his secret Communist activities; his trial ended in a hung jury. Two years later, when the Communist party surfaced to merge with the legal Workers party, he became the first Communist candidate for president of the United States. He ran in the next two presidential elections.

Foster and those who favored militant anticapitalism won control of the Communist party in 1929. But soon, plagued by poor health, Foster relinquished to Browder his post of general secretary and assumed the party chairmanship. Bedridden during most of the 1930s, Foster watched the party, on orders from the Stalin regime, swing from anticapitalism to close collaboration with non-Communist liberals and radicals in a ''popular front'' against fascism.

He dutifully endorsed each policy change: from official neutralism to support for American democracy. By 1945 the Browder-led party, as a result of its cooperation in the American war effort, enjoyed the largest membership and greatest influence in its history. Then Moscow returned to hard-line, revolutionary Marxism-Leninism, and Browder was ousted not only from his party post but even from party membership. Foster, ever the faithful party man, again became the head of the American Communist movement.

The emergence of incessant Soviet-American international rivalry in the years after World War II created an increasingly hostile climate for the Communist party in America. Foster held his dominant position as thousands of Communists quit the party. Even more quit after Stalin's death in 1953, the "thaw" in Soviet-American relations, the revelations of Stalinist terrors, and the brutal crushing of the Hungarian rebellion.

Foster and his supporters kept the party in close conformance with Moscow's wishes, but membership shrank to less than 3,000 by 1958. By that time Foster, seriously ill, was virtually inactive. After a protracted legal contest with the U.S. State Department, he secured permission to travel to the Soviet Union for medical treatment. Foster died in Moscow on Sept. 1, 1961, and was given a state funeral.

Further Reading

Two of Foster's autobiographical works are *From Bryan to Stalin* (1937) and *Pages from a Worker's Life* (1939). Also vital for understanding his career in the Communist party are Theodore Draper, *The Roots of American Communism* (1957) and *American Communism and Soviet Russia: The Formative Period* (1960); Irving Howe and Lewis Coser, *The American Communist Party: A Critical History, 1919-1957* (1957); and David A. Shannon, *The Decline of American Communism* (1959).

Additional Sources

Foster, William Z., *More pages from a worker's life,* New York: American Institute for Marxist Studies, 1979.

Johanningsmeier, Edward P., *Forging American communism: the life of William Z. Foster,* Princeton, N.J.: Princeton University Press, 1994.

Zipser, Arthur, *Workingclass giant: the life of William Z. Foster,* New York: International Publishers, 1981. □

Jean Bernard Léon Foucault

The French physicist Jean Bernard Léon Foucault (1819-1868) is remembered for the Foucault pendulum, by which he demonstrated the diurnal rotation of the earth, and for the first accurate determination of the velocity of light.

Léon Foucault, son of a Paris bookseller, was born on Sept. 18, 1819. He began to study medicine but turned to physics, probably as a result of becoming assistant to Alfred Donné, who was developing a pho-

toengraving process by etching daguerreotypes in connection with his anatomy lectures. This brought Foucault contact with the physicist Hippolyte Fizeau, who was at that time attempting to improve the daguerreotype process, and they collaborated for several years on optical topics. From 1845 Foucault was editor of the scientific section of the *Journal de débats*. In 1855 he was appointed physicist at the Paris Observatory; in 1864 he was elected a foreign member of the Royal Society of London; and in 1865 he became a member of the Académie des Sciences.

Rotating Frames of Reference

Foucault's first important experimental demonstration was of the earth's rotation, for which he used a pendulum. The plane of motion of a freely suspended simple pendulum appears to rotate; in fact, it is spatially fixed while the earth rotates. Foucault published his account of this in 1851, together with an equation connecting the apparent angular rotation of the pendulum's plane with the angular velocity of the earth and the latitude of the place of the experiment. It created great interest, and the experiment, readily repeatable with simple apparatus, was, and still is, frequently performed in public. In 1852 Foucault gave a further demonstration of the earth's rotation with a freely mounted gyroscope and derived some laws describing its behavior. These experiments, in combination with earlier theoretical work by Gustave Coriolis, led to a clearer understanding of rotating frames of reference. For his work Foucault was awarded the Copley Medal of the Royal Society in 1855.

Determining the Velocity of Light

In 1850 Foucault joined the debate over the then-competing particle and wave theories of light. D. F. J. Arago had demonstrated in 1838 that a crucial test could be made by comparing the velocities of light in air and in a dense medium, and he was experimenting to determine the velocity of light with a rotating-mirror method devised by Charles Wheatstone in 1834. Lack of success and ill health led Arago to pass the task on to Foucault in 1850. Success came in the same year, when Foucault observed a retardation of the velocity of light in water, giving support to the wave theory. He then saw how the rotating-mirror method could be refined to measure the absolute velocity of light in a restricted space. Foucault overcame the technical problems and in 1862 obtained a value of 2.98×10^{10} centimeters per second, the first accurate measure of this fundamental physical constant.

From 1855, as physicist at the Imperial Observatory, Foucault worked to improve the design of telescopes. As a member of the Bureau of Longitudes from 1862 he improved certain surveying instruments, particularly the centrifugal governor, which aided timekeeping in the use of field-transit instruments. The 1860s saw Foucault turning toward precision engineering and electricity, but he was incapacitated by a stroke in July 1867 and died in Paris on Feb. 11, 1868.

Foucault's ability to recognize fruitful lines of research, so sadly lacking in many of his contemporary countrymen, was combined with an experimental ability of the first order. His early death was a great loss to French science.

Further Reading

One of Foucault's experimental findings is reprinted in Harlow Shapley and Helen E. Howarth, *A Source Book in Astronomy* (1929). For general background see Henry Smith Williams, *The Great Astronomers* (1930). □

Michel Foucault

The French philosopher, critic, and historian Michel Foucault (1926-1984) was an original and creative thinker who made contributions to historiography and to understanding the forces that make history.

Michel Foucault was born on October 15, 1926, in Pottiers, France, the son of Paul (a doctor) and Anne (Malapert) Foucault. He studied at the Ecole Normale Superieure and at the University of Paris, Sorbonne, where he received his diploma in 1952. He served as director of the Institut Francais in Hamburg and held academic posts at the Universities of Clermont-Ferrand and Paris-Vincennes. In 1970 he became professor and chairman of the History of Systems of Thought at the College de France. A creative thinker, Foucault made substantial contributions to philosophy, history, literary criticism, and, specifically, to theoretical work in the human sciences. Often depicted as a "structuralist," a designation he disavowed, Foucault had something of a following among French intellectuals. He died from a neurological disorder on June 25, 1984, cutting short a brilliant career.

Foucault was known for tracing the development of Western civilization, particularly in its attitudes towards sexuality, madness, illness, and knowledge. His late works insisted that forms of discourse and institutional practices are implicated in the exercise of power. His works can be read as a new interpretation of power placing emphasis on what happens or is done and not on human agency—that is, he sought to explore the conditions that give rise to forms of discourse and knowledge. Foucault was particularly concerned with the rise of the modern stress on human self-consciousness and the image of the human as maker of history. He argued that the 20th century is marked by "the disappearance of man" because history is now seen as the product of objective forces and power relations limiting the need to make the human the focus of historical causation.

Throughout his studies Foucault developed and used what he called an "archeological method." This approach to history tries to uncover strata of relations and traces of culture in order to reconstruct the civilization in question. Foucault assumed that there were characteristic mechanisms throughout historical events, and therefore he developed his analysis by drawing on seemingly random sources. This gives Foucault's work an eclecticism rarely seen in modern historiography. His concern, however, was to isolate the defining characteristics of a period. In the *Order of Things* (1971) he claimed that "in any given culture and at any given moment there is only one *episteme* (system of knowledge) that defines the conditions of the possibility of all knowledge." The archeological method seeks to "dig up and display the archeological form or forms which would be common to all mental activity." These forms can then be traced throughout a culture and warrant the eclectic use of historical materials.

Foucault's archeological method entails a reconception of historical study by seeking to isolate the forms that are common to all mental activity in a period. Rather than seeking historical origins, continuities, and explanations for a historical period, Foucault constantly sought the epistemological gap or space unique to a particular period. He then tried to uncover the structures that render understandable the continuities of history. His form of social analysis challenged other thinkers to look at institutions, ideas, and events in new ways.

Foucault claimed that his interest was "to create a history of the different modes by which, in our culture, human beings are made subjects." By this he meant the way in which human beings are made the subjects of objectifying study and practices through knowledge, social norms, and sexuality. Thus he applied his archeological method to sexuality, insanity, history, and punishment. Just prior to his death, *Concern for the Self*, the third of his projected five volume *History of Sexuality*, was published in France. The first two volumes—*The Will to know* (published in English as *The History of Sexuality Volume I*, 1981) and *The Use of Pleasure* (1985)—explored the relation between morality and sexuality. *Concern for the Self* addresses the oppression of women by men. In these studies, as in his *Discipline and Punish* (1977) about the rise of penal institutions, Foucault isolated the institutions that are images of the *episteme* of modernity. His conclusion was that modernity is marked not by liberalization and freedom, but by the repression of sexuality and the "totalitarianism of the norm" in mass culture.

Foucault's work continues to have significance for historical, literary, and philosophical study. In his later years Foucault wrote and spoke extensively on varying topics ranging from language to the relations of knowledge and power. In the span of a short career Foucault had considerable impact on the intellectual world. Yet given the complexity, subtly, and eclecticism of his style, the full impact of his work has yet to be realized.

Further Reading

Foucault is included in *Contemporary Authors* (volumes 105, 113). Obituaries can be found in *Newsweek* (July 9, 1984) and *TIME* (July 9, 1984). For helpful works on Foucault see Alan Sheridan, *Michel Foucault: The Will to Truth* (Tavistock, 1980) and Hubert L. Dreyfus and Paul Rabbinow, *Michel Foucault: Beyond Structuralism and Hermeneutics* (1982).

Additional Sources

Macey, David, *The lives of Michel Foucault: a biography,* New York: Pantheon Books, 1993.
Eribon, Didier, *Michel Foucault,* Cambridge, Mass.: Harvard University Press, 1991. □

Joseph Fouché

The French statesman Joseph Fouché (1759-1820) served as minister of police under Napoleon and was influential in the return of Louis XVIII to the throne in 1815.

Joseph Fouché was born on May 21, 1759, near Nantes. He received an excellent education with the Oratorians, first at Nantes and then at Paris. He took minor religious orders and became a teacher. When the Revolution began to transform French society, he was teaching at the Oratorians' college at Nantes and became a prominent member of the local Jacobin club. Elected to the National Convention in August 1792, he voted for the establishment of the republic and the death of Louis XVI.

Upon entering public life, Fouché renounced his clerical vows and his religion. As a representative of the Convention, first in the Vendée and then at Lyons (1793-1794), he earned the name of terrorist by crushing all opposition to the Paris government. Because of a falling-out with Robespierre, he supported the Thermidorians in overthrowing the Jacobin regime on July 27-28, 1794.

During the 4 years of the Directory (1795-1799), Fouché had contacts with both the extreme left and the right

while remaining on good terms with the government. In 1798 he was ambassador to the Cisalpine Republic and in 1799 to Holland. By the summer of 1799 he was back in Paris as minister of police and placed his services at the disposal of Abbé Sieyès and Napoleon Bonaparte when, on 18 Brumaire (Nov. 9, 1799), they overthrew the government and established the Consulate. Fouché continued as minister of police, with but a 2-year interval (1802-1804), until he was relieved by Napoleon in 1810 after they had a falling-out.

The creation of the empire in 1804 led to his ennoblement with the title of Duke of Otranto. Furthermore, he amassed a large fortune during his years in office. In 1810 he settled at his estate at Point Carré until after the Russian campaign of 1812, when he again served Napoleon, first as administrator to the Illyrian provinces and then as a spy on Murat in Italy. He returned to Paris in April 1814 and vainly attempted to attach himself to the returning Bourbons.

During the Hundred Days, Fouché was once again minister of police. But believing that Napoleon could not survive the approaching war, he entered into correspondence with the royalists. Upon the Emperor's second abdication, on June 22, 1815, Fouché vigorously worked for the restoration of Louis XVIII, from whom he expected a high political position in return. The royalists, however, could not forgive the regicide and terrorist of the Revolution, and he finished his days in self-imposed exile first at Prague and then at Trieste, where he died on Dec. 25, 1820.

Further Reading

The best biography of Fouché is in French. Nils Forssell, *Fouché, the Man Napoleon Feared* (1928), is a good biography of Fouché and discusses his relationship with Napoleon. *The Memoirs of Joseph Fouché* (trans., 2 vols., 1825) was once thought to be the work of Fouché himself; it has since been attributed to Alphonse de Beauchamp, but it is based upon notes and papers left by Fouché and is worthwhile. *A Sketch of the Public Life of the Duke of Otranto* (trans. 1816) is a brief work thought to have been written by Fouché. See also Stefan Zweig, *Joseph Fouché: The Portrait of a Politician* (trans. 1930), and Ray E. Cubberly, *The Role of Fouché during the Hundred Days* (1969). □

Jean Fouquet

The French court painter and manuscript illuminator Jean Fouquet (ca. 1420-ca. 1480) was the leading 15th-century artist in France and the first painter in northern Europe to be vitally influenced by the Italian Renaissance.

A critic has aptly referred to Jean Fouquet as "a piece of France personified," so completely does his art reflect the sophisticated French temperament. Born at Tours, the illegitimate son of a priest, Fouquet probably received his early training in Paris as a manuscript illuminator. His leap to fame is attested to by the probability that he accompanied a French mission to Rome in 1446, for the Italian artist Antonio Filarete recorded that Fouquet portrayed Pope Eugenius IV with his two nephews. In Rome, Fouquet would have seen the frescoes (later destroyed) in the Vatican by Fra Angelico, and the style of the famous Florentine had a deep and lasting effect on his own.

When Fouquet returned to France, he opened a workshop in Tours. He received commissions from Charles VII and members of his court and from Louis XI, who made him official court painter in 1474. Fouquet died in Tours before Nov. 8, 1481, when a church document mentions his widow.

Panel Paintings

The earliest of Fouquet's several large panel portraits is probably *Charles VII*, painted about 1445 before Fouquet's trip to Rome, for it evinces no Italian influence. On the frame the monarch is described as "very victorious," probably a reference to the Truce of Arras, which was in fact one of very few victories enjoyed by the despondent Charles. The portrait is abstractly staged, objective, and unflattering. Fouquet manifested his sober clarity of vision in a self-portrait (ca. 1450; Paris), unusual in being a small, painted enamel roundel and notable as the first preserved independent self-portrait to be made north of the Alps.

About 1450 Fouquet undertook his most famous pair of pictures, the *Melun Diptych* (now divided between Berlin and Antwerp). On the left panel is Étienne Chevalier, treasurer of France in 1452, being presented by his name saint (Stephen) to the Virgin and Child on the right panel. The donor is placed before the variegated marble walls of a Renaissance palace, and the Madonna in three-quarter length is enthroned in an abstracted space, surrounded by nude, shining, chubby red and blue angels. Giant pearls bedeck the throne and Mary's crown. This image was surely scandalous in its own day, for the Virgin is a recognizable portrait of Agnes Sorel, the King's mistress, shown with a geometrically rounded, exposed breast. Chevalier had worked with Agnes Sorel in governing the shaky kingdom of Charles VII.

Similarly abstract and intellectualized is Fouquet's portrait *Guillaume Jouvenal des Ursins* (ca. 1455). This chancellor of France kneels in prayer before a highly ornamented wall, the figure placed close to the picture plane for immediacy. One other famous commission is far removed from the courtly milieu: a *Descent from the Cross* (ca. 1470-1475; Nouans). Monumental figures crowd the large panel, giving the effect of a sculptured frieze against a dark background. There is no overt expression of grief, and the mood of reverential dignity is conveyed in somber tones.

The Miniatures

Fouquet was especially adept in his miniature illustrations for manuscript books. Between 1452 and 1460 the master and his shop made for Chevalier a now-dismembered *Book of Hours* The miniatures are notable for showing Parisian architectural monuments, and there is a unique illustration of the contemporary staging of a mystery play. The donor's name and initials are decoratively, and pridefully, used throughout the compositions. Chevalier himself attends the anointing of the body of Christ for burial, and again he is shown, as in the *Melun Diptych*, being presented to the Madonna by St. Stephen. Italianate ornament and marble paneling occur frequently, and there are splendid landscape backgrounds reminiscent of the Loire Valley. Flickering highlights in many miniatures are rendered in gold, a touch of elegance that is typically French. Fouquet and his shop illuminated many other books; chief among them is the *Grandes chroniques de France* (1458).

Further Reading

The best monographic study of the paintings and miniatures of Fouquet is Paul R. Wescher, *Jean Fouquet and His Times* (1945; trans. 1947). See also Trenchard Cox, *Jehan Foucquet, Native of Tours* (1931), and Klaus G. Perls, *Jean Fouquet* (1939; trans. 1940). □

François Charles Marie Fourier

The French socialist writer François Charles Marie Fourier (1772-1837) was the prophet of a utopian human society.

Charles Fourier was born at Besançon on April 7, 1772. He studied at the local Jesuit high school, after which his family apprenticed him to various commercial concerns. During the early years of the Revolution, Fourier lived at Lyons, where he fought on the counterrevolutionary side and lost his inheritance in a series of business failures. Drafted in 1794, he was discharged for illness in 1796. He spent the remainder of his life in Lyons and Paris, earning a livelihood at odd jobs, living in cheap rooming houses, preaching his "universal harmony," and waiting for the financier who would subsidize his utopian community, but who never appeared.

Fourier first set forth his ideas in an article entitled "Universal Harmony," published in the *Bulletin de Lyon* (1803). For the next 34 years he expounded them in a mountain of books, pamphlets, and unpublished manuscripts; including *Theory of the Four Movements and General Destinies* (1808), *Treatise on Domestic and Agricultural Association* (2 vols., 1822), and *False Industry, Divided, Disgusting, and Lying, and Its Antidote* (2 vols., 1835-1836). Although these works were written in a bizarre style that often defied comprehension and incorporated many eccentric ideas, they gradually gained Fourier a small coterie of disciples.

Fourier believed he had discovered the laws that govern society just as Isaac Newton had discovered the laws of physical motion. Among people, Fourier thought, the analogy to gravitational attraction was passional attraction, a system of human passions and their interplay. He listed 12 passions in humans, which in turn were combined and divided into 810 characters. The ideal community should be composed of 1,620 persons, called a "phalanx," which would exhibit all the possible kinds of characters. In such a phalanx, if all activities were properly ordered, the passions of the individuals would find fulfillment in activities that would redound to their benefit. Fourier described in detail the ordering of these communities, the members' life routines, the architecture, even the musical notation. Moving from social reform to cosmological speculation, he also described the way in which the creation of such a harmony on earth would create a cosmic harmony.

One Fourierist experiment was attempted in France (without his approval) during his lifetime but quickly failed. Fourierist disciples appeared in time all over Europe and in the United States. Fragments of his ideas were eventually taken up by socialists, anarchists, feminists, pacifists, and educational reformers. Fourier died in Paris on Oct. 10, 1837.

Further Reading

Nicholas Riasanovsky presents a full discussion of Fourier's work in *The Teaching of Charles Fourier* (1969). Other views of his ideas and their early-19th-century environment are found in J. L. Talmon, *The Rise of Totalitarian Democracy* (1952), and Frank E. Manuel, *The Prophets of Paris* (1962).

Additional Sources

Beecher, Jonathan, *Charles Fourier: the visionary and his world*, Berkeley: University of California Press, 1986. □

Baron Jean Baptiste Joseph Fourier

The French mathematical physicist Jean Baptiste Joseph, Baron Fourier (1768-1830), was the first to discuss in a comprehensive manner the various aspects of the flow of heat in bodies.

On March 21, 1768, J.B.J. Fourier was born in Auxerre. At the age of 8 he lost his father, but the bishop of Auxerre secured his admission to the local military school conducted by Benedictine monks. After 2 years (1787-1789) in the novitiate of the Benedictine abbey of Saint-Benoît-sur-Loire, he left to serve as a lay teacher in his former school at Auxerre.

In 1789 Fourier's first memoir on the numerical solution of algebraic equations was read before the French Academy of Sciences. In 1794 a central teachers' college (École Normale) was established in Paris, and Fourier was one of its first students, but before long he was promoted to the faculty as lecturer. He then received an appointment to the newly founded École Polytechnique, where he first served as chief lecturer on fortifications and later as professor of mathematical analysis.

Fourier was 30 when Napoleon requested his participation as scientific adviser on an expedition to Egypt. Fourier served from 1798 to 1802 as secretary of the Institut d'Égypte, established by Napoleon to explore systematically the archeological riches of that ancient land. His papers, published in the *Décade* and the *Courrier d'Égypte,* showed him to be preoccupied with problems that ranged from the general solution of algebraic equations to irrigation projects.

Fourier proved himself a tactful diplomat, and upon his return to France Napoleon appointed him perfect of the department of Isère, with Grenoble as its capital, where he served from 1801 to 1814. There he wrote the work on the mathematical theory of heat conduction which earned him lasting fame. Its first draft was submitted to the academy in 1807; a second, much expanded version, which received the award of the academy in 1812, was entitled *Théorie des mouvements de la chaleur dans les corps solides.* The first part of it was printed in book form in 1822 under the title *Théorie analytique de la chaleur.* It was a masterpiece, not only because it covered the hitherto unexplored field of heat propagation but also because it contained the mathematical techniques which later were developed into a special branch of mathematics—Fourier analysis and Fourier integrals.

From 1815 Fourier served as director of the Bureau of Statistics in Paris. In the eyes of the new, royalist regime, Fourier's long service under Napoleon was offset by his opposition to Napoleon upon the latter's return from Elba.

In 1817 he became a member of the Academy of Sciences and served from 1822 as its perpetual secretary.

During the course of his career Fourier wrote several papers on statistics, but his lifelong love was the theory of algebraic equations on which he had just completed the manuscript of a book, *Analyse des équations déterminées,* and a lengthy memoir when he died in Paris on May 16, 1830.

Further Reading

The most detailed biography of Fourier in English is in François Arago, *Biographies of Distinguished Scientific Men* (trans. 1857). A later biography of Fourier is in Eric Temple Bell, *Men of Mathematics* (1937). The subsequent development and use of Fourier's outstanding contribution to mathematical physics is given in detail in H.S. Carslaw, *Introduction to the Theory of Fourier's Series and Integrals* (1906; 3d ed. 1930). Dirk J. Struik, *A Concise History of Mathematics* (1948; 3d rev. ed. 1967), is recommended for general background. ☐

John Fowles

John Fowles (born 1926) was an award winning post World War II novelist of major importance. While his works are reflective of literary tradition reaching back to Greek philosophy and Celtic romance, he was very much a contemporary existentialist, and his writings received both popular and critical acclaim.

John Fowles was born on March 31, 1926, to middle-class parents living in a small London suburb. He attended a London preparatory school, the Bedford School, between the ages of 14 and 18. He then served as a lieutenant in the Royal Marines for two years, but World War II ended before he saw actual combat.

Following the war, Fowles studied French and German at New College, Oxford. He later referred to this period as "three years of heaven in an intellectual sense," and it was during this time that he was exposed to the Celtic romances and the existential works of Albert Camus and Jean-Paul Sartre. After graduating from Oxford, Fowles began a teaching career that took him first to France where he taught English at the University of Poiters and then to Spetsai, a Greek island, where he taught at Anorgyrios College. It was on Spetsai that Fowles met Elizabeth Whitton. Three years later, on April 2, 1954, they were married in England.

Fowles continued to earn a living through a variety of teaching assignments until the success of his first published work, *The Collector,* allowed him to retire with his wife and her daughter to Lyme Regis in Dorset. He continued to live in this quiet sea-coast town—intentionally isolated from English literary circles—where he wrote, gardened, and pursued his interests in natural and local history.

It was not until Fowles was in his early 20s that he began his writing career. After translating a poem by Pierre de Ronsard he was able to overcome that fear of self-

to analyse, through a parable, some of the results of this confrontation.'' This theme, as well as a concern with freedom and authenticity and parallel realities, recurred in later novels. Miranda, according to Fowles, ''is an existential heroine although she doesn't know it. She's groping for her own authenticity.''

The commercial success of *The Collector* enabled Fowles next to publish *The Aristos: A Self-Portrait in Ideas.* As the title suggests, this volume consists of a collection of philosophical statements covering diverse areas but aimed at proposing a new, ideal man for our times—the Aristos. The publication of this book at that time probably owed something to the fact that *The Collector,* in spite of its popular reception, was denied critical consideration by many who failed to look past its thriller format.

Fowles' next published work, *The Magus,* was, according to its author, ''in every way except that of mere publishing date . . . a first novel.'' Using Spetsai as his model, Fowles created the island of Phraxos where Nicholas Urfe, a young English schoolmaster, meets Maurice Conchis, the enigmatic master of an island estate. Through a series of bizarre ''godgames,'' Conchis engineers the destruction of Nicholas' perception of reality, a necessary step in the achievement of a true understanding of his being in the world. While *The Magus* was first published in 1965, Fowles issued a revised edition in 1977 in which he had rewritten numerous scenes in an attempt to purify the work he called an ''endlessly tortured and recast cripple'' which had, nonetheless, ''aroused more interest than anything else I have written.''

Fowles was at work on a new manuscript when in 1966 he envisioned a woman in black Victorian garb standing on a quay and staring out at the sea. She ''was Victorian; and since I always saw her in the same static long shot, with her back turned, she represented a reproach on the Victorian Age. An outcast. I didn't know her crime, but I wished to protect her.'' The vision recurred, became an obsession, and led eventually to *The French Lieutenant's Woman,* a Victorian novel in manner and mores, but contemporary and existential in viewpoint. Fowles' rejection of the posture of omniscient narrator exhorted both characters and readers to grapple with possibilities and to grow through the pursuance of mystery which ''pours energy into whoever seeks the answer to it.'' The novel was made into a popular film of the same name in 1981.

In 1974 *Ebony Tower,* a collection of stories, appeared. The work was televised 10 years later. The title story is a concise re-evocation of the confrontation between the pseudosophisticated man of the world with the reclusive shaman who shatters his poorly conceived notions of reality, a theme more broadly enacted in *The Magus.* This volume contains a translation of a 12th-century romance written by Marie de France, and in a personal note preceding this translation Fowles paid tribute to the Celtic romance, stating that in the reading of these tales the modern writer is ''watching his own birth.'' Fowles' original title for this collection was *Variations* while these stories are original and unique, they are connected to each other and to the

expression that he once suggested is common to all Englishmen. Fowles' first serious attempts at writing took place on Spetsai, amidst the natural splendors of the Greek landscape. His experience of the mystery and majesty of this island was a powerful influence. Not only did he write poetry, which appeared later in his collection *Poems,* but this setting also provided the inspiration for *The Magus,* a work that would obsess the writer for many years. Leaving Greece was a painful experience for Fowles, but one that he saw as having been necessary to his artistic growth. ''I had not then realized that loss is essential for the novelist, immensely fertile for his books, however painful to his private being.''

While back in England and teaching in a variety of positions in the London area, Fowles worked on several manuscripts but was dissatisfied with his efforts and submitted none for publication until 1963, when *The Collector* appeared. *The Collector* is the story of Frederick Clegg, a poorly educated clerk of the lower-class and an amateur lepidopterist, who becomes obsessed with a beautiful young art student, Miranda Grey. Clegg wins a large sum of money in a football pool, enabling him to carry out a plan of kidnap and imprisonment. The narrative shifts, with the first part of the book told from Clegg's point of view and the second recounting the imprisoned Miranda's perspective. The characters of Miranda and Clegg, set in opposition, embody the conflict that Fowles, reaching back to Heraclitus, finds central to mankind—the few versus the many, the artistic versus the conventional, the *aristoi* versus *hoi polloi.* As Fowles noted, ''My purpose in *The Collector* was earlier works by an underlying sense of loss, of mystery, and of a desire for growth.

Daniel Martin, perhaps the most autobiographical of Fowles' novels, draws upon his early experiences of the Devonshire countryside as well as his later involvement in the Hollywood film industry. It appeared in 1974 to mixed reviews. While some critics faulted its rambling structure and lack of narrative suspense, others regarded it as a more honest, straightforward recounting of personal confrontation with one's own history. *Mantissa* (1982) though more cerebral, demonstrated a continuing concern with the artist's intrapersonal conflicts.

In 1996, a new edition of Fowles' essay *The Tree* was published, and along with it the essay *The Nature of Nature,* written some 15 years later when the author was approaching 70, suffering from a crippling illness and taking what one reviewer described as "a more immediate look at last things." In *The Nature of Nature,* Fowles wrote, "Illness has kept me even more alone than usual these last two years and brought me closer to being, though that hasn't always been very pleasant for my body. What has struck me about the acutely rich sensation of beingness is how fleeting its apprehension . . . the more you would capture it, the less likely that you will."

While Fowles' reputation was based mainly on his novels and their film versions, he demonstrated expertise in the fields of nature, art, science, and natural history as reflected in a body of non-fictional writings. Throughout his career, Fowles committed himself to a scholarly exploration of the place of the artist in contemporary society and sought the personal isolation and exile that he felt essential to such a search. While his roots in Western culture were broad and deep, he earned a reputation as an innovator in the evolution of the contemporary novel. He was a spokesperson for modern man, steeped in science, yet ever aware that what he more deeply needs is "the existence of mysteries. Not their solutions."

Further Reading

Non-fiction works by John Fowles included *Shipwreck* (1974); *Islands* (1978); *The Tree* (1979); and *The Enigma of Stonehenge* (1980). For further insights into the life and works of John Fowles see H. W. Fawkner, *The Timescapes of John Fowles* (1984), which contains a forward by Fowles himself; Robert Huffaker, *John Fowles* (1980); Barry Olshen, *John Fowles* (1978); and Peter Wolfe, *John Fowles* (1976).

Additional Sources

Loveday, Simon, *The Romances of John Fowles,* St. Martin's Press, 1985.
Pifer, Ellen, *Critical Essays of John Fowles,* G.K. Hall, 1986.
Tarbox, Katherine, *The Art of John Fowles,* University of Georgia Press, c1988.
Salami, Mahmoud, *John Fowles' Fiction and the Poetics of Postmodernism,* Associated University Presses, c1992.
Aubrey, James R., *John Fowles: A Reference Companion,* Greenwood Press, 1991.
Foster, Thomas C., *Understanding John Fowles,* University of South Carolina Press, c1994. □

Charles James Fox

The English parliamentarian Charles James Fox (1749-1806) won the reputation of being the champion of individual liberties against the oppressive tendencies of government and was known as the "Man of the People."

The third son of Henry Fox, 1st Baron Holland, Charles James Fox seemed destined almost from birth to follow his father's political career. Although he held high office for a shorter time than his father, he became more famous and far better loved. He also seemed destined to continue with William Pitt the Younger the intense political rivalry that their fathers had begun.

Of his two older brothers, one died in infancy and the other was sickly, so the father heaped affection and attention on Charles. Overindulged in his youth, Charles never developed the qualities of restraint or self-discipline. Indeed, Charles's father apparently preferred to encourage a lack of inhibition, for he introduced his son at a tender age to an extravagant and dissipated way of life that was to remain with him always.

Fox's carefree, easygoing manner and his great personal charm won for him a large number of friends, although many people were shocked by his wild and irresponsible behavior. He was completely self-indulgent and undisciplined, and his manner of life was thoroughly irregular. Nothing better typifies that aspect of his character than his later relationship with his mistress, Mrs. Elizabeth Armistead. After his connection with her had lasted more than 10 years, he married her in 1795 but kept the marriage a secret until 1802.

Early Career

Fox began his political career in 1768, when his father secured his election to Parliament as representative for the pocket borough of Midhurst. He was only 19, still technically too young to take his seat, but that did not deter him. For several years he voted with the government. Thus almost his first political act was to stand with the administration against John Wilkes, the popular symbol of liberty.

In 1770 Fox took a minor office in the new North ministry as a junior lord commissioner of the Admiralty. In this capacity he continued to support the government, speaking against the freedom of the press to report parliamentary debates. Following a disagreement with the ministry over the Royal Marriage Bill in 1772, he resigned his Admiralty post. Fox later held a position on the Treasury Board, but he remained there for less than a year; King George III dismissed him in annoyance over his conduct.

So began Fox's long period of opposition. During the following years he fought the government, chiefly over the American colonies, opposing measure after measure. When the American conflict ended and North's ministry fell, it seemed that Fox's time had arrived. But he had so antago-

nized the King that he could attain high office only with difficulty, and for a short time.

In 1782 Fox was secretary of state in Rockingham's ministry for a few months and was able to help pass a bill granting Ireland its legislative independence from Great Britain. When Rockingham died, Fox refused to serve under his successor, Shelburne. In 1783 Fox was again for a few months secretary of state, but this was in the notorious Fox-North coalition that was anathema to the King, who took the first opportunity to bring it down. In this period Fox succeeded in getting settled upon the prince regent enough money for his private establishment. He also introduced a bill for the reform of the East India Company, but over this issue the King managed to topple the coalition.

With William Pitt's advent to power, Fox once more began a long sojourn in opposition. He did support Pitt's unsuccessful bill to reform Parliament, but he opposed almost every other bill brought forward by the government. The role he played in pursuing the impeachment proceedings against Warren Hastings did not redound to his credit, nor did his stand in the Regency crisis speak well for his judgment.

Later Career

Fox greeted the outbreak of the French Revolution with rapture, as did many Englishmen. Later, the excesses of the Revolution caused many of its former English supporters to shake their heads, but Fox's admiration remained unabated. Even after Britain and France drifted into war, he continued

to praise the revolutionary events and principles. He opposed various security measures that Pitt brought forward, such as the Alien Act, the Treason Bill, the Seditious Meeting Bill, and the suspension of the Habeas Corpus Act. In popular esteem he became little better than a traitor, especially after his comment that he took pleasure in seeing France gain advantage over England while English policy remained so mistaken. His opposition to the war and his praise for France also cost him much of his parliamentary following.

On Pitt's death, in January 1806, Fox once more had a chance at high office, serving as foreign secretary in Grenville's ministry. In this capacity Fox managed to pass through Parliament the abolition of the slave trade—a bill that had been defeated when Pitt had introduced it years before. But at this point his career was cut short. He died on September 13 and was buried in Westminster Abbey beside Pitt.

Historical Perspective

Just as in his lifetime he aroused intense feelings, whether of adoration or of hatred, so after his death Fox continued to arouse intense feelings among his chroniclers. Some insist that he deserved his reputation as the champion of liberty, while others insist with equal conviction that he was a shallow opportunist whose oratory was mere posturing, an often successful attempt to gain notoriety and popularity.

Those who consider Fox sincere point to his long continuance in the political wilderness of opposition, while those who regard him as a charlatan point to the inconsistency of his stands on various issues. If he did come to believe sincerely in some of the principles he adumbrated, it is nevertheless only fair to add that he often acted thoughtlessly, irresponsibly, with excessive passion, and for the sheer delight of opposing governmental measures.

It is true that Fox never seriously utilized any of his vast fortune to further the reforms to which he professed so ardent an attachment. Furthermore, for the first 9 years of Pitt's ministry Fox really did not substantially differ from the minister on matters of principle and yet obdurately opposed almost his every measure. But after 1793 the French war constituted an issue which truly divided Fox and Pitt—and it was on just this issue that Fox stood most alone, indeed eventually almost without allies.

Further Reading

Memorials and Correspondence of Charles James Fox, edited by Lord John Russell (4 vols., 1853-1857), is very useful. Most of the biographies of Fox are strongly biased for or against him. Among the older studies are John Drinkwater, *Charles James Fox* (1928), and Christopher Hobhouse, *Fox* (1934; new ed. 1948). Another study is Loren Reid, *Charles James Fox: A Man for the People* (1969). Recommended for general historical background are J. Steven Watson, *The Reign of George III* (1960), and Archibald S. Foord, *His Majesty's Opposition: 1714-1830* (1964).

Additional Sources

Ayling, Stanley Edward, *Fox: the life of Charles James Fox,* London: J. Murray, 1991.

Mitchell, L. G. (Leslie George), *Charles James Fox,* Oxford; New York: Oxford University Press, 1992.

Powell, David, *Charles James Fox: man of the people,* London: Hutchinson, 1989. □

George Fox

The English spiritual reformer George Fox (1624-1691) was the chief inspirer of the Society of Friends, or Quakers.

The son of a weaver, George Fox was born in July 1624 at Fenny Drayton, Leicestershire. He became a cobbler with little book learning beyond the Bible. When he was 19, a voice told him to "forsake all"; so he became a dropout, wandering about England in a solitary quest for religious truth. Gradually he clarified his beliefs, convinced that he derived them from direct experiences of God's light within him, "without the help of any man, book, or writing."

Holding that every man and woman could be similarly enlightened by Christ, Fox began "declaring truth" in public and developed into a dynamic, fanatically sincere speaker. He preached in barns, houses, and fields and in churches "after the priest had done"; but because his zeal sometimes led him to interrupt services, he was imprisoned as a disturber of public order. Inspired by the "Inner Voice," he became spiritual leader of some Nottinghamshire former Baptists but then went to the north of England, preaching, praying, and protesting at every opportunity. In 1652 he trudged about Yorkshire, a sturdy figure in leather breeches wearing a broadbrimmed hat over the ringlets of hair which fell to his shoulders.

Though Fox denounced creeds, forms, rites, external sacraments, and a "man-made" ministry, he became something of a negative formalist, refusing to doff his hat to anyone or to call months and days by their pagan names; and he used "thee" and "thou" instead of "you." Such flouting of conventions provoked intense opposition. Fox was repeatedly beaten by rowdies and persecuted by the pious, and the forces of law and order imprisoned him eight times for not conforming to the establishment. But his indomitable courage and his emphasis on the spirit rather than the letter of religion won him converts, even among his persecutors.

Paradoxically, this opponent of institutional religion showed a genius for organizing fellowships of Friends complete with unpaid officers, regular meetings, and funding arrangements. As a result, though his message was universal, individualistic, and spiritual, Fox founded what, by 1700, became the largest Nonconformist sect in England. In 1654 he organized a team of some 60 men and women as a mission to southern England. After converting many there, he extended his own preaching to Scotland (1657-1658), Wales (1657), Ireland (1669), the West Indies and America (1671-1673), the Netherlands (1677 and 1684), and Germany (1677). By 1660 he was issuing epistles to the Pope, the Turkish Sultan, and the Emperor of China. He was a strange mixture of fanaticism and common sense, selflessness and exhibitionism, liberalism and literalism.

In 1669 Fox married the outstanding female leader in the Quaker movement, Margaret, widow of his friend and patron Thomas Fell. But God's service took priority over their partnership, which was interrupted by his missions, his imprisonments in 1673-1675, and his supervision of the movement. He died in London on Jan. 13, 1691.

Fox composed hundreds of tracts for his times, defending principles of the Friends and exposing other men as sinners and ministers of the "Great Whore of Babylon;" but it is by his *Journal,* a record of his day-to-day activities and thoughts, that he is best remembered.

Further Reading

The first edition of Fox's *Journal* (1694) was a revision of the original texts. The two-volume edition by Norman Penney, with an introduction by T. Edmund Harvey (1911), is based on the chief source manuscript; and there is a revised text of it, also by Penney (1924). The standard edition of the *Journal* is the revised edition of John L. Nickalls (1952). All of these editions contain the preface by William Penn. The eight-volume edition of Fox's *Works* (1831) is not readily accessible.

Among biographical studies, Vernon Noble, *The Man in Leather Breeches: The Life and Times of George Fox* (1953), is for the general reader. More specialized are Rachel Hadley King, *Fox and the Light Within, 1650-1660* (1940), and Henry E. Wildes, *Voice of the Lord: A Biography of George Fox* (1965). Isabel Ross, *Margaret Fell: Mother of Quakerism* (1949), is a study of Fox's wife. Hugh Barbour, *The Quakers in Puritan England* (1964), relates Fox to the historical background, including the findings of more recent research. There is more background detail in William C. Braithwaite, *The Beginnings of Quakerism* (1912; 2d ed. rev. 1955) and *The Second Period of Quakerism* (1919; 2d ed. 1961). □

Jean Honoré Fragonard

The work of the French painter Jean Honoré Fragonard (1732-1806) constitutes the final expression of the rococo style. He was famous for the fluid grace and sensuous charm of his paintings and for the virtuosity of his technique.

Jean Honoré Fragonard was born in Grasse on April 5, 1732; about 1738 his family moved to Paris. In 1747-1748 the young Fragonard worked as an apprentice in the studio of Jean Baptiste Chardin. In 1748 Fragonard began studying with François Boucher, and in 1752 Fragonard won the Prix de Rome, a prize awarded by the Royal Academy of Painting and Sculpture to allow promising artists to study at the French Academy in Rome. Between 1752 and 1756 he studied in Paris at the École des Élèves Protégés, a special school that educated young artists for work in Italy.

Early Career

In 1756 Fragonard left for Rome, and he remained in Italy until 1761. His career at the French Academy in Rome was not particularly successful, and his professors were displeased with him. He turned to drawing and to making landscape sketches, and during 1760 and 1761 he traveled about Italy making numerous romantic drawings of great gardens and the Italian countryside.

After his return to France in 1761 Fragonard occupied himself primarily with painting decorative landscapes; some were based on his Italian drawings, some were derived from the Dutch landscape of the 17th century, and others were in the popular 18th-century "pastoral" taste, that is, imaginary landscapes with shepherds and shepherdesses. These paintings were successful, but he was not accepted as an important professional artist until he was admitted to the Royal Academy in 1765 on the basis of a serious history painting which was not typical of either his taste or his temperament.

Mature Style

The rococo style in painting, which was established in France by Antoine Watteau in the early 18th century and which Fragonard exemplified so brilliantly, was aristocratic in nature, sensuous, intimate, and designed to provide pleasure; stylistically it depended upon soft, luminous colors, complex surfaces, refined textural contrasts, free brushwork, and asymmetrical compositions based upon the interplay of curved lines and masses. Produced for highly sophisticated patrons, rococo painting concentrated on aristocratic diversions, the game of love, decorative portraits, mythological and allegorical themes frequently treated in a playful manner, and idyllic pastoral scenes.

Between 1765 and 1770 Fragonard executed several portraits in which the sitters wear fanciful costumes, and many paintings of an erotic or suggestive nature. These works are characterized by the easy facility of his technique, rapid and delicate brushwork, glowing colors, a silvery or golden tonality of atmosphere, and an exuberant gaiety of mood. An excellent example of his painting from this period, and one which may be regarded as typical of the work usually associated with him, is *The Swing*. This scene depicts a lady in a pink dress seated on a swing on which she floats through the air, her skirts billowing, while a hidden gentleman observes from a thicket of bushes; the landscape setting emphasizes a bluish, smoky atmosphere, foaming clouds, and foliage sparkling with flickering light.

Pictures like *The Swing* brought Fragonard harsh criticism from Denis Diderot, a leading philosopher of the Enlightenment. Diderot charged the artist with frivolity and admonished him to have "a little more self-respect." By 1765, indeed, the rococo style was under critical attack, had entered its last phase, and was gradually being replaced by a return to the relative severity of the art of antiquity.

Fragonard, however, was unaffected either by criticism or by the encroaching neoclassicism. His work continued to be in demand, and during the early 1770s he received many commissions both from the royal government and from private persons. One of his most important patrons was the Comtesse du Barry, Louis XV's mistress, who commissioned several decorative paintings for Louveciennes, her château near Paris. The most famous paintings done for her comprise a set of four panels entitled *Loves of the Shepherds* (now in Frick Collection, New York); they show a pair of elegantly dressed lovers in a parklike setting and have titles which are self-explanatory: *Storming the Citadel, The Pursuit, The Declaration of Love,* and *The Lover Crowned.*

Later Career

In 1773 Fragonard made a second trip to Italy, one which lasted for a year. He painted some of his finest landscapes in 1775; the best of these, such as the *Fête at Saint-Cloud,* have a fantasy quality in which people are dwarfed into insignificance and the compositions are dominated by great fluffy green and golden trees melting into surging clouds. From about 1776 on Fragonard painted young girls reading, allegorical works on the theme of love, portraits, and rather sentimental genre scenes of family life. After about 1784 his production became relatively limited.

Fragonard's work was closely associated with the *ancien régime* in France, but he managed to make a successful personal adjustment to the French Revolution of 1789. His royal and aristocratic patrons were swept away in the political and social upheaval of the Revolution. He fled to his native Provence in 1790, but in 1791 he was back in Paris. From 1794 to 1797 he helped to create and administer the new National Museum, established by the Revolutionary government in the palace of the Louvre; in 1799 he was dismissed from his museum position. He died in Paris on Aug. 22, 1806.

Further Reading

The most important work on Fragonard is Georges Wildenstein, *The Paintings of Fragonard* (trans. 1960), a fully illustrated biography with a complete catalog of his work. An interesting evaluation of Fragonard's work within the context of 18th-century painting is presented in Michael Levey, *Rococo to Revolution* (1966). References to Fragonard can be found in Arno Schönberger and Halldor Soehner, *The Rococo Age* (1960), a handsomely illustrated work dealing with many facets of 18th-century culture.

Additional Sources

Thuillier, Jacques, *Fragonard,* Geneva, Switzerland: Skira; New York: Rizzoli, 1987.
Massengale, Jean Montague, *Jean-Honoré Fragonard,* New York: H.N. Abrams, 1993. □

Anatole France

The works of the French novelist and essayist Anatole France (1844-1924) combine classical pu-

rity of style with penetrating flashes of irony. He is a major figure in the tradition of liberal humanism in French literature.

Jacques Anatole François Thibault, who was to take the literary name of Anatole France, was born in Paris on April 16, 1844, the son of a self-educated bookseller. He attended the Collège Stanislas, a Catholic school, but was far from a brilliant pupil and emerged with a lasting dislike of the Church. Greater intellectual profit came to him from browsing among his father's books and from friendships with influential customers, which led to work for a publisher. France's first book was a study of the poet Alfred de Vigny and was followed by poetry and a verse drama, politely received but not particularly successful. At the same time he was pursuing a career in literary journalism, and in 1877 he married Valérie Guéin, the daughter of a well-to-do family, with whom he had a daughter, Suzanne, in 1881.

Early Career

France's first great literary success came in 1881 with *Le Crime de Sylvestre Bonnard* (*The Crime of Sylvestre Bonnard*). This story of an aging scholar betrays to the present-day reader an excessive sentimentality, but its optimistic theme and kindly irony were welcomed as a reaction against the brutal realism of the prevailing school of Émile Zola. The novel which followed, *Les Désirs de Jean Servien* (1882; *The Aspirations of Jean Servien*), was less well received. By the close of the 1880s France had established

himself as a literary figure and had also begun a liaison with Madame Arman de Caillavet, who had a celebrated literary salon. Their relationship ended only with her death in 1910. France's marriage was dissolved in 1893.

In 1890 appeared *Thaïs,* set in Egypt in the early Christian era, treating the story of the courtesan Thaïs and the monk Paphnuce with tolerant irony and skepticism. It was followed in 1893 by *La Rôtisserie de la Reine Pédauque (At the Sign of the Reine Pédauque),* another tale with philosophical implications, this time set in the 18th century; and in 1894 by *Le Lys rouge (The Red Lily),* a more conventional novel of love in the wealthier classes, set largely in Italy. *Le Jardin d'Épicure* (1884; *The Garden of Epicurus*) consists of reprinted articles but contains the essence of France's attitude to the world at that point: a weary skepticism redeemed by an appreciation of the delicate pleasures of the mind.

Elected to the French Academy in 1896, France was at the height of a successful career. But his journalistic articles had begun to include social as well as literary criticism, and when the Dreyfus case came to a head in 1897, he felt obliged to take sides with the Jewish officer, whom he considered to have been wrongly condemned. For the rest of his life France was to abandon the political skepticism of his earlier years, while the irony in his books turned sharply critical of the contemporary world. This becomes increasingly evident in four books of *L'Histoire contemporaine* (1897-1901; *Contemporary History*), in which the figure of Monsieur Bergeret acts as the representative of France's own views on the Dreyfus case and other social problems, and in the story *Crainquebille* (1901), in which the case was transposed into a parable of the unjust prosecution of a harmless and innocent street peddler.

Later Works

The book in which France's political irony reached its height was, however, *L'Île des Pingouins* (1908; *Penguin Island*), a penetrating glance at French history and life and perhaps the only satire in French literature which can be compared to Voltaire's *Candide.* The novel generally regarded as France's finest came out 4 years later: *Les Dieux ont soif (The Gods Are Athirst).* Set during the French Revolution, the book portrays the gradual development of a young artist, Évariste Gamelin, from his initial idealism and good nature to a point at which, through membership in a Revolutionary tribunal, his virtues have been transformed into a bloodthirsty and merciless fanaticism. France's own attitude is made clear through the character of Brotteaux, a formerly wealthy tax collector whose only possession is now his edition of Epicurus. Brotteaux, unjustly condemned by Gamelin's tribunal, meets the guillotine with stoic resolution. The novel ends with the overthrow of Robespierre and Gamelin's own execution.

France's last major work was *La Révolte des anges* (1914; *The Revolt of the Angels*), another satire, in which a group of angels attempt to free themselves from divine despotism. Less bitter than *L'Île des Pingouins* the book is also less successful. In France's later years he was increasingly involved politically with the extreme left and for a time became a supporter of the French Communist party. In 1921

he was awarded the Nobel Prize for literature; a year later his works were put on the papal Index. France, who had married again in 1920, died 6 months after his eightieth birthday, in 1924.

The many other books by France include collected articles on literary and social topics, volumes of autobiography, and a life of Joan of Arc. Regarded at the turn of the century as probably the most important French writer of his age, France lived too long for his reputation not to be viewed with impatience by a younger generation of writers who had little time for either his clarity of style or his polished irony. He himself had said, "People will reproach me for my audacity until they start reproaching me for my timidity." But if overvalued earlier, looked at in perspective, France's achievement as a novelist and satirist and his stand for the principles of justice and tolerance mark him as a major writer.

Further Reading

The most recent biography of France in English is David Tylden-Wright, *Anatole France* (1967). Among the older biographies, Edwin Preston Dargan, *Anatole France: 1844-1896* (1937), treats France's life until the Dreyfus case, and Jacob Axelrad, *Anatole France: A Life without Illusions, 1844-1924* (1944), deals with France's entire career. Up-to-date literary studies are Reino Virtanen, *Anatole France* (1968), and Dushan Bresky, *The Art of Anatole France* (1969). Alfred Carter Jefferson concentrates on France's political development in *Anatole France: The Politics of Scepticism* (1965). Useful earlier studies are James Lewis May, *Anatole France: The Man and His Work* (1924), and Haakon M. Chevalier, *The Ironic Temper: Anatole France and His Time* (1932). □

Francis I

Francis I (1494-1547) was king of France from 1515 to 1547. He continued the consolidation of monarchical authority and the expansionist foreign policy of his predecessors. He supported humanist learning and was a patron of the arts.

Born on Sept. 12, 1494, at the château of Cognac, Francis I was the son of Charles, Comte d'Angoulême, a member of the house of Orléans. Francis' mother was Louise of Savoy, who descended from a younger branch of the ruling house of Savoy and from the French noble house of Bourbon.

Francis was less than 2 years old when his father died and only 4 years old when he became heir apparent to the throne. He grew up as a ward of Louis XII. His education, which was primarily a training in arms, was supervised by Cardinal Georges d'Amboise, the most important councilor of Louis XII. The marriage of Francis to Claudia, daughter of Louis XII, was also arranged by the King. Francis' closest personal associations during his youth were with his mother and his sister Marguerite, the future queen of Navarre. Francis never outgrew his close relationship with the two women, and even after his accession to the throne he was influenced by them.

Rivalry with Charles V

The first major project undertaken by Francis I after he came to the throne in 1515 was the reconquest of the duchy of Milan. After defeating the Swiss at Marignano (1515) and taking Milan, Francis set out to assure the permanency of the French preponderance in northern Italy by signing treaties with the Pope, the Swiss Confederation, the Holy Roman emperor Maximilian I, and Maximilian's grandson Archduke Charles, ruler of the Netherlands and heir apparent to the kingdom of Aragon.

The treaties which Francis made with these individuals had barely been signed when the emperor Maximilian died. Francis I presented himself as a candidate for the imperial throne (it was an elective monarchy). But Archduke Charles, now king of Aragon and Castile, was elected Emperor Charles V in 1519. This election destroyed the settlement reached after Marignano and reopened the old rivalry of France and Aragon. Francis was now virtually encircled by territories belonging to his chief rival for influence in Italy (Charles V ruled Spain, the Low Countries, the Holy Roman Empire, and Franche-Comté). He was forced to embark upon new diplomatic initiatives. The cornerstones of his anti-imperial policy were alliances with the Lutheran princes of the Holy Roman Empire and with the sultan of Turkey. Francis' policies of keeping Germany disunited and of allying with powers on the eastern flank of Germany

would remain basic elements of French policy in Europe for centuries.

Four times (1522, 1527, 1536, and 1542) Francis went to war against Charles V, but at the end of their last encounter Francis had proved himself no better at keeping his Italian conquests than his predecessors had been. Milan was lost in 1522, and his attempt to regain it in 1525 ended in the disastrous defeat at Pavia. The French army was slaughtered, and Francis was taken prisoner by the Emperor. France itself was periodically invaded by the imperial armies during the wars. The two territorial acquisitions that Francis retained when the wars ceased following the Peace of Crépy (1544) were Savoy and Piedmont.

Cultural Activities

The rivalry of Francis I with his contemporary sovereigns also extended into the realm of learning and the arts. He retained the leading humanist scholars Jacques Lefèvre d'Étaples and Guillaume Budé and the poet Clément Marot in his service. Lefèvre, who acted as a spiritual councilor to the King's sister Marguerite, supervised the education of two of the King's sons, and Budé was instrumental in founding the Collège de France (1529-1530). The King also took steps to improve the royal library. The library was essentially a manuscript collection, but in 1536 and 1537 Francis ordered that henceforth a copy of all books printed in his realm be sent to it.

Francis derived more pleasure from, and certainly spent more money on, the arts than on the new learning. He commissioned and collected paintings by the great masters of Italy, but he was devoted most of all to architecture. He added a new wing to the château of Blois and created a wholly new château at Chambord. He carried out extensive remodeling at the château of Fontainebleau and at Saint-Germain-en-Laye and built a completely new château at Villers-Cotterets and another, now destroyed, just west of Paris in the Bois de Boulogne (the château of Madrid). He also commissioned the rebuilding of the Paris city hall.

Francis employed several Italian artists on these and other artistic projects. While the contributions of several, like Leonardo da Vinci, Andrea del Sarto, and Benvenuto Cellini, were few and their influence ephemeral, some, like Il Rosso and Francesco Primaticcio, who created the distinctive decoration at Fontainebleau, and Sebastiano Serlio, an architect and architectural writer, made lasting contributions to Renaissance art in France.

Reformation in France

Francis' attitude toward the growth of Protestantism was determined in part by his concern to play the role of protector of the new learning and in part by his foreign policy, both of which made him less anxious to persecute religious reformers and innovators than his theologians and judges would have liked. Because the educational and moral reform programs of the humanists made them appear to be religious innovators, Francis' support of the new learning made it seem that he favored some degree of religious innovation. Moreover, his sister Marguerite was very interested in the program of Christian renewal put forth by humanists such as Lefèvre d'Étaples, and she supported a number of them at her court.

But, although he was willing to allow the humanists to publicize their program, Francis I had no intention of actually supporting the establishment of Lutheranism in France. The French Church was already institutionally very much under his control as a result of the Concordat of Bologna, a bilateral accord he reached with the Pope in 1515. In return for disavowing formally the theory that an ecumenical council of the Church was superior to the Pope and for allowing the Pope a nominal role in the administration of the French Church, Francis obtained a formal statement guaranteeing his right to nominate the holders of the most important benefices in France (archbishops, bishops, and abbots), to tax the clergy, and to limit drastically the jurisdiction of Roman courts over French subjects.

The threat that Lutheranism posed to civil society and to traditional religious practice was clear in the 1520s, but Francis refrained from actively persecuting Protestants until the late 1530s. This course was in large measure imposed by his policy toward Charles V. Through most of the 1530s Francis was allied with the German Protestant princes, and he therefore could not persecute Protestants in France. Only once in this period did he turn sharply against the Protestants. On the night of Oct. 17-18, 1534, placards attacking the Mass were put up all over France, even upon the door to the King's bedchamber. This provocation led to a brief persecution of suspected Lutherans.

But when Francis changed his foreign policy and tried in 1538 to reach an accord with Charles V, persecution of Protestantism in France began more earnestly. The Edict of Fontainebleau (1540) brought the full machinery of royal government into action against suspected heretics. A second reversal in his foreign policy that reopened the alliance with the German Protestant princes in the early 1540s slowed the persecutions, but they began again after the accord with the Emperor reached in the Peace of Crépy (1544).

Internal Administration

The machinery of royal government was strengthened and extended in a number of different ways by this absolutist ruler, ably assisted by his equally tough-minded chancellor, Antoine du Prat. The Concordat of Bologna was one of the most important of their measures directed to this end. In this reign the last of the great semi-independent princely *appanages,* the duchy of Bourbon, was extinguished by a virtual act of confiscation that disinherited Charles de Bourbon (1523). The duchy of Brittany, administered separately by the first wife of Francis I, Queen Claudia, was brought under the direct administrative control of the King in 1535. Following a policy employed by his predecessors, Francis I also extended French administrative institutions into the territories he added to the realm.

The extent of the intrusion of the central administration into local society during this reign is best exemplified by the Ordinance of Villers-Cotterets (1539), in which the King commanded each parish priest to keep a record of all births, deaths, dowries, wills, and other significant exchanges of property. The clergy was taxed more regularly and more heavily than ever before, and the sale of government offices, once a private affair, was now conducted under the auspices of royal officials for the profit of the royal treasury. The first experiment in public credit, interest-bearing loans to the King, called *rentes,* which were guaranteed by the properties and revenues of the towns of France, was introduced in this reign. But the attempt to centralize the administration of all royal revenue, carried out with ruthlessness in 1522 and 1523, proved unsuccessful, and the collection and disbursement of the King's income remained a local operation.

As might be expected, there was resistance to some of the King's authoritarian policies and the procedures used to implement them. Constable Bourbon tried unsuccessfully to organize a revolt of the nobility, but throughout Francis' reign the nobility remained surprisingly quiet. In the early part of his reign, Francis faced opposition from within his administration. The Parlement of Paris resisted stoutly his new financial measures (especially the sale of offices), his protection of the religious innovators, and, above all, the Concordat of Bologna. The captivity of the King after the defeat at Pavia gave the Parlement an opportunity to demand reforms, but the judges had no real power behind them and Francis silenced them with his characteristic firmness when he returned from captivity. After that, with the exception of a tax rebellion in the west (1542), the internal politics of the reign consisted of little more than the rise and disgrace of different personages at the royal court.

Further Reading

The best introduction to the reign of Francis I is the short pamphlet of R. J. Knecht, *Francis I and Absolute Monarchy* (1969). Andrew C. P. Haggard, *Two Great Rivals (François I and Charles V) and the Women Who Influenced Them* (1910), and Francis Hackett, *Francis the First* (1935), are the only biographies, neither of which is scholarly. Dorothy M. Mayer, *The Great Regent: Louise of Savoy, 1476-1531* (1966), is a study of the King's mother and covers the early part of his life and reign. Other biographies of persons close to the King are Martha W. Freer, *The Life of Marguerite of Angoulême* (2 vols., 1854), and Christopher Hare (pseud. for Mrs. Marion Andrews), *Charles de Bourbon: High Constable of France, "The Great Condottiere"* (1911).

Information concerning the military and diplomatic activities of Francis I is in Karl Brandi, *The Emperor Charles V: The Growth and Destiny of a Man and of a World Empire* (1937; trans. 1939); Charles W. C. Oman, *A History of the Art of War in the Sixteenth Century* (1937); Jean Giono, *The Battle of Pavia* (1963; trans. 1965); and Joycelyne G. Russell, *The Field of Cloth of Gold: Men and Manners in 1520* (1969).

Henry M. Baird, *History of the Rise of the Huguenots of France* (2 vols., 1879), traces the beginnings of French Protestantism. On the Renaissance in France during Francis' reign see Arthur Tilley, *The Literature of the French Renaissance* (1885; 2 vols., 1904); Anthony Blunt, *Art and Architecture in France, 1500-1700* (1953); and Anne Denieul-Cormier, *The Renaissance in France, 1488-1559* (1969). William L. Wiley, *The Gentleman of Renaissance France* (1954), illustrates several aspects of the life of the court of Francis I.

Additional Sources

Knecht, R. J. (Robert Jean), *Francis I,* Cambridge; New York: Cambridge University Press, 1982. □

Francis II

Francis II (1768-1835) reigned as the last Holy Roman emperor from 1792 to 1806. As Francis I, he was emperor of Austria from 1804 to 1835. During his reign Austria became the principal bastion of European reaction.

Born in Florence on Feb. 12, 1768, Francis was the eldest son of Grand Duke Leopold of Tuscany. As his uncle Emperor Joseph II had no heirs, Leopold had been designated as his successor; and since Francis thus would someday succeed to the imperial throne, he was educated accordingly. At the age of 16, he was sent to Vienna, where Joseph himself supervised his introduction to the art of government. In 1789 he was given nominal command of the Austrian armies fighting against the Turks in the Balkans, but he showed no remarkable aptitude for military leadership.

In 1790 Leopold succeeded Joseph as emperor, and Francis began a long apprenticeship in which he was gradually to share equally in governing the empire. These plans were upset when Leopold died very suddenly on March 1, 1792, and Francis found himself elevated to the throne. In spite of his careful preparation for his responsibilities, he was neither remarkably mature nor very confident that he was equal to his task.

Conflict with France

Francis inherited an uncommonly difficult situation. In foreign affairs the Treaty of Pillnitz, which his father had negotiated with Austria's old antagonist Prussia just before his death, made war with revolutionary France likely, if not inevitable. Indeed, France declared war on the two German powers in April, beginning a struggle which, with some interruptions, would last over 2 decades and which would reveal the weakness of the Austrian monarchy. In the first phase the Austrians, after bungling the opportunity to inflict a rapid and decisive defeat on a still-disorganized France, suffered defeat on all fronts and lost all their Italian territories south of the Adige. The loss was only somewhat counterbalanced by Austria's share in the Third Partition of Poland (1795).

After Napoleon came to power in France, Francis attempted to muster patriotism to counter French pressure by proclaiming himself emperor of Austria in 1804. The attempt was a flat failure, but it did result in the preservation of an imperial title for the Hapsburgs after 1806, when under French pressure Francis agreed to the dissolution of the ancient Holy Roman Empire. Meanwhile, further defeats by France had resulted in the loss of Venetia, the Tirol, and Anterior Austria. Francis sought to rectify the losses by fight-

ing Napoleon in 1809. Again the results were catastrophic, for not only were the Austrians defeated, but Napoleon entered Vienna. Francis was constrained to give Napoleon his daughter Marie Louise in marriage and to supply an auxiliary corps for Napoleon's 1812 invasion of Russia. Only after Napoleon's defeat there did Francis draw back from this enforced alliance and join the great coalition against Napoleon in 1813.

Growing Conservatism

By the time the French had finally been defeated and the powers gathered in Vienna to make the peace (1815), Francis had had his fill of French radicalism. In internal affairs, too, he had moved steadily toward a more conservative pattern. His father had convinced him that the reforms of Joseph II were dangerous because they weakened the existing institutions of the monarchy; Leopold, however, had not lived long enough to establish the validity of his own, more restrained, but nevertheless enlightened system. Moreover, an Austrian Jacobin conspiracy had been discovered in 1794; it amounted to little, but it helped to convince Francis that French radicalism was an article for export, to be feared as much as French armies.

By the time of the Congress of Vienna, then, Francis believed that orderly society could be preserved only if France was permanently restrained from extending its influence beyond its borders and, more important, if political radicalism was stamped out wherever it appeared. In this belief he was reinforced by his brilliant chief minister, Prince Metternich. So, the last 2 decades of Francis' reign saw Austria, in association with Prussia and Russia, solidly lined up behind a policy devoted to the preservation of the status quo and to political reaction. This policy was formalized by the Carlsbad Decrees of 1819 and resulted in Austrian intervention to put down revolutions on several occasions.

Internally also, repression was the rule. Censorship was more strictly applied than at any time during the last three reigns, the peasantry continued to be oppressed by the great landowners, and every attempt by the various nationalities to assert themselves in any way was either suppressed or stifled in bureaucratic delay and inefficiency. Francis died in Vienna on March 2, 1835, leaving a feebleminded son, Ferdinand, to preside over this rickety structure.

Further Reading

A biography of Francis II is Walter Consuelo Langsam, *Francis the Good: The Education of an Emperor, 1768-1792* (1949). He is discussed in Carlile Aylmer Macartney, *The Habsburg Empire, 1790-1918* (1969). □

Francis Ferdinand

Francis Ferdinand (1863-1914) was archduke of Austria and heir apparent to the Austro-Hungarian throne. His assassination in 1914 was the immediate cause of World War I.

Born on Dec. 18, 1863, Francis Ferdinand (German, Franz Ferdinand) was the oldest son of Archduke Karl Ludwig, brother of Emperor Francis Joseph. He started a military career at the age of 15, serving in Hungary, Upper Austria, and Bohemia. The suicide of the crown prince Rudolf (1889) and his own father's death (1896) made him heir apparent.

Partly to cure a lung ailment and partly to enlarge his knowledge, Francis Ferdinand took several cruises during the 1890s, one of which brought him around the globe. Following his return he spent some time in Bohemia (1894-1895), but his illness soon forced him to spend several years on the Adriatic and the Mediterranean coasts. In the meantime he advanced in rank (becoming general of the cavalry in 1899), but this did not lessen his long-standing contempt for Viennese high society or his differences with the Emperor. He crowned his contempt by his morganatic marriage (July 1, 1900) to Countess Sophie Chotek.

Francis Ferdinand regarded the nationality question as the most serious problem of the empire. Initially he sought a solution in terms of "crownland federalism," with the historic borders more or less retained (except for Hungary). Later he favored the idea of the "United States of Greater Austria," which called for a thorough restructuring along ethnic lines. Simultaneously, Francis Ferdinand also toyed with the "trialistic" solution, which was to be achieved by granting the South Slavs an equal partnership with the Austrians and Hungarians in the empire. Finally, due largely to threatening Serbian irredentism, he returned to a modified dualism, calling for a special position for Bosnia-Herzegovina as the "Kingdom of Rama."

In foreign affairs Francis Ferdinand favored the pro-German orientation but also wished to restore understanding with Russia. This desire prevented him from advocating a policy of final solution against the growingly bellicose Serbia.

Francis Ferdinand's influence grew, and by 1913 he was inspector general of the combined armed forces. In this capacity on June 28, 1914, he visited Sarajevo and was assassinated by a group of Serbian conspirators. The fateful bullet, which unleashed the war, was fired by Gavrilo Princip.

Further Reading

The standard biography of Francis Ferdinand by Rudolf Kiszling, is available only in German. Fortunately there are also a number of good English-language works, most of which, however, place too much emphasis on the assassination and the "war guilt" questions. The best and most recent of these are Joachim Remak, *Sarajevo: The Story of a Political Murder* (1959); Hertha Pauli, *The Secret of Sarajevo: The Story of Franz Ferdinand and Sophie* (1965); and Vladimir Dedijer, *The Road to Sarajevo* (1966). □

Francis Joseph

Francis Joseph (1830-1916) was emperor of Austria and king of Hungary. He was the last noteworthy ruler of the Hapsburg Empire.

Born on Aug. 18, 1830, at Schönbrunn (Vienna), the elder son of Archduke Francis Charles, who was the second son of Emperor Francis I (Holy Roman emperor Francis II), Francis Joseph (German, Franz Josef) was not in direct line of succession. Yet, because his mentally impaired uncle Ferdinand I proved childless, Francis was immediately viewed and educated as an heir presumptive.

Proclaimed emperor after Ferdinand's abdication on Dec. 2, 1848, Francis Joseph began his rule by subduing a series of revolutions in his realm. The most serious of these, the Hungarian revolution, he crushed with Russian help. Then, after this dearly won victory, he had to reconstruct his near-defunct empire. Begun under the aegis of a constitution (March 4, 1849), this reconstruction continued throughout the 1850s, although in 1851 constitutionalism was replaced by a system of absolutist centralism.

Foreign-policy reverses during the 1850s, however, compelled Francis Joseph to reconsider his position on constitutionalism. Thus there soon ensued a period of constitutional experiments ("October Diploma" of 1860 and "February Patent" of 1861) which kept the empire's political life in a constant state of crisis up to 1867. These crises,

together with Austria's expulsion from Italy and Germany (1866), convinced Francis Joseph of the necessity of coming to terms with his subjects. He opted for a compromise with the strongest nationality, the Magyars. The result was the Austro-Hungarian Compromise (*Ausgleich*) of 1867, which brought about the dualistic reconstruction of the empire (Austria-Hungary), with both halves receiving their own constitutional governments and internal autonomy, and their common affairs being reduced to matters of foreign and military policy and some finances.

Although the new political structure was much more favorable for the evolution of political democracy and capitalism than the previous absolutist system, it still preserved the hegemony of the earlier ruling classes. Francis Joseph did not regard the compromise as an ideal solution, but he fought all attempts to alter it for fear of disrupting the unity of his empire. The weakness of this arrangement was revealed not only in the continued rivalry between the two partners but also in the growth of German-Czech national antagonism and extremism in Bohemia and in the increasingly bellicose Serbian irredentism.

Having been pushed out of Italy and Germany, the empire under Francis Joseph became increasingly active in the Balkans, which resulted in its occupation (1878) and later annexation (1908) of Bosnia-Herzegovina. This policy, however, soon placed Austria-Hungary on a direct collision course with Russia, forcing Francis Joseph to seek support in Bismarckian Germany in the form of the Dual Alliance (1879). This alliance later proved to be the first step in the direction of the political polarization of Europe, a polarization that, together with the nationality struggle in the Danubian and Balkan region, was of decisive importance in the outbreak of World War I and the dissolution of the empire.

Francis Joseph was a man of simple tastes. His political thinking was as uncomplicated and simple as his private life. He was basically a benevolent despot, unable to grasp the meaning and purpose of modern ideologies and popular political institutions. At the same time he was devoted to duty, to honor, and to the welfare of his people. Above all, he believed in the calling and destiny of his beleaguered dynasty. His death at Schönbrunn on Nov. 21, 1916, signaled the passing of an age.

Further Reading

The best works about Francis Joseph are the products of Austro-German historiography. Fortunately, a number of them have also appeared in English. Of these, Josef Redlich, *Emperor Francis Joseph of Austria: A Biography* (1929), is undoubtedly the best and most readily available account. Karl Tschuppik, *The Reign of the Emperor Francis Joseph, 1848-1916* (trans. 1930), is also excellent. Valuable, but not of the same caliber, are Albert Margutti, *The Emperor Francis Joseph and His Times* (1921), and Eugene Bagger, *Francis Joseph: Emperor of Austria, King of Hungary* (1927). Chester Wells Clark, *Franz Joseph and Bismarck: The Diplomacy of Austria before the War of 1866* (1934), and Charles W. Hallberg, *Franz Joseph and Napoleon III, 1852-1864* (1955), are excellent monographs, but they deal only with certain limited aspects of Francis Joseph's reign. Among the popular works on the Emperor's family and personal life is Bertita Harding, *Golden*

Fleece: The Story of Franz Joseph and Elizabeth of Austria (1937). □

St. Francis of Assisi

The Italian mystic St. Francis of Assisi (1182-1226) founded the religious order known as the Franciscans. He became renowned for his love, simplicity, and practice of poverty.

B ecause his father called him Francis, so did everyone else, although he was given the name Giovanni when he was baptized shortly after his birth in the town of Assisi in central Italy in 1182. His father, Pietro di Bernardone, was a successful cloth merchant, and Francis grew up with a love of fine clothes and good times. He led the other young men of the town in enjoying good food and drink, singing, and dancing.

When Francis was 20, he was taken prisoner in a war between Assisi and Perugia. A year later, sobered by jail and sickness, he underwent several religious experiences in quick succession. In one of these, while he was praying in the decrepit chapel of S. Damiano outside Assisi, he heard a voice from the crucifix telling him, "Francis, go repair my house, which is falling in ruins." Taking the words literally, Francis went quickly back to the city, sold his horse and some cloth from his father's shop, and came back to give the money to the priest at S. Damiano.

His father, furious at Francis' squandering money on churches and beggars, hauled him before the bishop to bring him to his senses. When the hearing began, Francis calmly took off all his clothes, gave them to his father (the astonished bishop quickly covered Francis with a cloak), and said that he was now recognizing only his Father in heaven, not his father on earth. His life from this time on was lived without money and family ties.

His Spirit

The 13th century was a time of troubadours, and Francis had their best characteristics. He was happy, he sang, he loved nature; he spoke to the birds and the animals as though they were his friends. In his "Canticle of Creatures" (also called "Canticle of the Sun") he wrote about Brother Sun and Sister Moon. Once he was heard to beg pardon of his own body, which he called Brother Ass, for having weighed it down with penances. Francis referred to his way of life as his marriage to Lady Poverty.

The 13th century was also a time when the Christian religion was taken very much for granted, and Francis felt the need to return to the original spirit of Christ. This meant living in poverty, and it also meant loving other people. A number of the young men of Assisi, attracted by Francis' example, joined him in his new way of life. In 1209 Francis and his companions went to Rome, where they presented their ideas to Pope Innocent III and received his approval. They found themselves influencing more and more people,

including a lady named Clare, whom Francis helped to enter a monastery of nuns and who later began the "second order" of Franciscans, the order for women.

In 1212 Francis left for the Holy Land. His ship ran into bad weather, and he had to return to Italy. Two years later his adventurous spirit and missionary zeal drove him to seek the Moors in Spain, but sickness prevented him from completing the trip. He tried once more, in 1219, going to Egypt with the Crusaders. At the siege of Damietta, Francis boldly walked through the battle lines into the camp of the Saracens and met the sultan of Egypt, who, apparently impressed with Francis' ideas about brotherly love, gave him permission to continue on to the Holy Land.

Franciscan Order

When Francis heard that trouble had started in Italy among some of his followers, now numbered in the thousands, he returned home. The group had been held together by the force of his own personality, but now Francis saw the need for a more practical guide to his kind of Christian life. He insisted that the new rule stress the poverty he felt was so important: the order could not possess money; all its houses must be simply furnished; and each friar could have only a tunic and cord (Francis himself wore an old sack tied at the waist), a pair of breeches, and, if really necessary, a pair of shoes. Francis went to Rome in 1223 to present the new rule to Pope Honorius III, who approved it wholeheartedly. It was during this visit that, according to tradition, Francis met Dominic. The Franciscan and Dominican religious orders have always felt a close relationship that dates back to the friendship between their founders.

The Stigmata

Francis returned to Assisi and began to spend more and more time alone, in prayer, leaving the decisions about his organization to others. While he was praying on Mt. Alvernia in 1224, he had a vision of an angelic figure, and when the vision disappeared Francis felt the wounds of Christ's stigmata in his hands, side, and feet. He was careful not to show them, but several close friends reported after his death that Francis had suffered in his body as Christ had suffered on the cross. His last 2 years were lived in almost constant pain and near-blindness. He died in 1226, and 2 years later he was canonized a saint.

Further Reading

Among the many biographies of St. Francis, Paul Sabatier, *Life of St. Francis of Assisi* (1894), remains a classic. G. K. Chesterton's excellent *St. Francis of Assisi* (1923) captures the spirit and style of the saint. *The Little Flowers of Saint Francis* (trans. 1887; new ed. 1958) is a collection of refreshing legends and stories about St. Francis written shortly after his death. □

St. Francis of Sales

The French prelate St. Francis of Sales (1567-1622) taught that spiritual perfection is possible for those leading a secular life.

The oldest of 13 children, Francis Boisy was born on Aug. 21, 1567, in the Sales castle in Thorens, Savoy, in eastern France. His wealthy father sent him to the best schools and prepared him for the life of a leisured gentleman. But when Francis was 11, he secretly decided to become a priest. At the Jesuit college of Clermont in Paris, he learned the Renaissance appreciation of art and literature, and at the University of Padua in Italy he studied law. In 1593, 2 years after he received his doctorate degree, he was ordained a priest.

The Roman Catholic Counter Reformation was vigorously under way at the time. Francis volunteered to travel with several other priests through the villages of Savoy to counteract Calvinism and win the people back to allegiance to Rome. For 4 years Francis used all his skills as a speaker and a writer in this cause. He was intelligent, personable, and sincere. The people with whom he came in contact were impressed by his deep spirituality, and gradually a large number of them accepted the Roman Catholic faith he preached.

In 1602 Pope Clement VIII consecrated the 35-year-old Francis bishop of Geneva, a city which until recently had been part of Savoy but which was now strongly Calvinist and developing ties with the Swiss Confederation. The young bishop worked energetically to organize and educate the relatively few Roman Catholics left in the city. He made

sure his priests received a sound training, and he established an organization to teach Catholic doctrine in the parishes of his diocese. Francis himself traveled to all of the churches, met with as many people as he could, and inspired them with his own energy and competence.

Francis' constant concern with a sound spirituality based on prayer led him to teach that union with God was not only possible but desirable for people living a life of business and family. His short book *Introduction to the Devout Life* gained widespread and lasting popularity, and his longer work, *Treatise on the Love of God,* is still considered a masterpiece of mystical theology.

In collaboration with a close friend, Jeanne Françoise de Chantal, he founded the Order of the Visitation of Our Lady (1610) for women. Francis preached more than 200 sermons a year for 20 years. He died suddenly of a cerebral hemorrhage at Lyons on Dec. 28, 1622. His writings—spiritual treatises, letters, tracts against the Calvinists—were collected after his death and published in 26 volumes. He was named the patron saint of writers.

Further Reading

St. Francis of Sales's *Introduction to the Devout Life* is available in an English translation by Michael Day (1956). Of the many biographies, Maurice Henry-Coüannier, *Saint Francis de Sales and His Friends* (trans. 1964), is a particularly interesting personal study. Of contemporary biographies, most interesting is Michael de la Bedoyere, *François de Sales* (1960). □

St. Francis Xavier

The Spanish Jesuit St. Francis Xavier (1506-1552) was a pioneer of Catholic missions in eastern Asia. Known as the Apostle of the East Indies, he has been acclaimed as one of the greatest missionaries in history.

Francis Xavier was born Francisco de Jasso y Xavier of a noble family of Basque stock on April 7, 1506. During his studies in Paris (1525-1536), he became involved in the small enthusiastic band that was organized by Ignatius of Loyola into the Society of Jesus. He and Ignatius were ordained priests in Venice in 1537. The following year Francis went to Rome, where he helped prepare the foundation of the Society of Jesus.

While in Rome, Xavier volunteered to fill a vacancy in a Portuguese delegation to eastern Asia. He spent from 1542 to 1549 in India, Ceylon, Malacca, and eastern Indonesia. In 1549 Japan became Xavier's mission field. While there he discovered that he had to change his missionary methods. No longer confronted with what he regarded as "barbarian" people, he traced the origins of Japanese culture to China, which was closed to foreigners. In a fantastic adventure Xavier tried to smuggle himself into this intriguing empire. Off the Chinese coast he died, with the promised land in sight, on March 19, 1552.

Xavier was a pathfinder who improvised missionary methods in the changing contexts of his life. In Goa, the Portuguese stronghold and capital of the East, he fought the scandalous vulgarity of colonial Christendom. In a second phase, working among lower-caste fishermen who accepted baptism to escape Moslem oppression, he devised Christian instruction for illiterates, focusing on children who taught their parents the message of the Gospel, preferably in songs. He baptized whole villages "until his hands gave up," leaving a summary of the faith and a government-protected catechist whenever he decided to move to regions beyond. His missionary methods remained basically the same during his apostolate in southeastern Asia.

After his adventurous journey to Japan, however, Xavier found himself in a new situation. He became engaged in dialogues with competent and self-confident partners and realized that a different approach was called for. He left this task to his successors, who before the end of the 16th century baptized almost ⅓ percent of the total population and inaugurated the "Christian century in Japan." Xavier went on to attempt his visit to China, which was the most important cultural influence on eastern Asia. His missionary voyage ended in an unfulfilled dream.

With the wisdom of hindsight, many people have criticized the superficiality of his methods. More important, however, many following generations have caught his vision of *amplius* ("further"). Xavier's commitment to the speedy dissemination of the Gospel has led many to call him a "St. Paul in modern style" who made the Society of Jesus into a missionary order. In 1622 he was canonized, and Pope Pius XI declared him (with St. Thérèse of Lisieux) the patron saint of all missions.

Further Reading

G. Schurhammer, *Saint Francis Xavier* (1928), is a scholarly study. James Brodrick, *St. Francis Xavier* (1952), is popular and thoughtful. See also Theodore Maynard, *The Odyssey of Francis Xavier* (1936). □

César Franck

The music of the French composer César Franck (1822-1890) is characterized by chromatic harmonies and skillful use of counterpoint. He frequently used a cyclic form, in which all the thematic material comes together in a climactic finale.

Born in Liège, Belgium, on Dec. 10, 1822, César Franck howed an unusual talent for music as a child. He began his studies at the Royal Conservatory, winning prizes for singing and piano playing. In 1835 his family moved to Paris. Franck attended the Paris Conservatory (1837-1842), where he won prizes for piano, counterpoint, fugue, and organ. He became known for the ease with which he improvised and performed difficult music at sight, transposing it to any key at will.

After a 2-year sojourn in Belgium, Franck settled permanently in Paris. He began composing and teaching. In 1858 he became organist at Ste-Clotilde, a post he held until his death. In 1872 he became professor of organ at the conservatory, where he attracted the devotion of some of the most promising students. Wielding a strong influence over younger composers like Vincent d'Indy, Ernest Chausson, and Henri Duparc, Franck seems to have turned his organ classes into composition courses and persuaded an entire generation of French composers to break away from opera (the only kind of music the French public seriously supported at this time) and to adopt a more serious attitude toward purely instrumental music. Franck died in Paris on Nov. 8, 1890.

Franck composed slowly and carefully, maturing through his lifetime. His total output is rather small, and his best works were written after his sixtieth birthday. The best-known of his choral compositions is *The Beatitudes,* completed in 1879, the same year he finished his Quintet for Piano and Strings, a characteristic work in the cyclic form. In 1884 he composed his most well-known piece for piano, the *Prelude, Chorale, and Fugue,* the title suggesting not only the religious tone that hovers over much of Franck's music but his own love of Johann Sebastian Bach.

The following year saw the appearance of Franck's Violin Sonata, with its effortlessly executed canon in the final movement, as well as the *Symphonic Variations* for piano and orchestra, a lyric quasi-concerto that treats piano and orchestra with equal consideration. The Symphony in D Minor, completed in 1888, follows the composer's preferred three-movement structure by combining the two traditional middle movements of the classical symphony, the andante and the scherzo, into a single movement. Again, all the principal themes return in the final movement.

Further Reading

Vincent d'Indy, *César Franck* (1906; trans. 1910), is a biography written by Franck's pupil. An excellent study of Franck and his artistic milieu is Laurence Davies, *César Franck and His Circle* (1970). Norman Demuth, *César Franck* (1949), discusses the music in detail.

Additional Sources

Davies, Laurence, *César Franck and his circle,* New York: Da Capo Press, 1977. □

James Franck

James Franck (1882–1964) studied the effects of an electron upon an atom. Along with Gustave Hertz, he was awarded the Nobel Prize in physics in 1925.

James Franck was a physicist whose experimental work with atoms and electrons proved Niels Bohr's theory that atoms are quantized—that they transmit and absorb energy in discrete quantities or packages. Along with collaborator Gustav Hertz, he was awarded the 1925 Nobel

Prize in physics. Franck was also known for his outspoken opposition to the use of the atomic bomb, which he helped develop during World War II.

Franck was born in Hamburg, Germany, on August 26, 1882, to Jacob Franck, a German Jewish banker, and Rebecka Nachum Drucker. Although Jacob Franck was deeply religious—he observed Jewish holidays with fasting and chanting—his spiritual devotion did not, on the whole, pass on to James, who would later declare science and nature as his true love and religion. He attended school at the Wilhelm Gymnasium in Hamburg before enrolling at the University of Heidelberg. Franck's father wanted him to study law and economics with the hope that his son would take over the family business. Out of a sense of duty, Franck complied, but after attending law lectures for a short time, he determined to follow his own path and enrolled in the faculty of chemistry.

Heidelberg was where Franck met Max Born, the German physicist with whom he formed his closest friendship. After two terms studying chemistry, Franck enrolled in the doctoral program at the University of Berlin. Under the influence of its physics professor, Emil Warburg, he became interested in physics and switched fields. He began a study to determine the mobility of ions using a method invented by Cambridge physicist Ernest Rutherford.

After graduating with a D.Phil. in 1906, Franck continued to pursue the same lines of research, exploring the forces between electrons and atoms at the physics faculty of the University of Frankfurt-on-Main. He returned to Berlin

in 1908 to become an assistant to Professor Heinrich Rubens. There, Franck began collaborating with the German physicist Gustav Hertz on a series of experiments that would provide direct proof of Bohr's theoretical model of atomic structure, demonstrate the quantized energy transfer from kinetic, or moving, energy to light energy, and establish both of their reputations.

Bohr had postulated that an atom's nucleus, or core, is surrounded by "orbits" of negatively charged electrons. Bohr theorized that these orbits revolve around the nucleus at set distances known as shells. The number of electrons and, thus, the number of shells vary according to the type of atom. Atoms ranking high on the periodic table of elements contain more electrons than simple elements such as hydrogen, which has just one proton and one electron. These extra electrons are contained in extra shells, according to a definite pattern. The first shell contains two electrons; the second, eight; the third, eighteen; the fourth; thirty-two; and fifth, fifty, and so on. As soon as the first shell is full, electrons begin to fill up the second shell, then the third, up to the last shell.

In their natural, unexcited state, the electrons try to stay as close to the nucleus as possible, that is, in an inner shell. Bohr suggested that electrons would jump from one shell to another if energy were applied to them. The distance they would jump would depend on the amount of energy supplied; when the energy source were withdrawn, they would fall back to their original position. The energy emitted by electrons falling back in toward the nucleus would be exactly equivalent to that absorbed by them when jumping to an outer shell. Most importantly, atoms receiving energy could not absorb just any amount but only the specific amount they would need to make a leap. Thus, Bohr spoke of the atom as being "quantized."

Franck and Hertz did not set out to prove Bohr's theory. In fact, they were not even familiar with his work at the time they were carrying out their experiments. Rather, they were interested in measuring the energy needed to ionize atoms of mercury. To this end, they bombarded atoms of mercury vapor with electrons moving at controlled speeds. Below a certain speed, the electrons would bounce off the atoms with perfect elasticity, indicating that the electrons did not possess sufficient energy to ionize the mercury atom, that is, to transfer enough energy to the mercury to enable *its* electrons to jump from one atomic shell into another. Above a certain speed, Franck and Hertz discovered that resonance occurred. At this point, energy was transferred from the electrons to the atoms, causing the mercury gas to glow. They found that energy had been transferred from the electrons to the atoms in discrete amounts. The energy value of the light emitted from the ionized atoms was equivalent to the energy given to them by the electrons. This experiment proved that the quantized energy had changed from the kinetic energy of the moving electrons to the electromagnetic energy given off by the glowing mercury. It also provided direct experimental evidence for Bohr's theory of the quantized atom, a crucial step in the development of twentieth-century physics.

This experiment was also significant because it led to the realization that the light spectrum of an atom holds the key to its atomic structure. The discontinuous bands of light in an atomic spectrum, each representing a particular energy level, correspond to the range of possible jumps that an excited electron could make as it drops from the outer shells, where the absorption of energy had sent it, back to its original inner shell.

Franck's work was unexpectedly interrupted with the outbreak of the First World War. He signed up and became an officer. He served through 1918, working with a group of physicists who prepared and later directed chemical warfare. Franck received the Iron Cross for his valor; he also received a serious leg injury, which almost claimed his life. Returning to academia in 1918, he was named as the head of the physics division at the Kaiser Wilhelm Institute for Physical Chemistry, later renamed the Max Planck Institute. There, Franck pursued his work on electron impact measurements. It was also at the institute that he met Niels Bohr, with whom he developed a lasting friendship. Franck always regarded Bohr as a physicist second to none and consulted him regularly. "I never felt . . . such hero worship as [I did] to[ward] Bohr," he said in an interview excerpted in *Redirecting Science: Niels Bohr, Philanthropy, and the Rise of Nuclear Physics.*

In 1920, with the influence of Born, Franck was appointed professor and director of the Second Physical Institute of the University of Göttingen. The friendship between Franck and Born blossomed into a close working relationship, with Franck the experimenter complementing Born the theorist. During their twelve years at Göttingen, the pair used one another as sounding boards for their ideas, discoveries, and publications, although they collaborated on only a few joint papers. The only contention between them was Franck's habit of holding frequent consultations with Bohr, a practice that tended to slow down their work. More than sixty letters between Franck and Born have survived from the 1920s.

In the spring of 1921, at Bohr's invitation, Franck paid a visit to Copenhagen in time for the March opening of Bohr's Institute of Theoretical Physics. By now, his reputation preceded him and his visit made front page news in Denmark. His meeting with the Swedish physicist Oskar Klein and Norwegian Svein Rosseland convinced him to continue his experimental work on Bohr's theories.

Back at the University of Göttingen a couple of months later, Franck concentrated on building a research facility of international repute. He afforded his students considerable academic freedom. Scientific discussions between teacher and pupils would occur as often during a walk or bicycle ride as in the laboratory. The standards for admission to his school were extremely high but once accepted, a student was assured of his unwavering support and friendship, both professionally and personally.

Franck continued to investigate collisions between atoms, the formation and disassociation of molecules, fluorescence, and chemical processes. In 1925, building on three previously unconnected theories, he published a paper dealing with the elementary processes of photochemical reactions. In it he set out the connection between electron transition and the motion of nuclei, and described a general rule for vibrational energy distribution. This rule was later expressed by the American physicist Edward U. Condon in terms of quantum mechanics (a mathematical interpretation of particle structures and interactions) and became known as the Franck-Condon principle, which is applied to a large number of chemical and spectroscopic phenomena. In 1926 Franck published a book summarizing his work in this area.

Also in 1926, Franck traveled to Sweden to accept the 1925 Nobel Prize in physics, awarded jointly to him and Hertz for their experiments proving Bohr's atomic theory. He returned to Göttingen to begin his next project, the study of photosynthesis, but had no sooner begun his experiments when Adolf Hitler's arrival on the German political stage changed his life.

When Hitler's anti-Semitic Nazi regime took control of Germany, a new law was declared that barred Jews from the civil service, excepting those who had served in the First World War. Although Franck's position was secure, he could not in good conscience continue to work for a regime dedicated to racism, so on April 17, 1933, he sent letters to the minister of education and to the rector of the university, announcing his resignation and decrying the government's discriminatory policy. Hoping to remain in Germany, Franck searched for another position. Two possibilities presented themselves, one being the chair of physics at the University of Berlin, which would shortly be open. Though it was a position Franck would have coveted under other circumstances, it would have meant working for the government. The other possibility was the directorship of the Kaiser Wilhelm Institute for Physical Chemistry, a position that retiring director Fritz Haber hoped Franck would accept. Internal problems in the institute, however, prevented Franck from assuming this post as well. Franck decided to accept a visiting lectureship at the Johns Hopkins University in America. After the three month period of that position he returned to Göttingen to contemplate his uncertain future. Tentative offers were made from universities in the United States, but they did not promise the permanency Franck was seeking. He decided to accept an offer from Bohr for a year's work at his Institute of Theoretical Physics.

Franck arrived in Copenhagen in April 1934, and, with his assistant Hilde Levi, set to studying the fluorescence of green plants, an extension of his previous work studying energy exchanges in complex molecular systems. Under Bohr's direction, he also began administering experimental nuclear research at the Institute. He was frustrated by poor facilities and slow coworkers and, as stated in *Redirecting Science,* wrote of this period: "My nuclear physics exhausts itself at present in work which is just about to be completed when someone else publishes it in *Nature.*" Working with a master theorist such as Bohr also proved difficult for Franck. "Bohr's genius was so superior. And one cannot help that one would get so strong inferiority complexes in the presence of such a genius that one becomes sterile," he later said in an interview quoted in *Redirecting Science.* After

being used to having his own laboratory and students, it was hard for Franck to get used to working in Bohr's shadow.

The combination of numerous frustrations spurred Franck to accept an offer to settle in the United States. In late 1935, he became a professor at Johns Hopkins University, where he spent three years before moving to the University of Chicago to fill its chair of physical chemistry. With the help of the Samuel Fels Fund, a laboratory dedicated to research into photosynthesis was built, which Franck directed until his retirement in 1949, though he continued to work there for many years subsequently. He became an American citizen in the early 1940s.

When the Second World War broke out, Franck played a leading role in the Manhattan Project, the American government-sponsored atomic bomb project. Like the other German scientists on the team, he was driven by a desire to beat Hitler to the production of a nuclear weapon. But he firmly believed that the bomb should be used as a mode of deterrence, not as a means of aggression. When the U.S. finally developed the bomb and subsequently deployed it against the Japanese, Franck was a harsh critic.

In 1942, a crisis struck in Franck's private life with the death of his wife, Ingrid Josephson, who had been sick for many years. He coped with the loss by immersing himself in his work. He chaired a committee of scientists charged with exploring the social and political implications of detonating an atom bomb. That committee's findings, titled the Franck Report, was submitted to the U.S. Secretary of War, Henry Stimson, in 1945, and warned the United States Government against the use of the bomb as a military weapon. The report also speculated on the dangers of embarking upon an arms race and also urged the U.S. to restrict nuclear testing to areas where human life would not be endangered. The Franck Report has been seen as a testament to Franck's integrity, conviction, and sense of scientific responsibility.

With the end of the war, Franck returned to his post at the University of Chicago where he continued his work with photosynthesis. He was particularly curious as to how plants are able to transform visible light into a form of energy that they use for sustenance and growth. He began experiments on the emanation of electromagnetic radiation of chlorophyll, a key ingredient in the photosynthesis process. Happy to be back at work, Franck experienced joy in his personal life as well. In 1946, he married Hertha Sponer, a professor of physics at Duke University in North Carolina, whom Franck knew from Göttingen and Berlin. They had two daughters, Dagmar and Elizabeth.

Franck was honored with numerous awards during his long career. In addition to the Nobel Prize, he was awarded the highest honor of the German Physical Society, the Max Planck Medal in 1953. Two years later, he received the Rumford Medal of the American Academy of Arts and Sciences. He became a foreign member of the Royal Society of London in 1964 and a member of the U.S. National Academy of Sciences.

During a visit in 1964 to Göttingen, the city where he had spent his most productive years and which had made him an honorary citizen in 1953, Franck died suddenly on May 21. He was eighty-three. He was remembered by his colleagues as a brilliant experimentalist, a dedicated scientist, and a kind and generous man.

Further Reading

Aaserud, Finn, *Redirecting Science: Niels Bohr, Philanthropy and the Rise of Nuclear Physics,* Cambridge University Press, 1990.

Biographical Memoirs of the Royal Society, Volume 11, Royal Society (London), 1965, pp. 53–74.

Born, Max, *My Life: Recollections of a Nobel Laureate,* Scribner's, 1975.

Cline, Barbara Lovett, *Men Who Made a New Physics,* University of Chicago Press, 1987, p. 108.

Levitan, Tina, *The Laureates: Jewish Winners of the Nobel Prize,* Twayne, 1960, p. 74.

Segre, Emilo, *From X-rays to Quarks,* W. H. Freeman and Co., 1980, p. 137.

Weber, Robert L., *Pioneers of Science: Nobel Prize Winners in Physics,* Institute of Physics, 1980, p. 75.

Bulletin of the Atomic Scientists, October, 1964, pp. 16–20.

Correspondence between Franck and Bohr is available on microfilm as part of the Bohr General Correspondence in the Niels Bohr Library of American Physics in New York.

The James Franck Papers, Joseph Regenstein Library, University of Chicago.

Kuhn, Thomas S., six sessions of interviews with Franck, July, 9–14, 1962, housed at the Archive for the History of Quantum Physics, microfilm 35, section 2 (available at the American Philosophical Society, Philadelphia, and the Niels Bohr Library of the American Institute of Physics, New York). □

and 1320 can be detected in many works. None of Franco's own compositions can be identified. Some motets are briefly quoted or cited in treatises; only one motet, in a German manuscript of the 13th century, has been tentatively ascribed to him.

Franco's treatise presents a new concept of musical notation, on which several other theorists were working at the time, about 1240-1270, but Franco gives the clearest and most logical exposition, and thus he had the widest and longest-lasting influence among all the authors of his period. He was the first to teach distinct note symbols for several clearly related note values, namely, the so-called *longa, brevis,* and *semibrevis,* the last of which developed into the modern whole note. Only with the help of this notation did it become possible to write musical lines of much rhythmic variety.

In addition, Franco's teachings of consonances and dissonances and their uses became standard for a long time thereafter, and his approach to composition and analysis of the musical styles created by Léonin and Pérotin and their successors was adopted by the following generations. His importance was such that music historians at one time spoke of an "epoch of Franco."

Further Reading

Perhaps the best accounts of Franco's teachings are in Gustave Reese, *Music in the Middle Ages* (1940), and in Homer Ulrich and Paul A. Pisk, *A History of Music and Musical Style* (1963), although the dates given in the latter work must be revised. □

Franco of Cologne

Franco of Cologne (active ca. 1250-1260), or Franco of Paris, was the outstanding music theorist of his century.

Thirteenth-century Paris was a cultural and political center that attracted numerous foreign artists and scholars. It was there that for longer or shorter periods of time men from many countries taught during the midcentury at the great new university: the German St. Albertus Magnus, the teacher of St. Thomas Aquinas and an outstanding philosopher, who in 1248 retired to Cologne; St. Thomas himself and his Italian compatriot St. Bonaventura; the English humanist John of Garland; and others. One of these scholars was Franco of Cologne, who received the honorary title of papal chaplain and became the preceptor, that is, head, of the Cologne branch house of the Order of St. John, probably in the early 1260s. These positions indicate that he was of noble birth, but no more is known of him.

Franco's fame derives from his treatise *Ars cantus mensurabilis* (The Art of Measurable Music), written about 1260. This treatise is preserved in seven manuscripts dating from the 13th to the 15th century and written in France, England, Sweden, and Italy. Numerous quotations from it and references to it appear in the literature of several countries, and its great influence on composition between 1250

Francisco Franco Bahamonde

The Spanish general and dictator Francisco Franco (1892-1975) played a major role in the Spanish Civil War and became head of state of Spain in 1939.

Born at El Ferrol, a town in the northeastern Spanish province of Galicia, on December 4, 1892, Francisco Franco was the second of five children born to Maria del Pilar Bahamonde y Pardo de Andrade and Don Nicolas Franco, who had continued the Franco family tradition by serving in the Naval Administrative Corp. The young Franco was rather active; he swam, went hunting, and played football. At 12, he was admitted to the Naval Preparatory Academy whose graduates were destined for the Spanish navy. However, international events conspired to cut short his anticipated naval career. In 1898, much of the navy had been sunk by the United States in the Spanish-American War. Spain was slow to rebuild, therefore many ports which had relied on naval contracts were plunged into an economic recession. El Ferrol was hit hard, and entrance examinations for the navy were cancelled, but not before Franco passed for entrance to the Toledo Infrantry Academy in 1907. Franco inherited the nicknames "Franquito" or "Frankie Boy," since he would not participate in the same activities as his fellow students. He became the object of malicious bullying and initiations, and graduated in the middle of his class in 1910. Until 1912, Franco served as a second lieutenant. He was first posted to El Ferrol but in 1912 saw service in Spanish Morocco, where Spain had become involved in a stubborn colonial war. By 1915, at age 22, he had become the youngest captain in the Spanish army. In 1916, he was severely wounded while leading a charge. He was decorated, promoted to major and transferred to Oviedo, Spain. During the next three years, he romanced Carmen Polo y Martinez Valdes, and delayed his plans for the Spanish Foreign Legion for marriage until 1923. Franco became commander in 1922 and rose to the rank of brigadier general (at the age of 33) by war's end in 1926.

During the next few years, Franco commanded the prestigious General Military Academy in Saragossa. In 1928 a daughter, Carmen, his only child, was born. He maintained friendships with the dictator, Miguel Primo de Rivera, and King Alfonso XIII, but when both were overthrown and the Second Republic began a radical reconstruction of Spanish society, Franco surprisingly remained neutral and avoided military conspiracies.

Military governorships in Corunna and the Balearic Islands were followed by promotion to major general in reward for his neutrality, but with the advent of a more conservative Cabinet Franco commanded the Foreign Legion in the suppression of the Asturias revolt (October 1934). Now identified with the right, in 1935 he was made commander in chief of the army.

The Spanish Civil War

In February 1936 the leftist government of the Spanish republic exiled Franco to an obscure command in the Canary Islands. The following July he joined other right-wing officers in a revolt against the republic which is when the Spanish Civil War began. In October they made him commander in chief and head of state of their new Nationalist regime. During the three years of the ensuing civil war against the republic, Franco proved an unimaginative but careful and competent leader, whose forces advanced slowly but steadily to complete victory on April 1, 1939. On July 18 Franco pronounced in the Nationalists' favor and was flown to Tetuán, Spanish Morocco. Shortly afterward he led the army into Spain. The tide was already turning against the Republicans (or Loyalists), and Franco was able to move steadily northward toward Madrid, becoming, on September 29, generalissimo of the rebel forces and head of state.

Franco kept Spain out of World War II, but after the Axis defeat he was labeled the "last of the Fascist dictators" and ostracized by the United Nations. Strong connections with the Axis powers and the use of the fascist Falange ("Phalanx") organization as an official party soon identified Franco's Spain as a typical antidemocratic state of the 1930s, but El Caudillo (the leader) himself insisted his regime represented the monarchy and the Church. This attracted a wide coalition linked to Franco, who, with the death of General Sanjurjo in 1936 and General Mola the next year, remained the only Nationalist leader of importance. By the end of the Civil War in March 1939, he ruled a victorious movement which was nevertheless hopelessly divided among Carlists, Requetés, monarchists, Falangists, and the army. Foreign opposition to Franco decreased and in 1953 the signing of a military assistance pact with the United States marked the return of Spain to international society.

The need to avoid immediate Axis involvement in order to begin recovery temporarily maintained the tenuous coalition. Franco's statement, "War was my job; I was sure of that," showed his hesitant attitude toward the prospect of civilian statecraft. Yet he maneuvered with finesse through World War II, beginning with his famous rebuff of Hitler at Hendaye on October 23, 1940.

Except for sending the Blue Division to the Russian front, Franco resisted paying off his obligations to Germany and Italy. Instead he allied with Antonio Salazar, the Portuguese dictator, who counseled neutrality. Negotiations with the United States solidified this stand, and in October 1943 relations with the Axis powers were broken. But Allied antagonism was only somewhat mollified by this belated effort, and on December 13, 1946, the United Nations recommended diplomatic isolation of Spain.

Peacetime Government

Franco met this new threat by dismissing Serrano Suñer from office, removing the overtly fascist content from the Falange, and limiting all factional political activity. In 1946 the newly created United Nations declared that all countries should remove their ambassadors from Madrid. He also issued a constitution in 1947 which declared Spain to be a monarchy with himself as head of state possessing the power to name his successor. This successor might be either king or regent, thus leaving the future unresolved, a tactic which Franco capitalized on throughout most of the postwar period to prevent any group or individual from making strong claims upon his government. Cabinet ministers were chosen with an eye to national balance, and so slowly Spain moved away from sectarianism.

The economic and diplomatic situation remained difficult. In 1948 France closed its border with Spain, and exile groups, sometimes supported by the U.S.S.R., maintained extensive propaganda campaigns. Flying the banner of anti-communism during the emerging Cold War served him well. In 1950, the United States returned its ambassador and three years later the Americans were allowed four military bases in Spain. President Dwight D. Eisenhower personally greeted Franco in Madrid in 1959. Indeed, considering his Concordat with the pope in 1953, Franco can be said to "have arrived." Franco's regime became somewhat more liberal during the 1950s and 1960s. It depended for support not on the Falange, renamed the National Movement. Almost as if this signaled the end of isolation, tourist trade began picking up until within a few short years Spain had a substantial surplus in international payments. Spain enjoyed rapid economic growth in the 1960s and by the end of the century, its previously agrigcultural economy had been industrialized.

This upsurge permitted Franco to engage in a slow process of modernization that contained a few liberal elements. In May 1958 he issued the principles of the National movement, which contained a new series of fundamental freedoms still dominated, however, by an absolute prohibition on political opposition or criticism of the government. On several later occasions control of the press was temporarily relaxed, and in 1966 the Cortes, up to then a purely appointive body, was made partially elective.

In matters of economic planning, however, Franco demonstrated more consistent liberal intent. He led a belated industrial recovery that raised the standard of living and decreased social unrest. Many of his later Cabinet technocrats, however, were members of Opus Dei, a relatively unknown Catholic laymen's organization reputed to have enormous economic power. Franco's reliance upon this group became obvious in 1969, when the Falange lost its official status.

Franco's health declined during the 1960s. In 1969 he designated Prince Juan Carlos, grandson of Spain's former king, Alfanso XIII, as his official successor. In 1973 Franco relinquished his position as premier but continued to be head of state. Such was the character of Franco's regime that the choice was rumored to have been made by the army, still the most important institution in Spanish society. In July 1974, Franco suffered an attack of thrombophlebitis, an attack that signaled a host of successive afflictions over the following 16 months: partial kidney failure, bronchial pneumonia, coagulated blood in his pharynx, pulmonary edema, bacterial peritonitis, gastric hemorrhage, endotoxic shock and finally, cardiac arrest. At one point, Franco exclaimed,

"My God, what a struggle it is to die." On November 20, 1975, when relatives asked doctors to remove his support systems, the 82-year-old Franco passed away. After Franco's death in Madrid, Juan Carlos became king.

Spain Today

The amazing reality for European integration is that just 20 years after the death of dictator Francisco Franco, Spain has become a mature, stable democracy in which power changes hands via ballot boxes and not bullets. "Electing a conservative government is a way of exorcising the specter of Francoism," says sociologist Victor Perez—Diaz. Gonzalez and his Spanish Socialist Worker's Party deserve most of the credit for moving the country out of the Franco era and into the modern world. Building on the foundations laid by King Juan Carlos and a transitional center-right regime, the Socialists consolidated Spanish democracy after coming to power in 1982. Refraining from widespread privatizations, they embraced free-market economics, modernized Spain's protected, antiquated industries and gave their once isolated country a respected international role with NATO membership and entry into the European Community in 1986. At home they upgraded health care, education and the welfare system, and reformed the old Franco-era army and got it out of politics.

Further Reading

Information on Franco is in George Hills, *Franco: The Man and His Nation* (1967), and Luis Bolin, *Spain: The Vital Years* (1967). See also Hugh Thomas, *The Spanish Civil War* (1961); Gabriel Jackson, *The Spanish Republic and the Civil War, 1931-1939* (1965); Rhea M. Smith, *Spain: A Modern History* (1965); and Stanley G. Payne, *Politics and the Military in Modern Spain* (1967). □

Anne Frank

Anne Frank (1929-1945) achieved world fame after her death from typhus in March 1945 in the Nazi concentration camp Bergen-Belsen through the publication of her diary in which she described the lives of eight Jews in hiding in the city of Amsterdam between June 1942 and August 1944.

Anne Frank was born on June 12, 1929, in Frankfurt, Germany. Her father, Otto, was the son of wealthy parents. He attended the classical gymnasium and served as a lieutenant of the German army in World War I. Following the loss of his parent's fortune during the 1920s' inflation in Germany, he was able to establish himself as a businessman in Frankfurt specializing in banking and in the promotion of name brands. Anne's mother also came from a well-to-do family. Anne had a close and warm relationship with her father and a more distant one with her mother. Anne's sister Margot, a pretty and feminine girl, was born in 1926 and also died in Bergen-Belsen.

Following the Nazi takeover of Germany in January 1933, the Frank's emigrated to Amsterdam, Holland, where Otto Frank became the managing director of a food company with a warehouse and office on the Prinsengracht, one of the city's canal/streets. Anne attended the Montessori school in Amsterdam. When the Nazis occupied Holland in May 1940 they began to institute anti-Jewish regulations which forced Anne to leave her school and to attend a Jewish secondary school. Jews were forced to wear the yellow Jewish star of David, and deportation of Jews from Holland to the Auschwitz extermination camp commenced. Margot received an order to report for deportation in early July 1942. Otto Frank, who had prepared for this eventuality by setting up a hiding place for his family, decided that the time had come. He moved his family into the hidden rear portion of the warehouse where he had prepared two apartments. He was joined there by Mr. van Daan, a co-worker, with his wife and 16-year-old son Peter. Eventually an eighth person joined them, an elderly Jewish dentist named Dussel.

The friends of the hidden Jews who worked in the office of the firm, Mr. Koophuis, Victor Kraler, Miep (de Jong) van Santen, Henk van Santen, and Elli Vossen, supplied them with food, black market ration cards, and other necessities. They were quiet during the day when the normal business of the firm was conducted downstairs. Life for the hidden began in the late day and evening hours.

Following a denunciation, probably by another member of the firm or by a night-time burglar, the police discovered the hidden persons and arrested them and their

helpers. The helpers were held by the Gestapo for a period and some were sentenced to forced labor. The Franks, van Daans, and Dussel were transported to the Dutch transit camp Wersterbork and from there to the extermination camp Auschwitz. It was the last major transport of Jews from Holland. When the Russians threatened to conquer the camp, Margot and Anne Frank were sent to Bergen Belsen where they perished. Of the eight Jews who were in hiding, only Otto Frank survived. (He died in 1980.)

Although Anne wrote a few short stories and started on a novel during her period in hiding, her most important literary achievement was a diary of the events taking place in Prinsengracht. When the German police raided the hiding place they scattered the pages of the diary on the floor. They were collected by Elli Vossen and Miep van Santen and handed to Otto Frank upon his return to Amsterdam.

The diary was forcefully written and tells the story of the living together of the eight persons in the Achterhuis, or the hidden back part of the house, in Prinsengracht. This was often done in a humorous way, displaying considerable talent of observation, originality, and description. Anne was well able to convey to the reader the fears about discovery and the hopes about an end to the war. She described the quarrels between the older van Daans and of the van Daans and the dentist, which often ended in the latter's refusal to further communicate with the van Daans for a week.

Anne's diary, originally published as *Het Achterhuis,* will be valuable to many readers for various reasons. Not the least of these is the story of a young girl growing up under the confining conditions on the Prinsengracht. She described the generation gap between the adults and their silly quarrels and how they tended to combine their forces in castigating her for all sorts of shortcomings. She told about her somewhat distant relationship with her mother and the close one with her father.

Her special attention was given to a budding puppy love with Peter van Daan. The harmless affair ended soon because it was difficult to maintain in the confined space of the hiding place and because she had a talk with her father who suggested ending the affair. But mainly it was because she was intellectually and emotionally the superior of Peter, a nice but rather colorless boy.

A good part of the chronologically-arranged diary entries, all addressed to a Kitty, are concerned with food, its preparation, hygiene, birthday parties and presents, and educating children in such adverse conditions. The cheerfulness of Anne's writing in such dangerous circumstances, as well as her sensitivity and talent to describe difficult circumstances and the tragedy of her short life, made her diary an instant success. The book was translated into over 30 languages, and a pocket book edition in Germany alone sold 900,000 copies, while several million copies of a United States publication of the diary were sold.

Today the house in Prinsengracht is an international youth center known as the Anne Frank House. There are Anne Frank centers devoted to her memory in several places, including Philadelphia and New York City.

Further Reading

Essential reading is the Doubleday edition of *Anne Frank: The Diary of a Young Girl* (1967) with its useful "Reader's Supplement." Also important is Ernst Schnabel, *Anne Frank* (1958), which presents important information relating to the Franks obtained by interviewing the survivors of the tragedy. Of interest also is the Broadway play *The Diary of Anne Frank* by Frances Goodrich and Albert Hackett. Hollywood made a motion picture of the diary of Anne Frank in 1959 which was adapted for television eight years later. The Dutch War Documentation Institute in Amsterdam published in 1986 a definitive, 714-page volume of the diaries complete with scientific endorsement of their authenticity. □

Helen Frankenthaler

The American painter Helen Frankenthaler (born 1928) was a central figure in the development of color-field abstraction during the late 1950s and the 1960s.

H elen Frankenthaler was born on December 12, 1928, in New York City. As a painter her earliest training was with the Mexican artist Rufino Tamayo at the Dalton School in New York. She studied with Paul Feeley at Bennington College, where she received her bachelor of arts degree in 1948. She then lived in New York City, although she traveled extensively throughout Europe. She was married to the painter Robert Motherwell.

In the early 1950s Frankenthaler participated in several important group shows and had her first solo exhibition in 1951. She exhibited regularly during this decade and by 1960 had begun to receive national and international recognition. Large exhibitions of her work were held at the Jewish Museum in New York City in 1960 and at Bennington College in 1962. In 1969 she enjoyed a major retrospective at the Whitney Museum of American Art.

Frankenthaler's style developed in ways counter to the better-known trends of abstract painting during the 1950s. Inspired by Jackson Pollock's black-and-white paintings of 1951, she began to stain thinned pigment into unprimed canvas. The paintings which resulted possessed a delicate, liquid appearance, and their surfaces were devoid of any hint of physical pigment. By contrast, most abstract painting of this time took inspiration from Willem de Kooning's work and emphasized dense surface face textures and aggressive brushwork. But Frankenthaler's direction gradually became influential. In 1953 she introduced the stain technique to Morris Louis and Kenneth Noland, both of whom adopted and developed it within the personal structures of their own painting. Along with Frankenthaler, these two painters profoundly influenced the direction of nonpainterly color abstraction in the 1960s.

The painting which Frankenthaler showed to Louis and Noland is called *Mountains and Sea* (1952). It clearly reveals the advantages of the staining technique, particularly in the flowing spontaneity of the color areas. Because the thinned pigment soaks naturally into the canvas ground, passages from one color to the next are experienced within a continuous optical field rather than as abrupt jumps from one discrete plane to another. In other words, the space is generated within the acknowledged limits of the two-dimensional canvas surface.

As its title suggests, *Mountains and Sea* bears a lingering resemblance to a natural landscape. In 1989 the editor-in-chief of *American Artist* referred to *Mountains and Sea* as one of the four "landmark paintings in the history of contemporary art." In her work after the early 1950s, Frankenthaler became more abstract in her imagery and devoted increasing attention to the development of her lyrical color sensibility.

During the 1960s and 1970s, Frankenthaler continued to develop her own style, one which emphasizes the notion of beauty. She explored the use of acrylic paints, and her work during this era tended to be larger, simpler, and more geometric than previous pieces. Still, her goal was to capture emotion through the use of color without using scenes or subjects. In the late 1970s she explored cubist ideas of space that she had learned in art school.

During the late 1980s critics began to realize more fully how significantly Frankenthaler's work had contributed to the art world. They credit her with many technical achievements and approaches to the use of color during her four decades of creativity. Retrospective exhibitions of her work began to tour museums, even as she continued to create. In late 1996 Eric Gibson noted in *ARTnews* that her latest round of prints, *Spring Run Monotypes,* "convey a wide array of sentiments that were barely noticeable in her earlier works."

Critics consider Frankenthaler one of the most highly regarded painters of the 20th century. Though she has experimented with a variety of techniques, her style has remained truly individual. She told *Newsweek* in 1989, "I continue to do the work I do." This beautiful and poetic work has assured her a place among the masters of contempory art.

Further Reading

For Helen Frankenthaler's position in relation to postwar American painting see Barbara Rose, *American Art since 1900: A Critical History* (1967). Two excellent retrospectives of her work are John Elderfield, *Frankenthaler,* Harry N. Abrams, Inc., 1997; and Ruth E. Fine, *Helen Frankenthaler: Prints,* Harry N. Abrams, Inc., 1993. Interviews with Frankenthaler are featured in Bradley W. Bloch, "Pigments of the Imagination," *New Leader,* September 4, 1989; and Carter Ratcliff, "Living Color," *Vogue,* June 1989. □

Felix Frankfurter

Felix Frankfurter (1882-1965), an associate justice of the U.S. Supreme Court, demonstrated a strong sense for civil liberties.

Felix Frankfurter was born in Vienna, Austria, on Nov. 15, 1882. At the age of 12 he and his six brothers and sisters were taken to the United States. Life on the East Side of New York City served as the background for Frankfurter's social interests.

Following graduation from the College of the City of New York in 1902, Frankfurter entered Harvard Law School. He became editor of the *Harvard Law Review* and earned his degree in 1906 with honors. Henry Stimson, the U.S. attorney for the Southern District of New York, appointed Frankfurter an assistant in 1906. When President William Howard Taft named Stimson secretary of war in 1911, Stimson took Frankfurter along as law officer of the Bureau of Insular Affairs.

Frankfurter returned to Harvard Law School as a professor in 1914. Eventually he was named the first Byrne professor of administrative law. His Harvard years were broken by government service during World War I. As a special assistant to the secretary of war, and later in the same capacity to the secretary of labor, he helped formulate policy. Again at Harvard, Frankfurter became involved in numerous cases of national prominence: the Scopes trial (1925), the silk strike in New Jersey, and the attempt to suppress the *American Mercury* in Boston. He fought for the release of Nicola Sacco and Bartolomeo Vanzetti in 1927 and helped found the American Civil Liberties Union. During Franklin D. Roosevelt's presidency Frankfurter worked on the Security Exchange Act of 1934 and helped formulate the Utility Holding Company Act.

Frankfurter was made a Supreme Court justice in 1939. From the beginning his opinions were challenged as extremely liberal. However, he took a resolute position on the Constitution and its place in American society. He understood that this document could survive only so long as the Court guarded its prerogatives.

Decisions in the civil rights area found Frankfurter strongly for the individual. His opinion on the movie *The Miracle* was typical. When the highest court in New York State ruled the film sacrilegious, Frankfurter saw this as an invasion of private rights. He was also strongly opposed to congressional committees and their investigating procedures.

Frankfurter had married Marion A. Denman after World War I. The marriage produced no children, and during World War II the Frankfurters adopted three English refugee children.

Further Reading

An excellent biography is Helen S. Thomas, *Felix Frankfurter, Scholar on the Bench* (1960). See also Wallace Mendelson, ed., *Felix Frankfurter: A Tribute* (1964), and Liva Baker, *Felix Frankfurter* (1969). Special studies are Patricia A. Edgeworth, *Mr. Justice Frankfurter and the Administration of Criminal Justice* (1955), which describes an area of law not usually associated with Frankfurter and offers a new view of him, and Clyde Edward Jacobs, *Justice Frankfurter and Civil Liberties* (1961). □

Aretha Franklin

Aretha Franklin (born 1942) had a modest beginning as a gospel singer in Detroit before becoming known as the "Queen of Soul."

When asked by Patricia Smith of the *Boston Globe* how she felt about being called the "Queen of Soul," Aretha Franklin's reply was characterized by grace but no false modesty. "It's an acknowledgment of my art," she mused. "It means I am excelling at my art and my first love. And I am most appreciative." Since she burst onto the public consciousness in the late 1960s with a batch of milestone recordings, Franklin has served as a standard against which all subsequent soul divas have been measured.

The combination of Franklin's gospel roots and some devastating life experiences have invested her voice with a rare—and often wrenching—authenticity. "It was like I had no idea what music was all about until I heard her sing," confessed singer-actress Bette Midler, as cited in *Ebony*. Though Franklin's work in later decades has rarely matched the fire—or the sales figures—of her most celebrated singles, she has remained an enduring presence in contemporary music. The release of several CD retrospectives and the announcement in 1995 that she would publish an autobiography and start her own record label seemed to guarantee that her influence would continue unabated.

Franklin was raised in Detroit, the daughter of famed minister C. L. Franklin and gospel singer Barbara Franklin, who left the family when Aretha was small and died shortly thereafter. The singer told *Ebony*'s Laura B. Randolph, "She was the absolute lady," although she admits that memories of her mother are few. The Reverend Franklin was no retiring clergyman; he enjoyed the popularity and, to some degree, the lifestyle of a pop star. He immediately recognized his daughter's prodigious abilities, and offered to arrange for piano lessons. However, the child declined, instead teaching herself to play by listening to records.

Gospel Roots

Franklin's talent as a singer allowed her to perform with her father's traveling gospel show. She sang regularly before his congregation at Detroit's New Bethel Baptist Church as well, where her performance of "Precious Lord," among other gospel gems, was captured for posterity. She was 14 years old but already a spellbinding performer. Producer Jerry Wexler—who shepherded Franklin to greatness on behalf of Atlantic Records some years later—was stunned by the 1956 recording. "The voice was not that of a child but rather of an ecstatic hierophant [a priest in ancient Greece]," he recalled in his book *Rhythm and the Blues*.

Franklin's life was no church social, however. She became a mother at age 15 and had her second child two years later. "I still wanted to get out and hang with my friends," she recollected to *Ebony*'s Randolph, "so I wanted to be in two places at the same time. But my grandmother

helped me a lot, and my sister and my cousin. They would babysit so I could get out occasionally."

Although first inspired by gospel music, Franklin soon became interested in non-religious music. After receiving her father's encouragement, she traveled to New York in 1960, embarked on vocal and dance lessons, and hired a manager. She then began recording demonstration tapes. Like singer-songwriter-pianist Ray Charles, who has often been credited with the invention of "soul music," Franklin brought the fire of gospel to pop music, her spiritual force in no way separated from her earthy sexuality.

Collaborations Launched Career

Celebrated Columbia Records executive John Hammond was so taken by Franklin's recordings that he signed her immediately. Her first Columbia album was issued in the fall of 1960. While a few singles made a respectable showing on the charts, it was clear that the label wasn't adequately showcasing her gifts, either in its choice of material or production. "I cherish the recordings we made together," remarked Hammond in *Rhythm and the Blues*, "but, finally, Columbia was a white company [that] misunderstood her genius."

Franklin's manager at the time, Ted White, was also her husband; they agreed that she should pursue other options when her contract expired. Wexler leapt at the opportunity to sign her to Atlantic, and eventually he, Arif Mardin, and Tom Dowd produced Franklin's first Atlantic sides.

Wexler brought Franklin to the Florence Alabama Music Emporium (FAME) studios in Muscle Shoals, Alabama, to record with a unique group of musicians adept in soul, blues, pop, country, and rock. This crew was stunned by Franklin's power and prowess. Accompanying herself on piano, she deftly controlled the tone and arrangement of the songs she performed. Backing vocals were provided either by her sisters Carolyn and Erma or by the vocal group the Sweet Inspirations, which featured Cissy Houston, mother of future singing star Whitney Houston. Wexler also brought in young rock guitarists Duane Allman and Eric Clapton for guest spots.

Unfortunately, only one of two songs—"I Never Loved a Man (the Way I Love You)"—was finished when White and one of the musicians had a drunken row; White grabbed Franklin and they vanished for a period of weeks. Wexler balanced jubilation with anxiety, as radio programmers around the country embraced "I Never Loved a Man," and distributors clamored for an album. But the artist was nowhere to be found. At last she surfaced in New York, where she completed the unfinished "Do Right Woman, Do Right Man," and in Wexler's words, "the result was perfection."

Franklin's first album for Atlantic, *I Never Loved a Man (the Way I Love You),* was released in 1967, and several hit-filled LPs followed. During this crucial period she enjoyed a succession of smash singles that included the rollicking "Baby I Love You," the pounding groove "Chain of Fools," the supercharged "Think," (which she wrote), the tender "(You Make Me Feel Like a) Natural Woman," and a blistering take on Otis Redding's "Respect." The latter two would become Franklin's signature songs.

R-E-S-P-E-C-T

Franklin's version of "Respect," coming as it did at a crucial point for black activism, feminism, and sexual liberation, was particularly potent. Wexler noted that Franklin took Redding's more conventional take on the song and "turned it inside out, making it deeper, stronger, loading it with double entendres." What's more, he noted, "The fervor in Aretha's magnificent voice" implied not just everyday respect but "sexual attention of the highest order," as implied by the "sock it to me" backup chorus she and her sisters devised.

Writer Evelyn C. White, in an *Essence* piece, referred to "Respect" as a revolutionary force in her own life. Franklin's "impassioned, soulful licks and sly innuendos about sexual pleasure made me feel good about myself," she wrote, "both as a black American and as a young girl about to discover sex." Eventually, the song would become an American pop standard. At the time of its release, however, it served primarily as a fight song for social change, and went on to score two trophies at that year's Grammy Awards.

Franklin's voice was crucial to the soundtrack of the era, and not just as a record playing on the radio. Franklin's father was a close friend of civil rights leader Rev. Martin Luther King, Jr. and his family. When the crusading minister was assassinated in 1968, Franklin was enlisted to sing at his funeral. Wexler described her performance of "Precious Lord" as "a holy blend of truth and unspeakable tragedy."

Franklin also sang the National Anthem at the Democratic Party's riot-marred 1968 convention in Chicago. Yet even as her soulful wail soothed a number of difficult national transitions and transformations, Franklin's own changes were hidden from view. "I think of Aretha as 'Our Lady of Mysterious Sorrows,'" Wexler wrote. "Her eyes are incredible, luminous eyes covering inexplicable pain. Her depressions could be as deep as the dark sea. I don't pretend to know the sources of her anguish, but anguish surrounds Aretha as surely as the glory of her musical aura."

Despite her inner turmoil, Franklin enjoyed phenomenal commercial success during these years. A number of other blockbuster Atlantic albums followed her debut on the label, and she proceeded to take home Grammys every year between 1969 and 1975. Instead of slowing down after all her overwhelming success, she continued to explore rock and pop records for new material and recorded cover versions of songs by the Beatles, Elton John, the Band, Paul Simon, Jimi Hendrix, and many others. "She didn't think in terms of white or black tunes, or white or black rhythms," noted Wexler. "Her taste, like her genius, transcended categories."

In 1972 Franklin sang at the funeral of gospel giant Mahalia Jackson, which suggested her stature in the gospel world; it was no surprise when *Amazing Grace,* an album of church music she recorded with Wexler, soared up the pop charts that year. At the inauguration of President Jimmy Carter in 1977, she provided an *a capella* rendition of "God Bless America."

Triumphed Despite Turmoil

Having parted ways with husband/manager Ted White some years earlier, Franklin married actor Glynn Turman in 1978. They divorced six years later. By the end of the 1970s, her record sales had dwindled, but she took an attention-getting turn in the *Blues Brothers* movie, in which she both acted and sang. The film and the Blues Brothers albums, recorded by *Saturday Night Live* funnymen and blues and soul fanatics Dan Aykroyd and John Belushi, helped fuel a new mainstream interest in 1960s soul.

In 1980 Franklin elected to leave Atlantic and sign with Arista Records. The label's slick production and commercial choice of material earned greater sales than she had enjoyed for some time, particularly for the single "Freeway of Love." She earned three more Grammys during the decade. Nonetheless, Dave DiMartino of *Entertainment Weekly* grumbled that most of her hits at Arista "have been assembled by big-name producers like Narada Michael Walden and might have easily featured another singer entirely—like, say, label mate Whitney Houston"; DiMartino also objected to the relentless pairing of Franklin with other stars for much-hyped duets, remarking, "Like . . . Aretha Franklin needs a *gimmick?*"

In 1979 Franklin's father was shot by a burglar in his home and fell into a coma. He died several years later, having never regained consciousness. As *Ebony*'s Randolph wrote, "When you've said as many goodbyes as

Aretha, it's impossible not to be palpably shaped by loss." The singer cited a point during her father's hospitalization as the most difficult decision of her life. "We had to have a trach [a tracheotomy, a procedure that involves cutting through the vocal chords]," she confided, "and we were afraid it would affect his voice, which was certainly his living."

But beyond this and other painful incidents, further triumphs lay ahead for Franklin. She was the first woman inducted into the Rock and Roll Hall of Fame, won a Grammy for best soul gospel performance, was the subject of an all-star documentary tribute broadcast on public television, sang at the inauguration of another president, Bill Clinton, in 1993, and won a lifetime achievement Grammy in 1995. Franklin might not have been the commercial powerhouse that some of her younger acolytes, like Whitney Houston and Mariah Carey, but she definitely had become an institution.

Franklin—who moved back to the Detroit area in the mid-1990s—announced plans for an autobiography and also made public her intention to start a record label, which would be called World Class Records. "I'm looking for space," she told the *Boston Globe*. "I'm the CEO." She continued to perform, her band by that time featuring two of her sons, Kecalf Cunningham and Teddy Richards.

Other projects, including film and television appearances, were also in the works. "I just strive for excellence pretty much across the board, whether it's as a producer, songwriter or singer," Franklin proclaimed to *Boston Globe* writer Smith. "I give people what I feel is best, not just what everyone says is 'hot.' I want to do things that are going to be meaningful and inspiring to them one way or another." Asked by the *Detroit Free Press* if she ever got tired of singing "Respect," the Queen of Soul replied, "Actually, no. I just find new ways of refreshing the song." Similarly, Franklin's voice continues to refresh new listeners.

Further Reading

Rees, Dafydd, and Luke Crampton, *Rock Movers & Shakers,* Billboard, 1991.
Wexler, Jerry, and David Ritz, *Rhythm and the Blues: A Life in American Music,* Knopf, 1993.
Boston Globe, June 14, 1991, p. 39; March 21, 1994, p. 30; September 29, 1995, p. 55.
Detroit Free Press, June 10, 1994, p. 3D; June 18, 1994, p. 2A.
Ebony, April 1995, pp. 28-33.
Entertainment Weekly, May 15, 1992, p. 64.
Essence, August 1995, pp. 73-77.
Jet, August 21, 1995, p. 33.
People, February 19, 1996, p. 22. □

Benjamin Franklin

Benjamin Franklin (1706-1790) was a leader of America's Revolutionary generation. His character and thought were shaped by a blending of Puritan heritage, Enlightenment philosophy, and the New World environment.

Benjamin Franklin was born in Boston into a pious Puritan household. His forebears had come to New England in 1683 to avoid the zealous Anglicanism of England's Restoration era. Franklin's father was a candle-maker and skillful mechanic, but, his son said, his "great Excellence lay in a sound Understanding, and solid Judgment." Benjamin praised his mother as "a discreet and virtuous Woman" who raised a family of 13 children. In honoring his parents and in his affection for New England ways, Franklin demonstrated the permanence of his Puritan heritage.

His Philosophy

Rejecting the Calvinist theology of his father, Franklin opened himself to the more secular world view of Sir Isaac Newton and John Locke. He read the deist philosophers, virtually memorized the English paper *Spectator,* and otherwise gave allegiance to the Enlightenment. Like his favorite author, Joseph Addison, Franklin sought to add the good sense and tolerance of the new philosophy to his Puritan earnestness. Thus, by the time he left home at the age of 17, his character and attitude toward life had already achieved a basic orientation.

The circumstances of his flight from home also reveal essential qualities. Denied a formal education by his family's poverty, Franklin became an apprentice to his brother James, printer of a Boston newspaper. While learning the technical part of the business, Franklin read every word that came into the shop and was soon writing clever pieces signed "Silence Dogood," satirizing the Boston establish-

ment. When the authorities imprisoned James for his criticisms, Benjamin continued the paper himself. Having thus learned to resist oppression, he refused to suffer his brother's petty tyrannies and in 1723 ran away to Philadelphia.

Successful Businessman

Penniless and without friends in the new city, Franklin soon demonstrated his enterprise and skill as a printer and gained employment. In 1724 he went to England, where he quickly became a master printer, sowed wild oats, and lived among the aspiring writers of London. He returned to Philadelphia and soon had his own press, publishing a newspaper (*Pennsylvania Gazette*), *Poor Richard's Almanack,* and a good share of the public printing of the province. He became clerk of the Pennsylvania Assembly and postmaster of Philadelphia, at the same time operating a bookshop and entering partnerships with printers from Nova Scotia to the West Indies. He was so successful that at the age of 42 he retired. He received a comfortable income from his business for 20 more years.

Franklin philosophized about his success and applied his understanding to civic enterprises. The philosophy appears in the adages of "Poor Richard" and in the scheme for moral virtue Franklin explained later in his famous *Autobiography*. He extolled hard work, thriftiness, and honesty as the poor man's means for escaping the prison of want and explained how any man could develop an exemplary character with practice and perseverance. Though sayings like "Sloth maketh all things difficult, but Industry all easy" do not amount to a profound philosophy of life (as Franklin knew perfectly well), they do suggest useful first steps for self-improvement. The huge circulation of both the sayings of "Poor Richard" (under the title "The Way to Wealth") and the *Autobiography,* plus their distorted use by miserly and small-minded apostles of thrift, led later to scathing assaults on Franklin by Nathaniel Hawthorne, Mark Twain, and D. H. Lawrence—but they in fact criticize a caricature, not the whole Franklin.

Civic Leader

Franklin became involved in civic improvement in 1727 by organizing the Junto, a club of aspiring tradesmen like himself, that met each week. In the unformed society of Philadelphia it seemed obvious to these men that their success in business and improvement of the city's life required the same thing: plans and institutions to deal with needs cooperatively. Thus, Franklin led the Junto in sponsoring civic improvements: a library, a fire company, a learned society, a college, an insurance company, and a hospital. He also made effective proposals for a militia; for paving, cleaning, and lighting the streets; and for a night watch. His simple but influential social belief that men of goodwill, organizing and acting together, could deal effectively with civic concerns remained with him throughout his life.

Work in Science

Franklin next turned to science. He had already invented the Pennsylvania fireplace (soon called the Franklin

stove). His attention fastened primarily on electricity. He read the new treatises on the subject and acquired ingenious equipment. In his famous kite experiment, proving that lightning is a form of electricity, he linked laboratory experiments with static electricity to the great universal force and made a previously mysterious and terrifying natural phenomenon understandable. Franklin's letters concerning his discoveries and theories about electricity to the Royal Society in London brought him fame. The invention of the lightning rod, which soon appeared on buildings all over the world, added to his stature. His scientific ingenuity, earning him election to the Royal Society in 1756, also found outlet in the theory of heat, charting the Gulf Stream, ship design, meteorology, and the invention of bifocal lenses and a harmonica. He insisted that the scientific approach, by making clear what was unknown as well as what was known, would "help to make a vain man humble" and, by directing the experiments and insights of others to areas of ignorance and mystery, would greatly expand human knowledge. Franklin the scientist, then, seemed to epitomize the 18th-century faith in the capacity of men to understand themselves and the world in which they lived.

Political Career

Competing with science for Franklin's attention was his growing involvement in politics. His election in 1751 to the Pennsylvania Assembly began nearly 40 years as a public official. He used his influence at first mainly to further the cause of his various civic enterprises. But he also became a leader in the long-dominant Quaker party, opposing the Proprietary party, which sought to preserve the power of the Penn family in affairs of Pennsylvania. Franklin devised legislative strategy and wrote powerful resolves on behalf of the Assembly, denying Proprietary exemption from taxation and otherwise defending the right of the elected representatives of the people to regulate their own affairs.

Colonial Rights within the Empire

At first Franklin had not the slightest thought about America's separation from Great Britain. He had grown up with allegiance to Britain and had a deep appreciation of the culture of the country of William Shakespeare, John Milton, Joseph Addison, and Alexander Pope. In 1751 he celebrated the rapid increase of colonial population as a great "accession of power to the British Empire," a big and happy family wherein the prosperity of the parent and the growth of the children were mutually beneficial.

Franklin expressed his patriotism by proposing a Plan of Union within the empire at Albany in 1754, and a year later in giving extensive service to Gen. Edward Braddock's expedition to recapture Ft. Duquesne from the French. To defend the empire during the French and Indian War (1754-1763), Franklin persuaded the Quaker Assembly to pass the first militia law in Pennsylvania, appropriate money for defense, and appoint commissioners (including himself) to carry on full-scale war. As the war progressed, he worked with British commanders to win a North American empire for Britain. For 3 decades or more Franklin allied himself in thought and deed with such men as William Pitt, who conceived of Britain as a vital, freedom-extending realm as dear (and useful) to its subjects in Boston and Philadelphia as to those in London or Bristol.

Even in this patriotism of empire, however, the seeds of disaffection appeared. The Albany plan, Franklin noted, dividing power between the king and the colonial assemblies, was disapproved by the Crown "as having placed too much weight in the democratic part of the constitution, and [by] every assembly as having allowed too much to [Royal] Prerogative." Franklin also thought it incredibly selfish for the proprietor of Pennsylvania to try to avoid taxation of his vast lands. He sided, he declared in 1756, with "the people of this province . . . generally of the middling sort." Thus, when he went to England in 1757 as agent of the Assembly, he was alarmed to hear the president of the Privy Council declare: "You Americans have wrong ideas of the nature of your constitution; you contend the King's instructions to his governors are not laws. . . . But those instructions . . . are . . . the Law of the Land; for the King is the Legislator of the Colonies." Though Franklin worked within the empire to resist this presumption, it was clear from the start that if it continued to dominate, Franklin's empire loyalty would wither and die.

Franklin lived in England from 1757 to 1762, seeking aid in restraining Proprietary power in Pennsylvania, meanwhile enjoying English social and intellectual life. He attended meetings of the Royal Society, heard great orchestras play the works of George Frederick Handel, made grand tours of the Continent, and was awarded honorary doctor's degrees by St. Andrews (1759) and Oxford (1762).

Back in America for nearly 2 years (1762-1764), Franklin traveled through the Colonies as deputy postmaster general for North America. In 20 years Franklin vastly improved postal service and at the same time made his position lucrative. He also continued his aid to poorer members of his family, especially his sister, and to the family of his wife, the former Deborah Read, whom he had married in 1730. They had two children, Frankie, who died at 4, and Sally, who married Richard Bache. Deborah Franklin also reared her husband's illegitimate son, William, often his father's close companion, who was appointed governor of New Jersey and was later to be notable as a loyalist during the Revolution. Franklin considered Deborah, who died in 1774, a good wife, mother, and helpmate, though she did not share his intellectual interests or even much of his social life.

Politics occupied most of Franklin's busy months at home. He opposed the bloody revenges frontiersmen visited on innocent Native Americans in the wake of Chief Pontiac's Conspiracy, and he campaigned to further restrict the proprietor's power. On this and other issues Franklin lost his seat in the Assembly (after 13 consecutive victories) in an especially scurrilous campaign. His Quaker party retained enough power, however, to return him to England as agent, commissioned especially to petition that Pennsylvania be taken over as a royal colony—a petition Franklin set aside when the perils of royal government loomed ever larger.

More Radical Position

Franklin played a central role in the great crises that led to the Declaration of Independence in 1776. He first advised obedience to the Stamp Act. But learning of the violent protest against it in America, he stiffened his own opposition, notably in a dramatic appearance before Parliament in 1766, when he outlined, plainly and bluntly, American insistence on substantial self-government. Encouraged by repeal of the act, Franklin again expressed his faith in the grand prospects for America within the empire and worked with Pitt, Lord Camden, and other Englishmen who wanted to liberalize both government at home and relations with the Colonies.

Yet Franklin mounted a strong propaganda assault on the Townshend Duties of 1767. In fact, Franklin's position was increasingly untenable. He was in countless official, personal, and sentimental ways committed to the British Empire, but he was more committed to the life-style he knew in America and which he now began to record in his *Autobiography*. The ideal solution, of course, was to find fulfillment for the life-style under the British flag. He only slowly realized that, at least under the policies of George III and Lord North, the two were incompatible.

Franklin's personal fame, as well as his appointment as agent for Georgia (1768) and for Massachusetts (1770), made him the foremost American spokesman in Britain for 10 crucial years, from 1765 to 1775. Protesting the Tea Act in 1773, he wrote two of his most skillful and famous political satires, *An Edict by the King of Prussia* and *Rules by Which a Great Empire May Be Reduced to a Small One*. These were merely the best of hundreds displaying Franklin's clever pen in aid of his chosen causes.

In 1774-1775 Franklin's agency in England came to an unhappy end. His friends in Massachusetts, against his instructions, published letters of Governor Thomas Hutchinson that Franklin had obtained in confidence. Exposed as an apparently dishonest schemer, Franklin was chastised before the Privy Council in 1774 and simultaneously deprived of his postmaster general's office. Then, in danger of being imprisoned as a traitor, Franklin continued to work with Pitt and others for conciliation, but the Boston Tea Party, the Coercive Acts, and the buildup of British troops in America doomed such efforts. When Franklin left England in March 1775, he was sure that "the extream corruption . . . in this old rotten State" would ensure "more Mischief than Benefit from a closer Union" between England and the Colonies.

The Revolutionary

In the next 18 months in America, Franklin reveled in the "glorious public virtue" of his compatriots. He served on the Pennsylvania Committee of Safety and in the Continental Congress, submitted articles of confederation for the united colonies, and helped draft a new constitution for Pennsylvania. He even went to Montreal to entice Canada to join the new union. He helped draft the Declaration of Independence and was among those who readily subscribed his name to it—at the age of 70 he had become a fervent revolutionist.

Franklin's skill was most in demand, though, as a diplomat to secure desperately needed aid for the new nation. In October 1776, appointed commissioner to France, he embarked with his two grandchildren. In France he began the most amazing personal success story in the history of diplomacy. His journey to Paris was a triumphal procession, and in the capital the literary and scientific community greeted him as a living embodiment of all the virtues the *philosophes* extolled.

Franklin played the role of the simple Quaker, exalted by his plainness amid the gaudy pomp of the court of Louis XVI. In a dramatic encounter at the French Academy, Franklin and the aged Voltaire embraced amid cheers. French intellectuals lionized Franklin, who, still a minister of an unrecognized country, established residence in the suburb of Auteuil, where he created friendships that became part of the legend of Franklin among the ladies of Paris. As usual, Franklin wrote witty letters, printed bagatelles, told stories, and otherwise displayed his brilliant personality.

Diplomatic Tasks in France

Franklin's diplomatic tasks proved more difficult. Though France was anxious that England be humbled, it could not afford openly to aid the American rebels unless success seemed probable. For a year (1777) Franklin worked behind the scenes to hasten war supplies across the Atlantic, block British diplomacy, and ingratiate himself with the French foreign minister and others who might help the United States. He also worked with the other American commissioners, Silas Deane and Arthur Lee, as those two strange compatriots quarreled with increasing bitterness. In December 1777 news of the American victory at Saratoga persuaded Louis XVI and his ministers to enter into an alliance with the United States, finally signed by Franklin and the other commissioners. Lee and Deane soon returned, quarreling, to America, leaving Franklin behind as the first American minister to the court of Versailles.

For 7 years Franklin was the premier American representative in Europe, conducting normal diplomacy and acting as purchasing agent, recruiting officer, loan negotiator, admiralty court, and intelligence chief. Nearly 80, Franklin carried his immense and varied burden effectively and in a way that retained French goodwill. He helped get French armies and navies on their way to North America, continued his efforts to supply American armies, outfitted John Paul Jones and numerous American privateers, and secured virtually all the outside aid that came to the American rebels.

Peace Commissioner

When, after Yorktown (1781), peace with independence became possible, Franklin made the first contact with British emissaries. During the summer of 1782 as the other peace commissioners, John Adams and John Jay, made their way to Paris, Franklin set terms close to those finally agreed to: independence, guaranteed fishing rights, evacuation of all British forces, and a western boundary on the Mississippi. Though Franklin insisted on working closely with French negotiators, he never subordinated American to French interests as his critics have claimed. In fact, the subtle Franklin, the intrepid Adams, and the resourceful Jay made an ideal team, winning for the United States a peace treaty of genuine national independence in 1783.

Viewing America's place in the world as his mission to France drew to a close, Franklin combined realism with idealism. "Our firm connection with France," he noted, "gives us weight with England, and respect throughout Europe." Thus balancing between the great nations, Franklin thought "a few years of peace will improve, will restore and increase our strength; but our future safety will depend on our union and our virtue." He stated many times there was "no such thing as a good war or a bad peace." Not the least isolationist or aggressive, he thought the peaceful needs of the United States required it to trade and cooperate honorably with nations all over the world.

Franklin left France in 1785 and landed in Philadelphia to the cheers of his countrymen. Honored as a living sage, he accepted election for 3 years as president of the Supreme Executive Council of Pennsylvania, became president of the Pennsylvania Society for Promoting the Abolition of Slavery, and resumed his activity in the American Philosophical Society, the University of Pennsylvania, and other civic projects. Though suffering from a physical disorder, he also maintained his large correspondence, wrote essays, and finished the last half of his *Autobiography*.

Framing of a New Government

Franklin's most notable service, however, was his attendance at the daily sessions of the Constitutional Convention during the summer of 1787. Too infirm to speak much in debate and less creative in political philosophy than some of his younger colleagues, he bolstered the confidence of the convention and, through good humor and suggestions for compromise, helped prevent its disruption in animosity. He gave decisive support to the "Great Compromise" over representation and dozens of times calmed volatile tempers and frayed nerves. At the convention's close, he asked each member, who like himself might not entirely approve of the Constitution, to "doubt a little of his own infallibility" and sign the document to give it a chance as the best frame of government human ingenuity could at that time produce. His last public service was to urge ratification of the Constitution and to approve the inauguration of the new government under his longtime friend George Washington. Franklin died peacefully on April 17, 1790.

Further Reading

Franklin's writings are in Albert H. Smyth, ed., *The Writings of Benjamin Franklin* (10 vols., 1905-1907), and Leonard Labaree and others, eds., *The Papers of Benjamin Franklin* (11 vols. to date, 1959-1968) and *The Autobiography of Benjamin Franklin* (1964). The best biography is Carl Van Doren, *Benjamin Franklin* (1938). For special studies see Carl and Jessica Bridenbaugh, *Rebels and Gentlemen: Philadelphia in the Age of Franklin* (1942); Verner W. Crane, *Benjamin Franklin and a Rising People* (1954), on Franklin's politics; Gerald Stourzh, *Benjamin Franklin and American Foreign Policy* (1954); I. Bernard Cohen, *Franklin and Newton* (1956), on Franklin's scientific work; Alfred O. Aldridge, *Franklin and*

His French Contemporaries (1957); Ralph L. Ketcham, *Benjamin Franklin* (1965), for Franklin's thought; and Claude A. Lopez, *Franklin and the Ladies of Paris* (1966). ☐

Sir John Franklin

The English explorer Sir John Franklin (1786-1847) is perhaps the most important figure in the search for the Northwest Passage.

In the 40-year period after the Napoleonic Wars, the British Admiralty took up the challenge of finding the elusive Northwest Passage, along the northern coast of North America between the Atlantic and Pacific oceans. The Royal Navy could afford to undertake the search at this time because of British predominance in naval power. Moreover, Arctic expeditions were seen as a good training ground for officers and men. The voyages themselves, the Admiralty believed, would yield important scientific information and strengthen the British imperial position in northern North America. Sir John Franklin was of major importance in these undertakings.

John Franklin was born on April 16, 1786, at Spilsby in Lincolnshire. His parents had intended that he enter the Church, but a holiday at the seashore aroused in him an inextinguishable desire to go to sea. His career in the Royal Navy began when he joined H.M.S. *Polyphemus,* which was about to play a significant part in the Battle of Copenhagen. Subsequent employment included a voyage in the *Investigator,* commanded by his cousin Capt. Matthew Flinders, to explore and map parts of the Australian coast, and service in H.M.S. *Bellerophon* and *Bedford* at the battles of Trafalgar and New Orleans, respectively. Franklin was promoted from midshipman to lieutenant on Feb. 11, 1808, and by the end of the Napoleonic Wars he had experienced much time at sea.

Early Exploration

Franklin's Arctic travels began in January 1818 with his appointment in command of the brig *Trent.* It was to accompany the *Dorothea,* commanded by Capt. David Buchan, on a voyage to the North Pole and Bering Strait, passing en route between Greenland and Spitsbergen. This expedition was unsuccessful.

In early 1819 Franklin was instructed to lead an expedition "to determine the latitudes and longitudes of the northern coast of North America, and the trendings of that coast from the mouth of the Coppermine River to the eastern extremity of the continent." The findings of this hazardous 5,550-mile expedition were published in 1823 in Franklin's *Narrative of a Journey to the Shores of the Polar Sea in the Years 1819-20,* a classic in the annals of exploration. By the time of his return to England in October 1822, he had been promoted to commander, and on Nov. 20, 1822, he was advanced to captain. His excellent service also brought him fellowship in the Royal Society.

Franklin's second journey to the Polar Sea was made via the Mackenzie River and Great Bear Lake in the years from 1825 to 1827. The object, Kotzebue Sound near Bering Strait, proved unattainable because of the lateness of the season; yet much of the northern coast of the continent was discovered by this expedition. Franklin was knighted in 1829 and thereafter achieved academic distinction.

In 1830-1833 Franklin commanded the frigate *Rainbow* in the Mediterranean Sea. In January 1837 he arrived at Hobart, Van Diemen's Land (Tasmania), to assume the position of lieutenant governor, which he held until 1843. His humanitarian sentiments toward the condition of the convicts restrained there resulted in judicious measures of social improvement.

Northwest Passage

At the time of his return to England in June 1844 Arctic exploration was of special interest, for the *Erebus* and *Terror* had just returned from a remarkable expedition to the Antarctic. The British Admiralty decided to use the *Erebus* and *Terror* to determine whether the Northwest Passage could be navigated by ship. Franklin, as senior naval officer with Arctic experience, obtained the command in spite of some protests that others were younger and perhaps more capable, and on March 3, 1845, Franklin, now 59, commissioned the *Erebus.* Both the *Erebus* and the *Terror* had been fitted with auxiliary screws (a new development in Arctic exploration) and supposedly provisioned for a 3-year voyage. The two ships sailed from England in May amid optimism that the mission's object would be met. They were last seen July 26, 1845, in Lancaster Sound.

It took many years to reconstruct the fate of Sir John Franklin. Some 50 expeditions were sent over 20 years to find him or his remains. They revealed that from Lancaster Sound the *Erebus* and *Terror* had passed through to the maze of islands known today as the District of Franklin. In May 1847 Franklin's party discovered the remaining gap in the Northwest Passage—between Victoria and Simpson straits. On June 11 Franklin died. There followed a third winter in the ice, at the end of which Capt. F. R. M. Crozier, now in command, and his men (105 in all) set out for the nearest Hudson's Bay Company post, Ft. Resolution. All perished miserably in this attempt.

Franklin's second wife (formerly, Jane Griffin) was responsible for sending a number of relief and search expeditions. That of the *Fox* in 1857, under Capt. Francis L. McClintock, discovered the main traces of the expedition, including important documents that tell the tragic tale.

Further Reading

Two biographies of Franklin are H. D. Traill, *Life of Sir John Franklin* (1896), and Geoffrey F. Lamb, *Franklin, Happy Voyageur: Being the Life and Death of Sir John Franklin* (1956). Details of the last expedition are in Capt. Francis L. McClintock, *The Voyage of the ''Fox'' in the Arctic Seas* (1859), and Richard J. Cyriax, *Sir John Franklin's Last Arctic Expedition: A Chapter in the History of the Royal Navy* (1939). A work on Lady Franklin, showing her importance in the search missions, is Francis J. Woodward, *Portrait of Jane* (1951). Recommended for general historical background is Laurence P. Kirwan, *A History of Polar Exploration* (1959). □

John Hope Franklin

A pioneer African American historian, John Hope Franklin (born 1915) was a highly respected scholar who wrote on many aspects of American history.

John Hope Franklin, the son of Buck and Mollie (Parker) Franklin, was born on January 2, 1915, in the small predominantly African American village of Rentiesville, Oklahoma. His father was a lawyer and his mother an elementary school teacher. Thanks to his mother, Franklin received his first taste of education when he was three years old. "Since there were no day-care centers in the village where we lived, she had no alternative to taking me to school and seating me in the back where she could keep an eye on me," Franklin recalled. When he was about five his mother noticed that he was no longer scribbling on the sheet of paper she gave him, but writing words and sentences.

After studying in the public schools of Rentiesville and Tulsa, he enrolled at Fisk University, intending to prepare himself for a career in law. But under the influence of a stimulating history professor, Theodore S. Currier, he changed to a history major. With Currier's strong encouragement, Franklin pursued graduate work at Harvard Uni-

versity, earning a doctorate in 1941. "The course of study was satisfactory but far from extraordinary," he commented in 1988. "Mark Hopkins was seldom on the other end of the log, and one had to fend for himself as best he could." His doctoral dissertation evolved into his first book, *The Free Negro in North Carolina, 1790-1860* (1943).

The Past Came First

Throughout his academic career John Hope Franklin made his first priority the study and teaching of history. Despite several opportunities to leave the classroom, he had "no difficulty in saying to anyone who raised the matter that I was not interested in deanships, university presidencies, or ambassadorships." This strong commitment to scholarship and teaching began with his first jobs after Harvard. At St. Augustine's College in Raleigh, North Carolina (1939-1943), and North Carolina College for Negroes in Durham (1943-1947), he managed to pursue extensive scholarly research while at the same time carrying the heavy teaching load characteristic of small liberal arts colleges. In 1947 he published his second book, *From Slavery to Freedom: A History of Negro Americans*. By the early 1990s in its seventh edition (with Franklin's former student Alfred A. Moss, Jr., as co-author), *From Slavery to Freedom* has been both a seminal work of scholarship helping to define the emerging field of African American history and a remarkably successful textbook.

Resisted Labeling

Despite the efforts of both admirers and critics, Franklin resisted being characterized as an African American who wrote solely on African American topics. Likewise, he did not want others to perceive him as a scholar who wished to present an African American view of the South, slavery, or Reconstruction. "The tragedy," Franklin told a *New York Times Book Review* writer in 1990, is that black scholars so often have their specialties forced on them. My specialty is the history of the South, and that means I teach the history of blacks and whites."

He followed up *From Slavery to Freedom* with a provocative study of the souls of white folk, *The Militant South, 1800-1860* (1956), a book that described the Old South as distinctively touchy, honor-conscious, and militaristic. He then turned to a pressing national issue. Writing in 1961 amid the commemoration of the centennial of the Civil War, Franklin wrote an influential interpretive essay (*Reconstruction: After the Civil War*) that challenged the then widely-held view that the Civil War had ended in an era of "national disgrace. "The book gave Franklin national prominence as one of the leading revisionists of Reconstruction historiography. Perhaps surprisingly, Franklin, in a 1995 *New York Times Magazine* interview, articulated an affection for the South. "Blacks, even when they left the South, didn't stop having affection for it. They just couldn't make it there.Then they found the North had its problems too, so you look for a place of real ease and contentment where you could live as a civilized human being. That's the South. It's more congenial; the pace is better; the races get along better. It's a sense of place. It's home." Nonetheless, Franklin left that place of ease for academic rigor.

Opportunity in the North

Franklin moved in 1947 from North Carolina College to Howard University, where he taught until 1956. When he accepted an appointment as chairman of the history department at Brooklyn College, the event was heralded on the front page of *The New York Times*: no African American historian had ever before held a full-time position in a predominantly white university. In 1964, shortly after publishing his fifth book, *The Emancipation Proclamation*, he was invited to join the history faculty at the University of Chicago.

A major consideration "in the move to Chicago was the opportunity to teach graduate students," said Franklin. "I realized that with all my frantic efforts at research and writing I would never be able to write on all the subjects in which I was deeply interested." In training a new generation of scholars, Franklin extended "immeasurably" his own "sense of accomplishment." In 18 years at the University of Chicago he supervised some thirty doctoral dissertations.

During the Chicago years Franklin was repeatedly honored by his scholarly colleagues, serving as president of the Southern Historical Association (1970), the Organization of American History (1975), Phi Beta Kappa (1973-1976), and the American Historical Association (1979). He was selected as the Jefferson Lecturer of the National Endowment for the Humanities in 1976 (publishing a revised version of his three lectures as *Racial Equality in America*). At the University of Chicago itself he served four years as chairman of the history department and was appointed John Matthews Manly Distinguished Service Professor in 1969.

He continued to be a prolific scholar, co-authoring a survey history of the United States (*Land of the Free*) and an illustrated history of African Americans. He edited several important works, including *Reminiscences of an Active: The Autobiography of John R. Lynch* and (with August Meier) *Black Leaders of the Twentieth Century* (1982). In addition, he wrote another well-received monograph, *A Southern Odyssey: Travelers in the Antebellum North* (1976). He was undeterred even by retirement, first from the University of Chicago in 1982 and then in 1985 from the James B. Duke Professorship at Duke University. He completed his biography of the 19th-century African American scholar George Washington Williams in 1985; continued his study of runaway slaves; and revised *From slavery to Freedom*. In 1992 he wrote *The Color Line: Legacy for the Twenty-First Century*, which was built on W.E.B. DuBois' prophesy that the problems of the 20th century would involve racial issues. In addition, he taught at the Duke University Law School from 1985 to 1992. In 1993 he was awarded the Charles Frankel Prize by President Bill Clinton for contributing to public understanding of the humanities. Two years later, Clinton honored Franklin again with the Presidential Medal of Freedom, the nation's highest civilian honor.

Race Relations Point Man

Recognition by Clinton was not limited to medals. In June 1997, Clinton appointed Franklin to chair a panel of eight to oversee a year-long initiative on race relations. At the time of his appointment, Franklin promised not to mince words in his talks with Clinton. "I think I'm valuable only to the extent that I am honest and candid," he told a writer for *The Atlanta Journal and Constitution.*

Over the course of his long academic career, Franklin was a visiting professor at many universities, including Cambridge University; twice held Guggenheim fellowships; and received honorary degrees from more than ninety colleges and universities.

A man of strong political ideals, Franklin once wrote, "I could not have avoided being a social activist even if I had wanted to." He played an important role in the historical research involved in the 1954 *Brown* v. *Board of Education* case, served as an informal adviser to Jesse Jackson, and actively campaigned against the confirmation of the appointment of Judge Robert Bork to the Supreme Court. At the same time he insisted that scholarship and politics must be kept separate and warned his fellow historians against the danger of allowing their concern with the "urgent matters of their own time" to distort their "view of an earlier period."

Despite his enviable march through the halls of academia, or perhaps because of it, Franklin still saw room for much improvement in U.S. race relations at the end of the twentieth century. "I'd be afraid to raise a black child in America today, not merely because of what would happen to him in the black community but in the white community too," he told *The New York Times Magazine.*

Franklin married his college classmate, the former Aurelia Whittington. They had one son, John Whittington, who became a program officer at the Smithsonian Institute. Franklin also had a foster son, Bouna Ndiaye, a native of Senegal. In addition to his scholarly pursuits, Franklin was an avid cultivator of orchids, including the officially registered hybrid phalaenopsis, John Hope Franklin.

Further Reading

In addition to Franklin's writing listed in the text see John Hope Franklin, "A Life of Learning," American Council of Learned Societies Occasional Paper, No. 4; "Revising the Old South," *U.S. News and World Report* (September 17, 1990); "Fifty Years of Exploring the Past: The Unfinished History of John Hope Franklin," *Ebony* (February 1990); Eric Anderson and Alfred A. Moss, Jr., *The Facts of Reconstruction: Essays in Honor of John Hope Franklin* (1991).

Additional Sources

Applebome, Peter, "Keeping Tabs On Jim Crow: John Hope Franklin," *The New York Times Magazine,* April 23, 1995, p.34.

Pomerantz, Gary M., "John Hope Franklin: Scholar With A Mission," *The Atlanta Journal and Constitution,* July 13, 1997, pp.A10. ☐

Rosalind Elsie Franklin

The British physical chemist and molecular biologist Rosalind Elsie Franklin (1920-1958) made her most outstanding contribution to molecular biology by establishing the crystallographic basis for the structure of DNA.

Rosalind Elsie Franklin was born in London, England, on July 25, 1920, the second child and first daughter of Ellis and Muriel (Waley) Franklin. Her family's background was in banking and the arts. Yet, by the age of 15 she had chosen science as her vocation. Years later she still debated this decision with her father, who eventually accepted it even though it meant, at that time, a choice of career over marriage and family life.

Following St. Paul's Girls' School in London, she went to Cambridge University in 1938 as a chemistry student at Newnham College. After graduation in 1941 she remained in Cambridge on a research scholarship to study gas-phase chromatography with Ronald G. W. Norrish, a Nobel Laureate for Chemistry in 1967.

Between 1942 and 1946 Franklin's expertise in physical chemistry was called upon to study the physical structure of coals as assistant research officer of the British Coal Utilization Research Association. In 1945 Franklin received her Ph.D. from Cambridge University for a thesis on "The Physical Chemistry of Solid Organic Colloids with Special Relation to Coal and Related Materials."

Early in 1947 Franklin left London for Paris where she was a researcher at the Laboratoire Central des Services Chimiques de l'État. There she worked closely with Jacques Méring until the end of 1950, having become an expert in X-ray crystallography. Her work was fundamental for what is now known as carbon-fiber technology.

As X-ray crystallography of biological compounds was rapidly expanding in Britain under the auspices of the Medical Research Council (MRC) in the early 1950s, Franklin returned to London. She joined the MRC Unit at King's College. There John Randall, who arranged for her to receive the Turner-Newall fellowship for three years, suggested that she work on DNA (deoxyribonucleic acid) structure.

The main outcome of the research Franklin conducted at King's College between January 1951 and March 1953 was published, with her research student Raymond G. Gosling as a co-author, in *Nature* on April 25, 1953. It included the X-ray photography of the B form of DNA ("Sodium deoxyribose nucleate from calf thymus. Structure B"), which provided the basis for the interpretation of DNA structure as a double helix by James D. Watson and Francis H. C. Crick. Their own famous paper appeared in the same issue also, in the section "Molecular Structure of Nucleic Acids." This joint publication, accompanied by yet another corroborating paper on DNA structure by Maurice H. F. Wilkins, A. R. Stokes and H. R. Wilson, also from King's College, conveys a misleading impression of the circumstances of the discovery of DNA structure. It appears as if this discovery resulted from a close cooperation linking the MRC Biophysics Research Unit and the Wheatstone Physics Laboratory, King's College, in London, and the MRC Unit for the Study of the Molecular Structure of Biological Systems at the Cavendish Laboratory in Cambridge, where Watson and Crick worked. Due to this contiguity, the experimental papers by Franklin and Gosling and by Wilkins, Stokes, and Wilson became "mere" corroborations, although they were independent interpretative efforts. In contrast, the double helix model gained further credibility from this juxtaposition, as it moved from the status of a "hypothesis" to that of a "proven" theoretical statement. All three papers professed advance knowledge of the general nature of the research performed both in King's College and in Cambridge.

By the time her DNA paper was published Franklin was no longer at King's College. She had found it imperative to leave because of Randall's unjustifiable injunction to abandon the DNA problem altogether. She moved to Birkbeck College in London, where John Desmond Bernal (1901-1971), a founder of British X-ray crystallography of biological compounds, welcomed her to work on the structure of TMV (tobacco mosaic virus), a project he had begun before World War II. In 1954 Franklin and Aaron Klug started a fruitful collaboration. Following her untimely death in 1958 he brought to completion their TMV work. He was awarded the Nobel Prize for Chemistry in 1982, in part for this work.

With the recognition of the fundamental importance of DNA structure for molecular biology in the 1960s, Franklin's work on DNA became a subject of great attention. In

1962 the Nobel Prize for Medicine or Physiology was awarded to Crick, Watson, and Wilkins, when Franklin was no longer alive. First clues about her role in the complex events which surrounded the discovery of DNA structure emerged in 1968 when Watson published his bestselling and highly controversial autobiography, *The Double Helix.* Nicknamed "Rosy" in a derogatory manner, Franklin was depicted there as the key obstacle to Watson and Crick's hunt for a helical interpretation of DNA. She was allegedly "anti-helical" and refused to disclose data she was in the course of interpreting herself. Franklin, Wilkins, and Linus C. Pauling, the Nobel Laureate for Chemistry (1954) and for Peace (1962) who had worked briefly on DNA in 1953, were portrayed as the "losers" in a "race" for the double helix, evidently won by Watson and Crick. As a result, both Franklin's work and her personality became the object of distortion.

Crick saw it differently: "After all, the structure was there waiting to be discovered—Watson and I did not invent it. It seems to me unlikely that either of us would have done it separately, but Rosalind Franklin was getting pretty close. She was in fact only two steps away. She needed to realize that the two chains were anti-parallel and to discover the base-pairing." Wilkins also acknowledged Franklin's contribution, posthumously, in his Nobel Lecture. Klug provided evidence, quoting Franklin's notebooks, that she was close to solving the DNA structure.

Her friend and biographer Anne Sayre suggested that Franklin might have been impeded in her progress on DNA by the problematic attitude towards women and minority researchers prevailing at King's College at that time. Although various authors lay emphasis on the clash of personalities at King's College, where Franklin was isolated, a key fact still remaining to be clarified concerns credit appropriation. Or, as F. R. Jevons put it: "Winner Takes All."

Franklin had too short a life to straighten the DNA record herself, having died of cancer on April 16, 1958, at the age of 37. How appropriate were J. D. Bernal's words: "Her early death is a great loss to science."

Further Reading

An assessment of Franklin's career was J. D. Bernal, "Dr. Rosalind E. Franklin" in *Nature* 182 (July 19, 1958). The three papers on DNA structure appeared in *Nature 171* (April 25, 1953). On Franklin, see: Edward Garber, editor, *Genetic Perspectives in Biology and Medicine* (1985); John Gribbin, *In Search of the Double Helix* (1985); Frederick Raphael Jevons, *Winner Takes All* (1981); Horace Freeland Judson, *The Eighth Day of Creation* (1980); James D. Watson, *The Double Helix. A Personal Account of the Discovery of the Structure of DNA,* Gunther S. Stent, editor (1980; the original version, without reviews and comments, appeared in 1968); Pnina G. Abir-Am, "Review of *A Century of DNA*" in *ISIS 69* (1978); Nicholas Wade, *The Ultimate Experiment* (1977); Maurice H. F. Wilkins, "The Molecular Configuration of Nucleic Acids," in *Nobel Lectures in Molecular Biology 1933-1975* (1977); Anne Sayre, *Rosalind Franklin and DNA* (1975); A. Klug, "Rosalind Franklin and the Double Helix," (published together with eight other papers for the 21 years of the double helix) *Nature* 248 (April 26, 1974); and Robert Olby,

The Path to the Double Helix (foreword by Francis Crick, 1974). □

Stella Maraia Sarah Miles Franklin

Stella Maraia Sarah Miles Franklin (1879-1954) was an Australian novelist. A sound chronicler and a satirist, she wrote with a sure but sensitive touch on the theme of her country's pioneer settlers.

Miles Franklin was born in Talbingo in the open rangelands of southern New South Wales on Oct. 14, 1879. She absorbed the lore of the upland grazing country before her father became a homesteader in 1891 and began dairy farming near Goulburn, where she attended public school and came to be more directly influenced by the emerging nationalism.

Franklin's first novel, *My Brilliant Career,* was written in its original version when she was 16. She submitted it to the *Bulletin,* a journal chronicling episodes of bush life, and received favorable comment and suggestions for revisions. The book was published in Edinburgh in 1901, and its authenticity, rich vernacular, and buoyant outlook earned it instant success in Australia. Appearing in the wake of a succession of ballads, short stories, and verse in the local idiom, it was quickly identified as "the very first" Australian novel, the first, that is, which "could not have been written by a stranger or a sojourner."

The author's achievement was in her down-to-earth portrayal of the pioneers' struggle and her treatment of the theme of the heritage handed on to later generations. Nevertheless, *My Brilliant Career* ruffled the young author's relatives and friends, who believed themselves parodied in it. Concerned and hurt, Franklin wrote a sequel, *My Career Goes Bung,* but withheld it from publication until 1946.

After working briefly in Sydney as a free-lance journalist and developing a more active sympathy with the underdog, Franklin moved to the United States in 1902. In Chicago she undertook social work with the National Women's Trade Union League and its journal, *Life and Labor. Some Everyday Folk and Dawn* (1909) had an Australian setting, but its strong political overtones, related to demands for woman's suffrage, robbed it of spontaneity. Moving to London, in World War I she worked as a hospital assistant and later as a political secretary.

After visiting Australia briefly in 1924, Franklin wrote three "photographic" novels of bush pioneering, *Up the Country* (1928), *Ten Creeks Run* (1930), and *Back to Bool Bool* (1931), all published under the pen name "Brent of Bin Bin." The third of the trio had a message in contemporary social problems. A humorous story of homestead-farm life, *Old Blastus of Bandicoot,* appeared under her own name in 1931.

In 1933 Franklin returned to live in Australia, and in 1936 her most widely acclaimed novel, *All That Swagger,* was published. An exposé of the frightening emptiness of the bush life and how its disappointments molded the lives of those trapped within it, the story is built around the indomitable character of a pioneer able to retain a zest for life in spite of setbacks.

Franklin's later writing included a literary biography, *Joseph Furphy: The Legend of a Man and His Book,* written in collaboration with Kate Baker (1944). Three "Brent of Bin Bin" books—*Prelude to Waking, Cockatoos,* and *Gentlemen at Gyang Gyang*—were published in the early 1950s; none broke new ground.

Miles Franklin died at Sydney on Sept. 19, 1954. She bequeathed extensive diaries to the Mitchell Library, Sydney, for eventual publication.

Further Reading

A comprehensive critical appreciation of Miles Franklin's work is given in H. M. Green, *A History of Australian Literature,* vol. 1 (1961). Concise sketches are given under "Brent of Bin Bin" and Miles Franklin, together with listings of her output, in Edmund M. Miller, *Australian Literature: A Bibliography to 1938; Extended to 1950,* edited by Frederick T. Macartney (1956).

Additional Sources

Coleman, Verna, *Miles Franklin in America: her unknown (brilliant) career,* London: Angus & Robertson, 1981.

Franklin, Miles, *Childhood at Brindabella: my first ten years,* Sydney: Angus and Robertson, 1974.

Roderick, Colin Arthur, *Miles Franklin: her brilliant career,* Adelaide; New York: Rigby, 1982. □

William Franklin

The American colonial administrator William Franklin (ca. 1731-1813) was the last of the royal governors of New Jersey. He chose to support Great Britain throughout the American Revolution.

William Franklin, the illegitimate son of Benjamin Franklin, was born in 1731 (possibly late 1730) and reared in his father's home. He obtained a militia commission with Pennsylvanians on the New York frontier and by 1750 had risen to captain.

When he returned to Philadelphia, Franklin became comptroller of the General Post Office, under his father, and clerk of the General Assembly. He accompanied the elder Franklin to England in 1757, studied law, and gained admittance to the bar. He traveled with his father in Europe and assisted in his scientific studies; Oxford awarded him a master of arts degree in 1762 at the same time his father was awarded an honorary degree. That year William married Elizabeth Downes. Personable and handsome, he fitted easily into English society. Through the influence of the Earl of Bute, he was appointed governor of New Jersey in 1763.

Despite the reservations of the proprietor of Pennsylvania, Franklin and his bride were at first popular in the colony. As governor, he tactfully avoided disputes with the Assembly and demonstrated genuine interest in improving roads, aiding agriculture, and reforming the legal code. But as differences grew between the colonists and the mother country, his position became difficult. He appreciated certain American grievances, but he had scant faith in popular government and supported the authoritarian stance his proprietor's instructions required.

After the extralegal Perth Amboy Convention (October 1765) chose delegates to the Stamp Act Congress, Franklin was in continual difficulties with New Jersey rebels. He became estranged from his father. Even after hostilities commenced, Franklin remained in office as a loyalist, forwarding information on the New Jersey situation to England. After January 1776 he was kept under guard by the Provincial Congress, which ordered his arrest on June 15 and had him imprisoned in Connecticut. Denied permission to visit his dying wife, he was exchanged in 1778.

For a time Franklin stayed in New York, where he served as president of the Board of Associated Loyalists. Soon he returned to England; the British commission on loyalist claims eventually awarded him £1,800 and a pension for the loss of his estates. He became reconciled with his father by letter in 1784 and died in England on Nov. 16, 1813.

Further Reading

Letters from William Franklin to William Strahan, edited by Charles Henry Hart (1911), is an illuminating source. Carl Van Doren's monumental *Benjamin Franklin* (1938) has much information on William. Other sources are Paul L. Ford, *Who Was the Mother of Franklin's Son* (1889); Francis Bazley Lee, *New Jersey as a Colony and and as a State,* vol. 1 (1902); and Donald L. Kemmerer, *Path to Freedom: The Struggle for Self-Government in Colonial New Jersey, 1703-1776* (1940).

Additional Sources

Gerlach, Larry R., *William Franklin, New Jersey's last royal governor,* Trenton: New Jersey Historical Commission, 1975.

Randall, Willard Sterne, *A little revenge: Benjamin Franklin and his son,* Boston: Little, Brown, 1984.

Skemp, Sheila L., *Benjamin and William Franklin: father and son, patriot and loyalist,* Boston: Bedford Books of St. Martin's Press, 1994. □

Lady Antonia Fraser

The British writer Lady Antonia Fraser (Pinter; born 1932), was a popular biographer, historian, and mystery novelist.

L ady Antonia Fraser was born on August 27, 1932, in London, England. She was the daughter of the seventh Earl of Longford, Francis Pakenham (born 1905), a statesman who had several cabinet posts under Labor Prime Minister Harold Wilson. He was also a famed public crusader and writer. Her mother was the Countess of Longford, Elizabeth Pakenham (born 1906), the author of a series of popular biographical studies of Queen Victoria, Wellington, Churchill, the Queen Mother, and Queen Elizabeth II.

It was natural that Antonia should become a writer, coming from a family of writers, the "literary Longfords." As well as her father and mother, Lady Antonia's sister Rachel Billington was a novelist; another sister, Judith Kazantzis, was a feminist poet; a brother, Thomas Pakenham, was an historian; and her two eldest daughters, Rebecca and Flora, were both writers.

Lady Antonia was educated at the Catholic convent and Oxford (Lady Margaret Hall, BA 1953). She converted to Catholicism in her teens, following her parents' lead, and at the age of 23 she married Sir Hugh Fraser, a handsome Catholic, Scots nobleman and war hero with the SAS (Special Air Services). He was 15 years her senior.

Sir Hugh Fraser had been a Conservative member of Parliament for Stafford since 1945 and had served in Conservative cabinets. They lived in London (when he was at the House of Commons) and in summer on an island in Inverness-shire, Scotland, owned by him. They had three sons and three daughters, but their marriage was dissolved in 1977. Already she was living with Harold Pinter, the playwright, whom she married in 1980. Her first husband died of cancer in 1984.

Her first job was in George Weidenfeld's publishing house as a general assistant. Lord Weidenfeld was a family friend and had Lady Antonia editing the expletives from Saul Bellow's *The Adventure of Augie March* for the British market. She published several juvenile items and *A History of Toys* (1966) before her major work, *Mary, Queen of Scots,* in 1969, which won the J. T. Black Prize for biography. Her mother, Lady Longford, had won the same prize five years before with a biography of Queen Victoria (1964).

Mother and daughter proceeded to carve up English history between them: Lady Longford taking the 19th century, Lady Antonia taking the 17th century. When Antonia wrote *Mary, Queen of Scots* she was pregnant with her fifth child. Two more biographies, *Cromwell, Our Chief Among Men* (1973) and *King James: VI of Scotland, I of England* (1974), came from her pen when she was still married to Hugh Fraser, and one biography, *King Charles II* (1979), between marriages. In the meantime she edited a series of writings: *Lives of the Kings and Queens of England* (1975), *Scottish Love Poems* (1975), *Love Letters: An Anthology* (1976), *Heroes and Heroines* (1980), *Mary, Queen of Scots: An Anthology of Poetry* (1981), and *Oxford and Oxfordshire in Verse* (1982).

The earlier books, from the historian's point of view, were more researched than the later works, maybe because she was thinking of becoming a mystery novelist. Her first book in this style, *Quiet as a Nun,* appeared in 1977. Her heroine, Jemima Shore, a television reporter, is intelligent and fashionable. The novel is set in a convent and the hysterical nuns are brought under control by Jemima with a sangfroid style and frank manner. In the second novel, *The Wild Island* (1978), a clique of crazy royalists on a Scottish island is mixed up with a motley crew, including a grandiloquent member of Parliament (M.P.) and a princess. These novels in their settings are reminiscent of scenes she knew from her own life—a convent and a Scottish island, the royalists, and even an M.P., her first husband. The novels starring Jemima Shore were successful and were televised in England. They were followed by *A Splash of Red* (1981) and *Cool Repentance* (1982).

More academic in character was her later book, *The Weaker Vessel* (1984), a volume about 17th-century women in England. It was based on primary documents rather than on other work by historians, and her organization is accomplished. Some reviewers of the book seemed to think that it was anecdotal and lacking analytical skills. *The Weaker Vessel* contains a hundred stories of mainly upper-class women and does not lend itself to theorizing, at least not according to Antonia Fraser. The limited emancipation of 17th-century women due to the influence of Oliver Cromwell peaked in mid-century. Women's status was set back after his death.

Fraser followed *The Weaker Vessel* with the mysteries *Oxford Blood* (1985), *Jemima Shore's First Case* (1986), and *Your Royal Hostage* (1987); *Boadicea's Chariot: The Warrior Queens,* in the United States *The Warrior Queens;* the mystery *The Cavalier Case* (1990); and *The Wives of Henry VIII* (1992). A more recent Fraser history is *Faith and Treason: The Story of the Gunpowder Plot,* an account of the 1605 conspiracy led by Guy Fawkes to blow up Parliament with King James I inside.

While Fraser has been justly celebrated for her literary prowess, her beauty has garnered much attention as well. "I suppose one's vanity is pleased by it, but if I could be born again with more beauty or more brains, I'd take the brains," Fraser is quoted in an article by Polly Samson appearing in *Harper's Bazaar,* November 1992, "Once you are called a beauty, then you are either an ex-beauty, a fading beauty, or 'still surprisingly beautiful.' But at least one gets more shortsighted, so when you remove your spectacles to put on makeup, the image in the mirror is pleasingly blurred."

Further Reading

For additional information on Lady Antonia see Mel Gussow, "Antonia Fraser: The Lady Is a Writer," *New York Times Magazine* (September 9, 1984); "Lady Antonia's Secret Garden," *House and Garden* (March 1985); *New Republic* (December 29, 1979); *Maclean's* (December 31, 1979); and *TIME* (September 17, 1984). □

Malcolm Fraser

Malcolm Fraser (born 1930), prime minister of Australia from 1975-1983, was regarded as one of the toughest and most successful leaders of the Liberal party.

John Malcolm Fraser was born and raised in "grazier" (sheep rancher) country in New South Wales and Victoria. His only profession outside of politics was that of grazier, running the family property of "Nareen." Indeed, Nareen remained his first home even while he was prime minister, and he returned to it after his defeat in the 1983 elections.

Fraser was educated at the elite Melbourne Grammar School and attended Oxford University, where he received an MA in 1952. In 1954 he was pre-selected as the Liberal party's candidate for the House of Representatives' seat of Wannon in Victoria, but he was defeated. In 1955 he recontested the seat successfully and retained it until he retired from politics.

At 24 he was the youngest member of Parliament and had the prime minister, Sir Robert Gordon Menzies, as his patron. However, his youth meant that his backbench apprenticeship was long. He served on numerous government committees but was not given a ministerial position until after Menzies had retired. Menzies' successor, Harold Holt, named Fraser minister for the army in 1966, from which position he became an outspoken advocate of the Vietnam War, a supporter of conscription, and a controversial figure. His penchant for "risk taking" became apparent. Under Prime Minister John H. Gorton, Fraser received the ministry for education and science and fought for increased federal aid to education. Following the 1969 election, during which the Liberals maintained the government but received their first serious electoral losses in eight years, Fraser was shifted

to the Ministry of Defense where he continued his support for a hawkish policy line.

Fraser continued in his aggressive style, fighting publicly with members of the military and coming into conflict with his prime minister. On March 8, 1971, Fraser resigned abruptly, accusing Gorton of "significant disloyalty to a senior minister." In fact, Fraser was distancing himself from a man whose leadership capacities were questionable. On March 10 Gorton was defeated as leader in a "spill" within the Liberal party, and William McMahon became prime minister. However, the Liberals were defeated in the 1972 election and became the Opposition for the first time in 23 years. Fraser became shadow minister on primary industry and later spokesman on labor and immigration.

Road to Prime Minister

The Opposition through its control of the upper house (the Senate) thwarted the Labor government, which called an election in 1974. Labor was returned, though with a reduced majority in the lower house and still lacking control of the upper. Nonetheless, the Liberals regarded the election as a setback and as a defeat for its then leader, Sir Bill Snedden. In March 1975 Malcolm Fraser defeated Snedden and became leader of the parliamentary Liberal party and the Opposition, a position he used to bring on the downfall of the Gough Whitlam Labor government. It was at Fraser's instigation that the Senate failed to pass the budget and created a constitutional crisis in what was possibly the biggest risk by Fraser in a risk ridden career. Fraser's popularity plummeted during October 1975 while the standing of the Labor party improved. However, the governor-general, Sir John Kerr, stepped in and dismissed Whitlam as prime minister, dissolved Parliament, and appointed Fraser "caretaker" prime minister pending an election. After he was sworn in as prime minister on November 11, 1975, Fraser directed the Senate to pass the budget and the cause of the crisis disappeared. Following a bitter election campaign Fraser became prime minister of Australia, having won the December 13 election with a record majority of 91 seats in the 125-member lower house and 35 seats in the 64-seat Senate.

Fraser became prime minister during a period of extreme economic difficulties with recession, inflation, and unemployment. His theme as prime minister was to blame the big spending previous Labor government and to attack the public sector as "parasitic" and the source of the Australian economic malaise. His aim was to reduce the size of the public sector and to stimulate the private. He was the first of the neo-conservatives and later advised Margaret Thatcher of England on electoral and policy strategy. He reduced the number of government departments and combined the functions of others; he introduced staff ceilings to control the size of the public sector and had revolutionary legislation passed which attacked public service tenure.

The period of the Fraser government was marked by bitterness and rancour between public service and government. The difficulties were not helped by the government's attacks on the integrity of its public servants. The most notorious of which was one of Fraser's ministers calling public servants pigs with their "snouts in the trough." Fraser also established a "razor gang" whose function was to investigate ways of cutting back on government functions. Despite promises to the contrary, Fraser disestablished the national health program of the Labor government and cut back dramatically spending in the areas of education and welfare. Pensions, unemployment benefits, and legal aid eligibility were all reduced.

Fraser's foreign policy centered on "hard line" anti-Communism, suspicion of the Soviet's intentions in the Indian Ocean, and general skepticism about detente with the Soviet Union. Following the Soviet Union's attack on Afghanistan, Fraser cut off all academic exchanges and withdrew official Australian presence at the Moscow Olympics—although, in defiance of the prime minister, an Australian team in fact competed. Internationally, his other main area was Africa. At a Commonwealth Heads of Government Meeting (CHOGM) he received international respect for his stance on Africa. He was an advocate for civil rights and a severe critic of the government of South Africa.

The Fraser Government

The Fraser period of government was one of high activity. It was not a traditional conservative government and, despite its cutbacks in public service, it demanded more of that service. Fraser also proceeded to revise the "Westminster" system of government and through various mechanisms placed more control into the hands of the prime minister, reducing the independence both of his senior public servants and his own party colleagues.

Fraser called elections in 1977 and in 1980 which he won. Despite his successes as leader and at three elections, Fraser was not a popular figure. He clashed with members of the mass media and was seen as arrogant, haughty, and ruthless. Despite his height (over six feet four inches), his style was neither imposing nor one which suited television. Moreover, the economy did not improve and the 1980 election saw the Labor party demonstrate some electoral success.

Fraser came under increasing criticism from within his own party and in particular from his most serious challenger for the leadership, Andrew Peacock. Peacock had taken a leaf from the Fraser book of tactics and had resigned as a minister with a blistering attack on the Fraser authoritarian style of governing. By so doing Peacock was able to distance himself from what he saw as the increasingly failing policies of the Fraser government. In what was generally seen as a frantic attempt to avoid electoral defeat, Fraser called an early election in March 1983. However, his move did not prevent the Labor party selecting as its leader the populist Robert Hawke. Hawke led the Labor party to victory. Peacock was elected leader of the Liberal party, and Fraser resigned from politics.

Critic of his own party

After his resignation Fraser was an outspoken critic of sections of his own party and in the election of 1984 was "waiting in the wings" should Peacock be resoundingly repudiated by the electorate. Despite the fact that the 1984 results demonstrated Peacock's electoral acceptance, Fraser maintained his criticisms. It should be remembered that Fraser was defeated while still young for a political leader (53), with plenty of time for a political revival. It should also be stressed that politics was his only real profession for 30 years. Fraser maintained a high profile internationally, having been an invited guest of honor at the prestigious conservative American Enterprise Institute in Washington, D.C. Moreover, he was involved in a number of meetings of "ex-leaders."

Fraser returned to farming in Nareen, but he did not abandon political life. He became involved in international affairs, particularly as a member of the Commonwealth Group of Eminent Persons, which worked to eliminate apartheid in South Africa. In 1996, Fraser was named special envoy to Africa by the Australian government to push Canberra's campaign for a temporary seat on the United Nations Security Council. At home in 1997, Fraser was an outspoken critic against consolidation of ownership of the country's print and electronic media. He also called for a national apology from Australia for the forced removal of Aboriginal children from their families, following the release of a human rights report on the matter. Fraser endorsed the report's finding that the removal of an estimated 50,000 Aboriginal children under a policy that existed until the 1970s amounted to genocide.

Further Reading

On the events of 1975, see Gough Whitlam, *The Truth of the Matter* (1979). See also, J. Edwards, *Life Wasn't Meant Easy* (1977), named after a famous quote by Fraser, and Anne Summers, *Gamble for Power* (1983). A detailed analysis of his period as prime minister is forthcoming under the tentative title of *First Amongst Equals* by Patrick Weller. Further material on Fraser can be found in A. Patience and B. Head (editors), *From Whitlam to Fraser* (1979) and A. Aitchison (editor), *Looking at the Liberals* (1974), which includes a chapter by Fraser. □

Peter Fraser

Peter Fraser (1884-1950) was a prominent socialist and Labour party politician of New Zealand. He emerged as a great wartime leader of his country and played an important part in the reconstruction following World War II.

Born in the village of Fearn in the Highlands of Scotland on Aug. 28, 1884, Peter Fraser was the son of a bootmaker of active liberal views. Young Fraser's education was curtailed so that he could help sustain his family, but in 1907 he went to London, where he became attracted to socialism and the Independent Labour party.

Socialist Leader

After a period of unemployment Fraser decided to emigrate to New Zealand and landed in Auckland in January 1911. There he joined the New Zealand Socialist party and spoke at political meetings as a supporter of the militant labor unions, which had rebelled against the more moderate Trades and Labour Councils. A laborer himself, Fraser was elected president of the Auckland General Labourers Union and in 1912 rose to be secretary of the "Red Federation" of Labour. The failure of a series of strikes by municipal workers and miners with which he was connected left him jobless and without influence.

In 1913 Fraser moved to Wellington to work on the docks. When the radical unions reorganized and a new political group, the Social Democratic party, was formed, Fraser became secretary treasurer. During the great wharf and mining strike of 1913 he was arrested. When World War I broke out in 1914, he attacked New Zealand's participation in an "imperialist" war and bitterly opposed conscription. In December 1916 he and other labor leaders were again arrested and charged with sedition. He was sentenced to a year's imprisonment and served the full term. Meanwhile, as secretary of the Social Democratic party, he had taken a leading part in the establishment of the New Zealand Labour party, formed in July 1916.

Labour Legislator

In October 1918 Fraser was elected to Parliament as Labour member for Wellington Central, and the next year he was made secretary to the parliamentary Labour party under H. E. Holland as leader. For the next 30 years he was rarely far from the center of the New Zealand political stage.

A sarcastic and telling debater, Fraser won respect for his industry and conscientious attention to the needs of the common man. Though his earlier industrial experience continued to prove invaluable to him, time blunted his radicalism, and he grew moderate with age and office. Land nationalization, for instance, which he supported in 1919, seemed politically unrealistic and somewhat naive to him when his party's platform was revised in 1927; and he came round to supporting the principle of industrial arbitration, which he had once rejected.

In 1933 Michael Joseph Savage became leader of the parliamentary party, and Fraser was elected his deputy. Two years later, in late 1935, Labour took office, and Fraser undertook the responsible portfolios of health, education, marine, and police. This period of his career established his claim as an imaginative and effective administrator as well as a powerful political personality. Some of his innovations—in health, education, and Maori affairs—had lasting results.

Prime Minister

In August 1939 Fraser became acting prime minister when Savage fell seriously ill; and when the latter died in March 1940, Fraser survived internal stresses within the Labour party to become prime minister. Fraser's executive difficulties were increased by political dissension and industrial unrest. The Opposition refused to take part in a national or coalition wartime government. In 1943, at the height of the war, he had to face a lively general election.

New Zealand's part in the war and its relations with Great Britain, Australia, and the United States offered Fraser a wide field in which to show his capacity and judgment. Though the victory of the Axis powers in Greece and Crete and the experience of fighting in the Middle East did not persuade him to remove his military strength to the Pacific theater of war, he otherwise collaborated very closely with the Australian Labour government.

Both New Zealand and Australia came to realize that the strategic and military role of the United States was as crucial in their area as it had been in Europe; and both accepted the challenge to participate in bringing about an improved postwar pattern in the Pacific. Their self-discovery and determination not to be overlooked was embodied in the Canberra Pact of 1944. Whereas he had once despised the League of Nations, Fraser had changed into a leading advocate of international organizations and cooperation. He attended the San Francisco Conference of 1945 and spoke vigorously, if unsuccessfully, in favor of collective security pacts within the United Nations framework; and he attacked the according of veto rights to the great powers. He had greater success in matters concerning international trusteeship and the setting up of the United Nations Economic and Social Council.

At home Fraser survived the general postwar election of 1946, but his established welfare policies were criticized from both left and right. The Labour party, divided over many issues, was defeated badly in the 1949 election. Fraser, whose wife had died childless in 1946, was exhausted, and he died after a short illness on Dec. 12, 1950.

A man of deep conviction, stubborn industry, and unspectacular but real breadth of talent, Fraser exemplified in his life and work many of the strengths and weaknesses of an active Labour politician in a modern democracy. His intelligence and office brought him into contact with many styles of socialist thought and action. The emphasis he placed on political and government activity and on the need for party discipline perhaps lessened his support among some more doctrinaire unionists, but he was accepted by his nation at a time of crisis in war and for years of peacetime reconstruction.

Further Reading

A biography of Fraser is James Thorn, *Peter Fraser* (1952). Fraser is discussed in these useful background works: F. L. Wood, *The New Zealand People at War* (1958), and Bruce M. Brown, *The Rise of New Zealand Labour* (1962). □

Simon Fraser

Simon Fraser (1776-1862) was a Canadian explorer and fur trader and the first man to follow the Fraser River from its source in the Rocky Mountains to the Pacific Ocean.

Simon Fraser was born at Bennington, N.Y., the son of Capt. Simon Fraser. The father, a loyalist, was captured by the rebels during the American Revolution and died in prison in Albany. His widow took their son to Canada immediately afterward. Placed in the care of his uncle Judge John Fraser of Montreal, young Simon was educated in that city. In 1792 he was apprenticed to the North West Company, the great Montreal fur-trading organization. For several years he was employed in the Athabasca Department.

In 1801 Fraser became a partner in the North West Company and 4 years later took charge of all the company's operations beyond the Rocky Mountains. The great adventure of his life took place in 1808, When he explored the Fraser River (named after him) to its mouth. It was almost foolhardy to try to shoot that wild and turbulent canyon in a frail canoe, but he persuaded his party to follow him, and the laconic report in his journal hardly does justice to the accomplishment.

Fraser's daring enterprise earned him a promotion, and he was placed in charge of the Red River Department, the largest in the western part of British North America, in 1811. In 1817 he was arrested by Lord Selkirk as an accessory to the Seven Oaks massacre near Red River the preceding year. Fraser had not been directly involved and was acquitted in the much-delayed trial held at York in 1819.

Shortly thereafter, Fraser retired from the service of the North West Company and settled among the Highlanders in St. Andrews, Upper Canada. The following year, 1820, he married at the age of 44. He eventually had five sons and three daughters. Little is known of this period in Fraser's life.

oseph von Fraunhofer, the son of a poor glazier, was born on March 6, 1787, in Straubing, Bavaria. An orphan by the age of 12, he became an apprentice to a mirror maker in Munich. He spent his first pennies at the flea market on an elementary textbook of geometry which he studied in his spare time. On July 21, 1801, two houses collapsed in Munich, and of the people buried under the ruins, Fraunhofer was the only one found alive. The incident brought him to the attention of J. Niggl, an optical instrument maker, and J. Utzschneider, a Benedictine from Benediktbeuern. In 1807, when Fraunhofer had already mastered through private studies the best German university textbooks on optics, he was invited to work with a new optical-instrument-making firm established largely through Utzschneider's efforts at Benediktbeuern.

Indicative of Fraunhofer's abilities was his first assignment: the making of achromatic lenses for telescopes. The task implied not only original theoretical work but also the production of highly homogeneous silicates. Fraunhofer's communication on the results of his research appeared in the *Denkschriften* (Memoirs) for 1814-1815 of the Academy of Sciences in Munich. The paper contained a description of the first use of the dark lines of the solar spectrum (Fraunhofer lines) as reference points for the measurement of refraction indexes.

Fraunhofer's other great achievement concerned the measurement of wavelengths in the optical spectrum. He transformed the spectroscope into a precision instrument, but his finest precision instrument was the micrometer, described in his memoir of 1824 to the Munich Academy.

He turned up again as a captain of militia during the rebellion of 1837-1838 in Upper Canada. He was then 62 years old, which might account for the permanent knee injury he suffered while on a night march. As a result, Fraser was awarded a government pension in 1841.

Fraser died, in relative poverty, on Aug. 18, 1862, one of the last survivors of the old "Nor'westers."

Further Reading

There is no definitive study of Fraser. The best account of his career is in the introduction to *The Letters and Journals of Simon Fraser, 1806-1808* (1960), edited by W. Kaye Lamb. Some useful information is also in Alexander Fraser, *The Clan Fraser in Canada* (1895), and Lawrence J. Burpee, *The Search for the Western Sea: The Story of the Exploration of Northwestern America* (1908; rev. ed. in 2 vols., 1935). See also John Spargo, *Two Bennington-born Explorers and Makers of Modern Canada* (1950). □

Joseph von Fraunhofer

The German physicist Joseph von Fraunhofer (1787-1826) was the first to solve the problem of constructing achromatic lenses of high magnitude.

By then he had been "extraordinary visiting member" there for 3 years, in due recognition of the talents of a first-rate physicist whose academic training consisted of spotty attendance of the lowest grades of elementary school.

Fraunhofer's success made his name synonymous with progress. Astronomers considered it a privilege to have their orders accepted by him. The famous refractor he made for the Dorpat Observatory and the heliometer he constructed for the Berlin Observatory gave both institutions positions of unchallenged leadership for several decades.

The privations of youth and his delicate constitution hardly equipped Fraunhofer for glassblowing, which caused in 1824 the first symptoms of a respiratory ailment. Proper attention to his health came too late. He died on June 7, 1826, in Munich at the height of a most promising scientific career.

Further Reading

Information on Fraunhofer is in Theodore F. Van Wagenen, *Beacon Lights of Science* (1924); Henry Smith Williams, *Great Astronomers* (1930); and Philip Lenard, *Great Men of Science* (1933). □

Sir James George Frazer

Sir James George Frazer (1854-1941), a British classicist and anthropologist, was the author of "The Golden Bough," a classic study of magic and religion. It popularized anthropology.

James Frazer was born in Glasgow, Scotland, on Jan. 1, 1854. He attended Glasgow University (1869-1874), where his major interest was the classics. He continued his studies in classics at Trinity College at Cambridge and was elected a fellow of the college in 1879. He remained at Cambridge the rest of his life, except for an appointment as professor of social anthropology at Liverpool University in 1907, which he resigned after a year.

Frazer continued his interest in classics, editing Sallust's *Catilina et Iugurtha* (1884), translating Pausanias's *Description of Greece* (1898), and editing and translating Ovid's *Fasti* (1929).

Frazer's early classical interests were considerably broadened through acquaintance with Sir Edward Tylor's *Primitive Culture.* Frazer decided that ancient rituals and myths could be illuminated by examination of similar customs of modern peoples living in a "savage" or "barbarous" stage. He borrowed Tylor's comparative method and developed his own method of comparison of customs of peoples of all times and places, which he retained throughout his lifelong research. His results have been criticized on the grounds that he took customs out of cultural context and that many of the customs compared were only superficially similar.

Early in his career as a fellow at Cambridge, Frazer met W. Robertson Smith, who stimulated his interest in comparative religion. Frazer's interest in totemism derived from Smith's invitation to write the article on the subject for the ninth edition of the *Encyclopaedia Britannica* (1888).

Frazer never did fieldwork. He spent all his life in the library, working 12, often 15, hours a day, almost every day. He obtained ethnographic information from the accounts of travelers, missionaries, and colonial administrators. To obtain desired information he prepared a questionnaire on "the manners, customs, religions, superstitions, etc., of uncivilized or semi-civilized peoples" (1887).

The first edition of *The Golden Bough* appeared in 1890. A second, expanded edition appeared in 1900, and a third, much expanded edition in 1911-1915. One reason for the great success of *The Golden Bough* is its excellent, if ornate, Victorian prose style. Today it is probably read as much for its literary merits as for its anthropological content.

Frazer was an inductivist; hence, his work is characterized by a sparsity of theory and much information. The general framework for the wealth of information, always so well phrased if too often oversimplified, is the idea that magic has given rise to religion, which in turn has given rise to science, in evolutionary stages. Magic is an attempt to control nature in which erroneous assumptions are made. When, in the course of time, the "savage" discovers that magic does not work, he gives up the attempt to control nature and instead seeks to propitiate or cajole the spirits or gods, which practice constitutes religion. Finally, in a higher state of civilization, man returns to the attempt to control nature, this time employing the experimental and objective techniques which constitute science. Frazer's distinction between magic and religion has proved valid, but the idea that an evolutionary stage of magic invariably preceded religion is invalid, as religious sentiments have been observed in very primitive peoples.

Frazer's *Totemism and Exogamy* (1910) is an expansion of his early work on totemism. His *Folk-lore in the Old Testament* (1923), *Man, God and Immortality* (1927), a collection of his writings on human progress, and many other works appeared in many volumes and in many editions. Though his ideas either have been disproved or amalgamated into more sophisticated theories, Frazer was perhaps the most honored anthropologist of all times. He was knighted in 1914 and awarded the British Order of Merit in 1925. He died in Cambridge on May 7, 1941.

Further Reading

An adulatory account of Frazer's life and work is given by his secretary, Robert Angus Downie, in *James George Frazer: The Portrait of a Scholar* (1940). A vivid description of Frazer and a more impartial analysis of his contributions constitute a chapter in Abram Kardiner and Edward Preble, *They Studied Man* (1961). Bronislaw Malinowski devotes a biographical appreciation to Frazer in *A Scientific Theory of Culture, and Other Essays* (1944). □

Edward Franklin Frazier

Edward Franklin Frazier (1894-1962), one of America's leading sociologists, specialized in studies of black people in North and South America and in Africa.

On Sept. 24, 1894, E. Franklin Frazier was born in Baltimore, Md. He took his bachelor of arts degree *cum laude* at Howard University in 1916. From 1916 to 1918 Frazier taught in secondary schools in Alabama, Virginia, and Maryland. In 1919 he began graduate studies at Clark University, Worcester, Mass., receiving a master of arts degree in sociology in 1920. As a research fellow at the New York School of Social Work (1920-1921), Frazier studied longshoremen in New York City. In 1921-1922 he studied folk high schools in Denmark. From 1922 to 1924 Frazier was an instructor in sociology at Morehouse College, serving also as director of the Atlanta School of Social Work (1922-1927). He married Marie E. Brown in 1922.

Frazier's essay "The Pathology of Race Prejudice" in *Forum* (June 1927) drew an analogy between race prejudice and insanity. As a result, Frazier had to leave Atlanta to avoid a white lynch mob. From 1927 to 1929 he pursued advanced study at the University of Chicago, receiving his doctorate in sociology in 1931 for *The Negro Family in Chicago* (1932). From 1929 to 1934 he worked under Charles S. Johnson, an outstanding African American sociologist, at Fisk University. Frazier returned to Howard University in 1934 as head of the department of sociology. In 1959 he became professor emeritus in the department of sociology and the African studies program.

From 1944 to 1951 Frazier served as part-time instructor at New York School of Social Work, Columbia University, and from 1957 to 1962 lectured at the School of Advanced International Studies, Johns Hopkins University. Frazier also served as visiting professor at several other colleges and universities. In 1948 Frazier served as president of the American Sociological Society, and he was chief of the Division of the Applied Social Sciences, Department of Social Sciences, United Nations Educational, Scientific, and Cultural Organization, in 1951-1953. Frazier published 8 books, 18 chapters in books, and at least 89 articles. His most significant work was on the African American family. In *The Negro Family in Chicago, The Free Negro Family* (1932), and *The Negro Family in the United States* (1939) Frazier offered pioneering interpretations of the character, history, and influence of the black family. His concept of the black matriarchy, despite recent challenges and new approaches, dominates work on the black family.

Frazier also offered candid, often polemical, analyses of the role of the black middle class, as in *Black Bourgeoisie* (1957). *The Negro in the United States* (1949; rev. ed. 1957) and *Race and Culture Contacts in the Modern World* (1957; rev. ed. 1965) contain Frazier's analysis of the black experience throughout the world.

Frazier's death on May 17, 1962, prevented completion of his study of the black church. Only an outline of his views, *The Negro Church in America* (1961), was published. G. Franklin Edwards, a colleague and friend, described Frazier as "a tough-minded intellectual" and "a fine exponent of the best tradition in American sociology and scholarship."

Further Reading

The best introduction to Frazier is his own works. G. Franklin Edwards edited and wrote an excellent introduction to Frazier's *On Race Relations: Selected Writings* (1968). St. Clair Drake's introduction to the 1967 reprint edition of Frazier's *Negro Youth at the Crossways* (1940) is also of great value. Howard W. Odum, *American Sociology: The Story of Sociology in the United States through 1950* (1951), contains a sketch of Frazier's life and works up to that date. There is a brief sketch of Frazier in Wilhelmena S. Robinson, *Historical Negro Biographies* (1968).

Additional Sources

Platt, Anthony M., *E. Franklin Frazier reconsidered,* New Brunswick N.J.: Rutgers University Press, c1991. ☐

Louis-Honoré Fréchette

Louis-Honoré Fréchette (1839-1908) was the best representative of the 19th-century patriotic manner in French-Canadian poetry. He was a less successful playwright and short-story writer.

Louis-Honoré Fréchette was born in Levis, Quebec, on Nov. 16, 1839. His turbulent vigor and lack of respect for conformists showed early in his interrupted schooling. So did his interest in writing poetry, and he soon frequented the bookshop of Octave Crémazie in Quebec. Fréchette went on to study law at Laval University and published his first collection of verse, *Mes Loisirs* (My Hours of Leisure), in 1863. Unable to make a business success of his journalism and law practice, he emigrated to Chicago in 1866.

The 5-year exile was fruitful. Fréchette responded both to the American dream of progress and to regret for his native land. He lost no time in starting *La Voix d'un exilé* (The Voice of an Exile; a collection eventually published in Chicago in 1868) and in founding French-language newspapers for the French Canadians in Chicago. He also wrote a play. The second newspaper lasted long enough to send him back to Canada as its correspondent in 1871. Here he began a political career, eventually gaining election to the federal Parliament (1874-1878). After the Liberal defeat of 1878, Fréchette returned to journalism and poetry, though standing for election again in 1882 (unsuccessfully). This was the period of his best work.

Fréchette's short stories and popular tales are entertaining, but his reputation rests mainly on his poetry. Fréchette was the best Canadian imitator of the French romantics and the most uncomplicated liberal patriot. *Les Oiseaux de neige* (Snowbirds) and *Les Fleurs boréales* (1879; Flowers of the North) celebrate Canadian nature in grandiose but harmonious verse. *La Légende d'un peuple* (1887; The Story of a People), although too servile an imitation of Hugo's *Légende des siècles,* attains some fine epic moments. Fréchette's success as a poet is due to the bold simplicity of his imagination. His regular but supple verse, rich rhymes, and fertile though too often conventional imagery make his symbols moving and memorable, though never profound or subtle. At his worst, Fréchette can be superficial, moralizing, and pompous, but the overall achievement of his best works completed the work of the Patriotic school, which was to add a sense of pride and dignity to the awareness of being a French Canadian.

Fréchette acquired renown and dignities in his lifetime. He was awarded the Prix Montyon of the Académie Française, and he held office as president of the Royal Society of Canada and of the École Littéraire de Montréal. Such honors earned him the nickname "Le Lauréat," sometimes used pejoratively. His success was late in relation to the Patriotic school, of which he was the youngest member. During his later years he was attacked for his many plagiarisms and was surpassed by the new fashion in poetry. He died in Montreal on May 31, 1908, with a definitive edition of his works still incomplete.

Further Reading

There is a short but rich study of Fréchette by David M. Hayne in Robert L. McDougall, ed., *Canada's Past and Present: A Dialogue* (1965). □

Frederick I

Frederick I (1123-1190), or Frederick Barbarossa, was Holy Roman Emperor from 1152 to 1190. He was one of the greatest monarchs of medieval Germany, and his strong rule set many patterns of future development.

The son of Duke Frederick II of Swabia, Frederick I was the nephew of Emperor Conrad III of the Hohenstaufen family. Frederick's mother, Judith, however, was a Welf, the sister of Henry the Proud, Duke of Saxony and Bavaria. Thus in his own person he united these rival families, whose feuding had torn Germany apart for some decades. He was brave, intelligent, and chivalrous and, in his later years, wore a long red beard, hence his name of Barbarossa, or Red Beard.

After Frederick was elected king of Germany in 1152, his first task was to negotiate a settlement with the Welf family in the person of his cousin Henry the Lion, Duke of Saxony. By 1156 an agreement between the two had been reached. Frederick gave Henry a free hand in Saxony, where Henry could exercise imperial powers and expand freely into Slavic lands beyond the Elbe River. Henry was

given almost the same authority in Bavaria, where he was also made duke.

With the Welfs conciliated, Frederick Barbarossa then proceeded to build up an imperial domain in western Germany along the Rhine near his ancestral Swabian holdings, giving special privileges to the towns, improving the status of the peasantry, and encouraging a well-structured feudalism among the nobility. He also gained control of the resources of Burgundy by marrying its heiress, Beatrice. Meanwhile Henry the Lion was behaving similarly in eastern Germany, where he advanced into Slavic lands, founded towns like Lübeck and Munich, cleared the Baltic of Wendish pirates, and encouraged Flemish and northern German peasants to settle lands beyond the Elbe. Their joint efforts resulted in Germany's making progress like that taking place in France and England during this same period.

Conflict with the Papacy

Frederick's concern with southern Germany and Burgundy, however, involved him in nearby Italy. He has been severely censured by many historians for his actions in this area. But it is hard to see how he could have avoided an interest in this part of the empire, where since the days of the emperor Henry V (reigned 1106-1125) German rulers had played little role and had allowed both the northern towns of Italy and the papacy to develop relatively undisturbed. Now all this changed.

Pope Adrian IV, at odds with his powerful vassal and protector the Norman king of Sicily, William I, asked assis-

tance from Frederick in getting rid of Arnold of Brescia, a religious reformer who had seized control of the city of Rome. In 1154-1155 Frederick answered this request by advancing on Rome and capturing and executing Arnold. In return he was crowned emperor by the Pope. Frederick, however, was obviously reluctant to accept the seeming subordination that this ceremony entailed.

By 1157 Pope and Emperor were definitely at odds, since, when Frederick held a diet in Besançon in Burgundy, he interpreted a papal letter as a slur upon his independence. From this time on he began to refer to his empire as a holy empire on a par with the Church. When he returned to Italy with a huge army in 1158, he was ready to challenge papal authority. He did so at a diet which he held at Roncaglia, where he claimed, as Roman emperor, complete authority over northern Italian cities, including both the right to appoint podestas, or imperial governors, for them and to levy heavy taxes upon them. He based such claims upon rights given emperors by the Roman law, which had newly been rediscovered and was being studied at Bologna and elsewhere in northern Italy. When Milan, the most powerful northern Italian city, resisted his claims and revolted, he captured it after a long siege and razed it. By 1161 he had crushed all resistance in northern Italy and seemed well on his way to organizing this rich area as an imperial domain under his direct rule.

Frederick's success, however, disturbed the papacy, which was now in the hands of a new pope, Alexander III. It also alarmed the Norman kings of Sicily to the south and the inhabitants of northern Italian towns who by 1168, with papal blessing, had organized the Lombard League to oppose Frederick's authority. Faced by this rising opposition, Frederick attempted to counter papal hostility by setting up an antipope and thus forced Alexander for a time to flee to France (1162-1165). He also planned an attack on the kingdom of Sicily. In the long run, however, his enemies proved too many for him to subdue. The Lombard League grew in power, and Milan was rebuilt while Frederick was unavoidably absent in Germany.

Finally, in 1174 Frederick returned again to Italy with a relatively small army, since he could rally only minimal support for his Italian plans among his German nobles. With this force he attempted several unsuccessful sieges of towns and then in 1176 was badly defeated by a Milanese force at the Battle of Legnano. Recognizing that this defeat had doomed his Italian prospects, Frederick made peace with Pope Alexander III and gave up his antipope. Alexander in return deserted his Lombard allies and allowed Frederick full control over the Church in Germany. In 1183 Frederick also came to terms with the Lombard League by signing the Peace of Constance, by which these centers were guaranteed self-government and the right to control their own taxes and judicial administration. Frederick's Lombard adventure had ended in failure.

Later Reign

Even before this final peace with the Lombard League, however, Frederick had decided to deal with the nobility of Germany, whose lack of support he blamed for his failure at Legnano, and especially with his cousin Henry the Lion. Henry was in a vulnerable position because many of the magnates of northern Germany had been alienated by his ruthlessness and high-handedness. In 1179 Frederick returned to Germany and ordered Henry to appear in court to answer charges brought against him by discontented vassals. Henry refused, his fiefs were declared forfeit, and he was driven into exile. His holdings in Saxony and Bavaria were broken up and divided among Frederick's supporters.

Victorious in Germany, in his last years Frederick finally won a great victory in Italy too—by marriage rather than by war. In 1186 he formed an alliance with King William II of Sicily to attack the weakening Byzantine Empire, which both coveted. William was young but childless, so to cement the alliance Frederick had his son Henry (later Henry VI) marry Constance, William's aunt and heiress to his throne. Three years later William died unexpectedly, and Henry found himself the ruler of the kingdom of Sicily, which had so long opposed his father's ambitions. Frederick then not only was supreme in Germany but had gained for his house in Italy the strong kingdom of Sicily.

In his last years Frederick took the cross and went on the Third Crusade. But on the way to Palestine in 1190 he died of a stroke while bathing in a stream in Cilicia. So great was his prestige among his contemporaries that a legend soon grew up in Germany that he had not died but was sleeping in a cave high in the Bavarian Alps. There, it was said, he sat on his throne, with his great red beard filling the cavern and ravens flying in and out. Someday, said the legend, he would awake and lead Germany again to glory.

The legend, however, differed considerably from the facts, for, although Frederick seemed to have won success in his later years, his reign was not what it might have been. His destruction of the territorial consolidation achieved by Henry the Lion benefited only the princes of Germany, while his loss of northern Italy set the stage for the later failure there of his able grandson Frederick II. Both Germany and Italy benefited little from his long reign.

Further Reading

The only good biography of Frederick I in English is Peter Munz, *Frederick Barbarossa* (1969). See also Austin Lane Poole, *Henry, the Lion* (1912). Valuable accounts of Frederick's reign can be found in James Westfall Thompson, *Feudal Germany* (1928); Geoffrey Barraclough, *The Origins of Modern Germany* (1946; 2d rev. ed. 1947); R. H. C. Davis, *A History of Medieval Europe: From Constantine to Saint Louis* (1957); and Christopher Brooke, *Europe in the Central Middle Ages, 962-1154* (1964). □

Frederick II

Frederick II (1194-1250) was Holy Roman emperor from 1215 to 1250. His unsuccessful effort to establish a strong centralized Italian state brought him into a long and bitter conflict with the papacy and the Italian urban centers.

Born in Iesi, Italy, Frederick II was the only son of Emperor Henry VI and of Constance of Sicily. His father died in 1197 and his mother, who served as regent for him, a year later. As the orphan king of Sicily, he was the ward of the great pope Innocent III, who ignored his education and training but kept his kingdom intact for him. Frederick grew up in Palermo, surrounded by factions who attempted to use him for their own ends and influenced by the Islamic and Greek culture that pervaded the dissolute Sicilian court.

At first Frederick was ignored in the empire of his father, where his able uncle Philip of Swabia and the Welf Otto IV, son of Henry the Lion, were quarreling over the imperial title. By 1211, however, Philip was dead and Otto IV had broken with Innocent III, who had previously supported him. So, when a group of German nobles asked him to go to Germany to assume the imperial crown, Frederick made his infant son, Henry, king of Sicily and hastened to Frankfurt, where in 1212 he was chosen ruler of Germany. He pacified the papacy, which feared a union between Sicily and the empire, by promising Innocent III that he would abdicate his Sicilian throne in favor of his son and that he would go on a crusade at the earliest opportunity. In 1214 Otto IV was defeated at Bouvines by Frederick's ally King Philip II (Augustus) of France, and in 1215 Frederick was recognized as emperor-elect by Pope Innocent III, who died a little while later.

Early Reign

Frederick began his reign as emperor in Germany by gaining the support of the magnates, both lay and ecclesiastical, by confirming in 1213 and 1220 their right to the privileges they had usurped in 1197 on the death of Emperor Henry VI. He then made his son, Henry, king of Germany and his viceroy and returned to Italy, which from this time on occupied most of his attention, for Germany never interested him except as a source of support for his Italian projects. Immediately upon his return he persuaded Pope Honorius III to crown him emperor and managed to put off giving up Sicily, as he had promised, on the grounds he needed to pacify it so that it could support his crusade.

The first task Frederick undertook was to establish firm control over the kingdom of Sicily, which had been in complete disorder since 1197. In 1220, in contrast with his actions in Germany, he revoked all privileges granted its towns and nobles since the death of King William II (1189), put down a Moslem revolt on the island of Sicily itself, and began to organize his realm into a tyrannical but well-administered kingdom. By 1225, prodded by Pope Honorius, he had married Yolande, heiress of the kingdom of Jerusalem (his first wife, an Aragonese princess, having died), and had made plans to proceed with his crusade to the East. He was still delaying on fulfilling this project when Pope Honorius died in 1227.

Honorius was succeeded by the aged pope Gregory IX (reigned 1227-1241), who, though over 80, was a vigorous, unrelenting foe of the young emperor. This aged pope almost at once excommunicated him for not going on crusade and, when Frederick then left for the East in 1228 without having the excommunication lifted, excommunicated him again and began planning a crusade against Frederick's Sicilian domains. Frederick proved very successful in the East, where he regained the city of Jerusalem from the Moslems by negotiation instead of war, crowned himself king of Jerusalem (a title which he retained until 1245), and built up his authority in the East. He returned in 1230 to find Pope Gregory IX attacking his kingdom of Sicily. After he had defeated the papal forces, he made Gregory lift his excommunication.

Policies in Italy

In 1231 Frederick promulgated the Constitutions of Melfi, an important code of laws that set up a nonfeudal state in Sicily. By this code the independence of towns and nobles was curbed, a centralized judicial and administrative system was established, mercenary armies were recruited, ecclesiastical privileges were limited, and commerce and industry were fostered by a uniform system of tolls and port dues and a common gold currency. At the same time his own revenues were increased by the establishment of royal monopolies over such things as salt production and the trade in grain. Sicily became one of the most prosperous realms in Europe.

Frederick then proceeded to attempt to extend his centralized rule to northern Italy, where in 1231 he made plans to subjugate its cities by appointing podestas, or imperial governors, over them. This alarmed the Pope, who saw the papacy, as in Henry VI's time, threatened between an imperial hammer in the north and the well-organized anvil of Sicily in the south. Gregory's answer was to reopen hostilities against Frederick II by attempting with some success to revive the Lombard League used against Frederick's grandfather Frederick Barbarossa. When these cities rose against him in support of a German revolt of his son King Henry, Frederick suppressed the revolt and in 1237 won a great victory over the Milanese at Cortenuova. As a result of this victory, the Lombard League temporarily collapsed and most of its cities submitted to him, as did the majority of the nobles of northern Italy.

While Frederick was establishing his authority firmly in Sicily and northern Italy, however, he was following quite a different policy in Germany. There in 1231 he issued the Constitution in Favor of the Princes, which had the result of making the magnates practically independent and even placed the towns under their rule. When his son Henry objected to this and revolted, Frederick suppressed his rising, threw him into prison, where he died, and replaced him as king in 1238 with his second son, Conrad. From this time on he made little attempt to exercise any real authority in Germany, whose princes, satisfied with their status, caused him no trouble. The only action of importance he took which affected Germany was his grant of a special charter to the Teutonic Knights, who, late in his reign, began their occupation of East Prussia, which they wrenched from the grasp of the kings of Poland.

In Italy, however, Pope Gregory IX still refused to accept Frederick's domination of northern Italy and excommunicated him. When his papal opponent died in 1241, Frederick reacted by using military force to keep a new pope from being elected for 2 years (1241-1243) and finally by procuring the election of a Ghibelline pope, Innocent IV (reigned 1243-1254). Innocent IV, however, soon broke with Frederick and fled from Italy to Lyons, where in 1245 he held a great Church council which condemned Frederick as the antichrist. The efforts of the Pope to enlist French and English support against this great Hohenstaufen ruler, however, proved abortive, and the war continued in Italy.

Frederick, relying on his able illegitimate sons and on lieutenants like Ezzalino, fought valiantly against the continuing resistance of the cities of Lombardy and the Papal States. Finally his army was badly defeated near Parma in 1248. By 1250, just as he was beginning to reverse the tide, he died suddenly, and his hopes of dominating all of Italy died with him. He left a number of illegitimate sons in Italy as his heirs, such as Manfred, Enzio, and Philip of Antioch, and one legitimate successor, the young Conrad across the Alps in Germany.

His Character

Frederick's character has long fascinated the historians and biographers who have studied him. He was married three times, first to Constance of Aragon, next to Yolande of Jerusalem, and finally to Isabelle of England. His real love was Bianca Lancia, with whom he carried on a lengthy liaison and who bore him several children. He had two legitimate sons and numerous illegitimate ones. He was reputed, probably with some justification, to have kept a harem in Palermo. His general lifestyle seemed to his contemporaries more Islamic than Christian; for instance, he maintained a force of Moslem mercenaries and scandalized his age by traveling with a private zoo. Though he remained formally a Christian, his spirit seemed more tolerant and skeptical than his age was ready to accept. In the cosmopolitan atmosphere of his Sicilian court, Arabic and Byzantine culture was highly prized.

Frederick proved an important patron of the arts throughout his entire reign. A poet himself, he prized southern French poetry highly, and he welcomed troubadour poets from this region when after the Albigensian Crusade they fled to his court. Through the influence of these poets, a new poetry began to be composed in the Sicilian vernacular tongue. He was also much interested in art and architecture, and under his aegis a classical artistic revival took place, anticipating that of later Renaissance Italy.

Frederick spoke a number of languages, and in 1234 he founded the University of Naples, the first state university in western Europe. He was much attracted to scientific ideas, perhaps because of his appreciation of Arabic culture. He is said to have conducted a series of experiments to determine how digestion took place, using the contents of the stomachs of executed criminals as his evidence. He also tried isolating children at birth to discover what language they would speak if untaught. He was also an enthusiastic falconer and wrote a book on the subject entitled *On the Art of Hunting with Birds,* which proved to be the most detailed scientific examination of ornithology written until the 19th century.

In short, Frederick deserves the title of Stupor Mundi (Wonder of the World), which his contemporaries bestowed upon him. This extraordinary man with all his faults, then, was a ruler who had the misfortune to be born before his time. He paid the price for this by seeing all his brilliance and ability brought to naught by a hostile papacy and a reluctant citizenry of the northern Italian communes. With his death Italy had to wait more than 600 years for the unity he had tried to bring about.

Further Reading

There are a number of excellent biographies of Frederick II. One of the best is Ernst Kantorowicz, *Frederick the Second, 1194-1250* (1927; trans. 1931). See also Lionel Allshorn, *Stupor Mundi: The Life & Times of Frederick II, Emperor of the Romans, King of Sicily and Jerusalem, 1194-1250* (1912); Georgina Masson, *Frederick II of Hohenstaufen* (1957); and Friedrich Heer, *The Holy Roman Empire* (1967; trans. 1968).

Frederick II

Frederick II (1712-1786), or Frederick the Great, was king of Prussia from 1740 to 1786. He combined the qualities of a warrior king with those of an enlightened despot.

The eldest son of Frederick William I of Prussia and of Princess Sophie Dorothea of Hanover, Frederick II was born in Berlin on Jan. 24, 1712. His father was a hardworking, unimaginative soldier-king, with no outward pretensions and no time to waste on superfluous niceties. Even as an adolescent Frederick, with the tacit support of his mother, rebelled against this mold. He preferred French literature to German and the company of young fops to that of old soldiers.

In 1730 Frederick and a young friend, Lieutenant Katte, planned a romantic escape to England, but their plot was discovered. The would-be escapees were arrested and condemned to death for desertion, and Katte was executed in Frederick's presence. The crown prince was spared upon the entreaties of Emperor Charles VI, although it is doubtful that his father ever intended to go through with the execution. Frederick, however, was imprisoned in the fortress of Küstrin in the most rigorous conditions until, after some 6 months, he voluntarily approached Frederick William with a request for pardon. For the next 2 years, although still nominally a prisoner, Frederick was employed in a subsidiary position of the local administration of Küstrin, thus learning the intricacies of the Prussian administrative system.

In 1732 Frederick was appointed commandant of an infantry regiment and, having decided to obey his father, he learned soldiering with all the thoroughness with which he had previously avoided it. In 1733, at his father's insistence, he married Elisabeth Christine of Braunschweig, but his

aversion to women was so pronounced that the marriage was, over the many years it lasted, never consummated.

Between 1733 and 1740 Frederick, who had grown into a young man whose unimposing stature was balanced by piercing blue eyes, an aquiline nose, and a good chin, exceeded even the expectations of his father in his dedication to hard, dull routine. But he also found time to devote himself further to French literature, to begin a lifelong correspondence with a number of French *philosophes,* and to try writing himself. One product of this period was the *Anti-Machiavel* (1739), a work in which he argued that the Italian's ruthlessly practical maxims for princes were no longer compatible with the more advanced ethics of a new age. He was soon given the opportunity to test his own conduct against these views.

War of the Austrian Succession

On May 31, 1740, Frederick William died, and Frederick became king of Prussia as Frederick II. Before he had time to accustom himself to his new position, the death of Emperor Charles VI on October 20 created a political crisis and presented Frederick with a unique opportunity. Like all the other leading powers of Europe, Prussia had subscribed to the Pragmatic Sanction, guaranteeing the succession of Charles's daughter Maria Theresa and the integrity of her dominions. But it was an open secret that at least France and Bavaria intended to make demands upon Austria as soon as the Emperor was dead, and Frederick saw no reason to stand by while others enriched themselves at Austria's expense. He offered to assist Austria in the maintenance of its possessions in exchange for the cession of the rich province of Silesia to Prussia. When this outrageous piece of blackmail was indignantly rejected, in December Frederick marched his troops into Silesia, thus launching the War of the Austrian Succession (1740-1748).

In the first phase of this struggle the combined onslaught of Prussian, French, and Bavarian forces threatened to overwhelm Austria. Not wishing to bring about a situation more favorable to his potential rivals than to himself, Frederick withdrew from the war in 1742 with most of Silesia as his price. When Austria, relieved of the necessity of fighting the Prussians, threatened to crush its remaining enemies, Frederick reentered the war in 1744. The conflict was finally ended in 1748 with Silesia still firmly in Prussian hands.

Seven Years War

Since the Austrians were antagonistic over the loss of Silesia, Frederick had reason to fear a renewal of the struggle. In the aftermath of the war both sides engaged in complicated diplomatic maneuvers. Austria, which had enjoyed a tentative alliance with Russia since 1746, tried to strengthen this while making overtures toward its old enemy France. Frederick in turn concluded the Treaty of Westminster (1755) with Great Britain, promising Prussian neutrality in the war that had just broken out between France and England. These maneuvers led directly to the Diplomatic Revolution, which in 1756 left Prussia facing an overwhelming Continental alliance of Austria, Russia, France, and Saxony. Rather than await inevitable death by constriction, Frederick attacked Austria, which he regarded as the weakest among the great powers facing him. Thus began the Seven Years War (1756-1763).

In this conflict Frederick distinguished himself by continually keeping at bay much more powerful antagonists. He took advantage of the natural lack of cohesion of coalitions and fought his enemies, so far as possible, one at a time. The superior discipline of the Prussian army allowed Frederick to march it to the theater of war in small detachments, from various directions, uniting only shortly before a battle was to be fought. He also made the most of the oblique order of battle which he had inculcated in the Prussian army and which allowed him to concentrate his forces against emerging weak spots in his enemies' more ponderous formations.

In spite of these advantages, by 1762 Prussia was on the verge of bankruptcy, its army was in no condition to continue the war, and Russian troops had occupied Berlin. At this juncture Empress Elizabeth of Russia died; her successor, the mad Peter III, an admirer of Frederick, pulled Russia out of the war. Thus saved, Frederick was able to conclude the Peace of Hubertusberg (1763), which restored the prewar status quo.

The Seven Years War taught Frederick that, while Prussia's recently acquired position as a great power had been successfully defended, any further adventures in foreign policy had to be avoided at all costs. Hereafter his policy was a strictly defensive one, bent primarily on preventing changes in the balance of power. This became evident when, in 1772, it appeared as if Austria and Russia were about to succeed in partitioning the Ottoman Empire. As there was no chance of securing reasonable compensation for Prussia, Frederick blustered and threatened until the principals agreed on a three-way partition of Poland. In 1778, when Joseph II of Austria attempted to acquire Bavaria, Frederick reluctantly went to war but engaged in no more than a halfhearted war of maneuver of which the Austrians at last tired; and in 1784, when Joseph tried to trade the Austrian Netherlands for Bavaria, Frederick organized the League of German Princes to preserve the status of Germany.

Domestic Policies

Frederick had inherited a well-run state from his father, a circumstance that allowed him to fight his major wars. But he worked as hard at internal administration as at military leadership. He very reluctantly delegated authority, took all important decisions himself, and ruled through ministers responsible only to him. His ruthless insistence on hard work and honesty resulted in a doubling of the revenues of the state in his reign and a tripling of the available reserve fund, this last in spite of the devastation associated with the Seven Years War.

Frederick continued the traditional Prussian policy of encouraging immigration of economically productive elements, particularly peasants, into the more backward and underpopulated areas of the state. In contrast, his policy toward the established peasantry tended to be restrictive. In

spite of the spirit of the times, he refused to abolish serfdom where it existed, fearing that such a measure would weaken the landed nobility, which produced both officers for his army and officials for his civil service.

In economics Frederick was a strict mercantilist, fostering the rather backward domestic industry with high tariffs wherever he could. He did not, however, extend these notions to the building of a fleet, so that Prussia did not participate in the great expansion of European overseas trade of the second half of the 18th century.

Apart from purely pragmatic measures, Frederick's reign was not a time of considerable reform. The one exception is the area of judicial procedure, where the efforts of his minister of justice, Cocceji, resulted not merely in a more extensive codification of the law but in the acceptance of the principle that the law is foremost the protector of the poor and the weak.

During his reign Frederick continued to concern himself with literature and music. He became, in a sense, the host of the most famous salon in Europe. Voltaire was only the best known of the *philosophes* to take advantage of his hospitality. The Prussian Academy of Sciences, which had long languished and which he renewed in 1744, provided much-needed subsidies for both major and minor luminaries of the French Enlightenment. At the same time Frederick had no use for those obstinate enough to persist in writing in "barbaric" German, and the young Goethe was not the only German author deprived of royal assistance for this reason.

But Frederick was not content to be merely a patron of literature. He found time to produce, besides *Anti-Machiavel*, the *Mirror of Princes* and a series of histories dealing with his own affairs that at his death filled 15 volumes.

An Assessment

Frederick was both lionized and vilified long after his death. In Germany his more nationally minded admirers produced a cult of Frederick the Great, the precursor of the all-German hero. In other countries he was blamed as the inventor of an implacable German militarism let loose upon the world. Both these views are gross distortions. Frederick was always a Prussian nationalist, never a German one. And while he was a soldier-king, his pervasive interests throughout his life were nonmilitary. The latter part of his reign was unquestionably pacific and in some cases even propitiatory in nature.

Frederick did not have a first-rate analytical mind, but Voltaire's denunciations of him after their famous quarrel do not sound much more convincing than his panegyrics when he still hoped to get some of the royal money. Frederick was parsimonious, perhaps to a fault, but his funds were in fact severely limited. His treatment of his queen, whom he refused even the right to reside near him, was perhaps unforgivable. Frederick II died at his beloved summer residence, Sans-Souci, near Potsdam on Aug. 17, 1786, and was followed on the throne by his nephew Frederick William II.

Further Reading

Among the older English biographies of Frederick, the best is probably W. F. Reddaway, *Frederick the Great and the Rise of Prussia* (1904). Other useful biographies are Edith Simon, *The Making of Frederick the Great* (1963), and D. B. Horn, *Frederick the Great and the Rise of Prussia* (1964). Gerhard Ritter, *Frederick the Great: An Historical Profile* (1936; 3d ed. 1954; trans. 1968), and G. P. Gooch, *Frederick the Great: The Ruler, the Writer, the Man* (1947), are both stimulating essays dealing with aspects of Frederick's life. See also John A. Marriott and Charles G. Robertson, *The Evolution of Prussia: The Making of an Empire* (1915; rev. ed. 1946); Hajo Holborn, *History of Modern Germany,* vol. 2 (1963); Peter Gay, *The Enlightenment: An Interpretation* (2 vols., 1966-1969); and Walter Henry Nelson, *The Soldier Kings: The House of Hohenzollern* (1970).

Additional Sources

Abulafia, David, *Frederick II: a medieval emperor,* London: Allen Lane, 1988; New York: Oxford University Press, 1992.

Duffy, Christopher, *Frederick the Great: a military life,* London: Routledge & K. Paul, 1985.

Duffy, Christopher, *The military life of Frederick the Great,* New York: Atheneum, 1986, 1985.

Mitford, Nancy, *Frederick the Great,* London; New York: Penguin Books, 1995.

Simon, Edith, *The making of Frederick the Great,* Westport, Conn.: Greenwood Press, 1977. □

Frederick III

Frederick III (1415-1493), Holy Roman emperor and German king from 1440 to 1493, was one of the longer-reigning and weaker of the Hapsburgs. His misfortunes spurred his family to strengthen their position. He was the last German emperor crowned by the pope in Rome.

Frederick III was born on Sept. 21, 1415, in Innsbruck. His father was Ernest, Duke of Austria, a title to which Frederick succeeded (as Frederick V) in 1424. The young prince developed interests in jewels, which he collected, and astrology, and study which did little to further his fortunes. Frederick was raised to the imperial office in June 1440, when he was crowned king of the Romans (that is, the Germans; the German king was not officially emperor until crowned by the pope) in Aachen to succeed his cousin, Albert II. Frederick was noted for his lack of leadership in the internal affairs of Germany. Rejecting the appeals of princes and cities for imperial reform, he rarely attended a meeting of the Imperial Diet. In his absence princes and cities organized or strengthened existing confederations, slowly undermining what was left of German unity and enhancing a princely power that no future emperor would ever overcome. And when princes fought and cities rebelled, Frederick again refused to intervene.

Despite this indolence, Frederick continued to collect precious stones and dignities. In 1452 he married Leonora of Portugal, and on March 16 he was crowned in Rome by Pope Nicholas V. The Pope had good reason to favor this Hapsburg. In 1448 Frederick and Nicholas had concluded the Vienna Concordat, which strengthened the power of Rome in the German Church, while it was beginning to wane elsewhere. Unwittingly, Frederick thus eased the way for that future collaborator with princely particularism, the German Reformation.

The Emperor did perform one positive act for his family. In order to head off aggressive moves by Duke Charles the Bold of Burgundy (1474), he arranged that his son, Maximilian, should marry Charles's daughter Mary. Charles died 3 years later; the French moved to absorb his heritage, but the richest Burgundian provinces in the Low Countries were preserved for Maximilian by his timely conclusion of the wedding arrangements. And it was this expansion to the West that created the nucleus of the future empire of Charles V.

Frederick was not so fortunate in the East. There, the Bohemians shook off his rule, while the Hungarian leader Mathias Corvinus actually occupied the Hapsburg capital of Vienna in 1485. Frederick had reached the end of his rope, and so had the Germans. They forced him to allow Maximilian to be elected king of the Romans. Frederick maintained the imperial office, but the empire was now in somewhat more capable hands. Frederick died at Linz on Aug. 19, 1493.

Further Reading

For the history of the empire during Frederick's reign see Geoffrey Barraclough, *The Origins of Modern Germany* (1947), and Denys Hay, *Europe in the Fourteenth and Fifteenth Centuries* (1966). □

Frederick William

Frederick William (1620-1688) was elector of Brandenburg from 1640 to 1688. Known as the Great Elector, he augmented and integrated the Hohenzollern possessions in northern Germany and Prussia.

Born in Berlin on Feb. 16, 1620, Frederick William was the only son of Elector George William and Elizabeth Charlotte of the Palatinate. He was raised in the Reformed faith of the Hohenzollern court and in 1634 went to the University of Leiden, where he dutifully, if unenthusiastically, attended lectures and more happily explored the vital commercial life of the harbor town. His experience in the Netherlands left him with a religious tolerance uncommon in his age and a firm impression of the commercial basis of Dutch power. He returned to Berlin in 1638 only to flee from an invading Swedish army with his ailing father. George William died in Königsberg on Dec. 1, 1640, and Frederick William succeeded him. He was quiet in manner, stocky and robust, with a face dominated by a nose of heroic proportions; in middle age he grew uncommonly corpulent.

The new elector of Brandenburg also inherited the duchies of Prussia in the east and Cleve-Mark on the Dutch frontier. His scattered possessions had widely different social and political systems, but they offered him potentially great influence in German affairs. In the beginning he directed his policy toward a cautious disengagement from his father's pro-Austrian diplomacy, which had led to the disastrous war with Sweden. At the same time he built up his own military forces to protect his exposed states and to give him diplomatic leverage. In these aims he succeeded well enough, and by the Treaty of Westphalia, ending the Thirty Years War in 1648, he acquired eastern Pomerania from Sweden, the bishoprics of Minden and Halberstadt, and the reversion of Magdeburg. From that time Hohenzollern possessions in Germany were second only to those of the imperial Hapsburg dynasty. Having failed to establish his hereditary claim to the duchy of Jülich-Berg, Frederick William turned after 1651 to the fiscal and administrative reorganization of his states. Each province sent agents to Berlin to attend the Privy Council, the central governing body over which the elector presided personally.

Domestic and Economic Policies

Like most absolutist rulers of the century, Frederick William had constantly to battle the opposition of the privileged aristocratic caste, the noble landlords who defended their "liberties" and special prerogatives through the estates and diets of the various provinces. Rather than risk rebellion by eliminating the diets, Frederick William whittled away at their influence, bargaining with each diet for the right to collect taxes, appoint officials of his own choosing, quarter troops, and exercise appellate jurisdiction. He took advantage of conflicts between the towns and the landed nobility, weakened the opposition, and created the financial base for a large standing army, which in turn became the instrument for imposing reforms on the institutions of the state. The organization of this army was the cornerstone of Prussian power. Though still a mercenary army on the old pattern, it was slowly nationalized so that by the end of his reign Frederick William's officer corps was largely made up of his own subjects.

Impressed by the economic success of the seafaring Dutch, the elector tried to build an active navy. He chartered Dutch ships to privateer in the Baltic during a war with Sweden from 1675 to 1679. In 1680 two chartered ships established a bridgehead colony on the Gold Coast, and his African Trading Company brought modest profits by trading in slaves with the West Indies. In this venture and in his internal economic policies he followed the mercantilist doctrines of the age. One of his main concerns was to bring new settlers to the land and skilled craftsmen to the towns, offering tax exemptions and subsidies to desirable immigrants. Nearly 20,000 French Huguenots settled in his territories after 1685, bringing important new manufacturing skills and a cultural refinement foreign to those frontier provinces.

Foreign Policy

Frederick William's foreign policy was governed by an unashamed territorial acquisitiveness. In the First Northern War between Sweden and Poland he allied himself first in 1655 with Sweden and then changed sides in 1657 to join the Poles. By the Treaty of Oliva in 1660 his duchy of Prussia won its freedom from Polish sovereignty. In 1672 and again in 1674 he joined the Austro-Dutch coalition against France, and in 1675 he turned against Sweden, France's northern ally. Although he captured Swedish Pomerania and its valuable seaport Stettin in 1677, the Treaty of Nijmegen returned it to Sweden in 1679. Frustrated by his allies, he reversed his policy once more and allied with France in 1679, sitting by quietly while Louis XIV established French dominance in the Rhineland. With the Turkish assault on Vienna in 1683, his friendship with France, which tacitly supported the Turks, cooled rapidly. After the expulsion of the Calvinist Huguenots from France in 1685 he once again cast his lot with the Austrian Hapsburgs and the Netherlands in the anti-French League of Augsburg.

During the later years of his reign Frederick William was plagued by painful rheumatism or arthritis complicated by asthma. In spite of his illness he kept a strict, almost military, working schedule. His tastes remained simple and his court frugal. He died at Potsdam on May 9, 1688, leaving his successors a state in place of the handful of scattered provinces he had inherited.

Further Reading

An excellent biography of Frederick William in English is Ferdinand Schevill, *The Great Elector* (1947). For historical background see David Ogg, *Europe in the Seventeenth Century* (1925; 6th rev. ed. 1952), and Cicely V. Wedgwood, *The Thirty Years War* (1939). □

Frederick William I

Frederick William I (1688-1740) was king of Prussia from 1713 to 1740. He inherited a state whose resources were meager and turned it into a leading German power.

The son of the elector Frederick III of Brandenburg and of Sophie Charlotte of Hanover, Frederick William I was born in Berlin on Aug. 15, 1688. In 1701 his father was named king of Prussia by Emperor Charles VI. Raised at a court which strove to achieve a cultivation and a level of material display rather beyond it means, Frederick William refused to participate in the elegant life around him and spent his leisure time hunting and drinking vast quantities of beer. When he came to the throne after his father's death in 1713, he moved his household into a handful of rooms in the corner of the palace; he turned the rest of the huge structure over to the use of various ministries and

transformed the pleasure gardens into a parade ground. Henceforth, hard work, parsimony, and the voice of the drill sergeant would characterize Prussia.

Partly for reasons of economy, partly because he trusted no one, Frederick William was determined to establish a purely personal government. His father's ministers were dismissed, and their successors were told to give their reports to the King in writing. Thus all major decisions were, in the last analysis, made by Frederick William himself.

Frederick William had come to the throne convinced that Prussia was in danger of being swallowed up by its more powerful neighbors. Determined to prevent this, he began strengthening his army. In 1715 he reentered the Great Northern War against Sweden. But although this campaign resulted in the gain of a part of western Pomerania, the deficiencies of the small (under 40,000) Prussian army were glaring. Unwilling to alienate the Prussian nobility, which insisted that its peasants could not be spared from their obligatory labor to do military service, Frederick William concentrated upon hiring troops abroad. Not until 1733 did he establish the canton system, which allowed regiments to recruit among the peasants and craft laborers of their home districts. By the end of his reign the size of the army had doubled and was second only to the imperial one in numbers. Two-thirds of the Prussian effectives, however, were foreigners.

To finance his military forces, Frederick William initiated new government procedures both for the spending and the collecting of revenue. The first was done by the creation of the General Finance Directory (1723), which was to approve all requests for money. The latter was achieved by replacing the feudal levy (an assessment that the nobility in practice no longer rendered) with a tax on land held by the nobles; by collecting taxes more efficiently from the peasantry; and by placing excise taxes not merely on luxury imports such as coffee, tea, and sugar but on most staple food items. Through these measures the yearly income of the state rose by 250 percent.

Apart from a general process of consolidation, the administrative reforms that made these financial gains possible were largely operational in nature. Spheres of responsibility were defined, and specific officials were made responsible for the functioning of various departments; in short, a class of amateur, part-time officials was transformed into a state-serving bureaucracy, staffed with newly chastened noblemen at the top and retired noncommissioned officers at the bottom. There were also minor judicial reforms and limited attempts to improve the lot of the peasants in the crown lands. Some 17,000 Protestants, expelled from Salzburg, were settled in East Prussia, to the considerable gain of that underpopulated province.

By the second half of the 1730s it was apparent to most contemporary observers that the work of 20 years had created a formidable army, backed by a full treasury. But the King, in spite of a developing quarrel with the empire over the province of Berg, could not be persuaded to use his resources. His last years were dominated by an increasingly bizarre concern with his palace guard of giants and with a running quarrel with his son and heir, Frederick. Frederick William I died in Potsdam on May 31, 1740.

Further Reading

The best biography of Frederick William I is Robert Ergang, *The Potsdam Führer* (1941). Also useful are Sidney B. Fay, *The Rise of Brandenburg-Prussia to 1786* (1937; rev. ed. by Klaus Epstein, 1964), and Hans Rosenberg, *Bureaucracy, Aristocracy and Autocracy: The Prussian Experience, 1660-1815* (1958). ☐

Frederick William III

Frederick William III (1770-1840) was king of Prussia from 1797 to 1840. A weak monarch, he presided first over the near-liquidation of the Prussian state in the Napoleonic Wars and then over its reconstruction.

Born in Potsdam on Aug. 3, 1770, Frederick William III succeeded his father, Frederick William II, as king of Prussia in 1797. He began his reign by sending his father's mistresses and favorites packing, and he let it be known that he intended to lift all existing restrictions on religion, to abolish censorship, and to improve the condition of the peasants. Soon, however, he retreated before the opposition of the conservative Prussian nobility.

During the War of the Second Coalition against France, Frederick William clung to a perilous and increasingly isolated neutrality. When at last Prussia joined the Third Coalition, it reaped only the catastrophic defeat of Jena (1806). In the subsequent Peace of Tilsit (1807) all of Prussia's Polish and western territories—roughly half its landmass—had to be surrendered. This disaster revealed the vulnerable position of a Prussia surrounded by more populous and powerful neighbors and thus gave impetus to the centralizing reforms carried out by Frederick William's ministers. These reforms enabled Prussia to reenter the war against Napoleon in 1813. In German history this renewal of the war is known as the War of Liberation, because of explicit representation on the part of the Prussian government that it was fighting to clear German soil of the foreign invader. In 1815 the Congress of Vienna awarded certain new lands to Prussia and restored most of its lost territories.

In spite of his numerous appeals to German patriotism and even nationalism during the war, upon its conclusion Frederick William joined the reactionary party that emerged during the Congress of Vienna. He refused to honor his promise to give Prussia a constitution and ordered the arrest of numerous liberals who had allowed themselves to be trapped into a careless revelation of their political philosophy. The later years of his reign were marked by undiminished reaction. The only positive achievements were the union of the Prussian Lutheran and Calvinist churches (1817), a reflection of the King's growing concern with religious questions, and the establishment of a northern German customs union (1834), a step that was to facilitate the extension of Prussian political dominion over this area some 3 decades later. Frederick William III died in Berlin on June 7, 1840.

Further Reading

Frederick William III's place in German history is examined in various works, including K. S. Pinson, *Modern Germany* (1954; 2d ed. 1966); W. M. Simon, *The Failure of the Prussian Reform Movement* (1955); Hajo Holborn, *A History of Modern Germany,* vol. 2 (1959); and K. Epstein, *The Genesis of German Conservatism* (1966). ☐

Frederick William IV

Frederick William IV (1795-1861) was king of Prussia from 1840 to 1861. Perhaps the most intelligent and artistically talented Prussian monarch, he proved to be an erratic and unreliable leader during the German Revolution of 1848.

On Oct. 15, 1795, Frederick William IV was born in Berlin, the oldest son of Frederick William III. Educated by the preacher-statesman J. P. F. Ancillon, he devoted most of his energies as crown prince to the ardent study and patronage of the arts. F. K. von Savigny, F. W. J. von Schelling, K. F. Schinkel, A. W. von Schlegel, L.

Tieck, L. von Ranke, A. von Humboldt, and other leaders of the romantic movement were among his closest friends.

Frederick William's ascension to the throne on June 7, 1840, was thus greeted with the expectation that he might help to realize the liberal-national aspirations of his distinguished friends. He soon alleviated press censorship and affirmed religious freedom for the independent Protestant sects and Rhineland Catholics. Yet personally he was devoted more to the ideals of the Holy Roman Empire and divine right of kings than to liberal constitutionalism, and he disillusioned liberals by delaying the promulgation of a constitution, which had been promised by his father. He finally yielded to pressure in February 1847, but rather than a popularly elected body he called only a united *Landtag* (diet)—a group of delegates from the traditional provincial diets.

With the outbreak of violence in March 1848 in Berlin, the King immediately lost his nerve and capitulated to the rebels, even to the point of riding through the streets of Berlin under the revolutionary German flag. But as soon as his armies had gained control again, he betrayed his promises, dissolved the popular assembly established by the revolution, and proclaimed a new reactionary constitution in December 1848. When the revolutionary all-German Parliament in Frankfurt offered him the imperial crown, he rejected it for ideological and political reasons as "unworthy." A subsequent attempt by his adviser J. von Radowitz to create a union of German princes under Prussian leadership failed when combined pressure by Austria

and Russia forced Frederick William to capitulate at Olmütz (1850).

During the remaining years of his reign the King withdrew increasingly to his artistic pursuits and left politics more and more in the hands of the ministers of the reaction. After he suffered a stroke in October 1857 and consequent mental collapse, his brother William ruled as regent until Frederick William's death in Potsdam on Jan. 2, 1861.

Further Reading

All of the major biographies of Frederick William IV are in German. The most extensive account of his reign in English is Heinrich Treitschke, *Treitschke's History of Germany in the Nineteenth Century,* vols. 6 and 7, book 5: *King Frederick William the Fourth, 1840-1848,* translated by Eden and Cedar Paul (1919). □

James Ingo Freed

James Ingo Freed (born 1930) was an American architect who designed many important structures, including the United States Holocaust Memorial Museum.

James Ingo Freed was born on June 23, 1930, in Essen, Germany. A Jewish refugee in Nazi Germany, Freed escaped to France in 1938 and emigrated to the United States with his younger sister in 1939. His parents emigrated in 1941. Freed became a naturalized American citizen in 1948.

In 1953 Freed received his Bachelor of Architecture degree from the Illinois Institute of Technology where he studied under Ludwig Mies van der Rohe, a renowned modernist architect who also escaped Adolf Hitler's Germany. After holding positions at Danforth & Speyer and Michael Reese Planning Association, both in Chicago, Freed worked under Mies' direction on the Seagram Building in New York City. Following a two-year appointment in the United States Army, Freed found a permanent position with I. M. Pei and Partners in 1956. He became a partner in 1980, and in 1989 the firm's name was changed to Pei Cobb Freed & Partners.

Throughout his lengthy career Freed sought projects that aimed to transform urban space into a pleasing and meaningful environment for the public. His structures include West Loop Plaza (Houston, Texas, 1980), Potomac Towers (Rosslyn, Virginia, 1990), and the New Warner Building on Pennsylvania Avenue (Washington, D.C., 1992). An architectural focus was the convention center, a structure Freed found particularly challenging due to its multiple and varied uses. Beginning in the late 1980s, Freed designed the New York Exposition and Convention Center, the Jacob Javits Convention Center in New York City, and the Los Angeles Convention Center in California. The latter is exemplary of Freed's desire to serve the urban populace. Giant towers of light are visible from the busy Los Angeles freeway, on which thousands of commuters travel each day, while the pedestrian side of the convention center is scaled to human size. Thus the building is functional for those attending convention center events, but also serves as a memorable landmark to travelers.

Noted for Holocaust Museum

In general, Freed sought challenging architectural commissions with extensive program requirements. One such commission, the United States Holocaust Memorial Museum, is perhaps his most notable project. Located just off the National Mall in Washington, D.C., the Holocaust Museum opened in April 1993, following more than 13 years of planning and construction. After visiting the sites of various concentration camps, Freed presented his architectural plan to the United States Holocaust Memorial Council in 1987. The design was unanimously approved. Construction commenced on the 1.9-acre site in September 1988.

Throughout the museum Freed made use of an industrial-type architecture of brick and steel. This type of modern construction, normally indicative of the benefits of a technologically advanced society, assumes haunting connotations in the context of the museum. While Freed did not aim to literally reproduce the Jewish ghettos or death camps in his design, certain referents to Nazi architecture are evident. For example, the tall, pointed structures on the exteriors of the museum may refer to the watchtowers from which concentration camp prisoners were monitored.

In planning the architectural transition from the exterior of the museum to its interior, Freed sought to separate the visitor both spatially and emotionally from the bustling city of Washington. The curved neoclassical façade, constructed of limestone, is nothing more than a false front for the "real" brick and steel structure inside. As such, it is symbolic of the gates to the concentration camps through which all Jewish prisoners passed.

Inside the museum, the Hall of Witness is a three-story rectangular room constructed of brick walls, boarded-up windows, and an intentionally warped skylight. The hall, through which all visitors pass upon entering the museum, is designed to disorient the visitor and to signify certain environmental components of Nazi Germany. The brick walls are a direct reference to the killing wall of Auschwitz. An immense steel staircase, narrower at the top and wider at the bottom, also disengages the visitor by its structural incongruities and skewed perspective. The skylight, set at a diagonal across the length of the hall, is constructed of steel and glass and is the main source of light for the room. As Freed noted, "Light is the only thing I know that heals. People at the camps said the sky was the only way out." Consequently, natural light, which Freed exploits through the design of the glass roof, is an important symbol for the architect.

The Hall of Remembrance is similarly symbolic in its design. The hexagonally-shaped room is also illuminated by a skylight. As a more subtle modernist construction, the Hall of Remembrance serves as a place for quiet contemplation once the visitor has passed through the entire museum. Installed on one side of the room is a steel box containing soil from various death camps, over which burns an eternal flame of remembrance. Candles line the perimeters of the remainder of the limestone walls. Small, triangular windows, perhaps referential to the similarly-shaped badges worn by the Jewish prisoners, permit limited view to the outside world. Through these windows the visitor may glimpse the Lincoln, Jefferson, and Washington Memorials, structures that, ironically, pledge freedom and democracy to all. In its design and installation, the Hall of Remembrance is a universal structure that serves to remind the visitor of the atrocities that occur by the hands of humanity.

Honored by President

Freed's Holocaust Museum is indicative of the quality of his work, for which he received abundant accolades. A fellow of the American Institute of Architects, Freed held several professorships at prestigious universities, including Columbia and Yale. He also served as dean and professor of architecture at the Illinois Institute of Technology from 1975 to 1978. Freed's numerous awards include the R.S. Reynolds Award for Excellence in Architecture, the Arnold W. Brunner Memorial Prize in Architecture, and the Thomas Jefferson Award for Public Architecture. Freed was awarded the National Medal of Arts in 1995. He was one of 13 honored that year by the annual award whose recipients are named by the president of the United States. The award honors distinguished artists who have offered inspiration to others, either through artistic achievement or exceptional work on behalf of the arts. His later projects include the San Francisco Main Public Library, California, and the United States International Cultural and Trade Center at Federal Triangle, Washington, D.C.

Freed's populist sensibility revealed itself when he discussed the San Francisco Library, which opened in 1996. "Old libraries told stories of power. But great tombs are no longer our forte. We needed a place for communities to celebrate their own essences."

Further Reading

No complete biography exists for James Ingo Freed. He is, however, cited in the 47th edition of Who's Who in America (1992-1993), volume 1; and in Les Krantz, editor, American Architects (1989). A good discussion of Freed's design for the Holocaust Museum may be found in Jim Murphy's article in Progressive Architecture (February 1993); for further commentary on the museum and a brief biography on Freed, see Kenneth Woodward, "We Are Witnesses," and Cathleen McGuigan, "He Built a Space of Terrible Beauty," in Newsweek (April 26, 1993).

Additional Sources

Knesl, John, "Accidental Classicists: Freed in Washington, Libeskind in Berlin," Assemblage: 1991, Dec., No. 16, p.98-101.

Cohen, Jean Lawlor, "James Ingo Freed: Architect of the U.S. Holocaust Memorial Museum," Museum & Arts Washington: 1988, Mar.-Apr., v.4, no.2, p.40-44.

Freed, James Ingo; Murphy, Jim; "Memorial to Atrocity: the United States Holocaust Memorial Museum," Progressive Architecture: 1993, Feb., v.74, n.2,p.60-73.

Sorkin, Michael, "The Holocaust Museum: Between Beauty and Horror," *Progressive Architecture: 1993,* Feb., v.74, n.2, p.74. □

Louis J. Freeh

Appointed director of the Federal Bureau of Investigation (FBI) in 1993, Louis J. Freeh (born 1950) was selected for this promotion because of the reputation he had earned in federal law enforcement. As an FBI agent and then a federal prosecutor, Freeh had helped win convictions in high-profile criminal cases. Despite controversy that swirled around the FBI during his watch, Freeh remained committed to running the bureau for as long as he could be effective.

The son of Beatrice and William Freeh, Sr., Louis Freeh was born on January 6, 1950, in Jersey City, New Jersey. Although a youth of considerable promise and ambition, Freeh came from a family of modest means. As a result he attended local public universities and worked to defray his expenses. His family lived in three rooms on the first floor of their house, renting the second story, after his father, a transplanted Brooklynite and real estate broker, moved the family to Hudson County. Graduating Phi Beta Kappa from Rutgers University in 1971, Freeh earned his law degree in 1974 from Rutgers Law School at Newark. In 1974-1975 he served as a law clerk in the Newark office of New Jersey's Republican senator, Clifford Case, leaving in 1975 to accept an appointment as an agent with the Federal Bureau of Investigation (FBI).

Assigned to New York Office

Assigned to the FBI's New York office, Freeh worked in the organized crime unit. His diligence and skills were fully demonstrated in a major investigation he headed of corruption on the New York waterfront that resulted in the conviction of 125 union and waterfront officials on federal racketeering charges. Anthony Scotto, the president of the International Longshoremen's Union, was one of those convicted. For this achievement Freeh was awarded a special FBI commendation and was promoted to supervisor in the Organized Crime Unit at FBI headquarters in Washington. While employed as an FBI agent Freeh met his future wife, Marilyn, at the time employed as a clerk at FBI headquarters. They became the parents of five sons.

Freeh's demonstrated skills and close cooperation with federal prosecutors earned him a further promotion in 1981 to assistant U.S. attorney in the Southern District of New York (New York City). Concurrent with this assignment, Freeh attended New York University Law School, earning the LLM degree in 1984. From 1988 to 1992 he served as adjunct associate professor at Fordham Law School. His matriculation and part-time teaching reflected his desire to enhance his knowledge of criminal law and his credentials for promotion in the federal judiciary.

Rose On His Record

His impressive record as prosecutor ensured such promotion, with his most important case involving the successful indictment and eventual conviction in 1987 of 16 of 17 crime leaders in the so-called Pizza Connection case. This complex criminal case involved a Sicilian-based drug-dealing (heroin) and money-laundering operation stretching from Turkey to Brazil that in the United States used pizza parlors as fronts for money laundering. Freeh not only won the respect of the law enforcement community for his skill in recruiting informers and tracing the elaborate ruses employed to sell drugs and launder money, but even defense attorneys praised his fairness when arguing the government's case in court. An innovative prosecutor, Freeh, for example, secured the cooperation of second-level criminals who provided the testimony that helped convict high-level Mafia leaders by setting up a U.S. witness protection program for foreign informers.

The successful prosecution of the Pizza Connection case led in 1987 to his promotions first to head the Organized Crime Unit in the New York office and then, in January 1989, to deputy U.S. attorney. In addition, in 1989 he received the Federal Law Enforcement Officers Achievement Award.

A Leading Prosecutor

Recognized as one of the leading prosecutors in the nation, Freeh was selected by Attorney General Richard Thornburgh in May 1990 to head a special federal investigation into the mail bombing deaths of Federal Judge Robert Vance of Birmingham, Alabama, and Savannah (Georgia) alderman and NAACP official Robert Robinson. Freeh masterminded a nationwide investigation that culminated in the arrest and conviction of Walter Lee Moody for terrorist acts (which also included sending mail bombs to other civil rights offices throughout the South). His handling of this investigation earned him the Attorney General's Award for Distinguished Service in 1991 and then, in July 1991, his nomination by President George Bush and Senate confirmation as federal district judge in the Southern District of New York.

Only 41 years old at the time of his appointment to the federal bench, Freeh's meteoric rise was based on his credentials as a skilled investigator and prosecutor and on his ability to work closely and effectively with others. Unlike others whose judicial appointments had been based on political connections, Freeh had never been directly involved in partisan politics.

His reputation for fairness and ability to provide leadership earned him the unprecedented promotion, given his youthful age of 43, to the post of FBI director. President Bill Clinton's decision to fire FBI Director William Sessions came on July 19, 1993, owing to questions raised beginning in October 1992 about Sessions' personal abuse of office. Sessions was known to travel in an armored limousine and in a private jet at taxpayers' expense. Now the president needed the appointment of someone who could lead the bureau at a transitional time in its history and at the same time win quick confirmation. Nominated on July 20, 1993, Freeh's reputation in the law enforcement community and with leaders of the Senate (notably Senators Daniel Moynihan, Sam Nunn, and Joseph Biden) resulted in a trouble-free and speedy Senate confirmation on August 6, 1993.

Freeh's appointment came at a critical time in the history of the FBI, confronting as he would the twin problems of redefining how the FBI should respond in the post-Cold War era to the international character of organized crime and religiously-based terrorism and at the same time finally settle the legacies of former FBI Director J. Edgar Hoover's controversial 48-year tenure. Under Hoover the FBI had strayed away from law enforcement to monitor and seek to contain the influence of dissident political organizations, had avoided hiring and promoting women and ethnic and racial minorities as agents, and had been constrained from instituting more innovative procedures and revised priorities to ensure successful prosecution of organized crime, political corruption, and white collar crime. Hoover's successors had moved slowly to contain FBI political surveillance, to increase the recruitment and promotion of women and minorities, and to adopt more flexible procedures and innovative strategies to address the more complex problems confronting the law enforcement community. Internal conflict within the bureau hierarchy, moreover, had slowed the pace of these administrative and personnel reforms.

Toward the end of 1993 Freeh traveled to Sicily to honor an Italian official assassinated by the Mafia. The visit and his words became a pledge to curb the Mafia.

Not Without Controversy

Further into his 10-year term, Freeh was beset by a series of embarrassments that tarnished the reputation of the FBI as well as his own. In 1996, the FBI was maligned for being overzealous in its pursuit of Richard Jewell, suspected of detonating a bomb at the 1996 Olympics in Atlanta. Jewell turned out to be innocent. The bureau's crime laboratory was found by the Justice Department's Inspector General in 1997 to be so sloppy in its practices that it potentially tainted hundreds of cases. "We're going to get hundreds, if not thousands, of motions that are going to encompass every part of the lab, from latent- fingerprint comparisons to tire-tread analysis," said one ranking FBI agent.

On a different front, Freeh quarreled with the Clinton White House over whether agents investigating possible Chinese influence on elected U.S. officials told National Security Council aides receiving information from the investigation that they could pass it on to their superiors. Clinton maintained the agents told the security council aides they could not pass the information, and Freeh contradicted the president. An associate of Freeh's leaked an advance copy of an unflattering book about the White House written by a former FBI agent. The same associate also provided "hundreds of personal files" to White House security aides. In response to the charges, Freeh made it harder for the White House to obtain sensitive material from the FBI. The director recruited a scientist to run the FBI lab and made numerous procedural changes as well.

Freeh also was criticized for showing favoritism to his friends, micromanaging bureau operations, and being aloof from the news media. Freeh's defenders lauded the director for cutting "chair-warmers" from bureau staff, streamlining the organization, getting in closer contact with agents working in the field, and fostering cooperation with the rival Central Intelligence Agency (CIA). It also was noted that Freeh abandoned the personal excesses of his predecessor, opting to ride in a minivan instead of a limousine and fly on commercial jets instead of a private plane.

Despite the controversies, Freeh had the support of agents in the field. "In spite of well-publicized difficulties, the director's support within the bureau is largely intact," John J. Sennett, president of the FBI Agents Association told *The New York Times* in 1997. "Yet agents are very disturbed by recent negative press. Freeh's most significant shortcoming in the minds of agents has been his apparent unwillingness to get the bureau's story out."

Despite the FBI's image problems, Freeh said he intended remain director until the end of his term or for as long has he can be effective running the large bureaucracy with an annual budget of about $3 billion and about 25,000 agents.

Further Reading

Freeh is the subject of a brief biographical sketch in *Who's Who in American Law, 1992-1993*. His role in the successful prosecution of the so-called Pizza Connection case is briefly described in Ralph Blumenthal, *Last Days of the Sicilians: The FBI's War Against the Mafia* (1988), and the controversy leading to Sessions' dismissal and Freeh's appointment as FBI director is sketchily surveyed in Ronald Kessler, *The FBI: Inside the World's Most Powerful Law Enforcement Agency* (1993). See also Leslie Grove's "The FBI's Freeh Agent" in *Vanity Fair* (December 1993). Researchers might more profitably consult the various news stories in national newspapers and periodicals (*New York Times, Washington Post, USA Today, Newsweek, TIME*) at the time of his nomination and confirmation as FBI director in July-September 1993 and the confirmation hearings held in August 1993 by the Senate Judiciary Committee on his nomination as FBI director. □

Douglas Southall Freeman

The American journalist Douglas Southall Freeman (1886-1953) was one of the major biographers in the United States during the 20th century.

Douglas Southall Freeman was born at Lynchburg, Va., on May 16, 1886, the son of a Confederate veteran. His family soon moved to Richmond, where Freeman was educated. After graduating from Richmond College in 1904, he proceeded to Johns Hopkins, where he received his doctorate in history at the age of 22. The only copy of his dissertation on the Virginia Secession Convention was lost in a fire.

Freeman returned to Richmond to work for the state tax commission as well as for local newspapers. In 1908 he edited the *Calendar of Confederate Papers,* demonstrating his continued interest in Southern history. In 1911 he joined the *News Leader,* the Richmond newspaper that was his employer for the rest of his journalistic career. The next year Freeman edited the *Reports on Virginia Taxation,* and in 1914 he married.

In 1915 Freeman took two major steps. He became editor of the *News Leader* and signed a contract for a biography of Robert E. Lee. He started the biography while fully employed as a newspaperman with side interests in lecturing and radio commentary. By 1926 Freeman had established his famous work schedule: mornings—4:30 A.M. to noon—on the newspaper, afternoons on history. His *R. E. Lee* (4 vols., 1934-1935) won a Pultizer Prize and made his reputation. It also resulted in Freeman's academic appointment as visiting professor of journalism at Columbia University (1934-1935). Freeman held the rank from 1936 to 1941 but was not in residence.

Lee's biography was a skillful amalgam of military history and biography which, according to historian Michael Kraus, has no superior in the "whole range of American biographical literature." Looking at the world through Lee's eyes and with no more information than Lee had, Freeman developed Lee's character and ideas.

In 1936, utilizing his leftover data, Freeman commenced a study of the Army of Northern Virginia which was published as *Lee's Lieutenants* (3 vols., 1942-1944). Re-

garded by Freeman as his best, though most difficult, work, it unraveled the complexity of the command structure of the army.

In 1945 Freeman began his most ambitious work, a biography of George Washington. Not until 1949 did he give up his newspaper position to become a full-time historian. Still he did not have enough time; only six of the seven proposed volumes were finished when he died on June 13, 1953. Freeman had not lived to hear the acclaim for *George Washington: A. Biography* (1948-1957).

Further Reading

The best short sketch of Freeman's life is in Dumas Malone's "The Pen of Douglas Southall Freeman" in Freeman's *George Washington* (7 vols., 1948-1957). Freeman is also treated briefly in Michael Kraus, *A History of American History* (1937) and *The Writing of American History* (1953). □

Roland L. Freeman

Roland L. Freeman (born 1936) was an American photographer devoted to recording the lives of rural and urban African Americans. His photographs comprised a social history beginning with the era of the civil rights movement.

B orn in Baltimore, Maryland, in 1936, Roland L. Freeman was sent from the streets of an urban environment to a southern Maryland tobacco farm at age 13 by a loving mother who foresaw disaster for him if he did not get away from the city. In 1954, as a member of the U.S. Air Force, he took his first pictures with a Brownie Hawkeye camera. However, he did not stick with photography at that point. Later, in 1963, he decided that photography would be his medium, and he had his first one-man show six years later.

Freeman's emphasis on documenting the African American urban and rural experience began with the March on Washington on August 28, 1963. On that date 200,000 African and white Americans gathered in a peaceful protest to pressure the U.S. government to guarantee African Americans legal equality. Inspired by that event, Freeman decided to use the medium of photography to report on the lives of ordinary people.

Began with Borrowed Camera

He became familiar with the photographs of Gordon Parks. His work was influenced by Roy DeCarava, whose pictures of family life in a Harlem tenement reminded Freeman of his own family. Through a chance meeting with photographer Burk Uzzle, Freeman began his photographic career with a borrowed camera. He began working for the *D.C. Gazette* in 1967 and was the newspaper's photo editor from 1968 to 1973.

In 1968, after the assassination of Martin Luther King, Jr., he photographed the mule-train march of the Poor Peo-

ple's Campaign from rural Mississippi to Washington, D.C., as a Southern Christian Leadership Conference photographer. That experience crystallized his commitment to be a witness documentarian of the changes in the lives of African Americans as new civil rights legislation opened doors that previously were closed to African Americans.

Documented the South

Using his camera as a tool of research as well as a form of creative expression, Freeman travelled through the backwoods of the rural South, gaining the trust of African American artisans and craftsmen who permitted him to photograph intimate details of their lives. He photographed African American congregations going to river baptisms, railroad workers laying tracks, blacksmiths at work and at home, and quilters with their wares. Presenting intimate closeups of their faces, homes, and daily activities, he presented not only a concentrated experience of the way African Americans view their world, but also a vision of a good life lived in small communities by loving people with satisfying work.

His sensitive portrayals were not, however, limited to one racial group. Some of his finest pictures were a "White Ghetto" series made in his native Baltimore. In those photographs, Native Americans and poor whites from Appalachia turn their backs or loll defiantly in front of Freeman's camera, touching each other reassuringly as they face his lens. One biting image shows a couple asleep on a dirty mattress in a dark room, arms entwined, mouths gaping as if dead or drugged.

During the 1970s Freeman became the Washington stringer for Magnum Photos, Inc. and worked for various magazines, such as *LIFE, Black Enterprise,* and *Essence.* These experiences helped give his work the journalist's succinctness. He also taught photography to students at such universities as George Washington and Howard and directed the Mississippi Folk Life Project.

Among his 12 one-man shows and eight group shows, two of Freeman's exhibitions were circulated nationally and internationally on extended tours. "Folkroots: Images of Mississippi Black Folklife" (1974-1976) opened in Mississippi and subsequently toured museums and galleries around the country. In 1981 "Southern Roads/City Pavements: Photos of Black Americans," one of his finest accomplishments, opened at the International Center of Photography in New York City. The result of a study of the African American experience from 1968 to 1980, it featured the Baltimore Arabers (street vendors), citified residents in fancy hats, close-ups of serious youth, and Mississippi folk life. This exhibition toured city and college museums across America during two separate national tours, gaining wide critical acclaim. According to the *New York Times,* "(Freeman's) pictures are in the tradition of Walker Evans and the other photographers of the Farm Security Administration." In 1982 the U.S. Information Agency sponsored a three-year African and European tour of the exhibition.

Quilts Caught Eye, Imagination

African American quilters captured Freeman's imagination and held it fast for more than two decades. In his 1996 book, *A communion of the Spirits: African-American Quilters, Preservers and Their Stories,* documents his foray into the world of African American quilts. The book describers the comfort Freeman found in quilts as a child and continues to explain how the man became intrigued and impassioned by quilts, quiltmakers, and their stories. In fact, when Freeman was diagnosed with cancer in 1991, he sought "healing" from quilts.

For his work behind the camera, Freeman was recognized by the National Endowment for the Arts, the National Endowment for the Humanities, and the National Black Arts Festival through its 1994 Living Legend Award. Freeman worked for *Time, Newsweek, National Geographic,* the *London Sunday Times,* and *Paris Match.* He was a research photographer for the Smithsonian Institution's Center for Folklife Programs and Cultural Studies. He also was invited to be the Eudora Welty Visiting Professor of Southern Studies at Millsaps College in Jackson, Mississippi for 1997.

Further Reading

Freeman's work appeared in the *Black Photographers Annual,* Vol. 2 (1974). More information can be found in two of his exhibit catalogues: *City Pavements/Country Roads* (1979) and *Southern Roads/City Pavements* (1981). See also Freeman, Roland L., *A Communion of the Spirits: African-American Quilters, Preservers, and their stories,* Rutledge Hill Press, 1996. □

Gottlob Frege

The German mathematician and philosopher Gottlob Frege (1848-1925) is considered the founder of modern mathematical logic. His work was almost wholly ignored during his lifetime but now exerts a great influence on the philosophy of logic and language.

Gottlob Frege was born on Nov. 8, 1848, at Wismar. He began his university studies at Jena in 1869 but after 2 years moved to Göttingen. He studied mathematics, the natural sciences, and philosophy and took his degree in 1873. Thereafter he taught at Jena in the department of mathematics. He was made a professor in 1896 and retired in 1918. Frege was married to Margarete Lieseberg, and the couple had one adopted son. Frege died on July 26, 1925, in Bad Kleinen.

Frege invented the concept of a formal system of mathematical logic, and in his first major work, *Begriffsschrift* (1879), he presented the first example of such a system in his formulation of a propositional and predicate calculus. He introduced the mathematical notion of function and variable into logic and invented the idea of quantifiers. He was also the first writer on axiomatic theory to make clear the distinction between an axiom and a rule of inference.

Further progress in this work convinced Frege that the basic ideas of arithmetic (but not of geometry) could be articulated solely in logical expressions. He expressed his new program first in a nonsymbolic work, *The Foundations of Arithmetic* (1884), which also featured a brilliant and devastating polemic against all previous attempts at the subject. The crown of his work was to be his *Basic Laws of Arithmetic.* The first volume of this work appeared in 1893; but in 1903, as Frege was about to issue the second volume, Bertrand Russell pointed out a contradiction in Frege's use of the concept of a "class," which undermined the proofs in the work. Frege hastily added an appendix that sought to remedy the defect (this effort was later proved defective), but thereafter he seemed to lose interest in the great project. Two decades later he regarded the whole enterprise as an error and fell back upon the Kantian interpretation of mathematical judgments as synthetic a priori.

Frege also made important contributions to the philosophy of logic. Concerning the old question: what is it for a proposition to have meaning?—he introduced a variety of distinctions that are being exploited by contemporary philosophers. Frege rejected epistemology as the starting point of philosophy and revived the classical view, dominant before René Descartes, that philosophical logic holds this place.

Further Reading

There are no biographies of Frege. His work, however, has been extensively studied, especially since translations of it have become available, beginning in the 1950s. A convenient collection of most of the important critical essays is in E. D. Klemke, ed., *Essays on Frege* (1968), which also has a complete bibliography. Two difficult but rewarding full-length studies are Jeremy D. B. Walker, *A Study of Frege* (1965), and Robert Sternfeld, *Frege's Logical Theory* (1966). □

Eduardo Frei Montalva

Eduardo Frei Montalva (1911-1982) was president of Chile and one of the most widely known and respected spokesmen for democratic reform in Latin America.

Eduardo Frei was born into a middle-class family in Santiago on January 16, 1911. His father was a Swiss immigrant, his mother, Chilean. Growing up, he was educated in Catholic elementary and secondary schools. In 1928 he entered Santiago's Catholic University to study law, graduating near the top of his class in 1933. Frei was a Chilean delegate in 1934 to the Congress of University Youth, a Catholic conference in Rome, a pivotal moment in Frei's life, for during this gathering he met Pope Pius XI; Eugenio Cardinal Pacelli, who was later to become Pope

Pius XII; and French social philosopher Jacques Maritain. These three men had a profound impact on the young Frei's political philosophy.

Deeply religious and increasingly drawn to politics, Frei became disenchanted with the orientation of the traditional representative of Chilean Catholic thought, the Conservative party. The Conservatives stubbornly resisted change, Frei believed, and were losing strength to new parties that postulated solutions to social problems. Active in the youth group of the party and editor of a newspaper in northern Chile, Frei and fellow youth group members finally broke with the Conservatives. The youth group grew into the National Falange, a party reflecting reformist Catholic thinking. Anti-Marxist and anticapitalist, the Falange sought inspiration in the writings of Maritain and the papal encyclicals of Leo XIII and Pius XI. Under the banner of the Falange, Frei ran in 1937 for a seat in the provincial legislature of Tarapacá, where he was managing the operations of a newspaper in the coastal town of Uquique. In his first run for office, Frei was unsuccessful.

Teaching, Political Inroads

In 1940 Frei became a member of the labor law faculty at the Catholic University while continuing to be an active participant in the affairs of the Falange party, taking the party's presidency in 1941. He was reelected to that post in 1943 and 1945. In May 1946 he was appointed minister of public works and communications in the Popular Front government of President Juan Antonio Ríos, but he resigned in January 1947 after the Ríos government brutally put

down a demonstration by Chilean workers. He later was reappointed to the public works post by President Gabriel Gonzalez Videla, who had succeeded Ríos. Frei was nationally respected for his efforts to improve Chile's antiquated transportation systems. After running unsuccessfully in several elections, he was finally elected to the Senate in 1949 and reelected in 1957. The Falange and Social Christian Conservative parties joined in 1957 to form the Christian Democratic party.

In 1958 Frei ran for the presidency and, maintaining the party's independence from electoral alliances, came in a third. From 1958 to 1964 the Christian Democrats attracted new recruits, while the rightist parties were discredited by their inability to deal effectively with the worsening national economic crisis. By 1964 Frei had emerged as a serious contender for the presidency and the only alternative to the well-organized and powerful leftist coalition, FRAP. In the election of 1964 Frei decisively defeated Salvador Allende Gossens, the FRAP candidate, receiving an absolute majority of the votes. For the nation Frei promised a "profound revolution within liberty and law": agrarian reform, an end to inflation, Chilean control of the foreign-owned copper industry, expansion of educational facilities, better housing, and incorporation of the masses into the political and economic life of the country. After victories in the congressional elections of 1965, Frei and his party had some degree of success in achieving these goals, although the nationalization of 51 percent of the nation's copper industry proved satisfactory to no one. His attempts at agrarian reform were largely a failure, only a small number of peasants having received their own plots of land by the end of Frei's term. In 1970 Frei was constitutionally unable to succeed himself and gave way to Allende.

Opposed Pinochet Regime

When Allende was overthrown and murdered in 1973 by Chile's right-wing military, led by General Augusto Pinochet Ugarte, Frei was initially supportive of the coup. Before long, however, he turned against the repressive Pinochet regime, speaking out against the ruling junta with a freedom accorded few in Chile at that time, a freedom to dissent that some felt was given Frei because of his international standing. In 1978, he led the unsuccessful campaign against Pinochet's plebescite to uphold the legitimacy of the junta's rule. The Pinochet forces carried the day, winning about two-thirds of the votes cast in the ballot.

In 1973, just after winning reelection to another term in Chile's Senate but before the coup against Allende, a probe in Washington by the U.S. Senate Foreign Relations Subcommittee on Intelligence disclosed that the Central Intelligence Agency of the United States had funneled $20 million into Frei's 1964 presidential campaign. These revelations, some of which were and continue to be suspect, came at a difficult time for Frei and for Chile and left many of his countrymen questioning the accuracy of Frei's portrayal of himself as a political centrist.

In his final years, Frei was active as a member of a global commission on international development led by German Willy Brandt. After complications from hernia sur-

gery, Frei died in Santiago on January 22, 1982, less than a week after his seventy-first birthday.

Further Reading

Selections from Frei's many publications can be found in *The Ideologies of the Developing Nations,* edited by Paul E. Sigmund (1963; rev. ed. 1967), and in sections of *Religion, Revolution and New Forces for Change in Latin America,* edited by William V. D'Antonio and Frederick B. Pike (1964). Leonard Gross wrote a popular and highly sympathetic study of Frei, *The Last, Best Hope: Eduardo Frei and Chilean Democracy* (1967). Federico G. Gil, *The Political System of Chile* (1966), details the development of the party system. A study of Christian Democracy in Latin America is Edward J. Williams, *Latin American Christian Democratic Parties* (1967).
Further information about Frei's later years can be found in *The Annual Obituary 1982,* edited by Janet Podell and published by St. Martin's Press, New York, in 1983. ☐

Paulo Freire

The Brazilian philosopher Paulo Freire (1921–1997) developed theories that have been used, principally in Third World countries, to bring literacy to the poor and to transform the field of education.

Paulo Freire was born on the northeastern coast of Brazil in the city of Recife in 1921. Raised by his mother who was a devout Catholic and his father who was a middle-class businessman, Freire's early years paralleled those of the Great Depression. Outward symbols, such as his father always wearing a tie and having a German-made piano in their home, pointed to the family's middle-class heritage but stood in contrast to their actual conditions of poverty. Reflecting on their situation, Freire noted, "We shared the hunger, but not the class." After completing secondary school and with gradual improvement in his family's financial situation, he was able to enter Recife University, preparing to become a teacher of Portuguese.

The Direction for his Later Life

The 15 years following World War II proved to be instrumental in giving direction to his later life. He had previously married a fellow teacher, Elza, in 1944. In addition to their shared careers in teaching, they worked together with middle-class friends in the Catholic Action Movement. This work became unsettling as they struggled with the contradictions between the Christian faith and their friends' lifestyles. In particular they faced strong resistance when suggesting that servants should be dealt with as human beings. Later they decided to work solely with "the people," the large population of the poor in Brazil.

A second experience that gave focus to Freire's later life came when he worked as a labor lawyer for the poor and involved a discussion with workers about the theories of Jean Piaget, a prominent psychologist. Evidently Freire's comments were not comprehended by one of the workers, who noted, "You talk from a background of food, comfort, and rest. The reality is that we have one room, no food, and have to make love in front of the children." Through such experiences and further study, Freire began to realize that the poor had a different sense of reality and that to communicate with them he had to use their syntax of meanings. This recognition served as a basis for his doctoral dissertation in 1959 at Recife University, where he was to soon become professor of history and philosophy of education.

Leading the National Literacy Program

In 1962 the mayor of Recife appointed Freire as head of an adult literacy program for the city. In his first experiement, Freire taught 300 adults to read and write in 45 days. This program was so successful that during the following year the President of Brazil appointed him to lead the National Literacy Program. This program was on its way to becoming similarly successful, with expected enrollments to exceed two million students in 1964. Under Brazil's constitution, however, illiterates were not allowed to vote. The *O Globe,* an influential conservative newspaper, claimed that Freire's method for developing literacy was stirring up the people, causing them to want to change society, and formenting subversion. As a consequence of a military overthrow of the government in 1964, Freire was jailed for 70 days, then exiled briefly to Bolivia and then to Chile for five years.

Providing Literacy in Exile

Freire met with opposition from some Chilian citizens who viewed him as a threat to their society. However, the director of a nationwide program for reducing illiteracy employed him to work in the Chilian Agrarian Reform Corporation. This provided him the opportunity over the next few years to become more involved in research and to write three books, the most noted of which is *Pedagogy of the Oppressed* (1970). In 1969 he accepted an invitation to be a visiting professor at Harvard. He quickly found a large audience of growing support in America primarily through the appearance in English of his publications. He left Harvard in 1970 to join the Office of Education at the World Council of Churches in Geneva. In this office his work over the next decade was marked by efforts to increase literacy and liberty in Third World countries through educational programs. Of particular note were his efforts to rethink and apply his theories in the West African country of Guinea-Bissau.

End of Exile

In 1979 Freire's exile status was lifted, allowing him to return home to Brazil where he became secretary of education in Sao Paulo. During the decade of the 1980s he published widely in the areas of education, politics, and literacy. In these writings he developed themes discussed previously and he continued to rethink their practical application to new situations.

Freire believed that poor peoples of the world are dominated and victims of those who possess political power.

What the poor need is liberation, an education giving them a critical consciousness, investing them with an agency for changing, and throwing off the oppressive structures of their society. Such an education would not conform and mold people to fit into the roles expected by society, but it would prepare them to realize their own values and reality, reflect and study critically their world, and move into action to transform it. When working with illiterate adults, Freire proposed the selection of words used by the poor in their everyday lives expressing their longings, frustrations, and hopes. From this list of words a shorter list is developed of possibly 16-17 words that contain the basic sounds and syllables of the language. These words are broken down (decoded) into syllables; afterwards, the learners form new words by making different combinations of syllables. In relatively a short period of time (a few days) they are usually writing simple letters to each other. During their studies a second and deeper level of analysis is occurring simultaneously. That is, the teacher using the very same words helps the students also to decode their cultural and social world. This deeper level of activity leads learners to greater awareness of the oppressive forces in their lives and to the realization of their power to transform them.

Freire wrote 25 books which were translated into 35 languages and was an honorary professor of 28 universities around the world. He maintained that he never would have been arrested or criticized had he stuck to teaching ABCs. He fell into disfavor, he said, because of his theory that illiteracy, not any religious reason, made people poor. He said, "Education is freedom." After his death in 1997, there was a three-day mourning in the state of Pernambuco.

Further Reading

There is a biography written by Denis Collins, *Paulo Freire: His Life and Thought* (1977). An earlier quotational bibliography compiled by Anne Hartung and John Ohliger is in Stanley M. Grabowshi's edited work, *Paulo Freire: A Revolutionary Dilemma for the Adult Educator* (1972). One of Freire's co-authors, Donaldo Macedo of Boston University, is writing an authorized biography.

The reader will find Freire's books *Pedagogy of the Oppressed* (1970) and *Pedagogy in Process: The Letters to Guinea-Bissau* (1978) excellent introductions to his thought. *Education for Critical Consciousness* (1974) contains concrete and practical examples of his teaching methods. The evolution of his thought and its application to world situation in the last two decades of the 20th century can be found in *The Politics of Education: Cultural Power and Liberation* (1985) and in *Literacy* (1987), written jointly with Donaldo Macedo. □

Theodorus Jacobus Frelinghuysen

Theodorus Jacobus Frelinghuysen (1691-ca. 1748), a Dutch Reformed clergyman, was a noted exhorter and revivalist who initiated the Great Awakening in America's Middle colonies.

A pastor's son, Theodorus Frelinghuysen was born at Lingen, Germany. His father and a minister friend gave him a thorough classical education. Frelinghuysen was licensed in 1717 by the Classis of Emden and the next year became a chaplain and then subrector in Friesland.

Having learned that four Dutch frontier congregations in New Jersey desired a pastor, Frelinghuysen left for America in 1719. In a guest sermon in New York (1720) he immediately offended influential clerics by deviating from established rubric and by advocating revivalism.

In his scattered settlements Frelinghuysen taught and preached passionately that religious performance without true conversion was an abomination. His zeal appealed to the young and the poor, but many parishoners resented criticism of their behavior and Frelinghuysen's stringent requirements for taking Communion. They allied themselves with New York clergymen who proclaimed baptismal regeneration instead. A long, bitter dispute produced publication of a lengthy *Klagte* (*Complaint*), signed by 64 family heads in the parishes. Some clerics, however, sided with Frelinghuysen, who defended himself ably in sermons published in several pamphlets. Gradually Frelinghuysen's influence grew; he was increasingly invited to preach to other New Jersey congregations.

Eloquent and vigorous, Frelinghuysen stimulated community intellectual life and trained several ministers. His presentation of the Gospel had a reforming effect, and significant revivals followed. The movement spread to other denominations, and Frelinghuysen (with the aid of Gilbert Tennent and later George Whitefield and Jonathan Edwards) led in generating the series of revivals called the Great Awakening.

Innovative and individualistic, Frelinghuysen worked to free the New World Dutch Church from the Classis of Amsterdam and urged greater authority for an American clerical tribunal than that granted by the Church in Holland. He also introduced private prayer meetings and lay preaching and advocated founding a college and theological seminary.

Frelinghuysen married Eva Terhune, a farmer's daughter; the couple had five sons and two daughters. The sons all entered the ministry, and both daughters married clergymen. Seven pamphlets of Frelinghuysen's sermons were published (several in English as well as in Dutch) during his lifetime.

Further Reading

William Demarest edited Frelinghuysen's *Sermons, Translated from the Dutch* (1856) and added a sketch of the pastor's life. The best account of Frelinghuysen's clerical activities is in Charles Hartshorn Maxson, *The Great Awakening in the Middle Colonies* (1920), which also provides insight into his character and struggles. Another study is James Tanis, *Dutch Calvinistic Pietism in the Middle Colonies: A Study in the Life and Theology of Theodorus Jacobus Frelinghuysen* (1967). Background studies are William Warren Sweet, *Religion in Colonial America* (1942), and Clifton E. Olmstead, *History of Religion in the United States* (1960). □

John Charles Frémont

John Charles Frémont (1813-1890) was an American explorer, politician, and soldier. Through his explorations in the West he stimulated the American desire to own that region. He was the first presidential candidate of the Republican party.

Born on Jan. 31, 1813, in Savannah, Ga., John C. Frémont was the illegitimate son of a French émigré, John Charles Frémon (*sic*), and Mrs. Anne Whiting Pryor. He was raised in Charleston, S. C. Frémont proved precocious, especially in mathematics and the natural sciences, as well as handsome. He attended Charleston College (1829-1831) but was expelled for irregular attendance.

Through the influence of Joel R. Poinsett, Frémont obtained a post as teacher of mathematics on the sloop *Natchez* and visited South American waters in 1833. In 1836 he helped survey a railroad route between Charleston and Cincinnati, and in 1836-1837 he worked on a survey of Cherokee lands in Georgia.

His Explorations

In 1838, through the influence of Poinsett, Frémont obtained a commission as second lieutenant in the Corps of Topographical Engineers of the U.S. Army. Assigned to the expedition of J. N. Nicollet which explored in Minnesota and the Dakotas, he gained knowledge of natural science and topographical engineering, as well as experience on the frontier. Also through Nicollet, he met the powerful senator from Missouri Thomas Hart Benton—and fell in love with Benton's daughter Jessie.

Benton secured an appointment for Frémont to explore the Des Moines River, which was accomplished in 1841. That fall he married Jessie Benton, gaining her father as protector. In 1842 Frémont was sent to explore the Wind River chain of the Rockies and to make a scientific exploration of the Oregon Trail. Employing Kit Carson as guide, he followed the trail through South Pass. His report was filled with tales of adventure and contained an excellent map. Frémont was on his way to becoming a popular hero with a reputation as the "Great Pathfinder," but, in reality, he had been following the trails of mountain men.

In 1843 Frémont headed an expedition that explored South Pass, the Columbia River, and the Oregon country, returning by way of Sutter's Fort in Mexican California. His report was printed just as James K. Polk became president, a time when expansionist feeling was high; the 10,000 copies of this report increased Frémont's heroic stature.

Mexican War

In 1845 Polk sent Frémont and soldiers (with Kit Carson as guide) to California. Expelled from California by its governor, Frémont wintered in Oregon. Polk's orders arrived in May. Frémont then marched to Sutter's Fort and there on June 14, 1846, assumed command of the American settlers' Bear Flag Revolt. Aided by commodores J. D. Sloat and

Robert F. Stockton, his forces were victorious, and he received the surrender of California at Cahuenga on Jan. 13, 1847.

Immediately Frémont became embroiled in a fight for the governorship of California with Gen. Stephen W. Kearny, who had marched overland from Missouri. Frémont was arrested, taken to Washington, D.C., and tried for mutiny, insubordination, and conduct prejudicial to good order. Found guilty, he was ordered dismissed from the Army. Polk remitted the penalty, but Frémont, in anger, resigned.

Political Career

Frémont moved to California, on the way conducting a private survey for a railroad route. In California he acquired land in the Sierra foothills, the Mariposa estate, and grew wealthy from mining. He bought real estate in San Francisco and lived lavishly, winning election as U.S. senator from California. He drew the short term and served only from Sept. 9, 1850, to March 4, 1851. Afterward he visited Paris and London, where he raised funds for ambitious schemes on the Mariposa. In 1853-1854 he conducted another private expedition surveying a railroad route, along the 37th-38th parallels.

In 1856 the newly formed Republican party named Frémont its first presidential candidate because of his strong stand on free soil in Kansas and his attitude against enforcement of the Fugitive Slave Law. His campaign suffered from a shortage of funds, and he lost, but he was at the peak of his career.

Subsequent Career

Frémont's overspeculation at the Mariposa led to his loss of this property. Then in 1861, at the outbreak of the Civil War, he performed disastrously as a major general at St. Louis and in western Virginia. In 1864 Radical Republicans approached Frémont about running for president in opposition to Abraham Lincoln; Frémont first accepted, then declined ungraciously.

After the war he was involved in promoting the Kansas and Pacific and the Memphis and Little Rock railroads. Both lines went bankrupt in 1870, leaving Frémont almost penniless. In 1878 his claim that the Republican party owed him a debt netted him appointment as governor of Arizona. He held the position until 1881, when angry protests from that territory led to his removal.

Frémont's old age was filled with frustrating schemes to recoup his fortune—while he was supported by his wife's authorship. In 1890 he was pensioned at $6,000 per year as a major general; he died 3 months later (July 13, 1890) in New York.

Further Reading

Only one volume of Frémont's autobiographical *Memoirs of My Life* (1887) was published. Jesse Benton Frémont wrote several works that give information about her husband's career, the best of which are *Souvenirs of My Time* (1887) and *Far-West Sketches* (1890). Good biographies include Frederick S. Dellenbaugh, *Frémont and '49* (1914), which has excellent sketches of his expeditions; Cardinal Goodwin's critical *John Charles Frémont: An Explanation of His Career* (1930); and Allan Nevins's laudatory *Frémont: The West's Greatest Adventurer* (2 vols., 1928) and his more balanced, one volume edition, *Frémont: Pathmaker of the West* (1939). □

Daniel Chester French

Daniel Chester French (1850-1931) was one of America's leading sculptors of the late 19th century and maintained his popularity and fame well into the 20th century.

Daniel Chester French was born in Exeter, N.H. He grew up in Concord, Mass., and came under the influence of the intellectual circle of Ralph Waldo Emerson and Louisa May Alcott. French chose to become a sculptor early in life and had the benefit of study with the painter William Morris Hunt and the sculptors William Rimmer and John Q.A. Ward—a particularly fortuitous group of instructors because of the variety of their esthetic approaches and their sympathetic professionalism.

With Emerson's assistance in 1874 French received the commission for the statue *Minute Man* for Concord. This immediately brought him fame. Though based upon the classical *Apollo Belvedere,* the sculpture was totally in keeping with the then-advanced style of historical bronze monuments. In 1876 French went to Italy and studied with

Thomas Ball, whose work combined the neoclassic heritage and the new naturalism.

Some of French's first works on his return to the United States were not unlike the plaster groups of John Rogers. However, French gained fame principally through the large public monuments he created for the custom houses in St. Louis and Philadelphia, the Boston Post Office, and, above all, the gigantic statue, *The Republic,* that dominated the World's Columbian Exposition in Chicago in 1893.

French evolved a type of allegorical figure which became his trademark, although it was emulated by other sculptors. This was the statuesque, somewhat sexless female in long flowing gown, as in the *Alma Mater* at Columbia University or the *Spirit of Life* at the Spencer Trask Memorial at Saratoga Springs, N.Y. The heavy, voluminous drapery often flowed over the heads of these figures as well, as can be seen in his most eloquent and personal work, *Angel of Death and the Young Sculptor,* a memorial to his friend and fellow sculptor Martin Milmore, who died young. The figure of Death confronts an idealized sculptor, who is at work on a relief of a sphinx.

French's best-known works are his two statues of Abraham Lincoln. The first, a standing Lincoln in Lincoln, Nebr., is similar to one by Augustus Saint-Gaudens in Chicago. The second, completed in 1922, and French's most famous sculpture, is the seated Lincoln in the Lincoln Memorial in Washington, D.C., done as one of several collaborative works with architect Henry Bacon.

Further Reading

A primary source on French is Mary French, *Memories of a Sculptor's Wife* (1928). Two biographies are Adeline Pond Adams, *Daniel Chester French: Sculptor* (1932), and Margaret Cresson, *Journey into Fame: The Life of Daniel Chester French* (1947). □

Philip Morin Freneau

Philip Morin Freneau (1752-1832) was an American poet, essayist, and journalist. Remembered as the poet of the American Revolution and the father of American poetry, he was a transitional figure in American literature.

Philip Freneau's life alternated between ardent political activity and attempts to escape to the solitude he thought necessary to a poet. Born in New York on Jan. 2, 1752, he graduated from Princeton in 1771, when with Hugh Henry Brackenridge he wrote a rousing poem, *The Rising Glory of America.* A period of schoolteaching and study for the ministry followed. At the outbreak of the American Revolution, Freneau composed vitriolic satires against British invaders and Tory countrymen. But then he withdrew to the Caribbean, writing his ambitious early poems, *The Beauties of Santa Cruz* and *The House of Night.*

Returning in 1778 to his home in New Jersey, Freneau joined the local militia and sailed as a privateer. In 1780, on release from British imprisonment, he wrote the bitter poem *The British Prison-Ship* and the enthusiastic *American Independence.* The next 4 years were dedicated to patriotic prose and verse in the *Freeman's Journal.* In 1784 he again went to sea as master of vessels which plied between New York and Charleston. His poetry at this time was concerned with native scene and character.

Though nurtured on English poets such as Alexander Pope, Freneau strove now for an "American" idiom, producing in *The Wild Honey Suckle* and *The Indian Burying Ground* verses of quiet distinction. His first two collections were *Poems* (1786) and *Miscellaneous Works* (1788). In 1790 he returned to partisan journalism, ultimately working as editor of the outspoken *National Gazette.* He so earnestly opposed Federalist policies that George Washington called him "that rascal, Freneau," though Thomas Jefferson credited him with saving the country when it was galloping fast into monarchy.

In the early 1800s, after another period at sea, Freneau retired to his farm in New Jersey. Collected editions of his poetry appeared in 1795, 1809, and 1815; new poems appeared in periodicals into the 1820s. He died on Dec. 18, 1832.

The most prolific poet of his generation, Freneau produced verse uneven in quality, often marred by anger, haste, or partisanship, but sometimes exhibiting original lyric power. He anticipated such American romantic poets as William Cullen Bryant and Edgar Allan Poe. His prose is less often successful.

Further Reading

Biographical and critical studies of Freneau include Samuel E. Forman, *The Political Activities of Philip Freneau* (1902); Lewis Leary, *That Rascal Freneau: A Study in Literary Failure* (1941); Nelson F. Adkins, *Philip Freneau and the Cosmic Enigma: The Religious and Philosophical Speculations of an American Poet* (1949); and Jacob Axelrad, *Philip Freneau, Champion of Democracy* (1967). □

Sir Henry Bartle Edward Frere

Sir Henry Bartle Edward Frere (1815-1884) was a British civil servant. The government sent him to South Africa to effect the unification of the Boer republics and the territories under British rule.

Bartle Frere was born into an old and religious family on March 29, 1815. In 1834 he sailed for Bombay, where the East India Company employed him as an assistant revenue clerk in Poona. He became the resident in the Deccan in 1847. While commissioner in Sind (1850-1859), his policy for dealing with the colonial peoples matured. He wanted Britain to be a good and effective neighbor with the Indian princes if they cooperated, but he advocated the use of the empire's resources to punish recalcitrance.

A self-willed aristocrat who read the Bible every morning, Frere was an aggressive champion of the imperial cause. He was appointed to the Viceroy's Council in 1859 and became governor of Bombay in 1862. A commercial crisis in 1866 in which the Bank of Bombay collapsed was partly blamed on Frere, and shortly after this he was transferred to London, where he sat on the Indian Council (1867-1877). Frere sought to make Afghanistan a buffer state between India and Russia and wanted a British resident in Kabul. The Afghans resisted and war broke out in 1878.

Frere in Africa

South Africa was becoming a major trouble center in the empire. Britain was not keen to involve itself too deeply in the affairs of a country it then believed poor in natural resources. The discovery of diamonds and the way in which this enabled the Africans to acquire guns forced Britain to change its mind. Policy then required the pacification of South Africa, the unification of the Boer republics— Shepstone annexed the Transvaal in 1877—and the British colonies, and the establishment of effective white control as preconditions for the exploitation of the country's mineral wealth. Frere was appointed high commissioner in South Africa to implement the new policy.

Shortly after Frere arrived at the Cape in 1877, war with the Gcaleka broke out. He deposed Kreli, the Gcaleka king,

proposed that German and Scottish farmers be settled on Gcaleka land, and sent his police to disarm the neighboring African kingdoms. Widespread bloodshed followed.

War with the Zulu

Crisis point had been reached in the relations between the Zulu and the British on one hand and the Zulu and the Boers on the other. The Zulu, under Cetshwayo, were reported to be organizing an African united front to drive the whites out of African lands. Frere's visit to Natal in 1878 reinforced his conviction that the destruction of Zulu military power was a prerequisite for establishing white supremacy in South Africa.

Britain lacked enthusiasm for war in South Africa at the time. Its cost, the conflict in Afghanistan, and a possible collision with the Russians necessitated a negotiated settlement with the Zulu. By 1878 the secretary of state, Sir Michael Hicks Beach, was urging Frere to negotiate. In Frere's view, however, the crisis in Natal called for a military solution and took precedence over the simmering Boer rebellion. He declared war on the Zulu in January 1879. Although British arms suffered a humiliating defeat at Isandlwana, Zulu power was finally broken.

Frere was censured for his disregard of Beach's instructions and was stripped of authority in Natal, Zululand, and the Transvaal. His recommendations for increased Boer participation in the Transvaal government were largely ignored. The Foreign Office at times suspected that he influenced the Cape administration against unification, and he was recalled in 1880. He died on May 29, 1884.

Further Reading

The two major biographies of Frere complement one another: John Martineau in *The Life and Correspondence of the Right Hon. Sir Bartle Frere* (2 vols., 2d ed. 1895) describes Frere's life in the light of contemporary assessments of his role in South Africa; while William Basil Worsfold, *Sir Bartle Frere* (1923), had access to documents which were unavailable to Martineau. For broader historical background see Frances E. Colenso and Edward Durnford, *The History of the Zulu War: Its Origin* (2d ed. 1881), and Lady Victoria Hicks-Beach, *The Life of Sir Michael Hicks Beach* (2 vols., 1932). □

Girolamo Frescobaldi

Girolamo Frescobaldi (1583-1643) was an Italian composer, teacher, and organist. His keyboard works are the culmination in the development from the Renaissance keyboard style to that of the baroque era.

Girolamo Frescobaldi was born in Ferrara, which, through his fifteenth year, was a rich cultural center under the Este court. He studied with the court organist Luzzasco Luzzaschi, who introduced him to a number of illustrious native and foreign musicians and to many species of music. Undoubtedly important among these contacts was a familiarity with the radical madrigals of Carlo Gesualdo, Prince of Venosa.

In 1598 Ferrara became an ecclesiastical state and the opulent cultural life of the court came to an end. Frescobaldi, perhaps influenced by these developments, went to Rome, possibly with the support of the Bentivoglio, a noble family of Ferrara. In 1604 he was organist and singer with the Congregation and Academy of S. Cecilia in Rome; in January and February 1607 he was organist of S. Maria in Trastevere. At that time Guido Bentivoglio went to Brussels as nunzio and Frescobaldi accompanied him. This gave him an opportunity to become acquainted with many important musicians of the Low Countries, including some of the English exiles resident there.

The year 1608 may be taken as the end of Frescobaldi's formative period; his first work, containing five-part madrigals, was published in Antwerp (such a work often signified the end of an informal apprenticeship). His music also made its first appearance in an anthology, one that included works by such renowned masters as Luzzaschi, Claudio Merulo, and Giovanni Gabrieli. Frescobaldi returned to Rome and in November 1608 became organist at St. Peter's.

Growth of His Reputation

Frescobaldi's reputation grew rapidly; his stipend, however, was small. He frequently received permission to be absent from his post. Undoubtedly he spent several periods in Venice, since many of his works were published

there. In 1614-1615 he was in the service of the Duke of Mantua, but, finding a cool reception, he returned to Rome, having neither resigned his position nor moved his family. In 1628 he accepted a position in Florence as organist to Ferdinand II de' Medici.

In 1634, possibly because of plague and civic upset, Frescobaldi returned to his position at St. Peter's, with an increase in stipend, and entered the most illustrious portion of his career. In 1635 he published what is probably now his best-known work, *Fiori musicali,* a collection of organ works to be played during various portions of the Mass. He remained at St. Peter's until his death.

His Works

At one time Frescobaldi was thought to have developed, almost single-handedly, the baroque keyboard style. More recent scholarship has shown that many of the stylistic innovations attributed to him already existed, and he must be seen as perfecting rather than introducing many of the elements that characterize his music. He brought to a high level the control of the form of the whole. Like others, he reduced the number of sections in multipartite forms, introduced thematic relations between the sections, and used other structural devices to relate the sections, thus strengthening the formal arch. He used various musical devices, such as pungent harmonic colors, in a baroque manner for expressive purposes, rather than for primarily esthetic satisfaction, as had been done in the Renaissance.

Although many of Frescobaldi's works have been lost, probably including a major part of his vocal music, his extant works are still numerous. His keyboard music in secular forms (*partite*), primarily for harpsichord, are outstanding examples of the use of the variation technique. His various forms for organ were intended for occasional use (such as introductory music) or as parts of the liturgy; they include toccatas, ricercars, and canzonas that are both structurally unified and highly expressive. In his vocal works—Masses, motets, arias, and the like—he used contemporary techniques but not the most advanced styles of his day.

Further Reading

Frescobaldi's music is discussed in Willi Apel, *Masters of the Keyboard* (1947), and Manfred F. Bukofzer, *Music in the Baroque Era: From Monteverdi to Bach* (1947).

Additional Sources

Hammond, Frederick, *Girolamo Frescobaldi,* Cambridge, Mass.: Harvard University Press, 1983. □

Augustin Jean Fresnel

The French physicist Augustin Jean Fresnel (1788-1827), through his analysis of interference, diffraction, and polarization, turned the wave theory of light into an integral part of exact physical science.

Augustin Jean Fresnel was born in Broglie on May 10, 1788. He received his elementary education on the family estate in Mathieu, Normandy, where his father, Jacques Fresnel, an architect, took refuge during the stormiest years of the Revolution. At the age of 16 Fresnel entered the École Polytechnique, where he excelled in mathematics but made little progress in physics. Following his graduation, Fresnel worked as an army engineer. In Nyons in early 1815, during the Hundred Days, he joined a group of royalists, and in the end he was decommissioned and sentenced to confinement. Because of ill health he was permitted to live in Normandy with his mother.

Fresnel began his research on light by attempting to understand the polarization of light, about which he read by chance in the newspaper. His knowledge of the subject was woefully inadequate, and not much better was his familiarity with physics in general. However, Fresnel persevered with his readings and carried out some experiments with simple apparatus. The first thing to be explained by the wave theory of light was the apparent failure of light waves to bend around a "corner" or edge, at complete variance with the behavior of water waves and sound waves. Fresnel showed that from the wave theory there followed a slight bending, and that it had to manifest itself in a succession of dark and luminous bands at the edge of the shadow. Most importantly, his mathematical formalism of the wave theory of light could predict the exact width of each of those bands.

Fresnel did not have a lens of short focal length, which he needed for the experimental verification of his theory. He found that an ingeniously suspended drop of honey would do the job!

Significance of Fresnel's Theory

Fresnel's *Memoirs,* which contained these important results together with his wave theory of light, were deposited at the Academy of Sciences in October 1815. According to the theory, the longitudinal waves, assumed by previous investigators such as Thomas Young, were replaced by transverse waves. Shortly afterward, Fresnel extended his idea of light as being the transversal vibration of an elastic medium (ether) to the problem of polarization. His ideas produced both admirers and opponents, but the theory had an unqualified effect on all future considerations of the geometrical and photometrical aspects of light and its relationship with space and matter. For this work Fresnel was elected in 1823 to the Academy of Sciences, and in 1825 he became a foreign member of the Royal Society of London, which in 1827 awarded him the Rumford Medal.

It was rare in the history of science that a most influential and solidly developed theory should emerge within a few years and in the hands of a newcomer to physics. Such a short span of time was also symbolic of the short life-span allotted to Fresnel. But those few years cast a long shadow on the subsequent history of physics. A starting point for modern relativistic physics was Fresnel's prediction of the change in the speed of light in moving media. The modern photon theory of light is also a development that left intact the validity of his basic insights into the mathematical formalism that alone can account for the most common features of the propagation of light.

Although Fresnel's health was rapidly deteriorating, he worked on the improvement of lighthouse lanterns. He replaced metal reflectors and thick lenses with lenses built from annular rings, the centers of curvature of which varied progressively and consequently eliminated spherical aberration. He also combined a fixed and a flashing light as a means of increasing the intensity of the light periodically. He died at Ville-d'Avray near Paris on July 14, 1827.

Further Reading

The most complete work on Fresnel is in French. A lengthy and informative eulogy of Fresnel is available in François Arago, *Biographies of Distinguished Scientific Men* (trans., 2 vols., 1859). The standard presentation of the full impact of Fresnel's ideas about light on 19th-century physics is in E. T. Whittaker, *A History of the Theories of Aether and Electricity*, vol. 1 (1910; rev. ed. 1951). □

Sigmund Freud

The work of Sigmund Freud (1856-1939), the Viennese founder of psychoanalysis, marked the beginning of a modern, dynamic psychology by providing the first systematic explanation of the inner mental forces determining human behavior.

Early in his career Sigmund Freud distinguished himself as a histologist, neuropathologist, and clinical neurologist, and in his later life he was acclaimed as a talented writer and essayist. However, his fame is based on his work in expanding man's knowledge of himself through clinical researches and corresponding development of theories to explain the new data. He laid the foundations for modern understanding of unconscious mental processes (processes excluded from awareness), neurosis (a type of mental disorder), the sexual life of infants, and the interpretation of dreams. Under his guidance, psychoanalysis became the dominant modern theory of human psychology and a major tool of research, as well as an important method of psychiatric treatment which currently has thousands of practitioners all over the world. The application of psychoanalytic thinking to the studies of history, anthropology, religion, art, sociology, and education has greatly changed these fields.

Sigmund Freud was born on May 6, 1856, in Freiberg, Moravia (now Czechoslovakia). Sigmund was the first child of his twice-widowed father's third marriage. His mother, Amalia Nathanson, was 19 years old when she married Jacob Freud, aged 39. Sigmund's two stepbrothers from his father's first marriage were approximately the same age as his mother, and his older stepbrother's son, Sigmund's nephew, was his earliest playmate. Thus the boy grew up in an unusual family structure, his mother halfway in age between himself and his father. Though seven younger children were born, Sigmund always remained his mother's favorite. When he was 4, the family moved to Vienna, the capital of the Austro-Hungarian monarchy and one of the great cultural, scientific, and medical centers of Europe. Freud lived in Vienna until a year before his death.

Youth in Vienna

Because the Freuds were Jewish, Sigmund's early experience was that of an outsider in an overwhelmingly Catholic community. However, Emperor Francis Joseph had emancipated the Jews of Austria, giving them equal rights and permitting them to settle anywhere in the monarchy. Many Jewish families came to Vienna, where the standard of living was higher and educational and professional opportunities better than in the provinces. The Jewish people have always had a strong interest in cultural and intellectual pursuits; this, along with Austria's remaining barriers to social acceptance and progress in academic careers, was influential in Freud's early vocational interests. Had it been easier for him to gain academic success, it might have been more difficult for the young scientist to develop and, later, to defend his unpopular theories.

Although as he grew older Freud never practiced Judaism as a religion, his Jewish cultural background and tradition were important influences on his thinking. He considered himself Jewish and maintained contact with Jewish organizations; one of his last works was a study of Moses and the Jewish people. However, at times Freud was unhappy that the psychoanalytic movement was so closely tied to Jewish intellectualism.

Freud went to the local elementary school and attended the humanistic high school (or gymnasium) from 1866 to 1873. He studied Greek and Latin, mathematics, history, and the natural sciences, and was a superior student. He passed his final examination with flying colors, qualifying to enter the University of Vienna at the age of 17. His family had recognized his special scholarly gifts from the beginning, and although they had only four bedrooms for eight people, Sigmund had his own room throughout his school days. He lived with his parents until he was 27, as was the custom at that time.

Prepsychoanalytic Work

Freud first considered studying law but then enrolled in medical school. Vienna had become the world capital of medicine, and the young student was initially attracted to the laboratory and the scientific side of medicine rather than clinical practice. He spent 7 instead of the usual 5 years acquiring his doctorate, taking time to work in the zoological and anatomical laboratories of the famous Ernst Brucke. At 19 he conducted his first independent research project while on a field trip, and at 20 he published his first scientific paper.

Freud received his doctor of medicine degree at the age of 24. An episode at about this time reveals that he was not simply the "good boy" his academic career might suggest: he spent his twenty-fourth birthday in prison, having gone AWOL from his military training. For the next few years he pursued his laboratory work, but several factors shifted his interest from microscopic studies to living patients. Opportunities for advancement in academic medicine were rare at best, and his Jewish background was a decided disadvantage. More important, he fell in love and wanted to marry, but the stipends available to a young scientist could not support a wife and family. He had met Martha Bernays, the daughter of a well-known Hamburg family, when he was 26; they were engaged 2 months later. They were separated during most of the 4 years which preceded their marriage, and Freud's over 900 letters to his fiancée provide a good deal of information about his life and personality. They were married in 1887. Of their six children, a daughter, Anna, became one of her father's most famous followers.

Freud spent 3 years as a resident physician in the famous Allgemeine Krankenhaus, a general hospital that was the medical center of Vienna. He rotated through a number of clinical services and spent 5 months in the psychiatry department headed by Theodor Meynert. Psychiatry at this time was static and descriptive. A patient's signs and symptoms were carefully observed and recorded in the hope that they would lead to a correct diagnosis of the organic disease of the brain, which was assumed to be the basis of all psychopathology (mental disorder). The psychological meaning of behavior was not itself considered important; behavior was only a set of symptoms to be studied in order to understand the structures of the brain. Freud's later work revolutionized this attitude; yet like all scientific revolutions, this one grew from a thorough understanding and acknowledged expertise in the traditional methods. He later published widely respected papers on neurology and brain

functioning, including works on cerebral palsy in children and aphasia (disturbances in understanding and using words).

Another of Freud's early medical interests brought him to the brink of international acclaim. During his residency he became interested in the effect of an alkaloid extract on the nervous system. He experimented on himself and others and found that small doses of the drug, cocaine, were effective against fatigue. He published a paper describing his findings and also participated in the discovery of cocaine's effect as a local anesthetic. However, he took a trip to visit his fiancée before he could publish the later findings, and during his absence a colleague reported the use of cocaine as an anesthetic for surgery on the eye. Freud's earlier findings were overshadowed, and later fell into disrepute when the addictive properties of cocaine became known.

During the last part of his residency Freud received a grant to pursue his neurological studies abroad. He spent 4 months at the Salpêtrière clinic in Paris, studying under the neurologist Jean Martin Charcot. Here Freud first became interested in hysteria and Charcot's demonstration of its psychological origins. Thus, in fact, Freud's development of a psychoanalytic approach to mental disorders was rooted in 19th-century neurology rather than in the psychiatry of the era.

Beginning of Psychoanalysis

Freud returned to Vienna, established himself in the private practice of neurology, and married. He soon devoted his efforts to the treatment of hysterical patients with the help of hypnosis, a technique he had studied under Charcot. Joseph Breuer, an older colleague who had become Freud's friend and mentor, told Freud about a hysterical patient whom he had treated successfully by hypnotizing her and then tracing her symptoms back to traumatic (emotionally stressful) events she had experienced at her father's deathbed. Breuer called his treatment "catharsis" and attributed its effectiveness to the release of "pent-up emotions." Freud's experiments with Breuer's technique were successful, demonstrating that hysterical symptoms could consistently be traced to highly emotional experiences which had been "repressed," that is, excluded from conscious memory. Together with Breuer he published *Studies on Hysteria* (1895), which included several theoretical chapters, a series of Freud's cases, and Breuer's initial case. At the age of 39 Freud first used the term "psychoanalysis," and his major lifework was well under way.

At about this time Freud began a unique undertaking, his own self-analysis, which he pursued primarily by analyzing his dreams. As he proceeded, his personality changed. He developed a greater inner security while his at times impulsive emotional responses decreased. A major scientific result was *The Interpretation of Dreams* (1901). In this book he demonstrated that the dreams of every man, just like the symptoms of a hysterical or an otherwise neurotic person, serve as a "royal road" to the understanding of unconscious mental processes, which have great importance in determining behavior. By the turn of the century

Freud had increased his knowledge of the formation of neurotic symptoms to include conditions and reactions other than hysteria. He had also developed his therapeutic technique, dropping the use of hypnosis and shifting to the more effective and more widely applicable method of "free association."

Development of Psychoanalysis

Following his work on dreams Freud wrote a series of papers in which he explored the influence of unconscious mental processes on virtually every aspect of human behavior: slips of the tongue and simple errors of memory (*The Psychopathology of Everyday Life,* 1901); humor (*Jokes and Their Relation to the Unconscious,* 1905); artistic creativity (*Leonardo da Vinci and a Memory of His Childhood,* 1910); and cultural institutions (*Totem and Taboo,* 1912). He recognized that predominant among the unconscious forces which lead to neuroses are the sexual desires of early childhood that have been excluded from conscious awareness, yet have preserved their dynamic force within the personality. He described his highly controversial views concerning infantile sexuality in *Three Essays on the Theory of Sexuality* (1905), a work which initially met violent protest but was gradually accepted by practically all schools of psychology. During this period he also published a number of case histories and a series of articles dealing with psychoanalysis as a therapy.

After 1902 Freud gathered a small group of interested people on Wednesday evenings for presentation of psychoanalytic papers and discussion. This was the beginning of the psychoanalytic movement. Swiss psychiatrists Eugen Bleuler and Carl Jung formed a study group in Zurich in 1907, and the first International Psychoanalytic Congress was held in Salzburg in 1908. In 1909 Freud was invited to give five lectures at Clark University in Worcester, Mass. He considered this invitation the first official recognition to be extended to his new science.

The new science was not without its difficulties. Earlier, Freud and Breuer had differed concerning their findings with regard to the role of sexual wishes in neurosis. Breuer left psychoanalysis, and the two men parted scientific company, not without some personal animosity. Ironically, Breuer saved his reputation at the time, only to be remembered by later generations because of his brief collaboration with Freud. During his self-analysis Freud developed a strong personal attachment to a philosophically inclined German otolaryngological physician, Wilhelm Fliess. From their letters one observes a gradual cooling of the friendship as Freud's self-analysis progressed.

At the same time Freud faced a major scientific reversal. He first thought that his neurotic patients had actually experienced sexual seductions in childhood, but he then realized that his patients were usually describing childhood fantasies (wishes) rather than actual events. He retracted his earlier statement on infantile sexuality, yet demonstrated his scientific genius when he rejected neither the data nor the theory but reformulated both. He now saw that the universal sexual fantasies of children were scientifically far more important than an occasional actual seduction by an adult.

Later, as psychoanalysis became better established, several of Freud's closest colleagues broke with him and established splinter groups of their own, some of which continue to this day. Of such workers in the field, Jung, Alfred Adler, Otto Rank, and Wilhelm Reich are the best known.

Later Years

In 1923 Freud developed a cancerous growth in his mouth that led to his death 16 years and 33 operations later. In spite of this, these were years of great scientific productivity. He published findings on the importance of aggressive as well as sexual drives (*Beyond the Pleasure Principle,* 1920); developed a new theoretical framework in order to organize his new data concerning the structure of the mind (*The Ego and the Id,* 1923); revised his theory of anxiety to show it as the signal of danger emanating from unconscious fantasies, rather than the result of repressed sexual feelings (*Inhibitions, Symptoms and Anxiety,* 1926); and discussed religion, civilized society, and further questions of theory and technique.

In March 1938 Austria was occupied by German troops, and that month Freud and his family were put under house arrest. Through the combined efforts of Marie Bonaparte, Princess of Greece, British psychoanalyst Ernest Jones, and W. C. Bullitt, the American ambassador to France (who obtained assistance from President Franklin D. Roosevelt), the Freuds were permitted to leave Austria in June. Freud's keen mind and ironic sense of humor were evident when, forced to flee his home at the age of 82, suffering from cancer, and in mortal danger, he was asked to sign a document attesting that he had been treated well by the Nazi authorities; he added in his own handwriting, "I can most warmly recommend the Gestapo to anyone." Freud spent his last year in London, undergoing surgery. He died on Sept. 23, 1939. The influence of his discoveries on the science and culture of the 20th century is incalculable.

Personal Life

Freud's personal life has been a subject of interest to admirers and critics. When it seemed necessary to advance his science, he exposed himself mercilessly, and, particularly in the early years, his own mental functioning was the major subject matter of psychoanalysis. Still, he was an intensely private man, and he made several attempts to thwart future biographers by destroying personal papers. However, his scientific work, his friends, and his extensive correspondence allow historians to paint a vivid picture.

Freud was an imposing man, although physically small. He read extensively, loved to travel, and was an avid collector of archeological curiosities. Though interested in painting, the musical charms of Vienna had little attraction for him. He collected mushrooms and was an expert on them. Devoted to his family, he always practiced in a consultation room attached to his home. He valued a small circle of close friends and enjoyed a weekly game of cards with them. He was intensely loyal to his friends and inspired loyalty in a circle of disciples that persists to this day.

Further Reading

The best English translation of Freud's works is *The Standard Edition of the Complete Psychological Works of Sigmund Freud* edited by James Strachey (24 vols., 1953-1964). Many of Freud's works have been published separately in other English-language editions. His brief *An Autobiographical Study* (1925), volume 20 of the standard edition, concentrates on his scientific work and almost ignores his personal life. More of his life is revealed, in a fragmented and incomplete way, in his *The Interpretation of Dreams,* volumes 4 and 5 of the standard edition. Freud's personality emerges most clearly from his letters, available in *Letters of Sigmund Freud,* selected and edited by Ernst L. Freud and translated by Tania and James Stern (1960). For an introduction to Freud's thought and style in his own words, the reader should begin with Freud's Clark University lectures, the *General Introduction to Psychoanalysis* (trans. 1920), or *Problems of Lay-analysis* (1927).

The definitive biography of Freud is Ernest Jones, *The Life and Work of Sigmund Freud* (3 vols., 1953-1957), also available in a one-volume edition edited and abridged by Lionel Trilling and Steven Marcus (1961). A balanced, somewhat negative discussion, which views Freud in relation to his predecessors and contemporaries, is Henri F. Ellenberger, *The Discovery of the Unconscious: The History and Evolution of Dynamic Psychiatry* (1970). □

Gilberto Freyre

Gilberto Freyre (1900-1987) was a Brazilian sociologist and writer who proposed a new interpretation of Brazil and its past based upon a modern anthropological understanding of race.

Gilberto de Mello Freyre was born into a distinguished Catholic family on March 15, 1900, in Recife, Brazil. The distinctive characteristics of this northeastern region were to shape all his life and work. His father, a college professor, was a great admirer of Anglo-Saxon traditions and, after teaching English to his son, enrolled him in a Baptist missionary school run by Americans. Freyre's intelligence and conversion to Protestantism led his teachers to arrange a scholarship for in 1918 him at Baylor University in Waco, Texas.

Upon graduation Freyre headed for Columbia University, where he lost his religion but acquired a new enthusiasm: cultural anthropology. Professor Franz Boas had an especially deep influence upon him, and as his disciple Freyre learned that race mixture, rather than being the cause of Brazil's lack of development (as taught by then-prominent social Darwinists) was probably its highest achievement, whereas social and cultural factors, especially slavery, could account for the country's retardation. Freyre also became enthralled at this time by the possibility of interpreting Brazil by looking at its past. His master's thesis on social life in Brazil in the mid nineteenth century was published in English immediately upon completion.

Regionalist Conference

After a year of traveling in Europe, Freyre returned to Brazil full of new ideas. One of them was the importance of regional differentiation within a country as large as Brazil. It was, he felt, by taking advantage of rich local traditions (from architecture to culinary arts) that Brazilians could maintain their identity in the face of an alienating modern world. With this in mind he organized a Regionalist Conference in Recife in 1925 and encouraged the development of local novelists, poets, and artists.

On a subsequent visit to the United States, Freyre traveled through the South, noted its similarities to his own northeast, and began to elaborate a broad thesis regarding the patriarchal origins of Brazil's social organization. In 1933 he published *Casa grande e senzala* (*The Masters and the Slaves*), in which he laid out this conceptual framework and richly illustrated it with primary documentation. He essentially described the relationship between Portuguese colonizers and their African slaves. He wrote in a personal style (almost stream of consciousness) that is sometimes repetitious and always disorganized but extremely effective in evoking a mood. In some ways Freyre tended to idealize the paternalistic relationship between masters and slaves, and this led to severe criticism. But the book won international acclaim for its author and gave all Brazilians a sense of national identity and of belonging together. It also made Freyre a household word among literate Brazilians.

Professor of Sociology

Freyre was named to a chair in sociology at the University of Brazil and in 1936 published *Sobrados e mucambos* (*The Mansions and the Shanties*), a sequel to the earlier book in 1933. A third work in the series, *Ordem e progresso,* followed in 1959. In addition, he wrote extensively on sociological and sociohistorical topics and even published a novel and a book of poetry. Freyre was the prime mover in the first Congress of Afro-Brazilian Studies in 1934.

He was in his sixties when he turned to fiction and published his first novel, *Doã Sinhá e o filho padre,* subsequently translated as *Mother and Son.* Freyre's regular columns in various Brazilian newspapers later took on a very conservative tone. Although it is easy to disagree with him today, his critics sometimes forget his success in dislodging racist theories from prominence in Brazil at the very time they were taking on their most sinister proportions in Europe.

Freyre continued to write and lecture into his eighties. He was well recognized by American and European scholars as a sociologist, politician, and writer. Moreover, he has been acknowledged as the most influential Brazilian intellectual of this century. Freyre died July 18, 1987, in Recife. He was 87.

Further Reading

Freyre and his place in Brazilian literature are analyzed in John A. Nist, *The Modernist Movement in Brazil: A Literary Study* (1967), and Afrânio Coutinho, *An Introduction to Literature in Brazil* (trans. 1969). Freyre and his historical work are discussed at length in John Mander, *The Unrevolutionary Society: The Power of Latin American Conservatism in a Changing World* (1969). See also Jean Franco, *The Modern Culture of Latin America: Society and the Artist* (1967).

Further information on Freyre can be found in Patricia Burgess, ed., *The Annual Obituary 1987* (1990). □

Gustav Freytag

The German novelist, dramatist, and critic Gustav Freytag (1816-1895) was perhaps Germany's most popular author from 1850 to 1870. He portrayed the struggles and triumphs of the rising middle class with engaging realism.

Born in Kreuzburg, Silesia, on July 13, 1816, Gustav Freytag read voraciously as a boy. At Breslau and Berlin he studied Germanic philology. He abandoned a teaching career after several years to devote his energies to writing and scholarship.

Turning first to drama, Freytag demonstrated outstanding talent for technique and theatrical effect and achieved popular success with *Die Valentine* (1846) and *Graf Waldemar* (1847), both of which were vehicles for his views on modern problems. In 1848 he moved to Leipzig, where for many years he was assistant editor of the *Grenzboten,* an influential liberal weekly devoted to literature and politics. His next play, *Die Journalisten* (1852; *The Journalists*), still delights audiences with its witty, animated dialogue and admirable characterizations, despite thematic material that is now irrelevant.

Freytag's reputation today rests on his narrative works. His first and finest novel, *Soll und Haben* (1855; *Debit and Credit*), contrasts the solid and energetic mercantile class with effete nobility and sees the mercantile class as destined to become the foundation for the "new state." His skillful portrait of class types, variety of characters, interest in detail, and humor reveal the influence of Charles Dickens. His second novel, *Die verlorene Handschrift* (1864; *The Lost Manuscript*), exhibits a similar concern for detail, this time in the realm of academic life, but is flawed by artificiality of plot and characterization.

Freytag's most lasting achievement probably is his cultural history, *Bilder aus der deutschen Vergangenheit* (5 vols., 1859-1862; *Pictures of German Life*), a matchless portrayal of Germany's entire past. This masterpiece combines careful historical study with an almost poetic style. Freytag based a cycle of eight historical romances on this material, entitled collectively *Die Ahnen* (1872-1880; *The Ancestors*), which depicts the varying fortunes of a single family through many centuries. He had hoped to achieve immortality with this "national epic," but his flagging creative powers become evident in the uneven and diminishing merit of the successive volumes. Also deserving mention are *Die Technik des Dramas* (1863; *The Technique of the*

Drama), *Lebenserinnerungen* (1886; *Reminiscences of My Life*), and a series of political essays (1887).

In 1879 Freytag moved to Wiesbaden, where he lived in comfortable retirement, showered with honors, until his death on April 30, 1895.

Further Reading

Biographical material in English on Freytag is still unavailable. For background see Benjamin W. Wells *Modern German Literature* (1895), and J. G. Robertson, *A History of German Literature* (1931; 6th ed. 1970). □

Henry Clay Frick

American industrialist and financier Henry Clay Frick (1849-1919) played leading roles in expanding the Carnegie Steel Company into the largest such enterprise in the world and in forming the United States Steel Company.

orn to a farming family in western Pennsylvania, Henry Clay Frick was the grandson of a wealthy miller and distiller. Although Frick received little formal education, he early showed an aptitude for business and at 19 became bookkeeper for his grandfather's businesses.

Frick was aware of the potential value of coking coal deposits for the burgeoning steel industry, and with financial backing from relatives and the Pittsburgh banker Thomas Mellon he began buying coal lands in the Connellsville region and constructing coke ovens. The enterprise brought handsome returns. Plowing all profits into acquiring more coal land and building more ovens, Frick and Company eventually controlled 80 percent of the output of this region.

Partnership with Carnegie

Meanwhile Andrew Carnegie, aware of Frick's abilities as financier and industrial manager and anxious to have a continuing supply of coke for his great steel company, took Frick in as a partner in 1882 and allowed him to purchase an 11 percent stock interest. At the same time, Carnegie purchased a controlling interest in the Frick Coke Company, though Frick continued as president.

Frick was one of the managing partners of the Carnegie Company until 1889, when Carnegie retired from active management and Frick was elected chairman. At this time the firm consisted of five or six mills and furnaces around Pittsburgh. There was no integration of production and no centralized management except the informal guidance supplied by the managing partners (a group of perhaps 6 out of about 25 owners of the business). In 1892, in accordance with a plan worked out by Frick, the productive units were reorganized as the Carnegie Steel Company, Ltd., capitalized at $25 million and, although not incorporated, probably the largest steel company in the world. Frick then

introduced centralized management procedures which greatly increased the firm's efficiency.

Homestead Strike

In 1892 occurred the Homestead strike, one of the most bitter labor conflicts of the decade; it cast a shadow over the rest of Frick's career, cooled his relationship with Carnegie, and almost cost Frick his life. In response to depressed business conditions and to compensate for expensive new machinery that greatly increased worker productivity, Frick proposed to lower the piecework wage rate. In response, the Amalgamated Iron and Steel Workers Union struck the Homestead plant. Frick recruited 300 strikebreakers through the Pinkerton Detective Agency, bringing them in armed barges down the Monongahela River. When the strikebreakers attempted to land, a day-long battle ensued. Ten men were killed and 60 wounded; order was restored only when the governor placed Homestead under martial law. Frick was widely denounced throughout the country for provoking the violence, but this criticism was soon followed by acclaim for his courage, when, with the help of a secretary, he subdued an assassin who shot him twice and stabbed him several times. Despite his wounds and loss of blood, Frick finished his day's work.

During the late 1890s the company prospered greatly. Between 1889 and 1899 annual production of steel rose from 332,111 to 2,663,412 tons, and profits advanced from about $2 million to $40 million in 1900. To secure a continuing supply of ore, Frick, in partnership with a Pittsburgh industrialist, acquired extensive ore properties in the newly opened Mesabi Range near Lake Superior, and Carnegie, at Frick's urging, leased other lands in an area belonging to John D. Rockefeller.

Formation of United States Steel

Although the company was extremely prosperous, its existence as a partnership was terminated in 1899 largely as a result of a quarrel between Frick and Carnegie. When Carnegie, acting on what he believed to be a binding agreement with Frick, set a price for coke from the Frick Coke Company that was considerably below the market price, Frick suspended deliveries, and the Carnegie Company faced a shutdown. Carnegie, as majority stockholder in both the coke and steel companies, forced Frick's resignation from both firms. By the terms of the "ironclad" partnership agreement of 1887 the Carnegie Company was obligated to purchase Frick's stock upon his resignation, but Carnegie refused to pay more than the valuation set by the "ironclad," although by 1899 the stock was worth three times that figure. Frick sued in equity to have the agreement set aside. Because of Frick's damaging revelations of the company's apparently exorbitant profits, Carnegie settled the suit by allowing the company to be incorporated at a figure which gave a value of $15 million to Frick's stock. Both men retired from management, and the two never spoke to each other again. In 1901, with the active participation of Frick, the Carnegie Corporation was merged into the United States Steel Company.

Until his death in 1919 Frick participated as a director in the affairs of many large corporations. He also formed a magnificent art collection, today housed in the Frick Museum in New York City. A large, handsome man with a powerful physique, Frick was hardworking, quiet, and reserved—the antithesis of the ebullient Andrew Carnegie. Frick left a fortune of about $50 million, five-sixths of it donated for public and philanthropic purposes.

Further Reading

The only complete biography of Frick is George Harvey, *Henry Clay Frick: The Man* (1928), which is laudatory, particularly in discussing his ability as a business manager. James Howard Bridge, a longtime friend of Frick and sometime secretary to Carnegie, favors Frick over Carnegie in *The Inside History of the Carnegie Steel Company* (1903); Bridge's *Millionaires and Grub Street* (1931) contains an intimate, laudatory description of Frick. A more critical treatment is Burton J. Hendrick, *The Life of Andrew Carnegie* (2 vols., 1932). More recent is Joseph Frazier Wall, *Andrew Carnegie* (1970), which also discusses Frick.

Additional Sources

Schreiner, Samuel Agnew, *Henry Clay Frick: the gospel of greed,* New York: St. Martin's Press, 1995.
Warren, Kenneth, *Triumphant capitalism: Henry Clay Frick and the industrial transformation of America,* Pittsburgh: University of Pittsburgh Press, 1995. □

Betty Friedan

Betty Friedan (born 1921) was a women's rights activist, author of *The Feminine Mystique,* and a founding member of the National Organization for Women, the National Abortion Rights Action League, and the National Women's Political Caucus.

Betty Friedan appeared suddenly in the national limelight with the publication of her first book, *The Feminine Mystique,* in 1963. It became a national best seller and propelled Friedan to a leadership position in the burgeoning movement for women's liberation. In that book Friedan identified a condition she claimed women suffered as the result of a widely accepted ideology that placed them first and foremost in the home. Attacking the notion that "biology is destiny," which ordained that women should devote their lives to being wives and mothers at the expense of other pursuits, Friedan called upon women to shed their domestic confines and discover other meaningful endeavors.

Friedan was herself well situated to know the effects of the "feminine mystique." She was born Betty Naomi Goldstein in 1921 in Peoria, Illinois, the daughter of Jewish parents. Her father was a jeweler, and her mother had to give up her job on a newspaper when she married. The loss of that potential career affected her mother deeply, and she urged young Betty to pursue the career in journalism that she was never able to achieve. The daughter went on to graduate *summa cum laude* from Smith College in 1942. She then received a research fellowship to study psychology as a graduate student at the University of California at Berkeley. Like her mother, she did some work as a journalist, but unlike her mother she did not end her career to build a family. She married Carl Friedan in 1947, and during the years that she was raising their three children she continued her freelance writing. After her husband established his own advertising agency they moved to the suburbs, where Friedan experienced what she later termed the "feminine mystique" first hand. Although she continued to write she felt stifled in her domestic role.

In 1957 Friedan put together an intensive questionnaire to send to her college classmates from Smith 15 years after graduation. She obtained detailed, open-ended replies from 200 women, revealing a great deal of dissatisfaction with their lives. Like Friedan herself, they tried to conform to the prevailing expectations of wives and mothers while harboring frustrated desires for something more out of life. Friedan wrote an article based on her findings, but the editors of the women's magazines with whom she had previously worked refused to publish the piece. Those refusals only spurred her on. She decided to investigate the problem on a much larger scale and publish a book. The result of her effort was *The Feminine Mystique*, which became an instant success, selling over three million copies.

Friedan began her book by describing what she called "the problem that has no name." In words that touched a sensitive nerve in thousands of middle-class American women, she wrote, "the problem lay buried, unspoken, for many years in the minds of American women. It was a strange stirring, a sense of dissatisfaction, a yearning that women suffered in the middle of the 20th century in the United States. Each suburban wife struggled with it alone. As she made the beds, shopped for groceries, matched slipcover material . . . she was afraid to ask even of herself the silent question—'Is this all?'"

With the publication of *The Feminine Mystique* Betty Friedan rose to national prominence. Three years later in 1966 she helped found the first major organization established since the 1920s devoted to women's rights, the National Organization for Women (NOW), and became its first president. Under Friedan's leadership NOW worked for political reforms to secure women's legal equality. The organization was successful in achieving a number of important gains for women. It worked for the enforcement of Title VII of the 1964 Civil Rights Act, which prohibited employment discrimination on the basis of sex. As a result of the organization's efforts, the Equal Opportunities Commission ruled that airlines could not fire female flight attendants because they married or reached the age of 35, nor could employment opportunities be advertised according to male or female categories.

NOW also lobbied for passage of the Equal Rights Amendment (ERA), which had remained dormant since it was first introduced in Congress by Alice Paul in 1923. In addition, the organization called for federally funded day care centers to be established "on the same basis as parks, libraries and public schools." NOW also worked to achieve the legalization of abortion and the preservation of abortion rights. Friedan was among the founders of the National Abortion Rights Action League in 1969. Finally in 1973 the Supreme Court legalized abortions. Deaths of women resulting from abortions dropped by 60 percent.

In 1970 Friedan was one of the most forceful opponents of President Nixon's nomination of G. Harrold Carswell to the Supreme Court. She argued before the Senate Judiciary Committee that in 1969 Carswell defied the Civil Rights Act by ruling in favor of the right of employers to deny jobs to women with children. That same year, at the annual meeting of NOW, she called for a Women's Strike for Equality, which was held on August 26—the 50th anniversary of the day women gained the right to vote. Women across the country commemorated the day with demonstrations, marches, and speeches in 40 major cities. Friedan led a parade of over 10,000 down Fifth Avenue in New York City.

The following year Friedan was among the feminist leaders who formed the National Women's Political Caucus. During the next several years she moved away from central leadership in the movement to concentrate on writing and teaching. She wrote a regular column for *McCall's* magazine and taught at several colleges and universities, including Temple University, Yale University, Queens College, and the New School for Social Research.

Friedan became an influential spokeswoman for the women's movement nationally as well as internationally. In 1974 she had an audience with Pope Paul VI in which she urged the Catholic Church to "come to terms with the full personhood of women."

As the women's movement grew and new leaders emerged with different concerns, Friedan's centrality in the movement dwindled. Nevertheless, she remained an outspoken feminist leader for many years. In 1977 she participated in the National Conference of Women in Houston, Texas, and called for an end to divisions and a new coalition of women. Her writing, teaching, and speaking continued throughout these years, as her ideas concerning the feminist movement evolved. In 1976 she published *It Changed My Life: Writings on the Women's Movement*, which was followed by her 1981 book, *The Second Stage*. In that publication Friedan called for a shift in the feminist movement, one that would address the needs of families and would allow both men and women to break from the sex-role stereotypes of the past.

In 1993, Friedan released *The Fountain of Age*, in which she began to explore the rights of the elderly and aging, just as she had once become attuned to women's issues. Friedan's focus is not on mere economics, but rather on helping the elderly find fulfillment in their latter years. In *The New York Times* she said, "Once you break through the mystique of age and that view of the aged as objects of care and as problems for society, you can look at the reality of the new years of human life open to us."

In 1996 new scholarship arose about Friedan's life when Daniel Horowitz published a controversial article in *American Quarterly*. Horowitz, who teaches at Friedan's alma mater, Smith University, draws a link between Friedan's feminism and her undergraduate years at Smith during the 1940s. Horowitz presents a new outlook on the work of Friedan, who has often said her feminism first emerged during the 1960s; in his article, Horowitz makes a strong case that it can be traced to the 1940s. But regardless of the time that Friedan's feminism first surfaced, she remains a significant influence on societal expectations and equality for women.

Further Reading

Betty Friedan's own writings are the best source of information on her life and work. She wrote extensively in popular magazines and was interviewed numerous times after 1963. She published four books: *The Feminine Mystique* (1963), *It Changed My Life: Writings on the Women's Movement* (1976), and *The Second Stage* (1981), and *The Fountain of Age* (1993). □

Milton Friedman

Milton Friedman (born 1912) was the founder and leading proponent of "monetarism," an economic doctrine which considers the supply of money (and changes therein) to be the primary determinant of nominal income and prices in the economy.

Milton Friedman, a native of Brooklyn, New York, was born July 31, 1912. After earning an undergraduate degree from Rutgers University in 1932 and a Master's degree from the University of Chicago the following year, Friedman became a research economist with the National Bureau of Economic Research in New York and later with the U.S. Treasury Tax Research Division. He earned a doctorate in economics from Columbia University in 1946 and after brief spells at Wisconsin and Minnesota universities returned to the University of Chicago to begin a long and distinguished career of teaching and research. After retiring in 1979 Friedman continued an active schedule of research and publishing at the Hoover Institute of Stanford University.

According to the monetarist view which Friedman developed and popularized, the private economy is basically stable unless disturbed by rapid money supply fluctuations or other government actions. Friedman advocated a "constant monetary rule" whereby the nation's money supply would grow by a fixed percentage each year, thereby avoiding overexpansion and inflation.

Blamed the "Fed" for Depression

Friedman's positions consistently put him at odds with the Federal Reserve System (often called the "Fed"), the central bank legislated by Congress in 1913 to create and control the nation's money supply. In his monumental *A Monetary History of the United States, 1867-1960* (with Anna J. Schwartz, 1963) Friedman provided a startling analysis of the Great Depression (1929-1933), arguing that the

Fed deserved considerable blame for allowing a dramatic fall in the money supply during this period. The traditional Keynesian view is that the Fed played an insignificant role and was powerless to stem the economic slide.

Although Friedman resisted offers to take government jobs himself, his ideas achieved considerable success in altering government policies. This was reflected, for example, in the historic setting of monetary growth targets by the Federal Reserve Board in 1979, a practice which Friedman had long advocated.

Friedman was also a staunch defender of the free enterprise system and a proponent of individual responsibility and action. In *Capitalism and Freedom* (1962) he outlined his concept of the proper role of government in a free society. These views were popularized through a regular *Newsweek* column starting in 1966 and through books such as *There Is No Such Thing As A Free Lunch*. His ideas were brought vividly home to the American public through an award-winning ten-part television series in 1980 entitled *Free to Choose* (co-authored with his wife, Rose Friedman).

Prolific Writer

As a scholar Friedman was prolific. Among his other well-known books are *Essays in Positive Economics* (1953), which included famous papers on the methodology of economics; *Studies in the Quantity Theory of Money* (1956), which revitalized the classic quantity theory of money as a foundation for monetarism; *A Theory of the Consumption Function* (1957), which provided a novel explanation for consumption decisions based on lifetime rather than current income; and *Monetary Trends in the United States and the United Kingdom* (co-authored with Anna J. Schwartz, 1982).

Friedman's articles in professional journals consistently challenged orthodox views and presented new ways of understanding economic data and events. In "The Role of Monetary Policy" in *American Economic Review* (1968) Friedman invented the now famous "long run natural rate of unemployment." This article provided strong arguments for refuting the simple Phillips Curve hypothesis that less unemployment could be achieved at the cost of higher inflation. The Phillips Curve analysis had been used by policy-makers to justify expansionary fiscal spending. Friedman's analysis, however, showed that attempts to lower the rate of unemployment below the "natural" level would cause only temporary reductions in unemployment and in the long run produce higher inflation along with higher unemployment.

In subsequent writings Friedman elaborated his views on these issues (*A Theoretical Framework for Monetary Analysis*, 1971, and "Nobel Lecture: Inflation and Unemployment," in *Journal of Political Economy*, 1977). Friedman's explanation for "stagflation," the existence of stagnant demand and high unemployment simultaneous with inflation, proved to be more convincing than orthodox Keynesian theories and provided tremendous impetus for defections from the Keynesian camp.

Nobel Prize Winner

Friedman's achievements were recognized early in his career. In 1951 he was awarded the John Bates Clark Medal of the American Economic Association, and in 1962 he was awarded the Paul Snowden Russell Distinguished Service Chair at the University of Chicago. In 1976 Friedman won his greatest honor, the Nobel Prize in Economics. Throughout his career Friedman earned numerous other awards and honorary doctorates from colleges and universities throughout the world.

In addition to his prolific writing, Friedman found time to be president of the American Economic Association (1967), vice-president of the Western Economic Association (1982-1983), and president of the Mont Pelerin Society (1970-1972). He was on the board of editors of the *American Economic Review* (1951-1953) and of *Econometrica* (1957-1969) and a member of the advisory board of the *Journal of Money, Credit, and Banking* (1968 into the mid-1980s).

In 1992 a reviewer breathlessly summarized the accomplishments of Friedman's book *Money Mischief: Episodes in Monetary History*, suggesting the economist has the rare ability to communicate his message to the non-academic. "Friedman compares inflation to alcoholism; blames the rise of Chinese communism, in large part, on an inadequately controlled money supply; defines and describes $MV = PT$ in four brief paragraphs; tells how three Scottish chemists ruined William Jennings Bryan's political career through their pioneering work with gold; and relates many other anecdotes befitting the book's subtitle, *Episodes in Monetary History*."

Held Strong Views

When Friedman would speak on, for instance, the woes of the U.S. education system, his free-market and anti-union views were readily apparent. "Why is it that our educational system is turning out youngsters who cannot read, write, or figure? The answer—simple but nonetheless correct—is that our current school system is a monopoly that is being run primarily by the teachers' unions: the National Education Association and the American Federation of Teachers. They are among the strongest trade unions in the country and among the most powerful lobbying groups.

"The people who run the unions aren't bad people; they're good people—just like all the rest of us. But their interests and the interests of a good school system are not the same."

Friedman was equally outspoken on the legalization of drugs. When an interviewer asked what good would come of it, the economist said, "I see America with half the number of prisons, half the number of prisoners, then thousand fewer homicides a year, inner cities in which there's a chance for these poor people to live without being afraid for their lives, citizens who might be respectable who are now addicts not being subject to becoming criminals in order to get their drug, being able to get drugs for which they're sure of the quality. You know, the same thing happened under prohibition of alcohol as is happening now (with drugs)."

Milton Friedman will be remembered as one of the most gifted economists of the 20th century. His iconoclasm often made him a controversial figure, yet unfolding events showed him to be ahead of his time, such as in resisting the spread of federal government power and in being a "watchdog" of the monetary authority. He excelled as an orator and debater. His popular writings in *Newsweek* and elsewhere provided succinct and novel solutions for economic ills which would allow the free market to work, such as the "negative income tax," an all-volunteer army, and floating exchange rates. While economists continue to debate the relevance of "monetarism" for policy decisions, there is little question that Friedman left the profession with and valuable new insights on economic behavior.

Further Reading

Additional information on Friedman can be found in L. Silk, *The Economists* (1976); Karl Brunner (editor), *Milton Friedman in Our Time* (1979); R. Sobel (author of four articles for this publication; see contributor list), *The Worldly Economists* (1980); Jr. Shackleton and G. Locksley (editors), *Twelve Contemporary Economists* (1981); and Mark Blaug, *Great Economists Since Keynes* (1985).

The opposing, in large part, Keynesian economics was developed by John Maynard Keynes in *The General Theory of Employment, Interest, and Money* (1936). See also Hirsch, Abraham, *Milton Friedman: Economics in Theory and Practice*, Harvester Wheatsheaf, 1990. □

Carl Joachim Friedrich

Carl Joachim Friedrich (1901-1984) was a German born educator whose writings on law and constitutionalism made him one of the leading American political theorists of the period after World War II.

Carl Joachim Friedrich was born on June 5, 1901, in Liepzig, Germany, the site of the first significant defeat of the Napoleanic armies. He attended several universities, receiving his doctorate from Heidelberg, and immediately began a distinguished career as a political theorist at Harvard University. He taught at Harvard until his retirement in 1971, although he also lectured at Heidelberg in the 1950s as well as at a variety of other schools, including Colby College, Duke University, and the University of Manchester in Great Britain, after his retirement.

In addition to his teaching and writing, Friedrich also served in a number of significant advisory positions. After World War II he advised Gen. Lucius Clay, then military governor of West Germany, on the issues of denazification, the visitation of American professors to newly reopened German universities, the writing of constitutions for the West German *landers* (or states), and the drafting of the 1949 Bonn Constitution for the Federal Republic of Germany. That constitution restored democracy to the people of West Germany. Later, in the 1950s, he also served as an adviser to the Commonwealth of Puerto Rico, assisting in

the reorganization of a semi-autonomous government there. He subsequently advised the European Constituent Assembly and in 1962 he served as president of the American Political Science Association.

Friedrich wrote upon a wide range of topics, once authoring a book on the Baroque Age. He spent most of his time and was best known, however, for his writings on political theory. In one sense, his work is difficult to classify, for although he vigorously opposed all forms of totalitarianism, he was also suspicious of the potential excesses of liberal democracy as it was practiced in the Western industrialized nations. He was best known for his famous statement on the rejection of a political society which would attempt to maximize personal freedom. He argued that "most people are very glad to leave a lot of things to other people," and he concluded, therefore, that democratic societies should not encourage everyone to try to have their own way politically.

In spite of these reservations, Friedrich nonetheless strongly endorsed the idea of democracy and argued particularly for the value of a constitutional democracy which placed strong institutions between an often unbridled citizenry and the policies which governments make. As a consequence, Friedrich believed greatly in the rule of law, arguing that it was only through a carefully designed system of legal protections that any democracy could choose its leaders, perform the public's business in a orderly manner, and prevent either the citizenry or the public office holders from excesses.

Friedrich's views on issues like democracy, law, constitutionalism, and justice were the result of his own extensive work on the history and the evolution of such ideas as well as his deep understandings of what had gone wrong in countries where democracy had failed. He had his biases, having little use for either the public's reliance upon a popular leader or for an over reliance upon mass institutions such as political parties as the key to democratic government. Certainly the rise of the National Socialists and Adolf Hitler in his native Germany had a great impact upon Friedrich's views.

Although Friedrich wrote extensively on such issues as power, community, liberty, and authority, he always returned to democracy, law, and constitutionalism as his main themes. He was hopeful that an increasing number of nation states would adopt constitutions which would guarantee democracy themselves, and he wrote extensively on the emerging need for what he called a "world community of law." His work on totalitarianism stressed the similarities of communism as practiced in the Soviet bloc with Hitler's fascism. He clearly identified communism as a threat to world peace and order.

Apart from more practical theories of politics, however, Friedrich also wrote extensively on the great modern age philosophers. Specifically, he wrote about theories of knowledge and how it was that people thought about things. He approved of the philosophy of Immanuel Kant, arguing that Kant's skepticism about people's knowledge was not only accurate but served as a worthwhile brake upon the arrogance of those who thought they understood too much. He did not approve of the philosophy of G. W. F. Hegel, feeling that Hegel's all-encompassing theories of knowledge permitted the righteous sense of ultimate insight that justified totalitarian political movements. He once wrote that Hegel was "the philosopher of war and the national authoritarian state."

He criticized Hegel as well for adopting a theory of knowledge which incorporated different perspectives as they originated from different observers. Again, he agreed with Kant on this issue, Kant maintaining that the difference in the perspective of different observers prevented universal understandings of the highest questions of philosophy. Friedrich also feared that acceptance of what he called the "relativist" position of Hegel on philosophical questions would inevitably lead to an ethical relativism which would undermine the acceptance of universal moral and legal principles. Though some writers disagree vigorously with Friedrich's interpretations of Hegel, it is clear that Friedrich's views upon knowledge and philosophy were closely related to his sincere desire to have legal and democratic values triumph over totalitarianism and injustice. Friedrich died in Lexington, Massachusetts, on September 19, 1984.

Further Reading

For additional information, particularly after World War II, see Edward N. Peterson, *The American Occupation of Germany—Retreat to Victory* (1977), which details Friedrich's role in interceding between his native German people and the sometimes poorly informed American occupation forces after World War II; John Gimbel, *The American Occupation of Germany* (1968) which includes references to Friedrich's role in reducing some of the excesses of denazification, which he felt had unfairly included too many Germans; and Jean Edward Smith, *The Papers of Lucius D. Clay* (1974) which describes Friedrich's relationship to Military Governor Lucius D. Clay and the confidence which General Clay had in Friedrich. □

Caspar David Friedrich

Caspar David Friedrich (1774-1840), one of the major artists of German romanticism, revived landscape painting in Germany, depicting through nature his own melancholy moods, pantheistic beliefs, and nationalistic feelings.

Born on Sept. 5, 1774, in Greifswald, Caspar David Friedrich was the son of a soap manufacturer. His mother died when he was 7; and when he was 13, his favorite brother died while the two boys were ice-skating, for which Caspar David suffered a lifelong sense of guilt. The painter's familiarity with death and his melancholy disposition were further affirmed by a suicide attempt.

Friedrich began studying drawing in 1788; in 1794 he entered the art academy in Copenhagen, one of the most liberal in Europe, notably in its unusual emphasis on drawing from nature rather than from older art. His teachers were masters of Danish neoclassicism, but they also transmitted the concepts of early English romanticism, notably Henry Fuseli's theories, before Friedrich left for Dresden in 1798.

Friedrich's early landscapes and engravings are much like his teachers' works, but constant sketching after nature released him from neoclassic formulations, and a careful realistic rendering asserted itself in vast, spacious landscapes at times populated by small isolated figures or heroic ruins. By 1806 he had developed an independent formal and iconological vocabulary.

Friedrich's reputation grew rapidly; he found patrons among Saxony's nobility and received the Prize of the Weimar Friends of Art. He became acquainted with the major writers of German romanticism and with the painters Phillip Otto Runge, Johan Christian Dahl, and Carl Gustav Carus. In 1808 the classicist critic F. W. B. von Ramdohr attacked Friedrich's painting *Cross in the Mountains* (also known as the *Tetschen Altarpiece*), demanding whether "it is a good idea to use landscape allegorically to represent a religious concept or even to arouse a sense of reverence." After criticizing the painting, depicting a crucifix on a mountain illuminated by the setting sun, Ramdohr concluded that a depiction of nature cannot properly be symbolical or allegorical, that "it is the greatest arrogance when landscape painting seeks to worm its way into the churches and crawl onto the altars." Several of Friedrich's friends answered these criticisms in detail, thereby causing a major argument that served ultimately to increase the artist's fame.

Friedrich himself interpreted the painting as representing man's continuous faith and hope in the person of Jesus Christ despite the decline of formalized religion. Whether populated by Christian symbols or not, Friedrich's landscapes all possess a spiritual quality, and such religious meanings reflect his own mystical convictions. Contact with the romantic writers had convinced him that "art must have its source in man's inner being; yet, it must be dependent on a moral or religious value." Among his aphorisms on art, he wrote: "The noble man (artist) recognizes God in everything. . . . Shut your corporeal eye so that you first see your picture with your spiritual eye. Then bring to light that which you saw in darkness so that it may reflect on others from the exterior to their spiritual interior." Like the romantic writers, he saw art as the mediator between man and the mystical sources of nature. His own time Friedrich viewed as being on the periphery of all religions, founded on the ruins of the temples of the past and building for a future of clarity and nondogmatic religious truth.

Contemporary political events formed the other major content of Friedrich's work. The Napoleonic Wars aroused in him a fierce hatred of France and an intense love of Germany. He expressed his patriotic support of the German liberation movements in mountain scenes depicting lost French soldiers or monuments to German freedom fighters. And his disappointment in the antidemocratic Prussian restoration after the wars was symbolized in a painting of an ice-encrusted ship named *Hope* (1822).

In 1816 Friedrich became a member of the Dresden Academy, which gave him a steady income and allowed him to marry in 1818. In 1820 the Russian czarevitch purchased several paintings from him, but Friedrich's popularity began to decline because of his political attitudes and increasing official attacks on his art. His mental and physical health steadily deteriorated. In 1837 a serious stroke terminated his career. He died on May 7, 1840, forgotten by all but a small circle of friends. His subjective, emotional art was rediscovered early in the 20th century, when German expressionism sought similar effects through more radical means.

Further Reading

A surprisingly balanced pamphlet on Friedrich was published by the German Library of Information, *Caspar David Friedrich: His Life and Work* (1940). More recent is Leopold D. Ettlinger, *Caspar David Friedrich* (1967). See also Marcel Brion, *Art of the Romantic Era* (trans. 1966).

Additional Sources

Bèorsch-Supan, Helmut, *Caspar David Friedrich,* London: Thames & Hudson, 1974.

The romantic vision of Caspar David Friedrich: paintings and drawings from the U.S.S.R., New York: Metropolitan Museum of Art; Chicago: Art Institute of Chicago; New York: Distributed by Abrams, 1990.

Jensen, Jens Christian, *Caspar David Friedrich: life and work,* Woodbury, N.Y.: Barron's, 1981. □

Bernard Patrick Friel

An Irish author, teacher, and playwright from Northern Ireland, Bernard Patrick Friel (born 1929) was noted for the powerfully realistic renditions of Irish life and culture found in his plays.

Bernard (Brian) Patrick Friel was born in Omagh, County Tyrone, to Patrick and Christina (Macloone) Friel. He moved to the city of Londonderry when he was ten, attended St. Columb's College there (1941-1946), and subsequently received his B.A. degree from St. Patrick's (theological) College in Maynooth. Instead of opting for a career in the Catholic priesthood, Friel entered the teaching profession. He graduated St. Joseph's Teacher Training School in Belfast in 1950.

His teaching career of ten years ended when he turned to full-time writing in 1960. That year the *New Yorker* had found a valuable resource in Friel. He could satisfy the appetite for "Irishness" that that publication's readers craved.

Friel, aside from his short stories, wrote two radio plays (*A Sort of Freedom* and *To This Hard House,* both in 1958) and three stage plays (*A Doubtful Paradise, The Enemy Within,* and *The Blind Mice,* each produced in 1959). These works gave Friel his start in the great tradition of Irish theater. He assigned no special theatrical import to those early efforts, but it was the successful depiction of an early churchman attracted to secular life in *Enemy Within* that encouraged Friel.

Characters Have Their Demons

Underneath such plays as *Philadelphia, Here I Come!, Faith Healer, Translations,* and later *Dancing at Lughnasa* lies an angry frustration. These frustrations result because of goals unrealized, things said, and more often than not things unsaid. The emotion that bubbled within him had no viable outlet other than the vivid Irish imagination and the Irish appetite for the marvelous. Brian Friel's characters constantly vie with alienation and emotive depravation.

W. B. Yeats' plays are compared to Friel's because they also stir the bottled-up emotion that seems to characterize the Irish people. Yeats' famous play *Catheleen Ni Houlihan* contributed to the flaming passions of the Easter uprising of 1916. In like manner, Friel's *Philadelphia, Here I Come!* (1965) ignited the same pent up passions within the play's lead character, Gareth (Gar) O'Donnel.

At age 27 O'Donnel is going to emigrate to America, Philadelphia to be exact. He muses over his past life in the (mythical) town of Ballybeg. With the aid of his alter ego, Private Gareth, Gar examines the failed life he has led thus far working in the general store of his father, S.B. (Screwballs) O'Donnel. He recalls the failed marriage proposal to his girl, Kate Doogan, and the failed provincial setting of County Donegal, which offers no hopeful prospects other than becoming a drunken hedge schoolmaster. Gar leaves for the States with a bleak sense of loss.

Faith Healer (1979) is made up of four monologues, the first and the last by Frank Hardy (the faith healer), and the second by his wife, Grace, an Englishwoman who quit the middle class to follow Frank. Teddy, a cockney showman who now serves as Frank's agent, narrates the third monologue. Disappointment, hope, and hopelessness, along with unvented emotion and unstated feelings, brim underneath the monologues of *Faith Healer.*

The four travel about England, Scotland, and Wales offering the chronically ill a miracle cure at the hands of Frank, but Frank has no control over his gift. When the gift works it can cure a whole congregation, but Frank can't predict when it will work. All he can do is hope. Upon his return to Ireland, Frank's gift fails him and he is brutally beaten to death in a bar for being unable to heal a person confined to a wheelchair.

Tales of Dreams Unrealized

Translations (1980) touches base on a theme that evokes much emotion in the context of Irish life, the death of the Irish language. Set in the 1830s, the play takes place during the period when the British Army Engineer Corps, in order to fully assimilate Ireland into the United Kingdom, commenced with its famous mapping and renaming of Ireland. *Translations* captures the loss to Irish culture that came with the upheaval in language.

Dancing at Lughnasa (1992), Friel's later success, portrays five Donegal sisters during the 1930s, spinsters that share their hopes and unfulfilled dreams of marriage and dancing. Friel's yearning for a return to pre-Christian values in Ireland is evident throughout. Four of the girls want to attend the pagan dance festival named after the fertility deity "Lugh" (pronounced "loogh"). We discover that the girls' brother (an ex-Catholic priest) was converted to African paganism while on missionary duty there, supposedly to convert the natives to Christianity. The denouement comes as the sisters are listening to their Marconi radio set and simultaneously break out in a flurry of wild, pagan style dancing. These are people trying to gain touch with their past selves.

In contrast to the acclaim *Lughnasa* garnered, *Wonderful Tennessee* (1993) was a bleak work, even though it showcased the same theme of intertwining pagan and Christian traditions. The virtues and dangers of connecting with one's animal self, loneliness within family, and the paralyzing loss of certainty in the modern world act as elements that demand a return to simpler ways of life. The play did not draw a mass public because its statement (which was private and encoded) did not connect with an audience that wanted entertainment, not introspection. *Tennessee* is all mood, nuance, and sudden turns of rapture and despair as four people take turns storytelling on a Donnegal dock. Some critics maintained the play was not as dynamic as *Dancing a Lughnasa*.

Friel's play *Molly Sweeney* had its American premier in January 1996 in New York City after it received positive reviews from British and Irish critics in Dublin in 1994. The play, said to be reminiscent in structure to Friel's earlier *Faith Healer,* is about a woman whose husband takes her to a failed surgeon in hopes of curing her blindness. At the crux of the drama is the idea that she may not want to be cured. Joe Dowling, who directed *Philadelphia, Here I Come* in New York City, described Friel as brilliant but essentially an emotional writer. "His writing comes out of a deep passion and instinct for human beings and how people interact with each other." Overall, Friel's writing is of the same high quality as Yeats, Synge, and O'Casey. An appraisal of his major works assures that the future of Irish literature holds a place of honor for Friel.

Further Reading

More information on Brian Friel may be found in the various biographical/critical sources. The *Dictionary of Literary Biography* (Vol. 13), *Contemporary Authors* ("New Revision Series," Vol. 33), and *Contemporary Literary Criticism* (Vol. 5) can furnish the reader with basic background on Friel. Two book-length biographies of the author are available: *Brian Friel: The Growth of an Irish Dramatist* by Ulf Dantanus (1987) and *Brian Friel* by D. E. S. Maxwell (1973). Background on Irish drama/theater in general can be found in the following sources: *The Modern Irish Drama: A Documentary History* by Robert Hogan et al., eds., which comes in six volumes and gives an overview of Irish dramatic history from 1899 to 1920; and D. E. S. Maxwell's *A Critical History of Modern Irish Drama, 1891 to 1980,* called "The fullest critical history of the Irish Drama," which is sure to give the reader further insight into the themes with which Irish drama deals.

Additional Sources

Pine, Richard, *Brian Friel and Ireland's Drama,* Routledge, 1990.

Andrews, Elmer, *The Art of Brian Friel: Neither Reality Nor Dreams,* St. Martins Press, 1995.
Kerwin, William, *Brian Friel: A Casebook,* Garland, 1997.
O'Brien, George, *Brian Friel: A Reference Guide, 1962-1992,* Prentice Hall International, 1995.
Peacock, Alan J., *The Achievement of Brian Friel,* C. Smythe, 1993. □

Jakob Friedrich Fries

The German philosopher Jakob Friedrich Fries (1773-1843), interested in the phenomenon of the mind, advanced psychological philosophy in the direction of psychological empiricism.

J akob Friedrich Fries, born in Barby, Saxony, on Aug. 23, 1773, studied at Leipzig and Jena. He became dozent at Jena in 1801, professor of philosophy and elementary mathematics at Heidelberg in 1805, and professor of philosophy in 1814. In 1816 Fries accepted the chair of theoretical philosophy at Jena.

Fries was one of the links in a chain which gradually transformed psychology from metaphysics to empiricism, from philosophy to science. A disciple of Immanuel Kant, he did not agree with Kant on all points but sought rather to reshape and elaborate the principles of critical philosophy. He was thus considered by some an opponent of Kant. Perhaps "semi-Kantian" describes him best, for the system which Fries developed was really midway between that of Kant and that of the "commonsense" school.

In his chief work, *Neue oder psychologische Kritik der Vernunft* (1807; New Critique of Reason), Fries tried to combine the teaching of Kant with elements from Friedrich Heinrich Jacobi's philosophy of faith, basing critical philosophy on psychology and substituting self-observation for the transcendental method. Fries maintained that only that which is sense-perceived can be known and that the principles of reason are immediately known in consciousness. Kant had sought to prove the principles of reason a priori. Fries, however, contended that human beings cannot know the supersensible, or things-in-themselves. They are objects of faith which satisfy the demands of the heart.

Like Kant, Fries discussed psychological facts under the heading of anthropology, considering them in the light of the customs of primitive peoples, and empirically thinking of the mental processes themselves as being the data that psychology had best study. The modern reader can possibly make more relevant sense of Fries by substituting "phenomenological" for Fries's "anthropological."

In 1821 Fries published the *Handbook of Psychical Anthropology,* in which he divided anthropology into mental and physical aspects. Under mental anthropology he studied the actual processes by which one perceives, remembers, and thinks. The mental processes, although depending upon a pure ego or self, are never known except through their effects. Similarly, the ego or self cannot be appreciated for itself but is known only through its effects.

Under physical anthropology Fries discussed the relationship between brain and mind. He distinguished three main faculties: knowledge, inner disposition (*Gemüth*) or feeling, and activity or will. He regarded each of these faculties as incorporated in or subordinated to the unitary self.

Further Reading

Virtually all of the important sources on Fries are in German. One of the few works in translation is Rudolf Otto, *The Philosophy of Religion Based on Kant and Fries* (1921; trans. 1931). For background material see George Sidney Brett, *Brett's History of Psychology*, edited and abridged by R. S. Peters (1953). □

Karl von Frisch

The Austrian zoologist Karl von Frisch (1886-1982) is noted for his studies of insect behavior and sensory physiology. His most famous discovery was that honeybees communicate by waggle dancing.

Karl von Frisch was born on November 20, 1886, in Vienna, the son of a university professor. He displayed an early interest in animals, which his family encouraged. His uncle, Sigmund Exner, the leading authority on insect vision at the time, channeled Frisch's earliest professional endeavors into a study of vision in honeybees.

Frisch studied under Richard von Hertwig at the University of Munich and received his doctorate in zoology in 1910. Early in his career he began to make important contributions to the analysis of animal behavior. It is said that every successful scientist has a small number of personal tools with which he levers discoveries out of nature, and Frisch had two in which he attained great mastery. The first was the repeated exploitation of the passage of honeybees from nest to flowers and back again, a complex sequence of behavioral events that is nonetheless easy to manipulate and monitor. The second was the method of training, developed by Ivan Pavlov, by which Frisch associated the stimuli to be studied with a subsequent reward of food. Animals trained in this fashion respond sharply to odd stimuli that they otherwise ignore, thus revealing ultimately their sensory capacities.

Using the training method, Frisch confounded C. von Hess in their famous debate on color vision in insects. He demonstrated the ability of fish to hear and of insects to perceive polarized light. Over the years Frisch sketched out in great detail the sensory physiology of the worker honeybee. In 1945 he made the astounding discovery that honeybee workers communicate symbolically about the location of food sources such as fields of flowers. They accomplish this deep within the hive by means of the "waggle dance," in which the entire body is vibrated as the bee runs through figure-eight patterns on the vertical surface of the comb. The middle part of the figure, the "straight run," provides the information; its angle with reference to the vertical indicates the angle the follower bees must take with

reference to the sun when they leave the hive; and its duration indicates the length of the trip. This mode of communication is the most complex ever discovered in invertebrate animals.

Frisch was director of the zoological institute in Munich from 1925 until World War II and again from 1950 to 1958. He received numerous honors, including the Balzan Foundation Award in 1963 and foreign memberships in the United States National Academy of Sciences and the Royal Society of London. He, along with Konrad Lorenz and Nikolaas Tinbergern, shared the 1973 Nobel Prize for physiology or medicine. In an article in *Science* regarding the Nobel Prize, Frisch was praised for teaching the world that human nature is "subject to the principles that mold the biology, adaptability and the survival of other organisms."

About his own work, Frisch philosophically wrote in *A Biologist Remembers,* "The layman may wonder why a biologist is content to devote 50 years of his life to the study of bees and minnows without ever branching out into research on, say, elephants, or at any rate the lice of elephants or the fleas of moles. The answer to any such question must be that every single species of the animal kingdom challenges us with all, or nearly all, the mysteries of life." Frisch died June 12, 1982, in Munich, Germany.

Further Reading

The best book on Frisch's life is his autobiography, *A Biologist Remembers* (1962; trans. 1964). He also reviewed his researches on honeybees in two beautifully written works available in English translation: the definitive treatise, *The Dance*

Language and Orientation of Bees (1967), and a shorter introductory work, *Bees: Their Vision, Chemical Senses and Language* (1950). □

Max Frisch

The Swiss novelist and dramatist Max Frisch (1911-1991) explored the nature of human identity, individuality, and responsibility. His work is characterized by an ironic depiction of the issues confronting man in a technological society.

Max Frisch was born May 15, 1911, in Zurich and raised in a conventional middle-class milieu. His father's sudden death in 1933 forced him to abandon his studies in Germanic philology and literature at the University of Zurich and become a journalist to support himself and his mother. He wrote primarily about sporting events for newspapers, but his work allowed him to travel widely. An assignment on the Dalmatian coast inspired his first novel, *Jürg Reinhardt: Eine sommerliche Schicksalsfahrt* (*Jürg Reinhardt: A Summer's Journey*) (1934), which later was shortened considerably to serve as the initial portion of the author's extended prose fiction *J'adore ce qui me brûle—oder die Schwierigen* (1943). These two narratives reveal Frisch's early concern with the theme of man's quest for his true identity.

In 1937, despondent because of a lack of critical notice, Frisch vowed never to write again and resumed his education with funding by a family friend. He earned a university diploma in architecture, a field he pursued successfully after his army service to 1954. One of his commissions was from the city of Zurich to create the Zurich Recreational Park. When he was drafted into the army in 1939, however, he started to keep a diary, which was published in 1940 as *Blätter aus dem Brotsack* (*Pages from a Knapsack*).

Wrote First Play

Four years later, encouraged by a drama critic, Frisch wrote his first play, the symbolic *Bin, or the Voyage to Peking,* followed by the baroque *Santa Cruz* (1944). The war years left their mark on the playwright, and his initial stage production, *Now They Sing Again* (1945), poignantly evokes the pathos and agony of the conflict. His grim farce, *The Wall of China* (1946), deals surrealistically with a man's impotence when confronted by the forces of history. *When the War Was Over* (1949), more conventional in structure, deals with Frisch's recurring theme of responsibility and guilt. The inability of intellectuals to expose evil and take a stand against it appears to Frisch to be a major factor in the rise and supremacy of Nazism.

In these productions various scenes at different locations may take place simultaneously with minimal stage sets. Influenced by Bertolt Brecht, the playwright believed that the stage should not allow the audience to escape into an illusion of reality. Characters alternately enact their roles and step out of them, thus confronting the audience directly with the issues. The actors portray allegorical figures, frequently wearing masks to conceal their real identities and thus achieving loss of individuality. To emphasize this absence of romantic personal expression, Frisch had four actors play 12 parts in *Count Oderland* (1951), a dramatic attempt to mirror the chaotic nature of the modern age. The mask projects a superficial image to the viewer. The image, whether created or accepted by the individual, is difficult to dispel; and the struggle to escape from this dilemma is the source of modern tragicomedy.

Frisch's ironic comedy, *Don Juan, or the Love of Geometry* (1953), deals with a man trapped by his public image who must free himself by escaping into marriage. In a more serious vein, Andri, the protagonist of *Andorra* (1962), is persecuted as an alleged Jew. Four years previously Frisch had plunged into black comedy and the theater of the absurd with *Biedermann and the Incendiaries,* a sardonic commentary depicting a world of meaningless habit and of never-ending production and consumption, with absurdity attached to any traditional value.

Return to Fiction

During the 1950s Frisch resumed his fiction writing, pursuing the same themes of his plays. *I'm Not Stiller* (1954), the author's best-known novel, portrays a sculptor who attempts to escape from his self-imposed prison and fulfill himself, only to capitulate in the end because his public will not accept the change. Similarly, Faber in *Homo*

Faber (1957) never really lives; rather he hides behind a mask. And the only way that Frisch's protagonist, Gontenbein, in *A Wilderness of Mirrors* (1962) can truly get to know and understand people is by pretending to be blind; only then do they feel sufficiently secure to remove their masks. This role playing, according to Frisch, is both misleading and fatal to love because it renders impossible the necessary adjustments and compromises involved in a constantly evolving relationship.

In 1975 he published *Montauk,* a novel that many critics felt was deserving of the Nobel Prize. In this work he draws from his relationship with Ingeborg Bachman, another writer. The book was described by Rüdiger Görner, a newspaper biographer, as "the most rigorous and tender, scrutinising and melancholic book Frisch wrote." When a journalist once asked him if he would like to correct any misinformation that had been published about him, he replied, "Fame is based on misstatements, so you should not correct them." He received many honors and awards for his plays and fiction from foundations and universities around the world. Among the later ones were: the German Book Trade Freedom Prize, 1976; commander, Ordre des Artes et des Lettres, 1985; Commonwealth Award, Modern Language Association, 1985; and the Neustadt International Prize for Literature, 1986. In 1986 Frisch stopped writing because of failing health. He died in Zurich at the age of 80 on April 4, 1991.

Further Reading

No critical biography of Frisch exists in English. Martin Esslin in *The Theater of the Absurd* (1961; rev. ed. 1969) considers several of Frisch's plays.

Further information on Frisch can be found in Deborah Andrews, ed., *The Annual Obituary 1991* (1992), Mark Hawkins-Dady, ed., *International Dictionary of Theatre: Playwrights* (1994), and Leonard S. Klein, ed., *World Literature: 20th Century* (1967; rev. ed. 1982). □

Otto Robert Frisch

The Austrian-British physicist Otto Robert Frisch (1904-1979) was recognized for his significant role in the discovery of nuclear fission.

Otto Robert Frisch was born on October 1, 1904, in Vienna, Austria, the son of Justinian and Auguste (Meitner) Frisch. Though his father had a doctorate in law, his mother was an accomplished musician, and the family had intellectual connections, his father was forced by financial circumstances to pursue a career as a printer. Young Frisch thus grew up in a hardworking bourgeois Jewish family of extensive education and high expectations. Educated in a Viennese *gymnasium,* he learned Latin, Greek, and some arithmetic, but most of his mathematical training was private and personal.

At the age of ten his father introduced him to Cartesian coordinates, and within a couple of days he had worked out for himself the equation of the circle. At the age of 12 his father again tutored him, this time in trigonometry. Upon learning the definition of sine and cosine, he was shown the equation $\sin^2 x + \cos^2 x = 1$, to which he replied, "Of course—it's obvious," thereby surprising his father and impressing those who heard the anecdote. Later, he was coached in calculus by Olga Neurath, a blind mathematician acquainted with many members of the Vienna circle of mathematicians and philosophers, with whom Frisch also came into contact. One of the most important events of his *gymnasium* days came when he had the opportunity to hear Albert Einstein speak on his theory of special relativity, scarcely hoping that one day he would meet him on a professional level.

In 1922 he entered the University of Vienna, graduating in 1926 with a Ph.D. in physics. For a few months he worked as a consultant for Siegmund Strauss, an Austrian inventor tinkering with x-ray dosimeters. From Strauss he must have learned a great deal about the construction of technical measuring apparatus, for this was to be a great strength of Frisch's throughout his long career. A few months later, in 1927, he was offered a research job in Berlin at the German National Physical Laboratory (*Physikalische Technische Reichsanstalt*), where he worked in the optics division under Carl Müller. Here he was also the colleague of his eminent aunt Lise Meitner, herself a physicist. She and Otto Hahn had collaborated for 20 years on work eventually to lead to the discovery of uranium fission. Frisch enjoyed his three years in Berlin, conducting research, making friends and contacts, even meeting his aunt's personal friend Einstein.

This period ended in 1930 when the German physics professor Otto Stern offered him a position as assistant, which Frisch later humorously described as a "high-class technician." There he conducted experiments upon molecular beams (that is, moving ionized gas molecules), deflecting them with magnets and measuring their deflection. Such controlled experiments necessitated the use of very delicate, very precise technical equipment which Frisch himself designed.

Germany in 1933 began to be dangerous for Jews. Hitler had come to power and racial laws were passed forbidding Jews to engage in certain activities, so Frisch began to look elsewhere for opportunities. He met Niels Bohr that summer at a conference in Copenhagen and became friendly with him. Then in October he visited England on a research grant, working at Birkbeck College in London under Patrick M. S. Blackett. With his grant nearing expiration in 1934, Bohr invited him back to Copenhagen with the compliment: "You must come to Copenhagen to work with us. We like people who can acutally perform thought experiments" Frisch went and remained for five years. There he continued work he had already begun on radioactivity, looking for new radioactive elements produced by alpha-ray bombardment—work requiring the use of more delicate measuring instruments which, again, he constructed. He also became more intimately acquainted with Bohr, whom he came to admire as the most profound thinker of all the modern physicists.

With Hitler's military successes in Austria in 1938 and Czechoslovakia in 1939, Frisch began to worry that he might be forced to return to Austria, now under German control, where he feared being placed in a concentration camp, so once more he put out feelers to England for possible work. Ironically, this most precarious time of his life also saw him play one of his most crucial scientific roles. Over the Christmas vacation of 1939 Frisch visited his aunt, now in Sweden. She and Otto Hahn were still collaborating—now by letter—in work on radioactivity. Having just received a letter from Hahn, she read it to Frisch while they were on an outing in the snow—she on foot, he on skis. Hahn had written to convey the startling information that uranium bombarded by neutrons produced the lighter element barium. Upon finishing the letter they sat down on a tree trunk, Frisch still in his skis, to calculate upon scraps of paper the possibility that uranium could split into barium. Between them, they were able to work out the probability.

Frisch returned to Copenhagen to inform Bohr and sent a short note of the discovery of nuclear fission (his coinage) to the British scientific journal *Nature*. In the excitement the concept of a chain reaction was totally missed by Frisch, though a Danish colleague, Christian Muller, quickly pointed it out. Frisch initially thought the idea absurd, suggesting that otherwise no uranium ore deposits could exist without exploding—until he recalled that the impurities within those ores acted as controls by blocking the reaction.

Also at this time (late in 1939) Frisch received a letter from Mark Oliphant, head of the Department of Physics at the University of Birmingham, offering him a nominal job as assistant, the real purpose being to get him further from Germany. His work consisted of meeting with Oliphant's beginning students to clarify whatever Oliphant may have confused them on. With little else to do he interested himself in problems related to uranium fission, especially that of separating U_{235} from the more common U_{238} (two forms of uranium differing in number of neutrons, and therefore in stability). Collaborating with Rudolph Peierls, he confirmed Bohr's suggestion that a chain reaction was more likely from U_{235} (because less stable). But his calculations upon the rapidity of a chain reaction and the amount of uranium needed for a critical mass disputed Bohr's belief that an atomic bomb was not feasible, for rather than tons of uranium being necessary, only one or two pounds were required. And with the perfection of his and Peierls' techniques for separating U_{235} from U_{238}, he realized that a more elaborate design with more separation tubes might enable one to produce one pound of uranium in a matter of weeks. This was startling. And it was frightening, for it opened the possibility that the Germans might be capable of constructing the bomb.

Later in 1940 Frisch transferred to the Liverpool Institute. From that base of research, for the next three years, he was to visit Oxford and Cambridge. At Liverpool he worked under James Chadwick, who in 1943 headed the British Atomic-Energy Commission to the United States. Frisch followed him there, first being naturalized as a British citizen—a process which took the remarkably short time of one week. In Washington, D.C., he met General Leslie Groves, who sent him to Los Alamos, New Mexico, to conduct secret research on the atomic bomb under Robert Oppenheimer. There he remained until 1945, seeing the Trinity test succeed in July of that year, near Alamogordo, New Mexico—the first atomic explosion.

After the war's end he returned to England, where from 1945 to 1947 he held the post of division leader in the Atomic Energy Research Establishment at Harwell, under Robert Cockburn. In 1947 he was given the Jackson Chair of Physics at Trinity College in Cambridge, where after a life as a travelling "scholar" he finally settled down, conducting research at the Cavendish Laboratory. In 1951 he married a graphic artist, Ulla Blau; they had two children—Monica Eleanor and David Anthony. Frisch remained at Cambridge, actively working until his retirement in 1972, continuing his research in physics through the use of newer techniques, including bubble chambers, lasers, and computers. The last years of his life were happy and fulfilling. He was, he said in 1979 shortly before his death, "a very lucky man." Among his awards and honors, the two bestowed upon him by his adopted home were most appreciated: the Order of the British Empire—Medal of Freedom (1946) and his election to the Royal Society (1948).

Further Reading

The only biography available is Frisch's autobiography, *What Little I Remember* (1979). This work is very rewarding—it does not pretend to be scholarly, but it conveys the excitement of Frisch's life, his humor, and his love of science and his fellow scientists. Frisch has also written works popularizing ideas of modern atomic physics. They are obsolete now, but still worth reading: *Meet the Atoms* (1947) and *Atomic Physics Today* (1961). □

Johann Jakob Froberger

The German composer and organist Johann Jakob Froberger (1616-1667) transmitted to Germany important style elements of Italian and French keyboard music.

Johann Jakob Froberger was the son of Basilius Froberger, musical director at the court in Stuttgart. Of Basilius's 11 children, 6 are known to have been musicians and, except for Johann Jakob, were employed at the court. Johann Jakob apparently received some musical instruction from his father and some from other court musicians. These included French, Italian, and English musicians as well as German ones, so that Froberger was probably well acquainted with the prevailing styles.

At some point Froberger went to Vienna, possibly as early as 1631. In 1637 he was employed as an organist there, and that year the court awarded him a stipend which allowed him to go to Rome to study with Girolamo Frescobaldi. Froberger returned to Vienna in 1641 as court organist and supervisor of chamber music and remained there until 1645.

Of Froberger's activities between 1641 and 1649 and of his whereabouts from 1645 to 1654 very little is known. Perhaps there occurred between 1641 and 1649 the reported competition in organ playing with the German musician Matthias Weckmann, which probably led to the extensive correspondence and exchange of compositions between the two. In 1649 Froberger dedicated a book of compositions to Emperor Ferdinand III, which would suggest that he was in Vienna. In 1650 he may have been in the service of Archduke Leopold, the governor of the Spanish Netherlands. During this period he probably made a trip to Paris, since a concert in his honor took place there in 1652.

In 1653 Froberger was back in Vienna, and again there is little information about his activities. In 1658 he was apparently dismissed from imperial service, probably on the accession of Leopold I. A trip to England is reported, but with such fantastic details as to be of doubtful authenticity. Froberger finally sought asylum with the dowager duchess Sibylla of Württemberg and spent the rest of his days at her residence at Héricourt in Burgundy.

Froberger's peripatetic career, together with his creative abilities, made him uniquely capable of shaping the future of German keyboard music. Through him the elements of the Italian style that he had learned from Frescobaldi were transferred to southern Germany. Through Froberger's connections with Weckmann and the Dutch musician Christian Huygens, these style elements were transmitted to the north as well, thus influencing composers down to the time of Johann Sebastian Bach and George Frederick Handel. Few of Froberger's works were published during his lifetime, but they were widely disseminated in manuscript (thus did Bach transmit them to his pupils).

Except for two vocal works, only Froberger's keyboard compositions are preserved. He employed forms similar to Frescobaldi's, but with French influences leading to more symmetrical structures and with his Germanic proclivity for counterpoint very evident.

Formerly Froberger was credited with giving to the keyboard suite its classical sequence of movements: allemande, courante, sarabande, and gigue. But this sequence was imposed on his suites at the time of the publication of his complete works in 1693. His true contribution, and it is an important one, is the synthesis of French, German, and Italian elements into a unique style that was influential for the entire baroque era.

Further Reading

No extensive study of Froberger exists in English. His significance is discussed in Manfred F. Bukofzer's excellent *Music in the Baroque Era: From Monteverdi to Bach* (1947). □

Sir Martin Frobisher

Sir Martin Frobisher (ca. 1538-1594), English explorer, naval commander, and soldier, initiated Eu- rope's search for a Northwest Passage to the Orient and discovered the Hudson Strait.

Martin Frobisher, born in Yorkshire, went to London as a boy to be educated by a relative. He showed no aptitude for book learning, so his kinsman sent him to sea. Before reaching manhood Frobisher had been on two voyages to the Guinea Coast. On the second he was captured and handed over to the Portuguese garrisoning São Jorge da Mina, who allowed him to return to England. For a time he engaged in piracy, though he never attacked English ships.

By the 1570s England had largely abandoned hope of finding a Northeast Passage to Asia, and thoughts turned to the Northwest. Frobisher formed a partnership with Michael Lok, a man of some means and learning. Frobisher's first voyage, in 1576, took him to Frobisher Bay in Baffin Island, which he at first claimed as the strait; he also captured an Eskimo whom Lok supposed was a Tatar from north of China.

English investors, including Queen Elizabeth, overlooked Frobisher's former piracy to pour money into Lok's Company of Cathay. Frobisher sailed again in 1577, this time to ship home what he mistakenly thought was gold-bearing ore. Lok still felt hopeful and sent Frobisher back in 1578. This time the mariner discovered the Hudson Strait, which he followed for nearly 200 miles and acknowledged to be a more promising Northwest Passage than Frobisher

Bay. He brought home more dirt and rocks, but English confidence had evaporated; Lok went to a debtors' prison and Frobisher sought other employment.

Frobisher accompanied Sir Francis Drake to the West Indies in 1585-1586. When Philip II's Spanish Armada entered the English Channel in 1588, Frobisher's part in the fighting was distinguished, and he received knighthood. He died of a bullet wound, received near Brest, where he had been sent to relieve the Spanish siege. He lived just long enough to be taken back to Plymouth.

Further Reading

William McFee, *Life of Sir Martin Frobisher* (1928), is an adequate biography. Highly recommended is George Best's 16th-century work, *The Three Voyages of Martin Frobisher in Search of a Passage to Cathay and India,* edited by Vilhjalmur Stefansson (2 vols., 1938). James A. Williamson, *Age of Drake* (1938; 5th ed. 1965), covers Frobisher's entire career, although this information is scattered throughout the work. Frobisher is also discussed in Samuel Eliot Morison, *The European Discovery of America: The Northern Voyages* (1971). □

Friedrich Wilhelm August Froebel

Friedrich Wilhelm August Froebel (1782-1852) was a German educator and psychologist who was a pioneer of the kindergarten system and influenced the growth of the manual training movement in education.

Friedrich Froebel was born on April 21, 1782, in Oberweissbach, a small village in Thuringia. His father was a Lutheran minister. His mother died 9 months after his birth. In 1797 Froebel was apprenticed to a forester in Thuringia. Two years later, while visiting his brother, Froebel took some courses at the University of Jena.

In 1801 Froebel returned home to be with his ailing father. After his father's death the following year he became a clerk in the forestry department of the state of Bamburg. From 1804 to 1805 he served as a private secretary to several noblemen.

Teaching Career

The year 1805 marked a turning point in Froebel's life. He went to Frankfurt intending to become an architect but instead ended up teaching in a preparatory school. The effect of this teaching experience on Froebel was such that he decided to make education his life's work. In 1808 he went to Yverdon, Switzerland, where he tutored boys attending Johann Pestalozzi's institute. Feeling somewhat lacking in his own educational background, he left Yverdon in 1811 and studied at the universities of Göttingen and Berlin until 1816. During this period he briefly served in the army raised by the German states to oppose Napoleon.

In 1816 Froebel opened the Universal German Educational Institute at Keilham, a school based on his own educational theories. Its curriculum was comprehensive in nature, covering all aspects of the student's growth and development—both physical and mental. In 1818 he married Henrietta Hoffmeister.

In Froebel's major educational work, *The Education of Man* (1826), he explained the basic philosophy which guided his educational undertakings—the unity of all things in God. This doctrine is evident in his work in the area of early-childhood education, to which he turned his attention in 1836. This culminated in the development of his famous kindergarten in 1840. That same year Froebel began to instruct teachers in the principles and methods of the kindergarten. His *Mutter- und Koselieder* (1843) is a song and picture book for children. He spent the remainder of his life elaborating, propagandizing, and defending the principles and practices embodied in the kindergarten.

In 1849, after spending approximately 5 years touring Germany and spreading the idea of the kindergarten, Froebel settled in Liebenstein. He spent the remainder of his life combating conservative forces critical of his educational theories. These forces managed in 1851 to get the Prussian government to ban the kindergarten on the grounds that it was an atheistic and socialistic threat to the state. This action was based not so much on what Froebel had done but rather on his followers' misrepresentation of his educational ideas. He did what he could to restore confidence in his kindergarten but died on June 21, 1852, some 8 years before the ban was lifted by the Prussian government.

The Kindergarten

This preschool experience for children grew out of Froebel's belief that man is essentially part of the total universe that is God. He felt that the only way for one to become one's real self, as God intended, was through the natural unfolding of the innate qualities that made up the whole person. This process should begin as soon as possible and under as natural conditions as possible. The program encouraged free activity, so that forces within the child could be released; creativeness, since man, being part of the creative God, should also create; social participation, since man must by nature act in society (a departure from Rousseau); and motor expression, which is related to activity and learning by doing.

Analysis of Educational Theories

The favorable aspects of his view of the kindergarten lie in Froebel's emphasis on the child, the view that education is growth, the recognition of the importance of activity in education, and the position that knowledge is not the end of education. Less favorable in terms of modern thought is the heavy emphasis he placed on object teaching. Froebel believed in an almost mystical way that an object could in some way create *symbolic* meaning for a child (for example, association with a ball teaches the meaning of unity). In later years the use of objects was to become a formalized and fixed part of the kindergarten curriculum. The "unfolding of innate qualities" in a mystical manner has also been criticized as being unscientific.

Further Reading

For an account of Froebel see his *Autobiography* (trans. 1886). For insight into the early growth of the kindergarten in the United States see Nina C. Vandewalker, *The Kindergarten in American Education* (1908). William Boyd, *The History of Western Education* (1921; 8th ed. 1966), and James Mulhern, *A History of Secondary Education in Pennsylvania* (1933), both place the kindergarten in relation to other educational developments. □

Charles Frohman

An American theatrical producer, Charles Frohman (1860-1915) saw the theater make its transition from stock companies to the star system. Primarily a pillar of "show business" rather than an artistic theatrical innovator, Frohman illuminated the theater with a bright gallery of stars under his personal management.

Charles Frohman was born on June 17, 1860 in Sandusky, Ohio, the son of a traveling peddlar. Frohman loved the theater from boyhood, when as an eight-year-old he hawked souvenir programs for a local production of *The Black Crook,* America's first musical show. From there he worked his way up through virtually every level of press agentry and theatrical management.

Leaving Ohio at age 12, he went to New York City and worked successively for two newspapers, the *Tribune* and the *Daily Graphic.* His love for the theater brought him to night work selling tickets at Hooley's Theater in Brooklyn. By 1877 he was an advance man for traveling shows, most notably Haverly's Minstrels. Frohman's sharp business sense and the support of his brothers, Daniel and Gustave, enabled the three of them to take on the management of Steele MacKaye's Madison Square Theater. There Frohman devised a touring company system that changed the American theater. Frohman hit upon the idea of sending out full companies to present road versions of plays that were hits in New York.

In 1888 Frohman was an agent for playwright Bronson Howard. The playwright's latest drama, *Shenandoah,* had only managed a limited run in Boston, but Frohman saw greater possibilities in it. He borrowed money from a few theatrical colleagues and produced the play in New York, achieving a great success. To clinch his recognition as the fastest rising theatrical entrepreneur on Broadway, he signed an exclusive contract with actor-turned-playwright William Gillette to produce all of that successful author's works. Gillette would become famous for plays such as *Sherlock Holmes* (1893) and *Secret Service* (1896).

Frohman wanted as much control over his theatrical enterprises as possible, and in 1890 he took over Proctor's

Theater and began his own stock company there. Three years later Frohman built his own theater, the Empire. With his brothers he became a leading theatrical impresario. By the turn of the century he was the most prominent producer in New York and London. In his transatlantic career Frohman was most successful in launching plays by English dramatists J.M. Barrie and Arthur Wing Pinero, Oscar Wilde, and Somerset Maugham. But his London theater ventures would ultimately cost him his life.

In 1895 Frohman, along with Al Hayman, Mark Klaw, Abe Erlanger, Sam Nixon, and Fred Zimmerman, formed the Theatrical Syndicate, also known as the Trust. This organization dominated the American theater from 1896 through World War I. Its alleged reason for being was to systematize haphazard theatrical booking networks across the United States, but it actually ended up exerting near total control over every aspect of theatrical production in the country. The syndicate had a majority interest in virtually every important theater in the country. Producers or performers who crossed the Trust found themselves unable to put on their plays.

The extent to which Frohman's personal influence shaped the development of the Theatrical Syndicate is disputed. His supporters maintain that he endured the high-handedness of his partners in order to present quality productions; Frohman's detractors charge him with having only a concern for projecting his own image as the "artistic" manager.

Many considered him a ruthless businessman who looked out only for himself, but this belies the fact that he died nearly penniless and that numerous actors and actresses were loyal to him and his management throughout their entire careers. Annie Russell, Margaret Anglin, Julia Marlowe, Otis Skinner, and Billie Burke were among the stars under his control. Maude Adams, the most popular actress of the turn of the century, literally owed her career to him (the role of Peter Pan was created for her) and went into eclipse after Frohman's death.

Even though Frohman was responsible for the proliferation of the star system, late in his career he realized that it had done much to destroy artistry in the theater. Frohman believed his great achievement had been to bring the best British plays to New York. Nonetheless, his theatrical acuity caused him to recognize that the reliance on stars made the script merely a dramatic property that was almost irrelevant because stars such as John Drew, Maude Adams, or Ada Rehan would attract crowds no matter what the play. Frohman's career lasted long enough to see later generations of his "family" succeed; for example, John Drew's young niece, Ethel Barrymore, emerged as a star (in the American playwright Clyde Fitch's *Captain Jinks of the Horse Marines*) in 1901.

Frohman exerted a tremendous influence on the commercial theater in the United States. He emphasized the production of new plays even though he was criticized for giving short shrift to the classics. He actively developed new stars, creating images for them and tenderly shepherding their careers. He constantly sought out untried playwrights and gave them encouragement. The financial cushion provided by the Trust enabled Frohman to profitably manipulate his theatrical system for over two decades. He created stars who created audiences for the works of Frohman's own playwrights. The controversy about his motivations and methods aside, it cannot be denied that Frohman's theatrical taste *was* respected and his concern for the theater as an institution revered.

Eager to free himself from what he considered to be prosaic origins, Frohman later in life adopted the code of behavior of an English gentleman of stiffest upper lip. His courtliness and reserve contrasted with his squat body and squinting countenance.

In 1915 his favorite playwright, J.M. Barrie, implored him to come to London to help out a faltering production. Frohman ignored warnings and sailed on the *Lusitania*. Calmly puffing a cigar as the ship was torpedoed on May 7, 1915, Frohman met his end as bravely as any stage hero, coolly intoning: "Why fear death, it's the greatest adventure of all." For his epitaph Frohman asked that he be remembered as "The man who gave *Peter Pan* to the world and *Chantecler* to America."

Further Reading

A sympathetic biography of Frohman, *Charles Frohman: Manager and Man,* was written in 1916 by Isaac F. Marcosson and Daniel Frohman. Daniel Frohman left two volumes of memoirs, *Memoirs of a Manager* (1911) and *Daniel Frohman Presents* (1935). These have scattered references to his brother.

Brooks Atkinson's *Broadway* (1970) contains an affectionate portrait of Frohman. Contemporary theater periodicals such as *Theatre, Green Book,* and *Dramatic Mirror* frequently featured articles about Frohman. □

Jean Froissart

The French priest, poet, and itinerate reporter Jean Froissart (c.1337-c.1404) is known primarily as a chronicler. During his wide travels, lodging in castles from Scotland to Italy, he recorded what he observed, leaving the best picture of 14th-century feudal life.

Jean Froissart was born in Valenciennes. Educated by and for the Church, he was later received into the priesthood, but his natural inclinations were somewhat opposed to the austerity of religious life, even though he was canon of the collegial church of Chimay and chaplain to the Count of Blois. After his arrival in England in 1361 he entered the service of Queen Philippa (she too a native of Valenciennes), wife of Edward III. His early poems and his heroic stories pleased the English court, but after the death of his protectress in 1369 he returned to Valenciennes.

Four years later Froissart was received by Wenceslas of Luxembourg, Duke of Brabant, a congenial poet who was his patron until 1384. His last patron on the Continent was the Count of Blois. From 1389 he was generally at Valenciennes or Chimay until he again left for England in 1394, where he was well received by Richard II but did not stay. Froissart was living in 1404, but the date of his death is unknown.

The poetry of Froissart fills three sizable volumes and ranges from *pastourelles,* to narrative and didactic poems, to courtly poetry. The best are *The Paradise of Love, The Pretty Buzzard of Youth,* and the long *Thornlet of Love,* on disappointments in love, and the bitter *Tale of the Florin* . His *Méliador,* in which are inserted 81 short poems of Wenceslas, contains over 30,000 lines; it is an attempt to revive the old Arthurian romance.

Froissart's *Chroniques de France, d'Engleterre et des païs voisins (Chronicles)* begins in 1327 and ends in 1400. His written source up to 1361 was Jean le Bel, whom he often copied directly. His main source derived from his art of getting people to tell him all they knew; no news correspondent ever equaled this medieval information magnet. Unlike Geffroi de Villehardouin and Jean de Joinville, Froissart was never involved in public affairs or military action, but he traveled and interviewed endlessly. He knew everyone and was at his best in describing the coronation of John II and the visit of Philip VI of France to Pope Benedict XII at Avignon. Indeed, the index to his chronicle constitutes a veritable "who's who" of western Europe for more than half a century, and yet Froissart was much more of a historian than a social reporter.

ership of such prominent Freudian analysts as Hanns Sachs and Theodor Reik. After pursuing a brief career as a psychoanalyst he left Nazi Germany in 1934 and settled permanently in the United States. Fromm taught in various universities such as Bennington College, Columbia, Yale, New School for Social Research, Michigan State, and the Universidad Autónoma de México. In 1962 he became professor of psychiatry at New York University.

Fromm wrote more than 20 books. Some of them became popular bestsellers: *Escape from Freedom* (1942); *Man for Himself* (1947); *Psychoanalysis and Religion* (1950); *The Forgotten Language* (1951); *The Sane Society* (1955); *The Art of Loving* (1956); *Marx's Concept of Man* (1961); *Beyond the Chains of Illusion: My Encounter with Marx and Freud* (1962); *The Dogma of Christ, and Other Essays on Religion, Psychology and Culture* (1963); *Zen Buddhism and Psychoanalysis* (1960); *The Life and Work of Sigmund Freud* (1963); *The Heart of Man* (1964); *Social Character in a Mexican Village* (1970); *The Revolution of Hope* (1968); *The Crisis of Psychoanalysis* (1970); and *The Anatomy of Human Destructiveness* (1973).

A sincere and profound humanism permeates all of Fromm's writings. He was genuinely concerned with the reality of human existence and the full unfolding of man's potentialities. He searched for the essence of man, the meaning of life, and the nature of individual alienation in the modern technological world. Deeply moved by the destruction and the suffering caused by two world wars, Fromm wrote extensively on the threats of technology and

Further Reading

The only work of Froissart in English is the *Chronicles,* the classic translation is Lord Berner's, edited by William P. Ker (6 vols., 1901-1903). Two good studies in English are G. G. Coulton, *The Chronicler of European Chivalry* (1976; 1977), and F. S. Shears *Froissart, Chronicler and Poet* (1974). □

Erich Fromm

Erich Fromm (1900-1980) achieved international fame for his writings and lectures in the fields of psychoanalysis, psychology, and social philosophy. He wrote extensively on a variety of topics ranging from sociology, anthropology, and ethics to religion, politics, and mythology.

Erich Fromm was born in Frankfurt am Main, Germany, on March 23, 1900, and died in Muralto, Switzerland, on March 18, 1980. He grew up in a devout Jewish family, but abandoned religious orthodoxy early in life when he became convinced that religion was a source of division of the human race. His academic career was impressive. He studied at the Universities of Frankfurt and Munich and received his Ph.D. from the University of Heidelberg. Later, he obtained psychoanalytic training at the prestigious Psychoanalytic Institute of Berlin under the lead-the insanity of the arms race. Faith in the future of man and the unity of humanity was the base of his humanistic vision.

Freud and Marx were the most decisive influences on Fromm's thinking. Originally Freudian in his intellectual orientation and clinical practice, he gradually grew more distant from Freudian therapeutic principles and later became a major critic of Freud. Along with Karen Horney, Harry Sullivan, and Karl Jung, Fromm was considered a Freudian revisionist and the founder of the neo-Freudian school. He rejected Freud's libido theory, the Oedipus complex, and the instincts of life and death as universally constant in the human species. Instead, he insisted on cultural variations and the influence of the larger context of history and social conditions upon the character of the individual. The concept of the unconscious and the dynamic conception of character were considered to be Freud's major achievements. The task of analytical social psychology, Fromm wrote, is that of understanding unconscious human behavior as the effect of the socio-economic structure of society on basic human psychic drives. Likewise, the character of the individual is rooted in the libidinal structure of society, understood as a combination of basic human drives and social forces. In the last analysis, Fromm rejected Freudian theory as authoritarian, repressive, and culturally narrow, enabling the individual to overcome the conflict between society and personal gratification and accept bourgeois norms.

In contrast, Fromm's admiration for Marx was complete. He considered Marx a sincere humanist who sought an end to human alienation and the full development of the individual as the precondition for the full development of society (*Marx's Concept of Man*). Marx's emphasis on the socio-economic base of society as a major determinant of human behavior was accepted as a given by Fromm. Marxism, though, needed to be completed by a dynamic and critical psychology—that is, a psychology which explained the evolution of psychic forces in terms of an interaction between man's needs and the socio-historical reality in which he lives (*The Crisis of Psychoanalysis*). Fromm never renounced his project of merging psycho-analysis and Marxism. This was his major work as a member of the Frankfurt School (The Institute for Social Research), a school committed to Critical Theory, a critique of the repressive character of bourgeois society. Psychological theory, he wrote, can demonstrate that the economic base of a society produces the social character, and that the social character produces ideas and ideologies which fit it and are nourished by it. Ideas, once created, also influence the social character and, indirectly, the socio-economic structure of society (*Socialist Humanism*).

In his popular book *Escape from Freedom* Fromm analyzed the existential condition of man. The source of man's aggressiveness, the human instinct of destructiveness, neurosis, sadism, and masochism were not viewed as sexually derived behavior, but as attempts to overcome alienation and powerlessness. His notion of freedom, in contrast to Freud and the critical theorists of the Frankfurt School, had a more positive connotation. It was not a matter of attaining "freedom from" the repressive character of the technologi-

cal society, as Herbert Marcuse, for instance, held, but "freedom to" develop the creative powers of man. In *Man for Himself* Fromm focussed on the problem of neurosis, characterizing it as the moral problem of a repressive society, as the failure of man to achieve maturity and an integrated personality. Man's capacity for freedom and love, he noted, are dependent upon socio-economic conditions, but are rarely found in societies where the drive of destructiveness prevails.

In the *Sane Society* he attempted to psychologize society and culture and showed that psychoanalytic principles can be successfully applied to the solution of social and cultural problems. In a society becoming increasingly insane, he wrote, only a concern for *ethics* can restore sanity. Each person needs to develop high ethical standards in order to rejuvenate society and to arrest the process of robotization of the human being. Technological domination is destructive of human personality. Man's need to destroy, for Fromm, stemmed from an "unlived life," that is, the frustration of the life instinct. Love becomes the only answer to human problems (*The Art of Loving*). He advocated a "socialist humanism" which in theory and practice is committed to the full development of man within the context of a socio-economic system that, by its rationality and abundance, harmonizes the development of the individual and society (*Socialist Humanism*).

In contrast to the pessimistic and deterministic conclusions of Freudian theory and the nihilistic implications of Critical Theory, Fromm functioned as a voice of conscience. He maintained that true happiness could be achieved and that a happiness-oriented therapy, through empathy, was the most successful one. He severely criticized established psychoanalysis for contributing to the dehumanization of man (*The Crisis of Psychoanalysis*). Also, consistent with his philosophy of love and peace, Fromm fought against nuclear weapons and helped organize a "sane society" movement to stop the insanity of the arms race.

His influence on humanistic psychology was enormous. Many later social analysts were inspired by Fromm's writings. An example would be the work of Christopher Lasch on the *Culture of Narcissism,* which continued in the United States Fromm's effort to psychoanalyze culture and society in a neo-Freudian and Marxist tradition.

Further Reading

Fromm is listed in most social science encyclopedias. For a general summary of his work, a more complete intellectual biography, and a critical assessment of his theories see: Jay Martin, *The Dialectical Imagination: A History of the Frankfurt School* (1973); Don Hausdorff, *Erich Fromm* (1972); B. Landis and E. Tauber (editors), *In the Name of Life: Essays in Honor of Erich Fromm* (1979) and "Erich Fromm: Clinician and Social Philosopher," in *Contemporary Psychoanalysis* (1979); and Richard Evans, *Dialogue with Erich Fromm* (1966).

Numerous dissertations have been written on Fromm. See J. Zimmerman, "Transcendent Psychology: Eric H. Erikson, Erich Fromm, Karen Horney, A. Maslow and Harry S. Sullivan and the Quest for a Healthy Humanity," Dissertation Abstracts International (1982); S. J. Dembo, "Synthesis of Liberation: Marx-Freud and the New Left, An Examination of the

Work of W. Reich, E. Fromm and H. Marcuse," Ph.D. Dissertation, Rutgers University (1975); and C. E. Daly, "The Epistemology and Ethical Theory of Erich Fromm as the Basis for a Theory of Moral Education," Ph.D. Dissertation, New York University (1977).

Additional Sources

Evans, Richard I. (Richard Isadore), *Dialogue with Erich Fromm*, New York, N.Y.: Praeger, 1981, 1966.
Knapp, Gerhard Peter, *The art of living: Erich Fromm's life and works*, New York: P. Lang, 1989. □

Arturo Frondizi

Arturo Frondizi (1908-1995) was a leader of the Argentine Radical party and the first legally elected Argentine president after the fall of Peron. He sought to restore constitutional government and to promote national economic development.

Arturo Frondizi, one of 14 children of Italian immigrant parents, was born on October 28, 1908, in Paso de los Libres in the northeastern province of Corrientes. His father was a road and bridge contractor who had moved his family and business to Buenos Aires. Arturo graduated from the University of Buenos Aires with a degree in law.

While a student, Frondizi became interested in the writings of Marx, but stopped short of becoming a Communist or Socialist, joining instead the Radical Civic Union (UCR) or Radical party of President Hipólito Irigoyen shortly before his ouster in a military coup in September 1930. Refusing to receive a diploma of honor from the leader of the coup, General José Félix Uriburu, Frondizi was briefly jailed for his vociferous opposition to the overthrow of Irigoyen.

Following graduation Frondizi practiced law. He also taught law and economics and became known as a writer and journalist. Politically, Frondizi gained a degree of prominence in the intransigent, or left wing, of the UCR, which called for economic and social reforms and supported the traditional Radical policy of abstention from the polls.

During the Conservative rule of the 1930s, Frondizi was a strong advocate of the policy of electoral abstention, but reversed his position after the removal from power of the Conservatives in 1943 and the Intransigent's take over of the UCR a few years later.

Rise and Fall of Peron

In the election of 1946 which brought Juan Perón to power, Frondizi ran for political office for the first time, winning a seat in the Argentine Chamber of Deputies, to which he was reelected in 1948. Frondizi was the unsuccessful candidate for the vice presidency on the Radical ticket headed by his colleague and rival Ricardo Balbín in 1951.

As a member of Congress Frondizi was a leader of the opposition to Perón, but he supported much of Perón's social and economic program. Strongly influenced by Marxism, Frondizi was known for his commitment to economic nationalism and was quite in accord with Perón's policy to reduce foreign influence in the Argentine economy. In 1955, however, Perón, confronted with increasing economic difficulties and in need of foreign investment capital, signed a contract with the Standard Oil Company of California to exploit Argentina's oil resources. Frondizi then became one of Perón's strongest critics.

Perón was overthrown in September 1955, and a caretaker government headed by General Eduardo Lonardi was established. Politically, the country was now divided between a strong anti-Peronist element that wanted to eliminate Peronism from the political scene altogether and the still loyal followers of Perón. Lonardi, who favored an accommodation with the Peronists, was replaced within two months as provisional president by the much less conciliatory General Pedro E. Aramburu, whose government adopted a harsh anti-Peronist policy, including the dissolution of the Peronist party, and pledged to hold elections as soon as possible.

By 1957, despite political and economic difficulties, the government of Aramburu carried out its promise to hold elections, and Frondizi, who had become a severe critic of the administration of Aramburu, won the nomination as the Radical party's candidate for the presidency in the forthcoming elections. But his candidacy caused a split in the UCR which led to the formation of two separate parties, the

Intransigent Radical Party (UCRI) and the Peoples Radical Party (UCRP). Frondizi, who advocated the reintegration of the Peronists into the political life of Argentina, was the uncontested leader and presidential candidate of the UCRI, while Ricardo Balbín became the compromise leader and presidential candidate of the UCRP, which was composed of various factions and individuals sympathetic to Aramburu's anti-Peronist measures and opposed to Frondizi. Frondizi, with the support of the Peronists, whose votes he courted with a promise to restore their party to legality, won not only the presidency but also control of the national congress and all of the provincial governorships in contention.

The Frondizi Presidency

Upon assuming the Argentine presidency on May 1, 1958, Frondizi inherited a number of serious economic problems, including an unfavorable balance of trade and severe inflation. These problems prevented him from carrying out the program outlined in his earlier writings and speeches. Disregarding his previous anti-imperialist pronouncements, in July of 1958, in an action reminiscent of Peron, he granted concessions to United States and European companies for the exploration of Argentina's petroleum resources. This was an effort to make Argentina self-sufficient in petroleum production and stem the out-flow of $300 million annually for petroleum imports. He was also forced to abandon his ideas on agrarian reform and independent industrial development and to seek outside aid to solve the country's economic difficulties. In December of 1958 he agreed with the International Monetary Fund (IMF) to put into effect a controversial stabilization and development program which imposed a regime of financial austerity on the country as a condition for receiving foreign investments and foreign loans. He hoped that this would stimulate the economy and develop Argentine industry.

Forced to Call Upon Military

Frondizi's economic program met with strong resistance on the part of the urban workers, and he was confronted with an outbreak of labor unrest. Compelled to call upon the military to maintain order, Frondizi found himself increasingly dependent on the military for support of his government.

Frondizi's term in office was plagued with political unrest and repeated coup attempts. Throughout his term, Frondizi's relations with the leaders of the military were strained, largely due to their distaste for his policy towards the Peronists. They repeatedly compelled him to dismiss from governmental posts officials suspected of having Peronist sympathies.

In March 1962, in fulfillment of his promise to restore the legality of the Peronist party, Frondizi allowed the Peronists to run their own candidates for the first time since 1955 in the congressional and local elections. The Peronists won a majority of the provincial governorships, including the most important one of Buenos Aires, and more than half of the available seats in the Chamber of Deputies. The leaders of the armed forces quickly responded, demanding federal intervention to annul the electoral victory of the Peronists, arrest their leaders, and form a coalition cabinet named by the military. Frondizi yielded to military pressure to the extent of intervening in five of the provinces won by the Peronists, but failed to gain the support he needed from the other political parties to form a coalition government. The military thereupon removed Frondizi from office in March of 1962 and set up a new provisional government under the president of the Senate, José María Guido.

Supported Peronist Candidate

After leaving the Argentine presidency, Frondizi continued to play an active role in the UCRI until 1964 when he and the minority faction broke away to form the Movement for Integration and Development (MID). The new party's goals were based upon his previous program for political integration and economic development; all reference to Radicalism was dropped. Frondizi and his followers maintained an alliance with Perón, and in the elections of 1973, which opened the door for Perón's brief return to power, Frondizi supported the Peronist candidate for the presidency, Héctor Cámpora.

Frondizi's personal charisma and his policies of economic development had won him a following among the professional and managerial element of Argentina's middle sector, and he remained an important figure in Argentine politics. Frondizi was also respected as an intellectual, reputed to be widely read and an articulate speaker. He wrote several books on Argentine politics and economics. At one time it was thought he was in line to be named economic minister of the Radical party should it be returned to power. Despite speaking out on pubic issues, Frondizi never returned to anything more than marginal prominence.

Frondizi died in Buenos Aires April 18, 1995, of a heart ailment. He was 86. His wife and only daughter died earlier, and Frondizi left no immediate survivors.

Further Reading

Frondizi's role in the Radical Party and the period of his presidency is dealt with in Peter G. Snow's, *Argentine Radicalism: The History and Doctrine of the Radical Civic Union* (1965). Robert A. Potash, *The Army and Politics in Argentina, 1945-1962* (1980) provides a thorough account of Frondizi's relations with the military and his removal from office in 1962. □

Comte de Frontenac et Palluau

Louis de Buade, Comte de Frontenac et Palluau (1622-1698), was a controversial governor general of New France, architect of French westward expansion, and commander of French forces against the Iroquois and the English colonies during King William's War.

The Comte de Frontenac was born on May 22, 1622, at Saint-Germain. His grandfather was equerry to Henry IV; his father was colonel of the Regiment of Navarre and an aide to Louis XIII; and his mother, Anne Phélypeaux de Pont-chartrain, was the daughter of an influential secretary of state. Louis XIII was his godfather.

Entering the army in his teens, Frontenac campaigned during the Thirty Years War and at the age of 21 was colonel of the Regiment of Normandy. He was also a courtier, lived extravagantly, and ran up huge debts. In 1669 he obtained a lucrative appointment with the Venetian forces defending Crete against the Turks, but within 3 months he was dismissed by the commanding general. Three years later he obtained the appointment of governor general of New France.

Administrator of New France

Plagued by an irascible temper and an exalted opinion of his own capacities, Frontenac quickly quarreled with the senior officials and the clergy. Many of these disputes centered about the fur trade. The minister of marine, Jean Baptiste Colbert, was striving to keep it within bounds to prevent its crippling his plans to diversify the colony's economy, while Frontenac encouraged the expansion of the western fur trade. This brought the French into conflict with the Iroquois, who were allied with the English of New York. By 1681, however, Frontenac had carried his internal disputes to such lengths that the civil administration was disrupted, and the following year he was dismissed.

Frontenac's successors struggled to curb the Iroquois and retain control of the west, with scant success. In 1689 England and France declared war. An assault on New York, by sea and from Canada, was planned. The governor general of New France had requested his own recall, and Frontenac was reappointed. Owing to delay, for which Frontenac was not responsible, the New York expedition had to be abandoned. That winter, as a reprisal against an Iroquois surprise attack that had inflicted heavy damage, Frontenac launched three war parties against the frontier settlements of New York and New England.

These raids did not deter the Iroquois, but they enraged the English colonies. They united their forces for a land and sea attack on Canada. The overland expedition against Montreal foundered, but a New England fleet reached Quebec only to find Frontenac with the entire armed strength of the colony waiting to oppose their assault force of untrained militia. After a few days of skirmishing they gave up and sailed away.

War against the Iroquois

The colony now came under constant attack by the Iroquois, but within 2 years the Canadians had mastered the art of guerrilla warfare and began carrying the war to the enemy. The Iroquois, also under attack by the western tribes, suffered heavy losses while French strength grew with the arrival of troop reinforcements from France. The Iroquois therefore tried to split the French alliance with the western tribes by a peace offensive. Frontenac's subordinates were convinced that he was being duped when he agreed to a cessation of hostilities pending peace talks; they demanded a full-scale invasion of the Iroquois cantons.

It was then discovered that the Iroquois diplomats had informed the western tribes that the French had abandoned them and made a separate peace. They were the more easily persuaded to abandon their alliance and make peace with the Iroquois because they were disgruntled with the French for economic reasons. French traders, with Frontenac's encouragement, had pushed farther west and were trading directly with the tribes that provided the furs to the middleman tribes in the French alliance. These, in turn, resented even more that the French were supplying firearms to their ancient foes, the Sioux.

The French found themselves in a precarious position, their allies defecting, and the Iroquois, their western flank secure, now reopening their attacks on the colony. In 1696 Frontenac was forced by pressure from his subordinates to launch a major campaign against the Iroquois. This crushed their offensive spirit and disrupted their negotiations with the French allies. The following year the war ended in Europe, and the Iroquois, denied English aid, were forced to treat for peace in earnest.

Canada had escaped the military consequences of Frontenac's inept policy, but the economic consequences could not be avoided. The amount of beaver traded in the west had increased during the war until there was a surplus approaching 1 million pounds, enough to manufacture half a million hats. The beaver trade, backbone of the Canadian economy, was bankrupt. Frontenac was by no means solely responsible for this condition, but despite repeated warnings he had done nothing to prevent it and not a little to engender it.

In civil affairs Frontenac's second administration was less turbulent than his first, but he frequently used his authority in a very despotic manner. By 1698 the minister, Louis de Pontchartrain, had become weary of excusing his kinsman's arbitrary conduct to Louis XIV. Frontenac was in imminent danger of again being recalled in disgrace. The aged governor, however, spared the King the necessity of making this decision. He was taken ill, and after making his peace with his subordinates, he died Nov. 28, 1698.

Further Reading

The most recent, and most critical, biography of Frontenac is W. J. Eccles, *Frontenac, the Courtier Governor* (1959). There are several others, all adulatory and all based on Francis Parkman, *Count Frontenac and New France under Louis XIV* (1877), a work which reflects the prejudices of the author and the values of his own society. General background studies which discuss Frontenac include Edgar McInnis, *Canada: A Political and Social History* (1947; rev. ed. 1959), and J. Bartlett Brebner, *Canada: A Modern History* (1960; rev. ed. 1970). □

Sextus Julius Frontinus

The Roman magistrate, soldier, and engineer Sextus Julius Frontinus (ca. 35-ca. 104) is known primarily as a technical writer.

Frontinus seems to have been of patrician descent, and his writings indicate that he had some knowledge of Alexandrian mathematics. In his role as magistrate, Frontinus served as *praetor urbanus* of Rome in the year 70 and as *consul suffectus* in 73. From 74 to 78 he served as governor of Britain, during which time he subdued the Silures, a powerful and warlike tribe from Wales. His instinct for public improvements, which dominated his whole career, led him to begin the construction of a public highway (Via Julia) in the conquered territory. Returning to Rome in 78, Frontinus served as *consul suffectus* in 98 and again in 100. It was during this latter period that most of his writings seem to have been composed.

Appointed *curator aquarum* (superintendent of the aqueducts) of Rome in 97, Frontinus embodied his knowledge of the water supply in a treatise, *On the Aqueducts of Rome,* a valuable source of information on the historical, legal, and technical life of the times. In this work Frontinus lists the names of the aqueducts, when and by whom they were constructed, and their size, height, and distribution, and he collects the many laws and penalties regulating their proper employment. The treatise portrays Frontinus as a faithful public servant who openly boasts that his reforms have made the city cleaner and the water and the air purer and removed the causes of pestilence which had formerly given Rome a bad reputation. In this work Frontinus shows himself aware of the relationship between the speed of outflow of water and its height.

Frontinus composed two treatises on military tactics. The first, *The Stratagems,* is a manual on military stratagems compiled from Greek and Roman military history. The book is divided into three parts—stratagems for use before the battle begins, those concerned with the battle itself, and those concerned with sieges and the raising of sieges. The other military treatise, *De re militari,* has not survived except in fragments quoted by other authorities.

Frontinus also composed a treatise on the art of surveying, of which only fragments are extant. It appears that this work was a pioneering effort in Roman surveying and that it was used as a standard authority for some years.

Further Reading

An early edition of Frontinus's work is *The Two Books on the Water Supply of the City of Rome,* translated and with explanatory chapters by Clemens Herschel (1899). A revised version of Herschel's work is *The Stratagems, and the Aqueducts of Rome,* edited by Mary B. McElwain (1925). Further information can be found in Thomas Ashby, *The Aqueducts of Ancient Rome,* edited by I. A. Richmond (1935). J. N. L. Myres, *Roman Britain* (1939), provides information on the political career of Frontinus as well as background information. □

Robert Lee Frost

Robert Lee Frost (1874-1963) was an intentionally American and traditionalist poet in an age of internationalized and experimental art. He used New England idioms, characters, and settings, recalling the roots of American culture, to get at universal experience.

Robert Frost was born in San Francisco on March 26, 1874. His father came from prerevolutionary Maine and New Hampshire stock but hated New England because the Civil War it had supported had robbed his own father of employment in the cotton mill economy. When Frost's father graduated from Harvard in 1872, he left New England. He paused in Lewistown, Pa., to teach and married another teacher, Isabelle Moodie, a Scotswoman. They moved to San Francisco, where the elder Frost became an editor and politician. Their first child was named for the Southern hero Gen. Robert E. Lee.

When Frost's father died in 1884, his will stipulated burial in New England. His wife and two children, Robert and Jeanie, went east for the funeral. Lacking funds to return to California, they settled in Salem, Mass., where Mrs. Frost taught school.

Transplanted New Englander

Robert had been a city boy, a proud Californian, and no student. Transplanted, he grew sensitive to New England's speechways, taciturn characters, and customs. He also be-

came a serious student and graduated from Lawrence High School as valedictorian and class poet in 1892. He enrolled at Dartmouth College but soon left. He had become engaged to Elinor White, classmate and fellow valedictorian, who was completing her college education. Frost moved from job to job, working in mills, at newspaper reporting, and at teaching, all the while writing poetry. In 1894 he sold his first poem, "My Butterfly," to the *New York Independent.* Overjoyed, he had two copies of a booklet of lyrics privately printed, one for his fiancée and one for himself. He delivered Elinor's copy in person but did not find her response adequate. Thinking he had lost her, he tore up his copy and wandered south as far as the Dismal Swamp (from Virginia to North Carolina), even contemplating suicide.

In 1895, however, Frost married Elinor and tried to make a career of teaching. He helped his mother run a small private school in Lawrence, Mass., where his first son was born. He spent 2 years at Harvard (1897-1899), but again undergraduate study proved uncongenial. With a newborn daughter as well as a son, he tried chicken farming at Methuen, Mass., and in 1900, when his nervousness was diagnosed as a forewarning of tuberculosis, he moved his poultry business to Derry, N.H. There his first son soon died. In 1906 Frost was stricken with pneumonia and almost died, and a year later his fourth daughter died. This grief and suffering, as well as lesser frustrations in personal life and business, turned Frost more and more to poetry. Once again he tried teaching, in Derry and then in Plymouth, N.H.

Creation of the Poet

In 1912, almost 40 and with only a few poems published, Frost sold his farm and used an annuity from his grandfather to go to England and gamble everything on poetry. The family settled on a farm in Buckinghamshire, and Frost began to write. Ezra Pound, the expatriate American poet, helped him get published in periodicals, but Frost resented Pound's excessive management.

Frost published *A Boy's Will* (1913), and it was well received. Though it contains some 19th-century diction, the words and rhythms are generally colloquial and subtly simple. Written in conventional rhymed stanzas and blank verse, the poems begin in delight and end in wisdom, as Frost later said poems should. They move through various subjective moods toward modest revelations. Such poems as "Into My Own," "Mowing," and "A Tuft of Flowers" convey an inclination toward nature, solitude, and meditation, toward the beauty of fact, and toward a New England individualism that acknowledges a need for love and community.

North of Boston (1914), also published in England, is more objective, made up mainly of blank verse monologues and dramatic narratives. "The Death of the Hired Man," soberly suspenseful and compassionate, with lyric moments of waiting, has more to do with the mutual understanding in a marriage than with death. "Mending Wall" is a bantering satire contrasting a tradition-bound farmer and his neighbor, a straight-faced tease. In "After Apple-picking" the picker asks quizzically whether he should settle for being plain tired or inflate his state by identifying it with the drowsiness of autumn. "Home Burial" and "A Servant of Servants" dramatize respectively a hysteria bred of loneliness and death, and the precarious sanity of a rural drudge.

North of Boston compounded the success of *A Boy's Will,* and the two volumes announced the two modes of Frost's best poetry, the lyric and the narrative. Although immediately established as a nature poet, he did not idealize nature. He addressed not only its loveliness but also the isolation, harshness, and anxiety its New England intimates had to endure. The reticence of his poetry, however, is not simply that of a taciturn New Englander; it restrains tremendous psychic and sexual forces, a violent and suicidal bent, and deep emotional needs that occasionally flashed out in his poetry and personal life.

Frost's place in literary tradition had also begun to clarify. His work led back to aspects of Thomas Hardy, Emily Dickinson, and Ralph Waldo Emerson, and Yankees Oliver Wendell Holmes, James Russell Lowell, and John Greenleaf Whittier, and to characteristics of William Wordsworth, English 18th-century meditators on landscape, John Donne, and the Latin idylls and eclogues of Theocritus and Virgil. But Frost's irony and ambiguity, his concreteness and colloquial tone, his skepticism and honesty bespoke the modern.

A Public Figure

When the Frosts returned to America in 1915, *North of Boston* was a best seller. Sudden acclaim embarrassed Frost, who had always avoided crowds. He withdrew to a small farm in Franconia, N.H., but financial need soon compelled him to respond to demands for readings and lectures. In 1915 and 1916 he was respectively Phi Beta Kappa poet at Tufts College and at Harvard. He conquered his shyness, developing an epigrammatic, folksy platform manner that made him one of the most popular performers in America and abroad. His tall muscular body and rugged face with its pale watchful eyes became a familiar sight; as the hair whitened, the face grew craggy, and the body thickened, those eyes remained the same.

From Frost's talks, his few published essays, and his poems, the outline of a poetic theory emerged. He strove for the sound of sense, for the colloquial, for a tension between the natural rhythm of speech and the basic iambic meter of English verse. He felt that the emotion that began a poem should generate a form through likenesses and contraries and lead to a clarification of experience. This was the way to spontaneity and surprise.

Mountain Interval (1916) brought together lyrics and narratives. The five dramatic lyrics of "The Hill Wife" look at a marriage dying on a solitary farm. On the other hand, "Meeting and Passing" uses a few vivid images to infuse a courtship walk with the promise of joy. The hilarious slide in "Brown's Descent" and the youthful tree-swinging of "Birches" (although its exuberance is restrained from hyperbole by "matter of fact") are countered by the deadly accident of "Out, Out—."

In 1917 Frost became one of the first poets-in-residence on an American campus. He taught at Amherst from 1917 to 1920, in 1918 receiving a master of arts, the first of many academic honors. The following year he moved his farm base to South Saftsbury, Vt. In 1920 he cofounded the Bread Loaf School of English of Middlebury College, serving there each summer as lecturer and consultant. From 1921 to 1923 he was poet-in-residence at the University of Michigan.

Frost's *Selected Poems* and a new volume, *New Hampshire,* appeared in 1923. For the latter Frost received the first of four Pulitzer Prizes. Though the title poem does not present Frost at his best, the volume also contains such lovely lyrics as "Fire and Ice," "Nothing Gold Can Stay," and "To Earthward." In "For Once, Then Something" Frost slyly joshes critics who ask for deep, deep insights; and in the dramatic narrative "The Witch of Coös" he turns a rustic comedy into a grotesque story of adultery and murder. "Two Look at Two" dramatizes a hushed encounter between human lovers and animal lovers.

Frost returned to Amherst for 2 years in 1923 and to the University of Michigan in 1925 and then settled at Amherst in 1926.

West Running Brook (1928) continued Frost's tonal variations and mingling of lyrics and narratives. The lyric "Tree at My Window" appeared along with "Acquainted with the Night," a narrative of a despairing nightwalker in a city where time is "neither right nor wrong." The title poem, recalling John Donne, is a little drama of married lovers and their thoughts upon a stream that goes "by contraries," a stream that itself contains a contrary, a wave thrown back against the current by a rock, a "backward motion toward the source" that emblems the lovers' own tendency.

Frost visited England and Paris in 1928 and published his *Collected Poems* in 1930. In 1934 he suffered another excruciating loss in the death of his daughter Marjorie. He returned to Harvard in 1936 and in the same year published *A Further Range.*

This volume contains considerable social comment, but in the context of a worldwide depression some of it seemed oversimplified and untimely. "Two Tramps at Mud Time," however, puts men's need, and therefore right, to work in dramatically personal terms. "The Drumlin Woodchuck" recommends a distrustful defensiveness in order to survive for love; and "Departmental," another fable, satirizes bureaucracy through the antics of ants. "Build Soil—A Political Pastoral" recalls Virgil's First Eclogue. Frost's character Depression Tityrus declares, "I'd let things take their course And then I'd take the credit." Among the shorter pieces, several speak of inadequacy, disillusion, or malevolence—"Desert Places," "Neither Out Far Nor In Deep," "Provide, Provide," and "Design."

Later Work and Personal Tragedy

Honors, forebodings, and tragedies continued to crowd in on Frost. Because of his weak lungs, his doctor ordered him south in 1936, and thereafter he spent his winters in Florida. Frost served on the Harvard faculty during 1936-1937 and received an honorary doctorate. After his wife died of a heart attack in 1938, Frost resigned from the Amherst faculty and sold his house. That same year he was elected to the Board of Overseers of Harvard College. In 1939 his second *Collected Poems* appeared, and he began a 3-year stay at Harvard. In 1940 his only surviving son committed suicide.

A Witness Tree (1942) included the lyric "Happiness Makes Up in Height for What It Lacks in Length" and "Come In," in which the speaker prefers the guiding light of stars to the romantic dark of the woods and the song of an unseen bird. *Steeple Bush* (1947) contained the beautiful elegy of decay "Directive." The monologist visits an abandoned village where he used to live and, through allusions to the Holy Grail, converts the visit into a journey back toward a source, a stream beside which he administers communion to himself: "Drink and be whole again against confusion."

In 1945 Frost essayed something new in *A Masque of Reason,* a verse drama, too chatty for the stage. A modernization of the biblical story of Job, it is theistic and sets forth good-humoredly the Puritanic conviction that man, with his finite mind, must remain separate from God. *A Masque of Mercy* (1947), a companion verse drama based on the story of Jonah, has a heretical or individualistic air about it but still comes out essentially orthodox, suggesting that man with his limited knowledge must try to act justly and mercifully, for action is his salvation if it complies with God's will. "Nothing can make injustice just but mercy."

Frost's *Complete Poems* appeared in 1949, and in 1950 the U.S. Senate felicitated him on his seventy-fifth birthday. In 1957 he returned to England to receive doctoral degrees from Oxford and Cambridge. On his eighty-fifth birthday the Senate again felicitated him. In 1961, at the inauguration of John F. Kennedy, Frost recited "The Gift Outright," the first time a poet had honored a presidential inauguration. A final volume, *In the Clearing,* appeared in 1962.

On Jan. 29, 1963, Frost died in Boston of complications following an operation. He was buried in the family plot in Old Bennington, Vt. His "lover's quarrel with the world" was over.

Further Reading

Lawrence R. Thompson has completed the first two volumes of an official Frost biography, *Robert Frost,* vol. 1: *The Early Years, 1874-1915* (1966), and vol. 2: *Years of Triumph* (1970). A useful critical biography is Philip L. Gerber, *Robert Frost* (1967). Margaret Bartlett Anderson provides an informal view in *Robert Frost and John Bartlett: The Record of a Friendship* (1963). An interesting biography by a friend is Louis Mertins, *Robert Frost: Life and Talks-Walking* (1965). An account of Frost's trip to the Soviet Union is Franklin D. Reeve, *Robert Frost in Russia* (1964).

Two sound introductions are Lawrence R. Thompson, *Fire and Ice: The Art and Thought of Robert Frost* (1942), and Sidney Cox, *A Swinger of Birches* (1957). The poet Amy Lowell includes a discussion of Frost in *Tendencies in Modern American Poetry* (1917). Reuben A. Brower concentrates on poetic criticism in *The Poetry of Robert Frost* (1963). More specialized studies are John F. Lynen, *The Pastoral Art of Robert Frost* (1960); James M. Cox, ed., *Robert Frost: A Collection of Critical Essays* (1962), which contains varied critical assessments of Frost; and James R. Squires, *The Major Themes of Robert Frost* (1963). □

Roman Catholic Church. He viewed the Anglo-Catholic revival of the 19th century as a later clash between the same forces.

In *The English in Ireland in the 18th Century* (1872-1874) Froude continued to show his admiration for strong rulers and strong government. This work was anti-clerical and anti-Irish. He played down English atrocities and attempted to show that English efforts to conciliate the Irish had been futile. His admiration for heroic figures was also shown in his work glorifying imperialism, *Life of Caesar* (1879), and in his further defense of Henry VIII, *Catherine of Aragon* (1891).

At his best Froude presented impressive and powerful accounts of history, laying before the reader a picture of the past magnificently conceived and painted. His descriptive style was most notable in his shorter essays, *Short Studies on Great Subjects* (1867-1882). However, his inaccurate use of documents brought ridicule from other historians, notably Edward Freeman. Froude's later work was devoted chiefly to a biography of Thomas Carlyle (4 vols., 1882-1884) and a collection of Carlyle's papers (2 vols., 1881).

Froude returned to Oxford in 1892 as regius professor of modern history. He died at Kingsbridge, Devon, on Oct. 20, 1894.

Further Reading

The best book on Froude is Waldo Hilary Dunn, *James Anthony Froude: A Biography* (2 vols., 1961-1963), which is based on family papers discussing Froude's controversial nature. Her-

James Anthony Froude

The English historian James Anthony Froude (1818-1894) specialized in Reformation and Tudor studies. His work is characterized by vivid description and an orderly narrative style.

James Froude was born in Dartington, Devon, on April 23, 1818. He was educated at Westminster and Oriel colleges, Oxford, and was elected fellow of Exeter College, Oxford, in 1842. He joined the High Church movement at Oxford and helped John Henry Newman with his *Lives of the English Saints.* He became disillusioned with the High Church party after 1845, and, influenced by the ideas of Thomas Carlyle, his religious views shifted toward Protestantism. He resigned his fellowship in 1849.

The first two volumes of Froude's *History of England from the Fall of Wolsey to the Death of the Spanish Armada* appeared in 1856, with the remaining 10 volumes completed by 1870. In this work, which altered the whole direction of Tudor studies, Froude condemned the scientific treatment of history, for he saw history as a great drama with emphasis upon personalities. Unlike his historical predecessors, he portrays Henry VIII as a hero of considerable historical importance and Elizabeth I as a weak and uncertain ruler. The Reformation he saw as a struggle of the forces of liberty against the forces of darkness, as represented by the

bert W. Paul, *The Life of Froude* (1905), is a biographical sketch. Lytton Strachey, *Portraits in Miniature, and Other Essays* (1931), identifies Froude as a mid-Victorian personality strongly influenced by Carlyle. □

Mikhail Vasilievich Frunze

The Soviet military leader Mikhail Vasilievich Frunze (1885-1925) reformed the Red Army and guided the militarization of the former U.S.S.R.

Mikhail Frunze was born on Feb. 2, 1885, in Pishpek (renamed Frunze), Kirghizia, the son of a medical orderly. He attended the St. Petersburg Institute of Technology and joined the Bolshevik party in 1904. He was an active party member, and his revolutionary ardor earned him a sentence of 8 years at hard labor.

During the civil war years Frunze distinguished himself, first against Adm. A. V. Kolchak on the eastern front in 1919 and later against Gen. P. N. Wrangel on the southern front in 1920. In what was perhaps the most brilliant military victory of the civil war, Frunze ordered his men to wade through the shallow sea of the narrow Perekop Isthmus past Wrangel's sleeping White Army. Cannon, men, and cavalry all floated silently by the enemy, and in the morning Wrangel's men were dumb-founded to find themselves surrounded by the Red Army.

Frunze conceived the "unitary military doctrine," combining ideology, determination, and aggressiveness in the promotion of world revolution. In January 1921, 2 months after the close of the civil war, Frunze astounded war-weary Russia by calling for total Soviet militarization for the war of the future. In June 1925 the U.S.S.R. Congress of Soviets passed the momentous law ordering the total economic mobilization of the Soviet state. The continual growth of his program of peacetime preparedness played no small role in enabling the U.S.S.R. to become one of the world's greatest military powers.

Frunze was appointed deputy commissar for military affairs in March 1924 and succeeded Leon Trotsky as commissar for military affairs in January 1925. His influence on the development of the Red Army was of decisive importance, as he proceeded to regularize the military organization. He was responsible for the circulation in November 1924 of a declaration that defined the duties of both the military commanders and the political commissars, thus resolving the difficult problem of the unity of command. Field-service regulations were redrafted, and he systematized the duties of the conscript in a recruitment law that served as the basis of all such subsequent legislation until 1936. Frunze believed in the importance of a sound officers' corps and stimulated the development of a countrywide network of advanced military schools.

This rise in the military was paralleled by Frunze's ascent in the party. In 1921 he was elected to the Central Committee, and in 1924 he was made a deputy member of the Politburo.

The circumstances surrounding Mikhail Frunze's premature death on Oct. 31, 1925, are rather mysterious. Stalin summoned Frunze to Moscow, where he was ordered to undergo surgery for cancer, from which he never recovered. His successor as commissar was Stalin's old friend K. E. Voroshilov.

Further Reading

A recent biography of Frunze is Walter Darnell Jacobs, *Frunze: The Soviet Clausewitz, 1885-1925* (1970). Another excellent source is John Erickson, *The Soviet High Command: A Military-Political History, 1918-1941* (1962). See also Michel Gardner, *A History of the Soviet Army* (1959; trans. 1966). □

Elizabeth Fry

Elizabeth Fry (1780–1845) was a British reformer and Quaker lay evangelist, who worked for prison reform, particularly to relieve the physical misery and moral degradation of women prisoners.

An evangelist who relied on prayer and Bible-reading to inculcate virtue, Elizabeth Fry epitomized the reformer inspired by religious motives. She also relied on her access to the politically powerful, an advantage she enjoyed as a member of a well-connected Quaker family and enhanced by the celebrity status that she quickly attained through her prison visits. Her work on behalf of women prisoners caught the popular fancy, and she enjoyed a prestige in her country and in other European countries that few women in a society ruled by men could match. On the other hand, England soon rejected her approach to prison reform.

People worried about the increase in crime that had started with the Industrial Revolution; it had increased even more after the end of the long wars with France brought extensive unemployment. A combination of the 18th-century Enlightenment critique of traditional institutions and a humanitarianism largely rooted in Evangelical (and Quaker) religion encouraged a fresh look at crime and punishment.

Fry inspired confidence as a devout, motherly woman of unquestionable sincerity. Her prison visits belonged to a tradition of well-off, benevolent women visiting the unfortunate, a kind of unpaid social work. Helping women prisoners appeared to be a respectable philanthropy for pious women with time, energy, and money to spare. Although the Society of Friends had an English membership of less than 20,000 during Fry's lifetime, Quaker women took a disproportionate role in charity and reform.

Elizabeth Fry was born into a happy, prosperous family, the Gurneys, at Norwich in eastern England, blighted only by the early death of her mother. Her father's relaxed Quakerism abandoned many of the restrictions identified with that religion, such as the requirement to wear only

simple clothing and to avoid worldly society. She grew up enjoying fashionable parties and dances that earlier Quakers would have avoided. Some of her sisters would eventually withdraw from Quakerism to join the state Anglican Church, and her banker brothers would greatly add to the family riches.

Fry was in her teens in 1798 when an American member of the Society of Friends attacked the luxurious "gayness" of the local Quakers and awakened in Fry a sense of God that began her conversion to a strict Quakerism. This was not the common Evangelical conversion experience—a realization of guilt, followed by a sense of God's forgiveness—but instead a mystical communion with God. She never desired religious ceremonies or theology or a highly organized church. Her religion was a very personal one, founded on silent meditation, aided by the reading of the Bible, that sometimes led to informal but eloquent sermons. Virtually alone among religious denominations of the early 19th century, the small Society of Friends allowed women and men an equal right to speak at religious services because of the Quaker principle of direct inspiration.

Fry gradually adopted the strict Quaker policies on dress and Quaker peculiarities of speech (such as saying "thee" and "thou" instead of "you"). She became what contemporaries called a plain Friend. By 1799, she rejected singing as a distraction from true piety. (Her younger brother Joseph John Gurney followed her in reviving many of the old distinctive practices of the Quakers that separated them from other people; although as the leader of the Evangelical

Quakers, he encouraged good relations with all Evangelical Protestants.)

After her father's death in 1809, Fry began to speak at Quaker meetings and was recognized officially as a full minister two years later. Her marriage in 1800 to a London Quaker, Joseph Fry, delayed her wider public career; she bore ten children between 1801 and 1816 (and an 11th in 1822).

Although at the urging of an American Quaker she had visited Newgate Gaol (jail) in London during 1813, it was at the end of 1816 that Elizabeth Fry began her systematic work as a prison reformer. She visited many prisons in the British Isles during the following years, but she made her special mission the reform of the women imprisoned in Newgate. Approximately 300 women and children were crowded in a women's ward comprising 190 square yards. Hardened criminals guilty of serious crimes were mixed with those jailed for minor offenses. Children lived in the prison with their mothers, in rags, filth, and idleness. As the prison furnished no uniforms, many poverty-stricken women existed half-naked. Prison policy combined occasional brutality with a permissiveness that allowed inmates considerable freedom—tolerating drinking and fighting—and made no attempt at rehabilitation, such as training the women for jobs outside prison walls.

In 1817, Fry organized the Association for the Improvement of Female Prisoners in Newgate. Two members visited the prisoners every day to read the Scriptures aloud. When Fry read from the Bible (and preached) at Newgate, so many people wanted to attend that the London magistrates authorized her to issue tickets. Association members adopted a personal approach toward women prisoners and tried to gain their active cooperation through kindness and persuasion. Fry's association put the women prisoners to work, sewing and knitting, under the supervision of prisoner monitors. With a prisoner as the instructor, it also organized a school for the women (and their children) to teach them to read the Bible. One of Fry's rules for the Newgate women declared "that there be no begging, swearing, gaming, card-playing, quarrelling, or immoral conversation."

Fry's work was not confined to Newgate. In 1818, she made a tour of prisons in northern England and Scotland with her brother Joseph John Gurney, described in a book published under his name, *Notes on a Visit Made to Some of the Prisons in Scotland and the North of England in Company with Elizabeth Fry.* Middle-class ladies' committees sprang up to visit prisons all over the country. In 1821, they joined together as the British Ladies' Society for Promoting the Reformation of Female Prisoners.

Fry was an activist, not in most respects an original thinker. Ironically, most of her ideas resembled that of Jeremy Bentham, an earlier prison reformer who often is contrasted with Fry because he despised religion. Like Bentham, Fry favored classifying prisoners (in contrast to the prevalent mixing of all types), providing productive work for them, and establishing healthful living conditions. Her more distinctive opinions favored the employment of matrons to supervise women prisoners, rejected capital punishment (and flogging) in principle, minimized the role of unproductive hard labor such as working the treadmill, and repudiated bread-and-water diets. She tried, with modest success, to mitigate the sufferings of the women sentenced to transportation to Australia, a form of penal exile. Above all, she insisted that women criminals could be redeemed.

For a few years, Fry had the ear of Cabinet ministers and parliamentary committees, but she soon lost her influence. Overestimating what she could do, she offended those whom she wanted to persuade. This was the case in 1818 when she lobbied the Home Secretary, Lord Sidmouth, to stop the execution of a Newgate prisoner.

By 1827, when she published the short book *Observations on the Visiting, Superintendence and Government of Female Prisoners,* based on her practical experience, her time of importance had already passed. She continued to argue for the importance of local ladies' committees; the influence of public-spirited women was needed to supplement and correct the laws and regulations established by men. For the prisoners themselves, she urged the women visitors to show a spirit of mercy: "Great pity is due from us even to the greatest transgressors among our fellow-creatures."

Fry lost prestige (and money for her prison charities) when her husband's businesses failed in 1828. As a bankrupt, he was excluded from the Society of Friends, and the Fry family became dependent on the financial generosity of the wealthy Gurneys.

By the mid-1820s, other prison reformers increasingly advocated policies contrary to Elizabeth Fry's. Many Quakers (including two of her brothers-in-law) were prominent in the Society for the Improvement of Prison Discipline and the Reformation of Juvenile Reformers (founded in 1818), but after a brief period when it supported her, the Society lobbied for a centralized professional prison administration and detailed bureaucratic rules that left no place for the visits of "meddlesome" ladies' committees. Fry's rivals campaigned for the harsh prison policies pioneered in the United States at Philadelphia, such as solitary confinement and exhausting hard labor. These principles became law when Parliament adopted the Prison Act of 1835.

Although lacking any practical influence, Fry remained a celebrity, particularly on the continent of Europe. Acclaimed in 1838 and 1841 when she visited France and the German states, she was also honored in 1842 by the king of Prussia who visited her Bible-reading at Newgate and lunched at her home.

Two years after Elizabeth Fry died in 1845, two of her daughters published a *Memoir of the Life of Elizabeth Fry with Extracts from her Journal and Letters,* an abridgment in two volumes of her 44 volumes of handwritten journals. The *Memoir* sought to make Fry a saint and left out whatever the daughters regarded as not fitting that image. Until 1980, Fry's biographers failed to read the original journals.

Fry was not the perfect woman that her daughters presented. She embodied many contradictions. She adhered to a strict Quakerism that required plain living and the rejection of worldly vanities; yet, as some fellow Quakers grumbled, her simple clothes were cut from expensive fab-

rics, and she rejoiced in her opportunities to mingle with politicians, aristocrats, and royalty. Nothing was more important for her than her religion, yet, to her great anguish, she failed to nurture a commitment to Quakerism among her children, nearly all of whom left the Society of Friends when they grew up.

Despite her limitations, Elizabeth Fry deserves to be remembered as a genuinely good woman, as her contemporaries acknowledged, and a much wiser one than the men who belittled her as a naive amateur realized. In the early 19th century, women reformers were loved more often than they were respected. Although far from perfect, Fry's philosophy of prison reform avoided numbing bureaucracy and dehumanizing brutality and encouraged the participation of members of the general public in the conduct of prison life.

Further Reading

Cooper, Robert Allan. "Jeremy Bentham, Elizabeth Fry, and English Prison Reform," in *Journal of the History of Ideas.* Vol. 42. (1981): 675-90.
Dobash, Russell P., R. Emerson Dobash, and Sue Gutteridge. *The Imprisonment of Women.* Basil Blackwell, 1986.
Kent, John. *Elizabeth Fry.* B.T. Batsford, 1962.
Rose, June. *Elizabeth Fry.* Macmillan, 1980.
Ignatieff, Michael. *A Just Measure of Pain: The Penitentiary in the Industrial Revolution, 1750-1850.* Pantheon, 1978.
Isichei, Elizabeth. *Victorian Quakers.* Oxford University Press, 1970.
McConville, Sean. *A History of English Prison Administration, 1750-1877.* Vol 1. Routledge and Kegan Paul, 1981.
Prochaska, Frank K. *Women and Philanthropy in Nineteenth-Century England.* Clarendon Press, 1980.
Punshon, John. *Portrait in Grey: A Short History of the Quakers.* Quaker Home Services, 1984. □

William Henry Fry

William Henry Fry (1813-1864) was the first American to compose a publicly performed grand opera, a critic, and an early champion of American composers.

William Henry Fry was born in Philadelphia on Aug. 10, 1813, son of the publisher of the *Philadelphia National Gazette.* He is said to have learned to play the piano by listening to instructions given his elder brother. He began formal study of harmony and counterpoint early in the 1830s with a Paris Conservatory graduate in Philadelphia. In 1836 Fry became secretary of the Philharmonic Society (organized 3 years earlier) and began his career as a music critic, reviewing concerts and writing articles for his father's newspaper.

In 1841 Fry completed *Aurelia the Vestal,* an opera he had worked on some 4 years. When attempts to have it produced failed, he turned his attention to *Leonora,* which was to become his best-known work. This opera, with a libretto adapted from a play by Edward Bulwer-Lytton, had its world premiere on June 4, 1845, in Philadelphia. It ran for 12 performances and was well enough regarded by the Seguin Opera Company to warrant a four-performance revival the next year.

Fry himself did not witness the revival, since he had departed for Europe as regular correspondent for the *Philadelphia Public Ledger* and the *New York Tribune* early in 1846. He remained abroad, mostly in Paris, for more than 6 years, returning to America in 1862 as political and general editor, as well as music critic, of the *New York Tribune*.

In New York, Fry gave a remarkable series of lectures on music; in the last he bitterly attacked Americans for their indifference to their own composers, emphasizing the need to encourage homegrown creators.

A high point in Fry's career came in 1853, when Louis Antoine Jullien's orchestra played three of his symphonies: *A Day in the Country, The Breaking Heart,* and *Santa Claus.* At his farewell benefit of May 31, 1854, Jullien performed yet another, *Childe Harold.* Fry's most notable orchestral achievement was perhaps the overture to *Macbeth,* completed in 1862.

A considerably revised version of *Leonora* with Italian text was presented at the Academy of Music in New York in 1858 with indifferent success. Another opera, *Notre Dame de Paris,* was produced in Philadelphia in 1864. Fry also composed a *Stabat Mater,* a Mass, and shorter compositions. He died in Santa Cruz, West Indies, on Dec. 21, 1864.

Further Reading

William T. Upton, *William Henry Fry: American Journalist and Composer-Critic* (1954), is an adequate full-length treatment. A chapter in Irving Lowens, *Music and Musicians in Early America* (1964), is devoted to Fry's nationalism. The biographical sketch in Frédéric Louis Ritter, *Music in America* (1883), was furnished by one of Fry's brothers. The most detailed account of Fry in a standard music history is in John Tasker Howard, *Our American Music: A Comprehensive History from 1620 to the Present* (1931; 4th ed. 1965). □

Northrop Frye

Northrop Frye (1912-1991) was a Canadian literary scholar. His literary theories, which outlined a science of literary criticism based on a core of identifiable mythic forms, had unusual importance internationally, particularly in the late 1950s to late 1970s.

Herman Northrop Frye was born in Sherbrooke, Quebec, on July 14, 1912. After the failure of his father's hardware business, his family moved to Moncton, New Brunswick, where he completed his primary and secondary education. His skill as a typist brought him to Toronto to compete in an Underwood-sponsored contest in 1929. He enrolled in Victoria College of the University of Toronto.

While still an undergraduate, he developed a deep fascination with the complex poetic prophecies of William Blake, particularly *Milton, The Four Zoas,* and *Jerusalem,* considered by many scholars to be the product of an eccentric, possibly insane, visionary. In Frye's first year of graduate work, in which he took concurrent training as a minister for the United Church of Canada (primarily Methodist), Frye decided to write a definitive book on Blake which would break Blake's difficult symbolic code. This near obsession sustained him through two unhappy years of graduate work at Merton College, Oxford, where he studied with poet Edmund Blunden in 1936-1937 and 1938-1939, after which he taught English at Victoria College for over four decades.

Ten-Year Labor on Blake

Heavily influenced by British scholars of myth, particularly James Frazer, he worked diligently on the Blake book from 1934 to 1945, finally producing *Fearful Symmetry.* Published in 1947, it is still considered the definitive reading of Blake. It shows that Blake's poetic universe was not psychotically personal but had close affinities with other major poetry. Basically Frye proposed that all literature fit into a grand apocalyptic pattern of heaven and hell. Aspects of literary expression such as tragedy (the Fall), irony (unrelieved hell), romance (resurrection), and comedy (communal reconciliation) form an interconnected circular pattern analogous to the Last Judgment or the wheel of fortune motifs common in medieval art.

Because Frye considered that the ideas he developed through Blake were unusually relevant to literary theory generally, he wrote a series of articles in the early 1950s suggesting how academic critics and students of literature could greatly improve their comprehension of their subject. He suggested the development of a standard symbolic and rhetorical terminology similar to that of musical studies. He spurned any evaluative, aesthetic factors as too subjective. Although Frye himself primarily studied Shakespeare, Milton, Blake, Yeats, T. S. Eliot, and Wallace Stevens, he considered all literature relevant, including folk tales, detective novels, and science fiction. He combined his ideas for the reform of literary studies in *Anatomy of Criticism* (1957), probably the most influential book of criticism written in English in the 20th century. It has been translated into many languages.

Shaped Literature Teachings

While important, the *Anatomy of Criticism* is a difficult book intended for professional scholars. Frye produced a much simpler book for general readers, *The Educated Imagination,* in 1963. He also developed a strong populist interest in the 1960s in reforming the way literature was studied and taught in the schools. A major New York publisher produced a series of readers for grades seven to 12, *Uses of the Imagination,* based on Frye's ideas. Two college anthologies were also developed.

Found Bible Influenced Literature

While Frye hoped to write a sequel to the *Anatomy of Criticism,* he became too busy with the practical implications of his ideas to concentrate on it. In 1971 he finally settled on a book on the Bible's influence on English literature as a third major work. As with his first two major books, he took a decade to produce *The Great Code* (1982), and, like the others, it was both controversial and bestselling in university circles. It was even number two on the Canadian non-fiction bestselling list for six weeks. Frye's basic point was that the Bible has provided the basic patterns of symbolism and imagery for nearly all of the literature of western cultures. As a result, the Bible must be carefully read and studied by all students of literature. Frye then began work on a sequel, *Words with Power* (1990), showing how English literature has heavily borrowed its structural forms from the Bible.

Words with Power was the last of forty books of literary criticism written by Frye. The work is a study of the relationship of Biblical language to the language and thought of mythology, literature, and everyday life. "In the course of this book, as he reverses direction from secularizing sacred scriptures to spiritualizing secular ones, his own language moves from the descriptive, the conceptual and the rhetorical to the language of proclamation and prophecy," wrote Steven Marx of Cal Poly University. "This confirms a sense that he is returning to his early vocation as a preacher and also suggests that like the authors he prefers, in interpreting the Bible, Northrop Frye is remaking it his owns."

Prolific in Later Years

In addition to *Words with Power,* a large volume of Frye's work met the public following *The Great Code,* including *Divisions on a Ground* (1982), *The Myth of Deliverance: Reflections on Shakespeare's Comedies* (1983), *Northrop Frye on Shakespeare* (1986), *No Uncertain Sounds* (1988), *Northrop Frye on Education* (1988), *Myth and Metaphor: Selected Essays 1974-1988* (1990), *Reading the World-Selected Writings 1935- 1976* (1990), and *The Double Vision* (1991). *A World in a Grain of Sand: Twenty-two Interviews with Northrop Frye* was published in 1991.

Intellectual but Humane

Frye died in Toronto Jan. 23, 1991 of an apparent heart attack following a recent diagnosis of cancer. He was 78. Writing in *America,* July 6, 1991, on the occasion of Frye's death, former student John P. McIntyre remembered the professor's ability for "showing off his students, letting them know that they really were better than they knew.

"As a teacher, he basically made sense. Not only could he put things together effortlessly, but in the doing he easily persuaded us of its rationale." McIntyre seems to credit this to Frye's methodical approach to analyzing literature. "Frye, the teacher, insisted that the study of literature provided a structure of knowledge no less systematic than the multiplication or periodic table. He approached literature deductively by using myth, patterns of imagery and genres. But he also approached literature inductively by talking about stylistics."

Reviewer John Bemrose, writing in *Maclean's* on *The Correspondence of Northrop Frye and Helen Kemp,* discovered a side of Frye his students could not have known—that which nurtured the romance with his wife that lasted from their first meeting in 1931 until her death in 1986. "With their wit, robust energy, lovingness and playful brilliance, these love letters are among the most fascinating ever published in this country—and should banish forever the notion of Frye as an intellectual iceberg." Reviewing *Northrop Frye: A Biography,* also for *Maclean's,* Bemrose wrote, "Frye's works often seem so much the product of a brilliantly functioning mind that it is easy to forget there is a struggling human behind them."

To honor Frye and his work, The Northrop Frye Centre was established in 1988 at Victoria University in the University of Toronto. The goals of the centre are to encourage research in the human sciences and the dissemination of humanist scholarship. The centre offers a fellowship program as well as programs by which scholars may become visiting fellows or associates of the centre. *The Collected Works of Northrop Frye* is expected to be published by the University of Toronto Press in 32 volumes. Drawing on the vast collection of Frye's papers in the Pratt Library of Victoria College, the collection will include an extensive selection of unpublished works, diaries, letters, early essays, speeches, fiction, and notebooks.

Further Reading

While Frye was a notable prose stylist, his writing is conceptually dense and difficult. General readers can approach Frye best through *The Educated Imagination* (1963) or *The Modern Century* (1967). Robert D. Denham prepared a bibliography (1973) and wrote an analysis of *Anatomy of Criticism, Northrop Frye and Critical Method* (1978).

Additional Sources

Ayre, John, *Northrop Frye: A Biography* Random House, 1989.
Denham, Robert D., *The Correspondence of Northrop Frye and Helen Kemp, 1932-1939,* University of Toronto Press, 1996.
Adamson, Joseph, *Northrop Frye: A Visionary Life,* ECW Press, 1993.
Kirkwood, Hilda, "Frye at the Forum" *The Canadian Forum,* March, 1991, v69, n797, p15. □

Fuad I

Fuad I (1868-1936) was the first king of modern Egypt. He assumed power in 1917 as sultan of Egypt, signifying the legally subordinate position of Egypt within the Ottoman Empire.

On March 26, 1868, Ahmed Fuad was born in Giza, the youngest son of Ismail Pasha, the notorious khedive of Egypt. Ismail Pasha's policies of modernization and Europeanization ultimately led to the bankruptcy of Egypt, the increasing intervention of European powers in Egyptian affairs, the outbreak of the first Egyptian revolution in 1879, and the consequent prolonged British occupation of the country. Upon his deposition in 1879 Ismail was accompanied by members of his immediate family into exile in Italy, where Fuad was brought up and educated. As a result, he acquired considerable knowledge of European affairs and proficiency in several languages.

Fuad returned to reside permanently in Egypt in the 1890s and began his education in Egyptian politics as aide-de-camp to Khedive Abbas II. This was a period in which the British administrator Lord Cromer exercised autocratic power and official Egyptian rulers were in effect subordinate to him. The rising Egyptian national movement seeking the liberation of the country from external control was gathering momentum, but Fuad learned the necessity of reconciling Britain's interests with Egypt's national aspirations. Two things affecting Fuad deeply during this period were the recognition of Britain's ascendancy in Egyptian affairs, and a tendency to utilize methods of ruling and administration that were autocratic. These were to play an important role in his discharge of his constitutional functions once Egypt was declared an independent sovereign state.

Egypt Independent

In 1917 Fuad assumed power as sultan, and barely 2 years later Egypt's second revolution broke out, this time led by Egypt's national hero and statesman Saad Zaghlul. Fuad apparently took no part in the uprising or in the political discussions that ensued between the nationalists and the British occupation. The outcome of that revolution compelled the British to grant Egypt nominal independence in 1922 and to conclude a treaty of alliance and friendship between them. Thus the way was paved for the drafting and ratification of an Egyptian constitution promulgated by royal decree on April 19, 1923, and for Fuad's accession as king of Egypt.

Though Egypt theoretically became a constitutional monarchy, the Egyptian constitution vested considerable powers in the king. Fuad could and did initiate legislation, convene and dissolve the Parliament, and actively interfere in the civil and military affairs of the state. His tendency toward autocratic control and the need for a manipulatable supreme power as perceived by Britain led to his perennial clash with nationalist forces in the country led by the newly organized populist party, the Wafd. From 1923 until his death the political struggle in Egypt was essentially between the palace, frequently supported by the British embassy and military presence, and the Wafd party, representing the interests of the Egyptian people.

Constitutional Crisis

This struggle led to the dissolution of the Egyptian Parliament, dominated by the Wafd, in 1930, and the abolition of the first constitution and its replacement by another—again by royal decree—in the same year. The Parliament "elected" in 1931 in accordance with the new constitution was boycotted by the nationalist forces, and its unrepresentativeness was so blatant that considerable social and political discord emerged. Tension and autocratic rule ultimately resulted in counterpressures, and in 1934 the royal constitution was dropped in favor of the one of 1923.

New elections brought the Wafd back to power. During his last year Fuad, along with other national forces, concentrated his energy on revising the treaty relationship between Egypt and Britain, and the negotiations initiated by him and his Egyptian supporters finally paved the way for the conclusion of a more favorable treaty between Britain and Egypt which was signed by Farouk, Fuad's successor, in 1936.

Farouk was Fuad's only son and the fruit of his second marriage, to Nazli, in 1919; Fuad's daughter Fawziyyah was the first wife of the shah of Iran and was divorced in 1948. Fuad died on April 25, 1936.

Further Reading

Useful background studies on Egypt include Hisham B. Sharabi, *Governments and Politics of the Middle East in the Twentieth Century* (1962); Mahmud Y. Zayid, *Egypt's Struggle for Independence* (1965); and Tom Little, *Modern Egypt* (1967; first published as *Egypt* in 1958). □

Sir Vivian Fuchs

Vivian Fuchs (born 1908) led the British expedition that was the first to cross Antarctica from coast to coast.

Vivian Fuchs was born February 11, 1908, in the English county of Kent, the son of a farmer of German origin. He was educated at Cambridge University, where he studied geology. Between the years 1929 and 1938 he went on four geological expeditions to East Africa. During World War II he was a major in the British Army and served in West Africa and Germany and received several medals for bravery.

After the war, Fuchs was put in charge of the Falkland Islands Dependencies Survey in 1947. The Dependencies were a group of islands near Antarctica and included Britain's claim to part of the mainland of Antarctica. Fuchs set up scientific bases on the Graham Peninsula and was marooned in one of them for a year when the supply ship could not land because of weather conditions. During that time he conceived of a plan to fulfill Ernest Shackleton's dream of crossing Antarctica from coast to coast.

Fuchs's plan was carried out by the British Commonwealth Trans-Antarctic expedition as part of the activities of the International Geophysical Year in 1957-1958. The plan involved two parties. One, led by Fuchs, left Shackleton Base on the Filchner Ice Shelf on November 24,

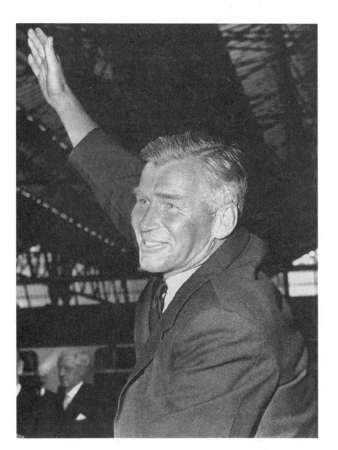

1957. In the meantime, a New Zealand team headed by Sir Edmund Hillary was establishing supply bases of food and fuel starting from McMurdo Sound on the other side of the continent.

Fuchs made slow progress in very bad conditions, with his heavy new Sno-Cat and Weasel vehicles frequently getting stuck in the snow. The British party had to cross a very dangerous region of crevasses at the place where the ice-shelf joined the Antarctic continent. Dog teams had to be sent ahead to find a safe route for the tractors, which were always in danger of falling into one of the crevasses. Furthermore, Fuchs's party was engaged in making seismic and gravity soundings all along their route, in order to determine the nature of the land underneath the Antarctic ice cap. This was extremely slow work although it was also extremely valuable. It showed, for example, that the ice reached depths of 9,000 feet and that there was a great valley at the South Pole. Establishing this information had been one of the main goals of the International Geophysical Year.

While Fuchs was engaged in this work, Hillary's teams made much faster progress. Originally, the New Zealand team had intended to go only as far as a place called Depot 700, 500 miles from the Pole, but Hillary continued on and reached the South Pole on January 3, 1958. He had made such good progress that he saw the possibility of completing the crossing himself. Early in January 1958, he radioed to London headquarters and to Fuchs to have Fuchs turn back in the face of the coming winter. This Fuchs refused to do. He carried on to the South Pole, which he reached on January 19, 1958. He was greeted enthusiastically by Hillary and the Americans who were stationed there at the Amundsen-Scott Base.

From the South Pole, Fuchs and Hillary continued on their very difficult trek as winter approached. They reached McMurdo Sound on March 2, 1958. It had taken Fuchs 90 days to cover the 2,180 miles from one side of Antarctica to the other. When they reached Scott Base in Victoria Land, Fuchs received word that he had been knighted as a result of his accomplishment. He and Hillary collaborated on writing the story of the expedition. Fuchs went on to be appointed director of the British Antarctic Survey in 1958 and headed it until his retirement in 1977.

Further Reading

The joint history of the Fuchs-Hillary expedition is *The Crossing of Antarctica* (London: Cassell, 1958). Fuchs later wrote a book about British activities in Antarctica and discussed his work there: *Of Ice and Men: The Story of the British Antarctic Survey, 1943-73* (London: Anthony Nelson, 1982). There is a good account of the Fuchs-Hillary expedition in Gerald Bowman, *Men of Antarctica* (New York: Fleet Publishing Corp., 1965) and in C.E.Fogg and David Smith, *The Explorations of Antarctica: The Last Unspoilt Continent* (London: Cassell, 1990). □

Carlos Fuentes

Carlos Fuentes (born 1928) was a Mexican short-story writer, novelist, essayist, and political writer whose works are a mixture of social protest, realism, psychological insight, and fantasy.

Carlos Fuentes was born on Nov. 11, 1928, in Mexico City. As the son of a Mexican diplomat, he went to school in Washington, D.C., where he became proficient in the English language. He held a law degree from the National University of Mexico and also studied at the Institute of Advanced International Studies in Geneva. He served in the Mexican diplomatic service and traveled in Cuba, Europe, the Soviet Union, the United States, and Latin America.

His first book, *Los días enmascarados* (1954; *The Masked Days*), consisted of a series of six stories in which the real world is mingled with the disquieting world of fantasy. He formed and directed, with Emmanuel Carballo, the *Revista méxicana de literatura* (1955-1958; *Mexican Review of Literature*). During 1956-1957 he held a scholarship at the Mexican Center for Writers.

Fuentes's first great novel, *La región más transparente* (1958; *Where the Air Is Clear*), caused a real sensation in literary circles and definitely established him as one of the best young writers. It portrays many grave social problems in contemporary Mexico City in a tone of bitter and violent

protest. The structure is developed by continuous juxtaposition of scenes from different social levels and from different epochs. Fuentes uses interior monologue and portrayal of the subconscious mixed with pages that resemble an essay more than a novel. His second novel, *Las buenas conciencias* (*The Good Conscience*), appeared in 1959. It undertakes a clarification of Mexican life in greater depth and broader perspective. It is a moral drama of Mexican society in which everyone appears both as victim and accomplice.

During 1959-1960 Fuentes edited *El espectador* (*The Spectator*). *Aura* (Dawn), a short novel, appeared in 1962, and that same year he saw the publication of *La muerte de Artemio Cruz* (*The Death of Artemio Cruz*). In this work Fuentes covers half a century of Mexican life, portraying the class which predominated in Mexico at the time, as represented by a man who took part in some of the skirmishes of the Revolution and, beginning in 1920, started to make a large fortune and acquire immense power. The death of this man and his 12 hours of agony constitute the theme of this novel. It was translated into numerous languages.

Fuentes's second volume of short stories, *Cantar de ciegos* (1964; *Song of the Blind*), is a synthesis of his literary worlds: magic, realistic, and humorous. In 1967 he won the Premio Biblioteca Breve, offered by the Seix Barral publishing company, for his novel *Cambio de piel* (*Change of Skin*).

Fuentes continued to write short stories, novels, plays, and essays which usually address political or social concerns of Mexico and central America. He was also an historian, of sorts, incorporating important figures of Mexican history into his fiction. Fuentes did this because it revealed Mexico—both past and present—to the world. He explained this view to George Kourous in *Montage*, "Mexico . . . made me understand that only in an act of the present can we make present the past as well as the future: to be a Mexican was to identify a hunger for being, a desire for dignity rooted in many forgotten centuries and in many centuries yet to come, but rooted, here, now, in the instant, in the vigilant time of Mexico."

Fuentes critical success reached new heights in 1975 with the release of *Terra nostra*. This novel about the evolution of Mexico earned Fuentes the Mexican Alfonso Reyes Prize. Fuentes's next fictions explored the spy novel and Mexico's place in the world. In 1985 Fuentes published *El Gringo Viejo,* a novel in which he combined an historical figure (American journalist Ambrose Bierce) with the supernatural, and Fuentes received some of the best reviews in his extensive literary career. Jane Fonda and Gregory Peck starred in a movie adaption of this novel.

Readers and critics both admired and despised Fuentes. Many critics cited his political views as a distraction to his literary talents; others wished he would focus only on writing fiction instead of exploring political commentary. Octavia Paz, one of Mexico's most recognized poets, was often an outspoken critic of Fuentes. However, his detractors did not prevent him from continually winning literary awards, including the Premio Cervantes in 1988.

In an interview in *Booklist* in 1996, Fuentes lamented the fact that in Mexico, "literature remains a minority affair.'' He was disappointed that culturally, the value of literature as its own entity does not exist. In 1997 in *World Press Review,* Fuentes claimed that Mexico had become the scapegoat for all of the problems in the United States. Throughout his career, Fuentes wrote his views and his opinions, not caring who he pleased or who he offended. Through all of this, the only consistent classification he has earned is the reputation as a master narrator. Fuentes himself challenged his critics, "Don't classify me, read me. I'm a writer, not a genre. Do not look for the purity of the novel according to some nostalgic canon.'' According to Fuentes, the canon, the collected body of prized literary works, needed to include more multicultural authors and texts. Because of his contributions to journalism, fiction, and non-fiction, Fuentes became an influential Hispanic writer who has expanded the literary canon.

Further Reading

Chalene Helmuth, *The Postmodern Fuentes,* Bucknell University Press, 1997, provides a contemporary analysis of Fuentes's work. Raymond L. Williams, *The Writings of Carlos Fuentes: History, Culture, and Identity,* Unviersity of Texas Press, 1996, provides a more complete overview of the writer. Fuentes was interviewed in *Publisher's Weekly,* October 25, 1991; *Montage,* September 1994; and *Booklist,* September 15, 1996. □

Athol Fugard

Athol Fugard (born 1932) was a South African playwright known for his subtle, poignant descriptions of the racial problems in his country.

Athol Fugard was born on June 11, 1932, in Middelburgh, a small village in the Karroo district in South Africa, of an English-speaking father and an Afrikaner mother. When he was three years old the family moved to Port Elizabeth, an industrial city on the Indian Ocean coast where Fugard was to spend, off and on, most of his life, and where he was to set most of his plays. He began his higher education studying motor mechanics at the technical college, but he transfered to Cape Town University to study philosophy and social anthropology.

Merchant Seaman

After three years he quit school, deciding instead to hitchhike up the African continent. He became a merchant seaman in North Africa and spent two years sailing around the Far East. In 1956 he returned to Port Elizabeth and found a job writing news bulletins for the South Africa Broadcasting Corporation. That year he also married Sheila Meiring, an actress. Together they started an experimental theater group for which Fugard wrote plays. In 1958 the couple went to Johannesburg, where Fugard secured a clerical position in the Native Commissioner's Court. It was while in Johannesburg that he made his first black friends and be-

came fully aware of the extent of the racial problems in his country.

Fugard drew on his experiences in the slums of Johannesburg to write his first full-length play, *No-Good Friday* (1959). His second play came out that same year; titled *Nongogo (A Woman for Twenty-Five Cents),* an account of a woman who had been a mineworker's whore. Following the production of the second play, Fugard obtained his first paying position in the theater as a stage manager in the National Theatre Organisation.

His first major play, *The Blood Knot,* was written in 1961. It is set in Korsten, a non-white slum near a factory area in Port Elizabeth, and concerns two brothers: Morrie, who is somewhat educated and light skinned enough to pass for white, though he chooses not to, and Zach, who is illiterate and dark skinned. The conflict between the two brothers, who live together, begins when Zach somehow acquires a pen-pal who turns out to be a white girl. He wants to meet her but cannot, and Morrie could meet her but does not want to.

The Blood Knot later became part of a triology known as *The Family.* The two other plays include *Hello and Goodbye* (1969) and *Boesman and Lena* (1969). These plays also deal with destitution in Port Elizabeth. *Hello and Goodbye* takes place on Valley Road, a poor white area near the center of town. It is about Hester Smit, a woman who returns after a long absence to claim money that she thought had been paid to her father after a crippling industrial accident. Her brother, Johnnie, experiences some difficulty in explaining to her that their father is dead and that the money was never paid. *Boesman and Lena* is about a black couple evicted from their home and forced to live in the mudflats near the Swartkops River. The play depicts the depths to which human existence can descend.

After *The Blood Knot* appeared, the South African government passed harsh censorship laws that forbade racially mixed casts and/or audiences in theaters. When the English television network BBC broadcast *The Blood Knot* in 1967 the South African government confiscated Fugard's passport for four years. He was not allowed to leave the country until 1971 when he went to London to direct *Boesman and Lena* at the Royal Court Theatre, where most of his plays have since been performed.

Politics without Dogma

The primary strength of Fugard's work lies in the way in which his works convey strong political messages without being dogmatic. He chose plays as his medium of speech because he felt that the theater enabled him to reach the largest number of people. His messages were discreet enough that his plays could be performed in South Africa, yet strong enough to have an important impact on the audience. While his plays were not explicitly anti-apartheid, the sorrows that arise in them do so as a result of apartheid. He said of his writing, "The sense I have of myself is that of a 'regional' writer with the themes, textures, acts of celebrations, of defiance and outrage that go with the South African experience. These are the only things I have been able to write about."

In 1974 Fugard published three plays. *Sizwe Bansi is Dead* is about a photographer, Styles, who wants to take a picture of Sizwe Bansi, a black whose work permit has been cancelled. Bansi, however, decides to exchange his identity for that of a corpse he finds in a ditch. *The Island* is about two black political prisoners, John and Winston, who share a cell on Robben Island. While they rehearse for a camp production of Sophocles' *Antigone,* they are struck with the contemporary relevance of the tragedy's message against tyranny. *Statements after an Arrest under the Immorality Act* depicts an affair between a white librarian and a black schoolteacher who are denounced to the police by their neighbors.

Appeared on Stage

Fugard's later works include *A Lesson from Aloes* (1978), *Master Harold . . . and the Boys,* perhaps his finest work (1982), and *The Road to Mecca* (1984). He also published a novel, *Isoti* (1979), based on notes taken on a voyage back from Europe in 1960. More recent plays are *A Place with the Pigs* (1987), *My Children! My Africa!* (1989), and *Playland* (1993). He published another novel, *Tsotsi* (1980), as well as film scripts. Fugard often directed and acted in his plays, as he did with 1995 and 1996 productions of *Valley Song*. In the play, Fugard played the character of the black grandfather, Jonkers, and the autobiographical character of the white author. Fugard stipulated that in subsequent productions, the two characters must be played by the same actor.

The stage was something of a pulpit for Fugard, and the actors in his plays preach with an artistic subtlety against the evils of apartheid. In *My Children! My Africa!,* friendship, idealism, and a young life are lost in the volatile political climate created by apartheid. In the mind of the public, Fugard's politics sometimes overshadowed the art of his plays. Writing in *Time* in 1994, William A. Henry III commented, "In his mind he is a poetic playwright, but the world has seen him as a political, even polemic one, and his works are valued more as a testimony against apartheid than for their subtle interplay of emotion and Beckettian sensitivity to the downtrodden."

Nelson Mandela biographer Mary Benson celebrated the lives of Fugard and another close friend, the late South African playwright Barney Simon, in her book *Athol Fugard and Barney Simon: Bare Stage, a Few Props, Great Theatre.* The subtitle came from a 1963 letter to Benson from Fugard describing plans for an upcoming production. Benson maintained the work of both playwrights could not be characterized simply as "protest theater." Speaking of her book to an interviewer, Benson remembered an interview once given by Simon. "He said, we should be going into people's lives, their souls, their ways of life. And if it brings in aspects of the struggle then that's okay. But it's good if it can go beyond just protesting the horrors, and inspire people to function constructively."

Though he traveled to direct and act in his plays, Fugard generally wrote when he was home in South Africa. During his later years he lived in his longtime home of Port Elizabeth.

Further Reading

Fugard is listed in *The Modern Encyclopedia of World Drama* (1984). A synopsis of South African theater that places Fugard in the context of his intellectual predecessors can be found in *The Oxford Companion to the Theatre* (1967). Selected portions of his journals are published under the title *Notebooks 1960-1967* (1983), edited by Mary Benson.

Additional Sources

Read, John, *Athol Fugard: A Bibliography,* National English Literary Museum, 1991. □

Alberto Keinya Fujimori

Alberto Keinya Fujimori (born 1938) was inaugurated president of Peru on his 52nd birthday, becoming the first person of East Asian descent to lead an American republic.

F ujimori was born in Lima on July 28, 1938—Peru's Independence Day. His parents, Naochi and Matsue Fujimori, had emigrated four years earlier from Shiyajama, Japan, to Peru, where they initially worked as agricultural field hands. This was an especially difficult period for Peru's 17,000-member Japanese community, which often faced racial hostility. During World War II Peru sent nearly 1,800 persons of Japanese extraction (many of them native-born Peruvian citizens) to the United States for internment.

The future president and his two brothers and two sisters were raised in La Victoria, a working-class district of Lima, and attended public schools. The valedictorian of his high school class, Fujimori in 1956 achieved the top score on the examination for admission to Peru's prestigious La Molina National Agrarian University. He graduated at the very top of the agricultural engineering program in 1961. The following year he returned to La Molina as a professor of mathematics. Fujimori received post-graduate training at the University of Strasbourg in France and in the United States, earning a Master's degree in mathematics from the University of Wisconsin at Madison in 1969. He was awarded honorary doctorates by the universities of Glebloux in Belgium and San Martin de Porres in Peru. Widely traveled in Peru and abroad, Fujimori spoke Spanish, Japanese, English, French, and German.

In 1984, shortly after becoming dean of the Faculty of Sciences at La Molina, that university's assembly elected him rector (president) of the school for a five-year term. The rectors of Peru's 30 other national universities chose Fujimori president of their council for the period 1987-1989.

Two years before the 1990 general election, Fujimori and several other politically independent professionals and businessmen founded the Cambio 90 (Change 90) move-

ment as a vehicle for their participation in the contest. Meanwhile, Fujimori increased his public visibility as the host of "Getting Together," a radio program devoted to public affairs. In this capacity he demonstrated his awareness of important issues and a notable ability to foster understanding among guests with opposing views.

The victor in Peru's 1990 presidential election would face a nearly impossible challenge. A $20-billion foreign debt had not been serviced regularly in several years. Peru's domestic economy was near collapse. A ten-year war with the Sendero Luminoso (Shining Path) guerrillas, fanatical Maoists, had taken 20,000 lives. International drug traffickers had established a powerful presence within the country. Nevertheless, nine candidates vied for the presidency.

For several months prior to the vote, internationally renowned novelist Mario Vargas Llosa, representing the conservative Democratic Front (Fredemo) coalition, was heavily favored to win. He seemed likely to trounce his mainly leftist challengers and achieve the 50 percent plurality required for direct election in the April 8 first round of balloting. But he frightened many citizens with his plan to attack the huge budget deficit and 3,500 percent inflation with a quick "shock therapy," which included the elimination of subsidies for staple foods, fuel, and utilities, and the firing of thousands of government workers. In the final months of the campaign Fujimori, a self-styled centrist whose "plan" consisted of little more than the slogan "honesty, hard work, and technology," surged from an obscure four percent standing in the polls to within three points of Vargas Llosa's 27 percent first-place finish, forcing a runoff.

In the second contest Fujimori charged that Vargas Llosa's "shock" would place too large a burden on poor Peruvians. He promised more gradual remedies for the nation's economic ills. Fujimori also criticized his opponent's emphasis on military solutions to the guerrilla and drug problems. The Cambio 90 candidate proposed to undercut support for the insurgents through economic development and to wean peasants away from the cultivation of coca (the source of cocaine) with a program of crop substitution.

On the June 8 election day, Fujimori won most of the votes that had gone to candidates eliminated in the first round, garnering 56.5 percent of the total to 34 percent for Vargas Llosa. Analysts noted that the light-skinned members of Peru's elite and middle-class voted heavily for Vargas Llosa, while Fujimori was favored by working-class citizens of Indian ancestry. Although himself a Roman Catholic, Fujimori received crucial support from the nation's small evangelical Christian community, whose members canvassed for him, missionary-like, door to door.

President Fujimori was inaugurated on July 28, 1990. He asserted in his inaugural address that he had inherited a "disaster" from his predecessor, Alan Garcia Pérez. The new administration quickly introduced its own economic "shock." The prices of many basic foods doubled and tripled overnight, while the cost of gasoline (which had been subsidized at seven cents per gallon) increased nearly 30-fold. Rioting occurred throughout the country, and Peru's major labor federations staged general strikes. Fujimori's popularity plummeted along with the purchasing power of civilians. But the spiraling rate of inflation slowed, allowing the administration to implement its other programs for economic recovery. Fujimori's autogolpe (self-coup) abolished Peru's constitution, Congress, and Supreme Court. It was after this point that he seized complete power. Undaunted amidst remarks of being a dictator, Fujimori insists that his leadership is within the realms of democracy.

Nicknamed "El Chinito" (The Little Asian) by the public, the diminutive and soft-spoken Fujimori held a black belt in karate and traced his ancestry to Samurai warriors. He was married in 1974 to civil engineer Susana Higuchi. They had four children. During his first term in office, Susana Higuchi became Fujimori's most vocal adversary. She announced in 1994 that she would seek office in an attempt to defeat him. Fujimori passed Peruvian law which prohibited her from running for office on the grounds that she was related to him. Their marriage ended with her being banned from the palace. Fujimori won the election in 1995 by a landslide.

In December of 1996 Peru and Fujimori became the center of attention once again as hundreds of foreign dignitaries were held hostage in the Japanese ambassador's mansion by an armed group of Tupac Amaru guerrillas. The hostage stance lasted for months, with the entire world waiting for a move to be made. On April 22, 1997, the seize ended when Peruvian commandos stormed the mansion. The resulting gunfire and ambush freed all remaining hostages and killed the 14 guerillas.

Further Reading

More information about Alberto Fujimori's Peru can be found in C. Harvey Gardiner, *The Japanese and Peru, 1873-1973* (1975); Felipe Ortiz de Zevallos, *The Peruvian Puzzle* (1989); Edmundo Morales, *Cocaine: White Gold Rush in Peru* (1989); and Gabriela Tarazona-Sevillano, *Sendero Luminoso and the Threat of Narcoterrorism* (1990). "President Alberto Fujimori—Talks Still Young," *The Indonesian Times* (1997). □

Fujiwara Kamatari

Fujiwara Kamatari (614-669) was the founder of the Fujiwara clan, which was influential in the Japanese imperial court for many centuries. He was instrumental in instituting the reform of the Taika era and establishing an imperial central government.

Originally surnamed Nakatomi, Fujiwara Kamatari was also known as Kamako. The Nakatomi clan was traditionally charged with Shinto priestly functions. Kamatari, together with the Mononobes, opposed the introduction and propagation of Buddhism in Japan and feuded with the Sogas, who became champions of Buddhism. Allied with Prince Naka-no oe (later Emperor Tenchi), Kamatari carefully planned to eliminate Soga-no

Iruka and Soga-no Emishi, who wielded great power in the imperial court.

In 645, taking advantage of the court function of receiving a Korean envoy, Prince Naka-no oe and Kamatari killed Iruka and Emishi. Emperor Kotoku ascended the throne in the same year and appointed Kamatari minister of the interior. Kamatari then initiated and carried out the reform of the Taika (great transformation) era.

The great nobles were summoned to the court, and the doctrine of absolute monarchy was proclaimed. Then followed certain practical measures, such as registration of households, the survey of arable land, rules for the supervision of monks and nuns, and some procedure for settling claims.

Taika Reform

In the second year of the Taika era, 646, the celebrated *kaishin-no cho,* or Reform Edict, was proclaimed. It consisted of four simple articles: Article I abolished private title to land and workers acquired by the formation of "namesake" or "succession" estates or by other means of appropriation. Article II established a metropolitan regime, called the *kinai,* or Inner Provinces, to include the center of government in a capital city; communications with the outer provinces were to be improved, and governors of provinces and districts within the *kinai* were to be appointed. Article III ordered the institution of registers of population, with a view to the allotment of rice land to cultivators on an equitable basis, and provided for the appointment of rural headmen. Article IV abolished old taxes and contributions of forced labor and introduced a new system of taxation.

After Emperor Tenchi ascended the throne, Fujiwara Kamatari also codified existing laws. Because of the location of the imperial palace at Otsu (Omi Province), the laws were called Omi laws. In the second year of Emperor Tenchi's reign, Kamatari was taken ill, and when his condition became serious, the Emperor appointed him minister of the left and conferred upon him the rank of *taishokukan,* the highest court rank, and the family name of Fujiwara.

Further Reading

The relationship between Emperor Tenchi and "Fujiwara-no Daijin," as Fujiwara Kamatari is sometimes called, is discussed in W. G. Aston's translation of *Nihongi: Chronicles of Japan from the Earliest Times to A.D. 697* (1956). The Taika era of reform and Kamatari's role in it are discussed in Ryusaku Tsunoda and others, *Sources of Japanese Tradition* (1958). There is an incisive analysis of the Taika reform and Kamatari's contributions in Sir George B. Sansom, *A History of Japan,* vol. 1 (1958). □

Fujiwara Michinaga

The Japanese noble Fujiwara Michinaga (966-1027) was one of the most powerful statesmen in the Heian period. Through his family, especially his daughters,

he exercised virtually complete control over the imperial court.

Fujiwara Michinaga was a son of Kaneiye, a powerful member of the Fujiwara clan who, as regent, had consolidated the power of the Fujiwaras. After Michinaga's elder brothers, Michitaka and Michikane, died young, he became the most powerful member of the Fujiwara clan. Michinaga caused his nephew, Korechika, and Korechika's younger brother, Takaiye, to be exiled. After being appointed Minister of the Left, he persuaded the emperor Ichijo to demote his consort, Sadako, the daughter of Michitaka, to the newly established rank of *chūgū* (consort below the empress) and make Akiko, his own daughter, the empress. It was the first time in the Heian court that the *chūgū* and *kōgō* (empress) stood side by side.

In this period of Japanese history, maternal relatives of the imperial family exercised great political power. Families with blood connections with the reigning house of Japan often occupied mansions of greater splendor than the palace of the emperors, but they also frequently contributed to the preservation of the imperial house and the protection of the throne.

Upon the death of Emperor Ichijo in 1011, Emperor Sanjo (reigned 1011-1016) ascended the throne. Michinaga made another daughter of his lady-in-waiting to the Empress. When the Emperor suffered from a disease of the eye, Michinaga used it as an excuse to force him to abdicate. Emperor Sanjo was succeeded by Emperor Goichijo (1016), a son of Michinaga's daughter. Michinaga was thus the maternal grandfather of the Emperor and thereafter acted much like a *kampaku* (adviser to the emperor).

Michinaga became *dajo daijin* (chancellor) in 1017 and made his son, Yorimichi, *sesshō* (regent); his daughter, Takeko, was made *chūgū* of Emperor Goichijo, and Michinaga thus enjoyed unrivaled prestige and power at the court. He was so powerful a figure that no one in the court dared criticize him.

Though Michinaga turned out to be the most powerful of the Fujiwara regents, his claim to the highest office was not strong on grounds of birth and court rank. He was obviously fortunate in that his older brothers died young and that he had several beautiful and strong-willed daughters. But he was a very adroit politician who knew how to deal with both friends and enemies.

Being alert to the changes that were taking place in the country, he foresaw the rise of the military families, who were then just beginning to dominate provincial life. Early in his career he allied himself with certain members of the Minamoto clan, by whose talents he was impressed, and it was their presence in the background that enabled him in the early days of his rise to power to defeat or intimidate his rivals.

Further Reading

For illuminating interpretations of the life and times of Fujiwara Michinaga see Sir George B. Sansom, *A History of Japan,* vol.

1 (1958). Some relevant facts are provided in Jean and Robert K. Reischauer, *Early Japanese History* (2 vols., 1937). ☐

Francis Fukuyama

A foreign policy expert and proponent of liberal democracy, philosopher Francis Fukuyama (born 1952) gained wide fame for his thesis that the present time may be "the end of history."

Francis Fukuyama was born October 27, 1952, in the Hyde Park neighborhood of Chicago. His father, Yoshio Fukuyama, a second-generation Japanese American, was trained as a minister in the Congregational Church and received a doctorate in sociology from the University of Chicago. His mother, Toshiko Kawata Fukuyama, was born in Kyoto, Japan, and was the daughter of Shiro Kawata, founder of the Economics Department of Kyoto University and first president of Osaka Municipal University in Osaka, Japan. Fukuyama's childhood years were spent in New York City. In 1967 his family moved to State College, Pennsylvania, where he attended high school.

Fukuyama received his B.A. in classics in 1974 from Cornell University where he studied under Allan Bloom. After spending a year in the Yale University Department of Comparative Literature in 1974-1975, he went on to receive his Ph.D. in political science from Harvard University in 1981, writing a dissertation on Soviet foreign policy.

RAND Researcher

Fukuyama was a member of the Political Science Department of the RAND Corporation, one of the oldest American "think tanks," researching public policy in Santa Monica, California, from 1979 to 1980, and then again from 1983 to 1989. There he did research on a variety of defense and foreign policy issues concerning the Middle East, East Asia, and elsewhere. In this period he wrote widely on Soviet foreign policy and regional security issues and edited the book *The Soviet Union and the Third World: The Last Three Decades* (with Andrzej Korbonski, 1987). Fukuyama was also a guest lecturer at the University of California, Los Angeles, during this time.

In 1981 and 1982 Fukuyama was a member of the Policy Planning Staff of the U.S. Department of State where he worked on Middle Eastern issues and served as a member of the U.S. delegation to the Israeli-Egyptian talks on Palestinian autonomy. He returned to the Policy Planning Staff in 1989, this time as deputy director for European political-military affairs.

While working on the Policy Planning Staff in 1989, Fukuyama published an essay entitled "The End of History?" in a small foreign policy journal, *The National Interest*. This essay suggested that with the spread of liberal political and economic ideas throughout the communist world and in much of the Third World, mankind had reached the end of its ideological evolutionary process. While history in the ordinary sense of "events"—even such important events as wars and revolutions—would continue, "history" in its Hegelian-Marxist sense of a broad evolution of human societies had reached its culmination not in socialism but in the ideals of the French and American revolutions.

Article Sparked Debate

The *National Interest* article, coming as it did five months before the fall of the Berlin Wall, sparked an extraordinary amount of debate and controversy both in the United States and abroad. Critics on the left argued that socialism remained a viable alternative; critics on the right charged that communism was still dangerous; and others said that the article underestimated the forces of religion and nationalism in the contemporary world.

After leaving the State Department in 1990, Fukuyama expanded the themes in the *National Interest* article into the book *The End of History and the Last Man*. Published in 1992, this book was translated into over 20 different languages. The American edition was awarded the Los Angeles Times Book Critics Award, and the Italian edition won the Premio Capri.

The End of History and the Last Man poses the question of whether it makes sense at the close of the 20th century to reconsider the possibility of writing a "universal history" of human development that in some way culminates in liberal democracy. Such a universal history—that is, a broad account of human social and political evolution, taking into account the experiences of all peoples in all times—was proposed by Kant, and versions were written by Hegel and Marx, among others. *The End of History and the Last Man* argues that there is in fact ground for such a project, based on two underlying forces driving the historical process: "modern natural science and the struggle for recognition." It concludes, however, on a more somber note. While many of the usually noted failings of contemporary liberal democracy (e.g., crime, poverty, racism, economic inequality, and the like) involve failure in the implementation of liberal principles rather than in the goodness of those principles themselves, the problem of the "last man"—that is, the individual whose horizons extend no further than the "equal recognition" that is the underlying ideal of modern democracy—is inherently unsolvable on the grounds of liberal principles.

Trust Essential to Prosperity

In his 1995 book *Trust: The Social Virtues and the Creation of Prosperity,* Fukuyama articulated the belief that faith in one's trading partners is necessary for commerce to prosper. "People who do not trust one another will end up cooperating only under a system of formal rules and regulations, which have been negotiated, agreed to, litigated, and enforced, sometimes by coercive means . . . Widespread distrust in a society, in other words, imposes a kind of tax on all forms of economic activity, a tax that high-trust societies do not have to pay," he wrote. In discussing his theories on trust with *Forbes,* Fukuyama noted the implications of trust,

or the lack thereof, for electronic commerce and the "virtual corporation" said to be a developing phenomenon of the Internet. "I resist the idea put forth by some of the information revolution enthusiasts that the technology itself will create communities. Obviously there's something to that in the way that it can empower people to communicate that's not dependent on geography. But trust relationships and the existing social networks remain basic to the success of computer networks."

From his home in McLean, Virginia, Fukuyama served as a resident consultant to the RAND Corporation in Washington, D.C. He was Hirst Professor of Public Policy at George Mason University. In 1986 he married Laura Holmgren, and they had three children, Julia, David, and John. He was a member of the American Association for the Advancement of Slavic Studies and of the Council on Foreign Relations.

Further Reading

For an introduction to the Hegelian source of Fukuyama's views, see Alexandre Kojève, *Introduction to the Reading of Hegel* (1969), and Leo Strauss, *On Tyranny, Including the Strauss-Kojève Correspondence* (1991). For an introduction to Kojève's Hegelianism, see Allan Bloom, "Alexander Kojève," in *Giants and Dwarfs* (1990). Also see Burns, Timothy, *After History?: Francis Fukuyama and His Critics,* Rowman and Littlefield, c1994. □

James William Fulbright

James William Fulbright (1905-1995) was as educator and politician, who, while a United States senator, sponsored the Fulbright Act of 1946, providing funds for the exchange of students, scholars, and teachers between the United States and other countries.

William Fulbright, politician, lawyer, educator, and writer, was born on April 9, 1905, in Sumner, Missouri. He received his bachelor of arts degree at the University of Arkansas in 1925. Attending Oxford University as a Rhodes scholar, he won a bachelor of arts degree (1928) and a master of arts degree (1931). During the following year's tour of Europe he developed his interest in international affairs. In 1932 he married Elizabeth Williams, and they had two daughters. George Washington University awarded Fulbright a bachelor of laws degree in 1934. After serving as a special attorney in the antitrust division of the U.S. Department of Justice (1934-1935), he joined the faculties of George Washington University (1935-1936) and the University of Arkansas (1936-1939). Fulbright served as president of the University of Arkansas from 1939 to 1941.

A member of the Democratic party, Fulbright entered the U.S. Congress as an Arkansas representative in 1943 during World War II. That September the House of Representatives adopted the Fulbright resolution that favored creation of the "appropriate international machinery with power adequate to establish and to maintain a just and lasting peace," as well as United States participation in that effort. Fulbright entered the Senate in 1944 and gained much influence during his long tenure (1959-1974) as chairman of the Senate Committee on Foreign Relations.

The Mutual Educational Exchange Program

The Mutual Educational Exchange Program, the Fulbright Act, was established by the U.S. Congress on August 1, 1946. This legislation authorized the use of U.S.-owned foreign currencies obtained from the sale of post-war surplus military equipment to finance grants for Americans to study, teach, or conduct research abroad, as well as for foreign citizens to study in the U.S. Since 1949 more than 100,000 nationals have participated in these exchange programs. It was later administered under the Mutual Educational and Cultural Exchange Act of 1961 which provides the legislative authority for the program. The main objective of this Act is "to enable the government of the United States to increase mutual understanding between the people of the United States and the people of other countries . . . and thus to assist in the development of friendly, sympathetic, and peaceful relations between the United States and other countries of the world." The program operates in more than 135 countries and binational commissions were established by executive agreements in 43 countries. The J. William Fulbright Foreign Scholarship Board (BFS) in Washington,

D.C. is composed of 12 educational and public leaders appointed by the President of the United States. It has statutory responsibility for the selection of all academic exchange grantees, the establishment of policies and procedures, and the supervision of the Fulbright Program worldwide.

Fulbright's Influence on Foreign Relations

Fulbright rose to prominence as a member of the Senate Banking and Currency Committee and the Foreign Relations Committee. As chairman of the former committee he conducted an investigation of the stock market in 1955. But Fulbright emerged primarily as one of the Senate's leading critics of American foreign policy, which he believed to be unnecessarily rigid and unproductive. In 1959, becoming chairman of the Foreign Relations Committee, Fulbright urged Congress to widen the scope of executive action and criticized the State Department for its rigidity in negotiations with the Communist powers. On domestic issues Fulbright remained moderate; on civil rights he was orthodox from a Southern point of view, yet without a trace of bigotry.

As a U.S. senator, Fulbright gained much influence during his long tenure (1959-1974) as chairman of the Senate Committee on Foreign Relations. He became a leading critic of U.S. foreign policy, particularly of U.S. involvement in the Vietnam War. By 1963 the problem of Vietnam was beginning to dominate America's external affairs. Long convinced that American fears of communism were being transformed into a positively antirevolutionary posture in Asia, Africa, and Latin America, Fulbright attempted to curb the foreign interventions of the Lyndon Johnson administration. In his 1965 committee hearings on Johnson's decision to send troops into the Dominican Republic, he argued that the President's advisors had exaggerated Communist participation in the Dominican revolution. In 1966 Fulbright's committee conducted a search investigating U.S. involvement in Vietnam and held hearings on U.S. relations with China. Eventually he denied the President's right to send American forces into hostilities without congressional approval. Despite his attacks on the Vietnam War, Fulbright won his fifth term as senator in 1968 with a surprising 59 percent of the Arkansas vote.

During the mid-1960s Fulbright published his foreign policy views in *Prospects for the West* (1963), *Old Myths and New Realities* (1964), and *The Arrogance of Power* (1967). Running for his sixth term as senator in 1974, Fulbright was defeated in the Arkansas Democratic primary, and he resigned from the U.S. Senate at the end of the year.

U.S.-Polish Educational Exchanges

The Office for U.S.-Polish Educational Exchanges was established on March 22, 1990, after a binational agreement was signed between the governments of Poland and the United States, later known as the Polish-U.S. Fulbright Commission. The Commission's mission is to offer qualified Polish and American nationals the opportunity to exchange significant knowledge and educational experience in fields of consequence to the two countries. It also aims to contribute to a deeper understanding of Polish-American relations and to broaden the means by which the two societies can further their understanding of each other's culture. The Polish government acknowledged the importance of the Commission's work by contributing to its funding. The Ministry of National Education provides the office space for the Commission, stipends for American students, salaries and housing for American scholars, travel costs for Polish grantees, and a two-week orientation program for U.S. grantees.

Polish Fulbright Alumni Association

In January 1992 the Polish-U.S. Fulbright Commission put notices in a number of Polish newspapers inviting former fulbrighters to contact the Commission. Some 160 alumni declared their wish to join the association. The Polish Fulbright Alumni Association (PFAA) and its Statute were registered by the Polish Court in February 1993. At its first meeting it was announced that Fulbright had been awarded Poland's highest award for a foreigner, the Order of Service of the Polish Republic. During a special ceremony at the Polish Embassy in Washington in December 1993, a delegation of PFAA and the Commission handed the Cross to Fulbright's wife, who represented her husband.

When Fulbright died in February of 1995, more than 250,000 scholarships had been awarded bearing his name.

Further Reading

The full-length biography of Fulbright is Haynes Johnson and Bernard M. Gwertzman, *Fulbright: The Dissenter* (1968). Karl E. Meyer, ed., *Fulbright of Arkansas: The Public Positions of a Private Thinker* (1963), contains a brief biography and a selection of Fulbright's public statements. □

Richard Buckminster Fuller

Richard Buckminster Fuller (1895-1983), American architect and engineer, was in a broad sense a product designer who understood architecture as well as the engineering sciences in relation to mass production and in association with the idea of total environment.

R. Buckminster Fuller was best known for his work on the Dymaxion House, Dymaxion Bathroom, and Dymaxion Car and as the inventor of the geodesic dome—as a means of attaining maximum space related to environment with minimal use of raw materials. "My philosophy," he wrote in *No More Secondhand Gods,* "requires of me that I convert not only my own experiences but whatever I can learn of other men's experiences into statements of evolutionary trending and concomitantly defined problem challenges and responses. My philosophy further requires that I at least attempt to solve the problems by inanimate invention." He also described himself as an "explorer in comprehensive anticipation design."

Fuller was born July 12, 1895, in Milton, Massachusetts, and attended Milton Academy. Even at an early age he was a nonconformist, and in 1913 he rejected formal education at Harvard, the college that had nurtured four generations of Fullers. During World War I he was commissioned in the U.S. Navy, where he had an opportunity to indulge his creative imagination; he designed a seaplane rescue mast and boom.

Dymaxion Concept

In peacetime Fuller's energies were channeled into the Stockade Building System, which failed because of ignorant contractors, inflexible building codes, and financial opposition. This failure, as well as the death of his daughter of rheumatic fever, forced him into an intense period of work, resulting in 1927 in the Dymaxion House. (The word Dymaxion is a compounding of the words "dynamism" and "maximum.") Circular in plan to prevent heat loss and with a tiny heating unit and air-conditioning unit, the house, 50 feet in diameter, weighed 6,000 pounds. It would have cost approximately $6,500 and could have been assembled from a 250-cubic-foot package transported anywhere. The cost of development would have been about $100 million.

In 1933 Fuller followed this with the three-wheel, front-wheel-drive Dymaxion Car. It was built like an airplane body, was air-conditioned, and could have traveled at 120 miles per hour.

Phelps Dodge Corporation developed the copper Dymaxion Bathroom in 1936. (Aluminum, plastics, and

such materials were not readily available or reasonably priced in the mid-1930s.) The quart of water necessary for a 10-minute bath would, in addition, provide an invigorating massage. The bathroom would have been free of sewage pipes, and waste material would have been stored for pickup and processing.

Following World War II, Beech Aircraft Company at Wichita, Kansas, wanted to convert their aircraft production plant into an assembly line for a Dymaxion House, which became known as the Wichita House of 1945-1946. Labor unions supported the project in order to retain full employment, but financial backers and the industry decided against it. In this failure America lost a chance, in 1945, to work toward solving housing and allied problems that came to plague the cities by the 1970s.

Geodesic Domes

Undaunted, Fuller began developing his ideas on geodesic domes, using the tetrahedron (of four triangular sides), economic in material and weight and thus of maximum efficiency, as a basic component. After numerous experimental prototypes, industry began to understand the advantages of such structures. In 1953 the Ford Company built a geodesic dome in Dearborn, Michigan, 93 feet in diameter; the Marine Corps built numerous smaller ones; and in 1958-1959 the Union Tank Car Company of Baton Rouge, Louisiana, constructed a dome 384 feet in diameter. Fuller's proposal for a hemispherical dome two miles in diameter to cover a portion of Manhattan Island, New York, to enclose a controlled environment was not acted on. But perhaps the best opportunity for a gigantic temporary structure of this kind was lost when the president of the 1964 World's Fair vetoed a proposed dome which would have covered 646 acres.

The United States Pavilion at Montreal's Expo 1967 was a three-quarter globe designed by Fuller, 200 feet high and 250 feet in diameter. Although the structure and its contents drew some sharp criticism, they represented "Creative America." Fuller's later experiments were geared toward an understanding of the world's resources and their efficient utilization.

Fuller's Influence

Fuller functioned primarily as a catalyst. He was important to the 20th century not only because of his own inventiveness but also for his influence upon the new generation. The pioneers of the modern movement, such as Ludwig Mies van der Rohe, have less influence than Fuller, who was the forerunner of concepts of the efficient utilization of materials and, with the Bauhaus, of mass production.

Fuller's philosophy of design contributed to the faith many contemporary architects have placed in the computer-age concept of "megastructure"—the idea of incorporating a city into a single giant structural complex, encompassing all functions of the urban environment, into which individual cells of habitation can be "plugged" or onto which they can be "clipped."

Although megastructure is impractical, with regard to structural feasibility and cost in the third quarter of the 20th century, when new structural techniques evolve and when the populace and its leadership understand the need for comprehensive planning then megastructure could be one possible solution to population growth and the habitation of man on a grand scale. Still, some critics argue that such an environment would be inhuman as well as impractical. British critic Kenneth Clark considers ideas such as megastructure "the most disreputable of all forms of public utterance," which "threatens to impair our humanity."

Fuller was elected to the American Academy and Institute of Arts and Letters and held more than 2,000 patents. From 1959 until his death, due to a heart attack, on July 1, 1983, Fuller was a research professor in design science and a professor emeritus at Southern Illinois University, as well as a popular lecturer. During his life, Fuller wrote 25 books.

Further Reading

Fuller's ideas are presented in his *Nine Chains to the Moon* (1938); *No More Secondhand Gods, and Other Writings* (1963); and *Ideas and Integrities: A Spontaneous Autobiographical Disclosure* (1963). Fuller's contemporary influence is examined in James T. Badlwin, *Buckyworks: Buckminster Fuller's Ideas Today,* John Wiley & Sons, Inc., 1996. A biography is Robert Snyder, *R. Buckminster Fuller: An Autobiographical Monologue/Scenario,* St. Martin's Press, 1980. The Fuller Research Foundation published *Dymaxion Index: Bibliography and Published Items Regarding Dymaxion and Buckminster Fuller, 1927-1953* (rev. ed. 1953). Other works that discuss Fuller's influence include Reyner Banham, *The New Brutalism; Ethic or Aesthetic?* (1966), and Royston Landau, *New Directions in British Architecture* (1968). □

Sarah Margaret Fuller

Sarah Margaret Fuller (1810-1850), an American feminist, cultural critic, and transcendentalist, fought for equality of the sexes.

Not long after her birth on May 23, 1810, in Cambridgeport, Mass., Margaret Fuller's father started to educate her as a wonder child. She was introduced to Latin at 6 and was reading literary classics when she might still have been playing children's games. By the time she was in her 20s, she could impress such transcendentalist leaders as Ralph Waldo Emerson and Bronson Alcott.

Fuller loved to talk, so she seized on the lyceum as a way to support herself and put forth her ideas. When she ran into masculine protest against a woman speaking to mixed audiences, she developed what she called "conversations." These systematic discussions with some of the most intelligent women in the Boston area were held from 1839 to 1844. Fuller had already begun publishing, but her most significant book, *Woman in the Nineteenth Century* (1845), developed from such "conversations." It proposed plans for relieving women's social restrictions and using their abilities to the fullest.

When the transcendentalists set up a journal, the *Dial,* in 1840, they chose Fuller as editor. Her incisive and decisive criticism of literature and the arts attracted the attention of Horace Greeley, editor of the *New York Tribune,* who brought her to New York as a critic for his paper in 1844.

Fuller's reviews for the *Tribune* demonstrated a first-rate esthetic intelligence. Though she found these duties satisfying, a trip to Europe so impressed her that in 1847 she settled in Rome. There she met and lived with a poor but handsome young Italian marquis, Angelo Ossoli, demonstrating her belief in love and in freedom for women. When the son she had by Ossoli in 1849 was a year old, they announced their marriage.

In the late 1840s, when the people of Rome were trying to shake off papal rule to form a city-state, Ossoli fought for the Roman Republic, while Fuller worked in the military hospitals. Throughout her stay abroad she had been writing for the *Tribune;* her descriptions of the Roman revolution were her most vivid work. When the revolution failed, the family fled, finally settling in Florence. Here she wrote the manuscript of a history of the revolution.

In May 1850 Fuller and her family embarked for New York. The ship was wrecked off Fire Island: wife, husband, and son all drowned on July 19, 1850, and in the catastrophe her manuscript was lost.

Further Reading

The most recent biography of Margaret Fuller is Arthur W. Brown, *Margaret Fuller* (1964). It should be supplemented by Mason

Wade, *Margaret Fuller: Whetstone of Genius* (1940). Joseph Jay Deiss, *The Roman Years of Margaret Fuller* (1969), illuminates one of her most important periods. □

Robert Fulton

Robert Fulton (1765-1815), American inventor, civil engineer, and artist, established the first regular and commercially successful steamboat operation.

Robert Fulton was born November 14, 1765, in Lancaster County, Pa. His father worked at farming, among other jobs, and died when Robert was a small boy. By the age of 10 Robert showed promise as an artist and was employed by local gunsmiths to make designs for their work. At 17 he went to Philadelphia, the cultural center of the Atlantic seaboard, and spent 4 years making portraits and doing miniatures. Financially successful, he was able to buy a farm near the city for his mother.

In 1786 Fulton went to London to study painting with Benjamin West, who had been a family friend and was by this time one of the leading American painters living in England. England was already in the midst of its industrial revolution, and Fulton was fascinated by the new engineering enterprises—canals, mines, bridges, roads, and factories. His interest became professional, and after about 1793 he gave up painting as a vocation, pursuing it only for his own amusement.

As early as 1794 Fulton considered using steam power to drive a boat. Seven years earlier John Fitch had successfully demonstrated his steamboat on the Delaware River at Philadelphia, but in the interim no one had been able to make both a mechanical and commercial success of the idea. Though the British government had banned the export of steam engines, Fulton wrote to the firm of Boulton and Watt about the possibility of buying a ready-made engine to be applied to boat propulsion.

Most of Fulton's energy during these years was devoted to more conventional problems of civil and mechanical engineering. He patented in England a "double-incline plane" for hauling canal boats over difficult terrain and machines to saw marble, to spin flax, and to twist hemp for rope. He built a mechanical dredge to speed the construction of canals and in 1796 published his illustrated pamphlet, *A Treatise on the Improvement of Canal Navigation.*

For the next 10 years Fulton devoted himself to the development of underwater warfare through the invention and improvement of a submarine and explosive torpedoes. It is thought that he believed that if warfare were made sufficiently destructive and horrible it would be abandoned—a fallacy often invoked by inventors of military devices. He tried to interest the French government in his experiments, and he obtained the promise of prizes for any British ships he might destroy with his devices. In 1801 he proceeded with his submarine, the *Nautilus,* against various ships but was unsuccessful. By 1804 his failure to win

death on February 24, 1815 he had erected a large boat works in New Jersey and directed the building of one ferry-boat, a torpedo boat, and 17 regular steamboats.

Fulton's success, where at least a dozen other American inventors had failed, had many causes. In Livingston he had a rich and politically powerful patron who was able to obtain a lucrative monopoly on the steam navigation of the state's waters. Fulton also began his work with a first-class engine, purchased from Boulton and Watt, the world's leading engine builders. Previous inventors, including John Fitch, had had to build their own engines. Also, Fulton was able to employ mechanics and experimenters who had, over the past 2 decades, gained considerable experience with steam engines. It was Fulton's luck and genius to be able to combine these elements into a commercially successful steamboat venture.

Further Reading

The first, and still useful, biography of Fulton is Cadwallader D. Colden, *The Life of Robert Fulton* (1817). The best biography is H. W. Dickinson, *Robert Fulton, Engineer and Artist: His Life and Works* (1913). Also useful is George Dangerfield, *Chancellor Robert R. Livingston of New York, 1746-1813* (1960). For the prehistory of steamboats see James Thomas Flexner, *Steamboats Come True: American Inventors in Action* (1944). □

French money for destroying British ships led him to offer to destroy French ships for the British government. Once again he failed in combat, although he was able to blow up one ship during an experiment.

In 1802 Fulton had met Robert R. Livingston, formerly a partner in another steamboat venture but recently appointed U.S. minister to the French government. Despite the failure of Fulton's earlier ventures, Livingston agreed to support Fulton's old idea of building a steamboat. In 1803 an engine was ordered (disassembled and with many duplicate parts) from Boulton and Watt, to be delivered in New York City. But it was 1806 before permission to export the engine was obtained, the parts were assembled, and Fulton was able to sail for America.

The engine was put together in New York and set aboard a locally built vessel. One of the problems was to determine the proper proportions for a steamboat. Fulton was convinced that science dictated a very long and narrow hull, though experience later proved him wrong. Although Livingston had been an advocate of a kind of jet propulsion for steamboats (that is, a jet of water forced out the back of the boat under high pressure), the two now settled on paddle wheels as the best method. On Aug. 17, 1807, the *Clermont* (as it was later named) began its first successful voyage up the Hudson River to Albany, N.Y. Under way it averaged 5 miles per hour.

After the voyage of the *Clermont,* steamboats appeared up and down the Atlantic Coast, and Fulton himself introduced the first steamboat on the western waters. Before his

Joseph Furphy

Joseph Furphy (1843-1912) was an Australian writer whose reputation rests on "Such Is Life," a major novel that gives accurate representations of the emerging national character and customs in colonial Australia's "age of gusto," the 1890s.

Joseph Furphy was born at Yering, a rural district outside Melbourne, on Sept. 26, 1843. He was educated at home, mainly by his mother, with the Bible and Shakespeare as his first readers. At 23 Furphy bought a threshing machine and at harvesttime took it through wheat areas. He became a homesteader in 1868 but after 5 years of hard times became a wool carrier. This occupation took him deep into the main pastoral areas, about which he was later to write so knowledgably. In slack times he tried his hand at gold mining. In his late 30s he joined his brother at Shepparton, in central Victoria, a rural town in which he spent the 1880s and 1890s.

Here, under the pen name Tom Collins, Joseph Furphy contributed regularly to the *Bulletin,* a weekly established in 1880 which reflected (and helped shape) the erupting Australianism of the day. In it, writers came forward to interpret Australians to themselves rather than to English readers. The movement had its roots in the back-country, where social tensions sprang from the sheep raisers' legal struggle to hold their estates against homesteading and, more immediately, from prolonged strikes involving rural workers.

phy appropriate to the developing frontier society. Supporting the view of the small landowner against that of the big sheep and cattle raisers, he admitted to something of the egalitarian approach. He picked up the prevailing views expressed in dissertations among shearers, drovers, teamsters, prospectors, and general roustabouts—men with a new political awareness sharpened by the varying "socialist" teachings of the American social writers Edward Bellamy and Henry George, whose books were being spread among ranch workers by union organizers. Furphy's writing possesses an intellectual content and background; yet it is narrow and parochial.

Two subsidiary novels taken from the great mass from which *Such Is Life* was quarried became *Rigby's Romance* and *The Buln Buln and the Brolga*. In 1905 Furphy submitted the former to a miners newspaper, where it was serialized; it came out in book form in 1921. *The Buln Buln and the Brolga* was not published until 1946. Both novels rely for their interest on their association with the greater work.

In 1905 Furphy moved to Western Australia, where two of his sons had established a business. He died at Claremont, a suburb of Perth, on Sept. 13, 1912.

Further Reading

The principal authority on Furphy's life is Miles Franklin in association with Kate Baker, *Joseph Furphy: The Legend of a Man and His Book* (1944 which, although sometimes vague and fragmentary, brings together good material on Furphy and his work. A concise sketch of Furphy and *Such Is Life* and an annotated list of his output are given (under his pen name, Tom Collins) in Edmund M. Miller, *Australian Literature: A Bibliography to 1938; Extended to 1950,* edited by Frederick T. Macartney (1956). A fuller appreciation of Furphy and his place in Australian literature is in H. M. Green, *A History of Australian Literature,* vol. 1 (1961).

Additional Sources

Barnes, John, *The order of things: a life of Joseph Furphy,* Melbourne; New York: Oxford University Press, 1990. □

Major Work

In this atmosphere Furphy wrote *Such Is Life,* delineating life in the pastoral lands of southeast Australia. It was the first rounded view of the Australian inland—a record written with a conscious rejection of romanticism. Furphy completed the long novel in 1897 and submitted it to the *Bulletin,* where its merit was immediately recognized. Accepting editorial advice, Furphy excised large sections; the reduced text was published in 1903. Reviews were excellent, but sales were meager. Through the efforts of a family friend, *Such Is Life* was again published in 1917; other editions were released in England and Australia.

Shrewd, proud and tolerant, Furphy had a quiet sense of humor and was self-effacing and devoted to his family—characteristics which were reflected in his writing. The warmth of his outlook and the richness of his experience add luster to *Such Is Life,* and in spite of some stylistic flaws it stands as "the most original and vigorous novel to come out of Australia." Discursive and laden with quotations and erudite allusions, it is marked by real humor in the presentation of character and scene, with an unfailing belief in and affection for the common man. *Such Is Life* is an extraordinary book in the ambitiousness and complexity of its structure. Furphy's editorial mentor, A. G. Stephens, described it as being like a riverboat, "carrying all manner of freight for all manner of people, and tieing up at a tree every night for tea, tucker [food], tobacco, and philosophical reflections."

Furphy was absorbed with the discussion going on among those trying to shape a political and social philoso-

Henry Fuseli

The Swiss painter Henry Fuseli (1741-1825) depicted the marvelous, the megalomaniac, supernatural horror, the irrational, the erotic, and the macabre, expressing violently romantic attitudes in a severe neoclassic style.

Henry Fuseli was the first artist to command the epic literature and heroic history of northern Europe as well as the Mediterranean countries, and by his wide reading and close study of the Old Masters he equipped himself to extend the scope of history painting far beyond the traditional limits of the Bible and classical antiquity. In his speculative boldness he was a child of the Enlightenment, but he was also a fierce critic of sterile rationalism and preached the gospel of the imagination with religious fervor.

Henry Fuseli was born Johann Heinrich Füssli (in 1764 he Anglicized his name) in Zurich on Feb. 6, 1741, the son of a painter with strong religious convictions who destined him for the Zwinglian ministry. After a period of intensive theological study Fuseli was ordained in 1761 and preached his first sermon. He was a friend of Johann Kaspar Lavater, whose *Aphorisms on Man* he later translated into English from manuscript. Fuseli became the favorite disciple of Johann Jakob Bodmer, who in 1740 had published an essay on the wonderful in poetry that led to a literary war with Johann Christoph Gottsched in Germany and the formation of a revolutionary Swiss school which used English literature, especially Milton and Shakespeare, as a spearhead in promoting romanticism.

Years in England

Fuseli's attack on corruption in high places made it prudent for him to leave Zurich in 1763. After a year in Germany, where he met most of the progressive writers of the day, he went to England. The idea was that he should act as a link between the English and the Swiss-German avant-garde movements, and his admirers confidently expected him to become the literary genius of the Continental coterie on his return. He earned his living by writing and translating and as a tutor to a young nobleman.

Like Voltaire earlier, Fuseli was attracted by the English tolerance of ideas, but it was the stirrings of romanticism

and especially the theater, in which David Garrick had pioneered a revolution in stagecraft, that captured his enthusiasm. Fuseli stayed in England for 6 years, by which time he had decided to become a painter. The story that Sir Joshua Reynolds told him he would become the greatest painter of the age if he studied in Rome for a few years is probably an exaggeration, but Fuseli was undoubtedly encouraged by Reynolds.

Years in Rome

Fuseli studied in Rome from 1770 to 1778. "Fuseli in Rome" wrote Lavater in 1773, "is one of the greatest imaginations." This sums up in a nutshell the fascination he exerted not only on Reynolds but on those who, like Johann Wolfgang von Goethe, never met him but heard about him from friends. Lavater described Fuseli's look as lightning, his word a thunderstorm, his jest death, and his revenge hell. These attributes of romantic genius had the unusual support of a Voltairean clarity of mind and incisiveness of expression. The elevation of the sketch as the spontaneous expression of genius also contributed to his reputation in romantic circles. He seems to have kept up his drawing from childhood, but his output was now prodigious, and the themes were precisely those that appealed to the early romantics: Milton, Shakespeare, Dante, the struggle for political liberty, attacks on religious bigotry, Greek tragedy, and Homer. He left many of his drawings with Lavater in Zurich, where Goethe and others eagerly sought them out.

Career as Painter and Teacher

In 1779 Fuseli returned to London, exhibiting regularly at the Royal Academy from 1780. His first outstanding success was *The Nightmare,* exhibited in 1782. Reynolds promoted his election as associate royal academician in 1788, the year Fuseli married Sophia Rawlins, but there was a temporary coolness when Fuseli was elected royal academician in 1790 over the head of Reynolds's nominee. In 1799 Fuseli became professor of painting at the academy, and his first three *Lectures on Painting* were published in 1801. In 1804 he obtained the key position of keeper, virtually head of the academy schools.

Parallel with Fuseli's career in the academy, and entirely in harmony with its goal, he threw himself with enthusiasm into every scheme for promoting the revival of history painting, including his illustrations of Homer (he collaborated with William Cowper from 1786); his paintings for John Boydell's Shakespeare Gallery; and above all his own Milton Gallery, 47 canvases on which he worked from 1790 to 1800.

Fuseli's last lectures—which put him in the forefront of those who pioneered art history in England by combining the analytical approach of Johann Joachim Winckelmann (whose *Reflections* he translated in 1765) with an even wider background of ideas—were delivered in 1825. On April 16 of that year he died in London.

Further Reading

The Life and Writings of Henry Fuseli, edited by John Knowles (3 vols., 1831), is valuable. By far the best introduction in English is Eudo C. Mason, *The Mind of Henry Fuseli: Selections from His Writings* (1951), a brilliantly annotated selection of Fuseli's major writings with an introductory study by Mason. Also useful is the essay on Fuseli in Ruthven Todd, *Tracks in the Snow: Studies in English Science and Art* (1946). An English translation of Paul Ganz, *The Drawings of Henry Fuseli,* appeared in 1949. Frederick Antal, *Fuseli Studies* (1956), is a scholarly monograph that reproduces some of Fuseli's finest drawings and is especially valuable for its critical apparatus and bibliographical references.

Additional Sources

Fuseli, Henry, *Henry Fuseli,* London: Academy Editions; New York: St. Martin's Press, 1974.
Fuseli, Henry, *The life and writings of Henry Fuseli,* Millwood, N.Y.: Kraus, 1982.
Schiff, Gert., *Henry Fuseli, 1741-1825: essay, catalogue entries and biographical outline,* London: Tate Gallery Publications, 1975. □

Numa Denis Fustel de Coulanges

The French historian Numa Denis Fustel de Coulanges (1830-1889) made a leading contribution to the study of ancient France and to the debate concerning Roman versus German influence on French institutions and society.

Numa Denis Fustel de Coulanges was born in Paris on March 18, 1830. He was admitted into the École Normale Supérieure in 1850, in the oppressive days preceding the collapse of the Second Republic. In 1853 Fustel was appointed a member of the French School in Athens and then spent 2 years in Chio, an opportunity which provided him with material for a contribution to the history of the island. He then returned to France to become a teacher in Amiens and Paris while taking his final degrees in 1857 and 1858. He was appointed professor of history in the University of Strasbourg in 1860. There he wrote and published at his own expense his first masterpiece, *La Cité antique* (1864), opening a fruitful line of research when he showed Greek and Roman city organization to have rested on kinship and the cult of the family hearth and ancestors.

But Fustel was to be lastingly diverted to another problem, the birth of his own country. In February 1870 Fustel came back to Paris as a professor of ancient history in the École Normale. The Sorbonne welcomed him in 1875, and in 1879 a professorship for the history of medieval France was created for him, thus acknowledging his achievements in this field. The German victory over France in 1870 had but given particular acumen to a problem whose political implications made it a passionate subject for historical controversy all over Europe: was Europe an issue of its Roman conquerors, or had it been broken and cast by the German invaders into a different mold, which had been the Middle

Ages? Fustel pointed out the living continuity of history, the blending of old and new into its flow, particularly stressing the facts about landed property. He argued his point in volume 1 of his *Histoire des institutions politiques de l'Ancienne France* (1874). His health, however, was now failing. In 1883 he had to resign the directorship of the École Normale, to which he had been appointed in 1880. His last years were spent in gathering new material and publishing some of it in *Recherches sur quelques problèmes d'histoire* (1885), *La Monarchie franque* (1888), and *L'Alleu et le domaine rural pendant la période mérovingienne* (1889). Fustel de Coulanges died near Paris in 1889.

Further Reading

A full-length study of Fustel is Jane Herrick, *The Historical Thought of Fustel de Coulanges* (1954). General works include George Peabody Gooch, *History and Historians in the Nineteenth Century* (1913; 2d ed. 1952), and Robert Latouche, *The Birth of Western Economy: Economic Aspects of the Dark Ages* (1956; trans. 1961). □

Johann Joseph Fux

Although the Austrian composer, conductor, and theoretician Johann Joseph Fux (1660-1741) was an important creative musician, he is best known for his treatise on counterpoint, "Gradus ad Parnassum."

ohann Joseph Fux was born in Hirtenfeld, Styria. There are no available details about his early training and career; he occupied his first known position in Vienna in 1696. In 1698 he was named composer to the imperial court. In 1704 he became second kapellmeister at the Cathedral of St. Stephen. He became second kapellmeister at the court in 1713 and, apparently in the same year, first kapellmeister. He occupied this prestigious post until his death on Feb. 14, 1741, in Vienna.

During Fux's tenure as kapellmeister the style at court was known for its so-called luxuriant counterpoint, even in such a predominantly melodic form as opera. His interest and scholarship in the theoretical discipline of counterpoint is captured in his *Gradus ad Parnassum* (1725). This work crystallizes the style distinction of the entire baroque era between an antique, learned, ecclesiastical style and a modern, more popular, predominantly secular style. Fux addresses himself to the details of writing in the learned style, which took as its supposed point of departure the contrapuntal writing of Giovanni Pierluigi da Palestrina. (The *Gradus* is written as a dialogue between Palestrina as master and Fux as pupil.) The *Gradus* preserves little of the essence of Palestrina's style, about which Fux could have had little firsthand knowledge; nevertheless it is an important musical document. It preserved important theoretical and practical details of contemporary musical thought; it was a tremendously influential work, which Haydn and Beethoven, among many others, studied; and its methodology prevailed into the 20th century.

Of the 405 extant works by Fux very few are available in modern publications, and these are mostly in scholarly editions. They include a large quantity of sacred music (50 Masses, 3 Requiems, 10 oratorios, vespers, psalms, and sacred sonatas) and 18 operas. The predominance of sacred music of an opulent kind befitting court use may explain the importance of contrapuntal writing in his operas, the most famous being *Costanza e Fortezza*, written for the coronation of the Emperor in 1723.

During this period Apostolo Zeno, who became court poet in 1718, was engaged in a reform of Italian opera in the interest of greater dignity and simplicity of organization. Since the imperial opera was not constrained by the economic austerity of the public opera houses of Italy, Fux could use choruses freely. For him, contrapuntal choruses in the sacred manner are organizing elements in the large scenic design. Unlike much Italian opera of the period, which concentrated on the solo aria, Fux's operas employ an ensemble of solo singers, while the large arias often use a concertizing solo instrument. His emphasis on contrapuntal structures was conservative and represented the older manner of treating musical texture.

Further Reading

The *Gradus ad Parnassum* is available as *Steps to Parnassus,* translated by Alfred Mann (1943). Also useful are Manfred Bukofzer, *Music in the Baroque Era* (1947), and Donald J. Grout, *A Short History of Opera* (1947; 2d ed. 1965). □

G

William Clark Gable

William Clark Gable (1901-1960), America's top male film star for nearly 3 decades, was idolized by millions as the symbol of ideal masculinity.

Clark Gable was born in Cadiz, Ohio, on Feb. 1, 1901, of Pennsylvania-Dutch farming stock. He quit high school to work in Ohio factories, Oklahoma oilfields, and Oregon lumber camps.

At 18 Gable determined to become an actor. Clumsy, untrained, and with little visible talent, he worked at various (often unpaid) jobs in stock companies. In 1923 Josephine Dillon, an acting teacher 11 years his senior, took him in hand. In 1924 they married and spent several difficult years in Hollywood. Gable worked as a movie extra and unskilled stage actor while being shaped for stardom by his wife. In 1927 the marriage collapsed. Gable left to play stock in Texas and in 1928 landed the lead in a New York production, *Machinal.* Unemployed thereafter for nearly a year, he returned to a West Coast stage role in *The Last Mile* and won his first real film part, in a western.

In 1930 Gable was finally given a contract at $350 a week by Metro-Goldwyn-Mayer (M-G-M). A small part led Gable to leading roles opposite stars Norma Shearer, Jean Harlow, and Greta Garbo. *It Happened One Night,* a 1934 comedy directed by Frank Capra, won Gable an "Oscar" and propelled him to "superstar" status, with a salary of $211,000 per year and mobs of women rioting hysterically at his public appearances.

Gable starred in a succession of critical and box-office triumphs, including *Boomtown, San Francisco, Mutiny on the Bounty,* and *Gone with the Wind.* He was a modest, hardworking "company man," and his playing mainly projected his own forceful personality and character, which, despite his success, remained essentially uncorrupted.

Marriage at 29 to Ria Langham, a wealthy 47-year-old divorcée, taught Gable social poise but did not alter his preference for simple outdoor living. He divorced his second wife. Marriage to young Carole Lombard, a top star of the 1930s, led to an extended idyll that ended tragically with her death in an air crash in 1942, just as Gable was enlisting—at 41—as a private in the Air Corps.

Gable returned to postwar prominence in a series of relatively undistinguished films. A brief marriage to Lady Sylvia Ashley ended in divorce. In 1954 he left M-G-M (after 23 years and 54 pictures) to become the most highly paid free-lance actor of the decade. Happily married to Kay Williams Spreckels, he remained the unchallenged "king" of Hollywood until his sudden death on Nov. 16, 1960, after completing a brutally strenuous performance in *The Misfits.*

Further Reading

Although a great deal was written about Gable while he was alive, all that remains useful are two posthumous volumes, Charles Samuels, *The King: A Biography of Clark Gable* (1962), and Chester Williams, *Gable* (1968). Additional material can be found in such reminiscences as Lionel Barrymore, *We Barrymores* (1951).

Additional Sources

Clark Gable, Boston: Little, Brown, 1986.
Garceau, Jean, *Gable: a pictorial biography,* New York: Grosset & Dunlap, 1977 1961.
Lewis, Judy, *Uncommon knowledge,* New York: Pocket Books, 1994.
Morella, Joe, *Gable & Lombard & Powell & Harlow,* London: W. H. Allen, 1976.

Scagnetti, Jack, *The life and loves of Gable,* Middle Village, N.Y.:
J. David Publishers, 1976.

Tornabene, Lyn, *Long live The King: a biography of Clark Gable,*
New York: Putnam, 1976.

Wallace, Charles B., *The young Mr. Gable: an illustrated account
of Clark Gable's early years in his native Ohio, 1901-1920,*
Cadiz, Ohio: Harrison County Historical Society, 1983.

Wayne, Jane Ellen, *Clark Gable: portrait of a misfit,* New York: St.
Martin's Press, 1993.

Wayne, Jane Ellen, *Gable's women,* New York: Prentice Hall,
1987; South Yarmouth, Ma.: J. Curley, 1987. □

Naum Gabo

**The Russian sculptor and designer Naum Gabo
(1890-1977) was a pioneer of the constructivist art
movement in Russia after the Revolution. He demonstrated in his work the potentialities of plastics and
threaded constructions.**

Naum Gabo changed his name from Naum Neemia
Pevsner to distinguish himself from his artist
brother, Antoine Pevsner. Gabo was born on August 5, 1890, in Briansk, Russia, an area now known as
Belarus. He was the son of an executive in a copper refinery.
In 1910 he went to Munich to study medicine, but after a
year he switched to engineering and physics. While in Munich he attended lectures in art history by the celebrated

scholar Heinrich Wölfflin. Gabo met Wassily Kandinsky
and was enthusiastic over the exhibitions of the Blaue Reiter
group, to which Kandinsky belonged.

In 1913 Gabo went to Paris to see Pevsner, who had a
studio there and who introduced him to friends involved in
the modern movement in art. Gabo and Pevsner went to
Oslo after World War I was declared, and there, in 1915,
Gabo made his first sculptures. These pieces were cubist.
He used sheet metal and celluloid to build abstract likenesses of human beings; one example is his *Head of a
Woman* (1916), composed of opaque celluloid cut, bent,
and attached to a flat plane to become a high relief extending from a flat surface.

In 1917 after the Revolution, Gabo and Pevsner settled
in Moscow. Gabo by this time had developed a distinct style
of his own. They renewed their acquaintance with
Kandinsky, who introduced them to Kasimir Malevich,
Vladimir Tatlin, and other avant-garde artists. Gabo established a studio and accepted students. At first he and his
brother supported the Revolution as a liberating force, not
only for social good but for the welfare of art. There was a
move, however, toward the use of art as propaganda to
further the aims of the state. Certain artists, Tatlin among
them, insisted that this was essential and supported the
politicians.

Published Art Philosophy

Gabo and Pevsner maintained that art must be autonomous and rise above temporary demands or it will cease to

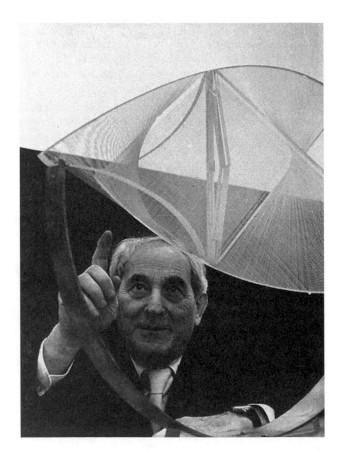

be art. In their *Realist Manifesto* published in the form of a broadsheet in 1920 they stated that space and time are fundamental to life and that art aimed at being one with the essence of the real must accept this basic premise. Art should concentrate on the dynamic aspects of life and reveal its energy, force, and rhythm. To accomplish this, mass must be abandoned as the basic element in sculpture and new materials used to make manifest the modern spirit. Consistent with the program of the manifesto, Gabo in 1920 produced *Kinetic Composition,* a construction that used a motor to rotate a steel blade; this piece is the earliest known example of kinetic sculpture.

In 1922 Gabo and Pevsner left Russia. Gabo spent the next decade in Berlin and exhibited regularly with the Novembergruppe. His work acquired architectural characteristics and monumentality. These developments are evident in his *Column* (1923), a shimmering upright sculpture of intersecting glass pieces on a metal base. He also used sheets of clear plastic scored to catch the light and create linear patterns. He and Pevsner collaborated in designing sets for Sergei Diaghilev's ballet *La Chatte* (1927).

Gabo lived in Paris from 1932 to 1936, exhibiting with the Abstraction-Création group, and then went to London and stayed for a decade. He was one of the editors of *Circle,* a periodical dedicated to promoting constructivist art. Gabo's sculptures at this time continued along the path established in Paris, but he exploited materials further. He was introduced to perspex, a new plastic from Imperial Chemical Industries, and used this material in some of his best-known works. He used transparent plastic tubing or plastic sheet made into warped, parabolic planes shot through with parallel nylon threading. The taut, delicate webbing of strings crisscrossed as the sculpture was moved. In some pieces he incorporated silver, gold, and aluminum wire; when set against a dark ground, they appeared ethereal. Gabo married Mariam Israels in 1937, and they had a daughter.

Arrived in United States

Gabo settled in America in 1946. Following an important exhibition of his works in 1948 he began to receive commissions for public works. He completed his Construction Suspended in Space for the Baltimore Museum of Art in 1951. He taught at the Harvard University School of Architecture (1953-1954). One of the monumental pieces he executed is his 81-foot construction that stands in front of the Bijenkorf Department Store in Rotterdam (1955-1957). This work is composed largely of a bronze-coated steel mesh that adheres to a skeletal frame resembling an upright seedpod. About the same time, he executed a wall relief for the U.S. Rubber Company in Rockefeller Center, New York City, and another one for the Baltimore, Maryland, museum. Also during the 1950s, Gabo took up wood engraving to explore the same concepts as his sculpture. He used this technique in his work through the mid-1970s.

Gabo's attempt to explore the fourth dimension, kinetic effects, as put forth in his *Manifesto,* was not literally followed up in most of his works. The *Monument for the Institute of Physics and Mathematics* (1925) contains rota-

ting elements, and the *Vertical Construction No. 2 (1964-64)* is rotated by a motor, but otherwise motion is generally restricted to hanging sculptures that rotate freely. He received many honors including the American Art Institute's Logan Medal (1954), the Brandeis Award (1960), and a Guggenheim Fellowship. A retrospective exhibition of his work toured Europe in 1965-66. Gabo died August 23, 1977, in Waterbury, Connecticut. He was 87.

Further Reading

The Museum of Modern Art catalog, *Naum Gabo—Antoine Pevsner* (1948), contains short texts by Ruth Olson and Abraham Chanin and an introduction by Herbert Read. *Gabo: Constructions, Sculpture, Paintings, Drawings, Engravings* (1957) has several fine plates and 10 stereoscopic color slides, and a bibliography by Bernard Karpel.
Further information on Gabo can be found in Jane Turner, ed., *The Dictionary of Art* (1996), and James Vinson, ed., *International Dictionary of Art and Artists* (1990). □

Dennis Gabor

The Hungarian-British physicist Dennis Gabor (1900-1979) received the Nobel Prize in Physics in 1971 for his invention of holographic photography.

Dennis Gabor was born on June 5, 1900, in Budapest, Hungary, to S. Berthold and Ady (Jacobovits) Gabor. The son of a businessman, he received his education at the technical universities of Budapest (1918-1920) and Berlin (1920-1927). He earned both his diploma and his doctorate in engineering from the Technische Hochschule, in Charlottenburg, Germany, the former in 1924, the latter in 1927. He remained in Berlin upon graduation, working as a research engineer for Siemens and Halske until Hitler's rise to power in 1933. At that point he left Germany for Britain, taking a job with the British Thomson-Houston Company in Rugby, England.

Gabor stayed with the British firm for 15 years, from 1933 to 1948, working on the improvement of the resolving power of the electron microscope. The electron microscope had increased resolving power a hundredfold over the finest light microscopes, yet it still fell short of allowing scientists to "see" atomic lattices (the patterned arrangement of atoms, not individual atoms, which are too small). The image was distorted in two ways—fuzziness (as if one's camera were out of focus) and sphericity (as though one were looking through a raindrop). If one improved the former, the latter worsened, and vice-versa.

In 1947 a brilliant solution occurred to Gabor. What if one were to use the diffraction pattern (the fuzziness) in a way which provided one with all the information about the atomic lattice. That is, why not take an unclear electron picture, then clarify that picture by optical means. This was the genesis of holography. Gabor proposed to take an electron beam of light and split it in two, sending one beam to an object, the other to a mirror. Both would initially have the

same wavelength and be in phase (coherent), but upon reflection from the object and the mirror back to the photographic plate, interference would be set up. Imagine ocean waves rolling in upon a long, sandy beach, one following another. Imagine them all equal in size, intensity, and timing. Now imagine you could split the beach in two, with two sets of waves coming in upon two different beaches. Tilt these two at an angle of your own choosing, superimpose them, and imagine the interference the waves would create for each other. This interference would not be completely chaotic, but would actually follow a pattern. From this "diffraction" pattern, one could reconstruct the initial waves. Now vary these initial waves in size, intensity, and timing (which might be imagined as due to different weather conditions out at sea). The diffraction pattern would differ correspondingly, and even the weather conditions might be hypothetically reconstructed. This is what Gabor wished to do with electron beams. The beam from the mirror would be unchanged, but the beam reflected from the object would contain all the irregularities imposed upon it by that object. Upon their meeting at the photographic plate, the two beams would be generally incoherent, and an interference pattern would occur. This interference could then be captured upon film, and if light were then shone through this film, it would take on the interference pattern and produce an image capable of three-dimensional reconstruction.

Gabor worked out the basic technique by using conventional, filtered light sources, not electron beams. The mercury lamp and pinhole were utilized to form the first, imprecise holograms. But because even this light was too

diffuse, holography did not become commercially feasible until 1960, with the development of the laser, which amplifies the intensity of light waves. Nevertheless, Gabor demonstrated mathematically that holography would work even with electron beams—just as his experiments showed it worked with ordinary light. The major practical problem remaining with the electron microscope prior to 1960, however, was not left unchallenged by Gabor—this was the double image incidentally obtained by the holographic process. Gabor was able to use the very defect of electron lenses—spherical aberration—to remove the second image.

Gabor published the principle of holography and the results of his experiments in *Nature* (1948), *Proceedings of the Royal Society* (1949), and *Proceedings of the Physical Society* (1951). This work earned him in 1948 a position on the staff of the Imperial College of Science and Technology, London. In 1958 he was promoted to professor of applied electron physics, and he held that post until his retirement in 1967. His other work consisted of research on high-speed oscilloscopes, communication theory, physical optics, and television, and he was awarded more than 100 patents. Yet Gabor was not the pure scientist or isolated inventor; many of his popular works addressed the social implications of technological advance, and he remained suspicious of assumptions of inevitable technological progress, nothing the social problems it could not solve as well as the ones it caused.

Gabor received many honors. In 1956 he was nominated to the Royal Society; he was made an honorary member of the Hungarian Academy of Scientists; and in 1971 he received the Nobel Physics Prize for his holographic work. He died in London on February 8, 1979.

Further Reading

There is little biographical information on Gabor, though some can be gleaned from *Who's Who in Science: Antiquity to Present,* edited by Allen G. Debus (1968) and other recent dictionaries of scientific biography. His own explanation—historical and scientific—of holography can be found in his Nobel Lecture (1971), contained in *Les Prix Nobel* (Stockholm, 1972). This French title nevertheless contains his English lecture, and a holographic photoplate is enclosed to further illuminate the subject. Of his popular works, *Innovations: Scientific, Technological, and Social* (1970), *The Mature Society* (1972), and *Proper Priorities of Science and Technology* (1972) are readable. They are also repetitive, and one would do well to choose only one of them, perhaps the most recent. □

Ange Jacques Gabriel

The buildings of the French architect Ange Jacques Gabriel (1698-1782) demonstrate elegant proportional relationships and superlative Gallic taste in the control of the dynamic expressiveness inherited from ancient Rome.

nge Jacques Gabriel was the most eminent 18th-century member of a family dynasty of architects descending from Jules Hardouin Mansart, first architect to King Louis XIV, with whom Ange Jacques's grandfather, Jacques IV Gabriel, and father, Jacques V Gabriel, had worked. Though Ange Jacques's early training is thought to have taken place under the architect Antoine Desgodetz, it was largely the execution of his father's designs for Paris town houses that formed his education.

At the age of 30 Ange Jacques Gabriel was launched professionally, having married Catherine de la Motte, daughter of the secretary of the Duc d'Antin, who had succeeded Mansart as superintendent of the royal buildings, and having received as a wedding gift from his father the influential post of controller of the king's buildings. Soon after his father became first architect to King Louis XV in 1734, Ange Jacques's grandiose architectural projects aroused the King's interest. Finances, however, restricted his activity to existing palaces: building the forecourt of the château at Fontainebleau (1737), restoring the Louvre in Paris (from 1755), and making internal adjustments at Versailles to create *les petits appartements* (1738-1753).

On his father's death in 1742 Ange Jacques Gabriel became first architect, a position he held until 1775. He lived in the Orangerie of the Tuileries Palace, and the King gave him a property at Versailles. His career was plagued by the bitter enmity of the new superintendent of buildings, the Marquis de Marigny, Madame de Pompadour's brother, and by a continual shortage of royal funds.

Gabriel's major works were executed between 1750 and 1774. The publication of J. D. Leroy's *Ruines des plus beaux monuments de la Grèce* (1758) coincided with Gabriel's adoption of a purer Greek style where, according to C. N. Cochin, "only the right angle makes a good effect." This was indicative of the abandonment of the curved and asymmetrical effects of the preceding rococo period. In truth, the French preference for more than a century had been the Greco-Roman esthetic of imposing weight with heavy ornamental adjuncts. Though this ideal remained apparent in Gabriel's works, his tendency was toward purifying the cubic mass and minimizing decorative accessories. This evolution is seen by comparing two of his works: the block pavilions flanking the entrance gates of the École Militaire in Paris (1751-1775) and the less ponderous, elegant sobriety of the Petit Trianon at Versailles (1762-1764), the most superb work of domestic architecture of the 18th century. Other major projects reveal experimentation within this basic, formulating inclination from Roman nobility toward Greek simplicity: the château at Compiègne (1752), the Place Louis XV (today Place de la Concorde) in Paris (1752-1765), the Salle de l'Opéra at Versailles (1753-1770), and the colonnaded terminating bays of the wings of the Cours d'Honneur at Versailles (1772).

All these works reveal bold assurance in the choice and arrangement of architectural forms and the harmonious integration of disparate parts of building complexes and terrains, gratifying the viewer with the sense of the conclusive correctness of the ensemble from any viewpoint, the result, no doubt, of Gabriel's experience with his father in city planning, notably the Place Royale (now Place de la Bourse) in Bordeaux (1731-1755).

Further Reading

Although the definitive monograph on Gabriel is in French, there are two satisfactory works in English. Sir Reginal Blomfield, *Six Architects* (1935), originally delivered as lectures at the University College of Wales, includes a delightful lecture on Gabriel that provides information on his life. H. Bartle Cox, *Ange-Jacques Gabriel* (1926), is a terse, objective study. □

Giovanni Gabrieli

The works of the Italian composer Giovanni Gabrieli (ca. 1557-1612) mirror the transition from the 16th-century Renaissance style to the 17th-century baroque. His compositions were very influential on Italian and German masters.

iovanni Gabrieli was born in Venice. He was associated with the court chapel of Roland de Lassus in Munich (1576-1580). Despite this important contact, the formative influence on the young Giovanni was his uncle Andrea Gabrieli, whose career as composer and organist anticipated his own. Giovanni's devotion to Andrea is witnessed by a collection of concerti (1587) issued by the younger man from among his own works and those of the older man, dead but a year.

Like his uncle, Giovanni worked in the Cathedral of St. Mark in Venice, first as deputy to the famed master Claudio Merulo (1584), then as second organist (1585), and finally as first organist (1586). He also composed vocal and instrumental pieces for church and state festivities and taught a young generation of composers the new musical idioms of the baroque. He died in Venice on Aug. 12, 1612.

Only a few of Gabrieli's secular vocal pieces have survived. But a collection of madrigals by his student Heinrich Schütz, printed in 1611 as the fruits of an apprenticeship with Gabrieli, suggests that the teacher was deeply interested in the genre. Among Gabrieli's madrigals is the eight-voice *Lieto godea* for two choruses. Here, as in the sacred pieces, antiphonal effects, created by means of vertical, chordal combinations, replace the linear movement of the older polyphonists.

Many more of Gabrieli's instrumental pieces have survived, including numerous canzonas, ricercars, and sonatas. Some early canzonas such as *La Spiritata* are conventional, sectional pieces in imitative, multithematic polyphony. Several of the monothematic ricercars, on the other hand, are virtually forerunners of the latebaroque fugue. Of particular interest is Gabrieli's *Sonata piano e forte,* the first composition ever to bear this title. In addition to marking dynamics throughout the individual parts, the composer prescribed the instrumentation of the sonata—a novel departure from Renaissance practice, in which instrumentation was usually an ad libitum matter. Among his late instrumental pieces is a *Sonata con tre violini e basso se piace,* for which the master made the decisive turn to the basso continuo, the foundation voice of most baroque music.

Of all Gabrieli's works, first place must go to the motets. Polychoral writing (*cori spezzati*), as promulgated by Adrian Willaert and continued by Andrea Gabrieli, found its most brilliant exponent in Giovanni Gabrieli. In his collection *Sacrae symphoniae* (1597) there were motets for six to sixteen parts and arranged for one to four choruses. For these works he replaced the older, imitative, melismatic polyphony of the Franco-Flemish school by syllabic, harmonic writing. Bass parts moving in fourths and fifths supported separated choirs responding antiphonally to one another in short, declamatory phrases. For Gabrieli, who designed his creations for large spaces, traditional counterpoint was less important than dramatic changes in texture and dynamics.

Gabrieli's second volume of *Sacrae symphoniae,* printed posthumously (1615), contains early as well as late pieces in the new concerted idiom. Characteristic of the late compositions are the juxtaposition of voices and instruments, virtuoso solo writing, and the basso continuo.

The motet *In ecclesiis* reveals most of the innovations of Gabrieli's late style: solos and duets supported by organ (basso continuo) or instrumental ensemble; a solo quartet of voices responding to or joining the chorus; and instrumental ensembles accompanying the singers or playing indepen-

dent sinfonie. With such a work resplendent with color, Gabrieli helped inaugurate a new musical epoch that was carried forward by many 17th-century Roman masters and, even more significantly, by the Germans Heinrich Schütz and Michael Praetorius.

Further Reading

Gabrieli's musical development is treated in Egon Kenton, *Life and Works of Giovanni Gabrieli* (1967). Information on Gabrieli is also in Manfred F. Bukofzer, *Music in the Baroque Era* (1947), and Gustave Reese, *Music in the Renaissance* (1954; rev. ed. 1959). □

Hans-Georg Gadamer

German philosopher, classicist, and interpretation theorist Hans-Georg Gadamer (born 1900) was the leading exponent of a comprehensive view of human beings as dialogue-partners with each other.

Gadamer was born in Marburg, Germany, son of a well-known professor of chemistry. His university studies at Breslau, Marburg, and Munich included ancient and modern languages and literature, history, art history, and philosophy. Further studies with Martin Heidegger led to the publication of his *Habilitation* in 1929, qualifying him to teach at a university. He taught at the Universities of Marburg, Kiel, Leipzig (where he was Rektor in 1946-1947), Frankfurt, and Heidelberg (where he succeeded Karl Jaspers in 1949 and was professor of philosophy until formal retirement in 1968). He married Kaete Lekebusch in 1950, and they had one daughter.

From his work as a teacher, his many writings, and his appearances and teaching abroad, Gadamer acquired a world reputation. His major work, *Wahrheit und Methode* (1960; translated as *Truth and Method,* 1975), was prepared for publication at the urging of students who first encountered his ideas in classes and seminars.

One of the few major German intellectuals to remain in Germany during the Hitler period and yet keep his distance from the Nazis, Gadamer represents the continuity of a European tradition linking the intellectual excitement of the 1920s to the 1960s, 1970s, and 1980s. Heidegger, Gadamer's teacher in the 1920s, was the greatest figure in existential philosophy, and Gadamer was closely associated with others who were to shape the course of theological, literary, and philosophical studies for decades to come. For today's students, Gadamer is a living witness of the vitality of the great teachers of his youth, as seen in his essays in Part II of *Philosophical Hermeneutics* (1976) and *Philosophical Apprenticeships* (1985).

Beginning in the 1950s, Gadamer himself represented a major position in philosophy of the humanities, counterposed to Marxists such as Jürgen Habermas, radically antimethodical interpreters such as Jacques Derrida, and the viewpoint represented by E.D. Hirsch that the meaning of a text is just what the author intended. Gadamer was the spokesperson for *philosophical hermeneutics*. The word "hermeneutics" has a long history in theology, literature, and the law. There it most frequently indicated an art of interpretation which could wrest secrets from difficult texts originally addressed to a past audience, such as the Bible. Following Heidegger's lead, Gadamer gave hermeneutics a broader meaning; it is a theory of human existence arising from study of the events of understanding and interpretation in which human beings are always involved.

Gadamer challenged the "scientific" view of the humanities which assumed that their task was to exploit *methods*, inspired by natural scientific method, to generate a single correct interpretation for every work. For Gadamer, the primary purpose of humanistic studies was deepening insight for the reader, viewer, or hearer. He focused on the dynamic by which the message of a work addresses its audience in his or her situation. The reader, he argued, never receives the message in precisely the same sense as the speaker's or author's intention, but always understands in ways shaped by prejudgments arising out of one's own experience and language-learning. Thus, nobody reads a text in precisely the same way as someone else. Differences will be especially significant when interpreters belong to different periods, since they will bring different questions and human interests to bear. The product will be the result of the "fusion of the horizons (or perspectives)" of the text and the interpreter.

But Gadamer did not propose an "anything goes" approach. Meaningful interpretation is limited by the fact that understanding always belongs to a *tradition*. The way conductors present a classical piece to contemporary audiences will be shaped not only by their perception of the audience's expectations, but also by inherited ways of interpreting the work and sets of assumptions, insights, and methods enriched, impoverished, and modified over the years. No one, Gadamer insisted, is immune to such an influence from the past. But a fresh interpretation becomes possible when an interpreter discovers some unexamined prejudgment at work, decides that it deserves to be challenged, and produces a new way of presenting the work. Moreover, the origin of the challenge may be the work itself. For Gadamer, a seminal work was a conversation-partner, a "Thou," addressing the self and calling its illegitimate biases into question.

Beginning in the 1970s Gadamer regularly taught part of the year in North America. He continued to pursue research, especially in classical Greek philosophy. He found that Plato's use of the dialogue form and Aristotle's description of moral insight suggest a viable alternative to the model of reason developed by uncritical admirers of the sciences of prediction and control. Some of his later work is available in *Dialogue and Dialectic* (1980), *The Idea of the Good in Platonic-Aristotelian Philosophy* (1986), and *Reason in the Age of Science* (1981).

Further Reading

There are no biographies of Gadamer. Richard Palmer, *Hermeneutics* (1969), places Gadamer's ideas in the German tradition of interpretation theory. David C. Hoy, *The Critical Circle* (1982), treats Gadamer against the background of contemporary literary theory. Richard Bernstein, *Beyond Objectivism and Relativism* (1983), connects Gadamer's hermeneutics to contemporary theory of knowledge. Gadamer's *Truth and Method* (1989, 1993) and introductions by David E. Linge and Frederick Lawrence to Gadamer's *Philosophical Hermeneutics* (1976) and *Reason in the Age of Science* (1981), respectively, can also orient readers to Gadamer's thought. □

Muammar Al-Gaddafi

Muammar Al-Gaddafi (born 1942) was head of the revolution that set up the Libyan Republic in 1969. In the Libyan *Jamahiriyya*, of which he was always the leader, Al-Gaddafi wanted to realize fully his concept of government by the masses.

Muammar Al-Gaddafi (also transcribed into other Western languages as Qaddafi, Gheddafi, and Khadafi, among others) was born in 1942, either in spring or in September. His birthplace was near Surt in the desert region of Libya bordering the Mediterranean along the Gulf of Sirte. He was the last child and only son in his family, people of modest means who belonged to the Bedouin tribe of the Qadhdhafa which was engaged in animal herding. The cultural traditions of the desert certainly influenced Gaddafi's and his sociopolitical ideas.

Involved In Student Movements

After receiving instruction in the teachings of the Koran, the sacred book of Islam, he attended the elementary school at Surt from 1953 to 1955. When his family moved to Fezzan, the region south of Tripolitania, he continued his education at Sebha from 1956 to 1961. Inspired by the ideas and political actions of Egypt's Gamal Abdel Nasser, he organized student demonstrations which led to his expulsion from the city. He then moved to the large coastal city of Misurata, to the east of Tripoli, where he completed his high school education between 1961 and 1963. At the same time he continued to organize a secret revolutionary movement.

In order to enable himself to fulfill his political plans, he entered the Military Academy of Bengasi in October 1963 and persuaded other members of the movement to join him there. Together with these men and other converted members of the military he set up the central committee of the Free Unionist Officers in 1964, which was organized along strictly collegial lines. In the same period Gaddafi was enrolled in the University of Bengasi for three years, attending courses for a degree in history. In 1966 he took part in a training course at the Beaconsfield Military Academy in Great Britain. Having been promoted to the rank of lieutenant and assigned to the army's Signal Corps based at Gariunis on the outskirts of Bengasi, Gaddafi broadened the base of the movement—the ramifications of which only he

was fully aware—and acquired at the same time an ever-growing personal prestige.

Kingdom to Republic

During the night of September 1, 1969, at a time when King Idris had already been abroad for several months for health reasons, Gaddafi gave the order—which had been deferred several times—for putting his long prepared plan into effect. The young officers easily seized power and proclaimed the Libyan Arab Republic. It was only on September 10 that it was noted that Gaddafi, now a colonel, was the president of the Revolutionary Command Council (RCC), the chief organ of the new regime.

The revolutionary will of the new leader soon expressed itself in a series of laws designed, among other things, to do away with the illegal benefits enjoyed by the representatives of the former regime and to overcome the traditional tribal differences. Following the example of Nasser, who had inspired his political development, Gaddafi called for the removal of the American (Wheelus Field) and British military bases; this was completed in June 1970. A series of measures affected the Italians still present in Libya in large numbers, ending in their mass expulsion in October 1970. At the same time extensive nationalization of the financial, industrial, and commercial sectors took place (in particular in the oil industry) and other significant reforms were commenced.

Among the modifications carried out within the institutions and political organization of Libya after the revolution

one could detect Gaddafi's determination, desperately tenacious in the face of difficulties, to involve the people as far as possible in the direct exercising of political power. In February 1971 he announced the creation of the Arab Socialist Union (ASU), which bore the same name as the sole Egyptian political party. The ASU, formally set up on June 11, 1971, held its first congress in April 1972. Rejecting all expressions of regional and class interests, the ASU intended to provide a large popular base for the revolution. In July 1972 Gaddafi vacated the office of president of the Council of Ministers, which he had occupied since January 1970, and dedicated himself from that time on to the theorization of the principles of the revolution which were later laid down in the "Green Book." In April 1974 Gaddafi also gave up all protocol and administrative duties associated with the head of state.

The People's Revolution

At a time when new legislation was being introduced in the labor and fiscal sectors with the aim of creating true "socialism," Gaddafi announced the "People's Revolution" in a speech at Zuara on April 15, 1973. By means of "elected people's committees" operating in various sectors it was intended that the principles of the revolution and of Islam should be increasingly put into practice. At the second general People's Congress in November 1976 Gaddafi proposed the creation of a direct democracy and the removal of the CCR; however, the delegates to the congress called for an adjournment, and during a special session of the congress on March 2, 1977, the Socialist People's Libyan Arab *Jamahiriyya* (a term which can be translated as "government by the masses") was proclaimed. With the intention of mobilizing the people, Gaddafi began in 1978 to encourage the creation of "revolutionary committees" which did not have clearly defined powers and which were called upon to "defend the Revolution." Starting in 1981 he began to impose a military character upon the organization of schools and universities.

Gaddafi's revolutionary policies affected many people both within Libya and elsewhere. Consequently, opposition emerged of varying types and intensities. A number of attempted plots organized against him in the early 1980s, probably with foreign involvement, failed and were quickly repressed by the regime. Other plots reported by foreign sources were perhaps only aimed at serving propaganda purposes. Gaddafi denied the legitimacy of all opposition and, in particular, issued warnings to Libyans resident abroad that opposed the revolutionary regime.

Gaddafi's idealistic aspirations guided Libya's foreign policy, which after the revolution was characterized by an unprecedented degree of activity. Gaddafi himself paid numerous visits to foreign countries, to virtually all Arab lands, and to many Communist states. Because of the many and various initiatives launched by Gaddafi in differing directions, his foreign policy was judged by some to be erratic. Indeed, it achieved only limited results and led to a great deal of mistrust. However, for Gaddafi it was important to affirm with insistence and vigor a number of essential policy points, such as his intransigent opposition to Israel and his quest for Arab unity. This quest involved successive attempts at forming political unions with Sudan, Egypt, Tunisia, and Syria, all of which ended, sometimes rapidly, in disastrous failures. A union with Morocco was announced in 1984.

In Chad, Libyan intervention beginning in 1980 led to Goukouni Oueddei being confirmed in power. But the search for political agreements and influence in other African countries had no success, and Gaddafi failed to convene the Organization of African Unity in Tripoli in 1982. The struggle against imperialism preached by Gaddafi along with the need for non-alignment led to Libya being diametrically opposed to the United States. Moreover, the United States accused Libya of supporting armed opposition and terrorist movements in other countries. Libya's relations with Western Europe improved, despite momentary crises.

Theory of Government

Gaddafi's claimed that his political concept, the Third Universal Theory, was derived from the principles of the Koran and hence in harmony with Islam. It was laid down with the purpose of providing an easily understood and complete approach in the "Green Book." The first part (published in 1976) concerned the political aspects of the organization of society. The second part (1977) concerned economic aspects and the third (1979) focused on social aspects. The first part denounced the representative democracies as hoaxes and claimed instead that only the direct participation of the masses in government, as laid down in the *Jamahiriyya,* offered a valid solution to political problems. In the economic sphere, Gaddafi intended to create a true socialist economy, completely opposed both to Western capitalism and to the Marxist-Communist concept; it was intended that workers become "partners, not employees," and there was opposition to all forms of exploitation (many tertiary services are considered exploitative, in particular in the commercial field). The social concept of the "Green Book" placed great emphasis on the role of the family, and women, equals to men in terms of dignity and rights, were seen in the first place as mothers.

The manner in which the "Green Book" was formulated, deliberately populist in approach and not strictly systematic, obviously presented difficulties of interpretation and application with respect to various concrete problems. The book was frequently discussed by the people and at congresses organized both in Libya and abroad by Libyan institutions. The "Green Book" was praised by some, often in a completely acritical manner, while others have subjected it to minute criticism. However, it would seem most valid to consider it as a manifesto for the revolution which Gaddafi was endeavoring to bring about in the Libyan *Jamahiriyya,* rather than as a treatise on political philosophy and economics.

Married and the father of three children, Gaddafi lived modestly, rejecting all luxuries and vices. Some considered him a messianic preacher who was intransigent and intolerant on the one hand, but sincere and even candid on the other. Others considered him an able politician who, though inclined to verbal excesses, was basically a clever man. In 1986 he made known to the press that he preferred the Western press to transcribe his name as Moammar Gadhafi.

As acts of international terrorism became more frequent in 1986, Gaddafi drew much attention as the source of training and financing such activities. On December 27, 1985, Palestinian terrorists attacked airports in Rome and Vienna. United States president Ronald Reagan accused Libya, but Gaddafi denied any involvement. On January 1, 1986, President Reagan ordered all U.S. citizens to leave Libya. Finally on April 14 the United States carried out a retaliatory bombing raid against several Libyan installations. Nearly 100 people were killed in the attack. Gaddafi claimed that he was innocent and that the raid was itself an act of terrorism. He cited as evidence that one of his children was killed during this raid.

Further Reading

For information on Gaddafi's personality (he was interviewed at length by the author) and for information concerning his activities during the first year of the revolution, see M. Bianco, *Kadhafi, mesager du désert* (1974). A journalistic, and well informed, source is J. K. Cooley, *Libyan Sandstorm* (1982). Detailed information is included in H. Bleuchot, *Chroniques et documents libyens, 1969- 1980* (1983). For information on relations with the U.S.A., see P. E. Haley, *Qaddafi and the United States since 1969* (1984). A biography is George Tremlett, *Gadaffi: The Desert Mystic* (Carroll & Graff Publishers, Inc., 1993). The story of the raid is told by pilot Col. Robert E. Venkius, *Raid on Qaddafi* (St. Martin's Press, 1992). □

James Gadsden

James Gadsden (1788-1858), American railroad promoter and a leading advocate of Southern nationalism, was the minister to Mexico responsible for the Gadsden Purchase in 1853.

James Gadsden was born in Charleston, S.C., on May 15, 1788, the grandson of a Revolutionary patriot. After graduating from Yale College in 1806, Gadsden entered business and then became a professional Army officer, rising to the rank of colonel by 1820. During the War of 1812 he served as an engineer and as an aide to Gen. Andrew Jackson. Later he fought against the Seminole Indians and was responsible for securing the evidence which led to the seizure, trial, and execution of two British agents.

In 1821 Gadsden served as adjutant general, but the Senate refused to confirm his appointment. Gadsden resigned from the Army and moved to Florida, where he was active in the territory's affairs. In 1823 he was responsible for placing the Seminoles on reservations and for building the state's first roads. He failed several times in bids to represent the Florida territory in Congress. Because in 1832 he backed nullification of President Jackson's earlier Tariff Act, he lost the support and friendship of the President.

During the 1830s Gadsden became an exponent of Southern nationalism and the expansion and integration of all Southern railroads. He proposed to end Southern economic dependency on the North by providing a direct link between the South and Europe, connecting all Southern railroads into one system, and connecting the Southern system with the Pacific Coast. He promoted these schemes at a number of Southern economic conferences between 1837 and 1850. Between 1840 and 1850 Gadsden served as president of the Louisville, Cincinnati and Charleston Railroad and greatly expanded its mileage. His ideas concerning Southern transportation were farsighted, but he was continually frustrated both by his devotion to Southern nationalism and by the general opposition of other Southern leaders whose notions of states' rights prevented effective regional development.

In 1853 Gadsden urged the purchase of territory along the Gila River from Mexico for the purpose of building a southern railroad between New Orleans and California. He won the support of U.S. Secretary of War Jefferson Davis and, through Davis's efforts, was appointed minister to Mexico. Gadsden next advocated purchasing extensive territory from Mexico, but he was successful in acquiring only a small strip (now parts of New Mexico and Arizona), which became known as the Gadsden Purchase. He died on Dec. 26, 1858.

Further Reading

There is no biography of Gadsden, but background information can be found in Paul Neff Garber, *The Gadsden Treaty* (1923). See also James Morton Callahan, *American Foreign Policy in Mexican Relations* (1932). □

Yuri Alexeivich Gagarin

The Russian cosmonaut Yuri Alexeivich Gagarin (1934-1968) was the first man to orbit the earth in an artificial satellite and thus ushered in the age of manned spaceflight.

Yuri Gagarin the third child of Alexei Ivanovich, a carpenter on a collective farm, and Anna Timofeyevna, was born on March 9, 1934, in the village of Klushino, Smolensk Province. Yuri attended an elementary school in Gzhatsk; in the sixth grade he began to study physics. At the age of 15 he became an apprentice foundryman in an agricultural machinery plant outside Moscow and enrolled in an evening school.

In 1951 Gagarin transferred to the Saratov Industrial Technical School. In 1955 he had to prepare a thesis in order to graduate. His problem was to design a foundry capable of producing 9,000 tons (metric) of castings a year. The state examining committee accepted his thesis, and he received his diploma.

Gagarin joined the Saratov Flying Club in 1955 and won his wings, learning to fly in the Yak-18. Late that year he was drafted and sent to the famous Orenburg Flying School, since he already had a pilot's license. He was disconcerted to learn that he would not be immediately put into jet planes. After he became an aviation cadet on Jan. 8, 1956, he was permitted to fly—but not in the jets he coveted. He started out all over again in the familiar Yak-18, learning to fly it the air force way. That year he also began flight training in the MIG jet.

Cosmonaut Selection and Training

On Oct. 4, 1957, *Sputnik 1,* the world's first artificial satellite, was orbited by the Soviet Union. Four days after *Sputnik 2,* on Nov. 7, 1957, Gagarin graduated from the flying school and was commissioned a lieutenant in the Soviet air force. On the same day he married Valentina Goryacheva.

Gagarin spent 2 years as a fighter pilot at an airfield above the Arctic Circle. By 1958 the Soviet government was asking for volunteers from the air force to pilot its spacecraft. On Oct. 5, 1959, Gagarin made formal application for cosmonaut training; he was selected in the first group of pilots. In 1960 the original group of 50 had been whittled down to 12, and these men moved to Zvezdograd (Star City), a newly built holding and training area in a suburb of Moscow.

For Gagarin and his 11 classmates training began in earnest. They were introduced to a bewildering curriculum of space navigation, rocket propulsion, physiology, astron-

omy, and upper atmospheric physics and were trained on special devices to accustom them to the physiological stresses of space flight. More to Gagarin's liking were the long hours spent in the mock-up of the *Vostok,* an exact replica of the spacecraft in which he would later orbit the earth. After only 9 months of training the cosmonauts were told that the first flight of the *Vostok* would be on April 12, 1961.

Orbiting Earth

The selection of Gagarin as the first man to orbit earth was assured when each cosmonaut was asked to designate who should be the one to make the flight; 60 percent named Gagarin. He was launched in *Vostok 1* on the planned date, and during the crowded 1 hour 48 minutes of his single orbit of the earth he proved that man could survive in space and perform useful tasks. His mission ended at 10:55 A.M., when he landed safely in a field near Saratov.

Following his mission, Gagarin became the commander of the cosmonaut detachment at Zvezdograd, a position he held until April 1965, when he briefly reentered mission training as a backup cosmonaut. During this period he also enrolled in the Zukovsky Institute of Aeronautical Engineering, where he began a 5-year course leading to a degree.

On March 27, 1968, Gagarin died in a plane crash outside Moscow while on a routine training flight. He was given a state funeral and was buried in the Kremlin wall facing Red Square. At the request of his wife, American astronauts Neil Armstrong and Edwin Aldrin left one of Gagarin's medals on the moon as a tribute to the world's first man in space.

Further Reading

The most accessible biography for the student is Mitchell R. Sharpe, *Yuri Gagarin: First Man in Space* (1969). Less readily obtainable is *Road to the Stars: Notes by Soviet Cosmonaut No. 1* (1961; trans. 1962), written by N. Denisov and S. Borzenko and printed in English by the Foreign Languages Publishing House in Moscow. Some biographical material is in William Shelton, *Soviet Space Exploration: The First Decade* (1968). □

Matilda Joslyn Gage

American reformer Matilda Joslyn Gage (1826-1898) was a leader in the struggle for women's rights in the nineteenth century. A onetime leader of the National Woman Suffrage Association, she wrote numerous speeches, essays, and books that analyzed the role of women throughout history and provided arguments for rejecting the traditions that perpetuated the oppression of women, African slaves, Native Americans, and other minorities in America.

Matilda Joslyn Gage was a leading figure in the women's suffrage movement of the late 1800s in the United States. A colleague of such prominent women's rights activists as Susan B. Anthony and Elizabeth Cady Stanton, Gage became a primary voice of the movement with her numerous speeches and feminist writings. Her works often stressed the historic accomplishments of women and the way in which men had frequently taken credit for or denied women's contributions. Gage herself was denied recognition of her achievements when she left the mainstream women's suffrage organization to form a more radical group; the resulting animosity led Anthony and Stanton to remove references to Gage in their book on the history of the suffrage movement. Because of this lack of documentation on Gage's role, she has often been overlooked by the generations that followed her.

Gage was born on March 24, 1826, in Cicero, New York. Her parents, Hezekiah and Helen Leslie Joslyn, were both supporters of liberal social reforms and took an active role in the education of their only child. Her father, who was a doctor, took charge of Gage's early schooling, instructing her at home in subjects such as Greek, physiology, and mathematics. Her learning was supplemented by her exposure to the ideas of scientists, philosophers, and theologians who were frequent guests of her parents. As she grew older, however, her parents decided she needed a more formal education and enrolled her in the Clinton New York Liberal Institute.

Used Literary Talents for Reform

Gage ended her schooling at the age of 18 when she married businessman Henry H. Gage. The couple, who eventually had four children, first settled in Syracuse, New York, but later moved to Fayetteville, New York. Gage continued to study independently to expand her knowledge, taking a particular interest in theology—a subject she would pursue throughout her life. In order to read original versions of the Bible, for instance, she furthered her studies of Greek and taught herself Hebrew. She also began to devote her energies to various social causes. An active abolitionist, she opened her home to escaped slaves as a stop on the Underground Railroad. As a supporter of the temperance movement to outlaw alcohol, she composed articles and gave speeches on the topic at meetings and conventions. The talent for organization and communication that she displayed in these activities were later devoted to the main work of her life—the fight for women's rights, including the right to vote.

Her days in the women's rights movement began when Gage delivered a speech at the Third National Women's Rights Convention in 1852 in Syracuse. Although, at the age of 26, she was the youngest speaker at the event, her words were so well-received that they were later published and circulated to gain support for the cause. Gage's talk focused on the numerous accomplishments of women throughout history and the need for women to escape the legal and economic shackles placed on them by society. She drew a parallel between the limited rights of women in America and the institution of slavery, stating that both forms of oppression stemmed from the same patriarchal attitudes. Over the next decade, Gage increased her stature in women's rights circles, holding a number of organization posts, writing articles, and giving speeches.

Elected Head of Suffrage Group

In 1869, Gage played a central role in the creation of the National Woman Suffrage Association (NWSA) and became a member of the group's advisory council. Throughout the 1870s, she was in the forefront of the increasingly radical statements and actions of the women's rights movement. In 1873, Susan B. Anthony was arrested for her illegal attempt to vote in New York. Gage joined Anthony in attempting to convince prospective jurors of the rightness of their struggle. Traveling to various townships across the state, she presented a reasoned and spirited speech titled "The United States on Trial, Not Susan B. Anthony." After her election to the top posts in both the National and New York suffrage organizations in 1875, Gage appeared before the U.S. Congress to testify in favor of a suffrage bill under consideration. When the government failed to pass the measure, she wrote a strongly worded protest that was circulated at the NWSA convention in Washington, D.C., in January of 1876. The essay declared that women should not participate in upcoming celebrations of the country's centennial because the nation was not a true democracy, but an inequitable power-system controlled by men. These statements raised the ire of government officials, and police were sent to close down the convention on the grounds that it was

an illegal assembly. Gage refused to put an end to the gathering, telling enthusiastic supporters that if arrested, she would continue the convention in jail.

In May of that year, Gage willingly handed over her national post to Elizabeth Cady Stanton, acknowledging the importance of having the most widely-known suffragist in the country represent the group during the centennial. She began to focus her efforts even more on writing in order to spread her ideas on women's rights and other social reforms. In 1878, she began a three-year tenure as editor of the NWSA newspaper, *National Citizen and Ballot Box.* Her articles covered such topics as the treatment of women prisoners, prostitution, the plight of Native Americans, and the role of Christianity in the oppression of women. These writings became the basis of many NWSA policies and inspired some court cases challenging the limits of women's rights.

Documented Women's Fight for Suffrage

With Stanton, Gage contributed a great deal of writing to the ambitious task of compiling a complete history of women's fight for suffrage. The first volume of the 3,000 page, three-part *History of Woman Suffrage* appeared in 1881. The two women also collaborated on a revised version of the Bible published under the title *The Women's Bible.* Gage applied her previous Biblical studies to research on the Old Testament for the project's Revising Committee. Her other literary work of that time included an 1880 pamphlet—"Who Planned the Tennessee Campaign of 1862?"—that showed how a woman by the name of Anna Ella Carroll had actually masterminded a critical military maneuver of the Civil War, but had not been given credit for the idea. Later in her life, Gage's writings would develop her ideas on religion and women's rights. In her 1893 book, *Woman, Church, and State,* she outlines a lengthy history of oppression of women by the Christian church, citing as evidence the burning of accused witches, the end of the early Church's allowance for women deacons, and the negative role of woman in the doctrine of original sin. Gage lamented the absence of the feminine in traditional concepts of God, and shocked one gathering of women in 1888 by opening a meeting with a prayer to a female God. Her attempts to extend feminist thought in this way did not find sympathy with many women activists, who found her concepts too radical.

In 1889, the NWSA merged with the other major national suffrage organization, the American Woman Suffrage Society, a more conservative body. Gage did not approve of the ideological compromises that the NWSA had made by joining the new organization, known as the National-American Woman Suffrage Association (NAWSA). She launched a more liberal organization, the Women's National Liberal Union (WNLU), which pushed for such measures as the abolition of prayer in public schools, the improvement of prisons, and the creation of labor unions. Cady and Stanton were angered by Gage's creation of the WNLU, feeling that the organization detracted from the goal of presenting a strong, unified women's lobby. Not only did they publicly condemn her efforts, they removed all references to her from the fourth volume of the *History of Woman Suffrage;* consequently, Gage would be ignored by many later historians.

In her final years, Gage was forced to retire from her reform activities due to her declining health. She moved to Chicago to stay in the home of one of her daughters and died there of a brain embolism on March 18, 1898. While her name has not been remembered as well as other suffragists such as Anthony and Stanton, Gage's extensive body of feminist literature serves as a record of the philosophy that drove the women's rights movement in her day. The rediscovery of these works by scholars is gradually reestablishing her reputation as one of the most influential voices among nineteenth-century woman reformers.

Further Reading

Gage, Matilda Joslyn, *Woman, Church, and State,* Persephone Press, 1980.
Spender, Dale, *Women of Ideas and What Men Have Done to Them,* Pandora Press, 1988.
Spender, Lynne, "Matilda Joslyn Gage: Active Intellectual," in *Feminist Theorists,* edited by Dale Spender, Pantheon Books, 1983.
Wagner, Sally Roesch, *A Time of Protest: Suffragists Challenge the Republic, 1870-1887,* Spectrum, 1987. □

Thomas Gage

The English general Thomas Gage (1719-1787) was commander in chief of British forces in North America and the last royal governor of Massachusetts.

Born at Firle, Sussex, Thomas Gage was a grandson of the 1st Viscount Gage, an Irish peer. On Jan. 30, 1741, Thomas purchased a lieutenancy in the 1st Northampton Regiment, and he obtained the rank of captain lieutenant when he transferred to Battereau's Foot in May 1742. Receiving his captaincy in 1744, he went to France as an aide to the Duke of Albemarle and participated in the battle of Fortenay. He saw action with Albemarle at Culloden in 1745 and was with the duke 2 years later in the Low Countries. In 1748 Gage purchased a majority in the 55th Regiment and became lieutenant colonel of that unit on March 2, 1751.

In 1754 Gage accompanied his regiment to America, where he distinguished himself in the French and Indian War, receiving a slight wound. In May 1757 he raised a provincial regiment and that same year commanded the light infantry in the strike against Ft. Ticonderoga. As a brigadier general, he led the rear guard of Commander Jeffery Amherst's forces at the capture of Montreal on Sept. 6, 1760, and then served as military governor of Montreal for a short period. In 1761 he was promoted to major general and 2 years later succeeded Amherst as commander in chief of all British forces in North America. During the next 10 years Gage remained in New York and was promoted to lieutenant general. In December 1758 he had married Margaret

Kemble, daughter of a member of the Council of New Jersey; they had five daughters and six sons.

Gage went to England in 1773 but returned to America immediately (because of the Boston Tea Party) with a commission as vice admiral and "captain general and governor in chief" of Massachusetts. He arrived in Boston on May 13, 1774, three days after news of England's punitive measures against Massachusetts had arrived. When the General Court convened in October, a number of towns sent delegates to a provincial congress meeting at Concord; thus did the colony develop two separate governments. Deteriorating relations between Britain and the American colonies were evident during the celebrations of Guy Fawkes Day, November 5, when Gage's effigy was publicly hanged and burned.

On April 14, 1775, Lord Dartmouth, Secretary of State for the Colonies, instructed Gage to take action against the colonial rebels. On the night of April 18 Gage sent out the expedition to the towns of Lexington and Concord that precipitated armed hostilities and the siege of Boston. On June 12 Gage issued a proclamation establishing martial law but holding forth amnesty to all rebels except Samuel Adams and John Hancock. Five days later came the Pyrrhic victory at Bunker Hill.

Gage's actions had received severe criticism in England, and on October 10 he was recalled. He was replaced as commanding general by William Howe. Gage remained in the army. In November 1782 he was made a full general, but participated in no further military activities. He died on April 2, 1787.

Further Reading

The definitive biography of Gage is John R. Alden's sympathetic *General Gage in America: Being Principally a History of His Role in the American Revolution* (1948). See also John Shy, *Toward Lexington: The Role of the British Army in the Coming of the American Revolution* (1965). □

Robert Mills Gagné

Robert Mills Gagné (born 1916) was an American educator whose studies of learning and instruction profoundly affected American schooling.

Robert Mills Gagné was born August 21, 1916, in North Andover, Massachusetts. He earned an A.B. degree from Yale in 1937 and a Ph.D. from Brown University in 1940. He was a professor of psychology and educational psychology at Connecticut College for Women (1940-1949), Pennsylvania State University (1945-1946), Princeton (1958-1962), and the University of California at Berkeley (1966-1969) and was a professor in the Department of Educational Research at Florida State University in Tallahassee starting in 1969. Gagné also served as a research director for the Air Force (1949-1958) at Lackland, Texas, and Lowry, Colorado. He was employed as a consultant to the Department of Defense (1958-1961) and to the United States Office of Education (1964-1966). In addition, he served as a director of research at the American Institute of Research in Pittsburgh (1962-1965).

Gagné's work had a profound influence on American education and on military and industrial training. Gagné and L.J. Briggs were among the early developers of the concept of instructional systems design which suggests that all components of a lesson or a period of instruction can be analyzed and that all components can be designed to operate together as an integrated plan for instruction. In a significant article titled "Educational Technology and the Learning Process" (*Educational Researcher,* 1974), Gagné defined instruction as "the set of planned external events which influence the process of learning and thus promote learning."

Gagné was also well-known for his sophisticated stimulus-response theory of eight kinds of learning which differ in the quality and quantity of stimulus-response bonds involved. From the simplest to the most complex, these are: signal learning (Pavlovian conditioning), stimulus-response learning (operant conditioning), chaining (complex operant conditioning), verbal association, discrimination learning, concept learning, rule learning, and problem solving.

Gagné argued that many skills may be analyzed into a hierarchy of behaviors, called a learning hierarchy. An instructor would develop a learning hierarchy for something to be taught by stating the skill to be learned as a specific behavior and then asking and answering the question "What would you have to know how to do in order to perform this task, after being given only instructions?"

Gagné tested the concept of learning hierarchies in studies, mainly using simple arithmetic skills. His findings tended to support the notion of learning hierarchies and indicated that individuals rarely learn a higher skill without already knowing the lower skill.

Gagné's approach to learning and instruction, especially the instructional systems design approach, was sometimes criticized as most appropriate for mastery learning of information and intellectual skill objectives, but less suited for attitude and cognitive strategy outcomes. Undoubtedly, Gagné's work had a tremendous impact on thinking and theories in educational circles. His hierarchical theory of prerequisite steps in learning had many implications for the sequencing of instruction, and many feel it contributed to the development of a more scientific approach to instruction. In the field of English, for example, it allowed teachers to break English language skills into successively simple components and to teach the components in an orderly sequence, reinforcing correct responses along the way. Gagné's focus on systematic precise instructions also helped to lay the groundwork for individualized instruction and school accountability in American society.

Further Reading

Gagné's work was conducted most closely with L.J. Briggs. Another researcher who worked closely with Gagné was W.P. Gephart. B.F. Skinner's work lends insight into one of the origins of Gagné's themes. *The Encyclopedia of Educational Research* (1982) places Gagné's contributions in the context of other related work, provides an historical perspective, and relates criticisms of his work. He is listed in *Who's Who in America* (1990-1991). Gagné wrote and edited many books and articles. Among them are: *The Conditions of Learning* (1965, 1970, 1977, 1985), perhaps already viewed as a classic text; *Principles of Instructional Design* (with L.J. Briggs, 1974, 1979, 1992); and *Psychological Principles in Systems Development* (1962), which is partly based on research in military training. His articles in the *Phi Delta Kappan* (May 1970) on new views on learning and instruction and in *Educational Psychologist* (May 1968) on learning hierarchies are significant manuscripts. □

Thomas Gainsborough

The English painter Thomas Gainsborough (1727-1788) ranks as one of the principal masters and innovators of the English school of landscape painting.

Thomas Gainsborough was baptized in Sudbury, Suffolk, on May 14, 1727. His father, a substantial cloth merchant, recognized Thomas's precocious artistic gifts and sent him at an early age, possibly 12, to London. Gainsborough was connected with the artists Francis Hayman and Hubert François Gravelot, possibly as apprentice to the former and assistant to the latter. Gainsborough is reported to have copied and restored

Dutch landscapes for dealers. At the age of 19 he married Margaret Burr, reputedly a natural daughter of the Duke of Beaufort, who is said to have brought him an income of £200 a year.

At the age of 21 Gainsborough was so much admired as a landscape painter that he was invited with the leading artists of the day to present a picture to the Foundling Hospital in London. His painting, *The Charterhouse,* shows a mature observation of reality and handling of light. From Hayman the scene painter and Gravelot the rococo decorator Gainsborough learned to approach pictorial composition on inventive principles, and the alternation between observation and invention henceforth became the basis of his artistic growth. The two approaches may be illustrated by comparing *Mr. and Mrs. Robert Andrews* (ca. 1749), with a deliciously observed Suffolk landscape dappled by sunlight and shadow of cloud, and *Henéage Lloyd and His Sister* (ca. 1750), shown against a limpid background of stage scenery.

Gainsborough's art after his early London studies falls into three main divisions: the Suffolk period, 1748-1759; the Bath period, 1759-1774; and the years of fame in London, 1774-1788. In Suffolk he combined the charms of the modern conversation piece with those of realistic landscape, thus making a strong appeal to the country gentry. Here too he painted the Suffolk countryside as faithfully and freshly as if he were a Dutch painter reborn in the 18th century.

The Portraits

Gainsborough's move to Bath was a flank attack to secure the patronage of the aristocracy, for he was not yet equipped to challenge Sir Joshua Reynolds in London. At Bath, Gainsborough had splendid opportunities to study Anthony Van Dyck, his central intermediary with the Old Masters and substitute for the grand tour, in the collections at Wilton and other great country houses within reach. *Mrs. Philip Thicknesse* (1760) is a daring adaptation of Van Dyck's great style to the new mode of rococo informality.

Once Gainsborough had found his model for elevated portraiture in Van Dyck's, he began to borrow attitudes as skillfully as Reynolds, but without any intellectual allusions, his preoccupation being with the visual. The pose of the *Blue Boy* (exhibited at the Royal Academy in 1770 under the title *A Young Gentleman*) is the reverse of that of the older boy in Van Dyck's *George Villiers, 2d Duke of Buckingham, and His Brother Francis.* The subject of Gainsborough's painting Jonathan Buttall, was a young man, not a boy, and it is as a haunting study of adolescence that the picture deserves its fame.

The Landscapes

The key to Gainsborough's artistic development is to be found in his practice as a landscape painter. Already at Bath he was conducting curiously modern experiments with materials and techniques, constructing models out of pieces of mirror, stones, cork, coal, lichen, dried weeds, and broccoli; applying a lump of whiting with a pair of tongs; and using a sponge or chalks. He worked on the same canvas in the near-dark, by candlelight, and in bright daylight. His "peep show" of the 1780s (preserved in the Victoria and Albert Museum, London) was a contrivance for showing colored transparencies of landscape in a box lighted by candles.

The transition in Gainsborough's painting to impressionistic abstraction, described by Reynolds as chaos assuming form by a kind of magic, may be followed by comparing the strongly Dutch *Gainsborough's Forest* (1748) with the *Cottage Door* (1780), a masterpiece which visually expresses the refinement of Thomas Gray's "Elegy Written in a Country Churchyard," and *Diana and Actaeon,* the ne plus ultra of Gainsborough's abstract style. In this late painting, which was unfinished at the time of his death in London on Aug. 2, 1788, he set out to challenge the old Masters by depicting a subject from classical mythology.

By the last decade of his life Gainsborough had evolved a common artistic language for both his portraits and his landscapes, and the *Morning Walk: Mr. and Mrs. William Hallett* (1785) is as poetically evocative as any of his pictures of cottage life, although the subject is taken from high society. The same impulse to refinement governs his "fancy pictures," or scenes of poetic genre, strongly influenced by the beggar boys and old peasants of Bartolomé Esteban Murillo and much admired by Reynolds.

Further Reading

The best illustrated, critical study of Gainsborough's art is Ellis K. Waterhouse, *Gainsborough* (1958), which includes a catalog. The standard biography is William T. Whitley, *Thomas Gainsborough* (1915). An excellent short monograph is Mary Woodall, *Thomas Gainsborough: His Life and Work* (1949).

Additional Sources

Lindsay, Jack, *Thomas Gainsborough, his life and art,* London; New York: Granada, 1982, 1981.

Potterton, Homan, *Reynolds and Gainsborough,* London: National Gallery, 1976.

Worman, Isabelle, *Thomas Gainsborough: a biography 1727-1788,* Lavenham Eng.: T. Dalton, 1976. □

Gaiseric

Gaiseric (died 477) was the ruler of the Germanic tribe of the Vandals who established a kingdom in North Africa and in 455 sacked Rome.

The Vandals were one of several tribes pushed into the Roman Empire by the attacks of the Huns. When Gaiseric, the son of King Godegiselus and a slave, succeeded his half brother Gunderic in 428, the Vandals were settled in southern Spain. However, the struggle for power among rivals in the Roman government, as in many other cases, provided new opportunities for the barbarians. The Roman governor of North Africa, Boniface, was under attack by forces of Emperor Valentinian III, and as Boniface's defeat seemed imminent, he was accused, perhaps unjustly, of calling in the Vandals in 429 to counter the Romans.

Gaiseric proved to be one of the most formidable of the barbarian leaders, skillful in both war and diplomacy. A contemporary account describes him of medium height, slightly lame, sparing of speech, but with a deep mind. As soon as he entered Africa, he turned his forces against the Romans, sacking and burning large sections of their territory. His hostility toward the Roman state was heightened by his adherence to the condemned heresy of the Arians. He tried to eradicate much of the orthodox Catholic influence from North Africa.

The conquest of Africa proceeded rapidly. In 430 Boniface was defeated, and in 431 Gaiseric took the city of St. Augustine, Hippo. In 435 the Romans were forced to make a treaty with Gaiseric which granted him much of eastern North Africa. This peace did not last, and in 439 he seized Carthage, the principal city of Roman Africa. In 442, he was recognized as king by the Roman emperor, Valentinian III.

By gaining control of North Africa, Gaiseric had gained control of the major granary of Rome. Furthermore, the Vandals now took to the sea and disrupted the commerce of the Mediterranean as far east as Greece. This type of activity culminated in the capture and sack of Rome in June 455.

Gaiseric was by now firmly established in North Africa, and a new treaty in 442 extended his area of control. He used his diplomatic skills to keep his enemies off guard. When enmity between the Goths and Vandals increased, he urged Attila to attack the Goths. Gaiseric's son married Eudocia, daughter of Valentinian III, who had been captured in Rome.

Meanwhile the rulers of the Eastern Empire were determined to recover North Africa. In 460 Emperor Majorian failed to conquer Gaiseric and was forced into a new treaty in 462. In 468 a massive new expedition was launched. Poorly led and outmaneuvered militarily and diplomatically, it was disastrously defeated. Gaiseric concluded peace with the East Romans in 468 and with the West Romans in 471. With these treaties he secured the Vandalic kingdom. After his death in 477 the kingdom was continued under his descendants until it was conquered by Belisarius in 533-534.

Further Reading

Some of the ancient sources on Gaiseric are translated in C. D. Gordon, *The Age of Attila: Fifth-Century Byzantium and the Barbarians* (1960). A good English account is J. B. Bury, *History of the Later Roman Empire from the Death of Theodosius I to the Death of Justinian, A.D. 395 to A.D. 565* (2 vols., 1923). □

Jorge Eliécer Gaitán

Jorge Eliécer Gaitán (1898-1948) was a Colombian political leader. Emerging from a humble background, he became the idol of the masses and a highly popular reformist leader. His assassination prevented his likely rise to the presidency of Colombia.

Born to an impoverished family on Jan. 23, 1898, Jorge Eliécer Gaitán was forced to struggle for his livelihood from an early age. After working his way through Colombian universities, he studied penal law in Italy under the noted Enrico Ferri. Returning home to a law professorship at the National University, he came to prominence with publication of *Las ideas socialistas en Colombia* in 1924. In addition to this statement of a progressive reform program for the Liberal party, to which he belonged, Gaitán achieved national prestige with his congressional investigation of a workers' strike and revolt in the Santa Marta banana zone in 1929. His documentation of the excesses of management and of the army's repressive intervention made him a hero to the Colombian peasantry.

Rebuffed by the Liberals for his reformist ideas, Gaitán organized his own Unión Nacional Izquierdista Revolucionaria (UNIR). This "Revolutionary Leftist National Union" met little success in challenging the domination of Colombia's two traditional parties, and by the close of the 1930s Gaitán disbanded the group and returned to the Lib-

politics in Robert H. Dix, *Colombia: The Political Dimensions of Change* (1967).

Additional Sources

Sharpless, Richard E., *Gaitán of Colombia: a political biography*, Pittsburgh: University of Pittsburgh Press, 1978. □

Hugh Gaitskell

The British politician Hugh Gaitskell (1906-1963) was chancellor of the exchequer from 1950 to 1951. He was leader of the Labour Party from 1955 to 1963.

Hugh Todd-Naylor Gaitskell was born in London on April 9, 1906, the son of Arthur Gaitskell, an Indian civil servant. He had a middle-class upbringing which included periods of time spent in Burma. He was educated at Winchester and New College, Oxford, where he received first class honors in "Modern Greats" (politics, philosophy, and economics) in 1927.

For the next ten years Gaitskell pursued a career in teaching. He lectured to Nottingham miners for a year (1927-1928) on behalf of the Workers' Educational Association, his first extended contact with working-class life. Then he taught economics and politics at University College, London, rising to the position of reader in political economy in 1938. In 1937 he married Dora Frost, with whom he had two daughters.

Gaitskell's interest in socialism was stimulated initially during his student days at Oxford, where he came under the influence of G. D. H. Cole, the socialist philosopher and historian. His first political act was to assist the workers in Oxford during the nine days' general strike of 1926. In 1935 he ran unsuccessfully as Labour Party candidate for a parliamentary seat at Chatham. He began to make speeches and to participate in party activities. He advocated collective security against fascism and took a moderate socialist line on economic questions, arguing in favor of social equality and against revolution.

During World War II Gaitskell joined the civil service on a temporary basis. He served in several important ministries and worked closely with the Labour politician Hugh Dalton. In the general election of 1945 he won the seat in Parliament for Leeds South, which he held for the remainder of his life. In the postwar government of Clement Attlee he was appointed to the positions of minister of fuel and power (1947-1950), minister of state for economic affairs (1950), and chancellor of the exchequer (1950-1951). As chancellor he introduced charges into the hitherto free National Health Service.

In 1951 the Conservative Party was returned to power, and Gaitskell never again held governmental office. Yet his political influence continued to grow, based as it was on a reputation for integrity and commitment to principle. In 1955, upon the resignation of Attlee, Gaitskell won the

eral party. Becoming an active leader of its left wing, he served successively as representative, senator, minister of education, and mayor of Bogotá. Continuing his law practice at the same time, Gaitán became an outstanding authority on Colombian penal law.

When mistrustful Liberal leaders refused to support his presidential candidacy in 1946, Gaitán ran for office on his own. Lacking organized support, he ran third in the race but soon afterward succeeded in capturing control of the Liberal party. When the party under his guidance won the March 1947 congressional elections, it was assumed that he would reach the presidency in the next contest.

Growing unrest under a Conservative minority government in 1948 aided Gaitán in strengthening his position as a champion of the people. On April 9, 1948, however, he was assassinated in downtown Bogotá during the convening of the Ninth Inter-American Conference. Although his shooting was not politically motivated, it provoked a severe wave of rioting, looting, and urban lawlessness which has gone down in history as the infamous *bogotazo*. Even in death a controversial figure, Gaitán is regarded by some as a selfish and opportunistic demagogue. Nonetheless, he remains the only 20th-century Colombian who reached the masses and gave them hope for a better life.

Further Reading

The best account of Gaitán's background and career appears in Vernon Fluharty, *Dance of the Millions: Military Rule and the Social Revolution in Colombia, 1930-1956* (1957). There is further consideration of his role in the evolution of Colombian

argued his case with intellectual distinction. It is generally conceded, even by his political opponents, that he would have been an effective, perhaps an outstanding, prime minister.

Further Reading

The best biography of Gaitskell is Philip M. Williams, *Hugh Gaitskell: A Political Biography* (1979, abridged and with new material, 1982). This should be read in conjunction with *The Diary of Hugh Gaitskell, 1945-1956,* edited by Philip M. Williams (1983). *Hugh Gaitskell, 1906-1963,* edited by W.T. Rodgers, contains interesting essays by people who knew him well at various times of his life. Carl Brand, *The British Labour Party: A Short History* (rev. ed., 1974) is a good introduction to the postwar history of the party. Two studies of the divisions within the Labour Party are Leslie Hunter, *The Road to Brighton Pier* (1959) and Stephen Haseler, *The Gaitskellites: Revisionism in the Labour Party, 1951-64* (1969), the latter written from a pro-Gaitskell perspective. Biographies of Labour politicians which contain useful material about Gaitskell are Ben Pimlott, *Hugh Dalton* (1985); Michael Foot, *Aneurin Bevan,* 2 vols. (1962, 1973); and Kenneth Harris, *Attlee* (1982).

Additional Sources

Williams, Philip Maynard, *Hugh Gaitskell,* Oxford Oxfordshire; New York: Oxford University Press, 1984. □

leadership of the Labour Party with a decisive victory over Herbert Morrison and Aneurin Bevan, a leader of the party's more radical wing.

Gaitskell steered the Labour Party in a moderate direction from 1955 until his death in 1963. He vigorously opposed the invasion of the Suez Canal by Britain, France, and Israel in 1956. He also tried to modify the party's commitment to the nationalization of industry, as embodied in clause four of its constitution. After losing the general election of October 1959 decisively to Harold Macmillan and the Conservatives, Gaitskell came under attack and the Labour Party began to divide into factions. At its annual conference at Scarborough a resolution was carried by the more radical faction led by Bevan endorsing unilateral nuclear disarmament. Gaitskell, a strong supporter of the North Atlantic Treaty Organization (NATO) alliance, made the most famous speech of his career on this occasion, vowing to "fight and fight and fight again to save the Party we love." The following year, at Blackpool, the party reversed the disarmament resolution by an overwhelming majority and re-established Gaitskell's authority as leader. It also gave him support on the clause four issue. In 1962 he used this authority to affirm the party's opposition to joining the European Common Market on the terms then being offered.

While at the peak of his influence Gaitskell became ill with a viral infection and died suddenly on January 18, 1963. His reputation as a political leader remained high. As both a conciliator and a vigorous fighter for his beliefs, he led the Labour Party in a moderate direction. He invariably

John Kenneth Galbraith

John Kenneth Galbraith (born 1908) was a leading scholar of the American Institutionalist school and arguably the most famous economist in the post World War II world. His views were a stinging indictment of the modern materialistic society that championed personal achievement and material well-being over public interest and needs. In spite of these views, he served as an advisor in both the American and Canadian governments from the 1930s onward.

John Kenneth Galbraith was born on October 15, 1908 in southern Ontario, Canada, on the shores of Lake Erie to a farming family of Scotch ancestry. He studied agricultural economics at the Ontario Agricultural College (then part of the University of Toronto; now, the University of Guelph) and graduated with distinction in 1931. He went on to study agricultural economics at the University of California, receiving his Ph.D. in 1934 after submitting a dissertation on public expenditures in California counties. In this year he also began his long, though frequently interrupted, tenure at Harvard University, where he became an emeritus professor. Galbraith's academic career frequently gave way to public service. He worked in the Department of Agriculture during the New Deal and in the Office of Price Administration and Civilian Supply during World War II, where, according to John S. Gambs, he was "virtually the

economic czar of the United States until he left in 1943" From his wartime work emerged a monograph, *The Theory of Price Control* (1952), which, though not widely influential, contained some of the seminal ideas of his major works.

After the end of the war in Europe, Galbraith worked with the Office of Strategic Services directing research on the effectiveness of the Allies' strategic bombing of Germany. In 1947 he was one of the liberal founders of the Americans for Democratic Action. After working prominently as a speechwriter in the presidential campaigns of Senator Adlai Stevenson, Galbraith went on to chair the Democratic Advisory Council during Dwight D. Eisenhower's Republican administration. In 1956 he visited India where his fascination with the country inspired his later works. He campaigned for President John F. Kennedy, and after Kennedy's victory he was named U.S. ambassador to India in the early 1960s. An outspoken critic of U.S. involvement in Vietnam, he campaigned on behalf of the presidential ambitions of Senators Eugene McCarthy (1968) and George McGovern (1972). Later he worked in the campaigns of Congressman Morris Udall (1976) and Senator Edward Kennedy (1980).

Galbraith's major intellectual contributions lie in the trilogy *The Affluent Society* (1958), *The New Industrial State* (1967), and *Economics and the Public Purpose* (1973). Along the way he published over 20 other books, including two novels, a co-authored book on Indian painting, memoirs, travelogues, political tracts, and several books on economic and intellectual history. He also collaborated on and

narrated a Public Broadcasting System television series, "The Age of Uncertainty."

American Capitalism

Other than his main trilogy, and perhaps *The Theory of Price Control,* Galbraith's *American Capitalism: The Concept of Countervailing Power* (1952) stands out in importance. The central argument of this book is that the growth of economic power in one economic sector tends to induce countervailing power from those who must bargain with the powerful. Hence, unionized labor and politically organized farmers rose in response to powerful manufacturers. The government is often involved in supporting the rise of this countervailing power and, in Galbraith's view, should be.

With its characteristic emphasis on the reality of economic concentration and on the microeconomics background of stabilization issues, this book solidified Galbraith's position as a continuing spokesperson for the New Deal perspective in economics. Galbraith coupled the new economics of John Maynard Keynes with the New Deal corporatist view, as did other Institutionalists of the time, notably C.E. Ayres and Allan G. Gruchy. With this book Galbraith's interest in power and his strong dissent from the neoclassical synthesis which was maturing at that time were set. The competitive modes so often used in economics textbooks, which had then been resurrected in the neoclassical synthesis which combined neoclassical microeconomics with Keynesian macroeconomics, maintain that good results follow from certain assumptions about the structure of the economy. Galbraith argued that such assumptions are not met in the actual economy, are unlikely to ever be met, and probably should not be met. He recognized power as an essential element of economic life and argued that only by examining the power of corporations, unions, and others could economists address the vital issues of social control and economic policy.

The Affluent Society

The Affluent Society examined the continuing urgency that affluent societies attach to higher consumption and production. The general explanation for this paradox, familiar to students of Veblen, is that obsolete ideas are held over from one historical period to another. These ideas persist not by inertia alone but also because they are convenient to powerful vested interests. *The Affluent Society* argued that the outmoded mentality of more-is-better impeded the further economic progress that would be possible if contemporary affluence were put to more reasonable use. Advertising and related salesmanship activities create artificially high demand for the commodities produced by private businesses and lead to a concomitant neglect of public sector goods and services that would contribute far more to the quality of life.

Galbraith's breakthrough as a best-selling author came with *The Affluent Society.* The widespread attention guaranteed some, albeit reluctant, hearing of his dissenting ideas in the economics profession. Indeed, he was eventually honored with the American Economic Association's prestigious presidency over the objections of some of the association's more conservative members. With its emphasis on the role of culture and history in economic life, and especially its review of the debilitating effects of an invidious pecuniary culture which seemingly had no higher social purpose than expanding material welfare, *The Affluent Society* gave a much needed awakening to the American Institutionalist school of economics. The book also influenced both the Great Society program and the rise of the American "counterculture" in the 1960s.

The New Industrial State

In *The New Industrial State* Galbraith expanded his analysis of the role of power in economic life. A central concept of the book is the *revised sequence.* The conventional wisdom in economic thought portrays economic life as a set of competitive markets governed ultimately by the decisions of sovereign consumers. In this original sequence, the control of the production process flows from consumers of commodities to the organizations that produce those commodities. In the revised sequence, this flow is reversed and businesses exercise control over consumers by advertising and related salesmanship activities.

The revised sequence concept applies only to the industrial system—that is, the manufacturing core of the economy in which each industry contains only a handful of very powerful corporations. It does not apply to the market system in the Galbraithian dual economy. In the market system, comprised of the vast majority of business organizations, price competition remains the dominant form of social control. In the industrial system, however, comprised of the 1,000 or so largest corporations, competitive price theory obscures the relation to the price system of these large and powerful corporations. In Galbraith's view, the principal function of market relations in this industrial system is not to constrain the power of the corporate behemoths but to serve as an instrument for the implementation of their power. Moreover, the power of these corporations extends into commercial culture and politics, allowing them to exercise considerable influence upon popular social attitudes and value judgments. That this power is exercised in the shortsighted interest of expanding commodity production and the status of the few is both inconsistent with democracy and a barrier to achieving the quality of life which the new industrial state with its affluence could provide.

The New Industrial State not only provided Galbraith with another best-selling book, it also extended once again the currency of Institutionalist economic thought. The book also filled a very pressing need in the late 1960s. The conventional theory of monopoly power in economic life maintains that the monopolist will attempt to restrict supply in order to maintain price above its competitive level. The social cost of this monopoly power is a decrease in both allocative efficiency and the equity of income distribution. This conventional economic analysis of the role of monopoly power did not adequately address popular concern about the large corporation in the late 1960s. The growing concern focused on the role of the corporation in politics, the damage done to the natural environment by an unmitigated commitment to economic growth, and the perversion of advertising and other pecuniary aspects of culture. *The New Industrial State* gave a plausible explanation of the power structure involved in generating these problems and thus found a very receptive audience among the rising American counterculture and political activists.

Third Book of the Trilogy

Economics and the Public Purpose, the last work in Galbraith's major trilogy, continued the characteristic insistence on the role of power in economic life and the inability of conventional economic thought to deal adequately with this power. Conventional economic thought, with its competitive model and presumptions of scarcity and consumer sovereignty—what Galbraith called the "imagery of choice"—serves to hide the power structure that actually governs the American economy. This obscurantism prevents economists from coming to grips with this governing structure and its untoward effects on the quality of life. Galbraith employed what he called "the test of anxiety" in this attack on conventional economics. He argued that any system of economic ideas should be evaluated by the test of anxiety—that is, by its ability to relate to popular concern about the economic system and to resolve or allay this anxiety. Galbraith contended that conventional economic thought failed the test of anxiety and again offered his basic model from *The New Industrial State* as an alternative approach to understanding the contemporary economy.

After the years he served in both the American and Canadian governments, Galbraith returned to scholarly activity, extensive travel, and writing, using Harvard University as his home base. Although "conventional economic wisdom" has remained firmly entrenched, Galbraith continued to kick at some of the props supporting it. In January 1997 Galbraith, delivering a lecture at the University of Toronto, again espoused his views that governments should create jobs by direct intervention in the economy. Although he represented the obscure Institutionalist school of economic thought, he nonetheless continued to convey his message that "there must be, most of all an effective safety net [of] individual and family support- for those who live on the lower edges of the system. This is humanely essential. It is also necessary for human freedom. Nothing sets such stern limits on the liberty of the citizen as the total absence of money." Only the future will likely force a resolution of Galbraith's principles. Either the visibility of the Institutionalist perspective will rise or Galbraith's work will experience the neglect common to other scholars of that school. Nonetheless, Galbraith's influence on the structure of the American economy will be felt for decades to come.

Further Reading

The best biographical work on John Kenneth Galbraith is his highly readable memoir, *A Life in Our Times* (1981). His influence and discussions of his work show up frequently in the *Journal of Economic Issues.* The book-length secondary literature on Galbraith includes Allan G. Grunchy, *Contemporary Economic Thought* (1972); Charles H. Hession, *John Kenneth Galbraith and His Critics* (1972); Myron E. Sharpe, *John Kenneth Galbraith and the Lower Economics* (1973, 2nd ed., 1974); John S. Gambs, *John Kenneth Galbraith* (1975); C.

Lynn Munro, *The Galbraithian Vision* (1977); Frederick J. Pratson, *Perspectives on Galbraith* (1978); and David Reisman, *Galbraith and Market Capitalism* (1980). ☐

Benito Pérez Galdós

The Spanish novelist and dramatist Benito Pérez Galdós (1843-1920) is best known for his masterly treatment of the vast panorama of Spanish society in a series of historical and contemporary novels.

Benito Pérez Galdós was born on May 10, 1843, in Las Palmas, Canary Islands. Due to a rigid upbringing he developed into a shy, quick-witted boy, interested in music, drama, and painting. He learned English from an American woman whose illegitimate daughter, Sisita, was his first cousin and childhood love. One of Galdós's most enduring remembrances concerned his affection for Sisita and the brusque intervention of his mother, who sent him away to Madrid in 1862 to study law.

In Madrid, Galdós felt irresistibly drawn to the turmoil of city life and soon abandoned his university courses for cafés, opera, theater, and long strolls through the streets. Intent upon understanding all classes and types of Spanish society, he frequented outlying districts, open-air markets, taverns, and tenement houses. By 1865 he had begun newspaper work. His articles on parliamentary sessions in *Las Cortes* made that newspaper famous.

Although Galdós was a perspicacious journalist, his ultimate aim was to give Spaniards not only a coherent picture of their daily lives but also a vision of a new Spain, reborn spiritually, culturally, and economically. He believed the novel best suited this purpose. In 1867 Galdós went to Paris, rediscovered the novels of Honoré de Balzac, and once back in Spain finished his first novel, *La sombra* (1870), and began a second, *La fontana de oro* (1867-1868).

Henceforth, except for his advocacy of liberal politics, Galdós lived immersed in literary activity. He wrote almost a hundred novels and plays, which may be classified into three groups. The first group includes his 46 *Episodios nacionales,* historical novels beginning with *Trafalgar* (1873) and ending with *Canovás* (1912). They retell in story form stirring episodes of 19th-century Spanish history and embody Galdós's conviction that the key to Spain's present and future betterment resides in a critical examination of the past.

The second group includes Galdós's realistic social novels, which divide into two subgroups. The first comprises the *Novelas de la primera época* (1867-1878). Among them are *Doña Perfecta* (1876) and *Gloria* (1876-1877), which boldly depict Spain's provincial hypocrisy and religious fanaticism. The second is made up of the 24 *Novelas españolas contemporáneas,* (1880-1915), which mark the maturity of Galdós's art. In such works as *La de Bringas* (1884), his four-volume masterpiece *Fortunata y Jacinta* (1886-1887), and *Misericordia* (1897), Galdós har-monized his passion for reform with the art of creating the illusion of reality. While treating many problems of Spanish life, he did not sacrifice character freedom to any social or moral teaching. Today, as then, his novels offer a compelling *imagen de la vida.*

The third group is made up of Galdós's plays. After writing novels for 20 years, Galdós turned to the theater. In 1891 he recast his novel *Realidad* into dialogue, staging it successfully the following year. He produced 22 plays, of which *La loca de la casa* (1893) and *El abuelo* (1904) are considered his best. The premiere of *Electra* (1901) unleashed a storm of controversy, earning Galdós the hatred of Spain's clergy and conservative class. Galdós was an authentic revolutionary of the Spanish theater. Reacting against José Echegaray's outmoded romantic melodrama, he confronted audiences with a frank portrayal of social conflicts. His plays anticipated the innovations of modern Spanish drama.

In 1897 Galdós was elected to the Spanish Academy, and by 1912 he had become totally blind. Beset by financial difficulties, he continued to write, although his health was failing. He died on Jan. 4, 1920, in Madrid.

Further Reading

The definitive biography in English of Galdós is Hyman Chonon Berkowitz, *Pérez Galdós: Spanish Liberal Crusader* (1948). Critical studies in English of his work include Walter T. Pattison, *Benito Pérez Galdós and the Creative Process* (1954); Sherman H. Eoff, *The Novels of Pérez Galdós* (1954); Alfred Rodriguez, *An Introduction to the Episodios*

Nacionales of Galdós (1967); and Michael Nimetz, *Humor in Galdós: A Study of the Novelas Contemporáneas* (1968). □

Galen

Galen (130-200), Greek physician, anatomist, physiologist, philosopher, and lexicographer, was probably the most influential physician of all time.

Throughout his life Galen was a prolific writer, producing his first books, *Three Commentaries on the Syllogistic Works of Chrysippus,* at the age of 13 and his last, *Introduction to Dialectics,* in the year of his death. His total output has been estimated at more than 2 1/2 million words. Those of his writings which survive make up over half the extant works of ancient medicine.

Various birth dates from 127 to 132 have been suggested, but 130 is generally accepted. Galen was born at Pergamon, Asia Minor, into a well-to-do family with strong scholarly traditions and influenced by the renaissance in Greek culture which had started at the end of the 1st century A.D. This renaissance had led to increasing Hellenization of the Roman world, the adoption of Greek models of learning, and the use of Greek as the cultural language.

Galen's father, Nicon, mathematician, architect, astronomer, philosopher, and devotee of Greek literature, was not only his sole instructor up to the age of 14, but the example of Stoic virtues on which Galen consciously modeled his own life. In his book *On the Passions and Errors of the Soul* he says he was "fortunate in having the least irascible, the most just, the most devoted of fathers," but of his mother he says "she was so very much prone to anger that sometimes she bit her handmaids; she constantly shrieked at my father and fought with him." Galen continues, "When I compared my father's noble deeds with the disgraceful passions of my mother I decided to embrace and love his deeds and flee and hate her passions." He defined passion as "that unbridled energy rebellious to reason" and had its control as one of his life's aims. Not surprisingly, perhaps, he himself remained unmarried.

Philosophical and Medical Training

In his fourteenth year Galen attended lectures given by Stoic, Platonic, Peripatetic, and Epicurean philosophers from Pergamon. Encouraged by Nicon, he refused to "proclaim [himself] a member of any of these sects" and said "there was no need for [the philosophy] teachers to disagree with one another, just as there was no disagreement among the teachers of geometry and arithmetic." Later in life he adopted the same attitude to the medical sects, and he urged physicians to take whatever is useful from wherever they find it and not to follow one sect or one man because that produces "an intellectual slave."

Galen relates that Nicon "advised by a dream made me take up medicine together with philosophy . . . if I had not devoted the whole of my life to the practice of medical and philosophical precepts, I would have learned nothing of importance . . . the great majority of men practicing medicine and philosophy are proficient in neither, for they were not well born or not instructed in a fitting way or did not persevere in their studies but turned to politics."

Galen, being well born, fittingly instructed, and eschewing politics, persevered with his studies at Pergamon for the next 4 years, as he puts it, "urging [myself] above [my] companions to such a degree that I was studying both day and night." His first anatomy teacher was Satyrus, a pupil of Quintus, who through his students played a major role in the resurgence of anatomical activity that culminated in Galen's work.

Nicon died in 150 and the following year Galen went to Smyrna. While there he wrote his first treatise, *On the Movements of the Heart and Lung.* In 152 he went to Corinth and on to Alexandria, where he remained for 4 years studying with Numisianus, Quintus's most famous pupil. Although Galen admired Numisianus and "the physicians [who] employ ocular demonstrations [of human bones] in teaching osteology," he tells us that "in Alexandria the art of medicine was taught by ignoramuses in a sophistical fashion in long, illogical lectures to crowds of fourteen-year-old boys who never got near the sick." He "went away surprised and sorrowful—sorrowful at [Julian the sectarian methodist's] lack of sense, and surprised . . . there could be sufficient stupid pupils to fill his classes."

To counteract the poor teaching and the misunderstandings of the students, Galen produced a number of dictionaries, both literary and medical. He also started a major work, *On Demonstration.* Unfortunately, no copy survives.

Physician to the Gladiators

In 157 Galen returned to Pergamon, where he "had the good fortune to think out and publicly demonstrate a cure for wounded tendons" which gained him, in 158, the position of physician to the gladiators. He was reappointed annually until the outbreak of the Parthian War in 161.

The traumatic injuries of the arena provided Galen with excellent opportunities to extend his knowledge of anatomy, surgery, and therapeutics, and throughout his life he drew on this fund of experience to illustrate his arguments. While physician to the gladiators, whose daily lives can be reconstructed from his writings, Galen produced some of his most original work, including his demonstration of the part played by the recurrent laryngeal nerve in controlling the production of the voice. This for him and his contemporaries had wide implications, since it impinged on their ideas of the soul.

Practice in Rome

In 163 Galen went to Rome, where he was befriended by the philosopher Eudemus and the consul Flavius Boethius. Galen's public anatomical demonstrations and his success as a physician so aroused the jealousies of the Roman physicians that Eudemus "warned him he was putting himself in danger of assassination." Galen, who accepted the Stoic teachings "to scorn honors and worldly goods and to hold only truth in esteem," scorned the self-seeking of his adversaries and deplored their inability to understand honesty of motive and intellect when they encountered it. He says "his training and studies [did] not fit him to cope with the ignorance and craftiness of his enemies," yet he felt it imperative "to continue to speak out freely." This passion to disseminate knowledge as widely and as publicly as possible is the key to understanding Galen and is the explanation of much of the polemical writing he directed at those who set themselves up as authorities and teachers and who either passed on false information or secretively withheld knowledge in their possession.

Galen returned to Pergamon in 166. However, a severe outbreak of plague among the Roman troops in Aquileia in 168 caused the emperors Marcus Aurelius and Lucius Verus to send for him and appoint him physician-in-ordinary. In 169 Marcus made Galen physician to his son, Commodus (emperor 180-192); and so until 175, when Commodus rejoined Marcus on his military campaigns, Galen lived in one or another of the imperial country houses. During this time he completed his major physiological work, *On the Usefulness of the Parts of the Body* in 17 books, and wrote another major physiological treatise, *On the Natural Faculties,* and many other treatises. In 176, as physician to Marcus, Galen returned to Rome permanently. Now under imperial protection, he continued his writing, lecturing, and public demonstrations.

In the winter of 191/192 a fire destroyed most of Galen's library. Yet in spite of this loss (which he met with Stoic calm, saying "no loss was enough to cause me grief"), we are very well informed about his writings, because he wrote two treatises on his own books and their order of production. The first he wrote as a young man when "a certain book . . . plainly inscribed 'Galenus Medicus' proved on inspection . . . to be a forgery." The second was compiled in 198. Both works provide authoritative information on the authenticity of his writings and are major sources of biographical detail.

From 179 to his death in 200, Galen continued his medical research and writings, producing such major works as *The Method of Cure.* However, during his last decade he wrote in a more philosophical vein, giving us such treatises as *On the Equality of Sin and Punishment, The Slight Significance of Popular Honor and Glory,* and *The Refusal to Divulge Knowledge.* His last work was titled *Introduction to Dialectics.*

Assessment of Galen

That Galen was a man of his time is shown by his success and rapid preferment, by his acceptance of dreams as sound directives for action and treatment, and by his acceptance of the Hippocratic tradition and of the social role of public prognostics. That he provoked such strong reactions shows him to have been a dominant individual in an age of individuals. Galen believed the Hippocratic writings were never wrong—merely obscure—and he saw his own work as the extension and clarification of the Hippocratic corpus; for example, he systematized the theory of the four humors. Nevertheless, Galen was aware of the intervening intellectual progress, saying "the fact that we are born later than the ancients and receive from them the arts in an advanced state, is no small advantage . . . things that took Hippocrates a long time to discover one can now learn in a few years and one can employ the rest of one's life in the discovery of the things that remain to be learned."

The change in medical thought that Galen produced in his own lifetime was much greater than the changes from Hippocrates's time to his own. When Galen commenced his studies, there were as many "medicines" as there were sects and no criteria for judging "the best sect." He showed that a major source of sectarian conflict and error was due to the lack of philosophical training, which in turn led to "the use of unproven principles," the misunderstanding of "demonstrations," and "a disdain of dissection." Because he accepted the mathematical model of truth, with its criterion of agreement, he claimed that "if conclusions in connection with the cure of disease [were properly] grounded, physicians would manifest an accord like that of geometricians, though it would require [their] learning at the very beginning the meaning of every term, and what undemonstrable propositions commonly called axioms will be accepted."

Galen saw the science of medicine as "based on two criteria, reason and experience," which guaranteed the truth or falsity of its propositions. His systematic anatomical experiments provided a means of demonstrating to the senses those things which no sane man could deny any more than he could deny the self-evident axioms of mathematics. However, among his self-evident axioms we find "Nature [and/or the Creator] does nothing in vain." His frequent appeal to this axiom for explanatory purposes is in part responsible for the overemphasis on the teleological aspects of his writings by both his followers and his critics. Galen's concept of Nature is subtle and complex, and his Creator differs from the Christian God in not being omnipotent but subject to both the laws of necessity and the nature of matter. It was the very success of his program of unification of medical theory that led to its "rigidity" and supremacy in the ensuing centuries.

Most surprisingly, we do not know Galen's family name, because, not wanting to trade on his forebears' reputations, he used only his given name; the name Claudius often associated with him is probably a Renaissance misunderstanding. Galen said of himself, "I have worked only for science and truth and for that reason I have avoided placing my name at the beginning of my books." On the other hand, he was pleased to record Marcus Aurelius's lavish praise that he was "the first of physicians and the only philosopher."

Further Reading

The translation by M. T. May, *Galen: On the Usefulness of the Parts of the Body* (2 vols., 1968), contains an excellent introduction and an extensive bibliography. Other translations of his works are R. Walzer, *Galen on Medical Experiences* (1946); R.M. Green, *A Translation of Galen's Hygiene* (1951); A.J. Brock, *Galen on the Natural Faculties* (1952); C. Singer, *Galen on Anatomical Procedures: The Later Books* (1962);

and P.W. Harkins and W. Riese, *Galen on the Passions and Errors of the Soul* (1964). A few selections can be read in M.R. Cohen and I.E. Drabkin, *A Source Book in Greek Science* (1948), and L. Clendening, *Source Book of Medical History* (1960). See also George Sarton, *Galen of Pergamon* (1954). □

Galileo Galilei

The Italian scientist Galileo Galilei (1564-1642) is renowned for his epoch-making contributions to astronomy, physics, and scientific philosophy.

Galileo was born in Pisa on Feb. 15, 1564, the first child of Vincenzio Galilei, a merchant and musician and an abrasive champion of advanced musical theories of the day. The family moved to Florence in 1574, and that year Galileo started his formal education in the nearby monastery of Vallombrosa. Seven years later he matriculated as a student of medicine at the University of Pisa.

In 1583, while Galileo was at home on vacation, he began to study mathematics and the physical sciences. His zeal astonished Ostilio Ricci, a family friend and professor at the Academy of Design. Ricci was a student of Nicolò Tartaglia, the famed algebraist and translator into Latin of several of Archimedes' works. Galileo's life-long admiration for Archimedes started, therefore, as his scientific studies got under way.

Galileo's new interest brought to an end his medical studies, but in Pisa at that time there was only one notable science teacher, Francisco Buonamico, and he was an Aristotelian. Galileo seems, however, to have been an eager disciple of his, as shown by Galileo's *Juvenilia,* dating from 1584, mostly paraphrases of Aristotelian physics and cosmology. Because of financial difficulties Galileo had to leave the University of Pisa in 1585 before he got his degree.

Early Work

Back in Florence, Galileo spent 3 years vainly searching for a suitable teaching position. He was more successful in furthering his grasp of mathematics and physics. He produced two treatises which, although circulated in manuscript form only, made his name well known. One was *La bilancetta* (The Little Balance), describing the hydrostatic principles of balancing; the other was a study on the center of gravity of various solids. These topics, obviously demanding a geometrical approach, were not the only evidence of his devotion to geometry and Archimedes. In a lecture given in 1588 before the Florentine Academy on the topography of Dante's *Inferno,* Galileo seized on details that readily lent themselves to a display of his prowess in geometry. He showed himself a perfect master both of the poet's text and of the incisiveness and sweep of geometrical lore.

Galileo's rising reputation as a mathematician and natural philosopher (physicist) gained him a teaching post at the University of Pisa in 1589. The 3 years he spent there are memorable for two things. First, he became exposed

through reading a work of Giovanni Battista Benedetti to the "Parisian tradition" of physics, which originated during the 14th century with the speculations of Jean Buridan and Nicole Oresme at the University of Paris. This meant the breakaway point in Galileo's thought from Aristotelian physics and the start of his preoccupation with a truly satisfactory formulation of the impetus theory. Second, right at the beginning of his academic career, he showed himself an eager participant in disputes and controversies. With biting sarcasm he lampooned the custom of wearing academic gowns. The most he was willing to condone was the use of ordinary clothes, but only after pointing out that the best thing was to go naked.

The death of Galileo's father in 1591 put on his shoulders the care of his mother, brothers, and sisters. He had to look for a better position, which he found in 1592 at the University of Padua, part of the Venetian Republic. The 18 years he spent there were, according to his own admission, the happiest of his life. He often visited Venice and made many influential friends, among them Giovanfrancesco Sagredo, whom he later immortalized in the *Dialogue* as the representative of judiciousness and good sense.

In 1604 Galileo publicly declared that he was a Copernican. In three public lectures given in Venice, before an overflow audience, he argued that the new star which appeared earlier that year was major evidence in support of the doctrine of Copernicus. (Actually the new star merely proved that there was something seriously wrong with the Aristotelian doctrine of the heavens.) More important was a letter Galileo wrote that year to Father Paolo Sarpi, in which he stated that "the distances covered in natural motion are proportional to the squares of the number of time intervals, and therefore, the distances covered in equal times are as the odd numbers beginning from one." By natural motion, Galileo meant the unimpeded fall of a body, and what he proposed was the law of free fall, later written as $s = 1/2(gt^2)$, where s is distance, t is time, and g is the acceleration due to gravity at sea level.

In 1606 came the publication of *The Operations of the Geometrical and Military Compass,* which reveals the experimentalist and craftsman in Galileo. In this booklet he went overboard in defending his originality against charges from rather insignificant sources. It was craftsmanship, not theorizing, which put the crowning touch on his stay in Padua. In mid-1609 he learned about the success of some Dutch spectacle makers in combining lenses into what later came to be called a telescope. He feverishly set to work, and on August 25 he presented to the Venetian Senate a telescope as his own invention. The success was tremendous. He obtained a lifelong contract at the University of Padua, but he also stirred up just resentment when it was learned that he was not the original inventor.

Astronomical Works

Galileo's success in making a workable and sufficiently powerful telescope with a magnifying power of about 40 was due to intuition rather than to rigorous reasoning in optics. It was also the intuitive stroke of a genius that made him turn the telescope toward the sky sometime in the fall of 1609, a feat which a dozen other people could very well have done during the previous 4 to 5 years. Science had few luckier moments. Within a few months he gathered astonishing evidence about mountains on the moon, about moons circling Jupiter, and about an incredibly large number of stars, especially in the belt of the Milky Way. On March 12, 1610, all these sensational items were printed in Venice under the title *Sidereus nuncius* (*The Starry Messenger*), a booklet which took the world of science by storm. The view of the heavens drastically changed, and so did Galileo's life.

Historians agree that Galileo's decision to secure for himself the position of court mathematician in Florence at the court of Cosimo II (the job also included the casting of horoscopes for his princely patron) reveals a heavy strain of selfishness in his character. He wanted nothing, not even a modest amount of teaching, to impede him in pursuing his ambition to become the founder of new physics and new astronomy. In 1610 he left behind in Padua his common-law wife, Marina Gamba, and his young son, Vincenzio, and placed his two daughters, aged 12 and 13, in the convent of S. Matteo in Arcetri. The older, Sister Maria Celeste as nun, was later a great comfort to her father.

Galileo's move to Florence turned out to be highly unwise, as events soon showed. In the beginning, however, everything was pure bliss. He made a triumphal visit to Rome in 1611. The next year saw the publication of his *Discourse on Bodies in Water.* There he disclosed his discovery of the phases of Venus (a most important proof of the truth of the Copernican theory), but the work was also the source of heated controversies. In 1613 Galileo published his observations of sunspots, which embroiled him for many years in bitter disputes with the German Jesuit Christopher Scheiner of the University of Ingolstadt, whose observations of sunspots had already been published in January 1612 under the pseudonym Apelles.

First Condemnation

But Galileo's real aim was to make a sweeping account of the Copernican universe and of the new physics it necessitated. A major obstacle was the generally shared, though officially never sanctioned, belief that the biblical revelation imposed geocentrism in general and the motionlessness of the earth in particular. To counter the scriptural difficulties, he waded deep into theology. With the help of some enlightened ecclesiastics, such as Monsignor Piero Dini and Father Benedetto Castelli, a Benedictine from Monte Cassino and his best scientific pupil, Galileo produced essays in the form of letters, which now rank among the best writings of biblical theology of those times. As the letters (the longest one was addressed to Grand Duchess Christina of Tuscany) circulated widely, a confrontation with the Church authorities became inevitable. The disciplinary instruction handed down in 1616 by Cardinal Robert Bellarmine forbade Galileo to "hold, teach and defend in any manner whatsoever, in words or in print" the Copernican doctrine of the motion of the earth.

Galileo knew, of course, both the force and the limits of what in substance was a disciplinary measure. It could be reversed, and he eagerly looked for any evidence indicating precisely that. He obeyed partly out of prudence, partly because he remained to the end a devout and loyal Catholic. Although his yearning for fame was powerful, there can be no doubt about the sincerity of his often-voiced claim that by his advocacy of Copernicanism he wanted to serve the long-range interest of the Church in a world of science. The first favorable sign came in 1620, when Cardinal Maffeo Barberini composed a poem in honor of Galileo. Three years later the cardinal became Pope Urban VIII. How encouraged Galileo must have felt can be seen from the fact that he dedicated to the new pope his freshly composed *Assayer,* one of the finest pieces of polemics ever produced in the philosophy of science.

The next year Galileo had six audiences with Urban VIII, who promised a pension for Galileo's son, Vincenzio, but gave Galileo no firm assurance about changing the injunction of 1616. But before departing for Florence, Galileo was informed that the Pope had remarked that "the Holy Church had never, and would never, condemn it [Copernicanism] as heretical but only as rash, though there was no danger that anyone would ever demonstrate it to be necessarily true." This was more than enough to give Galileo the necessary encouragement to go ahead with the great undertaking of his life.

The *Dialogue*

Galileo spent 6 years writing his *Dialogue concerning the Two Chief World Systems.* When the final manuscript copy was being made in March 1630, Father Castelli dispatched the news to Galileo that Urban VIII insisted in a private conversation with him that, had he been the pope in 1616, the censuring of Copernicanism would have never taken place. Galileo also learned about the benevolent attitude of the Pope's official theologian, Father Nicolò Riccardi, Master of the Sacred Palace. The book was published with ecclesiastical approbation on Feb. 21, 1632.

Its contents are easy to summarize, as its four main topics are discussed in dialogue form on four consecutive days. Of the three interlocutors, Simplicius represented Aristotle, Salviati was Galileo's spokesman, and Sagredo played the role of the judicious arbiter leaning heavily toward Galileo. The First Day is devoted to the criticism of the alleged perfection of the universe and especially of its superlunary region, as claimed by Aristotle. Here Galileo made ample use of his discovery of the "imperfections" of the moon, namely, of its rugged surface revealed by the telescope. The Second Day is a discussion of the advantages of the rotation of the earth on its axis for the explanation of various celestial phenomena. During the Third Day the orbital motion of the earth around the sun is debated, the principal issues being the parallax of stars and the undisturbed state of affairs on the surface of the earth in spite of its double motion. In this connection Galileo gave the most detailed account of his ideas of the relativity of motion and of the inertial motion. Bafflingly enough, he came to contradict his best-posited principles when he offered during the Fourth Day the tides as proof of the earth's twofold motion. The inconsistencies and arbitrariness that characterize his discourse there could not help undermine an otherwise magnificent effort presented in a most attractive style.

Second Condemnation

The *Dialogue* certainly proved that for all his rhetorical provisos Galileo held, taught, and defended the doctrine of Copernicus. It did not help Galileo either that he put into the mouth of the discredited Simplicius an argument which was a favorite with Urban VIII. Galileo was summoned to Rome to appear before the Inquisition. Legally speaking, his prosecutors were justified. Galileo did not speak the truth when he claimed before his judges that he did not hold Copernicanism since the precept was given to him in 1616 to abandon it. The justices had their point, but it was the letter of the law, not its spirit, that they vindicated. More importantly, they miscarried justice, aborted philosophical truth, and gravely compromised sound theology. In that misguided defense of orthodoxy the only sad solace for Galileo's supporters consisted in the fact that the highest authority of the Church did not become implicated, as the Catholic René Descartes, the Protestant Gottfried Wilhelm von Leibniz, and others were quick to point out during the coming decades.

The proceedings dragged on from the fall of 1632 to the summer of 1633. During that time Galileo was allowed to stay at the home of the Florentine ambassador in Rome and was detained by the Holy Office only from June 21, the day preceding his abjuration, until the end of the month. He was never subjected to physical coercion. However, he had to inflict the supreme torture upon himself by abjuring the doctrine that the earth moved. One hundred years later a writer with vivid imagination dramatized the event by claiming that following his abjuration Galileo muttered the words "Eppur si muove (And yet it does move)."

On his way back to Florence, Galileo enjoyed the hospitality of the archbishop of Siena for some 5 months and then received permission in December to live in his own villa at Arcetri. He was not supposed to have any visitors, but this injunction was not obeyed. Nor was ecclesiastical prohibition a serious obstacle to the printing of his works outside Italy. In 1634 Father Marin Mersenne published in French translation a manuscript of Galileo on mechanics composed during his Paduan period. In Holland the Elzeviers brought out his *Dialogue* in Latin in 1635 and shortly afterward his great theological letter to Grand Duchess Christina. But the most important event in this connection took place in 1638, when Galileo's *Two New Sciences* saw print in Leiden.

Two New Sciences

The first draft of the work went back to Galileo's professorship at Padua. But cosmology replaced pure physics as the center of his attention until 1633. His condemnation was in a sense a gain for physics. He had no sooner regained his composure in Siena than he was at work preparing for publication old, long-neglected manuscripts. The *Two New Sciences,* like the *Dialogue,* is in the dialogue form and the discussions are divided into Four Days. The First Day is largely taken up with the mechanical resistance of materials, with ample allowance for speculations on the atomic constitution of matter. There are also long discussions on the question of vacuum and on the isochronism of the vibrations of pendulums. During the Second Day all these and other topics, among them the properties of levers, are discussed in a strictly mathematical manner, in an almost positivist spirit, with no attention being given to "underlying causes." Equally "dry" and mathematical is the analysis of uniform and accelerated motion during the Third Day, and the same holds true of the topic of the Fourth Day, the analysis of projectile motion. There Galileo proved that the longest shot occurred when the cannon was set at an angle of 45 degrees. He arrived at this result by recognizing that the motions of the cannonball in the vertical and in the horizontal directions "can combine without changing, disturbing or impeding each other" into a parabolic path.

Galileo found the justification for such a geometrical analysis of motion partly because it led to a striking correspondence with factual data. More importantly, he believed that the universe was structured along the patterns of geometry. In 1604 he could have had experimental verification of the law of free fall, which he derived on a purely theoretical basis, but it is not known that he sought at that time such an experimental proof. He was a Christian Platonist as far as scientific method was concerned. This is why he praised Copernicus repeatedly in the *Dialogue* for his belief in the voice of reason, although it contradicted sense experience. Such a faith rested on the conviction that the world was a product of a personal, rational Creator who disposed everything according to weight, measure, and number.

This biblically inspired faith was stated by Galileo most eloquently in the closing pages of the First Day of the *Dialogue*. There he described the human mind as the most excellent product of the Creator, precisely because it could recognize mathematical truths. This faith is possibly the most precious bequest of the great Florentine, who spent his last years partially blind. His disciple Vincenzio Viviani sensed this well as he described the last hours of Galileo: "On the night of Jan. 8, 1642, with philosophical and Christian firmness he rendered up his soul to its Creator, sending it, as he liked to believe, to enjoy and to watch from a closer vantage point those eternal and immutable marvels which he, by means of a fragile device, had brought closer to our mortal eyes with such eagerness and impatience."

Further Reading

Galileo's chief works are available in excellent translations: *Dialogue concerning the Two Chief World Systems* (translated by Stillman Drake, 1953); *Dialogues concerning Two New Sciences* (translated by H. Crew and A. de Salvio, 1914; repr. 1952); and *The Discoveries and Opinions of Galileo* (edited and translated by Stillman Drake, 1957), which contains *The Starry Messenger,* the *Letters on Sunspots,* the *Letter to Grand Duchess Christina,* and the Assayer.

Stillman Drake also wrote *Galileo Studies: Personality, Tradition, and Revolution* (1970), which discusses Galileo and 16th-century science. An excellently written, relatively short biography is James Brodrick, *Galileo: The Man, His Work, His Misfortunes* (1965). Giorgio de Santillana, *The Crime of Galileo* (1955), and Jerome J. Langford, *Galileo: Science and the Church* (1966), treat Galileo's condemnation and trial. His philosophy of science is the principal consideration in Ludovico Geymonat, *Galileo Galilei* (1965). A Galileo bibliography of some 2,000 entries, covering the period 1940-1965, is in *Galileo: Man of Science* (1968), edited by Ernan McMullin, a volume of essays commemorating the four-hundredth anniversary of Galileo's birth. □

Albert Gallatin

Swiss-born Albert Gallatin (1761-1849) was U.S. secretary of the Treasury, as well as a diplomat, banker, and ethnographer.

Albert Gallatin was born in Geneva, Switzerland, on Jan. 29, 1761. His father was a prosperous merchant descended from an aristocratic family long politically prominent. Orphaned at the age of 9, Gallatin grew up in the home of a relative. He graduated from the Academy of Geneva in 1779. A young man of the age of the Enlightenment, he was sympathetic to the American Revolution and sailed for America in 1780, happy to be in "the freest country in the universe."

After a winter as a merchant in Maine, and a brief time with the colonial militia, Gallatin tutored in French in Boston in 1781. In 1782 he was appointed a tutor at Harvard College.

In 1783 Gallatin and a Frenchman planned to purchase western land and located an area in Virginia. Gallatin carried out surveying, mapped the interior, and registered land titles until an Indian uprising forced him to retreat. He took an oath of allegiance to the Commonwealth of Virginia in 1785.

Early Political Career

In 1786 Gallatin bought a 400-acre farm in western Pennsylvania and devoted himself to farming and land development. But his training and talents were unusual on the frontier, and he quickly became a political leader. In 1788 he was elected as a delegate to a meeting to propose amendments to the new U.S. Constitution. In 1789 he attended the Pennsylvania Constitutional Convention. He was elected to the Pennsylvania Legislature in 1790 and reelected the next 2 years. Quickly establishing a reputation for hard work and integrity, Gallatin became a skillful and logical orator. His greatest contribution came in the field of public finance. In 1793 he was elected to the U.S. Senate as a Republican.

However, when Gallatin took his Senate seat, the Federalists challenged his eligibility, based on the fact that he had not applied for citizenship early enough to meet technical citizenship requirements. The Senate ruled against him, and Gallatin returned to Pennsylvania, where the new excise tax on whiskey stills had stirred up the rioting known as the Whiskey Rebellion. Though he opposed the tax, Gallatin also opposed violence and tried to moderate the

local militia's use of force. He was largely responsible for persuading his comrades to submit to the new law.

Elected to Congress

Meanwhile, Gallatin had been elected to Congress again. He entered the House of Representatives in 1795 and became the most knowledgeable Republican on public finance. He proposed creation of the Ways and Means Committee—Congress's first permanent standing committee—to receive financial reports from the secretary of the Treasury and to superintend government finances. His *A Sketch of the Finances of the United States* (1796), a moderate, detailed analysis of the Federalist financial program, argued that a public debt was a public curse. Because the debt had grown since 1790, he proposed several new measures.

When James Madison retired in 1797, Gallatin became the Republican spokesman in the House. He opposed the Federalists' warlike measures against France and, when the Federalists passed the Alien and Sedition Acts (1798) to silence domestic political opposition, he resisted with powerful arguments defending basic civil liberties.

Secretary of the Treasury

With Thomas Jefferson's presidency in 1800 and the triumph of the Republicans, Gallatin was named to head the Treasury Department. He held this position longer than had any other secretary of the Treasury, serving from 1801 to 1814. Pledged to reduce the national debt and eliminate the excise tax, he projected a plan to pay off the debt by 1817, outlined proposals for appropriations for specified purposes, advocated promotion of manufacturing, and argued for constructing a nationwide network of roads and canals with Federal aid.

For 6 years Gallatin's policies worked. But after 1807 the Embargo Act and other American efforts at peaceful coercion to avoid involvement in the Napoleonic Wars wrecked his policies. Although Gallatin favored rechartering the Bank of the United States in 1811, Congress refused, and America entered the War of 1812 with its monetary system in disarray. The war dealt the final blow to Gallatin's financial system.

Diplomatic Career

President Madison granted Gallatin leave from the Treasury to join John Quincy Adams and James A. Bayard in exploring Russia's offer to mediate in the war. When Great Britain rejected this offer, Madison appointed Gallatin to the commission to negotiate directly with Britain. He became its most influential member. Adams, not much given to praise, rated him as the leading negotiator on both sides. Historian Henry Adams labeled the Treaty of Ghent "the special and peculiar triumph of Mr. Gallatin."

Gallatin continued in diplomatic service for most of the next decade. He served as American minister to France (1816-1823). In 1818 he joined Richard Rush in London to work out a treaty extending earlier commercial agreements, securing American fishing rights off Newfoundland, drawing the northern boundary between Canada and the United

States at the 49th parallel, and leaving the Oregon Territory open for joint occupation.

In 1823 Gallatin returned to the United States. Nominated for vice president on the Republican ticket headed by William H. Crawford, he withdrew when Crawford's manager attempted to substitute Henry Clay as the vice-presidential candidate. After Gallatin spent an interlude as a gentleman farmer, President John Quincy Adams appointed him minister to Great Britain in 1826. Gallatin's public career ended with his final report relating to the Maine boundary dispute.

Late Career

Settling in New York, Gallatin served as president of the National Bank from 1831 until his retirement in 1839. He unsuccessfully supported renewal of the charter of the Second Bank of the United States, but he was instrumental in obtaining the resumption of specie payments after their suspension following the economic panic of 1837. Although he criticized high tariffs and advocated free trade, he affirmed Congress's right to levy protective tariffs.

In his last years Gallatin was prominent in cultural affairs. He became president of New York University's council in 1830. In 1836 he was elected to the American Antiquarian Society, and in 1843 he headed the New York Historical Society. However, he devoted most of his attention to the ethnology of the American Indian and founded the American Ethnological Society in 1842.

In 1789 Gallatin had married Sophia Allegre, who died 5 months later. He married Hannah Nicholson in 1793, and they had two sons and three daughters. Gallatin died on Aug. 13, 1849.

Further Reading

A good biography of Gallatin is Raymond Walters, Jr., *Albert Gallatin: Jeffersonian Financier and Diplomat* (1957), though the older study by Henry Adams, *The Life of Albert Gallatin* (1879), remains useful. Special studies include Frederick Merk, *Albert Gallatin and the Oregon Problem: A Study in Anglo-American Diplomacy* (1950); Leonard D. White, *The Jeffersonians: A Study in Administrative History, 1801-1829* (1951); and Alexander Balinsky, *Albert Gallatin: Fiscal Theories and Policies* (1958).

Additional Sources

Adams, Henry, *Albert Gallatin,* New York: Chelsea House, 1983.
Aitken, Thomas, *Albert Gallatin: early America's Swiss-born statesman,* New York: Vantage Press, 1985.
Gallatin, James, *The diary of James Gallatin, secretary to Albert Gallatin, a great peace maker, 1813-1827,* West Port, Conn.: Greenwood Press, 1979, 1916.
Kuppenheimer, L. B., *Albert Gallatin's vision of democratic stability: an interpretive profile,* Westport, CT: Praeger, 1996. □

Thomas Hopkins Gallaudet

Thomas Hopkins Gallaudet (1787-1851), American educator, founded the first free school for the deaf in America.

Thomas Gallaudet was born in Philadelphia on Dec. 10, 1787. His family moved to Hartford, Conn., where he attended grammar school. He entered Yale College as a sophomore in 1802 and graduated the youngest in his class and with highest honors. He then tried his hand at law, teaching, and business but finally decided on the ministry. He attended Andover Theological Seminary from 1811 to 1814.

As a new pastor, Gallaudet encountered a deaf-mute child, Alice Cogswell, whose father set about to establish a special school for children like his daughter. Enlisted in the project to formalize this kind of education in America, Gallaudet went to Europe in 1815 to study established systems of symbolic instruction. He investigated the Braidwood method used in London and Edinburgh. Learning of advanced techniques practiced by Abbé Sicard with deaf-mutes in Paris, Gallaudet visited him and mastered his methods. When Gallaudet returned to the United States in 1816, accompanied by one of Sicard's assistants, he began seeking financial support for a school for the deaf and mute which had already been incorporated by the Connecticut Legislature. The school, inspired by the ability of Alice

Cogswell to overcome her handicap, opened in Hartford in 1817.

Gallaudet's direction, writings, and public appearances made the school successful. By 1830, when ill health forced him to retire, the school had 140 pupils, and its effectiveness had drawn public notice throughout the United States.

Gallaudet turned down offers to join university faculties or to lead other special schools so that he could devote himself to writing books for young children and promoting popular education. He worked on a speller and a dictionary and wrote *Book on the Soul* (1831), *Scripture Biography* (1833), and *Everyday Christian* (1835). These, along with numerous journal and magazine articles, gained him worldwide recognition.

The care of the insane became Gallaudet's new interest. In 1838 he became chaplain to the Retreat for the Insane in Hartford. From 1837 to 1844 he was also a volunteer chaplain of the Hartford county jail.

In 1821 Gallaudet had married Sophia Fowler, a deaf-mute and former pupil. They had eight children, one of whom, Edward, participated in founding the Gallaudet College for the deaf in Washington, D.C. Thomas Gallaudet died in Hartford on Sept. 10, 1851.

Further Reading

Heman Humphrey, *The Life and Labors of the Rev. T. H. Gallaudet* (1857), contains many letters, sermons, and addresses. The early chapters of Maxine T. Boatner, *Voice of the Deaf: A Biography of Edward Miner Gallaudet* (1959), provide a good, illustrated summary. See also Henry Barnard, *Tribute to Gallaudet* (1852; 2d ed. 1859). □

Rómulo Gallegos Freire

Rómulo Gallegos Freire (1884-1969) was Venezuela's most noted novelist, a teacher, and a political leader. Though he became president of his country, his fame rests on the vivid description of the Venezuelan people in his novels.

Rómulo Gallegos was born in Caracas on Aug. 2, 1884. He chose secondary school teaching as his vocation and during the 1920s instructed many young men who as university students mounted a rebellion against the tyranny of Gen. Juan Vicente Gómez and later became leaders in Venezuelan politics.

Literary Career

However, it was not as a teacher or political leader that Gallegos was to achieve greatest fame. In 1921, when he was 37, he published his first novel, *Reinaldo Solar*. Five years later his second work, *La Trepadora*, appeared. But *Doña Bárbara* (1930) brought him worldwide attention. This fictional portrait of a typical character of the Venezuelan interior was immediately popular in Venezuela and was widely read in other Spanish-speaking countries.

Among those who read and admired *Doña Bárbara* was Gómez, who offered Gallegos a seat in the Venezuelan Senate. However, unwilling to serve the dictator, Gallegos used an excuse to go abroad and did not return home until after the death of Gómez.

Meanwhile, Gallegos continued to turn out his novels. These included *Canaima* (1934) and *Pobre negro* (1937), which, like their predecessors, dealt with various groups in Venezuelan society. What is often considered his masterpiece is *Cantaclaro* , concerning the adventures of a wandering cowboy minstrel in the great plains of Venezuela. As did most of Gallegos's other works, it relied heavily on local dialect and the social circumstances of preindustrial Venezuela.

Political Involvement

With the death of Juan Vicente Gómez in 1935, Gallegos became increasingly involved in politics. He supported efforts of some of his former students to organize a nationalist left-wing party of democratic orientation, the Partido Democrático Nacional. In 1941 he agreed to be the party's symbolic candidate for president against the government's nominee, Gen. Isaias Medina Angarita. But Gallegos stood no chance of election.

During the next few years Gallegos devoted himself principally to literary activities, but he also supported the action of his party (now called Acción Democrática) in

joining with a group of young military men to seize power in October 1945. Thereafter, he served for some time as president of Acción Democrática.

In December 1947 Gallegos was the successful Acción Democrática candidate for president and was inaugurated 2 months later. However, almost from the beginning his government was faced with conspiracy by some military elements who opposed civilian control of the government. They deposed him on Nov. 24, 1948, and sent him into exile. He spent the next 9 years in Cuba and Mexico, where he wrote two new novels: *La brasa en el pico del cuervo* about Cuba and *La brizna de hierba en el viento* dealing with Mexico.

Upon the fall of the military dictatorship which had succeeded his regime, Gallegos returned to Venezuela in January 1958. In accordance with the new Constitution of 1960, Gallegos held a seat in the Venezuelan Senate as a democratically elected former president. However, he seldom attended Senate sessions, since his health did not permit this. After a long illness Gallegos died in Caracas on April 4, 1969.

Further Reading

There is no detailed study in English of Gallegos. Aspects of his political career are discussed in Robert J. Alexander, *The Venezuelan Democratic Revolution: A Profile of the Regime of Rómulo Betancourt* (1964), and John Martz, *Acción Democrática: Evolution of a Modern Political Party in Venezuela* (1966).

Additional Sources

Dunham, Lowell, *Rómulo Gallegos: an Oklahoma encounter and the writing of the last novel,* Norman, University of Oklahoma Press 1974. □

Joseph Galloway

Joseph Galloway (ca. 1731-1803), colonial American politician and lawyer, became a prominent loyalist at the outbreak of the American Revolution.

Joseph Galloway was born in Maryland. When he inherited his father's property, he moved to Philadelphia, studied law, and was admitted to the bar in 1749. He soon became one of the most prominent and wealthy lawyers in Pennsylvania and New Jersey. His marriage in 1753 to Grace Growden enhanced his social and financial position and gave him entrée to politics.

Elected in 1756 to the Pennsylvania Assembly, Galloway joined Benjamin Franklin's battle against the Penns' proprietary rule of the colony. When Franklin went to England to plead this cause, Galloway became spokesman of the "Popular party" (Philadelphia Quakers and their merchant allies).

Galloway was no democrat; his conservatism appeared in his public defense of the Stamp Act in 1765. Decrying the "spirit of disloyalty against the Crown" shown in the public riots after the Stamp Act, he proposed as alternatives a union of the Colonies and an American voice in the management of the empire.

As speaker of the Assembly from 1766 to 1774, Galloway tried to keep Pennsylvania out of colonial resistance to Parliament's imperial program. He was opposed by his bitter enemy, John Dickinson, spokesman of the Proprietary party. In 1774 both attended the First Continental Congress. Galloway introduced a sweeping plan to reorganize the empire that called for an American "Grand Council" elected by the colonial legislatures and possessing wide powers over intercolonial political affairs, a president general appointed by the Crown, and a mutual veto by Parliament and the Council over legislation passed by either affecting the Colonies. The plan was acceptable to many moderates. Had Galloway been more astute politically and secured Dickinson's support, it might have passed. Instead it was expunged from the official published proceedings of the Congress.

Embittered, Galloway declined to serve in the Second Congress and, fearing for his safety, fled to the British camp in New Brunswick. He returned to Philadelphia with Gen. William Howe's army in September 1777 and became civil governor of the city under British occupation. When Howe abandoned Philadelphia, Galloway sailed for England with him. His wife remained behind to save their property, but the Pennsylvania Assembly declared Galloway a traitor, confiscated his estate, and sequestered that of his wife.

Galloway's petitions to return after the Revolution were denied, and he was never reunited with his wife.

In England, Galloway pled the loyalist cause for restitution from the Crown. His *Historical and Political Reflections on the Rise and Progress of the American Rebellion* (1780) provides a loyalist interpretation of the Revolution. He died on Aug. 29, 1803, a pensioner of the Crown and an object of scorn to his countrymen.

Further Reading

Oliver C. Kuntzleman, *Joseph Galloway: Loyalist* (1941), is an inadequate biography of Galloway. His politics is treated satisfactorily in Theodore G. Thayer, *Pennsylvania Politics and the Growth of Democracy, 1740-1776* (1953). The Galloway-Dickinson rivalry is covered by David L. Jacobson, *John Dickinson and the Revolution in Pennsylvania, 1764-1776* (1965). See also Julian P. Boyd, *Anglo-American Union: Joseph Galloway's Plans to Preserve the British Empire, 1774-1788* (1941), and William H. Nelson, *The American Tory* (1962).

Additional Sources

Ferling, John E., *The Loyalist mind: Joseph Galloway and the American Revolution,* University Park: Pennsylvania State University Press, 1977. □

George Gallup

George Gallup (1901-1984) was a pioneer in the field of public opinion polling. He developed methods for perfecting the selection of sample populations, interviewing techniques, and formulation of questions. He also was a teacher and a proponent of educational reform.

George Horace Gallup was born on November 18, 1901, in the small town of Jefferson, Iowa. He was the son of George Henry Gallup, a farmer as well as a real estate dealer in agricultural land, and of Nettie Davenport. All of his higher education took place at the University of Iowa where he received a B.A. in 1923, an M.A. in 1925, and a Ph.D. in 1928. On December 27, 1925, he married Ophelia Smith Miller. They had two sons, Alec Miller and George Horace, Jr., who carried on their father's polling organization, and a daughter, Julia Gallup Laughlin.

From Teaching to Polling

Gallup's career as a teacher began after he received a bachelor's degree and stayed to teach journalism and psychology from 1923 to 1929 at his alma mater, the University of Iowa. He then moved to Drake University at Des Moines, Iowa, where he served as head of the Department of Journalism until 1931. In that year he moved to Northwestern University, Evanston, Illinois, as professor of journalism and advertising. The next year he moved to New York City to join the advertising agency of Young and Rubicam as director of research and then as vice-president from 1937 to

sections of both newspapers and magazines and then sharpened his survey methods to include radio audiences.

Gallup had firm beliefs in the validity of polling. In fact, he believed that polls made a positive contribution to the democratic process. He wrote that public opinion polls provided political leaders with an accurate gauge of public opinion, proved that the common people do make good decisions, focused attention on major issues of the day, uncovered many "areas of ignorance," helped administrators of government departments to make wiser decisions, made it more difficult for political bosses to pick presidential candidates "in smoke-filled rooms," revealed that the people are not motivated in their voting solely by self-interest, and helped define the "mandate" of the people in national elections.

During the 1930s and 1940s he improved the methods of pre-election surveys so as to gain accuracy. The results of polls taken in 392 elections in the United States and several foreign countries by his American Institute of Public Opinion achieved a mean average error of only 3.9 percent. Such a high degree of accuracy resulted from his methods of choosing population samples that are highly representative of the nation, of interviewing people rather than mailing out questionnaires, and of polling right up to election day in order to discover any changes in opinion over time.

In later life Gallup came to recognize that pre-election surveys had very little influence on politicians, many of whom expressed some contempt for them. He therefore dismissed the claim that polls were dangerous to a free political process because of their undue influence on politicians. Majority opinion, as made known by opinion polls, is "not necessarily a controlling factor in the legislation that emerges from Congress." In his view, "well-organized minorities can and do thwart the will of the majority." To safeguard the interests of the majority he recommended greater use of the initiative and referendum, both on a state and national scale. He firmly believed, however, that a carefully prepared opinion survey could be as accurate as a referendum and would be a lot cheaper.

1947. From 1933 to 1937 he was also professor of journalism at Columbia University, but he had to give up this position shortly after he formed his own polling company, the American Institute of Public Opinion (Gallup Poll), in 1935, where he concentrated on attitude research. He was also the founder (1939) and president of the Audience Research Institute. Other positions were: chief executive officer and chairman of the board of Gallup Organization, Inc., and president of Public Opinion Surveys, Inc., and of Gallup International Research Institutes, Inc., which had 35 affiliates doing research in over 70 foreign countries.

Apart from these business positions Gallup was active in professional and public service groups. He was president of the International Association of Public Opinion Institutes, 1947-1984, and of the National Municipal League, 1953-1956, and chair of the All-America Cities Award Committee, a jury which selects All-America cities on the basis of intelligent and effective citizen activity. He founded Quill and Scroll, an international honor society for high school journalists, and served as chair of its board of trustees. Gallup continued in nearly all of these offices until his death of heart failure on July 27, 1984, in Tschingel, Switzerland.

A Pioneer in Polling

By 1944 George Gallup was widely recognized as one of the major pioneers in public opinion polling and had participated in the creation of methods to achieve a high degree of accuracy in discovering the public's opinions on a wide variety of issues. He first developed his research techniques to test audience reaction to advertising and features

Always an Educator

George Gallup was best known as an entrepreneur in the business of discovering what people think about issues. But he was also an educator, and this experience, plus his study of the attitudes of millions of people, led him to formulate a philosophy of education which he described in *The Miracle Ahead* (1964). The collective views of people, he affirmed, are usually sound and logical; the people are not led by their emotions as elitists claim. However, their thinking about issues does not go deep enough. Humans have been slow to recognize the great power of the brain and make too little use of it. Thus far humanity has made real progress in enhancing its comfort and well-being, but in human relations we are no more advanced than the ancient Greeks. To achieve greater and more rapid progress, a new education system must be created to enhance our mental powers. The present system does not encourage in students a conception of education as a lifelong process. It does not provide mastery of the major fields of knowledge or essential communication skills nor the creative talents needed to find new and better solutions to the student's and society's problems. Training the mind involves the teaching of perception or awareness, concentration, organization of data, objectivity, problem solving, decision making, and creativity. Gallup was particularly affirmative toward the case history method of teaching, which offers "perhaps the best method that mankind has yet found to transmit wisdom as opposed to knowledge."

Awards and Publications

Gallup was widely honored for his creative work and enjoyed a long list of awards: distinguished achievement award, Syracuse University, 1950; honor award, University of Missouri, 1958; elected to Hall of Fame in Distribution, 1962; Distinguished Citizen Award, National Municipal League, 1962; Advertising Gold Medal, *Printers' Ink,* 1964; Parlin Award, American Marketing Association, 1965; Christopher Columbus International Prize, 1968; distinguished achievement award from New Jersey chapter of American Marketing Association, 1975; National Association of Secondary School Principals award, 1975; elected to Advertising Hall of Fame, 1977, and to Market Research Hall of Fame, 1978. He received honorary LL.D. degrees from Northwestern University, Drake University, Boston University, Chattanooga University, and the University of Iowa; an honorary D.Sc. from Tufts University; an honorary L.H.D. from Colgate University; and an honorary D.C.L. from Rider College.

His most important publications were: *The Pulse of Democracy: The Public Opinion Poll and How It Works* (1940, reprinted 1968); *A Guidebook to Public Opinion Polls* (1944); *Secrets of Long Life* (1960); *The Miracle Ahead* (1964); *A Survey of the Public's Attitudes Toward the Public Schools* (1969); *Attitudes of Young Americans* (1971); *The Gallup Poll: Public Opinion, 1935-1971* (1972); *Sophisticated Poll Watcher's Guide* (1976); and *The Gallup Poll: 1972-77* (1978). He was editor of *The Gallup Poll: Public Opinion* (1979–1983).

Further Reading

Gallup's books are the best sources for his opinions and philosophy. Books on opinion surveys and his role are Albert H. Cantril, editor, *Polling on the Issues* (1980) and A. H. Cantril and Charles W. Roll, *Polls: Their Use and Misuse in Politics* (1972). The following articles provide reviews of his books and some information on his career: *TIME* (May 3, 1948); *Newsweek* (August 20, 1956); *New Republic* (December 16, 1972; April 8, 1978); *Psychology Today* (June 1973); and *American Historical Review* (October 1973). The best obituary, with pertinent data on his career, was in the *New York Times* (July 28 and 29, 1984). □

John Galsworthy

The English novelist and playwright John Galsworthy (1867-1933) was one of the most popular writers of the early 20th century. His work explores the transi- tions and contrasts between pre- and post-World War I England.

Born on Aug. 14, 1867, in Coombe, Surrey, at the height of the Victorian era, John Galsworthy was educated at Harrow and New College, Oxford. He was admitted to the bar in 1890, and 8 years later, after his first novel *Jocelyn* appeared, he left law to continue writing. *The Island Pharisees* (1904) and *The Man of Property* (1906), which became the first novel in *The Forsyte Saga,* expanded his audience and his reputation.

As his popularity increased, Galsworthy published other novels of the Forsyte series: *Indian Summer of a Forsyte* (1918), *In Chancery* (1920), *Awakening* (1920), and *To Let* (1921). In *The Forsyte Saga* late Victorian and Edwardian England's upper-middle-class society is portrayed, dissected, and criticized. Although *The Man of Property* and *To Let* are widely separated in time, the Saga's theme and structure form a unit wherein three generations of the large, clannish Forsyte family rise and decay on realistic and symbolic levels.

The Country House (1907), *Fraternity* (1909), *The Patrician* (1911), and *The Dark Flower* (1913) are not novels in the sequence, but they are related to it in place and time. Galsworthy wove social history into his novels: he reproduced the values, classes, hierarchy, stability, and smugness of the Edwardian era.

After World War I Galsworthy produced another, less successful, cycle of novels about the Forsyte family in post-war England. *The White Monkey* (1924), *The Silver Spoon* (1926), and *Swan Song* (1928) were collectively published in 1929 as *A Modern Comedy.* This series is less firm than *The Forsyte Saga,* its characterizations are weaker, and its architectural quality is disjunctive. It reflects Galsworthy's own uncertainty about the years after the war, which were marked by a revolution in values whose outcome was uncertain. After the second cycle was completed, Galsworthy published two more novels, *Maid in Waiting* (1931) and *Flowering Wilderness* (1932).

Although Galsworthy is best known for his novels, he was also a successful playwright. He constructed his drama on a legalistic basis, and the plays typically start from a social or ethical impulse and reach a resolution after different viewpoints have been expressed. Like *The Silver Box* (1906) and *Strife* (1909), *Justice* (1910) is realistic, particularly in the use of dialogue that is direct and uninflated. Part of the realism is an awareness of detail and the minute symbol. That awareness is clear in the intricate symbols of *The Forsyte Saga;* it is less successful in the drama and his later novels because it tends to be overstated.

In *Justice* Galsworthy revealed himself as something of a propagandist or, according to Joseph Conrad, "a moralist." Galsworthy selected detail and character to isolate a belief or a judgment; he said, "Selection, conscious or unconscious, is the secret of art." The protagonists in his drama and his prose fiction generally typify particular viewpoints or beliefs. Explaining his method of characterization, he wrote, "In the greatest fiction the characters, or some of them, should sum up and symbolize whole streaks of human nature in a way that our friends, however well known to us, do not. . . . Within their belts are cinctured not only individuals but sections of mankind." He also stated that his aim was to create a fictional world that was richer than life itself.

John Galsworthy was awarded the Order of Merit in 1929 and the Nobel Prize for literature in 1932. He died at Hampstead on Jan. 31, 1933.

Further Reading

H.V. Marrot, *The Life and Letters of John Galsworthy* (1935), is valuable as a biographical source. Dudley Barker, *The Man of Principle* (1963), is the most comprehensive biography of Galsworthy. Ford Maddox Ford discusses him in *Portraits from Life* (1937). Other biographies are Sheila Kaye-Smith, *John Galsworthy* (1916); Leon Schalit, *John Galsworthy: A Survey* (1929); Hermon Ould, *John Galsworthy* (1934); and R. H. Mottram, *For Some We Loved: An Intimate Portrait of Ada and John Galsworthy* (1956).

Additional Sources

Dupre, Catherine, *John Galsworthy: a biography,* New York: Coward, McCann & Geoghegan, 1976; London: Collins, 1976.

Fabes, Gilbert Henry, *John Galsworthy: his first editions, points and values,* Norwood, Pa.: Norwood Editions, 1976.

Frechet, Alec, *John Galsworthy: a reassessment,* Totowa, N.J.: Barnes & Noble Books, 1982.

Gindin, James Jack, *The English climate: an excursion into a biography of John Galsworthy,* Ann Arbor: University of Michigan Press, 1979.

Gindin, James Jack, *John Galsworthy's life and art: an alien's fortress,* Ann Arbor: University of Michigan Press, 1987.

Ould, Hermon, *John Galsworthy: an appreciation together with a bibliography,* Folcroft, Pa.: Folcroft Library Editions, 1976. □

Sir Alexander Tilloch Galt

Sir Alexander Tilloch Galt (1817-1893) was a Canadian politician responsible for the financial provisions of Canadian federation as well as for some of Canada's first steps in diplomacy.

Alexander Galt was born in Chelsea, London, on Sept. 6, 1817, the youngest son of John Galt, the Scottish novelist. His father was the agent for a Canadian land company, and young Galt himself went to Canada in 1835 as a clerk in the British American Land Company, which owned half a million acres of land in the Eastern Townships, between the St. Lawrence River and the United States border. He rose to become secretary and later commissioner of the company. Through this work he became interested in railway promotion, first in the region owned by the company and, later, with the construction of the Grand Trunk Railway, in the St. Lawrence Basin.

Galt entered politics in 1849, representing Sherbrooke County, in the center of his company's holdings. This period in the legislature was brief, but he was reelected in 1853. As early as 1856 Galt began urging the federal union of the two Canadas rather than the legislative one.

Galt soon established himself as the leader of the English-speaking members of the Assembly from Canada East and in July 1858 was invited to enter the Macdonald-Cartier government as minister of finance. He accepted on condition that the ministry support a resolution favoring a federal union of British North America which would be pressed on the British government. The idea of federation was premature at this time, and Galt and his colleagues had no success in urging it on the Colonial Office. Galt laid the basis for a protective tariff during these years through providing additional duties on manufactured imports.

Out of office from 1862 to 1864, Galt returned to the finance portfolio in the coalition ministry that was formed to bring about a general federation of the British American colonies. In the confederation negotiations his financial skill was crucial in arranging the subsidy system intended to provide the necessary revenues for the poorer provinces of the new union.

On the formation of the first ministry of the new Dominion, in July 1867, Galt again became minister of finance. His tenure was short, however, for his independent nature brought him into disagreement with the leader of the government, John Alexander Macdonald, and he resigned in October. He retired from Parliament in 1872.

In the latter part of his life Galt made several ventures into diplomacy on behalf of Canada. In 1875 he served on the Halifax Fisheries Commission; in 1878 and 1879 Galt attempted unsuccessfully to negotiate commercial agreements with France and Spain; and he served as first high commissioner of Canada in London from 1880 to 1883. Galt's last years were spent in directing various enterprises in the western prairies in which his family was interested, notably irrigation, coal, and railroad ventures. He was knighted for public services in 1869 and died in Montreal on Sept. 19, 1893.

Further Reading

The standard biography of Galt is Oscar Douglas Skelton, *The Life and Times of Sir Alexander Tilloch Galt* (1920). His career is recounted in W.G. Hardy, *From Sea unto Sea: Canada, 1850 to 1910—The Road to Nationhood* (1962), and W.L. Morton, *The Critical Years: The Union of British North America, 1857-1873* (1964). Also useful is Donald Creighton, *John A. Macdonald* (2 vols., 1952-1956).

Additional Sources

Otter, A. A. den (Andy Albert den), *Civilizing the West: the Galts and the development of western Canada,* Edmonton, Alta., Canada: University of Alberta Press, 1982.
Timothy, Hamilton Baird, *The Galts: a Canadian odyssey,* Toronto: McClelland and Stewart, 1977-1984. □

Leopoldo Fortunato Galtieri

Leopoldo Fortunato Galtieri (born 1926) served as president of Argentina during the 1982 Falkland Islands War with Great Britain. After his country's defeat he was cashiered.

Had it not been for the Falklands Islands War of 1982, Leopoldo Galtieri would have become just another forgotten Latin American general. As a result of this war, though, he became the most memorable of the generals to rule Argentina since Juan Peron was driven from power in 1955.

Galtieri was born July 15, 1926, in Caseros, a suburb of Buenos Aires. He was the second of three children born into a working class family of Italian descent. In 1943 Galtieri entered the Argentine military academy, where he studied civil engineering. He graduated in 1945 and was commissioned a second lieutenant. For the next 35 years Galtieri steadily moved up through the ranks, eventually becoming commander-in-chief of the army. At six foot two inches, Galtieri was an imposing figure, often referred to as a "soldier's soldier."

There was little to distinguish Galtieri in his early career. His first assignment was to the Military School of Engineers in Concepción del Uruguay, in the Province of Entre Ríos. In 1949 he was promoted to lieutenant and attended a military engineering course at the U.S.-run military school in the Panama Canal Zone. In the 1950s he was promoted to captain and major, serving with the Fourth Battalion of Zapadores (Sappers) and as a staff officer assigned as professor in the Argentine Army War College.

Climbing the Promotion Ladder

In 1960 he spent six months studying advanced combat engineering at Fort Belvoir, Virginia. Upon his return to Argentina he served in the inspection office of military engineers. Then in 1962 he was appointed as staff officer of the Second Infantry Division. At the end of 1962 he was promoted to lieutenant colonel and assigned as professor of administration at the Army War College. In 1964 he became deputy commander of the Military School of Engineers. Then in 1967 he was promoted to colonel, and the next year he became commander of the military engineers 121st Construction Battalion.

Galtieri continued to advance through the ranks in the 1970s. He was appointed to deputy commander of the Engineer Corps in 1970, and two years later he was promoted to brigadier general and made commander of the Ninth Infantry Brigade. In 1973 he was made chief of staff of logistics and finance, and in 1974 he was appointed commander of the Seventh Infantry Brigade. The next year he became deputy commander and chief of staff of the Second Army Corps. Then Galtieri was made chief of staff for operations with the army general staff.

In the 1970s Argentina became increasingly unstable. Juan Peron returned from exile in 1973 and was elected president later that year. Upon his death in 1974 his wife (also the vice-president) assumed the presidency. She proved unable to resolve Argentina's economic problems or to respond effectively to leftist urban guerrillas. As a result, in 1976 a military coup by the heads of the army, navy, and air force removed her from office and installed General Jorge Rafael Videla, the army commander-in-chief, as president.

The Military Takes Over

At this time the army was conducting what is commonly known as the "Dirty War" against the guerrillas. During this period several thousands of suspected opponents of the government were secretly killed and buried by security forces. It remains unclear to what extent Galtieri was involved in the widespread abuses associated with this activity.

Galtieri's promotions continued. In 1977 he was promoted to the rank of major general and was named deputy commander of the Second Army Corps. Two years later he was named to command the First Army Corps. In December 1979 army commander-in-chief Roberto Viola announced his retirement, and Galtieri became commander-in-chief with the rank of lieutenant general.

March 1981 marked the end of the second three-year term General Videla had been appointed to by the junta. The junta, which included Galtieri as army commander, chose General Viola as president for the 1981-1984 term.

In 1981 Galtieri drew national attention for the first time by closing the border with Chile as part of the dispute with Chile over islands in the Beagle Channel. During that year he made two trips to the United States and was referred to by President Reagan as "a magnificent general."

On December 22, 1981, General Viola was forced from the presidency by the junta and was replaced by General Galtieri. Viola had proved incapable of dealing with the country's triple digit inflation and the sluggish economy. At the time he took office, Galtieri announced that he would finish the three-year term to which the junta had appointed Viola. In addition to becoming president, Galtieri retained his positions as army commander-in-chief and junta member. Serving with Galtieri on the junta were air force commander General Basilio Lami Dozo and navy commander Vice Admiral Jorge Anaya.

A War to Unite the Nation

Galtieri was known as a strong anti-Communist. A month before the coup placed him in the presidency he stated, "Argentina and the United States will march together in the ideological war being waged in the world." He shared the accepted idea of the time that the Argentine military should play a major role in directing the country. Galtieri's initial measures to deal with hyperinflation, including a freeze in public salaries and a cut in government spending, only added to the hardship of the Argentine people and increased popular dissatisfaction with military rule.

On April 2, 1982, faced with rising discontent, Galtieri took the classical way to divert attention from domestic problem. He started a foreign war, invading the Falkland Islands. Simply dismissing this as a desperate maneuver to cover domestic failure, though, is to over-simplify the situation. Viewed through Argentine eyes, the British occupation of the Falklands, some 300 miles off the Argentine coast in the South Atlantic, was an affront to national honor. The islands, called the Malvinas in Argentina, are felt to have been unjustly seized from Argentina in 1833. Their continued occupation by the British was a longstanding source of resentment. Some 20 years of talks with Britain had produced no results. Argentina held out for sovereignty over the islands. However, Britain noted that the 1,800 settlers of British origin vehemently opposed being ruled by Argentina, and so maintained control.

In this context the invasion produced euphoria in Argentina. The invasion itself hardly merited the word. After three hours of resistance by the small British garrison, the Argentines took control. On April 10 Galtieri called for a public demonstration of support for the invasion. One hundred thousand exuberant Argentines, forgetting their economic problems for the moment, appeared in the Plaza de Mayo in Buenos Aires.

It soon became apparent that Galtieri had made two serious miscalculations. He had felt that the United States would either back Argentina or at least remain neutral. He felt Argentine support of U.S.-backed governments in Central America and for the U.S.-funded Nicaraguan contra forces would gain him U.S. support. In addition, he felt that Reagan's attempt to lift the ban on military aid to Argentina reflected Reagan's support. However, after Secretary of State Alexander M. Haig, Jr. engaged in shuttle diplomacy between Buenos Aires and London in an unsuccessful attempt to resolve the dispute peacefully, the United States openly sided with Britain.

Galtieri's second miscalculation was his assumption that the British, in the twilight of their colonial role, would only respond to the invasion diplomatically. Again he proved to be wrong. Britain not only declared a naval blockade of the islands but sent an invasion fleet across the Atlantic, some 8,000 miles. To compound Galtieri's problems, the European Economic Community voted an arms embargo on Argentina. That was a serious blow, because after U.S. military aid stopped Argentina had become increasingly dependent on European arms suppliers.

However, once having occupied the islands Galtieri was determined to maintain Argentine control. On April 22 he visited the capital of the Falklands, Port Stanley, renamed by his government Puerto Argentina.

Defeat and Disgrace

Events early in May removed the last hope for peaceful settlement. On the second of May the British sank the Argentine cruiser *General Belgrano* even though it was outside the 200-mile exclusion zone declared by the British. The hundreds of Argentine lives lost made it even harder for Argentina to accept anything less than a clear victory in the dispute. Britain was placed in a similar position two days later when an Argentine-launched missile set the British destroyer *Sheffield* afire.

On May 21 the British established a beachhead on East Falkland. Heavy fighting continued until June 15, when the British finally took Port Stanley, capturing 15,000 Argentine soldiers. British training and equipment proved superior. In addition, at 300 miles off shore the Argentine air force was at the limit of its operational range and could not effectively support its troops.

The military defeat turned the euphoria of April into rage directed at the junta. Galtieri was forced from his positions as army commander-in-chief, junta member, and president. He stated, "I'm going because the army did not give me backing to continue as commander and president of the nation."

Had Argentina followed the normal pattern for Latin America, Galtieri would have simply faded from the scene. However, a remarkable event occurred. After election of Raúl Alfonsín in 1983, military officers were put on trial for offenses which occurred during the military rule. In December 1983 five former military leaders were convicted of crimes committed in the 1970s. Four other military officers on trial, including Galtieri, were acquitted.

In May 1986, however, the Supreme Council of the Armed Forces, Argentina's highest military tribunal, convicted Galtieri, Former Navy Commander Anaya, and former Air Force Commander Lami Dozo of the military crime of "negligence." All three received a prison sentence and were stripped of their military rank and the privileges of retired officers. All three were subsequently pardoned in 1989 by President Carlos Menem. Outraged by this action, human rights groups fought extensively for the Dirty War files in an effort to return Galtieri to prison. They succeeded in filing charges against the former general, and in May 1997 Spain issued an international warrant for his arrest. Argentine officials scoffed at the action by stating that those involved in the Dirty War had been appropriately tried and jailed for their crimes under Argentine law. Despite Argentine claims that their actions effectively closed the Dirty War case, the outstanding warrant exiled Galtieri in Argentina for the rest of his life.

Further Reading

Although no biography of Galtieri has appeared in English, information concerning him can be found in the following, Max Hastings and Simon Jenkins, *The Battle for the Falklands* (1983); Stephen Brown, "Spain vows to help expose truth of Dirty War," *Reuters* (April 22, 1997); Tito Drago, "Argentina-Human Rights: Spanish court cracks down on ex-dictator," *Inter Press Service English News Wire* (March 26, 1997). ☐

Sir Francis Galton

The English scientist, biometrician, and explorer Sir Francis Galton (1822-1911) founded the science of eugenics and introduced the theory of the anticyclone in meteorology.

Francis Galton was born on Feb. 16, 1822, at Birmingham, the son of Samuel Galton, a businessman, and Violetta Galton. After schooling in Boulogne and privately, he began to study medicine in 1838 but also read mathematics at Trinity College, Cambridge.

The death of Galton's father in 1844 left him with considerable independent means, and he abandoned further medical study to travel in Syria, Egypt, and South-West Africa. As a result, he published *Tropical South Africa* (1853) and *The Art of Travel* (1855). His travels brought him fame as an explorer, and in 1854 he was awarded the Gold Medal of the Geographical Society. He was elected fellow of the Royal Society in 1856.

Turning his attention to meteorology, Galton published *Meteorographica* (1863), in which he described weather mapping, pointing out for the first time the importance of an anticyclone, in which air circulates clockwise round a center of high barometric pressure in the Northern Hemisphere. Cyclones, on the other hand, are low-pressure centers from which air rushes upward and moves counterclockwise.

Meanwhile, Galton had developed an interest in heredity, and the publication of the *Origin of Species* (1859) by Charles Darwin won Galton's immediate support. Impressed by evidence that distinction of any kind is apt to run in families, Galton made detailed studies of families conspicuous for inherited ability over several generations. He then advocated the application of scientific breeding to human populations. These studies laid the foundation for the science of eugenics (a term he invented), or race improve-

ment, and led to the publication of *Hereditary Genius* (1869) and *English Men of Science: Their Nature and Nurture* (1874).

Finding that advances in the study of heredity were being hampered by the lack of quantitative information, Galton started anthropometric research, devising instruments for the exact measurement of every quantifiable faculty of body or mind. In 1884 he finally set up and equipped a laboratory, the Biometric Laboratory at University College, London, where the public were tested. He measured such traits as keenness of sight and hearing, color sense, reaction time, strength of pull and of squeeze, and height and weight. The system of fingerprints in universal use today derived from this work.

Galton's application of exact quantitative methods gave results which, processed mathematically, developed a numerical factor he called correlation and defined thus: "Two variable organs are said to be co-related when the variation of the one is accompanied on the average by more or less variation of the other, and in the same direction. Correlation must be the consequence of the variations of the two organs being partly due to common causes. If wholly due . . . the co-relation would be perfect." Co-relation specified the degree of relationship between any pair of individuals or any two attributes.

The developed presentation of Galton's views on heredity is *Natural Inheritance* (1889). A difficult work, with mathematics not beyond criticism, it sets out the "law of 1885," which attempts to quantify the influence of former generations in the hereditary makeup of the individual. Parents contribute each one-quarter, grandparents each one-sixteenth, and so on for earlier generations. Claims that Galton anticipated Mendel's ratios seem without foundation. For Galton, evolution ensured the survival of those members of the race with most physical and mental vigor, and he desired to see this come about in human society more speedily and with less pain to the individual through applying eugenics. Evolution was an unresting progression, the nature of the average individual being essentially unprogressive.

Galton used his considerable fortune to promote his scientific interests. He founded the journal *Biometrika* in 1901, and in 1903 the Eugenics Laboratory in the University of London. He died at Haslemere, Surrey, on Jan. 17, 1911, after several years of frail health. He bequeathed £45,000 to found a professorship in eugenics in the hope that his disciple and pupil Karl Pearson might become its first occupant. This hope was realized.

Further Reading

Galton's own account is *Memories of My Life* (1908). A full-length biography is Karl Pearson, *Francis Galton 1822-1911: An Appreciation* (1914-1930).

Additional Sources

Cowan, Ruth Schwartz, *Sir Francis Galton and the study of heredity in the nineteenth century,* New York: Garland Pub., 1985.
Forrest, Derek William, *Francis Galton: the life and work of a Victorian genius,* New York: Taplinger Pub. Co., 1974.
Galton Institute (London, England), Symposium (28th: 1991: London, England), *Sir Francis Galton, FRS: the legacy of his ideas,* Houndmills, Basingstoke, Hampshire: Macmillan, in association with the Galton Institute, 1993. □

Luigi Galvani

The Italian physiologist Luigi Galvani (1737-1798) is noted for his discovery of animal electricity.

L uigi Galvani was born at Bologna on Sept. 9, 1737. He studied theology for a while and then medicine at the University of Bologna. In 1762, upon completion of his studies, he was appointed lecturer of anatomy and surgery at Bologna. His interest focused on the animal senses, which led him into deep theoretical interest in the action of the nervous system.

By the middle of the 18th century various books on electricity were available in Italian, and in 1744 Benjamin Franklin's famous book on electricity appeared in Italian translation. Galvani was influenced by Franklin's "onefluid theory," according to which electrical phenomena were caused by an electric fluid that results in so-called positive electricity, while so-called negative electricity was the absence of fluid. What seemed especially important to Galvani was Franklin's explanation of the Leyden jar, the early form of condenser. According to Franklin, positive electricity accumulated on the inner conductor while the outer conductor became negatively charged. The whole setup was similar to an accumulation of fluid on the inside of the bottle. Galvani drew an analogy between the Leyden jar and animal muscle and carried out his experiments with this thought in mind. He studied the effects of electricity from lightning on muscular contractions in a frog and proved that the electricity produced muscular convulsions.

Galvani's first announcement of his experiments appeared in a paper, "On the Effect of Electricity on Muscular Motion," published in 1791. He also gave an account of convulsions produced in a frog, in the absence of an electrical machine, when the frog formed part of a circuit containing one or more pieces of metal. Galvani had observed motion of the nerve juices during these convulsions and proposed the theory that the convulsions were caused by electricity within the animal's body; the muscle fiber and the nerve were acting like a Leyden jar.

Galvani's great Italian contemporary Alessandro Volta began working on animal electricity in 1792 and came out in direct opposition to Galvani's theory of an animal electrical fluid. It was then that the famous controversy between the two began. Volta proved that the nerves were nothing but electrical conductors and that it was possible to get electrical effects by placing any two metals in contact with an intervening piece of moistened cardboard. In this controversy Volta was correct in his physical interpretations, yet it was Galvani's influence which fostered the flourishing sci-

ence of neurophysiology in the 19th century. However, the controversy between the two men spread into their personal relations and even into Italian politics of the time.

After the Cisalpine Republic was established in 1797, Galvani refused to swear allegiance to it on religious grounds and was dismissed from his university position. Volta swore allegiance and played a central role in the republic. Galvani was reinstated a year later, but by then he was a completely broken man. He died on Dec. 4, 1798.

Further Reading

Biographical material on Galvani is in Bern Dibner, *Galvani-Volta: A Controversy That Led to the Discovery of Useful Electricity* (1952). See also James R. Partington, *A History of Chemistry,* vol. 4 (1964). □

Bernardo de Gálvez

Bernardo de Gálvez (1746-1786), a Spanish colonial administrator, was captain general of Louisiana during the American Revolutionary War. His heroic exploits against the British during the war won him fame both in Spain and in America.

ernardo de Gálvez was born in Macharaviaya in the province of Malaga on July 23, 1746. Though poor, the Gálvez family belonged to the Spanish nobility, and young Gálvez was able to pursue an active and successful military career. At the outbreak of the American Revolution, Gálvez was assigned the post of commandant of the Spanish troops stationed in Louisiana, with the rank of colonel. He soon became governor and intendant of that Spanish province, assuming office in February 1777. Two years later the Revolutionary War became a world struggle as Spain joined its forces with those of France in the battle against Great Britain. Spain refused to ally itself directly with the United States or to recognize American independence because of its own position as a colonial power. Nevertheless Spain supplied the Americans with secret aid and undertook a vigorous military campaign of its own in America under the leadership of Gálvez.

Even before Spain came into the war, Gálvez had been actively engaged in providing arms to the Americans in the Louisiana area. On Spanish entry into the war, however, Gálvez took direct action against the British, and in three brilliant campaigns drove them out of West Florida, thus securing control of the mouth of the Mississippi River and the Gulf of Mexico for Spain. Of all his exploits in this period, the most famous was his daring conquest of Pensacola, in Florida, in May 1781. At the end of the war he returned to Spain to receive a hero's welcome; promotion to the rank of major general; appointment as captain general of Louisiana, East and West Florida, and Cuba; and elevation to the viceroyalty of New Spain.

In 1784 Gálvez went back to America, where he acted as principal adviser to Diego de Gardoqui in preliminary negotiations with the new United States over the Florida boundary question, a treaty of commerce, and the right of Americans to free navigation of the Mississippi River; it was these negotiations that led to the Jay-Gardoqui treaty in 1786. In 1785 Gálvez was responsible for ousting from Natchez, in Mississippi, the Georgia commissioners who had come to establish Bourbon County. That same year, however, he won the thanks of the American government for his part in releasing American merchants being held at Havana. Gálvez died in Mexico on November 30, 1786.

Further Reading

The standard account of Gálvez's career remains Alcée Fortier, *A History of Louisiana*, vol. 2 (1904). See also John Walton Caughey, *Bernardo de Gálvez in Louisiana, 1776-1783* (1934). □

José de Gálvez

José de Gálvez (1720-1787), Spanish statesman, reformer, and inspector general of New Spain (Mexico), recommended and introduced profound changes into the government and economy of the viceroyalty.

José de Gálvez was born in Málaga on Jan. 2, 1720. The son of an impoverished noble family, he came under the protection of two Málaga bishops who provided for his education. He attended schools in his hometown and Salamanca and graduated from the University of Madrid Law School. He became secretary to the Spanish minister of state, the Marquis de Grimaldi, and in 1764 was appointed *alcalde de casa y corte.*

In 1765 the Bourbon monarchs appointed Gálvez *visitador general* (inspector general) and sent him to New Spain. He soon found himself in conflict with the viceroy, who resented his extensive powers. To secure better viceregal support, Gálvez arranged for the appointment of the Marquis de Croix as new viceroy. Gálvez concerned himself with every aspect of administration. His actions and recommendations had a far-reaching impact on New Spain.

One of the major crises Gálvez faced in New Spain was the expulsion of the Jesuits. Spanish monarch Charles III ordered the wealthy and powerful Jesuits out of Spain and its domains in 1767. Gálvez and Viceroy Croix carried out the Crown's order rapidly and efficiently. The expulsion, however, brought much discontent. The Jesuits had developed a fine system of schooling, were highly regarded by many Indians and Creoles, and had established a powerful system of missions in northwest New Spain. Their expulsion was followed by outbreaks of protests which soon led to riots and violence. Gálvez responded harshly. Taking command of a small army of 600 men, he crushed the revolt, set up criminal courts, and dealt out summary justice.

Gálvez now turned to implement several important reforms. Import and export duties were sharply reduced, and New Spain was permitted to trade freely with other parts of the empire. The complex and archaic system of revenue collection was improved and modernized. Tax collection became more efficient, and treasury revenues increased. Gálvez promoted the organization of a tobacco monopoly, which proved to be very lucrative. In his general report after his tour of duty he recommended other reforms, including a new mining code and the organization of a mining guild for the protection and promotion of the mining industry. Following up his recommendations several years later, Spain issued a decree creating the guild, or Real Cuerpo de Mineria. Gálvez's measures bolstered the economy of New Spain, improved colonial administration, and brought increased revenues for the Crown.

Aware of the need to defend the northern territory of New Spain, Gálvez recommended an independent military government. After he returned to Spain (1771) and became minister of the Indies, he ordered that Mexico's northern states together with California, New Mexico, and Texas be placed under the control of a commandant general of the Provincias Internas, independent of the viceroy in Mexico City and directly responsible to the king. To guard against the Russians, who had begun colonies in northern North America, Gálvez organized an ambitious Spanish colonizing enterprise. He sent a group of friars into upper California to establish a chain of over 20 missions, which brought the limits of New Spain to San Francisco Bay.

Faced with constant involvement in European affairs and war with England, Spain needed local military bodies to defend its empire. Gálvez thus ordered the creation of a colonial militia composed of Indian and mestizo conscripts under Creole and Spanish officers. Perhaps his most significant suggestion implemented after his return to Spain was that the intendant system, already in use in Spain, be introduced in New Spain. This involved the creation of a much tighter hierarchical structure presided over by an intendant general in Mexico City, who was to supervise 12 intendants with specific territorial jurisdiction.

As minister of the Indies in Madrid, Gálvez continued to plan and implement new reforms. For his services he was awarded the title of Marquess of Sonora.

Further Reading

Herbert Ingram Priestly's scholarly and detailed *José de Gálvez: Visitor General of New Spain, 1765-1771* (1916), is still the standard work. Valuable background is provided by C. H. Haring, *The Spanish Empire in America* (1963); Charles Gibson, *Spain in America* (1966); and John H. Parry, *The Spanish Seaborne Empire* (1966). □

Vasco da Gama

The Portuguese navigator Vasco da Gama (ca. 1460-1524) was the first to travel by sea from Portugal to India. The term "Da Gama epoch" is used to de-

scribe the era of European commercial and imperial expansion launched by his navigational enterprise.

Little is known of the early life of Vasco da Gama; his father was governor of Sines, Portugal, where Vasco was born. He first comes to historical notice in 1492, when he seized French ships in Portuguese ports as reprisal for piratical raids. When he was commissioned for his famous voyage, he was a gentleman at the court of King Manuel I.

Manuel, against the advice of a majority of his counselors, had decided to follow up Bartolomeu Dias's triumphal voyage round the Cape of Good Hope (1487-1488) with a well-planned attempt to reach all the way to the Malabar Coast of India, the ports of which were the major entrepôts for the Western spice trade with southeastern Asia. This trade had fallen under the control of Moslem merchants; the Venetians were only the final distributors to Europe of these valuable commodities.

Manuel hoped to displace the Moslem (and thus the Venetian) middlemen and to establish Portuguese hegemony over the Oriental oceanic trades. He also hoped to join with Eastern Christian forces (symbolized to medieval Europeans by the legend of the powerful priest-king, Prester John) and thus carry on a worldwide crusade against Islam. Da Gama's voyage was to be the first complete step toward the realization of these ambitions.

Voyage to India

Da Gama, supplied with letters of introduction to Prester John and to the ruler of the Malabar city of Calicut, set sail from the Tagus River in Lisbon on July 8, 1497. He commanded the flagship *St. Gabriel,* accompanied by the *St. Raphael* and *Berrio* (commanded, respectively, by his brother Paulo and Nicolas Coelho) and a large supply ship. After a landfall in the Cape Verde Islands, he stood well out to sea, rounding the Cape of Good Hope on November 22. Sailing past the port of Sofala, the expedition landed at Kilimane, the second in a string of East African coastal cities. These towns were under Moslem control and gained their wealth largely through trade in gold and ivory. Proceeding to Mozambique, where they were at first mistaken for Moslems, the Portuguese were kindly received by the sultan. A subsequent dispute, however, led da Gama to order a naval bombardment of the city.

Traveling northward to Mombasa, the Portuguese escaped a Moslem attempt to destroy the small fleet and hurriedly sailed for the nearby port of Malindi. Its sultan, learning of the bombardment to the south, decided to cooperate with da Gama and lent him the services of the famous Indian pilot Ibn Majid for the next leg of the journey. On May 20, 1498, the Portuguese anchored off Calicut—then the most important trading center in southern India—well prepared to tap the fabulous riches of India.

Their expectations, however, were soon to be deflated. The Portuguese at first thought the Hindu inhabitants of the city to be Christians, although a visit to a local temple where they were permitted to worship "Our Lady"—Devaki, mother of the god Krishna—made them question the purity of the faith as locally practiced. The zamorin, the ruler of Calicut, warmly welcomed the newcomers—until his treasurers appraised the inexpensive items sent as gifts by King Manuel. In fact, the potentates of the East were at that time wealthier than the financially embarrassed Western kings, and the zamorin quite naturally had looked for a standard tribute in gold. The Portuguese merchandise did not sell well in the port, and the Moslem merchants who dominated the city's trade convinced the zamorin that he stood to gain nothing by concluding a commercial agreement with the intruders.

Amid rumors of plots against his life but with his ships stocked with samples of precious jewels and spices, da Gama sailed from Calicut at the end of August 1498. The trip back to Portugal proved far more difficult than the voyage out, and many men died of scurvy during the 3-month journey across the Arabian Sea. The *St. Raphael* was burned and its complement distributed among the other ships. The remaining vessels became separated in a storm off the West African coast, and Coelho was the first to reach home (July 10, 1499). The da Gamas had gone to the Azores, where Paulo died, and Vasco arrived in Lisbon on September 9.

Da Gama returned twice to India: in 1502, when he bombarded Calicut in revenge for an attack on a previous Portuguese expedition; and in 1524, when he was appointed viceroy. On Dec. 24, 1524, Vasco da Gama died in the southwestern Indian city of Cochin. He was richly rewarded for his services by his sovereign, being made

Count of Vidiguerira and Admiral of the Indian Seas and receiving pensions and a lucrative slice of the Eastern trade.

Da Gama's first voyage deserves to be compared with Columbus's more celebrated "discovery" of the New World. Neither man actually "discovered" unoccupied territories; rather, both linked anciently settled and developed parts of the world with Europe. The Spaniards subsequently conquered the "Indians" of the West, living in settler societies off their labor and natural resources; the Portuguese founded a seaborne commercial empire from which they tried to drain middlemen's profits from a trade still on the whole unfavorably balanced against Europe.

Further Reading

The best account of da Gama's enterprises remains K. G. Jayne, *Vasco da Gama and His Successors, 1460-1580* (1910). A contemporary account of the first voyage was translated and edited by E. G. Ravenstein, *A Journal of the First Voyage of Vasco da Gama, 1497-1499* (1898). This voyage also served as the theme of the great epic of Portuguese literature, Luis de Camões, *The Lusiads,* translated by William C. Atkinson (1952). The da Gama expedition led to the rise of a maritime empire, described in C. R. Boxer, *The Portuguese Seaborn Empire, 1415-1825* (1969), and to the "Da Gama epoch" of Europeans in the East, outlined from an Asian point of view in K. M. Panikkar, *Asia and Western Dominance: A Survey of the Vasco da Gama Epoch of Asian History, 1498-1945* (1954; new ed. 1959). □

Léon Gambetta

The French statesman Léon Gambetta (1838-1882) rallied his countrymen during the Franco-Prussian War. A founding father of the Third Republic, he was an influential figure during its formative years.

Léon Gambetta was born at Cahors on April 2, 1838, the son of a grocer from Genoa and his French wife. Educated at Montfaucon and Cahors, he studied law in Paris and was admitted to the Paris bar in 1860. Soon he became involved in the republican opposition to the Second Empire.

As a lawyer, Gambetta began to make his mark defending opponents of the regime, and in 1869 he was elected to the legislature on a radical program (the Belleville manifesto). He quickly became one of the leaders of the republican minority, and though he criticized the Empire's foreign policy, he was a vigorous patriot. After the capture of Napoleon III at Sedan during the Franco-Prussian War, Gambetta tried to rally the legislature to carry on the war but failed.

Gambetta became minister of the interior in the provisional government of national defense. After escaping from besieged Paris by balloon, he strove to rally the country to carry on the war. His impassioned oratory could not bring victory, but his efforts did help to save national honor and self-respect in defeat, and for this he has remained a national hero.

Elected to the National Assembly called to make peace, Gambetta protested the cession of Alsace-Lorraine. He campaigned for the republican cause and helped persuade the divided monarchists that they must frame a republican constitution. An astute parliamentary tactician as well as one of the greatest orators of modern France, Gambetta saw himself as a representative of the emerging lower middle classes into political prominence. His gradualism and talent for compromise were stigmatized as opportunism by his critics.

Gambetta played the key role in rallying republican forces during the May 16, 1877, crisis that led to President MacMahon's resignation, but it was his last important success. His great influence, prestige, and belief in strong government made him the object of republican suspicions, which kept him from forming a ministry until November 1881, a particularly difficult moment. The ministry was a disappointment to those who had expected a grand coalition of leading republican figures, and it lasted only 2 months. Although acknowledged as the foremost republican leader, he was never able to play the role his talents seemed to call for. Gambetta's death from peritonitis on Nov. 27, 1882, deprived the republic of a leader it would sorely miss in the years before World War I.

Further Reading

The definitive biography of Gambetta has yet to be written, but for the early and most exciting part of his career see J. P. T. Bury, *Gambetta and the National Defence* (1936). Although laudatory, the work of a young associate who was later presi-

dent of the republic, Paul Deschanel, *Gambetta* (1919; trans. 1920), is still useful, as is Harold Stannard, *Gambetta and the Foundation of the Third Republic* (1921).

Additional Sources

Bury, J. P. T. (John Patrick Tuer), *Gambetta's final years: 'the era of difficulties,' 1877-1882,* London; New York: Longman, 1982. □

George Gamow

The Russian-American physicist George Gamow (1904-1968) made important contributions to nuclear physics. He also did significant work in the fields of astrophysics and biology and wrote books popularizing science.

George Gamow was born in Odessa, Russia, on March 4, 1904. He became interested in physics at an early age, and when he was 18 he enrolled in the physico-mathematical faculty at Novorossia University in Odessa. After a year he transferred to the University of Leningrad, from which he eventually received a Ph.D. in 1928. That summer he visited the university in Göttingen, Germany. His work impressed the Danish physicist Niels Bohr so much that he was invited to be a fellow of theoretical physics at the University of Copenhagen. He remained in Denmark for one year, then spent the next year studying with Ernest Rutherford at the Cavendish Laboratory in England. He subsequently returned to the University of Copenhagen for another year.

In 1931 Gamow accepted the position of professor of physics at the University of Leningrad. After denying him permission to leave the country for two years, the Soviet government allowed him and his wife, Lynbov Vokhminzeva, to attend the 1933 Solvay Congress in Belgium; he took this opportunity to leave the Soviet Union forever. He spent the rest of the year at various scientific institutions all over Europe and was appointed professor of physics at the George Washington University in Washington, D.C., in 1934. Gamow remained there until 1956, when he transferred to the University of Colorado and divorced his wife. He married Barbara Perkins in 1958, and they remained in Colorado until his death in 1968. His career was extremely diverse: he delved into nuclear physics, astrophysics, biology, and writing.

Gamow's first major contribution to nuclear physics took place in Göttingen. He was intrigued by an unusual phenomenon that Rutherford had reported as a result of an alpha particle scattering experiment. When a uranium sample is bombarded with alpha particles (positively charged particles composed, like helium nuclei, of two protons and two neutrons), the particles are repelled by the electrostatic force exerted on them by the uranium nuclei, which are also positively charged. However, a uranium nucleus already contains alpha particles, and these remain there for a long time because the repulsive force exerted by a nucleus on alpha particles is overcome by the attractive force of the strong nuclear interactions at very close distances. The classical theories of physics maintained that the particles could never leave the nucleus because of the barrier that is created at the distance where the repulsive force becomes an attractive one. What puzzled Rutherford was that some alpha particles do leak out of the nucleus, though very slowly.

Gamow applied the new wave mechanics theories to this problem. In wave mechanics, the motion of particles is determined by "pilot waves," which are waves that can penetrate through any barrier. He showed that the alpha particles were in a sense "riding" on the pilot waves, enabling them to "tunnel" out through the barrier. This theory explained not only Rutherford's puzzle but also the relationship between the alpha particles emitted by different radioactive substances and the half-lives of the substances.

Gamow's second major contribution to nuclear physics was in the form of the Gamow-Teller selection rule for beta decay, a process whereby the nucleus of a radioactive atom emits an electron, thereby transforming itself into a different atom. In his theory of beta decay, Enrico Fermi had said that the electron leaves the nucleus straight out along the radius vector. Working with Edward Teller, Gamow showed that the electron could escape just as easily by moving in a hyperbolic trajectory. This discovery brought considerable insight into the magnetic interaction between the electron and the nucleus.

After this work Gamow turned his attention towards the application of nuclear physics to astrophysics. There had been previous, unsuccessful attempts to explain the abundance of nuclei in the cosmos in terms of thermodynamic equilibrium conditions. One of the problems with this approach was that the conditions for the formation of heavier nuclei were not the same as those for the formation of lighter nuclei. Gamow advocated the theory of the big bang and the expanding universe as a means of resolving the problem. He theorized that before the bang there was a fundamental state of matter he called "ylem" that consisted of a mixture of neutrons, electrons, and protons held together in a ball of high energy radiation. This ball then exploded and began to expand, allowing the fundamental particles to combine and form nuclei, and, eventually, elements—this is a process known as nucleosynthesis. He suggested that because such a universe was continually expanding, and hence changing, there would be sufficiently diverse conditions for elements of all different atomic weights to form in a non-equilibrium process. This theory also led Gamow to predict that there should be a certain level of remnant radiation from the big bang. This radiation was discovered accidentally almost 20 years later by researchers at Bell labs.

In 1954 Gamow turned to the field of biology, building on the work done by Francis Crick and James Watson on the helical structure of DNA (deoxyribonucleic acid). Gamow's work was in genetic coding theory, which deals with the way information is transferred in the genes. He used combinatorial mathematics to show that it was possible to establish the validity of certain proposed coding schemes by studying known sequences of amino acids.

Gamow also wrote many books popularizing science in an entertaining, innovative manner. This achievement won him the UNESCO Kalinga Award in 1956. He was a member of numerous scientific societies, among them the American Physical Society, the Washington Philosophical Society, the International Astronomical Union, and the Royal Danish Academy of Sciences and Letters.

Further Reading

Among the many books Gamow wrote to explain science to the layman are the well-known Mr. Tompkins books. *Mr. Tompkins in Wonderland* (1940) explains the theory of relativity, and *Mr. Tompkins Explores the Atom* (1944) discusses modern theories of the atom. He wrote several books on cosmology, including *The Moon* (1953) and a trilogy published in 1955 composed of *The Birth and Death of the Sun, Biography of the Earth,* and *The Creation of the Universe.* He had also been working on an autobiography, *My World Line,* at the time of his death. Incomplete, the book was published posthumously in 1970. □

Indira Priyadarshini Gandhi

Indira Priyadarshini Gandhi (1917-1984), a prime minister of India, was the most effective and powerful politician of her day in that country.

ndira Gandhi was born in the northern Indian city of Allahabad on November 19, 1917. She was the only child of Jawaharlal Nehru, a dominant figure in the nationalist movement and India's first prime minister. This association placed her at the center of India's struggle for freedom. After independence in 1947, she served as her father's hostess and confidante until his death. Throughout the period of her political association with her father, one of Gandhi's primary interests was social welfare work, particularly children's welfare.

Indira Gandhi attended Santiniketan University and Somerville College, Oxford University, in England. She married Feroze Gandhi (no relation to Mahatma Gandhi) in March 1942. Shortly thereafter they were both imprisoned for a period of 13 months for their part in the nationalist political agitation against British rule. Feroze Gandhi was a lawyer and newspaper executive and became an independent member of Parliament. He died in 1960. They had two sons, Rajiv and Sanjay.

Gandhi became president of the Indian National Congress in 1959. The Congress had led the country to freedom and had then become its major political party. She had joined the Congress in 1938 and subsequently served as a member of its Youth Advisory Board and chairman of its Woman's Department. Prior to assuming the presidency of the organization, Gandhi was named to its 21-member executive Working Committee and was elected with more votes than any other candidate to the powerful 11-member Central Election Board, which named candidates and planned electoral strategy.

In June 1964, following her father's death, Gandhi became minister for information and broadcasting in the Cabinet of Lal Bahadur Shastri and instituted an Indian television system. In January 1966, when Shastri died, she was elected leader of the Congress party in Parliament and became the third prime minister of independent India. She assumed office at a critical time in the history of the country. A truce had ended the 1965 war between India and Pakistan only a week before. The nation was in the midst of a two-year drought resulting in severe food shortages and a deepening economic crisis with rising prices and rising unemployment. The political repercussions of these difficulties were profound. In the fourth general elections of 1967 the Congress retained majority control (and reelected Gandhi as its leader) but lost control in half the state legislatures. After 20 years of political dominance, the Congress party experienced serious difficulty.

Gandhi immediately set about reorganizing the party to make it a more effective instrument of administration and national development. Her goal was to achieve a wider measure of social and economic justice for all Indians. As her left-of-center policies became clear, the Congress party split, with the younger, more liberal elements coalescing around Gandhi and the older, more conservative party leaders opposing her. This division came to a head in July 1969 when she nationalized the country's 14 leading banks in a highly popular move meant to make credit more available to agriculture and to small industry.

The split was formalized when Gandhi's candidate for the presidency of India, V.V. Giri, won over the party's official nominee. Although Gandhi took 228 members of Parliament with her into the New Congress, this was not a majority in the 521-member house, and she held power only with support from parties of the left. In December 1970 when Gandhi failed to get the necessary support to abolish the privy purses and privileges of the former princes, she called on the President to dissolve Parliament. Midterm elections were set for March 1971, one full year ahead of schedule.

A coalition of three parties of the right and an anti-Congress socialist party opposed Gandhi, who made alliances with parties of the left and some regional parties. Her platform was essentially one of achieving social and economic change more rapidly in an effort to improve the quality of life of India's people. Her party won a massive victory with over a two-thirds majority in Parliament.

Gandhi faced major problems in the areas of food production, population control, land reform, regulation of prices, unemployment, and industrial production. The problems were exacerbated by the influx of almost 10 million refugees as a result of the civil turmoil in East Pakistan. In November 1971 Indian troops crossed into East Pakistan to fight Pakistani forces. On December 6 Gandhi announced diplomatic recognition of the Bangla Desh government set up by East Pakistani rebel leaders. Ten days later Pakistan's commander in East Pakistan surrendered to India.

In the state elections held in India in March 1972, Gandhi's New Congress party scored the most overwhelming victory in the history of independent India; however, her

opponent accused her of violating election laws, and a high court upheld the charge in 1975. Because of this development, as well as domestic unrest, Gandhi declared a state of emergency and postponed elections. In the 1977 elections Gandhi and her party suffered major defeats; Gandhi lost her seat and the premiership.

The following year she headed the Congress party faction as she returned to Parliament. In 1979 she again became Prime Minister. In efforts to prove India's nonalliance in the global community, she visited both the United States and the USSR. Internally, riots broke out among Muslim, Hindu, and Sikh religious sects. Sikh separatists secured weapons within their sacred Golden Temple in Amritsar, assuming religious protection. Gandhi ordered government troops to storm the temple, leading to many Sikh deaths. This led to her assassination on the grounds of her own residence and office October 31, 1984, by her own Sikh security guards.

Further Reading

Biographies of Gandhi include Tariq Ali, *An Indian Dynasty: The Story of the Nehru-Gandhi Family,* Putnam, 1985; and Pupu Jayakar, *Indira Gandhi: An Intimate Biography,* Pantheon Books, 1993. □

Mohandas Karamchand Gandhi

Mohandas Karamchand Gandhi (1869-1948) was an Indian revolutionary religious leader who used his religious power for political and social reform. Although he held no governmental office, he was the prime mover in the struggle for independence of the world's second-largest nation.

Mohandas Gandhi was born on Oct. 2, 1869, in Porbandar, a seacoast town in the Kathiawar Peninsula north of Bombay. His wealthy family was of a Modh Bania subcaste of the Vaisya, or merchant, caste. He was the fourth child of Karamchand Gandhi, prime minister to the raja of three small city-states. Gandhi described his mother as a deeply religious woman who attended temple service daily. Mohandas was a small, quiet boy who disliked sports and was only an average student. At the age of 13 he was married without foreknowledge of the event to a girl of his own age, Kasturbai. The childhood ambition of Mohandas was to study medicine, but as this was considered defiling to his caste, his father prevailed on him to study law instead.

Gandhi went to England to study in September 1888. Before leaving India, he promised his mother he would abstain from eating meat, and he became a more zealous vegetarian abroad than he had been at home. In England he studied law but never became completely adjusted to the English way of life. He was called to the bar on June 10,

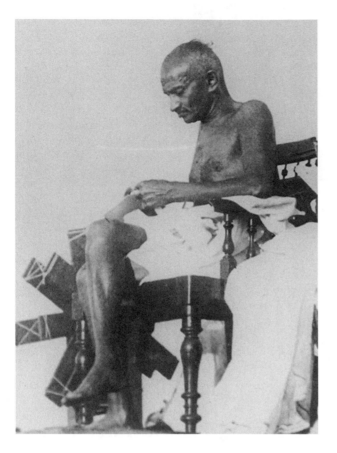

1891, and sailed for Bombay. He attempted unsuccessfully to practice law in Rajkot and Bombay, then for a brief period served as lawyer for the prince of Porbandar.

South Africa: The Beginning

In 1893 Gandhi accepted an offer from a firm of Moslems to represent them legally in Pretoria, capital of Transvaal in the Union of South Africa. While traveling in a first-class train compartment in Natal, Gandhi was asked by a white man to leave. He got off the train and spent the night in a train station meditating. He decided then to work to eradicate race prejudice. This cause kept him in South Africa not a year as he had anticipated but until 1914. Shortly after the train incident he called his first meeting of Indians in Pretoria and attacked racial discrimination by whites. This launched his campaign for improved legal status for Indians in South Africa, who at that time suffered the same discrimination as blacks.

In 1896 Gandhi returned to India to take his wife and sons to Africa. While in India he informed his countrymen of the plight of Indians in Africa. News of his speeches filtered back to Africa, and when Gandhi reached South Africa, an angry mob stoned and attempted to lynch him.

Spiritual Development

Gandhi began to do menial chores for unpaid boarders of the exterior castes and to encourage his wife to do the same. He decided to buy a farm in Natal and return to a simpler way of life. He began to fast. In 1906 he became

celibate after having fathered four sons, and he extolled *Brahmacharya* (vow of celibacy) as a means of birth control and spiritual purity. He also began to live a life of voluntary poverty.

During this period Gandhi developed the concept of *Satyagraha,* or soul force. Gandhi wrote: "Satyagraha is not predominantly civil disobedience, but a quiet and irresistible pursuit of truth." Truth was throughout his life Gandhi's chief concern, as reflected in the subtitle of his *Autobiography: The Story of My Experiments with Truth.* Truth for Gandhi was not an abstract absolute but a principle which had to be discovered experimentally in each situation. Gandhi also developed a basic concern for the means used to achieve a goal, for he felt the means necessarily shaped the ends.

In 1907 Gandhi urged all Indians in South Africa to defy a law requiring registration and fingerprinting of all Indians. For this activity Gandhi was imprisoned for 2 months but released when he agreed to voluntary registration. During Gandhi's second stay in jail he read Thoreau's essay "Civil Disobedience," which left a deep impression on him. He was influenced also by his correspondence with Leo Tolstoy in 1909-1910 and by John Ruskin's *Unto This Last.*

Gandhi decided to create a cooperative commonwealth for civil resisters. He called it the Tolstoy Farm. By this time Gandhi had abandoned Western dress for Indian garb. Two of his final legal achievements in Africa were a law declaring Indian marriages (rather than only Christian) valid, and abolition of a tax on former indentured Indian labor. Gandhi regarded his work in South Africa as completed.

By the time Gandhi returned to India, in January 1915, he had become known as "Mahatmaji," a title given him by the poet Rabindranath Tagore. Gandhi knew how to reach the masses and insisted on their resistance and spiritual regeneration. He spoke of a new, free Indian individual. He told Indians that India's shackles were self-made. In 1914 Gandhi raised an ambulance corps of Indian students to help the British army, as he had done during the Boer War.

Disobedience and Return to Old Values

The repressive Rowlatt Acts of 1919 caused Gandhi to call a general *hartal,* or strike, throughout the country, but he called it off when violence occurred against Englishmen. Following the Amritsar Massacre of some 400 Indians, Gandhi responded with noncooperation with British courts, stores, and schools. The government followed with the announcement of the Montagu-Chelmsford Reforms.

Another issue for Gandhi was man versus machine. This was the principle behind the Khadi movement, behind Gandhi's urging that Indians spin their own clothing rather than buy British goods. Spinning would create employment during the many annual idle months for millions of Indian peasants. He cherished the ideal of economic independence for the village. He identified industrialization with materialism and felt it was a dehumanizing menace to man's growth. The individual, not economic productivity, was the central concern. Gandhi never lost his faith in the inherent goodness of human nature.

In 1921 the Congress party, a coalition of various nationalist groups, again voted for a nonviolent disobedience campaign. Gandhi had come "reluctantly to the conclusion that the British connection had made India more helpless than she ever was before, politically and economically." But freedom for India was not simply a political matter, for "the instant India is purified India becomes free, and not a moment earlier." In 1922 Gandhi was tried and sentenced to 6 years in prison, but he was released 2 years later for an emergency appendectomy. This was the last time the British government tried Gandhi.

Fasting and the Protest March

Another technique Gandhi used increasingly was the fast. He firmly believed that Hindu-Moslem unity was natural and undertook a 21-day fast to bring the two communities together. He also fasted in a strike of mill workers in Ahmedabad.

Gandhi also developed the protest march. A British law taxed all salt used by Indians, a severe hardship on the peasant. In 1930 Gandhi began a famous 24-day "salt march" to the sea. Several thousand marchers walked 241 miles to the coast, where Gandhi picked up a handful of salt in defiance of the government. This signaled a nationwide movement in which peasants produced salt illegally and Congress volunteers sold contraband salt in the cities. Nationalists gained faith that they could shrug off foreign rule. The march also made the British more aware that they were subjugating India.

Gandhi was not opposed to compromise. In 1931 he negotiated with the viceroy, Lord Irwin, a pact whereby civil disobedience was to be canceled, prisoners released, salt manufacture permitted on the coast, and Congress would attend the Second Round Table Conference in London. Gandhi attended as the only Congress representative, but Churchill refused to see him, referring to Gandhi as a "half-naked fakir."

Another cause Gandhi espoused was improving the status of "untouchables," members of the exterior castes. Gandhi called them Harijans, or children of God. On Sept. 20, 1932, Gandhi began a fast to the death for the Harijans, opposing a British plan for a separate electorate for them. In this action Gandhi confronted Harijan leader Dr. Bhimrao Ambedkar, who favored separate electorates as a political guarantee of improved status. As a result of Gandhi's fast, some temples were opened to exterior castes for the first time in history. Following the marriage of one of Gandhi's sons to a woman of another caste, Gandhi came to approve only intercaste marriages.

Gandhi devoted the years 1934 through 1939 to promotion of spinning, basic education, and Hindi as the national language. During these years Gandhi worked closely with Jawaharlal Nehru in the Congress Working Committee, but there were also differences between the two. Nehru and others came to view the Mahatma's ideas on economics as anachronistic. Nevertheless, Gandhi designated Nehru his successor, saying, "I know this, that when I am gone he will speak my language."

England's entry into World War II brought India in without consultation. Because Britain had made no political concessions satisfactory to nationalist leaders, Gandhi in August 1942 proposed noncooperation, and Congress passed the "Quit India" resolution. Gandhi, Nehru, and other Congress leaders were imprisoned, touching off violence throughout India. When the British attempted to place the blame on Gandhi, he fasted 3 weeks in jail. He contracted malaria in prison and was released on May 6, 1944. He had spent a total of nearly 6 years in jail.

When Gandhi emerged from prison, he sought to avert creation of a separate Moslem state of Pakistan which Muhammad Ali Jinnah was demanding. A British Cabinet mission to India in March 1946 advised against partition and proposed instead a united India with a federal parliament. In August, Viceroy Wavell authorized Nehru to form a Cabinet. Gandhi suggested that Jinnah be offered the post of prime minister or defense minister. Jinnah refused and instead declared August 16 "Direct Action Day." On that day and several days following, communal killings left 5,000 dead and 15,000 wounded in Calcutta alone. Violence spread through the country.

Aggrieved, Gandhi went to Bengal, saying, "I am not going to leave Bengal until the last embers of trouble are stamped out," but while he was in Calcutta 4,500 more were killed in Bihar. Gandhi, now 77, warned that he would fast to death unless Biharis reformed. He went to Noakhali, a heavily Moslem city in Bengal, where he said "Do or die" would be put to the test. Either Hindus and Moslems would learn to live together or he would die in the attempt. The situation there calmed, but rioting continued elsewhere.

Drive for Independence

In March 1947 the last viceroy, Lord Mountbatten, arrived in India charged with taking Britain out of India by June 1948. The Congress party by this time had agreed to partition, since the only alternative appeared to be continuation of British rule.

Gandhi, despairing because his nation was not responding to his plea for peace and brotherhood, refused to participate in the independence celebrations on Aug. 15, 1947. On Sept. 1, 1947, after an angry Hindu mob broke into the home where he was staying in Calcutta, Gandhi began to fast, "to end only if and when sanity returns to Calcutta." Both Hindu and Moslem leaders promised that there would be no more killings, and Gandhi ended his fast.

On Jan. 13, 1948, Gandhi began his last fast in Delhi, praying for Indian unity. On January 30, as he was attending prayers, he was shot and killed by Nathuram Godse, a 35-year old editor of a Hindu Mahasabha extremist weekly in Poona.

Further Reading

Gandhi's *Autobiography: The Story of My Experiments with Truth* (2 vols., 1927-1929) covers the period to 1921. Of the numerous biographies, D. G. Tendulkar, *Mahatma* (8 vols., 1951-1954; rev. ed. 1960-1963), is most voluminous and utilizes

Gandhi's own writings. Other treatments include Romain Rolland, *Mahatma Gandhi* (trans. 1924); C. F. Andrews, ed., *Mahatma Gandhi: His Own Story* and *Mahatma Gandhi at Work* (both 1931); Louis Fischer, *The Life of Mahatma Gandhi* (1950) and *Gandhi: His Life and Message for the World* (1954); G. D. Birla, *In the Shadow of the Mahatma: A Personal Memoir* (1953); Rajendra Prasad, *At the Feet of Mahatma Gandhi* (1955); Pyarelal, *Mahatma Gandhi: The Last Phase* (2 vols., 1956-1958); and Martin Lewis, ed., *Gandhi: Maker of Modern India* (1965). Among the more provocative recent studies are Joan V. Bondurant, *Conquest of Violence: The Gandhian Philosophy of Conflict* (1958; rev. ed. 1965); Indira Rothermund, *The Philosophy of Restraint: Mahatma Gandhi's Strategy and Indian Politics* (1963); Erik H. Erikson, *Gandhi's Truth: On the Origin of Militant Nonviolence* (1969); and Penderel Moon, *Gandhi and Modern India* (1969). □

Rajiv Gandhi

Rajiv Gandhi (1944-1991) entered Indian politics after the death of his younger brother Sanjay in 1980, serving as adviser to his mother, Prime Minister Indira Gandhi, and as an elected member of Parliament. He became prime minister shortly after the assassination of his mother in 1984.

Rajiv Gandhi, India's sixth prime minister and general secretary of the Congress (I) party, was born on August 20, 1944, in Bombay, India. He was the grandson of India's first prime minister, Jawarharlal Nehru, and the eldest son of Prime Minister Indira Gandhi and her journalist, parliamentarian husband, Feroze Gandhi (no relation to Mahatma Gandhi). Brought up surrounded by politics, Rajiv Gandhi stayed out of the political world until the death of his younger brother Sanjay, who had been active politically as his mother's adviser and as a member of Parliament.

Gandhi's early years were spent at the prime minister's residence in New Delhi where his mother served as her father's official hostess. He was educated at Welham Preparatory and Doon schools, both elite Indian institutions. Following graduation from Doon School, Gandhi went to Britain where he attended the Imperial Scientific and Technical College in London and Cambridge University's Trinity College, studying mechanical engineering. His other interests included music (both Indian and Western), photography, ham radios, and flying.

While at Cambridge Gandhi met an Italian student studying English, Sonia Manio. They were married in New Delhi in 1968 and lived with his mother, who by then was prime minister. They had two children, a son, Rahul, and a daughter, Priyanka. Surrounded by political figures, the family nonetheless managed to keep its personal life out of the public eye.

Although he studied mechanical engineering, Gandhi chose to pursue a career as an airline pilot. Upon return to India he got his commercial pilot's license and joined Indian Airlines, the domestic carrier. He remained in this position until he entered politics.

Entrance into Politics

In June 1980 Sanjay Gandhi was killed while learning to fly when the plane he was piloting crashed in New Delhi. He had been instrumental as his mother's adviser in guiding Congress (I) party and governmental affairs from the mid-1970s on. He was also a member of Parliament elected from the Amethi district of Uttar Pradesh state of northern India.

After the death of his brother, his mother urged Gandhi to enter politics. Resigning his position with Indian Airlines, Gandhi served first as an adviser to his mother, and then, like his brother, entered Parliament by winning the seat made vacant by his brother's death. He was elected general secretary of the Congress (I) party and also supervised the completion of arrangements for the Asian Games which India hosted in 1982. Additionally, he remained one of his mother's chief advisers on a range of both domestic and foreign policy matters.

In dealing with party affairs, Gandhi showed little tolerance for those members who were incompetent, corrupt, or sycophantic followers of the Gandhi family. He started to streamline the Congress (I) organization by introducing modern managerial techniques and trying to bring younger, more dynamic people into the decision-making process. With these attempts and his rather gentle, soft-spoken personality, he gained an honorable reputation, although observers often wondered whether he had the political acumen and experience to deal with the knotty problems of state faced by his mother's administration, such as national integration and economic development.

The problem of national integration eventually catapulted Gandhi into the position of prime minister. In the northern state of Punjab demands by the predominant Sikh community had grown for more autonomy for the state, greater retention of the state's resources, and solution of border problems with neighboring states and had combined with what might be termed Sikh ethnic and religious revivalism. A small group of so-called "extremists" held what the government considered to be an untenable position on the issue of autonomy bordering on a call for complete independence. Talks between the government and Sikh leaders faltered, violence erupted, and some extremists were implicated in the murders of Punjab government officials. Those accused and some of their followers sought sanctuary in the Golden Temple, the most holy shrine of the Sikhs, in the city of Amritsar. They were protected essentially by the government's reluctance to violate holy places by sending in the police. The stalemate continued for about three years.

In the meantime, however, violence between various factions of the Sikh community escalated, and those hiding in the temple were accused of directing the murders of other Sikhs who disagreed with their position. Eventually the violence spread to the non-Sikh, primarily the Hindu population of Punjab. As it did, the government decided it had to act. In June 1984 troops were sent into the temple complex. During the armed confrontation most of those in the temple were killed, and hundreds of others throughout the Punjab were arrested. The government's action shocked the Sikh community and threats were made against the lives of the prime minister and other high ranking officials. The threat against Indira Gandhi was carried out on October 31, 1984, when Sikh members of her own bodyguard assassinated her.

Becomes Prime Minister

Rajiv Gandhi was then chosen by his party as prime minister. General elections to Parliament which normally would have been held in January 1985 were held one month early at the end of December 1984. The Congress (I) party won an overwhelming majority, securing 401 out of 508 contested seats. This was better than any previous electoral victory. Gandhi proved himself as a tireless and effective campaigner in the weeks preceding the election and was widely credited, along with an improved economy, with the party's success. His standing within the party was also improved by his denial of electoral districts to party members considered to be corrupt. In March 1985 elections were also held in 11 states for the states' assemblies. Although the Congress (I) party did not win in all 11, it did win in eight, and again Gandhi was credited with the success. He refused to let numbers of corrupt politicians run on the Congress (I) ticket.

Yet observers were skeptical. Gandhi entered politics and became prime minister as a result of his mother's death. Whether or not Gandhi's instincts about public policy could

compensate for a lack of experience remained to be seen. He appeared to be off to a promising start in 1985 by initiating new talks with the Sikhs and attempting to streamline and modernize the administration. However, the vexing issues of national integration and economic development were still of paramount concern. With only minor diplomatic successes, Sikh radicalism did not cease during Gandhi's term in office.

Under his 1986-1990 plan Gandhi launched India towards strong economic growth by removing many restrictions on imports and encouraging foreign investment. Beyond this effort, Gandhi was seen as indecisive. Despite the firing of his mother's aides and surrounding himself with a constantly changing array of cabinet members, government corruption continued, including accusations that Gandhi and his party members were receiving kickbacks from a Bofors arms deal.

In the November 1989 elections a former Gandhi loyalist, Vishwanath Pratap Singh, led a coalition to unseat the ruling party hurt by the numerous charges of corruption and incompetence. The Congress (I) party lost its majority and Gandhi was forced to resign as prime minister. Although displaced, Gandhi's opposition to Singh's administration proved tireless. His determination to return to office inspired a campaign in 1991 that political analysts believed would result in an absolute majority for Gandhi and his party. But he would not resume his former position. On May 21, 1991, Gandhi was assassinated by a terrorist bomb while campaigning in Tamil Nadu. Tamil separatists claimed the killing was an act of revenge for Gandhi's intervention in the Sri Lanka civil war of 1987.

Further Reading

For additional information see "Rajiv Gandhi, Super-salesman," *Newsweek* (June 17, 1985); "Rajiv the Son," *New York Times Magazine* (December 2, 1984); "India After Indira Gandhi," *MacLean's* (November 12, 1984); "Indira's Intrigues: India Elects a New Crown Prince," *The New Leader* (July 13, 1981); "Gandhi's Reluctant Heir," *MacLean's* (November 12, 1984); Underwood, N.-DeMont, J.al, et, "The End of a Dynasty?" *MacLean's* (June 3, 1991) □

Greta Garbo

The Swedish-born American film star Greta Garbo (1905-1990) became one of Hollywood's legendary personalities.

Born Greta Louisa Gustafsson on Sept. 18, 1905, in Stockholm, Sweden, Greta Garbo grew up in respectable poverty—inhibited, self-conscious, and oddly mature. She was one of three children who became a legendary actress and one of the most fascinating women of all time. Garbo was a woman of remarkable beauty, intelligence, and independent spirit. Despite her beauty, Garbo was somewhat reclusive and photophobic. She once told a gossip columnist in France, "I feel like a criminal who is hunted . . . when photographers come, they draw crowds. I am frightened beyond control. When so many people stare, I feel almost ashamed.''

She was a stagestruck girl of 14 when her job as a clerk in a department store led to photographic modeling for her employer's catalog. This in turn brought parts in two short advertising films and, at 16, a bathing beauty role in E.A. Petschler's film *The Vagabond Baron*. In 1923 Garbo was one of only seven students admitted to Sweden's prestigious Royal Dramatic Theatre Academy. While attending the training school, she chose her stage name and worked to develop her voice. Her studies at the academy served as both the foundation for her acting career and a source of several lifelong friendships with other actors and artists.

Within a year, one of Sweden's foremost film directors, Mauritz Stiller, recognized Garbo's unique beauty and immense talent. Stiller selected Garbo to play the role of Countess Elizabeth Dohna in the Swedish film *The Atonement of Gosta Berling* (1924). The film was considered a silent screen masterpiece and was a huge success throughout Europe. Garbo was soon cast in the leading role of *Joyless Street,* the definitive masterpiece of German realistic cinema, directed by G.W. Pabst. The film received international acclaim for its depth of feeling and technical innovations. The film and Garbo's performance were a critical success, shattering box office records.

Driving her unmercifully, Stiller molded her into an actress and insisted on bringing her with him to the Metro-Goldwyn-Mayer (MGM) studio in Hollywood in the sum-

mer of 1925. Through Stiller, she won an assignment in her first American film *The Torrent* (1926). Garbo quickly became the reigning star of Hollywood, due to both the box office success of her films and her captivating performances. She starred in eleven silent films. Her dramatic presence on the screen redefined acting. Garbo's aura created a unique balance between femininity and independence, proving that these qualities were not mutually exclusive. While many of her silent film contemporaries failed in making the transition to sound films, Garbo found artistic expression and thrived in this breakthrough medium. Her voice added a wonderful new dimension to her characters. She then starred in *The Temptress* (1926) and *Flesh and the Devil* (1927), which not only made her famous but introduced her to John Gilbert, with whom she conducted (both on and off the screen) a flaming romance which lasted several years. On the day they were to be married, Garbo left Gilbert standing at the altar.

Garbo's first sound picture was *Anna Christie* (1930), based on a play by American dramatist Eugene O'Neill. The sound scene was a tour de force, the longest, continuous sound take of the time. Because of the film's extraordinary success, MGM created a German language version with Garbo and an entirely new cast. Garbo's ability to act successfully in two languages demonstrates her remarkable range and linguistic talent.

Garbo's career continued to flourish. She starred in 15 sound films including such classics as *Mata Hari* (1932), *As You Desire Me* (1932), and *Queen Christina* (1933), one of her first classic roles. Director Rouben Mamoulian used Garbo's mask-like visage as a canvas upon which the audience ascribed an array of intense emotions. This use of her face as an expressive conduit became Garbo's signature style, and she created magic with it in her starring roles in *Susan Lennox—Her Fall and Rise* (1931 with Clark Gable), *Grand Hotel* (1932), *Anna Karenina* (1935), *Camille* (1936), *Conquest* (1937), and *Ninotchka* (1939).

Garbo gradually withdrew into an isolated retirement in 1941 after the failure of *Two-Faced Woman,* a domestic comedy. Her retirement was also partly because of World War II. She was tempted by a number of very interesting acting possibilities, but, unfortunately, none of the projects came to fruition.

Her twenty years of brilliant film portrayals created a cinematic legend characterized by financial success. During the mid-1930's she was America's highest paid female. Garbo's retirement from films did not mark the end of a very busy, independent life. Without the pressures of filmmaking, Garbo had the opportunity to turn to other creative pursuits such as painting, poetry, creative design of clothing and furnishings, gardening, and a rigorous daily exercise routine. In 1950 Garbo was chosen the best actress of the half-century in a poll conducted by the theatrical newspaper *Variety*. She became a U.S. citizen in 1951, and in 1954 she received (in absentia) a special Academy Award for ''her unforgettable screen performances.'' Garbo moved to New York city in 1953 and traveled extensively. She died at her home in New York on April 15, 1990.

Further Reading

The most informative works about Greta Garbo are John Bainbridge, *Garbo* (1955); Fritiof Billquist, *Garbo* (trans. 1960); and Raymond Durgat and John Kobal, *Greta Garbo* (1965). ☐

Carlos P. Garcia

Carlos P. Garcia (1896-1971) was the fourth president of the Republic of the Philippines. He was noted for the enunciation of the Filipino First Policy, intended to complete and guarantee Philippine economic independence and sovereignty.

Carlos P. Garcia was born in Talibon, Bohol, on November 4, 1896. He took law courses at Silliman University in 1918-1919 and graduated with a law degree from the Philippine Law School. He topped the bar examination in 1923. He was elected for three terms (1925-1931) as representative of the third district of Bohol. He served for three terms (1933-1941) as governor of Bohol Province. For 13 years (1941-1954) Garcia served in the Senate of the Philippines.

During World War II, in May 1942, Garcia was hunted by the Japanese military authority because of his loyalty to the Allied cause and his refusal to surrender and cooperate with the government. After the war he participated in several missions to Washington to work for the approval of the Philippine Rehabilitation and War Damage Claims. He was a delegate to the World Conference at San Francisco to draft the charter of the United Nations Organization in May 1945. He acted as presiding officer of the Southeast Asia Treaty Organization Conference in Manila in 1954, which produced the Manila Treaty and the Pacific Charter.

From 1947 to 1953 Garcia was vice president of the Nacionalista party directorate, and he also served in the Cabinet beginning in 1953 as vice president and secretary of foreign affairs. When he was in the Senate, he was chairman and member of numerous key committees, among them government reorganization, foreign affairs, public works, army and navy, and justice. He was also a member of the Senate Electoral Tribunal. From 1946 to 1951 Garcia served as minority floor leader of the Senate.

Succeeded President

When President Magsaysay was killed in an airplane accident on March 17, 1957, Garcia became his successor, having been elected vice president in November 1953. In the elections of 1957 Garcia won over three other candidates and became fourth president of the republic since its independence in 1946.

Garcia's main achievement before he became president involved his activities as foreign policy expert for the government. As secretary of foreign affairs, he opened formal reparation negotiations in an effort to end the nine-year technical state of war between Japan and the Philippines,

leading to an agreement in April 1954. During the Geneva Conference on Korean unification and other Asian problems, Garcia as chairman of the Philippine delegation attacked communist promises in Asia and defended the U.S. policy in the Far East. In a speech on May 7, 1954, the day of the fall of Dien Bien Phu, Garcia repeated the Philippine stand for nationalism and opposition of communism.

Garcia acted as chairman of the eight-nation Southeast Asian Security Conference held in Manila in September 1954, which led to the development of the Southeast Asia Treaty Organization, known as SEATO. Garcia's cardinal principles in foreign affairs, as announced in a speech on November 30, 1957, were "to maintain and improve Philippine-American relations" and "to foster closer ties with our Asian neighbors."

Stressed Austerity, Nationalism

Garcia's administration was characterized by its austerity program and its insistence on a comprehensive nationalist policy. On March 3, 1960, he affirmed the need for complete economic freedom and added that the government no longer would tolerate the dominance of foreign interests (especially American) in the national economy. He promised to shake off "the yoke of alien domination in business, trade, commerce and industry." Garcia was also credited with his role in reviving Filipino cultural arts.

The prevalence of graft and corruption in the government, institutional carryover from previous administrations, and U.S. disfavor of his Filipino First Policy put Garcia on the defensive and led partly to his defeat in the 1961 elections. Garcia died in 1971 at the age of 74.

Further Reading

Extensive information on Garcia is in Eufronio Alip, ed., *The Philippine Presidents from Aguinaldo to Garcia* (1958); Jesús V. Merritt, *Our Presidents: Profiles in History* (1962); and Pedro A. Gagelonia, *Presidents All* (1967). See also Hernando J. Abaya, *The Untold Philippine Story* (1967). Further information can be found in Ester G. Maring and Joel M. Maring, eds., *Historical and Cultural Dictionary of the Philippines* (1973). □

Gabriel García Márquez

Gabriel García Márquez (born 1928) was a Colombian novelist, short-story writer, and journalist whose works earned him the reputation of being the greatest living writer of Castilian in Spain and Latin America.

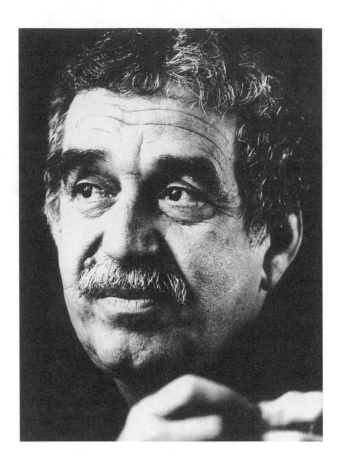

Born in Aracata, Magdalena, Gabriel García Márquez received his early education and baccalaureate degree from the Liceo Nacional of Zipaquirá in 1946. That year he started working as a newspaper editor for *El Universal* in Cartagena. In 1948 he moved to Barranquilla, where he was editor of *El Heraldo* until 1952. Then he became editor of the liberal newspaper *El Espectador* in Bogotá during repressive eras of the conservative dictators Laureano Gómez and his successor, General Gustavo Rojas Pinilla.

Between 1955 and 1960 several short stories and a novella had begun to establish García Márquez's fame in the Spanish-speaking world. *La hojarasca* (1955), a short novel, is set, like his later works, in the mythical town of Macondo in the swampy coastal area of northeastern Colombia known as the Ciénaga. The story reflects the changes the 20th century wrought in the life of this sleepy country town. Much of García Márquez's work centers on funerals. In *La hojarasca* mourners who knew the dead man in life contemplate the past, each from his own point of view. In three monologues these persons—an old colonel, his daughter Isabel, and Isabel's son—tell their story. The dead man, a doctor and former friend of the colonel, had committed suicide. The narrators do not entirely explain the motives of the suicide, but in the course of each story much of the past history of the village of Macondo is revealed. A strong premonition of imminent, relentless, and inevitable doom for Macondo permeates the novel.

Macondo and the Buendía family were further developed in *El coronel no tiene quien le escriba* (1961; *Nobody Writes to the Colonel and Other Stories*). The next short stories, *Los funerales de la Mama Grande* (1962), strengthened the growing reputation of García Márquez. The publication of *Cien años de soledad* (1967; *One Hundred Years of Solitude*) constituted something of a literary phenomenon

when it sold over 100,000 copies in 15 editions in Buenos Aires in 1969.

The story of *Cien años de soledad* depicts the rise and fall of a village as seen in the lives of five generations of one family—an almost biblical pentateuch—ending appropriately with flood and drought, climaxed by cyclonic winds of final destruction, which comes as the last living Buendía deciphers the ancient prophecies of doom and learns that "races condemned to 100 years of solitude did not have a second opportunity on earth." The setting of this novel is a microcosm for Colombia, and through extension, both South America and the rest of the world. Pablo Neruda, the most famous Chilean poet, called *Cien años de soledad,* "the greatest revelation in the Spanish language since the *Don Quixote* of Cervantes." This novel is generally considered García Márquez's masterpiece.

García Márquez considered his next novel, *El otono del patriarca* (1975; *The Autumn of the Patriarch*), "a perfect integration of journalism and literature." García Márquez continued to write novels, short stories, essays, and film scripts. In 1982 he was awarded the Nobel Prize for literature. In 1983, he wrote the film script *Erendira* adapted from his 1972 novella *La increible y triste historia de la candida Erendira y su abuela desalmada* (*Innocent Erendira and Her Heartless Grandmother*). García Márquez's other famous novel, *El amor en los tiempos del colera* (*Love in the Time of Cholera*) was written in 1985 (with an English translation published in 1988). This novel is an exploration of the manifestations of love and the relationship between aging, death, and decay. After *Cholera* he published the novels *El general en su laberinto* (1989; *The General in His Labyrinth,* 1990), *Doce cuentos peregrinos* (1992; *Strange Pilgrims,* 1993), and *Love and Other Demons* (1994).

García Márquez's fictional blend of history, politics, social realism, and fantasy has given rise to the term "magical realism." The use of magical realism was often imitated by other Latin American authors, most notably, Isabel Allende. His need to tell the story drives García Márquez's writing. In the July 1997 issue of *Harper's,* García Márquez writes, "the best story is not always the first one but rather the one that is told better." Because of his storytelling ability, García Márquez has assured himself a place in history as the greatest Latin American writer of the 20th century.

Further Reading

Critical interpretations of Gabriel García Márquez's work can be found in the series *Contemporary Literary Criticism,* Gale, Volume 2, 1974; Volume 3, 1975; Volume 8, 1978; Volume 10, 1979; Volume 15, 1980; Volume 27, 1984; Volume 47, 1988; and Volume 55, 1989. Interviews with García Márquez appeared in *PMLA: Publications of the Modern Language Association,* March 1989; *Variety,* March 25-31, 1996; *World Policy Journal,* Summer 1996; and *Booklist,* March 15, 1997.

□

Gabriel García Moreno

Gabriel García Moreno (1821-1875) was an Ecuadorian political leader whose dynamic leadership brought stability and improvement to his country. Though mostly governing as a dictator, he broke the power of the military and raised the influence of the Catholic Church.

On Dec. 24, 1821, Gabriel García Moreno was born in Guayaquil. His father, Gabriel García Gómez, was a Spaniard; his mother, Mercedes Moreno, belonged to one of the most distinguished and oldest families of that city.

At 15 García Moreno was sent to Quito to complete his education. At 17 he received minor orders in the Church; but he soon abandoned the idea of an ecclesiastical career and switched to law, in which he received his doctorate in 1844. In the meantime, his interest in politics arose. He was an admirer of Vicente Rocafuerte, whom he followed into opposition against Gen. Juan José Flores.

In 1846 García Moreno married Rosa Ascázubi, several years his senior. This marriage gave him a secure political base through membership in Quito's ruling class, a position his family already enjoyed in the port city of Guayaquil. In 1851 he was instrumental in the government's readmission of the Society of Jesus. When Gen. José María Urbina took over the presidency and expelled the order anew, García Moreno published a *Defense of the Jesuits.* He was forced into exile in Colombia, Peru, and Europe, and though he was elected to the Senate, the government did not allow him to return. Back in Ecuador by the end of 1856, the following year he was elected mayor of Quito and rector of the university, having won recognition by European scientific societies for his fieldwork in vulcanology.

Rise to Power

In 1857-1858 García Moreno was a member of the Senate. He led the opposition against the government while the country was being invaded by the Peruvian army. In January 1859 he fled to Peru but soon returned to Quito as one of the members of a newly formed revolutionary junta. Defeated by the regular Ecuadorian army, he had to flee once more to Peru. He offered his alliance to the Peruvian president, then sought French aid, in exchange for which Ecuador would have become a protectorate of France. Though all this scheming proved to be fruitless, the political situation within Ecuador suddenly changed. By September 1860 García Moreno was in control of the republic, having achieved military victory with the help of his old enemy Gen. Flores.

García Moreno's tenure as president was legalized by the Constituent Convention of 1861. During his first term, which ended in 1865, he maintained with harshness the government's stability in face of constant attacks on the part of Gen. Urbina and his Liberal followers and was able to wipe out militarism. Twice García Moreno undertook military intervention in Colombia, but both attempts ended in a fiasco. He negotiated with the papacy a concordat that regulated relations between the state and the Church; and to provide the country immediately with sorely needed teachers and at a limited cost, he arranged for the coming of various French teaching orders and the readmittance of the Jesuits.

Virtual Dictator

Since the 1861 Constitution did not allow immediate reelection, García Moreno arranged the election of Jerónimo Carrión (1865). After returning from a diplomatic mission to Lima and Santiago the following year, he found that political power had slipped from his hands. But in the face of mounting opposition President Carrión resigned, and García Moreno regained much of his former influence. Though he was instrumental in choosing the next president, Javier Espinosa, he lost patience with him after a year and led a barracks revolt that overthrew the government (Jan. 16, 1869).

García Moreno consolidated his power through a new constitution. His next 6 years in the presidency were the most positive of his record as chief executive. With practically no visible opposition, he concentrated on bettering higher education and building Ecuador's first railway. In a country that lacked highways, the construction of the paved road from Quito to the coast was of special significance.

On the expiration of his term in 1875, García Moreno chose to succeed himself. Four days before his new inauguration, on August 6, he was murdered by a disappointed Colombian office seeker.

Further Reading

For an interesting discussion of García Moreno see Lewis Hanke, ed., *Readings in Latin American History: Selected Articles from the Hispanic American Historical Review,* vol. 2 (1966). Biographies of García Moreno are also in Clinton Herring, *A History of Latin America from the Beginnings to the Present* (1955; 3d ed. 1968); James Fred Rippy, *Latin America: A Modern History* (1958; rev. ed. 1968); and George I. Blanksten, *Ecuador: Constitutions and Caudillos* (1964). □

Inca Garcilaso de la Vega

Inca Garcilaso de la Vega (1539-1616) was a Peruvian chronicler whose Spanish prose won him the designation as the first classic writer of America.

Inca Garcilaso de la Vega was born in Cuzco on April 12, 1539, the son of Capt. Sebastian Garcilaso de la Vega, a scion of a proud Spanish family distinguished in war and literature, and Chimpu Ocllo, niece of the last Inca emperor, Huayna Cápac. Named Gómez Suárez de Figueroa, he later changed his name to El Inca Garcilaso de la Vega. Reared by his mother, he learned the language, customs, myths, and legends of her people, while his father had him educated as a nobleman in the classical traditions of Spain.

Thus the mind of the bilingual child soon confused facts and fancies concerning the glories of the Incas, the triumphs of the Spaniards, and the splendors of classical Rome.

On his father's death the 21-year-old Garcilaso departed for Spain, where he vainly sought the aristocratic perquisites that he felt the public services of his sire deserved. Although he was disappointed in this pretension, a small legacy permitted him to settle down in 1571 near Cordova for the remainder of his life.

In 1572 the news of his mother's death and the stern measures of Spanish authorities in Peru to suppress her people apparently inspired in Garcilaso a resolve to prepare a defense of the Inca civilization and a record of its vanished grandeur. With tireless diligence he assembled information on all aspects of Inca history and culture and trained himself in the art of Castilian prose. The latter process began with 14 years spent on an arduous translation exercise which resulted in the best Spanish version of the Neoplatonist *Dialogues on Love,* a philosophical treatise written in Italian by the 15th-century Jewish humanist Leon Hebreo. To acquire narrative skill, Garcilaso wrote a novelesque account of Hernando de Soto's wanderings in the lower Mississippi Valley, called *The Florida of the Inca* (1605), which was based on information supplied by a veteran of that expedition.

Meanwhile, Garcilaso's masterwork, *The Royal Commentaries of the Incas* (1609), was taking shape. It was a systematic recital of the personalities, events, customs, rites, and the native dynasty of Peru from its beginnings to the

arrival of the Spaniards. The lyric descriptions of this work, written in poetic style, conjure up a vision of a utopian civilization. A literary achievement of genuine distinction, it is also a valuable historical record. A second part, *The General History of Peru* (1617), recounting events of the Spanish Conquest and published posthumously, is less impressive. Garcilaso died in April 1616.

Further Reading

Among the works on Garcilaso are Donald G. Castanien, *El Inca Garcilaso de la Vega* (1969), and John Grier Varner, *El Inca: The Life and Times of Garcilaso de la Vega* (1969). □

Samuel Rawson Gardiner

The English historian Samuel Rawson Gardiner (1829-1902) was a major historian of the Puritan revolution. His work is a lengthy, detailed, and well-researched study of a brief but significant period in English history.

Samuel Rawson Gardiner was born at Alresford, Hampshire, on March 4, 1829. Educated at Winchester and Christ Church, Oxford, he was professor of modern history at Kings College, London, from 1871 to 1885 and was elected fellow at All Souls College, Oxford, in 1884.

Gardiner's historical writings dealing with the Puritan revolution cover the years 1603 to 1660: *History of England from the Accession of James I to the Outbreak of the Civil War, 1603-1642* (10 vols., 1863-1882), *History of the Civil War, 1642-1649* (3 vols., 1886-1891), and *History of the Commonwealth and Protectorate, 1649-1660* (3 vols., 1895-1901). The last two volumes of his final work were completed by Charles Firth as *The Last Years of the Protectorate* (1909).

Perhaps Gardiner was interested in the Puritan revolution because of his own descent from Oliver Cromwell, although this relation in no way caused a biased account. While critics questioned his method and judgment in his earlier volumes, he was highly respected by the late 1870s, especially for his extensive use of manuscript sources from the archives and private collections in England and Europe. His treatment of the period 1603 to 1660 is exhaustive, and his handling of special areas shows sympathy and great breadth of imagination. His treatment of constitutional history shows knowledge of the political philosophy and the utopian idealism of the time. He was interested in the subject of religious toleration and made use of the works of obscure pamphleteers. In his analysis of the causes of the civil war he deals with human motives and political conduct with great perception. His careful analysis of human character is seen in his portrayals of James I, Archbishop Laud, and Cromwell. The work as a whole has a clear and unadorned style, but it lacks force and enthusiasm and often suffers from excessive detail.

Gardiner's lesser works, often more specialized treatments of 17th-century problems, include *Prince Charles and the Spanish Marriage* (1869), *What Gunpowder Plot Was* (1897), *Oliver Cromwell* (1901), and several edited collections of documents. His reputation as a historian was acknowledged by honorary degrees from Oxford, Edinburgh, and Göttingen. Gardiner died on Feb. 24, 1902, while still at work on the final volumes of the history of the Protectorate.

Further Reading

The best biographical work on Gardiner is Henry Barrett Learned, *Samuel Rawson Gardiner* (1902). Although out of date, it does provide an interesting account of his life and writings. Roland G. Usher, *A Critical Study of the Historical Method of Samuel Rawson Gardiner* (1915), is a more specialized study of Gardiner as a historian. □

John W. Gardner

John W. Gardner (born 1912) had a varied and productive career as an educator, public official, and political reformer. Perhaps best known as the founder of the lobby Common Cause, he was the author of several best-selling books on the themes of achieving personal and societal excellence.

John William Gardner was born in Los Angeles, California, on October 8, 1912. The younger of two sons born to William and Marie F. Gardner, Gardner's father died when he was one. Gardner was raised by his mother, who passed on to him a zest for literature and travel. After taking one year off to travel the world, Gardner graduated from high school in 1930. He attended Stanford as an undergraduate and became a Pacific Coast free-style swimming champion during this time. He graduated from Stanford in 1935 with a degree in psychology. The year before, he had married native Guatemalan Aïda Marroquin. They later had two daughters, Stephanie and Francesca.

In 1936 Gardner received an M.A. in psychology from Stanford, followed by a Ph.D. from the University of California, Berkeley, in 1938. His dissertation on "Levels of Aspiration" foreshadowed much of his later work on individual goal-setting and achievement.

World War II interrupted Gardner's budding teaching career (two years as an instructor at the Connecticut College for Women followed by two years as an assistant professor at Mount Holyoke College), but it allowed him to use his academic expertise. Assigned to intelligence in 1942, he initially monitored Axis radio propaganda, then was switched to the Office of Strategic Services (forerunner of the CIA), where he contributed to the development of OSS personnel assessment tests and helped test, process, and assign OSS agents. He was discharged from service in 1946 with the rank of captain.

Foundation Executive and Author

Gardner's public career began with his employment in 1946 as a staff member at the Carnegie Corporation, a foundation dedicated to the advancement and dissemination of knowledge. By 1955 he had become the foundation's president. He played a decisive role in awarding Carnegie grants supporting such activities as the Russian Research Center and Cognitive Studies Center at Harvard and what became known as the "new math." In 1958 he oversaw preparation of an important report published by the Rockefeller Brothers Fund, *The Pursuit of Excellence: Education and the Future of America.*

Gardner produced his best-known book in 1961 titled *Excellence: Can We Be Equal and Excellent Too?* In the book he discussed the dilemma of encouraging merit in a democracy, urging commitment to high standards in education, and rejection of "shoddiness" in any field, be it plumbing or philosophy. Three years later he published a book presenting the case for emphasis on a "common good" without sacrificing human individuality (*Self-Renewal: The Individual and the Innovative Society*).

Public Servant

While president of Carnegie, Gardner served frequently as a consultant to federal agencies. In 1961 he edited a collection of President Kennedy's political statements (*To Turn the Tide*), and in early 1964 he was appointed by President Johnson to chair a White House task force on education. The panel brought in a report favoring

federal aid to public schools to equalize education in areas of poverty and to encourage qualitative improvements and innovations in local communities. Many of its recommendations were enacted in the Elementary and Secondary Education Act of 1965.

In August 1965 Gardner became Johnson's secretary of health, education and welfare, remaining in that position until early 1968. While running the sprawling 90,000 employee department, he consolidated several of its social rehabilitation agencies and administered many of the newly enacted Great Society programs. After leaving the cabinet, he became chairman of the National Urban Coalition, a lobby working to halt the deterioration of inner cities. Frustrated with the opposition the NUC encountered from organized special interests, Gardner decided that a broader-based organization was needed to help bring about reform in an increasingly unresponsive political system.

Thus in 1970 he launched Common Cause, persuading several benefactors to finance a drive that netted 200,000 members within a year. A "public interest" lobby, Common Cause concerned itself with a wide range of issues including the Vietnam War, social welfare, and environmentalism. At first it drew substantial annual income from large contributions, but its base broadened quickly; in 1976 its governing board voted not to take donations exceeding $100 from corporations or unions. By the mid 1970s Common Cause had become closely identified with governmental reform generally, including campaign finance limits and disclosure laws, lowering of the voting age, and reform of the seniority system in Congress. Pragmatic in his view of politics as "a trading out of conflicting interests," however, Gardner insisted that influential positions in Common Cause be held by professional lobbyists and organizers. He stepped down as head of the organization in early 1977, remaining as chairman emeritus with an office in the same building. Common Cause membership declined after his departure, though the organization continued to be very active.

Gardner produced four books during the late 1960s and 1970s: *No Easy Victory* (1968), a study of the challenges confronting social reform, *The Recovery of Confidence* (1970), a plea for the restoration of moral values that some thought "sermonizing," *In Common Cause* (1972), a slim volume outlining the purpose of the new public interest lobby, and *Morale* (1978), an exhortation to individual citizens to return to traditional values of justice, freedom, and human dignity. Gardner also wrote the book *On Leadership*, which was published in 1990.

The Third Career

Gardner had once stated that everyone should have three careers, and in late 1979 he began his third, forming Independent Sector, aimed at insuring "the survival of the non-profit sector" in the face of federal encroachment. In the same year he was appointed by President Carter to the Commission for a National Agenda, whose task was to offer recommendations to deal with the likely issues of the 1980s. In 1981 Gardner was named to yet another presidential panel by Ronald Reagan, the Task Force on Private Sector

Initiatives, designed to find ways to make up for federal program cuts.

Some saw Gardner moving toward conservatism in his "third career," but there was consistency in his efforts to act in areas he felt had been vacated by the swing of the public policy pendulum. Also congruent with his earlier activities were Gardner's willingness and ability to serve presidents of both parties.

Gardner is the recipient of numerous honorary degrees and prestigious awards from the labor unions AFL-CIO and UAW and the Anti-Defamation League, as well as the Presidential Medal of Freedom. He is a fellow of both the American Academy of Arts and Sciences and the National Academy of Education. In 1996 Gardner received the James Bryant Conant Award for outstanding contributions to education in the United States.

In 1994 Gardner became chairman of the board of the nonpartisan, Denver based National Civic League. The organization launched an Alliance for National Renewal, hoping to foster a universal ethic of volunteerism and stimulate cities to tackle their own problems. In 1995 after one year with Gardner as its guide, the Civic League had brought together more than 100 organizations that worked at community development in numerous ways.

In the mid 1990s Gardner served as a professor of public service at the Stanford Business School. Gardner remained an active, visible symbol of civic reform and the national quest for excellence.

Further Reading

No biography of John W. Gardner has yet appeared. Gardner's own books (the full titles of which are included in the preceding article) collectively provide a profile of his personal beliefs and approach to public service: *Excellence* (1961); *Self-Renewal* (1964); *No Easy Victory* (1968); *The Recovery of Confidence* (1970); *In Common Cause* (1972); and *Morale* (1978). Andrew McFarland, *Common Cause: Lobbying in the Public Interest* (1984), is the most informative history of that organization and Gardner's role in it. Gardener's latest book, *On Leadership*, was published in 1990.

For periodical articles about John Gardner see *Commonwealth*, May 7, 1993; and *Knight-Ridder/Tribune News Service*, January 27, 1995. □

James Abram Garfield

James Abram Garfield (1831-1881) was an American Civil War general before becoming the twentieth president of the United States. He was assassinated after 6 months in office.

James A. Garfield was born in the log cabin of American myth on Nov. 19, 1831, near Cleveland, Ohio. Although his family dated back to the Massachusetts Bay Colony, his immediate ancestors had not prospered, and Garfield's

upbringing was plagued by dire poverty. His father died when James was 2 years old, and he was early put out to labor to help keep the family intact.

Garfield matriculated at the Western Reserve Eclectic Institute, later called Hiram College. He graduated from Williams College and, before he was 30, became a lay preacher for the Disciples of Christ. He taught school briefly and returned to Hiram as a professor and head of the college, but he did not enjoy the life. "You and I know," he wrote a friend, "that teaching is not the work in which a man can live and grow." Still, Garfield remained bookish throughout his life, and while by no means brilliant or original, he emerges as truly distinctive in his occasional writings, letters, and diary. These reveal a perspicacious mind, shrewd insight into his contemporaries' personalities, and a rare comprehension among politicos of the day of the vast changes through which the United States was going.

War and Politics

In 1859 Garfield was elected to the Ohio Senate and became a leading Union supporter in the Civil War. He accepted a commission as colonel and, typically, set about studying military strategy and organization. His readings must have been well selected because his rise in rank was rapid even for the Civil War era. An active role in the Battle of Middle Creek on Jan. 10, 1862, made him a brigadier general, and, in April, he fought during the bloody second day at Shiloh. After that he left the lines to become chief of staff through the Chickamauga campaign, organizing a divi-

sion of military information and being promoted to major general.

Garfield's military career reflected the dexterity with which he would later escape political crises unscathed, for although he was closely associated with several disasters that ruined associates, he himself escaped blame. Indeed, in December 1863 Garfield was elected to the House of Representatives in recognition of his military service and, until his death, was never again out of Federal office. His Ohio district was safe for Republicans, so Garfield could concentrate on the affairs of office, and he was the leader of his party in the House during the presidency of Rutherford B. Hayes.

Garfield was capable of neatly straddling a volatile issue. He was never so strong on the high-tariff issue as were most of his Republican colleagues and, as late as his presidential campaign of 1880, he remained publicly equivocal on the issue of Federal patronage. The Federal jobs at the disposal of the party in power were the life-blood of politics during the "gilded age." One wing of the Republican party—the "stalwarts"—called for no dalliance on the question, claiming the jobs as the just due of those who worked to put the party in power. Another wing of reformers, the "doctrinaires," felt that the quality of government would be improved if Federal jobs were assigned on the basis of merit. Garfield attempted to placate both sides.

On the money question Garfield was firm, standing unalterably for "hard" currency when many of his former constituents called for inflation. But he was less steadfast on the Southern question, alternating between "waving the bloody shirt"—exploiting Northern bitterness toward the South over the war—and supporting a more compromising attitude.

Monetary Scandal

Scandal nearly wrecked Garfield's career when he was accused of accepting money in return for supporting a congressional subsidy of the transcontinental railroad's construction company. But he managed to sidestep and survive the accusation, and he also weathered the revelation that he had accepted a legal fee from a company involved in government-contracted improvement of Washington streets. These lapses in ethics were more the result of carelessness than personal corruption, and Garfield in his last years was extremely careful to avoid any possible conflicts of interest. On the whole, he had a good record in the graft-sullied political world of the day, and reformers who could not support James G. Blaine were willing to accept Garfield.

In 1880 Garfield was elected to the U.S. Senate from Ohio, but before he took his seat, he agreed to manage John Sherman's campaign to win the Republican presidential nomination. The chief Republican candidates that year were former U.S. president Ulysses S. Grant and Senator James G. Blaine. Sherman's hopes were based on an anticipated deadlock between the two front-runners, which would force the convention to turn to him as a compromise candidate. The convention did, indeed, deadlock and settle on a third person, but that person was Garfield rather than Sherman. Toward the end of his life Sherman became convinced that his manager had actively betrayed him, but close examination of the records by several historians indicates that this was not so. Garfield knew before the convention that certain parties were working for him as a compromise candidate, but he neither encouraged nor effectively discouraged the talk. He certainly had presidential ambitions, but like a good party regular, he recognized Sherman's seniority among Ohio politicians and was willing to wait his turn. When the opportunity beckoned in 1880, he was more than ready.

Election to the Presidency

The immediate problem was the party's "stalwarts." Garfield had selected one of their number, Chester A. Arthur, as his vice-presidential candidate, but the leader of the "stalwarts," New York politician Roscoe Conkling, refused to work to get the important New York vote without specific promises from Garfield on patronage. Conkling believed that he received such promises and did help elect Garfield, but soon after the election, the two fell out. Garfield named Conkling's archenemy, James G. Blaine, to be his secretary of state and increasingly relied on Blaine's counsel. In a battle over the appointment of the collector of customs for the Port of New York (one of the richest plums in the Federal patronage), Conkling resigned his Senate seat and asked the New York Legislature, in effect, to rebuke the President by reelecting him. What might have happened under normal circumstances is impossible to tell, for on July 2, 1881, Garfield was shot in the back in a Washington railroad station by a deranged man named Charles Guiteau, who claimed he had killed the President in order to put Chester A. Arthur into office.

Garfield did not die immediately. But doctors could not locate one of the bullets, and infection eventually sapped his strength. Conkling was not reelected in the shocked aftermath of the shooting, and a civil service reform bill aimed at Conkling-style politics eventually passed Congress. But Garfield never left his bed; he died at Alberon, N.J., on Sept. 19, 1881.

A well-featured, heavily bearded man whose piercing eyes are the most striking feature of his photographs, Garfield was a significant figure in the development of congressional power during the 1860s and 1870s. His premature death precludes knowledge of how his perceptions of the changes America was undergoing might have impacted the successfulness of his presidency.

Further Reading

A primary source of information on Garfield is Theodore Clarke Smith, *The Life and Letters of James Garfield* (2 vols., 1925). An excellent biography is Robert Granville Caldwell, *James A. Garfield: Party Chieftain* (1931). Earlier works on Garfield tend to be absurdly laudatory, virtually ignoring problems connected with Garfield's military career and financial dealings. Garfield is discussed in Kenneth W. Wheeler, ed., *For the Union: Ohio Leaders in the Civil War* (1968). The best political survey of the age is H. Wayne Morgan, *From Hayes to McKinley: National Party Politics, 1877-1896* (1969). For the election of 1880 see Arthur M. Schlesinger, Jr., ed., *History of American Presidential Elections* (4 vols., 1971). □

Giuseppe Garibaldi

The Italian soldier Giuseppe Garibaldi (1807-1882) was the key military figure in the creation of the kingdom of Italy. An unflagging foe of all tyranny, he devoted his life to fighting oppression.

For the greater part of his life most of the native land of Giuseppe Garibaldi was under the control of foreigners. In the north Lombardy was held by Austria, and to the south of the States of the Church the kingdom of Naples was in the hands of the stagnant feudal regime of the Bourbons. Garibaldi was the embodiment of the Italian brand of 19th-century nationalism, which was impelled by the twin desires for unity and freedom.

Giuseppe Garibaldi was born on July 4, 1807, at Nice, which was at that time a French town. His father, Domenico, was a fisherman and modest tradesman, a fact that helped determine Giuseppe's early choice for a life at sea. At 17 he was already a sailor, journeying in the Mediterranean and Black seas, and in 1832 he earned certification as a merchant captain.

Garibaldi entered the Piedmontese navy and in 1833 joined Young Italy, the revolutionary organization of Giuseppe Mazzini, another Italian irredentist and patriot. As part of a larger republican plot of Mazzini, he became involved in a mutiny, attempting to seize his ship and take over the arsenal of Genoa. The plan failed and Garibaldi fled, taking refuge in France. He was condemned to death by default on June 3, 1834.

In 1836 Garibaldi sailed for Rio de Janeiro from Marseilles. For the next 4 years he fought as a soldier and naval officer and sometimes as a pirate for the province of Rio Grande in its attempt to free itself from Brazil. He then entered the service of Uruguay, becoming commander of the new Italian Legion at Montevideo in 1843. His victories at Cerro and Sant'Antonio in 1846 did much to ensure the liberty of Uruguay. Garibaldi's years in South America taught him the skills of war and steeled him for the Herculean tasks to come.

Revolt of 1848

His heart quickened by news of the uprising against Austria, Garibaldi returned to Italy with 80 men of his legion, landing at Nice on June 24, 1848. He offered his services in July to Charles Albert, King of the Piedmont, and in August was in command of a volunteer army at Milan. The following year, when the war was going badly for the revolutionaries and the Pope was away from Rome, Garibaldi was elected deputy of the Roman Assembly and worked for the creation of a Roman republic. Thus, against a French army aiding in the suppression of the general revolt, he defended the ephemeral republic, winning a brilliant victory at the San Pancrazio gate on April 30, 1849.

Garibaldi labored mightily during the next few months, inflicting defeats on Neapolitan and French armies. Only when it became clear that no power on earth could preserve the revolutionary movement from the superior forces of reaction did Garibaldi lead a handful of men on a retreat through central Italy. This movement was itself a masterpiece of military skill. He escaped to the Piedmont and in 1850 turned up in America, where he took a job making candles. He never intended to reside there permanently, and within the year he traveled to Peru, where he captained a ship under the flag of that country. In 1855 he returned to Italy and bought part of the island of Caprera, north of Sardinia, where he built a home.

War of Liberation

In 1858 a fateful meeting took place at Turin between Garibaldi and Camillo di Cavour, the prime minister of the Piedmontese kingdom. The count, looking forward eagerly to another war with Austria, asked the now-renowned soldier to form an army of volunteers. Cavour believed that this time, with boldness and planning, Austrian control could be broken. Garibaldi set himself to the task and was made a general in the Piedmontese army. In April 1859 he formed his corps, the Cacciatori delle Alpi, and in the same month war broke out. A rapid series of victories in May drove the Austrians out of northern Italy, all the way to the Tirol.

Dazzling as these accomplishments were, his greatest military feat lay yet before him. When the French, this time allies of the Piedmont, pulled out of the war in July 1859, Garibaldi shared Cavour's disappointment. But soldier and statesman were soon at odds with each other. Garibaldi was not permitted to attack the papal states in November and bitterly returned to civil life. He was quickly elected to the

Piedmontese Parliament, and in April 1860, he publicly attacked Cavour for ceding Nice to France. Meanwhile he was planning, with British encouragement, the invasion of Sicily. Neither he nor Cavour had given up on the national movement, even though the Piedmont had felt compelled to follow the lead of France and sign an armistice with Austria.

On May 11, 1860, Garibaldi landed at Marsala with a thousand men and on May 15, crushed an undisciplined Neapolitan army at Calatafimi. By May 25, Palermo, the capital of Sicily, was in his hands. Then, moving with remarkable speed and agility, his forces crossed the Straits of Messina, slipping past a formidable Neapolitan navy. On September 7, Garibaldi triumphantly entered Naples and proclaimed himself dictator of the Two Sicilies. A last major battle was fought a month later on the Volturno, a struggle that put an end to the Bourbon capacity for resistance. Garibaldi then punctuated these victories by holding plebiscites in Sicily and Naples.

These months of fevered and brilliant activity by Garibaldi in the south found their echo in the rest of Italy, as the foundations of tyranny were undermined. It was with jubilation that Italians greeted Victor Emmanuel, King of the Piedmont, as he traveled south through the country to meet Garibaldi near Naples. On Nov. 7, 1860, in one of the most generous acts in Western history, the soldier formally gave to Victor Emmanuel all of southern Italy and proclaimed him king of a united land.

All the problems had not been solved. Austria still possessed the Trentino, and the territory of the Church, protected by the French, still lay as an obstacle across central Italy. But Garibaldi withdrew to Caprera and once again entered politics. In April 1861, he castigated Cavour in Parliament because of the prime minister's failure to take his volunteers into the regular army. The bitterness between the two men was never fully assuaged, and it was only under Ricasoli, Cavour's successor, that Garibaldi's soldiers received satisfaction in the matter. By this time the fame of the great soldier had spread so far that Abraham Lincoln saw fit to offer him a command in the American Civil War. This he politely refused, preferring to remain as close as possible to events in Italy.

In the summer of 1862, at odds with the official position of the Italian government, Garibaldi began a march on Rome, only to be wounded in Calabria and taken prisoner. Moved by the general sympathy for the soldier and by the magnitude of his contribution to his country, the King granted him an amnesty. Garibaldi then returned to Caprera and in the following year resigned from Parliament over the issue of martial law in Sicily.

War of 1866

After traveling in 1864 to England, where he was given a hero's reception, Garibaldi formed another volunteer army with which to do battle once again with the Austrians. And again his army seemed invincible. He won battle after battle until, when about to attack the Trentino, he was ordered by his superior, Gen. Lamarmora, to withdraw. The order came on July 21, 1866, and Garibaldi's answer, "Ubbidisco" (I obey), has often been called a marvelous example of a soldier's subordination of his own wishes to the command of a superior, no matter how unpopular the command. This acquiescence should not be exaggerated since Garibaldi had already been told that Austria, because of Prussian pressure, could not under any circumstances yield the Trentino to Italy. Therefore no matter what his soldiers did, they would eventually be forced to withdraw for diplomacy's sake. The brief war ended with the cession of Venice to the new Italian kingdom.

Garibaldi returned to Caprera but not merely to savor the delights of victory. As the result of an agreement in 1864 between the French and Italian governments, French troops had been removed from Rome. Therefore he thought the time was right for another attack on the papal territory. Before he could put his plan into operation, he was once again arrested by the Italian government and brought back to Caprera. Almost at once he succeeded in escaping and went to Florence.

In spite of the government's official unwillingness to seize Rome by force, some members of the executive branch were fully in sympathy with Garibaldi's goals, and they furthered a second military effort. He was once again stopped, however, shortly after entering papal territory in October. It was ironic that when, in 1870, the Italian kingdom finally absorbed the remainder of the States of the Church, the great *condottiere* was not directly involved. He spent that year fighting for the French in the Franco-Prussian War.

Deputy for Rome

The last decade of Garibaldi's life was no less stormy than the earlier years. After the final humiliation of France by the Prussians he was elected to the Versailles Assembly; but he felt insulted by the French, mostly because they seemed unwilling to recognize the extent of his contribution to their war effort. He had, after all, won victories over the Germans at Châtillon and Dijon. He resigned his position in anger and returned to Caprera. In 1874 he was elected to Parliament as deputy for Rome. Garibaldi relished his position but was generally unhappy with the conservative cast of the government; when the ministry sought to confer upon him a large gift of money and an annual pension, he refused. It is revealing that when a government more oriented to the left took over and made the same offer, he accepted it gratefully. The generous gift was a recognition of the enormous debt owed by the new Italian kingdom to its greatest soldier.

Garibaldi, a handsome man with long hair, a full beard, and burning eyes, often disagreed violently with the government he had worked so hard to bring into existence. He was not an easy man to work with and his decisions were often rash, leading to the mercurial changes of his fortunes. But Giuseppe Garibaldi's contribution to Italy was of lasting significance, and when he died on June 2, 1882, his fellow citizens felt his passing deeply.

Further Reading

The two greatest authorities writing in English on Garibaldi are Denis Mack Smith and George M. Trevelyan. Smith's *Cavour* and *Garibaldi, 1860: A Study in Political Conflict* (1954) is an illuminating account of the character and historical significance of the two men and their strained relations with one another. A short biography by Smith is *Garibaldi: A Great Life in Brief* (1956). The three volumes by Trevelyan are very thorough: *Garibaldi and the Thousand* (1948); *Garibaldi and the Making of Italy* (1948); and *Garibaldi's Defence of the Roman Republic, 1848-9* (1949). The dates given for Trevelyan's books represent the latest of many editions. ☐

Hannibal Hamlin Garland

Hannibal Hamlin Garland (1860-1940), American author, augmented local-color writing by the new naturalistic techniques that combined realism with a sense of the individual's overwhelming struggle against a hostile environment.

In the late 1880s, when American local-color writers began to depict the brutal, dehumanizing aspects of life, the work which most effectively expressed the hardships of farmers of the northern prairies was Hamlin Garland's *Main Traveled Roads* (1891).

Garland was born near West Salem, Wis., on Sept. 14, 1860. Garland's father was an industrious farmer who moved his family from farm to farm in Wisconsin, Iowa, and South Dakota, hoping to wrest a better living from the fertile but unreliable fields. The successive homesteads—Garland later described them as "bare as boxes, dropped on the treeless plains"—provided little in the way of literature, but what little was available young Hamlin read with enthusiasm. His parents encouraged his literary interests and helped him get as much education as the area and his necessary work on the farm would allow. In 1882 he received a diploma from Cedar Valley Seminary in Osage, Iowa, where his family was then living. He took a brief trip to New England and then returned to teach school for 2 years in Illinois.

Garland's brief visit to Boston (which still kept up its pretense of being the literary capital of America) inspired him to return, and in 1884 he went to resume his education there. The only "university" he could afford was the Boston Public Library, but it proved ideal for him: whenever possible he devoted 14 hours a day to reading.

Garland entered Moses True Brown's Boston School of Oratory, working for his tuition. But, lacking money, he soon decided to give up his studies temporarily. When Brown heard that his brilliant pupil was quitting school, he proposed to make Garland a teacher. Consequently, in 1885 Hamlin Garland, "Professor of Elocution and Literature," presented public lectures on American, French, and German authors, the admission fee being his pay.

Early Career

His lectures brought Garland the attention of Boston literary people, and his reviews, articles, and stories were soon appearing in the *Transcript, Harper's Weekly,* and other publications. His admiring reviews of William Dean Howells eventually led to a meeting with that important novelist and critic, beginning what Garland called "the longest and most important friendship" of his life. Garland's praise of poet Walt Whitman similarly brought him the acquaintance and encouragement of that giant. Garland's appearance—he was a strikingly handsome young man with well-tended long brown hair and beard—prompted Whitman to comment, "Garland is much better mettle than his polished exterior would indicate."

"Main Traveled Roads"

However polished his exterior, Garland's stories were intentionally plain and rough. This was apparent in his first and best book, *Main Traveled Roads.* His objective was to convey the hard, unromantic truth of life on the plains, and he accomplished it effectively. His hostility toward landowners is manifest in one of the best stories in this collection, "Under the Lion's Paw." A poor man with a sick wife and hungry children rents a dilapidated farm from a greedy town merchant who turns farmers' misery to his profit. The tenant farmer has the owner's promise that he can buy the property at a reasonable price if he can make it pay, and so he and his family slave for 3 years to improve the house, barn, and fences which will one day be their own. But when they have doubled the value of "their" farm, the owner doubles the price, ensuring that both land and tillers will remain mortgaged to him forever. Garland dedicated the book to his parents "whose half-century pilgrimage on the main roads of life has brought them only toil and deprivation."

Commitment to Realism

Garland's commitment to realism in literature was expressed in his stories and also in his vigorous support of the new realistic drama and of many young realistic writers, most notably Stephen Crane. *Crumbling Idols* (1894) states Garland's theory of "veritism:" "The realist or veritist is really an optimist, a dreamer. He sees life in terms of what it might be, as well as in terms of what it is; but he writes of what is, and, at his best, suggests what is to be, by contrast." Garland seldom attained this ideal after 1891. His next novels, *Jason Edwards, A Member of the Third House,* and *A Spoil of Office* (all 1892), were hastily written propaganda pieces, not carefully wrought works of fiction. *Rose of Dutcher's Coolly* (1895) comes closer to fulfilling Garland's critical standard, although it is severely flawed.

Later Writing

In 1899 Garland married Zulime Taft, a beautiful woman with artistic training. Two daughters were born to the couple. After his marriage Garland consciously or unconsciously abandoned his bleak realism and in such books as *The Captain of the Gray-Horse Troop* (1902) achieved greater popularity at the cost of literary value. But if his fiction declined in quality, he found a new medium in which he could excell: autobiography. *A Son of the Middle Border* (1917) and *A Daughter of the Middle Border* (1921) treat his own life with honesty and understanding. The latter book received the Pulitzer Prize in 1922. Many honors came to Garland in his later years. He continued to write memoirs and accounts of psychic research until his death on March 4, 1940.

Further Reading

Jean Holloway, *Hamlin Garland* (1960), is a detailed and authoritative biography. Donald Pizer, *Hamlin Garland's Early Work and Career* (1960), is an excellent study. For a shorter treatment consult the chapter on Garland in H. Wayne Morgan, *American Writers in Rebellion: From Mark Twain to Dreiser* (1965). Larzer Ziff, *The American 1890s: Life and Times of a Lost Generation* (1966), places Garland in his period.

Additional Sources

Garland, Hamlin, *Back-trailers from the middle borde,* St. Clair Shores, Mich., Scholarly Press, 1974.

Garland, Hamlin, *Companions on the trail; a literary chronicl,* St. Clair Shores, Mich., Scholarly Press 1974, 1931.

Garland, Hamlin, *A daughter of the middle borde,* St. Clair Shores, Mich., Scholarly Press 1974, 1921.

Garland, Hamlin, *Roadside meeting,* St. Clair Shores, Mich., Scholarly Press 1974, 1930.

Garland, Hamlin, *A son of the middle border,* Lincoln: University of Nebraska Press, 197. ☐

Judy Garland

Judy Garland (1922-1969) starred in films, musicals, and on the concert stage. A superstar who never lost her waif appeal, she is best remembered for her performance in *The Wizard of Oz* and for the song "Over the Rainbow."

Judy Garland, born Frances Ethel Gumm on June 10, 1922, in Grand Rapids, Minnesota, began her show business career before she was three years old. By age six she was a veteran performer, appearing with her two older sisters in a vaudeville act. Mistakenly billed as "The Glum Sisters" in 1931, the sisters at the suggestion of a fellow performer changed their stage name to Garland (the name of a then-prominent drama critic). Shortly thereafter, at her own insistence, she changed her first name from Frances to Judy (after a popular song of the day).

In 1935 the head of MGM (Metro-Goldwyn-Mayer) was induced to hear her sing. Enthused, he signed her to a contract. There was some uncertainty at the studio on how to utilize her talents. A year passed before she made her first MGM film, a two reeler. Her first appearance in a feature did not come until 1937, when she was loaned to Twentieth Century-Fox. That same year at an MGM party for its star Clark Gable she was a hit singing a specialty number, "Dear Mr. Gable" adapted from the well-known standard "You Made Me Love You." As a result she and the song were incorporated into the 1937 feature *Broadway Melody of 1938.* Again she earned accolades.

MGM quickly put Garland into more films, each spotlighting her in song. In her next film—*Thoroughbreds Don't Cry* (1937)—she was cast with Mickey Rooney, with whom she subsequently appeared in eight films. MGM paired them in some of the Andy Hardy films, a series starring Rooney as an "average" American teenager. The duo was also winning in movies of the "c'mon kids, let's put on a show" type, including *Babes in Arms* (1939), *Strike Up The Band* (1940), *Babes on Broadway* (1941), and *Girl Crazy* (1943). Her most memorable film role (and the one which catapulted her to stardom) came in 1939 with *The Wizard of Oz.* She won a special Oscar as "best juvenile performer of the year." The film also provided her with the song ("Over the Rainbow") with which she was identified until her death.

During the 1940s she graced a number of outstanding musicals, including *Meet Me in St. Louis* (1944), *The Harvey Girls* (1946), and *Easter Parade* (1948). She was superb in a non-singing role in *The Clock,* a sentimental drama about a young girl and a serviceman on leave.

Garland's personal life, however, was less successful. She married music arranger David Rose in 1941, but that marriage ended long before the 1945 divorce. That same year she married director Vincente Minnelli, who guided Garland in some of her most notable films, including *The Pirate* (1948). Daughter Liza Minnelli (later a star in her own right) was born in 1946. This second marriage also faltered and was over well before the 1951 divorce. All during the 1940s she was plagued by a lack of self-confidence, strained by incessant work, hampered by weight problems.

She became heavily dependent on pills and in the the end broke down, her first known suicide attempt coming in 1950.

Once an admirable trouper, she became during the 1940s a problem artist. The filming of *In the Good Old Summertime* (1949) was repeatedly delayed, as was *Summer Stock* (1950). A pattern had been set which would increasingly debilitate her. She was replaced in a number of films and finally was fired by MGM in 1950.

Sidney Luft, a dynamic promoter who later became her third husband (1952), started Garland on a career on concert stages. She was a smashing success at the Palladium in London, at the Palace Theatre in New York City, and elsewhere. The magnificent film *A Star Is Born* (1954) capped her comeback, and she earned an Oscar nomination. But faltering health, increasing drug dependency, and alcohol abuse led to nervous breakdowns, suicide attempts, and recurrent breakups with Luft, by whom she had two children, Lorna (1952) and Joseph (1955). The Lufts finally divorced (1965) after years of legal wrangling.

Notwithstanding her troubles, Garland undertook a highly successful concert tour in 1961, which was capped by an enthusiastically received concert at Carnegie Hall: the live recording of that event sold over two million copies. That same year she won an Oscar nomination for best supporting actress for her dramatic performance in the film *Judgment at Nuremberg*. She had another non-singing role in the British film *A Child Is Waiting* (1963). Her last film role was in another British film, *I Could Go On Singing* (1963). Garland had made an auspicious television debut in 1955 on the *Ford Star Jubilee* and had done well in other guest appearances. Unfortunately, her long awaited television weekly series did not fare well, and CBS cancelled the variety show after one season (1963-1964).

Garland's personal and professional life continued to be a series of ups and downs, marked by faltering performances, comebacks, lawsuits, hospitalizations, and suicide attempts. After divorcing Luft she married Mark Herron, a younger, inconsequential actor with whom she had travelled for some time; the marriage lasted only months. Mickey Deans, a discotheque manager 12 years her junior, whom she married earlier that year, found her dead in their London flat on June 21, 1969. Death came from an "accidental" overdose of barbituates. She is buried in Hartsdale, New York.

Judy Garland was a superstar who, as one critic pointed out, "managed the considerable feat of converting herself into an underdog." Despite all the lows in her life she remained immensely popular and had a waif appeal that was never entirely lost.

Further Reading

There are biographies of Judy Garland by Anne Edwards (1975) and Christopher Finch (1975). There is an overview of her films and career by Joe Morella and Edward Z. Epstein (1970). More personal points of view are to be found in Mickey Dean's memoir (1972) and in Mel Tormé's less than kind recollection of working with Garland on her television show.

☐

François-Xavier Garneau

François-Xavier Garneau (1809-1866) was a French-Canadian historian whose "Histoire du Canada" was the first serious interpretation of Canada's past.

The parents of François-Xavier Garneau were illiterate, and his primary education was rudimentary. But he had the good fortune to go, at the age of 11, to a new school founded by Joseph-François Perrault, whose outstanding efforts to raise Quebec's educational level must have marked this pupil profoundly.

Travels and Early Employment

Thus at the age of 16 Garneau was apprenticed to the well-to-do lawyer Archibald Campbell, gaining professional status and considerable cultural enrichment. During this time he made his first journey to New York and published his first poem.

In 1831 Garneau embarked on a visit to England which lasted almost 2 years and included two trips to France. He thus had a firsthand view of the British constitution during the Great Reform period. He was actively involved in the constitutional progress of Canada and in the protection of French-Canadian rights. Garneau also made literary and intellectual contacts and kept a diary. This later furnished the substance of his *Voyage en Angleterre et en France* (1854 and 1855).

Returning to Quebec in 1833, Garneau spent the next 10 years at various occupations. He also founded two short-lived journals, *L'Abeille canadienne* (1833-1834) and *L'Institut* (1841), as well as contributing poems and political articles to Étienne Parent's *Le Canadien*. Garneau took no part in the rebellion of 1837 but reacted against the repressive measures which followed, taking up in particular the cause of preserving the French language in Canada.

Major Work

The year 1845 saw the publication of the first volume of Garneau's *Histoire du Canada depuis sa découverte jusqu'à nos jours* (The History of Canada from Its Discovery until Our Time), the two following volumes appearing in 1846 and 1848. Initial reception was mixed, but it included anonymous denunciations of the work as anti-Catholic and anti-Canadian (the latter term referring, at that time, exclusively to French Canadians). The cause of these attacks was Garneau's assessment of the *ancien régime*. According to Garneau's interpretation, the evils of absolutism, aggravated by distance from the metropolis, deprived the French settlers of the healthy independent growth enjoyed by their English neighbors. The Jesuits, though admired for their courage and discoveries, were blamed for the lack of enlightened education. Undeterred at first by criticism, Garneau completed his first edition and was voted £250 by the legislature in 1849.

A second edition in 1852 added a fourth volume on the period from 1792 to 1840, giving the author more ample

He died in 1866, leaving a growing reputation and a lasting influence on French-Canadian thought.

Further Reading

A rewarding general study with extracts of Garneau's work is Gustave Lanctôt, *François-Xavier Garneau* (1927). A shorter biography and general historical background is in Mason Wade, *The French Canadians, 1760-1967* (1955; rev. ed., 2 vols., 1968). □

Francis Garnier

Marie Joseph François, Garnier (1839-1873) was a French naval officer and adventurer who took a leading role in the exploration and colonization of Indochina.

The son of a disappointed royalist, Francis Garnier was born in Saint-Étienne on July 25, 1839, and was raised by maternal relatives in Montpellier. He entered the naval academy in 1855. After a short period of service in the South Atlantic and South Pacific, where he heroically saved the life of a fellow officer, he volunteered for service against China and Vietnam and saw action in 1860. In 1863 he entered the colonial administration of Cochin China (southern Vietnam) and by 1865 was in charge of the administration of Cholon, Saigon's Chinese mercantile quarter.

Quickly learning indigenous languages and studying the history and customs of the people among whom he worked, Garnier at the same time became an enthusiastic proponent of France's role in "civilizing" Indochina. His pamphlet *La Cochinchine française en 1864* (1864) was a protest against the retrocession of the colony to the Vietnamese empire and brought him to the attention of the Minister of the Navy and Colonies, Comte de Chasseloup-Laubat. When the ministry organized a mission to explore the upper Mekong River and the "back door" to southern China under Doudart de Lagrée in 1866, Garnier was assigned as his second in command. The party left Saigon in June 1866, paused to study the ruins of Angkor in Cambodia, and ascended the Mekong River through Laos into the Chinese province of Yunnan, where Lagrée died in March 1868. Renouncing his hopes of discovering the sources of the Mekong, Garnier led the party on to the Yangtze River and quickly down it to Shanghai.

Garnier returned to France to write his account of the mission, *Voyage d'exploration en Indochine* (1873), and participated in the defense of Paris (1870). Sailing again to China in 1872 he revisited Yunnan, intending but failing to reach Tibet. Returning to Shanghai, he found awaiting him a letter from Admiral Dupré, the governor of Cochin China, asking him to return to Saigon. Dupré sent him with 200 men to mediate a dispute between the Vietnamese government in Hanoi and the French merchant and adventurer Jean Dupuis, who had seized part of Hanoi on being refused

opportunity to display his patriotism, still coupled with his thought on constitutional liberalism. This Garneau was further able to develop in a third edition with a *Préface* and a *Discours préliminaire* (1859). By this time, however, he felt less sure of himself. Increased documentation had begun to cloud some of his bold assertions; the worldwide tide of liberal nationalism was ebbing; family and financial misfortunes had taken their toll of the man. Garneau retracted some of the anticlerical remarks from his text and inserted some more resonant declarations about language, religion, and national destiny. But the latent contradiction between conservative nationalism and enlightenment liberalism was not removed by such gestures. Garneau's wholehearted dedication to both of these provides the work with a tension which is not the least element in its success. In addition, his attempts to go back to prime sources constituted a pioneering step toward modern historiography, for his efforts were more limited by availability of documents than by his nationalist bias.

It is as a literary composition that the *Histoire* remains outstanding. Garneau's personal involvement and flowing rhetoric vie with his attempted objectivity to render the past dramatically present to the reader. Among the major themes are the military courage of the *habitants,* Canada's abandonment by France, the collective character of the people as a determinant in history, and the common Norman ancestry of the Canadians and the English. Garneau showed convincingly how political skill could replace military prowess to defend the interests and honor of the Canadians.

Charles Garnier was born on Nov. 6, 1825, in Paris. He attended the École de Dessin, the atelier of Louis Hippolyte Lebas, and the École des Beaux-Arts in 1841, and he also worked for Eugène Emmanuel Viollet-le-Duc. Garnier spent 5 years in Italy after winning the Grand Prix de Rome in 1848.

Garnier entered the competition for the Académie Nationale de Musique, better known as the Opéra, in Paris in 1861. He won fifth prize in the first stage of a two-phase competition and later that year won the commission. The Opéra was built from 1862 to 1867; the interiors were not completed until 1874. Sited on an irregular diamond adjacent to the Grand Boulevard, the structure was inspired, according to Garnier, by Michelangelo and Jacopo Sansovino. The Opéra provided a setting for Parisian society. The foyer, grand staircase, and auditorium are spacious, open, and rich in decoration. Empress Eugénie had favored the project by Viollet-le-Duc and did not admire Garnier's sumptuousness, even though it suited the period. When asked by the Empress whether the Opéra was in the style of Louis XIV, XV, or XVI, Garnier tactfully replied, "It is of Napoleon III."

The same plastic richness of effect was used by Garnier in his Casino in Monte Carlo (1878; extended 1881), even though the finish is in stucco. Its magnificent site facing the bay is again a stage setting, this time for the wealthy gamblers' game of roulette. The game rooms, salons, and waiting rooms are sumptuous.

permission to sell salt there. Reaching Hanoi early in November, Garnier found the officials unwilling to yield and so declared the Red River open to commerce. When the Vietnamese began making military preparations to evict him, Garnier seized the citadel of Hanoi, provoking an attack in which he was killed on Dec. 21, 1873.

Garnier, at Hanoi and in his explorations, gave voice to French colonial aspirations which were not to be denied, and most of the territory which he explored was under French control by 1893.

Further Reading

The only extensive biography of Garnier is in French, Albert de Pouvourville, *Francis Garnier* (1931). His life is seen in perspective in Joseph Buttinger, *The Smaller Dragon* (1958). □

Jean Louis Charles Garnier

Jean Louis Charles Garnier (1825-1898) was a French architect of the exuberant neobaroque style, an outgrowth of the effervescent but stricter classicism of Napoleon III's Second Empire style that began in the early 1850s.

After the Casino, Garnier's style mellowed considerably in a host of works ranging from churches, libraries, hotels, and houses to tombs, including the tombs of his musical contemporaries Bizet (1880) and Offenbach (1883) in Paris. Garnier died on Aug. 3, 1898.

Garnier did not fit into the emerging movements of functionalism or expressive structure, even though the structural innovations of the Opéra were of predominant significance. Structure for its own sake, as in the Eiffel Tower, he considered hideous. His plan for the Opéra, he freely admitted in his book *Le Nouvel Opéra de Paris* (1875-1881), was based upon no theory: "I leave success or failure to chance alone." The sweeping dynamic movement of Garnier's neobaroque can be found in the more linear forms of Art Nouveau.

Further Reading

There is no biography of Garnier in French or English. General histories do not discuss him extensively, but Henry-Russell Hitchcock, *Architecture: Nineteenth and Twentieth Centuries* (1958; 2d ed. 1963), describes his work in relation to the period. □

Elizabeth Garrett (Anderson)

Elizabeth Garrett Anderson (1836–1917) was an english physician who was the first woman to qualify in medicine in Britain and who pioneered the professional education of women.

Elizabeth Garrett was the second of ten children (four sons and six daughters) born to Newson Garrett, a prosperous businessman of Aldeburgh, Suffolk, and his wife Louisa Dunnell Garrett. Believing that all his children—girls as well as boys—should receive the best education possible, Garrett's father saw to it that Elizabeth and her sister, Louie, were first taught at home by a governess. In 1849, they were sent to the Academy for the Daughters of Gentlemen, a boarding school in Blackheath run by the Misses Browning, aunts of poet Robert Browning. Garrett would later shudder when she recalled the "stupidity of the teachers," but the rule requiring students to speak French proved to be a great benefit. On her return to Aldeburgh two years later, she continued to study Latin and mathematics with her brothers' tutors. Garrett's friend, educator Emily Davies (1830-1921), encouraged her to reject the traditional and limited life of the well-to-do English lady. Davies believed that women should be given the opportunity to obtain a better education and prepare themselves for the professions, especially medicine. But Davies, who later became the principal of Girton College, Cambridge, did not feel suited to becoming a pioneer in the field of medicine and encouraged Garrett to take on this role.

Visiting her sister in London in 1859, Garrett met Elizabeth Blackwell, the first woman in America to graduate from a regular medical school. Blackwell, who was then practicing medicine in England, had succeeded in having her name placed on the British Medical Register and was delivering a series of three lectures on "Medicine as a Profession for Ladies." Contrasting what she considered the useless life of the lady of leisure with the services women doctors could perform, Blackwell stressed the contributions female doctors could make by educating mothers on nutrition and child care, as well as working in hospitals, schools, prisons, and other institutions. Whereas Blackwell saw in Garrett a "bright intelligent young lady whose interest in the study of medicine was then aroused," Garrett had not yet decided on a career in medicine and was in fact somewhat overwhelmed by Blackwell's enthusiasm. "I remember feeling very much confounded," Garrett later explained, "and as if I had been suddenly thrust into work that was too big for me." Indeed, Garrett thought that she "had no particular genius for medicine or anything else." Nevertheless, Blackwell can be credited with having fueled Garrett's interest in becoming a fully accredited physician.

Despite his encouragement for his daughter to find some form of work outside the home, Garrett's father at first found the idea of a woman physician "disgusting." Her mother was too old-fashioned and inflexible to accept the idea that her daughter go to work, and she warned her family that if her daughter left home to earn a living, the disgrace would kill her. Seeking advice, Garrett was accompanied by her father on visits to prominent physicians; they were informed that it was useless for a woman to seek medical education because a woman's name would not be entered on the Medical Register, an official endorsement without which medicine could not be legally practiced in England. To guard against the circumstances that had made it possible for Blackwell to be entered on the register, foreign degrees had been ruled unacceptable. During their visits, one doctor asked Garrett why she was not willing to become a nurse instead of a doctor. "Because," she replied, "I prefer to earn a thousand rather than twenty pounds a year!" Indeed, throughout her life she remained vehemently opposed to the idea that women should be confined to nursing while men monopolized medicine and surgery.

Eventually, a meeting was arranged with Dr. William Hawes, a member of the board of directors of Middlesex Hospital, one of London's major teaching hospitals. This led to the suggestion that Garrett try a "trial marriage with the hospital" by working as a nurse for six months. Assigned to the surgical ward, she used the opportunity to attend dissections and operations, meet the medical staff of the hospital, and obtain some of the training provided to medical students. During this probationary period, Garrett found that she enjoyed the work immensely, that it was neither shocking nor repugnant to her feminine sensibilities, and that the difficulties against which she had been so seriously warned were quite trivial. "It is not true that there is anything disgusting in the study of the human body," she said. "If it were so, how could we look up to God as its maker and designer?" After a three-month probationary period, she abandoned the pretense of being a nurse and unofficially became a medical student, making rounds in the wards, working in the dispensary, and helping with emergency patients. She offered to pay the fees charged medical students but was told that no London medical school would admit her. The hospital staff accepted her as a guest, allowing her to study and carry out dissections, but would not accept her as a student.

In December of 1860, she took examinations that covered the work of the past five months and the results proved impressive. Then in May of the following year, she was accepted for some special courses of lectures and demonstrations; instead of providing new opportunities, this opening wedge stiffened the opposition and increased antifeminist hostility. When she received a certificate of honor in each of the subjects covered by her lecture courses, the examiner sent her a note: "May I entreat you to use every precaution in keeping this a secret from the students." When she answered a question in class that no other student could answer, the students drew up a petition calling for her exclusion on the grounds that she was interfering with their progress. The Medical Committee of Middlesex Hospital was glad to follow their recommendation and she left the hospital in July.

Despite further rejections from Oxford, Cambridge, and the University of London which, according to its charter provided education for "all classes and denominations without distinction whatsoever," Garrett would not be deterred. In 1862 the senate of the University of London had decided, however, that women were neither a class nor a denomination, which left the University without the power to admit them. Determined to secure a qualifying diploma in order to place her name on the Medical Register, she decided to pursue the degree of Licentiate of the Society of Apothecaries (L.S.A.); though the L.S.A. was not as prestigious as the M.D., its holders were duly accredited physicians. To qualify, an applicant had to serve a five-year apprenticeship under a qualified doctor, take certain prescribed lecture courses from recognized university tutors, and pass the qualifying examination. The Hall of Apothecaries was by no means an advocate of equal opportunity for women, but its charter stated that it would examine "all persons" who had satisfied the regulations, and—according to legal opinions obtained by Garrett's father—"persons" included women. An apothecary and resident medical officer at the Middlesex Hospital, who had been one of her tutors, accepted Garrett as an apprentice.

In October 1862, Garrett went to St. Andrews in Scotland where Dr. Day, the Regius Professor of Medicine, had invited her to attend his lectures. When university officials discovered that she had been permitted to secure a matriculation "ticket," the clerk was instructed to reclaim it. Garrett's refusal to return the ticket nearly sparked a lawsuit. It was finally decided that the university's constitution permitted the admission of women, but that the senatus had the discretionary power to exclude any particular person, male or female. Garrett was thus excluded. She remained in St. Andrews attending courses until December but had no chance of completing her studies there. Study in America might have been a possibility, but Garrett believed that her main task was to open the medical profession and medical education to women in England—even if the battle consumed much of her life and delayed her own career.

With great difficulty, she was able to piece together the elements of a course of instruction, including a summer spent studying with Sir James Simpson in Edinburgh and a very unhappy six-month period of service as a nurse in the London Hospital. But when Garrett presented her credentials to the Society of Apothecaries in the fall of 1865, the examining body refused to administer the examination. After Garrett's father threatened to sue, the apothecaries again reversed themselves. She passed the qualifying examinations to see her name enrolled in the Medical Register one year later. The Society of Apothecaries immediately revised their charter to require graduation from an accredited medical school—all of which excluded women—as a prerequisite for the L.S.A. degree. Another woman's name would not be added to the Medical Register for the next 12 years.

Garrett's goal was to establish a hospital for women staffed by women. Thus in 1866, she opened the St. Mary's Dispensary for Women in London "to enable women to obtain medical and surgical treatment from qualified medical practitioners of their own sex." For some years, she remained the only visiting physician and dispenser; three times a week, she attended outpatients, while also visiting patients in their own homes. The dispensary filled a great need; within only a few weeks, 60 to 90 women and children were seen each consulting afternoon. Serving an impoverished community as physician, surgeon, pharmacist, nurse, midwife, counselor, and clerk, Garrett's association with poverty-stricken families led to her involvement with the women's rights movement. In 1872, with a ward of ten beds, the dispensary became the New Hospital for Women and Children. Demand rapidly outgrew the original facilities, and three houses were purchased and converted into additional wards.

Like her friend Emily Davies, Garrett maintained a strong interest in the reform of education and the expansion of educational opportunities for women. At the time, free compulsory education was becoming a reality for the children of the working class, and Garrett was asked to run for election to the school board by the working men of the district in which she practiced. She was elected to the London School Board in 1870, the same year she obtained the M.D. degree from the University of Paris. Commuting back and forth from London to Paris, she passed all five parts of the examination and successfully defended a thesis on "Migraine" which showed her to be an excellent clinical observer who had treated a large number of patients suffering from migraine and other kinds of headache.

In 1869, Garrett applied for a staff position at the Shadwell Hospital for Children. James George Skelton Anderson, head of a large shipping firm, was one of the members of the hospital board of directors who interviewed her; he and Garrett began working together on reforms needed to improve the administration of the hospital. Their engagement was announced in December 1870. Many of her friends feared she would relinquish her work if married but, as Louisa Garrett Anderson explained in her biography of her mother, Garrett believed "that the woman question will never be solved in any complete way so long as marriage is thought to be incompatible with freedom and with an independent career." She was beginning to see her own life as a way of disproving this notion. They were married on February 9, 1871.

Garrett continued to practice medicine, contrary to the common expectation for married women. Like Garrett's father, Anderson supported his wife's commitment to combine marriage and family with a medical career. Their daughter wrote: "From 1871 to the close of her working life, some thirty-five years later, she proved that a married woman can succeed in a profession and that a medical woman need not neglect her family." Three children were born during their first seven years of married life, two of whom, Louisa and Alan, went on to distinguished careers of their own. The second daughter Margaret, however, died of tubercular peritonitis when only 15 months old.

The New Hospital for Women provided a demonstration of what trained professional women could accomplish. "No men or no hospital" served as Garrett's primary rule in guiding its development. In 1878, she became the first woman in Europe to successfully perform the operation of ovariotomy. Regarded as serious and dangerous, the first operation could not be performed in the hospital since the death of a patient would obviously injure its reputation. To deal with this problem, Garrett rented part of a private house and had the rooms thoroughly cleaned, painted, and whitewashed before the patient and nurses were brought in. The cost of the rooms and their preparation was contributed by James Anderson, who was proud of his wife's success but who noted, "We shall be in the bankruptcy court if Elizabeth's surgical practice increases." The next ovariotomy was performed in the hospital. Despite her successes, Garrett did not enjoy operating and was perfectly willing to turn this part of hospital work over to other skilled women surgeons as they joined her staff. The hospital moved to larger quarters at a new site in 1899, nearly two decades before being renamed the Elizabeth Garrett Anderson Hospital.

In 1874, along with Sophia Jex-Blake and others, Garrett helped establish the London Medical College for Women, where she taught for 23 years. As dean of the institution (1883-1903), she opposed the idea that women planning work as missionaries should come to the school and acquire a little medical knowledge. She "distrusted the capacity of most people to be efficient in two professions." Two years after its establishment, the London School of Medicine for Women was placed on the list of recognized medical schools, ensuring its graduates access to a registrable license. In 1877, the school was attached to the Royal Free Hospital and permitted to grant the degrees that were required for enrollment on the British Medical Registry. Garrett's son Alan was born just before the Royal Free Hospital opened its wards to women students; 50 years later he would become its chairman. The school became one of the colleges of the newly constituted University of London in 1901, and two years later, at the age of 67, Garrett resigned as dean to be appointed honorary president.

Whereas in controversial matters she took a quiet, professional position, Garrett was a suffragist and a member of the Women's Social and Political Union (founded 1903). Although she disagreed with women who were protesting against the Contagious Diseases Acts, which were instituted as an attempt to control venereal diseases, she was devoted to rebutting the pseudoscientific charge that intellectual activity harmed women's health and fertility; she was, regardless, condemned by some feminists for supporting the Contagious Disease Acts. Garrett's daughter suggests that her mother's training had provided little information about the venereal diseases and that her experience did not incite her to challenge the views of the medical profession in this particular matter. Later, the feminists were vindicated by evidence that the Acts were quite ineffective for their stated goals and offensive to many; they were repealed in 1886.

"Inadvertently" admitted to membership by the Paddington Branch (London) of the British Medical Association in 1873, Garrett was scheduled to read a paper on obstetrical section in 1875 at the annual meeting in Edinburgh when the error became known to Sir Robert Christison, then president of the association. Sir Robert proved unable to annul or expel Garrett, who was able to read her paper, but he and the association took steps to make sure no other women gained membership. A clause excluding females was added to the articles of the association in 1878, a prohibition not repealed until 1892. The only woman member of the association for 19 years, Garrett was elected president of the East Anglian branch of the British Medical Association in 1897.

In 1902 the Andersons retired to the Garrett family home in Aldeburgh, and six years later she became the first woman mayor of Aldeburgh. At the start of World War I, she traveled back to London to see her daughters Dr. Louisa Garrett Anderson and Dr. Flora Murray leave the city in charge of the first unit of medical women for service in France. "My dears," she said, "if you go, and if you succeed, you will put forward the women's cause by thirty years." During the war, Louisa Garrett Anderson was joint organizer of the women's hospital corps and served as chief surgeon of the military hospital at Endell Street from 1915-1918.

Elizabeth Garrett Anderson had lived a life full of firsts. She was England's first woman doctor, the first woman M.D. in France, the first woman member of the British Medical Association, the first woman dean of a medical school, and Britain's first woman mayor. Years after her death at Aldeburgh on December 17, 1917, her daughter wrote this tribute: "In her girlhood, Elizabeth heard the call to live and work, and before the evening star lit her to rest she had helped to tear down one after another the barriers which, since the beginning of history, hindered women from work and progress and light and service."

Further Reading

Bell, Enid Moberly. *Storming the Citadel: The Rise of the Woman Doctor.* Constable, 1953.

Garrett Anderson, Louisa. *Elizabeth Garrett Anderson, 1836-1917.* Faber & Faber, 1939.

Hume, Ruth Fox. *Great Women of Medicine.* Random House, 1964.

Manton, Jo Grenville. *Elizabeth Garrett Anderson.* Dutton, 1958.

Wilkinson, M. ''Elizabeth Garrett Anderson and Migraine'' in F. C. Rose and W. F. Bynum, eds. *Historical Aspects of the Neurosciences.* Raven, 1982, pp. 165-169.

Blackwell, Elizabeth. *Pioneer Work in Opening the Medical Profession to Women.* Longmans, Green, 1895, reprinted, Schocken Books, 1977.

Chaff, Sandra L., Ruth Haimbach, Carol Fenichel, and Nina B. Woodside, compilers and eds. *Women in Medicine: A Bibliography of the Literature on Women Physicians.* Scarecrow Press, 1977.

Hurd-Mead, Kate Campbell. *A History of Women in Medicine.* Haddam Press, 1938, reprinted, AMS Press, 1977.

Marks, Geoffrey, and William K. Beatty. *Women in White.* Scribner, 1972. □

John Work Garrett

The American railroad magnate John Work Garrett (1820-1884) made the Baltimore and Ohio Railroad a major line and dominated its affairs for almost 30 years.

John W. Garrett was born in Baltimore, Md., on July 31, 1820. After some college work he joined his father's mercantile firm. During the 1850s the Baltimore and Ohio Railroad extended its tracks westward and in 1852 reached Wheeling, Va., on the Ohio River. When this process created financial difficulties, a stockholders' committee was convened. Garrett's impressive analysis as a member of the committee resulted in his election as president of the railroad in 1858.

Garrett's railroad was a fundamental factor in the eventual Union triumph in the Civil War, because it straddled both Union and Confederacy territories and connected Washington, D.C., with the surrounding area. The railroad profited enormously from the wartime increase in its volume of freight and passengers.

Garrett's major effort after the war was aimed at linking Baltimore, Pittsburgh, Chicago, and New York by rail, thereby making the Baltimore and Ohio one of the four leading railroads serving the most vital, industrialized section of the country. He succeeded. Although in the process he employed some dubious competitive practices, his actions were probably not as reprehensible as those of his worst competitors.

A severe and prolonged depression began in 1873, and there was intensified pressure to reduce costs. Labor costs (in this essentially nonunion era) were the most vulnerable to downward pressure, so Garrett tried cutting wages (rather than dividends), simultaneously increasing the amount of work expected from his laborers. In response, the workers struck. The stoppage began on the Baltimore and Ohio in July 1877 and then spread, ultimately involving many railroads. The strike was marked by unprecedented violence; President Rutherford B. Hayes used Federal troops to end it by force. Since labor conditions were improved afterward, the strike was not a complete failure for the workers. Garrett,

aged by the strike, died on Sept. 26, 1884, in Deer Park, Garrett County, Md.

Further Reading

There is no authoritative biography of Garrett. His life must be approached through studies of his railroad, such as Paul Winchester, *The Baltimore & Ohio Railroad* (1927), and Edward Hungerford, *The Story of the Baltimore & Ohio Railroad* (1928). Both of these popular works have been replaced by scholarly monographs for selected topics: Festus P. Summers, *The Baltimore and Ohio Railroad in the Civil War* (1939), and Robert V. Bruce, *1877: Year of Violence* (1959). There are several general treatments of the railroad during Garrett's heydey: John Moody, *The Railroad Builders* (1919); John F. Stover, *American Railroads* (1961); and Carl N. Degler, *The Age of the Economic Revolution* (1967). □

Thomas Garrett

Thomas Garrett (1789-1871), American abolitionist, openly defied state and Federal statutes by giving aid to fugitive slaves, thus strengthening resistance to proslavery legislation.

Thomas Garrett was born of Quaker parents on Aug. 21, 1789, in Delaware County, Pa. His father, a farmer and scythe and edge-tool maker, taught his son his skills. Garrett married, raised a family, and made a career in the iron trades. He was early sympathetic to the antislavery movement, joined the Pennsylvania Abolition Society, and engaged in its work of aiding runaway slaves.

In 1820 Garrett moved to Wilmington, Del., where he became a wealthy iron merchant. He increased his abolitionist work, though Delaware was a slave state. Adjacent to Pennsylvania and New Jersey on one side and Maryland on the other, Delaware was a particular target for runaway slaves and offered many opportunities for Underground Railroad activities. Garrett explored all of these, aiding fugitives from several states and probing the various means for concealment and transportation. The State of Maryland set a reward of $10,000 for Garrett's arrest and employed all kinds of stratagems for surprising him in his illegal work.

Notorious for his antislavery campaign in this slave environment and vilified in the press, Garrett nevertheless managed to circumvent enemies and law officers until 1848, when a suit was brought against him in Federal court. His case was not helped by his bold declarations in court that he had aided fugitive slaves and would continue to do so. Judgment against him was rendered by U.S. Supreme Court Justice Roger B. Taney, and he was fined. The fine, coupled with business reverses, put Garrett into bankruptcy at the age of 60. However, friends helped him reestablish his business.

Garrett estimated that he had helped more than 2,700 slaves to freedom—a figure which became famous in antislavery annals. He was the prototype of Simeon Halliday in Harriet Beecher Stowe's *Uncle Tom's Cabin.* Abolition-

ists of all persuasions, as well as the African American community, admired Garrett. During the Civil War, African Americans protected his home from angry proslavery partisans. In 1870, when the African Americans in Wilmington were celebrating the passage of the 15th Amendment to the Constitution (which gave the vote to African American men), they drew Garrett through the streets in an open carriage preceded by a transparency on which the words ''Our Moses'' were inscribed.

Garrett died on Jan. 25, 1871. He had stipulated that he was to be carried to his grave by African Americans. They not only honored his request but participated in the Quaker services.

Further Reading

For a biography of Garrett see Thomas E. Drake's article ''Thomas Garrett, Quaker Abolitionist'' in *Friends in Wilmington, 1738-1938* (1938) and the section on Garrett in Larry Gara, *The Liberty Line: The Legend of the Underground Railroad* (1961). Other useful works for the study of Garrett include William Still, *The Underground Railroad* (1872; repr. 1968); Robert C. Smedley, *History of the Underground Railroad in Chester and the Neighboring Counties of Pennsylvania* (1883; repr. 1968); and Wilbur H. Siebert, *The Underground Railroad from Slavery to Freedom* (1898; repr. 1967).

Additional Sources

McGowan, James A., *Station master on the Underground Railroad: the life and letters of Thomas Garrett,* Moylan, Pa.: Whimsie Press, 1977. □

William Lloyd Garrison

William Lloyd Garrison (1805-1879), American editor, reformer, and antislavery crusader, became the symbol of the age of aggressive abolitionism.

William Lloyd Garrison was born on Dec. 10, 1805, in Newburyport, Mass. His father deserted the family in 1808, and the three children were raised in near poverty by their mother, a hardworking, deeply religious woman. Young Garrison lived for a time in the home of a kindly Baptist deacon, where he received the bare rudiments of an education. He was later apprenticed to a shoemaker, a cabinetmaker, and finally to the printer and editor of the *Newburyport Herald.*

Editor and Printer

Garrison borrowed money in 1826 to buy part of the *Newburyport Free Press;* it soon failed. He worked as a printer in Boston and in 1827 helped edit a temperance paper, the *National Philanthropist.* Seeing life as an uncompromising moral crusade against sin, and believing it possible to perfect a Christian society by reforming men and institutions, Garrison fitted easily into the evangelical currents of his time. In 1828 a meeting with Benjamin Lundy, the Quaker antislavery editor of the *Genius of Emancipa-*

tion, called his attention to that cause. Since 1828 was a presidential election year, Garrison accepted editorship of a pro-Jackson newspaper in Vermont, in which he also supported pacifism, temperance, and the emancipation of slaves. After the election, Garrison accepted a position with Lundy on the *Genius* in Baltimore.

Garrison's Brand of Abolitionism

The antislavery movement at this time was decentralized and divided. Some people believed slavery should be abolished gradually, some immediately; some believed slaves should be only partly free until educated and capable of being absorbed into society, others that they ought to be freed but settled in colonies outside the United States. There were those who saw slavery as a moral and religious issue; others considered abolition a problem to be decided by legal and political means. Garrison, like Lundy, at first favored gradual emancipation and colonization. But soon Garrison opposed both means as slow and impractical, asking in his first editorial in the *Genius* for "immediate and complete emancipation" of slaves.

Garrison's militancy got the paper and himself into trouble. Successfully sued for libel, he spent 44 days in jail, emerging in June 1830 with plans for an abolitionist paper of his own. Encouraged by Boston friends, he and a partner published the first number of the *Liberator* on Jan. 1, 1831, bearing the motto, "Our country is the world—our countrymen are mankind," adapted from Thomas Paine. Attacking the "timidity, injustice, and absurdity" of gradualists and colonizationists, Garrison declared himself

for "the immediate enfranchisement of our slave population." Promising to be "as harsh as truth, and as uncompromising as justice," he warned his readers, "I am in earnest—I will not equivocate—I will not excuse—I will not retreat a single inch—*and I will be heard.*"

The *Liberator,* which never had a circulation of over 3,000 and annually lost money, soon gained Garrison a national abolitionist reputation. Southerners assumed a connection between his aggressive journalism and Nat Turner's 1831 slave rebellion in Virginia and tended to see him as a symbol of unbridled Northern antislavery radicalism; Georgia, in fact, offered $5,000 for his arrest and conviction. Garrison, for his part, continued to pour invective not only on slaveholders but on those who failed to attack the system as violently as he; Northerners who equivocated were guilty of "moral lapses," Southerners were "Satanic man stealers." His bitter attacks on the colonizationists, summarized in *Thoughts on Colonization* (1832), and his running battle with the New England clergy (whose churches he called "cages of unclean birds") for their refusal to condemn slavery unconditionally probably lost more adherents for the antislavery cause than they gained. Garrison introduced discussions into his paper of "other topics . . . intimately connected with the great doctrine of inalienable human rights," among them women's rights, capital punishment, antisabbatarianism, and temperance (he also opposed theaters and tobacco). Thus by the late 1830s abolition was but one portion (albeit the most important) of Garrison's plan for the "universal emancipation" of all men from all forms of sin and injustice.

Organizing the Movement

Recognizing the need for organization, Garrison was instrumental in forming the New England Antislavery Society (later the Massachusetts Antislavery Society) in 1832 and served as its secretary and salaried agent. He visited England in 1833, returning to help found the national American Antislavery Society. In September 1834 he married Helen Benson of Connecticut, who bore him seven children, five of whom survived. When his friend George Thompson, the British abolitionist, visited Boston in 1835, feeling ran so high that a "respectable broadcloth mob," as Garrison called it, failing to find Thompson, seized and manhandled Garrison. Garrison's refusal to consider political action as a way of abolishing slavery (he felt it would delay it) and his desire to join the antislavery movement to other reforms gradually alienated many supporters. In 1840 his stand seriously divided the American Antislavery Society and led to formation of the rival American and Foreign Antislavery Society.

In 1844 Garrison adopted the slogan "No union with slaveholders," arguing that since the Constitution was a proslavery document, the Union it held together should be dissolved by the separation of free from slave states. Yet, despite his reputation, Garrison was a pacifist and did not believe in violence. He thought Harriet Beecher Stowe's *Uncle Tom's Cabin* important chiefly as a novel of "Christian non-resistance," and though he respected John Brown's aim, he did not approve of his method. He wanted, he wrote, "nothing more than the peaceful abolition of slavery, by an appeal to the reason and conscience of the slaveholder."

Civil War

Garrison supported the Civil War for he believed it an act of providence to destroy slavery, and his son served as an officer in a Massachusetts African American regiment. Critical at first of President Abraham Lincoln for making preservation of the union rather than abolition of slavery his chief aim, Garrison praised the President's Emancipation Proclamation and supported his reelection in 1864—as Wendell Phillips and some other abolitionists did not. Garrison favored dissolution of the American Antislavery Society in 1865, believing its work done, but he lost to Phillips, who wished to continue it. Garrison wrote his last editorial on Dec. 29, 1865, "the object for which the *Liberator* was commenced—the extermination of chattel slavery—having been gloriously consummated," and retired to Roxbury, Mass., writing occasionally for the press. He died on May 24, 1879.

Despite his reputation, Garrison's influence was restricted to New England (where it was not unchallenged), and his brand of immediatism was never the majority view. When the main thrust of abolition after 1840 turned political, pointing toward the Free Soil and Republican parties, Garrison remained outside, and in terms of practical accomplishment, others did more than he. Yet it was Garrison who became the general symbol of abolitionism. He was influential in relating it to issues of free speech, free press, and the rights of assembly and petition and to the powerful religious evangelism of the times. In his harsh and tactless way, he forced popular awareness of the gap between what the Declaration of Independence and the Constitution said and what the nation did, constantly challenging the country to put its ideals into practice.

Further Reading

The biography written by Garrison's sons, Wendell Phillips Garrison and Francis Jackson Garrison, *William Lloyd Garrison* (4 vols., 1885-1889), though not wholly trustworthy, is essential. Oliver Johnson, *William Lloyd Garrison and His Times,* with an introduction by John Greenleaf Whittier (1880), is unduly admiring. Ralph Korngold's study of Wendell Phillips and Garrison, *Two Friends of Man* (1950), is excellent. Russel B. Nye, *William Lloyd Garrison and the Humanitarian Reformers* (1955), is a useful short biography. Walter M. Merrill, *Against Wind and Tide* (1963), and John L. Thomas, *The Liberator: William Lloyd Garrison* (1963), are good recent studies. George M. Fredrickson, ed., *William Lloyd Garrison* (1968), is a three-part work comprising a selection of Garrison's writings, articles expressing opinions of him by his contemporaries, and articles by modern writers appraising his work. □

Marcus Mosiah Garvey

Marcus Mosiah Garvey (1887-1940), a black man from the West Indies, was the first to forcefully articulate the concept of African nationalism—of black people returning to Africa, the continent of their forefathers, to build a great nation of their own.

Marcus Garvey was born in St. Ann's Bay, Jamaica, on Aug. 17, 1887. He went to elementary school there and at the age of 14 became an apprentice in the printing trade. In 1903 he went to the capital, Kingston, to work as a printer. He soon became involved in public activities and helped form the Printers Union, the first trade union in Jamaica. He subsequently published a periodical called the *Watchman*.

In 1910 began a series of travels that transformed Garvey from an average person concerned about the problems of the underprivileged to an African nationalist determined to lift an entire race from bondage and debasement. He visited Costa Rica, Panama, and Ecuador. After briefly returning home, he proceeded to England, where contacts with African nationalists stimulated in him a keen interest in Africa and in black history. In each country he visited, he noted that the black man was in an inferior position, subject to the whim, caprice, and fancy of stronger races. His reading of Booker T. Washington's *Up from Slavery* at this time also had great effect upon him.

On his return in 1914 from England, where he had done further study, Garvey formed the Universal Negro Improvement Association (UNIA) and the African Commu-

nities League. These organizations were intended "to work for the general uplift of the Negro peoples of the world."

In 1916 Garvey went to the United States to raise funds to carry on the work of his Jamaican organizations. He was immediately caught up in the agitation of the times, and his voice thundered in the evenings on the streets of Harlem in New York City. A New York branch of the UNIA was established, soon followed by branches in other cities in the United States, in Central and South America, and in the Caribbean. The expansion of the UNIA was fostered by its official organ *Negro World,* a newspaper published in English, Spanish, and French. Published in New York City from 1918 to 1933, it was succeeded by the monthly *Black Man,* which ran through the 1930s, published after 1934 in London.

The *Negro World* reached out to black communities all over the world. It even penetrated into the interior of Africa, although it had been banned there by the white rulers. Garvey stressed the need for blacks to return to Africa for the building of a great nation, but he realized that until this was accomplished Africans needed to make themselves economically independent wherever they were. He encouraged blacks to start their own businesses, taking the commerce of their ghettos into their own hands.

Together with the American clergyman Archbishop George A. McGuire, Garvey formed the African Orthodox Church. This was in accordance with one of his basic principles, for he believed that each race must see God through its own racial spectacles. The Black Christ and the Black Madonna were proclaimed at the UNIA convention of 1924.

The Black Star Line shipping company and the Negro Factories Corporation were to be the commercial arms of the Garvey movement. It was the failure of the shipping venture that gave Garvey's enemies their chance to destroy him. Investments in the line were lost, and Garvey was imprisoned in 1925 in the United States. After serving 2 years 10 months of a 5-year sentence, he was deported to Jamaica. Previously, his plans for colonization in Liberia had been sabotaged by the colonial powers who brought pressure to bear on the Liberian government. As a result, the land which had been granted to the Garvey organization for the settlement of overseas Africans was given to the white American industrialist Harvey Firestone, and the expensive equipment shipped to Liberia for the use of Garvey's colonists was seized.

In Jamaica, Garvey attempted to enter local politics, but the restricted franchise of the time did not allow the vote to the black masses. He went to England and continued his work of social protest and his call for the liberation of Africa. He died in London on June 10, 1940.

Marcus Garvey was married twice. His second wife, Amy Jacques, whom he married in 1922, bore him two sons.

The Garvey movement was the greatest international movement of African peoples in modern times. At its peak, in 1922-1924, the movement counted over 8 million followers. The youngest cadres were taken in at 5 years of age

and, as they grew older, they graduated to the sections for older children.

Garvey emphasized the belief in the One God, the God of Africa, who should be visualized through black eyes. He told black people to become familiar with their ancient history and their rich cultural heritage. He called for pride in the black race—for example, he made black dolls for black children. His was the first voice clearly to demand black power. It was he who said, "A race without authority and power is a race without respect."

In emphasizing the need to have separate black institutions under black leadership, Garvey anticipated the mood and thinking of the future black nationalists by nearly 50 years. He died, as he lived, an unbending apostle of African nationalism. The symbols which he made famous, the black star of Africa and the red, black, and green flag of African liberation, continued to inspire younger generations of African nationalists.

Further Reading

For Garvey's views the definitive work is edited by his widow, Amy Jacques Garvey, *Philosophy and Opinions of Marcus Garvey* (2 vols., 1923-1925). Her *Garvey and Garveyism* (1963) is a biography. E. David Cronon, *Black Moses: The Story of Marcus Garvey and the Universal Negro Improvement Association* (1955), is a well-documented work which, however, fails to assess accurately Garvey's impact. A biographical sketch of Garvey is in Wilhelmena S. Robinson, *Historical Negro Biographies* (1967). See also E. Franklin Frazier, "The Garvey Movement" in August Meier and Elliott Rudwick, eds., *The Making of Black America: Essays in Negro Life and History* (1969), and C. L. R. James, *A History of Pan-African Revolt* (1969). □

Elbert Henry Gary

Elbert Henry Gary (1846-1927), American lawyer and industrialist, was responsible for organizing the U.S. Steel Corporation in 1901 and continued as its most influential figure until his death.

Elbert H. Gary was born on Oct. 8, 1846, near Wheaton, Ill. He became a lawyer in 1868, engaging in civil practice, and before long his clients included major business concerns, whose boards of directors he joined. Among his most important directorships was the Illinois Steel Company.

Gary had helped found the American Steel and Wire Company and the Federal Steel Company. His work in the latter task impressed the elder J. P. Morgan. The two men again collaborated in founding the U.S. Steel Corporation in 1901. U.S. Steel, as the largest industrial firm of its day, stayed under Gary's control for almost 3 decades.

The steel industry was characterized by competition among the few companies in it, and in 1909 Gary founded the American Iron and Steel Institute and the "Gary dinners" in order to stabilize prices. An antitrust suit was initiated against U.S. Steel, but the decision of the Supreme Court in 1919 vindicated Gary's policies.

The steel strike of 1919 thrust Gary into the limelight. The main issue was the right of independent unions to organize and to participate in collective bargaining. An advocate of the open shop, Gary held the attitude: "We are not obliged to contract with unions if we do not choose to do so." Gary rejected arbitration, and the workers eventually lost the strike. By his own lights, however, he was an enlightened and even a benevolent despot, for U.S. Steel offered its workers a welfare program that included pensions and a profit-sharing plan. Nonetheless, under Gary's direction the steel industry ran a 12-hour day and 7-day week that was not ended until 1923, and then only as a result of personal intervention by President Warren G. Harding. Gary's brand of paternalism guided his company and the industry until Franklin Roosevelt's New Deal administration.

Gary died (still chairman of the board of directors of U.S. Steel) on Aug. 15, 1927. His name is commemorated by the steel town of Gary, Ind., which was built by U.S. Steel.

Further Reading

The principal source on Gary is Ida M. Tarbell, *The Life of Elbert H. Gary* (1925), which, though useful, is uncritical. Arundel Cotter, *The Gary I Knew* (1928), contains reminiscences. James Howard Bridge, who was the personal secretary of Andrew Carnegie, is the author of *Millionaires and Grub Street* (1931), which includes a short chapter on Gary. Several

works deal with Gary's labor policy: Charles A. Gulick, Jr., *Labor Policy of the United States Steel Corporation* (1924), and David Brody, *Steel Workers in America* (1960) and *Labor in Crisis: The Steel Strike of 1919* (1965). □

Pedro de la Gasca

The Spanish priest and statesman Pedro de la Gasca (ca. 1496-1567) reestablished royal authority in Peru in the 1540s after the rebellious conquistador Gonzalo Pizarro overthrew the Spanish crown's representatives.

Trained in theology and a graduate of the University of Salamanca, Pedro de la Gasca showed himself throughout his life to be a prudent, energetic, and loyal servant of the powerful emperor Charles V. Appointed to the important Council of the Inquisition, Gasca first emerged in a significant role when, about 1540, he was sent to the Valencia region of Spain to investigate cases of heresy, to inspect the financial and judicial condition of the region, and to guide its defense against possible invasions by the French and the Turks.

In 1542 Charles V decreed the "New Laws" in an effort to administer more fairly the affairs of his Indian subjects, who were being abused by the Spaniards throughout the widespread American empire, and especially to bring peace to Peru, which was being torn by civil strife among the rapacious conquerors. The laws provided, among other matters, for an end to *encomiendas* (a system of tribute payment by Indians to Spaniards), for the establishment of an *audiencia* (supreme court) in Peru, and for the appointment of the first viceroy to the region.

The harsh enforcement of the New Laws by that viceroy precipitated rebellion by Gonzalo Pizarro, the half brother of the leader of the conquest, Francisco Pizarro. The viceroy was killed in battle by Gonzalo's troops (1545), and the rebellious *encomenderos,* or Spanish tribute holders, of Peru seized control of all of western South America from Panama south into Chile.

Such a grave and unprecedented challenge to the authority of Europe's mightiest monarch could not go unanswered. The dispatch of a powerful military force to Peru was considered but rejected because of the difficulties of sending and maintaining troops over such a great distance.

Departure for Peru

Charles V finally decided to send one man to try to win Peru back from the rebels. That man was Pedro de la Gasca. In an unprecedented exchange between a loyal official and his king, Gasca insisted on the grant of unlimited powers from the Crown before he would agree to undertake the mission to Peru. Gasca left for Peru in 1546. His retinue consisted of a secretary and a servant, but he was armed with decrees revoking the prohibition against *encomiendas;* he had full authority to draw unlimited revenues from the

began. The skirmish turned into a rout. Gonzalo Pizarro and his field marshal, Francisco de Carvajal, were made prisoners with all their troops. That same night Pizarro and Carvajal were tried and convicted by a two-man court appointed by Gasca. Both men were executed the following morning.

Gasca remained in command for another 2 years, busy in the reorganization and stabilization of the colony. He made an extensive redistribution of land, of *encomiendas,* and of honors, and he sent out exploring expeditions to remote regions of western South America, as much to keep disaffected conquistadores busy as to discover and settle new regions.

Return to Spain

In January 1550, Gasca departed from Peru for Spain, taking with him for the Crown a treasure estimated at several million dollars. Emperor Charles obtained for him first the bishopric of Palencia and then that of Sigüenza, and Gasca served in Spain for the rest of his life, not only as a churchman but also as a consultant on Peruvian matters and other colonial American affairs for the Crown and in his capacity as a member of the Council of the Inquisition.

Gasca's reconquest of Peru is significant in that it consolidated and institutionalized royal authority in what was to become the richest jewel in the Spanish imperial crown. On his death Gasca was buried in the Church of the Magdalena in Valladolid, a city that he loved and a church to which he had given much financial support.

Further Reading

The classic work of William H. Prescott, *History of the Conquest of Peru* (2 vols., 1847; many later editions), continues to be the best account in English of the conflict between Gasca and the conquistadores in Peru. Philip A. Means, *Fall of the Inca Empire and the Spanish Rule in Peru* 1530-1780 (1932), contains a lively restatement of the source materials used by Prescott. Chief among the early chronicles is that by Garcilaso de la Vega, *First Part of the Royal Commentaries of the Incas* (2 vols., 1964). See also James Lockhart, *Spanish Peru, 1532-1560* (1968), and John Hemming, *The Conquest of the Incas* (1970). □

royal treasury; he had total judicial power, ranging from the death sentence to amnesty; and he carried, as evidence of the royal confidence and authority vested in him, parchment papers that were blank except for the signature of Charles V.

Defeat of Pizarro

Because the Isthmus of Panama was under Pizarro's control, Gasca landed at the port of Santa Marta in Colombia. Soon, by judicious correspondence, he won over Pizarro's aides in Panama, partly by the immediate announcement of the repeal of the portion of the New Laws forbidding possession of *encomiendas* and partly because they saw little to fear in this lone priest.

Allowed to enter Panama, Gasca bombarded Pizarro and other rebel leaders in Peru with letters playing upon a variety of emotions: letters of promise of amnesty, letters of assurance of punishment, letters telling of the organization of powerful forces to reconquer the land should the rebels not submit to the Crown. Toward the middle of 1547 Gasca landed in northern Peru and there, joined by loyal Spaniards, he slowly gathered forces for the final contest with Pizarro.

On April 9, 1548, the small forces of the royalists and the rebels, probably numbering fewer than 1,500 on each side, faced each other on a plain near the ancient Inca capital of Cuzco. But the heart had gone from most of the rebels, and some of the principal officers and many of the troops crossed over to join the royal army as the battle

Elizabeth Gaskell

The English author Elizabeth Gaskell (1810-1865) wrote sociological novels that explored the ills of industrial England and novels of small-town life that are penetrating studies of character.

Elizabeth Cleghorn Stevenson was born on Sept. 29, 1810. Her mother died shortly thereafter, and she was sent to live with an aunt in Knutsford, a village in Cheshire. At the age of 15 she went to school at Stratford-on-Avon, where she remained for 2 years. She married the Reverend William Gaskell on Aug. 30, 1832.

The couple settled in industrial Manchester. There Elizabeth observed the extreme hardship of the workers and their struggles with the owners for a greater share in the profits of the mills. Her observations provided much of the background for *Mary Barton* (1848), her first novel. It was begun in 1845 to relieve her grief at the death of William, her fifth child and only son, and completed during intervals in a busy family life. It centers on a sensational murder but was written with the serious purpose of pointing out what John Barton, Mary's father, called the "right way" to remedy the ills of the workers. This is essentially a change of heart in worker and owner alike. The novel was both praised and damned, but it was an immediate success.

Because of *Mary Barton* Gaskell was asked to contribute stories to Charles Dickens's magazine *Household Words*. "Lizzie Leigh," which dealt with illicit love and illegitimacy, appeared in the first issue. Its themes were developed in *Ruth* (1853), in which Gaskell again called for a change of heart in the public.

Then Gaskell turned from the sociological novel to the novel of village life. Sketches which had appeared in *Household Words* were published as *Cranford* (1853). Drawn from the people and scenes known during her childhood in Knutsford, *Cranford* was far less sensational than her earlier books but no less interesting. The humorously depicted incidents and sharply observed characters capture the attention today as in the 19th century.

In *North and South* (1855) Gaskell returned to the sociological novel. Then, because of her friendship with Charlotte Brontë, Gaskell wrote *The Life of Charlotte Brontë* (1857). She was quite unlike the intensely introspective Charlotte but extremely sympathetic to her. Though the book did not tell the whole truth about Brontë's life, it was a remarkably revealing biography.

After the biography came *Sylvia's Lovers* (1863), a historical novel, and *Wives and Daughters* (1866), a novel of life in a quiet country town. Unfinished at her death, *Wives and Daughters* is Gaskell's most mature treatment of character. She died on Nov. 12, 1865.

Further Reading

The major biographical study of Mrs. Gaskell is Annette B. Hopkins, *Elizabeth Gaskell: Her Life and Works* (1952). Additional information appears in *The Letters of Mrs. Gaskell* (1966), edited by Arthur Pollard and J. A. V. Chapple. Sound criticism and a biographical sketch are in Pollard's *Mrs. Gaskell, Novelist and Biographer* (1966).

Additional Sources

Bonaparte, Felicia, *The gypsy-bachelor of Manchester: the life of Mrs. Gaskell's demon,* Charlottesville: University Press of Virginia, 1992.

Brodetsky, Tessa, *Elizabeth Gaskell,* Leamington, Spa: Berg, 1986.

Gerin, Winifred, *Elizabeth Gaskell: a biography,* Oxford: Clarendon Press, 1976.

Payne, George Andrew, *Mrs. Gaskell: a brief biography,* Folcroft, Pa.: Folcroft Library Editions, 1976.

Uglow, Jennifer S., *Elizabeth Gaskell: a habit of stories,* New York: Farrar Straus Giroux, 1993.

Whitfield, Archie Stanton, *Mrs. Gaskell, her life and work,* Norwood, Pa.: Norwood Editions, 1978. □

William Henry Gates III

Microsoft cofounder and Chief Executive Officer William (Bill) H. Gates III (born 1955) became the wealthiest man in America and one of the most influential personalities on the ever evolving information superhighway and computer industry.

William (Bill) Henry Gates III became the most famous businessman in recent history. His supreme accomplishment was to design and develop innovative software for the personal computer, making PC's universally popular machines. In user friendly language, communicating with computers is a matter of "translating" a person's native language into the codes that a computer understands. The easier this translation is to make, the easier it is to work with the computer and the more accessible and widely used the computer becomes. Gates' gift for software design, as well as his skills in business, made Microsoft, the company he cofounded with a high school friend in Richmond, Washington, a multi billion-dollar empire.

Love of Computer Technology

Gates was born on October 28, 1955 in Seattle, Washington. He was the second child and only son of William Henry Gates Jr., a prominent Seattle attorney, and Mary Maxwell, a former school teacher. Gates had two siblings. His sister, Kristi, one year his senior, became his tax accountant. Libby, nine years his junior, lived in Seattle raising her two children. Although Gates' parents had a law career in mind for their son, he developed an early interest in computer science and began studying computers in the seventh grade at Seattle's Lakeside School. Lakeside was a private school chosen by Gates' parents in the hopes that it would be more challenging for their son's intellectual drive and insatiable curiosity. At Lakeside Gates became acquainted with Paul Allen, a classmate with similar interests in technology who would eventually become his business partner.

Gates' early experiences with computers included debugging (eliminating errors from) programs for the Computer Center Corporation's PDP-10, helping to computerize electric power grids for the Bonneville Power Administration, and founding with Allen a firm called Traf-O-Data while still in high school. Their small company earned them $20 thousand in fees for analyzing local traffic patterns.

While working with the Computer Center's PDP-10, Gates was responsible for what was probably the first computer virus, a program that copies itself into other programs and ruins data. Discovering that the machine was connected to a national network of computers called Cybernet,

Gates invaded the network and installed a program on the main computer that sent itself to the rest of the network's computers and crashed. When Gates was found out, he was severely reprimanded and he kept away from computers for his entire junior year at Lakeside. Without the lure of computers, Gates made plans in 1970 for college and law school. But by 1971 he was back helping Allen write a class scheduling program for their school's computer.

The Article That Started It All

Gates entered Harvard University in 1973 and pursued his studies for the next year and a half. However, his life was to change in January of 1975 when Popular Mechanics carried a cover story on a $350 microcomputer, the Altair, made by a firm called MITS in New Mexico. When Allen excitedly showed him the story, Gates knew where he wanted to be: at the forefront of computer software design.

Gates and Allen first wrote a BASIC interpreter for the Altair computer. BASIC was a simple, interactive computer language designed in the 1960s. "Interpreter" describes a program that executes a source program by reading it one line at a time, performing operations one line at a time, and performing operations immediately. MITS, which encouraged and helped Gates and Allen, finally challenged them to bring their software in for a demonstration. Because they did not own an Altair (nor had they seen the 8080 microprocessing chip that was at the heart of the machine), Gates had to write and test his BASIC interpreter on a simulator program which acted like the 8080. Nonetheless, their BASIC ran the first time it was tested at MITS.

Gates dropped out of Harvard in 1975, ending his academic life and beginning his career in earnest as a software designer and entrepreneur. At this time, Gates and Allen cofounded Microsoft. They wrote programs for the early Apple and Commodore machines and expanded BASIC to run on microcomputers other than the Altair. One of Gates' most significant opportunities arrived in 1980 when he was approached by IBM to help with their personal computer project, code name Project Chess. Eventually asked to design the operating system for the new machine, Gates developed the Microsoft Disk Operating System, or MS-DOS. Not only did he sell IBM on the new operating system, but he also convinced the computer giant to shed the veil of secrecy surrounding the specifications of its PC so that others could write software for the machine. The result was the proliferation of licenses for MS-DOS as software developers quickly moved to become compatible with IBM. Over two million copies of MS-DOS were sold by 1984. Because IMB's PC architecture was opened up by Gates, MS-DOS and its related applications can run on almost any IBM-compatible PC. By the early 1990s, Microsoft had sold more than 100 million copies of MS-DOS, making the operating system the all-time leader in software sales. For his achievements in science and technology, Gates received the Howard Vollum Award in 1984 by Reed College in Portland, Oregon.

In 1987 Gates entered the world of computer-driven multimedia when he began promoting CD-ROM technology. CD-ROM is an optical storage medium easily connected to a PC, and a CD-ROM disc has an incredibly larger capacity that can store encyclopedias, feature films, and complex interactive games. Gates hoped to expand his business by combining PCS with the information reservoirs provided by CD-ROM and was soon marketing a number of multimedia products.

Gates' competitive drive and fierce desire to win has made him a powerful force in business but has also consumed much of his personal life. In the six years between 1978 and 1984 he took a total of only two weeks vacation. In 1985 a popular magazine included him on their list of most eligible bachelors. His status did not change until New Year's day 1994 when he married Melinda French, a Microsoft manager, on the Hawaiian island of Lanai. The ceremony was held on the island's Challenge golf course and Gates kept it private by buying out the unused rooms at the local hotel and by hiring all of the helicopters in the area to keep photographers from using them. His fortune at the time of his marriage was estimated at close to seven billion dollars. By 1997 his worth was estimated at approximately $37 billion, earning him the "richest man in America" title.

In *Hard Drive*, James Wallace and Jim Erickson quote Gates as saying, "I can do anything if I put my mind to it." His ambition has made him the head of a robust, innovative software firm and the richest man in America.

The Future for Microsoft

Gates emits the same competitiveness, drive, ambition, and need to win that was present 21 years ago when he dropped out of Harvard to start Microsoft. But some of the players have changed. Allen left Microsoft to become one of the country's most successful hi-tech venture-capital investors and owner of the Portland Trail Blazers basketball team. However, he returned to serve on Microsoft's board. Gates considers Steve Ballmer, a former Harvard classmate, his best friend and closest advisor. He hired Ballmer away from Proctor & Gamble in 1980 with the lure of a $50 thousand a year salary and a share of the business. In an interview with *Newsweek*, Gates is quoted as saying, "I think it's a phenomenal business partnership . . . And within the company, everyone has understood that we work very closely together and have a very common view of where we want to go." Gates shared his vision for the future of Microsoft with *Information Outlook*. Gates said, "We're in four businesses today, and in ten years we'll be in the same four businesses; desktop operating systems, productivity applications, server software, and interactive content business." He believes that speech recognition, natural language understanding, automatic learning, flat screen displays, and optic fiber will have the greatest technological impacts on the industry over the next 15 years.

Many of Gates' detractors criticize him not just for his success, but because they feel he tries to unfairly and maybe even illegally leverage his company's dominance of the desktop operating systems. Once Microsoft integrates its Internet browser, Explorer, and its Microsoft Network into its Windows Operating Systems, it will have the ultimate— Active Desktop—due out with Windows 97. Critics feel it will put all other entries at a disadvantage. "If improving a

product based on customer input is willful maintenance of trying to stay in business and not have Netscape turn their browser into the most popular operating system, then I think that is what we are supposed to do," was Gates' response to his critics as quoted by *Time* .

Gates and his wife had their first child, Jennifer, in April of 1996. Although many describe Gates as cold, relentless, and impersonal, his friends find him more reflective since his marriage and the birth of his daughter. Further, he recognizes his overall contribution. While he appears a little less exhausting and more civil, friends say he still pushes hard and keeps score.

Gates expects to run Microsoft for at least the next ten years at which time he plans to retire and focus on giving his money away. His philanthropic endeavors have been guided by his interests. He has directed those efforts primarily toward educational sources such as schools and libraries.

Further Reading

Since 1981 business magazine articles have described aspects of Gates' career. *Gates: How Microsoft's Mogul Reinvented an Industry—and Made Himself the Richest Man in America* by Stephen Manes and Paul Andrews (1994) is an authoritative and detailed biography. *Big Blues, The Unmaking of IBM* by Paul Carroll (1993) favorably compares Gates' entrepreneurial approach to business to IBM's management by committee approach. "E-Mail From Bill" by John Seabrook, *New Yorker* magazine (January 10, 1994) provides insight to Gates' goals and personality. *Architects of the Future, Microsoft Corporation 1993 Annual Report* contains product descriptions and marketshare analysis along with income statements and a discussion of litigation and federal agencies' inquiries. *PC Week* provides updates on the latest Microsoft products.
For books about Bill Gates see: *Encyclopedia of Computer Science,* Van Nostrand Reinhold, 1993 p 519. Gates, Bill with Nathan Myhevrold and Peter Rinearson, *The Road Ahead.* Ichbiah, David and Susan L. Knepper, *The Making of Microsoft,* Prima, 1991. Manes, Stephen and Paul Andrews, *Gates,* Doubleday, 1993. Slater, Robert, *Portraits in Silicon,* MIT Press, 1987. Wallace, James and Jim Erickson, *Hard Drive,* Wiley, 1992.
For periodical articles about Bill Gates see: *The Future of Microsoft.* Economist, V327, May 22, 1993, pp. 25-27. *Information Outlook,* May 1997. *National Review,* January 27, 1997. *New York Times,* January 3, 1994. *New Yorker,* January 10, 1994, pp. 48-61.*Newsweek,* June 23, 1997. *PC Magazine,* March 25, 1997. *Time,* January 13, 1997. □

Richard Jordan Gatling

Richard Jordan Gatling (1818-1903), American inventor, became famous for designing multiple-firing guns.

Richard Gatling was born on a large plantation in Hertford County, N.C., on Sept. 12, 1818. With his father he perfected machines to sow cotton and to thin out cotton plants. He worked in the county clerk's office from the age of 15 to 19, taught school briefly, and became a merchant. In 1839 he patented a rice planter. He moved to St. Louis in 1844, worked in a dry goods store, then made a wheat drill and manufactured seed planters.

Gatling studied medicine and became a doctor in 1850, although he never practiced. For a time he promoted railroad enterprises and real estate in Indianapolis, then he established farm-machinery factories in three midwestern cities. His inventions included a double-acting hemp break (1850), a steam plow (1857), a marine steam ram (1862), and a gunmetal alloy.

Soon after the Civil War began, Gatling designed the Gatling gun. The precursor of the modern machine gun, it could fire 350 rounds per minute. Later improvements raised the firing rate and extended the range to 1 1/2 miles. The Union's chief of ordnance was uninterested in Gatling's gun, so it was little used during the war. A few were procured by commanders, sometimes with private funds. Union naval officer David D. Porter used some, and three Gatlings guarded the *New York Times* building during the draft riots in 1863. In 1864 Gen. Benjamin Butler used 12. The Army Ordnance Department belatedly ordered 100 in 1866. The Colt Company produced these and all Gatlings thereafter.

The gun was not used officially during the war, partly because of Gatling's affiliation with the "Copperheads," a group of antiwar Democrats who opposed Lincoln's policies and were suspected of treason. Also, he had offered to sell the gun to anyone, including the Confederacy and foreigners. Many Gatlings were sold to England, Austria, and Russia and to South American nations. Until about 1900 they were used in small wars. The U.S. Army used them against the American Indians.

To compete with other machine gun manufacturers, in 1893 Gatling developed an electricity-driven gun that fired 3,000 rounds per minute. Later he built an automatic gas-operated gun. However, in 1911 the U.S. Army officially declared his weapon obsolete. He gained immortality of a sort with the word "gat," gangster slang for an automatic handgun.

In 1900 Gatling invented a motor-driven plow. Before it could be manufactured, he died in New York City on Feb. 26, 1903.

Further Reading

There is no biography of Gatling. For sketches of his life see William F. Moore, *Representative Men of Connecticut, 1861-1894* (1894), and Benjamin B. Winborne, *The Colonial and State Political History of Hertford County, North Carolina* (1906). For information on the Gatling gun see Paul Wahl and Donald R. Toppel, *The Gatling Gun* (1965).

Additional Sources

Johnson, F. Roy (Frank Roy), *The Gatling gun and flying machine of Richard and Henry Gatling,* Murfreesboro, N.C.: Johnson Pub. Co., 1979. □

Antoni Gaudí i Cornet

The Catalan architect and designer Antoni Gaudí i Cornet (1852-1926) merged Neo-Gothic and Moorish revival styles with the Art Nouveau style to form the most consistently original body of work by any architect of the late 19th and early 20th centuries.

Born on June 25, 1852, in the Catalan town of Reus near Barcelona, Antoni Gaudí studied at the School of Architecture in Barcelona (1874-1878) and also profited from reading the works of the French Neo-Gothic rationalist Eugène Emmanuel Viollet-le-Duc. Gaudí's first important commission was a house for Manuel Vicens in Barcelona (1878-1880; remodeled under Gaudí's direction, 1925-1926). Here, as in El Capricho, a summer house at Comillas near Santander (1883-1885), he drew upon Moorish sources in the polychromatic use of stone, brick, tiles, and wrought iron.

Sagrada Familia

In 1884 Gaudí succeeded Francesco Villar as the architect of the Church of the Sagrada Familia in Barcelona. Begun in 1875 and given a modest Neo-Gothic form by Villar in 1882, the church occupied Gaudí for the rest of his life. Built by private contribution rather than diocesan funds, it is still under construction from the architect's designs.

A small fragment of the huge project, the Transept of the Nativity with its four carrot-shaped stone towers capped by fantastic free-form terminals of glazed tile, is the most prominent feature of the unfinished church, as it is indeed of the Barcelona skyline. In the Sagrada Familia, Gaudí joined the Neo-Gothic and Art Nouveau styles to produce one of the most dramatic architectural compositions of the 19th century.

Güell Buildings

In 1885 Gaudí also began a series of works for Eusebio Güell, a textile manufacturer. These include the Güell Palace in Barcelona (1885-1889); a chapel for the Güell Colony, or settlement of textile workers, at Santa Coloma de Cervelló just west of Barcelona (1898-1915; left unfinished); and an unsuccessful housing development in the city, now known as the Park Güell (1900-1914).

The Güell Palace, with basement stables of vaulted masonry, a multistory hall covered by a pierced, conical vault, exquisite ironwork, and brightly colored tile chimney pots, combines Moorish and Art Nouveau designs and is one of Gaudí's most impressive achievements. The inclined piers of the chapel for the Güell Colony, of which only the crypt was built, were based upon Gaudí's studies of structural forces by means of leaded models hung from his studio ceiling. These piers, like those in the large model of the Sagrada Familia that Gaudí built to show the completed church, assume the lines of inverted catenary curves and thus eliminate the need for buttressing. In the Güell chapel, as in the finished portions of the Park Güell, Gaudí's mastery

of materials, textures, and colors is fully demonstrated. On the benches of the square in the Park Güell, for example, he used ceramic fragments to create abstract compositions of dynamic shapes and colors.

Battló and Milá Houses

Two residential projects in Barcelona are among Gaudí's major works. He remodeled a building as a home for the Battló family (1905-1907). The Battló House is locally known as the "house of bones" because the balconies of its front facade resemble bones and skulls. The facade is covered with iridescent tiles, and the roof is wavelike in form. The Milá House (1905-1910) with its undulating facades and wrought-iron balconies in the form of sea weed suggests the Mediterranean that washes the shores of Catalonia.

For the Battló House, as for the earlier Güell Palace, Gaudí designed furniture in the curvilinear patterns of Art Nouveau, but the parabolic arches in the attic of the Milá House, as well as the undulating walls and roof of the school building on the grounds of the Sagrada Familia (1909), are more than merely formal effects. Here Gaudí relied upon traditional Catalan vaulting techniques to create maximum stability through the use of warped-plane, tile-masonry construction.

Gaudí was a lifelong bachelor, a religious zealot, a Catalan nationalist, and, to some, an uncanonized saint. After 1914 he refused all commissions, to devote himself full time to the Sagrada Familia, even living in his basement workshop there. He was struck down by a streetcar while on his way to church one evening. Dressed in old clothes and unrecognized, he was taken to a charity ward. By the time he was identified it was too late. He died on June 10, 1926, and was buried in the crypt of his beloved Sagrada Familia.

Further Reading

George R. Collins's scholarly *Antonio Gaudí* (1960) has a brief but excellent text, a chronology, a bibliography, and many illustrations. There are several other appreciative interpretations of Gaudí's work, the best of which are James Johnson Sweeney and Josep Lluis Sert, *Antoni Gaudí* (1961; rev. ed. 1970), and E. Casanelles, *Antonio Gaudí A Reappraisal* (1965; trans. 1968), both well illustrated. Juan Eduardo Cirlot, *The Genesis of Gaudian Architecture* (1966; trans. 1967), has a brief general text and many photographs.

Additional Sources

Descharnes, Robert, *Gaudí, the visionary*, New York: Viking Press, 1982.
Martinell, Caesar, *Gaudí: his life, his theories, his work*, Cambridge, Mass.: MIT Press, 1975.
Sterner, Gabriele, *Antoni Gaudí—architecture in Barcelona*, Woodbury, N.Y.: Barron's, 1985. □

Paul Gauguin

The French painter and sculptor Paul Gauguin (1848-1903), seeking exotic environments, first in

France and later in Tahiti, frequently combined the people and objects in his paintings in novel ways, evoking in the process a mysterious, personal world.

Paul Gauguin was born in Paris on June 7, 1848, to a French father, a journalist from Orléans, and a mother of Spanish-Peruvian descent. When Paul was 3 his parents sailed for Peru after the victory of Louis Napoleon; his father died on the way. Gauguin and his mother remained in Peru for 4 years and then returned to Orléans, where he attended a seminary. At the age of 17 he enlisted in the merchant marine.

In 1870 Gauguin began a career as a stockbroker and remained in this profession for 12 years. He married a Danish girl, Mette Sophia Gad, and seemed destined for a comfortable middle-class existence.

Beginnings as an Artist

Gauguin was an enthusiastic Sunday painter. The Salon of 1876 accepted one of his pictures, and he started a collection of works by impressionist painters. As time went on, his desire to paint became ever stronger, and in 1883, Gauguin, now 35, decided to give up business and devote himself entirely to painting. His wife, wishing to economize, took their five children to live with her parents in Copenhagen. Gauguin followed her, but he soon returned with his eldest son, Clovis, to Paris, where he supported himself by pasting advertisements on walls.

In 1886, with Clovis enrolled in a boarding school, Gauguin lived for a few months in the village of Pont-Aven in Brittany, then left for the island of Martinique, first stopping to work as a laborer on the Panama Canal. He returned to Pont-Aven in February 1888, gathered about him a group of painters, including Émile Bernard, and preached and practiced a style he called synthetism, which involved pure color patterns, strong, expressive outlines, and formal simplifications.

In October, Vincent van Gogh invited Gauguin to join him at Arles. Gauguin, proud, arrogant, sarcastic, and urbanely sophisticated, and Van Gogh, open and passionately needing human companionship, did not get along. When Van Gogh threatened him with a razor, Gauguin hurriedly left for Paris. There he resumed his bohemian existence until 1891, when he left France and the Western civilization he had come to deride and went to Tahiti.

Pre-Tahitian Paintings

Among Gauguin's masterpieces of this period are the *Vision after the Sermon—Jacob Wrestling with the Angel* (1888) and the *Yellow Christ* (1889). In both paintings Breton peasants, to whom Gauguin was attracted as exotic, noncultivated types, figure prominently. Gauguin's usual bright colors and simplified shapes treated as flat silhouettes are present, but these paintings also reveal his symbolist leanings. Objects and events are taken out of their normal historical contexts. In the *Vision* Breton women observe an episode described in Genesis: Jacob wrestling with a stranger who turns out to be an angel. Gauguin suggests thereby that the faith of these pious women enabled them to see miraculous events of the past as vividly as if they were occurring before them. In the *Yellow Christ* Gauguin, using as his model a yellow wooden statue from a church near Pont-Aven, depicts Breton women as if they were in the presence of the actual Crucifixion.

Two Periods in Tahiti

When Gauguin arrived in Tahiti, he did not settle in the capital, Papeete, which contained Europeans, but lived with the natives some 25 miles away. He took a native girl as his wife, and she bore him a son. Ill and poor, he returned to France in August 1893, where to his delight he found that he had inherited a small sum from an uncle. In Paris he lived with flair, accompanied much of the time by a Javanese girl named Annah, who later disappeared with the contents of his studio. The exhibition of his Tahitian work in November was not successful financially. In early 1894 he went to Denmark and then to Brittany.

In 1895 an unsuccessful auction of Gauguin's paintings was held. He sailed for Tahiti that spring. He settled again among the natives, this time in the north. His health grew poorer; an ankle he had broken in Brittany did not heal properly, and he suffered from syphilis and strokes. He was harassed by the government authorities, whom he flouted but upon whom he had to depend for menial jobs in order to support himself. In 1901 he moved to the Marquesas Islands. He died there, alone, of a stroke on May 8, 1903.

Tahitian Paintings

Gauguin once advised a friend to avoid the Greek and choose rather "the Persian, the Cambodians, and a little of the Egyptian." He epitomized the disenchantment of several postimpressionist painters with bourgeois Parisian existence; but whereas Henri de Toulouse-Lautrec sought the Parisian demimonde and Van Gogh fled to Arles, Gauguin achieved what was perhaps the most extreme break when he left Europe for a non-Western culture.

Gauguin's Tahitian paintings celebrate the lushness and mysterious splendor of his new environment. At the same time they are seldom correct pictures of Tahitian life, from an anthropological standpoint, but rather feature recastings and recombinations of objects and persons taken out of their normal settings, as was the case with several of his paintings done in Brittany. In *La Orana Maria* (1891) a Tahitian woman, her young son, and two women standing nearby are shown in the obvious attitudes of the Virgin and Child with attendant saints or worshiping angels. In *Where Do We Come From? What Are We? Where Are We Going?* (1898), Gauguin's most ambitious painting in terms of size, number of figures, and probable overlay of meanings, there are Tahitian natives in unusual and probably contrived meditative poses and a foreboding primitive idol. In a way yet to be explained, the painting has to do with human destiny.

Gauguin's art, in several ways, anticipated trends in 20th-century modernism. For example, his unusual juxtapositions and startling anachronisms can be seen as precursors of the dislocations in the surrealist art of the 1920s and later. His whole life, as well as the style and subject matter of most of his art, was instrumental in paving the way for the positive acceptance of primitive art objects on the part of German expressionist and other 20th-century artists.

Further Reading

Dennis Sutton, ed., *Paul Gauguin's Intimate Journals* (1958), contains poignant accounts of Gauguin's struggle to survive after he left France. John Rewald, *Gauguin* (1938), has little analysis of the paintings but extensive quotations from Gauguin's writings. Robert Goldwater, *Gauguin* (1957), contains beautiful illustrations, including watercolors seldom seen, and good analyses of the paintings. Christopher Gray, *Sculpture and Ceramics of Paul Gauguin* (1963), is the authoritative work on this aspect of the artist. Wayne Andersen, *Gauguin's Paradise Lost* (1971), is a psychological interpretation of Gauguin's art and life. An important background study is John Rewald, *Postimpressionism,* vol. 1 (1956; 2d ed. 1962). □

Giovanni Battista Gaulli

The Italian painter Giovanni Battista Gaulli (1639-1709) is known for the drama of his illusionistic ceiling paintings in fresco and the brilliance of his color harmonies in oils.

Giovanni Battista Gaulli, called Baciccio, was born in Genoa and was baptized on May 10, 1639. When he was 18 years old, his entire family died of the plague. Soon afterward he left for Rome, where he spent the rest of his life. There he met Gian Lorenzo Bernini, with whose help Baciccio's career flourished. He received many commissions to execute frescoes in the churches of the papal city and mythologies in its palaces. "He painted all the cardinals," Lione Pascoli wrote in 1730, "all the important people of his day who came to Rome, and the seven popes who reigned from Alexander VII to Clement XI."

In 1674 Baciccio was president of the painters' guild, the Academy of St. Luke. After Bernini's death in 1680 Baciccio's prestige declined somewhat owing to the increasing popularity of the cooler, quieter art of Carlo Maratti, but he never lacked commissions. He died in Rome on March 26, 1709.

Baciccio's earliest identifiable works, such as the oil sketches for the frescoes at S. Agnese, show the natural style he brought with him from Genoa. In these sketches he often used colors at top saturation—the brightest, purest blue, the reddest red—and applied paint rapidly in almost explosive brushstrokes filled with energy and vigor.

Baciccio's most famous work is the *Triumph of the Name of Jesus* in the Church of the Gesù (1672-1679), which covers most of the nave ceiling of the massive church. Gazing upward, we have the illusion that the roof is open at the center. High in the sky are cherubim and angels

who circle around the light emanating from the monogram of Jesus. Below on cloud banks are throngs of saints and churchmen who kneel in adoration. At one end is a group of the damned being cast down to hell by the same mystical light that draws the blessed up to heaven.

The most striking aspect of this work is the way in which large groups of figures spill over the edge of the frame and seem to hover above our heads and underneath the roof of the church. Thus they exist in the same zone of space that we do, only higher up. In this way Baciccio stresses the smallness of the distance that separates heaven from earth and therefore the immediacy of the celestial. These figures on clouds that seem to float inside the church take on the sense of mass, clarity of contour, and bright colors with which we are familiar in the material world. The figures gazing down from the higher regions of heaven assume a less physical, more spiritual existence. Their outlines blur, their solidity dissolves, and their colors drain as they sink back into the divine light.

Further Reading

The standard book on Gaulli is Robert Enggass, *The Painting of Baciccio: Giovanni Battista Gaulli* (1964). There is an excellent essay on him in Ellis K. Waterhouse, *Italian Baroque Painting* (1962). □

Jean Paul Gaultier

French designer Jean Paul Gaultier (born 1952) became world famous for his avant-garde designs, usually first displayed in runway shows that are themselves media events.

Jean Paul Gaultier was born in France in 1952. Not interested in sports or any of the usual childhood pleasures, he was a prodigy when it came to fashion design. Young Gaultier designed a collection of clothing for his mother and grandmother at age 13. At age 15 he invented a coat with bookbag closures. When he reached the age of 17, he boldly sent his design sketches to Paris designer Pierre Cardin. Cardin appreciated his talents enough to hire the young man as design assistant. Gaultier worked for Cardin for two years. He then spent a year designing for Jacques Esterel before joining the House of Patou in Paris, working with designers Angelo Tarlazzi and Michael Goma for three years.

In 1976 several of Gaultier's sketches were published in *Mode Internationale,* a French fashion magazine. The sketches were favorably received by the design world. That same year Gaultier launched his design career under his own label for a company called Mayagor, as well as continuing to design free-lance ready-to-wear furs, swimwear, and leather clothing.

When Kashiyama, a well-funded Japanese clothing manufacturing conglomerate, caught wind of Gaultier's growing reputation, his career was launched. They signed him to an exclusive contract for men's and women's collections under his own name. Renowned as perhaps the most avant-garde fashion designer of his time, Gaultier was sometimes called the Prince of Perversity. He was known for keeping a keen winking eye on young London and New York street fashions, reinterpreting them with a dash of Parisian panache, then pushing them out on his runways. Some of his most recognizable cutting-edge designs are jackets, dresses, and jumpsuits with indiscreet cutouts that make the garments resemble cages. His unique designs also include dresses and tops with sliced open breasts and bra-like torpedo inserts, fichu off-the-shoulder tops, multi-colored Lycra, vinyl and leather bike pants, and kilt-ish skirts for men.

His always outrageous shows were held in an amphitheater that was actually a converted slaughterhouse outside of Paris. The shows were considered the media events of each fashion season partly because tickets for the collection were so coveted. Ultra-fashionable throngs of Gaultier groupies, dressed in both his latest and now-classic designs, and masses of the fashion press vie, sometimes violently, for seats to see his innovative, thought-provoking parade of new designs. Even nonfashion celebrities show up—actor Jack Nicholson, former model Verushka, singers Grace Jones and Ninah Cherry, and exiled film director Roman Polanski.

In 1997 Gaultier displayed couture for the first time in a Paris show. In an article in *Interview,* he stated that "We are in a world where many people are staying at home on the Internet, not doing anything. I think the moment now for couture is right because it's a small fantasy. It's special, and for only one customer at a time." Gaultier was the only designer in the show to feature couture for men as well as women. Also noteworthy in the 1997 Paris show were corsets for men. Gaultier rationalized in *Interview* that, "I am for equality of gender. I say there's couture for women, so why not for men?" Although Gaultier derived his inspiration for design from the street in the past, and couture is generally perceived to be in the realm of the elite, he attempted to respect the tradition of couture with fabrics not normally used in couture.

Gaultier has been known for using unique looking models in his shows of all different shapes, sizes and ages. In *Interview* he explained that, "I have never really cared about what fashion's ideal was. There are different kinds of beauty and I always try to show that."

In 1987 Gaultier received the coveted French designer of the year award. In 1988 he launched a lower-priced sportswear line called Junior Gaultier, at first carried exclusively in a small store located in Les Halles, a funky area of Paris, and later sporadically sold in U.S. department stores. His other store, located on the chic Right Bank of Paris, contained his men's and women's ready-to-wear bearing high price tags ($1,200 for a suit). These clothes were also carried in boutiques in New York, Los Angeles, and Miami. In 1990 Gaultier's talents were viewed by a wider, less fashion-conscious audience when he designed the entire wardrobe for the controversial British director Peter Greenaway film "The Cook, The Thief, His Wife and Her Lover." Long a fan of Greenaway's films, Gaultier and he decided that the clothing for this modern day morality play should change colors as the characters moved from set to set. Four sets of clothing were made: red for the dining room, blue for the parking lot, white for the bathroom, and green for the kitchen. One of his most devoted fans was singer Madonna, who on her 1990 Blonde Ambition international tour wore nothing but Gaultier suits with sliced open breasts covering a torpedo bra corset over menswear pants. She was also one of the first to adopt his lingerie-over-clothing trend in 1985.

In 1997, Gaultier collaborated with French movie director Luc Besson to design costumes for the movie "The Fifth Element", a futuristic sci-fi thriller. Although the film received less than enthusiastic reviews, the costumes were referred to as "body-conscious" and "outlandish" in reviews in *National Review* and *People Weekly*.

Although Gaultier's designs are sometimes considered over-the-edge, there is no question among the fashion historians or the retail fashion world that his multiple talents greatly influence the work of other designers. Gaultier imitations and sometimes blatant thefts of his somewhat insane designs often appear in more moderately priced department stores mere months after his runway shows.

Further Reading

Additional information on designers and fashions can be found in the *Fairchild Dictionary of Fashion* (1988), *McDowell's Directory of 20th Century Fashion* (1987), and Catherine McDermott's *Street Style* (1987). See also Andrew Edelstein's *The Pop Sixties* (1985), Alison Lurie's *The Language of Clothes* (1983), and Melissa Sones' *Getting into Fashion* (1984).

For periodical articles about Jean Paul Gaultier see: *The New York Times*, April 10, 1994; May 8, 1997; July 1, 1997; *Vogue*, October, 1994; *Interview*, April 1997; *People Weekly*, May 19, 1997; *Entertainment Weekly*, May 23, 1997; *Rolling Stone*, May 29, 1997; *National Review*, June 16, 1997. □

Karl Friedrich Gauss

The German mathematician Karl Friedrich Gauss (1777-1855) made outstanding contributions to both pure and applied mathematics.

Karl Friedrich Gauss was born in Brunswick on April 30, 1777. At an early age his intellectual abilities attracted the attention of the Duke of Brunswick, who secured his education first at the Collegium Carolinum (1792-1795) in his native city and then at the University of Göttingen (1795-1798). In 1801 Gauss published *Disquisitiones arithmeticae,* a work of such originality that it is often regarded as marking the beginning of the modern theory of numbers. The discovery by Giuseppe Piazzi of the asteroid Ceres in 1801 stimulated Gauss's interest in astronomy, and upon the death of his patron, the Duke of Brunswick, Gauss was appointed director of the observatory in Göttingen, where he remained for the rest of his life. In 1831 he collaborated with Wilhelm Weber in the establishment of a geomagnetic survey in Göttingen.

Apart from his books Gauss published a number of memoirs, mainly in the journal of the Royal Society of Göttingen. Generally, however, he was reluctant to publish anything that could be regarded as controversial, so that some of his most brilliant work was found only after his death.

Gauss married twice, but both wives died young. Of his six children, his youngest daughter remained to take care of him until his death on Feb. 23, 1855.

Theory of Numbers

Gauss always strove for perfection of form in his writings. Consequently his finest work, *Disquisitiones arithmeticae,* in which he integrated the work of his predecessors with his own, by its elegance and completeness rendered previous works on the subject superfluous. Quadratic residues, which led to the law of quadratic reciprocity that Gauss had discovered before he was 18, and indeed power residues in general, are treated extensively. Gauss made three more outstanding contributions to the theory of numbers: the theory of congruences, the theory of quadratic forms, and researches on the division of the circle into equal parts. Gauss also introduced the notation $a\ b$ (mod c) for congruences; he developed the theory of congruences of the first and second degrees and showed that all problems of indeterminate analysis can be expressed in terms of congruences. Also he investigated the representation of integers by

binary and ternary quadratic forms. However, neither the work on quadratic forms nor that on second-degree congruences had any impact until the importance of these contributions was later recognized by K. G. J. Jacobi.

On the other hand, Gauss's results on the division of the circle were received with enthusiasm, for these were immediately recognizable as the solution of a famous problem in Greek geometry, namely, the inscription of regular polygons in a circle. First, Gauss proved that a regular polygon with 17 sides can be constructed with ruler and compasses; he then generalized the result by showing that any polygon with a prime number of sides of the form $2^{2m} + 1$ can be constructed with these instruments.

Algebra and Analysis

Albert Girard was the first to surmise in 1629, but was unable to prove, that every algebraic equation has at least one root. Gauss gave three proofs for this: the first of these, given in his thesis, assumes that a continuous function which takes positive and negative values is necessarily zero for some value of the variable.

It is clear from Gauss's notebooks that he recognized the double periodicity of the elliptic functions; however, the work was unpublished, and discovery of the property is credited to N. H. Abel, a later mathematician who gave the first published account. Gauss was the first to adopt a rigorous approach to the treatment of infinite series, as illustrated by his treatment of the hypergeometric series. This series, $1 + ab/c\, x + a\,(a + 1)b\,(b + 1)/c\,(c + 1)\, x^2/2! + \ldots$, had

been introduced earlier by Leonhard Euler, but it was Gauss who devised a test to establish the conditions for the convergence of this series. He also brought to light the important property that nearly all the functions then known could be expressed as hypergeometric series.

The theory of biquadratic residues was developed by Gauss in two memoirs which he presented to the Royal Society of Göttingen in 1825 and 1831. These investigations, an extension of his earlier work on quadratic residues, involved the use of complex numbers. Gauss recognized that all numbers are of the form $a + ib$ and represented such numbers by points in a plane. Besides deriving the law of biquadratic reciprocity with the help of complex numbers, Gauss opened up a new line of research by modifying the definition of a prime number. According to the new definition, the number 3, for example, remains a prime, while the number 5 becomes composite, since it can be expressed as a product of complex factor $(1 + 2i)\,(1 - 2i)$.

Astronomical Calculations

After the discovery of Ceres in 1801, the body was lost to observers, but from Piazzi's observations before it disappeared, Gauss successfully determined the orbit of this asteroid and was able to predict accurately its position. Gauss's success in these calculations encouraged him to develop his methods further, and in 1809 his *Theoria motus corporum coelestium* appeared. In it Gauss discussed the determination of orbits from observational data and also presented an analysis of perturbations.

In his calculation of planetary orbits Gauss used the method of least squares. This method enables all the data to be used when more observations are available than the minimum needed to satisfy the equations. In attempting to justify the method, Gauss derived the Gaussian law of error, familiar to students of probability and statistics as the normal distribution.

Non-Euclidean Geometry

Since the time of the Greeks many attempts had been made to prove Euclid's postulate concerning parallels; the postulate is equivalent to the supposition that the sum of the angles of a triangle is two right angles. In 1733 an attempt to prove the postulate was made by Girolamo Saccheri, who, in fact, invented two non-Euclidean geometries only to reject them for unsound reasons. Gauss envisaged the possibility of developing a geometry without the parallel postulate and on one occasion even measured the angles of a triangle formed by three mountains, finding the sum to be two right angles within the limits of experimental error. Although he published nothing on the subject, Gauss was almost certainly the first to develop the idea of non-Euclidean geometry.

As adviser on geodesy to the Hanoverian government, Gauss had to consider the problem of surveying hilly country. This led him to study differential geometry, and he developed the concepts of curvilinear coordinates and line-element and parametric representations. In 1827 he published a memoir in which the geometry of a curved surface was developed in terms of intrinsic, or Gaussian, coordinates. Instead of considering the surface as embedded in a three-dimensional space, Gauss set up a coordinate network on the surface itself, showing that the geometry of the surface can be described completely in terms of measurements in this network. Defining a straight line as the shortest distance between two points, measured along the surface, the geometry of a curved surface can be regarded as a two-dimensional non-Euclidean geometry. The Gaussian coordinates thus provided an instrument for the analytical development of non-Euclidean geometries.

Further Reading

An extract from Gauss's memoir on magnetic measurements is given in William Francis Magie, *A Source Book in Physics* (1955). The best book on Gauss is G. Waldo Dunnington, *Carl Friedrich Gauss, Titan of Science: A Study of His Life and Work* (1955). A good account of Gauss's life and work is William L. Schaaf, *Carl Friedrich Gauss: Prince of Mathematicians* (1964). A simple introduction to the application of non-Euclidean geometry in relativity theory is in Max Born, *Einstein's Theory of Relativity* (trans. 1922; rev. ed. 1962).

Additional Sources

Beuhler, W. K. (Walter Kaufmann), *Gauss,* Berlin; New York: Springer, 1986.
Beuhler, W. K. (Walter Kaufmann), *Gauss: a biographical study,* Berlin; New York: Springer-Verlag, 1981.
Reich, Karin, *Carl Friedrich Gauss: 1777/1977,* Meunchen: Moos, 1977.
Reich, Karin, *Carl Friedrich Gauss: 1777-1977,* Bonn-Bad Godesberg: Inter Nationes, 1977. □

Cesar Augusto Gaviria Trujillo

Cesar Augusto Gaviria Trujillo (born 1947) entered politics at age 23, serving as a Liberal party representative and in various cabinet positions before being elected president of Colombia from 1990-1994. In 1994 he was elected secretary general of the Organization of American States (OAS).

Cesar Augusto Gaviria Trujillo was born in Pereira (which in 1966 became the capital city of the newly created Department of Risaralda, Colombia) on March 31, 1947. His father was a middle-class coffee grower, sometime journalist, and avowed free-thinker affiliated with the Liberal party. His mother, in contrast, came from a family closely identified with the Conservative party. Gaviria married Ana Milena Munoz, also a native of Pereira from a wealthy family. They had two children: Maria Paz and Simon.

An excellent student, Gaviria attended the prestigious, private University of Los Andes in Bogota where he majored in economics. After graduating first in his class in 1970 at age 23, he launched his political career by winning a city council seat (1970-1974) in his hometown of Pereira as a candidate from the Liberal party. In 1971, during the administration of Conservative President Misael Pastrana Borrero (1970-1974), he was appointed assistant director of the National Planning Department. In 1972 and 1973 he served as general manager of a private-sector company, Transformadores T.P.L., S.A., based in the Department of Risaralda.

In 1974 he was elected to the House of Representatives from Risaralda. Less than a year later, during the presidency of Liberal Alfonso Lopez Michelsen (1974-1978), he was appointed mayor of his native city. He served as mayor for one year (1975-1976). He then reassumed his position in the House, becoming an active member of that chamber's Economic Affairs Committee (Tercera Comision).

In August 1978, following the inauguration of Liberal Julio Cesar Turbay Ayala to the presidency (1978-1982), he was named vice-minister of economic development, a post which he occupied for almost two years. Upon his return to Congress in 1980 he resumed his participation in the House Economic Affairs Committee, over which he presided as chairman in 1981-1982. In 1983, during Conservative President Belasario Betancourt's term in office (1982-1986) he was elected by a bipartisan majority of his colleagues to a one-year term as president of the House of Representatives.

During the early-and mid-1980s Representative Gaviria combined his successful parliamentary career with forays into the field of journalism. In 1982 he served as director of the newspaper *Diario de la Tarde,* a regional daily published in Pereira. Between 1983 and 1986 he frequently wrote economic and political commentaries for the national daily, *El Tiempo,* published in Bogota.

During 1985-1986 he acted as campaign director for the successful Liberal party presidential candidate, Virgilio Barco Vargas (1986-1990). In 1986 he was named adjunct director of the Liberal party.

Upon Barco's assumption of the presidency on August 7, 1986, Gaviria was appointed as the new government's finance minister (Hacienda y Credito Publico). During his tenure in this key cabinet post, he was responsible for drawing up major legislative initiatives on agrarian reform and tax reform, both of which were subsequently enacted by Congress. His tax reform bill was particularly noteworthy because for the first time in Colombia's modern history it exempted low-income citizens from the obligation of filing income tax reports, thereby reducing the administrative load on the nation's overburdened tax authorities, while it simultaneously modernized the tax collection system and increased overall tax revenues collected by the national government. During his term as finance minister he also served on two occasions as acting minister of justice.

Having discharged the duties of finance minister for just under 10 months, in May 1987 he was named minister of government by President Barco. In this ministry he was responsible for guiding the administration's peace initiative that brought the M-19 guerrillas to the negotiating table in 1988 and ultimately led to their historic demobilization in 1989. As minister of government he also served as acting president of the republic on nine separate occasions while President Barco was absent from the country on state visits.

In February 1989, although widely recognized as one of the Barco administration's most effective and respected cabinet officers, he resigned from the government ministry to accept the position of campaign director for Liberal Senator Luis Carlos Galan, the front-running candidate for the presidency in the 1990 elections. Galan was brutally assassinated on August 18, 1989, by hitmen (known as Sicarios) from the notorious Medellin Cartel, one of several powerful drug trafficking organizations operating in Colombia. Gaviria then acceded to the requests from Galan's family and his former supporters within the Liberal party to run for the party's presidential nomination.

After his sweeping victory in the Liberal party's nominating convention in March 1990, Gaviria won the presidency in May 1990, garnering 47 percent of the popular vote (versus 23 percent for the Conservative candidate, Alvaro Gomez Hurtado, his closest rival). The electoral race was marked by extensive terrorism and violence sponsored primarily by the Medellin drug traffickers. In all, three presidential candidates were assassinated during Colombia's traumatic 1989-1990 electoral campaign. In addition to Senator Galan, the left-wing Patriotic Union party candidate, Senator Bernardo Jaramillo Ossa, and the former M-19 guerrilla chieftain and Democratic Alliance candidate, Carlos Pizzaro Leongomez, were also murdered. Upon his assumption of office on August 7, 1990, among the major challenges that the 43-year-old president had to face was how to end the wave of drug-related terrorism convulsing his country and thereby assure the survival of civilian and democratic rule in Colombia during his term (1990-1994) and beyond.

In 1994 Columbia's constitutional court voted 5-4 that it was legal to possess small amounts of hard drugs for personal consumption including marijuana, cocaine, and hashish. Alarmed by the implications, Gaviria and the government cracked down on drug use in public, signing a decree that banned drug consumption in public places and imposed penalties on two dozen categories of people who use narcotics, such as government employees or drivers of vehicles. Gaviria also appealed to church leaders, professional organizations, peasant groups, and students to support a referendum to amend the constitution and ban drug use. Although it appeared that such a referendum would be difficult legally to implement, Gaviria's actions apparently influenced the populace. Opinion polls showed a large majority of people opposed to legalization of drugs in Columbia.

In 1994 Gaviria was elected secretary general of the Organization of American States (OAS). The OAS, a 35 nation organization and the world's oldest regional forum, had raised its profile in defense of democracy in Guatemala, Peru, and Haiti. Gaviria assumed OAS duties after his presidential term ended in August 1994. Surprising those who assumed he would lead a comfortable life as secretary general of a staid and sleepy forum, Gaviria launched an overhaul of the OAS, including a 30 percent reduction in staff. He defended the action, saying that the savings would free up resources for technical forays into areas such as trade and narcotics suppression. The OAS had no binding authority and no troops to dispatch, even though the organization assisted in reversing executive coups in Guatemala and Peru. Nonetheless, Gaviria pushed for change in the OAS, stating in *The Miami Herald* that "We just cannot accept becoming a diplomatic antique."

Further Reading

There are no English language biographies of President Cesar Gaviria currently available. Nevertheless, relevant information on the man, his times, and his country can be found in the following books and articles: Robert Dix, *The Politics of Colombia* (1987); Jonathan Hartlyn, *The Politics of Coalition Rule in Colombia* (London: 1988); Bruce Michael Bagley, "Colombia and the War on Drugs," in *Foreign Affairs* (Fall 1988); Jenny Pearce, *Colombia: Inside the Labyrinth* (London: 1990); and Bruce Michael Bagley, "Dateline Drug Wars: Colombia: Wrong Strategy," in *Foreign Policy* (Winter 1989-1990).

For periodical articles about Cesar Augusto Gaviria Trujillo see: *Knight-Ridder/Tribune News Service,* February 9, 1994; *Knight-Ridder/Tribune News Service,* March 27, 1994; *Knight-Ridder/Tribune News Service,* May 27, 1994; *Knight-Ridder/Tribune News Service,* June 12, 1994; and *Knight-Ridder/Tribune News Service,* January 6, 1997. □

John Gay

The English playwright and poet John Gay (1685-1732) is best known for "The Beggar's Opera," a skillful blend of literary, political, social, and musical satire.

John Gay was born on June 30, 1685, in Barnstaple, Devonshire. Orphaned at age 10, he was sent to the local grammar school until, aged about 17, he was apprenticed to a silk dealer in London. Possibly because of illness, he was released from this apprenticeship in 1706 and returned to Barnstaple. In 1708 he became Aaron Hill's secretary, helping especially with Hill's question-and-answer periodical paper, the *British Apollo*. That year Gay published his first poem, *Wine;* his first published prose, *The Present State of Wit,* a critical account of all the current journals, appeared in 1711.

Gay was domestic steward in the household of the Duchess of Monmouth from 1712 to 1714. Something between a secretary and a wit in residence, Gay gained financial security and freedom to write without loss of independence. As a result, 1713 was a most productive year for him, with the publication of six poems, at least two essays, and a play. The play, *The Wife of Bath,* was a failure; one poem, *The Fan,* was popular enough to establish a poetic fad.

The Shepherd's Week (1714) is a set of six pastorals in which English rural life is realistically portrayed. Gay's literary burlesque *The What D'ye Call It* (1715) was moderately successful. His wonderful three-book poem *Trivia: or, the*

Additional Sources

Melville, Lewis, *Life and letters of John Gay (1685-1732), author of "The beggar's opera,"*, Norwood, Pa.: Norwood Editions, 1975.
Melville, Lewis, *Life and letters of John Gay (1685-1732), author of "The beggar's opera"*, Philadelphia: R. West, 1977.
Nokes, David, *John Gay, a profession of friendship,* Oxford; New York: Oxford University Press, 1995. □

Helene Doris Gayle

Helene Doris Gayle (born 1955) is an AIDS researcher and epidemiologist for the Centers for Disease Control in Atlanta, Georgia.

Helene Doris Gayle is a specialist in the epidemiology of acquired immune deficiency syndrome (AIDS) and the human immunodeficiency virus (HIV) in children and teenagers. She is the coordinator of the AIDS Agency and chief of the HIV/AIDS Division at the U.S. Agency for International Development, Office of Health. In her position she has travelled to Africa and Asia to investigate the ways the disease affects different societies and to help coordinate international efforts to study it.

Born the third of five children on August 16, 1955, in Buffalo, New York. Her father, Jacob Sr., was an entrepreneur and her mother, Marietta, was a psychiatric social worker. Gayle was influenced by her parents from an early age, for her parents impressed upon their children the importance of making a contribution to the world. Gayle was also affected by growing up during the Civil Rights movement, and served as head of the African American student union in her high school.

Gayle pursued a bachelor of arts degree in psychology in 1976 at Barnard University, followed by a medical degree from the University of Pennsylvania in 1981. Medical school opened the door for Gayle to the "social and political aspects of medicine," she told *Ebony* writer Renee D. Turner. After hearing a noted researcher speak on the efforts to eradicate the deadly smallpox virus, Gayle decided to seek a masters of public health, which she received from Johns Hopkins University in 1981. She then began a residency and internship in pediatrics at Children's Hospital Medical Center in Washington, D.C., where she worked for three years.

In 1984, Gayle was accepted to the epidemiology training program at the Centers for Disease Control and Prevention (CDC) in Atlanta, where she focused on the AIDS virus. She held various positions at the CDC, concentrating her efforts on the effect of AIDS on children, adolescents and their families, both in the United States and worldwide. Gayle has found that the U.S. African American community, especially its women, is at high risk of contracting the fatal disease. In the late 1980s, African American women made up 52 percent of the female AIDS population

Art of Walking the Streets of London, published by subscription in 1716 to much acclaim and to the financial relief of the unemployed Gay, was deservedly praised for its originality, humor, and vivid accuracy.

Another play, *Three Hours after Marriage,* was produced in 1716 without great success. The next few years were marked by the successful publication of his collection *Poems* (1720), the libretto for G. F. Handel's *Acis and Galatea* (1722), and a tragedy, *The Captives* (1724). *Gay's Fables* (1727) was long popular with both adults and children.

The Beggar's Opera opened on Jan. 29, 1728, and ran for 62 nights—an unprecedented number—in its first season. This ballad opera, with music by John Pepusch, is a satirical picture of life among London's pickpockets, prostitutes, and highwaymen. Though the sequel, *Polly* (1729), also with music by Pepusch, was banned from performance, its publication brought Gay £1,000. Plagued by ill health, he died on Dec. 4, 1732.

Further Reading

Henry Lee, ed., *Gay's Chair* (1820), contains some spurious early poems but a genuine memoir by Gay's nephew, Joseph Buller. William E. Schultz, *Gay's Beggar's Opera: Its Content, History, and Influence* (1923), is the definitive study of that work. The fullest biography is William H. Irving, *John Gay, Favorite of the Wits* (1962). Patricia M. Spack *John Gay* (1965), is a convenient and reliable critical study, and Sven Armens, *John Gay, Social Critic* (1966), has the emphasis its title suggests.

nationwide even though they only constituted 11 percent of the entire population. Gayle is an advocate for education as an important tool for the prevention of HIV/AIDS; as she told Turner, "Learning more about the spread of the disease also will provide some ammunition" in combating it. Gayle has traveled extensively studying the risk factors which contribute to the spread of HIV/AIDS in her position with the AIDS division for the Agency for International Development. The author of many articles and studies on HIV/AIDS risk factors, Gayle has received numerous awards, including the Henrietta and Jacob Lowenburg Prize, the Gordon Miller Award, and the U.S. Public Health Service achievement medal. She taught at various universities and is on the editorial board of the *Annual Review of Public Health.* Gayle is unmarried and has no children. As she told Turner, "I don't regret having placed a high priority on a career that enables me to make a contribution to mankind." Besides, she added, "we have no choice but to try to make an impact."

Further Reading

Burgess, Marjorie, "Helene D. Gayle," in *Contemporary Black Biography,* Volume 3, Gale, 1993, pp. 74–76.
Black Enterprise, October, 1988.
Turner, Renee D., "The Global AIDS Warrior," in *Ebony* □

Joseph Louis Gay-Lussac

The French chemist and physicist Joseph Louis Gay-Lussac (1778-1850) is distinguished for his work on gas laws and for his studies of the properties of cyanogen and iodine.

B orn at Saint-Léonard in the department of Vienne, Joseph Gay-Lussac came from a solidly bourgeois family. The storms of the French Revolution delayed his education, but largely by his own disciplined self-teaching, he passed the examinations and was admitted to the prestigious École Polytechnique in 1797. Here he became the protégé of Claude Louis Berthollet.

In these early years Gay-Lussac's skill as an experimenter and scientific instrument maker was well developed. In 1802 he published a law of the expansion of gases by heat, which became known as Charles' law. In 1804 he made an ascent of 23,000 feet in a balloon to collect samples of the atmosphere for chemical analyses and to measure the dependence of the earth's magnetic field on elevation. In 1806 Gay-Lussac was elected to the Institut de France, and in 1809 he became a professor of chemistry at the École Polytechnique and professor of physics at the Sorbonne. He invented the portable barometer, steam injector pump, and air thermometer and improved the spirit lamp and the chemist's furnace. In addition to his work on these laboratory devices, he contributed to the production and improvement of industrial chemical machinery and processes, above all in the important sulfuric acid tower which bears his name.

In 1805-1806, through the intervention of Berthollet, Gay-Lussac accompanied the scientific explorer Alexander von Humboldt on his expedition through Italy and Germany making measurements of terrestrial magnetism. While in Rome, the young chemist was able to use the laboratory of Wilhelm von Humboldt, on which occasion he discovered the presence of fluorides and phosphates in the bones of fish. Not long after this, Gay-Lussac met a beautiful girl in a Paris draper's shop, soon became engaged, and then sent his fiancée to school to complete her chemistry education. In 1808 he married her. The marriage lasted for 40 years and was marked by the closest collaboration of hearts and minds.

In addition to his well-known work on the combining properties of gases, Gay-Lussac also worked on the determination of vapor densities, and the coefficients of expansion of gases, in which he pioneered the procedures, and contributed to the careful quantitative measurements that in later years were so useful for grounding the kinetic theory of gases and thermal physics. He published his most influential work in 1808, the law of combining volumes of gases.

Electrolysis and Iodine

Some of Gay-Lussac's best work, however, was done in close collaboration with Louis Jacques Thénard, the chemist who created the foundations of organic analysis. Together they produced the alkali metals in quantity by reacting fused alkalis with red-hot iron. Napoleon made considerable sums available to the École Polytechnique to support their work on electrolysis. However, though aware of the theoretical importance of the electrolytic process, they elaborated a more efficient method of producing the alkali metals.

Gay-Lussac investigated (1813-1814) the chemical properties of iodine and described his findings in a number of papers presented to the Institut de France. However, Sir Humphry Davy, visiting in Paris at the time, wrote a particularly insulting note to the scientific world claiming priority for the discovery of the elemental nature of iodine, asserting that Gay-Lussac had learned the fundamental properties of iodine from him. In yet another controversy Gay-Lussac and Thénard claimed a priority of 36 hours for their isolation of boron. They claimed that the experiment was completed on June 21, 1800, and the results sent to Geneva for publication, whereas Davy's announcement was supposedly dated June 30. It should be noted that the potassium that Davy used to treat borax was produced by using the Thénard-Gay-Lussac method.

Other Achievements

The French partners also carried out extensive investigations on the composition of hydrochloric acid. Individual work by Gay-Lussac on the properties of the sulfates and sulfides, as well as other salts, was an important step in the perfection of what later became known as volumetric analysis. He compiled extensive solubility charts for numerous compounds. Classic work on cyanogen compounds was carried out by him largely on his own. He was also the first to recognize that the CN combination was stable and behaved as a radical in the various combinations into which it entered.

Gay-Lussac served in 1818 as superintendent of the government gunpowder plant and as chief assayer of the national mint in 1829. King Louis Philippe raised him to the peerage in 1839. The honor had been delayed for 17 years, for, argued the old aristocracy, Gay-Lussac worked with his hands. He died on May 9, 1850.

Further Reading

Gay-Lussac is discussed in Sir William A. Tilden, *Famous Chemists: The Men and Their Work* (1921); Edward Farber, ed., *Great Chemists* (1961); and Maurice Crosland, *The Society of Arcueil: A View of French Science at the Time of Napoleon I* (1967). □

Sir Patrick Geddes

The Scottish sociologist, biologist, educator, and town planner Sir Patrick Geddes (1854-1932) is famous for his concepts and achievements in town planning.

P atrick Geddes, born in Ballater on Oct. 2, 1854, was brought up near Perth. Through boyhood explorations of Perthshire and the Highlands, Patrick learned to see rural and urban life as a whole and began to study all living things, including man, in relation to their environment. He graduated from Perth Academy at 16.

After an 18-month apprenticeship in a local bank, Geddes began studies of chemistry, geology, and biology, along with drawing and cabinetmaking. At 20, however, he found his real goal—zoology under T. H. Huxley. Then, while on an expedition to Mexico, a crisis of temporary blindness turned him from "eye-minded" extrovert into philosophical classifier of sciences and inventor of graphic "thinking machines" from folded sheets of paper. Thus arose his combination of Auguste Comte's sociology with Frédéric Le Play's occupational economics of Place-Work-Family into his own graphic double-action formula of Place→Work→Folk::Folk→Work→Place.

Returning to Scotland in April 1880 with weakened eyes which thereafter kept him from the microscope, Geddes became an inspiring lecturer in botany at Edinburgh University and carried on an incredibly varied intellectual and practical life. He urged the application of energy and biology concepts to statistics and economics; lectured on cooperation and socialism, capital, and labor; and campaigned for university extension and other educational reforms.

In 1886 Geddes married Anna Morton, a gifted musician, and they founded the Edinburgh Social Union. Moving into a workers' tenement, they cleaned up by example and

personal labor many of the worst slum dwellings along the Royal Mile.

Accepting a part-time professorship in botany at University College, Dundee, in 1888 (held until 1919), Geddes organized the first summer schools in Europe at Edinburgh (1887-1898) and founded the Outlook Tower (1892) as "the world's first sociological laboratory." Here also came into focus his town planning concepts of civic and regional survey, or "diagnosis before treatment," and of "conservative surgery" instead of wholesale destruction of slum areas. Though biology was being crowded into the background, Geddes did publish the milestone *Evolution of Sex* (1889), in collaboration with his later-famous pupil, J. Arthur Thomson.

In 1897 Geddes and his wife went to Cyprus as private "economic missionaries," reclaiming arid farmlands and starting rural industries as realistic answers to the unsolved "Eastern question" of blundering colonial politicians. In 1899 and 1900 he made lecture tours of the United States, organizing meanwhile the American Section of the International School at the Paris Exposition of 1900. In Paris he launched a bold plan for preserving the best national pavilions of the "Rue des Nations" as permanent international museums and institutes—a UNESCO nearly 50 years ahead of its time! Impossible of realization then, the project has since been termed the greatest of Geddes's "magnificent failures." Another of these was his epoch-making survey of Dunfermline in 1903-1904 for the Scottish trustees of Andrew Carnegie's $2,500,000 gift to his birthplace. Rejected by them but published at Geddes's own expense, the result-

ing *Study in City Development* is today a classic of Geddesian thought and planning methods.

The decade 1914-1924 took Geddes to India and Palestine. He made diagnosis-and-treatment surveys of some 50 Indian urban areas. Among these his 2-volume *Town Planning towards City Development* for Indore in 1918 vies with his 1915 classic, *Cities in Evolution*, in awakening citizens as well as planners to the practical significance of his P→W→F::F→W→P formula. Both works are seasoned with neologisms coined to express new concepts, such as "paleotechnics," "neotechnics," "biotechnics," "conurbation," "megalopolis," "kakatopia," and "eutopia."

In 1919 he gave his farewell address at Dundee, then accepted the chair of sociology and civics at the University of Bombay. Returning to India via Jerusalem, he there made city plans for the military governor and designed a university for the Zionists which, had they built it, would have given the world a model of interdisciplinary and interfaith higher education that might well have provided solutions to age-old Arab-Jewish-Christian conflicts.

In 1924 serious illness forced Geddes's return to Europe, but on reaching southern France he made a remarkable recovery and was soon building a small-scale Outlook Tower and University Hall near Montpellier. In 1925 he could thus open his final project, the Scots College, as the first unit of a Mediterranean "Cité Universitaire." The New Year's Honors of 1932 listed Geddes as Sir Patrick for his services to education. He died in Montpellier on April 17, 1932.

Further Reading

The most recent book on Geddes is Philip Mairet, *Pioneer of Sociology: The Life and Letters of Patrick Geddes* (1957). Philip Boardman, *Patrick Geddes: Maker of the Future* (1944), contains some semifictional material now being weeded out for a revised edition. The first book on Geddes, Amelia Defries's *The Interpreter Geddes: The Man and His Gospel* (1927), is rather disorganized but contains authentic transcriptions of some of his "teaching talks." Another important document is Lewis Mumford's evaluation of Geddes in *The Condition of Man* (1944).

Additional Sources

Boardman, Philip, *The worlds of Patrick Geddes: biologist, town planner, re-educator, peace-warrior,* London; Boston: Routledge and K. Paul, 1978.

Kitchen, Paddy, *A most unsettling person: the life and ideas of Patrick Geddes, founding father of city planning and environmentalism,* New York: Saturday Review Press, 1975.

Mairet, Philip, *Pioneer of sociology: the life and letters of Patrick Geddes,* Westport, Ct.: Hyperion Press, 1979.

Meller, Helen Elizabeth, *Patrick Geddes: social evolutionist and city planner,* London; New York: Routledge, 1990.

Meller, Helen Elizabeth, *Patrick Geddes: social evolutionist and city planner,* London; New York: Routledge, 1993.

Patrick Geddes: a symposium, 1 March 1982, Dundee: Duncan of Jordanstone College of Art: University of Dundee, 1982. □

Geertgen tot Sint Jans

Geertgen tot Sint Jans (ca. 1460-1490) is one of the most beloved Netherlandish primitive painters, noted for his charming naiveté and the purity and simplicity of his style.

The principal source of knowledge concerning Geertgen tot Sint Jans, also called Geertgen van Haarlem, is the Dutch biographer Karel van Mander, who wrote about him in 1604. According to Van Mander, Geertgen was born and lived in Haarlem and was a lay brother in the local Order of St. John as well as a pupil of Albert van Ouwater. Van Mander records that Geertgen died at the age of 28. More recent discoveries, however, suggest that he was actually born in Leiden and that he served a portion of his apprenticeship in Flanders, probably at Bruges. In any case, his paintings display a marked Flemish influence, especially from the works of Hugo van der Goes.

The earliest painting attributed to Geertgen is the *Holy Kinship* (ca. 1480), which shows a strong reliance upon Van Ouwater both in the treatment of the static, doll-like figures and in the construction of the luminous architectural setting. Geertgen's *Adoration of the Magi* in Cleveland, from a few years later, reveals the added inspiration of Van der Goes for the composition and the quality of the continuous landscape recession.

Geertgen's later works are characterized by feelings of intense devotion as well as increasing formal innovation. A small *Nativity* in London, for example, is not only profoundly emotive but highly original, representing as it does the first true nocturne in Western art. In much the same way, the famous *St. John the Baptist in the Wilderness* is expressive of deep religious sentiment yet also reveals the "most advanced conception of landscape to appear in 15th-century Flemish painting" (Charles D. Cuttler, 1968). For the high altar of the Commandery of the Order of St. John in Haarlem, Geertgen executed a gigantic altarpiece of which two major fragments survive. Entitled the *Lamentation* and the *Burning of the Bones of John the Baptist*, these works are noted for their unified landscape spaces and the contrived and elaborate grouping of the figures. A section of the latter painting, in particular, contains the first posed group portrait in Dutch art, the persons depicted being members of the artist's own monastic community.

Geertgen's late style is represented by the painting *Man of Sorrows*. In this shockingly original and emotional panel, the brutally beaten figure of Christ, surrounded by the instruments of his Passion, is posed against a stark gold background that transports the event outside of earthly time and space. In this, one of the most richly creative products of the artist's imagination, Geertgen expressed his deep individual piety and his spiritual kinship to the great religious mystics of the late Middle Ages.

Further Reading

There is no full-length work on Geertgen in English. With the exception of short accounts in Erwin Panofsky, *Early Netherlandish Painting* (2 vols., 1953); Charles D. Cuttler, *Northern Painting* (1968); and a few articles in journals, all other material on Geertgen is in German or Dutch. □

Clifford Geertz

The American cultural anthropologist Clifford Geertz (born 1926) did ethnographic field work in Indonesia and Morocco, wrote influential essays on central theoretical issues in the social sciences, and advocated a distinctive "interpretive" approach to anthropology.

Clifford Geertz was born in San Francisco on August 23, 1926. After serving in the U.S. Navy during World War II, he received a B.A. from Antioch College in 1950 and a Ph.D. from Harvard University in 1956. Having held a number of brief appointments early in his career, he took a position at the University of Chicago in 1960, where he was rapidly promoted to associate and then full professor. In 1970 he joined the Institute for Advanced Study in Princeton, New Jersey, as professor of social science, a position of rare distinction which he still occupied in 1995. Over the years Geertz received a considerable number of honors and awards, including honorary degrees from several institutions. In 1958 and 1959 he was a fellow at the Center for Advanced Study in the Behavioral Sciences (Stanford) and in 1978-1979 he served as Eastman Professor at Oxford University. His books won major prizes, including the prestigious 1988 National Book Critics Circle Award for Criticism for *Works and Lives: The Anthropologist as Author.*

In 1952 Geertz first went to Indonesia with a team of investigators to study Modjokuto, a small town in east central Java, where he and his wife lived for more than a year. On the basis of his research there Geertz wrote his dissertation, later published in 1960 as *The Religion of Java.* A comprehensive analysis of Javanese religion in its social context, this book presents a picture of a highly religious culture composed of at least three main strands (related to different population groups). These include a traditional kind of animism, Islam (itself internally diverse), and a Hindu-influenced refined mysticism.

In later years Geertz returned to Java but also spent extensive periods in Tabanan, a small town in Bali. Initially treated with complete indifference by the Balinese, Geertz and his wife gained significant access to their community. He presented his interpretation of his time there in a classic essay on the Balinese cockfight. Both in the matching of the cocks and in the bets surrounding the fight, the Balinese dramatized their concern with maintaining a definite hierarchy of rivalries and groups in which everyone had his or her fixed place.

Geertz carried out field work in Sefrou, a town in north central Morocco, in the 1960s and early 1970s, enabling him to compare two "extremes" of Islamic civilization: homogeneous and morally severe in Morroco and blended with other traditions and less concerned with scriptural doctrine in Indonesia. In both countries he found traditional religion affected by the process of secularization; whereas people used to "be held" by taken-for-granted beliefs, in modern societies they increasingly have to "hold" their beliefs in a much more conscious (and anxious) fashion. Geertz published *Islam Observed in 1968* .

In his early work Geertz investigated why certain communities achieved greater economic growth and modernization than others. For example, he found that the "ego-focused" market peddlers of Modjokuto, who only looked out for their own and their families' gain, were in a less favorable position than the "group-focused" Tabanan aristocrats. The latter group could use their traditional prestige to mobilize communal resources for new investments, even though they had to temper their modern entrepreneurial drive with concern for the well-being of their community.

Geertz also authored a number of essays which elaborate on his theories, including *The Interpretation of Cultures* in 1973 and *Local Knowledge* in 1983.

In 1995, Geertz published *After the Fact: Two Countries, Four Decades, One Anthropologist*. In the book, he charted the transformation of cultural anthropology from a study of primitive people to a multidisciplinary investigation of a culture's symbolic systems and its interactions with the larger forces of history and modernization. Geertz used the greatest strength of anthropology (the ability to compare cultures). His periods of extended fieldwork in Indonesia and Morocco enabled him to view each through the lens of the other. He also used anecdotes in the book of non-western countries tackling the same social questions as Western countries: national identity, moral order, and competing values.

Throughout his career Geertz tried to make sense of the ways people live their lives by interpreting cultural symbols such as ceremonies, political gestures, and literary texts. Geertz was also interested in the role of thought (especially religious thought) in society. Analyzing this role properly, he argued, requires "thick description," a probing appraisal of the meanings people's actions have for them in their own circumstances—a method Geertz tried to demonstrate in his own work. Skeptical of attempts to develop abstract theories of human behavior but sensitive to issues of universal human concern, he emphasized that anthropologists should focus on the rich texture of the lives of real human beings. Yet he showed that in writing about others one necessarily transforms "their" world; the very style in which social scientists write conveys their distinctive interpretation. Geertz' own highly sophisticated, but dense and occasionally convoluted writing style exemplifies his influential "interpretive" approach to cultural anthropology.

Further Reading

The titles and publication dates of Geertz' main works clearly show the focus and evolution of his interests: *The Religion of Java* (1960), *Agricultural Involution: The Process of Ecological Change in Indonesia* (1963), which explains the colonial background of and economic constraints inherent in labor-intensive Japanese agriculture; *Peddlers and Princes: Social Change and Economic Modernization in Two Indonesian Towns* (1963), a readable comparative study; *Person, Time, and Conduct in Bali: An Essay in Cultural Analysis* (1966); *Islam Observed: Religious Development in Morocco and Indonesia* (1968), a small but elegantly written near-classic comparative analysis; *The Interpretation of Cultures* (1973), a well-crafted set of highly influential theoretical essays and illustrative case studies; *Meaning and Order in Moroccan Society* (1979), with L. Rosen and H. Geertz; *Negara: The Theatre State in Nineteenth-Century Bali* (1980); *Local Knowledge: Further Essays in Interpretive Anthropology* (1983); and *Works and Lives: The Anthropologist as Author* (1988), a subtle analysis of the works of four outstanding anthropologists.

For autobiographical resources see: Geertz, Clifford, *After the Fact: Two Countries, Four Decades, One Anthropologist*, Harvard University Press, 1995. For biographical resources see: Morgan, John H., *Understanding Religion and Culture—Anthropological and Theological Perspectives*, University Press of America, 1979 and Rice, Kenneth, *Geertz and Culture*, University of Michigan Press.

For periodical articles about Clifford Geertz see: *Publishers Weekly*, January 2, 1995; *The New York Times Magazine*, April 9, 1995; *The Chronicle of Higher Education*, May 5, 1995; and *New Statesman and Society*, June 2, 1995.

For on-line resources about Clifford Geertz see: http://userwww.sfsu.edu/~rsauzier/Geertz.html asnd http://www.biography.com. □

Frank O. Gehry

Frank O. Gehry (Frank O. Goldberg; born 1929) was an American architect whose sculptured designs and use of vernacular materials won him somewhat belated but widespread recognition.

Frank O. Gehry was born in 1929 in Toronto, Canada, and moved to Los Angeles in 1947 with his parents, Irving and Thelma Goldberg (he changed his name in the mid-1950s). He studied at the University of Southern California from 1949 to 1951. After receiving practical experience as a designer in a Los Angeles firm, he returned to USC to complete his Bachelor of Architecture degree in 1954. Gehry studied City Planning at the Harvard Graduate School of Design in Massachusetts, an important center for the dissemination of the International Style. Leaving Harvard in 1957, the architect returned to the West Coast to work for a variety of firms before opening his own practice, Frank O. Gehry and Associates, Inc., in Los Angeles in 1962.

In retrospect it seems understandable that Gehry would move quickly to establish himself as an independent because he was a highly individual designer and talent. Gehry's childhood idol was Frank Lloyd Wright, who created a number of homes in the Los Angeles area during the 1920s. The bold individuality of Wright's California dwellings had an impact on Gehry's attitude toward house design. Also as a result of living and working in California, Gehry was exposed to the so-called "California progressives". Prominent in this group were Bernard Maybeck, Irving Gill, and Charles and Henry Greene; these designers were interested in experimentation with structure, materials, or form. Yet any suggestion that Gehry is a direct descendant of the progressive movement in California radically underestimates his own unique nature.

Critics falter when attempting to label or categorize Frank Gehry's work and attitudes. While some have called his architecture "post-modern" (referring to a movement that rejects the International Style in favor of pre-modernist ideas and models), Gehry's attitude is neither modern nor post-modern. Others have labeled him a deconstructivist, pairing him with such contemporary figures as Peter Eisenman who dismember (or "deconstruct") traditional shapes and forms in an attempt to free architecture from its theoretical and historical past. In short, what makes Gehry difficult to classify is his freedom from the constraints of popular theories, both past and present.

While Gehry rejects the minimalism of International Style architecture, he does appreciate the movement's love of man-made materials. Gehry goes further than International Style designers in embracing corrugated metal, chain link, and plywood. He celebrates these 20th-century materials in what he calls "cheapscape architecture." Gehry used these materials in his "Santa Monica Place", a low-budget shopping mall and parking garage of 1979-1981, as well as in his own home, also in Santa Monica, of 1977-1979. Yet through the years these inexpensive materials have become common in his work and are even regarded by some as his "signature".

If some of Gehry's buildings, including his residence in Santa Monica, appear to display qualities of deconstructivist architecture, they are created without the intellectual baggage of that movement. In his house project, the architect purchased a quaint 1920s suburban home, and wrapped it in chain link, other metals, plywood, and glass, thus creating the effect of an old house carefully preserved inside a newer one. Here his impulse was anything but deconstructivist; the "old" house gave meaning to the "new," and vice versa.

Gehry's architecture is characterized by an inclusive approach. He designs his buildings with a concern for the way people move through them. They are able to live and work comfortably within the spaces that he has created. His buildings are created to address the culture and context of their sites. In 1995 Gehry designed a building for the Department of Art at the University of Toledo, Canada; the building's architectural form was intended to represent the students' creative energy. In 1997 Gehry worked with the Experience Music Project (EMP) to design a 110,000 square foot complex scheduled to open in 1999 and comprised of an interactive museum, education center, and restaurant/nightclub showcasing live music. In the spirit of capturing the nature of contemporary music, the design for the building calls for fractured forms that will resemble guitar bodies. Exhibition spaces will resemble industrial rooms with pull down doors - a tribute to contemporary bands' beginnings in warehouses and garages. "I share EMP's goal of creating a place where the exhibits and the building treat music as a living and evolving art form," Gehry said in an article in *TCI,* March 1997.

Gehry stated once that "I approach each building as a sculptural object." In keeping with his sensitivity to sculpture and painting, Gehry enjoyed working with other artists in creating multimedia pieces. Perhaps the most famous of these projects was his collaboration with Claes Oldenburg and Coosje van Bruggen in an outdoor theater spectacular in Venice in the mid-1980s. The architect has said that the irreverent Oldenburg was a continuing source of inspiration. Gehry also worked with the sculptor Richard Serra. An outgrowth of their contact was a furniture series in which Gehry created a number of lamps that resembled coiled fish. Other official contacts with the arts community have included the designing of homes for artists, as in Gehry's 1972 Malibu studio for the painter Ron Davis.

Partly because of his irreverent approach to design, Gehry belatedly received recognition from the official world of art and architecture. An important showing of his work at the Whitney Museum of Art in 1988 signaled the beginning of this new attitude of respect and appreciation. The following year he received the Pritzker Architecture Prize, the profession's top international award. In 1991 Gehry won two awards from the American Institute of Architects for a "spunky and provocative" nine-story warehouse in Boston and a "village-like" sequence of low buildings for a furniture maker in Rocklin, California. In 1992 Gehry was awarded the Wolf Prize in Art, as well as the

Imperiale Award in Architecture given by the Japan Art Association. In October 1994, Gehry became the first recipient of the Lillian Gish Award for lifetime contribution to the arts.

Gehry's models, drawings, sketches and furniture designs have been collected in important museums all over the world and presented in numerous exhibitions. One of the most important exhibitions was presented in 1986 by the Walker Art Museum in Minnesota. The exhibit toured throughout the U.S. and Canada.

Further Reading

To learn more about the architecture of Gehry and his peers—and see excellent illustrations of their works—consult *Postmodern Visions,* edited by Heinrich Klotz (1985) and *The Language of Post-Modern Architecture* by Charles Jencks (1987). Two fine collections of writings on contemporary architecture that feature chapters on Gehry's house in Santa Monica are *The Secret Life of Buildings* (1985) by Gavin Macrae-Gibson and *The Critical Edge* (1985) by Tod Marder. Two monographs devoted to the life and works of Gehry are *The Architecture of Frank Gehry* (1988) and *Frank Gehry: Buildings and Projects* (1986), edited by Peter Arnell and Ted Bickford. Paul Goldberger has written several interesting articles on the architect, including "Studied Slapdash" in the *New York Times Magazine* (January 18, 1976). A perceptive appraisal of Gehry's place in the contemporary architectural scene is Janet Nairn's "Frank Gehry: the Search for a 'No Rules' Architecture" in *Architectural Record* (June 1976).

For autobiographical works see: Gehry, Frank O., *Individual Imagination and Cultural Conservatism, Volume I,* Academy Editions, 1995. For biographical resources about Frank Gehry see: Eisennan, Peter and Gehry, Frank, *Peter Eisennan and Frank Gehry,* Rizolli International Publications, 1991 and Steele, James, *Schnabel House: Frank Gehry (Architecture in Detail),* Phaidon Chronicle Books, 1993.

For periodical articles about Frank Gehry see: *Architectural Record,* July 1993; May 1994; and *TCI,* March 1997.

For on-line resources about Frank Geertz see: http://www.bm30.es/proyectos/gugge_uk.html, http://www.cf.ac.uk/uwcc/archi/jonesmd/la/index.html, http://www.cf.ac.uk/uwcc/archi/jonesmd/la/surf/chiat.html, http://hudson.acad.umn.edu/Frankbio.html, http://ted.com/ghery.html, and http://www.x-com.de/busstops/gehry.bio.html. □

Hans Geiger

Hans Geiger (1882–1945) invented the Geiger counter.

Hans Geiger was a German nuclear physicist best known for his invention of the Geiger counter, a device used for counting atomic particles, and for his pioneering work in nuclear physics with Ernest Rutherford.

Johannes Wilhelm Geiger was born in Neustadt an-der-Haardt (now Neustadt an-der-Weinstrasse), Rhineland-Palatinate, Germany, on September 30, 1882. His father, Wilhelm Ludwig Geiger, was a professor of philology at the

University of Erlangen from 1891 to 1920. The eldest of five children, two boys and three girls, Geiger was educated initially at Erlangen Gymnasium, from which he graduated in 1901. After completing his compulsory military service, he studied physics at the University of Munich, and at the University of Erlangen where his tutor was Professor Eilhard Wiedemann. He received a doctorate from the latter institution in 1906 for his thesis on electrical discharges through gases.

That same year, Geiger moved to Manchester University in England to join its esteemed physics department. At first he was an assistant to its head, Arthur Schuster, an expert on gas ionization. When Schuster departed in 1907, Geiger continued his research with Schuster's successor, Ernest Rutherford, and the young physicist Ernest Marsden. Rutherford was to have a profound influence on young Geiger, sparking his interest in nuclear physics. Their relationship, which began as partners on some of Geiger's most important experiments, was lifelong and is documented in a series of letters between them.

In addition to supervising the research students working at the lab, Geiger began a series of experiments with Rutherford on radioactive emissions, based on Rutherford's detection of the emission of alpha particles from radioactive substances. Together they began researching these alpha particles, discovering among other things that two alpha particles appeared to be released when uranium disintegrated. Since alpha particles can penetrate through thin walls of solids, Rutherford and Geiger presumed that they could move straight through atoms. Geiger designed the

apparatus that they used to shoot streams of alpha particles through gold foil and onto a screen where they were observed as scintillations, or tiny flashes of light.

Manually counting the thousands of scintillations produced per minute was a laborious task. Geiger was reputedly something of a workaholic, who put in long hours recording the light flashes. David Wilson noted in *Rutherford: Simple Genius* that in a 1908 letter to his friend Henry A. Bumstead, Rutherford remarked, "Geiger is a good man and work[s] like a slave. . . . [He] is a demon at the work and could count at intervals for a whole night without disturbing his equanimity. I damned vigorously after two minutes and retired from the conflict." Geiger was challenged by the haphazardness of their methodology to invent a more precise technique. His solution was a primitive version of the "Geiger counter," the machine with which his name is most often associated. This prototype was essentially a highly sensitive electrical device designed to count alpha particle emissions.

Geiger's simple but ingenious measuring device enabled him and Rutherford to discern that alpha particles are, in fact, doubly charged nuclear particles, identical to the nucleus of helium atoms traveling at high velocity. The pair also established the basic unit of electrical charge when it is involved in electrical activity, which is equivalent to that carried by a single hydrogen atom. These results were published in two joint papers in 1908 entitled "An Electrical Method of Counting the Number of Alpha Particles" and "The Charge and Nature of the Alpha Particle."

In bombarding the gold with the alpha particles Geiger and Rutherford observed that the majority of the particles went straight through. However, they unexpectedly found that a few of the particles were deflected or scattered upon contact with the atoms in the gold, indicating that they had come into contact with a very powerful electrical field. Rutherford's description of the event as recorded by Wilson revealed its importance: "It was as though you had fired a fifteen-inch shell at a piece of tissue paper and it had bounced back and hit you." These observations were jointly published by Geiger and Marsden in an article entitled "On a Diffuse Reflection of the Alpha-Particles" for the *Proceedings of the Royal Society* in June of 1909.

Thirty years later Geiger recollected, "At first we could not understand this at all," Wilson noted. Geiger continued to study the scattering effect, publishing two more papers about it that year. The first, with Rutherford, was entitled "The Probability Variations in the Distribution of Alpha-Particles." The second, referring to his work with Marsden, dealt with "The Scattering of Alpha-Particles by Matter." Geiger's work with Rutherford and Marsden finally inspired Rutherford in 1910 to conclude that the atoms contained a positively charged core or nucleus which repelled the alpha particles. Wilson noted Geiger's recollection that "One day Rutherford, obviously in the best of spirits, came into my [laboratory] and told me that he now knew what the atom looked like and how to explain the large deflections of the alpha-particles. On the very same day, I began an experiment to test the relation expected by Rutherford between

the number of scattered particles and the angle of scattering."

Geiger's results were accurate enough to persuade Rutherford to go public with his discovery in 1910. Nonetheless, Geiger and Marsden continued their experiments to test the theory for another year, completing them in June of 1912. Their results were published in German in Vienna in 1912 and in English in the *Philosophical Magazine* in April of 1913. Wilson noted that Dr. T. J. Trenn, a modern physics scholar, characterized Geiger's and Marsden's work of this period: "It was not the Geiger-Marsden scattering evidence, as such, that provided massive support for Rutherford's model of the atom. It was, rather, the constellation of evidence available gradually from the spring of 1913 and this, in turn, coupled with a growing conviction, tended to increase the significance or extrinsic value assigned to the Geiger-Marsden results beyond that which they intrinsically possessed in July 1912."

In 1912 Geiger gave his name to the Geiger-Nuttal law, which states that radioactive atoms with short half-lives emit alpha particles at high speed. He later revised it, and in 1928, a new theory by George Gamow and other physicists made it redundant. Also in 1912 Geiger returned to Germany to take up a post as director of the new Laboratory for Radioactivity at the Physikalisch-Technische Reichsanstalt in Berlin, where he invented an instrument for measuring not only alpha particles but beta rays and other types of radiation as well.

Geiger's research was broadened the following year with the arrival at the laboratory of James Chadwick and Walter Bothe, two distinguished nuclear physicists. With the latter, Geiger formed what would be a long and fruitful professional association, investigating various aspects of radioactive particles together. However, their work was interrupted by the outbreak of the First World War. Enlisted with the German troops, Geiger fought as an artillery officer opposite many of his old colleagues from Manchester including Marsden and H. G. J. Moseley from 1914 to 1918. The years spent crouching in trenches on the front lines left Geiger with painful rheumatism. With the war over, Geiger resumed his post at the Reichsanstalt, where he continued his work with Bothe. In 1920, Geiger married Elisabeth Heffter, with whom he had three sons.

Geiger moved from the Reichsanstalt in 1925 to become professor of physics at the University of Kiel. His responsibilities included teaching students and guiding a sizable research team. He also found time to develop, with Walther Mueller, the instrument with which his name is most often associated: the Geiger-Mueller counter, commonly referred to as the Geiger counter. Electrically detecting and counting alpha particles, the counter can locate a speeding particle within about one centimeter in space and to within a hundred-millionth second in time. It consists of a small metal container with an electrically insulated wire at its heart to which a potential of about 1000 volts is applied. In 1925, Geiger used his counter to confirm the Compton effect, that is, the scattering of X rays, which settled the existence of light quantum, or packets of energy.

Geiger left Kiel for the University of Tubingen in October of 1929 to serve as professor of physics and director of research at its physics institute. Installed at the Institute, Geiger worked tirelessly to increase the Geiger counter's speed and sensitivity. As a result of his efforts, he was able to discover simultaneous bursts of radiation called cosmic-ray showers, and concentrated on their study for the remainder of his career.

Geiger returned to Berlin in 1936 upon being offered the chair of physics at the Technische Hochschule. His upgrading of the counter and his work on cosmic rays continued. He was also busy leading a team of nuclear physicists researching artificial radioactivity and the by-products of nuclear fission (the splitting of the atom's nucleus). Also in 1936 Geiger took over editorship of the journal *Zeitschrift für Physik,* a post he maintained until his death. It was at this time that Geiger also made a rare excursion into politics, prompted by the rise to power in Germany of Adolf Hitler's National Socialist Party. The Nazis sought to harness physics to their ends and engage the country's scientists in work that would benefit the Third Reich. Geiger and many other prominent physicists were appalled by the specter of political interference in their work by the Nazis. Together with Werner Karl Heisenberg and Max Wien, Geiger composed a position paper representing the views of most physicists, whether theoretical, experimental, or technical. As these men were politically conservative, their decision to oppose the National Socialists was taken seriously, and seventy-five of Germany's most notable physicists put their names to the Heisenberg-Wien-Geiger Memorandum. It was presented to the Reich Education Ministry in late 1936.

The document lamented the state of physics in Germany, claiming that there were too few up-and-coming physicists and that students were shying away from the subject because of attacks on theoretical physics in the newspapers by National Socialists. Theoretical and experimental physics went hand in hand, it continued, and attacks on either branch should cease. The Memorandum seemed to put a stop to attacks on theoretical physics, in the short term at least. It also illustrated how seriously Geiger and his associates took the threat to their work from the Nazis.

Geiger continued working at the Technische Hochschule through the war, although toward the latter part he was increasingly absent, confined to bed with rheumatism. In 1938 Geiger was awarded the Hughes Medal from the Royal Academy of Science and the Dudell Medal from the London Physics Society. He had only just started to show signs of improvement in his health when his home near Babelsberg was occupied in June of 1945. Suffering badly, Geiger was forced to flee and seek refuge in Potsdam, where he died on September 24, 1945.

Further Reading

Beyerchen, Alan D., *Scientists under Hitler: Politics and the Physics Community in the Third Reich,* Yale University Press, 1979.
Dictionary of Scientific Biography, Volume 5, Scribner, 1972, pp. 330–333.
Williams, Trevor I., *A Biographical Dictionary of Scientists,* John Wiley & Sons, 1982, p. 211.
Wilson, David, *Rutherford: Simple Genius,* MIT Press, 1983.
"Geiger and Proportional Counters," in *Nucleonics,* December, 1947, pp. 69–75.
"Hughes Medal Awarded to Professor Hans Geiger," in *Nature,* Volume 124, 1929, p. 893.
Krebs, A. T., "Hans Geiger: Fiftieth Anniversary of the Publication of His Doctoral Thesis, 23 July 1906," in *Science,* Volume 124, 1956, p. 166.
"Memories of Rutherford in Manchester," in *Nature,* Volume 141, 1938, p. 244. □

Ernesto Geisel

Ernesto Geisel (1908-1996) was a Brazilian army general, president of Brazil's national oil company (Petrobras), and president of the Republic (1974-1979). As president he began the process of disengaging the military from control of the Brazilian government.

Ernesto Geisel was the fourth general to serve a term as president of Brazil during the so-called Military Republic (1964-1985). He belonged to a group of officers known as Castellistas (after President [General] Humberto de Castello Branco, 1964-1967) who did not favor continued military rule but who had lost out to those who did. Geisel's selection signaled the beginning of a nine-year process aimed at establishing a civilian presidency. He had the distinction of being the first Protestant to preside over the largest Catholic population in the world.

Son of a German Lutheran immigrant, Geisel and his brother, Orlando, used the military as the means of upward social and economic mobility. Both he and his brother achieved generals' stars, the latter serving as minister of the army (1969-1974). Born on August 3, 1908, in Bento Gonçalves, in the heart of Rio Grande do Sul's wine country where his father taught in the Lutheran school, Ernesto Geisel received his secondary education in the military school in Porto Alegre (1921-1924). He acquired his military preparation in the Escola Militar do Realengo, from which he was graduated first in the class of 1928 as an *Aspirante* in artillery.

Early Military Career

As a lieutenant he participated in the Revolution of 1930 on the side of the victorious forces of Getúlio Vargas. His early career mixed military and civilian assignments: as battery commander, as general secretary of the Rio Grande do Norte state government (1931), and as treasury and public works secretary in Paraiba (1934, 1935). This activity identified him with the military reformers known as *tenentes* (lieutenants). He helped suppress the revolt of São Paulo (1932) and the Communist uprising of 1935. He taught at the Realengo military school between 1938 and 1941 and completed the general staff course in 1943.

In early 1945 he was one of a large group of Brazilian officers who took a special course at the U.S. Army's Command and General Staff School at Fort Leavenworth, Kansas. In October 1945 he was chief of staff of an important armed unit in Rio de Janeiro which played a key role in the deposition of Vargas. In the next decade, as he advanced in rank, he served on the National Security Council staff (1946-1947), as military attache in Uruguay (1948-1950), on the Armed Forces General Staff (1950-1952), on the faculty of the Escola Superior de Guerra (1952-1955), and on President João Cafe Filho's military staff.

As a Military/Political Leader

In 1957, while chief of the Army General Staff's intelligence section, he sat on the National Petroleum Council, beginning a long association with Brazilian oil. Promoted to brigadier general in March 1960, he was in command of the military zone in which Brasília is located when Brazil entered into political crisis with the resignation of President Janio Quadros and the military's subsequent resistance to Vargas' protegé Vice President João Goulart assuming the presidency. Though Goulart became chief of state, the crisis continued until he was deposed by a combination of political, business, and military opponents at the end of March 1964.

Geisel was one of the high-ranking officers linked to the Escola Superior de Guerra in Rio de Janeiro who played an important role in the conspiracy, seizure of power, and planning for the political, economic, and administrative reorganization of Brazil. He successfully worked with sev-

eral other like-minded generals for the selection of Army Chief of Staff Humberto de Castello Branco to complete Goulart's term of office. As chief of Castello's military staff, Geisel was intimately involved in the administration's decision-making processes.

Under Castello, he worked to stop the use of torture and other extreme methods by hard-line officers who believed that "bad Brazilians" wanted to turn the country toward Communism and so had to be dealt with harshly. Geisel and Castello Branco believed that the military should clean up the government, reform the economy, and then turn power back to civilians at the end of the term in March 1967. The subsequent struggle for control of this conservative revolution saw the Castellistas forced to cede ground to the radical demands of the hard-liners.

In October 1965 when the Congress refused to approve a law that would have given the government greater power to intervene in the states, to judge civilians in military courts, and to suspend political rights of adversaries, Castello Branco decreed Additional Act II to the constitution abolishing political parties and establishing indirect presidential elections. Over Geisel's objections, Castello, seeking to preserve military unity, agreed to hard-liners' demands that instead of a civilian, the next president would be Minister of War Artur Costa e Silva. Geisel argued that "we are selling the future for a precipitous solution to a present [problem]." He was correct; giving in to the right only prolonged military rule and only preserved a superficial military unity.

Years with Petrobras

During the Costa e Silva administration (1967-1969), Geisel, now a four-star general, sat as a judge on the Supreme Military Tribunal. Retiring from the army in 1969, he was appointed president of the national oil company, Petrobras, which he turned toward the production and distribution of derivatives and toward extensive exploration abroad and in Brazilian coastal waters. While a nationalist, he took the reasonable position that Petrobras was a means to supply Brazil with sufficient petroleum and not a barrier against foreign investment.

His years at Petrobras coincided with a period of economic growth during which annual rates rose to 12 percent. Unhappily, the investments in Brazil's productive capacity came out of savings resulting from low wages, while criticism and labor unrest were suppressed with arrests, torture, and censorship. The military hard-liners formed an organizational structure outside the normal command structure. A so-called "intelligence community" comprising the National Intelligence Service (SNI) and the intelligence services of the army, air force, and navy grew up after 1968. Army intelligence set up a network throughout Brazil of Departments of Internal Operations (DOIs). Government agencies and universities all had special agents assigned to them. Spies and informers proliferated. Institutionalized violence became the order of the day, as interrogation in a DOI commonly included torture. Within the armed forces this "outside" parallel activity generated divisions, irritation, and shame, while among civilians it made the military an object of distrust and contempt.

As President

It was in this atmosphere that Geisel came to the presidency. Nomination as the government party's candidate was tantamount to election, and the choice was in the hands of President Emílio Garrastazu Médici, who the military had put in office when Costa e Silva suffered a stroke in 1969. Preceding the official decision there was an intense behind-the-scenes struggle between the hard-liners and the more moderate Castellistas, now led by Geisel. He was helped by the fact that his brother, Orlando, was minister of the army and that a close ally, General João Figueiredo, was chief of Médici's military staff.

Though not immediately understood by civilians or by the United States government analysts, Geisel's rise to power marked a shift away from repression and toward the path to democratic rule. The hard-liners contested his authority over the repressive apparatus in several incidents of torture and/or disappearance. Geisel replied vigorously to such challenges, replacing various commanders with trusted subordinates. He labelled his political program *distenção*—"the slow, gradual, and secure relaxation" of control measures. It would be "the maximum of development possible with the minimum of indispensible security."

His economic policy sought to maintain high rates of growth while attempting to deal with the effects of the oil price shocks. His national development plan called for massive investments in basic infra-structure such as highways, telecommunications, hydro-electric dams, mineral extraction, factories, and atomic energy. At the risk of bruising nationalist sentiments, the government opened Brazil to prospecting by foreign oil companies for the first time since the early 1950s. The massive Itaipu dam on the Paraná river border with Paraguay symbolizes the era. Brazil borrowed billions of dollars to pour into concrete and steel as investment in future development.

The economic necessities resulted in a markedly different foreign policy. Strict alignment with the United States and a world view based on ideological frontiers and blocs gave way to "responsible pragmatism." Accepting its then 80 percent dependence on imported oil and American inability to assist, Brazil modified its pro-Israeli stance and called for Israel to withdraw from Arab lands occupied in the 1967 war. Closer ties were established with Saudi Arabia and Iraq. Brazil recognized China, Angola, and Mozambique and moved closer to Latin America, Europe, and Japan. Its 1975 agreement to build nuclear reactors with what was then West Germany led to conflict with the Carter administration, which was also, oddly enough, criticizing the Geisel government for the very human rights abuses that it was struggling to stop. In frustration at American high-handedness and lack of understanding, the Geisel administration renounced Brazil's military alliance with the United States.

Politically, Geisel's last two years as president centered on the question of succession, which led to further confrontations with the hard-liners. Admitting that Brazil enjoyed only "relative democracy," Geisel did not hesitate in April 1977 to rewrite the rules of the political game to contain the opposition parties and to dismiss the far-right minister of the army, General Sílvio Frota, in October 1977. Curiously, though distenção presupposed a more open, decentralized political system, Geisel employed a highly centralized decision-making process in his administration.

In 1978 with the Frota crisis behind him, Geisel had to deal with the first labor strikes since 1964 and successive election victories by the opposition Brazilian Democratic Movement party. He eased restrictions on exiles, reestablished *habeas corpus,* annulled the government's extraordinary powers decrees, and imposed João Figueiredo as his successor.

When he left office in March 1979 Brazil was less dependent on foreign imports and was a major industrial goods exporter, but on the negative side it was suffering a 42 percent inflationary rate and was over $43 billion in debt to foreign lenders. His determination to disengage the military from control of government, while gradually reestablishing democratic practices, marked his administration. The basic economic infrastructure that the Geisel years provided will carry Brazilian development into the 21st century. Geisel died of cancer in September 1996.

Further Reading

There are no biographies of Geisel in English. There is a good summary of 20th-century Brazilian history in Thomas E. Skidmore and Peter H. Smith, *Modern Latin America* (1984) and a useful review of recent decades in Robert Wesson and David V. Fleischer, *Brazil in Transition* (1983); Jerry Dubrowski, "Brazilian ex-military ruler Ernesto Geisel dies" *Reuters* (September 12, 1996) □

Theodor Geisel (Dr. Seuss)

Theodor Geisel (1904–1991), better known as Dr. Seuss, wrote the popular children's book *The Cat in the Hat*.

Theodor Geisel, better known to millions of children as Dr. Seuss, brought a whimsical touch and a colorful imagination to the world of children's books. Before Geisel, juvenile books were largely pastel, predictable, and dominated by a didactic tone. Though Dr. Seuss books sometimes included morals, they sounded less like behavioral guidelines and more like, "listen to your feelings" and "take care of the environment," universal ideas that would win over the hearts of youngsters from around the world; Geisel's 47 books were translated into 20 languages and have sold more than 200 million copies. Of the ten bestselling hardcover children's books of all time, four were written by Geisel: *The Cat in the Hat, Green Eggs and Ham, One Fish, Two Fish, Red Fish, Blue Fish,* and *Hop on Pop.*

Wrote for Adults as well as Children

Geisel's last two books spent several months on the bestseller lists and include themes that appeal to adults as well as children. "Finally I can say that I write not for kids but for *people*," he commented in the *Los Angeles Times*. Many of his readers were surprised to learn that Geisel had no children of his own, though he had stepchildren from his second marriage to Audrey Stone Dimond; he once said, "You make 'em, I amuse 'em," as quoted in the *Chicago Tribune*. According to the *Los Angeles Times*, the author also remarked, "I don't think spending your days surrounded by kids is necessary to write the kind of books I write. . . . Once a writer starts talking down to kids, he's lost. Kids can pick up on that kind of thing."

Practiced Drawing at the Zoo

When he was a child, Geisel practiced sketching at the local zoo, where his father was superintendent. He went on to graduate from Dartmouth College in 1925 and subsequently studied at the Lincoln College of Oxford University. After dropping out of Oxford, he traveled throughout Europe, mingling with emigres in Paris, including writer Ernest Hemingway. Eventually returning to New York, he spent 15 years in advertising before joining the army and making two Oscar-winning documentaries, *Hitler Lives* and *Design for Death*.

Geisel began writing the verses of his first book, *And to Think That I Saw It on Mulberry Street,* in 1936 during a rough sea passage. Published a year later, the book won much acclaim, largely because of its unique drawings. All of Geisel's books, in fact, feature crazy-looking creatures that are sometimes based on real animals, but usually consist of such bizarre combinations of objects as a centipede and a horse and a camel with a feather duster on its head. Unlike many puppeteers and cartoonists who have capitalized on their creations by selling their most familiar images to big-time toymakers, though, Dr. Seuss concentrated his efforts on creating captivating books.

"Basically an Educator"

Admired among fellow authors and editors for his honesty and hard work, the Pulitzer Prize-winning author, according to Ruth MacDonald in the *Chicago Tribune,* "perfected the art of telling great stories with a vocabulary as small as sometimes 52 or 53 words." "[Geisel] was not only a master of word and rhyme and an original and eccentric artist," declared Gerald Harrison, president of Random House's merchandise division, in *Publisher's Weekly,* "but down deep, I think he was basically an educator. He helped teach kids that reading was a joy and not a chore. . . . For those of us who worked with him, he taught us to strive for excellence in all the books we published."

Further Reading

See *Chicago Tribune,* 9/26/91; *Entertainment Weekly,* 10/11/91; *Los Angeles Times,* 9/26/91; *People,* 10/7/91; *Publishers Weekly,* 10/25/91; and the *Times* (London) 9/27/91. □

Margaret Joan Geller

Margaret Joan Geller (born 1947) discovered the existence of a Great Wall of galaxies in space that stretches at least 500 Million light-years.

Margaret Joan Geller, an astronomy professor at Harvard University and a senior scientist at the Smithsonian Astrophysical Observatory, helped discover a "Great Wall" of galaxies in space stretching at least 500 million light-years. The existence of this structure, the largest ever seen in the universe, presents a conundrum for theorists dealing with the early universe. She has been mapping the nearby universe for the past sixteen years and has produced the most extensive pictures yet.

Geller was born in Ithaca, New York, on December 8, 1947, to Seymour Geller and Sarah Levine Geller. She received her bachelor's degree at the University of California at Berkeley in 1970, and was a National Science Foundation fellow from 1970 to 1973. Her M.A. followed at Princeton University in 1972, and her Ph.D. thesis, entitled "Bright Galaxies in Rich Clusters: A Statistical Model for Magnitude Distributions," was received at Princeton University in 1975. She was a fellow in theoretical physics at the Harvard-Smithsonian Center for Astrophysics from 1974 to 1976, and a research associate at the center from 1976 to 1980. She was a senior visiting fellow at the Institute for

Astronomy in Cambridge, England, from 1978 to 1982, and an assistant professor at Harvard University from 1980 to 1983. Geller became an astrophysicist with the Smithsonian Astrophysical Observatory in 1983 and a professor of astronomy at Harvard University in 1988.

Since 1980 Geller has collaborated with astronomer John P. Huchra on a large-scale survey of galaxies, using redshifts to measure the galaxies' distance. (A redshift is a shift toward the red or longer-wavelength end of the visible spectrum that increases in proportion to distance.) Cosmologists have long predicted that galaxies are uniformly distributed in space, despite recent evidence of irregularities. Geller and Huchra hypothesized that three-dimensional mapping of galaxies beyond a certain brightness over a large-enough distance—500 million light-years—would confirm the predictions of uniformity. In January 1986 Huchra and Geller published their first results. But instead of the expected distribution, their "slice" of the cosmos (135 degrees wide by 6 degrees thick) showed sheets of galaxies appearing to line the walls of bubblelike empty spaces.

Geller and Huchra's so-called Great Wall is a system of thousands of galaxies arranged across the universe—its full width was indeterminable because it fell off the edges of the survey map. The wall contains about five times the average density of galaxies; but "what's striking," Geller told M. Mitchell Waldrop of *Science Research News* in 1989, "is how incredibly *thin* [—fifteen million light-years—the bubble walls] are." Large structures such as the Great Wall pose a problem for astronomers—they are too large to have formed as a result of gravity since the big bang (a cosmic explosion that the universe was born out of and expanded from over time), unless a significant amount of clumpiness was present at the origin of the cosmos. This theory, however, is contradicted by the smoothness of the cosmic microwave background, or "echo" of the big bang. Dark matter, invisible elementary particles left over from the big bang and believed to constitute 90 percent of the mass of the universe, is another possible explanation. But even dark matter may not be capable of producing so large an object as the Great Wall. "There is something fundamentally missing from our understanding of the way things work," Geller told Waldrop. Between January 1986 and November 1989, Geller and Huchra published four maps (including the first), and in each found the same line of galaxies perpendicular to our line of sight. Geller and Huchra's survey will eventually plot about fifteen thousand galaxies.

Geller won a MacArthur fellowship—also known as a "genius award"—in 1990 for her research. She received the Newcomb-Cleveland Prize of the American Academy of Arts and Sciences that same year. In addition to galaxy distributions, Geller is interested in the origin and evolution of galaxies and X-ray astronomy. She is a member of the International Astronomical Union, the American Astronomical Society, and the American Association for the Advancement of Science.

Further Reading

Bartusiak, Marcia, "Mapping the Universe," in *Discover,* August, 1990, pp. 60–63.

Powell, Corey S., "Up against the Wall," in *Scientific American,* February, 1990, pp. 18–19.

Waldrop, M. Mitchell, "Astronomers Go up against the Great Wall," in *Science Research News,* November 17, 1989, p. 885. □

Murray Gell-Mann

The American physicist Murray Gell-Mann (born 1929) coined the definition "quarks" to describe the triplets of particles that form the cores of atoms. The Nobel Prize winner for Physics in 1969, he helped to develop the Stanford model, which describes the behavior of subatomic particles and their forces.

Murray Gell-Mann was born on September 15, 1929, in New York City of Austrian immigrant parents. A precocious child, he attended a special school for gifted children, where he took a physics course. "It was the dullest course I've ever taken," he told *Omni* magazine in 1985, "and the only course I've ever done badly in!"

Early Academic Career

Gell-Mann graduated from school at the age of 15 and entered Yale University, where he sailed through a bachelor's degree to earn his diploma in 1948. Next came graduate study at the Massachusetts Institute of Technology (MIT), where he claims to have found out, for the very first time, what true scientific research can achieve. Totally committed to his work, he completed his doctorate in 1951, and proceeded to the Princeton Institute for Advanced Studies, where he had been awarded a research grant.

Gell-Mann's first academic appointment was in 1952 with the Institute for Nuclear Studies at the University of Chicago, where he started the work on elementary particles that was to bring him the Nobel Prize in physics in 1969. In 1955 he moved to the California Institute of Technology (CalTech). A member of the National Academy of Sciences and the American Academy of Arts and Sciences, Gell-Mann was the recipient of the Dannie Heineman Prize of the American Physical Society in 1959 and of numerous special lectureships and honors.

Order out of Chaos

Gell-Mann was one of the young physicists of the 1950s who tried to bring order into the chaotic field of elementary particles. In 1953 he proposed the invariant quality of "strangeness" to explain the behavior of some of the elementary particles. This quality, he noted, was conserved in strong and electromagnetic interactions but not in weak interactions. Strangeness proved useful in ordering the particles to form a classification chart somewhat analogous

consultant to the Institute for Defense Analysis, especially with regard to the detection of nuclear test detonations.

His formal place of employment, however, was the University of Chicago, where he remained until 1955. The following year he took a professorship at CalTech.

A settled home on the coveted west coast notwithstanding, Gell-Mann left California in 1993 to work at the Santa Fe Institute—an institution he co-founded in 1984—to focus on complex adaptive systems, an interdisciplinary field.

Gell-Mann has written and co-authored many papers. His longer works include: *The Discovery of Subatomic Particles,* (1983) and *The Quark and the Jaguar.*

A Man of Many Interests

A man of wide interests, Gell-Mann speaks 13 languages fluently, is an accomplished ornithologist, and is very knowledgeable about the archeology of the Southwestern United States. A passionate conservationist, he helped to establish a nonprofit organization called the World Resources Institute.

Further Reading

Information on Murray Gell-Man can be found in *Omni* (May, 1985) and *The Scientific Life* (1962), contains an interesting interview with Gell-Mann. For background information on elementary particle physics see David Park, *Contemporary Physics* (1964). □

to the periodic table of elements. The chart not only listed families of particles, but by means of it Gell-Mann was able to predict the existence of a hitherto unknown particle, omega-minus, which was detected in 1964.

Physicists began using the term "strange particles" to describe a group of particles, inclusive for K-mesons and hyperons, that exhibited several peculiarities. To explain the anomalously long lifetimes of these particles, Gell-Mann advanced the theory of "associated production": the strong forces responsible for strange particles could act to create them only in batches of more than one at a time. Using his strangeness formulations, Gell-Mann also gave descriptions in detail of numerous decay events of strange particles, as well as prophesying the existence of the neutral xi particle.

In his continuing search for a more general elementary particle theory, Gell-Mann introduced a hypothetical particle, the quark, which is viewed as the fundamental stable constituent of the other particles and therefore is possibly the ultimate building block in the physical universe. Although quarks were not known to exist in the early 1960s when he began to work on particle physics, by the mid-1990s six types, forming three pairs, had been positively identified, and Gell-Mann does not rule out the possibility that there may be many more waiting for discovery.

During the Cold War years, Gell-Mann's work on particle physics was useful to the U.S. defense industries and the military. Notable among his assignments was his antisubmarine work for the Rand Corporation, and his service as a

Amin Gemayel

Amin Gemayel (born 1942) was a Lebanese nationalist and Christian political leader who became president of the Republic of Lebanon in September 1982.

B orn in Bikfayya, Lebanon, in 1942, Amin Gemayel was the eldest of Pierre and Genevieve Gemayel's five children. Amin grew up in the Christian right-wing nationalist Lebanese Union Party (known as the Phalangists) founded by his father in 1936. A lawyer by profession, Gemayel had a long political experience as a partisan starting in his youth and as a member of parliament for 12 years before he was elected president in September 1982. His diligence and managerial talent accounted for his success in the realm of business, mass communication, and civic activities. He ran a successful law firm, established the House of the Future (a center for documentation and research), and published the French-language newspaper *Le Reveil* and a trilingual quarterly (*Panorama de L'Actuelite*) during the 1970s. His main function as a member of the Political Bureau of the Phalangists was to oversee the party's civic activities and network of business holdings.

Amin commanded a private police unit during the Lebanese war (1975-1982), but his major involvement in the conflict was political and relatively conciliatory. Hence, he maintained contact with Muslim and Palestinian leaders throughout the war and nurtured a moderate disposition, knowing that in a democratic pluralistic society national leadership presupposes mutual responsiveness. Therefore, he was his party's logical nominee for the presidency after his strong and charismatic brother, President-elect Bashir Gemayel, was assassinated on September 14, 1982. Having kept a distance from Israeli temptations, especially after Israel invaded Lebanon in June 1982, Amin emerged as a "consensus candidate," almost unanimously supported internally and received with partially guarded but explicit Arab support.

Gemayel labeled his charge as president the "vast adventure," setting his goals as: "the withdrawal of the Israeli (and all non-Lebanese) forces, reconstruction of the Lebanese army, political reconciliation and reform, and socioeconomic reconstruction and development." To avail this task, he had the backing of impressive supporters, including most major Arab states, the United States of America, Western Europe, and the goodwill of the United Nations. Internally, he was supported by a consensus among leaders and factions, excluding leftist associations and extreme radicals across the political spectrum.

But there were political problems. Amin's election was met with a cool reception by Israel, Syria, Iran, Libya, and the Palestine Liberation Organization (PLO), each of whom had found and exploited partners in Lebanon itself ready to thwart the regime's declared objectives. All five actors pursued goals that were better served by holding a "Lebanese card" in the Middle East conflict. In addition, Gemayel himself made moves that were misconceived. He made numerous unprecedented partisan appointments to high-ranking civil service and quasi-political posts, thus inviting accusations of hegemony; allowed the recently reconstructed army to be used in security operations, involving anti-Phalangists in the civil strife, without ensuring external cooperation, particularly from Syria and Israel; totally relied on the "American option" before ascertaining American willingness and ability to support his "adventure;" and negotiated an abortive withdrawal agreement with Israel, the implementation of which involved Israeli conditions not acceptable even to Gemayel himself.

As a result, none of the goals he set for his government were satisfactorily attained: staggered Israeli withdrawal was more disruptive than occupation itself and was never completed. Syrian influence in Lebanon became stronger than ever, especially after Gemayel declined ratification of the May 1983 agreement with Israel. The Lebanese Army stood badly divided. After two abortive National Reconciliation Conferences in Geneva (1983) and Lucerne (1984), and the formation of a National Unity Cabinet, political reconciliation and reform were as elusive as ever. Socioeconomic problems were more acute than they had ever been during the ten years of war in Lebanon.

Gemayel was a "progressive rightist." He viewed Lebanon's distinctiveness in its way of life, which values human rights, entrepreneurship, moderation, "revulsion with totalitarianism," and a yearning for unity in diversity. Gemayel believed that Lebanon was an Arab state with values and a distinct identity of its own. It lived in, and depended on, the Arab world for its prosperity. Therefore, while it should never deviate from its independence and conciliatory role among the Arab states and between them and the Western world, Lebanon ought to share in the peaceful pursuit of Arab causes and serve as a "roadblock" between Israel and Syria. Gemayel believed that Lebanon should maintain a "special" relationship of "cooperation and coordination" with Syria despite the discrepancy "in their social, economic and political systems," because they share "a long historical experience and wide-ranging interests."

Gemayel disavowed the 1983 constitutional system because it "concealed double-dealing and created a marginal state void of any nationalistic sentiment." In its place, he proposed a politically centralized system based on "regional units" with broad administrative autonomy. This system would be managed by all religious communities "through their sharing in the highest posts of government." Gemayel rejected classical numerical democracy in favor of "compound democracy," where decisions are made by concurrent majority reflecting society's pluralism.

Unfortunately, the constant state of turmoil in Lebanon left Gemayel virtually powerless to accomplish anything. As the Chamber of Deputies were unable to elect a new president when his term was up, before leaving office and ultimately the country, Gemayel appointed the commander of the Lebanese army Major General Michel Aoun as his successor.

Gemayel attended French-oriented schools throughout his educational career. From Jesuit primary and secondary schools, he went to the Universite Saint Joseph in Beirut where he earned an LL.B. in 1966. He was fluent in French and Arabic and, to a lesser extent, mastered the English language. He was an avid tennis player, reader of history, and good listener to classical music. He was married to the former Joyce Tayyan late in 1967. They had three children, two boys and a girl, named Pierre, Sami, and Nicole. After his term in office, Amin Gemayel went into exile in Paris, France.

Further Reading

Little has been written on Amin Gemayel beyond news literature, including *The New York Times, Newsweek, TIME* magazines (August-September 1982), and *Reuters* (May 21, 1996; Aug. 12, 1996). He is listed in the *International Who's Who* 1983-1984 and in *Who's Who in Lebanon,* 1983. His article "The Price and the Promise" in *Foreign Affairs* (Spring 1985) is a valuable source on his thinking. Equally valuable are three documents authored by him (two in Arabic) about his vision of future Lebanon published in *Umara al-Tawaef* (Princes of the Sects) in 1984, and finally, *Rebuilding Lebanon* New York: University Press of America (1992). □

Pierre Gemayel

Lebanese leader Pierre Gemayel (1905-1984) founded the Lebanese Phalanges, a political and military force which he led for almost 50 years. The Phalangist Party, geared toward Lebanese Christians,

focused on the need for a strong Lebanese state. Gemayel's sons both served as president of Lebanon.

Pierre Gemayel was born in 1905, in Bikfaya, a small town in the Northern Matn region of Mount Lebanon. He was a descendant of a family of local notables which in the first half of the 19th century had acquired the hereditary title of *shaykh*. He studied at the Jesuit St. Joseph University in Beirut, where he graduated with a degree in pharmacy from the French Faculty of Medicine and Pharmacy.

During his studies and while practicing his profession he was strongly involved in athletics and especially football (soccer), for which he founded the Lebanese Football Federation. As a representative of this sport he was sent to the Olympic games in Berlin in 1936. He expressed some admiration for the discipline and the strong national identity exhibited by the Germans. During his stay in Europe he studied the Czech athletic society the Sokol (Falcon), which inspired him to establish a similar organization in Lebanon. In November 1936 Pierre Gemayel and four other prominent Lebanese—two members of each of the major political parties then, the Constitutional Bloc and the National Bloc—founded the Lebanese Phalanges.

Although the Lebanese Phalanges emphasized discipline, insisted on a strong attachment to the nation, and wore a distinctive attire, its ideology was totally opposed to fascism and totalitarianism. In fact, the Lebanese Phalanges was formed as a reaction to the emergence of a fascist party, the Syrian Social Nationalist Party (SSNP), founded by Antun Sa'adah, which had a Pan-Syrian ideology that had some appeal to the secularly-minded Christians. The ideology of the Lebanese Phalanges, which was primarily geared toward the Lebanese Christians, centered on Lebanon as a separate national identity imbued with the values of freedom and democracy as the best guarantee for the survival of the Christian community in a predominantly Arab and Muslim Middle East.

The Lebanese Phalanges under the charismatic leadership of Pierre Gemayel became by 1942 a major political force, claiming 35,000 members among the Maronite Christian community. Gemayel's cooperation, based on a common understanding about the nature of Lebanon, with the prominent Sunni politician (and a founding father of Lebanon), Riyad al-Sulh was crucial to Gemayel's ability to convince and mobilize the Maronite youth in support of the independence of Lebanon rather than retaining the French mandate. Gemayel was arrested by the French as an instigator of demonstrations and was released when the struggle for independence succeeded on November 22, 1943.

Gemayel and his party began in 1943 to follow a policy of consistently supporting the Lebanese political system and the Lebanese presidency in particular as essential for the survival of Lebanon. When opposition to the first Lebanese president after independence, Bishara al-Khoury, rose by leaps and bounds and eventually forced him to resign in 1952, Gemayel was the last to abandon him. Similarly, when the next president, Camille Chamoun, was faced with

a revolt in 1958 led by major Muslim leaders and backed by President Gamal Abdel Nasser of the United Arab Republic (Egypt and Syria), Gemayel sided with Chamoun, fearing that the independence of Lebanon would be compromised if dominated by Nasser. The civil war of May to October 1958 was instrumental in making Gemayel and his Phalangist Party an indispensable part of the Lebanese political establishment. Gemayel himself served frequently in the Cabinet throughout the period 1958-1975. After the expansion of the Chamber of Deputies into 99 members in 1960, Gemayel and several members of his party were elected in each of the four Chambers of Deputies of 1960, 1964, 1968, and 1972.

In the turbulent period that followed the Arab-Israeli (Six-Day) War of 1967, Gemayel feared that the rising tide of Palestinian guerrilla operations across the Lebanese-Israeli border (especially after the expulsion of the Palestine Liberation Organization [PLO] from Jordan in 1970) would again undermine Lebanese independence and sovereignty. The PLO's military presence in Lebanon was depicted by Gemayel as a state within a state. There is no doubt that this issue triggered the conflict in Lebanon which began in April 1975 and which in turn transformed Gemayel's Phalangist Party and particularly its militia, the Lebanese Forces, into the most formidable indigenous military force in Lebanon.

In the first phase of the conflict, Gemayel was at loggerheads with the PLO and its Muslim-Leftist allies. In January 1976 Gemayel formed, with former president Chamoun and other Christian politicians, the Lebanese Front, which basically represented the vast majority of the Christians in Lebanon. After the disintegration of the Lebanese Army in early 1976, Syrian President Hafiz Assad sent his troops to Lebanon and managed to convince Gemayel and the Lebanese president at the time, Suleiman Frangie, that the sole purpose of the Syrian troops was to make the PLO abide by its agreements with the Lebanese Government. By early 1978, however, the commander of the militia of the Phalangist Party, the Lebanese Forces, Pierre Gemayel's younger son Bashir Gemayel, had realized that Assad was interested in neither curbing the PLO in Lebanon nor withdrawing his troops. Consequently, Bashir fought the Syrians, sought an alliance with the Israelis, and consolidated his power within the Christian community by either eliminating or undermining his rivals. By 1981 Bashir upstaged both his father and his elder brother, Amin Gemayel, within the Phalangist Party and Lebanese Forces as well as within the Christian community at large. When the Israelis waged their war against the PLO in Lebanon in 1982, Bashir Gemayel became the only possible candidate for the presidency. The ambition that had eluded Pierre Gemayel was achieved by his son Bashir, who was elected president of Lebanon in August 1982. As Bashir's chief program was to force the Syrian troops out of Lebanon, he was duly assassinated on orders from Assad himself. Subsequently, the elder son of Pierre Gemayel, Amin Gemayel, was elected president in September 1982. Pierre Gemayel was able in the last two years of his life to keep the Phalangist Party and the Lebanese Forces under control. He tried to assist his son Amin by serving in the so-called National Unity Cabinet formed in April 1984 after the abrogation, due to Syrian military pressure, of the U.S.-sponsored Israeli-Lebanese Accord of May 1983. He died on August 29, 1984, while he was serving in the Cabinet. His legacy, comprised of many elements—namely, his heir, former President Amin Gemayel, the Lebanese Forces, and the Phalangist Party itself—will most probably remain an integral part of the Lebanese polity.

Further Reading

For additional information on Pierre Gemayel see John P. Entelis, *Pluralism and Party Transformation in Lebanonal Kata'ib, 1936-1970* (Leiden: 1974), a scholarly work on the ideology and organization of Gemayel's Phalangist Party prior to the conflict in Lebanon; Marius Deeb, *The Lebanese Civil War* (1980), an authoritative scholarly work which covers the prominent role of the Phalangist Party during the civil war phase of the conflict in Lebanon; and Thomas L. Friedman, *From Beirut to Jerusalem* (1989), an honor-winning journalist's account of 10 years in the Middle East. Jacques Nantet, *Pierre Gemayel* (Paris: 1986) is a comprehensive biography of Pierre Gemayel. In Arabic, there is an indispensable two-volume history of Gemayel's Phalangist Party during its formative years which is based on the party's archives: *Tarikh Hizb al-Kata'ib al-Lubnaniya* (History of the Lebanese Phalangist Party) Vol. I: *1936-1940* (Beirut: 1979) and Vol. II: *1941-1946* (Beirut: 1981). □

Edmond Charles Genet

Edmond Charles Genet (1763-1834), known as Citizen Genet, French emissary to the United States, influenced American foreign relations as well as the formation of America's early two-party system.

Edmond Genet was the scion of prerevolutionary French gentry. After an aristocratic upbringing and education, in 1781 Genet followed his father into the French Foreign Ministry. He was fortunate to be posted in Russia when the French Revolution began and was able to retain his position until 1792. After a brief hiatus he emerged as Citizen Genet to accept a Girondist appointment as French minister plenipotentiary to the United States. He was specifically told to use his compelling personality and diplomatic skill to convince America to side with the French Republic in the French Revolutionary wars.

Genet's arrival in America in 1793 precipitated a crisis in Franco-American relations. Pro-French Secretary of State Thomas Jefferson, already at odds with the neutral Federalist administration, successfully insisted that Genet be accorded full diplomatic recognition. Genet, meanwhile, operating on the assumption that the American government and its people would look the other way while he chartered American vessels as privateers to prey on British shipping in the West Indies, set out to enlist popular support.

The Federalist administration's icy reaction to Genet's pursuit was quite the reverse of the adulation accorded him by American citizens at large. His journey from Charleston to New York in search of funds and private naval support was a triumphal tour. His undiplomatic activities in Phila-

delphia, however, coupled with his growing popularity, moved the administration to action.

The Federalists had noted that, along Genet's entire route on his tour through the states, the dynamic envoy had organized and left behind functioning political organizations known as "democratic societies." The creation of these societies justifiably alarmed the Federalists, for eventually they became key components of opposition, against the Federalists, in the expanding Jeffersonian-Republican party organization. This activity of Genet's, along with the diplomatic embarrassment he imposed on President George Washington by his repeated violations of the Neutrality Proclamation of 1793, resulted in the revocation of his diplomatic credentials in December 1793. Even Jefferson had come to view Genet with increasing mistrust.

Rather than return to France, Genet married the daughter of New York governor George Clinton and settled on Long Island. He is remembered as a central figure in the establishment of a firm line of demarcation between Federalists and Jeffersonian-Republicans during the 1790s.

Further Reading

There is no satisfactory full-length study of Genet. His diplomatic activities in the United States are discussed in Alexander DeConde, *Entangling Alliance: Politics and Diplomacy under George Washington* (1958). For his political activities in America see Eugene P. Link, *Democratic-Republican Societies, 1790-1800* (1942). There is a useful summary of Genet's mission in John C. Miller, *The Federalist Era, 1789-1801*

(1960). See also George Gates Raddin, *Caritat and the Genet Episode* (1953). ☐

Jean Genet

Dubbed "the Black Prince of letters," by his discoverer, Jean Cocteau, the French novelist and playwright Jean Genet (1910-1986) was obsessed with the illusory, perverse, and grotesque elements of human experience. His works present the world of the isolated and despairing outcast.

According to his own version of events, Jean Genet was born on Dec. 19, 1910, to a Parisian prostitute, who soon abandoned him. Placed in a foster home, Jean was raised in the Morvau region by a farming family. At the age of 10 he began pilfering articles from his benefactors and their neighbors, perhaps to arouse the parental concern he knew to be absent in his life. His ploy failed and, according to Jean Paul Sartre, his resolution to remain a thief constituted a significant existential act:"Thus I decisively repudiated a world that had repudiated me."

At the age of 16 Genet was sent to the Mettray Reformatory, where the impressionable boy cultivated an admiration for evil and a taste for homosexuality. Escaping from his confinement after five years, Genet contracted for an extended enlistment in the Foreign Legion, collected his bonus and a few days later deserted. During the next decade Genet wandered across Europe, immersing himself in the underworld and surviving as a beggar, thief, narcotics smuggler, forger, and male prostitute. Arrested several times, Genet spent most of World War II in prison, where he began to write.

Genet, however, often lied about his past, and Edmund White took about the task of dispelling many of the clouds surrounding Genet and propagated by Sartre. As even Sartre himself acknowledged, Genet practiced certain economies when it came to self-revelatory truth so White relentlessly seeks out corroboration. Many of the documents, it turns out, refuse to corroborate. White first shows how thoroughly Genet's own version of his childhood—drawn in sharp lines of poverty and abuse—was a myth, an affectation given credibility by Sartre. Born in Paris in 1910, Genet had been abandoned by his unwed mother and made a ward of the state. But the carpenter's family that was entrusted with his care gave Genet ample attention and affection. Raised in a farming village, he was not made to work, prospered in school, had plenty of books, and scored high on examinations. Contrary to his later claim, he did not have to steal to survive. ("You couldn't call them thefts," recalls one classmate. "He took some pennies from his mother to buy sweets, all kids do that.")

The effect of White's first chapters is to suggest Genet largely fabricated a grim childhood to fit his chosen persona as a renegade. Precocious and rebellious, the dandified Genet refused, as he put it, "to become an accountant or a petty official." And so he escaped from every apprenticeship, opting to become a petty thief. This eventually landed him in the notorious reform penitentiary at Mettray, a society of male outcasts governed by a counter-code of homosexuality, theft, and betrayal which Genet would later celebrate.

Concentrating on the ambiguity of morality in a society characterized by repression and hypocrisy, his novels and plays portray the individual trapped in a state of enforced dissolution. *Our Lady of the Flowers,* composed under almost impossible conditions in Fresnes prison, was published in Lyons in 1943. The novel, peopled by pimps and prostitutes, depicts the author's erotic world of homosexuality, masturbation, bizarre fantasies, and violent murder. Marked by nonconformity and exoticism, the work uses a lyrical delicacy of language to describe an incredibly sordid milieu.

The Miracle of the Rose (1943), written in Santé prison, is an autobiographical narrative in which Genet proclaims a cult of the criminal, praising both crime itself and the perpetrators of it. The religious imagery of the earlier work is intensified, and the ceremony of prison life is closely identified with the satisfactions derived from religious rites. *Funeral Rites* (1945) and *Quarrel of Brest* (1946) continue these themes.

Genet's works composed in prison, to which he had been sentenced for life, attracted critical acclaim; such literary notables as Sartre and Jean Cocteau successfully petitioned for his pardon, and he was released in 1948. *The*

Thief's Journal (1949), recounting Genet's adventures in the European underworld of the 1930s, was proclaimed by Sartre to be the author's finest work in both form and substance.

In his drama *The Maids* (1948) Genet explores the sequence of masks, roles, and conditions assumed by two maids to maintain their constantly shifting identities. Moral values are reversed throughout, with evil achieving a reverence traditionally assigned to goodness. *Death-watch* (1949) describes the sadomasochistic relationship of three prisoners, ending in nightmarish death. Genet's ritualistic theater continued to explore the deceptive relationship between illusion and reality in *The Balcony* (1957), *The Blacks* (1959), and *The Screens* (1961).

His heart leaned from his "'religious nature'' as he confessed in his autobiographical *Thief's Journal* (1949, English 1965). "I am alone in the world, and I am not sure but that I may not be the king . . . ''

On September 19, 1982, Genet visited the Palestinian refugee camp of Shatila near Beirut. Two nights earlier, Israel had permitted its Lebanese allies to enter the surrounded camp, and they had massacred its Palestinian inhabitants. A walk through Shatila, wrote Genet, "resembled a game of hopscotch . . . . A photograph doesn't show how you must jump over the bodies as you walk along from one corpse to the next.

The "thick white smell of death" in Shatila inspired Genet to one self-invention. He would be reborn as a witness for the Palestinians. *Prisoner of Love,* his book-length memoir of the Palestinian fedayeen, appeared a month after his death in 1986. This was the first new writing Genet had produced in years, and it rekindled an interest in his life and work.

Genet's work, while involved with social issues, rejects any form of political commitment. His confrontation with the world has both deeply stirred and repulsed his readers and audiences. Composed outside literary tradition in terms of plot, characterization, and thematic implications, his personal projections possess a psychological truth fused with dramatic imagery.

According to White, Genet, rather than embodying some collective disorder of his time, acted largely upon his own disorder. But his death was as bland as his life was colorful. His obituary, after listing his many credits, simply states, "died in Paris".

Further Reading

Jean Paul Sartre, *Saint Genet* (1952; trans. 1963), is an exceptionally revealing analysis of the man and his art. Other full-length studies in English include Bettina Knapp, *Jean Genet* (1956); Tom F. Driver, *Jean Genet* (1966); Richard N. Coe, *The Vision of Jean Genet* (1968); and Philip Thody, *Jean Genet: A Study of His Novels and Plays* (1969). Focusing on the author's plays are critical sections in Wallace Fowlie, *Dionysus in Paris* (1960); Martin Esslin, *The Theatre of the Absurd* (1961); David I. Grossvogel, *Four Playwrights and a Postscript* (1962); and Lionel Abel, *Metatheater* (1963). A good resource for his life's work can be found in: *Genet: A Biography.* Knopf, 728 pp., $35.00. Edmund White as cited by Marin Kramer. Many of his life's accomplishments can be found in *Current Biography*
(1974). His obituary ran in the *New York Times,* April 16, 1986. □

Genghis Khan

Genghis Khan (1167-1227) was the creator of the Mongol nation and the founder of one of the vastest empires the world has ever seen.

Genghis Khan, whose original name was Temüjin, was born on the banks of the river Onon in the extreme northeast corner of present-day Mongolia. He was left an orphan at the age of 9, his father, a nephew of the last khan of the Mongols, having met his death at the hands of the Tatars, who in the second half of the 12th century had displaced the Mongols as the dominant tribe in eastern Mongolia. Temüjin's mother was deserted by her husband's followers at the instigation of the Taichi'uts, a rival clan who wished to prevent his succeeding to his father's position, and she was reduced to bringing up her family in conditions of great hardship.

Rise to Power

When Temüjin had grown into young manhood, he was taken prisoner by the Taichi'uts, whose intention it was to keep him in perpetual captivity. However, he succeeded in escaping and soon afterward became the protégé of Toghril, the ruler of the Kereits, a Christian tribe in central Mongolia. It was with the aid of Toghril and a young Mongol chieftain called Jamuka that Temüjin was able to rescue his newly married wife, who had been carried off by the Merkits, a forest tribe in the region which is now the Buryatiya in present-day Russia. For a time after this joint operation Temüjin and Jamuka remained friends, but then, for some obscure reason, a rift developed between them and they parted company. It was at this time that certain of the Mongol princes acclaimed Temüjin as their ruler, bestowing upon him the title by which he is known in history, Chingiz-Khan (Genghis Khan), which bears some such meaning as "Universal Monarch."

Genghis Khan's patron Toghril was driven into exile and then restored to the throne by the efforts of his protégé 2 years later, in 1198, the first precise date in Genghis Khan's career. The two chieftains allied themselves with the Chin rulers of North China in a campaign against the Tatars, Toghril being rewarded for his share in the joint victory with the Chinese title of *wang* (prince), whence his Mongol title of Ong-Khan, while Genghis Khan received a much inferior title. In 1199 they took the field against the Naimans, the most powerful tribe in western Mongolia, but the campaign was unsuccessful owing to Ong-Khan's pusillanimous conduct. In the years 1200-1202 the allies won several victories over a confederation of tribes led by Genghis Khan's former friend Jamuka; and in 1202 Genghis Khan made his final reckoning with the Tatars in a campaign which resulted in their total extinction as a people.

Relations with Ong-Khan had in the meanwhile so deteriorated that it came to open warfare. The first battle, though represented as indecisive, seems in fact to have been a defeat for Genghis Khan, who withdrew into a remote area of northeastern Mongolia. He soon rallied, however, and in a second battle (1203) gained a complete victory over Ong-Khan, who fled to the west to meet his death at the hands of the Naimans, while his people, the Kereits, lost their identity, being forcibly absorbed by the Mongols.

Genghis Khan now turned against his enemies in western Mongolia: the Naimans allied with Jamuka and the remnants of the Merkits. The Naimans were finally defeated in 1204, and Küchlüg, the son of their ruler, fled westward to find refuge with the Kara-Khitai, descendants of the Chinese Liao dynasty, who after their expulsion by the Chin had founded a new empire in the area of present-day south Kazakhstan and Xinjiang region of China. Jamuka, now a fugitive, was betrayed by his followers and was put to death by Genghis Khan, his former friend, who found himself at last in undisputed control of Mongolia. In 1206 a *kuriltai,* or diet, of the Mongol princes, meeting near the sources of the Onon, proclaimed him supreme ruler of the Mongol peoples, and he was now able to contemplate the conquest of foreign nations.

Conquest of China

Already, in 1205, Genghis Khan had attacked the Tanguts, a people of Tibetan origin in what is today Kansu and the Ordos Region of China, and two further campaigns against that people in 1207 and 1209 cleared the way for a frontal assault on China proper. In 1211 the Mongols invaded and overran the whole of the region north of the Great Wall; in 1213 the wall was breached, and their forces spread out over the North China plain; in the summer of 1215 Peking was captured and sacked, and the Chin emperor fled to Kaifeng on the southern banks of the Yellow River. Leaving one of his generals in charge of further operations in North China, Genghis Khan returned to Mongolia to devote his attention to events in central Asia.

Küchlüg the Naiman, who had taken refuge among the Kara-Khitai, had dethroned the ruler of that people and had possessed that kingdom. An army dispatched by Genghis Khan chased him from Kashghar across the Pamirs into Afghanistan, where Küchlüg was captured and put to death; and the acquisition of his territory gave the Mongols a common frontier with Sultan Muhammad, the hereditary ruler of Khiva, who as the result of recent conquests had annexed the whole of central Asia as well as Afghanistan and the greater part of Persia.

Campaign in the West

War between the two empires was probably inevitable; it was precipitated by the execution of Genghis Khan's ambassadors and a group of merchants accompanying them at the frontier town of Otrar on the Syr Darya. Genghis Khan set out from Mongolia in the spring of 1219; he had reached Otrar by the autumn and, leaving a detachment to lay siege to it, advanced on Bukhara, which fell in March 1220, and on Samarkand, which capitulated a month later, the victors of Otrar having taken part in the siege. From Samarkand, Genghis Khan sent his two best generals in pursuit of Sultan Muhammad, who crisscrossed Persia in flight until he met his end on an island in the Caspian Sea. Continuing their westward sweep, the generals crossed the Caucasus and defeated an army of Russians and Kipchak Turks in the Crimea before returning along the northern shores of the Caspian to rejoin their master on his homeward journey. Genghis Khan, in the meantime, having passed the summer of 1220 in the mountains south of Samarkand, attacked and captured Termez in the autumn and spent the winter of 1220/1221 in operations in what is now Tajikistan.

Early in 1221 he crossed the Oxus to destroy the ancient city of Balkh, then part of the Persian province of Khurasan, and dispatched his youngest son, Tolui (Tulë), the father of the Great Khans Mangu (Möngkë) and Kublai, to complete the subjugation of that province, which he subjected to such devastation that it has not fully recovered to this day. In the late summer Genghis Khan advanced southward through Afghanistan to attack Sultan Jalal al-Din, the son of Sultan Muhammad, who at Parvan near Kabul had inflicted a defeat upon a Mongol army. He gave battle to Jalal al-Din on the banks of the Indus; the sultan was decisively defeated and escaped captured only by swimming across the river.

With Jalal al-Din's defeat the campaign in the west was virtually concluded, and Genghis Khan returned by slow stages to Mongolia, which he did not reach till the spring of 1225. In the autumn of the following year he was again at war with the Tanguts; he died, while the campaign was still in progress, in the Liupan Mountains in Kansu on Aug. 25, 1227.

Further Reading

René Grousset, *The Conqueror of the World* (1944; trans. 1967), is still the best biography, though clearly no longer abreast of contemporary research. Other biographies include Henry Desmond Martin, *The Rise of Chingis Khan and His Conquest of North China* (1950), and Franklin MacKenzie, *The Ocean and the Steppe: The Life and Times of the Mongol Conqueror Genghis Khan, 1155-1227* (1963). Several original sources are available in English translation; the work of the Persian historian Juvaini is available as *The History of the World-Conqueror* (trans. 1958), and extracts of the native chronicle, *The Secret History of the Mongols,* are in Arthur Waley, *The Secret History of the Mongols and Other Pieces* (1963). For details of the campaigns in central Asia and eastern Persia see Wilhelm Barthold, *Turkestan down to the Mongol Invasion* (trans. 1928), and John Andrew Boyle, ed., *Cambridge History of Iran,* vol. 5 (1968). □

Hans-Dietrich Genscher

A long-time leader of West Germany's liberal party, the FDP, Hans-Dietrich Genscher (born 1927) was also his country's foreign minister beginning in 1974. While firm in his support of West Germany's ties to the United States and Western Europe, Genscher's tenure in office was also marked by persistent efforts to keep *Ostpolitik* and detente alive.

Hans-Dietrich Genscher was born March 21, 1927, to a middle-class family in the small Saxon town of Reideburg, Germany. In the last months of World War II he was drafted into the *Wehrmacht* (German army). After his release as a prisoner of war, Genscher studied law and economics at the Universities of Halle and Leipzig, graduating with a law degree in 1949. As the Stalinist regime in the German Democratic Republic (GDR) became increasingly oppressive in the early 1950s, Genscher became one of the thousands of refugees who moved to West Germany. In 1952 he settled in Bremen and took up private law practice in that city.

The future foreign minister developed an early interest in politics, and he remained a life-long Liberal. While still a student at Halle and Leipzig, he joined the East German Liberal Democratic Party (LDDP). Perhaps because he had to leave his home at an early age, Genscher showed little interest in state or regional politics. Instead, he concentrated on national and international affairs.

At the end of the 1950s Genscher became one of the proteges of Walther Scheel, a rising Liberal leader. Scheel became chairman of the FDP in 1961, succeeding the right-wing politician Erich Mende, who had led the FDP in virtual lock-step with the Christian Democrats since the early 1950s. In 1968 Genscher became vice-chairman of the FDP, and a year later, after Scheel's election as president of

the Federal Republic, Genscher succeeded his mentor as leader of West Germany's Liberals.

Scheel and Genscher led the FDP away from its position as junior partner of the Christian Democrats (CDU) and opened the way for a coalition with the Social Democrats (SPD). When the 1969 elections gave the FDP and the SPD a majority of the seats in the Bundestag (parliament), the two parties formed a coalition cabinet under the leadership of Willy Brandt. In this first "Social-Liberal" cabinet Genscher served as minister of the interior. Five years later when Helmut Schmidt succeeded Brandt as chancellor, Genscher became foreign minister and vice-chancellor, positions which he held continuously through the mid-1980s.

In attempting to steer a course as a Liberal leader in postwar West Germany, Genscher had to juggle the desire to preserve the classic principles of liberalism with the pragmatic need to assure the survival of his party. In the early 1980s the two major parties—the Social Democrats and the Christian Democrats—between them obtained well over 90 percent of the popular vote, so that the FDP repeatedly faced the danger of not attracting the minimum 5 percent necessary for representation in the Bundestag. They avoided disaster at the national level during those years, but in a number of state elections the Liberals failed to clear the 5 percent hurdle.

Genscher's liberalism found its expression primarily in a particularly strong commitment to maintaining individual rights and civil liberties. As minister of the interior he effectively met the challenge of the terrorist attacks by the

Baader-Meinhoff gang and other groups without violating the norms of the *Rechtsstaat.*

The FDP attempted to cope with the danger of political oblivion by being open to coalition agreements with both the political right and the political left. The result was to give the party and Genscher himself reputations as chameleons who change political partners for purely opportunistic reasons. In the 1960s the FDP abandoned its longtime coalition with the CDU and formed a government with the SPD. A decade later Genscher was instrumental in dissolving this partnership and leading his party back into the conservative camp.

In 1982, prodded by the then Liberal minister of economics, Count Lambsdorff, Genscher made possible the *Wende* (change of direction) which resulted in bringing Helmut Kohl and a CDU/FDP coalition to power. The turn to the right enabled the FDP to retain its influence in the national executive, but the abruptness of the shift also had severe repercussions for the party. Some well-known Liberal leaders resigned their party memberships rather than support the Kohl government. The party also failed to clear the 5 percent hurdle in a number of state elections. To appease the intra-party turmoil Genscher at the beginning of 1985 resigned as national chairman. He was succeeded by Martin Bangemann, Count Lambsdorff's successor as minister of economics in the Kohl cabinet.

Genscher's careers as party leader and cabinet minister were not marked by ideological or programmatic innovations. Rather, he acquired well-deserved reputations as a pragmatist and clever tactician. This is particularly true of his long-term service as West Germany's foreign minister. Genscher was head of West Germany's Foreign Office beginning in 1974 and became one of the most senior among the foreign ministers of the major powers. In the SPD/FDP coalition Genscher's administration of West Germany's foreign policy was strongly identified with the *Ostpolitik,* the efforts to improve West Germany's relations with the Eastern bloc. Genscher did not originate the *Ostpolitik,* but he became an effective supporter of this initiative. At the same time he did not neglect good relations with the United States and the Federal Republic's West European neighbors.

After joining the Kohl cabinet, Genscher was one of the focal points of continuity in West Germany's foreign policy. He attempted to conduct the Federal Republic's foreign policy along many of the same lines as before the *Wende.* This effort at times exposed him to severe criticism from some of the more doctrinaire Christian Democrats, who preferred a more confrontational course, especially in relations with the Soviet Union.

On May 17, 1992, Genscher, with surprising abruptness, resigned from his post as Foreign Minister providing little to no explanation for his decision. His rapid exit ignited a bitter power struggle as to who would fill his position in the FDP which some speculated would lead to the collapse of Germany's coalition government. Eventually, former Justice Minister Klaus Kinkel was chosen and pledged to continue Genscher's course of foreign policy.

In the years that followed his departure from government, Genscher continued to play an active role in world politics. Despite publishing his decidedly lengthy and somewhat erratic memoirs in 1995, critics say Genscher provided little true insight about the dynamics of the German government he was such an integral part of.

Further Reading

Literature in English on Genscher is scant; no full-scale biography of the foreign minister has appeared. Genscher himself has provided accounts of his foreign policy aims and ideas in two collections of speeches and papers: *Bewährung: Diplomatie in Krisenzeiten* (*Test: Diplomacy in Times of Crisis*) (1980), and *Deutsche Aussenpolitik 1975-1980* (*German Foreign Policy 1975-1980*) (1981). General accounts of Genscher's influence on West Germany's foreign policy include Wolfram Hanrieder, *West German Foreign Policy 1949-1979* (1980); Helga Haftendorn, *Security and Detente: Conflicting Priorities in German Foreign Policy* (1985); and Ekkehart Krippendorf and Volker Rittberger, editors, *The Foreign Policy of West Germany: Formation and Content* (1980). Additional references include Bilski, A.-Hollander, J. "A one two punch."*,Macleans* (May 5, 1992); Josef Joffe, "Rocking Germany's Boat," *U.S. News and World Report* (May 11, 1992); Tom Heneghan,"Genscher bores Germany with diplomatic memoirs,"*Reuters* (September 19, 1995). □

Gentile da Fabriano

Gentile da Fabriano (ca. 1370-1427) was the leading Italian painter of the International Gothic style.

Gentile da Fabriano, whose real name was Gentile di Niccolò di Giovanni di Massio, came from Fabriano in the Marches. According to tradition, his family was an old one and moderately prosperous. His father, who was said to have been a scholar, mathematician, and astrologer, became an Olivetan monk when a monastery of that order was established in Fabriano in 1397. Gentile's brother, Ludovico, was a monk of the same order in Fabriano, and Gentile himself was living in the Olivetan monastery of S. Maria Nuova in Rome at the time of his death. A document of Oct. 14, 1427, speaks of him as dead.

Gentile's art indicates that he was probably trained in Lombardy, perhaps in Milan. He worked in the then current International Gothic style, to which he brought his own personal quality. His earliest works display the decorative rhythmic drapery patterns preferred by the International Gothic masters, which Gentile tempered and ultimately abandoned after his contact with Florentine art.

In a document of 1408 Gentile is recorded in Venice, where he painted an altarpiece (now lost) for Francesco Amadi. Testifying to his high reputation was his commission in 1409 for frescoes in the Doges' Palace in Venice (painted over in 1479). Pandolfo Malatesta commissioned Gentile to decorate a chapel (destroyed) in Brescia in 1414. The artist is last recorded in Brescia on Sept. 18, 1419, when he departed for Rome to answer the summons of Pope Martin V. Gentile's name first appeared on the roll of painters in

Florence in 1421. He was in Siena in 1420 and 1424-1425 and in Orvieto late in 1425. From 1426 until the time of his death he was in Rome.

Typical of Gentile's early style is the polyptych (ca. 1400) from the convent of Valle Romita in Fabriano, in which Gentile displays the International Gothic love for naturalistic detail in the floral turf beneath the feet of the graceful, slender saints whose figures are swathed in rhythmic, linear drapery. The central panel, the *Coronation of the Virgin,* shows the love for calligraphic drapery so characteristic of Gentile's early style. Other noteworthy early works include the much damaged *Madonna* in Perugia and the *Madonna with Saints and Donor* in Berlin.

The altarpiece *Adoration of the Magi,* signed and dated 1423, was Gentile's major work in Florence. In remarkably good condition, with its original frame still intact, it shows Gentile's Gothicism now tempered by his contact with the more austere art of Florence. The rich display of gold leaf and brilliant colors were favorite International Gothic traits, but in the interest in perspective and foreshortening and especially in the exquisite predella panels Gentile shows the influence of the Florentines.

The altarpiece for the Quaratesi family, signed and dated 1425, also demonstrates the composite quality of Gentile's art. The fresco *Madonna Enthroned* in Orvieto Cathedral of late 1425 has few traces of the International Gothic style and displays a corporeality and fullness in keeping with his evolution after Florence. His last works, the frescoes in St. John Lateran in Rome depicting the life of John the Baptist and grisaille portraits of saints, were destroyed in 1647, when Francesco Borromini reconstructed the interior.

Further Reading

The best work in English on Gentile is the chapter on the artist in Raimond van Marle, *The Development of the Italian Schools of Painting,* vol. 8 (1927). Luigi Grassi, ed., *Tutta la pittura di Gentile da Fabriano* (1953), in Italian, is useful for its illustrations.

Additional Sources

Christiansen, Keith, *Gentile da Fabriano,* Ithaca, N.Y.: Cornell University Press, 1982. □

Giovanni Gentile

The Italian philosopher and politician Giovanni Gentile (1875-1944) was influential in reviving Hegelian idealism in Italy. He made significant contributions to the Italian educational system and participated in the formation of the Fascist corporate state.

On May 30, 1875, Giovanni Gentile was born at Castelvetrano, Sicily. He earned a scholarship to the University of Pisa in 1893. There his interests were turned from literature to philosophy by the influence of Donato Jaja. Enthusiastically responding to this new stimulation, Gentile determined to revive the idealist doctrine of the autonomy of the mind.

After 5 years of teaching in secondary schools, Gentile began his university career in Naples with an inaugural lecture entitled "The Rebirth of Idealism" (1903). Subsequently he taught at Palermo and, after Jaja's death, inherited the chair at Pisa in 1914. The next few years were filled with intense work, culminating in three major volumes: *The Theory of Spirit as Pure Act* (1916), *Foundations of the Philosophy of Law* (1916), and the first volume of his *Logic* (1917). During the years 1903-1922 Gentile and Benedetto Croce collaborated in editing a periodical, *La critica.*

After the Italian defeat at Caporetto, Gentile became increasingly involved in public life. Together with a group of friends he founded a review, the *New Liberal Politics,* in order to promote political and educational reforms. After Mussolini's march on Rome in 1922, Gentile became minister of public instruction, with full powers to reform the school system. He now had the authority to begin the second part of his life's dream: the rejuvenation of Italian culture. After the enactment of his plan, Gentile's political influence lessened, although he received appointments to several political positions and cultural organizations. His duties as president of the National Fascist Institute of Culture and director of the new *Enciclopedia italiana* took most of his energies during the next 15 years, but Gentile continued to teach, now at the University of Rome, and published a major work, *The Philosophy of Art.*

Gentile supported Mussolini's Ethiopian adventure but became increasingly disaffected with the party after Mussolini allied Italy with Germany in 1940. However, he saw Mussolini as the only man who could rescue Italy from civil war and from the warring foreign armies on Italian soil.

In spite of the turmoil and the constant dangers of his last years, Gentile managed to finish the final aspect of his idealist philosophy: *The Genesis and Structure of Society.* On April 15, 1944, after interceding on behalf of some students whose loyalty was suspect, Giovanni Gentile was shot by a band of partisans.

Further Reading

The definitive study of Gentile is by H. S. Harris, *The Social Philosophy of Giovanni Gentile* (1960), a sympathetic account which also provides all the necessary background information. Harris also translated *Genesis and Structure of Society* (1960), which contains a biographical essay and an exhaustive bibliography of Gentile studies in English. See also Roger W. Holmes, *The Idealism of Giovanni Gentile* (1937), and Pasquale Romanelli, *Gentile: The Philosophy of Giovanni Gentile* (1938).

Additional Sources

Romanell, Patrick, *Croce versus Gentil,* New York: AMS Press, 1982. □

Geoffrey of Monmouth

The English pseudohistorian Geoffrey of Monmouth (ca. 1100-1155) is known for his "History of the Kings of Britain," through which he contributed greatly to the dissemination of the Arthurian legend throughout Europe.

Geoffrey was born in or near Monmouth, Wales. By 1129 he was residing in Oxford, probably as a member of a nonmonastic ecclesiastical community. He stayed at Oxford at least until 1151 and during this period wrote his two extant works, *Historia regum Britanniae* (1136-1138; *History of the Kings of Britain*) and *Vita Merlini* (ca. 1148; *The Life of Merlin*). Geoffrey was a keen observer of contemporary trends in historical writing and combined his observations with a fertile imagination and a consistent, if not profound, philosophical outlook about history to produce his brilliant pseudohistory of the Britons, the Celtic people which inhabited the island of Britain before being conquered by the Anglo-Saxons.

Historia regum Britanniae purports to be a Latin translation of a "very old book" recounting the story of the rise and fall of the Britons. In composing his legendary history, Geoffrey utilized material from British legend and folklore. He also borrowed from earlier Latin accounts of the Britons but treated all his sources with great imaginative freedom. *The Historia* begins with the story of Brutus, grandson of Aeneas and founder of Britain; there follow accounts of many mythical monarchs (including King Lear). The climax of the work is Geoffrey's invention of a glorious reign of King Arthur and his description of Arthur's tremendous victories over the invading Saxons and the hostile Roman Empire. Here Geoffrey was influenced by contemporaneous historians' accounts of the Anglo-Norman kings and by the English civil war which raged as he wrote. The main themes of the *Historia* are that history is cyclic, that civil strife brings national disaster, and that the goals of the individual and those of society often clash.

In the *Vita Merlini,* a 1,500-line Latin poem, Geoffrey tells the story of Merlin, a legendary Welsh prophet and prince, whose prophecies formed one part of the *Historia.* Merlin goes mad as he watches a ferocious battle and flees to the forest, thwarting all attempts to make him return to the court, whose follies he bitterly reveals. This work carries further Geoffrey's concern with the hero who finds antagonism between his own desires and the values of society.

In 1151 Geoffrey was designated bishop of St. Asaph on the border of England and Wales. In the years following his death, his *Historia* became widely, though not unanimously, accepted as factual and influenced serious historians of the Britons and the English for centuries.

Further Reading

The most thorough, though controversial, study of Geoffrey's art is J. S. P. Tatlock, *The Legendary History of Britain* (1950). Also useful is the chapter on Geoffrey in Roger S. Loomis, ed., *Arthurian Literature in the Middle Ages* (1959). For a recent analysis of the themes and intellectual context of the *Historia regum Britanniae* see Robert W. Hanning, *Vision of History in Early Britain from Gildas to Geoffrey of Monmouth* (1966). □

George I

George I (1660-1727) was king of Great Britain and Ireland from 1714 to 1727. Founder of the Hanoverian dynasty, he was the first English monarch whose claim to reign depended upon an act of Parliament.

Born at Hanover on March 28, 1660, George Lewis, of the house of Brunswick-Lüneburg, was the son of Ernest Augustus and Sophia, granddaughter of James I of England. George's marriage to his cousin Sophia Dorothea in 1682 united the Hanoverian possessions of the house of Brunswick. He answered his wife's suspected infidelity by divorcing her in 1694 and confining her to her castle for life. He succeeded his father as elector of Hanover in 1698.

George's role in British history stemmed from two circumstances: he was the great-grandson of James I, and he was a Protestant. In 1701 the English Parliament, recognizing that neither William III nor his successor, Anne, would leave an heir and fearing reversion of the crown to a Roman Catholic, passed the Act of Settlement; it conferred the inheritance on Sophia of Hanover and "the heirs of her body being Protestants." By this statute George became king in 1714—to the exclusion of some 57 persons with superior hereditary claims.

Understandably, George proved unpopular in Britain. A shy, rather sour man, he preferred to avoid crowds and royal pageantry. Ignorant of the language, bereft of intellectual gifts, and unmoved by the arts, save music, he showed no appreciation of English culture. Hanover remained undisguisedly his first love. He showered his German mistresses with estates and pensions and showed favoritism to his German courtiers. In foreign affairs he was rightly suspected of giving priority to the interests of Hanover, but fortunately those interests were usually congruent with Britain's.

Yet, fundamentally, George I was the right man at the right time for Britain. He possessed a quality the Stuart kings had lacked—steadiness. He knew his friends from his enemies and rewarded them accordingly; nothing was more essential in defending the new dynasty against treason. He quickly learned to find his ministers among the Whigs, who had supported his succession to the throne.

Though ignorant of English politics, George I did have experience in European foreign affairs. For 6 years he relied chiefly on his Hanoverian ministers, Bernstorff and Bothmer; the English ministers, led by Lords Townshend and Stanhope, usually had to work through the German advisers on matters requiring royal assent. The main weak-

George I died suddenly of a stroke on June 11, 1727, while journeying to Hanover. Unmourned by his family and his English subjects, he had nevertheless done his duty. His instincts were authoritarian, yet he had managed to stifle rebellion without imposing tyranny. Above all, he learned to accommodate himself to a system of constitutional rule that the more energetic William III had found frustrating and distasteful.

Further Reading

The most penetrating account of George I's relationship with his ministers can be found in J. H. Plumb, *Sir Robert Walpole* (2 vols., 1956-1961). A detailed history of the reign by Wolfgang Michael is partially translated from the German under the title *England under George I* (2 vols., 1936-1939). John M. Beattie, *The English Court in the Reign of George I* (1967), contains a valuable chapter on the court in politics.

Additional Sources

Hatton, Ragnhild Marie, *George I, elector and king,* Cambridge, Mass.: Harvard University Press, 1978.

Mangan, J. J., *The king's favour: three eighteenth century monarchs and the favourites who ruled them,* New York: St. Martin's Press, 1991. □

George II

George II (1683-1760) was king of Great Britain and Ireland and elector of Hanover from 1727 to 1760. During his long reign the system of governing Britain through an oligarchy of powerful political managers solidified.

George II, born Nov. 10, 1683, followed a military career as a young man. As Prince of Wales, he displayed hostility to his father—which was amply returned—and counted his father's advisers as enemies. Thus, when he became king in 1727, he did not wish the incumbent leading minister, Robert Walpole, to continue in office. But Walpole stayed on all the same. The new queen, Caroline of Ansbach, whose close friendship Walpole had secured 10 years earlier, made George II see that Walpole could provide what others could not: stable government and a lavish budget for the court.

The Queen ruled her husband. Although George II took mistresses, his enduring passion was for his wife. Her ample physique attracted him; her management of his ego enslaved him. They were quite unalike. He was meticulous, industrious, and orderly in his habits, yet lacking in self-confidence. She was bold and charming. He had no time for ideas, though he loved music and read history; the religious and philosophical subjects that she delighted in discussing were to him "lettered nonsense." It was a stormy marriage; the King shouted, but the Queen got her way. Walpole, who ignored the mistresses, had indeed "taken the right sow by the ear," and although the Queen's death in 1737 diminished his certainty of royal favor, he was kept on until war

ness of this arrangement lay in its tendency to isolate the King's government from its parliamentary support. When the King visited Hanover in 1716, his most influential men in Parliament, Townshend and Sir Robert Walpole, were left behind and fell victim to intrigue. Blamed for opposing the King's foreign policy and, quite unfairly, for conniving with George's son, the Prince of Wales, Townshend lost royal favor and resigned in April 1717. Walpole followed him. Finding allies among the Tories, they led a vigorous parliamentary opposition. The lively court of the Prince of Wales became a gathering place of dissident politicians. Although the government, increasingly dominated by Bernstorff until 1719, survived these onslaughts, the political turmoil provoked by the outcast Whigs goaded the King into action.

It has been said that George I reigned but did not rule. However, he could be energetic and ruthless when his power seemed threatened. To overshadow the prince's court, he suppressed his aversion to courtly entertainments and conversed with ambitious men. The King's inability to speak English was not a serious hindrance; nearly everyone at court was fluent in French.

In 1720 the bursting of the "South Sea Bubble" raised stormy protests in Parliament. The goverment badly needed men who could tame the House of Commons, and chief among these was Walpole. Gaining access to George I through his aging but most trusted mistress, Madame Schulenberg, now Duchess of Kendal, Walpole and Townshend successfully negotiated a reentry to office. By 1722 Walpole was the King's leading minister and retained royal confidence to the end.

ment was unsettled until 1757, when he agreed to accept the combined leadership of Pitt and Lord Newcastle. George II disliked both men, but under them Britain achieved its greatest triumphs in 18th-century warfare. Amid these triumphs the old king died of a heart attack on Oct. 25, 1760.

Clearly, George II's role in the great victories of the Seven Years War was at best a marginal one. It was not that he was lazy or stupid; he understood government business and took it seriously. If during his reign the power of monarchy seemed to diminish, it was mainly because he preferred to avoid difficult situations. Power flowed to those with stronger wills. ''Ministers are kings in this country,'' he grumbled. It was not true, but he generally acted as though it were.

Further Reading

J. D. Griffith Davies, *A King in Toils* (1938), is a study of George II. R. L. Arkell, *Caroline of Ansbach: George the Second's Queen* (1939), and Peter Quennell, *Caroline of England: An Augustan Portrait* (1939), offer good introductions to life at George II's court. Lord Hervey's *Memoirs* provides a colorful eyewitness account of the court; Romney Sedgwick's abridged edition (1952; rev. 1963) retains most of the material relating to the King and Queen. For reliable accounts of politics during George II's reign see Basil Williams, *The Life of William Pitt, Earl of Chatham* (2 vols., 1913); J. H. Plumb, *Sir Robert Walpole* (2 vols., 1956-1961); and John B. Owen, *The Rise of the Pelhams* (1957). □

eroded his parliamentary position in 1742. Even after Walpole retired, George II sought his advice.

George II was the last English monarch to lead his troops in battle, but, ''for all his personal bravery,'' he was, as Walpole observed, ''as great a political coward as ever wore a crown.'' When pressured by his ministers he quarreled and complained but yielded. Thus he gave up the one minister who completely captured his heart, John Carteret, because the Pelhams brought to bear their parliamentary power. Carteret's intellectual gifts and his zeal for a strong diplomatic posture attracted George II, but the man had no parliamentary base, and when the Pelhams sought his dismissal in 1744, the King acquiesced. The new broad-based ministry that was then formed insisted, in 1746, on giving office to William Pitt the Elder. George II detested Pitt and vowed never to show him favor, but when nearly all his ministers threatened to resign, he capitulated.

It was the habit of the Georges to hate their sons. George II's strangely intense loathing for Frederick, Prince of Wales—''that monster''—was fully shared by the Queen, who once asserted: ''My dear first-born is the greatest ass, and the greatest liar, . . . and the greatest beast in the whole world.'' To avoid employing the dissident politicians who, since 1737, had gathered around the prince at Leicester House, the King gladly put up with the Pelhams. There was no sorrow at court when the prince died in 1751, but there was regret when Henry Pelham died in 1754.

''Now I shall have no more peace,'' George II remarked on learning of Pelham's death. He was right. His govern-

George III

George III (1738-1820) was king of Great Britain and Ireland from 1760 to 1820. His long reign witnessed the American Revolution, the defeat of Napoleon, the founding of the "second British empire," and the decline of monarchical power.

B orn on June 4, 1738, in London, George III was the eldest son of Frederick, Prince of Wales. Frederick's death in 1751 left the young George heir apparent to the throne, to which he ascended when his grandfather, George II, died in 1760.

As a youth, George was a poor student whose emotional immaturity matched his mental underdevelopment. He formed strong attachments to older men whom he could respect as figures of authority. Abstemious, economical, and morally upright, he worked conscientiously, though unimaginatively, at being king, at preserving the Crown's dignity, and at maintaining England's power and honor. He knew the constitutional limits of monarchical power and had no wish to exceed them. With experience he grew adept at using all the Crown's considerable political influence, supporting one faction against another and employing ''secret service money.'' Indeed, his skill at these activities lent color to Opposition cries that he exercised ''personal rule'' and ''subverted'' the English constitution.

Early Reign

One of the first matters to occupy the new king's attention was his own marriage. Suppressing his preference for an English woman, George chose, as was expected of him, a German Protestant princess, Charlotte Sophia of Mecklenburg-Strelitz. Although she was homely and dull, George remained faithful to her after their marriage in 1761, and they had 15 children.

Early in his reign George made himself unpopular by ousting William Pitt the Elder (1761) and installing in the Treasury his adviser, Lord Bute. As a Scot, Bute was despised and distrusted by the English even before he made an unpopular peace with France. George relied utterly upon Bute, but his confidence was misplaced, for Bute had neither sagacity nor courage and soon resigned (1763).

Thus began the King's long search for a minister in whom he had confidence and who could also control the government. After Bute came George Grenville (1763-1765) and Lord Rockingham (1765-1766). Then George brought Pitt back and created him Earl of Chatham (1766). But Chatham suffered a mental breakdown, and George then entrusted the government to the Duke of Grafton (1768-1770). Grafton proved incompetent, and when he resigned in January 1770, the King appointed Lord North first lord of the Treasury (1770-1782). At last George III had a "prime minister" whom he liked and trusted. By this time experience had made George a master politician. His strength and determination kept the increasingly reluctant

(and increasingly unsuccessful) North at the head of the government for 12 years.

Several explosive issues buffeted George and his government during the first 2 decades of his reign. Most significant were the turbulences created by the political reformer John Wilkes and by the American colonies. The pious King regarded the disreputable Wilkes with horror and hatred. By prosecuting the popular Wilkes, George further increased both his personal unpopularity and the public's lack of confidence in his government. But the exercise of power depended not on mob approval but on the favor of the gentry in the House of Commons. As the American war dragged on, the government's lack of success together with the haranguing of the Opposition alienated many of the gentry who had formerly voted for the King's policies. Furthermore, large segments of influential public opinion outside Parliament disapproved of the American war and of government policy and wished for administrative reform and economy. North's ministry fell in 1782, and the American colonies won their independence. These two events ushered in a new phase in British government and in the life of George III.

Later Reign

Once more George had to tolerate ministries headed by persons whom he detested: first Rockingham, until his death in 1782 brought Lord Shelburne to power, and then the "infamous" Fox-North coalition nominally headed by the Duke of Portland. By exceeding the strict bounds of his constitutional authority, George managed to bring down the coalition over the issue of Fox's East India Bill. To head the new ministry, he picked William Pitt the Younger.

Pitt was strong and capable, and his long tenure of office was markedly successful. His strength rebuffed, just as North's weakness had invited, the King's political maneuvering. While Pitt devoted himself to financial and administrative reforms and then to the struggle with France, George III retired more and more from political life into domestic concerns. He still had occasional political impact, most notably when by his adamant opposition to Catholic emancipation in Ireland he caused Pitt's resignation (1801). His domestic tranquility was disturbed by the coarse extravagances of his two eldest sons (George, Prince of Wales, and Frederick, Duke of York) and by his own ill health.

George III experienced mental incapacity on a number of occasions. His mental aberration, long deemed manic-depressive insanity, has recently been diagnosed by medical experts as the result of a rare metabolic disorder called porphyria. George had four major attacks: October 1788 to February 1789; February-March 1801; January-March 1804; and October 1810 to his death on Jan. 29, 1820. The last illness led to the establishment of Prince George's regency (February 1811). In his last years George III was also totally blind and deaf, a proper object of sympathy, even affection, for the public who despised the Regent's profligacy.

Further Reading

A full-length biography of George III is J. C. Long, *George III: The Story of a Complex Man* (1961). An interesting biographical essay is provided in J. H. Plumb, *The First Four Georges* (1956). For the King's mental condition, the long-accepted view of Manfred S. Guttmacher, *America's Last King: An Interpretation of the Madness of George III* (1941), has now been authoritatively challenged by Ida Macalpine and Richard Hunter, *George III and the Mad-Business* (1969). For an understanding of George III's political role, a number of special studies are invaluable: L. B. Namier, *The Structure of Politics at the Accession of George III* (2 vols., 1929; 2d ed., 1 vol., 1957); Romney Sedgwick's long introduction to his edition of the *Letters from George III to Lord Bute, 1756-1766* (1939); Richard Pares, *King George III and the Politicians* (1953); and John Derry, *The Regency Crisis and the Whigs, 1788-89* (1964). A general history of the period is J. Steven Watson, *The Reign of George III, 1760-1815* (1960).

Additional Sources

Andrews, Allen, *The King who lost America: George III and independence,* London: Jupiter Books, 1976.

Delany, Mrs. (Mary), *The autobiography and correspondence of Mary Granville, Mrs. Delany: with interesting reminiscences of King George the Third and Queen Charlott,* New York, AMS Press, 1974.

Gattey, Charles Neilson, *"Farmer" George's black sheep: the lives and loves of George III's brothers and sister,* Abbotsbrook, Bourne End, Buckinghamshire: Kensal Press, 1985.

Pain, Nesta, *George III at home,* London: Eyre Methuen, 1975.

Plumb, J. H. (John Harold), *New light on the tyrant George III,* Washington: Society of the Cincinnati, 1978.

Van der Kiste, John, *George III's children,* Far Thrupp, Stroud, Gloucestershire: A. Sutton, 1992. □

George IV

George IV (1762-1830), the king of Great Britain and Ireland from 1820 to 1830, was one of the most detested British monarchs. He was also a man of exquisite taste who profoundly influenced the culture of his age.

Regency England, roughly the first 3 decades of the 19th century, takes its name from George's title of prince regent, which he held from 1811 to 1820. It was a period of great elegance in art, architecture, and the style of aristocratic life, and also one of unrestrained indulgence and moral laxity. The prince regent set the example in both respects.

The future George IV was born on Aug. 12, 1762. His father, George III, an extremely moral and pious man, loved his eldest child as a son, but hated him as his heir. For both reasons the young prince was kept under a very tight rein and carefully insulated from the outside world. In 1783, when the prince came of age, he violently reacted against these restraints and entered society with a great splash. George was tall and handsome, with a tendency toward

portliness, which in maturity was to become gross obesity. He entered into the pleasures of life with gusto, and Mrs. Fitzherbert soon emerged as the first of a succession of mistresses. He began to indulge his passion for building, and the Royal Pavilion at Brighton was begun in 1784. By 1787 the prince was already hundreds of thousands of pounds in debt and had to be bailed out by Parliament, the first of many such occasions.

The prince's escapades strained relations with his father, and political differences increased the tension between them. The prince became the intimate friend of George III's bitterest political enemies, the Whigs, led by Charles James Fox. Fox was a man of immense personal charm, and Whig society was the most glittering group of the day. The Whigs fought the prince's battles for money in Parliament; he entered fully into their political schemes. Together they waited in 1788 in ill-disguised anticipation that the King's insanity would prove permanent and that the prince would become regent.

George III, however, recovered. The prince had not been able to grasp power, and his reputation had suffered. It suffered still further from a secret, and illegal, marriage to the Catholic Mrs. Fitzherbert, which soon became common knowledge. In 1795, at his father's urging, the prince decided to regularize his position and increase his income by making a legitimate marriage. The choice of Princess Caroline of Brunswick could not have been more unfortunate; she was coarse, vulgar, and wildly eccentric. It was an arranged marriage, and the prince detested her from first sight. The marriage was barely consummated when the

couple separated. Princess Charlotte, their only child, died in 1817. Caroline's notorious affairs in England and abroad only served to underline George's own sexual irregularities, and their interminable bickering until her death in 1821 surrounded the monarchy with scandal.

Patron of the Arts

Without Caroline, George's reputation might well have been higher. He was warm-hearted and generous, and devoted to his often motherly mistresses. He was also a man of superb taste. England is in his debt for some of its most famous and beautiful architectural treasures. Regent Street and Regent's Park owe their beauty to him, and he rebuilt Buckingham Palace and Windsor Castle. The beautiful classical portico of the National Gallery came from Carlton House, his residence as heir to the throne.

George made a magnificent collection of 17th-century Dutch paintings, and, as king, he persuaded his government to spend a fortune for a collection that formed the nucleus of the National Gallery. He filled his palaces with the finest examples of 18th-century French and contemporary English furniture. No British monarch, except possibly Charles I, ever added so much to the nation's cultural heritage. But George's tastes were expensive, and at a time when most of his subjects were experiencing extreme privation during the wars with France and their aftermath, his extravagance caused bitter resentment.

Regent and King

In 1811 his father became permanently insane, and George was declared prince regent. The Whigs, however, did not come to power with him, for the prince's relations with the Whigs had become increasingly strained since Fox's death in 1806. In 1812 George did make an attempt to bring some of the Whigs into a coalition ministry, but they would not accept a compromise. George had never been a Whig by conviction, and thereafter he settled comfortably with his father's Tory ministers and advisers. He, however, was never the strong political influence George III had been in his prime. The blunt Duke of Wellington, his last prime minister, called George and his brothers "the damnedest millstones about the neck of any Government that can be imagined."

In 1820, when he came to the throne on his father's death, George IV persuaded a reluctant government to undertake a divorce from his detested queen. This caused a national outcry, less because the Queen was loved than because George was hated, and the action had to be dropped. On occasion the King exerted his prerogatives, as when he chose George Canning over Wellington for prime minister in 1827, but in general George followed the advice of his ministers. He enjoyed his public role, and though old, overweight, and corseted, he played it with great dignity and a real sense of drama until he died, unlamented, on June 26, 1830.

Further Reading

Roger Fulford, *George the Fourth* (1935; rev. ed. 1949), is a fine modern biography. See also J. H. Plumb's delightful *The First*

Four Georges (1956). R. J. White, *Life in Regency England* (1963), is recommended for general historical background.

Additional Sources

Foord-Kelcey, Jim., *Mrs. Fitzherbert and sons,* Sussex, England: Book Guild, 1991.

Hibbert, Christopher, *George IV,* Harmondsworth: Penguin, 1976.

Hibbert, Christopher, *George IV: Prince of Wales, 1762-181,* New York, Harper & Row 1974, 1972.

Hibbert, Christopher, *George IV, regent and king, 1811-1830,* New York: Harper & Row, 1975 1973.

Palmer, Alan Warwick, *The life and times of George IV,* London: Cardinal, 1975, 1972.

Richardson, Joanna, *The disastrous marriage: a study of George IV and Caroline of Brunswick,* Westport, Conn.: Greenwood Press, 1975, 1960. □

George V

George V (1865-1936) was king of Great Britain and Northern Ireland and emperor of India from 1910 to 1936. He maintained the monarchy as a stabilizing influence in a period of rapid international and domestic changes.

Born June 3, 1865, at Marlborough House, London, George V was the second son of the Prince and Princess of Wales (later King Edward VII and Queen Alexandra). Though over the years the royal family had several homes, it was to Sandringham in Norfolk, constructed by his father, that George as prince and later as king was especially attached. His early education was by private tutors, but the strongest influence on him was his mother. As the second son, he was to have a naval career, and in 1877 he became a naval cadet. He trained at sea, passed his examination to become a midshipman, attended the Royal Naval College at Greenwich, and served from 1886 to 1888 in the Mediterranean. In 1890 he was given personal command of a first-class gunboat with the West Indies and North American Squadron and was promoted to commander in August 1891.

Only with the death of his elder brother, the Duke of Clarence, in January 1892, did George, now 26, come into direct line of succession to the throne. He was at once created Duke of York, introduced into the House of Lords, and provided with living quarters in St. James's Palace. The next year he married his cousin, Princess Mary of Tech, who had been betrothed to his brother. To this union were born five sons and one daughter.

Accession to Throne

For some years George spent much of his time on official visits—to Russia in 1894 to attend the funeral of Alexander III; in 1897 to Ireland; in 1901 to Australia (where he opened in Melbourne the first Commonwealth Parliament), South Africa, and Canada; and in 1905-1906 a nota-

and some 300 visits to hospitals, as well as personally distributing 58,000 decorations. He and the Queen also followed the fortunes of two sons in the armed services. Due to the hostilities with Germany, a royal proclamation in 1917 changed the official name of the royal family from Hanover to Windsor. It was to Buckingham Palace that crowds turned on Armistice Day, Nov. 11, 1918. Soon after, the King visited battlefields, cemeteries and devasted areas in France and then received President Wilson of the United States in London. In vain he advised David Lloyd George in 1918 to postpone a general election. Outwardly, at least, he was more successful when he sought to be a symbol of unity in opening the new Ulster Parliament in June 1921.

Later Reign

In various ways George's role affected events as the reign continued. In 1923, partly on the advice of elder statesmen and partly through his own decision, he chose Stanley Baldwin as prime minister, passing over Lord Curzon, who had more seniority. He accepted the advent of Labour to power in 1924 as natural and their due. With the end of the general strike in 1926 his influence was important in the decision not to punish strike leaders. In the financial and constitutional crisis of 1931 the role of King George was more controversial. The necessity of a national (nonpartisan) government, if Labour failed, was urged upon him by Sir Herbert Samuel, the Liberal leader. In the words of his private secretary, the King successfully impressed upon Ramsay MacDonald (who had been Labour prime minister) "that he was the only man to lead the country through the crisis." MacDonald formed a national coalition. It was perhaps as much a matter of the King advising his ministers as they advising him.

As his life developed, these qualities began to be associated with George V—dignity, frankness, occasional obstinacy and irritability, sense of duty, and fair play. His latter years were somewhat clouded by the differences with his eldest son, the Prince of Wales, who rebelled against tradition. But this did little to obscure the royal family as a symbol of British unity, particularly evident in the ceremonies of the King's Silver Jubilee in 1935. There was solemnity in St. Paul's and pageantry in Westminster Hall. Huge crowds massed in the streets as the King and Queen drove through London each day, and before Buckingham Palace as they appeared on the balcony each evening for a week.

But it soon became clear that the King's old bronchial ailment which nearly took his life in 1929 had returned, this time fatally. After a brief illness he died on Jan. 20, 1936, at the age of 70. His tomb is in the nave of St. George's Chapel, Windsor.

Further Reading

There are two excellent biographies of George V: John Gore, *King George V: A Personal Memoir* (1941), treats his private life; Harold Nicolson, *King George the Fifth: His Life and Reign* (1952), covers his public life. Another personal account is in James Pope-Hennessy, *Queen Mary, 1867-1953* (1959).

ble visit to India. With Victoria's death in 1901 he was created Prince of Wales. And Sir Arthur Bigge, Victoria's principal private secretary since 1896, became his private secretary, a role which continued when the prince became king and lasted until 1931. Bigge, created Lord Stamfordham in 1911, had great influence on George's official life. On Stamfordham's death in 1931 George V said, "He taught me how to be a King."

Edward VII and his son George V were two quite different personalities, the former an extrovert who enjoyed ceremonial pageantry, the latter a shy man who put himself on display only as an act of duty. George ascended the throne in May 1910. His coronation came in June 1911; in December in Delhi he received homage from the native Indian rajas. Meanwhile, in England he had inherited a constitutional crisis, the consequence of the attack of the Commons, controlled by the Liberal government, upon the Lords, controlled by the Conservatives. Upon the insistence of Prime Minister Asquith, King George agreed to create enough new peers to force the Parliament Bill, limiting the legislative power of the Lords, through that House. The Lords eventually gave way without the mass creation of new peers. In an even more serious crisis, involving national unity, over the Third Home Rule Bill for Ireland, King George brought the party leaders together at Buckingham Palace in 1914 in hopes of resolving the problem. The outcome was postponed by the advent of World War I.

During the war the King had no direct responsibility. But his duties, nonetheless, were manifold. He made some 450 recorded inspections of military and naval installations

Additional Sources

Halperin, John, *Eminent Georgians: the lives of King George V, Elizabeth Bowen, St. John Philby, and Nancy Astor,* New York: St. Martin's Press, 1995.

Hough, Richard Alexander, *Born royal: the lives and loves of the young Windsors,* Toronto; New York: Bantam Books, 1988.

Rose, Kenneth, *King George V,* New York: Knopf: Distributed by Random House, 1984.

Rose, Kenneth, *King George V,* London: Weidenfeld and Nicolson, 1983.

Sinclair, David, *Two Georges: the making of the modern monarchy,* London: Hodder and Stoughton, 1988.

Van der Kiste, John, *George V's children,* Far Thrupp, Stroud, Gloucestershire; Wolfeboro Falls, NH: A. Sutton, 1991. □

George VI

George VI (1895-1952) was king of Great Britain and Northern Ireland from 1936 to 1952. He guided his country through World War II and the years of rapid transformation that followed.

Prince Albert, as George VI was generally known during his early years, was the second son of the Duke of York (later George V); he was born at York Cottage, Sandringham, on Dec. 15, 1895. Although a sensitive, shy, and at times nervous child, he was happy and possessed a determined spirit. In 1909 he entered the Royal Naval College at Osborne and 2 years later went on to Dartmouth. At both institutions he won the respect of his teachers and his classmates. Afterward he entered the navy professionally.

During the first years of World War I the prince served on the battleship *Collingwood* and later on the *Malaya* and while on the former participated in the Battle of Jutland (May 1916). Periods of illness, however, interrupted his service. Later in the war he was appointed to the Royal Naval Air Service, and in 1919 he became the first member of the royal family to receive a pilot's certificate.

After the war Prince Albert spent a year at Trinity College, Cambridge, where he proved to be a keen and diligent student. In 1920 George V created him Duke of York, and in this capacity he developed a special interest in industrial problems. His famous youth camps, where schoolboys and boys from industrial areas could spend weekends, were inaugurated in 1921. In 1923 he married Lady Elizabeth Bowes-Lyon, and the two became a model royal couple. They had two children: Princess Elizabeth (April 21, 1926) and Princess Margaret (Aug. 21, 1930).

Throughout the years between 1919 and his accession the Duke of York traveled widely. He gained a new confidence in himself and won the esteem of others. When his brother, Edward VIII, abdicated in 1936, the duke ascended to the throne as George VI. The new king brought to the monarchy a dignity, a compassion, and a broad understanding of human problems which served him well and compensated for his limited knowledge of political matters.

As king, George VI continued to display the qualities that characterized his earlier life. He proved to be a valuable source of advice for his ministers. In 1939 the King and Queen went to Canada in a precedent-breaking trip which was successful beyond expectations. As a result of this visit all talk of Canadian neutrality in the event of war ceased. That June the royal family proceeded to the United States, and the King became the first reigning British sovereign to enter that country. Throughout World War II he furthered Anglo-American unity. During the war he painstakingly carried out his many responsibilities and, together with the Queen, became a frequent visitor to the devastated areas of England. He identified with his people in their common suffering and gained their admiration. In postwar years he presided over far-reaching changes in the domestic and colonial realms. He died on Feb. 6, 1952.

Further Reading

Sir John W. Wheeler-Bennet, *King George VI: His Life and Reign* (1958), is a superb official biography that includes numerous samplings of the King's letters and diary comments. *A King's Story: The Memoirs of the Duke of Windsor* (1951) is useful for intimate reflections, and Harold G. Nicolson, *King George V: His Life and Reign* (1953), is an excellent companion volume. □

Henry George

The American economist and social reformer Henry George (1839-1897) popularized the "single-tax" reform movement.

Henry George was born in Philadelphia, Pa., on Sept. 2, 1839. He left school when he was 13 years old and spent 2 years as a clerk before becoming a seaman. After his arrival in San Francisco in 1858, he worked as a laborer, gold prospector, and printer. He married and started to raise a family and for several years experienced a desperate, grinding poverty.

In 1865 George became a journalist. In several newspapers, including the *San Francisco Daily Evening Post,* which he founded and edited (1871-1875), he criticized and exposed some of the major inequities of his day, such as speculation in public lands, the illegal actions of monopolies, and the exploitation of new Chinese immigrants in California. As a deeply religious and moral man, he felt that America could not condone such actions.

George studied economics and slowly systemized his thinking. In his editorials and writings he proposed various economic reforms, including public ownership of utilities and public-oriented industries such as railroads and the telegraph system. Still, he never embraced the ideology of socialism. His major work was *Progress and Poverty* (1879), which he infused with his strong moral passion for justice

and his hatred of poverty. George claimed that private ownership of land was the root cause of poverty and also held up progress. It was morally wrong for people to become wealthy without working, but just from ownership of a natural resource that should be accessible to all people. He claimed that the rise of rents that went along with the growth of industry and progress forced wages to fall. For a "remedy" he proposed the nationalization of land or the taxing of land so highly that the economic rent would go to the community and be used for the public good.

George's simple solution, the "single tax," and his moral questioning of society's values and actions appealed to the people, though not to most economists, and made George famous. In the 1880s the single tax became the focus of a powerful reform movement. Local clubs were formed, and George propagandized for acceptance of the single tax. The idea even had a formidable impact on British radicalism in that decade.

George moved to New York in 1880, where his fame was such that he was asked to run for mayor as a reform candidate in 1886; he was narrowly defeated by Abram Hewitt but ran ahead of the Republican candidate, Theodore Roosevelt. Though in poor health, he was persuaded to run again, but he died before the election, on Oct. 29, 1897.

Further Reading

Charles Albro Barker, *Henry George* (1955), is a thorough study of George's life, and Edward J. Rose, *Henry George* (1968), is a good, shorter biography. Other studies include Henry George, Jr., *The Life of Henry George* (1900); Elwood P. Lawrence, *Henry George in the British Isles* (1957); and Steven B. Cord, *Henry George: Dreamer or Realist?* (1965). Robert L. Heilbroner discusses George in the context of 19th-century economic thought in *The Wordly Philosophers: The Lives, Times, and Ideas of the Great Economic Thinkers* (1953; 3d ed. rev. 1967).

Additional Sources

Barker, Charles A. (Charles Albro), *Henry Georg,* Westport, Conn., Greenwood Press 1974.

Cord, Steven B., *Henry George, dreamer or realist?,* New York: Robert Schalkenbach Foundation, 1984.

Geiger, George Raymond, *The philosophy of Henry George,* Westport, Conn.: Hyperion Press, 1975, 1933.

George and the scholars: a century of scientific research reveals the reformer was an original economist and a world-class social philosopher, New York: Robert Schalkenbach Foundation, 1991.

Jones, Peter d'Alroy, *Henry George and British socialism,* New York: Garland Pub., 1991.

Rather, Lois, *Henry George—printer to author,* Oakland Calif.: Rather Press, 1978. □

James Zachariah George

The American politican and jurist James Zachariah George (1826-1897) was one of Mississippi's strongest white-supremacy statesmen in the Reconstruction era.

James George was born on Oct. 20, 1826, in Monroe County, Ga. After his father's death his mother moved to Mississippi, where George spent the bulk of his life. His early education was limited, but by diligence and long study he acquired an above-average classical knowledge.

After service in the Mexican War (1846-1848) in Jefferson Davis's 1st Mississippi Volunteers, George gained admittance to the Mississippi bar. He was a member of the state convention that passed the 1861 ordinance of secession. Commissioned a captain of the Confederate infantry at the Civil War's outset, he ultimately rose to the rank of colonel of cavalry. Yet his military career was limited by 2 years spent as a war prisoner.

George resumed his law practice in 1865. His *Digest of Supreme Court Decisions* (1872), a compilation of court summaries dating back to Mississippi's statehood, still remains a basic reference guide. Meanwhile his law partnership became Mississippi's leading legal firm. In politics he soon gained the important post of chairman of the State Democratic Committee. His championship of the restoration of white supremacy in Mississippi prevented his election to Congress during the period of military reconstruction. In 1879, however, he was appointed to the Mississippi Supreme Court and was immediately elected chief justice. In 1881 he was elected to the U.S. Senate and held this office until his death.

Throughout his senatorial career, George consistently fought Federal interference in Mississippi affairs. He was ever the champion of the common people; despite his wealth and social prestige, he took pride in being called "the Commoner" by the admiring small-farmer element of Mississippi.

George was prominent in framing and passing the 1890 Mississippi Constitution. He was the only Senate Democrat who supported the Sherman Antitrust Act (1890). In his last years he began writing *The Political History of Slavery in the United States.* The unfinished text was published 18 years after his death in Mississippi City on Aug. 14, 1897.

A contemporary wrote that George's "robust physique, virile mind, tireless industry, firm will and capacity for sustained effort" made him "a type of the self-made men who have created and been created by this great republic."

Further Reading

No substantive biography of George exists. His *Political History of Slavery in the United States* (1915) contains personal references, and he is mentioned in such histories of Mississippi as Charles S. Sydnor and Claude Bennett, *Mississippi History* (1939), which includes a short biography, and Albert D. Kirwan, *Revolt of the Rednecks: Mississippi Politics, 1876-1925* (1951). □

Stefan George

The German symbolist poet Stefan George (1868-1933) strongly influenced a group of brilliant and idealistic disciples, thus manifesting his revolt against the materialism of his time.

Born in Rüdesheim near Bingen on the Rhine, Stefan George graduated from a gymnasium in Darmstadt and spent several years traveling throughout western Europe. While in Paris in 1889, he was admitted to Stéphane Mallarmé's soirées, where he met Paul Verlaine, Émile Verhaeren, and Auguste Rodin; and in Berlin, as a student of Romance languages, he came to know Carl August Klein, who was the first to recognize him as a poet. With Klein's help he founded and edited *Blätter für die Kunst* (1892-1919; Periodical for Art), the mouthpiece for the distinguished George circle of esthetes. This intellectual élite included not only poets and critics such as Friedrich Gundolf, Ernst Bertram, Max Kommerell, Karl Wolfskehl, and Norbert von Hellingrath but also men of action like Count Claus von Stauffenberg.

George's life may be divided conveniently into five major creative periods. During the first of these (1886-1889) he wrote verses which remained unpublished until 1901, when they appeared in his book *Die Fibel.* It was in his second period (1890-1896) that George emerged as a symbolist poet writing in strong contrast to the naturalistic trend then prevailing in German literature. His first work, a collection of 18 poems, *Hymnen* (1890; *Hymns*), was dedicated to his friend Klein. It was followed by *Pilgerfahrten* (1891) and *Algabal* (1892). Illustrated by Melchior Lechter, these

books appeared only in limited private editions of less than 200 copies.

Solitude and lack of companionship characterize George's third creative period (1897-1902) as evidenced by his collections of melancholic poems full of despair, *Das Jahr der Seele* (1897; *The Year of the Soul*) and *Teppich des Lebens* (1899; *The Carpet of Life*). Like his earlier writings, they were unavailable to the general public. Only at the turn of the century, when the Berlin publisher Georg Bondi brought out a one-volume edition of *Hymnen, Pilgerfahrten,* and *Algabal,* did his books begin to appear through regular trade channels. His contemporaries, however, considered his poetry exclusive and aristocratic and marked by the flaws of fin-de-siècle literature. Thus he was, in general, alienated from his fellow poets in Germany and abroad.

George's fourth period (1903-1913), often called the classical one, comprises not only *Der siebente Ring* (1907; *The Seventh Ring*) and *Der Stern des Bundes* (1913; *The Star of the Order*) but also his only volume of prose, *Tage und Taten* (1903; *Days and Deeds*). At this time George finally found the companion whom he had been seeking—young Maximilian Kronenberger. Their relationship, however, was short-lived; just a year after their first meeting Maxim died, one day before his sixteenth birthday. Nevertheless, his role in the poet's life may be compared to that of Beatrice in the life of Dante.

The fifth and last phase (1914-1933) finds George in the role of a judge and seer. He deals explicitly with the problems of his age in a collection of poetry, *Das neue Reich* (1928; *The New Reich*). Very much against his will, he was acclaimed by the Nazis as their champion and forerunner. But no movement could have been more alien to him than theirs, and when they attempted to honor him, he left the country and settled in Switzerland, where he died, a voluntary exile, in Minusio outside Locarno. In addition to his achievements as a lyrical poet, George became known as a gifted and productive translator.

Further Reading

The best commentaries on George in English are Edwin Keppel Bennett, *Stefan George* (1954), and Ulrich K. Goldsmith, *Stefan George: A Study of His Early Work* (1959). □

Richard Andrew Gephardt

United States Congressman Richard Andrew Gephardt (born 1941) has served in the U.S. House of Representatives since 1977 and was a candidate for the Democratic nomination for president in 1988. His protectionist campaign theme failed to win him the nomination. In 1989 he became Democratic majority leader in the House.

Richard A. Gephardt, first elected to Congress in 1976 from Missouri's Third Congressional District, epitomized the new breed of Democratic politicians which emerged in the 1970s and 1980s. These politicians, often labeled Atari Democrats, sought to wed the traditional party concern for social issues with new technology and fiscal conservatism. Gephardt's record reflects this new political pragmatism, which borrows from both liberal and conservative beliefs. The south St. Louis congressman endorsed constitutional amendments to ban abortion and school bussing; he supported tuition credits for parents of children in private schools, and school prayer; and he opposed gun control legislation. Yet he also supported a freeze on nuclear weapons and led the opposition to the MX missile. He also worked to stop military aid to the Nicaraguan Contras during the 1980s.

Richard Andrew Gephardt was born in St. Louis, Missouri, on January 31, 1941, to Louis Andrew and Loreen (Cassell) Gephardt, both the grandchildren of German immigrants. After completing high school in St. Louis, Gephardt enrolled at Northwestern University in Evanston, Illinois, majoring in speech and drama. He received a B.S. degree in 1962. He obtained a J.D. degree from the law school at the University of Michigan in 1965. One year later, in August 1966, Gephardt married Jane Ann Byrnes, formerly of Nebraska, whom he had met when both were undergraduates at Northwestern.

Early Political Career

Returning to south St. Louis where he was raised, Gephardt became active in ward politics and in 1971 was elected to the St. Louis board of aldermen. Five years later Gephardt ran for the Third District congressional seat vacated by retiring Congresswoman Leonor Sullivan. The middle-class, predominately white district, composed of Roman Catholic ethnic neighborhoods in south St. Louis, suburbs in St. Louis County, and a section of primarily rural Jefferson County, mirrored his centrist political philosophy. The 35-year-old Gephardt easily defeated his opponent, State Senator Donald Gralicke, in the Democratic primary and took 64 percent of the vote in the general election against his Republican opponent, Joseph Badaracco.

After his arrival in Washington in 1977, Representative Gephardt quickly rose to prominence. Fellow Missouri Congressman Richard Bolling, then chairman of the House Rules Committee, arranged his assignment on the House Ways and Means Committee, a rare honor for a freshman legislator. Two years later Gephardt won a seat on the House Budget Committee. Through service on the Budget Committee Gephardt established his reputation as a fiscal conservative. In 1982 he and New Jersey Senator Bill Bradley sponsored the Fair Tax Act, popularly known as the Bradley-Gephardt Bill, which eventually became the Tax Reform Act of 1986. By 1984 Gephardt had joined the "inner circle" of House Democratic leadership with his selection as chairman of their caucus, the fourth-highest post behind speaker, majority leader, and majority whip.

Gephardt also organized attempts to reestablish the centrist position in the national Democratic Party following presidential party nominee Walter Mondale's overwhelming defeat by President Ronald Reagan in the 1984 campaign. In 1985 he announced the creation of the Democratic Leadership Council, composed of younger Democrats from the South and West including Georgia Senator Sam Nunn and Governors Bruce Babbitt of Arizona and Charles S. Robb of Virginia.

The Gephardt Amendment

Gephardt's best-known initiative was the Gephardt amendment, which directed the federal government to identify those nations with large trade surpluses with the United States and take action against any country that has achieved its advantage by unfair practices. The amendment called for negotiation, but if that failed, the president would be required to impose tariffs and take other punitive action that would reduce the trading partner's surplus by 10 percent per year. The Gephardt amendment proved particularly popular among blue collar workers threatened by the loss of employment in the automobile and steel industries and among Americans dissatisfied with the rapid rise of Japanese economic power. The amendment passed in the House by a four-vote margin and was added to the Omnibus Trade Bill of 1987. The Senate, however, rejected the controversial proposal aided by President Ronald Reagan's threat to veto the measure if it reached his desk.

Ran For the Presidential Nomination

Riding on the popularity of his amendment and his prestige as chair of the Democratic Leadership Council, Gephardt on February 23, 1987, became the first Democrat to declare his candidacy for the 1988 presidential nomination. In a 30-minute speech in St. Louis he established his campaign theme when he declared before the audience, "The next president must be as tough in negotiating the terms of trade as this president has been in negotiating with the Russians." When reminded that Democratic presidential nominee Walter Mondale came under sharp attack in the 1984 campaign for taking a protectionist stance, Gephardt replied, "The facts have changed. Mondale was talking about an issue that was about to happen. Now it has happened."

Gephardt plunged energetically into the race, particularly in the crucial Iowa caucus campaign. After months of dogged determination and some good fortune following the political demise of former Colorado Senator Gary Hart, Gephardt won the caucus contest on February 8, 1988. He then emerged as the frontrunner until his defeat by Massachusetts Governor Michael Dukakis in the New Hampshire primary one week later. Undaunted, Gephardt continued his campaign, winning the South Dakota primary on February 23 and hoping for a breakthrough on "Super Tuesday," the March 8 primary held simultaneously in 20 states. He won only in Missouri, his home state. Hoping to capitalize on the disaffection of blue collar automobile workers because of Japanese competition, the faltering and nearly broke Gephardt campaign focused all of its remaining energy on the March 23 Michigan primary. Rev. Jesse Jackson, however, staged a stunning upset, winning 53 percent of the vote; Dukakis got 29 percent, and Gephardt only 13 percent. Two days later Gephardt withdrew from the race.

Became House Majority Leader

Easily reelected to his congressional seat in 1988, Gephardt, who had campaigned in Iowa, New Hampshire, and Michigan as the populist outsider, quickly resumed his rapid ascent in the House Democratic leadership hierarchy. In 1989 he succeeded Congressman Thomas Foley to become House majority leader. In that role Gephardt continued to garner public attention with his spirited attacks on the Bush administration. In March 1990, for example, Gephardt criticized what he termed President Bush's failure to capitalize on the political changes sweeping across Eastern Europe. Unveiling a Democratic alternative on Eastern Europe, Gephardt, in a speech before the Center for National Policy, outlined a broad initiative to support the reforms of Soviet President Mikhail S. Gorbachev through increased aid to emerging Eastern Bloc democracies and through a proposal to send U.S. food aid to the Soviet Union. Moreover, Gephardt continued to espouse the theme of economic nationalism, which was the center of his unsuccessful presidential campaign. However, he began to link trade policy with incentives to improve American education and the quality of American manufactured products.

Gephardt did not make another bid for the presidency in 1992. He often bumped heads with President Clinton. He opposed Clinton's North American Free Trade Agreement (NAFTA) because he believed it exported U.S. jobs overseas. In 1994 when Republicans became House majority, Gephardt was elected minority leader. According to the *New York Times,* Gephardt said he hoped to develop "a strategy to represent the workers, the middle-income families, the poor families of this country." That year he announced a middle-class tax cut and, later, a plan to simplify tax rates. Both announcements came days before Clinton was to reveal his own plans for similar ideas. These actions were a source of friction between Clinton and Gephardt.

Further Reading

No book-length biographies currently exist on Richard Gephardt. However, brief discussions of his life and political accomplishments can be found in H. Rinie, "The Gephardt File: Rebel Without A Cause," *U.S. News and World Report* (February 8, 1988); Elizabeth Drew, *Election Journal: Political Events of 1987-1988* (1989); and the *New York Times Biographical Service,* Vol. 18 (February 1987). See also Morton Kondracke, "Man for All Seasons," *The New Republic* (July 3, 1989) and the *Los Angeles Times* (March 8, 1990). For Gephardt's vision for the Democratic Party, see David Corn, "Beyond 'Too Far,'" *The Nation* (April 10, 1995). Information about the Gephardt/Clinton clash over NAFTA is in Amy Borrus, "The Latest Trade War: Democrat vs. Democrat," *Business Week* (March 10, 1997) ☐

Jean Louis André Théodore Géricault

The French painter Jean Louis André Théodore Géricault (1791-1824), by virtue of his subject matter and style, is generally considered the first true romanticist. In his short career he established the most viable direction for the immediate future of painting.

Théodore Géricault was born in Rouen on Sept. 26, 1791, the son of a lawyer who did not approve of the boy's wish to become a painter. Upon leaving the Lycée Impérial in 1808, Géricault clandestinely entered the studio of the famous painter of horses Carle Vernet. Géricault had a great love for horses and this alone, no doubt, explains his choice of a master, for Vernet's elegant, rather bloodless animals have very little in common with the vigorous creations of his student. Géricault remained in Vernet's studio for 2 years and formed a lasting friendship with the master's son, Horace.

Géricault then studied with Pierre Narcisse Guérin, who, steeped in neoclassic principles, could not understand the turn his student's art was taking. With reference to Géricault's simplification of form, Guérin is said to have remarked, "As for your figures, they resemble nature the way a violin case resembles a violin." And Géricault's penchant for strong value contrasts elicited the criticism that all

Géricault's pictures seemed to have been painted by moonlight. Yet Guérin, in the opinion of Géricault's biographer Charles Clément, was tolerant of his pupil's forceful originality.

Early Works

In 1812 the Salon accepted Géricault's *Chasseur Officer on Horseback Charging,* the first of only three paintings to be publicly exhibited in France during his lifetime. The picture was well received and was awarded a gold medal, but it was not purchased by the state. Géricault had less success 2 years later at the Salon with his *Wounded Cuirassier,* equally colossal in size but less finished in execution as well as in planning. The artist himself was dissatisfied with it.

Shortly after the restoration of the Bourbons in 1815, Géricault joined the royal musketeers and was stationed at Versailles for 2 or 3 months. During this period he had a love affair with an unidentified woman who bore him a son, Hyppolyte Georges.

Géricault had always been an admirer of the Old Masters and had copied their work at the Louvre. In 1816 he embarked upon a trip to Florence and Rome, where he studied the painting of Raphael and, even more, of Michelangelo, whose temperament was much closer to his own. In Rome, Géricault undertook the painting of a major work, the *Race of Riderless Horses on the Corso,* inspired by a tumultuous local event. He never completed it, but two of the preparatory oils reveal that he sought a fusion of the

excitement of the experienced, contemporary event with the notion of timelessness inherent in the art of classical antiquity.

"Raft of the Medusa"

Upon his return to Paris in 1817, Géricault made his first lithographs and brought a degree of his free style to the medium. The following year he began work on what was to become his largest and best known composition, the *Raft of the Medusa*. The subject was suggested by an actual event of 1816 which had captured the public's imagination and stimulated their political sensibilities: a raft with survivors from the sunken frigate *Medusa* was recovered after 12 days of unspeakable agony; only 15 of the original 149 passengers were alive. Blame was put on the incompetent, politically reactionary captain and, through him, on the government itself. Géricault belonged to a liberal group which met at the house of his friend Horace Vernet, but his interest in the event was primarily in the human drama of anguish and survival, and he complained when a critic saw in the expression of one of his figures a criticism of the Ministry of the Navy.

While the *Raft of the Medusa* did not receive the expected acclaim at the Salon of 1819, it did earn Géricault a great deal of money, for he toured the English provinces with it. In England he produced his famous set of lithographs known as the "Great English Series," and he painted the *Races at Epsom,* based largely on an English racing print but invigorated by the richness of Géricault's palette and stroke. This picture is often noted as a prefiguration of impressionism. While the modernity of the racing theme and the interest in atmosphere may justify such a view, it should be observed that the theatricality of the impossible "flying gallop" is entirely alien to the impressionists' handling of the subject.

Portraits of the Insane

Perhaps Géricault's most enduring achievement consists of the portraits of mental patients at the Hospital of the Salpêtrière in Paris, painted in 1822. These pictures were intended as representations of the "ten classic types" established by the pioneering psychiatrist Dr. Georget, and the five extant paintings have the distinction of showing not a trace of mockery. The artist may well have seen in these cases heightened states of normal emotions and, in this sense, found them akin to his art as a whole.

In his last years Géricault planned a number of ambitious works, among them the *Slave Trade* and *Victims of the Inquisition,* but he did not complete them. After a series of unfortunate accidents and, possibly, as a result of a generally dissolute life, Géricault's health deteriorated steadily for a period of almost a year, and he died in Paris at the age of 32, on Jan. 26, 1824.

Further Reading

The basic work for all Géricault studies is still Charles Clément, *Géricault* (1868), which is in French. A good modern study in English is Klaus Berger, *Géricault and His Work* (1952; trans. 1955), which contains a catalog of works and many illustra-

tions. Geraldine Pelles, *Art, Artists and Society—Origins of a Modern Dilemma: Painting in England and France, 1750-1850* (1963), is recommended for general background.

Additional Sources

Clement, Charles, *Géricault: a biographical and critical study with a catalogue raisonne of the master's works,* New York: Da Capo, 1974.
Eitner, Lorenz, *Géricault, his life and work,* London: Orbis Pub., 1983. □

Geronimo

The career of Apache warrior Geronimo (1829-1909) was symbolic of the struggle for a Native American way of life in conflict with that of the advancing American frontiersmen.

Geronimo was born in No-doyohn Canyon in Arizona in June 1829. As he grew to manhood, he was apparently indolent, for he was called Goyakla, "He Who Yawns." In 1858 his mother, wife, and three children were killed by Mexican bounty hunters, seeking scalps. "I could not call back my loved ones, I could not bring back the dead Apaches, but I could rejoice in . . . revenge," he later declared. During the next 15 years he rose steadily as a war leader among the Apaches. Apache agent John Clum, who arrested Geronimo in 1877, described him as "erect as a mountain pine, while every outline of his symmetrical form indicated strength and endurance. His abundant ebony locks draped his ample shoulders, his stern features, his keen piercing eye, and his proud and graceful posture combined to create in him the model of an Apache war-chief."

Forced onto the reservation at San Carlos in Arizona, Geronimo was a minor leader in the 1881 Apache outbreak. Gen. George Crook pursued the Apaches and forced them to return. In 1885 they fled San Carlos again, angry at being cheated on their rations and unhappy with rules which forbade many of their tribal customs; Geronimo led the renegades. Pursued by American and Mexican troops, the Apaches nevertheless conducted numerous raids on both sides of the international boundary. In 1886 they met to discuss surrender terms but reneged and escaped again.

For 4 months these 39 renegades were pursued by 5,000 American soldiers, an equal number of Mexican troops, plus many bounty hunters, but they never were forced into battle. In September, Geronimo agreed to surrender to Gen. Nelson A. Miles on the condition that after 2 years' imprisonment he would be returned to Arizona. President Grover Cleveland ignored these terms, however. Geronimo and his followers were imprisoned at Ft. Pickens, Fla. In 1894, moved to Ft. Sill in Oklahoma, they were interred as prisoners of war, although allowed to prosper as farmers.

Geronimo later toured with a "Wild West" show, was an "attraction" at the Omaha and Buffalo expositions, and

was exhibited at the St. Louis World's Fair (1904). He died at
Ft. Sill in 1909, still a prisoner of war.

Further Reading

Geronimo's reminiscences, *Geronimo's Story of His Life,* were
recorded and edited by S. M. Barrett in 1906. The best account of Geronimo's career by one of his contemporaries is
John G. Bourke, *On the Border with Crook* (1891). More
recent and comprehensive is O. B. Faulk, *The Geronimo
Campaign* (1969). □

Elbridge Gerry

**Elbridge Gerry (1744-1814), American patriot and
statesman, signed the Declaration of Independence
and was vice president under James Madison.**

Elbridge Gerry was one of 12 children born to Thomas
and Elizabeth Gerry. Little is known of his youth, from
his birth on July 17, 1744, in Marblehead, Mass., to
his 1758 entrance to Harvard College. Upon graduation in
1762, he entered his father's prosperous mercantile firm. He
joined a Marblehead social group that became increasingly
political as Massachusetts felt the impact of Britain's imperial policy. In 1765 Gerry argued publicly that Americans
might in conscience evade the new Stamp Act duties. In

1770 he served on the local Committee of Inspection to
enforce the boycott of the Townshend Act, and 2 years later
he aided Sam Adams in setting up committees of correspondence. With John and Sam Adams, Gerry made up the
patriot triumvirate in the Bay Colony.

Prelude to Revolution

Gerry early became militantly anti-British. He opposed
British efforts to place judges out of reach of public control,
to send Anglican bishops to America, and to enlarge the
royal civil and military establishment in the Colonies. He
was equally hostile to popular democracy: when Marblehead mobs in 1774 destroyed a local hospital he had helped
establish, he denounced the "savage mobility" and
withdrew from politics.

Gerry returned to public life when the Coercive Acts
(1774) closed the port of Boston, and Marblehead became
the port of entry for donations from other Colonies. He
organized the relief effort and sought to prevent profiteering.
He resumed his place on the local committee of correspondence and became one of the leading figures in the Provincial Congress. Active with John Hancock in collecting
military stores, Gerry was almost captured by the British
troops en route to Concord on April 18, 1775.

With the Revolutionary War under way, Gerry labored
in the Second Continental Congress to prepare his colleagues for separation from Britain. He urged state taxes
adequate to maintain a stable currency and preserve public
credit and worked to create an effective military establish-

ment, although he preferred a citizen militia in peacetime. He considered the new national government under the Articles of Confederation "the finishing stroke of our Independence."

An Antifederalist

In 1780 Gerry left Congress in a huff over what he considered an affront to his state and did not resume his seat until 1783. In the interim he tended to his personal fortune. He bought a large confiscated Tory estate in Cambridge and retired from active business. In 1786 he married Ann Thompson, daughter of a New York merchant.

At the Constitutional Convention (1787) Gerry favored congressional payment of the national debt and assumption of state debts. He expressed fears of excessive democracy and opposed popular election of Congress. But, equally fearful of aristocracy, he demanded annual elections, an enumeration of the powers of the national government, and, especially, a Bill of Rights. He refused to sign the Constitution and spoke vigorously against ratification in Massachusetts on the ground that without a safeguard such as a Bill of Rights, Federal government would eventually subvert republicanism. What Gerry sought was a workable balance between governmental power and popular liberty.

National Politics

Despite his objections, Gerry accepted a seat in the Federal Congress in 1789, where he endorsed Alexander Hamilton's funding scheme, demanded full justice for the public creditors, and bought shares in the Bank of the United States. He returned to private life from 1793 until 1797, when President John Adams appointed him to a three-member delegation to France. Gerry was as shocked as his colleagues by the French government's demand for a bribe as a precondition for treaty negotiations. But, convinced that hostility between the two republics must be avoided, Gerry remained after his colleagues departed. Publication of the "XYZ" papers at home, while he was still attempting to negotiate with Talleyrand, damaged Gerry's reputation. However, Adams defended his conduct as opening the door to the later and more successful mission which produced the Franco-American Convention of 1800.

Governor and U.S. Vice President

Elected governor of Massachusetts in 1810, Gerry followed a moderate policy toward Federalist officeholders but later turned more partisan. In addition to large-scale replacement of Federalist by Republican officials, Gerry approved a bill in 1812 to redistrict the state so as to give Republicans disproportionate representation in the legislature. (The new shape of Essex County, roughly similar to a salamander, was caricatured by opponents with Gerry's profile at its head, thus coining the word "gerrymander.") In the 1812 election Gerry lost the governorship. He was made vice president under James Madison and held this post until his death on Nov. 23, 1814.

Further Reading

An early biography is by Gerry's son-in-law, James T. Austin, *The Life of Elbridge Gerry*, 2 vols. (1828-1829). It has been superseded by a modern scholarly biography by George A. Billias (see below). Two collections of source materials provide valuable information on Gerry's congressional career and the "XYZ" affair: Russell W. Knight, ed., *Elbridge Gerry's Letterbook: Paris, 1797-1798* (1966), and C. Harvey Gardiner, ed., *A Study in Dissent: The Warren-Gerry Correspondence, 1776-1792* (1968). Gerry's role in the "XYZ" affair is treated fully in Alexander De Conde, *The Quasi-War: The Politics and Diplomacy of the Undeclared War with France, 1797-1801* (1966). His activities in the Constitutional Convention are traced in Max Farrand, ed., *Records of the Federal Convention*, 4 vols. (1911-1937). A perceptive account of Gerry's career is Samuel E. Morison's essay, "Elbridge Gerry, Gentleman Democrat" (1929), which was republished in Morison's *By Land and by Sea* (1953).

Additional Sources

Billias, George Athan, *Elbridge Gerry, founding father and republican statesman*, New York: McGraw-Hill, 1976. □

Gershom ben Judah

The German rabbi, scholar, and religious poet Gershom ben Judah (ca. 950-1028) exerted a great influence on Jewish social institutions. He is also known as Rabbenu Gershom and Meor Ha-Golah, "Light of the Exile."

The places of the birth and death of Gershom ben Judah are not known with certainty, but he passed most of his adult life at Mainz, Germany. Gershom's importance arose from the fact that his teaching career as a rabbinical authority came just after the extinction of the rabbinical centers in Babylonia. With the consolidation of the Moslem Empire, the Babylonian scholars drifted across to Europe, bringing with them their manuscripts, their scribal tradition, their teaching, and their authority. The Palestinian centers had long ceased. As a result, central Europe and for a time Spain became the heartland of Jewish life and evolution. Later, Spain was to cease and only central European Jewry remained.

Gershom's distinction lay in the fact that he was one of the first and most successful rabbis to transplant and establish the Talmudic learning of Babylonia to Europe. Gershom was an excellent rabbinical scholar, was steeped in all the ancient traditions, and was a natural teacher and organizer of studies. He had, in addition, a consummate judgment in deciding moral and ethical matters concerning the ordinary actions of life. These qualities assured him his success and his popularity.

Gershom's foundational work was his treatment of the Talmud text. He established correct readings, provided illuminating commentaries, drew up exegetical rules, and taught exact methods of interpretation. Gradually, from being merely an academic center of attraction for rabbinical students from all over Europe, he and his school became the guide, mentor, and judge for the autonomous Jewish communities of France, Germany, and the Low Countries. Participating in meetings of community leaders, he helped to shape their social and cooperative institutions, and he defined local laws and customs.

Gershom's influence was profound and felt far beyond his time. It was not merely that he was the educator and molder of the rabbis who then went back to their home communities. It lay much more in the enduring legislation which was enacted under his guidance. The prohibition of polygamy, the limitation of the husband's right to divorce, the treatment of apostates returning to Jewry, the privacy of personal letters, the promulgation of the principle of majority rule in the local communities—these were but a few of his major enactments. Violation of these laws he proposed and had had enacted were punished by excommunication from the community of Israel; this was known in time as the ''*herem* (ban) of Rabbenu Gershom.'' He was author of many *responsa,* or answers, to knotty legal questions and problems which arose in the everyday life of the communities and which entailed apparent conflict of law and commandment. The formation of community cohesion and the strengthening of the community's self-awareness were of powerful consequence for the subsequent fate of European Jewry. These communities were able to withstand and survive the 700 years of persecution and ostracism that were in store for them until the Hitlerian terror swept their underpinnings away forever.

Gershom was author also of penitential prayers (*selihot*), and he prepared a copy of the biblical *Masorah,* or traditional method of reading and pronouncing, and therefore of interpreting, the Bible.

Further Reading

Background works that discuss Gershom ben Judah are Israel Abrahams, *Jewish Life in the Middle Ages* (1896; rev. ed. 1932), and Cecil Roth, *A Short History of the Jewish People* (1936; rev. ed. 1959). ☐

George Gershwin

American composer George Gershwin (1898-1937) was eminently successful in popular music, as well as in the classical field with several concert works and an opera that have become standards in the contemporary repertory.

Georg e Gershwin played a prominent role in one of the most colorful eras of American popular music: the so-called age of Tin Pan Alley—roughly 1890-1930—when popular music became big business. In Tin Pan Alley (28th Street between Broadway and Fifth Avenue in New York City) numerous music publishing houses poured forth popular songs each year. The musical theater

and the private parlor rang with the sounds of ragtime, romantic ballads, and comedy songs. Talented composers such as Gershwin, Irving Berlin, and Jerome Kern, among dozens of lesser figures, fed this lucrative music-making machine and flourished.

George Gershwin was born in Brooklyn in New York City on Sept. 26, 1898, the son of Rose and Morris Gershovitz, immigrants from Russia. After settling in New York's Lower East Side, his father changed the family name to Gershvin; when George entered the professional world of music, he altered the name to Gershwin.

When George was 12, the moderately well-off family purchased a piano; he soon showed a marked inclination for improvising melodies and was given piano lessons. Later he studied the theory of music and harmony. Though Gershwin was not interested in formal education and never finished high school, he continued to study music. Even after his success in musical comedy, he studied with composer Henry Cowell and with music theorist Joseph Schillinger.

Music Business

When Gershwin was 15, he went to work for a large publisher of popular music as a try-out pianist (or ''song plugger''). He began writing his own songs about this time (mostly with lyricist Irving Caesar), none of which his employer was interested in publishing. Finally, in 1916, his first song appeared: ''When You Want 'Em You Can't Get 'Em.''

Gershwin also began to get a few songs set into current musical shows, a common practice of the day. By 1918 he

had shown enough promise to be hired by Harms, Inc., as a songwriter at a weekly salary. Gershwin scored his first big success in 1919 with the song "Swanee" (words by Irving Caesar), introduced by Al Jolson in *Sinbad*. In the same year he composed his first complete score, for the successful musical *La, La, Lucille*.

Musicals of the 1920s

During the 1920s Gershwin established himself as one of the musical theater's most talented and successful composers. He wrote five scores for successive editions of George White's Scandals (1920-1924) and began a series of shows with his brother, Ira, as lyricist, which included *Lady Be Good* (1924), *Primrose* (1924), *Tell Me More* (1925), *Tip Toes* (1925), *Oh Kay* (1926), *Funny Face* (1927), *Rosalie* (1928), *Treasure Girl* (1928), *Show Girl* (1929), and *Strike Up the Band* (1929).

Concert Works

In 1924 the prominent bandleader Paul Whiteman asked Gershwin to write an original "jazz" work for a concert. The result, *Rhapsody in Blue* for piano and jazz band, was Gershwin's debut in the concert hall as pianist and composer, his first attempt at writing an extended piece, and the first time jazz rhythms and blues-oriented melodies were used successfully within a classical framework.

Reviewing the premiere, Olin Downes wrote that the "composition shows extraordinary talent, just as it also shows a young composer with aims that go far beyond those of his ilk. . . ." These aims were demonstrated again in the Piano Concerto in F (1925), commissioned by Walter Damrosch for his New York Symphony; *Three Preludes* for piano (1926); and *An American in Paris* (1928), premiered by Damrosch and the New York Philharmonic. After *Rhapsody in Blue,* Gershwin himself scored all his orchestral works.

In the 1930s Gershwin composed four more musicals with Ira: *Girl Crazy* (1930); *Of Thee I Sing* (1931), which was the first musical awarded a Pulitzer Prize; *Let 'Em Eat Cake* (1933); and *Pardon My English* (1933). He also wrote film scores, including *Damsel in Distress* and *Shall We Dance*. He spent 2 years on his last major work, the opera *Porgy and Bess* (1935), based on a novel by DuBose Heyward about a ghetto in Charleston, S. C. The composer died of a brain tumor in Beverly Hills, Calif., on July 11, 1937.

Gershwin's best songs have proved to be some of the most durable of his era, and his classical works give his career a dimension shared by none of his Tin Pan Alley companions. His fondness for African American music is responsible in part for the rhythmic vitality and blues-tinged lyricism of all his works. His best scores, especially those utilizing Ira Gershwin's trenchant and sympathetic verses, are as fresh, vigorous, and unconventional as any written for the American musical theater. Moreover, Gershwin's music has a peculiar American stamp recognized the world over.

Further Reading

David Ewen, *George Gershwin: His Journey to Greatness* (rev. ed. 1970), is the most detailed and accurate of the biographies. Isaac Goldberg, *George Gershwin: A Study in American Music* (1931; new enlarged ed. by Edith Garson, 1958), the earliest biography, was written with Gershwin's cooperation and is of special interest. See also Edward Jablonski and Lawrence D. Stewart, *The Gershwin Years* (1958). □

John Gerson

The French clergyman John Gerson (1363-1429) was a leader of the Conciliar movement. He is known for his efforts in ending the Great Schism.

John Gerson was born Jean Charlier at Gerson on Dec. 13, 1363. He attended the College of Navarre at the University of Paris, where he was taught by Pierre d'Ailly, who became his close friend. He became chancellor of the University of Paris in 1395, when d'Ailly resigned the post. Gerson's early actions at the university were not particularly notable, but they reflect the general opinion of the times. Thus in 1387 he demanded the condemnation of the Dominican monk Jean de Montson, who denied the Immaculate Conception; and he warned students away from "immoral" popular literature.

Gerson emerged as a firebrand reformer only when the university took a leading role in ending the Great Schism. Since 1378 the Church had been divided between rival popes, one at Rome and one at Avignon, and by 1409 the initiative in ending this schism was taken by the Conciliarists. They argued that a general council of the Church had the right to choose a new pope, and this was attempted, without success, at the Council of Pisa (1409). The University of Paris was a strong base for the Conciliarists, and Gerson had joined the movement by the time of the Council of Constance (1414-1418). At Constance he led the successful drive to end the schism, in which the Council deposed the rival popes and elected Martin V.

But Gerson's influence was fleeting. He alienated much of the Council by his stubborn insistence on the condemnation of Jean Petit (who had written that the assassination of the Duc d'Orléans by Burgundian partisans was justifiable tyrannicide). The Council refused to condemn Jean Petit, and under threats from the Duke of Burgundy, Gerson had to flee to Germany at the end of the Council. Later he was able to return to France and spent his last days at Lyons, where he taught children and wrote devotional works and hymns. He died there on July 12, 1429.

John Gerson ranks as one of the outstanding Conciliar pamphleteers. He wrote that the authority of the universal Church (as represented by a general council) is greater than that of the pope and that therefore a general council may depose and elect popes. He was also a proponent of Gallicanism and a supporter of a strong monarchy in France. In philosophy he adopted the Ockhamist position,

and in theology he was attracted by the mysticism of the Devotio Moderna—in both cases following the late medieval trend against rational investigation of the faith.

Further Reading

The established biography of Gerson is J. L. Connolly, *John Gerson, Reformer and Mystic* (1928). A more recent study is J. B. Morrall, *Gerson and the Great Schism* (1960). For information on Gerson's Conciliar theories and his part in healing the schism see J. N. Figgis, *Studies in Political Thought from Gerson to Grotius* (1907; 2d ed. 1931); E. F. Jacob, *Essays in the Conciliar Epoch* (1943; rev. ed. 1963); and Brian Tierney, *Foundations of the Conciliar Theory* (1955). □

Arnold Lucius Gesell

Arnold Lucius Gesell (1880-1961) was an American psychologist and pediatrician whose pioneering research on the process of human development from birth through adolescence made a lasting mark on the scientific investigation of child development.

Arnold Lucius Gesell was born on June 21, 1880, in Alma, Wisconsin. His parents highly valued education, and early in his life, Gesell decided he wanted to become a teacher. He graduated from the University of Wisconsin in 1903 and then became a high school teacher and principal before entering graduate school at Clark University, where he received a Ph.D. degree in 1906. Gesell believed that in order to do research in child development, he also needed medical knowledge, so he studied medicine at Yale, receiving an M.D. in 1915. Early in his career he taught psychology and child hygiene at the Los Angeles State Normal School.

Gesell joined the faculty at Yale as assistant professor of education in 1911 and established and directed the Yale Clinic of Child Development from 1911 to 1948. The Yale Clinic became the focal United States center for the study of child behavior in its time. From 1948 until his death, Gesell served as director of the famous Gesell Institute of Child Development in New Haven, Connecticut, which continued the work begun in the Yale Clinic. Gesell died in New Haven on May 29, 1961.

Gesell was one of the first to attempt a quantitative study of child development. Louise Bates Ames, one of his co-workers, described his work as "painstaking" and "controlled." Developing his own methods of observation and measurement, Gesell had children, including infants, of different ages respond to different stimulus objects such as cubes and pellets and bells while he observed their behavior and responses. After 1926 he used the motion picture camera as the main means of observing children, filming about 12,000 children.

Gesell's initial work focussed on retarded children, but he believed that it was necessary to understand normal infant and child development in order to understand nonnormality. He also studied Down's syndrome, cretinism, and cerebral palsy.

Gesell's pioneer work on infant mental development led him to conclude that the mental development of children appears to follow certain regularities comparable to the kind of regularities in physical development. He documented patterns and similarities in children's mental development and claimed that individuals go through an identifiable sequence of stages. Gesell's work is often cited as supporting a belief in predetermined natural stages of mental development in the later heated controversy over nature versus nurture in educational readiness.

Some of the data Gesell obtained were integrated into schedules which could be used to calculate the Gesell Development Quotient, or DQ. For a while the DQ was widely used as a measure of the intelligence of young children.

Later researchers raised questions about some of Gesell's findings. The DQ is no longer used, and some say Gesell's conclusions were based on a limited number of cases and a restricted sample of all white, middle-class children in one New England city. Others believe he made too little allowance for individual variations in growth and for cultural influences on child behavior.

There is no question, however, about Gesell's pervasive influence on American psychology and education and on child-rearing practices. Gesell sometimes spoke directly to parents, advocating "discerning guidance" rather than rigidity with rules or, on the other hand, overpermissiveness. He also considered questions such as the psychological factors in adoption and the effect of premature birth on mental development. His books gave norms for behavior at successive stages of development. Three books widely read by parents in the 1940s and 1950s were: *Infant and Child in the Culture of Today* (with Francis L. Ilg, 1940), *The Child from Five to Ten* (with Frances L. Ilg, 1946), and *Youth: The Years from Ten to Sixteen* (with Frances L. Ilg and Louise Bates Ames, 1956).

Further Reading

Among the many books that Gesell wrote are: *Guidance of Mental Growth in Infant and Child* (1930), *How a Baby Grows* (1945), and *Studies in Child Development* (1948).

Gesell is listed in *Webster's American Biographies* (1979). Irvine provides a brief biographical sketch of Gesell in "Pioneers in Special Education," in *Journal of Special Education* (Winter 1971). *The International Encyclopedia of the Social Sciences* (1968) gives insight into his work and life.

Additional Sources

Ames, Louise Bates, *Arnold Gesell: themes of his work,* New York, N.Y.: Human Sciences Press, 1989. □

Konrad von Gesner

The Swiss naturalist Konrad von Gesner (1516-1565) wrote "Historia animalium," which is considered the basis of modern zoology.

Konrad von Gesner was born on March 26, 1516, in Zurich. The man who was to become known as the German Pliny and to be ennobled by the Hapsburg emperor Ferdinand I began his life inauspiciously. His father, a poor furrier, perished in the battle of Kappel in 1531, as the wars spawned by the Reformation laid bloody hands on the Swiss cantons.

Young Gesner came under the protection of Heinrich Bullinger, Huldreich Zwingli's successor, and Oswald Myconius, the Protestant classics scholar. Their generosity permitted Gesner to undertake studies at the University of Strassburg, where he displayed great linguistic talent and interest in nature. Although he angered his guardians by marrying a beautiful but impoverished lady, Gesner was allowed to continue his studies at Basel, where he also studied medicine.

Gesner secured the professorship in Greek at Lausanne in 1537 and speedily compiled a dictionary in that language. The city physician of Zurich prevailed upon the young scholar to resume his medical studies so after wandering across France, Gesner settled down at the medical school of Montpellier and became a doctor of medicine. For his degree he successfully defended an anti-Aristotelian thesis on the nature of sensation.

Sometime after 1540 Gesner began teaching Aristotelian physics at the Collegium Carolinium. In his spare time he composed his *Bibliotheca universalis,* a vast encyclopedia in which he listed alphabetically all of the authors who had written in Greek, Latin, and Hebrew, with a listing of all their books printed up to that time. This work made Gesner famous, and offers of scholarly employment poured in, including one from the Fuggers, the richest family of Europe. The Fuggers, however, attached the condition that Gesner embrace Catholicism, which he refused. He spent the rest of his life as a practicing physician at Zurich, leaving only for short expeditions to study flora and fauna.

In 1551 Gesner began work on the most comprehensive survey of nature undertaken during the Renaissance epoch, his monumental *Historia animalium,* an illustrated encyclopedia of the entire domain of living creatures: birds, fish, and animals. The work was an improvement of earlier European efforts of this kind but reflected the transitional nature of Renaissance scientific thought. Though including descriptions of creatures from remote America, Asia, Russia, and Africa, Gesner also described a host of mythical beasts. Although he had used such taxonomic devices as "genus, species" and "class, order" in his description of plants, Gesner showed little advance over Aristotle in discerning a pattern of biological order, a task to be delayed for almost 2 centuries. His book was beautifully illustrated by artists of the time and included drawings by Albrecht Dürer.

In 1555 Gesner wrote a tome on his first love, languages, entitled *Mithridates.* In 1564 the emperor Ferdinand conferred the title of nobility on Gesner, who designed his coat of arms to portray the books he had written and those that he still planned, including one on nine classical authors and one on gems. In 1565 the plague, which has been identified from Gesner's description as a form of pulmonary bubonic, came to Zurich, and on December 13 he died. A true child of his turbulent times, Gesner was still enthralled by a semireligious vision of nature, a vision composed of an unstable mixture of Aristotle, Scripture, and a passionate desire to explore and observe nature directly and personally.

Further Reading

There is no biography of Gesner in English. Useful studies are Henry Morley, *Clement Morot and Other Studies* (2 vols., 1871; repr. 1970); Frank Dawson Adams, *Birth and Development of the Geological Sciences* (1938); and George Sarton, *Six Wings: Men of Science in the Renaissance* (1957).

Additional Sources

Braun, Lucien, *Conrad Gessner,* Geneve: Editions Slatkine, 1990. □

Don Carlo Gesualdo

Don Carlo Gesualdo, Prince of Venosa (ca. 1560-1613), was an Italian composer famed for his chromatic madrigals and motets. Few matched him in writing music so removed from traditional modal theory and practice.

Carlo Gesualdo was born in Naples. He studied music at the academy founded by his father, Don Fabrizio of Gesualdo, where he heard the works of Giovanni Macque, Bartolomeo Roy, and Pomponio Nenna. Nenna's madrigals, in particular, influenced Gesualdo's style.

After the death of his older brother in 1585, the composer became heir to the Gesualdo title. With the title came an arranged marriage to his cousin, a marriage that was a catastrophe for both parties. Donna Maria d'Avalos, twice married before she became Gesualdo's wife, openly preferred the love of another. In 1590, to avenge his honor, Gesualdo ordered the guilty pair murdered, together with his second child, whose legitimacy was suspect.

In 1594 Gesualdo married Eleonora d'Este, the daughter of Alfonso II, Duke of Ferrara, at whose court lived Torquato Tasso, Nicolò Vicentino, and Luzzasco Luzzaschi. On several occasions Gesualdo set to music the lyrics of his friend Tasso, whose morbid nature was so similar to his own; and hearing the chromatic experiments of Luzzaschi and Vicentino may well have reinforced the direction of his own musical development. Gesualdo remained at Ferrara for 2 years, frequently taking trips to Florence, where he heard the music of the Camerata. Shortly before the death of his father-in-law in 1597, Gesualdo left northern Italy and returned to Naples, where he remained for the rest of his life. He died on Sept. 8, 1613.

Gesualdo's extant works in the collected edition issued by Wilhelm Weismann and Glenn E. Watkins (Hamburg, 1957—) comprise 19 *sacrae cantiones* for five voices and 20 for six and seven voices, 27 Holy Week responsories for six voices, and 125 madrigals for five voices. Not only were the madrigals the most numerous part of his production, but they were also reissued more frequently than the sacred pieces.

Gesualdo's melancholy nature often led him to lyrics of overwhelming sadness. By using chromatic tones, even earlier associated with intense feelings, he heightened the expressiveness of the poetry through music. Although his chromatic passages were sometimes mere pictorial "madrigalisms," Gesualdo more often delineated the overall mood of the text rather than individual words. He employed chromaticism harmonically as well as melodically. By means of chromatic tones he constructed numerous triadic combinations foreign to the mode and then arranged them in unconventional and exciting ways.

Chromaticism in a melodic line was of course not new at this time, but Gesualdo's exaggerated use of it did much to weaken the modal core of his pieces. By so doing, he stretched the limits of the old style even when he remained within the fold of the polyphonists. In this sense Gesualdo was more conservative than the Florentine Camerata, a group who deliberately overthrew the older structures. While their experiments reached forward to the new monodic style, Gesualdo's chromatic madrigals and motets remained the most fevered and impassioned examples of the old practice. To some Gesualdo remains a bizarre experimenter, but to others he is a genius whose art is only now receiving its due recognition.

Further Reading

Gesualdo's life is outlined in Cecil Gray and Philip Heseltine, *Carlo Gesualdo: Prince of Venosa, Musician and Murderer* (1926), and in Cecil Gray, *Contingencies and Other Essays* (1947). Useful background studies are Alfred Einstein, *The Italian Madrigal* (trans. 1949), and Gustave Reese, *Music in the Renaissance* (1954; rev. ed. 1959). □

Jean Paul Getty

Jean Paul Getty (1892-1976) was a billionaire independent oil producer who founded and controlled the Getty Oil Company and over 200 affiliated companies.

Jean Paul Getty was born on December 15, 1892, in Minneapolis, Minnesota. His father, George Franklin Getty, was a lawyer, but in 1904 he moved his wife, Sarah Risher Getty, and his son to the Oklahoma territory to begin a successful career as an independent oilman. Two years later the family moved to Los Angeles, California, where young Getty attended private school before graduating from Polytechnic High School in 1909. After a European tour he attended the University of Southern California and the University of California at Berkeley; he spent his summers working on his father's oil rigs as a "roustabout." In 1912 Getty enrolled in Oxford University in England, from which he received a degree in economics and political science in 1914.

In 1914 Getty arrived in Tulsa, Oklahoma, determined to strike it rich as a wildcat oil producer. Although he operated independently of his father's Minnehoma Oil Company, his father's loans and financial backing enabled him to begin buying and selling oil leases in the red-bed area of Oklahoma. Getty saw himself as a modern oil man, relying on geological data and not simply on the instinct of the experienced veterans, but he also thrived on the excitement, gamble, risks, and high stakes of the oil business. Getty's own first successful well came in in 1916, and by the fall of that year he had made his first million dollars as a wildcatter and lease broker.

For the next two years Getty "retired" to the life of a wealthy playboy in Los Angeles, but he returned to the oil business in 1919. During the 1920s he and his father continued to be enormously successful both in drilling their own wells and in buying and selling oil leases, and Getty became more active in California than in Oklahoma. He amassed a personal fortune of over three million dollars and acquired a third interest in what was to become the Getty Oil Company.

After his father's death in 1930 Paul Getty became the president of the George Getty Oil Company (successor to Minnehoma Oil), but his mother inherited the controlling interest, as his father had been upset with his son's profligate personal life. During the 1930s Getty followed several paths to both short-term and long-term success. His wells contin-

ued to produce, and profits poured in. He also bought a controlling interest in the Pacific Western Oil Corporation, one of the ten largest oil companies in California. After a series of agreements with his mother he obtained the controlling interest in the George Getty Oil Company, and he began real estate dealings, including the purchase of the Hotel Pierre in New York City.

The Getty Oil Company

Getty's ambition was to build up an independent, self-contained oil business involving refining, transporting, and selling oil as well as exploration and drilling. To that end he began in the 1930s to gain control of the Tidewater Oil Company. Getty pursued that goal in a series of complicated maneuvers, which involved tilting with the giant Standard Oil of New Jersey, until in the 1950s he had control of Tidewater, Skelly Oil, and the Mission Corporation. In 1967 these companies merged into the Getty Oil Company, the foundation of Getty's fortune. Getty had a majority or controlling interest in Getty Oil and its nearly 200 affiliated and subsidiary firms, and he remained its president until his death in 1976.

At the outbreak of World War II, Getty, a yachtsman, volunteered for service in the Navy, but his offer was rejected. At the request of Naval officers, however, he took over personal management of Spartan Aircraft, a Skelly and Getty subsidiary. The corporation manufactured trainers and airplane parts, and it later converted to the profitable production of mobile homes.

After the war Getty took a lucrative gamble on oil rights in the Middle East. In 1949 he secured the oil rights in Saudi Arabia's half of the Neutral Zone, a barren tract between Saudi Arabia and Kuwait. He made major concessions to King Saud, which shocked the large oil companies, but after three years and a $30 million investment, Getty found the huge oil deposits which helped make him a billionaire.

In his business career, Getty continued to invest and reinvest; his fortune consisted not of cash, but stocks, corporate assets, and real estate. A loner, he saw himself as a solitary knight in fierce battle with the giant "Seven Sisters" oil firms, and that competitive urge fueled his desire to build a larger and larger fortune.

A "Public" Personal Life

In 1957 *Fortune* magazine published a list of the richest men in America. Getty's name headed the list, and the resultant publicity turned the reclusive Getty into an object of public fascination and legend. Getty complained about the fame, the requests for money, and the assumption that he would pick up every restaurant check, but he also furthered his own legends: he wrote articles on such topics as "How To Be Rich" and pretended to poverty by wearing rumpled suits and threadbare sweaters. The public was fascinated by Getty's wealth and extravagance and also by his reputed stinginess. After 1959 he stopped living out of hotel rooms and established his home and offices at Sutton Place, a 16th-century, 700-acre manor outside London. The huge estate, with its gardens, pools, trout stream, and priceless furnishings, was also a near garrison, with elaborate security arrangements. Giant Alsatian dogs had the run of the estate, and there were also two caged lions, Nero and Teresa. Numerous stories circulated about Getty's penny-pitching; the most famous incident was the installation of a pay telephone on the Sutton Place grounds. Getty offered various explanations, but the public preferred to see the phone booth as a symbol of his stinginess.

The public also seemed to like to read into Getty's life the lesson that money does not buy happiness. Getty was married five times: to Jeannette Dumont (1923), Allene Ashby (1925), Adolphine Helmle (1928), Ann Rork (1932), and Louisa Lynch (1939); each marriage ended in divorce. He had five sons, two of whom predeceased him, and his relationship with each of them was difficult. His grandson, J. Paul Getty III, was kidnapped in Italy in 1973. Although he was returned for a ransom, part of his ear had been cut off. Getty was a celebrity, and public interest, fueled by envy and admiration, focused on Getty's tragedies as well as his billions.

Besides oil, Getty's major interest was art. He began serious collecting in the 1930s—European paintings, furniture, Greek and Roman sculptures, 18th-century tapestries, silver, and fine Persian carpets, including the 16th-century Ardabil carpet from Tabriz. He housed his collection at Sutton Place and at his ranch house at Malibu, California, one wing of which he opened as the J. Paul Getty Museum in 1954. In 1969 construction began on a new Getty Museum, also on his Malibu property. The huge building is a replica of an ancient Roman villa found near the ruins of

Pompeii, and the extensive Getty collection was moved there after his death.

Jean Paul Getty died at Sutton Place on June 6, 1976; he is buried on his Malibu estate.

Further Reading

Getty wrote two autobiographies, *My Life and Fortunes* (1963) and *As I See It* (1976). He wrote about his art collection in *The Joys of Collecting* (1965) and published such advice books as *How To Be Rich* (1965) and *How To Be A Successful Executive* (1971). A biography written with Getty's cooperation is Ralph Hewins, *The Richest American: J. Paul Getty* (1960); the *New York Times* obituary of June 6, 1976, also provides useful information. In *The Seven Sisters: The Great Oil Companies and the World They Shaped* (1975) Anthony Sampson discusses Getty's role as an independent oil producer. Two biographies in 1986 added little new information: *The House of Getty* by Russell Miller and *The Great Getty: The Life and Loves of J. Paul Getty—Richest Man in the World* by Robert Lenzner. □

Abu Hamid Muhammad al-Ghazali

Abu Hamid Muhammad al-Ghazali (1058-1111) was one of the foremost intellects of medieval Islam. Personal discontent with scholastic orthodoxy led him to mysticism and the writing of a monumental work which harmonized the tendencies of both orthodoxy and mysticism within Islam.

The vast area now known as the Islamic world had been quickly conquered by the Moslem Arabs in the century following the death of the prophet Mohammed in 632. The period to 945 had seen a demographic change in Islam, from being a religion adhered to almost exclusively by the conquering Arab minority to the faith held by the majority of the inhabitants of the caliphal empire.

During the period from 750 to 945, however, the empire had disintegrated into petty states ruled by Moslem governors turned dynasts, each only theoretically subordinate to the increasingly powerless caliph in Baghdad, whose chief prerogative came to be the issuing of certificates of legitimacy in exchange for having his name retained on the local coinage and mentioned in the Friday congregational prayers. Beginning with the Buwayh family in 945, who were supplanted in 1055 by the Seljuks, the disintegrating empire of the caliphs was partially restored by secular rulers who took power in Baghdad, eventually claiming the title of sultan while retaining the caliphs of the Abbasid dynasty as useful figureheads.

This appears to have led to a sense of alienation on the part of the influential class of scholar-jurists, steeped in the best of Islamic religion and culture. Al-Ghazali was to point in directions which would relieve this sense of frustration for Moslem thinkers.

Al-Ghazali was born in the town of Tus in eastern Persia, not far from the modern city of Meshed, in 1058. His father appears to have been a pious merchant of modest means. Al-Ghazali was orphaned at an early age, but funds were found for him to pursue the lengthy course of study which led to recognition as a doctor of the sacred law, and to a career as a scholar and lawyer in the well-endowed theological colleges (Arabic, *madrasa*) which were being established in the Seljuk domains during al-Ghazali's lifetime.

At the age of 27 al-Ghazali moved from eastern Persia to Baghdad and attached himself to Nizam al-Mulk, the powerful minister of the Seljuk rulers and a generous patron of scholarship and letters. Nizam al-Mulk appointed al-Ghazali professor in the chief college which he had founded in Baghdad, the Nizamiya Madrasa, and for the next 4 years he was at the summit of the legal and scholarly profession. But discontent with the general corruption of his professional colleagues and perhaps also political fears of the Assassins (who had killed his patron, Nizam al-Mulk, in 1092) led al-Ghazali to give up his brilliant career very suddenly in 1095.

The next 11 years in al-Ghazali's life are obscure; it is known that he went on a pilgrimage to Mecca, stayed a while in Syria, and then retired to Tus. During this period he lived the life of an ascetic Sufi, or mystic, preoccupied with spiritual matters and almost oblivious to the world. He also wrote his most important book during this period, *The Revivification of the Religious Sciences.*

The last years of his life saw a brief return to teaching, the composition of his autobiography, and the foundation of a retreat for the training of mystics in his native town of Tus.

His Works

As a highly educated *alim*, or scholar (Arabic plural, *ulama,* popularly spelled *ulema* in the West), al-Ghazali wrote several works on jurisprudence and on dogmatic theology, as well as polemics against various heresies. These more or less conventional books are overshadowed by his works on philosophy and mysticism. After embarking on his brilliant career in Baghdad at the Nizamiya, al-Ghazali became dissatisfied with the conventional scholarship of the traditionists and jurists and embarked on a deep study of philosophy. This was a subject not widely known, and rather suspect in the view of the orthodox. His conclusions were that the Moslem philosophers al-Farabi and Ibn Sina were too preoccupied with philosophy as such and had virtually placed themselves outside the community of Moslems.

At the same time, al-Ghazali felt strongly drawn to Greek philosophical logic, to which his study of philosophy had exposed him. His major philosophical contributions are twofold: *The Aims of the Philosophers,* in which al-Farabi's and Avicenna's Neoplatonist ideas were described without criticism, and *The Incoherence of the Philosophers,* in which the works of these Moslem thinkers were shown to be either impossible to square with orthodox Islam or poorly reasoned from a philosophical point of view. The reason why al-Ghazali presented *The Aims of the Philosophers* without comment and then demolished their ideas in a second book may be that he felt that philosophy, the logic of which strongly attracted him and which he felt was valuable, had never been explained by a nonphilosopher, that is, by a truly orthodox scholar.

But al-Ghazali's greatest contribution to medieval Moslem thought was his *The Revivification of the Religious Sciences,* a four-volume work composed in his period of withdrawal from the academic milieu of Baghdad. Its importance—long recognized in the Moslem world—lies not so much in its advocacy of mysticism as in its harmonious fusion of the whole body of Moslem ritual and culture, including mysticism, into a pattern preparing the believer for the world to come. Al-Ghazali's insistence upon intelligent observance of Moslem cultic practices relieved the tension between the stricter orthodox and the majority of those drawn to Islamic mysticism. The antinomians could be rejected without alienating the many who felt the need of both traditional Moslem ritual and of a more personal religious experience.

Further Reading

W. Montgomery Watt translated al-Ghazali's autobiography, *The Faith and Practice of al-Ghazali* (1953). The best study of al-Ghazali is Watt's *Muslim Intellectual: A Study of al-Ghazali* (1963). Also valuable are Margaret Smith, *Al-Ghazali, the Mystic* (1944); Watt's general work *Islamic Philosophy and Theology* (1962); and Fadlou Shehadi, *Gazali's Unique Unknowable God* (1964), which presents a thorough discussion of al-Ghazali's philosophy. □

Lorenzo Ghiberti

Lorenzo Ghiberti (ca. 1381-1455) was an Italian sculptor, goldsmith, architect, painter, and writer. His east doors, called the Gates of Paradise, of the Baptistery of Florence are a supreme monument to the age of humanism.

Lorenzo Ghiberti was born in Florence about 1381. He learned the goldsmith's trade from Bartoluccio de Michele; though many small sculptural pieces have been attributed to Ghiberti, no goldsmith's article mentioned in contemporary documents is extant. He was accepted in the goldsmiths' guild in 1409, in the painters' guild in 1423, and in the stonemasons' guild in 1427.

In 1400 Ghiberti went to the Romagna to escape the plague in Florence and assisted another painter in executing frescoes (since destroyed) on the walls of the castle of Carlo Malatesta. On his return to Florence in 1401 Ghiberti took part with seven other Tuscan sculptors (including Filippo Brunelleschi and Jacopo della Quercia) in the historic competition for the gilded bronze north doors of the Florence Baptistery and won it. The theme was the sacrifice of Isaac, and both Ghiberti's and Brunelleschi's trial reliefs are pre-

served. In style Ghiberti's line suggests classical antiquity, but in the little gilded figure of Isaac he created the first truly Renaissance nude.

Baptistery North Doors

When the commission was given to Ghiberti in 1403 (and renewed in 1407), the subjects were changed from the Old to the New Testament. There are 28 scenes, placed within Gothic quatrefoils, as on the bronze south doors (1330-1336) of the Baptistery by Andrea Pisano. The figures are gilded and set in high relief against a neutral ground. Border strips separating the panels are filled with a rich continuity of vegetable and animal life, and 48 heads of male and female prophets occur at the intersections. Ghiberti formed a large workshop to carry out his great undertaking, and it was a training ground for the next generation of Florentine painters and sculptors, including Donatello, Masolino, and Paolo Uccello. The doors were completed in 1424.

Ghiberti made several other works during the period from 1403 to 1424, including two larger-than-life bronze statues of saints for the niches on the exterior of Orsanmichele in Florence. *John the Baptist* was completed for the cloth merchants' guild in 1416, and *St. Matthew* was installed in its niche in 1422 by the bankers' guild. *John the Baptist* still reflects the International Gothic style, as do the earlier panels of the north doors. *St. Matthew* represents the culmination of Ghiberti's new classical style; in pose the figure reflects an ancient Roman philosopher type.

Between 1417 and 1427 Ghiberti made two bronze reliefs for the font of the Baptistery in Siena. In these a new pictorial treatment of the relief, probably influenced by the contribution of his former pupil Donatello to the font, foreshadows Ghiberti's own east doors of the Florence Baptistery. During this period he also became involved in the most important architectural enterprise of the time in Florence: the completion of the dome of the Cathedral. In 1418 he was paid for a model, though his share in the dome as built by Brunelleschi (1420-1436) remains open to question.

Gates of Paradise

After a trip to Venice in 1424, Ghiberti returned to Florence, and in 1425 he received the commission for the east doors of the Baptistery. The doors open on *paradiso,* the area between an Italian baptistery and its cathedral. Michelangelo is said to have remarked that the doors were worthy of being the gates of Paradise, and since then they have been called the Gates of Paradise. For this pair of doors Ghiberti was permitted to alter the whole layout and reduce the number of Old Testament scenes from 28 to 10. The constricting Gothic quatrefoils and the bronze background were abandoned; each large square was totally gilded, so that the sculptor could represent landscape and architectural depth as though he were a painter. All 10 scenes plus the surrounding sections of frieze (which includes in a medallion a self-portrait of the sculptor) were modeled in wax between 1425 and 1437, at which time they were cast in bronze. Finishing and gilding took longer, and not until 1452 were the doors installed.

In each panel there are several scenes, which flow from one to the next in correct perspective depth (owing to the contemporary researches of Brunelleschi and Leon Battista Alberti). Thus in the first panel, the story of Adam, occur the episodes of the Creation of Adam, the Creation of Eve, and their Expulsion from the Garden, from left to right in the foreground, and the Temptation in the far distance, in very low relief. The nude figures of Eve in this composition are among the first sensuous female nudes of the Renaissance. Likewise advanced is the artist's study of drapery forms throughout the panels. They reveal a new grace and beauty rarely surpassed in all of Western sculpture.

Other works in bronze by Ghiberti include a tomb slab (1423) for Fra Leonardo Dati in S. Maria Novella, Florence, and the reliquary shrine of the Three Martyrs (1428), commissioned by Cosimo de' Medici for S. Maria degli Angeli, Florence (now in the Bargello). In 1428 he was enlisted to create another statue, *St. Stephen,* for Orsanmichele. Between 1432 and 1442 the artist designed and supervised the casting of another bronze reliquary, that of St. Zenobius, in the Cathedral, Florence, and also designed a number of stained-glass windows for the Cathedral.

Ghiberti's works in marble include the tomb slabs for Lodovico degli Obizi (died 1424) and Bartolommeo Valori (died 1427), both in Sta Croce, Florence. He also designed the tabernacle that encloses Fra Angelico's *Linaiuoli Madonna* of 1433.

The "Commentarii"

During the last years of his life Ghiberti wrote his *Commentarii,* in which he reveals his knowledge, shrewdness, and cultivated sensitivity. This work, begun about 1447, was not completed at the time of his death in Florence on Dec. 1, 1455. The first commentary deals with the relative merits of artists of classical antiquity, whom Ghiberti knew solely through literary sources. The second commentary, in which he describes works of art in various cities that he had visited, is the principal source of our knowledge of 14th-century art in Florence and Siena; this section also includes Ghiberti's autobiography, the earliest by an artist that has survived. The third commentary takes up more than half the volume and deals with an analysis of the eye, its makeup and functions, and the relation of sight to the behavior of light.

Ghiberti in his writing as well as in his art was a vital link between the medieval Gothic past and the new world outlook he helped to create, the Renaissance. A son, Vittorio (1416-1496), continued the workshop after his father's death.

Further Reading

There are two fine books in English on Ghiberti: a volume with large photographic details by Ludwig Goldscheider, *Ghiberti* (1949), and a lengthy scholarly study by Richard Krautheimer in collaboration with Trude Krautheimer-Hess, *Lorenzo Ghiberti* (1956).

Additional Sources

Krautheimer, Richard, *Lorenzo Ghiberti,* Princeton, N.J.: Princeton University Press, 1982. □

Domenico Ghirlandaio

The Italian artist Domenico Ghirlandaio (1449-1494) was the leading fresco painter in Florence in the late 15th century.

Domenico Ghirlandaio, born in Florence, was the son of the goldsmith Tommaso Bigordi. According to Giorgio Vasari, Tommaso was called Ghirlandaio (the garland maker) because he made metal garlands. Vasari also declared that Domenico studied painting with Alessio Baldovinetti. Twice married, Ghirlandaio had nine children, one of whom, Ridolfo (1483-1561), was also a painter. Ghirlandaio died of the plague in Florence on Jan. 11, 1494.

Ghirlandaio painted sweeping, well-filled but uncrowded compositions and easy portrait likenesses. He was interested in classical antiquity and aware of contemporary Flemish painting. He supervised a large shop of assistants, chief among whom were his brothers Davide and Benedetto and his brother-in-law, Bastiano Mainardi. The chief problem in Ghirlandaio scholarship is the sorting out of his work from that of his various associates.

Early Work

A recently uncovered fresco, the *Madonna of Mercy* and the *Lamentation over Christ,* in the Church of Ognissanti, Florence, is among Ghirlandaio's earliest (ca. 1475) extant works. The fresco, painted for the Vespucci family, displays Ghirlandaio's characteristic skill at portraiture and includes a portrait of Amerigo Vespucci.

In the frescoes (ca. 1475) in the Chapel of S. Fina in the Collegiata, San Gimignano, Ghirlandaio blended painted with real architecture to create open designs filled with portraits of the local citizens. One scene, the *Funeral of St. Fina,* includes a cityscape depicting the towers of San Gimignano.

In the *Last Supper* (1480) in the Church of Ognissanti refectory Ghirlandaio painted an extra bay into the scene, which appears to continue the real architecture of the refectory into the fresco. This device is remarkably effective, though it somewhat detracts from the story. The iconography is traditional, with Judas seated opposite Christ, but Ghirlandaio seems to anticipate Leonardo da Vinci in his arrangement of the disciples into groups of twos and threes.

Ghirlandaio's fresco, the *Calling of Peter and Andrew,* in the Sistine Chapel (1481-1482), Rome, is especially successful in its sense of openness and is one of the clearest and most easily read in the chapel. Characteristically, the "calling" is witnessed by crowds of onlookers and contains numerous contemporary portraits.

Sassetti Chapel

The Sassetti Chapel frescoes (1486) in Sta Trinita, Florence, are among Ghirlandaio's best work. The episodes, of the life of St. Francis, are embellished by contemporary Florentine settings and personalities. In the lunette scene depicting Francis receiving the rules of the order, the setting is the Piazza della Signoria with a view of the Loggia dei Lanzi. Among those witnessing the event are Lorenzo the Magnificent, Francesco Sassetti (the donor), and the writer Angelo Poliziano. The scene showing Francis resuscitating a child is set in the Piazza Sta Trinita with views of the bridge and Church of Sta Trinita.

S. Maria Novella

The most extensive fresco cycle Ghirlandaio executed, in the choir of the church of S. Maria Novella, Florence, was commissioned on Sept. 1, 1485, by Giovanni Tornabuoni. The artist promised to complete the project by May 1490. The frescoes tell the stories of St. John the Baptist and the Virgin Mary in 14 separate scenes arranged in four registers along the sidewalls of the choir. The style makes it clear that much of the actual painting was done by assistants. Recently restored, the frescoes are exceptionally effective decoration.

Panel Paintings

Ghirlandaio did a number of panel paintings. He preferred working in tempera, although he undoubtedly was familiar with the oil technique. In the *Adoration of the Shepherds* (1485) the swarthy peasant types seem to derive from Hugo van der Goes's *Portinari Altarpiece.* One of Ghirlandaio's most appealing panels is the *Adoration of the Magi* (1488). As in most of his work, the colors tend to be rather harsh and contrasty; nonetheless, the scene has a quiet piety and charm. It includes a particularly fine landscape viewed through the posts of the shed behind the Virgin and Child. Two portraits, *Francesco Sassetti and His Son* and the *Grandfather with His Grandson,* are noteworthy for their restrained gentleness. Ghirlandaio's last panel, the *Visitation* (1491), is rather simple in design and seems to anticipate the balanced compositions of the High Renaissance.

Further Reading

A full-length study of Ghirlandaio is Gerald S. Davies, *Ghirlandaio* (1908; 2d ed. 1909). A detailed study is in Raimond van Marle, *The Development of the Italian Schools of Painting,* vol. 13 (1931). See also Sydney Joseph Freedberg, *Painting of the High Renaissance in Rome and Florence* (2 vols., 1961). □

Aurobindo Ghose

The Indian nationalist extremist leader, poet, and philosopher Aurobindo Ghose (1872-1950) abandoned his radical political activities to develop a religious teaching for the spiritual benefit of all men.

urobindo Ghose was born in Calcutta, the third of six children. His father—of high-caste background—was a distinguished physician in the employ of the civil service, thoroughly Anglicized and a persuaded atheist. In 1879 Aurobindo was sent to England with his brothers for higher education to prepare for the Indian civil service. Though forced to live in near poverty, he excelled in his academic studies, especially in the classics, English literature, and European languages.

At King's College, Cambridge, Ghose joined an association of fellow Indians, expressing a deep interest in Indian nationalism. In 1893 he returned to India and resolved to strive for Indian independence. He served the maharaja of Baroda from 1893 to 1907, becoming successively professor of English, vice-principal at Baroda College, and finally principal of the National College of Calcutta.

During this period Ghose began to associate with radical Indian nationalists and revolutionaries, openly criticizing the Indian National Congress for its moderation, and founding a revolutionary newspaper so skillfully written that no pretext could be found for his arrest. However, in 1908 after a series of bombings he was arrested along with other suspects. Though he was acquitted soon after, it was during this short period that he became increasingly preoccupied with the spiritual dimensions of Indian cultural and corporate life.

Ghose experimented with Yoga, read extensively, and meditated on the *Veda* and *Bhagavad Gita*. In 1910 he openly abandoned active politics and went to the French settlement at Pondicherry, where he established the Aurobindo Ashram (retreat) to develop and promote his teaching, though he did not give up his interest in the political affairs of India. He was joined by his wife and a number of his friends—including several suspected revolutionaries—and remained continually under the surveillance of the English secret service. In 1914 he founded the magazine *Arya,* designed to promote his philosophical and religious teachings.

Ghose's basic spiritual goal was "to make the truth dynamic in the soul of man." For this he proposed an "integral Yoga" designed not for spiritual withdrawal from the world but for the purpose of transforming earthly human life "here in the individual and the community." Man must be opened to a supramental divine consciousness which can create a spiritual "superman" and a new order of life in the world, transforming moribund human institutions into "free forms" of strength, love, and justice. The emphasis of his teaching was on the spiritualization of the phenomenal world and all human activity through the emergence of a disciplined religious elite, extending widely to touch all mankind.

Among Ghose's writings published in English are *The Yoga and Its Objects* and *Love and Death* (both 1921), *The Life Divine* (1949), *Essays on the Gita* (1950), and *The Message and Mission of Indian Culture* and *The Mind of Light* (both 1953).

Further Reading

Studies of Ghose include George Langley, *Sri Aurobindo: Indian Poet, Philosopher and Mystic* (1949); A. B. Purani, *The Life of Sri Aurobindo* (1958; 3d ed. 1964) and *Sri Aurobindo: Some Aspects of His Vision* (1966); and Vishwanath P. Varma, *The Political Philosophy of Sri Aurobindo* (1960).

Additional Sources

Feys, Jan, *The life of a yogi,* Calcutta: Firma KLM, 1976.

Ghose, Aurobindo, *Tales of prison life,* Calcutta: Sri Aurobindo Pathamandir, 1974.

Heehs, Peter, *Sri Aurobindo, a brief biography,* New York: Oxford University Press, 1989.

Joshi, Kireet, *Sri Aurobindo and the Mother: glimpses of their experiments, experiences, and realisations,* New Delhi: Mother's Institute of Research in association with Motilal Banarsidass, Delhi, 1989.

Purani, Ambalal Balkrishna, *The life of Sri Aurobindo,* Pondicherry: Sri Aurobindo Ashram, 1978.

Rishabhchand, *Sri Aurobindo, his life unique,* Pondicherry: Sri Aurobindo Ashram, 1981.

Roshan, *Sri Aurobindo in Baroda,* Pondicherry: Sri Aurobindo Ashram, 1993.

Satprem, *Sri Aurobindo, or, The adventure of consciousness,* New York: Institute for Evolutionary Research, 1984.

Srinivasa Iyengar, K. R., *Sri Aurobindo: a biography and a history,* Pondicherry: Sri Aurobindo International Centre of Education, 1985. □

Alberto Giacometti

The recurring themes of the Swiss sculptor and painter Alberto Giacometti (1901-1966) are time, movement, and transparence. He is best known for his elongated figural structures.

he son of a painter, Alberto Giacometti was born in Stampa on Oct. 10, 1901. He began to draw and model at an early age, and in 1919 he enrolled at the École des Arts-et-Métiers in Geneva. He traveled in Italy in 1920-1921. He studied with the sculptor Émile Antoine Bourdelle at the Académie de la Grande-Chaumière in Paris from 1922 to 1925. After sharing a studio in Paris with his brother Diego from 1925 to 1927, Giacometti set up on his own.

Giacometti's early work derived from cubist (*Torso*, 1925), African, and Cycladic sculpture (*Spoon Woman*, 1926). But by 1928 he began to develop a personal treatment of the medium, moving to more original ideas—in part a result of his meeting that year with the surrealists, with whom he later became affiliated. In his *Man* and *Reclining Woman Who Dreams* (both 1929) he created open structures concerned principally with establishing a viable language of form and solving the technical difficulties of armature and support.

Giacometti occasionally returned to figural themes in the 1930s and early 1940s, as in *Nude, Femme qui marche* (1933-1934), the first of the elongated torsos, and *Woman*

with *Chariot I* (1942-1943). The latter work, evocative and immobile, is an extension of the expressive qualities stated in the major work of this period: the surrealist constructions of 1929 to 1945.

These constructions imply or state movement— *Suspended Ball* (1930-1931) and the *Captured Hand* (1932)—and sometimes border on the fantastic, as in the well-known *Palace at 4 A.M.* (1932-1933). They are quasi-realistic, as in the *Woman with Her Throat Cut* (1932), and at times allusive, as in the *Project for a Passage* (1932). In *Hands Holding the Void* (1934) Giacometti brought together the figural and the fantastic and prefigured the metaphysics articulated in his postwar work.

Giacometti lived in Switzerland from 1942 until 1945, when he returned to Paris. In Switzerland he met Annette Arm, who became his wife.

Giacometti's work after 1945 was almost exclusively figural, ranging from numerous portraits of his brother and his wife to sculptures of the anonymous and universal man, pointing, standing, or walking. He found a new means of modeling and painting. In his sculpture small, anonymous patches are laid over a skeletal structure; in his paintings he used short nervous lines and monochromatic low-keyed hues. In both mediums he employed elongated proportions, either in individual parts of the figure or throughout the body as a whole.

Giacometti's compositions narrowed down to four themes: one person in an environment, as in *Walking Quietly under the Rain* (1949), or several people encoun-

tering each other, as in *City Square* (1948); single figures gesturing, such as the *Man Pointing* (1947); figures placed atop a pedestal or support, such as *Chariot* (1950); and single, gazing portraits that concentrate on the head, as in *Portrait of Diego* (1954) and *Monumental Head* (1960). Regarding this last theme, Giacometti once remarked that "all the rest of the head is a prop for the gaze." He died in Chur, Switzerland, on Jan. 12, 1966.

Further Reading

The most recent and thorough monograph on Giacometti is David Sylvester, *Alberto Giacometti* (1965). Peter Selz, *Alberto Giacometti* (1965), the exhibition catalog for the Museum of Modern Art, is short but useful. The most profound interpretation of Giacometti's imagery can be found in two essays of Jean Paul Sartre, "The Quest for the Absolute" (1948) and "The Paintings of Giacometti" (1954), both translated into English and published in Sartre's *Essays in Aesthetics* (1964). For another interpretation see Jacques Dupin, *Alberto Giacometti* (trans. 1963).

Additional Sources

Juliet, Charles, *Giacometti,* Paris: Hazan, 1985.
Lord, James, *Giacometti, a biography,* New York: Farrar, Straus, Giroux, 1985. □

A. P. Giannini

Within the pantheon of 20th-century American business leaders stands the Italian-American A. P. Giannini (1870-1949). As financier and banker he transformed the nature of banking in large and small ways; as an Italian-American he became a symbol of legitimate success and a source of practical help to immigrants and an inspiration to their descendants.

Amadeo Peter Giannini was born May 6, 1870, in San Jose, California, to Virginia and Luigi Giannini, immigrants from Genoa. The Gianninis possessed enough resources to lease a hotel in San Jose. After several years of successful hotel-keeping, Luigi purchased a 40-acre farm. He was killed in 1877 by a disgruntled worker in a quarrel over a one dollar debt. The following year Virginia married Lorenzo Scatena, who had worked his way to America from Lucca as a sailor. The Scatena family moved in 1882 to San Francisco, where Lorenzo took a job with a fruit wholesaling company in the district of North Beach. Success followed, and within a year Scatena had formed his own fruit company.

Amadeo was a good student, but the excitement of the business life—first tasted after school and on Saturdays in his stepfather's company—lured him into the adult work world after a brief course of study at Heald's Business College. His initiative and enthusiasm quickly resulted in greater responsibility, and by the age of 17 he was making regular business trips for the company. Amadeo, later to be known as A.P., exhibited at 17 many of the traits that would

characterize his career as a banker. He worked long hours, was a careful observer of the business environment, and extended his personal and professional assistance to clients he deemed worthy. His efforts as a travelling commission man were eventually rewarded with a half-interest in Scatena & Co.

The rising young businessman married Clorinda Agnes Cuneo in 1892. Her father, Joseph, was one of North Beach's richest men, his fortune having been established in real estate. For nine years after his marriage A.P. continued in the commission produce business, retiring at the age of 30. His savings and real estate, together with $100,000 that he received from the sale of his interest in Scatena & Co., allowed him to support his family in a satisfactory manner. He summed up his attitude toward personal wealth: "I don't want to be rich. No man actually owns a fortune; it owns him."

Early Banking Career

After a brief flirtation with reform politics in Long Beach, Giannini began his banking career upon the death of his father-in-law in 1902. Joseph Cuneo died intestate and the family asked A.P. to manage the estate. Among the Cuneo holdings was an interest in a North Beach bank, Columbus Savings and Loan, which had been founded and was controlled by Italian-American John Fugazi. This first bank in the North Beach community preferred to make large loans, a practice which not only encouraged competition and the establishment of another Italian-American bank, but also gave rise to criticism by Giannini, who was a director of

the bank. A.P. argued that the bank was not making enough small loans to the area's newcomers. He advised the bank to actively solicit their business.

Failing to convince the board of directors, A.P. resigned from the Columbus Savings and Loan in 1904 and set out to organize a bank which would follow his business strategies. By the summer of 1904 Giannini, along with other businessmen of Italian origin, organized the Bank of Italy, capitalized at $300,000, half of which was paid in immediately. A major portion of the bank's first day deposits came from small tradesmen who had been actively solicited by A.P. and other members of the bank. Often their ignorance of English or bank procedure required that deposit slips and checks be filled out by the bank's personnel.

The personal reputation and solicitation of Giannini and his associates were the main reason for the bank's growth. Giannini tramped the streets of North Beach explaining in Italian the functions of a bank, his bank, to people who had never used one. Giannini was making banking services available to people who had either been turned away or ignored by the larger, unfriendly banks. North Beach deposits remained in the community in the form of real estate loans as small as $375 or personal loans as small as $25.

Growth During Disasters

A.P.'s imaginative behavior during the great San Francisco earthquake and fire of 1906 furthered his reputation and that of his bank. Although the quake occurred at 5 a.m., the Bank of Italy opened its doors at 9 o'clock and conducted business as usual. Giannini closed the bank at noon, however, fearing the worst as the fires spawned by the ruptured gas lines spread closer to the financial district. Securing horses and wagons from Scatena & Co., Giannini loaded the bank's cash and gold onto a wagon, hid them beneath a crate of oranges, and transported them to his home outside the city. There he hid the bank's assets in the ash trap of the living room fireplace.

A.P. saw in the city's destruction not only a chance to service his customers but another opportunity for the Bank of Italy. Nine days after the quake a newspaper advertisement announced the temporary location of the bank's operations. The city's larger banks were unable to respond as quickly. Giannini's foresight in removing his bank's cash together with his personal knowledge of his customers' accounts (he needed no records) allowed him to resume operations quickly. Deposits exceeded withdrawals in less than six weeks after the earthquake.

Giannini demonstrated similar ingenuity and foresight when in mid-1907 he picked up rumblings about future financial uncertainty despite the nation's prosperous economy. He began a campaign to increase the bank's gold reserves, build up deposits, and reduce outstanding loans after personal review. Thus, when the financial panic struck the Bank of Italy was able to meet it head on. Its stock of gold piled high in the teller's cage inspired confidence, and the bank did not have to invoke rules limiting withdrawals or requiring advance notice as other, larger institutions did.

Once again the bank had weathered a major crisis due to the foresight of A. P. Giannini.

Pioneer in Branch Banking

It was this same readiness to listen and to anticipate the future needs of his bank and customers that led Giannini to his greatest achievement—the pioneering of branch banking.

In 1908 Giannini heard several officials extol the virtues of branch banking as a solution to the various defects of American banking and as a means of bringing banks closer to the people. A.P. familiarized himself with Canadian branch banking practices and thus was prepared to act in 1909 when California enacted a law authorizing the establishment of branches. On Columbus Day, 1909, the directors of the Bank of Italy authorized the opening of such a branch in San Jose. When the Bank of Italy acquired control of a local San Jose bank A.P. sought local investors and retained many of the local personnel so that the branch would be seen as part of the community. By 1918 the Bank of Italy had become the first statewide branch banking system in the United States, with 24 branches throughout California and possessing more than $93 million.

The following year Giannini began to develop a transcontinental system. Leaders of New York City's Italian community had sought his assistance in establishing a regularly chartered depository of their own. Using proven techniques, A.P. first acquired the East River National Bank, and later the Banca Meridionale, a branch banking system in Italy. Thus he acquired the first elements in a transcontinental and worldwide banking system. Through reorganization and restructuring of these and other banks Giannini eventually formed the Bank of America, which possessed assets of $6 billion by 1939 and became the world's largest bank in 1945.

The Bank of America

Giannini's efforts were not without opposition and hostility. In 1919, for instance, California's superintendent of banks raised objections to A.P.'s opening of additional branches. He relented only after Giannini was able to convince him of the reasonableness of his motives and the falsity of the "whispering campaign" which had raised the doubts. The last great challenge to A. P. Giannini's banking empire came in 1948 when the Federal Reserve began an investigation into charges that his holding company had violated the anti-monopoly provisions of the Clayton Anti-Trust Act. A.P. died on June 3, 1949, however, before the board returned its findings and ordered that his corporate structure be dismantled. Later the U.S. Court of Appeals set aside the order, declaring that the Federal Reserve had failed to prove its charges of monopolistic practices.

A. P. Giannini's contributions were as a businessman and as an Italian-American. As a banker he established and refined branch-banking, and his bank became a model for the nation and the world. He stressed services for the "little fellow." Through his introduction of such practices as the repayable monthly home loan he brought home ownership within the reach of the multitudes. His concern for those previously ignored also included giving them representation in the management of his banks.

Giannini's success allowed him to assist fellow Italian-Americans in several ways. In addition to providing financial services, he is credited with having helped save alien Italians from the loss of their property and civil rights in California at the outbreak of World War II.

Further Reading

A. P. Giannini is listed in the *Biographical Dictionary of American Leaders* (1983) and in the *Dictionary of American Biography* Supplement. The most complete and authoritative account is Marquis and Bessie James, *Biography of a Bank* (1954). Andrew F. Rolle, *The Immigrant Upraised* (1968) sets Giannini's accomplishments in the context of the western American experience, as does Erik Amfitheatrof, *The Children of Columbus* (1973).

Additional Sources

Bonadio, Felice A., *A.P. Giannini: banker of America,* Berkeley: University of California Press, 1994.
James, Marquis, *Biography of a bank; the story of Bank of America N.T. & S.A,* Westport, Conn., Greenwood Press 1971, 1954.
Nash, Gerald D., *A.P. Giannini and the Bank of America,* Norman: University of Oklahoma Press, 1992. □

Vo Nguyen Giap

Vo Nguyen Giap (born 1912) was a Vietnamese Communist military strategist and architect of the 1954 defeat of the French at Dien Bien Phu. He also directed the Communist campaign of the 1960s and 1970s against the government of South Vietnam.

Born in Quang Binh in what was to become the Communist state of North Vietnam, Vo Nguyen Giap was raised in a middle-class family of high educational attainment. He joined the anti-French movement as a student at Quoc Hoc College in Hue, becoming a Communist after reading some of the writings of Nguyen Ai Quoc (Ho Chi Minh's earlier alias).

Giap was a founding member of the Indochinese Communist party organized by Ho in Hong Kong in 1930. Subsequently detained by the French in prison (where he met his wife), Giap afterward obtained a doctorate of law from Hanoi University and became a history teacher at Thang Long College. His study and teaching of Vietnamese stimulated his growing nationalism as well as his resentment of both China and France as oppressors of the Vietnamese people in historical and modern times. He also developed a great admiration for Napoleon, with whom, as a military leader, he was later said to identify.

Fleeing to China at the beginning of World War II after the French banned the Communist party, Giap joined Ho Chi Minh's Vietnam Independence League (Viet Minh) and assumed responsibility for guerrilla activities in northern

Tonkin (in present-day North Vietnam). Giap's wife and sister were subsequently arrested by the French and died in prison, increasing Giap's anti-French feelings.

In 1945 Giap became defense minister in the government formed by Ho Chi Minh before the return of France to Vietnam. Giap's inability to control himself from passionately expressing his hatred of France caused Ho to exclude him from the 1946 delegation to the unsuccessful Fontainebleau negotiations. Giap's ruthlessness also antagonized many of his Viet Minh comrades.

Triumphed Against the French

The military successes of his eight years' leadership of the People's Army of Vietnam (PAVN) against the French, however, made Giap virtually indispensable to the cause of the Communists. Not all of his strategy against the French succeeded, but Giap learned valuable lessons from his setbacks at the hands of French forces. In a tactical blunder in 1951, Giap ordered a general counteroffensive and lost some 20,000 men in battles in the Red River delta. His great triumph at Dien Bien Phu in May 1954 after a 55-day siege boosted him to a position second only to Ho Chi Minh in the eyes of his countrymen. Considered by many to be a military genius, Giap probably would have driven the French from the country had Ho not acquiesced to Soviet and Chinese pressures for a political settlement.

Following the 1954 Geneva partition of Vietnam, Gen. Giap served as a vice premier of North Vietnam as well as defense minister and army chief. He was also a member of the politburo of the Lao Dong (Workers') party. When a major war erupted between South Vietnam and North Vietnam and U.S. armed forces came to the defense of the Saigon regime, Giap split again with Ho and the majority of the North Vietnamese leadership in arguing against conventional warfare in the south. He expressed serious doubt that the PAVN could win against the better equipped U.S. and South Vietnamese forces and argued instead for the same sort of guerrilla warfare that had succeeded against the French.

Mapped Tet Offensive

Ho remained firmly convinced that aggressive conventional warfare would win the day in the south. Giap and a handful of Politburo members who sided with him steadfastly argued for first-phase revolutionary warfare, consisting of guerrilla assaults and the covert buildup of a political base in the south. Badly outnumbered, Giap barely managed to retain his position as head of the PAVN, though he was demoted a couple of notches in the Politburo, moving from fourth highest rank to sixth highest. A series of stinging defeats for PAVN forces in 1965 and 1966 helped to redeem Giap in the eyes of the majority of North Vietnamese party officials. When a key political adversary, Nguyen Chi Thanh, died in 1967, Giap regained control of strategy for the People's Army. He was the architect of the Tet Offensive in 1967, which represented textbook "people's" warfare, coordinating political and military initiatives. The offensive failed, however, when the general population in South Vietnam failed to rise up in support of their northern liberators, as had been expected. In the four years from 1968 to 1972, Giap mapped guerrilla attacks by small units, frustrating their U.S. and South Vietnamese opponents and doubling U.S. combat casualties. Emboldened by high-tech weaponry supplied by the Soviet Union and the apparent weakness of South Vietnamese armed forces, Giap in 1972 finally endorsed the idea of conventional warfare in the south. However, his Easter Offensive was thwarted by decisive U.S. power in the air and on the sea and the inability of the People's Army to better coordinate its operations.

Surrendered Army Command

The following year, Giap gave up direct command of North Vietnamese armed forces, reportedly because he was suffering from Hodgkin's disease. In 1980, he resigned as defense minister. Two years later, he assumed the leadership of the Science and Technology Commission and lost his seat in the Politburo. The North Vietnamese people, however, continued to look upon Giap with great affection. In 1992, Giap was given North Vietnam's highest honor, the Gold Star Order, for his contributions "to the revolutionary cause of party and nation."

Author of various books and articles, Giap extended his views to a worldwide audience. For many, his series of articles published in 1961 as *People's War: People's Army* became a virtual bible of guerrilla warfare. In 1970, Giap's *The Military Art of a People's War,* edited by Russell Stetler, was published.

Further Reading

Glimpses of Giap are all that can be obtained from much of the literature on Vietnam in the years since he became prominent. Exceptions are Giap's own collected articles, *People's War: People's Army* (1961) and *Big Victory, Great Task: North Viet-Nam's Minister of Defense Assesses the Course of the War* (1968), both of which provide considerable insight into his military ability. P. J. Honey, ed., *North Vietnam Today: Profile of a Communist Satellite* (1962), offers a somewhat dated but still valuable overview of Communist-ruled North Vietnam, including some perceptive insights into Giap himself, while Australian Communist journalist Wilfred G. Burchett, *Vietnam North* (1966), presents a later, if highly partisan, picture. For good background to both Giap's triumph at Dien Bien Phu and his subsequent direction of the assault against South Vietnam see Bernard Fall, *The Two Viet-Nams: A Political and Military Analysis* (1963; 2d rev. ed. 1967). A more recent assessment of Giap's contributions during the Dien Bien Phu offensive against the French and the war for the political reunification of Vietnam can be found in *Encyclopedia of the Vietnam War,* edited by Stanley I. Kutler and published by Scribner's, New York, in 1996. See also *Britannica Online,* at http:www.eb.com, for its entries on Giap and the Vietnam War. □

Edward Gibbon

The English historian Edward Gibbon (1737-1794) wrote "The Decline and Fall of the Roman Empire." Although superseded in part as history, this work is still read for its clarity, accuracy, and brilliant style. Gibbon's "Autobiography" is a classic of the genre.

Edward Gibbon was born May 8, 1737, in Putney. A sickly child, he had tutors and spent two brief intervals at school, but he owed most of his early education to his voracious reading. In April 1752 he was sent to Oxford, where he learned little. In his summer vacation he began his first book, a chronological inquiry called *The Age of Sesostris,* which he later destroyed. Back at Oxford, he found a new subject of inquiry and in June 1753 told his horrified father that he had become a Roman Catholic.

The elder Gibbon immediately sent his son to Lausanne in Protestant Switzerland. M. Daniel Pavilliard, a Calvinist minister, was Edward's tutor and reclaimed him for Protestantism. Gibbon remained in Switzerland until 1758, shortly before he came of age. There, at first with Pavilliard's help and later alone, he acquired his classical learning and developed his scholarly bent. He also learned French thoroughly, made some lifelong friends, and fell in love. The French and the friends endured, but the romance foundered. Neither parent would permit his child to settle permanently in another country. Without parental aid there was no money, and Gibbon puts it, "I sighed as a lover; I obeyed as a son."

Student, Soldier, Traveler

In 1758 Gibbon's father settled a small income on him in exchange for his help in ending the entail on their estates. To his surprise, Gibbon found his stepmother kind and friendly, so he spent much of his time with his father and stepmother. Both Gibbons were officers of the Hampshire militia, which was embodied in May 1760. Gibbon's militia duties prevented his devoting all his time to scholarship, but he published (July 1761) an *Essay on the Study of Literature,* written in French, and considered possible historical subjects.

Earlier in 1761, at his father's request, Gibbon made an unsuccessful attempt to enter Parliament. In December 1762 his active service with the militia ended, and in January 1763 he began a tour of the Continent. Reaching Rome in October 1764, he there first thought of writing his history. But he did not yet begin it.

Gibbon returned to England in 1765, where he continued his studies, but his only publications were two volumes of a French literary journal, edited with his friend G. Deyverdun, *Mémoires littéraires de la Grande-Bretagne* (1768 and 1769) and an attack on Warburton's interpretation of the sixth book of the *Aeneid.* He began a history of the Swiss republics in French (1767), which he abandoned. David Hume, who read this work, urged him to write history, but in English. By this time Gibbon may already have begun preliminary work for the *Decline and Fall,* but he was preoccupied with domestic matters; his father died in November 1770.

Parliament and History

In 1772, having straightened out some of the tangles in his father's finances, Gibbon settled in London with his sources comfortably around him in an extensive library. He joined the famous Literary Club and became a member of Parliament in 1774, and in February 1776 he published the first volume of his *Decline and Fall*. The fifteenth and sixteenth chapters seemed so devastating an account of the early Christian Church that attackers hurried into print. Gibbon ignored them until a rash young man named Davis added plagiarism and the falsification of evidence to the charges against Gibbon. Gibbon's superb *Vindication* (1779) can be read with delight by those who know nothing about either the history or Davis's attack; in passing, Gibbon answered his other critics.

After a brief visit to France (1777) Gibbon continued to work on his history, which was enjoying a large sale. In 1779 he was appointed a lord of trade, and he was a conscientious member of that Board and of Parliament, but his real work was writing; volumes 2 and 3 were published in 1781. Gibbon had lost his seat in Parliament in 1780 but was elected to another in 1781. A new ministry abolished the Board of Trade in 1782, and Gibbon left Parliament forever in 1784.

In September 1783 Gibbon returned to Lausanne to share a house with his old friend Deyverdun and to write the concluding volumes of his history. Much of volume 4 had been written before he left England, but its completion and volumes 5 and 6 occupied Gibbon until June 1787. He then returned to England to see the volumes through the press; they were issued on his fifty-first birthday. While in England, Gibbon had the pleasure of hearing R. B. Sheridan refer, in a famous Parliamentary speech, to Gibbon's "luminous pages," and he enjoyed public applause and the company of his English friends. Nevertheless, Lausanne was now his home and in 1788 he returned to Switzerland.

Last Years

Various literary projects, especially six attempts to write his own memoirs, occupied Gibbon upon his return. His happiness was seriously marred by Deyverdun's death (July 4, 1789), which left him, in his words, "alone in Paradise." The cause of his return to England (1793), however, was concern for his friend John Holroyd, Lord Sheffield, whose wife had died suddenly. A long-standing illness of Gibbon's own was temporarily relieved by surgery in November but Gibbon died on Jan. 16, 1794. After Gibbon's death Lord Sheffield compiled and published his friend's memoirs and other miscellaneous works (1796 and 1814).

Further Reading

J. B. Bury edited the standard edition of *The History of the Decline and Fall of the Roman Empire* (7 vols., 1896-1902; 3 vols., 1946). The best edition of Gibbon's autobiography was edited by Georges A. Bonnard (1966). Bonnard also edited *Gibbon's Journey from Geneva to Rome: His Journal from 20 April to 2 October 1764* (1961). Jane Elizabeth Norton, *A Bibliography of the Works of Edward Gibbon* (1940), and her edition of Gibbon's *Letters* (1956) are exemplary. The standard biography is David M. Low, *Edward Gibbon, 1737-1794* (1937). An excellent short critical biography is George Malcolm Young, *Gibbon* (1948). Gibbon is praised in Harold L. Bond, *The Literary Art of Edward Gibbon* (1960). Rewarding critical studies are John B. Black, *The Art of History: A Study of Four Great Historians of the Eighteenth Century* (1926); Joseph W. Swain, *Edward Gibbon the Historian* (1966); and David P. Jordan, *Gibbon and His Roman Empire* (1971). □

James Gibbons

James Gibbons (1834-1921), an American Roman Catholic cardinal, did much to reconcile the Church with national institutions when American Catholicism was faced with momentous transformation and crisis.

James Gibbons was born on July 23, 1834, in Baltimore, Md., of Irish immigrant parents. His boyhood was spent in Ireland, where he received his education; he returned to America to study at a Catholic college and seminary in Baltimore. Ordained in 1861, he rose rapidly in the councils of the Church and by 1868 was consecrated vicar apostolic of North Carolina.

In 1877 Gibbons became archbishop of Baltimore, the oldest and most prestigious archdiocese in the United States (which included Washington, D.C.). In 1886 he was created a cardinal, the second American to receive the red biretta. From that time until his death in 1921, he was the unofficial leader of the Church in the United States, honored and extolled by all Americans. In 1917 Theodore Roosevelt wrote to him, "Taking your life as a whole, I think you now occupy the position of being the most respected, and venerated, and useful citizen of our country." When the United States entered World War I, Gibbons gave unstinted support to President Woodrow Wilson.

Gibbons was a staunch defender of the Church, and his *The Faith of Our Fathers* (1876) was one of the most successful apologetics written in the English language. Yet he respected all faiths, and at the 1893 Parliament of Religions he led the assembly in the Protestant version of the Lord's Prayer, to the consternation of Catholic conservatives. Gibbons successfully defended the Knights of Labor (a union considerably Catholic in membership) from papal censure, thereby winning a reputation as labor's friend, though in fact he deplored class consciousness and condemned industrial violence. He unalterably opposed the fragmentation of American Catholicism into ethnic divisions. He championed the American separation of church and state and never ceased to praise America's democratic institutions.

There was little of the ascetic, the mystic, or the scholar about Gibbons. He was not a bold innovator, brilliant orator, or masterful administrator. Yet such was the transparency of his piety and patriotism and such were the depths of his love for Church and nation, that he remains to this day

of Carlo Fontana. Gibbs became acquainted with many members of the English aristocracy, for whom he made drawings and who were helpful to him in later life. He returned to England in 1709.

Through the influence of Edward Harley, Earl of Oxford, Gibbs was made one of the surveyors to the commissioners for building 50 new churches in London in 1713, and in this capacity he designed St. Mary-le-Strand (1714-1717), his first public building. Here he expressed not only influences of Sir Christopher Wren but also ideas absorbed from Italian baroque and mannerist architecture. Gibbs was employed by Lord Burlington in rebuilding the east block of Burlington House, Piccadilly, before that patron embraced Palladianism, but was superseded by the earl's protegé, Colen Campbell.

When the Whigs, who supported the Palladians, came to power, Gibbs as a Tory of baroque tendencies lost his official post in 1715, but his private practice among Tory patrons continued to be exclusive and remunerative. He built Cannons House, Middlesex (1716-1719; demolished 1747) for the Duke of Chandos; added a chapel and library at Wimpole Hall, Cambridgeshire (ca. 1720), for Lord Harley; built the exquisite Octagon Room at Twickenham, Middlesex (1720), with beautiful plasterwork by Italian stuccoworkers; and erected Ditchley House, Oxfordshire (1720-1725), probably his most splendid house, for the Earl of Lichfield, again with remarkable plasterwork by Italian craftsmen.

the greatest and most beloved Catholic leader America has known.

Further Reading

John T. Ellis, *The Life of James Cardinal Gibbons Archbishop of Baltimore, 1834-1921* (1952), impressively researched and brilliantly written, is superior to Allen S. Will's fine *Life of Cardinal Gibbons* (1922). Ellis's *American Catholicism* is the best brief treatment of Gibbons. For the crucial era of Gibbons's leadership see two splendid, scholarly works: Robert D. Cross, *The Emergence of Liberal Catholicism in America* (1958), and Thomas T. McAvoy, *The Americanist Heresy in Roman Catholicism, 1895-1900* (1963; formerly titled *The Great Crisis in American Catholic History, 1895-1900,* 1957).
□

James Gibbs

The highly individualistic achievement of the British architect James Gibbs (1682-1754) stands between the English baroque school and the Palladian school.

James Gibbs was born at Footdeesmire near Aberdeen, Scotland, in December 1682, the younger son of a Scottish gentleman. As a young man, he traveled on the Continent, pursuing his fondness for drawing. In Rome he determined to become an architect and entered the school

But public commissions were not entirely lacking. In 1720 Gibbs designed St. Martins-in-the-Fields (built 1722-1726), one of his outstandingly beautiful works. Like St. Mary-le-Strand and many of his houses, the interior was decorated with plasterwork by the fashionable Italian stuccoworkers, who probably came to England through his encouragement. St. Martins was followed by another building of extreme elegance and dignity, the Senate House at Cambridge (1722-1730), as well as the new buildings of King's College. Many of the ornamental buildings in the park at Stowe House, Buckinghamshire, are his work, including the Temple of Diana (1726), the Temple of Friendship (1739), the Gothic Temple (1740), and the Column with a statue of Lord Cobham.

Gibbs's general influence among architects and clients was great because of his exhaustive knowledge of architecture acquired through long study in Rome, an experience rare among architects of that generation, although later more common. This influence he extended by means of his *Book of Architecture* (1728), a record of both his executed and unexecuted work, and especially his *Rules for Drawing the Several Parts of Architecture* (1732), a work used by countless architects, students, scholars, and builders up to the present day.

Of Gibbs's later works the circular Radcliffe Library at Oxford (1737-1749) is his most ambitious and monumental achievement; it shows much influence of Nicholas Hawksmoor. Gibbs published the designs in the large folio volume *Bibliotheca Radcliviana* in 1747, and he received from the university the honorary degree of master of arts. He designed the new decorations of Ragley Hall, Warwickshire (ca. 1750-1755), in the rococo taste then becoming fashionable. A distinguished late work is the church of St. Nicholas at Aberdeen (1751-1755). In his last years Gibbs held the sinecure post of architect to the Office of Ordnance. He died in London on Aug. 5, 1754.

In his early buildings, especially in his churches, Gibbs displayed that discreet form of the baroque which he had absorbed from Carlo Fontana in Rome and also from Wren's example. Characteristic features of his work are window architraves interrupted by prominent rustication blocks, *oeil de boeuf* (oxeye) windows, boldly projecting cornices, and parapets topped by urns. In his later buildings the exterior form conformed more closely to severe Palladian principles, but the interiors retained a baroque exuberance.

Further Reading

The only monograph on Gibbs and his work is Bryan D. Little, *The Life and Work of James Gibbs, 1682-1754* (1955). There are brief discussions of him in Peter Kidson and Peter Murray, *A History of English Architecture* (1962; rev. ed. 1965), and John Gloag, *The English Tradition in Architecture* (1963). Gibbs's relationship to contemporary baroque and Palladian architects is dealt with in John Summerson, *Architecture in Britain, 1530-1830* (1955; rev. ed. 1963). See also K. A. Esdeile, *St. Martins-in-the Fields, New and Old* (1944), and Christopher Hussey, *English Country Houses: Early Georgian, 1715-60* (1955). □

Josiah Willard Gibbs

Josiah Willard Gibbs (1839-1903) was an American mathematical physicist whose pioneer work in statistical mechanics laid the basis for the development of physical chemistry as a science.

When Josiah Willard Gibbs began his work, thermodynamics had become a true science, firmly based on recently formulated laws of the conservation of energy. These included the law that equated heat and energy and the law of the dissipation or degradation of energy (first and second laws of thermodynamics), which had been worked out mathematically.

Gibbs began with the known thermodynamic theory of homogeneous substances and worked out the theory of the thermodynamic properties of heterogeneous substances. It was this work which, some years later, provided the basic theory for the new branch of science known as physical chemistry. Gibbs's great contribution, "On the Equilibrium of Heterogeneous Substances," was published in the *Transactions of the Connecticut Academy of Arts and Sciences* in 1876 and 1878. Before the end of the 19th century it had been translated into French and German, and Gibbs was widely recognized as one of the greatest mathematical physicists since Isaac Newton. He was one of the few American physicists of that century to achieve an international reputation and the only one to make a theoretical contribution of fundamental importance.

Early Life and Education

Josiah Willard Gibbs was born Feb. 11, 1839, in New Haven, Conn., of a distinguished and learned family. His father was professor of sacred literature in the Yale Divinity School for many years and a well-known linguist. Gibbs graduated from Yale College in 1858 with prizes in mathematics and Latin. He continued his studies at Yale, earning his doctorate of philosophy in 1863. Afterward he was appointed tutor in the college, where he taught Latin for 2 years and natural philosophy for a third year. From 1866 to 1869 he studied in Paris, Berlin, and Heidelberg, where his teachers were some of the world's most distinguished mathematicians and physicists. This period in Europe constituted his only residence outside of New Haven, for in 1871 he was appointed professor of mathematical physics in Yale College—the first such chair in an American college—and he served in that capacity for the rest of his life.

Work in Thermodynamics

From the beginning of his professorship, Gibbs devoted himself to the development and presentation of his theory of thermodynamics. His first two scientific papers made an exhaustive study of geometrical methods of representing by diagram the thermodynamic properties of homogeneous substances. These early papers brought Gibbs to the attention of England's leading physicist, James Clerk Maxwell. Maxwell constructed a model illustrating a portion of the work and sent a plaster cast to Gibbs. After investigating

Although Gibbs received many honors during his lifetime, including the Royal Society's Copley Medal and the Rumford Medal of the American Academy of Arts and Sciences, his immediate influence was limited to a small circle of advanced physicists. The esoteric nature of his work made him practically unintelligible to students. Shy and retiring by nature, he made no effort to attract followers or to communicate to a wider audience. The first impact of his work, both theoretical and applied, was in Europe, for America had neither physicists nor a chemical industry capable of taking advantage of the many insights his work provided.

Gibbs never married. He died on April 28, 1903, in New Haven.

Further Reading

There are two book-length biographies of Gibbs: Muriel Rukeyser, *Willard Gibbs* (1942), studies Gibbs as a creative thinker from a poet's point of view, and Lynde P. Wheeler, *Josiah Willard Gibbs: The History of a Great Mind* (1951), deals best with the technical side of Gibbs's work. Solid studies of Gibbs are in James Gerald Crowther, *Famous American Men of Science* (1937); Bernard Jaffe, *Men of Science in America* (1954; rev. ed. 1958); and Mitchell Wilson, *American Science and Invention* (1954). □

homogeneous substances, Gibbs went on to his great work, "On the Equilibrium of Heterogeneous Substances." It was this thesis that contained the "phase rule," which has been of such great practical value in industrial chemistry.

Later Work

Gibbs's subsequent work in thermodynamics was valuable but not on the same order as the earlier papers. During the 1880s his interests began to turn in other directions. He modified his earlier work on quaternions and geometric algebra into a system of vector analysis especially suited to the needs of mathematical physicists, and he developed his own theory of optics based on electricity rather than electromagnetism. His theory was built chiefly upon the hypothesis that light is a periodic disturbance propagated through media whose structures are more fine-grained than the wavelength of light. The theory was published in the *American Journal of Science* between 1883 and 1889. As in his paper on thermodynamics, Gibbs relied to an unusual degree upon mathematical logic and avoided all special hypotheses concerning the constitution of matter.

During the 1890s Gibbs published nothing at all. His last and perhaps his greatest contribution, *The Elementary Principles of Statistical Mechanics,* was published in 1902. The book, termed by one authority "a monument in the history of physics which marks the separation between the nineteenth and twentieth centuries," laid the foundation for a new branch of theoretical physics that ultimately developed into quantum mechanics.

Kahlil Gibran

Lebanese writer and artist Kahlil Gibran (1883-1931) influenced modern Arabic literature and composed inspirational pieces in English, including *The Prophet*.

Kahlil Gibran, baptized Gibran Khalil Gibran, the oldest child of Khalil Gibran and his wife Kamila Rahme, was born January 6, 1883, in Besharri, Lebanon, then part of Syria and the Ottoman Turkish Empire. His childhood in the isolated village beneath Mt. Lebanon included few material comforts and he had no formal early education. However, he received a strong spiritual heritage.

Surrounded for centuries by members of the Moslem and Druze religions, residents of Maronite Christian villages like Besharri evolved a mystical philosophy of life. His later work was influenced by legends and biblical stories handed down for generations in the scenic region near the ancient Cedars of Lebanon.

Seeking a better future, the family, except for their father, moved to America in 1895. They joined relatives and shared a tenement in South Boston, Massachusetts. Kamila Gibran sold lace to support her four children and opened a small dry goods store. While registering for public school, Gibran's name was shortened and changed.

His life changed when a settlement house art teacher noticed his artistic skill. Florence Peirce with Jessie Fremont Beale, a philanthropist, arranged for Gibran's introduction to Fred Holland Day in December 1896.

A Boston patron of literature and fine arts who was also an "artistic" photographer, Day used Gibran, his younger sisters Marianna and Sultana, half-brother Peter, and Kamila as models. After discovering Gibran's aptitude for literature and art, Day proclaimed him a "natural genius" and became his mentor. Gibran designed book illustrations, sketched portraits, and met Day's friends. He then went to Beirut, Lebanon, in 1898 to attend Madrasat-al-Hikmah, a Maronite college where he studied Arabic literature and cofounded a literary magazine.

Returning to Boston in 1902, he experienced family tragedy. During 1902 and 1903 Kamila, Sultana, and Peter died from disease. Marianna, a seamstress, supported both herself and Gibran, who resumed his art work and renewed his friendship with Day.

In 1903 Josephine Preston Peabody, a poetess and friend, arranged for an exhibition of his work at Wellesley College; in 1904 Gibran and another artist exhibited their work at Day's Boston studio. Here, Gibran met Mary Elizabeth Haskell, who became his patron and tutor in English for two decades. The owner of Miss Haskell's School for Girls and, later, headmistress of the Cambridge School, she believed he would have an outstanding future. She aided several talented, needy people and was a major factor in Gibran's success as an English writer and artist.

From 1908 to 1910 Haskell provided funds for Gibran to study painting and drawing in Paris. Before going to France, he studied English literature with her and had an essay, "al-Musiqa" (1905), published by the Arabic immigrant press in New York City.

Diverse influences, including Boston's literary world, the English Romantic poets, mystic William Blake, and philosopher Nietzsche, combined with his Besharri experience, shaped Gibran's artistic and literary career. Although his drawings depict idealized, romantic figures, the optimistic philosophy of his later writing resulted from a painful personal evolution. Understanding Gibran's attitude towards authority gives greater insight to his work in English.

Gibran opposed Ottoman Turkish rule and the Maronite Church's strict social control. After "Spirits Rebellious," an Arabic poem, was published in 1908, Gibran was called a reformer and received widespread recognition in the Arabic world. Other Arabic writings, including "Broken Wings" (1912), were published in New York where a large Syrian-Lebanese community flourished. He became the best known of the "Mahjar poets" or immigrant Arabic writers. His most respected Arabic poem is the "The Procession" (1919). He was president of Arrabitah, a literary society founded in New York in 1920 to infuse "a new life in modern Arabic literature."

Gibran sought and won acceptance from New York's artistic and literary world. His first work in English appeared in 1918 when *The Madman* was published by the American firm of Alfred A. Knopf. The sometimes cynical parables and poems on justice, freedom, and God are illustrated by three of Gibran's drawings. In 1919 Knopf published Gibran's *Twenty Drawings;* in 1920 *The Forerunner* appeared. Each book sold a few hundred copies. In October 1923 *The Prophet* was published; it sold over 1,000 copies in three months.

The slim volume of parables, illustrated with Gibran's drawings, is one of America's all-time best selling books; its fame spreads by word of mouth. Critics call it overly sentimental. By 1986, however, almost eight million copies—all hard-bound editions—had been sold in the United States alone. Several of his other works enjoyed substantial sales. Gibran bequeathed his royalties to Besharri; ironically, the gift caused years of feuding among village families.

Gibran's views on the brotherhood of man and man's unity with nature appeal primarily to young and old readers. The parables present a refreshing, new way of looking at the world that has universal appeal. By 1931 *The Prophet* had been translated into 20 languages. In the 1960s it reached new heights of popularity with American college students.

Although in failing health, Gibran completed two more books in English—*Sand and Foam* (1926) and *Jesus, The Son of Man* (1928)—that illustrate his philosophy. After his death earlier essays were compiled and published, and his Arabic work has been translated into many languages.

Gibran was 48 when he died in New York City on April 10, 1931, of cancer of the liver. The Arabic world eulogized him as a genius and patriot. A grand procession greeted his body upon its return to Besharri for burial in September 1931. Today, Arabic scholars praise Gibran for introducing Western romanticism and a freer style to highly formalized

Arabic poetry. "Gibranism," the term used for his approach, attracted many followers.

In America, the West Tenth Street Studio for Artists in Greenwich Village, where he lived after 1911, has been replaced with a modern apartment building. But Gibran's books are in countless libraries and book stores. Five art works, including a portrait sketch of Albert Pinkham Ryder, are at New York City's Metropolitan Museum of Art, the gift of his patron Mary Haskell Minis.

The young emigrant from Lebanon who came through Ellis Island in 1895 never became an American citizen: he loved his birthplace too much. But he was able to combine two heritages and achieved lasting fame in widely different cultures. These two aphorisms from *Sand and Foam* convey Gibran's message:

> Faith is an oasis in the heart which will never be reached by the caravan of thinking.

> How can you sing if your mouth be filled with food? How shall your hand be raised in blessing if it is filled with gold?

Further Reading

The definitive biography of Gibran in English by Jean Gibran and Kahlil Gibran, *Kahlil Gibran, His Life and World* (1974), documents his life through letters, notebooks, and diaries. *Beloved Prophet, The Love Letters of Kahlil Gibran and Mary Haskell and Her Private Journal* (1972), edited by Virginia Hilu, reveals the complex relationship between Gibran and his longtime patron. An early biography, *This Man from Lebanon* (1945) by Barbara Young, presents an uncritical view. A more realistic but undocumented study is Mikhail Naimah, *Kahlil Gibran, A Biography* (1950). Khalil S. Hawi, *Kahlil Gibran: His Background, Character, and Works* (1963) is a detailed study, but the author lacked access to important sources. Studies on Arabic literature that discuss Gibran include: Salma Khadra Jayyusi, *Trends and Movements in Modern Arabic Poetry* (1977), Vol. I; M. M. Badawi, *A Critical Introduction to Modern Arabic Poetry* (1971), Ch. 5, "The Emigrant Poets."

Additional Sources

Gibran, Jean, *Kahlil Gibran, his life and world,* Boston: New York Graphic Society, 1974.
Gibran, Jean, *Kahlil Gibran, his life and world,* New York: Interlink Books, 1991.
Hawi, Khalil S., *Kahlil Gibran: his background, character, and works,* London: Third World Centre for Research & Publishing, 1982, 1972. □

Althea Gibson

Althea Gibson is noted not only for her exceptional abilities as a tennis player, but for breaking the color barrier in the 1950s as the first African American to compete in national and international tennis.

Born in Silver, South Carolina, in 1927, Althea Gibson became the dominant female athlete of the late 1950s in a sport well known for its custom of racial segregation. Tennis was not Gibson's first sport; instead, she shot pool, bowled, and played basketball. She even boxed a little.

Childhood in Harlem

During the Depression the Gibson family moved north to Harlem. When she was ten years old, Gibson became involved with the Police Athletic League (PAL) movement known as "play streets." Essentially, PAL was an attempt to help troubled children establish work habits they would use later in life. In 1940 in Harlem, PAL promoted paddleball. After three summers of paddleball competition Gibson was so good that the Cosmopolitan Tennis Club sponsored her to learn the game of tennis and proper social behavior.

In 1942 Gibson began winning tournaments sponsored by the American Tennis Association (ATA), the black counterpart to the United States Lawn Tennis Association (USLTA). In 1944 and 1945 Gibson won the ATA National Junior Championships. In 1946 Gibson was recognized by politically astute blacks as a player who could help break down institutionalized racism in the United States. Sponsored by Hubert Eaton and Walter Johnson and inspired by Sugar Ray Robinson, Gibson soon dominated every event on the ATA schedule. By the beginning of the 1950s she was ready to endure the hardship of breaking the color barrier in tennis.

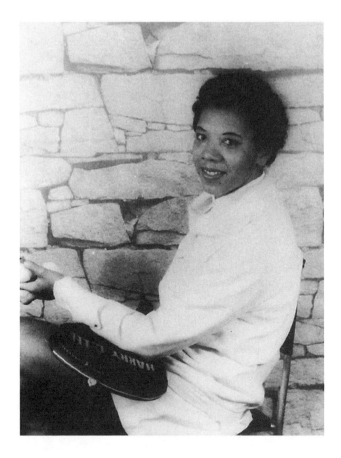

Breaking the Color Barrier

Gibson had a powerful ally: four-time U.S. singles and doubles champion Alice Marble. The USLTA finally allowed Gibson to play in the 1950 Nationals when Marble intervened on her behalf. Gibson lost her first match of the tournament, but the entrance had been made. Over the next several years Gibson rose in the USLTA rankings (ninth in 1952, seventh in 1953). After a year of touring the world, playing special events for the U.S. State Department, Gibson staged a full-scale assault on the tennis world in 1956. That year she won the French Open in both singles and doubles.

Tennis Dominance

Over the next two years Gibson was the dominant women's tennis player in the world. In 1957 and 1958 she won both Wimbledon and the U.S. Nationals. In 1958 she wrote a book about her life called *I Always Wanted to Be Somebody*.

Further Reading

Tom Biracree, *Althea Gibson* (New York: Chelsea House, 1989).

Betty Millsaps Jones, *Wonder Women of Sports* (New York: Random House, 1981).

Pat Ross, ed., *Young and Female: Turning Points in the Lives of Eight American Women, Personal Accounts* (New York: Random House, 1972). □

William Gibson

An author of plays, poetry, fiction, and criticism, Gibson (born 1914) is best known for his drama *The Miracle Worker* (1959). Praised for its honest, unsentimental treatment of the relationship between Helen Keller, a woman born deaf, blind and mute who grew up to became a nationally celebrated writer and public figure, and Annie Sullivan, the nurse who teaches Helen language and morals, *The Miracle Worker* remains Gibson's most admired and revived work.

A lthough Gibson's works have been variously faulted as superficially realistic dramas that sentimentalize the serious issues they raise, Gibson is praised for his accurate ear for dialogue and strong command of dramatic conflict. Robert Brustein observed: "Gibson possesses substantial literary and dramatic gifts, and an integrity of the highest order. In addition, he brings to his works authentic compassion, wit, bite, and humor, and a lively, literate prose style equalled by few American dramatists."

Gibson was born in New York City, where he attended City College of New York from 1930 to 1932. Following his graduation, he supported himself as a piano teacher in Kansas while pursuing an interest in theater. His earliest

plays, produced in Topeka, were light comedies that Gibson revised and restaged during his later career. The first, *A Cry of Players* (1948), concerns a sixteenth-century English playwright named Will who is prompted to leave his wife and family for the life of the London theater, while the second, *Dinny and the Witches* (1948), features as its eponymous protagonist a Faustian character who is sentenced to death by three comic witches for having stopped "the clock of eternal time." Gibson first achieved widespread popular success with *Two for the Seesaw* (1958), his first major play produced in New York City. Set in New York in the 1880s, this work combines humor and melodrama to depict the relationship between Gittel Mosca, an overgenerous, unemployed dancer, and Jerry Ryan, a selfish Nebraska lawyer who becomes involved in a love affair with Gittel while preparing to divorce his wife. Although Jerry leaves Gittel to return to his wife, Gibson concludes the play by implying that Gittel has gained from the brief relationship by becoming more self-assertive, while Jerry has learned humility and concern for others. Characterizing *Two for the Seesaw* as a casual entertainment, most critics praised the play's brisk dialogue and Gibson's compassionate treatment of his characters. Brooks Atkinson commented: "By the time the curtain comes down, you are not so much aware that Mr. Gibson has brought off a technical stunt as that he has looked inside the hearts of two admirable people and made a charming full-length play out of them."

Gibson achieved his greatest success with *The Miracle Worker*. Originally written and performed as a television drama, the play was later adapted for stage and film. Al-

though realistic in tone, *The Miracle Worker* often makes use of cinematic shifts in time and space to illuminate the effect of the past on the present in a manner analogous to Arthur Miller's *Death of a Salesman*. Using innovative lighting and onstage set changes, Gibson juxtaposes Helen's present quest for language and meaningful human connection with the past experiences of Annie Sullivan, the "miracle worker" of the title who was partially cured of childhood blindness through surgical operations during her adolescence. Summoned to the Keller home in Tuscumbia, Alabama, Annie becomes locked in a test of wills with Helen as well as her family, who have allowed Helen to become spoiled and uncooperative due to their pity for her and attendant refusal to administer discipline. Although faulted as superficial or exploitative by some reviewers, *The Miracle Worker* has been praised for Gibson's alternately heroic, humorous, and sympathetic treatment of Annie and Helen's struggle for human language and love. Walter Kerr asserted: "[Gibson has] dramatized the living mind in its incredible energy, in its determination to express itself in violence when it cannot arrange itself into thought. . . . When it comes, the physical contact of the child and the teacher—a contact that is for the first time meaningful and for the first time affectionate—is overwhelming."

In his nonfiction volume *The Seesaw Log and Two for the Seesaw* (1959), Gibson combines the text of *Two for the Seesaw* with a chronicle of his participation in initial productions of that play and *The Miracle Worker*. Asserting that the producer and director of both productions had taken commercial liberties that obscured the artistic integrity of his plays, Gibson largely withdrew from the New York theater during the 1960s and 1970s. His last major play for the New York stage, *Golden Boy* (1964), is a musical adaptation of Clifford Odets's book of the same title about the moral consequences that confront a talented black boxer after he accidentally kills a man in the boxing ring. Gibson's miscellaneous works of the 1960s and 1970s also include *A Mass for the Dead* (1968), a family chronicle about Gibson and his ancestors; *A Season in Heaven* (1974), a chronicle of specific events in Gibson's immediate family; and *Shakespeare's Game* (1978), a volume of theoretical drama criticism that borrows terminology from chess and psychology to explain relationships between scenes and between author and audience.

Further Reading

Contemporary Literary Criticism, Volume 23, Gale, 1983.
Dictionary of Literary Biography, Volume 7: *Twentieth Century American Dramatists*, Gale, 1981.
America, November 10, 1990, p. 350.
Cosmopolitan, August, 1958.
Los Angeles Times, October 19, 1982.
Nation, December 2, 1968.
New England Theatre, Spring, 1970. □

Franklin Henry Giddings

Franklin Henry Giddings (1855-1931) was an American sociologist, educator, and one of the leading writers in the social sciences in the late 19th century.

Franklin Giddings was born on March 23, 1855, in Sherman, Conn. After graduation from Union College, he turned to newspaper work in Connecticut, and during the next 10 years he developed great skill in analyzing public issues. He began to publish articles in scholarly journals, mainly on economic questions, and received favorable notice from the academic world. In 1888 he was made lecturer on politics at Bryn Mawr College and soon became a full professor. In 1894 he was invited to a new chair in sociology and the history of civilization at Columbia University, where he developed one of the nation's leading departments until his retirement in 1928.

"Consciousness of Kind"

The major themes in Giddings's work were fully presented in his *Principles of Sociology* (1896), where he clearly described sociology as a special basic social science, rather than the sum of other social sciences. Specifically, he conceived of sociology as the study of developing forms of human society, based on the changing intensity of "consciousness of kind," or collective feelings of similarity and belonging. These feelings are expressed in two complementary kinds of associations: relatively cohesive and intimate groups, and groups designed for highly specialized interests. Societies develop through normal conflicts and readjustments between these two forms. These themes were illustrated in *Inductive Sociology* (1901) and *Readings in Descriptive and Historical Sociology* (1906).

In subsequent years Giddings gave greater emphasis to processes of social causation and collective achievement. One application of this approach was crucial to the essays in *Studies in the Theory of Human Society* (1922), where he asserted that the environment affects the character of a population and, indirectly, its ability to overcome environmental limitations and to create more complex techniques and solutions. Another application was Giddings's controversial espousal of United States imperialism in *Democracy and Empire* (1900). Finally, in a posthumous work called *Civilization and Society* (1932), Giddings analyzed the practical conflict between government and formal rules, on the one hand, and custom and folkways, on the other, in periods of rapid social change.

Toward the end of his career, Giddings was a pioneer in encouraging the use of careful quantitative and experimental methods in studying social phenomena (*The Scientific Study of Human Society*, 1924). Among his most famous students were F. Stuart Chapin, Howard W. Odum, and Donald Taft, who transmitted his orientation to more than 3 decades of sociological research and training. He died on June 11, 1931.

Further Reading

The best survey of Giddings's career is John L. Gillin's chapter on Giddings in Howard W. Odum, ed., *American Masters of Social Science* (1927). A shorter account is Odum's *American Sociology* (1951). Another review of some scope is by Clarence H. Northcott in Harry Elmer Barnes, ed., *An Introduction to the History of Sociology* (1948). □

André Gide

The works of the French author André Gide (1869-1951) reveal his passionate revolt against the restraints and conventions inherited from 19th-century France. He sought to uncover the authentic self beneath its contradictory masks.

André Gide was born in Paris on Nov. 22, 1869, to Paul Gide, a professor of law at the Sorbonne, and his wife, Juliette, both of the Protestant upper middle class. After the death of his father when André was 11, the boy was dominated by his mother's love and grew up in a largely feminine environment. His fragile health and nervous temperament affected his education, which oscillated between formal schooling and a combination of travel and private tutoring. At 15 he vowed a lifelong spiritual love to his cousin, Madeleine Rondeaux.

Symbolist Period

In 1891 Gide published his first book, *Les Cahiers d'André Walter* (*The Notebooks of André Walter*), in which dream is preferred to reality, spiritual love to the physical. It did not succeed, however, in winning over the reluctant Madeleine, as Gide had intended. During this period he was introduced into the symbolist salons of Stéphane Mallarmé and José de Heredia by his friend Pierre Louÿs. In the symbolist vein Gide wrote *Le Traité du Narcisse* (1891; *Treatise of the Narcissus*) and *Le Voyage d'Urien* (1893).

In 1893 Gide set out for Africa with his friend Paul Laurens in the hope of harmonizing imperious sensual desires and inherited puritanical inhibitions. At Susa he had his first homosexual experience. There Gide fell ill with tuberculosis and was forced to return to France, where he was shocked to find the symbolist salons unchanged. Retiring to Neuchâtel for the winter, he wrote *Paludes* (*Marshlands*), a satire on stagnation and a break with symbolism.

In 1895 Gide returned to Africa, where he met Oscar Wilde and Lord Douglas. Wilde obliged Gide to acknowledge his pederasty, to which he now passionately acquiesced. This was indeed a pivotal year for Gide for it also brought the death of his mother and his marriage to Madeleine, who continued to symbolize for him the pull of virtue, restraint, and spirituality against his cult of freedom and physical pleasure. Gide's life was a constant effort to strike a balance between these opposite imperatives.

Middle Years

Gide articulated his doctrine of freedom in 1897 in *Les Nourritures terrestres* (*Fruits of the Earth*), a lyrical work advocating liberation through sensuous hedonism. *L'Immoraliste* (1902), a novel transposing many autobiographical elements, dramatizes the dangers of Michel's selfish quest for freedom and pleasure at the ultimate cost of death to his pious wife, Marceline. In this, perhaps Gide's greatest novel, as in various other works, the portrait of the virtuous, devoted heroine was inspired by Madeleine.

Conceived at the same time as *L'Immoraliste*, *La Porte étroite* (1909; *Strait Is the Gate*) is a critique of the opposite tendency of excessive restraint and useless mysticism. Again patterned after Madeleine, the heroine, Alissa, renounces her love for Jérôme to devote herself entirely to God and the spiritual life. The final pages of her diary suggest the futility of her self-denials in the face of solitude without God. This was Gide's first success.

In the relatively sterile years between these two novels, Gide was a cofounder of *La Nouvelle revue française*. After publishing in 1911 another highly polished though less autobiographical work, *Isabelle,* Gide was ready to challenge the principle of order in art. This he accomplished in *Les Caves du Vatican* (1914; *The Vatican Swindle*), a humorous satire on bourgeois complacency, be it orthodox or anticlerical, and on relativism and chance. The work defies conventional psychology's insistence on motivated acts. Instead Gide carries to the extreme the idea of freedom, for the hero, Lafcadio, murders a total stranger by pushing him out of a moving train. Thus Gide evolved the notion of the "gratuitous act," an expression of absolute freedom, unpremeditated, seemingly unmotivated. He was no doubt influenced by his reading of Henri Bergson, Friedrich Nietzsche, and Fyodor Dostoevsky.

In *La Symphonie pastorale* (1919), a pastor's free interpretation of Christ's words to legitimize his love for the heroine is pitted against his son's orthodox adherence to the restrictions of St. Paul. This work reflects Gide's religious crises of 1905-1906, which had been precipitated by his disturbing meetings with the fervent Catholic poet, playwright, and diplomat Paul Claudel, and of 1916, after the conversion of his friend Henri Ghéon to Catholicism. The latter crisis was also caused by the beginning of Gide's love affair with Elisabeth van Rysselberghe, who later became the mother of his only child, Catherine. This religious crisis also inspired *Numquid et tu . . . ?*, which retraces Gide's effort to seek and find his own truth in the Gospels.

Gide risked his reputation by publishing *Corydon* (1924), an apology of homosexuality, and *Si le grain ne meurt . . .* (1926; *If It Die . . .*), his well-known autobiography which treats the years 1869-1895, the period of his homosexual liberation.

"The Counterfeiters"

Gide's *Les Faux-monnayeurs* (*The Counterfeiters*) appeared in 1926. It is the fruit of a 30-year meditation on a twofold esthetic freedom: freedom from subjective, autobiographical fiction and freedom from the limitations of the traditional novel. In order to convey a true impression of life, chaotic, elusive, perceived subjectively and individually, Gide devised a technique of disorder. Gide underscores this innovation by means of the character Édouard, who is also writing a book called *Les Faux-monnayeurs* and who fails to achieve the same goal. *Les Faux-monnayeurs* is a landmark in the general revolt against realism, defying the reader's conventional expectations and forcing him to reflect on the technical problems which face the modern novelist.

Also in 1926 appeared *Dostoevsky*, a collection of lectures and articles on the Russian novelist, whom Gide greatly admired and helped bring to the attention of the French public. Like the *Lettres à Angèle* (1900) and *Prétextes* (1903), which contains an admirable study of Oscar Wilde, *Dostoevsky* is a book of criticism which retains its interest chiefly because it reveals Gide's own thoughts on literature and philosophy.

Later Years

In 1925-1926 Gide traveled in the Congo with his friend Marc Allégret. He was deeply distressed by the colonial exploitation of the natives that he witnessed there. Upon his return he published accounts of his trip and issued a call for action. This experience undoubtedly facilitated his conversion to communism in the 1930s. Disillusioned by a visit to the U.S.S.R. in 1936, he admitted his mistake in *Retour de l'U.R.S.S.* (1936; *Return from the U.S.S.R.*) and *Retouches à mon Retour de l'U.R.S.S.* (1937; *Afterthoughts on the U.S.S.R.*).

Gide had long since ceased to feel at ease with intellectual conformity. In 1931 he had insisted in the play *Oedipe* on the individual's obligation to draw his own ethical conclusions (Oedipus) rather than follow the path of blind discipleship (Eteocles and Polynices).

In 1935 *Les Nouvelles nourritures* (*Later Fruits of the Earth*) had reiterated the ideal of liberation, now tempered by consideration of others, a sense of social duty, and self-discipline. During the German Occupation, Gide was forced to flee to Tunisia. In *Thésée* (1946) the adventures and accomplishments of the old Theseus parallel Gide's own. The optimistic mood betrays the author's serene confidence in the path he had chosen. The following year Gide was awarded an honorary degree from Oxford and the Nobel Prize for literature.

Probably the most important publication of Gide's later years was his *Journal, 1889-1939*, released in 1939, one year after the death of his wife. The final volume (1950) carries the journal through 1949. Considered by some his best work, the *Journal* is the moving self-portrait of a man whose mind mirrored the crisis of the modern intellectual. It also contains precious information on his curious platonic marriage to Madeleine, who quietly endured her husband's homosexual adventures by taking refuge in a world of piety and domesticity. Her mute suffering was a great source of guilt and pain to Gide, who loved her deeply. *Et nunc manet in te*, published posthumously in 1951, is Gide's testimony to that love and a frank account of their unspoken tragedy. Gide died in Paris on Feb. 19, 1951, and was buried at Cuverville in Normandy.

Further Reading

There are two major critical biographies of Gide: Justin O'Brien, *Portrait of André Gide: A Critical Biography* (1953), and George D. Painter, *André Gide: A Critical Biography* (1968). Also useful is Harold March, *Gide and the Hound of Heaven* (1952). The best general studies in English of Gide's works are Albert J. Guerard, *André Gide* (1951; 2d ed. 1969); Germaine Brée, *Gide* (1953; trans. 1963); and George W. Ireland, *André Gide: A Study of His Creative Writings* (1970). Less ambitious but worthwhile introductions to Gide are Enid Starkie, *André Gide* (1953), and Wallace Fowlie, *André Gide: His Life and Art* (1965). Recommended for general background on the 20th-century French novel are Henri Peyre, *The Contemporary French Novel* (1955); Germaine Brée and Margaret Guiton, *An Age of Fiction: The French Novel from Gide to Camus* (1957); and Victor Brombert, *The Intellectual Hero: Studies in the French Novel, 1880-1955* (1961).

Additional Sources

Cordle, Thomas, *André Gide,* New York: St. Martin's Press, 1975 1969.

Mann, Klaus, *André Gide and the crisis of modern thought,* New York: Octagon Books, 1978, 1943.

O'Brien, Justin, *Portrait of André Gide: a critical biography,* New York: Octagon Books, 1977, 1953.

Tolton, C. D. E., *André Gide and the art of autobiography: a study of Si le grain ne meurt,* Toronto: Macmillan of Canada, 1975. □

John Gielgud

One of the 20th century's most distinguished actors, John Gielgud (born 1904) was noted for his Shakespearean roles for the stage, especially Hamlet, and appeared in numerous theatrical and television films and on recordings of classic books and plays. He also authored several theatrical "reminiscences" throughout his career.

John Gielgud ranks among the foremost interpreters of Shakespeare in the 20th century and was one of the most prolific theater artists; continuing to work in theater, film, and television abundantly into his eighties. He was often ranked with Ralph Richardson and Laurence Olivier as comprising the "Triumvirate" of English actors which dominated the acting world of the English theater from the 1930s through the 1960s; with Gielgud branching into a significant directing career in the 1950s.

The third of four children of Frank Gielgud, a stockbroker, and his wife, the former Kate Terry-Lewis; Gielgud was born in London, England, on April 14, 1904, into a family with theatrical roots. On his mother's side he was descended from the great Terry acting family, one of his great aunts being Ellen Terry, one of the most famous actresses of the 19th century; on his father's side, his great grandparents were leading actors in 18th-century Poland. Young John took an early interest in performance; designing and inventing plays in a toy theater along with his siblings.

After finishing his secondary education, he decided to try his luck on the stage, promising his father that if he did not succeed by age 25 he would study to be an architect. Fortunately he was offered a scholarship to Lady Constance Bennett's Drama School, and through this experience made his first professional debut as an unpaid walk-on in *Henry V* at the Old Vic. Gielgud became involved in managing and understudying with James Fagan's Company in 1922. He obtained a scholarship to the Royal Academy of Dramatic Art (RADA), and after leaving there in 1923 he played a number of parts, the most significant of which were Trofimov in Chekhov's *The Cherry Orchard* and understudying, then taking over for Noel Coward in Coward's play *The Vortex*. Both roles guaranteed his success as an actor.

Gielgud joined the Old Vic company in 1929, where he began to develop his elegant style and expressive "cello-like" voice. He won immediate acclaim in his Shakespearean roles, and over the course of his career he played most of Shakespeare's leading men including: Angelo, Oberon, Lear, Julius Caesar, Romeo, and Mercutio (which he alternated with Laurence Olivier in 1935), Prospero, Antony, Macbeth, Hotspur, and Richard II. He was most famous for his role as Hamlet, which he played first in 1930 and which he played over 500 times in his career, being fixed in the tradition of significant English "Hamlets" since the 18th century. Of his Hamlet the critic John Mason Brown wrote: "Such a voice, such diction, and such a gift of maintaining the melody of Shakespeare's verse even while keeping it edged from speech to speech with dramatic experience, is a new experience." The *Literary Digest* called his Hamlet "cerebral" and "intellectual," "sensitive, disciplined, disdaining rant and the roaring traditions."

In addition to the classics, Gordon Daviot's *Richard of Bordeaux* (1932, which Gielgud also directed) established him as a popular star in the West End. He was also noted for his performances of Jack Worthing in *The Importance of Being Earnest* (1939). About his early career, in a 1983 interview he noted that: "I played a lot of very neurotic young men. I might have been typed as an hysterical juvenile. I was lucky to get Shakespeare, Chekhov, and Congreve early on and develop an appetite for really good stuff that showed I could do something outside my own range. One is inclined to trade on the qualities that brought one's reputation. . . ."

In the 1950s, 1960s, and 1970s Gielgud alternated acting with directing, helping to promote many new playwrights such as Terence Rattigan, Graham Greene, and Enid Bagnold, as well as directing opera. He created a one-man show based on the works of Shakespeare entitled *Ages of Man*, which toured Britain and was seen in New York and on American television. He appeared with lifelong friend Ralph Richardson in two acclaimed plays in the early 1970s: David Storey's *Home* and Harold Pinter's *No Man's Land*. He won the Tony Award in 1961 for his direction of *Big Fish, Little Fish*, a special Tony Award for *Ages of Man* in 1959, and a Drama Desk Award and Tony nomination for best actor for *Home* (1971).

Gielgud made his film debut as Daniel in the silent 1924 film *Who Is the Man?* and appeared in dozens of films, more notably in Hitchcock's *The Secret Agent* (1936), as Disraeli in *The Prime Minister* (1941), *Around the World in 80 Days* (1956), *Saint Joan* (1957), *Becket* (1964), *Murder on the Orient Express* (1974), *The Elephant Man* (1980), and *Chariots of Fire* (1980). As Hobson in *Arthur* (1981), he won the American Academy Award for Best Supporting Actor.

Gielgud's more recent film credits include: *Arthur 2: On the Rocks, Shining Through, The Best of Friends, The Power of One, First Knight,* and *Shine.*

Gielgud's career has been multifaceted. In 1996 he worked with actors Jane Seymour and Christopher Reeve to provide voices for the lead characters in Warner Bros. Feature Animation's *The Quest for Camelot.* Gielgud's numerous and recent television credits include: *Brideshead Revisited, Wagner, The Far Pavilions, The Master of Ballantrae, Oedipus, War and Remembrance, A Man for All Seasons,* and *Inspector Alleyn.* In the early 1980s Gielgud appeared as a spokesman for Paul Masson wines on television. In 1996 he recited poetry with Alan Bates and Ben Kingsley for a television advertisement for the Union Bank of Switzerland.

Although he wrote several books about his life in the theater, he admitted to enjoying reading "trashy" American novels and listening to opera in his elegant country home in Buckinghamshire, England. Gielgud was knighted in 1953 and held honorary degrees from St. Andrew's University, Oxford University, and Brandeis University. He continued to be active in the arts in the 1990's.

Further Reading

John Gielgud wrote six autobiographical works: *Early Stages* (1939), *Stage Directions* (1963), *Distinguished Company* (1973), *An Actor in His Time* (1979, republished in 1996), *Backward Glances* (1989), and *Acting Shakespeare* (1991). Two good biographies exist in *John Gielgud: A Celebration* (1984) by Gyles Brandmeth and Ronald Hayman's *John Gielgud* (1971). See the *Columbia Encyclopedia* (Edition 5, 1993, p14870) for a short biography on John Gielgud. Other considerations of his career can be found in *Poet at the Piano* by Michiko Kakutani, *The Player* by Lillian Ross, *John Gielgud's Hamlet* by Rosamund Gilder, and Sir Laurence Olivier's autobiography, *Confessions of an Actor* (1982).

For additional biographical resources about John Gielgud see: Redfield, William, *Letters from an Actor,* Proscenium Publications, 1984; Harwood, Ronald, *The Ages of Gielgud: An Actor at Eighty,* Proscenium Publications, 1984; Findlater, Richard, *These Our Actors: A Celebration of the Theatre Acting of Peggy Ashcroft, John Gielgud, Laurence Olivier and Ralph Richardson,* Elm Tree Books; and *The Columbia Encyclopedia, Edition 5,* 1993.

For periodical articles about John Gielgud see: *America,* August 13, 1994; and *Entertainment Weekly,* September 6, 1996.

For on-line resources about John Gielgud see: http://www.mpx.com.au/~zaphod/ProsperoGielgudIdea.html, http://www.flf.com/shine/allnotes.htm, http://www.ocean-fm.com/magazine.text/camelot.txt, and http://moviereviewmagazine.com/029704c5.htm. □

Otto von Gierke

The German jurist Otto von Gierke (1841-1921) was a leader of the Germanistic school of legal historians and is best known for his theory of the nature and role of associations, called the Genossenschaft theory.

Otto von Gierke, born on Jan. 11, 1841, in Stettin, was the son of a Prussian official. He spent his early years in a family atmosphere that was highly respectable, cultured, and intensely Prussian. The latter part of his university training was at Berlin, where he was strongly influenced by George Beseler, a Germanist in juristic theory. Gierke's early career was interrupted by wartime service in the army. After holding professorships at the universities of Breslau (1872-1884) and Heidelberg (1884-1887), he succeeded to Beseler's chair at the University of Berlin in 1887. He remained in that post until his death on Oct. 10, 1921.

In Gierke's early years the dominant influence in German legal history and jurisprudence was that of the Romanists, led by Friedrich Karl von Savigny. Writers of this school looked back to the Justinian Code and to later students of Roman law for guidance in interpreting the development and meaning of German law. As an ardent Germanist, Gierke tried to seek out those legal principles that were "truly German." In the first of his famous four volumes on the German law of association (*Das deutsche Genossenschaftsrecht,* (1868-1913), he began his painstaking study of the development of the German concept of association. This study occupied much of the rest of his life. The massive research and perceptive analysis that went into the four volumes made the study an acknowledged classic in the literature of legal and political theory.

In his historical study Gierke found support for his conception of associations as having a real personality of their own, rather than a fictitious personality that is merely attributed to them by law. He argued that modern law, when it deals with such groups as joint-stock companies, trade unions, or churches, should recognize that such associations, like medieval guilds or local communes, organize themselves for their own purposes, have their own system of social law, and are capable of collective willing and acting. In the complex pattern of associations, which includes the state itself, the humblest and most narrow of them has some of the same dignity and value as the highest and most comprehensive.

Gierke's Germanism appeared also in a series of articles criticizing the first draft of a new civil law code for its neglect of Germanic principles, and in three books (1895-1917) on German civil law in which he undertook "to penetrate the new code with a Germanistic spirit."

The American philosopher Morris R. Cohen called Gierke "a sort of patron saint of political pluralists." The British legal historian Frederic Maitland did much to cultivate this view when he introduced Gierke to British academic circles in 1900 and emphasized Gierke's legal doctrine of the autonomous real personality of associations. But Gierke was definitely not a political pluralist. He never questioned the need for a sovereign state. The pluralistic elements of his theory were always balanced by the dominant role that he assigned to the state and its law. Nor was he an advocate of any sort of functional federalism for Germany. His devotion to Prussia and the monarchy and his concern for assured unity of the German people moved him steadily toward centralized authority and made him a vigorous critic of the Weimar Constitution of post-World War I Germany.

Further Reading

A section of *Das deutsche Genossenschaftsrecht* by Gierke was translated with an introduction by Frederic W. Maitland as *Political Theories of the Middle Age* (1900). Other sections were translated with an introduction by Sir Ernest Barker as *Natural Law and the Theory of Society, 1500-1800* (2 vols., 1934). A study of Gierke, which includes translations of several portions of his books and articles, is John D. Lewis, *The Genossenschaft-Theory of Otto von Gierke: A Study in Political Thought* (1935). □

Romeo Gigli

Italian designer Romeo Gigli (born 1949) won renown for almost singlehandedly causing the renaissance of elaborate beading, drapery, and the use of luxury fabrics such as velvet, brocade, and silks, all in a modern manner.

Romeo Gigli was born in Faenza, Italy into a wealthy aristocratic family. One need only look at his childhood to find the beginning of his love of luxury. Gigli's father was in the antiquarian book business and Gigli himself acknowledged: "My ideas are all from pictures I have in my head from 15th and 16th century books." But inspired as he was by his father's trade, Gigli did not go into the family business. Instead, he studied architecture for two years, traveling regularly to the European capitals of London and Paris. In 1972, a store in Bologna, Italy, asked Gigli to design clothes based on the avant-garde street fashions he had seen in these two capital cities.

In 1978, Gigli traveled to New York to design a collection of menswear for Piertro Dimitri. Although Dimitri wanted him to stay and sign an exclusive design contract, Gigli remained in New York for only one season. He then returned to Italy and began work as a design consultant for several Italian clothing companies, including Timmi.

Gigli launched his own company in 1983 and set up his own label, manufactured by the Novara based company Zamasport. Notices of favor from the fashion press were swift and loud. His unstructured and anachronistic designs brought a refreshing air of romance and simplicity back to fashion, and Gigli soon stood bare shoulders above the rest of the Italian fashion pack, including Giorgio Armani. In 1989 Gigli made a controversial move, taking his style presentations from Milan to Paris, where he continued to show under the tents outside the Louvre and under the auspices of the French fashion organization, Le Chambre du Syndicale, before moving into a showroom in the Marais district. In 1991, Gigli separated from his two business partners, restructured his business, and created "Romeo World" - turning over 200 billion lire in the first year.

Gigli's shows were populated by wan, pale models, watched by cultist gatherings of his fashion fans. His designs were sought after by slender, fashion-conscious, wealthy women around the world. To describe Gigli's designs one must think of a combination of Renaissance regality, Japanese severity, and disheveled punk-oriented street chic. Gigli's distinctive style has grown more pronounced with each collection since 1986 - it is characterized by a close fit that follows the lines of the body; soft, romantic draping; a tendency towards asymmetry; and an overall look of grace and fluidity. His colors are muted but rich and he works mostly in stretch linen, silk, chiffon, cotton gauze, wool, cashmere, and silk gazar.

"Gigli was the first designer to rediscover femininity in a modern way," says Chris Gilbert, president of The Fashion Service, a retail adviser and trend tracking agency in New York. "His influence on fashion has impacted strongly already: the smaller shoulders, longer earrings, the rounded hiplines and the mix of delicate and luxurious fabrics in stretch formations: all of that is from Gigli."

Gigli was one of the first designers to show a mix of other designers' work in his stores. For instance, in his Milan boutique his designs were combined with those designed by Jean Paul Gaultier and Sybilla. He found clothing as fascinating as fine art. One season after a fabric-buying trip to India, Gigli came back and ripped out everything in his showroom to put up a display of saris, just for people to come and look at.

Gigli came out with a lower-priced line to be available in chic boutiques and high fashion department stores in the early 1990s. Some fashion critics have criticized Gigli for being slightly overbearing with, for example, the voluminous layers of luxury and crystal beaded ball gowns in one 1990 collection. Naysayers called him more of an "interior decorator" than a fashion designer. But many observers will admit that his early work was possibly the most influential fashion design of the late 1980s. And his avant-garde otherworldly fashion influence is expected to continue to grow into the 1990s.

Further Reading

Additional information on designers and fashions can be found in the *Fairchild Dictionary of Fashion* (1988), *McDowell's Directory of 20th Century Fashion* (1987), and Catherine McDermott's *Street Style* (1987). See also Andrew Edelstein's *The Pop Sixties* (1985), Alison Lurie's *The Language of Clothes* (1983), and Melissa Sones' *Getting into Fashion* (1984).

For on-line resources about Romeo Gigli see: http://made-in-italy.com/fashion/fashion/gigl/gigl.htm and http://www.firstview.com/Spring 96/Romeo Gigli. □

Sir Humphrey Gilbert

Sir Humphrey Gilbert (ca. 1537-1583), English soldier and colonizer, failed in his attempt to settle Newfoundland. Nevertheless he took the first step toward building a British colonial empire in America.

Humphrey Gilbert was born at Greenway, Devonshire. His family was well-to-do, but as a younger son he inherited only enough to pay for his education. He entered the service of Elizabeth before she became queen, and her friendship endured until his death.

Gilbert accompanied the Earl of Warwick's expedition to France in 1562 to aid the Huguenots, then hard pressed by their own government. It is supposed that Gilbert's interest in America dated from this experience and that he here met André Thevet, the French geographer who had visited the New World and written two books about Brazil.

By 1565 Gilbert had become interested in a northern route to the Pacific. He petitioned the Queen for permission to discover a passage to China and wrote *A Discourse of a Discoverie for a New Passage to Cataia,* advocating an English colony on the west coast of North America. Nothing came of this. Gilbert then served in Ireland, intermittently, until 1570, for which he was knighted. During the next few years Gilbert represented Plymouth in Parliament and saw military service in the Netherlands. In 1576 his *Discourse* was published.

In 1578 Gilbert received letters patent from the Crown empowering him to make Western discoveries on the condition that he not harm Spanish subjects. The Northwest Passage is not mentioned in this grant. Gilbert probably wished to establish a colony between the Hudson River and Cape Hatteras. What actually happened on his voyage of 1578 is uncertain; he may have attacked the West Indies, but he founded no colony and was back in England by April 1579. Unable to sail again immediately, he went once more to Ireland, then returned to England to prepare for another voyage of colonization.

Gilbert's small ship sent out for reconnaissance in 1580 does not seem to have visited Newfoundland. After much trouble with the financing, he embarked from a point near Plymouth with five ships and about 260 men in June 1583. Reaching St. John's Bay in Newfoundland in August, he took possession for the Queen. During an exploration of the adjacent mainland coast he lost a ship and all the prospective colonists. It seemed necessary to take what was left of the expedition back to England and return the following spring. Against others' advice, Gilbert insisted on sailing in the *Squirrel,* a tiny ship that was too heavily laden to be seaworthy. On the night of Sept. 9, 1583, watchers on a nearby ship saw the *Squirrel* 's lights vanish, and it and Gilbert were seen no more.

Gilbert is remembered as the first English colonizer. He was not a sailor, and although he studied and understood navigation he felt uncomfortable on shipboard. Before his last voyage the Queen wrote suggesting he not go along, being "a man of not good hap by sea."

Further Reading

A biography of Gilbert and essential documents, including his own writings, are contained in David Beers Quinn, ed., *The Voyages and Colonising Enterprises of Sir Humphrey Gilbert* (2 vols., 1940). William G. Gosling, *The Life of Sir Humphrey Gilbert, England's First Empire Builder* (1911), still has value. A. L. Rowse, *The Expansion of Elizabethan England* (1955), has interesting sections on Gilbert. E. G. R. Taylor, *Tudor Geography, 1485-1583* (1930), provides useful information about Sir Humphrey's plans and aspirations.

Additional Sources

Public Archives of Canada. British Archives., *What strange new radiance: Sir Humphrey Gilbert and the New World: exhibition, brochure, and catalogue,* Ottawa: Public Archives, Canada, 1979. □

William Gilbert

The English physician and physicist William Gilbert (1544-1603), an investigator of electrical and magnetic phenomena, is principally noted for his "De magnete," one of the first scientific works based on observation and experiment.

William Gilbert was born in Colchester, Suffolk, on May 24, 1544. He studied medicine at St. John's College, Cambridge, graduating in 1573. Four years later he began practicing in London. He was prominent in the College of Physicians and became its president in 1599. The following year he was appointed physician to Queen Elizabeth I, and a few months before his death on Dec. 10, 1603, physician to James I.

In 1600 Gilbert published *De magnete* (*On the Magnet, on Magnetic Bodies, and Concerning That Great Magnet, the Earth: A New Physiology*), in Latin. The first major scientific work produced in England, it reflected a new attitude toward scientific investigation. Unlike most medieval thinkers, Gilbert was willing to rely on sense experience and his own observations and experiments rather than the authoritative opinion or deductive philosophy of others. In the treatise he not only collected and reviewed critically older knowledge on the behavior of the magnet and electrified bodies but described his own researches, which he had been conducting for 17 years.

In electrostatics Gilbert coined the word "electricity," greatly extended the number of known materials exhibiting electric attraction, and suggested that static electric attraction was due to a subtle electric effluvium emitted by electrified bodies. The greater bulk of the work, however, is devoted to magnetism. Although the compass had been known in Europe for at least 4 centuries, Gilbert's was the first important study on the detailed behavior of compass needles, their variation from true north, and the tendency of the north pole of the needle to dip. From experiments involving a spherical lodestone, the most powerful magnet then available, Gilbert concluded that the earth was a huge magnet, with a north and south magnetic pole coinciding with the rotational poles. The variation in compass readings from true north, he believed, was due to land masses.

Gilbert also speculated on the nature of magnetism, suggesting that magnetic bodies had a kind of soul which spontaneously attracted other bodies. He pointed out that gravity might be a sort of magnetism, or was at least analogous to it, and that the motions of the planets might well be explained by considering their mutual influence.

Gilbert's studies were so complete and comprehensive that as late as 1822 it was asserted that *De magnete* contained almost everything known about magnetism. Today the unit of magnetomotive force is called the gilbert.

Further Reading

Gilbert's *De magnete* (*On the Magnet*) is available in several translations, such as those of S. P. Thompson and P. Fleury Mottelay. The only complete biography of Gilbert is Silvanus P. Thompson, *Gilbert of Colchester: An Elizabethan Magnetizer* (1891), which is now difficult to obtain. Romano Harré, *Early Seventeenth Century Scientists* (1965), has a full chapter on Gilbert. A brief biography is given in George Sarton, *Six Wings: Men of Science in the Renaissance* (1957). Most standard histories of science discuss Gilbert's contributions. See particularly Abraham Wolf, *A History of Science, Technology, and Philosophy in the 16th and 17th Centuries* (2 vols., 1939; 2d ed. 1959). □

Sir William Schwenck Gilbert

The English playwright and poet Sir William Schwenck Gilbert (1836-1911) collaborated with Sir Arthur Sullivan to create a famous series of comic operas.

William Gilbert was born in London, the son of a retired naval surgeon who became a prolific novelist. As an infant, he traveled to Germany and Italy with his parents, was kidnaped by brigands in Naples, and was later ransomed—almost a scenario for his later operettas. After receiving a fine education at Boulogne, France, and then at the University of London, the young man was granted a military commission in the Gordon Highlanders. He spent 4 years as a clerk in the education department of the Privy Council, studied law with no particular distinction, and drifted into journalism.

Gilbert contributed drama criticism and humorous verse to various London periodicals under his boyhood nickname "Bab" and also illustrated several of his father's novels. His artwork for his own "Bab Ballads" (1866-1871) possesses a direct and quaint humor. In 1866 Gilbert began his career as a playwright. His penchant for satire was revealed in *Dulcamara* (1866), in which he ridiculed grand opera, and in several shorter burlesques. He had a series of dramatic successes, including *The Palace of Truth* (1870) and *Pygmalion* and *Galatea* (1871).

Gilbert's association with Sullivan was initiated in 1871. Their first major production, *Trial by Jury* (1875), produced under D'Oyly Carte's able management, contained Gilbert's characteristically gay and jibing wit, well accentuated by Sullivan's score. So popular was this work that a company was formed, and in rapid succession *The Sorcerer* (1877), *H. M. S. Pinafore* (1878), *The Pirates of Penzance* (1880), and *Patience* (1881) were performed in London and New York. The Savoy Theatre was constructed by Carte for their works, and the Savoyard productions included *Iolanthe* (1882), *The Mikado* (1885), *Ruddigore* (1887), *The Yeoman of the Guard* (1888), and *The Gondoliers* (1889).

The comic operas of Gilbert and Sullivan are characterized by sharply satirical attacks on Victorian bureaucracy, the grotesquely sentimental qualities of currently popular art and amusements, and contemporary topics such as the estheticism of Oscar Wilde. The cleverness of form and the acerbic wit gave their plays—especially *The Mikado* and *H. M. S. Pinafore*—a transcendent reference, and time has not diminished their relevance. Gilbert and Sullivan developed a new dramatic art form. No longer was the narrative subordinated to the music, as in formal opera, but rather through the integration of the two the characterizations and plot structure are rendered more meaningful. Gilbert's lyrics with their unique rhythms and internal rhymes suggested the music Sullivan provided for them.

After 20 years of fruitful collaboration a conflict developed, and the two severed their relationship. The quarrel was actually between Gilbert and Carte over finances, but Sullivan had been drawn into the disagreement. A reconciliation was effected, but their subsequent productions fell short of their major accomplishments. Gilbert was knighted in 1907 and subsequently retired to Middlesex, where he lived as a country squire; he accidently drowned in 1911 near his estate there.

Further Reading

Sidney Dark and Rowland Grey, *W. S. Gilbert: His Life and Letters* (1923), is the most substantial biography of Gilbert. Hesketh Pearson, *Gilbert and Sullivan: A Biography* (1935), and William A. Darlington, *The World of Gilbert and Sullivan* (1950), are excellent accounts of the two men and the Victorian musical world. John Bush Jones, ed., *W. S. Gilbert: A Century of Scholarship and Commentary* (1970), is an anthology of critical opinion from 1869 to 1968.

Additional Sources

Baily, Leslie, *Gilbert and Sullivan, their lives and times,* Harmondsworth, Eng.; New York: Penguin Books, 1979, 1973.

Eden, David, *Gilbert & Sullivan, the creative conflict,* Rutherford N.J.: Fairleigh Dickinson University Press; London: Associated University Presses, 1986.

James, Alan, *Gilbert & Sullivan,* London; New York: Omnibus Press, 1989.

Pearson, Hesketh, *Gilbert and Sullivan: a biography,* London: Macdonald and Jane's, 1975.

Pearson, Hesketh, *Gilbert, his life and strife,* Westport, Conn.: Greenwood Press, 1978.

Stedman, Jane W., *W.S. Gilbert: a classic Victorian and his theatre,* New York: Oxford University Press, 1995. □

Lillian Gilbreth

Lillian Gilbreth reared the 12 children portrayed in the best-selling book "Cheaper by the Dozen. She is a prominent consultant in time-motion studies.

L illian Gilbreth was one of the founders of modern industrial management. She brought psychology to the study of management in the early twentieth century and then brought them both to the forefront of the business world. She broke new ground with her book *The Psychology of Management,* which concerned the health of the industrial worker. An outstanding academician who developed new curricula for major universities throughout the United States, Gilbreth became widely known for making human relations an integral part of management theory and practice.

Gilbreth was born Lillian Evelyn Moller on May 24, 1878, in Oakland, California. She was the oldest of nine children of William and Annie Delger Moller, who ran a devout household of strong German influence. Her mother was the daughter of a prominent Oakland businessman, and her father was a dedicated husband who had sold his New York business to buy into a partnership in the hardware industry in California. Because of her mother's poor health, Gilbreth's public school education did not begin until she was nine, but she progressed quickly and was academically successful in high school. Her passions at the time were literature and music, which she studied with composer John Metcalfe. She was well traveled as a high school student, visiting New York, Boston, and Chicago with her father.

Although very proud of his daughter's talents, Gilbreth's father did not believe that women should attend college. She convinced him, however, to let her enter the University of California and live at home, continuing to care for her sisters. She studied modern languages and philosophy, and her goal was to teach English. Gilbreth was the first woman in the university's history to speak on commencement day in 1900, when she received her B.A. in literature. After graduation, Gilbreth entered Columbia University to pursue a master's degree in literature, but illness forced her to return home in her first year. She reentered the University of California, finished her master's degree in literature in 1902, and began work on a Ph.D.

In 1903, Gilbreth took a break from her studies to travel abroad. She stopped first in Boston, where she met Frank Gilbreth. Ten years her senior, he owned a construction business and was working on the development of motion-study techniques—methods to minimize wasted time and energy and increase productivity in industry. They corresponded through the mail for ten months after they met, and they were married on October 19, 1904. They would have

twelve children, two of whom would later record their humorous memories of family life in the popular books *Cheaper by the Dozen* and *Belles on Their Toes.*

Work was the focus of Frank Gilbreth's life. He wanted a complete partnership with his new wife and began to teach her about construction. He saw that her interest in the human aspects of industry complemented his ideas and he encouraged her to work with him. Their goals and their personalities influenced each other so strongly that both of their careers were redirected into new areas. The mental and physical health of workers was then largely neglected, and Lillian Gilbreth became increasingly interested in her husband's work as she recognized her potential contribution. Her doctoral studies shifted from literature to psychology.

Lillian Gilbreth's marriage began with several major responsibilities—her academic work, starting a large family, and becoming acquainted with the business world. She started as a systems manager in her husband's consulting business and was soon acknowledged as an expert in the study of worker fatigue and production. Her reputation was partially due to her precise measurements when collecting data. Among her contributions were the analysis of machinery and tools, the invention of new tools and the methods to simplify their use, and the standardization of tasks. Most importantly, her work led to a greater understanding of the importance of the welfare of individual in business operations. This was instrumental in broadening acceptance of her husband's work on increasing productivity.

In 1910, the Gilbreths moved their growing family to Providence, Rhode Island, where Lillian Gilbreth entered Brown University to continue her doctoral studies in psychology. She began writing about industrial management from a scientific and psychological perspective. A lecture she delivered at the Dartmouth College Conference on Scientific Management in 1911 on the relationship between management and psychology became the basis for her doctoral dissertation.

In 1913, Frank and Lillian Gilbreth started the Summer School of Scientific Management. The school trained professionals to teach new ideas about management, and it emphasized the study of motion and psychology. Tuition was free, admission was by invitation, and classes were well attended by professors and business people from the United States and abroad. The Gilbreths ran the summer school for four years. Lillian Gilbreth received her Ph.D. from Brown in 1915. Her dissertation had already been published as a book, *The Psychology of Management,* in 1914. She was the first theorist in industrial management to emphasize and document the importance of psychological considerations in management.

After Frank Gilbreth's death in 1924, Lillian Gilbreth moved her family to her home state of California, where she provided a new home and college educations for her children, maintained a consulting business, and continued teaching and researching on efficiency and health in industry. Gilbreth became a well respected businesswoman; Johnson & Johnson hired her consulting firm to train their employees, and Macy's in New York had her study the working conditions of their salespeople to investigate techniques to reduce fatigue. The Dennison Co. and Sears & Roebuck were also clients, among many others. She started a new school called Gilbreth Research Associates, which catered to retail interests and went international in 1926. But by 1929, several universities were modeling motion in their engineering schools, using laboratories complete with photographic devices and movement measurement tools. Convinced that her ideas would now be carried on, she closed Gilbreth Research Associates. That same year she traveled to Tokyo to speak at the First World Power Congress. Gilbreth was now lecturing at universities such as Stanford, Harvard, Yale, and the Massachusetts Institute of Technology. She joined the Purdue University faculty in 1935 as a professor of management, becoming the first woman professor in the engineering school.

When America entered World War II, Gilbreth consulted at the Arma Plant in Brooklyn, New York, which handled huge Navy contracts. The staff at the plant grew from a few hundred to eleven thousand men and women, and she managed the personnel restructuring and worker training for this enormous expansion. Especially notable was her development of an exercise program for the women; although white-haired and over sixty years old, she kept up with the younger women.

In 1948, Gilbreth began teaching at the Newark College of Engineering in New Jersey. She was the first woman professor in this school of engineering as well, and she stayed there for two years. She went on to teach in Formosa from 1953 to 1954 and at the University of Wisconsin in 1955. Gilbreth remained active professionally well into her eighties, speaking and writing on management issues. She also became a widely sought speaker on human relations problems in management. Gilbreth received over a dozen honorary degrees. She was the recipient of the Hoover Medal from the American Society of Civil Engineers in 1966, and other engineering and management professional organizations around the world bestowed many awards upon her for her pioneering work. She died in Phoenix, Arizona, on January 2, 1972.

Further Reading

Carey, Ernestine G., and Frank B. Gilbreth, Jr., *Cheaper by the Dozen,* Crowell, 1948, expanded edition, 1963.
Carey, Ernestine G., and Frank B. Gilbreth, Jr., *Belles on Their Toes,* Crowell, 1950.
Haas, Violet B. and Carolyn C. Perrucci, editors, *Women in Scientific and Engineering Professions,* University of Michigan Press, 1984.
Spriegel, W. R. and C. E. Meyers, editors, *The Writings of the Gilbreths,* Richard D. Irwin, 1953.
Yost, Edna, *Frank and Lillian Gilbreth, Partners for Life,* Rutgers University Press, 1949.
"Lillian Moller Gilbreth: Remarkable First Lady of Engineering," in *Society of Women Engineers Newsletter,* Volume 24, 1978.
Trescott, M. M., "A History of Women Engineers in the United States, 1850–1975: A Progress Report," in *Proceedings of the Society of Women Engineers 1979 National Convention,* New York Society of Women Engineers, 1979. □

colleagues, forced him to abandon the attempt in late October. A second expedition organized a year later ended in failure and the death of his companion, Alfred Gibson, whom he commemorated in naming the Gibson Desert. To make matters worse, a party led by Peter Warburton succeeded in crossing the desert, winning a race that Giles had hoped to win.

Giles was determined to persevere even though yet another explorer, John Forrest, also preceded him. In 1875 Giles organized a third expedition, this time starting farther south and using camels instead of the horses that had not stood up to dry conditions. Leaving from Beltana on May 6, 1875, he arrived at Perth, after a harrowing journey, on Nov. 10, 1875. Not content with this achievement, he determined to become the first to cross both ways. The more northerly route he selected was one that would take him through the Gibson Desert, which had previously defeated him. On Jan. 13, 1876, he left Perth and headed northeast before striking inland. On this occasion he crossed the desert and accomplished his goal by reaching the telegraph line on Aug. 23, 1876.

This was the peak of Giles's life. He carried out no further major explorations, though in 1882 he did carry out some investigations near the Musgrave Ranges. In the 1890s he found employment at Coolgardie on the Western Australian goldfields as a clerk in the mines office. Wealth eluded him, and he died a man of no material substance on Nov. 13, 1897.

Ernest Giles

The Australian explorer Ernest Giles (1835-1897) was the first man to cross the desert wilderness between central and western Australia both ways.

Ernest Giles was born in Bristol, England, on July 20, 1835, and educated at Christ's Hospital, London. In 1850 he followed his parents, younger brother, and five sisters who had migrated to South Australia in 1848. An adventurous young man, he was unable to settle for long in one place and after trying his hand on the Victorian goldfields and working in Melbourne as a post office clerk, he eventually found employment as a stockman on the Darling River in New South Wales. The constant need to find additional pasture took him on several expeditions, aroused his interest in exploration, and developed his knowledge of bushcraft.

The late 1860s was a period in which growing interest was being shown in the region between central and western Australia. Although the coastal route around the Great Australian Bight had been traversed, no one had yet crossed the inland wilderness.

On Aug. 4, 1872, Giles set out from the Charlotte Waters Telegraph Station, but the harshness of terrain and climate, combined with the uncooperativeness of one of his

Further Reading

For Giles's account of his work see his *Geographic Travels in Central Australia* (1875) and *Australia Twice Traversed* (2 vols., 1889). A useful brief biography is Louis Green, *Ernest Giles* (1963). Interesting accounts of Giles's work are in J. H. L. Cumpston, *The Inland Sea and the Great River* (1964), and in William Joy, *The Explorers* (1964).

Additional Sources

Dutton, Geoffrey, *Australia's last explorer, Ernest Giles,* Adelaide: Rigby, 1974.

Ericksen, Ray, *Ernest Giles: explorer and traveller, 1835-1897,* Melbourne: Heinemann Australia, 1978. □

Langdon Brown Gilkey

Langdon Brown Gilkey (born 1919) was the preeminent American ecumenical Protestant theologian in the last half of the 20th century. A thinker of diverse interests and profound existential, ethical, historical, and scientific insights, his theology mirrored the rise and fall of the dominant Protestant neo-orthodoxy of the middle years of this century and proposed a theological agenda for the new religious and cultural pluralism appearing on the horizon toward the end of the century.

Langdon Brown Gilkey, Shailer Mathews Professor of Theology at the University of Chicago Divinity School since 1977, formally retired in March 1989 after 25 years at the school where he taught with distinguished theologians and students of religion as Mircea Eliade, Bernard Loomer, Bernard Meland, Paul Ricoeur, Joseph Sittler, Paul Tillich, and David Tracy. The author of fourteen books and more than one hundred articles, Gilkey's theological method, like Tillich's, was "correlational," a discussion that reflected a more basic pattern of thinking, namely, "to ponder the character of our existence, both personal and historical, before God in the light of the historical and social situation, the massive contours of events, in which we find ourselves." He characterized the half-century in which he self-consciously matured and worked as a "theologian" as a "Time of Troubles," the apparent beginning of a process of social disintegration and historical decline. It was within this context of personal and social crisis that Gilkey thought, wrote, and spoke forcefully and creatively; reinterpreting the classical Christian symbols of the transcendence and mystery of God, the fall and sin of humans, and divine providence and the direction of history in relation to a secular and scientific culture and the plurality of religions as they encounter the post-Christian and postmodern culture of the West.

Gilkey was born in Chicago, Illinois, on February 9, 1919; the son of Charles Whitney and Geraldine Gunsaulus (Brown) Gilkey. He attended the famous University of Chicago Laboratory School before graduating from the Asheville (North Carolina) School in 1936 and enrolling at Harvard where he received his A.B. in philosophy *magna cum laude* in June 1940. Looking back on that prewar period, Gilkey wrote that in college "Religion, or interest in it, played absolutely no part in my personal or my intellectual life. . . . I was, I suppose, an ethical humanist if I was anything." This despite being raised in an exhilarating atmosphere of theological (American Baptist) and political "liberalism" in Hyde Park, where his father was the first dean of the university's Rockefeller Chapel and his mother an equally prominent and successful early feminist.

In September 1939 while touring France with the Harvard-Yale tennis team, Gilkey saw the early manifestations of Hitler's Third Reich. Although he and his student generation detested Hitler, many detested war more. However, in the spring of 1940 something quite unpredictable happened. Gilkey went to the Harvard Chapel to hear a friend of his father, the noted Protestant neo-orthodox theologian Reinhold Niebuhr. He left that service "converted" to an entirely new view of the power struggles among nations; shortly leaving behind the optimistic illusions of his humanistic idealism.

A major turning point in Gilkey's life was his departure in mid-August 1940 for Peking to teach English to Chinese students at Yenching University. This experience in the Orient—he did not return to the United States for five years—was unquestionably the most significant and formative experience of his life. After the Japanese attack on Pearl Harbor in December 1941, Gilkey and other "enemy nationals" were placed under house arrest. Fifteen months later, in March 1943, they (mostly British and Americans) were sent to an internment camp in Shantung province, where Gilkey remained until the war ended in August 1945. At the camp Gilkey served as helper to the camp mason, the cook and the kitchen administrator. The extraordinary impact that captivity with some 1,500 to 2,000 men, women, and children had on his future theological reflection is powerfully recorded in *Shantung Compound* (1966).

After returning to the United States and experimenting with the possibility of a career in law and international diplomacy; Gilkey began the formal study of theology, philosophy of religion, and ethics at Union Theological Seminary in New York City under the tutelage of his "spiritual father," Reinhold Niebuhr. From 1951 to 1954 he taught at Vassar, and after receiving his Ph.D. in Religion from Columbia University in 1954 he moved to Vanderbilt University in Nashville, Tennessee, where he remained for nearly a decade. The years at Vanderbilt were memorable for his participation with the divinity school faculty in the university's civil rights struggle over the expulsion of a Black divinity school student, James Lawson, for "coaching" neighboring protesters in the techniques of nonviolent resistance. In the end, virtually the entire divinity school faculty and five medical school faculty resigned over this issue.

Gilkey moved to a new teaching position at the University of Chicago in the fall of 1963. During his years at Vanderbilt Gilkey received a Guggenheim Fellowship to travel to Germany in 1960-61. For the next 23 years Langdon Gilkey exercised an extraordinary influence as a member of the theological faculty of the divinity school there. His brilliant lectures, concern for students, and social activism added renewed vigor to the "Chicago School." He completed three distinctively neo-orthodox books—*Maker of Heaven and Earth* (1959), *How the Church Can Minister to the World Without Losing Itself* (1964), and *Shantung Compound* (1966).

Gilkey' was challenged by the Second Vatican Council, which had been called by Pope John XXIII in 1961. In the summer of 1965 Gilkey received a second Guggenheim Fellowship and moved to Rome for the next several months to study the "new theology" in Roman Catholic circles that was making this extraordinary ecumenical event possible. A decade later after continuous research, public lectures in Catholic colleges and universities, and teaching many Catholic students entering the divinity school, Gilkey published the results of his ecumenical inquiry in *Catholicism Confronts Modernity* (1975).

Another unforeseen development during the 1960s and early 1970s was Gilkey's involvement with the "Death of God" theological movement. His earlier philosophical pursuits at Harvard—his senior thesis had explored the atheistic naturalism of George Santayana—alerted him to the novelty of Protestant *theologians* affirming secular humanism's central thesis regarding the loss of religious transcendence in the post-Enlightenment world. However, Gilkey's personal and social experience had assured him of the continuing relevance and validity of the classical Christian theological symbols. Indeed, his next four major theological works—*Naming the Whirlwind: The Renewal of God-Language* (1969), *Religion and the Scientific Future* (1970), *Reaping the Whirlwind: A Christian Interpretation of History* (1976), and *Message and Existence: An Introduction to Christian Theology* (1979)—are each a deliberate attempt to respond to these arguments and show that religious discourse is meaningful in interpreting our uniquely human experience and our quest for existence, meaning, and value. According to Gilkey, civilization remains as precarious and as ambiguous a venture as ever, requiring faith in a grace and providence to address *religious* conflicts brought about by the disintegration of modern secular faith. This cultural critique is developed in his collection of essays *Society and the Sacred: Towards a Theology of Culture in Decline* (1980).

In the late summer of 1981, Gilkey was unexpectedly invited to be a witness for the American Civil Liberties Union (ACLU) in the "Creationist Trial" in Little Rock, Arkansas. What was surprising about this trial was the mutual support provided the ACLU plaintiffs by the local Protestant, Catholic, and Jewish communities versus the Creationist proponents' defense based on the testimony of witnesses well trained in the method and content of modern science! "Creation Science" thus bore all the marks of earlier forms of religious absolutism rooted in a cultural crisis when social, political, and historical anxieties mount in search of reliable moral authority. In response to this theocratic urge of religious fundamentalism, Gilkey argued that genuine science always needs the protection of the legal, political, moral, and religious constraints of the cul-

ture within which it functions to preserve itself from ideological distortion. The details of this trial and argument appeared in his book *Creationism on Trial: Evolution and God in Little Rock* (1985).

Gilkey published three more books: *Gilkey on Tillich* (1990), *Through the Tempest: Theological Voyages in a Pluralistic Culture* (1991), and *Nature, Reality, and the Sacred: The Nexus of Science and Religion* (1993). In the most recent book, Gilkey proposes that theology and science depend on each other for their completion. He demonstrates that science draws its presuppositions from a broad cultural context that includes religious perceptions about the power, life, order and unity of nature.

Gilkey's thought later moved in the direction of a "liberal" or "post-liberal" interest in the post-Christian dialogue with other world religions, especially Buddhism and modern Sikhism; stimulated by the writings of Mircea Eliade, the opportunity to teach at Kyoto University (Japan) in 1975, and his own active participation in yoga classes and Sikh summer retreats in New Mexico. What he called the "rough parity" among religions was first manifest to him in these experiences and, together with his earlier interest in the relations of science and religions and the relativity of our historical, political, and cultural judgments, formed his theological agenda at the end of the 1980s.

In 1997, Gilkey remained active on the faculty at Georgetown University in the Theology Department. His main pedagogical concern, as he once stated in *Reader's Advisor, 14th Edition* (1994) continued to be "not will religion survive as much as will we survive and with what sort of religion, a creative or a demonic one?"

Further Reading

An excellent overview of Langdon Gilkey's career is available in Joseph L. Price, "The Ultimate and the Ordinary: A Profile of Langdon Gilkey," in *Christian Century* (April 12, 1989). The best single introduction to Gilkey's life and thought is the *Festschrift, The Whirlwind in Culture,* edited by Donald W. Musser and Joseph L. Price (1988), which contains a detailed autobiographical essay and a complete bibliography of Gilkey's work through 1985. *Shantung Compound* (1966) is the most popular and accessible guide to the existential roots of Gilkey's religious sensibility, and his theological methods are summarized in his short systematic theology *Message and Existence* (1979).
For biographical resources about Langdon Gilkey see: Walsh, Brian J., *Langdon Gilkey—Theologian for a Culture in Decline,* 1991; *Who's Who in America, 46th Edition,* 1990-91; *Who's Who in Religion, 4th Edition,* 1992-93; and Sader, Marion, *Reader's Advisor, 14th Edition,* R.R. Bowker, 1994.
For periodical articles about Langdon Gilkey see: *Commonwealth,* May 20, 1994.
For on-line resources about Langdon Gilkey see: http://www2.uchicago.edu/divinity/fac.html and http://www.georgetown.edu/departments/theology/faculty/gilkeyl. □

Dizzy Gillespie

Fifty years after helping found a new style of progressive jazz that came to be known as bebop, Dizzy Gillespie's (1917-1993) music is still a major contributing factor to the development of modern jazz.

As a trumpet virtuoso Gillespie stands firmly as a major influence in the development of the jazz trumpet. His band was a virtual training ground for younger musicians. In 1990 he led and wrote the arrangements for a group that included bassist John Lee, guitarist Ed Cherry, drummer Ignacio Berroa, conga drummer Paul Hawkins, and saxophonist Ron Holloway. More than 40 years earlier Gillespie was the first bandleader to use a conga player. Employing Latin rhythms and forging an Afro-Cuban style of polyrhythmic music was one of Gillespie's many contributions to the development of modern jazz.

Before Gillespie there was New Orleans musician Buddy Bolden—the earliest known jazz cornetist—who was followed by King Oliver, Louis Armstrong, and Roy Eldridge. In his memoir, *To Be or Not to Bop,* Gillespie described the influence of Armstrong and Eldridge on his trumpet playing: "Roy Eldridge was a French-style trumpet player. Eldridge was in a direct line from Louis Armstrong, and he was the voice of that era, the thirties. I hardly ever listened to Louis, but was always aware of where Roy's inspiration came from. So I was looking at Louis Armstrong,

you see, because they are one and the same. My inspiration came through Roy Eldridge, from Louis Armstrong and King Oliver and Buddy Bolden. That's the way it happened."

Gillespie played with bands in Philadelphia from 1935 to 1937 before moving to New York. In Philadelphia, where his family had moved from Cheraw, South Carolina, Gillespie learned Eldridge's trumpet solos from fellow trumpeter Charlie Shavers. It was then that Gillespie earned his nickname for his erratic and mischievous behavior. When Gillespie was in the Frankie Fairfax band in Philadelphia he carried his new trumpet in a paper bag; that inspired fellow musicians like Bill Doggett to call him "Dizzy." While Gillespie himself acknowledged the paper bag incident, but he said the nickname didn't stick until later.

Gillespie's basic style of solo trumpet playing at that time involved "running them changes"—improvising on chord changes in a song and introducing new chord changes based on the song's melody. He had taught himself piano and used the instrument to experiment with new melodies and chord changes. When he went to New York in 1937 he did not have a specific job, but was introduced to other musicians by Shavers. Gillespie joined in jam sessions, sometimes after hours at clubs in Harlem like Monroe's Uptown House and Dicky Wells's. He would also sit in with bands; while jamming one night with Chick Webb's band at the Savoy Ballroom, Gillespie met Mario Bauza, a Cuban trumpeter who introduced him to Latin rhythms.

Within a year Gillespie was hired by the Teddy Hill Orchestra for a European tour when the regular trumpet player didn't want to go. Hill probably liked Gillespie's style, which was similar at that time to Roy Eldridge's; Eldridge had left Hill's band to join Fletcher Henderson. By 1937—when he was only 19—Gillespie had already made a name for himself among New York musicians, who couldn't help but notice his radically fresh take on solo trumpet playing: he utilized the upper register of notes above high C, played with great speed, and used new rhythms and chord changes. Gillespie made his first recordings with the Teddy Hill Orchestra just prior to leaving for Europe on "The Cotton Club Show."

Gillespie joined the Cab Calloway Orchestra in 1939 and stayed until 1941. Gillespie wrote in his memoir, "It was the best job that you could possibly have, high class." Calloway played the Cotton Club and toured extensively. During this period Gillespie continued to play all-night jam sessions at Minton's and Monroe's Uptown House to develop his musical knowledge and style. In 1939 the most in-demand trumpet players for recording dates in New York were Eldridge, Shavers, and Buck Clayton. Gillespie was fourth on the list, but somehow managed to land a recording date with Lionel Hampton, which resulted in the famed "Hot Mallets" session. In this session Gillespie became the first musician to record in the modern jazz style with a small group. Lionel Hampton said of the session, as quoted in Gillespie's book, "[Gillespie] came out with a new style, came out with a bebop style. He came out with a different style than we'd ever heard before. A lot of people don't know that was the creation of bebop, the beginning of bebop." Of course, it wasn't called bebop just yet.

Gillespie left Calloway in 1941 following a misunderstanding. During a performance someone from the vicinity of the trumpet section was having fun aiming spitballs at the bandleader, who was singing in front of the band at the time. Naturally Calloway assumed Gillespie was responsible. By most accounts, however, Gillespie was completely innocent and had been set up. Words led to action; Gillespie pulled a knife on Calloway and actually cut him a few times. While the two later reconciled and remained friends, Gillespie was forced to leave the band. This well-known incident illustrates the flip side of Gillespie's jovial personality; he often found himself in situations where he might need to defend himself, and was fully prepared to do so.

Gillespie joined the Earl "Fatha" Hines band in 1942, about the same time Charlie Parker did. Although Parker became famous as an alto saxophonist, he was playing tenor sax at that time. Gillespie first met Parker in Kansas City in 1940 when he was on tour with Cab Calloway. The two of them jammed together at the Booker T. Washington Hotel for several hours. Gillespie ventured in *To Be or Not to Bebop,* "I guess Charlie Parker and I had a meeting of the minds, because both of us inspired each other." They spent a lot of time together during their stint with the Hines band.

By the time he joined Hines, Gillespie had composed "A Night in Tunisia," one of his most famous songs. He was also writing arrangements for other bandleaders, including Hill, Calloway, Jimmy Dorsey, and Woody Herman. He wrote bebop arrangements, as most bandleaders at that time were interested in having one or two bebop numbers in their repertoires. Several musicians have commented that even if Gillespie had not been able to play the trumpet, he could have made a name for himself on the basis of his original compositions and arrangements. Other jazz standards credited in whole or in part to Gillespie include "Groovin' High," "Manteca," "Woody 'n You," "Con Alma," and "Salt Peanuts."

A large part of the Earl Hines band departed in 1943 to form a new group headed by Billy Eckstine. Former Hines members who joined Eckstine included Sarah Vaughan, Gillespie, Parker, and others. The band also featured saxophonists Gene Ammons and Dexter Gordon. Gillespie became musical director for Eckstine, whose backers got him a job on 52nd Street. Gillespie stayed with Eckstine for about seven months, touring and playing on 52nd Street. "The Street," as it was described by critic Pete Migdol in Gillespie's memoir, "was the hippest block with regard to its short distance and that amount of music. . . . This was the top talent street, and it was, of course, discoverer of a lot of the new people for that era."

After leaving Eckstine, Gillespie substituted in the Duke Ellington Orchestra for about four weeks, then formed his own group to play at the newly opened Onyx Club on 52nd Street. Gillespie had been playing bebop whenever he could since 1940, the year he married Lorraine Willis. Now he was able to play it full time. 52nd Street became the proving ground for a new jazz style that had previously been played primarily at late night jam sessions.

"The opening of the Onyx Club represented the birth of the bebop era," Gillespie recalled in his book. "In our long sojourn on 52nd Street we spread our message to a much wider audience." His first quintet at the Onyx Club in 1944 included Oscar Pettiford on bass, Max Roach on drums, George Wallington on piano, and Don Byas on tenor sax. Gillespie had tried to get Parker to join, but he had temporarily returned to Kansas City.

Also in 1944 Gillespie received the New Star Award from *Esquire* magazine, the first of many awards he would receive in his career. Describing the new style his quintet played, Gillespie wrote, "We'd take the chord structures of various standard and pop tunes and create new chords, melodies, and songs from them." For example, Tadd Dameron's composition "Hothouse" was based on "What Is This Thing Called Love," and Parker's "Ornithology" came out of "How High The Moon." Gillespie also noted, "Our music had developed more into a type of music for listeners." There would be little dancing to bebop. Rhythm and phrasing, however, were also important to the new jazz style. "The most important thing about our music was, of course, the style, how you got from one note to another, how it was played. . . . We had a special way of phrasing. Not only did we change harmonic structure, but we also changed rhythmic structure."

Gillespie's quintet also played other clubs, including the Downbeat and the Three Deuces, where the group included Charlie Parker—by then on alto sax—and Bud Powell on piano. Gillespie also played for two months in Hollywood with Parker, vibraphonist Milt Jackson, bassist Ray Brown, pianist Al Haig, and drummer Stan Levy. This was the West Coast debut of bebop and it was very well received. In fact, it was around this time that the term "bebop" came into use. Gillespie recalled, "People, when they'd wanna ask for one of those numbers and didn't know the name, would ask for bebop. And the press picked it up and started calling it bebop. The first time the term bebop appeared in print was while we played at the Onyx Club."

Gillespie's quintet and the presentation of modern jazz in that format reached its apex in 1953—with a concert at Massey Hall in Toronto that featured Gillespie, Parker, Powell, Roach, and legendary jazz bassist Charles Mingus. As Roach recalled in Gillespie's memoir, "The five people that Dizzy had originally thought about in the group at the Onyx didn't really materialize until we did Jazz at Massey Hall, that album, in 1953." Billed by jazz critics as "the greatest jazz concert ever," it was recorded by Mingus—a last-minute substitute for Pettiford—and later released on Debut Records.

From the big bands and orchestras that he first organized in the late 1940s, to the small combos of the early 1950s that served as incubators for young musicians like saxophone giant John Coltrane, Gillespie's influence consistently defined modern jazz. Though the enterprise was short-lived, Gillespie had his own record label, Dee Gee Records, from 1951-53. He appeared at the historic first Newport Jazz Festival in 1954. And he later played the role of unofficial ambassador of jazz, beginning with a 1956 world tour sponsored by the U.S. State Department. These are just a few of the many accomplishments highlighting the career of this remarkably accomplished titan of contemporary American music.

In 1989, the year he became 72 years of age, Dizzy Gillespie received a Lifetime Achievement Award at the National Association of Recording Arts and Sciences' Grammy Award ceremonies. The honor—one of many bestowed on the trumpet virtuoso—recognized nearly 50 years of pioneering jazz performances. That same year he received the National Medal of Arts from President George Bush "for his trail-blazing work as a musician who helped elevate jazz to an art form of the first rank, and for sharing his gift with listeners around the world."

Not letting age slow him down, in 1989 Gillespie gave 300 performances in 27 countries, appeared in 100 U.S. cities in 31 states and the District of Columbia, headlined three television specials, performed with two symphonies, and recorded four albums. He was also crowned a traditional chief in Nigeria, received the Commandre d'Ordre des Artes et Lettres—France's most prestigious cultural award—was named regent professor by the University of California, and received his fourteenth honorary doctoral degree, this one from the Berklee College of Music. The next year, at the Kennedy Center for the Performing Arts ceremonies celebrating the centennial of American jazz, Gillespie received the American Society of Composers, Authors, and Publishers' Duke Award for 50 years of achievement as a composer, performer, and bandleader.

Although his health was failing due to pancreatic cancer, Gillespie continued to play the music that he loved late in his life. His last public appearance was in Seattle in February of 1992. Gillespie passed away quietly in his sleep on October 6, 1993 at the age of 75.

Further Reading

Feather, Leonard, *The Encyclopedia of Jazz in the Sixties,* Horizon, 1966.

Feather, Leonard, *The Encyclopedia of Jazz in the Seventies,* Horizon, 1976.

Horricks, Raymond, *Dizzy Gillespie and the Bebop Revolution,* Hippocrene, 1984.

Koster, Piet, and Chris Sellers, *Dizzy Gillespie, Volume 1: 1937-1953,* Micrography, 1986.

McRae, Barry, *Dizzy Gillespie,* Universe Books, 1988.

New Grove Dictionary of Jazz, Macmillan, 1988.

Detroit Free Press, January 7, 1993; January 8, 1993.

Down Beat, December 1985; January 1986; September 1989; August 1990.

Entertainment Weekly, January 22, 1993.

IAJRC Journal, Winter 1991.

Maclean's, March 20, 1989.

New Yorker, September 17, 1990.

New York Times, January 7, 1993; January 13, 1993; January 17, 1993.

Time, January 18, 1993.

Times (London), January 8, 1993.

Washington Post, January 7, 1993; January 10, 1993. □

Sam Gilliam

Sam Gilliam (born 1933) merged aspects of action painting, color field painting, and postpainterly abstraction with his own unique approach to the shaped canvas. The result is color structured by the form of the canvas itself.

Sam Gilliam was born in Tupelo, Mississippi, in 1933. He received a B.A. degree in fine arts and an M.A. degree in painting (1961) from the University of Louisville, Kentucky. He later resided in Washington, D.C. and taught in public schools there as well as prominent art schools and universities in Washington D.C., Maryland, and Pennsylvania. Throughout his career, Gilliam was concerned with problems of color, atmosphere, and structure. His interest in color staining was inspired, in part, by the work of "Washington color artists" such as Morris Louis and Kenneth Noland. A strong philosophical influence also came from the sculptor Rockne Krebs, with whom Gilliam shared a studio building.

Gilliam's work is rich and varied and involves juxtapositions of color and monochrome, thin stains of paint, and impasto. His early work from the 1960s is geometric and hard-edged. In 1966 he became interested in color staining, pouring paint in broad, translucent flows, thereby creating interpenetrating areas of saturated color.

A year later he began experimenting with a new technique which involved staining a canvas with acrylic paints and then folding or rolling it to create a series of vertical striations. The canvases were then stretched on beveled stretchers in such a way that the painting formed its own frame. These folded paintings of 1967 recall Barnett Newman's work with the repeating vertical stripe.

In 1968 Gilliam responded to the general movement towards "painting as object" with his own brand of shaped paintings: large-scale (30 to 40 foot) suspended canvases with paint flowed and folded on. In these highly sculptural works, gravity and the flexibility of the fabric give the paintings their structure. The way the painting is hung can also determine the color arrangement, by placing noncontiguous areas of the canvas side by side through draping and folding the fabric. These "freed" canvases are not bound by stretchers or frame and are designed to unite with their architectural settings. Not only are spatial variations created by looping and draping the cloth, but also by the interaction of the work with the containing space of the room. The effect from a distance is one of interweaving arcs of color, much like the aurora borealis.

Autumn Surf, a work created in 1973 for the San Francisco Museum of Art, was designed to be entirely free of wall support. One hundred and fifty yards of polypropylene were spread and draped over wooden beams attached to vertical posts and were also hung from ceiling hooks. The overall effect was of waves crashing on the shoreline.

Gilliam's first outdoor piece, an installation at the Philadelphia Museum of Art entitled *Seahorses,* dates from

1975. It was a vast project utilizing 16,800 square feet of material and 250 gallons of acrylic paint.

Later Gilliam experimented with a variety of armatures for his draped paintings, including sawhorses, poles, and screens.

During the 1970s Gilliam continued to work with stretched canvases, experimenting with folding, staining, pouring, and splashing as methods of paint application. During this period his work reveals an increasing interest in the effects of translucent paints. The *Ray Series* (1970-1972) uses a wide range of colors, tones, and intensities. The *Ahab Series* (1973) tends towards a monochrome of silvery white.

Gilliam's 1973 work with assemblages incorporating buttons, photos, and laundry tickets gave way in the mid 1970s to textured canvases with wedge-shaped color insets which appear as though suspended in a fluid-like atmosphere. Gilliam painted canvas, cut it into geometric shapes, then collaged these pieces onto other canvases. The "white collage paintings" of 1976 were created by building up layers of paint in a variety of colors and tones, then covering the whole with a textured white impasto and overglazing. In these works color appears almost as pure light.

The "black paintings" begun in 1977 are similarly heavily textured by layering black paint over other hues and then raking the surface of the painting. These linear configurations, and the geometric planes created by the cutcanvas collage technique, add unity and focus. The juxtaposition of dark tones with areas of color and the mixture of opaque and translucent paints result in a work where warm tones pervade and the vitality of the surface is enhanced.

By 1980, Gilliam applied sculptural elements to the surface of his canvases, making three dimensional sculptural paintings. Later he created multimedia installations and used brightly stained polypropylene, layers of color, computer generated imaging, metallic and iridescent acrylics, hand made paper, aluminum, steel, and plastic. Gilliam's art was an example of evolution through aesthetic exploration.

Sam Gilliam frequently exhibited at the Fendrick Gallery in Washington, D.C. In 1969 eight of Gilliam's suspended canvases were included in a group exhibition at the Corcoran Gallery. In 1971 he had a one-man show at the Museum of Modern Art and also created works for New Spaces, the Walker Art Center, Minneapolis. His 1975 work *Seahorses* was part of the Philadelphia Festival Project at the Philadelphia Museum of Art, and in 1977 he had an installation at Artpark in Lewiston, New York.

Gilliam has been the recipient of many commissions, grants, awards, and honorary doctorates since his first grant in 1967 from the National Endowment for the Arts. He has exhibited internationally and is known all over the world.

Gilliam married Dorothy Butler, a syndicated columnist for *The Washington Post* and the author of *Paul Robeson, All-American* (1976). The Gilliams had three daughters. As a hobby the artist collected antique toys, especially mechanical banks, and pieces of marble from around the world. They reside in Washington D.C. where Gilliam operates a large studio in the historic Shaw district

and continues to create art which embellishes its surroundings and entices viewers with its daring diversity.

Further Reading

The best sources of information about contemporary artists are exhibition catalogues and journal articles. Among the former, the following contain useful information about Gilliam's work: Wadsworth Atheneum, *Gilliam/Edwards/Williams: Extensions* (1974); University of Pennsylvania, Institute of Contemporary Art, *Material Pleasures; the Fabric Workshop at ICA* (1979); Smithsonian Institution, National Museum of American Art, *Across the Nation: Fine Art for Federal Buildings, 1972-1979* (1980); University Gallery, University of Massachusetts at Amherst, *Sam Gilliam: Indoor and Outdoor Paintings, 1967-1978* (1978); and the Studio Museum in Harlem, *Red and Black to "D": Paintings by Sam Gilliam* (1982).
Helpful articles in periodicals include: Keith Morrison, "Interview with Sam Gilliam," *New Art Examiner* (June 1977); Jay Kloner, "Sam Gilliam: Recent Black Paintings," *Arts Magazine* (February 1978); Hugh M. Davies, "Sam Gilliam," *Arts Magazine* (March 1979); and Carrie Rickey, "Art from Whole Cloth," *Art in America* (November 1979).
For periodicals about Sam Gilliam see: *Scholastic Art,* December 1995.
For on-line resources about Sam Gilliam see: http://www.crosstownarts.com/CrosstownArts/client_art/sam/html and http://www.speedmuseum.org/sam_gilliam/westlou.html. □

Charlotte Anna Perkins Gilman

Charlotte Anna Perkins Gilman (1860-1935) was a writer and lecturer who tried to create a cohesive body of historical and social thought that combined feminism and socialism.

Charlotte Perkins was born on July 3, 1860, in Hartford, Connecticut. She was raised by her mother, Mary A. Fitch Perkins, because her father left his wife and children soon after Charlotte's birth and thereafter provided little support, emotional or financial, to his family. Frederick Beecher Perkins, her father, was the grandson of the noted theologian Lyman Beecher, which made Charlotte's great aunt the famous Harriet Beecher Stowe, author of *Uncle Tom's Cabin*. The Beecher family was perhaps the most famous family in America, but when Charlotte's father left he took his family connection with him. She and her brother grew up in an unhappy, cheerless home. Mother and children lived on the edge of poverty, moving 19 times in 18 years to 14 different cities.

Charlotte studied art for a time and later earned her living by designing greeting cards, teaching art, and, for a brief time, tutoring children. At the age of 24, after a long period of uncertainty and vacillation, she married Charles Walter Stetson, a handsome and charming local artist. Their only child, Katharine, was born the following year.

From the beginning of the marriage Charlotte Perkins Stetson suffered from depression. She became so seriously depressed that she was persuaded by her husband to consult the well-known Philadelphia neurologist, S. Weir Mitchell, a specialist in women's nervous diseases. His treatment stipulated extended bed rest to be followed by a return to working as a wife and mother. She was to give up all dreams of a career, she was never to write or paint again, and she was never to read for more than two hours a day. She followed his regimen for a time and almost experienced a mental breakdown. Calling upon some inner sense of survival, she rejected both husband and physician and fled to the house of the Channings, friends in Pasadena, California, whose daughter, Grace Ellery Channing, was Charlotte's dearest friend. Charlotte and Walter were eventually divorced, and Walter married Grace Channing. The three remained friends thereafter and jointly raised Katharine.

For a time Charlotte Stetson barely managed to support herself and Katharine, and later her mother, by running a boarding house. During these difficult years she launched her writing and lecturing career. In 1892 *The Yellow Wallpaper* appeared, a chilling story of a young woman driven to insanity by a loving husband-doctor, who, with the purest motives, imposed Mitchell's rest cure. The next year she published a book of verse, *In This Our World*. In 1894 she co-edited *The Impress*, a journal of the Pacific Coast Woman's Association. She was soon earning her living by lecturing to women's clubs and men's clubs, to labor unions and suffrage groups, to church congregations and Socialist organizations.

Soon after Walter Stetson remarried, both parents agreed that their child should live with her father and his new wife. Charlotte Stetson, moderately well known by this time, was vigorously attacked in the press for being "an unnatural mother" and abandoning her child. Unnerved, she fled from her home, and from 1895 to 1900 she led a nomadic existence, ceaselessly lecturing and writing, endlessly travelling across the country. Out of this environment came her most famous book, *Women and Economics,* which appeared in 1898, was soon translated into seven languages, and won her international recognition. In 1900 she published *Concerning Children;* in 1903, *The Home: Its Work and Influence;* in 1904, *Human Work;* in 1911, *Man Made World: Or Our Androcentric Culture;* and in 1923, *His Religion and Hers: A Study of the Faith of Our Fathers and the Work of Our Mothers.* From 1909 to 1915 she edited a monthly magazine, *The Forerunner,* for which she wrote all the copy. Each year two books were serialized; the full seven-year run of *The Forerunner* equalled in number of pages 28 full-length books.

In 1900, after a long and carefully examined courtship, Charlotte married George Houghton Gilman, her first cousin. They lived happily until 1934 when Houghton died suddenly. Charlotte Gilman, aware now that she suffered from terminal cancer, moved back to Pasadena to be with her daughter. Grace Channing Stetson, also a widow, joined her there, reuniting the women of the family. In 1935 Gilman completed her autobiography, *The Living of Charlotte Perkins Gilman.* She said good-bye to her family, and, with the chloroform she had been long accumulating, she ended her life. The note she left appears in the last pages of her autobiography.

> No grief, pain, misfortune or 'broken heart' is excuse for cutting off one's life while any power of service remains. But when all usefulness is over, when one is assured of unavoidable and imminent death, it is the simplest of human rights to choose a quick and easy death in place of a slow and horrible one. . . . I have preferred chloroform to cancer.

Charlotte Perkins Gilman had an enormous reputation in her lifetime, but she is almost unknown today. A serious critic of history and society, she tried to create a cohesive body of thought that combined feminism and socialism. She struggled to define a human social order built upon the values she identified most closely as female values, life-giving and nurturing. She constructed a theoretical world view to explain human behavior, past and present, and to project the outlines of her vision for the future.

The most important fact about the sexes, men and women, is the common humanity we share, not the differences that distinguish us, Gilman said repeatedly. But women are denied autonomy and thus are not provided the environment in which to develop. Women are forced to lead restricted lives, and this serves to retard all human progress. Men, too, suffer from personalities distorted by their cultural habits of dominance and power. A healthy social organism for both men and women, therefore, requires the autonomy of women. She saw herself as engaged in a fierce struggle for the minds of women. She wrote historical treatises, sociological essays, short stories, novels, plays, and poems in an effort to win over women to her view of the past and, more important, to project a vision of the future. In sociological and historical works she analyzed the past from her peculiar humanist-socialist perspective. (Gilman insisted she was not a feminist; rather the world was "masculinist," and it was she who sought to introduce a truly humanized concept.) In her fiction she suggested the kind of world we could have if we worked at it.

Charlotte Perkins Gilman's life remains as an inspiration to subsequent generations. Her daily living, her ideas, her writing, her lectures are all of a piece. She wrote about the need for women to achieve autonomy, and she struggled in her own life to achieve autonomy. She drew upon the painful and debilitating elements in our own inner and outer experiences as a central focus of her world. In a sense she studied history and sociology, economics and ethics, in order to understand where she came from, why her parents were the way they were, why her life took the form it did, and ultimately how to learn to control her destiny and to manage her life.

Further Reading

The best way to become familiar with Charlotte Perkins Gilman's work is to begin with her books in print: *Women and Economics* (reprinted 1966), *The Home* (reprinted 1972), *The Living of Charlotte Perkins Gilman* (reprinted 1975), and *Herland* (1979). "The Yellow Wallpaper" is available in pamphlet form published by The Feminist Press. It is also included in a collection of fiction by Gilman entitled *The Charlotte Perkins Gilman Reader,* edited by Ann J. Lane (1980). *The Forerunner,* Gilman's monthly journal which ran from 1909 to 1916, was reprinted by Greenwood Press in 1968.

There are also manuscript collections of Gilman letters, diaries, lectures, and notes. The largest collection is at the Arthur and Elizabeth Schlesinger Library on the History of Women in America, at Radcliffe College, Cambridge.

There is as yet no complete published biography of Charlotte Gilman. The early years of her life are covered in Mary A. Hill, *Charlotte Perkins Gilman: The Making of a Radical Feminist 1860-1896* (1980). Carl N. Degler wrote the biographical essay on Gilman in *Notable American Women.* For further critical assessment consult Carl N. Degler, "Charlotte Perkins Gilman on the Theory and Practice of Feminism," *American Quarterly* (Spring 1956), and Ann J. Lane's introductions to *Herland* (1979) and *The Charlotte Perkins Gilman Reader* (1980). □

Daniel Coit Gilman

An educator and pioneer in the American university movement, Daniel Coit Gilman (1831-1908) today remains recognized for his accomplishments as the first president of Johns Hopkins University in Baltimore. From 1875 until his retirement in 1901 he helped make Johns Hopkins one of America's first major graduate schools.

Daniel Coit Gilman was born in Norwich, Connecticut, on July 6, 1831, of old New England ancestry. He spent his early youth in Norwich but later lived and attended school in New York, where his parents moved when he was of high school age. He entered Yale as a member of the class of 1852, and while there began a life-long friendship with fellow student Andrew D. White, who was later to become the first president of Cornell University.

In 1853 Gilman and White sailed for Europe as attachés of the American legation in St. Petersburg. While in Europe Gilman travelled in England, France, and Germany digesting stores of knowledge regarding European education. He spent the winter of 1855 attending lectures at the University of Berlin.

Near the end of 1855 Gilman returned to New Haven and Yale to accept employment with the Sheffield Scientific School. As chief administrator and secretary of the school's board of directors Gilman became a leading spokesman promoting instruction and research in science and technology. Demonstrating what was to become known as the "new education" in his writings and addresses, his experience with the Sheffield School was to set the tone of the rest of his career. While in this position Gilman came to know the geologist James Dwight Dana, whose biographer he subsequently became. At Dana's request he proposed a plan for the complete organization of a school of science. In this plan, published in 1856, Gilman acknowledged how far ahead Europe was in providing opportunities for the study of

"science for its own sake" as well as training in the professions.

While at Yale Gilman became professor of physical geography and remained in that position until he left for the University of California. In spite of his duties, he found time to serve as school visitor for the New Haven Public Schools. He became active in a number of reforms, among which were the promotion and creation of a public high school in New Haven. Later he was made a member of the newly created Connecticut State Board of Education.

In 1872, following the election of Noah Porter to the presidency of Yale, Gilman accepted the presidency of the University of California. While in California he introduced improvements in spite of the obstacles interposed by the California legislature and those who wanted the university to become chiefly a school of agriculture. Gilman remembered his experience in California as "brief but significant" because he was there at a time "when it was important to show the distinction between a university and a polytechnic institute."

Gilman's main career achievement was the creation and development of Johns Hopkins University, which grew out of the university bequest of Johns Hopkins, Baltimore financier. At Hopkins' death in 1874 the $3,500,000 bequest passed into the control of 12 trustees whom he had chosen seven years previously. The trustees sought the advice of three well known university presidents—Charles Eliot of Harvard, James B. Angell of Michigan, and Andrew White of Cornell—who agreed that Gilman should be president of this new undertaking.

Gilman accepted the position in 1875 and spent the summer of that year in Europe seeking ideas and searching for a faculty. From the beginning his purpose, as well as that of the trustees, was to establish an institution, national in scope, where intellectual training would be of a higher order than that available in other American colleges and universities. In February 1876 Johns Hopkins University opened with a faculty of six well chosen men, aided by a number of younger associates. Part of the early success of Johns Hopkins was the method of choosing students to match the abilities of the faculty. Scholarships of $500 each were offered to 20 college graduates chosen by examination. Candidates for the degree of doctor of philosophy were to have as "severe a course of training as would be required at a German University."

Early Gilman biographers have emphasized the strong German influence on Gilman during the formative years at Johns Hopkins, saying it was the "German doctorate" that became the aim of the graduate school and the "German seminar" that became its method. It has been generally held that Johns Hopkins started primarily as a graduate school and later developed its undergraduate program. More recently it has been argued that Gilman was not as "single eyed" in his interest in graduate education and research as tradition envisions and that he placed the effect of higher studies on students over their contributions to the advancement of knowledge. Gilman's success, it is said, came "because his aims were plural." Nevertheless, the establishment of graduate education emphasizing research and scholarly publications as a leading element in American universities dates from the founding of Johns Hopkins University. Seventeen years after its founding funds became available for the opening of the Johns Hopkins Medical School, offering one of the most advanced programs for the training of doctors existant at that time.

Gilman, at age 70, resigned the presidency in 1901 and between 1902 and 1904 served as president of the newly formed Carnegie Institution, where he continued as a trustee until his death. Interested in public improvement throughout his life, he succeeded Carl Schurz as president of the National Civil Service Reform League and was also connected with the Peabody Fund, the Slater Fund, and the Russell Sage Foundation. On October 13, 1908, he died at his place of birth—Norwich, Connecticut.

Further Reading

Gilman is listed in the *National Cyclopaedia of American Biography,* the *Biographical Dictionary of American Educators,* and the *Dictionary of American Biography.* A biography which merits attention is Abraham Flexner's *Daniel Coit Gilman: Creator of the American Type of University* (1946). Francesco Cordasco's *Daniel Coit Gilman and the Protean Ph.D: The Shaping of American Graduate Education* (1960) provides a critical perspective on Gilman's contributions to American higher education. An interpretation of Gilman's years at Johns Hopkins is Hugh Hawkins' *Pioneer: History of the Johns Hopkins University, 1874-1889* (1960), winner of the Moses Coit Tyler Prize in American Intellectual History. Gilman's contributions to periodical literature include his *Life of James D. Dana* and a volume on *James Monroe* in the "American Statesmen Series." Especially helpful in understanding Gilman as a university president is his *Launching of a University,* published in 1906. □

Laura Gilpin

Laura Gilpin (1891-1979) was an American photographer best known for her southwestern landscapes and for her photographic studies of the Pueblo and Navajo Indians.

Laura Gilpin was born in Austin Bluffs, Colorado, on April 22, 1891. Although she briefly attended eastern boarding schools, she grew up in Colorado Springs and always thought of herself as a westerner. Even as a child she enjoyed exploring the mountains around her home. In 1903 Gilpin got a Brownie camera, which she used the following year to photograph the St. Louis World's Fair, and about 1909 she began experimenting with autochromes, a new color photographic process developed in France. Living on her family's ranch on the western slope of the Rockies from 1911 to 1915, Gilpin raised poultry and continued making pictures. By the time she went to New York in 1916 to study at the Clarence H. White School of Photography (with money saved from her poultry business) she was an accomplished amateur photographer.

Gilpin studied with White for two years, then returned home to Colorado to set up a commercial photography studio. While earning her living doing portraits and advertising work, she began exploring the Southwest and making pictures of the Pueblo Indians and the ruins of their Anasazi ancestors. These early, atmospheric pictures showed the influence of her training with White, a leading pictorial photographer who emphasized mood rather than detail in his photographs. Gilpin later moved away from this soft-focus approach and adopted a more straightforward, hard-edged style for photographing the Southwest.

Gilpin's long-term involvement with the Navajo began in 1930 when she ran out of gas on their reservation while on a camping trip with her companion Elizabeth Forster.

Deeply impressed by the Navajo people who came to their aid, Forster became a field nurse on the reservation. She lived in Red Rock, Arizona, for two years. Gilpin later became a frequent visitor to the reservation and, through the contacts made by her friend, began to photograph the Navajo people. Her pictures of families, trading posts, hogans, and ceremonies form a compassionate record of traditional Navajo life.

After Forster lost her job in 1933 financial difficulties and a number of photographic projects kept Gilpin away from the reservation for 16 years. In 1941 she published her first major book, *The Pueblos: A Camera Chronicle,* based on a series of lantern slides she had made of archaeological sites. During World War II (1942-1944) she worked as a public relations photographer for the Boeing Company in Wichita, Kansas, and then moved to Santa Fe, New Mexico, where she resumed making photographic books. *Temples in Yucatan: A Camera Chronicle of Chichen Itza* appeared in 1948 and *The Rio Grande: River of Destiny,* her monumental study of the Rio Grande and the people along its banks, came out the following year.

In 1950 Gilpin returned to the Navajo reservation to gather more pictures for a book. Although she initially thought it would be a quick and easy job, her work on the project took 18 years. She travelled all over the reservation, as she could spare time away from her commercial business, gathering information and pictures that would help her tell the story of the Navajo peoples' adaptation to modern American life. Eventually, she came to realize the great importance of traditional beliefs to the Navajo people, and her project began to focus on how traditions could be maintained in a rapidly changing world. *The Enduring Navaho,* which finally appeared in 1968, was widely hailed by anthropologists and by the Navajo people themselves as a truthful and compassionate record of Navajo life.

During the 1970s, Gilpin regained much of the recognition in national photographic circles that she had enjoyed in the 1920s. She was at work on a photographic book about the Canyon de Chelly and its Navajo inhabitants when she died in Santa Fe on November 30, 1979.

Further Reading

The only one of Gilpin's books that is still in print is *The Enduring Navaho* (1968). A full-length biography and wide selection of pictures can be found in Martha A. Sandweiss, *Laura Gilpin:*

An Enduring Grace (1986). Gilpin's photographic estate is now housed in the Amon Carter Museum, Fort Worth, Texas.
□

Étienne Henry Gilson

The French Roman Catholic philosopher Étienne Henry Gilson (1884-1978) was an important modern exponent of Thomism. He stressed the importance of rigorous philosophical reasoning corrected and expanded by Christian revelation.

On June 13, 1884, Étienne Gilson was born in Paris. He was educated at the Petit Séminaire de Notre-Dame-des-Champs and the Sorbonne (1895-1907). In 1908 Gilson married Thérèse Ravisé they later had one son and two daughters. He spent several years as a high school teacher and pursued research at the Sorbonne, receiving a doctoral degree in 1913 for a dissertation on the philosophy of René Descartes. The same year Gilson began teaching at the University of Lille. During this period he moved from a thorough training in modern philosophy to the study of medieval philosophy on the advice of his teacher at the Sorbonne, the distinguished philosopher Lucien Lévy-Bruhl.

Gilson served in the French army in World War I. He was captured at the Battle of Verdun in 1915 and spent the remainder of the war as a prisoner.

From 1919 to 1921 Gilson taught at the University of Strasbourg. In 1921 he became professor of the history of philosophy at the Sorbonne, and during the next ten years he achieved an international reputation as a philosopher and medieval scholar. In 1932 he was made first holder of the chair of the history of medieval philosophy at the Collège de France.

Distinguished visiting lectureships and honors marked Gilson's career. His Gifford Lectures at the University of Aberdeen (1930-1931) became perhaps his best-known book, *The Spirit of Medieval Philosophy* (1932). His William James Lectures at Harvard in 1935 were published as *The Unity of Philosophical Experience* (1937). In 1947 he was honored by the highest distinction attainable by the French scholar: membership in the French Academy.

While a visiting professor at Harvard in 1927, Gilson was invited to Toronto to establish an institute of medieval studies. The institute was established in 1929 in connection with St. Michael's College of the University of Toronto and, under Gilson's direction, became perhaps the finest center in the Western world for research on the Middle Ages. After years of "commuting" between France and Canada, Gilson resigned from his chair at the Collège de France in 1951 and devoted the remainder of his active career to directing the institute in Toronto.

Among Gilson's prolific writings were *The Christian Philosophy of Saint Thomas Aquinas* (1919), *The Philosophy of Saint Bonaventure* (1924), *The Mystical Theology of*

Saint Bernard (1934), *Christianity and Philosophy* (1936), *God and Philosophy* (1941), and *Being and Some Philosophers* (1949).

Anton Pegis summed up the relevance of Gilson's resolute preoccupation with the philosophy of the 13th-century St. Thomas Aquinas in these words: "In this new age, full of historical pressures and conflicts, of new and unexplored philosophical horizons, Thomism is for Gilson a philosophy equipped to deal with man in all the concreteness of his life and in all the existential dimensions of his thought." Gilson died on September 19, 1978, in Cravant, France.

Further Reading

There is no full-length biography of Gilson in English. Biographical material appears in *A Gilson Reader: Selected Writings,* edited by Anton Pegis (1957), which is also a good sampling of the range of Gilson's thought. His obituary apeared in the October 2, 1978 issue of *Time*. □

Alberto Evaristo Ginastera

The composer Alberto Evaristo Ginastera (1916-1983) employed both national idioms of his native Argentina and a variety of avant-garde techniques in developing a unique style.

Of Spanish-Italian ancestry, Alberto Ginastera was born in Buenos Aires on April 11, 1916. At the age of five, he became frustrated when he was unable to play his country's national anthem on a toy flute, because the instrument's range was too narrow. His musical talent was recognized early on, and he entered the Williams Conservatory in Buenos Aires to study music at age 12. He graduated from the National Conservatory of Music with honors in 1938, and three years later he returned to the conservatory as professor of composition. Ginastera set extremely high standards for himself, destroying some of his early compositions because he wanted to be remembered only for his best work.

Not Always Politically Correct

In his early years, Ginastera was not widely known outside Argentina, and even there, his political views sometimes got him into trouble with the country's leaders. The composer was particularly critical of the country's military governments, which he felt inhibited artistic expression. Twice, he was forbidden to teach, even at a music school he had founded, the Conservatory of Music and Scenic Arts at La Plata.

Ginastera's three *Danzas argentinas* for piano and the one-act ballet *Panambí* date from 1937. A second ballet, *Estancia (Ranch),* was commissioned by the American Ballet Caravan in 1941. His first symphony, *Sinfonia porteña* (1942), established him as a leading Latin American composer.

During an extended stay in the United States on a Guggenheim fellowship Ginastera's *Duo for Flute and Oboe* (1945) was premiered. Returning to Argentina, he organized in 1948 the Conservatory of Music and Scenic Art of the province of Buenos Aires. Later he became dean of the faculty of arts and musical science of the Catholic University of Argentina. In 1962 he was named director and professor of composition at the Latin American Center for Advanced Musical Studies in Buenos Aires.

Identified as Musical Nationalist

Ginastera was early identified with musical nationalism. Such works as *Overture for the Creole Faust* (1943), *Pampeana No. 1* for violin and piano (1946), *Pampeana No. 2* for cello and piano, *Pampeana No. 3* for orchestra (1954), as well as his piano pieces and Argentine songs, reflect national characteristics.

However, the First String Quartet (1948) and the popular *Variaciones concertantes* for chamber orchestra (1953) are more formal and nonassociative. The Sonata for Piano (1952) employs polytonal and twelve-tone techniques. Extensive serialism is found in the extraordinarily difficult Violin Concerto (1963) commissioned for the opening of Philharmonic Hall at Lincoln Center. With the opera *Don Rodrigo* (1964) and the cantata *Bomarzo* (1964), commissioned by the U.S. Library of Congress, he emerged as one of the leaders of the avant-garde, making effective use of microtones, aleatory passages, and electronic effects.

Most of Ginastera's major works were commissioned. These include the Second String Quartet (1958), Piano Concerto (1961), Concerto for Harp and Orchestra (1965), and the Cello Concerto (1968). The Juilliard String Quartet performed his Second String Quartet in 1958 at the International American Music Festival in Washington, D.C. This was the first major serial composition from Ginastera and did much to establish his international reputation. Critic Howard Taubman said Ginastera created "an original and exciting synthesis of contemporary trends . . . employing polytonality, serial technique, and a variety of novel timbres with compelling naturalness." Aside from the perseverance of certain Argentinian rhythmic patterns, there is little that might be labeled either traditional or ethnic in the composer's mature works. They established him not only as a master craftsman of great originality but one uncommitted to any particular "school" of contemporary music.

Second Opera Made Headlines

Ginastera's second opera, *Bomarzo* made headlines upon its international debut in Washington, D.C., in 1967. Like the composer's first opera *Don Rodrigo,* it was atonal, but there the resemblance ended. The story line for the second opera was based on the final 15 seconds of life of the Duke of Bomarzo and featured scenes of sex, voyeurism, impotence, violence, and nudity. The opera was a stunning success in the United States, but Argentina banned its performance in that country until five years after its U.S. premiere, citing the composer's "obsession" with sex.

Ginastera often found inspiration in literature for his musical works. His cantata for soprano and orchestra, *Milena* was based on the letters of Franz Kafka, while Pablo Neruda supplied the text for another vocal work called *Serenata.* Of the importance of the classics of art, literature, and music to his own work, Ginastera once said, "I think that when an artist feels lost with too much speculation, he should re-read the works of Shakespeare, look at Fra Angelico's paintings or listen to Beethoven's symphonies, and then I am sure he would return to the right path."

Ginastera first married in 1941, wedding Mercedes de Toro. Their marriage ended in divorce in 1969 and produced two children, Alejandro and Georgina. In 1971, Ginastera married again, this time to Aurora Natola. The couple moved to Switzerland shortly after their marriage, but the move did little to alter the basic character of Ginastera's music. In 1980 his symphonic piece *Iubilum,* written to mark the 400th anniversary of Buenos Aires' founding, was first performed. Three years later in Geneva, Ginastera died at the age of sixty-seven on June 25, 1983.

Further Reading

A doctoral dissertation by David Edward Wallace, *Alberto Ginastera: An Analysis of His Style and Techniques* (1964), is available in duplicated book form. David Ewen, *World of Twentieth Century Music* (1968), has a short biography of Ginastera and a valuable analysis of 11 compositions. Otto Deri, *Exploring Twentieth Century Music* (1968), evaluates the composer's contributions. Suggestions for further investigation are in Gilbert Chase, *A Guide to the Music of Latin America* (1945; 2d ed. rev. 1962).

Further information about the later years of Ginastera's life can be found in *The Annual Obituary 1983,* edited by Elizabeth Devine and published by St. James Press, Chicago and London, in 1984. The entry on Ginastera also contains a brief appraisal of his life's work, as does Britannica Online's entry on the composer, which can be found at http://www.eb.com. □

Newt Gingrich

Hailed as *Time*'s "Man of the Year" in 1995 and touted by some historians as this century's most influential Speaker, U. S. Representative Newt Gingrich (born 1943) held on to his Speaker's post by a narrow margin of only three votes in 1997. "For better or worse, he has changed the language and substance of American politics perhaps like no other politician in recent history," said Time magazine's editor James Gaines. The man who felled the former Speaker of the House Jim Wright on ethics violations was himself charged and fined for his own violation of House ethics in 1996. His "Contract with America" fell short of its promises and his conservative stance has taken on a liberal hue. The Speaker now faces his greatest challenge from within his own party. The question many are asking is whether he can survive his current tenure as Speaker of the House.

Bomb Thrower or Visionary?

"Our view is that Newt Gingrich is a bomb thrower," *Time* reported. A fire-breathing Republican Congressman from Georgia, he is more interested in right-wing grandstanding than in fostering bi-partisanship. . . . Another view is that Newt Gingrich is a visionary. An impassioned reformer . . . {who} innovative thinking and respect for deeply felt American values to the House." In any case, Congress has not been quite the same since Gingrich was first elected to represent Georgia's Sixth Congressional District in 1978.

Born in Harrisburg, Pennsylvania to 19-year-old mechanic, Newton C. McPherson, and 16-year-old, Kathleen Daugherty, Newt's life had a rough start. His parents split within days of their marriage. His mother remarried Robert B. Gingrich, a career soldier, three years later. Gingrich maintained his ties to the McPherson family. Even as a political figure, he wore a McPherson tartan tie.

As the stepson of an Army officer, Newt Gingrich moved from town to town attending five schools in eight years both here and abroad. Gingrich recalls how his experience formed his political approach to Howard Fineman in *Newsweek.* "Politics and war are remarkably similar systems," said Gingrich. "You grow up an Army brat named Newton, and you learn about combat."

In 1960, the Gingrich family moved from Fort Benning, Georgia. Not long after, Gingrich pursued his political career in Columbus. In fact, within a few months in Georgia, he ran a successful campaign for his friend's election to class president. At Emory University in Atlanta, Gingrich established a Young Republicans club.

Fired Up Republicans in Washington

From the time he landed in Washington in 1978, he gained a national reputation for his combative style and his leadership of a collection of young, aggressive, conservative House Republicans. "For his first five years in office," the New York Times said, "Mr. Gingrich, along with a band of young conservative Republicans turned their junior status to advantage and waged guerrilla warfare against democratic House leadership and even their own party's leaders. Under Mr. Gingrich's tutelage, about a dozen of the insurgents formed a group known as the Conservative Opportunity Society (COS) Republicans. Mr. Gingrich maintains, have become so accustomed to their minority status that they need to be prodded to challenge the status quo."

The tenets of Gingrich's philosophy were echoed by the COS—the antithesis of the "liberal welfare state," a state that he regularly criticizes. In 1984, "he turned preliminary sessions of he Republican national convention into a battleground until the Conservative Opportunity Society was inserted into the platform," the Atlantic said.

Gingrich was also well-known for his special taste for colleagues roasted on the moral spit of an ethics committee

investigation. In 1979, during his first term, he called for the expulsion of Representative Charles Diggs, a Democrat from Michigan, who had been convicted of embezzlement. In 1983, he called for the expulsion of two representatives who allegedly had sexual relations with teenagers working as pages in the House. And later, of course, Gingrich spearheaded the movement to oust Jim Wright.

Grabbed Public Attention

In the early 1980's, Gingrich launched a new weapon, taking advantage of a rule allowing House members to read items into the record after Congressional sessions. He gave frequent speeches criticizing Democrats for their position on a wide range of issues, from communism to school prayer to Central America—speeches given before an empty House chamber, but broadcast nationwide on the cable network C-SPAN. This tactic was also used by Gingrich's followers—a group of conservative Republicans elected mostly in the 1980s and labeled the party's "young Turks," in contrast to the GOP's less aggressive old guard.

In the spring of 1984, an angry Thomas P. "Tip" O'Neill, then Speaker of the House, ordered the cable TV cameras to periodically pan the chamber to show that Gingrich was speaking to an empty House. O'Neill called Gingrich's tactics "the lowest thing I have seen in my 32 years in the House." The confrontation resulted in a rare House rebuke to the Speaker and wide coverage for Gingrich—something he valued highly. Newsweek defined what it called Gingrich's Newtonian law: conflict equals exposure equals power. "If you are in the newspaper everyday and on the TV often enough then you must be important."

Gingrich wrote in the Conservative Digest: "The Democratic Party is now controlled by a coalition of liberal activists, corrupt big city machines, labor union bosses and House incumbents who use gerrymandering, rigged election rules and a million dollars from taxpayers per election cycle to buy invulnerability. When Republicans have the courage to point out just how unrepresentative, and even weird, liberal values are, we gain votes. . . . Fear and corruption now stalk the House of Representatives in a way we've never witnessed before in our history."

Proved Wright Wrong

Gingrich's battle against Jim Wright began in 1987; a one-man crusade which few in Washington took seriously. Before Gingrich was through, however, more than 70 House Republicans signed his letter asking the House's ethics committee to investigate Wright. The accusations were related to Wright's links to a Texas developer, to his favors to savings and loan operators, and the way in which he published and sold a book of his speeches and writings Reflections of a Public Man. Wright received unusually large royalties and sold the book to political contributors—an arrangement seemingly designed to circumvent ceilings on donations.

Gingrich was ruthless on the offensive. His dramatic contentions won him necessary Congressional allies and his rhetorical skills made him eminently quotable, thus a media darling. "I'm so deeply frightened by the nature of the corrupt left-wing machine in the House that it would have been worse to do nothing," he was quoted as saying in the *New York Times.* "Jim Wright has reached a point psychologically, in his ego, where there are no boundaries left." Following the investigation, the ethics committee said it had reason to believe Wright had violated House rules 69 times. Less than two months later, on June 6, 1989, Wright resigned as Speaker.

In March 1989, in the midst of his war with Wright, Gingrich's Republican colleagues elected him to the post of Minority Whip by a narrow 87-85 margin. The vote signaled "a wake-up call to incumbent GOP leaders from younger members who want a more aggressive, active party," said the *Congressional Quarterly Weekly Report.* "Gingrich's promotion from backbench bomb thrower to Minority Whip was an expression of seething impatience among House Republicans with their seemingly minority status."

Gingrich's supporters pointed to his energy, communication skills, and commitment to capturing a majority of House seats. "A year ago, no one would have predicted that this enfant terrible of the Republican Party could mount a credible bid for the leadership—let alone snag its No. 2 slot," the *Weekly Review* said, "But Republicans became particularly frustrated with their decade-old minority status in the House when the Reagan era came to an end: Even the eight year reign of a president as popular as Reagan couldn't deliver them from their plight. Gingrich's call for radical change fell on responsive ears."

Gingrich's high-profile role put his personal moral standards in the spotlight. His opponents resurrected the contradictions between Gingrich's ethics-and-traditional-values stand and his messy divorce from his first wife, who was cancer stricken. Democrats *Newsweek* said, also point out "his management of a political action committee that raised $200,000—and gave $900 to candidates." After Gingrich took on Wright, the Democratic Congressional Campaign Committee publicized a 1977 deal in which Gingrich received $13,000 from a group of friends to write a novel. He wasn't in Congress at the time, although he had run twice unsuccessfully for the seat which he eventually won in 1978. Democrats say the arrangement allowed Gingrich's backers to support him financially and get a tax shelter in the bargain. Gingrich said he did research in Europe and wrote three chapters, but the book was rejected by publishers.

In addition to these charges, two days before Gingrich was elected Minority Whip, the *Washington Post* reported that he had persuaded 21 supporters to contribute $105,000 to promote *Window of Opportunity: A Blueprint for the Future,* which he co-authored in 1984 with his second wife, Marianne, and science fiction writer David Drake. The book sold only 12,000 hardcover copies; the investors reaped tax benefits and Gingrich and his wife made about $30,000. Gingrich acknowledged that this book deal was "as weird as Wright's," but was on the up and up because "we wrote a real book for a real (publisher) that was sold in real bookstores." The book deal remained a question mark in Gingrich's past that did not stall his political career in the 1990s.

In October of 1990, Gingrich gained headlines again when he opposed—and led 105 fellow Republicans in voting down—a proposed budget package. His defiance and disregard for the presidential endorsement angered Senate Minority Leader Robert Dole, who was quoted in *Newsweek:* "You pay a price for leadership. If you don't want to pay the penalty, maybe you ought to find another line of work." Dole felt Gingrich, fearful of his personal popularity, fought the budget in ignorance of the bi-partisan agreements that had been the fruit of hard work.

Reached Career-Long Dream

In November 1990, despite his growing reputation on the national level, Gingrich had a scare in his home district at the election. He won by a narrow margin of 983 votes of the nearly 156,000 cast in Georgia's Sixth District. The root of Gingrich's trouble at home was his blockage of federal mediation in the 1989 strike at Eastern Airlines. The Atlanta airport is of great importance to the surrounding communities, and 6,000 employees of Eastern lived in his district. Obviously shaken, Gingrich told his constituents that he had received their warning in the close re-election, and would more closely carry out their mandate in his coming term in office.

Gingrich spent the next four years pursuing his goal of achieving a Republican Majority in Congress. He reached his dream in 1994. On September 27, 1994, Gingrich and his associates presented his brainchild—the "Contract with America," a 100-day House Republican plan to revolutionize Congress, spending, and federal government operations. With Gingrich's consistent campaign support for Republican candidates all over the country, they received the partisan majority in the November elections.

As a result, Newt Gingrich took over as Speaker of the House in January of 1995. During his first year, he faced the challenge of living up to the promises detailed in the "Contract" and also once again confronted ethics charges but did not receive any convictions. He published two books in 1995—the nonfiction *To Renew America* and the fiction novel *1945.*

A Tenuous Second Term

Unlike his first election to the House as Speaker in 1995, Newt Gingrich won his second term by a narrow margin of three votes. Not only was the Speaker under investigation by the ethics committee for allegedly violating House standards by knowingly abusing the tax code in raising tax-deductible funds for a college course he taught, he was also criticized for his book deal with HarperCollins. Gingrich was originally offered a $4.5 million advance for two books, due to very strong criticism, he declined the offer and settled for royalties instead.

While exonerated from 74 of the 75 ethics charges levied against him, the one that he was charged with, admitted to, and levied a $300,000 fine for was enough to tarnish the rising star enough to put his second term as Speaker on shaky ground. Gingrich's greatest challenge was now coming from within his own Party.

Gingrich has come under intense fire from within the Republican Party. Many claim that he has damaged the Party beyond repair and the best thing for him to do is step down. The problem with that scenario is that the Republican Party has no successor that they feel strongly enough about to force a "coup" although there has been much talk of it. Unlike 1995 and 1996 when the Republican majority was united, they are currently a House divided. "The way some Republicans tell it," according to an account in the *Economist* "their troubles are wrought by Newt Gingrich. Two years ago Mr. Gingrich was celebrated {among those with short memories} as the most powerful Speaker of this century; now a fellow House Republican describes him as 'road kill on the highway of American politics.'" Mr. Gingrich is said to be a man with no agenda, who cannot decide if he is conservative or liberal. The lackluster start of the 105th Congress, when compared to the 104th, clearly defines the state of affairs within the Republican Majority-held House and the Party itself. Mr. Gingrich, who has a resilience that few politicians have, has lost his political power base. The question on everyone mind is can he get it back?

Further Reading

Anderson, Alfred F., *Challenging Newt Gingrich Chapter by Chapter* (1996).
Wilson, John K., *Newt Gingrich: Captial Crimes and Misdemeanors* (1996).
Warner, Judith, *Newt Gingrich: Speaker to America* (1995).
Gingrich, Newt, *Newt Gingrich's Renewing American Civilization* (audio cassette, 1997). □

Allen Ginsberg

The American poet Allen Ginsberg (1926-1997) was one of the most celebrated figures in contemporary American literature. He was a leading member of the "Beat Movement" and helped lead the revolt against "academic poetry" and the cultural and political establishment of the mid-20th century.

Allen Ginsberg was born on June 3, 1926, in Newark, New Jersey, to Russian-Jewish parents. He had an emotionally troubled childhood that was later reflected in his poetry. His mother, Naomi, suffered from various mental illnesses, and was periodically institutionalized during his adolescence. Contributing to Ginsberg's growing confusion during these years was his growing awareness of his homosexuality, which he concealed from both his peers and his parents until he was in his twenties.

Ginsberg enrolled at Columbia University with the intention of becoming a lawyer. At Columbia, he fell in with a crowd that included writers Jack Kerouac and William Burroughs, as well as Lucien Carr and Neal Cassaday. Around the time he was a student at Columbia, Ginsberg got into some trouble with the police. His apartment was used as a base for a robbery, and in order to avoid being charged as

an accomplice, he pleaded insanity. He ended up spending several months in a mental hospital.

After graduating with a bachelor of arts from Columbia in 1948, Ginsberg worked as a market researcher in New York and then migrated to San Francisco, where he became a principal figure in the "Beat Generation" literary movement. The Beat movement was an American social and literary movement originated in the 1950s where artists, derisively called "beatniks," expressed their alienation from conventional society by adopting a style of seedy dress, detached manners, and a "hip" vocabulary. Generally indifferent to social problems, they advocated sensory awareness that might be induced by drugs, jazz, sex, or the disciplines of Zen Buddhism. Ginsberg's *Howl and Other Poems* (1956), along with Kerouac's *On the Road* ultimately became the "Beat" movement's twin scriptures.

Howl's raw, graphic language dealt with human discontent and despair, moral and social ills, Ginsberg's homosexuality, and his mother's communist beliefs. Many traditional critics were astonished. While some commentators shared the attitude of Walter Sutton, who considered *Howl* "a tirade revealing an animus directed outward against those who do not share the poet's social and sexual orientation," others echoed the opinion of Paul Zweig, who argued that the poem "almost singlehandedly dislocated the traditional poetry of the 1950s." The publisher, poet Lawrence Ferlinghetti, became a defendant in an obscenity trial, but was later acquitted after testimony led Judge Clayton W. Horn to rule that *Howl* was not obscene. Still, leading literary and popular journals typically complained

that *Howl* was vulgar and undisciplined. Another critic complained that "Ginsberg made it seem like anybody could write poetry.

Nevertheless, Ginsberg's triumphant synthesis of sociology and mysticism, Blake and Walt Whitman, and the Bible and Marxism, had found an audience. Declaiming his poems in coffeehouses, jazz clubs, and colleges, Ginsberg (with a thick, untrimmed beard and his balding head heavily fringed with hair) reinforced his dual image: a saint to the underground minority, a freak to the mainstream majority.

Ginsberg's next volume *Kaddish and Other Poems 1958-1960* (1961), delved further into his past. Based on the "Kaddish," a traditional Hebrew prayer for the dead, it poignantly expressed the anger, love, and confusion felt towards his mother while rendering the social and historical milieu which informed his mother's troubled life. Some critics considered this piece to be his most important work. John Tytell explained "*Kaddish* testified for Ginsberg's capacity for involvement with another human in torment, for the acceptance of another's weirdness."

Ginsberg had visions while reading the poetry of William Blake. These visions led him to experiment with drugs, and he took LSD under the guidance of the late Timothy Leary in the 1960s. He said that some of his best poetry was written under the influence of drugs: the second part of *Howl* with peyote, *Kaddish* with amphetamines, and *Wales - A Visitation* with LSD. However, after a trip to India in 1962, where he was introduced to yoga and meditation, he, generally, changed his mind about drugs. He believed that yoga and meditation were far superior to raising one's consciousness, but still believed that psychedilcs could prove helpful in writing poetry.

Ginsberg was a visible political activist in the 1960s and 1970s. He coined the term and advocated "flower power," a strategy in which antiwar demonstrators promoted positive values like peace and love to dramatize their opposition to the death and destruction caused by the Vietnam War. He protested at the 1968 Democratic Convention in Chicago and later testified on behalf of the "Chicago Seven" who were prosecuted on conspiracy charges. Ginsberg was later jailed after demonstrating against President Richard Nixon at the 1972 Republican Convention in Miami. He was also a staunch advocate for gay rights. When asked to describe his social and political views, he simply responded "Absolute defiance." These experiences, as well as his conversion to Buddhism, his concerns about aging, and the anguish over the deaths of close friends Kerouac and Cassaday, heavily influenced Ginsberg's work.

Ginsberg was a survivor, as he outlived enemies like J. Edgar hoover who thought he was a threat to the establishment. He remained durable, and was an icon of American counterculture for four decades. It could be said that if one generation outgrew him, a new one rose to show their interest. In the 1990s, he was a favorite on MTV, and collaborated with the band *Sonic Youth* and singer Bono of *U2*.

In later years, Ginsberg's health began to fail. He suffered from cirrhosis of the liver, bouts of hepatitis, diabetes, and Bell's palsy, which left his face partially paralyzed. As he continued his relentless self-promotion and an exhausting schedule, Ginsberg accomplished what few writers attain: his acclaim and celebrity were at their height at his death. He had always said he wanted to die peacefully, and on April 5, 1997, at the age of 70, just days after being diagnosed with terminal liver cancer, he died, surrounded by "close friends and lovers" in his New York apartment. Ferlinghetti stated, "He went the way he wanted to go." Longtime friend and former California lawmaker Tom Hayden told CNN, "Allen was like a prophet of the 1960s." His most recent works before his death were *Selected Poems, 1947-1955* and a rock cd *The Ballad of the Skeletons*.

There are also excellent pieces in his other collections: *Empty Mirror* (1962); *Reality Sandwiches* (1963); *The Yage Letters* (1964), written with William Burroughs; *The Marihuana Papers* (1966); *TV Baby Poem* (1968); *Planet News 1961-1967* (1969); *Ankor Wat* (1969); and *Indian Journals* (1970).

Further Reading

Serious attention to Ginsberg's work is lacking, but Jane Kramer, *Allen Ginsberg in America* (1969), is a sympathetic, excellent biography. Obituaries which extensively detailed Ginberg's life and his writings appeared in the April 6, 1997 editions of the *New York Times* and the *Los Angeles Times* . □

Ruth Bader Ginsburg

Supreme Court Justice Ruth Bader Ginsburg (born 1933) is known as the legal architect of the modern women's movement.

In 1960 a dean at Harvard Law School recommended one of his star pupils, Ruth Bader Ginsburg, to serve as a clerk to Supreme Court Justice Felix Frankfurter. Though Frankfurter, like others familiar with Ginsburg, acknowledged her impeccable academic credentials, he confessed that he was not ready to hire a woman. This was neither the first nor the last instance where Ginsburg was defined by her gender rather than her formidable intellect. But the rejection galvanized in Ginsburg a fighting spirit to right the wrongs that women suffered so routinely in American society. Thus, much as lawyer and former Justice Thurgood Marshall had converted the prejudice he faced as a black into the engine fueling his crusade to topple institutional racism, so did Ginsburg act on the lessons she had learned from her life. As the legal architect of the modern women's movement, Ginsburg, more than any other person, exposed a body of discriminatory laws anathema to the spirit and letter of the United States Constitution.

When President Bill Clinton announced the nomination of Ginsburg to fill the seat being vacated by retiring Supreme Court Justice Byron White, the initial reaction focused less on her qualifications and more on whatever the president had botched during the selection process. Clinton was accused of indecisiveness and insensitivity, as he had publicly dangled the names of other candidates—in one

instance asking a Boston judge to prepare an acceptance speech—before giving the nod to Ginsburg. But once the political dust settled, Ginsburg's record guided the discussion. With few exceptions, legal observers praised her for both ground breaking advances she had won as a litigator and for the scholarly precision that had marked her 13-year tenure on the bench.

Faced Gender Discrimination

Ruth Joan Bader was born March 15, 1933, to Nathan and Cecelia (Amster) Bader in the Flatbush section of Brooklyn, New York to a comfortable middle-class family. Cecelia Bader was the driving force in her daughter's life, a role model at a time when women had to fight for the privileges and rights that men enjoyed by default. "I pray that I may be all that she would have been had she lived in an age when women could aspire and achieve and daughters are cherished as much as sons," the *New York Times* quoted Ginsburg as saying in her acceptance of Clinton's nomination.

After graduating from high school, Ginsburg attended Cornell University where she graduated with high honors in government, and subsequently Harvard Law School, where she distinguished herself academically and served on the Law Review. In the "good old boy" male-dominated world of upper crust law, Ginsburg was told that she and her eight female classmates, out of a class of 500, were taking the places of qualified males. She transferred to Columbia University after two years, when her husband, who would become one of the country's preeminent tax attorneys, took a

job in New York. But gender discrimination continued to overshadow her scholastic achievements. Although she graduated at the top of her class, law firms, which normally enter fierce bidding wars for such a star, refused to hire her.

First Tenured Female at Columbia Law

After a clerkship for District Judge Edmund L. Palmieri in New York, Ginsburg joined the faculty of Rutgers University where, in order to elude the Draconian employment policies covering child-bearing women, she concealed her second pregnancy by wearing clothes too big for her. At Rutger's she was only the second female on the school's faculty and among the first 20 women law professors in the country. In 1972, after teaching a course on women and the law at Harvard, which denied her tenure, she was snatched up as the first female faculty member in the law school's history. Although she wasted no time making a name for herself as a legal scholar, it was a litigator—she was counsel to the American Civil Liberties Union (ACLU), where she directed the Women's Rights Project—that her keen, laser sharp mind found its greatest outlet.

The women's movement took off in the early 1970s due to a confluence of factors, including the inspiration provided by the victories recently won by civil rights activists, the increasing number of working women outside the home and encountering employment discrimination, and a growing feminist awareness that the United States, though progressive in some areas, was laden with gender-discriminating institutions. For Ginsburg the central issue was the strategy she and others would use to force the desired changes in society. Just as years earlier the National Association for the Advancement of Colored People (NAACP) had recognized that racism needed to be tackled in the courts and not in the political arena—where, after all, the Jim Crow laws had been born—Ginsburg found her target in those laws by which society's inequalities were both tolerated and promoted. But, on a more basic level, Ginsburg turned to cases in which men and families, in addition to women, were victimized by government policies that discriminated on the basis of gender. A former ACLU colleague was quoted as telling *Legal Times,* "We were young and very green. She had it all so carefully thought through. She knew exactly what she needed to do."

Argued Women's Rights before Supreme Court

In a 1973 case before the Supreme Court, Ginsburg successfully argued against a federal statute that gave more housing and medical benefits to men within the armed service than to women. The statute allowed a man to automatically claim his wife as a dependent, even if she did not depend on his income, and thus claim the benefits, while the woman in uniform would qualify for those benefits only after showing that her husband received more than half his support from her. Speaking before an all-male court, Ginsburg expertly blew out of the water a government statute that, on the one hand, disadvantaged a man who is a dependent and, on the other, minimized the economic contributions of women. In another case, Ginsburg convinced the court that a provision of the Social Security Act discriminated against men and the families of women because it gave certain benefits to widows and not widowers. Ginsburg also convinced the court to strike down a law ostensibly benefiting women—an Oklahoma statute that women over the age of 18 could purchase alcohol while men needed to be at least 21.

By most accounts, had Ginsburg gone the route of arguing only those cases in which women were the victims of discriminatory laws, she would not have effectively revealed the absurdity and unconstitutionality of all laws that treat men and women differently. Indeed, the crux of her legal philosophy—that the law cannot proscribe rights to one group and not to another—would have surely collapsed if she sought to protect women more than men. She had little patience for the claim of some feminists that women think differently than men and are inherently better suited for certain activities, be it child-rearing or government service.

Having won five of the six cases she argued before the Supreme Court and showing, more than any other lawyer, that the equal protection provision of the Fourteenth Amendment applies not just on the basis of race but on gender, Ginsburg, in the waning days of President Jimmy Carter, was named a judge on the United States Court of appeals for the District of Columbia. Though Ginsburg has been hailed as the Thurgood Marshall of the women's movement, she unlike Marshall (who saw his judgeship as an opportunity to continue the activism and advocacy he practiced as a lawyer), brought a cautious, measured disposition to the court. Her belief, shared by many conservatives, is that, with few exceptions, the courts should interpret laws and leave policy-making in the electoral, political domain. Ginsburg further delighted rightists with her vote to dismiss an appeal by a homosexual sailor who was contesting his discharge from the Navy, and with her statement that affirmative action policies can backfire by demeaning the achievements of blacks. In 1987 cases that produced a division on the court, Ginsburg voted 85 percent of the time with Judge Robert Bork, an arch conservative whose nomination to the Supreme Court would be torpedoed by Democrats, and 38 percent of the time with Judge Patricia Wald, one of the court's staunchest liberals. Still, Ginsburg curried favor with liberals with her votes supporting freedom of speech and broadcasting access to the courts.

Supreme Court Justice

With the retirement of Justice Byron White, President Clinton reportedly sought out a replacement with the intellect to counter the court's chief conservative, Antonin Scalia, and the political skills to pull toward the left members of the court's pivotal centrist block. The first choice was New York Governor Mario Cuomo, who declined the nomination. When the name of Interior Secretary Bruce Babbit was floated, environmental groups successfully lobbied to keep him in his present position. The frontrunner in the final days was Boston Judge Stephen Breyer, who according to reports, had been told to draft an acceptance speech. But

Clinton decided not to proceed with Breyer, evidently because the president was less impressed with the judge after the two met in the White House. Following that meeting, Clinton asked to see the results of the preliminary background check on Ginsburg, who had been on the short list for nomination.

While some commentators criticized Clinton for zig-zagging and for turning his back on Breyer, Ginsburg received the accolades of the legal community. Court observers praised her commitment to the details of the law, her incisive questioning of lawyers arguing before her, and her talent for winning over colleagues with dispassionate and well-reasoned arguments. Clinton was quoted in the *New York Times* as saying, "I believe that in the years ahead she will be able to be a force for consensus-building on the Supreme Court, just as she has been on the court of appeals, so that our judges can become an instrument of our common unity in their expression to their fidelity to the Constitution." Conservatives, grateful that a liberal ideologue had not been nominated, rallied behind Ginsburg, as did liberals, believing that they had found a foil to Scalia, even though the two jurists are good friends. In a widely reported joke, when Scalia was asked with whom he would want to be stranded on a desert island, Mario Cuomo or Harvard law professor Laurence Tribe, his answer was Ruth Bader Ginsburg.

Ironically, the loudest concerns about the nomination of this champion of equality came from some women's and abortion rights groups. Although pro-choice, Ginsburg, in articles and speeches, has questioned the reasoning underlying "Roe vs. Wade," the 1973 Supreme Court decisions protecting abortions under a right to privacy not explicitly mentioned in the Constitution. According to Ginsburg and a growing number of legal scholars, abortion rights are most convincingly grounded in the equal protection provisions of the Constitution rather than in a nebulous right to privacy. In keeping with her legal philosophy of judicial restraint—that is, minimizing the political activism of the court—Ginsburg has argued that state legislatures should have more flexibility than "Roe" provides, and that, at the time of the decision, the political atmosphere was favoring a liberalization of strict abortion laws, a claim disputed by some abortion rights advocates.

Confirmation to the Supreme Court often involves more a political brawl than a deliberative review of a nominee's record, but the Senate Judiciary Committee hearings on Ginsburg were remarkably free of rancor and partisanship. Setting the tone for the friendly hearings, Committee Chairman Joseph Biden, echoing statements of his Democratic and Republican colleagues, said according to the *Boston Globe,* that Ginsburg had "already helped to change the meaning of equality in our nation."

On August 3, 1993, Ginsburg was confirmed by the Senate in a vote of 96 to 3, becoming the 107th Supreme Court Justice, its second female jurist, and the first justice to be named by a Democratic president since Lyndon B. Johnson. She was then sworn in during August 10 ceremonies held at the White House and the Supreme Court itself. The three senators to oppose her confirmation were Republicans

Jesse Helms of North Carolina, Don Nickles of Oklahoma, and Bob Smith of New Hampshire. President Clinton said in a statement quoted by the *Detroit Free Press,* "I am confident that she will be an outstanding addition to the court and will serve with distinction for many years."

Her First Term

According to the *Tribune News Service,* "In her rookie year on the Supreme Court, Ruth Bader Ginsburg proved to be anything but a novice. . . . {Ginsburg} proved assertive from the outset." Yet some Court observers, comparing her to former Justices Thurgood Marshall and William J. Brennan Jr., felt that she had not championed the underdogs as the former justices had and that her prose lacked compassion or combativeness.

In his nomination of Ginsburg, President Clinton felt that she would be a good counter balance for the conservative Antonin Scalia and an equalizing replacement for the conservative Justice Byron White. Since joining the Supreme Court, Justice Ginsburg, it is felt, has moved the court leftward, but not as much as the liberals had hoped. In her first term as a junior justice, according to Aaron Epstein of Knight-Ridder Newspapers, "Ginsburg strongly backed gender equality, solidly supported separation of church and state, opposed an expansion of property rights, argued to preserve protection of workers and opposed police, and prosecutors more often than most of her colleagues."

Women in the Judiciary

In a rare public appearance together, Justices Ruth Bader Ginsburg and Sandra Day O'Connor attended a program sponsored by the University of Pennsylvania Law School and the University's Annenberg Public Policy Center entitled *Women and the Bench* celebrating women in the judiciary. During the introduction of Ginsburg and O'Connor, Colin Diver, dean of the law school said, "every single woman who has ever served on the U.S. Supreme Court" was in attendance. This venue allowed some distinguished alumnae along with the justices and other women in the judiciary to recount their experiences and careers for their primarily law student oriented audience. While being appointed to the Supreme Court by President Bill Clinton, Justice Ginsburg attributed former President Jimmy Carter with changing the judicial landscape for women forever. She said, "He appointed women in numbers such as there would be no going back."

According to U.S. District Court Judge Phyllis A. Kravitch, "When Carter took office in 1977 there were only two women presiding over federal appeals courts and eight ruling in federal district courts. Now, besides the two women on the Supreme Court, 25 women judges sit in U.S. appeals courts and 100 in district courts. . . . And the states have all followed suit." Sandra Day O'Connor added, "About eight percent of the nation's judges are women."

While being applauded for stepping into her position as Supreme Court Justice without hesitation, some observers feel that she hasn't yet found her voice. Christian Kellett, law professor at Dickinson College in Carlisle, Pennsylvania feels, "She hasn't struck out on her own yet, but she is far

more confident of her opinions than other junior justices have been. I think her influence has brought justices in the conservative middle over to the liberal side in some instances." Since taking office Justice Ruth Bader Ginsburg has written 35 significant opinions, two important concurring opinions, and three selected dissenting opinions.

Further Reading

Italia, Bob, and Paul Deegan, *Ruth Bader Ginsburg,* (1994).
Ayer, Eleanor H., *Ruth Bader Ginsburg: Fire and Steel on the Supreme Court* (1994, 1995).
Bredeson, Carmen, *Ruth Bader Ginsburg: Supreme Court Justice* (1995). □

Asher Ginzberg

Asher Ginzberg (1856-1927), better known by his pen name Ahad Ha-Am (one of the people), was an intellectual leader whose impression on the writers, politicians, and culture of modern Judaism was profound. His view of cultural Zionism was the inspiration for a rebirth of Hebrew literature and for a renewed interest in the history of Jewish philosophy and ethics.

Ahad Ha-Am was born in a small Ukranian town to a Hasidic family. (Hasidism is a Jewish pietistic sect begun in the 18th century.) He became disillusioned with Hasidism at the age of 13 (the age of Bar Mitzvah, Jewish maturity). For a time he was attracted to the Jewish Enlightenment that advocated integrating Judaism and modern thought. He rejected this thinking because it scorned the traditional forms of Judaism and its cultural tradition, which he considered important. While joining the early Zionists (called "Hovvevi Zion" or "Lovers of Zion"), he looked beyond their political program to its cultural innovations. In Odessa, the center of Jewish life in the Ukraine, he found kindred souls whom he influenced even as they influenced him.

This early experience of moving from one world of thought to another taught him to look skeptically at "causes." He wrote that Jewish intellectuals were advancing and retreating without any sense of order. At one moment they called upon the Jewish people to abandon the tradition; at another they summoned them to reaffirm national culture; at still other times they looked to modern educational systems. He suggested that Jewish intellectuals look to their past, find a continuity with the heart of Judaism, and become not a people "of the book" but a "literary people" whose intellectuals write as a reflection of a vivid cultural life rather than as a substitution for it.

A Spiritual Mentor

Ahad Ha-Am became a mentor for an entire generation of Jewish intellectuals through his writings, which expressed these ideas. In 1889 he published his first essay, "Lo Zo Ha

Derech'' (This Is Not the Way). From then until his reflective ''Sakh Ha-Kol'' (Summing Up) he wrote on topical issues correcting and chastising the Jewish intellectual. His collection of essays *At the Crossroads* demonstrates his responsive creativity: he investigated the meaning of Jewish ethics as an answer to an English Reform rabbi's essay on Christianity. Essays on Jewish ritual, the Sabbath, and the meaning of tradition came in response to criticisms by Reform and Enlightened Jewish leaders. His view of Zion as a cultural center rather than as merely a political or practical reality was advanced in dialogue with Zionist congresses, speeches, and books.

In 1896 he founded a new type of Hebrew periodical—*Hashiloah*. The name is that of the river mentioned by Isaiah as one that flows slowly, a symbol of Ahad Ha-Am's Zionism. In that journal the leading Jewish intellectuals—Chaim Nahman Bialik, later Israel's poet laureate; Chaim Weizmann; and others—published their views. In 1899 Ahad Ha-Am founded a secret society, the B'nai Moshe (Sons of Moses). The name reflected his view of the prophetic role. Moses, unlike Aaron the priest, stood as a prophet to chastise and rebuke the people. Priests serve the people and give them what they need. Prophets are a creative opposition party. Although the secret society soon disbanded, Ahad Ha-Am's model of creative opposition was influential among Jewish leaders.

A Zionist Leader

Not only did Ahad Ha-Am act as a spiritual mentor to Jewish thinkers and writers, but he was also an involved activist. He visited the land of Israel (then Palestine) four times—in 1891, 1896, 1899, and 1911—and finally settled there in 1921 until his death on January 2, 1927. Each of these visits occasioned a critical essay. He became more convinced of the possibility of a Jewish cultural revival in the land, but he clearly saw problems others neglected. He recognized the ethical question raised by the Muslim population, but few listened to him. He was also active in the Zionist congresses, although he counted himself as a ''mourner at the wedding'' at the first congress in 1897. He was an influential force acting against Theodor Herzl's territorialism in the famous Sixth (or Uganda) Congress in 1903, holding out for Israel as the only land in which the Jews could have a homeland. From 1903 to 1921 he lived in London. He was active working against the rabid anti-Zionist faction among assimilated British Jews. He had close ties with Chaim Weizmann and was involved in the negotiations that led to the Balfour Declaration in November 1917, although he was cautious about its real importance.

When Ahad Ha-Am died he was honored by Jews around the world. He was a force that moderated the practical elements of Zionism so that the spiritual and cultural concerns could be given primacy. His revival of Jewish literature and a study of Jewish ethics made him a leader in Jewish thought, and his work for Zionism won him recognition.

Further Reading

There is a fascinating biography of Ahad Ha-Am which reveals the life experience behind his thought: Leon Simon, *Ahad Ha-am: A Biography* (1960). A study of his ideas and their importance in Zionism can be found in Norman Bentwich, *Ahad Ha-am and His Philosophy* (Jerusalem, 1927). A good selection of his essays and a fine analysis of his work is found in Arthur Hertzberg, *The Zionist Idea: A Historical Analysis and Reader* (1959). The continuing relevance of Ahad Ha-Am is expressed in the critical and insightful collection of essays *At the Crossroads: Essays on Ahad Ha-Am,* edited by Jacques Kornberg (1983). This volume contains chapters on Ahad Ha-Am as editor of Hashiloah, on the B'nai Moshe, and on his relationship with disciples and colleagues in the Zionist movement. □

Louis Ginzberg

The Lithuanian-born Jewish scholar Louis Ginzberg (1873-1953) was a professor at the Jewish Theological Seminary of America for over 50 years and was among the foremost Talmudic and rabbinic students of his time.

Louis Ginzberg was born in Kovno on Nov. 28, 1873, into a family with a tradition of distinguished scholarship. After studying at various rabbinic academies in Lithuania, Ginzberg pursued his studies at German universities, receiving a doctorate in Semitic languages from the University of Heidelberg in 1897. Emigrating to America in 1899, he served as editor of rabbinic literature for the Jewish Encyclopedia. In 1902 he became professor of Talmud at the Jewish Theological Seminary in New York, where he remained until his death. He was a founder and the first president of the American Academy for Jewish Research and was among those awarded honorary degrees at Harvard University's Tercentenary Celebration in 1936. He married Adele Katzenstein in 1909.

Ginzberg authored over 500 books and articles on Talmudic and rabbinic literature; the earliest work was a study of Talmudic folklore (1899) in the writings of the Church Fathers. His *Legends of the Jews* (7 vols., 1909-1938) is an encyclopedic compilation of almost all the folkloric material in the Talmud and Midrash dealing with biblical episodes and personalities. (In 1956 a one-volume edition was published posthumously under the title *Legends of the Bible.*) This material was again the subject of the first volume of the series *Genizah Studies in Memory of Dr. Solomon Schechter* (1928).

Ginzberg's chief area of interest, however, was the Halakah (Jewish religious law). His earliest book on this subject, *Geonica* (1909), dealt with the Halakah in the period of the Geonim (heads of Talmudic academies in Babylonia in the 6th to 11th century). He dealt with this period again in volume 2 of the *Genizah Studies.* The Talmud Yerushalmi (Jerusalem or Palestinian Talmud) was his specialty within Halakic research. His earliest work in this area is a collection of texts, *Yerushalmi Fragments from the Genizah* (1909); his major work is a commentary on the Palestinian Talmud (1941 and 1961).

Research emphasizing Halakic literature was a reflection of Ginzberg's belief that only in the Halakah could one find "the mind and the character of the Jewish people exactly and adequately expressed." As the teacher of generations of Conservative rabbis, Ginzberg was mentor to Conservative Judaism in America for half a century. He died on Nov. 11, 1953.

Further Reading

Two collections of Ginzberg's essays are *Students, Scholars and Saints* (1928) and *On Jewish Law and Lore* (1955). A bibliography of his writings from 1894 to 1945 is in the American Academy for Jewish Research, *Louis Ginzberg: Jubilee Volume on the Occasion of His Seventieth Birthday* (1945). The biography written by his son, Eli Ginzberg, *Keeper of the Law: Louis Ginzberg* (1966), gives an intimate portrait. □

Natalia Levi Ginzburg

Italian novelist, essayist, playwright, and translator, Natalia Ginzburg (née Levi; 1916-1991) was famous for her portraits of family life and for her spare style.

Natalia Ginzburg was born in Palermo in 1916, the daughter of Guiseppe Levi, a prominent anatomy professor. She grew up in Turin where she married the translator and anti-Fascist leader Leone Ginzburg. During the early years of World War II she and her family lived in forced residence in the mountainous Abruzzi region. (Her father and two brothers were arrested by the Fascists; one brother escaped.) In 1943 Ginzburg, her husband, and three children moved to Rome where he was soon arrested for editing an underground newspaper and tortured to death by the Nazis. After his death she returned to Turin where she worked as an editor with the famous Einaudi publishing house and wrote. In 1950 she married Gabriele Baldini, a musicologist and professor of English literature (who died in 1969).

Although Ginzburg was a playwright ("I Married You for Fun") and a translator (Proust and Flaubert), she was best known for her autobiography, her fiction, and her essays. Among her novels (dates are for English translations) are *The Road to the City* (1949), *All Our Yesterdays* (1956), *A Light for Fools* (1957), *Voices in the Evening* (1963), *No Way* (1974), and *The City and the House* (1985).

Ginzburg's favorite theme was families. In one of her best-loved works, *Family Sayings* (1963), she offered glimpses into her own childhood and family life. As the youngest of five children, she was always being told to be quiet. Her need to say things in a hurry if she was to be heard at all perhaps helped form her telegraphic style, she once remarked. In *The Manzoni Family* (1983) she wrote a history of the family of writer Alessandro Manzoni, whose *The Betrothed* ranks as one of the classics of Italian and world

literature. Ginzburg intended her history, based on Manzoni family letters, "to be read as a novel—a novel, however, in which nothing is invented."

Her novel *Voices in the Evening* is another example of her concern with family. In the story, Elsa, a young unmarried woman, recounts the tragedies, loves, and social entanglements of an unnamed north Italian village from the days of Fascism through to the postwar era. As the title suggests, we hear the voices of the lovers, Tommasino and Elsa, and of their families, but sometimes so briefly, so minimally, that they seem faint, distant, as if we were overhearing snatches of conversation in the evening.

With great patience and precision, Ginzburg records the day-to-day concerns of her characters' lives: what to eat, who was invited to the party, what the bus schedule is, whether or not the new young doctor is competent. Yet Ginzburg's story also has its ironies. Home, hearth, family circle, the "little things" so dear to the author, so seemingly safe and desirable, can also be lethal. If Tommasino marries Elsa, he will join her family's domestic circle and that intimacy will destroy him, he fears. Already he has begun to drive his thoughts "underground," to "bury" them, so that when he is with Elsa "we say things of no account." Ginzburg's relentless piling on of carefully selected detail after detail, with all the dispassion of a reporter, gives this novel an extraordinary ring of truth.

True to her concern for families and children, Ginzburg published *Serena Cruz or True Justice* (1990), a book of her reflections about the widely disputed and publicized adoption case of a little Filipino girl in Italy.

Ginzburg's simplicity, her integrity, her passion for truth, and her concern for family come through best in her essays collected in *The Little Virtues* (1962). In "The Son of Man" she explained how the experiences of Fascism and World War II scarred her and her generation. The horrors of homelessness, the fears of seeing loved ones snatched in the night, as she experienced with Leone Ginzburg, continue to haunt her. Her rage erupts against an earlier generation that allowed Fascism to come to power and to thrive on a world of lies: "We cannot lie in our books and we cannot lie in any of the things that we do. And perhaps this is the one good thing that has come out of the war. Not to lie and not to allow others to lie to us." In "Silence" she discussed one of the "strangest and gravest vices of our time," our inability to communicate meaningfully with each other, and some of the reasons for "this bitter fruit of our sick times."

No matter what she wrote—fiction, essays, history, autobiography—her style was spare and lean. She wrote "through clenched teeth, as it were, giving away as little as possible," an exasperated American reviewer once commented. Ginzburg's images are so few that when they appear, they blaze like shooting stars on a summer night. Yet her intent was certainly not "to give away as little as possible." Her aim was concreteness and, above all, truth and integrity.

Her style reflects these concerns. Her sentences, her words are so few and so carefully chosen that we feel she would not release a single one unless she was convinced of its artistic and moral truth. Yet, unlike some of the American minimalists, there is nothing fragmented or indeterminate about her fiction. She was an old fashioned storyteller who believed in clearly defined plots. Reading Ginzburg's novels is like going to an exhibit of drawings. It's exciting to study the lines, to appreciate her draftsmanship. If "writing is a struggle against silence," as Mexican writer Carlos Fuentes once wrote, then Ginzburg's art lies in knowing where and how to break that silence.

Ginzburg's work also teaches us "the little virtues" that she describes in her essays. The great themes, the great truths, she tells us, can be found at home, in our family lives, in the familiar day to day, in a world that we all know. In the little virtues we'll find the great ones, she tells us. All we have to do is look.

In 1983 Ginzburg was elected to the Italian Parliament, and served one term. She lived near the Pantheon in old (central) Rome, until she died of cancer on October 7, 1991.

Further Reading

English translations of Natalia Ginzburg's works are reviewed regularly in major newspapers such as *The New York Times, Washington Post,* and *New York Review of Books,* which occasionally also publish extracts. For interviews in English see Laura Furman, "An Interview with Natalia Ginzburg," *Southwest Review* (Winter 1987), and Mary Gordon, "Surviving History," *The New York Times Magazine* (March 25, 1990). Anne Marie O'Healy, "Natalia Ginzburg and the

Family," *Canadian Journal of Italian Studies* (1986) deals with Ginzburg's interest in families.

Additional Sources

Ginzburg, Natalia, *Family sayings,* Manchester: Carcanet, 1984, 1967.
Ginzburg, Natalia, *Family sayings,* New York: Seaver Books: Distributed by H. Holt, 1986, 1967.
Ginzburg, Natalia, *Family sayings,* New York: Arcade Pub., 1989, 1967. □

Giovanni Giolitti

The Italian statesman Giovanni Giolitti (1842-1928) enacted an extensive program of constructive social legislation. He has been criticized for his manipulation of Italian political factions.

B orn on Oct. 27, 1842, at Mondovi in Piedmont, Giovanni Giolitti was the son of mountain peasants. Finishing his juridical studies at the University of Turin in 1861, he entered government service, specializing in financial administration. In 1882 he was elected to the Chamber of Deputies. In 1889-1890 he served as minister of treasury. In 1892 he first became prime minister. His government, consisting mainly of the representatives of the left, lasted 18 months. It ended with Giolitti's resignation because of his involvement in the enormous scandal of the Bank of Rome.

In 1897 Giolitti resumed his political career. Between 1901 and 1903 he was minister of the interior. In 1903 he organized his second Cabinet, which lasted until 1905. In May 1906 he became prime minister for the third time, but now for a full 3-year term. He gave priority to economic problems, organized public works on a large scale, and, having adopted much of the program of the Socialists, promoted a policy of significant reforms which included legislation on public health, housing, work conditions, woman and child labor, workers' disability, and old-age pensions.

In 1911 Giolitti formed his last prewar government, but it became increasingly difficult for him to maintain the balance in his parliamentary coalition. In the midst of growing domestic difficulties, in October 1911 he involved Italy in a war with Turkey. However, this conflict did not mitigate the mounting conflicts inside the country. Therefore, for fear of a revolution, Giolitti made further concessions to the lower classes, including the enactment of almost universal manhood suffrage. Following the general elections in October and November 1913, the parliamentary majority set up by Giolitti from heterogeneous elements proved to be excessively difficult to handle. Therefore, although having won the election in March 1914, he chose to resign once more.

After the outbreak of World War I, Giolitti became a spokesman of the political neutrality of Italy. But after the disaster of Caporetto he pleaded for an all-out effort in the defense of the country. In the difficult postwar situation

Giolitti's long political experience seemed to promise that he would be able to check the threatening anarchy. In 1920 he organized his fifth Cabinet, which lasted until the following year. He stopped the wave of strikes and the occupation of factories in August and September 1920 by promising to enact reforms demanded by the workers. But his actions satisfied neither the industrialists nor the Socialists. Moreover, he incurred the disfavor of Nationalists because of the Treaty of Rapallo in 1920, which dealt a terrible blow to Italian aspirations on the Dalmatian coast. He antagonized the Church by his tax policy and the big landowners by his proposal for agrarian reform.

Giolitti granted his silent approval to the Fascists, and he supported Benito Mussolini. But after 1924 he openly attacked Fascist policies. Giolitti died on July 17, 1928, in Cavour in Piedmont.

Giolitti is a most controversial figure. Severely criticized, he has also been defended as a great statesman. He was an expert at manipulating party combinations, and his enemies contemptuously called his tactics the "Giolittian manner." But this method of government, which he had inherited from his predecessors, proved to be the only workable one in Italy at that time. His constructive social legislation gave the Italians a period of real advance and prosperity. His role as a liberal statesman can be properly assessed only against a background of the totalitarian state that then emerged.

Further Reading

Much material on Giolitti's life and political activities is in his autobiography, *Memoirs of My Life,* translated by Edward Storer (1923). There is no biography of Giolitti in English. A. William Salomone, *Italy in the Giolittian Era: Italian Democracy in the Making, 1900-1914* (1945; 2d ed. 1960), contains an exhaustive study of Giolitti's political activities before World War I. George Terhune Peck, *Giovanni Giolitti and the Fall of Italian Democracy, 1919-1922* (1945), deals with Giolitti's postwar activities.

Additional Sources

Peck, George Terhune, *Giovanni Giolitti and the fall of Italian democracy, 1919-192,* 1942. □

Giorgione

The Italian painter Giorgione (1477-1510) was one of the first masters of the Venetian High Renaissance. His works are notable for their poetic qualities.

Although the career of Giorgione occupies a very short period of time, his creation of mood through color, light, and atmosphere, giving a dreamlike character to his paintings, established a style of poetic romanticism that influenced numerous Venetian contemporaries, particularly Titian and Palma Vecchio, but also secondary masters such as Cariani, Vincenzo Catena, and Il Romanino. Because of the paucity of documents and of signed pictures by these masters, many attributions are difficult to establish, and various critics differ radically in assigning works to Giorgione himself and to the so-called Giorgionesque painters who followed him.

The painter called Giorgione, whose name was Giorgio (Zorzi) da Castelfranco, was born in the town of Castelfranco near Venice in 1477. No information exists as to his family or his early years. Because of his early death of the plague in Venice at the age of 33 and because of the poetic nature of his pictures, the legend grew that he was handsome, a fine musician, and an ardent lover. The name Giorgione ("Big George") implies that he was a tall man.

Giorgione became a pupil of the greatest Venetian artist of the day, Giovanni Bellini, entering his studio about 1490. Bellini himself began to develop the effects of light and atmosphere, suggesting the warmth of a late summer afternoon and establishing a tranquil contemplative mood in such late works as the *Religious Allegory* (ca. 1490) and the *Madonna of the Meadow.*

Early Works

Two cassone panels, the *Judgment of Solomon* and the *Judgment of the Baby Moses by Fire,* are generally accepted as Giorgione's early works (ca. 1495-1500). In them the landscape backgrounds are already developed, but the figures retain a rather rigid archaistic stance reminiscent of the

works of Vittore Carpaccio. More mature are Giorgione's *Adoration of the Kings,* the little *Holy Family,* and the *Adoration of the Shepherds,* in the last of which the deep landscape corridor to the left and the group of figures to the right establish a formula for Venetian composition that survived throughout the century.

Mature Works

The brevity of Giorgione's career limits the importance of chronology, since his mature production fell within one decade. The *Madonna with Saints Francis and Liberale* can be reasonably placed about 1500-1504. Here the artist elongated the high throne to a much greater degree than usual in northern and central Italian painting in order to establish an equilateral triangle, thus revealing his Renaissance feeling for strong geometric relations in formal structure. The mellow landscape distance and the dreamlike contemplative attitude of the figures provide a notable example of the Giorgionesque mood.

The *Tempest* is Giorgione's most personal excursion into the realm of idyllic landscape, an evocation of the pastoralism of ancient Greece and Rome, represented in ancient literature by the poetry of Theocritus and Virgil and comparable with the Renaissance poetry of Pietro Bembo in *I Asolani* (1505) and Jacopo Sannazzaro in *Arcadia* (1502). The enigma of the precise literary meaning of the picture has invited a variety of explanations, none of which has been universally accepted. The latest is Edgar Wind's book *Giorgione's Tempest* (1969), which interprets the male figure as Fortitude and the female as Charity, but this is inconsistent with the very poetic nature of the composition.

The pictures by Giorgione that are mentioned by a near contemporary, Marcantonio Michiel (ca. 1532), include the *Tempest, the Boy with an Arrow, the Three Philosophers, the Sleeping Venus,* and possibly the *Shepherd with Pipe.* Michiel says that after Giorgione's death Titian completed the landscape of the *Venus,* this most admired of all evocations of the ideally beautiful goddess, and that Sebastiano del Piombo finished the *Three Philosophers.* Giorgione's hand in the *Judith* has not been challenged, although undocumented. The *Christ and the Adulteress,* the *Madonna and Saints,* and the *Pastoral Concert* seem to most Anglo-Saxon writers to belong to Giorgione, but recent Italian critics have preferred to transfer them to the young Titian.

The Frescoes

The close relationship between Giorgione and Titian is epitomized by the lost frescoes, dated 1507-1508, on the exterior of the German Merchants' Exchange (Fondaco dei Tedeschi) in Venice, where the two artists collaborated. Titian, presumed to be the younger man, appears to have worked under Giorgione's direction at this time. Lodovico Dolce (1557), a friend of Titian, records that Titian painted the *Allegory of Justice* over the side portal and Giorgione the nude figures on the main facade. Known today through 18th-century prints and a few archeological fragments, these frescoes only increase the problem of distinguishing between the work of the two men at this period.

The Portraits

Giorgione's portraits provide the greatest problems in the matter of attribution since none is signed or documented. By general agreement he is assigned several half-length portraits: the *Young Man* (Berlin), the so-called *Antonio Broccardo, the Laura,* dated by an old inscription on the back 1506, and *La Vecchia.* The more doubtful *Portrait of a Man* (San Diego, Calif.) has an old attribution to Giorgione on the back of the panel, and the *Self-portrait* (Brunswick, Germany) is probably a damaged original, much reduced in size. The famous group portrait *The Concert,* formerly given to Giorgione, is now generally accepted as a youthful work by Titian.

Further Reading

There are two excellent accounts of Giorgione in English. Terisio Pignatti, *Giorgione* (trans. 1971), is a documented study of his career and examines the complexities of Giorgione attributions. George Martin Richter, *Giorgio da Castelfranco, Called Giorgione* (1937), is a scholarly work in which all important documents and original sources are reprinted, including the accounts of Marcantonio Michiel (1532), Giorgio Vasari (1568), and Carlo Ridolfi (1648). A brief, more popular book is Duncan Phillips, *The Leadership of Giorgione* (1937). There is an excellent appreciation of Giorgione in A. Richard Turner, *The Vision of Landscape in Renaissance Italy* (1966). □

Giotto

The Florentine painter, architect, and sculptor Giotto (ca. 1267-1337) evolved a revolutionary new style and was the greatest and most influential Italian painter before the Renaissance.

An outline of the life of Giotto may be deduced from documents and literary sources. At the time of his death in 1337 he was said to be 70 years old. Traditionally his birthplace is given as Colle di Vespignano in Mugello, though some scholars now believe that he was a native of Florence. According to a legend recorded by Lorenzo Ghiberti in his *Commentaries* (ca. 1450), the painter Cimabue discovered Giotto. The account states that while traveling in the countryside Cimabue came upon a shepherd drawing with chalk on a flat stone. Cimabue was so impressed that he offered to take the shepherd, Giotto, to Florence and train him in the artist's craft.

Giotto married in 1290; his wife bore him four sons and four daughters. Pope Boniface VIII called him to Rome in 1300. Between 1302 and 1306 Giotto was in Padua, painting the Arena Chapel frescoes. In 1327 he was enrolled in the painters' guild in Florence. Between 1328 and 1333 he was in Naples, working for Robert of Anjou. On April 12, 1334, Giotto was appointed *capomastro* of the Cathedral of Florence and city architect. In 1335-1336 he was called to Milan to serve Duke Azzone Visconti. He died on Jan. 8, 1337, in Florence.

His Background

Stylistic trends at the beginning of the 14th century aimed at greater realism. The abstraction and poetic beauty of the Italo-Byzantine style had reached a culmination in the paintings executed by Cimabue in Florence and Duccio in Siena. Artists after them abandoned the Italo-Byzantine style for the aristocratic elegance and decorativeness of the Gothic style, which originated in France. This style had other qualities that were even more significant for the development of Italian painting. It was more emotional and markedly more naturalistic than the Italo-Byzantine style. Both of these qualities were reinforced by the teachings of the preaching orders, the Franciscans and the Dominicans, who sought to make Christ more accessible to the uneducated and illiterate by emphasizing his humanity rather than his divinity. The effect of this doctrine was to replace the lyrical poetry of medieval art with the vernacular prose of the newly emerging realism of the 14th century. If the urge toward greater realism needed further support, it was found in the artifacts of classical antiquity—the buildings and statues of ancient Rome. In Roman art early-14th-century artists discovered monumentality and, again, realism. Giotto's art brought these trends to their culmination: he was at once a superb decorator, a creator of monumental and heroic types, and a profound storyteller, whose work expressed genuine human emotions.

S. Francesco, Assisi

There is no consensus on what constitutes Giotto's early work. Scholars are divided, and the debate is vigorous over what Giotto may have painted before he executed the frescoes in the Arena Chapel. The principal question is, what did Giotto paint in Assisi?

Soon after the canonization of St. Francis (1228) the church of S. Francesco in Assisi was begun. Built on the side of a hill, it is divided into two levels: the Upper Church, with a lofty vaulted single aisle and simple transept and apse, and the Lower Church, with a low vaulted ceiling. By the last quarter of the century the building was complete enough for painters to work in the Upper Church. The most renowned artists in Italy were called to Assisi.

The walls along the nave are divided horizontally into two registers, stories from the Old and New Testaments decorating the upper register and the story of St. Francis decorating the lower register. The St. Francis cycle is painted in a Giottesque manner and was attributed traditionally to Giotto. In 1312 the chronicler Riccobaldi Ferrariensis observed that Giotto had painted in the Franciscan church in Assisi. Later Ghiberti in his *Commentaries* observed that Giotto had painted nearly all of the lower part of the church. This remark could mean that Giotto painted all of the Lower Church or all of the lower register in the Upper Church, that is, the story of St. Francis. The numerous Giottesque paintings in the Lower Church can be dated after Giotto's murals in Padua, that is, after about 1305, and are not to be considered early works. Few critics, in fact, consider any of the Giottesque painting in the Lower Church as authentic work by Giotto.

The story of St. Francis must date before 1307 and probably dates in the 1290s. If these are the works referred to by Ghiberti, they would be among the earliest extant examples of Giotto's art. In the second edition of his *Lives* (1568) Giorgio Vasari specifically attributed the St. Francis cycle to Giotto. This viewpoint became the traditional one and was not questioned until the 20th century, though some critics noted discrepancies between the frescoes in Assisi and those in Padua.

In 1912 F. Rintelen declared that Giotto did not paint the story of St. Francis. Critics quickly polarized into Giotto and non-Giotto camps, and the debate began. Those who attributed the works to Giotto cited their obvious Giottesque character and the centuries-old tradition that associated them with the artist. The non-Giotto critics listed numerous stylistic discrepancies between the St. Francis cycle and the Arena Chapel frescoes, which, they declared, were too fundamental to be explained by the time span that separated them. Most of the non-Giotto critics looked to the scenes depicting the Old and New Testaments for evidence of Giotto's hand, though most of these scenes are in poor condition, making stylistic judgments difficult.

The story of St. Francis has been subjected to close physical examination, including an elaborate analysis of the fresco method employed. Similar analyses continue on those frescoes universally accepted as by Giotto. A comparison with some of the Arena Chapel frescoes revealed differences in the fresco method employed in Assisi and in Padua, which would seem to support the non-Giotto viewpoint, although it is too sketchy to be conclusive.

Among those who attribute the St. Francis cycle to Giotto, there is general agreement that *St. Francis Honored by a Simpleton* and the scenes on the left wall in the bay nearest the crossing are not by Giotto but by his contemporary, the St. Cecilia Master. There is, furthermore, general agreement that Giotto's role in the St. Francis cycle was that of a master supervising a large shop of assistants. This may explain some of the stylistic discrepancies noted by the non-Giotto critics. Among the other paintings in S. Francesco commonly associated with Giotto's name are the story of Isaac, the story of Joseph, the *Lamentation over Christ,* the *Resurrection,* and the *Church Doctors* in the vaults of the first bay.

Giotto went to Rome in 1300, and scholars include the fresco fragment in St. John Lateran among his early works. In poor condition and extensively restored, it depicts Pope Boniface VIII announcing the Jubilee Year. A panel painting, the *Stigmata of St. Francis* (Louvre, Paris), is signed with Giotto's name, though few now accept it as an authentic work. The *Madonna Enthroned* in S. Giorgio alla Costa, Florence, in poor condition, is widely but not universally given to Giotto. Vasari mentioned a panel by Giotto in that church, and this picture is usually thought to be the one Vasari knew. The painted cross in S. Maria Novella, Florence, is the finest of the early Giotto panel paintings to have survived. As with all the early works, there is no universal agreement on its authenticity. The scholars who accept it as

a work by Giotto date it before 1300. A polyptych, the *Madonna with Saints,* from the Badia (Uffizi, Florence) was mentioned by Ghiberti as a work by Giotto. Most critics accept Ghiberti's statement and attribute it to Giotto.

Arena Chapel

All attributions to Giotto must be compared with the fresco cycle (1302-1306) he painted in the Arena Chapel, Padua, for Enrico Scrovegni. These works, universally accepted as Giotto's, are in good condition with little overpainting.

The Arena Chapel is a modest single-aisle, barrel-vaulted structure, with a semicircular apse. The entire interior is frescoed from the vaults down the sidewalls and across the triumphal arch and entrance wall. The narrative scenes relate the life of the Virgin and the life and Passion of Christ in a total of 37 individual scenes. They are arranged in three registers along the sides, with the *Annunciation* and two episodes from the Passion continuing across the triumphal arch. On the entrance wall is the *Last Judgment;* Scrovegni is depicted among the blessed, presenting a model of the chapel to the Virgin. On the sidewalls in a fourth register below the narrative scenes are painted allegorical representations, the *Virtues and Vices,* as though they were bits of sculpture set in illusionistically rendered niches. The vault is painted blue with golden stars and includes a series of medallions of the Madonna, the Redeemer, and various prophets.

Giotto's style in the Arena Chapel is simple and direct. The narrative scenes are dominated by figures which move along the foreground plane before bits of landscape or architecture. The backgrounds serve to establish the setting without attempting to be accurate in scale or overly elaborate in detail. The elements of the setting are usually arranged to frame and augment the figure groups. Strong undulating rhythms are created by the contour of the architecture and landscape, leading the beholder's eye with an almost irresistible strength across the walls. The sky, painted a deep blue, provides an excellent foil for the figures and settings. The blue of the sky can be read as the picture plane, thus pushing the figures forward so that they seem to swell off the surface of the wall itself and bring the actors of the religious drama into the three-dimensional, corporeal world.

Giotto's figures have a sense of corporeality that is overwhelming. Swathed in great folds of drapery, their silhouettes are seldom broken by extraneous elements. They move across the wall with a measured slow pace that by itself suggests solemnity and dignity. The figures, which are kept to a minimum, are modeled with simple highlights and shadows that emphasize their fullness.

Giotto expressed the drama of the unfolding religious story with understatement and simplicity which heightens rather than diminishes the drama. Where other artists might have had the figures gesticulate and grimace, Giotto has them merely turn their wrist or shift their glance. In the scene showing Joachim, the father of Mary, walking among his flocks after his rejection from the temple, Giotto suggests Joachim's overwhelming disappointment and dejection by a simple nod of Joachim's head and by the wrapping of his hands within his cloak. Similarly, in the *Betrayal of Christ,* the glance that passes between Christ and Judas as Judas kisses him is far more dramatic than all the waving torches and spears of the arresting soldiers. Through such understatement Giotto makes the life of Christ understandable and human by expressing it in comprehensible terms.

Another device Giotto used frequently was to paint some figures viewed from behind. We seem to be witnessing an event as part of a crowd, the crowd in the painting. We are forced to look over someone's shoulder to see what is happening, as in the *Lamentation over Christ,* where a large portion of Christ's body is obscured by a figure in the foreground.

Giotto's use of color in the Arena Chapel frescoes was descriptive. He took care to be consistent, that is, the costumes of the various people remained the same whenever they appeared; but he seemed to ignore the expressive potential of color that Duccio exploited so well in his *Maestà* (1311). The blue sky that fills a great portion of many scenes provides a unifying element, which is saved from monotony by the richly colored geometric fillets that divide the narrative scenes.

Other Mature Works

Giotto's frescoes in Padua are the most extensive and best-preserved example of his mature style. Some other works from roughly the same period have survived. The large *Madonna Enthroned,* painted shortly after the frescoes in Padua for the Church of Ognissanti, Florence (Uffizi), is universally accepted as an authentic work by Giotto. Restoration of the painting, after it had been damaged by a bomb explosion at the Uffizi museum in 1992, provided further evidence that it was indeed Giotto's work. Some scholars date it before the Arena Chapel frescoes and others as late as 1310. It shows the Madonna and Child seated on a canopied Gothic throne encircled by saints and angels. The Madonna looks directly at the beholder with an unflinching gaze; the Child, who has an incongruously mature expression on his face, raises his hand in benediction. All traces of the Italo-Byzantine style have disappeared. Giotto's style is austere, focusing on the establishment of full bulky forms in a believable space. The sense of space is emphasized by the perspective rendering of the throne and the overlapping rows of saints beside the Madonna.

About 1310 Giotto designed a mosaic showing the calling of St. Peter for old St. Peter's in Rome. The mosaic, called the *Navicella,* was completely reworked when the new St. Peter's was built in the 16th century. A pair of mosaic medallions depicting angels may have been made by Giotto at this same time.

Giotto painted a number of works between 1310 and 1320. Among them is a painted cross made for the Tempio Malatestiano in Rimini, now partially dismembered. Somewhat later Giotto made another painted cross in Padua, which is entirely intact. A low horizontal gabled altarpiece in Berlin, the *Dormition of the Virgin* (ca. 1320), is probably a workshop piece.

Peruzzi Chapel

Giotto painted another major fresco cycle in the Peruzzi Chapel in Sta Croce, Florence. These frescoes, which probably date about 1320, relate the lives of John the Baptist and St. John the Evangelist. A tall Gothic chapel with a vaulted ceiling, it is open on the side toward the nave with windows on the wall behind the altar. The frescoes are in three registers along the sides with the topmost scene set within a lunette. They are in bad condition, having been painted in *fresco secco,* or tempered pigments on dry plaster. Recent restorations have removed most of the overpainting so that the frescoes are now more or less pristine, though faint.

In these frescoes Giotto went beyond his designs for the Arena Chapel in terms of spatial organization. The figures in the Peruzzi Chapel move about in realistic architectural settings; they are usually drawn at a slight angle to the picture plane to emphasize their recession into space. As in the Arena Chapel, Giotto continued to use backgrounds to frame figure groups. In the *Raising of Drusiana,* for instance, the city walls and the clustered city towers call attention to the figures arranged before them.

The figures have the same simple fullness and restrained dignity of Giotto's earlier figure types, but they are somewhat taller and more slender. Giotto continued his use of understatement to heighten the drama. In the *Feast of Herod,* for example, Giotto shows Salome beckoning to the servant carrying the charger with the head of the Baptist rather than dancing. She seems eager to present to her mother the grisly prize. The Peruzzi Chapel frescoes reveal Giotto's growth as an artist. They are far more complex in design and composition than those in Padua, yet they retain a sense of clarity and simplicity.

Bardi Chapel

Giotto also decorated the Bardi Chapel, adjacent to the Peruzzi Chapel in Sta Croce and similar in format. The frescoes depict the story of St. Francis in six scenes with a seventh, the *Stigmata,* painted on the wall above the entrance to the chapel. They are in much better condition than the Peruzzi Chapel works, having been executed in true fresco rather than *fresco secco.* These paintings invite comparison with those of the same subject in Assisi. Indeed, critics who attribute the Assisi story of St. Francis to Giotto often cite the Bardi Chapel frescoes as evidence that Giotto was the author of both. In the scene *Francis Renouncing His Patrimony* the similarities are striking, but in the other scenes they are less so. One critic has suggested that Giotto was not the artist of the Bardi Chapel frescoes, a theory that has attracted little support.

Architecture and Sculpture

In 1334 Giotto became *capomastro* of the Cathedral in Florence and chief architect to the city. The design for the Cathedral campanile is usually attributed to Giotto, though only the two lowest stories were completed by the time of his death in 1337. The Ponte alla Carraia in Florence (1334-1337) may have been designed by Giotto in his role as city architect, but it has been so extensively modified that it is impossible to verify this theory. The two lowest stories of the Cathedral campanile include a series of reliefs on all four sides. Most of these reliefs are now thought to have been carved by Andrea Pisano.

Further Reading

The literature on Giotto is extensive. For a complete bibliography up to 1937 see Roberto Salvini, *Giotto-Bibliografia* (1938), in Italian. Giovanni Previtale's monograph, *Giotto e la sua bottega* (1907), also in Italian, is well organized and has exceptionally fine color and black-and-white reproductions and a good bibliography. Cesare Gnudi's monograph, in English, *Giotto* (1958), is considered the standard modern work. For good discussions of Giotto's style see Bernhard Berenson, *The Florentine Painters of the Renaissance* (1896; rev. ed. 1909), and Evelyn Sandberg Vavala's *Uffizi Studies: The Development of the Florentine School of Painting* (1948) and *Studies in the Florentine Churches*, vol. 1 (1959). Some of the arguments against Giotto's authorship of the St. Francis cycle in Assisi are given in Millard Meiss, *Giotto and Assisi* (1960). For an analysis of the fresco method used in Assisi see Millard Meiss and Leonetto Tintori, *The Painting of the Life of St. Francis in Assisi, with Notes on the Arena Chapel* (1962). □

Giovanni da Bologna

The Flemish-Italian sculptor Giovanni da Bologna (1529-1608) was, after Michelangelo, the most important and original 16th-century sculptor. One of the supreme exponents of the mannerist style, Giovanni was an important influence in the development of the baroque.

Giovanni da Bologna, also known as Giambologna and Jean de Boulogne, was born in Douai, Flanders. He received his early training in the studio of the Flemish sculptor Jacques Dubroeucq. About 1554 Giovanni traveled to Italy and spent 2 years studying in Rome. During Giovanni's stay in Florence on his way back to Flanders, the collector and connoisseur Bernardo Vecchietti recognized his talent and offered to support him while he pursued his studies in Florence. Within 2 years Giovanni received his first commission from the Medici grand dukes, and he remained in Florence in the service of the Medici until his death on Aug. 13, 1608.

In 1560 Giovanni competed unsuccessfully for the commission of the Fountain of Neptune in Florence. Three years later he signed the contract for his first major work, the Fountain of Neptune in Bologna (completed 1567). This was followed by a series of fountains for Medici villas and gardens in which Giovanni succeeded in making the sculpture an integral part of the patterns created by the flowing water.

In 1581 a contemporary wrote of Giovanni, "His dearest ambition is to equal Michelangelo, and in the view of many connoisseurs, he has already done so, and may surpass him if he lives." This need to compete with Michelan-

gelo was a vital element in the early part of Giovanni's career. This was made most obvious when Francesco de' Medici commissioned him in 1561 to produce a group, *Florence Triumphant over Pisa,* to act as a pendant to Michelangelo's *Victory* group. The survival of the wax model, the intermediate full-scale model in plaster, and the final marble group (now in the Museo Nazionale, Florence) enables us to follow the progressive transformation of Michelangelo's forms into the graceful and sinuous lines so characteristic of Giovanni's style.

His Bronzes

Giovanni's remarkable technical virtuosity is particularly evident in his small bronzes. Designed to be appreciated by connoisseurs, statuettes like *Venus after Her Bath* (ca. 1564-1565) and *Astronomy* (ca. 1572) are brilliantly conceived to form an almost incredible variety of subtly interrelated views. The extreme attenuation and delicate balance of the *Mercury* (several versions produced between 1564 and 1580) would have been impossible in any other medium. The *Apollo* (1573-1575), one of eight bronze statues executed for the study of Francesco de' Medici in the Palazzo Vecchio, Florence, shows Giovanni's preeminence over his Florentine contemporaries. The Medici sometimes sent the autograph small bronzes as diplomatic gifts, and these, together with their numerous copies and the reproductions of Giovanni's other works, were largely responsible for the dissemination of his style throughout Europe.

Late Works

The *Rape of the Sabines* (1582) in the Loggia dei Lanzi, Florence, is another of Giovanni's masterpieces whose genesis is well documented by the survival of wax models and, in this case, two small versions in bronze. In a covering letter to the Duke of Parma in 1579, Giovanni writes of one of these small bronze groups that "it might represent the Rape of Helen or perhaps of Proserpine or even one of the Sabines. The subject was chosen to give scope to the science and accomplishment of Art." According to Rafaello Borghini (1584), it was in response to a challenge that Giovanni subsequently worked up this composition into the large marble group, solely to demonstrate his "excellence in Art." In the *Rape* the characteristic mannerist device of the serpentine figure is extended in a masterly way to embrace the group so that from every angle it retains its graceful poise and balance both as a group and as an abstract interwoven pattern of flowing lines.

Giovanni's equestrian monument of Cosimo I in the Piazza della Signoria, Florence (1581-1595), resulted in three further commissions for similar monuments; they established a standard type of equestrian statue for the 17th and 18th centuries. His last major marble sculpture, *Hercules and a Centaur,* in the Loggia dei Lanzi, Florence (1594-1599), reveals the full extent of his development and shows his great dramatic power.

Further Reading

The most recent monograph on Giovanni da Bologna is in Flemish. A very good introduction to the sculpture of the 16th century, which includes valuable information about Giovanni's major works, is John Pope-Hennessy, *Italian High Renaissance and Baroque Sculpture* (3 vols., 1963). John Shearman, *Mannerism* (1967), is a stimulating discussion of the esthetic ideals of mannerism. □

Yolande Cornelia Giovanni Jr.

American poet Yolande Cornelia (Nikki) Giovanni, Jr. (born 1943), initially wrote poetry from a revolutionary Black's standpoint in the 1960s, but later moved to more traditional themes and softer attitudes.

Nikki Giovanni, née Yolande Cornelia Giovanni, Jr., was born on June 7, 1943, in Knoxville, Tennessee, to Gus and Yolande Giovanni. When she was still an infant, the family moved to a suburb of Cincinnati, Ohio, where both her parents worked as social workers. In1957 Giovanni moved to Knoxville to live with her grandparents—the southern influence of Tennessee and her grandmother, Louvenia Terrell Watson, were strong factors in Giovanni's development.

Giovanni attended an Episcopal school as a child and was a voracious reader of literature from T. S. Eliot to Richard Wright. In September 1960 she was an early entrant into the freshman class at Fisk University in Tennessee. At the time a conservative in her political views, she nevertheless rebelled against the paternalistic attitude of the historically Black colleges of the era. After ignoring a number of Fisk's social rules, she was placed on probation and, unwilling to change her behavior, suspended before completing her freshman year. Giovanni returned to Fisk in 1964 and became a militant participant in the cultural and political movements on campus. She fought the administration to establish a chapter of the Student Non-Violent Coordinating Committee (SNCC) on campus, edited the campus literary magazine *Elan,* and participated in John Killens' legendary creative writing workshop. While in Killens' workshop, Giovanni published her first article in a national publication, *Negro Digest.* She graduated *magna cum laude* from Fisk in 1967 with a B.A. in history.

Back in Cincinnati during the summer of 1967, Giovanni organized the first Black Arts Festival and founded The New Theatre, a Black drama group. She left Cincinnati at her mother's urging to enroll in the University of Pennsylvania's School of Social Work with a Ford Foundation fellowship in 1967. In 1968 she moved to New York, where she enrolled in Columbia's School of Fine Arts with a grant from the National Foundation of the Arts. In 1968 she taught in the SEEK program, a pre-college enrichment program for minority students at Queen's College.

Giovanni formed her own publishing company to publish her first book of poetry, *Black Feeling, Black Talk* (1968). Her second volume, *Black Judgement* (1969), was distributed by Broadside Press. In 1970 the two books were combined into one volume and published by William Morrow. Giovanni's first books created quite a sensation in the political and collegiate worlds that constituted the audience for Black Arts poetry. Her most notorious poem from *Black Feeling . . .* is "True Import of the Present Dialogue, Black vs. Negro," which asks, "Nigger/Can You Kill" and ends with a directive for "niggers" to learn how to kill in order to become "Black Men." Similar exhortations to violence appear in *Black Judgement* with calls for the destruction of oppressive whites and middle-class Black collaborators.

Giovanni's early radical poems often use ironic parodies of biblical quotes and influences. For instance, "The Great Pax Whitie" in *Black Judgement* uses lines from Genesis and the gospel song "Peace Be Still" to denounce America's practice of Christianity and democracy. This same volume, however, includes love poems; an early almost feminist poem, "Woman Poem"; and tributes to rhythm and blues singers. One of Giovanni's best-known poems, "Nikki-Rosa," is a sentimental tribute to Black family life and southern culture.

The strain of being a revolutionary, at least in print, had begun to show even in *Black Judgement.* "Adulthood" catalogues the many assassinations of the 1960s and ends with Giovanni wondering why she had not chosen a safe middle-class existence. In 1969 Giovanni gave birth to her son, Tommie, an event that seemed to move her further away from her militant stance. By the time of *Re-creation* (1970) the focus of the poetry was love songs, tributes to Black music, and ironic statements about racism. A most revealing poem, "Revolutionary Dreams," argues that a revolution would take place if she "dreamed natural/ dreams of being a natural woman." In 1970 Giovanni also established NikTom, Ltd., a communications company, and edited and published *Night Comes Softly,* an anthology of poetry by black women.

In 1971 Giovanni published *Gemini: An Extended Autobiographical Statement on My First Twenty Years of Being a Black Poet,* a collection of prose pieces which was nominated for a National Book Award. Her other publications include poetry volumes: *The Women and the Men* (1975); *Cotton Candy on a Rainy Day* (1978); and *Those Who Ride the Night Winds* (1983), tributes to Giovanni's heroes from John Lennon to Phillis Wheatley. Her prose works are *A Dialogue: James Baldwin and Nikki Giovanni* (1973); *A Poetic Equation: Conversations Between Nikki Giovanni and Margaret Walker* (1974); and *Sacred Cows . . . and Other Edibles* (1988), rambling and light essays in the tradition of Erma Bombeck. Giovanni's publications for children include *Spin a Soft Black Song* (1971), *Ego-tripping and Other Poems for Young People* (1973), and *Vacation Time: Poems for Children* (1980).

Giovanni's move away from radicalism in the early 1970s earned her recognition in more traditional circles. She recorded her poetry with the New York Community Choir, and the album *Truth Is on Its Way* was chosen the best spoken album in 1972 by the National Association of Radio and Television Announcers. Giovanni was given a Woman of the Year award by *Mademoiselle* and appeared on national television. Black middle-class organizations such as Omega Psi Phi fraternity and PUSH honored her work. Her quick wit and feisty personality made her a much sought after speaker on the college circuit. However, the new popularity in the white world won her the contempt of such radicals as Amiri Baraka (LeRoi Jones), who condemned her in a highly profane poem. Giovanni remained controversial. She visited South Africa at a time that progressive forces were calling for a cultural boycott—her opposition to the boycott of South Africa led to her being blacklisted by TransAfrica and she received bomb and death threats. Giovanni wrote in opposition to affirmative action (*Sacred Cows . . .*). She glibly dismissed questions about her radical past and categorized herself as a rugged individualist similar to the heroines of the conservative novelist Ayn Rand.

Giovanni taught at Rutgers' Livingston College from 1968 to 1972 and was a professor of English at Virginia Polytechnic Institute in Blacksburg, Virginia, in 1990. She continued to receive awards and recognition and continued to publish into the 1990s. Recent works include: *Racism 101* (1994) and *The Genie in the Jar* (1996).

Further Reading

For additional biographical information see the *Dictionary of Literary Biography* (Volume 41) and Giovanni's works *Gemini* and *Sacred Cows*. For critical information see Claudia Tate, *Black Women Writers at Work* (1983); Eugene Redmond, *Drum Voices* (1976); Mari Evans, editor, *Black Women Writers: 1950-1980* (1984); and Margaret McDowell, "Groundwork for a More Comprehensive Criticism of Nikki Giovanni" in *Belief vs. Theory in Black American Literary Criticism* (1986).

For biographical resources about Nikki Giovanni see Tate, Claudia, *Nikki Giovanni,* Twayne Publications, 1992. For autobiographical resources or works see: Baldwin, James, *A Dialog,* Lippincott; Giovanni, Nikki and Walker, Margaret, *A Poetic Equation: Conversations Between Nikki Giovanni and Margaret Walker,* Howard University Press, 1983; Fowler, Virginia C., *Conversations with Nikki Giovanni,* University Press of Mississippi, 1992; Giovanni, Nikki, *Racism 101,* Quill, 1995; Giovanni, Nikki, *The Selected Poems of Nikki Giovanni,* William Morrow and Company, 1996; and Giovanni, Nikki, *Love Poems,* William Morrow and Company, 1997.

For on-line resources about Nikki Giovanni see: http://www.ulspvt.k12mi.us/ELibrary/ELGiovanni.html, http://athena.english.vt.edu/Giovanni/Giovanni_biog.html, http://athena.english.vt.edu/Giovanni/Giovanni_pubs.html, and http://athena.english.vt.edu/Giovanni/Giovanni_awards.html. □

Stephen Girard

Stephen Girard (1750-1831), French-born American merchant and philanthropist, had a successful career in business and banking and became one of the wealthiest men in America.

S tephen Girard was born near Bordeaux on May 20, 1750. Although his father, a burgess of the city and a pensioner of the Crown, exercised considerable influence in Bordeaux, Girard's early life was not pleasant. At the age of 14 he left home, signing on as a cabin boy on a trading vessel sailing for Santo Domingo. He made numerous trips to the West Indies. In 1771 the 21-year-old Girard was licensed as an acting captain. His first voyage as a commanding officer was not financially profitable, and he found himself in debt to his Bordeaux creditors. He was able to repay his debts, but the venture helped convince him that his future lay in America.

At the outbreak of the American Revolution, Girard was engaged in the coastal trade. Forced into Delaware Bay by the British blockade, he brought his ship to Philadelphia. There he sold the vessel and in 1776 opened a small store. The following year he married Mary Lum, daughter of a local shipbuilder.

After the British evacuated Philadelphia, Girard became an American citizen and began to establish himself as a merchant. After early disappointments, his sense of business and willingness to work hard paid off. At the height of his career he was one of the richest men in America.

Girard's success as a merchant stimulated interests in real estate, insurance companies, and banking. He had been a strong supporter of the First Bank of the United States and worked to get the bank's charter renewed. When Congress refused to recharter the bank, he purchased the building and in 1812 opened the Bank of Stephen Girard in

Philadelphia. Because of his connections with the Federal Treasury and other banks in the United States and Europe, he was able to help the government during the financial crisis caused by the War of 1812. The government's efforts to obtain a loan of $16 million proved unsatisfactory until Girard, John Jacob Astor, and David Parish took over the unsubscribed portion and sold it to the public. Following the war, Girard played a major role in the chartering of the Second Bank of the United States.

Girard's humanitarianism became apparent early in his career. During the French Revolution he had provided valuable assistance to French refugees, and when a yellow fever epidemic hit Philadelphia in 1793, he not only helped care for the sick but also worked to clean up the conditions that had created the epidemic. Girard's will clearly indicated his philanthropy: the bulk of his estate, over $6 million, went to the city of Philadelphia in the form of a trust fund to be used for educating poor, white orphan boys. As a result, Girard College was founded.

Further Reading

One of the most interesting accounts of Girard's life is Cheesman A. Herrick, *Stephen Girard, Founder* (1923). Harry Emerson Wildes, *Lonely Midas: The Story of Stephen Girard* (1943), is a sympathetic biography.

Additional Sources

Wilson, George, *Stephen Girard: America's first tycoon,* Conshohocken, Pa.: Combined Books, 1995. □

François Girardon

The work of the French sculptor François Girardon (1628-1715) reflected the French taste for a restrained, classical version of the dominant baroque style.

François Girardon was born at Troyes on March 17, 1628. He studied in Rome for an undetermined period of time between 1645 and 1650. He then studied at the Royal Academy in Paris and was admitted to the academy as a member in 1657. Much of Girardon's most important work was executed for King Louis XIV and consisted of major commissions for the palace and gardens of Versailles. One of Girardon's most famous productions is *Apollo and the Nymphs of Thetis* in Versailles (1666-1672), originally designed for a grotto there. This elaborate project of seven separate marble statues depicts the god Apollo surrounded by nymphs, and it exemplifies with exceptional clarity the French interpretation of the baroque style in sculpture, an interpretation that rejected the fluid, dramatic, and emotional Italian baroque in favor of a cooler, more sober approach based upon the sculpture of antiquity. The *Apollo* group is filled with references to Hellenistic and Roman sculpture, and while Girardon was working on the

commission he made a second trip to Rome for inspiration from antique sources. The ancient world, however, had never attempted to assemble several large pieces of freestanding sculpture into one unified composition, and in solving this problem Girardon had recourse to the paintings of Nicolas Poussin, the great French baroque classicist.

The classicism of the *Apollo* group conformed fully to the official style of the French Academy and the personal taste of Louis XIV, but the composition has many baroque elements. The vigor and variety in the movement of the figures, the rich textural contrasts, the grand scale of the project, and the dramatic use of space are all stylistic qualities that firmly link the work to the international baroque style.

One of Girardon's most important works is the tomb of Cardinal Richelieu in the church of the Sorbonne, Paris (1675-1677). This monument shows the dying prelate in a semireclining position, his vestments falling in broad curves that are echoed in the draperies of the allegorical figures at the head and foot of the tomb. As originally placed in the church, the monument was freestanding so that the spectator was compelled to enter into the action of the work—a typical baroque compositional device.

Girardon's most significant late work was a majestic bronze equestrian statue of Louis XIV (1683-1692) executed for the Place Vendôme in Paris and based upon the famous Roman equestrian monument of the emperor Marcus Aurelius. Girardon's work was destroyed during the French Revolution, but several small-scale copies of it exist.

During the 1690s French taste shifted from Girardon's classicism to the more expressive baroque manner of Antoine Coysevox. Girardon died in Paris on Sept. 1, 1715.

Further Reading

The most important work on Girardon, Pierre Francastel, *Girardon* (1928), is in French. For a brief but thorough and excellent analysis of Girardon's place in 17th-century French art see Sir Anthony Blunt, *Art and Architecture in France, 1500-1700* (1954; 2d ed. 1970). □

Jean Giraudoux

The plays and novels of the French author and diplomat Jean Giraudoux (1882-1944) are marked by the use of myth, fantasy, and an original, somewhat precious style.

Jean Giraudoux was born on Oct. 29, 1882, in the little town of Bellac in the Limousin, the second son of a provincial employee of the highway department and a gentle, reserved mother whose letters show a natural gift for writing. Although the family moved to Pellevoisin when Jean was only 7, Bellac remained for him the symbol of a certain ideal way of life. Several of his most appealing characters are also natives of Bellac, for example, l'Apollon de Bellac and Suzanne.

In 1893 Giraudoux received a scholarship at the lycée of Châteauroux, where he was an excellent pupil for 7 years. His partly autobiographical novel *Simon le pathétique* (1926) and memories of his classmates give a picture of a polite, sensitive, aloof adolescent with a certain elegance in dress and language and a passion for excelling in both studies and sports. He received in this provincial school a solid humanistic education from excellent, idealistic teachers. His last 2 years of secondary school were spent in Paris, where he stood first in his class.

In 1903, after a year of military service, Giraudoux was admitted to the École Normale Supérieure in Paris, where he maintained his brilliant record. His study of German literature, his major field of interest, and his subsequent contact with German civilization during a year on scholarship in Germany had a lasting effect on his intellectual and artistic life. While hesitating before committing himself to the career of a scholar, he spent a happy year as an assistant in French at Harvard University, a year which proved to be his last formal contact with the academic world.

Prose Writings

Upon his return to France in 1908, Giraudoux took a position as assistant literary editor on the paper *Le Matin*. For several years, free at last from the discipline of school and examinations, he led a carefree life and kept postponing a decision on a career. Through his position he began to meet writers and eventually tried his own hand at writing short stories. Some of these were completely traditional and undistinguished, but others, published in 1909 in the volume entitled *Les Provinciales*, already showed signs of his original style and his peculiar vision of the world.

In these stories, based on childhood memories, Giraudoux gives a universal dimension to commonplace events by setting them in a cosmic context, a formula that was to become his most characteristic manner. Another volume, of three novellas, *L'École des indifférents* (1911), reflects his own existing mood of uncommitted detachment.

In 1910 Giraudoux took and passed the examination that would allow him to train for the consular service. Before the war he was never promoted beyond the rank of diplomatic courier and vice-consul. At the outbreak of hostilities, he was drafted and subsequently served on the French front and at the Dardanelles. Twice wounded and finally discharged, he was sent in 1916 as a military instructor to Portugal and later to Harvard. His war books, *Lectures pour une ombre* (1917) and *Adorable Clio* (1920), are meditations on the war rather than descriptions of it. In *Amica America* (1919) Giraudoux paints the New World with a good deal of fantasy but with genuine sympathy.

In 1918 Giraudoux married Suzanne Boland, who the following year bore his only child, Jean Pierre. Another examination entitled him to the post of embassy secretary, but he accepted instead the directorship of a government service which was eventually to become the Department of Cultural Relations. This position may have inspired his first nonautobiographical work, the novel *Suzanne et le Pacifique* (1921), whose heroine, a newstyle Robinson Crusoe, rejects the temptation to abandon her native culture as she grows to understand it better alone on her desert isle.

Ever since his student days Giraudoux had been concerned with the Franco-German question. This is the problem he takes up in his novel *Siegfried et le Limousin* (1922). Quite characteristically he treats it not in political or economic (that is, realistic) terms but in a poetic, almost mystical consideration of national character and cultural inheritance.

While serving as chief of the Information and Press Services of the Ministry of Foreign Affairs (1926-1934), Giraudoux was appointed to the commission to settle Turkey's war claims. He assumed the post of inspector of diplomatic and consular positions in 1936. In this office he wrote *Pleins pouvoirs* (1939), a remarkable double-headed work that outlines, on the one hand, the political, economic, and moral reforms he proposed to Édouard Daladier, and defines, on the other, his understanding of the cultural heritage and destiny of France. At this critical moment of its history, Giraudoux saw France's salvation in a preservation of the humanistic ideal. Profoundly affected by the events of 1939-1940, he retired from public life and died on Jan. 31, 1944.

The Playwright

For this statesman whose official vocation always seemed more like an avocation, Giraudoux's meeting in 1928 with the great actor-director Louis Jouvet was to have momentous repercussions. He wrote with Jouvet's encouragement and technical advice the play *Siegfried,* adapted from *Siegfried et le Limousin*. With its immediate success under Jouvet's direction, Giraudoux found himself launched in a new career, the one for which he is the most famous. His close association with Jouvet continued as he henceforth wrote almost entirely for the stage.

Although the basic conflicts of this theater are contemporary—conflicts, for example, between war and peace, freedom and destiny, man and woman, or man and the supernatural—the plots are often inspired by classical literature (*La Guerre de Troie n'aura pas lieu, Amphitryon 38, Electre, Pour Lucrèce*), German legend (*Ondine*), or the Bible (*Judith, Sodome et Gomorrhe*). Giraudoux's treatment of character is at the farthest pole from the psychological or sociological studies of the realistic theater. His young women, civil servants, ragpickers, or military heroes arrive before the audience in full possession of their essences and evolve no more than the gods against whom they are pitted. And yet so great is Giraudoux's magic of style that he enchanted a whole generation, weary of "bourgeois" drama and "well-made" plays, into believing that there was another way of dealing with reality. His popularity was challenged only by the ideological theater of the existentialists and the even more fantastic plays of the so-called theater of the absurd.

Further Reading

The best general studies of Giraudoux in English are Donald Inskip, *Jean Giraudoux: The Making of a Dramatist* (1958), and Laurent LeSage, *Jean Giraudoux: His Life and Works* (1959). Recommended for general background are Germaine Brée and Margaret Guiton, *An Age of Fiction: The French Novel from Gide to Camus* (1957); Wallace Fowlie, *A Guide to Contemporary French Literature* (1957) and *Dionysus in Paris: A Guide to French Contemporary Theatre* (1959); Jacques Guicharnaud, *Modern French Theatre from Giraudoux to Genet* (rev. ed. 1967); and Henri Peyre, *The Contemporary French Novel* (rev. ed. 1967). □

Simon Girty

Simon Girty (1741-1818), American frontiersman and one of American history's infamous renegades, defected to the British during the Revolution and led Indian raids on his own people.

Simon Girty was born near Harrisburg, Pa. His father was killed by Indians, Simon was held prisoner by the Seneca for 3 years, and at 15 he was forced to watch his stepfather being tortured to death at the stake. Yet Girty almost became a Seneca and was close to the Delaware Indians, too. After his release from captivity, he worked for the British as an interpreter of the Seneca language. However, he had no qualms about serving in Lord Dunmore's War against the Shawnee.

After 1776 Girty acted as an interpreter for the Continental Congress until he was discharged for "ill behavior." He served with Indian fighters and led a small expedition in 1778. Then, suddenly, he turned against the American

cause and fled to Detroit to work for the British. He interpreted for lieutenant governor and Indian superintendent Henry Hamilton, the notorious "Hair Buyer," who traded goods with his Indian allies for Yankee scalps.

Girty acquired such strong influence over Indian war parties that he accompanied and even led them on raids into Pennsylvania and Kentucky settlements. On a foray in 1782 his reputation for cruelty was documented by a witness who reported Girty's participation in the torture-murder of Col. William Crawford. Girty particularly wanted the scalp of Col. John Gibson because the colonel had repulsed Girty's siege of Ft. Laurens and in a captured letter had bragged that he would trepan Girty—that is, open his skull—if he caught him.

After defeating David Rogers' force on the Ohio River in 1779, Girty and his warriors helped capture Ft. Liberty, where despite British assurances of safety many prisoners were slaughtered. After the Revolution, Girty participated in the defeat of Gen. Arthur St. Clair on the Wabash in 1791 and fought against Gen. Anthony Wayne at Fallen Timbers in 1794. Girty had to flee to Canada after the Americans occupied Detroit in 1796.

When Oliver Hazard Perry's 1813 victory on Lake Erie opened Canada to American forces, Girty fled to his friends the Mohawks. His house was overrun but not destroyed because the Americans did not realize that the renegade had lived there. He returned to it in 1816, old and blind, and died on Feb. 18, 1818.

Further Reading

The best book on Girty (and his brothers) remains Consul Willshire Butterfield, *History of the Girtys* (1890), although it is sometimes difficult to read. A newer work is Thomas Boyd, *Simon Girty: The White Savage* (1928). Richard Elwell Banta, *The Ohio* (1949), has a solid biographical sketch of Girty. For general historical background see Dale Van Every, *A Company of Heroes: The American Frontier, 1775-1783* (1962).

Additional Sources

Truman, Timothy, *Wilderness: the true story of Simon Girty, the renegade,* Lancaster, Pa.: 4Winds Pub. Group, 1989. □

Valéry Giscard d'Estaing

The third president of the French Fifth Republic, Valéry Giscard d'Estaing (born 1926) was the architect of France's economic return as one of the leading nations of the world.

Valéry Giscard d'Estaing was born in Koblenz, Germany on February 2, 1926, during the French occupation of the Rhineland. Most of his childhood was spent in Clermont-Ferrand, which had been his family's home for generations. Like many upper class young men of his day, Giscard (he is commonly known by the traditional family name) moved to Paris as a teenager to continue his studies at the Lycées Jeanson de Sailly and Louis-le-Grand.

World War II interrupted his studies. At the age of 16 he joined the resistance against the Germans and collaborationist Vichy government and participated in the 1944 liberation of Paris. He then joined the French army and continued in the fight against the Germans in northern France and later in Germany.

After the war Giscard resumed his studies and was admitted to the prestigious engineering school Ecole polytechnique in 1946. After graduating he went on to the new Ecole national de l'administration established to train future bureaucrats to carry out major economic and civil responsibilities with modern management techniques. He received high academic honors. His education also included a year at the Harvard Business School.

A Rapid Rise in the Bureaucracy

In 1952 Giscard was named *inspecteur des finances* and began a meteoric bureaucratic career. He was one of the leaders of a new generation of civil servants who eschewed traditional norms of both neutrality and maintaining the status quo. Rather, they were committed to modernizing the French economy and thereby avoiding the problems that had afflicted France since the 1870s.

Young Giscard turned to politics earlier than many of his bureaucratic colleagues. In 1956 he was elected to parliament from his home department of the Puy-de-Dome,

which he continued to represent into the 1980s. Meanwhile, he was building his career in Paris as well. In 1955 he was named deputy director of Prime Minister Edgar Faure's personal staff.

Like many bureaucrats of his generation, Giscard was ready to participate in General de Gaulle's first government of the Fifth Republic in 1959 because the general's goal of grandeur meshed neatly with his desire for economic growth. Because of his political as well as bureaucratic background, Giscard was able to start near the top. He was named deputy finance minister in that first government and was the youngest member of the cabinet.

For the first 23 years of the Fifth Republic, Valéry Giscard d'Estaing held a variety of critical posts. In 1962 he was named minister of finance and economic affairs. He resigned that post in 1966, but served as chair of the National Assembly Finance Committee for the next two years. President Georges Pompidou reappointed Giscard minister of the economy and finance after his election in June 1969. Giscard held that post until Pompidou's death in 1974. Giscard d'Estaing then ran for president (as a member of the Independent Republican Party) against the Socialist leader François Mitterrand, and won the election held immediately thereafter. He served a full term as president but in seeking re-election in 1981 he was defeated by Mitterrand.

More Successes than Failures

Throughout his career, Giscard d'Estaing was known for three things. First, he was a loyal, if occasionally critical, ally of the Gaullists. In 1962 Giscard and his new political party, the Independent Republicans (*Républicains indépendents*) supported the referendum on the direct election of the president and then threw their support to the Gaullists in the subsequent legislative elections. That support was critical for the formation of the first stable parliamentary majority in French republican history. The Gaullists and Giscardians were allied thereafter. There were moments of serious disagreement—for example, prompting Giscard's resignation from the cabinet in 1966—but those problems never threatened the life of a Gaullist cabinet.

Second, Giscard was the politician of the center and right most open to progressive socio-economic reform. In his book *French Democracy* (1977) he advocated a more open, pluralistic system than that provided by the Gaullists. In addition, he strongly supported environmental protection, expansion of the social services, and loosening government control over economic forces and at least hinted at the possibility of a coalition government with the Socialists.

Finally, Giscard was probably best known as an economic reformer, as the leader of a generation of politician-bureaucrats who transformed France from one of the most backward into one of the most dynamic economies in Europe. Though more of a free-market capitalist than his Gaullist colleagues, Giscard was not reluctant to use the state to provide investment funds and other incentives, to encourage firms to merge, and to generally create what he called "national champions"—one or two large firms in each industrial sector that could compete effectively in international markets.

Giscard's career was not a total success. His presidency never produced the results he had hoped for in each of these areas. His alliance with the Gaullists—including his growing rivalry with Jacques Chirac, who served as his first prime minister—limited his ability to embark on political or economic reforms. Most notably, they made it impossible for him to make the kind of opening to the center left envisioned in *French Democracy*. He began his presidency with a series of important symbolic changes—dining with immigrant workers, stopping plans for an expressway on Paris' left bank, and holding cabinet meetings outside of Paris. Those symbols did not turn into substantive improvement in the lot of immigrants or in the quality of urban life nor into decentralization. President Giscard d'Estaing and his second prime minister, the economist Raymond Barre, did succeed in removing many state controls over the economy, but their liberalization reforms helped push France into a recession by the later 1970s.

Late in his term Giscard and those around him became embroiled in a series of scandals and were accused of high-handed leadership. As a result, Giscard lost the 1981 presidential election to the man he had defeated seven years earlier, François Mitterrand. The Gaullist and Giscardian parties then lost the subsequent legislative elections as well, and for the first time in a quarter of a century, Giscard d'Estaing found himself in opposition.

His career was in limbo after that. In 1984 he was reelected to the National Assembly in a by-election in his old district. Still, a return to the top was unlikely given his defeat in 1981 and the fact that other center and right wing politicians had become more popular.

After losing the election, Giscard remained active in political and economic arenas. In 1990, Giscard played a major role in establishing the Union for France (UPF), a right-wing political organization. In 1996 Giscard participated in The Fortune Global Forum—a world gathering of leading companies and political leaders who discussed the challenges of the global marketplace. In 1997 Giscard served as president of the Auvergne Regional Development Agency—a regional institution focusing on regional development and economic promotion and composed of forty members including local and regional collectivities, financial establishments, large companies, small and medium-sized businesses

Giscard reflected as much as any one individual could the personality of the group that dominated the Fifth Republic's first quarter century. Though he came from the "old France" of the nobility and small town politics, he also personified the "new France" of technically competent bureaucrats who sparked the modernization that turned France into one of the most powerful and dynamic countries in the world.

Further Reading

For an overview of Valéry Giscard d'Estaing's career, see J. R. Frears, *France in the Giscard Presidency* (London, 1981). For his own ideas, see Valéry Giscard d'Estaing, *French Democracy* (1977).

For biographic resources about Valéry Giscard d'Estaing see: *The Columbia Encyclopedia, Edition 5*, Columbia University Press, 1993.
For on-line resources about Valéry Giscard d'Estaing see: http://www.biography.com, http://web.w2line.fr/ard-auvergne/gb/default.html, and http://web.w2line.fr/ard-auvergne/gb/brochure.html. □

Christopher Gist

The American frontiersman Christopher Gist (ca. 1706-1759) was one of the first explorers of the Ohio and Kentucky wilderness. He also accompanied George Washington on missions to the French in the Ohio Valley.

Christopher Gist was born in Maryland. He probably did some surveying as a young man because he wrote and drew maps well in later life. But nothing is known of his youth in general. In 1750 he was living with his family on the Yadkin River of North Carolina not far from Daniel Boone. He married Sarah Howard (the date is not known) and raised five children.

The Ohio Company chose Gist to explore the country of the Ohio River as far as the Louisville area, and he carried out a careful examination of the territory in 1750. When he returned to North Carolina, he found that his family had fled to Roanoke, Va., because of Indian attacks. He rejoined them but went west again in the summer of 1751 to explore the Pennsylvania and western Virginia country south of the Ohio River and between the Monongahela and Great Kanawha rivers. About 1753 he settled briefly in the Pennsylvania wilderness near modern Brownsville.

Gist accompanied George Washington on his journey to French forts in the Ohio Valley in the winter of 1753; he is said to have saved Washington's life twice. He was with Washington when he defeated a small band of French soldiers in May 1754. Gist also accompanied Washington when he unsuccessfully attempted to repel a French force from Ft. Necessity the following July. Later Gist acted as guide to British general Edward Braddock in the march on the French Ft. Duquesne. Before reaching the French outpost, their force was ambushed and defeated by French and allied Indians. On July 9, 1755, Braddock was mortally wounded, and Gist and the remnants of the British troops were led to safety by Washington, who had command of a company of militia.

Later Gist served as captain of a company of scouts and as an Indian agent. His plan to recruit Indian auxiliaries from among the Cherokee of eastern Tennessee in 1756 proved to be premature and failed. Much later, of course, Indian scouts were essential to Army operations on the western frontier.

Gist died of smallpox in either Georgia or South Carolina in 1759. He was highly regarded by his contemporaries as a woodsman, explorer, and map maker, and although his fame was eclipsed by Daniel Boone's, it must be remembered that he examined the Ohio and Kentucky wilderness a full 18 years before Boone ever saw it.

Further Reading

An interesting account of Gist's life and the period is Richard Elwell Banta, *The Ohio* (1949). Gist's explorations in Ohio are covered extensively in Kenneth P. Bailey, *The Ohio Company of Virginia and the Westward Movement, 1748-1792* (1939). See also Charles H. Ambler, *George Washington and the West* (1936), and Hugh Cleland, *George Washington in the Ohio Valley* (1955).

Additional Sources

Powell, Allan, *Christopher Gist, frontier scout,* Shippensburg, PA: Burd Street Press, 1992. □

Rudolph William Giuliani

Former U.S. Attorney Rudolph Giuliani became the 107th mayor of New York City in 1994 on the Republican ticket. He was the first non-Democrat to become mayor in 24 years.

In January 1994, Rudolph William Giuliani became New York City's first Republican mayor since John Lindsey was elected in 1965. Giuliani's tough-on crime platform perhaps clinched the victory for the former U.S. attorney for the state of New York. In the years since his election, this tough stance seems to have paid off; in 1995, Giuliani announced that the murder rate in New York City had dropped by nearly one-fifth, the biggest annual decline in decades. However, he remains a controversial political figure, and on at least one occasion he has committed a widely-criticized breach of diplomacy—when he ejected Yasser Arafat Leader of the Palestine Liberation Organization (PLO) and winner of the Nobel Peace Prize, from a New York concert.

Started in Courts

Giuliani was born into a second-generation immigrant Italian family in Brooklyn, New York, on May 28, 1944. He was the only child of Harold and Helen Giuliani. As a child, the young Giuliani sometimes worked in his parent's bar and grill. The elder Giuliani was determined that his son attend college and rise above the family business. Rudolph Giuliani was educated in Catholic schools and then attended the all-male, Roman Catholic Manhattan College. There he seriously considered entering the priesthood, but eventually decided on law. He graduated from New York University's law school in 1968, and went on to have an impressive career in government, working first as a law clerk for a federal judge, and then as an assistant United States attorney for the Southern District of New York. Giuliani took on sensational corruption cases, and his reputation as a dogged prosecutor grew.

In 1975 Giuliani went to Washington, DC to work in President Gerald Ford's administration, under Judge Harold Tyler, deputy attorney general in the Justice department. Giuliani originally a liberal Democrat, had recently defected to the Republican party. When President Jimmy Carter took office in 1977, Giuliani followed Tyler to work for his law firm. Giuliani moved back to Washington under President Ronald Reagan, as associate attorney general in the Justice department. There, Giuliani took considerable flak for refusing asylum to Haitian refugees, deeming that the Duvalier regime was merely economically—not politically—oppressive to its people.

Became U.S. Attorney in New York

In 1983 Giuliani returned to New York for good, this time as U.S. attorney for the Southern District. In that position, Giuliani enjoyed some high-profile successes. He infiltrated some of the most powerful Mafia crime families and indicted a New York parking violations bureau official as part of a bribery ring. In the spring of 1986, uncovered the New York insider trading scandal, handing down indictments against several Wall Street investors. Among those arrested was Ivan Boesky, who turned himself in before Giuliani could indict him. In exchange for a lesser charge, Boesky agreed to pay $100 million and to secretly tape record conversations with other insider traders.

However, Giuliani has often been criticized for his grandstanding style. One of the lost legendary examples during his years as U.S. attorney was the arrest of three men involved in the insider trading scandal—Richard B. Wigton, a Kidder, Peabody executive; Timothy L. Tabor, a former employee of Kidder, Peabody; and Robert M. Freeman of Goldman, Sachs. Two of the men had been handcuffed at work and paraded in front of their colleagues, to the media's delight. The charges against all three were later dropped.

Mayoral Hopes

Giuliani eventually left the U.S. attorney's office, but still remained one of the most prominent and controversial figures in New York politics, going before the polls in 1989 in his first hotly contested mayoral race against David Dinkins. In that election, the main issue was racial strife, which was threatening to tear the city apart. Giuliani's conservative political stance was less appealing to voters than that of Dinkins, a liberal Democrat.

But in one of the most racially charged events to occur in New York City, Mayor Dinkins stumbled badly. In 1992, in the mostly Jewish section of Crown Heights in Brooklyn, a car in a Hasidic motorcade hit a young black child. After, a mob of angry blacks descended on a Jewish scholar visiting from Australia, stabbing him to death. Riots followed, in which 80 Jews and 50 policemen were injured. A jury later acquitted the man charged with the killing, following which Dinkins issued a lukewarm statement "expressing faith in he jury system . . . roundly denounced as insensitive to Jewish concerns," wrote Todd S. Purdum in the *New York Times Magazine*. Dinkins's Crown Heights blunder opened the door for Giuliani to the Jewish vote.

Still, Giuliani's tough-guy approach has been difficult for New Yorkers to embrace. In the fall of 1992, Giuliani made an appearance at a rally for the Policemen's Benevolent Association (PBA), a gathering of "raucous, beer-drinking, overwhelming white police officers"outside City Hall, wrote Purdum in the same article. Crowd members bore racially offensive signs critical of Dinkins, among the now legendary, "Dump the washroom attendant!" The demeanor of the crowd, which later moved in droves to block traffic on the Brooklyn Bridge, reflected badly on Giuliani. But what tainted him the most was his address to the PBA, in which he used expletives that Dinkins had originally used to respond to an officer's charge that the mayor did not support the police.

The rally was a major political fiasco for Giuliani. According to writer Purdam, he probably gained no votes from it—the police officers either were already supporters or lived outside of the city. And it damaged the reputation he was trying to build—that of a peacemaker. The speech he made after his loss in the 1989 election also damaged him. He announced that Dinkins had won, and in response, his election aides started booing. Giuliani began screaming, "Shut-up!" repeatedly. Later he said he feared that the crowd was out of hand, and their remarks would seem racially motivated.

Prior to the 1993 elections, many New Yorkers were horrified by a Giuliani plan to put 90-day limits on stays at homeless shelters. He remarked that he thought offering, unlimited access was actually "very cruel." "It sounds generous and compassionate," Giuliani was quoted as saying in a *New York* magazine article, "but it isn't. There's an understanding of human psychology that's missing. The less you expect of people, the less you get. The more you expect, the more you get." Giuliani also alienated liberal voters by his statement that he would bar controversial Muslim leader Louis Farrakhan from speaking at Yankee stadium, depriving him of his First Amendment rights.

Many political analysts say that Giuliani's attitudes seem to be a throwback to earlier times, that they distort and oversimplify the growing complexity of urban problems. Wrote Catherine S. Manegold in the *New York Times* after the election, "Throughout this year's campaign, Mr. Giuliani spoke tirelessly about the need to 'clean up' a city that he sees in moral and physical decline. To his supporters, he came across as a tough-edged iconoclast bent on bringing order out of urban chaos, a crusading Batman to New York City's gritty Gotham."

Yet other pundits call Giuliani a candidate for the future, and one who transcends political lines. "With his emphasis on individual responsibility, Giuliani is much closer in political philosophy to the New Democrat Bill Clinton claims to be than to David Dinkins is," said Fred Siegel, a professor of humanities, quoted in a *New York* magazine article.

To save Giuliani from his gaffes, he hired campaign mastermind David Garth, who was on the winning side in five of the last seven New York mayoral contests.Garth also went to bat for Vice-President Al Gore during the 1988 presidential primary, and handed a victory to Arlen Specter in a 1992 Republican senatorial race in which he was trailing. Garth helped solidify Giuliani's image as a "fusion candidate" just as Garth had done for John Lindsey's election in 1965, assembling minority candidates and representatives of minority districts to run on the same ticket.

With Garth maneuvering what a *New York Times Magazine* article dubbed "the race race," Giuliani was also able to capitalize on his anti-crime reputation. Dinkins maintained that crime decreased during hid term and according to John Taylor in a *New York* magazine piece, they had. Murders fell from 2,262 in 1990 to 2,055 in 1992, Taylor wrote. But to New Yorkers, the prevailing perception was that crime was on the rise. "One reason is the increasing brutality and capriciousness committed," wrote Taylor. "Entire families are executed in drug wars. Teenagers kill each other over sneakers. Robbers casually shoot victims even if they have surrendered wallets. The proliferation of carjackings means people are no longer safe even in their automobiles." One of Giuliani's campaign promises, along with creating jobs through tax cuts, and reducing administration in schools in order to increase money spent on teachers and students, was to crack down on such crimes, and he had the resume to back it up.

Still, many New Yorkers expressed dissatisfaction with both candidates. *Time* magazine ran a short article entitled "The Politics of Disgust," in which Janice C. Simpson claimed that "The only movement [in the polls] is the rising disapproval rating for both [candidates]. Neither candidate is getting across a message that he can be an urban Mr. Fixit. Dinkins comes off as a courtly but unimaginative bureaucrat with a taste for fussy clothes and fancy ceremonies. Giuliani has a reputation as a humorless autocrat with an abrasive management style that involves shooting first and asking questions later." An editorial in the *New York Times* began its editorial for David Dinkins with an expression of voter sentiment just before the election: "Something must be badly wrong with a system that can't produce candidates better than David Dinkins and Rudolph Giuliani. The real issues are being oversimplified. It doesn't really matter who wins."

Time writer Janice Simpson predicted that in a race "with no candidate who stands out as a clear vote for competence," that voting would break down along racial lines. That happened in the 1989 election, and also in the 1993 election. According to Felicia R. Lee in the *New York Times,* Simpson was correct. More than 90 percent of blacks voted for Dinkins, and so did most Hispanic voters. But very three out of four white votes went to Giuliani.

Lee wrote that New York City's black population was deeply disappointed by the election results, which indeed turned out to be a race based on race. "None interviewed said that Mr. Dinkins was a great mayor, but they said he tried to delve into the social factors behind problems like crime during a time of dwindling resources. Most said that despite his flaws, Mr. Dinkins would have won re-election had he been white. "Beyond that," Lee continued, "their concern was that Mayor-elect Rudolph W. Giuliani has surrounded himself with mostly white males with little understanding of issues of concerns to blacks, poor people, or other special interests."

Mayor Giuliani

According to Alison Mitchell writing in the *New York Times,* Giuliani addressed those concerns in his victory speech. Standing at the lectern with David Dinkins, the mayor-elect said it was time for the city to join as one, "whether you voted for me, for David Dinkins or you decided not to vote or you voted for any of the other candidates, we are all New Yorkers."

Tough on Crime

In the years since he was elected, Giuliani has maintained his emphasis on crime-fighting, using a range of methods—Comstat, a computerized analysis of crime statistics and police accountability, low tolerance for misdemeanor crimes especially gun and drug possession, targeting high-crime areas, holding local commanders responsible for results in their precincts, and implementing corporate management techniques in the police force.

In an article printed in *American City and County* Janet Ward said that it wasn't easy to shock New Yorkers—especially with good news. However, at a New Year's Eve (1996) press conference in Time Square, Mayor Giuliani and Police Commissioner Safir did just that. "When the ball comes down in Times Square tonight," said Giuliani "it will be coming down in one of the safest cities in America." Ward went on to say that it had been a long time since "one of the safest cities" and "New York" were used in the same sentence, but the facts support the claim. The city had realized double-digit decline in crimes for the past three years. New York had 48,016 or 15.7 percent fewer crimes in 1996. Overall, Giuliani said, "the city has seen 163,428 fewer felonies since 1993, a drop of almost 40 percent. Additionally, 1996 saw the city's lowest number of crime complaints in 27 years. The big crime, murder, dropped 16 percent in 1996 and has fallen nearly half since 1993."

Giuliani called the decline "a very significant success," and proof that New York is becoming safer. "People outside of New York City are very often almost shocked by the notion that it is not the most dangerous city in America," Giuliani was quoted as saying in *The Daily Telegraph.* "That's a reputation that the city, despite all of the statistical information to the contrary, can't quite shake." However, the drop in crime has not been attributed to any one factor. Some have suggested that it may be due to a demographic shift—a decline the population of teenage males, the group that is statistically most likely to commit crime. Another is that the crack epidemic, which hit the city in the mid-1980s, began to ease up in the early 1990s. But the New York City police commissioner says that police effectiveness has more to do with it than the media and other observers are willing to give them credit for.

Giuliani has also continued to harass the Mafia. In September of 1995, he appointed a monitor to inspect the books of the five-day Feast of Saint Gennaro, the annual carnival of New York's Little Italy. Few New Yorkers were surprised when the Grand Jury investigating the case announced that the Mafia skimmed the profits of the street vendors at the festival. However, only the most cynical were not surprised when it was revealed that the dollar bills which the devout pinned to the statue of Saint Gennero—intended for the Catholic church and its charities—also ended up in the pockets of the Mob.

Giuliani has sometimes committed mistakes in international diplomacy. In October 1995, Giuliani ejected Yasser Arafat, leader of the Palestine Liberation Organization (PLO) and winner of the Nobel Peace Prize, from a concert at New York's Lincoln Center, which was part of the UN's 50th anniversary celebrations. Despite intense criticism from the White House, the State Department, the UN, and even some Jewish groups, Giuliani defended his decision, claiming that Arafat had "never been held to account for the murders [for which] he was implicated." Just a few days earlier, when Cuba's President, Fidel Castro, was in New York, Giuliani had refused to invite him to a gala dinner. "It's my party and I'll invite who I want," he was quoted as saying in *The Daily Telegraph.* □

William Glackens

American painter William Glackens (1870-1938) reacted against the academic restrictions of his period, combining a vivid impressionism with a firm sense of structure in his work.

William Glackens was born in Philadelphia on March 13, 1870. After he completed high school (where John Sloan and Albert C. Barnes were his classmates), he became an artist-reporter for Philadelphia newspapers. He attended night classes at the Pennsylvania Academy of Fine Arts, studying with Thomas Anshutz. Glackens shared a studio with Robert Henri; in 1895 they worked their way to Europe on a cattle boat. In Holland and Paris they studied the Dutch masters, Diego Velázquez, and Francisco Goya. On his return to New York in 1896, Glackens worked for newspapers and commenced a long career as a magazine illustrator. *McClure's Magazine* sent him to Cuba in 1898 to cover the Spanish-American War, which he did brilliantly.

Glackens began exhibiting his paintings in 1901, attracting attention among critics and patrons who were turning away from the conventional standards of the academy. His subjects were café scenes, crowds on city streets, in parks, and on beaches, and people at play in outdoor settings. The influence of Pierre Auguste Renoir and other French impressionists is apparent.

In 1904 Glackens married, and 2 years later he traveled in France and Spain. His work was rejected by the National Academy of Design in 1907. He was one of the group of painters called "The Eight" who exhibited at the Macbeth Gallery in 1908. This show marked the end of the ascendancy of academic painting in the United States. Some of the painters in this group specialized in realistic social comment; Glackens remained fundamentally a romantic, his work reflecting a healthy and joyous view of life.

Glackens was influential in helping Albert C. Barnes form his great collection of modern art; the two traveled to Europe in 1912, returning with canvases by Édouard Manet, Edgar Degas, Paul Cézanne, Paul Gauguin, Vincent Van Gogh, Henri Matisse, and Renoir. Glackens was one of the organizers of the famous Armory Show of 1913, and he served as chairman of the committee that selected the American entries. Three of his own paintings were shown. He was one of the organizers of the Society of Independent Artists in 1916, which presented exhibitions without juries or prizes.

Throughout the 1920s and 1930s Glackens's work received wide recognition. The late paintings include imposing nudes, flower pieces, and portraits of members of his family. Basically impressionistic but with a strong sense of structure, these paintings combine sumptuous color, spontaneity of handling, and an increasingly architectural sense of compositional organization in a decidedly contemporary manner. His illustrations, particularly those involving animated crowds of people, exhibit brilliant and expressive draftsmanship, as do a smaller series of etchings of urban subjects. He was not a radical technically; his work was gay, pleasant, and elegant.

Glackens died suddenly on May 22, 1938.

Further Reading

Ira Glackens, *William Glackens and the Ashcan Group* (1957), is a delightful personal account by the artist's son. The best critical and biographical summary is in the catalog of the St. Louis exhibition, *William Glackens in Retrospect* (1966). There are picture books edited by Forbes Watson, *William Glackens* (1923), and Guy Pène du Bois, *William J. Glackens* (1931). Memorial exhibitions in Pittsburgh and New York during the 1930s produced valuable catalogs. Interesting personal sidelights appear in Bennard B. Perlman, *The Immortal Eight* (1962).

Additional Sources

Gerdts, William H., *William Glackens,* Fort Lauderdale: Museum of Art; New York: Abbeville Preress, 1996. □

Washington Gladden

The American clergyman Washington Gladden (1836-1918) was a pioneer of the Social Gospel and a key spokesman for liberal Protestantism.

On Feb. 11, 1836, Washington Gladden was born in Pottsgrove, Pa. Much of his childhood was spent in western New York, a district famous for its religious enthusiasms. This fact, coupled with his family's piety, aroused in young Gladden strong spiritual interests. In the mid-1850s he entered Williams College, where he received a degree preparatory to entering the ministry. In 1860 Gladden accepted his first pastorate in a Congregational church in Brooklyn. For the remainder of his life he devoted his principal energies to ministerial duties in urban areas, first in New York City, then in Massachusetts, and finally for over 30 years at the First Congregational Church in Columbus, Ohio.

From the outset Gladden was influenced by the new theological and social concerns animating American Protestantism in the late 19th century. Though lacking formal theological training beyond college, he kept abreast of current developments through wide and systematic reading. He was deeply affected by the writings of Horace Bushnell. Gladden preached the need to adapt Protestant theology to the new developments in biblical criticism and the natural sciences, especially Darwin's theory of evolution. He published several books espousing these views; as a member of the staff of a national journal, the *Independent,* he disseminated his ideas to a broad national audience. He also contributed frequently to the *Congregationalist,* a widely respected periodical.

Gladden quickly recognized some of the more destructive tendencies of city living. He urged that the church minister to the needs of working people, the poor, and those hurt by the impersonality of urban life. Thus he was an early exponent of what was eventually called the Social Gospel. He urged support for labor unions to protect the working man, identified with the settlement house movement, and entered into politics in Columbus, Ohio, to represent those seeking reform of municipal government.

Gladden's most spectacular act in support of the Social Gospel occurred in 1905, when he roundly condemned the American Board of Commissioners for Foreign Missions, a powerful national body of the Congregationalists, for accepting a $100,000 gift from John D. Rockefeller, Jr. He denounced the gift as "tainted money," an attack similar to those being leveled by secular "muckraking" journalists at big business and the great captains of industry.

Although not an originator of new ideas and trends, Gladden nevertheless pioneered in the theological views he adopted and in the social causes he espoused. By the time of his death in Columbus on July 2, 1918, he was considered one of the leading spokesmen for liberal Protestantism and the Social Gospel.

Further Reading

Gladden's autobiography is *Recollections* (1909). A sound, comprehensive biography of Gladden is Jacob Henry Dorn, *Washington Gladden: Prophet of the Social Gospel* (1967). An interpretive account of the man and his influence is Richard D. Knudten, *The Systematic Thought of Washington Gladden* (1968). □

William Ewart Gladstone

The English statesman William Ewart Gladstone (1809-1898) led the Liberal party and served as prime minister four times. His strong religious sense was an integral part of his political and social policies.

William Gladstone was born in Liverpool on Dec. 29, 1809. His parents were of Scottish descent. His father, Sir John Gladstone, was descended from the Gledstanes of Lanarkshire; he had moved to Liverpool and become a wealthy merchant. William's mother, Anne Robertson of Stornaway, was John Gladstone's second wife, and William was the fifth child and fourth son of this marriage. He was educated at Eton and Christ Church, Oxford; he took from his school days a sustained love for the classics and experience in debating. He was president of the Oxford Union and denounced the Parliamentary Reform Bill in a speech in 1831.

Gladstone graduated in December 1831, and a parliamentary career followed a brief sojourn in Italy in 1832. He, who was to become the great Liberal leader, was originally elected as a Tory from the pocket borough of Newark, and his major interest at the beginning was the Church of England, which he had seriously considered as a career. His maiden speech in June 1833 was a defense of West Indian slave owners with examples drawn from his father's plantations. His first book, *The State in Its Relations with the Church* (1838), was a defense of the established Church. In 1839 he married Catherine Glynne; the marriage was a happy one and gave to Gladstone important connections with the old Whig aristocracy.

Conversion to Liberalism

The 1840s saw Gladstone begin his move from right to left in politics. This meant a shift from High Tory (Conservative) to Liberal and a change in primary interest from defending High Church Anglicans to a concentration on financial reform. This change in Gladstone's outlook came in Sir Robert Peel's ministry of 1841-1846, in which Gladstone served as vice president and finally (1843) as president of the Board of Trade. The budget of 1842 was a move toward free trade with duties on hundreds of articles repealed or reduced, and Gladstone contributed much to this new tariff schedule. He resigned in 1845 on a religious issue—the increased grant to the Roman Catholic Maynooth College in Ireland—but returned to office in the same year as secretary of state for the colonies. The Corn Law repeal brought the Peel ministry down in 1846 and temporarily ended Gladstone's political career.

At the same time Gladstone severed his connections with Newark, which was controlled by the protectionist Duke of Newcastle, and in 1847 was elected member of Parliament for the University of Oxford. On the death of Peel in 1850 Gladstone moved to a new position of strength in the ranks of the Peelites (Tory liberals). His brilliant speech in 1852 attacking the budget proposed by Benjamin Disraeli brought about the fall of Lord Derby's government, and Gladstone became chancellor of the Exchequer in a coalition government headed by Lord Aberdeen. He could now apply his considerable financial talents to the economic policies of the nation, but this opportunity was

curbed by the Crimean War, which Britain formally entered in 1854. The laissez-faire budget of 1853 was nevertheless a classic budget in the British commitment to economic liberalism.

Gladstone's religious views were also growing more liberal, more tolerant of Nonconformists and Roman Catholics. He voted to remove restrictions on Jews in 1847, and he opposed Lord John Russell's anti-Catholic Ecclesiastical Titles Bill in 1851. Gladstone was clearly shaken by the Oxford movement and the conversion of some of his Oxford friends (among them Henry Manning) to Roman Catholicism. This experience, however, served to broaden his understanding and respect for individual conscience. A trip to Naples (1850-1851), where he witnessed the terrible poverty in the reactionary Bourbon Kingdom of the Two Sicilies, also helped turn him away from his innate Toryism, and the conversion to liberalism was complete.

Prime Minister

In the 1850s and 1860s Gladstone moved toward a position of leadership in a newly formulated Liberal party. He had served as chancellor of the Exchequer in Lord Palmerston's coalition government (1859-1865), but following the death of Palmerston in 1865, a realignment of the parties took shape which saw the old Tory and Whig labels replaced by Conservative and Liberal. Thus the Peelites and the Whig Liberals came together in a new party under Gladstone's leadership. He introduced a bill in 1866 to expand the parliamentary electorate, but it failed. Disraeli then scooped the Liberals with his famous "Leap in the Dark" Reform Bill of 1867, which passed, enfranchising most of the adult males in the urban working class. But Disraeli's "Tory Democracy" did not return immediate dividends at the polls. In the election of 1868 Gladstone and the Liberals were returned with a comfortable majority.

Gladstone's first Cabinet (1868-1874) was one of the most talented and most successful of the four he headed; he considered it "one of the finest instruments of government that ever were constructed." The legislation passed was extensive, and the reforming theme was to reduce privilege and to open established institutions to all. The universities and the army were two of the targets. The removal of the religious tests for admission to Oxford and Cambridge and the abolition of the purchase of commissions in the army were liberal victories of 1871.

The Education Act of 1870, which provided for the creation of board schools at the elementary level, was the first step in the construction of a national education system. Competitive exams were introduced for most departments of the civil service in the same year. Other commitments to democracy included the realization of old Chartist dreams, such as the secret ballot in 1872. With these reforms Gladstone won some support but also antagonized powerful interests in the Church and the aristocracy. His opponents said that he was a wild demagogue and a republican; the government was defeated in the election of 1874.

Ireland and the Empire

The "Irish question," which was to dominate Gladstone's later years, received considerable attention in the first Cabinet. Responding to the Fenian violence of the 1860s, the government moved to disestablish the Irish Episcopal Church in 1869 and pass a Land Act in 1870. But the Irish problem remained, and the home-rule movement of Isaac Butt and Charles Stewart Parnell demanded a solution in the 1870s.

Gladstone emerged from a temporary retirement in 1879 in the celebrated Midlothian campaign to attack Disraeli's pro-Turkish foreign policy. The theme of his attack was that Disraeli's Near Eastern policy was morally wrong. The Turkish atrocities in the Balkans outraged Gladstone just as the prisoners of Naples had provoked his earlier attack against Bourbon injustice in Italy. Gladstone's direct appeal to the British voter in this campaign was a first in a more democratic approach to electioneering, and his eloquence was triumphant as the Liberals won the general election of 1880.

The major concern of Gladstone's second Cabinet was not foreign policy but Ireland and the empire. A Second Land Act was passed in 1881, which attempted to establish a fair rent for Irish tenants and tenure for those who paid rent. The act was not popular with the landlords or tenants, and a series of agrarian riots and general violence followed. The high point of this was the assassination of Lord Cavendish, the chief secretary for Ireland, and Thomas Burke, the undersecretary, in Phoenix Park, Dublin, in 1882. The Fenians, rather than the Home Rule party, were responsible for this act, but Gladstone was forced to suspend discussion of Irish reform and resort to harsh measures of suppression in a Prevention of Crimes Bill (1882).

Gladstone's commitment to Ireland was coupled with a consistent opposition to imperialism. He considered imperialism a Conservative ruse to distract the masses from the real issues. He believed that the "infamy of Disraeli's policy was equalled only by the villainy with which it had been carried out." For Britain to seize power in Africa to exploit the native population would be as unjust as the Turkish rule in the Balkans. But Gladstone's second ministry coincided with a worsening agricultural depression in which England's free trade policy seemed a liability rather than an asset. New market areas unencumbered with tariffs had an appeal, and imperialism became a popular crusade. Egypt and the Sudan were the main concerns in the 1880s following Britain's purchase of the Suez Canal (1875). A riot in Alexandria brought a British occupation in 1882, and a rebellion in the Sudan brought the death of Gen. Gordon in 1885, when Gladstone's dilatory tactics failed to rescue him in time. The popular reaction to Gordon's death was a clear indication of Gladstone's misreading of this issue.

The Irish question reached its climax in Gladstone's third and brief (February to July) Cabinet of 1886. The Home Rule Bill was the sole program. It was designed to give Ireland a separate legislature with important powers, leaving to the British Parliament control of the army, navy, trade, and navigation. Gladstone's Liberal party had the votes to carry the bill, but the party split on the issue. Joseph Chamberlain led a group known as the Liberal Unionists (loyal to the Union of 1801) to oppose Gladstone's policy; the bill failed and Gladstone resigned. He had been correct in his premise that home rule or some degree of self-government was essential to the solution of the Irish question, but he failed to face up to the problem of the other Ireland, the Ulster north that lived in fear of the Catholic majority.

Gladstone was to remain in Parliament for another decade and to introduce another Home Rule Bill in 1893, but after the defeat of 1886 he was no longer in command of his party or in touch with the public he had led and served so long. His insistence on home rule for Ireland combined with his opposition to imperialism and social reform was evidence of this. The meaningful legislation in behalf of trade unions was sponsored by the Conservatives. His opposition to the arms buildup in the 1890s was consistent with his sincere desire for peace but doomed to failure given the German military expansion of the same period. Gladstone retired in 1894 and died on May 19, 1898; he was buried in Westminster Abbey.

Evaluation of His Career

Gladstone is still seen today as the epitome of the Victorian statesman. His industry (he often worked 14 hours a day), powerful sense of moral purpose, appetite for sermons, and lack of wit made him an easy target for the disciples of Lytton Strachey. But Gladstone was at the same time a major force in the shaping of British democracy. No single politician of the 19th century ever matched Gladstone's ability to mobilize the nation behind a program. Only Gladstone could make a budget sound like the announcement of a crusade. His sympathy for the oppressed people of the world—the Irish, the Italians, the Bulgarians, and the Africans—was genuine.

Gladstone lacked the tact to get along with Queen Victoria and with some of his colleagues but, like William Pitt the Elder before him, he could reach out of Parliament and arouse the public. In appearance and bearing this gaunt figure, whose speeches were marked by evangelical fire, might have belonged to the 17th century, but in parliamentary tactics he anticipated the 20th century. His achievements are impressive by any standard. The respect and affection that the British reserved for Gladstone is summed up in the nicknames they gave him; he was the "Grand Old Man" and the "People's William."

Further Reading

The standard biography of Gladstone was written by a fellow Liberal, John Morley, *Life of William Ewart Gladstone* (1903; new ed., 1 vol., 1932). A more analytical portrait is in Sir Philip Magnus, *Gladstone: A Biography* (1954; repr., with corrections, 1960). Discussions of special issues in his career are Paul Knaplund, *Gladstone and Britain's Imperial Policy* (1927); R. W. Seton-Watson, *Disraeli, Gladstone and the Eastern Question: A Study in Diplomacy and Party Politics* (1935); and J. L. Hammond, *Gladstone and the Irish Nation* (1938). Recommended for general historical background are R. C. K. Ensor, *England, 1870-1914* (1936); Herman Ausubel, *The Late Victorians: A Short History* (1955); H. J. Hanham, *Elections and Party Management: Politics in the Time of*

Disraeli and Gladstone (1959); and Ronald Robinson and John Gallagher, *Africa and the Victorians* (1961).

Additional Sources

Chadwick, Owen, *Acton and Gladstone,* London: Athlone Press, 1976.

Feuchtwanger, E. J., *Gladstone,* New York: St. Martin's Press, 1975; London: A. Lane, 1975.

Gladstone, Penelope, *Portrait of a family: the Gladstones, 1839-1889,* Ormskirk, Lanc.: T. Lyster, 1989.

Matthew, H. C. G. (Henry Colin Gray), *Gladstone, 1809-1874,* Oxford; New York: Oxford University Press, 1986; 1988.

Ramm, Agatha, *William Ewart Gladstone,* Cardiff: GPC, 1989.

Shannon, Richard, *Gladstone,* London: Hamilton, 1982; Chapel Hill: University of North Carolina Press, 1982, 1984.

Stansky, Peter, *Gladstone, a progress in politics,* Boston: Little, Brown, 1979; New York: W. W. Norton, 1979, 1981. □

Ellen Glasgow

The works of American novelist Ellen Glasgow (1873-1945) constitute a social history in fiction of Virginia from the Civil War to World War II. Her novels are distinguished in style and conception.

Ellen Glasgow was born on April 22, 1873, in Richmond, Va. Her father was a Scotch-Irish Presbyterian who "never committed a pleasure." His wife was a woman of "laughing spirit" whom he neither understood nor appreciated. Ellen's childhood was marred by her parents' misalliance (a subject her fiction frequently reflected), but her youth was secure and privileged, and she acquired a good education under private tutors.

Political economy was Glasgow's special interest. Before she was 20 Henry George's book *Progress and Poverty* converted her to Fabian socialism, though she remained hostile to the idea of revolution. Cruelty, greed, and intolerance were the real adversaries of mankind, she believed. Her novels led Southern fiction away from the accepted lies that the enemy was the North, the nouveau riche, or black people; they showed that the foe was not without but within.

Shortly after her mother's death in 1893, Glasgow finished her first novel, *The Descendant,* which was published anonymously in 1897. Perhaps the young woman approached writing with such professional dedication because an affliction, deafness, seemed to make "normal" life impossible. "At twenty-two," she later wrote, "I told myself that marriage was not for me."

Love was another matter, however. When Glasgow returned from a trip abroad in 1899, she met a man in New York, whom she calls Gerald B———in her autobiography. She almost forgot her deafness and made the most of her personal gifts: beauty, gaiety, and wit. Gerald B———was married, but the affair evidently brought the young writer a new sense of her power. The novels of this period, *The*

Voice of the People (1900), *The Battleground* (1902), and *The Deliverance* (1904), reflect this new-found power.

Gerald B———died in 1905. Glasgow's next books may reflect that loss, but by 1909, when *The Romance of a Plain Man* appeared, she was clearly in control of her art. The year her father died, 1916, saw the publication of *Life and Gabriella,* which studied the character of Southern women. In 1917 she became engaged to Henry W. Anderson, but the engagement was finally broken.

Barren Ground (1924), *The Romantic Comedians* (1926), and *The Sheltered Life* (1932) are three of Glasgow's best novels. *In This Our Life* (1941), her last novel, received the Pulitzer Prize. *A Certain Measure* (1943), her critical writings, was the last book published before her death in Richmond on Nov. 21, 1945.

Further Reading

Miss Glasgow's *The Woman Within* (1954), a frank autobiography, is splendid. Blair Rouse, *Ellen Glasgow* (1962), combines biography and criticism. Fine brief accounts of her work are Van Wyck Brooks, *The Confident Years, 1885-1915* (1952); Jay B. Hubbell, *The South in American Literature, 1607-1900* (1954); and Louis Auchincloss, *Ellen Glasgow* (1964), reprinted in his *Pioneers and Caretakers* (1965). Miss Glasgow's relation to Southern literary traditions is discussed by C. Hugh Holman in R. C. Sinonini, Jr., ed., *Southern Writers: Appraisals in Our Time* (1964).

Additional Sources

Glasgow, Ellen Anderson Gholson, *The woman within,* New York: Hill and Wang, 1954, 1980; Charlottesville: University Press of Virginia, 1994. ☐

Sheldon Lee Glashow

The theoretical work of American physicist Sheldon Lee Glashow (born 1932) made an important contribution to the unification of elementary particles and forces. He shared the 1979 Nobel Prize in Physics.

Sheldon Lee Glashow was born on December 5, 1932, in the northern tip of Manhattan in New York City. He was the youngest of three children of two Russian immigrants, Lewis Gluchovsky, a plumber, and Bella Rubin. He graduated from the Bronx High School of Science in 1950; one of his classmates was Steven Weinberg, with whom Glashow later shared the Nobel Prize. He received his B.A. from Cornell (1954) and Ph.D. from Harvard (1958). A post-doctoral fellow at CERN (European Council for Nuclear Research) and at the Niels Bohr Institute in Copenhagen from 1958 to 1960, Glashow taught at Stanford (1961-1962) and Berkeley (1962-1966) before assuming a professorship at Harvard in 1966, where he remained into the 1990s. Beginning 1979 he was the Higgins Professor of Physics there. In 1972 he married Joan Alexander, with whom he had two children, Bryan and Rebecca, and two step-children, Jason and Jordan.

Glashow's principal contribution was to the unification of elementary-particle forces. "Unification" refers to the process by which scientists learn to describe apparently disparate phenomena as different manifestations of the same thing. Lightning, static electricity, the aurora borealis, and St. Elmo's fire, for instance, are different forms of electricity. Significant progress in science is often tied up with acts of unification. When in the 17th century Isaac Newton showed that the force pulling objects to the ground and the one keeping planets in motion around the sun is the same force, gravitation—it was an act of unification. So was James Clerk Maxwell's discovery, in the 19th century, that electricity and magnetism were different aspects of one phenomenon, electromagnetism. Subsequently, numerous attempts were made to achieve further unifications, such as Einstein's failed attempt to link gravity and electromagnetism, but when Glashow arrived at Harvard as a graduate student in 1954, little progress had been realized.

Elementary Particle Forces

At that time, four fundamental forces (or interactions) were known—gravitation, electromagnetism, and the strong and the weak forces—and every other force had been shown to be a manifestation of one of these. The last three are called elementary-particle forces, because they govern the behavior of the subatomic world, and a number of physicists had given thought to their unification. A pre-

requisite, however, for unification was the existence of a common mathematical "language," and the mathematics in which each was then couched were very different.

Glashow was put on the track of elementary-particle unification by his mentor at Harvard, Julian Schwinger. In the late 1940s Schwinger had helped solve certain extremely troublesome problems that beset the mathematical language, called quantum field theory, in which electromagnetism was then couched. For this work he was awarded the 1965 Nobel Prize in Physics. According to quantum field theory, a force is carried by a type of particle called a vector boson; electromagnetism, for instance, is carried by the photon. Schwinger conveyed to Glashow his intuition that electromagnetism might be unified with the weak force if the latter, too, could be written in the language of quantum field theory. Schwinger tried to do this by assuming the weak force to be carried by two vector bosons, one positively, one negatively charged. The scheme, however, was plagued with difficulties.

Glashow examined vector bosons in his Ph.D. thesis, and then, between 1958 and 1960 while on a post-doctoral fellowship abroad, studied their possible role in the weak interaction. In March of 1960, in Paris, he met another advocate of unification, Murray Gell-Mann, and accepted the latter's invitation to become a research fellow at the California Institute of Technology. At Caltech, Glashow composed the paper that first set forth the ideas on which his Nobel Prize is based. "At first sight," the paper began, "there may be little or no similarity between electromagnetic effects and the phenomena associated with weak interactions. Yet certain remarkable parallels emerge with the supposition that the weak interactions are mediated by unstable bosons." The paper developed these parallels, proposing that not two but three vector bosons—positive, negative, and neutral—carried the electroweak force. This proposal solved many problems Schwinger's theory had not and provided a scheme for unifying the weak electromagnetic interactions. Glashow's "electroweak" unification, however, had two embarrassing features. One was that the version of quantum field theory on which the scheme was based, called gauge theory, contained certain inconsistencies (it was apparently not "renormalizable"). The other was that the scheme implied that so-called "neutral" weak interactions (in which no charge was exchanged) ought to exist, and they had not been seen.

Refining the Theory

The first of these two problems was solved in 1971 by the work of two Dutch theorists, Gerard Hooft and Martinus Veltman. The second problem was solved by Glashow himself, through another important contribution to particle physics. This one was based upon an idea of Gell-Mann. In 1964 Gell-Mann proposed that most types of particles, including protons and neutrons, consisted of different combinations of a type of particle that came in three varieties called a "quark." In the summer of 1964 Glashow proposed (with colleague James Bjorken) the existence of a *fourth* variety of quark, whimsically named "charm." This created a symmetry between the two fundamental families of elementary particles: leptons (which include electrons and muons) and quarks. Incorporated into Glashow's unified scheme of weak and electromagnetic forces, the charmed quark also eliminated the problem of neutral weak interactions, reducing them to a much smaller rate.

Glashow's electroweak scheme (similar schemes were also proposed by Glashow's school colleague Steven Weinberg and Pakistani physicist Abdus Salam) made certain predictions, which were confirmed in short order: neutral weak interactions at the reduced rate (1973), the existence of a charmed particle (1974), and an effect known as atomic parity violation (1978). Glashow's Nobel Prize came the following year, 1979, shared with Weinberg and Salam. Their work forged a major part of what has come to be known as the standard model of elementary particle physics, which is a comprehensive picture of the basic units of matter and their behavior.

Meanwhile, Glashow had already been at work on the next logical step, the unification of the electroweak and strong forces. In 1974, in collaboration with Harvard colleague Howard Giorgi, he proposed a "Grand Unified Theory" that used a gauge theory to unify the electroweak and strong interactions. This theory, however, had some disquieting implications, cosmologically speaking. The most notable one was that protons, the basic building blocks of atomic nuclei, were unstable and would ultimately all decay—that matter, in short, was mortal. So far, experiments have failed to detect proton decay, which may only mean, however, that more complex versions of Grand Unification are involved. Glashow's work in the late 1980s

and early 1990s was concerned with cosmology and in particular with the nature of the so-called "dark" matter in the universe.

Glashow spoke out as an advocate of mathematics in 1995 when the University of Rochester, New York proposed a plan to dismantle the math graduate program and reduce it to a "mere service facility." In a letter to the president of the University, Glashow stated that, "Americans, whether college educated or not, often lack the critical quantitative skills fostered by the study of mathematics." He worried that the action by the University would send the message that math played no significant role in education.

Polemical, witty, and rarely without a trademark cigar, Glashow was a striking character among contemporary physicists. More than many, he loved collaborations and did much of his best work with others, including Murray Gell-Mann and his fellow Nobel laureates Abdus Salam and Steven Weinberg. Though a theorist concerned with the fundamental structure of matter, Glashow was temperamentally and philosophically inclined toward areas of physics that have experimental consequences and devoted much time to examining how high-energy processes could be made experimentally observable.

Further Reading

Aside from scientific articles, Glashow wrote a number of popular articles, as well as a book, *Interactions* (1988), a potpourri of tales, charts, cartoons, and poems about physics and physicists. Glashow was the subject of an extensive profile in the *Atlantic Monthly* in August 1984. A narrative account of the drive toward unification, with a long description of Glashow's role, is provided in *The Second Creation: Makers of the Revolution in Twentieth Century Physics,* by Robert P. Crease and Charles C. Mann (1986).

For on-line resources about Sheldon Lee Glashow see: http://144.26.13.41/phyhist/sglash.htm or http://www.biography.com. □

Philip Glass

The American composer Philip Glass (born 1937) had a tremendous impact on all contemporary music. His brand of music, called minimalism, merged Eastern concepts of time with Western musical elements, altering the perception of music. He has been one of the most provocative, visible, and controversial composers of his generation.

Philip Glass was the leading composer/performer of the musical movement called minimalism, which emphasized musical process rather than complex musical structures. He simplified the traditional organizing factors of Western music—such as harmony, melody, modulation, and rhythm—and concentrated on creating complex layers of sound through a minimum of musical manipulation. His pieces utilized repetitive cycles of rhythm, similar to Hindu *ragas,* which change slowly over long periods of time and are said to produce a trance-like state in some listeners. In fact, Glass's works can be described as the grafting of Eastern concepts of space, time, and change on Western musical elements such as diatonic harmony. Divisive rhythm (that is, rhythm organized according to one unit of duration and its divisions) is replaced by the addition of rhythmic cycles that, when joined, move like wheels within wheels—everything precisely organized but constantly changing.

Philip Glass was born in Baltimore, Maryland, on January 31, 1937. His youth was characterized by a number of remarkable successes. A precocious child, he advanced quickly as a scholar and student of the flute and entered the University of Chicago at the age of 14. After receiving a bachelor of arts in 1956, he entered the Juilliard School of Music in New York City in 1958 and pursued composition studies with William Bergsma and Vincent Persichetti. By 1965 Glass had composed over 100 works, 40 of which had been published. He was the recipient of numerous awards, including a Broadcast Music Industry Award (1960), the Lado Prize (1961), two Benjamin Awards (1961, 1962), a Ford Foundation grant (1962), and a Young Composers' Award (1964).

Despite these achievements, Glass increasingly felt that his compositional style, based on the 12-tone and advanced rhythmic and harmonic forms popular at Juilliard, was no longer a meaningful outlet for his creativity. In hopes of revitalizing his music, the composer left for Paris in 1964 to study composition with Nadia Boulanger on a Fulbright Fellowship.

Reliance on Cyclic Rhythm

Lessons with this famous teacher had less of an impact on Glass than did his later exposure to non-Western music. He travelled extensively to India, Tibet, and Tunisia, and in 1965 he became a working assistant to the virtuoso sitar player, Ravi Shankar. Through notating Eastern music for a film and studying tabla music with the well known Indian percussionist, Alla Rakha, Glass gained an understanding of the modular-form style of Indian music. Shortly thereafter he completely rejected his earlier compositional style and began to rely solely on the Eastern principle of cyclic rhythm to organize his pieces. Harmony and modulation were added later, but these usually consisted only of a few static chords.

After returning from Europe in 1967 the composer organized the Philip Glass Ensemble, a seven-member group consisting of three electric keyboarders and three wind players with one sound engineer. They made their debut in New York on April 13, 1968, and embarked on the first of several European tours the following year. Notable works from this period include *Pieces in the Shape of a Square* (1968), *Music in Fifths* (1969), *Music for Voices* (1972), *Music in Twelve Parts* (1971-1974), and *Music with Changing Parts* (1970), which was the first album released by Glass' recording company, Chatham Records.

Glass' reputation as a serious composer suffered during this experimental period. Support from the academic community dropped off almost completely. However, a small cult following continued to grow. The appearance of the ensemble at the Royal College of Art in London in 1970 drew support from the visual arts. And in 1974 the first parts of *Music in Twelve Parts* were released on Virgin Records, a progressive rock label, thereby increasing his exposure to the popular music audience. Before long Glass counted such popular performers as David Bowie and Brian Eno among his fans, and the effects of his works could be seen in the rock music of Tangerine Dream and Pink Floyd. His ability to appeal to numerous musical factions caused him to be described as a "crossover" phenomenon—an artist with a small following who suddenly connects with a mass audience. Indeed, according to David Ewen, he is the only composer ever to have received standing ovations at three such varied musical venues as Carnegie Hall, the Metropolitan Opera House, and the Bottom Line (a New York City rock club).

Einstein on the Beach

Glass' alliance with the visual arts prompted a collaboration with Robert Wilson, the painter, architect, and leader in the world of avant-garde theater. *Einstein on the Beach,* Glass' best known work, was enthusiastically received at its premier in Avignon, France, on July 25, 1976. More a series of "events" than an opera, this full-length stage work explores through dance and movement the same concepts of time and change that Glass investigated through music. Several characters appear as Einstein, one playing repetitive motives on a violin; a chorus intones repetitive series of numbers and clichés; dancers and actors perform repetitive actions such as moving back and forth across the stage in slow motion. *Einstein on the Beach* has less to do with meaning than concept. "Go to *Einstein* and enjoy the sights and sounds," advises Robert Wilson in one interview, "feel the feelings they evoke. Listen to the Pictures." The opera was successfully produced throughout Europe and in 1984 it played to sold-out houses in New York. Its artistic success, however controversial, rests with its ability to consistently engage audience attention, to alter mood and provoke thought, and to force the theater-goer to actively supply the organization, structure, and meaning of the opera.

Glass followed this work with other theater successes. *Satyagraha*, commissioned by the city of Rotterdam in 1980, is the ritual embodiment of pacifist spirituality. Based on the life of Gandhi, the opera unfolds as a series of tableaux tracing his early life. The libretto is derived solely from the *Bhagavad Gita* and is sung in Sanskrit. It is said to be one of Glass' most lyric works.

Glass' later compositions included *The Photographer*, a chamber opera based on the life of the early 20th-century inventor Eadweard Muybridge (Amsterdam, 1982). *Akhnaton*, Glass' third opera, was produced at the Stuttgart Opera in 1984. In addition, Glass scored for films: the music for *Mark di Suvero, Sculptor*, directed by François de Ménil, was issued by Virgin Records as *North Star* in 1977. And *Koyaanisqatsi* was successfully received at the New York Film Festival in 1982. Glass composed numerous works for the Mabou Mines theater productions and choreographers Lucinda Childs, Alvin Ailey, and Jerome Robbins have incorporated his pieces into their repertoires.

Glass also collaborated with Robert Wilson on another opera, *The Civil Wars: (a tree is best measured when it is down)* and worked on a piece based on the writings of Doris Lessing called *The Making of the Representative of Planet 8*. In 1985 Glass teamed with composer Robert Moran and director Andrei Serban to produce the opera *The Juniper Tree* based on a Brothers Grimm fairytale.

Glass continued his collaborative efforts into the 1990's. He composed three operas based on films by the deceased Jean Cocteau, French author and movie director. *Orphee*, composed by Glass in 1993, followed the soundtrack of the film closely. In *La Belle et la Bete* (1994), Glass went one step further, stripping the film of its soundtrack and creating a live and carefully synchronized operatic accompaniment that took its place among his finest and most exciting works. In *Les Enfants Terribles* (1996) Glass teamed with choreographer Susan Marshall to tell the story through instrumental music and dance rather than singing.

In 1997 Glass composed and recorded a symphony based on the David Bowie album *Heroes*. One reviewer remarked in *New Statesman* (February 14, 1997) that Glass needed to be given credit for helping take a giant hammer to the wall that traditionally separated classical and rock music. In the same article Glass commented that, "Just as composers of the past have turned to music of their time to fashion new works, the work of Bowie became an inspiration for symphonies of my own."

Further Reading

Most of the information on Philip Glass is available in periodicals such as *TIME* (June 19, 1978), *High Fidelity/Musical America*

(April 1979), and *People* (October 6, 1980). Two particularly good articles appear in *Contact,* no. 11 (1975) and no. 13 (1976). An excellent, detailed essay on Glass can be found in David Ewen's *American Composers* (1982). Robert Palmer's discussion of the composer's background and development in the record insert for *Einstein on the Beach* (Tomato Records, 1978) is noteworthy. Most of Glass' works can be obtained on Chatham, Virgin, Tomato, or CBS records.

For periodical articles about Philip Glass see: *American Record Guide*, September-October 1996; *Time,* December 9, 1996; and *New Statesman*, February 14, 1997.

For on-line resources about Philip Glass see: http://www.biography.com. □

Owen Glendower

The Welsh national leader Owen Glendower (c. 1359?-c.1415) led Welsh opposition to English rule during the early 1400s.

Owen Glendower, also known as Owain ap Gruffydd and Glyndyfrdwy, Lord of Glyndwr and Sycharth, claimed descent from Bleddyn ap Cynvyn and from Llewelyn ap Gruffydd, the last native Prince of Wales. After inheriting estates in Merioneth, Glendower probably studied law at one of the Inns of Court in London. By 1385 he was serving as a squire with King Richard II against the Scots. Possibly knighted in 1387, he also served the Earl of Arundel under Henry of Lancaster (who became Henry IV in 1399). Glendower headed a Welsh rebellion in 1399, and, after being captured at Flint Castle, he was pardoned, but some of his lands were not restored to him. After an unsuccessful appeal to Parliament, Glendower turned to rebellion and in 1400 took the title of Prince of Wales.

As a rebel, Glendower gained considerable support because of agrarian discontent. He and his followers seized south Wales and gained control of Conway, Ruthin, and Hawarden; they also attacked the royal army in the north. In 1402 Glendower was crowned at Machynlleth, and he simultaneously negotiated with the English for peace and with Ireland and Scotland for help. Aided by the weather, Glendower checked the royal forces sent against him, and at Pilleth he captured Reginald de Grey and Sir Edmund de Mortimer. This action paved the way for a treaty with the Mortimers and the Percys for the overthrow of the King. After his daughter married Mortimer, Glendower released him, and during the next few months he gained control of Carmarthen, Usk, Caerleon, and Newport. This alliance ended with the Battle of Shrewsbury (1403), in which Glendower failed to join the Percys. For the next few years Glendower and his followers controlled Wales; they ravaged the English border, regulated Church appointments, and sent the bishop of St. Asaph as an ambassador to France. Capturing Harlech and Cardiff, Glendower controlled the area west of Worcester, and in 1405 he called for a Welsh Parliament.

From 1405 onward, Glendower's power started to decline, and his sons were captured by Prince Henry. Glendower recaptured Carmarthen with the help of the French, but he was defeated in battle in 1406, deserted by his ally the Earl of Northumberland the following year, and then lost Aberystwyth in 1408 and south Wales. Glendower's wife and several of his relatives were captured by the English in 1413, and although King Henry V made several offers of full pardon in an attempt to calm the border on the eve of his French campaign, Glendower never submitted to the English.

Glendower is believed to have died on Sept. 20, 1415, at Monnington, Herefordshire. His sons concluded negotiations with the English the following spring, but the terms of their pardons were less favorable than those that had been offered to Glendower.

The main aim of Glendower and his followers was to secure the political and ecclesiastical independence of Wales. They also wanted to preserve the native language and culture of Wales.

Further Reading

The standard biography of Glendower is Sir John E. Lloyd, *Owain Glyn Dwr (Owen Glendower)* (1932). Other biographies include Arthur G. Bradley, *Owen Glyndwr and the Last Struggle for Welsh Independence* (1901), and John D. G. Davies, *Owen Glyn Dwr* (1934). For general historical background see Ernest F. Jacob, *The Fifteenth Century, 1399-1485* (1961).

Additional Sources

Davies, R. R., *The revolt of Owen Glendower,* Oxford, England; New York: Oxford University Press, 1995.

Henken, Elissa R., *Fulfilling prophecy: Owen Glendower, legend and symbol,* Ithaca, N.Y.: Cornell University Press, 1996.

Sale, Richard, *Owen Glendower's way,* London: Hutchinson, 1985.

Skidmore, Ian, *Owen Glendower, Prince of Wales,* Swansea: C. Davies, 1978.

Williams, Glanmor, *Owen Glendower,* Cardiff: University of Wales Press, 1993. □

John Herschel Glenn Jr.

John Herschel Glenn, Jr. (born 1921) was a military test pilot, astronaut, businessman, and U.S. senator from Ohio. In 1984 he unsuccessfully sought the Democratic nomination for president.

John Glenn was born in Cambridge, Ohio, on July 18, 1921, to John Herschel Glenn, Sr., a plumbing contractor, and Clara Sproat Glenn. His parents had two other children who died in infancy, and they later adopted his sister Jean. He was reared nearby in the small town of New Concord and graduated from high school in 1939. Glenn credits his parents for instilling his deep rooted Presbyterian faith and its accompanying philosophy that everyone is given certain talents and has a duty to use them to the fullest. He enrolled at Muskingum College, a Presbyterian school in New Concord, to study chemical engineering, but left there to enlist for naval aviation training following America's entry into World War II. He married his high school sweetheart, Anna Margaret (Annie) Castor, in April 1943. They had two children, John David and Carolyn Ann.

Commissioned in the Marine Corps Reserve in March 1943, Glenn was assigned to squadron VMO-155 and ordered to the Pacific. The squadron, equipped with F4U Corsairs, was based on Majuro in the Marshall Islands and flew a variety of bombing and strafing missions against Japanese garrisons on other islands in the area. Glenn flew 59 combat missions while stationed there. After returning to the United States, he served principally as a flight instructor and was promoted to captain in July 1945. He remained on active duty after the war and was brought into the regular Marine Corps in 1946.

In the Korean conflict Glenn flew jets in ground support missions for the Marines and in air-to-air combat in the Air Force's new F-86 fighters as an exchange pilot, completing a total of 90 missions between February and September 1953. He gained a reputation for taking the battle to the enemy at such close range that often he would come back with a seemingly unflyable aircraft. Once, he returned in a plane with more than 200 holes in it, and it was immediately nicknamed "Glenn's flying doily."

Test Pilot to Astronaut

He was promoted to major in February 1953 and after his return from Korea worked tirelessly to make up for his lack of a college degree (awarded 1962) by self-study in engineering subjects and attending service schools. He was assigned to the Navy's Patuxent River test pilot school and later to the Bureau of Aeronautics. Glenn developed a project in which an F8U Crusader jet fighter would try to break the non-stop transcontinental speed record, refueling in mid-air three times. He received permission to make the attempt himself and on July 16, 1957, flew from Los Angeles to New York in 3 hours, 23 minutes. For this feat a fifth Distinguished Flying Cross was added to the many medals he had earned in wartime.

Spurred by the successful Russian Sputnik satellite, the U.S. government in 1958 began Project Mercury, a top-priority plan to place a man in orbit around the earth. Glenn went through a selection process of strenuous and exacting physical and psychological testing and was named one of the seven Mercury astronauts in April 1959. Promoted to lieutenant colonel the same month, Glenn was the senior astronaut in rank and age. Motivated by a deep religious faith and a tenacious devotion to duty, he reflected an earnest confidence that helped win the space program widespread public support.

Glenn was backup pilot for both the suborbital flights of Alan Shepard and Virgil "Gus" Grissom in 1961. He was chosen for the first orbital mission, "Friendship 7," circling the earth three times on February 20, 1962. It was a technological triumph, but part way through the nearly five-hour flight a data sensor indicated that his space capsule's protective heatshield had become dislocated. On these early missions no repairs could be made in space, and if the heatshield actually had slipped, Glenn would have perished without a trace in the fireball of re-entry into the atmosphere. The next week a relieved nation celebrated his safe return with parades in New York and Washington, D.C., as well as New Concord; not since Charles Lindbergh had the public so acclaimed a peacetime hero. Glenn responded on behalf of all the astronauts with a simple and moving speech before a joint meeting of Congress.

President John F. Kennedy admired the astronauts and their deeds and became Glenn's personal friend. He advised Glenn to finish his Marine career and seek public office, but after Kennedy's death Glenn's political future became more difficult. Moreover, in February 1964 Glenn suffered a severe inner-ear injury in a fall in the bathroom of his Columbus, Ohio, apartment. When he was taken to a military hospital in San Antonio for treatment speculation circulated that his problem was a delayed result of his space flight, but these rumors were dispelled when initial reports of the accident were clarified. His lengthy convalescence forced postponement of his retirement from the Marines and made him abandon as well his declared plans to run in the Democratic primary for U.S. senator from Ohio. By late 1964 he had recovered and was even able to fly jet fighters once again. Glenn asked that the Marine Corps not consider him for higher rank as he still intended to retire. President Lyndon Johnson set aside his request, however, and pro-moted him to full colonel at a White House ceremony in October 1964. Glenn then retired in January 1965.

Businessman to Politician

Glenn became an executive of Royal Crown Cola International from 1965 to 1969, when he resigned to try again for the Senate. Although his political organization was inexperienced, he was narrowly defeated in the Democratic primary of 1970 by Howard Metzenbaum, who was himself defeated by Robert A. Taft, Jr., in the general election. Between 1970 and 1974 Glenn became a partial owner of motels near Orlando, Florida. Along with other investments, they made him a wealthy man.

In 1974 Glenn made his third try for the Senate, again opposing Metzenbaum in the primary. This time Glenn's campaigning and organization were much improved. Glenn defeated Metzenbaum and went on to win the general election by one million votes. (Metzenbaum later won election as Ohio's second senator.) In the Senate Glenn was a member of the Foreign Relations and Governmental Affairs committees. He was respected as a hard-working senator, at his best when dealing with technical issues. His voting record tended to be conservative on national defense and foreign affairs, but more liberal on domestic social issues. He was the principal author of the Nuclear Nonproliferation Act of 1978, which sought to limit the spread of nuclear weapons. In 1980 he was re-elected by a margin of 1.6 million votes—the largest in Ohio history—in the face of a nationwide Republican trend.

In April 1983 Glenn announced his intention to seek the Democratic presidential nomination. He had been called "a Democratic Eisenhower," and many expected him to have the best chance to defeat the acknowledged front-runner, former Vice President Walter Mondale, in the primaries. Unlike Ike, however, Glenn somehow could not convey his charming and warm private personality to voters nationwide. His political organization suffered from frequent changes in key personnel and was inept in the timing of campaign events. Almost everywhere Glenn was enthusiastically received, but often disappointed his audiences with long, overly detailed speeches. His campaign steadily lost momentum as Mondale, a seasoned politician, racked up many endorsements among the diverse groups that comprise the national Democratic Party. Glenn's best showing was a second-place finish in Alabama, and he withdrew in March 1984, leaving the race to Senator Gary Hart, who had captured much of the vote of the "baby-boom" generation; the Reverend Jesse Jackson, who was forging a coalition among minorities; and Mondale, ultimately selected as the party's nominee.

After again winning his seat both in the 1986 and 1992 elections, Senator Glenn remained a strong voice in the Congress for a permanent research station in space, and supported increased funding for education, scientific research and space exploration. He announced in 1997 that he would not seek another term in the senate, but retire to pursue other interests. He was then assigned to the Senate Campaign Finance Reform Committee as vice-chair. He also approached NASA with the proposition that he be sent back into space again so that they could study the effects of exposure to weightlessness on older Americans.

John Glenn spent most of his adult life serving the nation. The ending of his 1962 address before Congress shows why he won the admiration of millions with his modesty and quiet patriotism: "We are all proud to have been privileged to be part of this effort, to represent our country as we have. As our knowledge of the universe in which we live increases, may God grant us the wisdom and guidance to use it wisely."

Further Reading

Most information about Glenn is found in periodicals; the only biography yet published was written before his entry into politics. *John H. Glenn: Astronaut,* by Lt. Col. Philip N. Pierce, USMC, and Karl Schuon (1962), covers his early life, his Marine career, and his orbital flight. Anyone wishing to find out more about Glenn's Marine career is advised to consult the History and Museums Division, Headquarters, U.S. Marine Corps, Washington, DC 20380. *We Seven* by The Astronauts (M. Scott Carpenter, et al., 1962) includes writings by Glenn on his flight, as well as detailed descriptions of his training. Among official government publications is the National Aeronautics and Space Administration's *This New Ocean: A History of Project Mercury* (1966) by Lloyd S. Swenson, Jr., et al. A best-selling, rather irreverent look at Project Mercury is *The Right Stuff* by Tom Wolfe (1979). A motion picture based on Wolfe's book appeared in 1983, but affected Glenn's candidacy little. Of value for those interested in Glenn's political career is the 1983 pamphlet *John Glenn,* published by Political Profiles, Inc., of Washington, DC, which includes a biographical sketch written by Jon Margolis. *Letters to John Glenn John Glenn: Astronaut* (1962) by Philip Pierce and Karl Schuon, Van Riper's *Glenn: The Astronaut Who Would Be President* (1983) examines Glenn's political years. Also a visit to Senator Glenn's website on the Internet at http://little.nhlink.net/john-glenn/jglenn.htm yields much information on his current activities □

Kiro Gligorov

Kiro Gligorov (born 1917) became the first president of the Republic of Macedonia in January 1991. He led the newly established state to international recognition, independence, and sovereignty.

Kiro Gligorov was born on May 3, 1917, in the city of Shtip (Stip), in the Republic of Macedonia, a part of Yugoslavia. He came from a family that was actively involved in the struggle for the national liberation of Macedonia from the Ottoman Turks. Most historians agree that until the beginning of the 20th century a majority of the Slav population of Macedonia considered themselves Bulgarians. However, after the establishment of an independent Bulgarian state and changes in the social and political conditions in the Balkans, a Macedonian national consciousness and separatism developed rapidly. This process was enhanced by the ideology and tactics adopted by the Inter-

nal Macedonian Revolutionary Organization, which, founded in 1893, fought for "Macedonia for the Macedonians" and the creation of an independent Macedonian state.

During the first Balkan War of 1912 an alliance composed of Bulgaria, Greece, Montenegro, and Serbia defeated the forces of the decaying Ottoman Empire and brought an end to five centuries of Turkish rule in Macedonia. However, the victors could not agree among themselves on the division of Macedonia, and a second Balkan War ensued a year later in which Romania and Turkey joined the three former allies in a war against Bulgaria. By the Treaty of Bucharest the territory of Macedonia was apportioned among Bulgaria, Greece, and Serbia, which later became part of Yugoslavia. Aegean Macedonia, the largest part, was attached to Greece; Vardar became part of Yugoslavia; and Pirin, the smallest area, was given to the defeated Bulgaria. In addition, a small number of Macedonians were included in Albania.

'The Apple of Discord'

Each of the Balkan states adopted a policy of de facto assimilation, the Greeks regarding Macedonian Slavs as Slavophones (Slav-speaking Greeks), the Serbs calling them "Southern Serbs," and the Bulgarians considering them Bulgarians. For the Macedonians themselves the division was but one more event in a long history of subjugation and imposed division. Throughout most of the 19th and 20th centuries most Balkan and foreign observers referred to Macedonia as "the apple of discord" and "the powder

keg of the Balkans." It was in this social, political, and cultural environment in Vardar Macedonia that Kiro Gligorov grew up.

As a youngster Gligorov attended the local primary school in his native town and then moved to Skopje, now the capital of the Republic of Macedonia, where he completed his secondary education. He received his higher education at the Law Faculty of the University of Belgrade, graduating in 1938. As a university student Gligorov was active in left-wing politics and in 1937 was arrested and jailed for a time. After graduation he returned to Skopje, where he worked as an attorney for a private bank.

Service in the Government of Yugoslavia

The greatest political challenge of his generation was the struggle against fascism and the construction of a new socialist society in post-World War II Yugoslavia. In 1941 Gligorov joined the antifascist national liberation movement and actively participated in the struggle against the foreign invaders. In 1943 he became secretary of the Initiative Committee for the convocation of the Antifascist Council for the People's Liberation of Macedonia (ASNOM) and then as a member of the Council of ASNOM fought against foreign occupation forces as well as for the overthrow of the old regime. On August 2, 1944, representatives of the people of Vardar Macedonia proclaimed an independent and sovereign Macedonian state as an equal member of the six constituent republics of the People's Federal Republic of Yugoslavia (PFRY). In the new Macedonian Republic, Gligorov, who, it seems, until then was also known by the name of Kiril Gligorov, was appointed secretary of finances of the Presidium of ASNOM (1944-1945).

During and immediately after the war Gligorov was active in the Antifascist Council for the People's Liberation of Yugoslavia (AVNOJ) and was a delegate to the third assembly of AVNOJ as well as a member of the Presidium of the newly-established Provisional Government of PFRY. In 1944 Gligorov joined the Communist Party of Yugoslavia, subsequently called the League of Communists of Yugoslavia (LCY).

Recognized by the party and the government for his ability and expertise, Gligorov soon moved to Belgrade, where for more than four decades he occupied several significant positions of responsibility in the federal government. At the same time, Gligorov was a professor in the Faculty of Economics at the University of Belgrade.

As an economics expert responsible for the finances of the country and vice president of the Federal Executive Council from 1967 to 1969, Gligorov was one of the influential economists who initiated and supported the introduction of reforms designed to give the government, LCY, and society at large a more democratic foundation. As head of a federal government team, he was one of "the architects of the economic reform" and was instrumental in implementing the first market-based modification of the Yugoslav economy. It is noteworthy that these were the first such reforms not only in Yugoslavia but anywhere in the then socialist bloc.

Most historians agree that Gligorov was one of the most capable pro-reform officials in the federal government during the 1960s and early 1970s. In the 1970s he occupied a number of high positions in the federal structure. From 1969 to 1972 Gligorov was a member of the presidency of the Socialist Federal Republic of Yugoslavia (SFRY). From 1974 to 1978 he was president of the National Assembly (Skupstina) of the SFRY. While occupying these posts Gligorov was also elected to the National Assembly of the Republic of Macedonia as well as to the Federal Assembly.

Gligorov was also active in party work and was elected to many leadership positions in the LCY. At the Eighth Congress of the LCY in 1965 he was elected to the Central Committee, and at the Ninth Congress in 1969 he became a member of the party presidency and of the Executive Bureau of the LCY. At both the Tenth and Eleventh LCY Congresses he was reelected to the Central Committee. As in his governmental work, Gligorov also demonstrated his democratic and liberal commitment within the party organs. At the Tenth LCY Congress in May 1974 liberalism, pluralism, and the federalization of the party were strongly condemned by many delegates. However, in his keynote speech to the Commission for Socioeconomic Relations Gligorov gave what one historian described as "a spirited defense of the necessity and virtues of a market economy."

After 1978, although Gligorov continued for some time to serve as a member of the Council of the Federation and the National Defense Council of the presidency of SFRY, he was effectively removed from the political life of the country. However, as earlier, he continued to do research on social and economic questions, participate in scholarly conferences, and publish his findings. Throughout most of his years in Belgrade Gligorov was a member of the Council of the Institute of International Politics and Economics and of the Federal Planning Institute and served as president of the Institute for Social Sciences. For his services, Gligorov was awarded many Yugoslav and foreign decorations.

Helping To Found a New Nation

Gligorov's greatest contribution to the history of Macedonia and to his people came in the late 1980s and early 1990s. In 1989, when the transformations emanating from the Soviet Union and Eastern Europe reached Yugoslavia, Gligorov was called to serve on a team of experts in the last Yugoslav government to oversee the implementation of a market economy and the building of a "new type of socialism." Events, however, outpaced political reforms. With the onset of the crisis in Yugoslavia, Gligorov made a successful political comeback, this time in his native land, the Republic of Macedonia.

When the former Yugoslavia seemed on the verge of collapse, Gligorov sided with those who called for moderation and a peaceful solution of the crisis. Together with the president of Bosnia and Herzegovina, he put forward a realistic proposal for an alliance of equally sovereign states. However, it was not accepted by the other Yugoslav leaders. There is no doubt that the end of the Cold War and the changes in the social, political, and economic system in the former Yugoslavia and the Soviet Bloc not only influenced but produced changes in Gligorov's ideology as well as his tactics as a politician.

In Macedonia Gligorov advocated the democratization of the country, the establishment of a civil society with independent institutions, the introduction of legality, and a free market economy as well as a multi-party system and free elections. Inaugurated as president of the Republic of Macedonia on January 27, 1991, Gligorov managed to guide the Macedonian Republic through a difficult period and to place the presidency at the forefront of Macedonia's national consolidation.

He supported the Macedonians who, on September 8, 1991, voted overwhelmingly in a general free referendum for the independence of their country. Following the vote, on September 17, 1991, the Macedonian Parliament proclaimed the independence and sovereignty of the Republic of Macedonia. The Macedonian Republic, therefore, was the only state of the former Yugoslav republics to attain independence through peaceful means.

Despite the country's economic difficulties, the tensions the country's ethnic diversity created, and the problems associated with the politics of transition to a market economy and democracy, Gligorov kept domestic peace by observing the new constitution, which guaranteed human and civil rights to all. He earned the respect of many world leaders and was instrumental in gaining United Nations' recognition, albeit under the awkward title of former Yugoslav Republic of Macedonia. He succeeded, moreover, despite strong Greek opposition to the name of the republic, in convincing the European Union, the United States, Russia, China, and other states to grant recognition to Macedonia.

The Macedonian Republic had many domestic problems to solve and foreign issues to overcome. Despite the fact that there were people who were critical of Gligorov's past activity and did not approve of many of his presidential policies, he became a national symbol of determination, pragmatism, and moderation for the majority of Macedonians. Through his efforts he strengthened the Macedonian people's will to overcome obstacles and enhanced their optimism in building their own authentic, democratic republic. To keep the civil war in the former Yugoslavia from spreading into Macedonia, the United States sent troops to patrol the northern border.

Reelection followed by car bomb

Gligorov was reelected to a second five-year term in October 1994. A president of the republic may serve two terms at most. One year later, however, Gligorov's fortunes turned when the president was gravely wounded in a car bomb attack in early October 1995. Gligorov lost an arm and was partially blinded. Parliamentary Speaker Stojan Andov was appointed acting president. Extreme nationalists were blamed for the bombing at first, followed by the Bulgarian mafia. Many viewed the assassination attempt as being spawned by an agreement signed in New York in September 1995 with the goal of normalizing relations with Greece. The agreement was expected to result in increased trade with Greece and the restoration of Macedonian access

to its main sea port, Thessaloniki. However, sanctions against Serbia remained a problem.

With Gligorov off the scene, at least temporarily, it was thought by some that the Alliance for Macedonia, a fragile ruling coalition of (formerly communist) Social Democrats and free-market Liberals, would dissolve. Gligorov surprised skeptics with an extraordinary recovery, returning to his office to put in full days of work while wearing tinted glasses to conceal the loss of his eye. Gligorov expressed a desire on Macedonia's part to avoid Slav or Orthodox alliance and join NATO and the European Union. For his efforts to bring peace to the Balkans, Gligorov was nominated for the Nobel Peace Prize by an American university professor and a group of Macedonian academic institutions in 1996.

In June 1997, Gligorov traveled to the United States and met with President Bill Clinton. According to a White House statement, Clinton "praised President Gligorov for his statesmanship in resolving differences with his neighbors and promoting ethnic tolerance at home." During the meeting, Gligorov urged Clinton to extend the mission of 500 U.S. troops stationed in Macedonia as part of a United Nations peacekeeping mission. "No one in the Balkans can remain impassive or quiet and peaceful and tranquil in terms of all the developments we have seen in Bosnia and the ones we're now seeing in Albania, and the possible dangers of any kind of involvement on the part of Kosovo (in Serbia) in this situation," Gligorov said following his meeting with Clinton.

Further Reading

The writings and speeches of Kiro Gligorov are scattered in various periodicals and publications of the former Yugoslav Parliament. Since 1989 most of his speeches and interviews have been translated into English and published in the Foreign Broadcast Information Service *Daily Report* (Eastern Europe). For his role in the introduction of reforms in the 1960s and 1970s see Dennison Rusinow, *The Yugoslav Experiment, 1948-1974* (1978). For brief notes on Gligorov and the events in Macedonia see the following articles in Radio Free Europe/ Radio Liberty, *Research Report:* Duncan M. Perry, "Politics in the Republic of Macedonia: Issues and Parties" (June 4, 1993); Hugh Poulton, "The Republic of Macedonia after UN Recognition" (June 4, 1993); and Stefan Troebst, "Macedonia: Powder Keg Defused? (January 28, 1994). For Gligorov's role in the fall of the former Yugoslavia see Lenard J. Cohen, *Broken Bonds: The Disintegration of Yugoslavia* (1993). □

Mikhail Ivanovich Glinka

The composer Mikhail Ivanovich Glinka (1804-1857) was the earliest important musical figure of 19th-century musical nationalism in Russia—indeed, Russia's first musical personage of importance. He is known as the father of Russian music.

Mikhail Glinka was born on May 20, 1804, in Novospasskoe, a village in Smolensk Province. From the age of 13 he was raised in St. Petersburg. His training was in the upper-class traditions of the capital. He moved in the circles that passed as enlightened for the time, and he experienced the atmosphere of ferment and question that prevailed in Russia with Western exposure, military and social, after 1812. He was said to have been sympathetic toward the Decembrist uprisings of 1825, yet later times found him politically conservative.

A prodigy, Glinka studied music with visiting foreigners in St. Petersburg. Of them, John Field should be mentioned as a strong influence, although the close relationship reported between the two is doubtful. He also studied in Italy, and in Berlin at the age of 33 he studied theory and composition with Siegfried Dehn.

Glinka adopted the practice of the numerous Italians dominating music in St. Petersburg: using stories and tunes from Russian historical and folk sources. Thus, his first opera, *A Life for the Czar, or Ivan Susanin* (1836), told the story of a Russian peasant's sacrifice as he misled Polish troops marching against the Czar. Although willing to accept the occasional folk reference from visiting Italians, many St. Petersburg opera goers found Glinka's effort "music for coachmen." Others, however, approved, and among them was the Czar.

With *A Life for the Czar*, Glinka not only opened Russia's first significant musical chapter but became one of the important figures of European 19th-century romantic nationalism. This coincidence of Russia's first musical efflorescence with the romantic-national phase of Western musical history has left an indelible mark on Russian and Soviet musical thinking to this day.

In his second opera, *Ruslan and Ludmilla* (1842), Glinka's effort at a "national" style was more marked. The same effort is heard in his numerous songs, a number of which are settings of texts by Aleksandr Pushkin. Glinka ventured also into symphonic music with overtures, the popular *Kamarinsky* (a fantasy on two Russian folk songs), and music for what has latterly been hailed as the "first Russian symphony" (1834; finished in 1948 by Vissarion Shebalin). His devotion to folk idiom was not limited to the Russian; he treated Middle Eastern, Finnish, Polish, Italian, and Spanish tunes as well. *Ruslan and Ludmilla*'s disappointing reception led Glinka to spend more and more time abroad.

Glinka's influence on all subsequent Russian musical development was profound, not just as romantic and nationalist but also as essentially conservative in means. He encouraged Aleksandr Dargomyzhsky and Mily Balakirev on the one hand, Anton Rubinstein and Peter Ilyich Tchaikovsky on the other. That he was not as distinctly "Russian" as was fondly held in earlier decades is no slur on his talent, which was great. He died in Berlin, on his way to confer further with Dehn, on Feb. 3, 1857.

Further Reading

The newest view of Glinka in English is in Mikhail O. Zetlin, *The Five: The Evolution of the Russian School of Music*, translated and edited by George Panim (1959). Chapters on Glinka appear in M. D. Calvocoressi and Gerald Abraham, *Masters of Russian Music* (1936) and Donald Brook, *Six Great Russian Composers* (1946). Paul Henry Lang, *Music in Western Civilization* (1941), attempts to place Glinka in some historical perspective.

Additional Sources

Brown, David, *Mikhail Glinka: a biographical and critical study*, New York: Da Capo Press, 1985, 1974.
Glinka, Mikhail Ivanovich, *Memoirs*, Westport, Conn.: Greenwood Press, 1980, 1963.
Montagu-Nathan, M. (Montagu), *Glinka*, New York: AMS Press, 1976. □

Duke of Gloucester

The English statesman Humphrey, Duke of Gloucester (1391-1447), was a leader of the strong expansionist policy against France. His lasting importance, however, lay in his patronage of learning and his benefactions to Oxford University.

Humphrey, Duke of Gloucester, whose other titles were Earl of Hainaut, Holland, Zeeland, and Pembroke; Lord of Fresia; Great Chamberlain of England; and Defender of the Realm, was popularly known as the "Good Duke." He was the fourth and youngest son of Henry IV. Possibly educated at Balliol College, Oxford, he was made a knight of the Garter at the age of 9 and was created Great Chamberlain of England in 1413 and Duke of Gloucester the following year. During the French campaign he served on the War Council, supervised the plundering of Harfleur, and was wounded in the stomach by a dagger while fighting beside his brother Henry V at Agincourt (1415).

While recovering, Humphrey was made constable of Dover and warden of the Cinque Ports. He returned to military service in the second campaign of Henry V, where he led the forces that entered Bayeux without opposition and took Lisieux in 1417 and Cherbourg the next year. Made governor of Rouen, he also acted as regent in 1420-1421, when Henry was on his last French campaign; and, though named sole regent by Henry V on his deathbed, Humphrey was given the title of Protector with power to act only as the deputy of John, Duke of Bedford, his older brother.

In 1422 Humphrey recklessly married Jacqueline of Hainaut and reconquered her lands only to lose them to Philip of Burgundy in 1425 and to alienate Burgundy from the English cause. In spite of interfamily feuds with his uncle, Henry Beaufort, a cardinal and the bishop of Winchester, he was reconciled through the efforts of his brother and became Protector again in 1427-1429 and Lieutenant of the Kingdom in 1430-1432. After his first marriage was annulled, he married his mistress, Eleanor Cobham, who

was convicted of witchcraft in 1441, sending his influence into decline.

Serving as captain of Calais and lieutenant of the army in the 1430s, Humphrey became the champion of the English claims against France, where he tried to arrange an Armagnac marriage for Henry VI, and in 1445 he argued for a violation of the truce. When the King came of age in 1442, the protectorate ended, and Humphrey was replaced as the chief adviser to the Crown by William Pole, 1st Duke of Suffolk. Suspected of planning to kill the King and seize the throne for himself, Humphrey was arrested on Feb. 18, 1447, soon after Parliament met at Bury St. Edmunds. He was found dead in his bed 5 days later. Foul play has never been proved, but popular belief claimed that the Duke of Suffolk was responsible. There are, however, strong reasons to believe Humphrey's death was natural.

Humphrey's influence on English politics was limited and of passing importance as he won support from the masses for his nationalistic antipapal policies. The epithet "Good" derives from this and from his support of literature and men of letters, and his protégés included John Lydgate, John Capgrave, and Titus Livius of Ferrara, the historian, who wrote *A Life of Henry V*. As a strong churchman, he endowed monasteries, including St. Albans. Humphrey had a reading knowledge of Latin and Italian literature as a result of a visit to Italy, and he made large gifts of books (his own library had over 600 works) and money to augment the small university library at Oxford, as well as founding temporary lectureships that terminated at his death. His donations remained at Oxford until the Reformation, when, in 1550, the commissioners under Edward VI ordered them removed. The room where the library was kept, known as "Duke Humfrey's Room," was restored by Sir Thomas Bodley and in 1602 again became the public library of the university.

Though he was buried at St. Alban's, a tradition developed that Humphrey was buried at St. Paul's Cathedral, London, where the poor would gather to solicit food, giving rise to the expression "to dine with Duke Humphrey."

Further Reading

The standard biography is Kenneth Hothman Vicker, *Humphrey, Duke of Gloucester* (1907), which, though dated, is still valuable. A recent, general work on the period is Ernest Fraser Jacob, *The Fifteenth Century, 1399-1485* (1961), in the "Oxford History of England" series. The best work on the wars is Édouard Perroy, *The Hundred Years War* (1945; trans. 1951). For Humphrey's patronage of literature see the essay by Roberto Weiss in Donald James Gordon, ed., *Fritz Saxl, 1890-1948: A Volume of Memorial Essays from His Friends in England* (1957). □

Sir John Bagot Glubb

The British soldier John Bagot Glubb (1897-1986) effectively created and commanded the Arab Legion military force in Transjordan and Jordan from 1939

to 1956; subsequently he wrote books and lectured widely.

John Glubb was born on April 16, 1897, at Preston, Lancashire, and educated at Cheltenham College and the Royal Military Academy at Woolwich. He then entered the army as a second lieutenant in the Royal Engineers. In World War I he served on the Western front and was wounded three times.

When Glubb arrived in the Middle East in 1920, the area was emerging from centuries of control by the Ottoman Turks and possessed an uncertain and turbulent atmosphere. Glubb quickly earned a reputation as a friend of the Arabs. He lived among the Bedouins, studying their customs and learning their language. The native police force that he organized played a large part in bringing order to the troubled frontiers of Iraq.

In 1926 Glubb resigned his British commission and became an administrative inspector for the government of the new state of Iraq. After serving brilliantly for 5 years in this capacity, he was transferred to the British mandate of Transjordan and attached to the Arab Legion, the small army of that state. As the commander of the Desert Patrol of the Legion, he ended the Bedouin raids and restored order to the area. In 1939 Glubb was appointed commander of the Arab Legion. He remained a devoted friend to the Arab people and tried to introduce European skills and methods to them. He never, however, ceased to respect Arab traditions; indeed, he became captivated by the customs of these people, whose dress and speech he had adopted and whose confidence he had won.

In World War II Glubb's Arab Legion gained a reputation for outstanding and spirited performance. Shortly after the British mandate ended and Transjordan became independent (it was renamed Jordan in 1949), riots broke out between the Arabs and Jews in Palestine, and the Arab Legion was called on to help maintain order. Later, in 1948, when the Arab League (of which Transjordan was a member) declared war on Israel, the Arab Legion spearheaded the attack.

Glubb's position with the Jordanian government became uneasy, however, and in 1956 Jordan's young king, Hussein, shocked the Western world by dismissing him. Glubb then returned to England and was knighted. His publications include *Story of the Arab Legion* (1948), *A Soldier with the Arabs* (1957), *Britain and the Arabs* (1959), *War in the Desert* (1960), *The Great Arab Conquests* (1963), *The Empire of the Arabs* (1963), *The Course of Empire* (1965), *The Lost Centuries* (1967), *Syria, Lebanon and Jordan* (1967), and *Short History of the Arab Peoples* (1968).

Further Reading

The most useful book on Glubb is his own *A Soldier with the Arabs* (1957), which is in part autobiographical. The volume underscores Glubb's own work with the Arabs and explains why he was dismissed in 1956. Also recommended are George Antonius, *The Arab Awakening: The Story of the Arab National Movement* (1939); Sir Reader W. Bullard, *Britain and the Middle East, from the Earliest Times to 1950* (1951); and Neijla M. Izzeddin, *The Arab World: Past, Present, and Future* (1953). □

Christoph Willibald Gluck

Christoph Willibald Gluck (1714-1787) was an Austrian composer and opera reformer. His operas represent an end to the older style of the opera seria and the beginning of the modern music drama.

Christoph Willibald Gluck was born of German-Bohemian stock on July 2, 1714, at Erasbach in the Upper Palatinate. His father was a forester. In 1726, according to some sources, Gluck was sent to a Jesuit college where he received formal music lessons as part of his education. At the age of 19 he enrolled in the university in Prague, where he was also actively engaged in musical activities.

After a short stay in Vienna in 1736, Gluck went to Milan, where he was in the employ of the Melzi family from 1737 to 1739. At this time he studied with the composer Giovanni Battista Sammartini. In 1741 Gluck's first opera, *Artaserse,* after a libretto by Pietro Metastasio, was produced.

During the next 20 years Gluck pursued the career of the typical 18th-century opera composer. He was active in Vienna, traveled extensively to serve his various patrons, and produced one or two new operas a year. In 1762, however, his dramatic ballet *Don Juan* was performed in Vienna; this event marked a significant change in Gluck's career. *Don Juan* is a ballet which narrates a story rather than presents a series of abstract geometric patterns. Most significantly, the music for *Don Juan* reflects the action onstage, thereby paving the way for Gluck's "reform" operas. In 1766, in Vienna, Gluck returned to the "reform" ballet, producing *Semiramide,* in which music and plot complement one another.

Collaboration with Calzabigi

Gluck came under the influence of the Italian dramatist and man of letters Ranieri Calzabigi, active in Vienna as court poet following Metastasio's long, brilliant career. Gluck and Calzabigi collaborated on three operas. Their first collaboration was *Orfeo ed Euridice,* produced in Vienna in 1762. They severely modified the legendary tale and abandoned the traditional "dry" recitative; the opera is one of great simplicity and directness in which nothing extraneous hinders the presentation of the drama. Calzabigi and Gluck thus opened the way for the possibilities for reform of the old-fashioned Italian *opera seria.* Their second collaborative effort, *Alceste,* modeled on the Euripides drama, premiered in 1767 in Vienna. Three years later *Paride ed Elena,* their last collaboration, was produced in Vienna.

Career in France

In 1770 Gluck was at the height of his fame. François du Roullet, attaché to the French embassy in Vienna, wrote a libretto for Gluck, but in the French style, based on Racine's famous drama *Iphigénie en Aulide.* Du Roullet's drama proved to be the means which brought Gluck to France. In 1773 he agreed to compose several French operas and moved to Paris at the instigation of his former pupil, Marie Antoinette, to supervise the productions. *Iphigénie en Aulide* was premiered the following year, which also saw the production of the French version of *Orfeo ed Euridice.* In 1775, as an act of homage to the memory of Jean Baptiste Lully and as a diplomatic gesture to French sensitivities, Gluck undertook to compose an opera based on Philippe Quinault's drama *Armide,* which had already been composed by Lully.

The French version of Gluck's *Alceste* was mounted at the Paris Opéra in 1776, and *Armide* was presented in 1777. His career came to a close with *Iphigénie en Tauride* in 1779. He retired from public life that year and returned to Vienna, where, following a stroke, he died on Nov. 15, 1787.

Opera Reform

Gluck was a very practical man of the theater, and during the 2 decades he was involved with opera reform he continued to compose other operas and entertainments in the old-fashioned, traditional style. It was largely due to Calzabigi's and Gluck's efforts that a general reexamination of the condition of the musical theater in the mid-18th century resulted in a series of masterpieces. Gluck's major accomplishment was to prove the efficacy of a lofty, serenely neoclassic style for the music drama. The reform operas were intended to demonstrate the possibilities the music theater held for the presentation of great, sublime ideas, and Gluck's efforts must be considered a success.

Gluck was very conscious of the precise role music was to play in the theater. "I sought to restrict music to its true function, namely to serve the poetry by means of the expression—and the situations which make up the plot—without interrupting the action or diminishing its interest by useless and superfluous ornament. . . . I have not cherished the invention of novel devices except when they were demanded by the situation and the expression. There was, finally, no rule which I did not gladly violate for the sake of the intended effect" (Dedicatory Letter, *Alceste,* 1769). In his five major reform operas there are no distracting subplots or senseless comedy scenes; the dramas move irrevocably toward the denouement, and Gluck always made the music entirely suitable for the intention of the drama.

Gluck's impact was tremendous. He received the ultimate accolade in France by precipitating several literary and critical "wars." During his lifetime there were many imitators and disciples, especially in France. The perfection of Gluck's operatic vision haunted the imaginations of composers as diverse as Hector Berlioz and Richard Wagner a century later. In Gluck's creations the genesis of modern opera composition is to be found.

Further Reading

The best biography of Gluck in English is Alfred Einstein, *Gluck* (trans. 1936; rev. ed. 1964). The operas are discussed in depth by Donald J. Grout, *A Short History of Opera* (2 vols., 1947; rev. ed., 1 vol., 1965). See also Joseph Kerman, *Opera as Drama* (1956). □

Max Gluckman

A distinguished British anthropologist, Max Gluckman (1911-1975) pioneered the study of traditional African legal systems. His research stressed social conflict and mechanisms for conflict resolution while studying urbanization and social change in colonial Africa.

A member of the second generation of great British anthropologists, Max Gluckman was born in Johannesburg, South Africa, in 1911. His parents, Russian-Jewish immigrants to South Africa, later resettled in the newly-formed state of Israel, where Gluckman died in 1975. Originally intending to study law, he chose instead to pursue a degree in anthropology at the University of the Witwatersrand. In 1936 Gluckman, a lifelong scholar-sportsman, was awarded a Transvaal Rhodes Scholarship to Exeter College, Oxford. Though he attended Kaspar B. Malinowski's famous seminars at the London School of Economics, it was the structural analyses of Edward Evans-Prichard and A. R. Radcliffe-Brown that most strongly influenced him. Gluckman was trained in structural analysis of social systems as dynamic but ultimately balanced systems of conflicting forces.

In 1936-1938 Gluckman carried out fieldwork in Zululand. His chief interests were the study of African legal systems and the dynamics of local conflict and its resolution. While remaining within the tradition of structural analysis, Gluckman's work had a distinct orientation. Rather than viewing African societies as closed, stable systems, Gluckman recognized the sometimes chaotic changes brought about by colonialism and race relations. He distinguished between the relatively stable forms of conflict characteristic of pre-colonial Zululand and the much more complicated and volatile colonial situation. This early work attempted to apply structural analysis to social situations much more complex and unstable than was the practice for anthropologists at that time.

In 1939 Gluckman joined the staff of the Rhodes-Livingston Institute in what was then Northern Rhodesia. From 1942 to 1947 he was the institute's director, shaping its research interests through the force of his powerful personality and through his intellectual and moral sensibilities. His links to the elegant structuralism of Evans-Prichard and Radcliffe-Brown grew weaker. Here in central Africa Gluckman developed his interests in the complexities of social and political relations that took for granted racial, political, and cultural pluralism. He encouraged research in the urbanizing areas of southern and central Africa. In addition to scholarly papers, Gluckman supported the publication of works that would be of practical help to local administrators.

Never having fully abandoned his interest in law, Gluckman produced during this period a classic treatise on the principles of jurisprudence among the Barotse of central Africa. In this detailed analysis, Gluckman examined the legal concept of the "the reasonable man" in the context of an indigenous central African legal system.

Despite his interest in conflict and in culturally complex settings, Gluckman always assumed that social systems could be analyzed as integrated systems. Thus his most enduring work is on rituals of rebellion, demonstrating how ritualized forms of hostility can serve ultimately to promote social cohesion by providing controlled expression of hostility to authority.

In 1947 Gluckman returned to England to teach at Oxford but almost immediately accepted an offer to head up a new anthropology department at Manchester University. What Gluckman established, however, was more than a new department. Gradually he assembled a group of colleagues and students that collectively became known as the Manchester School of Anthropology. Most of these anthropologists continued to carry out work in sub-Saharan Africa as did many other British anthropologists of the time. Yet the work of the Manchester School was distinctive for its emphasis on detailed village studies examining various social mechanisms for dealing with conflict.

Among Gluckman's numerous distinguished students perhaps Victor Turner is the most famous. In Turner's brilliant early work in the 1960s, *Schism and Continuity in an African Society*, Gluckman's interest in the dynamics of structural contradictions in society was carried out with particular success. As with many of Gluckman's students, Turner retained a strong interest in cultural outlets for such conflicts and contradictions. Witchcraft accusations, disease and curing rituals, rites of status reversal, or the role of village headmen as mediators with outsiders were all cultural themes that interested Gluckman and his students at Manchester.

In stressing the role of conflict in social life and in taking into account the role of colonialism and race relations in modern African societies, Gluckman moved social anthropology in Britain in a Marxist direction. Yet he never completely abandoned the more traditional British interest in societies as stable self-regulating systems. His ethnographic analyses were distinguished by the use of a detailed single case study to illustrate general structural principles. Moreover, Gluckman and his students refined the use of statistics in the analysis of social structure and the introduction of historical materials as evidence for the contrast between periods of social stability and change. In all his work, Gluckman insisted on the highest standards of scholarship.

Max Gluckman published numerous books and articles. Among the most important of his works are *Custom and Conflict in Africa* (1955), *Order and Rebellion in Tribal Africa* (1963), *The Ideas in Barotse Jurisprudence* (1967),

Essays on the Ritual of Social Relations (1962), and *Closed Systems and Open Minds* (1967). His Frazer lecture, "Rituals of Rebellion," is the most famous and succinct treatment of his approach to the structural study of conflict.

Less well-known is Gluckman's longtime commitment to the development of anthropology in Israel. He cooperated in the development of joint research projects between his own university and several Israeli universities. Israeli students were encouraged in these efforts to carry out community studies of Bedouin populations in their country.

Max Gluckman's prodigious energies were not restricted to his anthropological research. He remained throughout his life a strong supporter of organized sports and became an acknowledged expert on soccer and an avid soccer fan in Manchester. Perhaps such an active interest in organized sports was an understandable extension of Gluckman's lifelong interest in the delicate balance between social conflict and order.

Further Reading

An extensive analysis of Gluckman's work is contained in chapter 6 of *Anthropology and Anthropologists: The Modern British School* by Adam Kuper (1983). Briefer treatments are contained in *A History of Ethnology* by Fred Voget (1975) and *An Introduction to a Social Anthropology* by Lucy Mair (1965). The *London Times* of April 13, 1975, carried a long, informative obituary of Max Gluckman. Of Gluckman's numerous published works, *Essays on the Ritual of Social Relations* (1962) and *Closed Systems and Open Minds* (1965) are of particular interest to a general audience. □

Comte de Gobineau

Joseph Arthur, Comte de Gobineau (1816-1882), was a French diplomat, man of letters, and racial theorist. He was the first to propound the idea of Aryan superiority as a scientific theory.

Joseph Arthur de Gobineau was born on July 14, 1816, at Ville d'Avray near Paris, the scion of a noble family that remained loyal to the Bourbons. He attended school at the College of Bienne in Switzerland. From 1835 until his diplomatic sojourns he lived in Paris, where he occupied himself with literary work and a wide range of studies.

The Comte de Gobineau's aristocratic connections led to a meeting with Alexis de Tocqueville. When Tocqueville became foreign minister for a brief time in 1849, he made Gobineau his private secretary and, soon after, chief of his Cabinet. Later, Gobineau was made first secretary in the embassy at Berne, and later he held posts at Hanover and Frankfurt.

Gobineau's Theory

Gobineau's most important work, *Essay on the Inequality of Human Races* (1853-1855), partly translated into English in 1856, was an expression of his basic understanding of the meaning of his own life and of the events of his times. He was a royalist who despised democracy. He believed he was a descendant of a noble race of men, and he saw the French Revolution as a direct result of the bastardization of the race to which he belonged.

Gobineau sought to create a science of history by explaining the rise and fall of civilizations in terms of race. There were three races—the blacks, who were stupid and frivolous, but in whom the senses were well developed; the yellows, who craved mediocrity; and the whites, who were strong, intelligent, and handsome. Of the whites, the Aryans were superior, with the Germans being the purest of the Aryans. "German" did not refer to the entire German nation, *die Deutschen,* but rather to a tribe of Aryans, *die Germanen,* or Teutons, who had invaded Europe and set themselves up as an aristocracy to rule over the indigenous Celts and Slavs, who were inferior.

Gobineau did not believe that there are any modern pure races, nor was he set against all race mixing. He believed that civilization arose as the result of conquest by a superior race, virtually always Aryan, over inferior races. While Aryans were brave, strong, and intelligent, nevertheless they were a bit unimaginative and weak in sense perception. A small amount of infusion of black blood would heighten the senses and improve the imagination. Such an infusion, by way of Semites, explains the flowering of art and philosophy in ancient Greece.

However, Gobineau held that while some race mixing is good, too much is very bad, as it leads to the stagnation of civilization. Because Aryans have an appetite for race mixing, which made civilization possible in the first place, race mixing will eventually go too far, leading to the eventual destruction of civilization.

Gobineau was no nationalist. He associated nationalism with democracy and believed that both promoted excessive mixing of Aryan with inferior bloods. The disturbances of 1848 and 1871 increasingly convinced him that race mixing already had gone too far and European civilization was doomed. Today one can only wonder at this French count's fantastic version of the Germanic concept of the twilight of the gods!

Diplomatic and Literary Career

In 1854 Gobineau went to Teheran as first secretary, becoming minister to Persia in 1861. Several works on Persian society resulted, as well as a number of stories with a Persian setting.

In 1864 Gobineau represented France at Athens and in 1868 at Rio de Janeiro, where he became a friend of the Brazilian emperor, Dom Pedro II. Gobineau's last post was at Stockholm in 1872. He was forced to retire from the diplomatic corps in 1876 and spent most of his remaining years in Italy.

Gobineau continued his literary career. *The Pleiads* (1874) is considered his finest novel. Many of his literary writings were published posthumously. He met Richard Wagner in Rome in 1876 and subsequently made several trips to his home in Bayreuth. Gobineau's racial theories had not been well received in France, but Wagner was very much impressed by Gobineau's views. Partly through the influence of the Bayreuth circle, Gobineau's racial ideas became popular in Germany in the decades after his death in Turin on Oct. 13, 1882.

Further Reading

A recent work on Gobineau is Michael D. Biddiss, *Father of Racist Ideology* (1970). Two older works are Arnold H. Rowbotham, *The Literary Works of Count de Gobineau* (1929), and Gerald M. Spring, *The Vitalism of Count de Gobineau* (1932). See also Jacques Barzun, *Race: A Study in Modern Superstition* (1937). ☐

Robert Hutchings Goddard

The American pioneer in rocketry Robert Hutchings Goddard (1882-1945) was one of the founders of the science of astronautics.

obert Goddard was born on Oct. 5, 1882, in Worcester, Mass., the son of Nahum Danford Goddard, a businessman, and Fannie Hoyt Goddard. From his earliest youth Goddard suffered from pulmonary tuberculosis. Although he remained out of school for long periods, he kept up with his academic studies, and he read voluminously in *Cassell's Popular Educator* and science fiction.

In 1904 Goddard enrolled at Worcester Polytechnic Institute and received his degree in physics in 1908. He then entered the graduate school of Clark University, where he was granted a master's degree in 1910 and received his doctorate a year later.

Early Investigations in Rocketry

Goddard went to the Palmer Physical Laboratory of Princeton University as a research fellow in 1912. He proposed a research project he described as "the positive result of force on a material dielectric carrying a displacement current." In the course of his experimentation he developed a vacuum-tube oscillator that he subsequently patented in 1915, well before that of Lee De Forest.

While Goddard's days in the laboratory were given over to his research in radio, his nights were free to work upon the fundamentals of rocketry. Approaching the problem theoretically, he was able by 1913 to prove that a rocket of 200 pounds' initial mass could achieve escape velocity for a 1-pound mass if the propellant was of gun cotton at 50 percent efficiency or greater. He began patenting many of the rocket concepts that ultimately gave him a total of more than 200 patents in this particular field of technology. They were to cover many of the fundamentals in areas such as propellants, guidance and control, and structure. For example, his patent granted on July 7, 1914, clearly identifies the concept of multistaging of rockets, without which the landing of men on the moon or sending probes to Mars and Venus would not be possible.

When his health permitted, Goddard returned to teaching and research at Clark University. By this time he was wholly devoted to rocketry. He built a vacuum chamber in which he fired small, solid-propellant rockets to study the effects of different types of nozzles in such an environment. Having exhausted his own funds and not wishing to draw further on the resources of the university, he applied to the Smithsonian for a grant of $5,000, which he was awarded in 1917. With these funds he began the study of rocketry in earnest.

During World War I the U.S. Army Signal Corps provided $20,000 to the Smithsonian Institution for research in applied rocketry by Goddard. He moved to the Mt. Wilson Observatory in California and set up a workshop in which to experiment with solid-propellant rockets as weapons. There, with two assistants, Henry C. Parker and Clarence N. Hickman, he set to work on two projects.

Parker worked on a rocket with a single charge that could be launched from an open tube. This was the forebear of the World War II bazooka. Meanwhile, Hickman devoted his energies to one of Goddard's pet but more complex problems—a rocket propelled by the injection of successive solid charges into its motor. Parker's rocket proved to be successful, but Hickman's was simply unworkable. However, both rockets were demonstrated for military officials, but despite the success and the obvious enthusiasm of the military, the armistice 4 days after the demonstration canceled all Army interest in Goddard and his rockets. It was not revived for 26 years.

Liquid-propellant Rockets

In 1919 the Smithsonian Institution published Goddard's monograph "A Method of Reaching Extreme Altitudes," which he had submitted earlier to that organization with a request for research funds. The newspapers, seeing a casual reference to the moon and the prospect of hitting it with a rocket loaded with flash powder, pushed Goddard into the headlines. Being a reticent man as well as a dedicated physicist, he recoiled from the unwanted publicity and resisted further attempts by publications to present the subject.

During the decades of the 1920s and 1930s Goddard's research was supported by erratic and unpredictable funding from Clark University, the U.S. Navy, the Smithsonian Institution, and the Carnegie Foundation. From static testing of small solid-propellant rockets Goddard graduated to liquid-propellant motors. His long experimentation with solid-propellant rockets had by the early 1920s convinced him that the efficiency of such motors was simply too low ever to be of use in space travel. Indeed, by the early 1920s he had daringly mentioned liquid hydrogen (not then obtainable) and liquid oxygen, that is, nuclear and ionic propulsion for rockets.

Goddard's first liquid-propellant rocket was launched in 1926 from a farm near Auburn, Mass. Present on the occasion as photographer was the young Mrs. Esther Goddard, whom Goddard had married in 1924. The rocket reached an altitude of 41 feet and a range of 184 feet and traveled the distance in only 2 1/2 seconds. It was not a statistically impressive performance, but neither was that at Kitty Hawk, N. C., on Dec. 17, 1903.

Work in New Mexico

Needing more room and a milder outdoor climate for his experiments, Goddard moved to New Mexico, near Roswell, in 1930. His Mescalero Ranch was only 100 miles from the White Sands Missile Range. There, in a well-equipped machine shop, Goddard and a small team of assistants began work on the design and fabrication of liquid-propellant rockets that were the direct forebears of the Saturn 5 and Titan 3C space boosters of the 1960s.

The first launching in New Mexico took place in 1930. In 1932 a rocket with a gyroscopic stabilizer was flown. In that same year Goddard returned to Clark University because of the economic depression. During the succeeding 2 years at Clark he continued his research as well as he could and received several patents that grew out of his work in New Mexico.

After Goddard returned to the ranch, the rockets grew larger and flew higher. On March 31, 1935, a 15-foot-tall model reached an altitude of 7,500 feet under gyroscopic control. Goddard's research continued here until 1942. During these years he turned his attention to a high-speed turbopump for delivering the propellants to the combustion chamber of the motor. It was a component that had long held up his development of a really efficient rocket.

Return East

On May 28, 1940, Goddard met with officers of the U.S. Army Air Corps and Navy in Washington, D.C., to brief them on his rockets and their potential as weapons. In 1941 he finally received a small contract from the Army Air Corps and Navy to develop a liquid-propellant jet-assist-takeoff rocket for aircraft. In July 1942 he left Roswell to continue his research at the Navy Engineering Experimental Station at Annapolis, Md. There his experiments met with technical success, but an attempt to demonstrate the motor on an actual aircraft ended in failure and the loss of the plane. As rockets of all types, especially the V-1 and V-2, began making the headlines, Goddard received offers of jobs from many companies; he accepted the invitation from Curtiss-Wright, where he worked until his death on Aug. 10, 1945.

Further Reading

The Papers of Robert H. Goddard was edited by Esther C. Goddard and G. Edward Pendray (3 vols., 1970). The only full-length biography of Goddard is Milton Lehman, *This High Man: The Life of Robert H. Goddard* (1963). Anne Perkins Dewey, *Robert Goddard, Space Pioneer* (1962), is a biography for younger readers. For general reading on rocketry during the period in which Goddard figured prominently see Willy Ley, *Rockets Missiles, and Men in Space* (1952; rev. ed. 1968); Beryl Williams and Samuel Epstein, *The Rocket Pioneers on the Road to Space* (1955); and Wernher von Braun and Frederick I. Ordway III, *History of Rocketry and Space Travel* (1966). Useful books on astronautics in general include Frederick I. Ordway, James P. Gardner, and Mitchell R. Sharpe, *Basic Astronautics: An Introduction to Space Science, Engineering, and Medicine* (1962), and Mitchell R. Sharpe, *Living in Space: The Astronaut and His Environment* (1969). □

Kurt Gödel

The Austrian-American mathematician and philosopher-scientist Kurt Gödel (1906-1978) developed the celebrated "Gödel's proof" which provided extraordinary insight into the basis of mathematical thought and revolutionized modern logic.

Kurt Gödel was born on April 28, 1906, in Brno, now in the Czech Republic but then part of Austria-Hungary. His father was a well-off textile manufacturer and his life with his parents and brother has been described as "happy." His inquisitive nature by age 6 earned him the family name "Mr. Why." By age 14 he had become interested in mathematics, and a year later, in philosophy. At 17, he mastered university-level mathematics and excelled at other subjects as well his brother Rudolph said, "it was rumored that in the whole of his time at high school not only was his work in Latin always given the top marks but that he had made not a single grammatical error."

Gödel entered the University of Vienna to study theoretical physics; two years later, he shifted to mathematics, and then to mathematical logic. He joined the university faculty in 1930 after receiving his doctorate. In 1931 Gödel published "On Formally Undecipherable Propositions of *Principia Mathematica* and Related Systems". It was an extremely specialized paper but it attracted early attention and became famously known as Gödel's proof. Gödel was 25.

Gödel's proof denies the possibility that a mathematical system supported on axioms can be verified within that system and ends 100 years of attempts by previous mathematical inquiry to establish a system of axioms which might embody the whole of mathematical reasoning that is, to put all of mathematics on an axiomatic base. This work had been brought to a high level of attainment in the sections on the elementary logic of propositions in Bertrand Russell's *Principia Mathematica,* and it had been apparently completed in the brilliant achievements of David Hilbert in his "axiomatic period" from 1922 to 1930.

Gödel devised a method of converting the symbols of mathematical logic into numbers (Gödel numbers) so as to achieve the arithmetization of metamathematical statements, that is, statements about mathematical arrangements and formulas. He was able to illustrate how a metamathematical statement could be shown to be demonstrable even when postulating its own indemonstrability. From this it would follow that any arithmetical formula is undecidable on the basis of any metamathematical reasoning which could be represented arithmetically. At the

same time it could be shown that an undemonstrable formula can nevertheless be established as an arithmetic truth.

Gödel showed in this highly complex chain of reasoning that it is not possible to prove the self-consistency of a system on the basis of metamathematical statements except by going outside that system for the methods of proof. Further, he showed that statements can be constructed within such a system which can be neither proved nor disproved within that system but which can be shown to be arithmetical truths. These conclusions revolutionized mathematical thinking and stimulated the branch of mathematics known as proof theory.

Gödel's life was devoted to the activity of doing fundamental theoretical work. His work in mathematical logic lasted until 1942, when he became primarily occupied with philosophy, intensely studying Leibniz (with whom he closely identified), Kant, and Husserl, until his death in 1978. Gödel arrived at the Institute for Advanced Study in Princeton, NJ, in the fall of 1933, where he met Einstein for the first time, and lectured there for several months in 1934. He married in Adele Porkert in Vienna in 1938. After several commutes between Princeton and Vienna, the Gödel's moved to Princeton permanently in 1940. He became a permanent member of the Institute in 1946 and was appointed to a professorship in 1953.

Gödel distanced himself from the affairs of the world and took part in almost no practical activities: such were the demands of his concentration on fundamental theoretical work. He restricted himself to few contacts with the outside world and most of its inhabitants. He was inclined to caution and privacy; he avoided controversies and appeared to be "exceptionally sensitive" to criticism. He published little (but left a large body of notes and unpublished works), lectured infrequently, accepted few invitations, and disliked travel to the point of declining several honorary degrees because accepting them meant traveling. He was not interested in operating motor vehicles. His few interests were in surrealist and abstract art, his favorite writers included Goethe and Franz Kafka, he enjoyed light classics and some 'pop' music and Disney films, especially Snow White.

Gödel and Einstein found each other to be intellectual equals, and as it happened they shared the same cultural background. Beginning in 1942 in Princeton, they saw and talked with each other almost daily until Einstein's death in 1955. Einstein told a colleague that in the later years of his life, his own work no longer meant much and "that he came to the Institute merely to have the privilege to be able to walk home with Gödel"

Gödel's physique was frail and he was in relatively poor health for much of his life, suffering at times from depression enough to be hospitalized. Gödel's brother, a physician, observed that Kurt's diet was excessively stringent and was harmful. Gödel did not obey doctor's orders, "even at the point where most people would," and he himself admitted that he was a difficult patient. It was widely believed that he was paranoid and constantly worried about food poisoning. In 1978, he died of malnutrition and "inanition" (starvation) caused by "a personality disorder" (according to his death certificate).

Since his death, Gödel's fame has spread more widely, beginning almost immediately with the 1979 publication of Douglas R. Hofstader's *Godel, Escher and Bach*. The mathematician John von Neumann has called Gödel's achievement in modern logic "a landmark which will remain visible far in space in time." George Zebrowski had said that "No other example of human thought is as far-reaching as Gödel's proof." Gödel's friend and biographer Hao Wang observes that to find work of comparable character in both science and philosophy, "one has to go back to Descartes (1596-1650) and Leibniz (1646-1716), and he adds that it may take "hundreds of years" for the more definite confirmation or refutation of some of [Gödel's] larger conjectures."

In layman's terms, what Gödel did was show conclusively that humans do not live in a universe in which they can solve all problems and learn everything. It can never be done because the universe is infinite and human minds are not. In a way, Gödel's proof is a truth about systems of thought, not about the universe; it is about maps, and not about the territory they represent. What Gödel set out to prove is that the actual territory will always transcend the map.

As one writer has put it, "Unpredictable things happen to finite beings." Gödel's proof suggests a universe that is an open-ended, infinite, eternal existence, requiring no beginning, and in this universe our knowledge may become extensive and significant but will never be complete. An unfalsifiable idea is complete within itself; little green men may live in all refrigerators, but we can't know that since they disappear when the door is opened. Religious dogma is another example of an unfalsifiable idea, for part of its appeal is that it has its own internal resistance to answering questions about its truth. Dogmas are outside Gödel's universe because they try to end all discussions and tests of truth, whereas Gödel's universe asks that we appreciate the practical value of imperfection, serendipity, and wildness. Open-endedness: legal systems can never be more than "good enough;" political systems which are closed impoverish cultural and economic lives, and ultimately fail.

In even simpler terms, as Zebrowski puts it, Gödel's proof can be explained this way: an elderly woman attends a meeting of philosophers concerned with the nature of the universe and tells them that the world rests on the back of a turtle. The chairman asks her to explain what this turtle stands on; she snaps back that it stands on the back of yet another turtle. "And what does that turtle stand on?" demands the chairman. The elderly woman shakes her finger and replies, "You can't fool me, sonny it's turtles all the way down!"

Further Reading

For a model of expository biography, see Hao Wang, *Reflections on Kurt Gödel* (1987); also, Pelle Yourgrau, *The Disappearance of Time* (1991), and John W. Dawson, *Logical Dilemmas: The Life and Work of Kurt Gödel*. George Zebrowski's "Life in Gödel's Universe: Maps All The Way" *Omni* (April 1992) is very helpful for non-mathematicians. □

Godfrey of Bouillon

The French crusader Godfrey of Bouillon (ca. 1060-1100) was one of the chief lay leaders of the First Crusade and the first ruler of the newly formed state of Jerusalem.

Godfrey was the second son of Eustace II, Count of Boulogne, and Ida, daughter of Godfrey II, Duke of Lower Lorraine. After years of delay Emperor Henry IV finally confirmed him in the duchy of Lower Lorraine. When he and his brothers, Eustace and Baldwin, joined the First Crusade, Godfrey was nevertheless obliged to pledge his castle in Bouillon, as well as the lordship of Verdun, to the bishop of Liège, presumably to help finance the expedition.

The crusaders reached Constantinople shortly before Christmas, 1096. For several months there were promises and betrayals and armed skirmishes with the Byzantine troops. Finally the whole force of crusaders, now swelled by the Norman contingent and Bohemund's army, crossed the Bosporus and set out for Nicaea. When Jerusalem was captured in July 1099, the higher clergy and the greater barons offered the crown to Godfrey, having failed to convince Count Raymond to take it. Godfrey accepted the leadership but claimed instead the title of Advocatus Sancti Sepulchri (Defender of the Holy Sepulcher). This made him lay warrantor of the newly won lands, allowing the Church to preserve, initially, its own interests. The ecclesiastical claims to Jerusalem and its dependent towns were advanced by the forceful Daimbert, Archbishop of Pisa, who, backed by Bohemund, became patriarch a short time later. Godfrey, who in reality had little effective power, took an oath of homage to Daimbert and managed to retain control of his small state until his death on July 18, 1100, near Tiberias. According to Moslem sources, he was killed in battle.

Godfrey was the first Western ruler in Jerusalem, and this undoubtedly helped form the legend in later literature in which he was transformed into the model for the valorous Christian knight, the Chevalier au Cygne (Swan Knight). Dante, in the *Divine Comedy*, places him with the warrior-saints in Paradise. There is, however, no reliable evidence for his unusual piety or for his extraordinary chivalric qualities. His chief accomplishment remains the establishment of a workable feudal administration in Jerusalem based on customary fief holding and oaths of loyalty. That he was able to do this in the face of overt and continual hostility from friends and enemies says much about the character of the man.

Further Reading

The most satisfactory and dispassionate biography of Godfrey is John C. Anderssohn, *The Ancestry and Life of Godfrey of Bouillon* (1947). Sir Steven Runciman, *A History of the Crusades* (1951-1954), and Kenneth M. Setton, ed., *A History of the Crusades* (1955-1962; 2d ed. 1969), provide helpful background material. □

tended to isolate him from the mass of Americans, especially politicians. The philosopher William James, who acknowledged an intellectual debt to Godkin, wrote that Godkin "couldn't imagine a different kind of creature from himself in politics," and an opponent once said that Godkin approved of nothing since the birth of Christ.

In the early 1880s Godkin's sphere of influence expanded when the *Nation* merged with a daily newspaper, the *New York Evening Post,* and he became editor of both. The *Evening Post* and the *Nation* led the bolt of the so-called Mugwumps, who refused to support the Republican party's somewhat-tarnished 1884 candidate for president, James G. Blaine. Godkin continued his battles until failing health forced his retirement in 1899. He died in May 1902.

Further Reading

Rollo Ogden edited the *Life and Letters of Edwin Lawrence Godkin* (2 vols., 1907). An anthology of the *Nation,* with an introductory history favorable toward Godkin, is *Fifty Years of American Idealism: The New York Nation, 1865-1915,* edited by Gustav Pollak (1915). Allan Nevins, *The Evening Post: A Century of Journalism* (1922), concentrates on the career of William Cullen Bryant, a previous editor, but deals with Godkin as well. See also W. M. Armstrong, *E. L. Godkin and American Foreign Policy, 1865-1900* (1957).

Additional Sources

Armstrong, William M., *E. L. Godkin: a biography,* Albany: State University of New York Press, 1978. ☐

Edwin Lawrence Godkin

The British-born American journalist Edwin Lawrence Godkin (1831-1902) edited the *Nation,* a politically influential weekly magazine.

E dwin Lawrence Godkin was born in Ireland, the son of English parents. He studied in an English public school and at Queen's College in Belfast before moving to London to study law. He soon began work in publishing and later became a correspondent for the *London Daily News.* From 1853 to 1855 he covered the Crimean War and then toured the United States, traveling through the South and West writing articles on slavery. He moved to New York City, completed his law studies, and was admitted to the New York bar in 1858.

Godkin continued writing for the *London Daily News* and also penned editorials for the *New York Times.* He soon conceived of founding a political and intellectual journal patterned after England's famous *Spectator.* By 1865 he had raised the money and the first issue of the *Nation* appeared.

The circulation of the *Nation* was never large, rarely rising above 10,000, but it rapidly became influential. It was read by a select company of American opinion makers: editors, politicians, professors, and writers. Godkin used it to advocate low tariffs, civil service reform, and reduced government expenditures and to attack political corruption. His ideas had force and influence, but his doctrinaire mind

Sidney Godolphin

The English statesman Sidney Godolphin, 1st Earl of Godolphin (1645-1712), was head of the Treasury during the first great 18th-century war against France and successfully financed the most costly military and naval operations undertaken by England to that time.

Y ounger son of an old Cornish family, Sidney Godolphin was born about June 15, 1645. While a young man he served in the royal household, on two diplomatic missions, and as a member of Parliament before finding his real vocation at the Treasury. He was given a peerage by Charles II in 1684, and Charles relied on him during the last years of his reign. "Sidney is never in the way," he said, "and never out of the way."

During the reign of James II, which followed that of Charles, Godolphin was overshadowed by that king's Catholic advisers. He was, however, one of the last to desert James II, who was deposed during the Glorious Revolution of 1688. James's Dutch successor, William III, also recognized Godolphin's ability and twice made him head of the Treasury (1690-1696, 1700-1701). The Godolphin and Marlborough families had great influence with Princess

Anne, the heiress to the throne, and in 1698 Godolphin's son was married to Lord Marlborough's daughter.

Soon after Anne became queen (1702), England plunged into war with France. The Queen placed Marlborough in charge of the war and Godolphin at the head of the Treasury, where he had the important task of financing Marlborough's campaigns. Relying on long-term borrowing, he successfully found ways and means to conduct a long and successful war without endangering the government's credit—a notable achievement. He was also a leader in negotiating the Treaty of Union with Scotland, whereby that country became an integral part of the new United Kingdom of Great Britain (1707).

Godolphin was less successful as a politician. Known as a churchman and Tory in previous reigns, he was forced to break with the Tories over the conduct of the war. As he relied more heavily on the Whigs, with their support among Nonconformists and the commercial and financial interests, he lost the support of his Church and Tory associates. Eventually he was forced to break with his most useful political associate, Robert Harley, Speaker of the House of Commons and later secretary of state. Disliking Godolphin's growing alliance with the Whigs, Harley schemed to supplant the Marlborough-Godolphin administration with one of his own. He finally succeeded, using his influence with the Queen and profiting from general discontent over the prolonging of the war. Godolphin, who had been made an earl in 1706, was dismissed in August 1710. Two years later, on Sept. 15, 1712, he died at the London home of his friend Marlborough.

Further Reading

Sir Tresham Lever, *Godolphin: His Life and Times* (1952), a biography, is not adequate on the financial aspects or on the party politics of the period. P. G. M. Dickson, *The Financial Revolution in England* (1967), is excellent. Robert Walcott, *English Politics in the Early Eighteenth Century* (1956), and Geoffrey Holmes, *British Politics in the Age of Anne* (1967), cover party politics from contrasting viewpoints. Many of Godolphin's letters to Marlborough are printed in William Coxe, *Memoirs of John, Duke of Marlborough* (3 vols., 1818-1819; 2d ed., 6 vols., 1820).

Additional Sources

Dickinson, William Calvin, *Sidney Godolphin, Lord Treasurer, 1702-1710,* Lewiston: E. Mellen Press, 1990.

Sundstrom, Roy A., *Sidney Godolphin: servant of the state,* Newark: University of Delaware Press; London: Associated University Presses, 1992. □

Manuel de Godoy y Álvarez de Faria

The Spanish statesman Manuel de Godoy y Álvarez de Faria (1767-1851) was the favorite of Maria Luisa, Queen of Spain, and her husband, Charles IV. He was the most important political figure in Spain between 1792 and 1808.

Manuel de Godoy was born in Badajoz on March 12, 1767, of noble but poor parents. He received a limited education, and in 1784, at the age of 17, he went to Madrid, where he was admitted to the Royal Guards. At this time he was an unusually handsome young man, with a gracious smile and bold, black eyes.

In September 1788 the young guardsman came to the attention of Maria Luisa of Naples, the domineering wife of the heir to the throne of Spain. She became extremely fond of Godoy, a fondness which her husband came to share. In later years Godoy was accused of being Maria Luisa's lover, but there is no real evidence to support this allegation.

In December 1788 Charles III died and was succeeded by his son Charles IV. Godoy's rise in the new reign was meteoric. He was created Duke of Alcudia and a grandee of Spain, and in 1792, at the age of 25, he replaced the Count of Aranda as head of the government. Godoy held that post until 1798, when he was forced to resign; in 1801 he returned to office.

In 1796 Godoy worked out an alliance with France, and from then until 1808 Spain and England were almost continuously at war. It was a costly and unsuccessful war, and as the years passed Godoy became more and more unpopular. By 1807 a conspiracy to overthrow him, centered on the heir to the throne, Ferdinand, had developed. In

March 1808, at Aranjuez, the conspirators acted. With the help of a well-organized riot, they frightened Charles into dismissing Godoy and abdicating in favor of his son, who now became Ferdinand VII.

By this time Napoleon had decided to replace the Spanish Bourbons, his allies, with a member of his own family. Ferdinand was lured to Bayonne in April 1808. Soon Maria Luisa, Charles, and Godoy were also sent there by the French, who had been moving into Spain since autumn 1807. At Bayonne, Napoleon forced the Spanish royal house into abdicating in his favor. A few months later Napoleon's younger brother entered Spain as Joseph I.

After the events at Bayonne, Maria Luisa, Charles, and Godoy went to live in Italy. Maria Luisa died there on Jan. 2, 1819, and Charles died a few weeks later. Godoy was with them to the end.

After the withdrawal of the French armies from Spain in 1814, Ferdinand returned as king. While he lived, Godoy was not allowed back in his country. On Ferdinand's death in 1833 Godoy went to Madrid in the hope that he would have his properties restored to him, but he failed. He finally settled in Paris and died there on Oct. 4, 1851.

Further Reading

The most useful biography of Godoy in English is Edmund B. D'Auvergne, *Godoy: The Queen's Favorite* (1912). For a scholarly and readable account of the political, social, and economic situation in Spain during this period see Raymond Carr, *Spain, 1808-1939* (1966). □

Boris Feodorovich Godunov

Boris Feodorovich Godunov (ca. 1551-1605) was czar of Russia from 1598 to 1605. Although an able and intelligent ruler, he came to suspect widespread subversion and treason and more and more resorted to political terror.

B oris Godunov was born in Moscow. He was a member of the ancient Russian family of Saburov-Godunov of Tatar origin, which migrated from the Golden Horde in the 14th century. The family was close to the Moscow court, and Boris became a favorite of Ivan IV. Although he could probably do no more than sign his name and during his whole life never read a book, Godunov had a natural wit and intelligence which the relatively learned Ivan appreciated. While not an *oprichnik,* (member of the nobility associated with the court) Godunov was linked with the *oprichnina* by his marriage to the daughter of Maliuta Skuratov, perhaps the most notorious *oprichnik* of all and a favorite of Ivan. In 1580 Godunov was promoted to the rank of boyar on the marriage of his sister to Feodor, the son of Ivan IV.

The Regent

When Ivan IV died in 1584, Feodor became czar of Russia. Feodor, however, had the mentality of a child and was temperamentally incapable of taking initiative. Rule, therefore, passed to a dual regency of Nikita Romanovich Yuriev, the Czar's uncle, and Boris Godunov. With the death of Yuriev in 1586, Godunov became Russia's new master in all but name.

Godunov kept a separate court of his own and dealt directly with foreign powers. He is believed to have controlled completely the machinery of the government, especially the security police, headed by his cousin, Simon Godunov, which he used to eliminate his political rivals.

During Godunov's regency, Muscovy's warlike operations dating back to the reign of Ivan IV continued on the various frontiers. In 1590 the Russians became engaged in a war with Sweden that lasted until 1595 and resulted in Moscow's recovery of the territories on the shores of the Gulf of Finland lost under Ivan IV. Sweden, however, retained the port of Narva, which was the real object of Russian ambitions.

Russia also resumed its advance in western Siberia and strengthened its hold there by establishing new military and trading outposts. Russian infiltration in the northern Caucasus continued, and in 1598 Moscow established relations with Georgia.

Significant developments also took place in domestic affairs. Taking advantage of the visit to Moscow by the Patriarch of Constantinople, who came to Russia in quest of alms, Godunov obtained his consent to the elevation of the head of the Russian Church to the rank of patriarch. Job, a nominee of Godunov, was elected by a Russian Church Council in 1589 as the first incumbent of the new office.

Godunov was interested in learning from the West and even thought of establishing a university in Moscow, but he had to abandon the idea because of opposition from the clergy. He did, however, send 18 young men to study abroad. He also promoted foreign trade, concluding commercial treaties with England and with the Hansa.

The Czar

It was not surprising that after Feodor's death in 1598 the head of the Russian Church offered Godunov the crown on behalf of the nation. Although Godunov was well fitted by experience and ability to become czar, he refused the crown, insisting on the convocation of a national assembly. The assembly met in 1598 and duly elected Godunov to the throne. Godunov acquired, however, unlimited autocratic power like any hereditary autocrat.

In spite of all his efforts, Godunov's brief reign witnessed tragic events. In 1601 famine brought disaster to the people. The crops failed again in 1602 and also, to a considerable extent, in 1603. Although the government tried to feed the population of Moscow free of charge, send supplies to other towns, and find employment for the destitute, its measures availed little against the calamity. It has been estimated that more than 100,000 people perished in the capital alone. More and more peasants fled from the center of Muscovy to join the Cossacks. Godunov's attempts to restrain them failed, and mass banditry developed.

The people blamed Godunov for these problems. Rumors spread that he was a criminal and a usurper and that Russia was being punished for his sins. It was rumored that Godunov had plotted to kill Prince Dimitry, the son of Ivan IV, but had mistakenly murdered another boy. It was further alleged that the true prince had escaped and would return to claim his rightful inheritance.

In 1603 a claimant to the throne did appear, professing to be Czarevich Dimitry. The true identity of the Pretender is not known, but it was as Grishka Otrepyev, a runaway monk and former serf of the Romanov family, that Godunov officially denounced him. The Pretender spent the year 1603 canvasing help in Poland. In 1604 he crossed into Muscovy at the head of over a thousand adventurers, chiefly Poles. He proclaimed himself rightful heir to the Russian throne and denounced Godunov as a usurper. A measure of Godunov's unpopularity was the fact that Cossacks and disaffected elements in southwest Russia rallied to the invader in large numbers. As Dimitry marched toward Muscovy, many towns went over to him without a shot being fired.

Czar Godunov himself seemed paralyzed in the Kremlin. He did not personally take the field against the Pretender, although he did attempt to confirm that Prince Dimitry was dead. When it seemed that his efforts might succeed, Godunov died suddenly on April 23, 1605. He was succeeded by his son Feodor II. But in a few months riots broke out in Moscow, and Feodor and his mother were murdered. In June 1605 the Pretender entered the capital in triumph.

Further Reading

One biography of Boris Godunov is Stephen Graham's inadequate *Boris Godunof* (1933). A fictionalized account is Aleksandr Pushkin's drama, *Boris Godunov* (1831; trans. 1918). A good study of the Pretender episode is Philip L. Barbour, *Dimitry, Called the Pretender: Tsar and Great Prince of All Russia, 1605-1606* (1966). Sergei F. Platonov, *The Time of Troubles* (1923; trans. 1970), is a classic study of the period. George Vernadsky, *A History of Russia,* vol. 5, 2 parts (1969), is recommended for general background.

Additional Sources

Emerson, Caryl, *Boris Godunov: transpositions of a Russian theme,* Bloomington: Indiana University Press, 1986. □

William Godwin

The English political theorist and writer William Godwin (1756-1836) was a libertarian anarchist and utopian proponent of a natural, rational, secular society.

William Godwin, son of an Independent minister, was born on March 3, 1756, at Wisbeck, Cambridgeshire. Trained for the ministry at Hoxton Academy, a Dissenting college, he became a Sandemanian minister in East Anglia and the Home Counties from 1778 to 1783. The Sandemanians, a radical, fundamentalist sect expelled by the Presbyterians and accepted by the Independents, continued to influence Godwin's secular thought even after he became an atheist. In particular, he retained Sandemanian doctrines of communal property, of opposition to the authority of church and state, and of the progressive reform of individual character and conduct.

Godwin's earliest work, published anonymously, was a prospectus for a private school, *An Account of the Seminary That Will Be Opened . . . in Surrey* (1784). This revealed his characteristic belief in an egalitarian society which would form human nature through a continuous educational process, benevolently encouraging individual reason, justice, and moral law. Godwin developed these principles in his most important work, *An Enquiry concerning the Principles of Political Justice and Its Influence on General Virtue and Happiness* (1793). In part a refutation of Edmund Burke's *Reflections on the French Revolution* (1790), the *Enquiry* rejected property and power as just foundations for political society. Living in a time of rapid industrial development, Godwin longed for a simple communal economy in which individuals would progress indefinitely toward increasing rationality and equity.

Of Godwin's 35 other works the most important are *The Adventures of Caleb Williams* (1794), a social novel;

The Enquirer (1797); *History of the Commonwealth of England* (1824); and *Thoughts on Man* (1831). He died in London on April 7, 1836.

Godwin's personal life seldom approached his philosophical ideals of individual nobility and generosity. In 1797 he married the radical feminist Mary Wollstonecroft, who died 6 months later. Left with an infant daughter, he married Mary Jane Clairmont in 1801. His life was rarely conventional, but he was outraged when his daughter, Mary, went to live with the married Percy Bysshe Shelley, long Godwin's financial supporter and committed disciple.

The influence of Godwin's writings on his younger contemporaries was considerable. Such disparate figures as the utopian socialist Robert Owen, the radical Francis Place, the socialist economist William Thompson, and even Karl Marx were impressed by Godwin's political and economic thought.

Further Reading

The two most acceptable studies of Godwin in the context of his time are George Woodcock, *William Godwin* (1946), and David Fleisher, *William Godwin: A Study in Liberalism* (1951). Other works include H. N. Brailsford, *Shelley, Godwin, and Their Circle* (1913; 2d ed. 1954); Ford K. Brown, *The Life of William Godwin* (1926); and A. E. Rodway, ed., *Godwin and the Age of Transition* (1952). Godwin is placed in the tradition of anarchist thought in George Woodcock, *Anarchism: A History of Libertarian Ideas and Movements* (1962), a fine study of thought and society.

Additional Sources

Brown, Ford Keeler, *The life of William Godwin*, Norwood, Pa.: Norwood Editions, 1975; Philadelphia: R. West, 1977.

Grylls, R. Glynn (Rosalie Glynn), *William Godwin & his world*, Folcroft, Pa. Folcroft Library Editions, 1974.

Marshall, Peter H., *William Godwin*, New Haven: Yale University Press, 1984.

Robinson, Victor, *William Godwin and Mary Wollstonecraft*, Folcroft, Pa.: Folcroft Library Editions, 1978.

Woodcock, George, *William Godwin: a biographical study*, Folcroft, Pa.: Folcroft Library Editions, 1975. □

Joseph Paul Goebbels

The German politician Joseph Paul Goebbels (1897-1945) directed the extensive system of propaganda in Nazi Germany.

Joseph Goebbels was born on Oct. 29, 1897, in the Rhenish textile city of Rheydt, the son of a pious Catholic bookkeeper of modest means. With the support of stipends granted by Catholic organizations, the young Goebbels attended the university and earned a doctorate in literature in 1922.

After a number of unsuccessful attempts as writer, journalist, and speaker, Goebbels joined the National Socialist organization in northern Germany under Gregor Strasser in 1924 and edited various publications of this group from 1924 to 1926. In the late summer of 1925 Goebbels first met Hitler, was immediately enamored with the Führer, and broke with Strasser in November 1926 to go to Berlin as *Gauleiter* (district leader) upon Hitler's request. Here he founded and edited the party weekly, *Der Angriff* (The Attack). He took over the propaganda machine of the party in 1928 and became minister of popular enlightenment and propaganda with Hitler's rise to power in 1933.

From this position Goebbels built a machinery of thought control, which not only served as an effective support for the Nazi regime and later the war effort, but also actively limited and shaped all forms of artistic and intellectual expression to conform to the ideals of National Socialism and, most particularly, racist anti-Semitism. This involved the control of the press through censorship and removal of Jewish and non-Nazi editors and the establishment of government-sponsored radio stations, newspapers, and magazines. Jewish artists, musicians, writers, and even natural scientists—many of Germany's ablest men and women—were removed and often sent to concentration camps. Works by Jewish composers and writers were burned and outlawed. "Decadent" modern art was replaced by a Nazi standard of pseudoromantic, sentimental art. Education on all levels was similarly controlled.

Mass rallies, ever-present loudspeaker systems, and the mass production and distribution of "people's radios" ensured wide dissemination of Hitler's demagogic appeals to the nation. Goebbels, who had an unusually appealing speaking voice, increasingly became the Führer's channel of communication with the population. Most notorious was Goebbels's speech in August 1944 in the Sports Palace of Berlin, in which he fanatically called for total war.

His fanaticism lasted to the end. In 1945 Goebbels called for the destruction of the German people since they had not been able to win victory. He stayed with Hitler even after Hermann Göring and Heinrich Himmler had sought contacts with the Allies. Goebbels killed himself and his entire family in Berlin on May 1, 1945, only hours after Hitler's suicide.

Further Reading

Both sets of Goebbels's diaries are available in English: Louis P. Lochner, ed. and trans., *The Goebbels Diaries, 1942-43* (1948), and Helmut Heiber, ed., *The Early Goebbels Diaries, 1925-26*, translated by Oliver Watson (1962). Of Goebbels's books, only his early diary-memoir *My Part in Germany's Fight* (trans. 1940) is readily available in English. The most extensive biography of Goebbels in English, Ernest K. Bramstedt, *Goebbels and National Socialist Propaganda, 1925-1945* (1965), is also a brilliant study of the totalitarian propaganda machine. A shorter, more biographical study by journalist-historians Roger Manvell and Heinrich Fraenkel, *Dr. Goebbels: His Life and Death* (1960), is perhaps more accessible and exciting for the general reader. The older biographies—Rudolf Semmler, *Goebbels: The Man next to Hitler* (1947); Curt Riess, *Joseph Goebbels* (1948); and Erich Ebermayer and Hans-Otto Meissner, *Evil Genius: The Story of Joseph Goebbels* (trans. 1953)—are less scholarly but still useful and interesting.

Additional Sources

Goebbels, Joseph, *The Goebbels diaries, 1939-1941,* London: H. Hamilton, 1982.

Goebbels, Joseph, *My part in Germany's fight,* New York: H. Fertig, 1979.

Heiber, Helmut, *Goebbels,* New York: Da Capo Press, 1983, 1972.

Semmler, Rudolf, *Goebbels, the man next to Hitler,* New York: AMS Press, 1981. □

Maria Goeppert-Mayer

In 1963, Maria Goeppert-Mayer became the first woman to receive the Nobel Prize in physics. She earned the prize for her work on the structure of the atomic nucleus.

Maria Goeppert-Mayer was one of the inner circle of nuclear physicists who developed the atomic fission bomb at the secret laboratory at Los Alamos, New Mexico, during World War II. Through her theoretical research with nuclear physicists Enrico Fermi and Edward Teller, Goeppert-Mayer developed a model for the structure of atomic nuclei. In 1963, for her work on nuclear structure, she became the first woman awarded the Nobel Prize for theoretical physics, sharing the prize with J. Hans D. Jensen, a German physicist. The two scientists, who had reached the same conclusions independently, later collaborated on a book explaining their model.

An only child, Goeppert-Mayer was born Maria Göppert on July 28, 1906, in the German city of Kattowitz in Upper Silesia (now Katowice, Poland). When she was four, her father, Dr. Friedrich Göppert, was appointed professor of pediatrics at the University at Göttingen, Germany. Situated in an old medieval town, the university had historically been respected for its mathematics department, but was on its way to becoming the European center for yet another discipline—theoretical physics. Maria's mother, Maria Wolff Göppert, was a former teacher of piano and French who delighted in entertaining faculty members with lavish dinner parties and providing a home filled with flowers and music for her only daughter.

Dr. Göppert was a most progressive pediatrician for the times, as he started a well-baby clinic and believed that all children, male or female, should be adventuresome risk-takers. His philosophy on child rearing had a profound effect on his daughter, who idolized her father and treasured her long country walks with him, collecting fossils and learning the names of plants. Because the Göpperts came from several generations of university professors, it was unstated but expected that Maria would continue the family tradition.

When Maria was just eight, World War I interrupted the family's rather idyllic university life with harsh wartime deprivation. After the war, life was still hard because of postwar inflation and food shortages. Maria Göppert at-

tended a small private school run by female suffragists to ready young girls for university studies. The school went bankrupt when Göppert had completed only two of the customary three years of preparatory school. Nonetheless, she took and passed her university entrance exam.

The University of Göttingen that Göppert entered in 1924 was in the process of becoming a center for the study of quantum mechanics—the mathematical study of the behavior of atomic particles. Many well-known physicists visited Göttingen, including Niels Bohr, a Danish physicist who developed a model of the atom. Noted physicist Max Born joined the Göttingen faculty and became a close friend of Göppert's family. Göppert, now enrolled as a student, began attending Max Born's physics seminars and decided to study physics instead of mathematics, with an eye toward teaching. Her prospects of being taken seriously were slim: there was only one female professor at Göttingen, and she taught for "love," receiving no salary.

In 1927 Göppert's father died. She continued her study, determined to finish her doctorate in physics. She spent a semester in Cambridge, England, where she learned English and met Ernest Rutherford, the discoverer of the electron. Upon her return to Göttingen, her mother began taking student boarders into their grand house. One was an American physical chemistry student from California, Joseph E. Mayer, studying in Göttingen on a grant. Over the next several years, Maria and Joe became close, going hiking, skiing, swimming and playing tennis. When they married, in 1930, Maria adopted the hyphenated form of their names. (When they later moved to the United States, the spelling of her family name was anglicized to "Goeppert.") Soon after her marriage she completed her doctorate with a thesis entitled "On Elemental Processes with Two Quantum Jumps."

After Joseph Mayer finished his studies, the young scientists moved to the United States, where he had been offered a job at Johns Hopkins University in Baltimore, Maryland. Goeppert-Mayer found it difficult to adjust. She was not considered eligible for an appointment at the same university as her husband, but rather was considered a volunteer associate, what her biographer Joan Dash calls a "fringe benefit" wife. She had a tiny office, little pay, and no significant official responsibilities. Nonetheless, her position did allow her to conduct research on energy transfer on solid surfaces with physicist Karl Herzfeld, and she collaborated with him and her husband on several papers. Later, she turned her attention to the quantum mechanical electronic levels of benzene and of some dyes. During summers she returned to Göttingen, where she wrote several papers with Max Born on beta ray decay—the emissions of high-speed electrons that are given off by radioactive nuclei.

These summers of physics research were cut off as Germany was again preparing for war. Max Born left Germany for the safety of England. Returning to the states, Goeppert-Mayer applied for her American citizenship and she and Joe started a family. They would have two children, Marianne and Peter. Soon she became friends with Edward Teller, a Hungarian refugee who would play a key role in the development of the hydrogen bomb.

When Joe unexpectedly lost his position at Johns Hopkins, he and Goeppert-Mayer left for Columbia University in New York. There they wrote a book together, *Statistical Mechanics,* which became a classic in the field. As Goeppert-Mayer had no teaching credentials to place on the title page, their friend Harold Urey, a Nobel Prize-winning chemist, arranged for her to give some lectures so that she could be listed as "lecturer in chemistry at Columbia."

In New York, Goeppert-Mayer made the acquaintance of Enrico Fermi, winner of the Nobel Prize for physics for his work on radioactivity. Fermi had recently emigrated from Italy and was at Columbia on a grant researching nuclear fission. Nuclear fission—splitting an atom in a way that released energy—had been discovered by German scientists Otto Hahn, Fritz Strassmann, and Lise Meitner. The German scientists had bombarded uranium nuclei with neutrons, resulting in the release of energy. Because Germany was building its arsenal for war, Fermi had joined other scientists in convincing the United States government that it must institute a nuclear program of its own so as not to be at Hitler's mercy should Germany develop a nuclear weapon. Goeppert-Mayer joined Fermi's team of researchers, although once again the arrangement was informal and without pay.

In 1941, the United States formally entered World War II. Goeppert-Mayer was offered her first real teaching job, a half-time position at Sarah Lawrence College in Bronxville, New York. A few months later she was invited by Harold Urey to join a research group he was assembling at Columbia University to separate uranium–235, which is capable

of nuclear fission, from the more abundant isotope uranium–238, which is not. The group, which worked in secret, was given the code name SAM—Substitute Alloy Metals. The uranium was to be the fuel for a nuclear fission bomb.

Like many scientists, Goeppert-Mayer had mixed feelings about working on the development of an atomic bomb. (Her friend Max Born, for instance, had refused to work on the project.) She had to keep her work a secret from her husband, even though he himself was working on defense-related work, often in the Pacific. Moreover, while she loved her adopted country, she had many friends and relatives in Germany. To her relief, the war in Europe was over early in 1945, before the bomb was ready. However, at Los Alamos Laboratory in New Mexico the bomb was still being developed. At Edward Teller's request, Goeppert-Mayer made several visits to Los Alamos to meet with other physicists, including Niels Bohr and Enrico Fermi, who were working on uranium fission. In August of 1945 atomic bombs were dropped on the Japanese cities of Hiroshima and Nagasaki with a destructive ferocity never before seen. According to biographer Joan Dash, by this time Goeppert-Mayer's ambivalence about the nuclear weapons program had turned to distaste, and she was glad she had played a relatively small part in the development of such a deadly weapon.

After the war, Goeppert-Mayer returned to teach at Sarah Lawrence. Then, in 1946, her husband was offered a full professorship at the University of Chicago's newly established Institute of Nuclear Studies, where Fermi, Teller, and Urey were also working. Goeppert-Mayer was offered an unpaid position as voluntary associate professor; the university had a rule, common at the time, against hiring both a husband and wife as professors. However, soon afterwards, Goeppert-Mayer was asked to become a senior physicist at the Argonne National Laboratory, where a nuclear reactor was under construction. It was the first time she had been offered a position and salary that put her on an even footing with her colleagues.

Again her association with Edward Teller was valuable. He asked her to work on his theory about the origin of the elements. They found that some elements, such as tin and lead, were more abundant than could be predicted by current theories. The same elements were also unusually stable. When Goeppert-Mayer charted the number of protons and neutrons in the nuclei of these elements, she noticed that the same few numbers recurred over and over again. Eventually she began to call these her "magic numbers." When Teller began focusing his attention on nuclear weapons and lost interest in the project, Goeppert-Mayer began discussing her ideas with Enrico Fermi.

Goeppert-Mayer had identified seven "magic numbers": 2, 8, 20, 28, 50, 82, and 126. Any element that had one of these numbers of protons or neutrons was very stable, and she wondered why. She began to think of a shell model for the nucleus, similar to the orbital model of electrons spinning around the nucleus. Perhaps the nucleus of an atom was something like an onion, with layers of protons and neutrons revolving around each other. Her "magic numbers" would represent the points at which the various layers, or "shells," would be complete. Goeppert-Mayer's likening of the nucleus to an onion led fellow physicist Wolfgang Pauli to dub her the "Madonna of the Onion." Further calculations suggested the presence of "spin-orbit coupling": the particles in the nucleus, she hypothesized, were both spinning on their axes and orbiting a central point—like spinning dancers, in her analogy, some moving clockwise and others counter-clockwise.

Goeppert-Mayer published her hypothesis in *Physical Review* in 1949. A month before her work appeared, a similar paper was published by J. Hans D. Jensen of Heidelberg, Germany. Goeppert-Mayer and Jensen began corresponding and eventually decided to write a book together. During the four years that it took to complete the book, Jensen stayed with the Goeppert-Mayers in Chicago. *Elementary Theory of Nuclear Shell Structure* gained widespread acceptance on both sides of the Atlantic for the theory they had discovered independently.

In 1959, Goeppert-Mayer and her husband were both offered positions at the University of California's new San Diego campus. Unfortunately, soon after settling into a new home in La Jolla, California, Goeppert-Mayer suffered a stroke which left an arm paralyzed. Some years earlier she had also lost the hearing in one ear. Slowed but not defeated, Goeppert-Mayer continued her work.

In November of 1963 Goeppert-Mayer received word that she and Jensen were to share the Nobel Prize for physics with Eugene Paul Wigner, a colleague studying quantum mechanics who had once been skeptical of her magic numbers. Goeppert-Mayer had finally been accepted as a serious scientist. According to biographer Olga Opfell, she would later comment that the work itself had been more exciting than winning the prize.

Goeppert-Mayer continued to teach and do research in San Diego, as well as grow orchids and give parties at her house in La Jolla. She enjoyed visits with her granddaughter, whose parents were daughter Marianne, an astronomer, and son-in-law Donat Wentzel, an astrophysicist. Her son Peter was now an assistant professor of economics, keeping up Goeppert-Mayer's family tradition of university teaching.

Goeppert-Mayer was made a member of the National Academy of Sciences and received several honorary doctorates. Her health, however, began to fail. A lifelong smoker debilitated by her stroke, she began to have heart problems. She had a pacemaker inserted in 1968. Late in 1971, Goeppert-Mayer suffered a heart attack that left her in a coma. She died on February 20, 1972.

Further Reading

Dash, Joan, *The Triumph of Discovery: Women Scientists Who Won the Nobel Prize,* Messner, 1991.
Opfell, Olga S., *The Lady Laureates: Women Who Have Won the Nobel Prize,* Scarecrow, 1978, pp. 194–208.
Sach, Robert G., *Maria Goeppert-Mayer, 1906–1972: A Biographical Memoir,* National Academy of Science of the United States, 1979. □

George Washington Goethals

U.S. Army officer and engineer George Washington Goethals (1858-1928) succeeded in building the Panama Canal after many others had failed.

On June 29, 1858, George W. Goethals was born in Brooklyn, N.Y., to a Dutch immigrant family. Intending to become a physician, he attended the City College of New York for 3 years. He then won a coveted appointment to the U.S. Military Academy at West Point, from which he graduated in 1880, second in a class of 52. He was one of two members of his class selected to go on to engineering school.

From 1882 to 1903 Goethals served with distinction on projects dealing with river and harbor improvements. He taught engineering at West Point (1885-1889, 1898-1900) and was assistant to the Army chief of engineers (1894-1898). During the Spanish-American War he was chief engineer of the I Army Corps, and from 1903 to 1907 he was on the general staff of the Army.

Meanwhile the United States had begun construction of the Panama Canal, but the Isthmian Canal Commission and the two civilian engineers who headed the project had made slow progress. In 1907 President Theodore Roosevelt decided to place a military engineer in complete charge, picking Goethals over many other talented engineering officers.

Combining administrative ability with professional skill, Goethals overcame enormous obstacles of engineering, climate, disease, and living conditions before the canal was officially opened in 1914. The most difficult part of building the canal, Goethals later wrote, was the problem caused by the "human element." As many as 45,000 persons, of many nationalities and speaking a variety of languages, worked on the canal. Goethals made himself accessible to all, heard complaints, visited every aspect of the project, and had an uncanny mastery of the smallest details. In the process, sanitary officer William C. Gorgas succeeded in eliminating yellow fever.

Goethals served as governor of the Canal Zone from 1914 to 1917. During World War I he was in charge of the purchase, storage, and transport of all supplies and the movement of all troops within the United States and overseas, winning the Distinguished Service Medal for his achievements. After retiring from the Army in 1919, he was a private consulting engineer on many important projects, including the Holland Tunnel and the George Washington Bridge, connecting Manhattan and New Jersey, and the Goethals Bridge, connecting Staten Island and New Jersey. He died on Jan. 21, 1928, and was buried in the Army West Point cemetery.

Further Reading

Goethals's life is best described in Joseph Bucklin Bishop and Farnham Bishop, *Goethals: Genius of the Panama Canal* (1930). See also Gerstle Mack, *The Land Divided: A History of the Panama Canal and Other Isthmian Canal Projects* (1944). □

Johann Wolfgang von Goethe

The German poet, dramatist, novelist, and scientist Johann Wolfgang von Goethe (1749-1832), who embraced many fields of human endeavor, ranks as the greatest of all German poets. Of all modern men of genius, Goethe is the most universal.

The many-sided activities of Johann Wolfgang von Goethe stand as a tribute to the greatness of his mind and his personality. Napoleon I's oft-quoted remark about Goethe, made after their meeting at Erfurt—"Voilà un homme!" (There's a man!)—reflects later humanity's judgment of Goethe's genius. Not only, however, does Goethe rank with Homer, Dante Alighieri, and William Shakespeare as a supreme creator, but also in his life itself— incredibly long, rich, and filled with a calm optimism— Goethe perhaps created his greatest work, surpassing even his *Faust,* Germany's most national drama.

Goethe was born in Frankfurt am Main on Aug. 28, 1749. He was the eldest son of Johann Kaspar Goethe and Katharina Elisabeth Textor Goethe. Goethe's father, of Thuringian stock, had studied law at the University of Leipzig. He did not practice his profession, but in 1742 he acquired the title of *kaiserlicher Rat* (imperial councilor). In 1748 he married the daughter of Frankfurt's burgomaster. Of the children born to Goethe's parents only Johann and his sister Cornelia survived to maturity. She married Goethe's friend J. G. Schlosser in 1773. Goethe's lively and impulsive disposition and his remarkable imaginative powers probably came to him from his mother, and he likely inherited his reserved manner and his stability of character from his stern and often pedantic father.

Early Life

Goethe has left a memorable picture of his childhood, spent in a large patrician house on the Grosse Hirschgraben in Frankfurt, in his autobiography *Dichtung und Wahrheit.* He and Cornelia were educated at home by private tutors. Books, pictures, and a marionette theater kindled the young Goethe's quick intellect and imagination.

During the Seven Years War the French occupied Frankfurt. A French theatrical troupe established itself, and Goethe, through his grandfather's influence, was allowed free access to its performances. He much improved his knowledge of French by attending the performances and by his contact with the actors. Meantime, his literary

proclivities had begun to manifest themselves in religious poems, a novel, and a prose epic.

In October 1765 Goethe—then 16 years old—left Frankfurt for the University of Leipzig. He remained in Leipzig until 1768, pursuing his legal studies with zeal. During this period he also took lessons in drawing from A. F. Oeser, the director of the Leipzig Academy of Painting. Art always remained an abiding interest throughout Goethe's life.

During his Leipzig years Goethe began writing light Anacreontic verses. Much of his poetry of these years was inspired by his passionate love for Anna Katharina Schönkopf, the daughter of a wine merchant in whose tavern he dined. She was the "Annette" for whom the collection of lyrics discovered in 1895 was named.

The rupture of a blood vessel in one of his lungs put an end to Goethe's Leipzig years. From 1768 to the spring of 1770 Goethe lay ill, first in Leipzig and later at home.

It was a period of serious introspection. The Anacreontic playfulness of verse and the rococo manner of his Leipzig period were soon swept away as Goethe grew in stature as a human being and as a poet.

Study in Strasbourg

Goethe's father was determined his son should continue his legal studies. Upon his recovery, therefore, Goethe was sent to Strasbourg, the capital of Alsace and a city that lay outside the German Empire. There his true Promethean self and his poetic genius were fully awakened. One of the most important events of Goethe's Strasbourg period was his meeting with Johann Gottfried von Herder. Herder taught Goethe the significance of Gothic architecture, as exemplified by the Strasbourg Minster, and he kindled Goethe's love of Homer, Pindar, Ossian, Shakespeare, and the *Volkslied*. Without neglecting his legal studies, Goethe also studied medicine.

Perhaps the most important occurrence of this period was Goethe's love for Friederike Brion, the daughter of the pastor of the nearby village of Sesenheim. Later Goethe immortalized Friederike as Gretchen in *Faust*. She also inspired the *Friederike Songs* and many beautiful lyrics. *Kleine Blumen, kleine Blätter* and *Wie herrlich leuchtet mir die Natur!* heralded a new era in German lyric poetry.

During this Strasbourg period Goethe also reshaped his Alsatian *Heidenröslein*. His lyrical response to the Gothic architecture of Strasbourg Minster appeared in his essay *Von deutscher Baukunst* (1772). Goethe also probably planned his first important drama, *Götz von Berlichingen*, while in Strasbourg. In August 1771 Goethe obtained a licentiate in law, though not a doctor's degree. He returned to Frankfurt in September and remained there until early 1772.

"Sturm und Drang" Period

From spring to September 1772 Goethe spent 4 months in Wetzlar in order to gain experience in the legal profession at the supreme courts of the empire. However, Goethe found a more genial society in a local inn among the "Knights of the Round Table," calling himself "Götz von Berlichingen."

Goethe's passionate love for Charlotte Buff—who was the daughter of the Wetzlar *Amtmann* (bailiff) and was engaged to Johann Christian Kestner, the secretary of legation and a member of the Round Table—created a crisis. Out of its agony—Goethe's obsession with Charlotte led him almost to suicide—the poet created the world-famous novel *Die Leiden des jungen Werthers* (1774). A Rhine journey in the autumn of 1772 and intense preoccupation with his literary projects on his return to Frankfurt brought partial recovery to Goethe.

Goethe remained in Frankfurt until the autumn of 1775, and these were years of fantastic productivity. *Götz von Berlichingen* was finished in 1773. This play established the Shakespearean type of drama on the German stage and inaugurated the *Sturm und Drang* movement. Another play—*Clavigo*—soon followed. A tragedy, *Clavigo* marked considerable advancement in Goethe's art.

Die Leiden des jungen Werthers appeared in 1774. This novel, written in the epistolary style, brought Goethe international fame and spread "Werther fever" throughout Europe and even into Asia. A sentimental story of love and suicide, *Werther* utilized the private and social experiences of its author's months in Wetzlar, molding them into one of the most powerful introspective novels of all time. Its psychological impact upon Goethe's contemporaries and its influence on German literature can scarcely be exaggerated.

Many unfinished fragments—some of them magnificent—also date from these years. Goethe worked on the dramas *Caesar* and *Mahomet* and the epic *Der ewige Jude*. A fragment of *Prometheus,* a tragedy, ranks among the poet's masterpieces. Perhaps the greatest work from these years was Goethe's first dramatization of the Faust legend.

During these years Goethe's poetic genius found its own unique self. The masterpieces of this great *Sturm und Drang* period include *Wanderers Sturmlied* (1771); *Mahomets Gesang* (1772-1773); *An Schwager Kronos* (1774); *Prometheus* (1774), a symbol of the self-confident genius; and *Ganymed* (1774), the embodiment of man's abandonment to the mysteries of the universe.

In 1775 Goethe fell in love with Lili Schönemann, the daughter of a Frankfurt banker. Goethe became formally betrothed to her, and Lili inspired many beautiful lyrics. However, the worldly society Lili thrived in was not congenial to the poet. A visit to Switzerland in the summer of 1775 helped Goethe realize that this marriage might be unwise, and the engagement lapsed that autumn. *Neue Liebe, Neues Leben* and *An Belinden* (both 1775) are poetic expressions of Goethe's happiest hours with Lili, while *Auf dem See,* written on June 15, 1775, reflects his mood after he broke the spell that his love for Lili had cast upon him. Goethe also conceived another drama during these Frankfurt years and actually wrote a great part of it. However, he did not publish *Egmont* until 1788. Graf Egmont, its protagonist, is endowed with a demonic power over the sympathies of both men and women, and he represents the lighter side of Goethe's vision—a foil to Faust—and his more optimistic outlook.

Career in Weimar

On Oct. 12, 1775, the young prince of Weimar, Duke Karl August, arrived in Frankfurt and extended an invitation to Goethe to accompany him to Weimar. On November 7 Goethe arrived in the capital of the little Saxon duchy that was to remain his home for the rest of his life. The young duke soon enlisted Goethe's services in the government of his duchy, and before long Goethe had been entrusted with responsible state duties.

As minister of state, Goethe interested himself in agriculture, horticulture, and mining, all fields of economic importance to the duchy's welfare. Eventually his many state offices in Weimar and his social and political commitments became a burden and a hindrance to his creative writing. Perhaps Goethe's most irksome responsibility was the office of president of the Treasury after 1782.

Goethe made his first long stay at Weimar from November 1775 until the summer of 1786. In 1782 Emperor Joseph II conferred a knighthood on him. During these 12 years Goethe's attachment for Charlotte von Stein, the wife of a Weimar official and the mother of seven children, dominated his emotional life. A woman of refined taste and culture, Frau von Stein was 7 years Goethe's senior and was perhaps the most intellectual of the poet's many loves.

The literary output of the first Weimar period included a number of lyrics (*Wanderers Nachtlied, An den Mond,* and *Gesang der Geister über den Wassern*), ballads (*Der*

Erlkönig), a short drama (*Die Geschwister*), a dramatic satire (*Der Triumph der Empfindsamkeit*), and several *Singspiele* (*Lila; Die Fischerin; Scherz; List und Rache;* and *Jery und Bätely*). Goethe also planned a religious epic (*Die Geheimnisse*) and a tragedy (*Elpenor*). In 1777 Goethe began to write a theatrical novel, *Wilhelm Meisters theatralische Sendung.* In 1779 the prose version of his drama *Iphigenie auf Tauris* was performed.

Under Frau von Stein's influence Goethe matured as an artist as well as a personality. His course toward artistic and human harmony and renunciation was mirrored in several poems written during this period: *Harzreise im Winter* (1777); *Ein Gleiches* (1780), *Ilmenau* (1783), and *Zueignung* (1784).

Italian Journey

In September 1786 Goethe set out from Karlsbad on his memorable and intensely longed-for journey to Italy. He traveled by way of Munich, the Brenner Pass, and Lago di Garda to Verona and Venice. He arrived in Rome on Oct. 29, 1786, and soon established friendships in the circle of German artists. In the spring of 1787 Goethe traveled to Naples and Sicily, returning to Rome in June 1787. He departed for Weimar on April 2, 1788.

It would be almost impossible to overstate the importance of Goethe's Italian journey. Goethe regarded it as the high point of his life, feeling it had helped him attain a deep understanding of his poetic genius and his mission as a poet. No longer in sympathy with *Sturm und Drang* even before his departure from Weimar, Goethe was initiated into neoclassicism by his vision of the antique in Italy. Goethe returned to Weimar not only with a new artistic vision but also with a freer attitude toward life. He recorded this journey in his *Italienische Reise* at the time of his trip, but he did not publish this volume until 1816-1817.

Return to Weimar

Goethe returned from Italy unsettled and restless. Shortly afterward, his ties with Frau von Stein having been weakened by his extended stay in Italy and by lighter pleasures he had known there, Goethe took the daughter of a town official into his house as his mistress. Christiane Vulpius, although she could offer no intellectual companionship, provided the comforts of a home. Gradually, she became indispensable as a helpmate, although she was ignored by Goethe's friends and unwelcome at court. Their son August was born in 1789, and Goethe married her in 1806, when the French invasion of Weimar endangered her position.

Goethe had finished *Egmont* in Italy. Additional literary fruits of his trip were the *Römische Elegien,* which reflected Italy's pagan influences, written in 1788-1789; the iambic version of *Iphigenie auf Tauris* (1787); and a Renaissance drama, *Torquato Tasso* (1790). Goethe also planned an epic *Nausikaa* and a drama *Iphigenie auf Delphos.* *Faust* was brought an additional step forward, part of it being published in 1790 as *Faust, Ein Fragment.*

Meanwhile, two new interests engrossed Goethe and renewed his Weimar ties. In 1791 he was appointed director of the ducal theater, a position he held for 22 years; and he became increasingly absorbed in scientific pursuits. From his scientific studies in anatomy, botany, optics, meteorology, and mineralogy, he gradually reached a vision of the unity of the outward and inward worlds. Not only nature and art but also science were, in his view, governed by one organic force that rules all metamorphoses of appearances.

It is absolutely misleading, however, to suggest as some critics have that after his Italian journeys Goethe became a scientist and ceased to be a poet. In 1793 Goethe composed *Reineke Fuchs,* a profane "World Bible" in hexameters. He also took up his abandoned novel of the theater. His projected study of a young man's theatrical apprenticeship was transformed into an apprenticeship to life. *Wilhelm Meisters Lehrjahre,* varying between realism and poetic romanticism, became the archetypal *Bildungsroman.* Its influence on German literature was profound and enduring after its publication in 1795-1796.

Goethe's unique literary friendship with Friedrich von Schiller began in 1794. To it Goethe owed in great degree his renewed dedication to poetry. Goethe contributed to Schiller's new periodical *Die Horen,* composed *Xenien* with him in 1795-1796, received Schiller's encouragement to finish *Wilhelm Meisters Lehrjahre,* and undertook at his urging the studies that resulted in the epic *Hermann und Dorothea* and the fragment *Achilleis.* Schiller's urging also induced Goethe to return once more to *Faust* and to conclude the first part of it. *Xenien,* a collection of distichs, contains several masterpieces, and *Hermann und Dorothea* (1797) ranks as one of the poet's most perfect creations.

From Goethe's friendly rivalry with Schiller issued a number of ballad masterpieces: *Der Zauberlehrling, Der Gott und die Bajadere, Die Braut von Korinth, Alexis und Dora, Der neue Pausias,* and the cycle of four *Müller-Lieder.*

Goethe's classicism brought him into eventual conflict with the developing romantic movement. To present his theories, he published, in conjunction with Heinrich Meyer, from 1798 to 1800 an art review entitled *Die Propyläen.* Goethe also defended his ideals of classical beauty in 1805 in *Winckelmann und sein Jahrhundert.* But the triumphant publication of the first part of Faust in 1808 defeated Goethe's own classical ideals. It was received as a landmark of romantic art.

Last Years

The last period of Goethe's life began with Schiller's death in 1805. In 1806 he published his magnificent tribute to Schiller *Epilog zu Schillers Glocke.* In 1807 Bettina von Arnim became the latest (but not the last) of Goethe's loves, for the poet soon developed a more intense interest in Minna Herzlieb, the foster daughter of a Jena publisher.

The publication of the first part of *Faust* in 1808 was followed by the issuance the next year of a novel, *Die Wahlverwandtschaften,* an intimate psychological study of four minds. The most classical and allegorical of Goethe's works, *Pandora,* was published in 1808. The scientific treatise *Zur Farbenlehre* appeared in 1810.

In 1811 Goethe published the first volume of his auto-biography, *Aus meinem Leben, Dichtung und Wahrheit.* Volumes 2 and 3 followed in 1812 and 1814. The fourth, ending with Goethe's departure from Frankfurt in 1775 for Weimar, appeared in 1833, after his death. Additional materials for a continuation of *Dichtung und Wahrheit* into the Weimar years were collected in *Tag und Jahreshefte* (1830).

Increasingly aloof from national, political, and literary partisanship in his last period, Goethe became more and more an Olympian divinity to whose shrine at Weimar all Europe made pilgrimage. In 1819 Goethe published another masterpiece, this one a collection of lyrics inspired by his young friend Marianne von Willemer, who figures as Sulieka in the cycle. Suggested by his reading of the Persian poet Hafiz, the poems that constitute *Westöstlicher Diwan* struck another new note in German poetry with their introduction of Eastern elements.

Meanwhile, death was thinning the ranks of Goethe's acquaintances: Wieland, the last of Goethe's great literary contemporaries, died in 1813; Christiane in 1816; Charlotte von Stein in 1827; Duke Karl August in 1828; and Goethe's son August died of scarlet fever in Rome in 1830.

In 1822 still another passion for a beautiful young girl, Ulrike von Levetzow, inspired Goethe's *Trilogie der Leidenschaft: An Werther, Marienbader Elegie,* and *Aussöhnung.* The trilogy is a passionate and unique work of art written in 1823-1824, when Goethe was approaching the age of 75. Between 1821 and 1829 Goethe published the long-promised continuation of *Wilhelm Meisters Lehrjahre—Wilhelm Meisters Wanderjahre,* a loose series of episodes in novel form. His *Novelle* appeared in 1828.

However, the crowning achievement of Goethe's literary career was the completion of the second part of *Faust.* This work had accompanied Goethe since his early 20s and constitutes a full "confession" of his life. The second part, not published until after Goethe's death, exhibited the poet's ripe wisdom and his philosophy of life. In his *Faust* Goethe recast the old legend and made it into one of Western literature's greatest and noblest poetic creations. The salvation of Faust was Goethe's main departure from the original legend, and he handled it nobly in the impressively mystical closing scene of the second part.

Goethe died in Weimar on March 22, 1832. He was buried in the ducal crypt at Weimar beside Schiller.

Further Reading

Goethe reveals himself in *Goethe's Autobiography: Poetry and Truth from My Life* (trans. 1932) and *Italian Journey, 1786-1788* (trans. 1962). An excellent introduction to Goethe the man is David Luke and Robert Pick, eds., *Goethe: Conversations and Encounters* (1966), a collection of writings by his contemporaries. Biographies of Goethe include John G. Robertson, *The Life and Work of Goethe, 1749-1832* (1932), and Richard Friedenthal, *Goethe: His Life and Times* (1963; trans. 1965). Among the best introductions to Goethe's work are Barker Fairley, *A Study of Goethe* (1947); Henry Hatfield, *Goethe: A Critical Introduction* (1963); and Ronald Gray, *Goethe: A Critical Introduction* (1967). Georg Lukács, *Goethe and His Age* (1948; trans. 1968) analyzes him from a Marxist viewpoint. His writings and thought are examined in Barker

Fairley, *Goethe as Revealed in His Poetry* (1932; rev. ed. 1963); Ronald Peacock, *Goethe's Major Plays* (1959); Elizabeth M. Wilkinson and L. A. Willoughby, *Goethe: Poet and Thinker* (1962); and Hans Reiss, *Goethe's Novels* (1963; trans. 1969).
Contemporary scholars discuss Goethe in Victor Lange, ed., *Goethe: A Collection of Critical Essays* (1968). Specialized studies include Humphry Trevelyan, *Goethe and the Greeks* (1941); Adolf I. Frantz, *Half a Hundred Thralls to Faust: A Study Based on the British and the American Translators of Goethe's Faust, 1823-1949* (1949); and Stuart Pratt Atkins, *The Testament of Werther in Poetry and Drama* (1949) and *Goethe's Faust: A Literary Analysis* (1958). □

Nikolai Gogol

With the works of the Russian author Nikolai Gogol (1809-1852) the period of Russian imitation of Western literature ended. He found inspiration in native materials and combined realistic detail with grotesque and otherworldly elements.

Nikolai Gogol was born on March 20, 1809, in the little Ukrainian town of Sorochincy. He was, as a child, dreamy and withdrawn and was deeply affected by the death of a younger brother. When he was 9, Gogol went away to school, where he spent 7 years. He was a mediocre student but well behaved. He left school in June 1828 and apparently intended to make a career for himself in the Russian civil service. But despite financial difficulties, he delayed entry into the civil service and attempted to make a name for himself in literature. He published the poem "Italy" on March 23, 1829, in the journal *Son of the Fatherland;* it was a clumsy effort, however, and received no critical attention. In 1829 he published at his own expense a more ambitious narrative poem, *Gants Kiukhelgarten,* which recounted the attempts of a romantic hero to escape from an idyllic but stifling environment. The poem was badly received by the critics, and Gogol attempted to retrieve and destroy all the extant copies.

Because of the failure of his first literary efforts Gogol turned to a career in the civil service and worked in several government offices. He then became a teacher in a girls' boarding school in 1831, a vocation that bored him and at which he was not very good. He persisted in his writing, and his work began to gain some attention. He attracted the interest of Vassily Zhukovsky, an important contemporary Russian poet, and in May 1831 was introduced to Aleksandr Pushkin, Russia's greatest poet. With the writing and publication of *Evenings on a Farm near Dikanka* in 1831-1832, Gogol had arrived at a position of importance in literary matters. The stories in this collection are a mixture of realistic detail from Ukrainian folk life and bizarre and supernatural detail.

Shorter Works

Arabesques (1835) consists of essays, art criticism, fragments of novels, and three short fictional masterworks: "The

Mirgorod (1835) is a collection of four stories. The first tale, "Old World Landowners," is a description of the vegetable existence of two old people who live in an idyll of comfort, peace, and love. Tragedy and death, however, intrude on their existence. The second tale of this cycle is the pseudohistorical narrative "Taras Bulba," an unconvincing love story set against the background of the Ukrainian-Polish wars of the 16th and 17th centuries. The third tale of the cycle is "Viy," a supernatural tale about a student who kills a witch who turns out to be a young and beautiful woman. The last tale is "The Story of How Ivan Ivanovich and Ivan Nikiforovich Quarrelled," a story about an absurd argument between two honorable citizens of the town of Mirgorod.

In 1836 Gogol published "The Nose," a grotesque tale about a nose that disattaches itself from a certain major's face and insists on leading an independent existence to the major's dismay. The tale is a narrative of grotesque and bizarre incidents against a background often painted with minute and objective realism.

The Theater

Gogol wrote his dramatic masterpiece *The Inspector General* between October and December 1835, and it seems probable that Gogol received the idea for the play from Pushkin. The play is about an impostor who is mistaken for a true but incognito inspector general and who is showered with favors and servility so as to mask the corruption and dishonesty of the civil servants. The play was at first rejected by the censor, but upon appeal to the Czar himself it was permitted to be staged. The success of the play was immediate and overwhelming. In considering Gogol's theater, one should mention too the comedy *The Marriage,* which was published in 1842 after 9 years of work.

Gogol loved to travel and was convinced that travel was beneficial to his health. During the last 16 years of his life he spent more time abroad than he did in Russia. He was particularly attracted to Rome, which he loved with an abiding passion. In the summer of 1836 he stopped at Vienna for his health and there experienced an important creative outpouring. He worked on *Dead Souls,* revised "Taras Bulba," and wrote "The Overcoat." He also experienced a religious vision which had shattering importance for him and influenced his subsequent view of art and his religious duty.

Portrait," "Nevsky Prospect," and "The Diary of a Madman." "The Portrait," which Gogol wrote in 1833-1834, is concerned with the relationship of art and religion. Specifically, it is about the selling of one's artistic soul to the evil spirit for money. Gogol was to become increasingly concerned with the moral implications of his craft. In this respect "The Portrait" anticipates the crisis about the relationship between art and religion that he was to experience in the last decade of his life.

"Nevsky Prospect" was completed in October 1834 and is based on the contrast of two loves pursued by two young men and the contrast between an ideal and a common view of love. Both love stories end in banality, and Nevsky Prospect, the street on which the adventures begin, is the marketplace of the world's vanity. "The Diary of a Madman" was written in 1833-1834 and is a faintly sketched work about a minor civil official who is frustrated over a love and becomes possessed by delusions of grandeur. Using the visions of a madman, Gogol shows the senselessness of striving and the vanity of the world.

Despite considerable success in his writing by 1834, Gogol was still not fixed in his mind about a career and harbored notions about being a professor and a scholar. In the fall of 1834 he was appointed lecturer in history at St. Petersburg University. He obtained this position by grace of the influence of important friends, and he was supremely unqualified to hold the post, both by way of temperament and background. This career, which lasted from the fall of 1834 to December 1835, was a dismal failure.

"Dead Souls"

Gogol began to work on *Dead Souls* in the fall of 1835. He spent about 6 years writing it and did most of the writing abroad. He experienced difficulties with the censors, but the book was finally published on May 21, 1842. The work is of stunning originality and tells of Chichikov, a con man who travels about Russia buying serfs who have died but who are still carried on the tax rolls and then using the dead serfs as collateral for loans. On another level Chichikov's journey is a descent into the comic hell of Russian reality. General and typical failings of humanity are embodied in the types that Chichikov meets on his journey. Chichikov himself is the personification of banality and lack of character. The picture that Gogol paints of provincial Russia is one of oppressive banality, stupidity, and corruption.

"The Overcoat," published in 1842, is without doubt the masterpiece of Gogol's short pieces of fiction. It has had an enormous influence on the subsequent development of Russian fiction. The plot is about an insignificant copying clerk who saves up for an overcoat which is stolen from him on the first day of possession. Shortly after the theft the clerk falls ill and dies.

Final Period

With the publication of "The Overcoat" and *Dead Souls,* Gogol's great contribution to Russian letters came to an end. The bold intention to continue *Dead Souls* was never realized, for Gogol burned most of the second part, and what he left is markedly inferior to the first part. Gogol became progressively convinced that he had the duty to use his art for the betterment of humanity. His moralizing tendencies are seen in the volume he published on Dec. 31, 1846, *Selected Passages from Correspondence with Friends,* a work that was badly received by critics.

During the course of the 1840s Gogol became more and more convinced that he must purify his own soul, and he came increasingly under the influence of the clergy. He made a pilgrimage to Jerusalem in the Spring of 1848. During the last 9 months of his life, his health deteriorated and he suffered from severe depression. The priest Matthew Konstantinovsky, a strong and intolerant person, gained considerable influence over Gogol's mind and persuaded him to fast more severely than was good for Gogol's weakened constitution. Gogol died on Feb. 21, 1852.

Further Reading

Translations of Gogol's works are available in many editions. Bernard Guilbert Guerney's translations are recommended. David Magarshack, *Gogol: A Life* (1957), is a competent and interesting critical biography. Biographical data are mixed with critical analysis in Janko Lavrin, *Gogol* (1926) and *Nikolai Gogol (1809-1825): A Centenary Survey* (1951). Vladimir Nabokov, *Nikolai Gogol* (1944), is an amusing and entertaining analysis of some aspects of Gogol's work, while Vsevolod Setchkarev, *Gogol: His Life and Works,* translated by Robert Kramer (1965), is a sober and trustworthy analysis of individual works. A specialized study of Gogol's short stories is Frederik Driessen, *Gogol as a Short Story Writer: A Study of His Technique of Composition* (trans. 1965). Prince D. S. Mirsky, *A History of Russian Literature* (2 vols., 1926-1927), is recommended for general literary and historical background. An abridged one-volume edition of Mirsky's work was edited by Francis J. Whitfield (1949; rev. ed. 1958).

Additional Sources

Gogol, Ann Arbor: Ardis, 1981.
Troyat, Henri, *Gogol: the biography of a divided soul,* London: Allen and Unwin, 1974. □

Goh Chok Tong

A leader of the People's Action Party and an activist for more consultative mechanisms of government, Goh Chok Tong (born 1941) became Singapore's prime minister on November 28, 1990.

Goh Chok Tong's appointment as the first deputy prime minister after the victory of the People's Action Party (PAP) in the December 1984 general election was the first indication to Singaporeans that he would succeed Lee Kuan Yew, the only prime minister of Singapore since June 1959, when the PAP government first assumed office. After the September 1988 general election, which reelected the PAP government for the seventh time, Goh informed Singaporeans that he would succeed Lee as prime minister in two years' time. Later, Goh confirmed that while Lee would step down as prime minister on November 28, 1990, he would still be a senior cabinet minister.

In a sense, the political renewal of the PAP and the search for the second generation leaders to replace the old guard began in September 1972, when Ong Teng Cheong (the second deputy prime minister in 1990) and Ahmad Mattar (minister for the environment in 1990) were among the ten new PAP candidates who were elected into Parliament. Similarly, Goh, S. Dhanabalan (minister for national development in 1990), and Tan Soo Khoon (speaker of Parliament in 1990) were part of the second batch of ten new PAP Members of Parliament (MPs), winning their seats in the December 1976 general election. Goh, who entered politics at the age of 35, would become Singapore's second prime minister 14 years later.

Education in Singapore and the United States

As Goh was born in Singapore in 1941, he was an infant during the Japanese occupation years of 1942-1945. He came from a humble background, and in one of his parliamentary speeches he admitted that his two children were much better off than he was when he was young, as he was then living in a house with several families. Because Goh's father died when he was very young, his mother worked as a teacher in a Chinese school to support him and his sister. Both of them were raised by their mother with the help of their grandmother, an uncle, and an aunt.

Like Lee Kuan Yew, Goh was educated at Raffles Institution. He excelled in his studies and in sports. He was interested in writing and was described by his schoolmates as a good writer. At the 30th anniversary reunion dinner of the Raffles Institution Class of 1958, in December 1988, Goh confessed that he had become a politician by default, because in his youth, he had aspired to be a journalist. After completing his school certificate examinations, he switched from the science stream to the arts stream for his higher school certificate examinations. This decision was a turning point as it enabled him to study economics at the University of Singapore in 1961.

Goh spent three years at the University of Singapore and topped his class of 19 students by obtaining a B.A. (Honours) Class I in economics in 1964. As partial fulfillment for his degree, he wrote a 108-page thesis on "A Statistical Analysis of the Production Response of Malayan Fisherman to Price Changes." He joined the Singapore Civil Service (SCS) as an administrative officer after graduation. In 1966 he won a fellowship to Williams College in the United States and successfully completed the M.A. program in development economics.

From Business to Politics

On the completion of his graduate studies in the United States, Goh returned to his job in the SCS and worked as an economic planner and research economist. In August 1969 he was seconded to the Neptune Orient Lines Ltd. (NOL), a newly incorporated government company and Singapore's national shipping line, as its planning and projects manager. He resigned from the SCS about a year later and became part of NOL's permanent staff. His rise up NOL's corporate ladder was rapid. He was appointed as a financial controller and later as a financial director on the NOL board of directors. His appointment as NOL's managing director in November 1973, after only four years' service, was a tribute to his managerial skills. Indeed, his ability to transform NOL into a profitable enterprise caught the eye of the minister for finance, Hon Sui Sen, who succeeded in persuading him to enter politics.

Accordingly, Goh left NOL and participated in the December 1976 general election as the PAP candidate for the electoral constituency of Marine Parade. He won his seat with a convincing majority of 10,496 votes and captured 76.8 percent of the valid votes. He was appointed senior minister of state in the Ministry of Finance in September 1977. He held that post until March 1979, when he was promoted to the position of minister for trade and industry. In January 1981 he was given the additional portfolio of health. He relinquished the trade and industry portfolio in May 1981 and devoted the remaining year as the minister for health to the introduction of the Medisave scheme, which enabled Singaporeans to use their Central Provident Fund to pay their medical bills. He was appointed as minister for defence in June 1982 and as first deputy prime minister in January 1985. He indicated that he would retain the defence portfolio after succeeding Lee as prime minister in November 1990.

Developing a Leadership Style

Unlike Lee, Goh believed in a consultative style of leadership. He and his colleagues were responsible for a change in leadership style after the December 1984 general election that resulted in the PAP winning 77 of the 79 parliamentary seats, but its share of the votes had unexpectedly declined by 12.6 percent, from 75.5 percent in the 1980 general election to 62.9 percent in 1984. The election also demonstrated that 37 percent of the voters who voted for the opposition wanted a change in both the style of government and the substance of some of its policies. Perhaps the most important signal sent by the electorate to the PAP government was that Singaporeans wanted to be consulted and involved in the public policy-making process and to have more control over those decisions that affected their lives directly.

Goh and his colleagues responded to this signal by creating a Feedback Unit in March 1985 and launching the National Agenda in February 1987. However, the shift toward a consultative style of government became more pronounced when the National Agenda (which was renamed the Agenda for Action) was adopted at the PAP convention on January 24, 1988. It was presented by Goh to Parliament three weeks later as a Green Paper for debate and consultation before a final government decision was made. The PAP had conducted a massive exercise in consultation, public education, and consensus building in 1987 to enable all Singaporeans to participate in formulating the means for attaining the goals envisaged in its Vision of 1999. Goh contended that such an exercise was useful because "the ties between the elected leaders and the people . . . must be constantly nurtured through continual discussion, feedback and explanation" so that the government "will have a close feel of the mood of the people, and the people will understand thoroughly what is at stake and what needs to be done."

Consultation in the Office of Prime Minister

Another indicator of Goh's commitment to consultation also became evident on January 11, 1988, when he referred the two bills providing for the establishment of the

Group Representation Constituency (GRC) scheme to a select committee for scrutiny. This scheme was designed to ensure that the minority groups would always be represented in Parliament by requiring a GRC to be represented by three teams of three MPs each, which must include at least one MP from a minority group in each team. The select committee on the GRC scheme received 99 written representations from Singaporeans of varied backgrounds. Twelve representors gave oral evidence to the select committee, and the proceedings of the three-day public hearing were telecast in the evening by the Singapore Broadcasting Corporation.

The same mechanism of the select committee was also used for the discussion of the land transportation issue in 1989 and of the Maintenance of Religious Harmony and Elected Presidency bills in 1990. This reliance on the select committee to obtain the public's views on controversial legislation in recent years indicates clearly Goh's departure from Lee's paternalistic style of governing Singapore. The select committee was rarely used by Lee, as he did not believe in consulting public opinion.

In short, as Goh became Singapore's second prime minister on November 28, 1990, he was not expected to make any drastic change in policies; but he and his colleagues were expected to rely on a more persuasive and consultative style of leadership more in tune with the aspirations of the younger generation of Singaporeans.

In 1993, Goh spoke in *Forbes* about IT2000, Singapore's plan to place information technology as a top priority for the country. "We use technology," he explained, "to overcome the disadvantages of a limited labor force, small domestic market and lack of natural resources. We aim to be a developed country by the end of the century and can succeed only if we harness technology effectively for the economy." He admitted that in order to foster the greater entrepreneurship needed to move to the next phase, that Singapore would need to loosen up on rules that would impede on development. However, the government would draw the lines on information flow that included pornography, religious literature, or foreign publications engaging in domestic political debate about Singapore.

In August 1994, on National Day, Goh's speech was reminiscent of his paternalistic predecessor Lee. Goh declared that Singapore's economic success would be undermined if it followed the ways of the west. He urged young Singaporeans to avoid materialism and condemned single mothers, saying that he would make it harder for them to buy government flats. Although older Singaporeans were more impressed with Goh's statements than the younger and ambitious middle class, few Singaporeans seemed concerned about the future of the country. At that time, unemployment claimed less than 2% of the workforce and incomes were rising at an average of 6% a year.

As 1997—the end of Goh's five year term and the next election—approached, Goh postponed calling an election date. Although the PAP's share of the vote dropped from 76% in 1980 to 61% in the last election, the PAP still dominated the popular vote. Singapore continued to thrive economically, with an economic growth rate of 6% in 1996

and ranking sixth in the world in terms of GNP per person. Goh and the PAP won the election with the party's best showing in 16 years—65% of the vote and all but two of the parliamentary seats.

Further Reading

Many of Goh Chok Tong's speeches are available from the Information Division, Ministry of Communications and Information: "The Second Long March," in *Singapore into the Nineties* (1986); *A Nation of Excellence* (1986); "The Vital Importance of Leadership," in *Speeches* (March-April 1989); and "Spirit of Singapore," in *Speeches* (January-February 1990). The bibliography and four books on politics in Singapore which cover some of the policies formulated by Goh and his colleagues are discussed in: Stella R. Quah and Jon S. T. Quah (compilers), *Singapore* (Oxford: 1988); R. S. Milne and Diane K. Mauzy, *Singapore: The Legacy of Lee Kuan Yew* (1990); Jon S. T. Quah, Chan Heng Chee, and Seah Chee Meow (editors) *Government and Politics of Singapore* (Singapore: 1987); Jon S. T. Quah (editor), *In Search of Singapore's National Values* (Singapore: 1990); and Raj Vasil, *Governing Singapore: Interviews with the New Leaders* (Singapore: 1988).
For a biography of Goh Chok Tong see: Chong, Alan, *Goh Chok Tong: Singapore's New Minister,* Eureka Publications, 1991.
For periodical articles about Goh Chok Tong see: *Forbes,* March 29, 1993; *The Economist,* August 27, 1994; *The Economist,* September 14, 1996; *The Economist,* December 21, 1996; *Macleans,* January 13, 1997; *Macleans,* June 9, 1997; and *The Wall Street Journal,* June 20, 1997. □

Mehmet Ziya Gökalp

Mehmet Ziya Gökalp (c. 1875-1924) was a Turkish publicist and pioneer sociologist. He was influenced by modern western European, especially French and German, thought and elaborated an ideology of Turkish nationalism which was largely implemented, after his death, by Kemal Atatürk.

Ziya Gökalp (this last name, Old Turkish "Sky hero," was originally a pen name;) was born in Diyarbakir in southeastern Anatolia either on an unknown date in 1875 or on March 23, 1876. After attending a local secondary school, he arrived in the capital, Constantinople (Istanbul), in 1896. He had already imbibed the liberal and reformist ideas which were associated with what became the Committee of Union and Progress, and his attitudes soon attracted the attention of the despotic Sultan Abdul-Hamid II's secret police, leading to Gökalp's imprisonment for a year.

The Young Turk Revolution of 1908 enabled Gökalp to openly advocate his views and to act as a cultural and educational adviser to the government. In 1915 he became the first professor of sociology at Istanbul University. In 1919 his identification with the party which had led Turkey into World War I resulted in his being exiled to Malta for 2 years, but he subsequently returned and spent the last part of his life in endeavoring to provide an intellectual basis for the new regime of Mustapha Kemal (Kemal Atatürk). Gökalp died in Constantinople on Oct. 25, 1924.

Gökalp was primarily exercised by the problems of how far Turkey should adopt Western culture and how far the traditional Islamic civilization should accordingly change in the direction of a European-type nation-state. He rejected the religious and political conservatism of the pan-Islamists, regarding traditional Islam as a brake on the nation's progress. He was for a while attracted by Ottomanism, the ideal of a multinationalism made up of the separate nationalities within the Ottoman Empire; but as political and military events demonstrated the impossibility of this, he evolved his idea of "Turkism," the realization of the Turkish national spirit and culture, to be achieved through a revival of Turkish popular culture and literature and a purification of the language by ridding it of extraneous elements.

Gökalp flirted only briefly with pan-Turanianism, the union of all Turkic peoples in Asia. His views on the social ideals which should mold a nation he derived above all from the French sociologist Émile Durkheim. Thus, while he was neither a very original nor a very clear thinker, Gökalp's teachings came after his death to have a profound influence on the evolution of Turkey under Atatürk.

Further Reading

Much of Gökalp's work appeared as essays and articles in journals; there is no complete edition of his work. A good general survey of the man and his significance is in Uriel Heyd, *Foundations of Turkish Nationalism: The Life and Teachings of Ziya Gökalp* (1950).

Additional Sources

Heyd, Uriel, *Foundations of Turkish nationalism: the life and teachings of Ziya Gökalp,* Westport, Conn.: Hyperion Press, 1979. □

Gopal Krishna Gokhale

Gopal Krishna Gokhale (1866-1915) was an Indian nationalist leader. President of the Indian National Congress, he also served in the Imperial Legislative Council and founded the famed Servants of India Society.

On May 9, 1866, Gopal Krishna Gokhale was born in the Ratnagiri District of the Bombay Presidency into a poor but eminently respectable Chitapavan Brahmin family. At age 18 he secured a bachelor's degree from Elphinstone College and joined the illustrious Deccan Education Society. At 22 Gokhale became secretary of the famous Sarvajanik Sabha, the leading political organization of Bombay. He also became a professor at Fergusson College and, in 1891, secretary of the Deccan Education Society.

In 1895 Gokhale was chosen secretary to the Indian National Congress. In the same year he was elected to the senate of Bombay University. He was 29 years old. From 1898 to 1906 Gokhale was a member of the Poona Municipality and served as its president in 1902 and 1905. Under his leadership the municipal government was effectively reformed and democratized. In 1899 he was elected to the Bombay Legislative Council, in which he played a prominent role until his election to the Imperial Legislative Council in 1902.

In the Imperial Legislative Council, Gokhale demonstrated a breadth of knowledge as well as a painstaking mastery of all relevant details on pending legislation, which soon marked him as the most distinguished member of the Council. He was particularly noted for his impressive participation in the annual debate upon the budget.

The year 1905 saw Gokhale at the apex of his career. He was elected president of the Indian National Congress, and he founded the prestigious Servants of India Society, dedicated to advancement of the nation's welfare and to the "spiritualization" of politics. In the same year he was sent by the Congress on a special mission to England to air India's constitutional demands before British leaders. While there he had several important interviews with Lord Morley, secretary of state for India. In 1908 Gokhale was again deputed to visit England in connection with the impending Morley-Minto constitutional reforms of the government of India.

In 1912 Gokhale visited South Africa, where he met Mohandas Gandhi in connection with Gandhi's campaign for rights for Indians. Gokhale also met with Gen. Jan Smuts to assist in securing a satisfactory agreement regarding the position of Indians. His involvement in so wide a range of public and legislative bodies and his strenuous commitment to the advancement of education had, however, worn him out, and he died in Poona on Feb. 15, 1915.

Further Reading

The *Speeches and Writings* of Gokhale were edited by R. P. Patwardhan, D. G. Karve, and D. V. Ambekar (2 vols., 1962-1966). The best volume in English on Gokhale is D. B. Mathur, *Gokhale: A Political Biography* (1966). A brief study is T. R. Deogirikar, *Gopal Krishna Gokhale* (1964). There is an interesting collection of articles on Gokhale in *Gopal Krishna Gokhale: A Centenary Tribute* (1966), published by the Maharashtra Information Centre. See also Stanley A. Wolpert, *Tilak and Gokhale: A Revolution and Reform in the Making of Modern India* (1962).

Additional Sources

Nanda, Bal Ram, *Gokhale: the Indian moderates and the British raj,* Princeton, N.J.: Princeton University Press, 1977.
Wolpert, Stanley A., *Tilak and Gokhale: revolution and reform in the making of modern India,* Delhi: Oxford University Press, 1989. □

Arthur Joseph Goldberg

Arthur Joseph Goldberg (1908-1990), a leading American lawyer and public official, was U.S. secretary of labor, ambassador to the United Nations, and activist Justice of the U.S. Supreme Court.

Arthur J. Goldberg was born on August 8, 1908, the youngest of 11 children whose immigrant parents were Russian Jews. He worked as a delivery boy for a shoe factory while acquiring an education in the Chicago public schools. Goldberg at times labored with construction gangs as he attended first Crane Junior College of the City College of Chicago, then Northwestern University, from which he received a B.S.L. degree in 1929.

Following graduation Goldberg was admitted to the Illinois bar and worked as an associate lawyer in a Chicago law firm. Law practice provided an income which enabled him to earn a law degree from Northwestern University in 1930. Shortly thereafter—on July 18, 1931—the young lawyer married Dorothy Kurgans; in the years to come two children, Barbara and Robert Michael, were born and raised. Until the United States entered World War II in 1941 Goldberg enjoyed a growing reputation in Chicago, particularly in the field of labor law after he represented the Newspaper Guild in a bitter strike in 1938.

Labor's Advocate

During World War II Goldberg established a distinguished record in the Office of Strategic Services as chief of the Labor Division in Europe. After victory in 1945 he returned to the practice of labor law, which was a growing field during the post-war years. As chief counsel for the United Steelworkers of America Goldberg achieved national stature as a champion of organized labor. Building on this experience he overcame enormous obstacles to bring about the merger of the American Federation of Labor (A.F. of L.) and the Congress of Industrial Organizations (C.I.O.). This and other victories revealed the accuracy of one observer's assessment that Goldberg "proved to be an exceptionally able practitioner of the art of negotiating the terms of collective agreements at both the bargaining table and, on occasion, in the White House."

The leading role in the AFL-CIO merger brought Goldberg national preeminence. By 1958 he became a confidant of Sen. John F. Kennedy of Massachusetts, who had proposed significant labor reforms. During the senator's successful campaign for the presidency in 1960 Goldberg was one of Kennedy's closest advisers. It came as no surprise, then, that the new president appointed Goldberg as secretary of labor in 1961. Although he served for less than two years, he was extraordinarily effective in a wide range issues. Besides continued success as a labor negotiator, particularly with respect to strikes, Goldberg fought unemployment and worked for an increased minimum wage and for the elimination of racial discrimination in employment. He also initiated both a pilot program to train and place youths in jobs and the White House Conference on National Economic Issues and shaped the policies of the President's Advisory Committee on Labor-Management Relations. The motive behind all these efforts was the attainment of peace and the preservation of the public interest. What Secretary Goldberg said of the labor-mediating role was true for other areas as well: The secretary, as a mediator, "inevitably is driven to seeking peace. . . . He can *hope* that the settlement will prove fair and equitable to the public as well as to the involved parties, but this can be no more than hope, since sanctions are lacking and strong-willed parties are involved."

Became Supreme Court Justice

In 1962, after more than 20 years of exemplary service, Justice Felix Frankfurter resigned his seat on the U.S. Supreme Court. Kennedy nominated Goldberg to fill this vacancy. Following Senate confirmation he exchanged the politically-charged environment of cabinet office for the more austere, but no less high-pressured, chambers of the nation's highest court. Although Goldberg served at this post for just three terms, from 1962 to 1965, he nonetheless left an indelible imprint on American constitutional law. He took his seat during a tumultuous era in which the Court pursued a course of almost unprecedented judicial activism. Goldberg joined a group of liberal Justices, led by Chief Justice Earl Warren and including William O. Douglas, Hugo L. Black, and William J. Brennan, Jr., who believed that the Court possessed a constitutional duty to actively pursue a course of social and legal change. In case after case the new Justice helped make a majority whose decision rested not upon precedents alone, but, as he said, on those principles so rooted in the "traditions and conscience" of the American people that they "ranked as fundamental." Several of the most significant areas in which the Warren Court adhered to an activist policy included racial desegregation, voting rights, the rights of criminal defendants, and freedom of expression.

A basic feature of the Warren Court's activism was an expansive reading of the 14th Amendment to the Constitution, which applied federal guarantees of equal protection of the law and due process to the states. The substance and scope of these guarantees was, however, uncertain. Goldberg and the other liberal Justices were often criticized for reading their own opinions as to what was fair or right into the meaning of these vague provisions. Yet they often did so in order to protect the rights of the dispossessed and unfortunate, and, as in the case of African Americans, those of persecuted minorities in general. At the same time, the liberals took controversial positions in decisions because they believed that in shielding the rights of the poor and weak, they were defending the individual rights of all Americans.

Perhaps no case illustrates Goldberg's and the Warren Court's judicial activism better than *Escobedo* v. *Illinois* (1964). In 1963 the Court decided that through the due process clause of the 14th Amendment the Sixth Amendment's guarantee of the right to counsel applied in all cases involving poor defendants in state courts. But this decision did not state how early in the criminal justice process the right to counsel existed. Did the right extend beyond the trial to the point of arrest, accusation, and interrogation? This question raised the issue of whether the right to counsel could be combined with the Fifth Amendment's guarantee against self incrimination. In the *Escobedo* case the police questioned the defendant, Danny Escobedo, in connection with the murder of his brother-in-law. Escobedo had not been indicted, and during this interrogation he repeatedly asked to talk with his lawyer, who at one point he saw in a nearby room. Yet the police rejected each request; eventually, he made an incriminating statement that the state used to convict him during the trial. On appeal, Escobedo claimed that the prejudicial statement should not have been allowed because he was denied the assistance of counsel. In the Supreme Court the State of Illinois argued that the state should not be required to provide counsel until the preliminary stages of the trial. Justice Goldberg, writing for the Court, rejected this contention, stressing that it would make the trial essentially an appeal from an unrestrained interrogation, rendering the protection of the Fifth and Sixth amendments "a very hollow thing."

Escobedo opened the way to other far-reaching and controversial decisions which enlarged the rights of those investigated for suspicion of or charged with crimes. To those cases, however, Justice Goldberg would not contribute.

Continued Public Service

In 1965 Goldberg resigned from the Court to become the U.S. ambassador to the United Nations. President Lyndon B. Johnson, embroiled in an increasingly complex and tragic war in Vietnam, had asked Goldberg to accept the U.N. post, hoping that he might through his effective negotiating skills help achieve a just peace. Goldberg left the Court with reluctance. "I shall not, Mr. President, conceal the pain with which I leave the Court after three years of service," he wrote. "It has been the richest and most satisfying period of my career." Nevertheless, Goldberg, as he had throughout a lifetime of public service, approached the new responsibilities with resolution and enthusiasm. But although he achieved several significant accomplishments, particularly during the Arab-Israeli War of June 1967, the central goal of peace in Vietnam eluded him. Early in the summer of 1968 the former labor lawyer, U.S. secretary of labor, and Justice of the Supreme Court resigned the ambassadorship and returned to legal practice as a partner in a well-known New York law firm. In 1970 he was an unsuccessful candidate for governor of New York. After that, though no longer in public office, Goldberg maintained involvement in public affairs. He held faculty positions at Columbia, American University, Hastings College of Law, and the University of Alabama School of Law and remained an influential expert on labor law. Goldberg died on January 20, 1990.

Further Reading

There is a good survey of Arthur J. Goldberg's career, particularly as a Supreme Court Justice, in Leon Friedman and Fred L. Israel, editors, volume IV, *The Justices of the United States Supreme Court, 1789-1969: Their Lives and Major Opinions* (1969). His major opinions and speeches are collected in D. P. Moynihan, editor, *Defenses of Freedom* (1956). His book *AFL-CIO: Labor United* (1956) and essay "Law and the United Nations," 52 *American Bar Association Journal* 813 (1966) provide valuable insights into the man, his ideas, and his times. Good studies including a discussion of the Warren Court and Goldberg's contribution as an activist Justice are Henry Julian Abraham, *Freedom and the Court: Civil Rights and Liberties in the United States* (1967) and John Paul Frank, *The Warren Court* (1964). □

Whoopi Goldberg

Whoopi Goldberg has been called Hollywood's most uncategorizable star. The high-energy actress, who has appeared in such films as *The Color Purple* and *Sister Act* was the first African American to host the Academy Awards.

Whoopi Goldberg's life and career have followed similar circular journeys: both began with ingenuous hope then slipped dangerously toward extinction, only to be resurrected by a rediscovery of the dormant initial promise. Throughout her acting career, she has not forgotten the lessons she learned in her early, difficult life. There is, in a sense, no division between Goldberg the actress and Goldberg the person, as Paul Chutkow pointed out in *Vogue:* "She seems much the same way she has often appeared on-screen: fresh, direct, exuberant, no cant, no can't." Goldberg's unpretentiousness and determination imbue her best characterizations—they are direct and empathetic. She is committed to her art. "Simply, I love the idea of working," she admitted to Aldore Collier in *Jet.* "You hone your craft that way." And she is committed to rectifying disparaging social conditions affecting the unfortunate, and to which she was once subjected. Her success is earned, and she offers no platitudes for its achievement, only a realistic vision: "Take the best of what you're offered," she told Chutkow, "and that's all you can do."

Born Caryn E. Johnson in New York City in 1955, Goldberg wanted to be a performer from the very beginning. "My first coherent thought was probably, I want to be an actor," she recounted to Chutkow. "I believe that. That's just what I was born to do." She was acting in children's plays with the Hudson Guild Theater at the age of eight and throughout the rest of her childhood immersed herself in movies, sometimes watching three or four a day. "I liked the idea that you could pretend to be somebody else and nobody would cart you off to the hospital," Goldberg explained to *Cosmopolitan*'s Stephen Farber.

But by the time she reached high school, Goldberg had lost her desire and vision. It was the 1960s, and she was hooked on drugs. "I took drugs because they were available

to everyone in those times," she told Farber. "As everyone evolved into LSD, so did I. It was the time of Woodstock, of be-ins and love-ins." Goldberg dropped out of high school and became lost in this culture, delving further into the world of drugs and ending up a junkie. Finally she sought help, cleaned herself up, and, in the process, married her drug counselor. A year later, Goldberg gave birth to her daughter, Alexandrea. Less than a year afterward, she was divorced. She was not yet twenty years old.

In 1974 Goldberg headed west to San Diego, California, pursuing her childhood dream of acting. She performed in plays with the San Diego Repertory Theater and tried improvisational comedy with a company called Spontaneous Combustion. To care for her daughter, Goldberg had to work as a bank teller, a bricklayer, and a mortuary cosmetologist. She was also, for a few years, on welfare. During this period, she went by the name "Whoopi Cushion," sometimes using the French pronunciation "Ku*shon.*" After her mother pointed out how ridiculous the name sounded, Goldberg finally adopted a name from her family's history.

Developed Insightful Comic Routine

In a significant step, Goldberg moved north to Berkeley, California, in the late 1970s and joined the Blake Street Hawkeyes Theater, a comedic avant-garde troupe. With this group, Goldberg was able to realize her powerful acting and comedic abilities, developing a repertoire of 17 distinct personae in a one-woman show that she labeled *The Spook Show.* She performed the show on the West Coast, then toured the country and Europe in the early 1980s before landing in New York City.

Among her sketches were four rueful—and sometimes sublime—characters: Fontaine, a profanity-spewing drug dealer with a Ph.D. in literature who travels to Europe looking for hashish, only to openly weep when he comes across Anne Frank's secret hiding place; a shallow thirteen-year-old surfing Valley Girl who is left barren after a self-inflicted abortion with a coat hanger; a severely handicapped young woman who tells her prospective suitor who wants to go dancing, "This is not a disco body"; and a nine-year-old black girl who bathes in Clorox and covers her head with a white skirt, wistfully hoping to become white with long blonde hair so she can appear on *The Love Boat.*

Although Brendan Gill of the *New Yorker* decided Goldberg's sketches were "diffuse and overlong and continuously at the mercy of her gaining a laugh at any cost," the majority of critical and popular reaction was positive. Cathleen McGuigan writing in *Newsweek* believed that Goldberg's "ability to completely disappear into a role, rather than superficially impersonate comic types, allows her to take some surprising risks." And Enid Nemy, in a review of Goldberg's show for the *New York Times,* found the performer's abilities extended beyond mere comic entertainment and that her creations—seamlessly woven with social commentary—"walk a finely balanced line between satire and pathos, stand-up comedy and serious acting." These realistic and ranging performances also caught the attention of famed film director Mike Nichols (*Who's Afraid of Virginia Woolf, The Graduate*). After seeing Goldberg's premiere performance in New York, Nichols offered to produce her show on Broadway in September of 1984.

Film Debut Earned Critical Praise

Another Hollywood figure entranced by Goldberg's sensitive performances was director Steven Spielberg, who at the time was casting for the film production of author Alice Walker's *The Color Purple*. Spielberg offered Goldberg the lead role of Celie—her first film appearance. Goldberg told Audrey Edwards of *Essence* how badly she wanted to be a part, any part, of the film: "I told [Alice Walker] that whenever there was an audition I'd come. I'd eat the dirt. I'd play the dirt, I'd *be* the dirt, because the part is perfect."

"As Celie, the abused child, battered bride, and wounded woman liberated by Shug's kiss and the recognition of sisterhood's power, Whoopi Goldberg is for the most part lovable and believable," Andrew Kopkind wrote in a review of the movie for the *Nation*. "She mugs a bit, pouts and postures too long in some scenes, and seems to disappear in others, but her great moments are exciting to behold." *Newsweek* 's David Ansen concurred in assessing Goldberg's film debut: "This is powerhouse acting, all the more so because the rage and the exhilaration are held in reserve." For this performance, Goldberg received a Golden Globe Award and an Academy Award nomination.

But the film itself failed to receive the praise bestowed on Goldberg. "The movie is amorphous," Pauline Kael wrote in the *New Yorker*. "It's a pastoral about the triumph of the human spirit, and it blurs on you." Much criticism was aimed at the selection of Spielberg, a white male, to direct a story that focuses on the Southern rural black experience, has a decidedly matriarchal point-of-view, and offers cardboard representations of its male characters. Even Goldberg herself was criticized when she defended Spielberg and the film. In an interview excerpted in *Harper's,* director Spike Lee questioned Goldberg's allegiances: "Does she realize what she is saying? Is she saying that a white person is the only person who can define our existence? . . . I hope people realize, that the media realize, that she's not a spokesperson for black people." Goldberg countered by defining for Matthew Modine in *Interview* the breadth of her social character: "What I am is a humanist before anything—before I'm a Jew, before I'm black, before I'm a woman. And my beliefs are for the human race—they don't exclude anyone."

Increased Exposure Allowed Social Activism

Despite the lukewarm reception to the film as a whole, Goldberg's fortunes rose. In addition to her awards for her film portrayal, she won a Grammy Award in 1985 for her comedy album *Whoopi Goldberg* and received an Emmy nomination the following year for her guest appearance on the television show *Moonlighting*. The increased exposure, recognition, and acceptance allowed Goldberg to pursue social activities focusing on issues that affected her when she required public assistance and that she has tried to call attention to since her early stand-up routines.

Beginning in 1986, Goldberg hosted, along with Billy Crystal and Robin Williams, the annual *Comic Relief* benefit that raises money for the homeless through the Health Care for the Homeless project. "People would like the United States to be what we're told it can be, without realizing that the price has gone up—the price, you know, of human dignity," she explained to Steve Erickson in *Rolling Stone*. "Homelessness in America is just disgusting. It's just disgusting that we could have this big, beautiful country and have families living in dumpsters. It makes no sense." Goldberg appeared on Capitol Hill with Senator Edward Kennedy in a forum that opposed the proposed cuts in federal welfare. *Jet* reported her remarks in December 1995. She told the forum, "The welfare system works. I know it does because I'm here." Her protests are not limited to any one social imbalance; Goldberg also campaigns on behalf of environmental causes, the nation's hungry, AIDS and drug abuse awareness, and women's right to free choice. She has been recognized with several humanitarian awards for her efforts.

Increased exposure, though, did not translate into increased success for Goldberg, as she went on to star in a succession of critically assailed movies: *Jumpin' Jack Flash, Burglar, Fatal Beauty, The Telephone, Clara's Heart,* and *Homer and Eddie.* It seemed that as soon as she had risen, she had fallen. "On the strength of her past work as a stand-up comic, Goldberg deserves better," Lawrence O'Toole wrote in a review of *Burglar* for *Maclean's*. "If she keeps making thumb-twiddling movies like this one, she is unlikely to get it." And in a review of *Clara's Heart* for *People,* David Hiltbrand noted that ever since her debut film, Goldberg "has barely kept her head above water while her movies went under. After this, she'll need her own lifeboat."

Goldberg was vexed by gossip and rumors that Hollywood was ready to write her off. "In less than five years she went from Hollywood's golden girl to a rumored lesbian/Uncle Tom with a bad attitude and a career on the skids," Laura B. Randolph described in *Ebony*. "In Hollywood, that combination is almost always terminal, and insiders whispered that she should pack it in and be happy to do guest spots on the *Hollywood Squares*."

Goldberg remained steady, though, disavowing critical displeasure. "I've just stopped listening to them," she explained to Chutkow. "I've taken crazy movies that appeal to me. I don't care what other people think about it. If it was pretty decent when I did it, I did my job." And that seems to be the tenuous thread that connects her box-office disappointments: her strong performance marred by poor direction or a poor final script. The *New York Times* 's Janet Maslin, reviewing *Fatal Beauty,* wrote what could be taken as an overall assessment of Goldberg's failed showings: "It isn't Miss Goldberg's fault, because Miss Goldberg is funny when she's given half a chance."

Ghost Revived Career

Goldberg seemed simply to need the right vehicle to transport to the audience her comic approach underscored by biting social and tender humanitarian elements. Her chance came with the 1990 film *Ghost*. "Thank God

Whoopi finally has a part that lets her strut her best stuff," Ansen proclaimed. Although some critics didn't fully embrace the film (the *New Yorker*'s Terrance Rafferty called it a "twentysomething hybrid of *It's a Wonderful Life* and some of the gooier, more solemn episodes of *The Twilight Zone*"), most critical and popular response was overwhelmingly positive—especially to Goldberg's portrayal of the flamboyant yet heroic psychic, Oda Mae. It was a part for which she lobbied studio executives for more than six months, and her persistence paid off. Considered a sleeper when it was released, *Ghost* was the highest-grossing movie of 1990. And Goldberg won an Oscar for her performance, becoming only the second black female in the history of the Academy Awards to win such an honor (the first was Hattie McDaniel, who won for *Gone with the Wind* in 1939).

In a decisive indication of her acting range, Goldberg immediately followed her comedic role in *Ghost* with a substantive dramatic role in *The Long Walk Home*. The film is a poignant evocation of the bus boycott in Montgomery, Alabama, in 1955—a pivotal event in the American civil rights movement. Goldberg portrays Odessa Cotter, a housekeeper who, because of the boycott, is forced to walk almost ten miles to work, regardless of blistering or bleeding feet. Throughout, the character maintains her composure and integrity. Chutkow quoted Richard Pearce, the director of the film, on Goldberg's successful characterization: "What her portrayal of Odessa revealed about Whoopi was a complex inner life and intelligence. Her mouth is her usual weapon of choice—to disarm her of that easy weapon meant that she had to rely on other things. It's a real actress who can bring off a performance like that. And she did."

Goldberg also confirmed her far-reaching, unassailable talent in the arena of television. Beginning in the 1988-89 season, she earned accolades for appearing on an irregular basis as a crew member on the successful series *Star Trek: The Next Generation*. And while her 1990 stint in the series *Bagdad Cafe* was short-lived, Goldberg in 1992 secured the coveted position of late-night talk show host. *The Whoopi Goldberg Show* devoted each program to just one guest; Goldberg interviewed actress Elizabeth Taylor on the show's debut, and subsequent programs featured such celebrities as heavyweight boxing champion Evander Holyfield. The show was canceled in 1993.

The year 1992 also brought a series of successful film roles to Goldberg. She began the year portraying a homicide detective in director Robert Altman's highly anticipated and subsequently acclaimed Hollywood satire *The Player*. In mid-year Goldberg donned a nun's habit as a Reno lounge singer seeking refuge from the mob in a convent in the escapist comedy *Sister Act;* one of the biggest box-office draws of the summer of 1992, the film, according to *Detroit Free Press* film critic Judy Gerstel, worked "as summer whimsy mainly because of Goldberg's usual witty, lusty screen presence." And in the fall she turned again to a dramatic role, starring in *Sarafina: The Movie;* a film adaptation of the musical about Black South African teenagers' struggle against apartheid, *Sarafina* was shot entirely on location in Soweto, South Africa.

Goldberg went on to appear in several more films including *Made in America, Sister Act II* (for which she was paid eight million dollars), *Corrina, Corrina,* and *Boys on the Side.* These films received mixed reviews, but as Janet Maslin stated in the *New York Times* in her review of *Boys on the Side ,* "Ms. Goldberg, still reigning as Hollywood's most uncategorizable star, finally finds a role that suits her talents."

The Academy Awards

Goldberg took a break from acting to host the Academy Awards in 1994 and 1996. This took a great deal of courage considering she was the first African American and first female to host the event solo. The awards show is scrutinized by more than one billion people. In 1994, she had big shoes to fill because Billy Crystal had hosted the event for four years previously and the public was upset that he did not return. She performed to the critics' approval. *Jet* reported, "Critics and industry observers who had expressed wariness and reservation . . . hailed her for her tasteful comments, good jokes and ability to keep the three-hour show moving merrily along."

In 1996, the academy faced public protest by the Rev. Jesse Jackson for the lack of African American voters and nominees. The protest did not seem to bother Goldberg, who joked that she would wear Jackson's ribbon of protest, but she knew he was not watching. Maslin of the *New York Times* commented, "With Whoopi Goldberg as its quick-witted host, the show soon established an energetic tone and a refreshing impatience with Oscar traditions."

Love Life Makes Headlines

Goldberg has been linked with several of her movies costars: Timothy Dalton, Ted Danson, and most recently Frank Langella, her costar in a Disney release called *Eddie.* Her reported romance with Langella comes after a brief one-year marriage to Lyle Trachtenberg, a movie and television technicians' union organizer, whom she met on the set of *Corinna, Corinna.* A friend of Goldberg's admitted to *People,* "They've been mismatched from the beginning." Mismatched is a curious description, considering Goldberg once told Larry King, "Lyle's a real normal guy."

Her divorce happened quietly compared to what happened at the end of her romance with Ted Danson, whom she met on the set of *Made in America.* At a Friars Club Roast of Goldberg, Danson showed up tastelessly in blackface. His face appeared totally black with very large white lips. Danson roasted Goldberg by presenting a routine that included the word "nigger" several times, and included details of their sex life. Although many do not believe Danson is a racist, *Jet* commented, "Danson's routine stirred memories of days when white actor Al Jolson performed black caricature, which many found offensive." Many prominent African Americans expressed their disgust—Jackson, Spike Lee, and Montel Williams. At first, Goldberg defended Danson, claiming that she hired the makeup artist for Danson and wrote some of the jokes. However, Goldberg later told *Jet* magazine, "Well, we had already split up by then, but it ruined our friendship—it certainly did—which was sad. It was real painful, and it was very public. And the loss of this friendship hurts a great deal. We can never go and have a soda, anywhere." The incident drew so much attention that Goldberg probably wished the press would only report on her acting.

Goldberg's constant quest for a range of roles—what led Maslin to label her "one of the great unclassifiable beings on the current movie scene"—is not the mark of a Hollywood prima donna but of an actor committed to her craft. "None of my films cure cancer," Goldberg explained to Chutkow. "But they have allowed me to not just play one kind of person, which is important to me. Nobody knows how long this stuff is gonna last, and you want to have it and enjoy as much of it and be as diverse as you can."

In 1997, after appearing in the comedy film *The Associate,* Goldberg left Hollywood and returned to the theater, starring on Broadway in *A Funny Thing Happened on the Way to the Forum.* The hit production of this 1963 musical classic is a vaudevillian spin on the classic Roman comedies of Plautus.

Further Reading

Christian Science Monitor, March 27, 1986.
Cosmopolitan, December 1988; March 1991; April 1992.
Detroit Free Press, May 29, 1992.
Ebony, March 1991.
Essence, March 1985.
Harper's, January 1987.
Interview, June 1992.
Jet, April 24, 1989; August 13, 1990; April 22, 1991; January 13, 1992; June 1, 1992.
Maclean's, April 6, 1987.
Nation, February 1, 1986; December 10, 1990.
New Republic, January 27, 1986.
New Statesman, August 23, 1991.
Newsweek, March 5, 1984; December 30, 1985; October 20, 1986; July 16, 1990.
New York, December 12, 1988; April 2, 1990.
New Yorker, November 5, 1984; December 30, 1985; July 30, 1990.
New York Times, October 21, 1984; October 30, 1987; February 14, 1988; February 9, 1990; March 7, 1997.
Parade, November 1, 1992.
People, October 17, 1988; April 2, 1990.
Rolling Stone, May 8, 1986; August 9, 1990.
Time, December 17, 1990; June 1, 1992.
Vogue, January 1991. □

Harry Golden

The Jewish-American humorist Harry Golden (1902-1981) was writer and publisher of the *Carolina Israelite* and author of many popular books including *Only in America.*

Harry Golden, born in 1902, was the son of Leib and Anna Klein Goldhirsch. Although many references identify Golden's birthplace as New York City, his autobiography says that his father and his oldest brother left their home in Milulintsy, a village in eastern Galicia, then part of the Austria-Hungary Empire, and migrated to Canada and, after brief stays in other places, saved money to bring Golden and his mother and sister to New York City in 1905. Immigration officials at Ellis Island changed the surname to Goldhurst. Golden grew up in the poor but culturally rich Jewish ghetto of New York City's Lower East Side, where his father earned a living as a teacher of Hebrew and as a freelance writer. His mother, born in Rumania, was pious and prayerful, but illiterate. The father, a rationalist in religion, nonetheless kept strict Sabbath observances and greatly influenced his son's intellectual development.

Golden attended Public School 20 and found especially exciting the lively evening classes for immigrant children. He was an eager learner and prolific reader and carried his enthusiasm through the completion of his formal education at the City College of New York. Thereafter, Golden engaged in several kinds of work, most significantly as a floor boy with the furrier company owned by Oscar Geiger, a devotee of the reformer Henry George. Golden worked for Geiger's senatorial campaign as candidate of the Single Tax party in 1924.

Golden soon found himself in the stock market business, employed in his sister Clara's firm. In 1926 Golden began his own business, Kable and Company, selling stocks and bonds on the partial payment plan. But Golden turned this operation into a lucrative "bucket shop" that speculated on the stock purchases of his clients and skimmed off profits on the rise and fall in the market value of the stocks.

The best-known client of the firm was Bishop James Cannon, Jr., of the Methodist Episcopal Church, who was morally compromised with Golden in these speculations. Golden was brought to trial and served a three-year prison sentence from 1929 to 1932.

A Base in North Carolina

Upon completion of his sentence Golden worked at his brother's Hotel Markwell on Manhattan's west side. Throughout the 1930s, as the menace of Nazism grew in Germany, Golden took a new and deep interest in Jewish history and culture, immersing himself in the literature of these subjects. Then in 1941 he left New York, moved to Charlotte, North Carolina, and changed his name to Golden. He joined the staff of the Charlotte *Labor Journal* and became familiar as a partisan of the union movement in a part of the country where that cause was often equated with communism. He then became a successful salesman of advertising space for the Charlotte *Observer* and decided on a bold adventure in publishing his own newspaper.

The Carolina Israelite, which first appeared in October 1942, became an exceptional and noteworthy publication. Golden produced the paper in two old homes in Charlotte, writing all of it, often in a fit of energy, and issued it when he was ready. It was a Jewish enterprise that grew to influence in a part of the country where Jews were not in great number, and in fact most of its circulation, soon reaching 16,000, was in the major cities—New York, Chicago, Los Angeles, and Philadelphia. Also, the *Carolina Israelite* espoused liberal social and political views, most controversially on racial integration and labor, in an area where these issues were explosive. But Golden was developing at the same time the soft touch and humor that enabled him to support these causes in a manner that did not induce hatred toward him in return. Golden spoke at different places in the South as he worked for the civil rights movement, and in Atlanta he was asked a familiar question: "What's a Jew doing down here trying to change the Southern way of life?" Golden replied: "I am trying to organize a Jewish society for the preservation of Christian ethics." The Atlanta audience, Golden reported, cheered.

Golden gathered many of his *Carolina Israelite* essays into a book, *Only in America,* published in 1958. It was a success and made Golden a national name. The earnings from the book supported the newspaper at a time when Golden's unpopular views on integration prompted withdrawal of advertising and loss of support from worried merchants, many of them Jewish. Also, in the midst of his newly won fame Golden's background and real identity were exposed in an anonymous letter to his publisher. But Golden outrode the revelation and continued in the national limelight. He was a frequent guest on national television programs, a contributor to journals such as *The Nation* and *Commentary,* with special assignments from *LIFE,* and a popular lecturer around the country. The television exposure also swelled the subscription lists of his newspaper.

Humor in Social Problems

Only in America and other books that followed in similar format placed Golden in the traditions both of the native humorist, such as Will Rogers, and the ethnic humorist, such as Peter Finley Dunne and Sam Levenson. Golden seemed to appeal to an American reading audience that felt the necessity for conformity and affirmation of its way of life and at the same time feared the decline of cultural pluralism. Golden's Jewish identity to that extent enhanced his appeal. He symbolized the contemporary Jew who had left the ghetto behind and was at home in middle-class America. If his humor chastized, it did so with a loving touch and always with a moral lesson that reminded Americans of their traditional idealism.

Golden's various schemes for solving the racial problem in America were most memorable. Observing that white Southerners were loathe to sit with African Americans on busses or in restaurants, but noting that whites often stood in line with African Americans at grocery stores and other places, Golden called on the public school to remove all chairs from their classrooms. This "Vertical Negro Plan" would thereby overcome Southern reservations about sitting in the same room with the other race. Golden's "White Baby" plan would pave the way for integration of Southern theaters and movie houses by arranging for African Americans to enter these places carrying a white baby.

By the end of the 1960s Golden had turned away from the extremist side of the African American movement, denouncing the militant voices in it. He closed the *Carolina Israelite* in 1968. He also resigned from the Student Nonviolent Coordinating Committee (SNCC) because of its opposition to Israel. But Golden remained a committed Democratic party liberal and, having assisted earlier in the campaigns of Adlai Stevenson, he supported the candidacies of John F. Kennedy and Robert Kennedy. Although an immensely popular writer, Golden was criticized, most often by other Jewish spokesmen who found his manner of addressing social problems and anti-Semitism too frivolous, disarming, and sentimental. Harry Golden died in 1981.

Further Reading

Golden once said that he was assisted throughout his writing career by an unfailing memory. That quality of mind characterized his autobiography, *The Right Time,* which is often rich with observations of Jewish life in New York City and of Southern mores, but which suffers from an excess of detail. Golden books that followed *Only in America* include *For 2 Plain* (1959), *You're Entitle'* (1962), and *Ess, Ess Mein Kind* (1966). *The Best of Harry Golden* (1967) is an anthology of his writings. A handsome book with many photographs is Golden's *The Greatest Jewish City in the World* (1972) about Jewish culture in New York. Other subjects on which Golden wrote are found in *Carl Sandburg* (1961), *Mr. Kennedy and the Negroes* (1964), and *The Israelis* (1971). An essay on the Harry Golden phenomenon is Theodore Solotaroff, "Harry Golden & the American Audience," in *Commentary* (March 1961). □

Sir George Dashwood Taubman Goldie

The British trader and empire builder Sir George Dashwood Taubman Goldie (1846-1925) created the Royal Niger Company, which secured British claims to the lower Niger and Northern Nigeria.

The son of the Speaker of the Manx Parliament, George Goldie was born on the Isle of Man. His family were influential landowners on the island. The family name was Taubman, but Goldie adopted his mother's family name when he was knighted in 1887.

In the 1860s Goldie trained as a royal engineer at Woolwich but afterward used a legacy to visit Egypt, where he took an Arab mistress. He went to the Sudan, living an idyllic and isolated life for 3 years, learning Arabic and reading extensively in African travel literature. He also met Hausa pilgrims from Nigeria and began studying that country.

Returning to England, Goldie ran away to Paris with the family governess, Mathilda Elliot, and they were caught in the Prussian siege of 1870 and were married in July 1871. Goldie's escapades and an avowed atheism cut him off from an official career and the highest circles of Victorian society.

In 1875 the Taubman family purchased a near-bankrupt firm which traded on the Niger River. Goldie was given the task of putting its affairs in order and visited the Niger for the first time. He concluded that overcompetition was ruining all the British firms on the river, and he set out to create a single monopolistic organization. By 1879 he had succeeded in amalgamating the British firms into the United African Company but thereafter had to face competition from the Africans and French.

Goldie then decided to secure administrative rights by treaty from Africans to establish his company as a government which could exclude competitors by administrative measures. In 1882 he formed the National African Company for this purpose and began treaty making. By 1884 Goldie had ruined the French competition, and at the Berlin Conference (1884-1885) Britain was given the task of administering the lower Niger. The British government was unwilling to spend money for such a purpose and in 1886 gave a royal charter to Goldie's company, which was renamed the Royal Niger Company.

By 1892 the company had established a complete monopoly of trade. The British government ignored the opposition this provoked because the company was expanding and establishing British territorial claims in Nigeria at no cost to the taxpayer. In 1895, however, a commission of inquiry investigated the company, and Joseph Chamberlain, the new colonial secretary, determined to take over Goldie's administration. This was delayed by struggles with the French on Northern Nigeria's frontiers, but eventually in 1900 the Protectorate of Northern Nigeria took over the company's administrative functions.

Thereafter Goldie played little part in public life, rejecting various offers of colonial governorships and turning down an offer to take control of the British South Africa Company after Cecil Rhodes's death. He died in London on Aug. 25, 1925.

Further Reading

Goldie destroyed his papers during World War I and never wrote his intended memoirs. His views on African administration and indirect rule are expressed in the introduction he wrote for Seymour Vandeleur, *Campaigning on the Upper Nile and Niger* (1898). His niece Dorothy Wellesley wrote *Sir George Goldie, Founder of Nigeria: A Memoir* (1934) as a personal portrait. The definitive study, based largely on British government sources, is John E. Flint, *Sir George Goldie and the Making of Nigeria* (1960). □

William Golding

The winner of the 1983 Nobel Prize in literature, Golding is among the most popular and influential British authors to have emerged after World War II.

Golding's reputation rests primarily upon his acclaimed first novel *Lord of the Flies* (1954), which he described as "an attempt to trace the defects of society back to the defects of human nature." A moral allegory as well as an adventure tale in the tradition of

Daniel Defoe's *Robinson Crusoe* (1719), R. M. Ballantyne's *The Coral Island* (1857), and Richard Hughes's *A High Wind in Jamaica* (1929), *Lord of the Flies* focuses upon a group of British schoolboys marooned on a tropical island. After having organized themselves upon democratic principles, their society degenerates into primeval barbarism. While often the subject of diverse psychological, sociological, and religious interpretations, *Lord of the Flies* is consistently regarded as an incisive and disturbing portrayal of the fragility of civilization.

Golding was born in St. Columb Minor in Cornwall, England. He enrolled in Brasenose College, Oxford, in 1930, initially intending to obtain a degree in the sciences. After several years of study, however, he decided to devote himself to the study of English literature. He published a volume of poetry, *Poems,* in 1934 to scant critical notice; he himself later repudiated the work. Receiving a degree in English in 1935, he worked in various theaters in London, and in 1939 he moved to Salisbury, where he was employed as a schoolteacher. He served five years in the Royal Navy during World War II, an experience that likely helped shape his interest in the theme of barbarism and evil within humanity. Following the war Golding continued to teach and to write fiction. In 1954, his first novel, *Lord of the Flies,* was published to much critical acclaim in England. He continued to write novels, as well as essays, lectures, and novellas, throughout the next three decades. Most of these works, however, were overshadowed by the popular and critical success of *Lord of the Flies.*

Golding's *Lord of the Flies* presents a central theme of his oeuvre: the conflict between the forces of light and dark within the human soul. Although the novel did not gain popularity in the United States until several years after its original publication, it has now become a modern classic, studied in most high schools and colleges. Set sometime in the near future, *Lord of the Flies* is about a group of schoolboys abandoned on a desert island during a global war. They attempt to establish a government among themselves, but without the restraints of civilization they quickly revert to savagery. Similar in background and characters to Ballantyne's *The Coral Island, Lord of the Flies* totally reverses Ballantyne's concept of the purity and innocence of youth and humanity's ability to remain civilized under the worst conditions.

While none of Golding's subsequent works achieved the critical success of *Lord of the Flies,* he continued to produce novels that elicit widespread critical interpretation. Within the thematic context of exploring the depths of human depravity, the settings of Golding's works range from the prehistoric age, as in *The Inheritors,* (1955), to the Middle Ages, as in *The Spire* (1964), to contemporary English society. This wide variety of settings, tones, and structures presents dilemmas to critics attempting to categorize them. Nevertheless, certain stylistic devices are characteristic of his work. One of these, the use of a sudden shift of perspective, has been so dramatically employed by Golding that it both enchants and infuriates critics and readers alike. For example, *Pincher Martin* (1956) is the story of Christopher Martin, a naval officer who is stranded on a rock in the middle of the ocean after his ship has been torpedoed. The entire book relates Martin's struggles to remain alive against all odds. The reader learns in the last few pages that Martin's death occurred on the second page—a fact that transforms the novel from a struggle for earthly survival into a struggle for eternal salvation.

Golding's novels are often termed fables or myths. They are laden with symbols (usually of a spiritual or religious nature) so imbued with meaning that they can be interpreted on many different levels. *The Spire,* for example, is perhaps his most polished allegorical novel, equating the erecting of a cathedral spire with the protagonist's conflict between his religious faith and the temptations to which he is exposed. *Darkness Visible* (1979) continues to illuminate the universal confrontation of Good and Evil; Golding was awarded the James Tait Black Memorial Prize for this novel in 1980. Throughout the 1980s Golding's novels, essays, and the travel journal *An Egyptian Journal* (1985) have received general praise from commentators. *Lord of the Flies,* however, remains central to Golding's popularity and his international reputation as a major contemporary author.

Further Reading

Allen, Walter, *The Modern Novel,* Dutton, 1964.
Anderson, David, *The Tragic Past,* John Knox Press, 1969.
Authors and Artists for Young Adults, Volume 5, Gale, 1991.
Axthelm, Peter M., *The Modern Confessional Novel,* Yale University Press, 1967.

Babb, Howard S., *The Novels of William Golding,* Ohio State University Press, 1970.

Baker, James R., *William Golding: A Critical Study,* St. Martin's, 1965.

Biles, Jack I., *Talk: Conversations with William Golding,* Harcourt, 1971. □

Emma Goldman

The career of the Lithuanian-born anarchist Emma Goldman (1869-1940) drew attention to American problems in civil liberties at the turn of the century.

E mma Goldman was born on June 27, 1869, in Kovno of Jewish parents. She emigrated to the United States in 1885 and worked in clothing factories in Rochester, N.Y. In 1887 she married, quickly divorced, remarried, and finally separated. Inspired by the libertarian writings of Johann Most, she moved in 1889 to New York City. An attractive and intellectual woman, she now began her long association with the Russian anarchist Alexander Berkman.

Goldman's radical activities culminated in a plan with Berkman to commit an anarchist "deed" against Henry Frick, of the Carnegie Steel Company, who was resisting his employees' unionist efforts. Though she was not with Berkman when he shot and wounded Frick (and was sentenced to prison), she herself went to prison the following year in New York for allegedly urging the unemployed to take "by force" the food they required.

Though Goldman ceased advocating violence, she continued defending those who did. Upon her release from prison, she became a nurse and a midwife. Trips to Europe in 1895 and 1899-1900 broadened her perspectives. She became notorious again in 1901 and suffered unwarranted harassment when the disturbed assassin of President William McKinley said her speeches had influenced him.

When Berkman came out of prison, he joined Goldman's publication *Mother Earth* (1906-1917). Mature, bespectacled, but still attractive and magnetic in personality, she spoke on drama and literature, as well as on issues of the day. Her book *The Social Significance of the Modern Drama* (1914) was superficial; stronger and more varied was *Anarchism and Other Essays* (1910).

Goldman gained new fame during the "youth movement" of radicals and social experimenters in the 1910s. Her battle for birth control information and related matters of special concern to women was notable. Charged with obstructing operation of the Conscription Act during World War I, she and Berkman were fined and sentenced in 1917 to 2 years' imprisonment. Long, recriminatory proceedings culminated in her being deprived of citizenship on technical grounds, and she was deported to Russia.

Emma Goldman had hailed the Russian Revolution, she found herself repelled by the Bolshevik dictatorship and left Russia. *My Disillusionment in Russia* (1923) and *My Further Disillusionment in Russia* (1924) stirred world controversy. She married a Welsh miner to obtain British citizenship, and friends bought her a home in France. Her distinguished autobiography *Living My Life* appeared in 1931.

During the Spanish Civil War (1936) Goldman actively supported her anarchist comrades. She died in Toronto, in Canada, on May 14, 1940. Though she had been barred from the United States (except for a 90-day visit in 1934), her body was permitted entry, and she was buried in Chicago.

Further Reading

Emma Goldman is represented in Charles Hurd, ed., *A Treasury of Great American Speeches* (1959). Her career is fully reviewed in Richard Drinnon, *Rebel in Paradise: A Biography of Emma Goldman* (1961). Eunice Minette Schuster, *Native American Anarchism* (1932), helps place her in perspective.

Additional Sources

Chalberg, John, *Emma Goldman: American individualist,* New York, NY: HarperCollins, 1991.

Drinnon, Richard, *Rebel in paradise: a biography of Emma Goldman,* Chicago: University of Chicago Press, 1982, 1961.

Falk, Candace, *Love, anarchy, and Emma Goldman,* New Brunswick N.J.: Rutgers University Press, 1990.

Ganguli, Birendranath, *Emma Goldman: portrait of a rebel woman,* New Delhi: Allied, 1979.

Goldman, Emma, *Living my life: an autobiography of Emma Goldma,* Salt Lake City, Utah: G.M. Smith, 1982.

Goldman, Emma, *A woman without a country,* Sanday Scot.: Cienfuegos Press, 1979.

Morton, Marian J., *Emma Goldman and the American left: "Nowhere at home"*, New York, N.Y.: Twayne Publishers, 1992.

Solomon, Martha, *Emma Goldman,* Boston: Twayne Publishers, 1987.

Wexler, Alice, *Emma Goldman in America,* Boston: Beacon Press, 1984.

Wexler, Alice, *Emma Goldman in exile: from the Russian Revolution to the Spanish Civil War,* Boston: Beacon Press, 1989. □

Josephine Goldmark

Josephine Goldmark (1877-1950), believing that most political and economic problems could be resolved by disciplined intelligence, devoted her life to helping agencies of government improve the lot of women and children.

Josephine Goldmark was the youngest of ten children. Her father, a chemist, had been forced to flee from Vienna after the Revolution of 1848; her mother had been brought to the United States from Prague about the same time. The children, proud of their European background, became enthusiastic Americans. Josephine received her BA from Bryn Mawr College. While doing graduate work at Barnard she volunteered for the New York branch of the Consumers' League, where her older sister Pauline was secretary.

The Consumers' League had been founded in 1891 to try to influence employers to improve the working conditions of shopgirls. A decade later, under the direction of Florence Kelley, the league was concerned with women working in factories, sweatshops, and homes, as well as in stores. Until Kelley's death in 1932, Goldmark was a friend and ally. Without Kelley's penchant for public agitation, Goldmark contributed painstaking research, and her writings were all the more powerful because they were understated and unrhetorical.

In the early 20th century some states were beginning to regulate the hours, or the wages, or the "conditions of labor" of children, or women, or all workers. Some of the legislation was poorly drafted or based on slight knowledge of the facts; there were seldom provisions for effective administration. Even more important, employers found the federal courts sympathetic to their protests that labor legislation "unreasonably" abridged the ability of employers and employees to contract freely with each other. In 1905, for example, the Supreme Court declared that a New York law was unreasonable in limiting to ten the number of hours in a day which a man could be employed in a bakery.

Goldmark's first publication was a compilation in 1907, for the benefit of state legislatures, of the laws already passed regulating child labor. The next year, learning that the Supreme Court was going to review an Oregon law limiting. The number of hours a woman could work in a laundry (or a factory), Goldmark was able to persuade Louis D. Brandeis, her brother-in-law, to help defend the law. The result was the now-famous "Brandeis brief." In only two pages Brandeis discussed the legal issues; Goldmark had supplied him with more than 100 pages of documents—laws, parliamentary investigations, the findings of social theorists—to show that reasonable people reasonably concluded that women in the workforce required special protections. The Supreme Court accepted this novel mode of argument, declaring that, given woman's "disposition and habits of life," some legislation "to protect her seems necessary" to secure the "real equality" to which she is constitutionally entitled.

In 1912 Goldmark published an 800-page study, *Fatigue and Efficiency,* which argued that reducing hours not only increased output, but also improved the quality of life of the worker and the worker's family. A realistic legislature and judiciary would, she argued, consider such reasonable goals as fully justifying intelligent labor legislation. In rejecting the arguments of "critics"—mostly male, mostly employers—Goldmark anticipated the protests of some feminists in the 1920s and later that any legislation specifically "protecting" women made them second-class citizens. To argue that way, she declared, was "superficial"; anyone who faced "the facts" had to acknowledge that women were different enough to require special consideration.

Goldmark was executive secretary of a special committee on nursing convened by the Rockefeller Foundation immediately after World War I; she was the principal author of the report *Nursing and Nursing Education in the United States* (1923). Public interest in nursing had soared during the war and the devastating epidemic of influenza in 1918-1919. In previous decades major reforms had been accomplished in the training of doctors, lawyers, and engineers, but many nurses-in-training were still regarded as apprentices at best, cheap labor at worst. Goldmark carried out an exhaustive survey of nursing education in America and abroad, and she called for a basic liberal arts education, carefully supervised clinical training, and professional work for such key specialties as public health nursing. Subsequently Goldmark served as a director of the New York Visiting Nurses Service.

Always a private person, Goldmark in her later years, while maintaining her friendship with such leaders as Frances Perkins and Eleanor Roosevelt, devoted an increasing amount of her time to writing. In 1930 she published *Pilgrims of '48,* a discursive account of her parents' experiences in Austria-Hungary and the United States. In 1936 she showed her admiration for the "social engineering" that sustained *Democracy in Denmark.* At her death she was at work on a biography of Florence Kelley (published posthumously in 1950 as *Impatient Crusader.*

Further Reading

There is a good biographical sketch in *Notable American Women* (1971). See the obituary in the *New York Times* for December 16, 1950. An excellent account of a generation of reformers, including Goldmark, is Robert Bremner, *From the Depths: The Discovery of Poverty in the United States* (1956). A recent survey of the difficult experiences of wage-earning women in the United States is Alice Kessler-Harris, *Out to Work* (1982). ☐

Carlo Goldoni

The plays of the Italian dramatist, poet, and librettist Carlo Goldoni (1707-1793) brought new realism and more credible characterization to the Italian stage. He wrote more than 250 works in Italian, Venetian dialect, and French.

B orn to a prosperous middle-class family, Carlo Goldoni displayed a theatrical inclination from early childhood. As a university student, he often put aside his law books to attend performances. In 1734, after 3 years in the diplomatic service, Goldoni became poet of the Imer company in Venice and successively was appointed director of the S. Samuele and S. Giovanni Crisostomo theaters. Goldoni's marriage in 1736 to Nicoletta Connio, daughter of a prominent Genoese family, dates from this formative period.

Although he interrupted theatrical activities in 1744 to practice law, Goldoni returned to Venice in 1748 as poet of the S. Angelo theater, then under the leadership of Girolamo Medebac. Overworked and underpaid—his contract for 1750 demanded 16 new plays—Goldoni accepted a competing offer from the Vendramin brothers, impresarios of the S. Luca theater.

The years 1748-1762 represent the most successful of Goldoni's career because now he was able to incorporate his views on dramatic reform into the fabric of his works. Until Goldoni, the prevailing commedia dell'arte style depended upon actors who improvised their roles from a list of stock characters. Therefore drama revolved about the actors and the success with which their talents impressed the audience. Goldoni's works signaled a new direction in which primacy was soon restored to the playwright, whose scripts—not an actor's improvisations—determined the play.

By observing society and providing plausible motivation for his characters, Goldoni's more credible and more realistic works soon gained an immense following. Among his most successful are *The Crafty Widow* (1748); *The Antiquarian's Family* (1749), in which Goldoni points to the conflict between the rising bourgeoisie and the decaying nobility; *The Comic Theatre* (1750), which he calls "less a Comedy than a Foreword to all my Comedies"; and *La Locandiera* (1753; *Mine Hostess*), in which the protagonist Mirandolina astutely manages to keep the affections and services of the headwaiter at her inn, while igniting the interest of two noble guests, one a professed woman hater, the other an old miser. From these and other works emerges the ethical content of Goldoni's character plays. A believer in modernity and progress, he championed the rights of women and the equality of all classes. In espousing these views, Goldoni frequently satirized the aristocracy and their courts.

Goldoni's successes did not spare him from criticism. During the period 1748-1753, while Goldoni was creating more realistic and thoughtful plays for the S. Angelo theater, he was often attacked by Pietro Chiari, then a writer of sentimental, romantic dramas at the S. Samuele theater. An example of their rivalry was Chiari's parody, *The School for Widows*, which appeared shortly after Goldoni's *The Crafty Widow*. After moving to the S. Luca theater, Goldoni faced the more formidable hostility of Count Carlo Gozzi. Irascible and title-conscious, Gozzi endeavored to discredit Goldoni in any possible way, for the democratic, progressive Goldoni held views diametrically opposite to those of the aristocratic conservative. Disguised as a defense of traditional dramatic forms, Gozzi's criticism of Goldoni's realism was an extension of this personal antagonism.

Goldoni, a mild-mannered, pleasant person with no desire to continue this bitter polemic, left Venice for the prestigious directorship of the Italian theater in Paris. However, after 2 unhappy years (1762-1764) he accepted appointment as tutor in Italian (1764-1768) to the daughters of King Louis XVI. While maintaining residence in Paris, Goldoni furnished new material in Italian and dialect for the Venetian stage. Also from this period come his works written in French. Especially noteworthy are the comedy *Le Bourra bienfaisant* (1771) and *Memoirs of His Life and Theatre* (1787), from which the reader gains a view of Goldoni's evolving dramatic style and detailed accounts of artists, directors, and theaters of his time.

The French Revolution brought an end to the pension Goldoni had been receiving from the French government. Already in his 80s and nearing blindness, Goldoni spent his last years in penurious suffering. Ironically, news of the reinstatement of his pension in 1793 arrived the day after his death.

Further Reading

For English texts of Goldoni's works see Carlo Goldoni, *Three Comedies* (1961), which contains *Mine Hostess, The Boors,* and *The Fan;* and his play *The Comic Theatre: A Comedy in Three Acts* (1750; trans. 1969). The best book in English on Goldoni is Joseph Spencer Kennard, *Goldoni and the Venice of His Time* (1920). For background information see Giacomo Oreglia, *The Commedia dell'Arte* (1961; trans. 1968).

Additional Sources

Holme, Timothy, *A servant of many masters: the life and times of Carlo Goldoni,* London: Jupiter, 1976. □

James Michael Goldsmith

James Michael Goldsmith (born 1933), British-French industrialist and financier, achieved international renown as a corporate raider after a successful career in manufacturing and distributing consumer products.

James Michael Goldsmith was born in Paris, France, on February 26, 1933, to Frank Goldsmith, manager of a luxury hotel chain and former British Parliament member, and Marcelle Mouiller Goldsmith. *Tycoon,* the title of Goldsmith's biography, reported that he is a descendant of the Goldschmidts, German Jewish bankers of Frankfurt, and of French Catholics on his mother's side. Seeking greater freedom and opportunities, his wealthy grandfather left Germany and settled in England; his father was educated at Oxford, was elected to Parliament, and served in World War I. However, anti-German views in England caused the father to lose his parliamentary seat, and the family moved to France. During World War II the family fled France to escape from the Nazis and lived in the Bahamas. The series of family dislocations were to give Goldsmith, who later owned luxurious homes in four countries, a cosmopolitan outlook. With his wealth he established an almost private world where he could pursue new business and personal goals.

James, known as "Jimmy" to his friends, enjoyed a privileged upbringing, attended Eton for several years, and was independent-minded and adventure-seeking. He enjoyed betting on horse races and playing poker. At age 16 he left school after deciding a formal education was not needed to achieve financial success.

Several years of high society life were followed by military service before Goldsmith entered business in partnership with his older brother in 1953. The next year his young wife, Isabella, died, leaving him with an infant daughter to raise; this tragedy made him more serious about pursuing a career. In 1955 he founded Laboratoires Cassene, a French pharmaceutical manufacturing company. When over-expansion brought him to the brink of bankruptcy in 1957, he was forced to sell the firm. But Goldsmith remained in the same line of business, becoming more fiscally conservative.

Goldsmith's new companies, Laboratoires Laffort and Laboratoires Lanord, known as Gustin-Milical outside France, grew into a profitable pharmaceutical chain. With the assistance of a banker, Selim Zilkha, Goldsmith established Ward Casson Ltd. in Great Britain to distribute similar products; next, he acquired and expanded British pharmaceutical and children's furniture store chains. Goldsmith succeeded primarily by marketing a popular slimming product, a self-tanning lotion, a disinfectant, and lower-priced antibiotics and by making other health products widely available and less expensive.

In 1964 Goldsmith entered the grocery distribution business with the founding of Cavenham Foods Ltd. in Britain. He also purchased the rights to some of Britain's best-known food brand names. The turning point of his career came in 1971 when he succeeded in a hostile takeover of Bovril, a long established British food company. The bitter fight, disapproved of by London's financial elite, led Goldsmith to offer increasing higher bids and to incur a large debt. However, his restructuring and selling of Bovril's subsidiaries resulted in great profits. This deal earned Goldsmith his reputation for financial expertise, but establishment status eluded him.

In 1972 he continued his expansion in the food industry by acquiring Allied Suppliers, Britain's fourth largest chain of grocery stores. Also, as early as 1973 Goldsmith began investing in American companies. In December 1973 he announced that Cavenham Holdings had acquired control of Grand Union, the tenth largest supermarket chain in America, for $62 million.

By the mid-1970s, when Goldsmith had achieved his goal of financial success, new endeavors, including politics in England and publishing in France, attracted his attention. In the early 1970s he became an active supporter of Conservative party efforts, even offering advice on reforming the party. In 1976 he was granted a knighthood. However, Goldsmith's fame and wealth led to public criticism of his business methods and personal life. In 1977 he left England and reestablished his business headquarters in France. Goldsmith's business and personal life was still considered unconventional, however, and, to a degree, anti-authoritarian. He followed the Social Darwinist "survival of the fittest" theory in business, and he openly maintained two families, one in England and one in France.

During the financial boom of the 1980s Goldsmith was the ideal person to pursue corporate restructuring of conglomerates. He believed the corporate raider brought more success to the acquired company. In 1980 his international business empire included some of his earlier holdings plus a 24 percent ownership of Diamond International Corporation (a timber company) and control of Basic Resources International. Goldsmith angered environmentalists by selling the rest of his holdings in Diamond International, which included 96,000 acres in New York's Adirondack Park, for development.

In 1985 Goldsmith acquired Crown Zellerback, a California-based paper and timber company, after a bitter bidding war. However, in 1986 he was thwarted in his hostile bid for Goodyear Tire and Rubber Company of Akron, Ohio. Nonetheless, he made a $93 million profit by selling his holdings back to Goodyear.

By the mid-1980s Goldsmith had joined the ranks of the renowned American corporate raiders T. Boone Pickens, Carl Icahn, Saul Steinberg, and Irwin Jacobs. Like them, he believed his actions were improving the American economy.

Although Goldsmith's complex business empire at one time consisted of three levels of holding companies, by 1988 his organization was based in the Cayman Islands, West Indies, under the name General Oriental Investments. A small group of long-time associates were his principal advisers and management team, although investment banks, including Lazard Freres, also gave advice.

When the business climate changed after the stock market crash in October 1987, Goldsmith did not change his strategy. However, the withdrawal in April 1990 of his hostile bid for the British conglomerate B.A.T. temporarily halted his takeover activities. Nonetheless, Goldsmith's financial resources and his manufacturing and distributing

experience enabled him to benefit from new opportunities provided by the economic unification of Europe.

In 1993, Goldsmith did an abrupt about-face and left business to devote himself to environmental causes. In 1994 he published *The Trap,* setting forth the thesis that social stability was being destroyed by global free trade, intensive agriculture, and nuclear energy. Goldsmith continued to be concerned with trade issues, speaking out against GATT (General Agreement on Tariffs and Trade) in 1994. He argued that GATT could lead to social chaos because low-wage foreign workers, augmented by the collapse of communism, would displace workers in America and Europe. Competition for cheap labor, in his opinion, would enrich big corporations, dislocate people in poor countries, and deprive European workers of needed jobs. Goldsmith suggested local continental trading blocs as an alternative. In 1995 Goldsmith self published *The Response,* which presented evidence to support his thesis in his first book.

Using his anti-free trade agenda, and his finances, Goldsmith established two political parties. "L'Autre Europe" campaigned for a European Union that refuted Nafta and GATT and that fostered corporate rules for the environment. In 1995 Goldsmith was elected to the European Parliament, along with 12 other like-minded individuals. In 1995, Goldsmith also formed and financed the Referendum Party in order to force a referendum on the issue of the European Union, to run candidates in the next British election and to extend his views to that country's parliament. Although, in 1997, it seemed unlikely that the Referendum Party would win many votes in the general elections, Goldsmith undermined efforts by other British parties to garner support for participation in a European Union that supported free trade.

Goldsmith's character and personal life have puzzled some people, but his ancestry and childhood experiences help explain his personality. His loyalty has always been given to individuals and not to countries or corporations; this was a lesson he learned from his father's life.

Further Reading

The best source on Goldsmith is Geoffrey Wansell's biography, *Tycoon. The Life of James Goldsmith* (1987). An apparently authorized biography, it describes Goldsmith's career, business views, and personal philosophy in detail, but does not analyze his character or motives. Goldsmith's career as a corporate raider has been well documented by contemporary articles in the *Wall Street Journal, New York Times,* and business magazines; dozens of stories describe his 1990 thwarted B.A.T. takeover. Goldsmith is listed in *Who's Who 1990* [a British Who's Who].
For biographical resources about James Goldsmith see: Fallon, Ivan, *Billionaire: The Life and Times of Sir James Goldsmith* (1992); Ingrams, Richard, *Goldenballs;* Wansell, Geoffrey, *Sir James Goldsmith.* Books written by James Goldsmith include: Goldsmith, James, *The Trap* (1992) and Goldsmith, James, *The Response.*
Periodical articles about Sir James Goldsmith include: *Backpacker* (February 1993); *New Statesman and Society* (March 12, 1993); *Barron's* (May 17, 1993); *Business Week* (May 24, 1993); *The New Yorker* (May 31, 1993); *New Statesman and Society* (November 25, 1994); *Business Week* (De-

cember 5, 1994); *The Economist* (April 29, 1995); *Gentlemen's Quarterly* (June 1995); *The Economist,* (September 2, 1995); *Financial World* (November 7, 1995); *National Review* (November 27, 1995); *The Economist* (May 4, 1996); *The American Spectator* (July 1996); *The New York Review of Books* (October 17, 1996); *New Statesman* (October 18, 1996); *The Economist* (October 19, 1996); *The Nation* (November 25, 1996); and *Business Week* (January 27, 1997). ☐

Oliver Goldsmith

The Canadian poet Oliver Goldsmith (1794-1861) is remembered primarily for "The Rising Village," the first book of verse to be written by a native Canadian, published in London.

Oliver Goldsmith, a grandnephew of the British poet of the same name, was born of United Empire loyalist stock in St. Andrews, New Brunswick. When he was a small boy, the family moved to Halifax, Nova Scotia. At the age of 11 he began work in the dispensary of the Naval Hospital at Halifax and then became successively an assistant in an ironmonger's shop, a bookseller's helper, and a merchant's clerk. He interrupted his work to attend the Halifax Grammar School and in 1810 entered the commissariat department of the British army; he spent almost the whole of the remainder of his life in that department, becoming eventually deputy commissary general. In connection with his duties he spent some time in England, Hong Kong, and Corfu, but his base was usually in the Atlantic Provinces. He died in Liverpool.

Goldsmith's literary career began in 1822, when he joined an amateur theater group in Halifax and tried his hand at writing an opening address. The address was rejected, but, as Goldsmith puts it in his *Autobiography:* "Encouraged by some friends I wrote a poem called *The Rising Village....* The celebrated author of *The Deserted Village* [his granduncle] had pathetically displayed the anguish of his countrymen, on being forced, for various causes, to quit their native plains, . . . and to seek a refuge in regions at that time but little known.... I, therefore, endeavoured to describe the sufferings they experienced in a new and uncultivated country, the difficulties they surmounted, the rise and progress of a village, and the prospects which promised happiness to its future possessors."

The Rising Village is of historical interest. It has also been hailed as a great document of pioneer life, but it is in fact not nearly as accurate in its account of conditions in early Nova Scotia as were the writings of Thomas Chandler Haliburton. As a poem, it follows *The Deserted Village* in meter and general structure but falls far short of its model in artistic merit. It lacks both the wit and the passion of the older poem, is less specific in its details, employs mainly conventional epithets, and has very few striking figures of speech. The picture it gives of a flourishing Nova Scotian

economy is greatly idealized, but it does express the growing pride and self-esteem of the colony in the 1820s.

Further Reading

There is no book on Goldsmith. The chief source is the *Autobiography of Oliver Goldsmith,* discovered and edited by the Reverend Wilfrid E. Myatt (1943). Goldsmith's life and work are examined in John P. Matthews, *Tradition in Exile: A Comparative Study of Social Influences on the Development of Australian and Canadian Poetry in the Nineteenth Century* (1962), and Carl F. Klinck, ed., *Literary History of Canada: Canadian Literature in English* (1965).

Additional Sources

Goldsmith, Oliver, *Autobiography of Oliver Goldsmith: a chapter in Canada's literary history,* Hantsport, N.S.: Lancelot Press, 1985. ☐

Oliver Goldsmith

The British poet, dramatist, novelist, and essayist Oliver Goldsmith (1730-1774) wrote, translated, or compiled more than 40 volumes. The works for which he is remembered are marked by good sense, moderation, balance, order, and intellectual honesty.

The fifth child of a country rector in Ireland, Oliver Goldsmith entered Trinity College, Dublin, in 1745 and earned a bachelor of arts degree in 1749. He studied medicine at the University of Edinburgh in 1752-1753 but did not take a degree. After further medical training at the University of Leiden, he traveled on the Continent, not to return to London until 1756, when he attempted to establish a medical practice.

Goldsmith soon began to supplement his meager income from medicine by contributing reviews and essays to such popular journals as the *Monthly* and the *Critical.* His first book, *An Enquiry into the Present State of Polite Learning in Europe* (1759), included an important essay on the English stage. By the mid-1760s Goldsmith, or "Goldy" as Dr. Johnson fondly nicknamed him, had established a steady income as a compiler. An original member of the famous "Club" founded by Dr. Johnson in 1764, Goldsmith enjoyed the friendship of such 18th century notables as Edmund Burke and Sir Joshua Reynolds, who later wrote a brief biographical sketch of him. Goldsmith's inability to handle his money, his extravagance, his generosity, and his habit of borrowing money from his friends kept the stocky, pockmarked author in debt until the end of his life. Indeed, he is said to have left debts amounting to £2,000.

Goldsmith made his early literary reputation as an essayist. The eight weekly numbers of the *Bee* (1759), which contain some excellent small poems, dramatic criticism, moral tales, and serious and fanciful discourses, exhibit his preoccupation with vivid and rich human detail and his

felicitous style. Perhaps his finest sustained work as an essayist, however, was *The Citizen of the World* (1762), which had appeared serially in the *Public Ledger* in 1760-1761. Goldsmith employed the popular 18th-century device of a foreign traveler commenting in letters to his home country upon the strange customs of the lands through which he passed. These "Chinese Letters" exhibit Goldsmith at his relaxed, playful, and graceful best.

Poetry and Fiction

The Traveller (1764), Goldsmith's first major poem, expresses such conventional ideas of his age as the vanity of human wishes and despair in the search for happiness. Best described as a philosophic-descriptive lyric, the poem is a panoramic, imaginative tour through Italy, Switzerland, and France. His poetic masterpiece, *The Deserted Village* (1770), has often and erroneously been mistaken as a wholly autobiographical poem. Picturing the economic difficulties of rural life, the dangers of luxury, and "trade's unfeeling train," the poem expresses current 18th-century ideas in so personal, moving, and aphoristic a fashion that it remains one of the most frequently quoted poems in the English language. Both poems exhibit Goldsmith's mastery of the heroic couplet, the major poetic form of the period. He left a third long poem entitled *Retaliation* unfinished at his death.

Goldsmith's one novel, *The Vicar of Wakefield,* was received indifferently upon its publication in 1766 but soon became popular and remained the most widely read of all the 18th-century novels for the next 100 years. According to

James Boswell, Dr. Johnson saved the distraught Goldsmith from a debtors' prison by selling this manuscript, the only one he could find in Goldsmith's lodgings, for £60.

The brief novel, which leads Dr. Primrose and his family from disaster to fresh disaster, has greater structural and thematic unity than most critics have acknowledged. Its greatest appeal, however, lies in its gentle and tolerant humor, the attractiveness of Dr. Primrose's character, the combined pathos and irony of the narrative, and Goldsmith's graceful prose style.

Plays and Other Works

Goldsmith's first play, *The Good Natur'd Man,* found little favor when it was finally produced in 1768. While it has important historical interest because it marks a major turn away from the sentimental comedy that had dominated the 18th-century stage, it preaches a prudent benevolence throughout which has little appeal for the modern reader.

The second of his plays, *She Stoops to Conquer* (1773), is by far the more impressive of the two. Despite a farcical plot and the patent absurdities of Young Marlowe's mistaken assumption that the Hardcastle mansion is an inn and of Mrs. Hardcastle's delusion that her husband is a highwayman, the play's wit, good humor, and lively characterizations made it an immediate success and have given it continuing popularity. In their search for marriage and social position, the characters have a warmth and charm quite atypical of most plays of the period.

As compiler, author, and translator, Goldsmith participated in a host of commercial publishing ventures during his lifetime. He was involved, for example, in the publication of a five-volume abridgment of Plutarch's *Lives* (1762), a two-volume *History of England* (1764) followed by a four-volume continuation (1771), two volumes of *The Beauties of English Poesy* (1767), two volumes of *Roman History* (1769), two volumes of *Grecian History* (1774), and eight volumes of *An History of the Earth and Animated Nature* (1774).

Further Reading

The authoritative biographical study of Goldsmith is Ralph Wardle, *Oliver Goldsmith* (1957; rev. ed. 1969). Other studies include Ricardo Quintana, *Oliver Goldsmith: A Georgian Study* (1967), a scholarly though sometimes uneven work, and Robert H. Hopkins, *The True Genius of Oliver Goldsmith* (1969), an excellent critical commentary on Goldsmith's writings. Useful discussions of Goldsmith's work are in Alan D. McKillop, *The Early Masters of English Fiction* (1956), and in Ian Watt, *The Rise of the Novel: Studies in Defoe, Richardson and Fielding* (1957). Recommended for general historical and social background are J. H. Plumb, *England in the Eighteenth Century* (1951; rev. ed. 1966); A. R. Humphreys, *The Augustan World: Society, Thought, and Letters in Eighteenth Century England* (1954; rev. ed. 1963); Ian Watt, *The Augustan Age* (1968); and R. J. White, *The Age of George III* (1968).

Additional Sources

Freeman, William, *Oliver Goldsmith,* Philadelphia: R. West, 1977 c1952.

Gamble, William, *Two Irish poets: Goldsmith and Moore,* Philadelphia: R. West, 1977.

Ginger, John, *The notable man: the life and times of Oliver Goldsmith,* London: Hamilton, 1977.

Goldsmith: interviews and recollections, Houndmills, Basingstoke, Hampshire: Macmillan Press; New York: St. Martin's Press, 1993.

MacLennan, Munro, *The secret of Oliver Goldsmith,* New York: Vantage Press, 1975.

Sells, A. Lytton (Arthur Lytton), *Oliver Goldsmith: his life and works,* New York: Barnes & Noble Books, 1974.

Wibberley, Leonard, *The good-natured man: a portrait of Oliver Goldsmith,* New York: Morrow, 1979. □

Barry Goldwater

Barry Goldwater (born 1909) was elected as a Republican to the U.S. Senate five times between 1952 and 1980, leaving temporarily to run unsuccessfully for president in 1964. His outspoken conservatism gained him the label "Mr. Conservative" in American politics. He was considered the most important American conservative between Senator Robert Taft's death in 1953 and Ronald Reagan's election as governor of California in 1966.

Barry Morris Goldwater was born in Phoenix, Arizona, on January 1, 1909, the first child of Baron and Josephine Williams Goldwater. His Polish-born grandfather and great-uncle had migrated to the Arizona territory from the California Gold Rush fields. They discovered that there were easier ways to make a fortune - such as operating a bordello and bar. They also founded a small general store, J. Goldwater & Bro., in La Paz in 1867. Soon the brothers opened stores throughout Arizona with the Phoenix branch, established in 1872, becoming the flagship of the family operation. This store was headed by Barry Goldwater's father, Baron. Barry was an indifferent student at Phoenix's Union High school, where he showed early leadership abilities when his classmates elected him as President of the Freshman class. His principal suggested that he might be happier elsewhere, so young Barry was sent by his family to finish his last four years at Staunton Military Academy in Virginia. There he won the medal as best all-around cadet and began his lifelong interest in the military. Although he hoped to attend the U. S. Military Academy at West point, his ill father insisted enroll at the University of Arizona. He completed only one year, dropping out to join the family department store business when his father died in 1929.

Successful Businessman

Goldwater showed good aptitude for the retail business, rising from a junior clerkship to the presidency of the firm by 1937. He was an innovative manager, setting up the first employees' health-hospitalization plan of any Phoenix mercantile firm, forming a flying club for his employees, introducing a number of novel product lines, and creating a national reputation for the store by taking out advertisements in the *New Yorker.* In addition to being the most prestigious store in Phoenix, the Goldwater enterprise shared the city's booster spirit, cooperating in civic initiatives to improve the city and attract new residents.

He was the first Phoenix businessman to hire African-Americans as sales clerks, thereby breaking the "color barrier" in the city's hiring practices. It was during this time as well that Goldwater overworked himself into two nervous breakdowns and began to have trouble with alcohol, two issues that his later political opponents wee always quick to recall.

In September 1934 Goldwater culminated a brief courtship by marrying Margaret (Peggy) Johnson, daughter of a successful Indiana businessman whose firm later became part of Borg-Warner. The couple had four children, Joanne (1936), Barry Jr. (1938), Michael (1940), and Peggy (1944).

Goldwater eagerly interrupted his business career to take part in World War II. Though his age seemingly disqualified him from the air combat assignment he coveted, Goldwater parlayed his decade-old reserve commission into an assignment in the Army Air Force. He served first as an instructor in the gunnery command. Then, for most of the war, he used the flying skills he had leaned in the late 1920's to pilot supply runs in the India-Burma theater and across the Atlantic as well. When the war ended he accepted the task of organizing the Arizona Air National

Guard, eventually achieving the rank of brigadier general in the Air Force Reserve.

By the late 1940s Goldwater was a locally prominent figure, winning acclaim as Phoenix "Man of the Year" in 1949. He had joined in a citizens' reform effort resulting in a revised city charter that gave extensive powers to a city manager and called for at-large election of the city council. When suitable council candidates failed to emerge in 1949 Goldwater ran for a council seat himself, leading the city-wide ticket in the nonpartisan election.

"Mr. Conservative"

Goldwater soon outgrew local politics. Frustrated with the policies of the New and Fair Deals, in 1950 he devoted his energies to managing the successful gubernatorial campaign of Howard Pyle. Sensing an opportunity for the Republican party to become truly competitive in the state for the first time, he decided to challenge Democratic Senate Majority Leader Ernest McFarland in the 1952 election. Campaigning as a staunchly conservative critic of "Trumanism," excessive federal spending, the "no win" U.S. strategy in the Korean War, and what he saw as a weak and futile foreign policy toward the Soviet Union, Goldwater eked out a narrow victory. He squeaked by on the coattails of Republican presidential candidate Eisenhower by over 35,000 votes and began his long and distinguished national political career.

Goldwater's entry into the Senate was at a critical time for conservatives. The twenty years that had passed since Republicans held power had seen the New Deal Domestic Reforms, World War II and the rise of the Cold War. The American political landscape was very different from when Herbert Hoover promised a "chicken in every pot". Many questioned if conservatism with its emphasis on state's rights and limited central government was even relevant in the new atmosphere Initially a supporter of the Robert A. Taft over Eisenhower for the 1952 Republican nomination, Goldwater maintained independence from Eisenhower's programs and was one of his most outspoken critics. Notably he criticized foreign aid spending and supported Senator Joseph McCarthy's campaign against "Communism-in-government" even after McCarthy clearly lost favor with Eisenhower. In December 1954 the Arizonan was one of only 22 senators (all Republicans) who took McCarthy's side in the vote to censure the Wisconsin senator. Though he agreed with Eisenhower on most domestic issues, Goldwater often took more extreme positions than the president—especially in his condemnation of labor unions, his opposition to federal action in civil rights matters, and his advocacy of a strongly nationalist foreign policy. At one point castigating the Eisenhower policies as a "dime-store New Deal," he opposed Eisenhower's use of federal troops in the Little Rock integration crisis and criticized the administration for producing balanced budgets in only three of its eight years.

Goldwater gained in influence during the 1950s. Through his effective leadership of the Republican Senatorial Campaign Committee he won affection and respect from his party colleagues. After his solid re-election victory (with 56 percent of the vote) in 1958 Goldwater began to receive considerable media attention as the leader of the conservative movement. He enhanced this image through a thrice-weekly syndicated newspaper column and by publishing in 1960 an extended statement of his political creed, *The Conscience of the Conservative* (which eventually sold 3.5 million copies). He was viewed, despite often contradictory and inconsistent casual remarks, as a straight-from-the-gut conservative whose appeal stemmed from the fact that his own profound confusion somehow reflected his supporter's anxiety. Wisely foregoing a political battle with Republican liberals in 1960, he settled for exercising behind-the-scenes influence on the platform while supporting Richard Nixon for the presidential nomination. His loyalty to the party ticket won him Nixon's support for the future.

Presidential Candidate

Goldwater later contended that he was not eager for the 1964 nomination against the popular Kennedy, but he came increasingly to be regarded as his party's likely nominee. Friendly rivals from their years together in the Senate, he and Kennedy even discussed the type of campaigns they might wage against each other. Kennedy's assassination and the accession of Texas-born Lyndon B. Johnson to the presidency further reduced Goldwater's enthusiasm for the nomination; as Johnson's appeal in the South and West threatened to keep Goldwater from capitalizing on his own natural strengths in those areas. By the end of 1963, however, he succumbed to pressures from the informal "Draft Goldwater" group that had been in existence since 1961; he announced his candidacy on January 3, 1964.

Goldwater chose to enter only selected primaries, while building support in states where delegates were selected by other means. After a damaging loss in the New Hampshire primary at the start of the campaign, he won important victories in Illinois and Nebraska; then, in early June he defeated his only real competition for the nomination—New York Governor Nelson Rockefeller—in the crucial California primary. Goldwater's nomination was then inevitable. He won on the first ballot at the convention in San Francisco, but events revealed the depth of division in the party: Rockefeller was booed by the predominantly conservative delegates, while nominee Goldwater was pilloried by his liberal foes (and the press) for a statement in his acceptance speech: "I would remind you that extremism in the defense of liberty is no vice. And let me remind you that moderation in the pursuit of justice is no virtue."

While Goldwater added to his own problems by making some gratuitous and inappropriate statements in the campaign, he never had a chance to defeat Johnson. Public perception of Goldwater as an extremist was fed by events at the GOP convention and by his well-known opposition to federal civil rights laws (he did not oppose integration, but thought that states properly had jurisdiction in such matters). The result was a Johnson landslide: Goldwater received only 38.8 percent of the vote and carried only five states in the deep South and Arizona. Goldwater's appeal to persons who wanted a return to a prewar American way of life was swept aside in view of Johnson's progressive Great Society.

Elder Statesman

Goldwater was never again considered a viable presidential candidate, but his stature in the party and as a spokesman for the conservative cause was firmly established. Back in private life (he had given up the chance to run for re-election in 1964), he announced that Nixon was his choice for the presidency in 1968 and then set about putting his own career back on track. In 1968, as Nixon narrowly won the presidency, Goldwater was elected once again to the Senate (with 57 percent of the vote).

His White House ambitions put aside, Goldwater re-established himself as a forceful presence in the Senate. He strongly backed the American military involvement in Vietnam and, as a prominent member of the Armed Services Committee, he gave strong support to the Nixon administration's aggressive defense policies. He was more critical on domestic issues, where he again thought Nixon too inclined to temporize; in particular, he felt the wage-price guidelines of the early 1970s were a "disaster."

Never one to waver in a political cause, Goldwater remained loyal to Nixon, suspending judgment while the Watergate crisis unfolded in 1973 and early 1974. He did not finally break from Nixon until the revelation, on August 5, 1974, that the president had indeed acted to obstruct justice in the Watergate case. Because of his stature and unquestioned integrity, Goldwater's defection was a symbolic final blow to Nixon, who resigned from the presidency four days later.

Goldwater won his most convincing re-election victory in 1974, being returned to the Senate by a 58 percent vote. He was impatient with what he regarded as President Ford's vacillations on policy—as he had been with Nixon—but again he was a loyal (if outspoken) follower, supporting the president over Ronald Reagan for the 1976 Republican nomination. Ford's defeat placed in the White House a president for whom Goldwater developed genuine contempt, Jimmy Carter. He opposed Carter on nearly every major issue, including defense cutbacks, diplomatic recognition for the People's Republic of China, and the Panama Canal treaties. In 1980 he was an early, enthusiastic backer of his fellow conservative, Ronald Reagan, for the Republican nomination. Reagan's easy victory over Carter was accomplished on a platform echoing many of Goldwater's earlier positions. Goldwater himself was again re-elected in 1980, though with a narrower margin of victory than ever before. His age (71) and frequent hospitalizations apparently played a part in making the result so close, a fact suggesting that his fifth term in the Senate would be his last.

Although he regained his seat in 1988, Goldwater nevertheless was never again a power in the conservative movement. His libertarian streak made him uncomfortable with his own party's New Right social agenda. The strong desire of this New Right to use coercive power of the state to influence morality were at odds with what Goldwater believed were matters of personal choice. In 1979 Goldwater published his political memoir, *With No Apologies;* he wrote it early, he said, because he believed "the Republic is in danger" and "time is short." With Reagan's re-election in 1984, Goldwater's fears for the future abated somewhat. Yet he remained curiously unconnected to the upsurge of political conservatism reflected in Reagan's successes. Fiercely independent and seemingly out of step with the majority throughout his political career, he somehow seemed apart even from the "New Conservatives" dominating his party in the 1980s.

Nearing the end of 30 years in the Senate, Goldwater seemed to take special pleasure in the license afforded an elder statesman, daring to speak out against spokesmen for the Moral Majority whom he thought too self-serving as well as against his more traditional moderate-to-left targets.

After his retirement in 1987, Goldwater returned to Phoenix where he was still considered an asset to any political campaign. During the 1996 Presidential campaign, Goldwater's opinions and endorsements were continually sought. He eventually supported the candidacy of Senate majority leader Robert Dole, he was highly vocal in his praise of the possibility of former Joint Chiefs of Staff Colin Powell as president. One of Goldwater's major interests as Chairman of the Armed Services Committee was the passage of the Goldwater-Nichols Military Reform Act, which authorized the chairman of the Joint Chief's of Staff's ability to order other branches of the military to cooperate with one another. This act cut through bitter interservice rivalry that often crippled military operations, and enabled theater commanders to simply order different services under their command to work together without first going up the chain of command in Washington.

Though he suffered one of the worst electoral defeats in history when he sought the presidency, Barry Goldwater will certainly be considered one of the leading political figures of his era as he was responsible for ushering the conservative wing of the Republican party and relegating the moderates to a secondary position, thereby changing the face of American politics for decades.

Further Reading

The best account of Goldwater's life and career is his autobiography, *With No Apologies: The Personal and Political Memoirs of United States Senator Barry Goldwater* (1979). In the 1960s, when he was considered a presidential possibility, two biographies appeared; the more valuable is Jack Bell, *Mr. Conservative: Barry Goldwater* (1962); *Barry Goldwater: Freedom Is His Flight Plan* (1962), written by his long-time political aide Stephen Shadegg, is naturally very favorable in its view. Goldwater's 1964 presidential campaign is treated in John H. Kessel, *The Goldwater Coalition: Republican Strategies in 1964* (1968); Richard Rovere, *The Goldwater Caper* (1965); F. Clifton White, *Suite 3505: The Story of the Draft Goldwater Movement* (1967); and Theodore H. White, *The Making of the President 1964* (1965). In addition, Goldwater wrote a number of books expressing his political credo, including *The Conscience of a Conservative* (1960), *Why Not Victory? A Fresh Look at American Foreign Policy* (1962), *The Conscience of a Majority* (1970), and *The Coming Breakpoint* (1976). Finally, a number of studies of the Republican Party in recent times give considerable attention to his political impact, including Michael W. Miles, *The Odyssey of the American Right* (1980) and David W. Reinhard, *The Republican Right Since 1945* (1983). A lively interview in *Jet* describes Goldwater's ongoing independence July 24, 1995. □

Samuel Goldwyn

Polish-born American film producer Samuel Goldwyn (born 1882) was notable among Hollywood executives for his belief that artistic aspirations need not conflict with commercial success.

Samuel Goldwyn (original surname, Goldfish) was born in Warsaw on Aug. 17, 1882, ran away from home at the age of 9, and arrived in the United States 4 years later. He learned English in night school, supporting himself as a glove salesman.

In 1913 Goldwyn joined vaudeville producer Jesse L. Lasky and theatrical director Cecil B. DeMille in forming the first feature motion picture company on the West Coast. Their initial production, *The Squaw Man* (1913), was an instant success, as was *Carmen* (1915). When Lasky and DeMille merged with another film producer in 1916, Goldwyn became an independent producer and distributor. In 1919 he was instrumental in importing the European masterpiece *The Cabinet of Dr. Caligari,* which, despite its box office failure, helped establish Goldwyn's reputation.

Among Goldwyn's early films were *Jubilo* (1919), a drama about farm life; *The Penalty* (1922), a story of drug addiction; *Stella Dallas* (1925), a mature domestic drama; and *The Winning of Barbara Worth* (1927), the western that introduced Gary Cooper. Goldwyn was credited with making Cooper—and later Laurence Olivier and Danny Kaye—a movie star.

Goldwyn met the challenge of talking pictures by seeking writers who could furnish literate dialogue. Such literary figures as Lillian Hellman, Ben Hecht, Robert E. Sherwood, and Sidney Howard wrote scripts worthy of the talented directors Goldwyn chose. Goldwyn's first talking picture, *Bulldog Drummond* (1929), was a witty satire by Howard. *Arrowsmith* (1931), adapted from Sinclair Lewis's novel, was directed by John Ford. *The Wedding Night* (1935), about a strife-torn New England family, was powerfully directed by King Vidor.

With the highly acclaimed film of Lewis's *Dodsworth* (1936), Goldwyn began his long association with director William Wyler, collaborating on such excellent films as *These Three* (1936); Lillian Hellman's adaptation of her controversial play *The Children's Hour; Wuthering Heights* (1939), brilliantly acted by Laurence Olivier; *The Little Foxes* (1941), also written by Hellman; and *The Best Years of Our Lives* (1946), which won nine Academy Awards.

Other important Goldwyn productions included *The Secret Life of Walter Mitty* (1947), *Hans Christian Andersen* (1952), and *Guys and Dolls*. His last film was *Porgy and Bess* (1959). His impact and influence on the movie industry was significant.

Goldwyn was also known for his quick wit and humor. He was reported to have commented, "Pictures are for entertainment, messages should be delivered by Western Union." When asked about his autobiography, Goldwyn reportedly replied, "I don't think anybody should write his autobiography until after he's dead."

Further Reading

Goldwyn's *Behind the Screen* (1923) gives historical and autobiographical information. A well-written and entertaining biography is Alva Johnston, *The Great Goldwyn* (1937). Background information is in Richard Griffith and Arthur Mayer, *The Movies: The Sixty-year Story of the World of Hollywood and Its Effect on America* (1957), and Richard Schickel, *Movies: The History of an Art and an Institution* (1964). Arthur Marx chronicles the life of the famed film producer in *Goldwyn: the Man Behind the Myth* (1976). □

Nicolas Gombert

The Franco-Flemish composer Nicolas Gombert (ca. 1500-1556) introduced fully imitative treatment in the motet, and his method of composing the parody Mass remained the most important one throughout the Renaissance.

Almost nothing is known of the origin and early training of Nicolas Gombert. One edition of his four-voice motets with the ascription *Nicolai Gomberti Flandri Brugensis . . .* identifies his birthplace as Bruges, but other indirect evidence suggests the town of La Gorgue in Flanders. If the German music theorist Hermann Finck (*Practica musica,* 1556) is correct when he names Gombert a student of Josquin des Prez, such training probably occurred at Condé, where Josquin ended his illustrious career.

Gombert spent a large part of his creative life in the imperial chapel of Charles V. Gombert's name first appears on a *rolle des benefices* of Oct. 2, 1526, written in Granada, Spain, where Charles was temporarily sojourning. By 1529 Gombert was charged with training the royal choristers and composing music for court and chapel functions. He performed these duties until shortly before Dec. 28, 1540, when he is no longer mentioned in the chapel archives.

During these years Gombert and the choir accompanied the Emperor on many trips to Spain, Italy, Austria, Germany, and Flanders. The Hapsburgs rewarded the composer with income from several large churches, including those at Courtrai and Tournai. Since Finck speaks of him as alive in 1556, but he is no longer listed the following year in the records of Tournai Cathedral, it can be assumed that he died sometime in 1556 or 1557.

Gombert's extant works comprise 41 French chansons, 8 Magnificats, 159 motets for four to six voices, and 10 Masses. Most of these compositions support Finck's opinion that Gombert "has shown to all composers the method of writing imitation. . . . He avoids rests and his composition is both full of harmony and imitation." Imitation was not new with Gombert, for Josquin had made it an important part of musical architecture. But while the older man merely added it to a battery of other structural devices, Gombert restricted himself more completely to imitation. Unlike Josquin, whose music has an airy quality resulting from numerous rests given to all parts, Gombert avoids them by keeping all voices singing almost continuously. As a result, his pieces sound "fuller" and more "harmonic" than those of the previous generation.

Gombert avoids constructive techniques such as phrase repetition, canon, and *cantus firmus*. In the motets where long passages are often little more than an ongoing imitation of the same motive, he alters each repetition. Following Josquin, he favors the large two-part motet structure (AB:CB) in which the close of each part employs identical music and text.

Of Gombert's 10 Masses, 8 can be classified as "parodies" of preexisting models. For these parody Masses, in part a creation of Gombert, he replaced the older *cantus firmus* tenor with polyphonic chansons and motets, some of which were from his own hand. Motives from the model were joined succesively in one voice or simultaneously in several, and strategically alternated with freely composed material.

Further Reading

A discussion of Gombert's style is in Gustave Reese, *Music in the Renaissance* (1954; rev. ed. 1959). For background see Donald Jay Grout, *A History of Western Music* (1960). □

Juan Vicente Gómez

The Venezuelan dictator Juan Vicente Gómez (1857-1935) presided over the transformation of his country from a backward nation into one of the globe's major oil producers and an important force in international commerce.

Juan Vicente Gómez was born in the mountain state of Tachira and had virtually no formal education. He started to work as a cowboy, and within a few years he was the owner of a substantial landed property in his native state. He had also become involved in the turbulent local politics of his region.

In politics Gómez associated himself with another Tachira native, Cipriano Castro, who led contingents in several civil wars of the last decades of the 19th century. When Castro organized, from exile in Colombia, an invasion of his homeland, Gómez accompanied him in the effort, and when it was successful and Castro became president of Venezuela, Gómez was rewarded with the vice presidency.

Although Gómez had already acquired an extensive reputation as a plotter and schemer, Castro was injudicious enough to go to Europe for medical attention in 1908. Gómez promptly seized power and told the President not to return. From then until his death, Gómez completely dominated the government, although he served as president only part of the time.

During Gómez's regime oil was discovered and began to be exploited on a large scale. The first oil well was brought in 1914, and during the next decade and a half there was a frantic scramble for concessions by the big international oil companies. Gómez bargained astutely with these firms, perhaps more to his own advantage than to that of Venezuela. By the 1930s the country had become one of the world's major oil producers, and the finances of the Venezuelan government had expanded dramatically.

A man of marked native shrewdness and utter ruthlessness, Gómez took advantage of this change to build up what was said at the time to be the largest fortune in South America, while treating Venezuela largely as his personal plantation.

With the increased government revenues Gómez paid off the whole foreign debt of the republic; he mounted an appreciable road-building program in the interior; and he modernized the armament of the military, upon whom he largely depended for his continuance in power. In the meantime, his regime was so arbitrary that Gómez became widely known as the "tyrant of the Andes." Opponents were ruthlessly eliminated by being put in jail, where they were frequently tortured or killed. Thousands of people fled into exile to avoid the wrath of the regime.

Power remained essentially in the hands of the rude mountain folk who had descended upon the capital at the turn of the century. The Venezuelan army was top-heavy with generals who had won their rank by loyalty to Gómez and shared with him the proceeds from the exploitation of

the country. They were allowed to seize land and other goods so long as they did not challenge the dictator. Gómez himself acquired plantations all over the country and was reported to have actually assigned various army units to cultivate a number of these on his behalf. He munificently endowed many of the scores of children whom he was reported to have sired during his long bachelor life.

There were numerous plots against the Gómez regime. On several occasions, invasions were mounted by oppositionists from such offshore islands as Trinidad and Curaçao. In May 1928 university students in Caracas revolted and seized the presidential palace—where Gómez seldom stayed—but were finally suppressed. However, none of these attempts to oust the dictator prospered, and he died peacefully in bed in Maracay on Dec. 17, 1935.

Further Reading

There are two full-length biographies of Gómez in English: Thomas Rourke, *Gómez, Tyrant of the Andes* (1936), is hostile; while John Lavin, *A Halo for Gómez* (1954), is an attempt to revise the established view of Gómez and portray him in a more favorable light. □

Máximo Gómez

A Dominican by birth, Máximo Gómez (1836-1905) became a general in Cuba's independence army and a hero of the struggle which ended Spanish domination over Cuba.

Máximo Gómez was born in the small town of Baní in the Dominican Republic on Nov. 18, 1836. The son of a lower-middle-class family, he entered a religious seminary, but his religious instruction was soon interrupted by a Haitian invasion of the Dominican Republic in the mid-1850s. Joining the forces of Dominican patriots, he fought bravely in the battle of Santomé in 1856 and in numerous subsequent battles. When Dominican general Pedro Santana invited Spain to reestablish control over the Dominican Republic in 1861, Gómez accepted a commission as captain in the Dominican army reserve. He retained that post until the end of the Spanish domination in 1865, when he moved to Santiago de Cuba.

Cuba's Ten Years War

Cuba was then experiencing revolutionary turmoil, as Cuban patriots conspired to rid the island of Spanish control. Unhappy with the treatment he and other Dominicans had received from Spain and horrified by the exploitation of the black slaves, he started to conspire with Cuban revolutionaries. When, on Oct. 10, 1868, Carlos Manuel de Céspedes and other leaders began Cuba's Ten Years War for Independence, Gómez joined the rebellion. His experience in military strategy was of importance to the revolutionary cause, and he was soon promoted to the rank of general and later to commander of Oriente Province. A master of guer-

rilla warfare, Gómez organized the Cuban rebels into highly mobile small units which could operate independently, harassing the Spanish troops continually.

Although at first the Cuban forces were successful, the Spaniards soon gained the offensive. By 1871 the rebels had been pushed back to Oriente Province, and the rebellion was contained in that part of the island. In a meeting with rebel president Céspedes, Gómez argued for an invasion of the western part of the island. He pointed out that the rebellion should be made an unbearable economic burden for Spain and that this could be accomplished through an invasion that would emancipate all black slaves in the island and cripple the sugar industry. "If liberty is not given to the slaves," Gómez wrote in his campaign diary, "and if production of the great sugar plantations is not impeded, the revolution is destined to last much longer and rivers of blood will flow unfruitfully in the fields of the island."

Gómez's plan met with strong opposition from conservative and landed groups. Although they supported the Cuban cause, they feared for their economic interests, and after much discussion the plan was finally rejected. The Dominican leader returned to the zone of Guantánamo, where he continued to engage victoriously with the Spanish forces. In 1872 Gómez prevailed upon the government to accept his plan. But before it could be implemented, dissension again broke out within the revolutionary ranks and Céspedes relieved him as commander of Oriente Province. Although in 1873 Céspedes was removed from the presidency and Gómez was restored to his position of command, the invasion had to wait until 1875.

Even after the invasion got under way, it reached only Las Villas Province in central Cuba. Gómez's destruction of sugar plantations met with much opposition from the landed and sugar interests. Some officers also resented a foreigner in command. Others were jealous of Gómez's position and actions. Furthermore, supplies, weapons, and money failed to arrive from exiles in the United States. Finally, in 1876, Gómez was forced to resign his military post. Though he was appointed secretary of war shortly after, his plan of action in western Cuba had failed.

Disappointed and disillusioned, Gómez left Cuba just prior to the signing of the Peace of Zanjón in February 1878, which ended the Ten Years War. From Cuba, Gómez traveled to Jamaica and then to Honduras, where he was appointed army general. From Honduras he supported the ill-fated "Guerra Chiquita" (Little War, 1879-1880), an attempt by several Cuban rebel leaders led by Gen. Calixto García, to continue the war against Spain.

New Attempts at Liberation

In 1884 Gómez left Honduras for the United States to organize and collect funds for a new rebellion in Cuba. In New York he met with veteran general Antonio Maceo and with José Martí, then engaged in mobilizing the Cuban exiles in support of the war against Spain. But Gómez and Martí soon clashed, and the latter, fearful of Gómez's authoritarian attitude, withdrew from the movement. Martí's withdrawal, desertion from the revolutionary ranks, disillusionment among exiled Cubans, lack of capital and weapons, and poor organization all doomed the new movement to failure. Gómez traveled to Panama for a short stay and then settled back in the Dominican Republic.

There he received a new call from Martí in 1892 for a final effort to liberate Cuba. Martí had organized a revolutionary party in exile and now offered Gómez the post of military chief. Forgetting old differences, Gómez accepted promptly and joined Martí and Maceo in their revolutionary endeavors. For the next few years the three men worked tirelessly, organizing Cubans in and out of the island until finally, on Feb. 24, 1895, the War for Independence began. In April of that same year Gómez, Martí, and other leaders landed in Cuba and joined Maceo, who was already in the battlefield.

War for Independence

Now Gómez finally was able to implement his invasion plan. Although Martí's tragic death in Dos Ríos on May 19, 1895, in one of the early combats of the war dealt a strong blow to the morale of the rebellion, Gómez and Maceo did not waver. In repeated attacks the two generals undermined and defeated the Spanish troops and carried the war to the western provinces. By 1896 the Spanish troops were retreating and the Cubans seemed victorious throughout the island. Then came a change in the Spanish command and the more conciliatory Spanish marshal Arsenio Martínez Campos was replaced by Gen. Valeriano Weyler, a tough and harsh disciplinarian.

Weyler's policy of concentrating the rural population in garrisoned towns, the increasing numbers of Spanish troops, and Maceo's death allowed the Spaniards to regain the initiative. Yet they were unable to defeat the Cuban rebels or even engage them in a major battle. Gómez retreated to the eastern provinces and from there carried on guerrilla operations. He rejected any compromise with Spain, and in January 1898, when the Spanish monarchy introduced an autonomy plan that would have made Cuba a self-governing province within the Spanish Empire, Gómez categorically opposed it.

This was the existing condition in Cuba when the United States declared war on Spain on April 25, 1898, following the explosion of the battleship *Maine* in Havana's harbor earlier that year. The Cuban forces collaborated with the U.S. Army in the short campaign against Spain. By August hostilities had ceased, and Spain agreed to relinquish sovereignty over the island. Gómez and his troops retired to the sugar mill Narcisa in Las Villas Province and there awaited the departure of Spanish troops. After the withdrawal Gómez made a triumphant tour of the island and amid general joy entered Havana on Feb. 24, 1899.

Postwar Difficulties

But Gómez, the most popular hero of the war, soon got into trouble. He requested that the Americans pay the Cuban veterans for their services since 1895 and at a higher rate than American soldiers had received. The United States refused and offered $3 million, or an estimated $75 for each soldier who turned in his weapons. Gómez also clashed with the Cuban Assembly, composed of army delegates,

over a proposed United States loan. Gómez opposed the loan as well as its onerous terms and criticized the Assembly for considering it. The Assembly in turn resented Gómez's high-handed manner and the secret conversations he held with representatives of the U.S. government to secure payment for the war veterans. The Assembly finally dismissed Gómez as commander in chief of the army.

Gómez's dismissal only increased his popularity. As the end of the American occupation approached and candidates emerged for the presidential election of 1901, Gómez was the most popular figure. Yet the old general refused to be considered, claiming, "I would much rather liberate men than govern them." Instead, he campaigned for and helped elect Tomás Estrada Palma, former rebel president and delegate-in-exile of the Cuban Republic in Arms. Gómez supported Estrada Palma's administration, but when the President announced his intention to reelect himself, he met with Gómez's stiff opposition. Old and sick, Gen. Gómez went on a speaking tour but could do little, for he died on June 17, 1905.

Further Reading

Valuable information on Gómez as well as on Cuba's wars for independence is in Charles E. Chapman, *A History of the Cuban Republic* (1927), and Philip Sheldon Foner, *A History of Cuba and Its Relations with the United States,* vol. 2 (1963). □

Laureano Eleuterio Gómez Castro

Laureano Eleuterio Gómez Castro (1889-1965) was leader of the Colombian Conservative party and spokesman of its right wing. He was the fiercest partisan in recent Colombian history and symbolized clerical and authoritarian values.

Born in Bogotá on Feb. 20, 1889, Laureano Gómez attended the National University and received an engineering degree in 1909. Turning immediately to a public career, he founded the periodical *La Unidad* and served as its director from 1909 to 1916. Joining the Conservative party, he was first elected a national representative in 1911, serving until 1918 and again from 1921 to 1923. Subsequently a cabinet minister on various occasions in the 1920s and 1930s, Gómez assumed the leadership of the Conservative party in 1932 and remained its dominant figure until his death. Running the party with iron discipline and intellectual force, he became an admirer of Hitler and of Franco, criticized the United States relentlessly, and attacked a series of Liberal governments while also directing the daily *El Siglo,* which he founded in 1936.

As a spokesman of the ultraright wing of his party, Gómez personified the Spanish tradition of authoritarian government and clericalism. Representing the feudalistic and aristocratic landed gentry of Colombia, he became a brilliant parliamentarian and political tactician. His polemical attacks on the Liberals were extreme in their vehemence and contributed to a deterioration of political consensus within the ruling elite. When the Liberals divided over the presidential candidacy of Jorge Gaitán in 1946, Gómez shrewdly manipulated the election of a minority Conservative president. In 1950 he successfully campaigned for the presidency when the Liberals refused to participate.

As president, Gómez proceeded to institute an authoritarian right-wing regime which resembled European corporativist governments. Although stricken by a heart attack in 1951, he continued to control the government through a handpicked successor. The increasing breakdown of public order and the apparent establishment of civilian dictatorship precipitated a military seizure of power in 1953, and Gómez went into exile in Spain. In July 1956 he negotiated with Liberal leader Alberto Lleras Camargo the Pact of Benidorm, which called for bipartisan collaboration in opposition to the military dictatorship. On July 20, 1957, following the collapse of the regime, he and Lleras also signed the Declaration of Sitges, which committed the two parties to an equal division of authority from 1958 until 1974. They agreed to divide political posts equally, the 4-year presidential terms alternating between the two parties.

Although ill health and advanced age prohibited his return to the presidency, Gómez continued to dominate the Conservative party until his death on July 13, 1965, in Bogotá.

Further Reading

There is no full-length biography of Gómez. The best review of his personality and political career is in Vernon L. Fluharty, *Dance of the Millions: Military Rule and the Social Revolution in Colombia, 1930-1956* (1957). An account which includes the final years of Gómez's career is Robert H. Dix, *Colombia: The Political Dimensions of Change* (1967). □

Samuel Gompers

The American labor leader Samuel Gompers (1850-1924) was the most significant single figure in the history of the American labor movement. He founded and was the first president of the American Federation of Labor.

Few great social movements have been so influenced by one man as was the American labor movement by Samuel Gompers. He virtually stamped his personality and viewpoint on the American Federation of Labor (AFL). This heritage included both Gompers's social conservatism and his truculent firmness on behalf of the organized skilled workers of the country. His is a unique success story, of an utterly penniless immigrant who became the confidant of presidents and industrialists.

Gompers was born on Jan. 27, 1850, in east London, England. His family was Dutch-Jewish in origin and had lived in England for only a few years. The family was extremely poor, but at the age of 6 Gompers was sent to a Jewish free school, where he received the rudiments of an education virtually unknown to his class. The education was brief, however, and Gompers was apprenticed first to a shoemaker and then in his father's cigar-making trade. In 1863, when Gompers was 13, the family moved to the tenement slums of the Lower East Side of New York City. The family soon numbered 11 members, and Gompers again went to work as a cigar-maker.

Cigar-makers' Union

Naturally gregarious and energetic, Gompers joined numerous organizations in the bustling immigrant world of New York City. But from the start nothing was so important to him as the small Cigar-makers' Local Union No. 15, which he joined with his father in 1864. Gompers immediately rose to leadership of the group. At the age of 16 he regularly represented his fellow workers in altercations with their employers, and he discussed politics and economics with articulate workingmen many years his senior.

This was a time of technological flux in cigar-making, as in practically every branch of American industry. Machines were being introduced which eliminated many highly skilled workers. The cigar-makers were distinguished, however, by the intelligence with which they studied their problems. The nature of the work—the quietness of the process, for example—permitted and even encouraged discussion of economic questions, and this environment

whereas the AFL unions were interested only in improving the day-to-day material life of their members. The socialists' attempt to capture the AFL in 1894 did succeed in unseating Gompers for a year, but he was firmly back in power by 1895 and, if anything, more bitterly hostile to socialism in the unions than ever.

"Socialism holds nothing but unhappiness for the human race," Gompers said in 1918. "Socialism is the fad of fanatics . . . and it has no place in the hearts of those who would secure the fight for freedom and preserve democracy." Throughout his career he inveighed against the flourishing Socialist party and the numerous attempts to form revolutionary unions. Although many forces account for the failure of socialist thought among American unions, Gompers's influence at the head of the movement for 40 years cannot be discounted.

Devotion to Unionism

However, if Gompers was hostile to the socialists, he was as devoted to the cause of unionism as any other American labor leader before or since. He was the first national union leader to recognize and encourage the strike as labor's most effective weapon. Further, when issued an injunction in 1906 not to boycott the antilabor Buck Stove and Range Company, he defied the courts (albeit gingerly) and was sentenced to a year in prison for contempt (a conviction later reversed on appeal). Gompers spent only one night in jail (a rare distinction among labor leaders of his day) and, characteristically, was contemptuous of, rather than sympathetic with, those with whom he shared his cell. But his devotion to unionism and the rhetoric with which he denounced avaricious industrialists matched anything of his time.

National Prominence

Although the leader of a socially disreputable movement, Gompers had good relations with several presidents and became something of an adviser to president Woodrow Wilson. In 1901 he was one of the founders of the National Civic Federation (an alliance of businessmen willing to tolerate unions and conservative union leaders), and Wilson found it politically expedient and worthwhile to have the support of the AFL during World War I. Gompers supported the war vigorously, attempting to halt AFL strikes for the duration and denouncing socialists and pacifists. He served as president of the International Commission on Labor Legislation at the Versailles Peace Conference and on various other advisory committees.

During the 1920s, though in failing health, Gompers served as a spokesman for the Mexican revolutionary government in Washington and considered himself instrumental in securing American recognition of the new regime. He was received with high honors by President Plutarco Elias Calles in 1924, but, realizing that the end was near, Gompers returned early to the United States and died in San Antonio, Tex., on December 13. Characteristically, his last words were: "Nurse, this is the end. God bless our American institutions. May they grow better day by day." What had begun as expedient for Gompers—acceptance of the

provided Gompers with an excellent social schooling. The most significant influence upon his life was a formerly prominent Scandinavian socialist, Ferdinand Laurrel, who had become disillusioned with Marxism and taught Gompers that workingmen ought to avoid both politics and utopian dreaming in favor of winning immediate "bread and butter" gains in their wages, hours, and conditions.

In fact, Gompers had many contacts with socialists, though, from his earliest days, he had little time for their ideals. Basing his own unionism on a "pure and simple" materialistic approach, he built the Cigar-makers' International Union into a viable trade association despite technology and unsuccessful strikes.

American Federation of Labor

With Adolph Strasser, the head of the German-speaking branch of the Cigar-makers' Union (Gompers led the English-speaking branch), and several other trade union leaders, Gompers helped to set up in 1881 a loose federation of trade unions which, in 1886, became the AFL. Founded during the heyday of the Knights of Labor, the AFL differed from the older organization in nearly every respect. The Knights emphasized the solidarity of labor regardless of craft and admitted unskilled as well as skilled workers to membership. The AFL, with Gompers as its president, was a federation of autonomous craft unions which admitted only members of specific crafts (carpenters, cigar-makers, and so on) and made no provision for the unskilled. The Knights looked forward to a society in which the wage system would be abolished and cooperation would govern the economy, capitalist system and working within it—had become his gospel. Indeed, he was one of the makers of the modern institutions of which he spoke in that he won for capitalism the loyalty of labor and for labor a part in industrial decision making.

Gompers the Man

Among friends, Gompers was gregarious and convivial. He enjoyed eating and drinking, sometimes excessively (he was a vociferous enemy of prohibition), and at home he was the classic 19th-century paterfamilias with a retiring, worshipful wife and a large brood of deferential children.

Gompers first made his reputation as an orator and always delivered a speech well. He spoke widely in the cause of the AFL, rose to great heights of eloquence on occasion, and thanks to an agile mind and sharp tongue was rarely bested in debate. He mixed with equal ease among awkward workmen and in the polished society of Washington's highest circles. He had been a militant anticlerical in his youth and never attended a church or synagogue except to speak on labor's behalf. Although of Jewish heritage and education, he did not think of himself as a Jew or, for that matter, as a member of any religion. None of his books was distinguished except his autobiography, *Seventy Years of Life and Labor* (1925).

Further Reading

Gompers's autobiography, *Seventy Years of Life and Labor* (2 vols., 1925; rev. ed. in 1 vol., 1943), is indispensable. The most comprehensive and authoritative biography is Bernard Mandel, *Samuel Gompers* (1963). Also valuable are Philip Taft, *The A. F. of L. in the Time of Gompers* (1957), and Marc Karson, *American Labor Unions and Politics, 1900-1918* (1958). The best among the brief surveys of American labor are Foster Rhea Dulles, *Labor in America* (1949; 3d ed. 1966); Henry Pelling, *American Labor* (1960); and Thomas R. Brooks, *Toil and Trouble: A History of American Labor* (1964). □

Wladislaw Gomulka

Wladislaw Gomulka (1905-1982) ruled Poland for 14 years as first secretary of the Communist party. His career in politics reflected the difficult relationship between nationalism and international communism in Eastern Europe after 1945.

Wladislaw Gomulka was born in February 1905, into a working-class family in Krosno, in southern Poland. He began work as a plumber at the age of 14 and soon became involved in political agitation. He joined the clandestine Polish Communist party in 1926 and became an active and effective organizer of strikes. After 2 years in prison for conspiracy, he went to Moscow in 1934; after returning in 1936, he was imprisoned again but escaped when the Germans invaded Poland 3 years later, and again went to the Soviet Union. During his two years

there, he had no significant involvement in communist politics, and he remained a home-grown and locally oriented Communist more Polish than Soviet. His appointment in 1942 to a top executive position on the Central Committee of the Polish Workers' party encouraged other local party activists to believe that local control of the party might be possible.

During the war, Gomulka was a very active member of the Communist section of the resistance to the German occupation. In 1943, Stalin appointed him general secretary of the Polish Workers' (Communist) Party, and in 1944 he became deputy premier in the new Polish government formed under Soviet auspices. In the same year, he became party secretary of the newly formed Politburo, the party's ruling executive committee.

Gomulka and his associates were purged from the party in 1949, essentially because they were nationalists who refused to accept without question policies dictated by Moscow. Oddly, he was not arrested until 1951 and was kept in seclusion until 1954 but no case was brought against him in a show trial, as had been common in other communist-ruled Eastern European countries, and he was not executed. Stalin died in March, 1953, and pressure on the Polish leaders to be harsh died with him.

The "de-Stalinization" which occurred in early 1956 at the famous twentieth congress of the Communist Party of the Soviet Union helped loosen Moscow's ideological and operational control of other communist parties, and Gomulka's ideas of a specifically "Polish road to socialism"

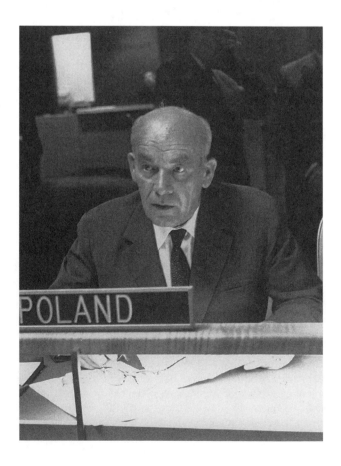

came back into favor. In the summer and autumn of 1956 the wave of strikes and riots centered on Poznan facilitated Gomulka's return to the Central Committee and to the Politburo. At a crucial meeting in Warsaw on October 19/ 20, he convinced Nikita Khrushchev, general secretary of the CPSU, and other Soviet leaders that Poland's independence would have to be respected, a remarkable achievement given that Soviet troops were within striking distance of Warsaw. On October 21, Gomulka was unanimously elected the party's first secretary, effectively, the head of state.

One consequence of this dramatic turn of events was that for the first time in the history of communism in Poland, the party became supported by the masses. This was unsettling for some of the party veterans, for it meant that policies in Poland would have to be devised with greater attention to Polish public opinion and Polish social needs. In the next several months, Gomulka and Khrushchev remained in direct communication, and concessions granted to the Poles during Gomulka's official November visit to Moscow (cancellation of Poland's debts to the USSR, extension of new credits, and some Polish control over Soviet troop movements in Poland), significantly strengthened Gomulka's political position at home. He became a symbol of political change and patriotic renovation.

Gomulka began his regime as a moderate; he moved quickly to improve relations with the Catholic Church, among other things, by releasing Cardinal Wyszynski and numerous bishops and priests from detention; in return, the Church urged all Catholics to take part in the January 1957 parliamentary elections, which Gomulka's party won with an absolute majority.

With solid support in the country, Gomulka turned to strengthening discipline within the party, first by attacking those who opposed his stability-oriented measures, then by changing the editorial staffs of all party publications, imposing censorship, and establishing permanent commissions for control of science, culture and education within the Central Committee apparatus. Next came intraparty purges, which eliminated more than 261,000 members from party ranks (about 20 percent of the total). After two years of such measures (in 1958 the tasks of political and organizational consolidation appeared to have been completed) Gomulka's agenda turned to resuming the process of socialist construction.

Gomulka was cautious, lest he rekindle tensions with major changes; he never elaborated boldly about "the Polish road to socialism," and his regime gradually grew into authoritarianism at home and loyal obedience to the Soviet Union in foreign relations. His popularity eroded; discontent and dissatisfaction grew. Ironically, in time his political strength became based on his close personal relationship with top Soviet leaders Khrushchev, followed by Leonid Brezhnev and Aleksei Kosygin and in time, Gomulka became an isolated leader within his own party.

Gomulka's rule had become highly personalized and restrictive, another irony, for he had years earlier condemned Stalin's "cult of personality." His personal characteristics became the defining elements of the political system in Poland: "stubbornness, arrogance, manipulation, a finger in every pie and a sense that he would be ruler for decades to come."

In early 1968, intellectuals and students began protests against the party's restrictive cultural policy, precipitated by the regime's banning a theatrical production. In March, several hundred students were arrested at Warsaw university for demonstrating; many were tried immediately and sentenced on charges of "hooliganism and insulting the police." This provoked violent confrontations between police and students throughout the country.

In a speech that same month, Edward Gierek, a party official and Politburo member, gave his semi-official blessing to the campaign of purge and intimidation that was to spread throughout the county. A week later in a speech to Warsaw party activists, Gomulka attempted to take a relatively moderate position, but militant party members interrupted him continuously in front of national television cameras, chanting Gierek's name; in many ways, party members were actively in revolt against the stagnation of Gomulka's rule.

Gomulka's authority was strengthened somewhat by the August 21 invasion of Czechoslovakia by Warsaw Pact military forces, including some Polish troops, out of grave concerns that the liberal Czech model of "socialism with a human face" was destabilizing other Eastern European communist regimes; Soviet leader Brezhnev later praised Gomulka as "the faithful son of the Polish working class and leading activist of the international communist movement" but ultimately, this did little to solidify Gomulka's power.

From late 1968 on, the party's attention turned toward redefining economic policy, including proposals to reform the industrial wage system by tying it to hoped-for increases in efficiency and productivity specifically by forcing greater productivity with threats of increased unemployment and economic deprivation. Inevitably, tensions among workers increased. In December, 1970, the government announced increases in the prices of food and fuels ranging from 15 to 30 percent. Workers' protested; government suppression of workers set off a chain reaction of demonstrations and strikes, and ultimately a national political crisis. Two months later, the food price increases were revoked, but it was too late; Gomulka associates' suppression of workers (particularly in Gdansk) led to thousands wounded and hundreds dead. Protests spread throughout the country, and to party officials, generalized revolt seemed imminent. Given this, several Politburo members and numerous Central Committee members announced their opposition to Gomulka. The split in the party hierarchy came to a head on December 19, 1970, when Gomulka suffered a sudden heart attack. After seven hours of deliberations, Gomulka was asked to resign from the Politburo and the Secretariat. He was replaced by Edward Gierek.

Further Reading

The best work on Gomulka is Nicholas Bethell, *Gomulka: His Poland, His Communism* (1969), an admirably concise and objective work which is both a biography of Gomulka and a history of modern Poland. Other important works are M. K.

Dziewanowski, *The Communist Party of Poland* (1959); Richard Hiscocks, *Poland: Bridge for the Abyss* (1963); and Hansjakob Stehle, *The Independent Satellite* (1963; trans. 1965). See also Jan B. de Weydenthal, *The Communists of Poland: An Historical Outline* (1978). □

Ivan Aleksandrovich Goncharov

The Russian novelist Ivan Aleksandrovich Goncharov (1812-1891) is one of the great realists of Russian literature. His novel "Oblomov" is a classic of Russian fiction.

Ivan Goncharov was born of a well-to-do family. Although the family background was of the merchant class, he was brought up in the patriarchal atmosphere of Russian manor life. After leaving the University of Moscow, he entered the civil service, where he labored patiently for many years without conspicuous success. His rise to literary prominence came in 1847, when he published his first novel, *A Common Story.* Hailed enthusiastically by the great Russian critic Vissarion Belinsky, this work dealt with the transformation of a young provincial idealist into a somewhat vulgar and practical young man.

In 1849 Goncharov published "The Dream of Oblomov," a short sketch that became the core of his greatest novel. In 1853 he accompanied an expedition on a 2-year voyage to the Far East. He did not enjoy the trip, but he was a perceptive reporter and his account of the journey appeared as *The Frigate Pallas* in 1856.

In 1858 Goncharov finished the novel *Oblomov,* and it was published the following year. Oblomov has become an archetypal character, the embodiment of vegetable comfort, of disinclination to action, and of lassitude. He is the dreamer rather than the doer, and he is contrasted with Shtolz, the new man, the energetic, self-willed man, who unsuccessfully attempts to inspire Oblomov to a more active existence. As a superfluous man, Oblomov is part of a gallery of great Russian fictional creations, which includes Aleksandr Pushkin's Eugene Onegin, Mikhail Lermontov's Pechorin, and Ivan Turgenev's Rudin. The word *Oblomovshchina* (Oblomovism) has passed into the Russian language to signify a special kind of high-minded indolence.

Goncharov's last important novel, *The Ravine,* appeared in 1869. The theme of the novel, as in *A Common Story,* has to do with the new and the old, the ideal and the useful. The novel expresses what is perhaps the most important conflict in Goncharov's work: the conflict between a love for the patriarchal, leisurely, fixed ways of old Russia and an interest and curiosity in the liberal and radical elements that were breaking through the crust of old Russia.

Goncharov also wrote an autobiographical apologia, *Better Late than Never* (1870, published in 1879), in which

he attempted to prove to the younger generation that he understood the spirit of his age as well as they. Among his other publications are *My University Reminiscences* (1870); *A Million Torments* (1872), a work of criticism; and *Notes on Belinsky's Personality* (1874). A posthumous work entitled *An Uncommon Story* came to light in the 1920s and confirmed the psychopathic side of his personality; it is an account of imagined plots against him and imagined attempts by others to plagiarize his work.

Further Reading

Janko Lavrin, *Goncharov* (1954), is a short and useful study. The chapter on Goncharov in D. S. Mirsky, *A History of Russian Literature, from Its Beginnings to 1900,* edited by Francis J. Whitfield (1958), is informative and interesting and provides the best background information on the period available in English. □

Natalia Goncharova

The Russian painter and theatrical scenery designer Natalia Goncharova (1881-1962) was pivotal in the development of avant-garde Russian art during the decade prior to World War I and thereafter was an important and innovative designer of costumes and stage flats.

Russian art during the first two decades of the 20th century absorbed the new styles and philosophies of Western European art and moved to the cultural forefront. Goncharova and her husband, Mikhail Larionov (1881-1964), through their work and their efforts organizing shows and artist's groups were at the center of this artistic revolution which preceded and was concurrent with that country's political upheaval.

Natalia Goncharova (sometimes spelled Gontcharova) was born in Nagaevo in central Russia. The Goncharova family had lost its fortune, based on the manufacture of linen, by the late 18th century. The renowned poet Pushkin had married one of her ancestors, Natalia Goncharova, after whom she was named. Her father was an architect. Natalia's mother's family, the Belyaevs, had produced a number of priests and were noted for being patrons of music. From 1891 to 1896 Goncharova attended the gymnasium in Moscow. In 1898, having formed her decision to be an artist, Goncharova entered the College of Painting, Sculpture and Architecture (Moscow) where she studied sculpture under Pavel Troubetskoi, who worked in the style of Auguste Rodin. Three years later she left the college despite having won a silver medal and not having completed the ten-year period of study of that curriculum. This coincided with her adoption of painting as her preferred medium of expression.

A Career and a Husband

By 1900 Goncharova had met her future husband, Mikhail Larionov. He had also enrolled in the college in 1898, but in the Department of Painting. Her decision to take up painting was encouraged by Larionov and by her fascination with the play of light and the harmonies of color. Like many Russian artists of her time, the first few years of the 20th century was a period of exposure to and adoption of the styles that had evolved in the capitals of Western Europe. At the time she was drawn to Impressionism and Divisionism, styles associated respectively with Monet and Seurat. Both styles emphasized not the recording of solid objects but the capturing of light (color) that was reflected back from the object to the eye. As a result, drawing tended to be loose and there was an emphasis on color, the strokes of paint. This led to a consciousness of the paint, the strokes, and the texture and pattern on the canvas. These two styles were important for freeing art from being purely representational. Artists were acquiring an awareness of art being an esthetic expression inspired by, but not dependent on, the appearances of the physical world.

In 1906 the great Russian ballet impressario Diaghilev arranged for a selection of paintings by Goncharova and Larionov to be included in the Russian section of the Salon d'Automne in Paris. Their inclusion in this recently established yearly showing of new radical art (the Fauves had their first group showing there that year) indicates that both artists were considered exemplars of trends in the avant-garde of their country. Over the next nine years, prior to her emigration from Russia, Goncharova participated in a number of important exhibitions, many of which she and Larionov organized. During this period she was also represented in the 1912 Post-Impressionist exhibition organized by Roger Fry at London's Grafton Gallery, in a one-person show (1913) of 761 works in Moscow (reduced to 249 pieces the following year when shown in St. Petersburg), and in a show at the Paul Guillaume Gallery of Paris with a catalogue by the noted critic Apollinaire.

The Style of Rayonism

The half decade which preceded the outbreak of the war was a period of rapid development in the visual arts in Russia. Goncharova was at the forefront of this. Amazingly, three distinct trends simultaneously appeared in her work: Rayonism, Neo-Primitivism, and Cubo-Futurism. The first of these is an original style conceived by Larionov and was extensively explored by Goncharova as well. Rayonism was among a number of completely abstract styles at the time in Western art. Like Impressionism, Rayonism concentrates on the light rays reflecting off objects. The space in a Rayonist painting is not measurable but is an atmosphere charged with the energy of an infinite number of light rays either directly from the sun or, more likely, rays bouncing back and forth from the physical objects around one. From this infinity of rays were selected particular ones—the title often revealing the objects from which they had been reflected. The guiding principle is purely esthetic in that the colors are chosen for their harmony or visual effect.

For over three decades artists had been fascinated by the idea of creating a non-objective art based on the orchestration of color. If music was completely abstract and yet infinitely expressive, could not there be an art using color (instead of sound) which was equally abstract and expressive. Goncharova was among the 11 artists who signed Larionov's Rayonist Manifesto when it was published in 1913, at which time she showed Rayonist works at the *Donkey's Tail* and *Target* exhibitions *Cats: Rayonist Apprehension in Pink, Black and Yellow* of 1913 (New York, Solomon R. Guggenheim Museum) approaches Braque and Picasso's Analytical Cubism in its overall animated and crystalline effect, though with rich color. Instead of the fragmented interlocked shapes found in Cubism, *Cats* is based on long, slashing colored strokes. Rayonism was a short-lived style, having reached its end by 1914. Franz Marc, associated with the Blaue Reiter of Munich (with whom Goncharova exhibited in 1912), admired her work and painted in a manner inspired by Rayonism in 1913, perhaps due to her influence.

The Neo-Primitivism Style

Concurrent with Rayonism, Goncharova painted in a style now referred to as Neo-Primitivism. This was a phenomenon that had occurred earlier in France and elsewhere and seems related to changing political, social, and cultural aspirations. In conjunction with a democratization of political and social thought, there was often a tendency to try to discover the underlying character of national cultures by looking to traditional folk or peasant art for inspiration. Because of her family's clerical background and her having spent her youth living at a country estate, Goncharova would have been drawn to traditional religious and folk art as part of her formative experience and as the fine arts of the masses of her countrymen. This was a period when the intelligentsia came to look upon icons (Russian devotional images) as an important national cultural heritage. The great Romanov exhibition of icons (1913), many of which had been cleaned for the first time, excited many esthetically sensitive people.

Goncharova had painted religious themes for a number of years, having felt that the intensely religious sense and meaning of icons was one of the most important goals for an artist to capture in his or her work. The rich colors, dazzling decorative effects, and highly formalized and stylized character of icons had already inspired her work. *Archangel* (Paris, private collection) of about 1909 to 1911, the left panel of a triptych titled *The Savior,* in facial type and drapery pattern bears resemblance to typical aspects of icons. The emphasis on broad flat patterning, as in the angel's wings or the large rhythms of the fabric, suggests influence of folk arts. This led Goncharova to employ a manner that was unrelated to academic practice. Besides emphasizing flat, decorative qualities, at times the paint was seemingly splashed on the surface or was applied rapidly for spontaneity of effect. The charm and naiveté that had earlier been acclaimed in the painting of Henri Rousseau appeared in Goncharova's work and were, very importantly to her, derived from native sources.

Cubo-Futurism Style

Between 1913 and 1914 Cubo-Futurism, aspects of the then-contemporary styles of Cubism and Futurism, appeared in Goncharova's painting. Cubism would have been known to Russian artists through publications, exhibitions, and collections such as those of Morozov and Shchukin. Cubism was ambivalent to color to the benefit of a new sense of structure—the fragmentation and interlocking of form and shape resulting in a uniformly animated composition in which the figure/ground relation is eliminated.

Italian Futurism also had a following in Russia in the years immediately preceding World War I. Futurism's glorification of dynamism as a constant in modern experience often led to the use of images such as large scale industry, trains, and race cars as emblems of the world rapidly transforming culturally and technologically. This is reflected in Goncharova's work *Airplane over Train* (Kazan Art Museum) of 1913, for example. Her Futurism, like that of the Italians, was alive with color. The sensations of motion were suggested by rhythmic repetitions of shapes or lines. The inclusion of painted words or word fragments, as if they were from signs and part of an environment through which one was passing, further aided this perception. Sound waves were similarly implied by rhythmic effects and occasionally by the use of musical notations.

A Solid Place in Art History

In 1915 Goncharova and Larionov, who had been released from service in the Russian Army for medical reasons, moved to Lausanne, Switzerland, to continue their collaboration with Diaghilev's Ballets Russes. This lasted until 1929 when Diaghilev died, after which Goncharova worked for other ballet companies. Her travels of 1916 and 1917 to San Sebastian (Spain), Paris, and Rome formatively brought her into contact with traditional Spanish culture and with a wide range of important contemporary styles. In 1919 Goncharova permanently settled in Paris. The year before the Galerie Sauvage (Paris) had held an exhibit of the theatrical work of Goncharova and Larionov. To Goncharova, painting and theatrical work were closely related, both being forms of esthetic expression. Her theatrical sketches and flats have frequently been exhibited and collected. The vision or interpretation of the ballets on which Goncharova and Larionov worked resulted in a close involvement of the visual with the performing arts. Their costumes and settings often determined the tone of the performance.

By the 1950s growing interest in the flowering of radical Russian art prior to the revolution established Goncharova as one of the pioneers of modern art. Her paintings were acquired by important museums, such as the Tate Gallery, London, and there were a number of exhibitions, that of the Galerie de l'Institut (Paris, 1956) having included new Rayonist paintings and drawings. Despite almost crippling arthritis, Goncharova continued to be productive during the last decade of her life. Her final works moved away from the interpretive and the decorative and sought to explore the infinite, as if at the end of her career Goncharova was returning to her earlier interest in expression through abstraction.

Further Reading

Mary Chamot's *Goncharova-Stage Designs and Paintings* (London, 1979) is invaluable for the study of Goncharova's art, particularly in that it reviews her seldom treated theatrical work. John E. Bowlt's *Russian Art of the Avant-Garde: Theory and Criticism, 1902-1934* (1976) is equally important for an understanding of the intellectual bases of her early work and the climate in which it was conceived. □

Edmond de and Jules de Goncourt

The brothers Edmond de (1822-1896) and Jules de (1830-1870) Goncourt collaborated on novels which originated the Naturalist school in France. Their "Journals" provide a fascinating picture of Parisian literary life in the 19th century.

Edmond de Goncourt was born at Nancy on May 26, 1822, and his younger brother, Jules, in Paris on Dec. 17, 1830. Their father, a member of a recently ennobled family, who had fought with distinction under Napoleon, died in 1834 and their mother in 1848, leaving the brothers a comfortable private income. Neither married, and the two were virtually never separated until Jules's premature death on June 20, 1870.

Initially the Goncourts intended to become painters, but during a trip to Algeria in 1849 they began to make travel notes and decided to make their career in literature. Their early attempts at plays and a novel were unsuccessful, and they turned to art criticism and works of history dealing with the 18th century and Revolutionary age. Their first success in fiction was *Charles Demailly* (1860), a novel describing the unscrupulous literary world of Paris and the intrigues which finally drive the hero insane. The careful documentation of a pathological case, intended to give an impression of extreme realism, marks all the Goncourts' novels. In 1861 there followed *Soeur Philomène* (Sister Philomène), a somewhat morbid study of hospital life built round the career of a nun; and in 1864 *Renée Mauperin,* a vigorous portrait of a middle-class family, ending once again somewhat melodramatically with the deaths of the son in a duel and of the daughter by heart disease brought on by remorse.

The novel which is often considered the Goncourts' masterpiece and which had most influence on the young Émile Zola and the Naturalist school is *Germinie Lacerteux* (1865). Here, the plot is based very closely on the life of the brothers' own housekeeper who had died in 1862. Regarded by them as an ideal servant, she had in fact been leading a double life for years, robbing them and indulging in drink and promiscuous sexual relationships which had brought her two illegitimate children and finally caused her

Edmond de Goncourt

brothers and later of Edmond, running from 1851 to 1896, was published only in the late 1950s. Edmond died on July 16, 1896, and by the terms of his will endowed in 1900 the Goncourt Academy, a group of 10 writers who enjoy great prestige in France and who annually award the Goncourt Prize, the most famous French literary award, to the prose work which they consider to be the best to have appeared during the year.

Further Reading

An edition of the 1851-1870 diaries was published as *The Goncourt Journals, 1851-1870,* edited by Lewis Galantière (trans. 1937); selections from the full version running from 1851 to 1896 are contained in *Pages from the Goncourt Journal,* edited by Robert Baldick (trans. 1962). There are two studies in English of the Goncourt brothers: a short book by Robert Baldick, *The Goncourts* (1960), and a translation from the French, André Billy, *The Goncourt Brothers* (1960). ☐

early death. With the transposition of the brothers themselves into the single character of an old lady, the novel follows fact very closely and furnishes a convincing and horrifying picture of degradation.

In 1867 the Goncourts published *Manette Salomon,* often considered the finest novel dealing with the life of the artist in France. The main theme, reflecting a certain misogyny apparent in both brothers, is the destructive effect of a woman on the creative genius of an artist. The last novel the Goncourts wrote together was *Madame Gervaisais* (1869), the story of a religious conversion, treated again pathologically as a form of insanity and described with documentary realism.

After Jules's death Edmond, deeply affected both by this and the Franco-Prussian War of 1870-1871, gave up writing for some time but later took up again the novel already planned by the brothers, *La Fille Élisa,* which appeared in 1877. This is another story of degradation, this time of a poor girl who becomes a prostitute, commits a murder, and is condemned to death but is reprieved only to die in the prison hospital. Other novels followed, notably *La Faustin* (1882), the psychological study of a successful actress.

Throughout Edmond's lifetime he also continued to bring out works on art, especially on that of the 18th century and of Japan, while selections of the *Journal* appeared from 1887 to 1896. The full version of the diaries, which contain a remarkably frank and colorful account of the life of the

Luis de Góngora y Argote

The Spanish poet Luis de Góngora y Argote (1561-1627) caused a furor with his use of complex metaphor, Latinized vocabulary, unconventional syntax, and metaphysical subtleties. His baroque style became known as Gongorism.

Born in Cordova on July 11, 1561, Luis de Góngora was educated there and at the University of Salamanca, where, without much enthusiasm, he studied law while preferring literature and music. No evidence exists that he obtained his degree. An unfortunate love affair is said to have given origin to one of his best-known sonnets, LXXXVI, *La dulce boca que a gustar convida* ("The sweet mouth that invites one to taste"), a caustic prognostic to lovers that "all that is ever left of love is its venom."

As early as 1580 Góngora manifested some predilection for *culto,* or euphuistic, poetry—as is shown by his use of proparoxytonic verse, his Latinizations, and his exploitation of classical mythology. Even so, during these early years and later, he retained a liking for the popular, for the picaresque, and even for waggery.

By his middle 20s the precocious Góngora was well enough known to be complimented by Miguel de Cervantes in a poem of literary criticism, *Canto de Calíope* (1585; "Song of Calliope"). Sponsored by an uncle, and after providing the customary evidence that he was a *cristiano viejo* (that is, untainted with Jewish or Moorish blood), Góngora obtained remunerative prebendaries and took minor orders toward the priesthood. Income now assured, he began to live a rather carefree life, to which an austere bishop soon put a stop. The bishop accused Góngora of unchurchly fondness for bullfighting, music, and theater, fined him 4 ducats, and forbade his further attendance at bullfights.

A Góngora maturer in years, if not in financial practices, moved in 1601 to Valladolid, temporary seat of the royal court, where he wrote a great deal of festive verse, fell out with Francisco de Quevedo, spent money too freely, and plunged into debt. Vicissitudes, however, did not check his growing prestige, which by 1606 had earned him the reputation of being an illustrious poet.

The years 1612-1613, when Góngora wrote *Fábula de Polifemo y Galatea* ("The Fable of Polyphemus and Galatea") and *Las soledades* ("Solitudes"), were the most important in his literary life, and the controversy attendant on the publication of these poems has continued until today. Góngora's strongest apologist, Dámaso Alonso, eloquently defends Gongorism and challenges its defamers: "Obscurity, no: radiant clarity, dazzling clarity. Clarity of language of hard perfection and exact grammatical enchasing . . ."; while Elisha Kane (1928) attacks Gongorism as a physician a pestilence: "Gongorism is the disease of an age and a culture." Kane does not attribute to Góngora the "disease" of Gongorism but rather blames the 17th century, a "barren, baroque epoch."

In 1617 Góngora was appointed chaplain to Philip III over the objections of the Duke of Lerma, who questioned the desirability of appointing a poet to a position so close to the King. In spite of his salary from this post and from his prebendaries, Góngora, who frequently gambled and lived beyond his means, seemed always short of funds. In 1625, to his despair, he was in danger of losing to creditors even his horse and carriage; in July he wrote to a friend, "I feel like jumping in a well." His debts continued to accumulate, and his pride suffered a heavy blow when his residence in Madrid was auctioned and purchased by his implacable literary enemy Francisco de Quevedo. One setback followed another. The Conde-Duque de Olivares offered to underwrite the costs of publishing Góngora's poetry but reneged on his promise, leaving Góngora largely unpublished, although his writings circulated in manuscript.

Before his death in Cordova on May 23, 1627, Góngora gave all his manuscripts to his nephew, Luis de Saavedra, who never bothered to have them published, presumably being occupied in grabbing his late uncle's prebendary income. Because of this negligence by an unconcerned beneficiary, Góngora's prose (excepting his letters) has disappeared. Only his poetry survives.

His Poetry

Góngora's major poems, those that have aroused the most controversy, are *Polifemo* (1613), based on the thirteenth book of the *Metamorphoses* of Ovid, and *Las soledades* (1613). *Polifemo* tells the story of the love of the one-eyed Cyclops, Polyphemus, for the charming, mocking sea nymph Galatea. The scene is a bat-haunted cave on the Sicilian coast, where jealous Polyphemus slays the handsome Acis, and a grief-stricken Galatea beseeches the goddess of the sea to transform Acis into a river. Of the four *soledades* he planned to write, Góngora completed only the first; the second was never finished and no trace exists of the third and fourth. *Las soledades* tells the story of a youth shipwrecked among goatherds, of a flower-bedecked village, of fireworks and athletic contests, of the youth's encounter with a beautiful maiden, and of their subsequent marriage.

In *Polifemo* and *Las soledades* Góngora sought beauty of language in lines of abstruse complexity and tried to create a "new reality" by means of new metaphor. To him, to call things by their common names was to tread on old treadmills: he gave things new names to exalt and enliven them. His defenders would say Góngora's was "the poet's eye, in a fine frenzy rolling, seeking to give airy nothing a local habitat and a name."

Concerning the enduring quality of Góngora's sonnets and his other conventional poems, there is no controversy, and no anthology of Spanish poetry would appear without a selection of them. Sonnet CLXVI is the lyrical Spanish counterpart of Robert Herrick's "Gather ye rosebuds while ye may," although more overcast with sorrow, especially in the final word, *nada* (nothing).

Few poets have conveyed the elemental sorrow of a young bride whose beloved is going off to war as Góngora does in the *romancillo* XLIX, whose first stanza reads: La más bella niña/ de nuestro lugar/ hoy viuda y sola,/ y ayer por casar,/ viendo que sus ojos/ a la guerra van/ a su madre dice,/ que escucha su mal:/ *Dejadme llorarl orillas del mar.* (The loveliest girl in our village, today a widow and alone, yesterday still single, seeing her beloved depart for war, says to her mother, listening to her lamentation: *Let me pour forth my grief on the shore of the sea.*)

Further Reading

The most thorough study of Góngora in English is antagonistic, Elisha K. Kane, *Gongorism and the Golden Age: A Study of Exuberance and Unrestraint in the Arts* (1928). Background information is in George Tyler Northup, *An Introduction to Spanish Literature* (1925; 3d ed. rev. by Nicholson B. Adams, 1960), and in Richard E. Chandler and Kessel Schwartz, *A New History of Spanish Literature* (1961). □

Julio González

The Spanish sculptor Julio González (1876-1942) pioneered welded iron constructions and gave the medium an unprecedented expressiveness and range.

Julio González was born on Sept. 21, 1876, in Barcelona. He learned his craft from his father, a goldsmith and sculptor. González exhibited sculpture in metal at the Barcelona International Exposition in 1892 and at the World's Columbian Exposition in Chicago in 1893. He studied painting as an evening student at the Barcelona School of Fine Arts.

In 1900 González moved to Paris, where he renewed his acquaintance with Pablo Picasso. At this time González devoted himself to painting. His brother Joan, also a painter, died in 1908. González, grief-stricken, abandoned all artistic activity for many months. When he recovered, he returned to his first love, sculpture, but his work was intermittent and dispirited. Anguish over his brother's death had abated, but González was haunted by it, and he also suffered from a sense of personal inadequacy.

In 1926, when he was approaching 50, González acquired sufficient confidence to begin working full time. His sculpture of the next 4 years was cubistic, modest in scale, and reminiscent of the so-called transparencies of Jacques Lipchitz. In 1930 González began to instruct Picasso in welding. The collaboration of González with perhaps the most powerful innovator in modern art led, as one would expect, to a vitalization of his own artistic conceptions. González's *Head* (1934) and *Standing Figure* (1932) show Picasso's influence. These works are linear in conception, with forms and attitudes as agile and intense as a grasshopper's body, and yet they are totally expressive of welded iron.

González became a member of the constructivist group Cercle et Carré at this time, and in 1934 he exhibited with the Abstraction-Création group. Some of his last works, such as *Woman Combing Her Hair* (1936) and *Monserrat* (1936-1937), have expressionist characteristics and a monumentality unlike anything he had done before. *Monserrat,* which represents the starkly simple figure of a woman with a scarf on her head, is essentially naturalistic in terms of proportion and sense of bulk despite the meagerness of descriptive detail. In a sense, this sculpture, thought by many to be his finest, is uncharacteristic, for González combined abstraction and surrealism in his two versions of *Cactus Man,* spiky, gesturing, anthropomorphic vegetations.

During World War II, because of war shortages, González was forced to abandon welding and instead model in plaster. He executed a number of sketches for *Monserrat II,* but he finished only the head: it is that of a woman, her hair covered by a bandana. She appears to be crying out as if confronted by an unspeakable atrocity. This piece was his last work. He died in Paris on March 27, 1942. Though his output was small, his influence on such sculptors as David Smith, Theodore Roszak, Reg Butler, and Lynn Chadwick is testimony to the eloquence of his art.

Further Reading

There are few studies of González's art in English. There are two exhibition catalogs, one by Hilton Kramer for the Galerie Chalette in New York (1961) and another by Andrew Ritchie for the Museum of Modern Art (1956). The latter received wider distribution; it provides a basic text and adequate plates. Vincente Aguilera Cerni, *Julio González* (1962), includes a text in Italian and English. The Galerie de France of Paris published *Joan González 1868-1908, Julio González 1876-1942, Roberta González, Peintures et dessins inédits* (1965), with a text in French, English, and German.

Additional Sources

Withers, Josephine, *Julio Gonzalez: sculpture in iron,* New York: New York University Press, 1978. □

Felipe González Márquez

Prime Minister of Spain from 1982 to 1996, Felipe González Márquez (born 1942) helped lead Spain into the European community of nations.

Birth and Childhood

Felipe González Márquez was born on March 5, 1942, in Seville, the largest city in western Andalusia in the south of Spain. His father, Felipe González Helguera, bought and sold cattle and owned a small dairy in a lower-middle-class district of Seville. His mother, Juana Márquez, was, in her son's words, "the driving force of the family."

The particular period of Spanish history in which González grew up had a decisive influence on what were later to be his ideological beliefs. Between 1936 and 1939 Spain had suffered an horrific civil war, resulting from a military rising that overthrew the reformist government elected to power in February 1936. Under the ultraconservative regime established by General Francisco Franco at the end of the war in 1939, all political parties and trade unions were banned except those organized by the state. All forms of dissent were prohibited. González was born at a time when Spanish prisons were full to overflowing with political prisoners. Thousands of people had been executed since the end of the war because of their liberal beliefs. In his neighborhood in Seville lived a number of former political prisoners who had served their sentences in a nearby Francoist labor camp. Finally, the 1940s were years of extreme hardship. The combined effects of the civil war, the subsequent world war, the Francoist policy of economic autarchy, and a long, severe drought brought shortages of even the most basic necessities of life. Spaniards refer to the 1940s as "the hungry years."

During those years González attended a school run by Claretian priests, then entered the Faculty of Law at Seville University. There he was soon influenced by the highly politicized atmosphere which characterized Spanish (and other European) universities in the 1960s. In 1962 he joined the illegal and secret Socialist Youth movement and, two years later, the equally clandestine Spanish Socialist Workers' Party (PSOE). It was also at Seville University that he met Carmen Romero López, whom he married in 1969.

By the mid-1960s the economic and social situation in Spain had changed considerably from the hunger and scarcities of the 1940s. The Franco regime had abandoned autarchy and Spain had been reincorporated into the world capitalist system. Politically, however, the regime had not changed at all. Strikes were illegal, but became increasingly frequent in these years, as did demonstrations, go-slows, lock-outs, unfair dismissals, and numerous other manifestations of conflict between employers and workers. When González graduated from Seville University in 1966, he set up the city's first labor counseling office and, as a lawyer specializing in labor cases, acted on behalf of the employees in various parts of the country in some of the most important disputes of the time.

Early Political Career

While he was advancing his professional career, González was also gaining a name for himself as a member of the clandestine Socialist party. In 1939 most of the party's surviving leaders had left Spain for exile. Inside the country a minimal organizational structure managed to keep going, from which new leaders began to emerge. Felipe González was one of this new generation of activists. In 1965 he became a member of the Seville provincial committee and, later, of the national committee. In 1970 the PSOE held its 11th congress and González was elected to the party's most important internal body, the executive commission. By then González and his contemporaries in the PSOE felt increasingly uncomfortable with an aging exiled party leadership that seemed to be divorced from the realities of contemporary Spain.

In 1974 at the 13th party congress held at Suresnes near Paris, González was elected as the party's first secretary-general. His election represented the triumph of the "new" PSOE over the "historic" sector. It also constituted the recognition of González as a major figure within the Spanish socialist movement and the beginning of a new phase in his political career. As leader of the PSOE (with the *nom de guerre* "Isidoro") his political responsibilities and activities had already increased when, in November 1975, General Franco died, opening the way to the legalization of a multi-party system in Spain. Throughout 1976 González traveled widely in Europe discussing the political future of Spain and of the PSOE with the leaders of other European socialist

parties. He established particularly strong links with the West German Social Democratic party. At home he participated in negotiations between the centrist government of Adolfo Suárez and the opposition parties which were designed to achieve consensus on the need for moderate reformist policies, rather than radical change, in order to ensure a peaceful transition to democratic rule. When the first free elections in 41 years were held in June 1977 the PSOE became the main opposition party in the Spanish Cortes (parliament).

Under the leadership of González, the PSOE worked to consolidate Spain's nascent democracy and to increase its own appeal to the progressive, but moderate, sectors of Spanish society. In May 1979 at the 28th party congress, González resigned as secretary-general when the majority of the delegates rejected his motion that the word "Marxist" be dropped from the party's definition of itself. Four months later, however, at an extraordinary congress, he was reinstated and the motion was carried. Giving the party a social democratic image earned González criticism from the left wing of his party, but it paid dividends with respect to the electorate. In October 1982 the PSOE won a landslide victory at the polls and González became Spain's first Socialist prime minister since 1939.

Spain's First Socialist Prime Minister

González' personal charisma, his prestige as a politician, and his control of the PSOE's executive apparatus subsequently enabled him to weather a number of internal storms and to implement controversial policies. Most notably, the leader of the PSOE altered decisively the party's position on Spanish membership of NATO. The PSOE was strongly opposed when Spain joined the North Atlantic Treaty Organization (NATO) in 1981. After the 1982 election, however, the González government and the majority of the PSOE advocated remaining in the alliance. In a referendum held in March 1986 the question was decided in favor of retaining NATO membership. Three months later González again led his party to victory in a general election. He won his third term in office in the elections held on October 29, 1989, although this time, unlike the two previous occasions, the PSOE did not secure an absolute majority in the Cortes.

During González's mandate, Spain definitively left behind the international isolation of the Franco years, becoming a member of the European Economic Community in 1986 and of the Western European Union in 1988. Prime Minister González maintained close relations with a number of Latin American leaders and, as vice-president of the Socialist International, took a particular interest in national and international efforts to resolve the problems occasioned by economic and political instability in Central America.

After serving his forth consecutive term, González announced in June 1997 that he would not seek re-election. His withdrawal followed a series of financial and political scandals. The most serious were charges against some 20 political and police officials under González, including a former Interior Minister, over organizing squads that killed Basque separatists in the 1980s.

Further Reading

The history of the PSOE from 1879 to 1982 is competently recounted by Richard Gillespie in his *The Spanish Socialist Party* (1989). There is, as yet, no analysis in English of the PSOE in power, but Paul Preston's *The Triumph of Democracy in Spain* (1986) provides *inter_alia,* an acute analysis of the role of the Spanish Socialist party in the transition from dictatorship to democracy. See also Santos Juliá, "The Rights and Wrongs of Self-Avowed Marxism: The Ideological Conversion of the Leaders of the PSOE between 1976 and 1979" in Frances Lannon and Paul Preston, editors, *Elites and Power in Modern Spain* (1990). A good history of the Spanish Civil War is Gabriel Jackson, *The Spanish Republic and the Civil War, 1931-1939* (1965). □

Manuel González Prada

The Peruvian essayist and poet Manuel González Prada (1848-1918) was one of the most dynamic and aggressive polemicists of the late 19th century in Spanish America. He fought for change and progress and denounced the vestiges of Spanish colonialism.

Manuel González Prada was born on Jan. 6, 1848, in Lima, the son of a wealthy and conservative family. A rebellious child from his early years, he ran away from the seminary where he had been placed by his devout mother and began his university career studying German poets. Later he switched to law, the field in which his family wanted him to take a degree, but then made up his mind to become a farmer.

González Prada began writing poetry during this period, and in 1871 his verses were included in José Domingo Cortés's anthology, *América poetica.* González Prada married a Frenchwoman, Adriana de Verneuil; they had three children, of whom only one, Alfredo, survived. In 1879 González Prada enlisted for duty in the War of the Pacific (1879-1883) between Chile and Peru. When Peru was defeated, he remained in his house during the entire 3 years of Chilean occupation, determined not to lay eyes on the conquerors of his homeland.

After 1883 González Prada traveled to Europe and spent some time in Paris, reading and absorbing the ideas of modern German, Italian, and French writers, as well as the theories of the French writers of the Enlightenment and those of many of the positivists.

Call for Reforms

When González Prada returned to Lima, he immediately assumed a prominent place in the vanguard of Peruvian national awareness. Writers and political figures alike caught the contagious fire of his revolutionary fervor. He spoke out eloquently not only against the stagnant aristocratic class from which he had come, but also against the rejection of the Indian as an element of the national character and against the clergy and the ruling military oligarchy, which he viewed as the sources of many of the country's chronic ills.

González Prada became the articulate standard-bearer for a new generation of Peruvians who gathered about him, answering the call he had put forth in these lines from one of his early essays: "The decayed and wormeaten tree trunks have already produced their flowers of poisonous fragrance and their bitter-tasting fruits! Let new trees grow and yield new flowers and new fruits! Old men to the tomb, young men to work!"

Principal Works

The principal works of prose published in González Prada's lifetime are *Páginas libres* (1894) and *Horas de Jucha* (1908). After his death in 1918, more than half a dozen volumes of his prose writings appeared. His most celebrated collections of poetry are *Minúsculas* (1901), *Presbiterianas* (1909), and *Exóticos* (1916). Other important volumes of his poetry are *Trozos de vida* (1933), *Libertarios* (1938), and *Baladas peruanas* (1939).

Despite his intensely active public career, which included forming the first Peruvian Radical party (1891) and directing the National Library in Lima (1912-1918), González Prada possessed sufficient compulsive renovating energies to bring the enrichment of new French, English, and Italian verse forms to Spanish-American poetic expression. Critic Orlando Gómez-Gil has observed, "In his writings as much as in his life, González Prada demonstrates an innovative and revolutionary spirit that is peculiarly and unmistakably his alone." González Prada died in Lima, on July 22, 1918.

Further Reading

There is no book-length study of González Prada in English. A good sketch of his life and work is in William Rex Crawford, *A Century of Latin American Thought* (1944). González Prada's influence on the Aprista movement is analyzed in Harry Kantor, *The Ideology and Program of the Peruvian Aprista Movement* (1953), in Robert E. McNicoll, "Intellectual Origins of Aprismo," and in Harold A. Bierck, ed., *Latin American Civilization: Readings and Essays* (1967). See also German Arciniegras, *Latin America: A Cultural History* (1965; trans. 1967). □

Gonzalo de Berceo

The Spanish author Gonzalo de Berceo (ca. 1195-c 1252) wrote narrative religious poems and is considered the foremost poet of the Castilian language in the 13th century.

Gonzalo de Berceo was born in Berceo near Navarre in the wine-rich region of La Rioja, which figures prominently in his works. He was raised and educated in the monastery of San Millán de la Cogolla, an important shrine in that region. It is also possible that he studied in the short-lived institute of Palencia. He joined the priesthood at an unknown date, but by 1221 he was already a deacon in San Millán. Of the six documents known of him, four are dated in San Millán, the last one Dec. 20, 1246. He died after 1252, the date of the death of King Ferdinand III of Castile, which is mentioned in *Milagros XXV.*

Gonzalo's extant works are all in *cuaderna vía* (the learned poetic form, imported from France, consisting of 14-syllable verses arranged in quatrains with a single rhyme) and can be divided into three groups: lives of the saints (*Vida de San Millán de la Cogolla, Vida de Santo Domingo de Silos, Martirio de San Lorenzo,* and *Vida de Santa Oria*), Marian works (*Loores de Nuestra Señora, Milagros de Nuestra Señora,* and *El duelo que fizo la Virgen*), and doctrinal works (*El sacrificio de la Misa, Los signos del Día del Juicio,* and *Los tres Himnos*). The chronology of these works has not been fully established. A few other works have been lost, and the long narrative poem *Libro de Alexandre* (ca. 1240) has been attributed to him in one of its two extant manuscripts, though the attribution is open to question.

The subject of Gonzalo's poetry is religious and international (lives of the saints and miracles of the Virgin, many of them with known French sources), and traditionally his poems have been considered the lyrical outpourings of a simple soul. But the fact remains that these poems always find a way of centering upon his monastery of San Millán de la Cogolla. Obviously, naiveté was no more a trademark of Gonzalo than it was of the Middle Ages in general. The factor of religious propaganda, therefore, should not be neglected when considering the wellsprings of his poetry, which in fact uses many of the technical traits of the *juglares* (minstrels), who would be the logical broadcasters of his poems. But his works are remembered, and read, as much more than the religious propaganda so common in his day. His poetic language shows a surprising maturity; his poetic technique is near perfect; and his creative mind gives concrete and plastic reality to his subject.

Further Reading

The most recent and complete English work on Berceo is Brian Dutton's introduction to his edition of Berceo's *Vida de San Millán.* ☐

George Peabody Gooch

The British historian and political journalist George Peabody Gooch (1873-1968) is noted for his work on historiography and diplomatic history.

Born to a middle-class London family in 1873, George Gooch was fortunate, as he once remarked, to have been born with ''a warm heart, an inquiring mind, and an adequate income.'' After studying at Eton, London, and Trinity College, Cambridge, he spent the autumn of 1895 in Berlin. That same year he made the ac-

quaintance of Lord Acton, who guided the young historian's work for the next 5 years. In 1896 Gooch attended lectures at the Sorbonne and the School of Political Science in Paris. In 1903 he married Sophie Schoen.

Gooch's first work, *English Democratic Ideas in the Seventeenth Century* (1898), in which he viewed even the most fanatical of his historical subjects with liberal toleration, is a classic in its field. Politics, however, soon drew him away from scholarly pursuits. The crisis of the Boer War brought Gooch into the company of other young Liberals who attacked the imperialism of Joseph Chamberlain. In 1903 Gooch stood for member of Parliament from Bath and in 1906 was elected. His defeat for reelection in 1910 brought his active political career to a close, but the experience had confirmed his liberalism and given him personal knowledge of the leading personalities of his time.

Gooch was editor of the *Contemporary Review* from 1911 until 1960. He contributed many essays to the *Review,* using it to attack Nazism after 1934. To its pages he welcomed refugees from Fascist Italy and Nazi Germany.

In *History and Historians in the Nineteenth Century* (1913), Gooch's most lasting achievement, he assessed the writings of over 500 historians, tracing the emergence of the scientific method in historical research, portraying the masters of the craft, and analyzing their influence on their times. His other major contribution to historiography was *Recent Revelations of European Diplomacy* (1927; revised periodically until 1940), in which he discussed authors and sur-

veyed the publication of documents and memoirs concerned with pre-1914 diplomacy.

Between World Wars I and II Gooch wrote numerous books on diplomatic history, edited *British Documents on the Origins of the War* with Harold Temperley (11 vols., 1926-1938), and published essays on current political questions. As president of the National Peace Council (1933-1936), he tried to convince other pacifists that peace could be maintained only by opposing the dictators on the Continent.

After World War II Gooch's interests turned to the 18th century, and he wrote *Frederick the Great* (1947), *Maria Theresa* (1951), *Catherine the Great* (1954), and *Louis XV* (1956). He died on Aug. 31, 1968.

Further Reading

For an understanding of Gooch, the best work is his autobiography, *Under Six Reigns* (1958). There is an essay on Gooch by F. L. Hadsel in Samuel William Halperin, ed., *Some 20th-Century Historians: Essays on Eminent Europeans* (1961).

Additional Sources

Eyck, Frank, *G.P. Gooch: a study in history and politics,* London: Macmillan; Atlantic Highlands, N.J.: Distributed by Humanities Press, 1982. □

Jane Goodall

Jane Goodall (born 1934) was a pioneering woman primatologist. Her holistic methods of fieldwork, which emphasized patient observation over long periods of time of social groups and individual animals, transformed not only how chimpanzees as a species are understood but also how studies of many different kinds of animals are carried out.

In July of 1960, 26-year-old Jane Goodall set out for the first time for Gombe National Park in southeastern Africa to begin a study of the chimpanzees that lived in the forests along the shores of Lake Tanganyika. Her mother traveled with her as officials thought it unseemly that a young, unmarried woman would set off on such a venture alone. She thought at the time that the study might take three years. She ended up staying for more than two decades.

Goodall seemed an unlikely candidate for such a task. The elder of two daughters, she had been born into a middle-class British family. Her father, Mortimer Herbert Morris-Goodall, was an engineer. Her mother, Vanna (Joseph) Morris-Goodall, was a successful novelist. She had little formal training when she set out for Gombe, having worked previously as a secretary at Oxford and as an assistant editor in a documentary film studio in London. Otherwise, she brought to her work a life-long love of animals, a strong sense of determination and a desire for adventure.

This was not her first trip to Africa. In 1957 she had sailed to Mombasa on the East African coast where she met Louis Leakey, who would become her mentor. With his wife Mary, Leakey had discovered what were then the oldest known human remains. These discoveries substantiated Leakey's claim that the origins of the human species were in Africa, not in Asia or Europe as had been previously thought.

Leakey hoped that studies of the primate species most closely related to human beings—chimpanzees, gorillas, and orangutans—would shed light on the behavior of human ancestors. He chose Goodall because he believed that as a woman she would be more patient and careful than a male observer and that as someone with little formal training she would be more inclined to describe what she saw rather than what she thought she should be seeing.

In her earliest days at Gombe, Goodall worked alone or with native guides. She spent long hours working to gain the trust of the chimpanzees, tracking them through the dense forests and gradually moving closer and closer to her subjects until she could sit in their midst—something which had not been achieved by her predecessors. Her patience produced a stunning set of discoveries about the behaviors and social relations of her subjects. Chimpanzees had previously been thought to be violent, aggressive animals with crude social arrangements. Researchers had given their subjects numbers rather than names and had ignored the differences in personality, intelligence, and social acumen that Goodall's studies revealed. Chimpanzees, Goodall showed, organized themselves in bands that had complex social structures. They were often loving and careful parents and also formed attachments to their peers. They hunted and ate meat. And, perhaps most startling, they used primitive "tools"—twigs or grasses that they stripped of leaves and used to get termites out of termite mounds. This discovery helped force scientists to abandon their definition of homo sapiens as the only animals that use tools.

In 1962 Leakey arranged for Goodall to work on a Ph.D. at Cambridge University, which would give scientific legitimacy to her discoveries. Despite bitter disagreements with her adviser, who belonged to the older school of ethologists (people who study animal behavior), she managed to complete the necessary work in brief visits to England. In 1965 she became the eighth person ever to take a Ph.D. from Cambridge without having previously earned a B.A.

By 1964 the Gombe Stream Research Center had become the destination of choice for graduate students and other scientists wishing to study chimpanzees or to learn Goodall's methods. The general public was also becoming acquainted with Goodall's work through a series of articles in *National Geographic* magazine and later through National Geographic television specials. In 1964 Goodall married Hugo Van Lawick, a Dutch wildlife photographer who had come to Gombe at the invitation of Leakey to take pictures for the magazine. Goodall's son by that marriage, Hugo (more often referred to as "Grub"), was her only child.

The 1970s were marked both by changes in Goodall's understanding of the chimpanzees and by the way in which research was carried out at Gombe. In 1974 what Goodall referred to as a "war" broke out between two groups of chimpanzees. One group eventually succeeded in killing many members of the other group. Goodall also witnessed a series of acts of infanticide on the part of one of the mature female chimps. These revelations of the darker side of chimpanzee behavior forced her to revise her interpretation of these animals as being fundamentally gentle and peaceloving.

In May of 1975 four research assistants were kidnapped from the research center by Zairean rebels. After months of negotiations, the hostages were returned. Because of continued risk, almost all of the many European and American researchers left Gombe. Goodall continued to carry out her work with the help of local people who had been trained to conduct research.

Later, Goodall turned her attention to the plight of chimpanzees in captivity. Because of their close physiological and genetic resemblance to humans, chimpanzees have been widely used as laboratory animals to study human diseases such as AIDS. Goodall used her expertise and fame to lobby for limitations on the number of animals used in such experiments and to convince researchers to improve the conditions under which the animals are kept. She also worked to improve conditions for zoo animals and for conservation of chimpanzee habitats. In 1986 she helped found the Committee for the Conservation and Care of Chimpanzees—an organization dedicated to these issues.

For her efforts, Godall received a great many awards and honors, among them the Gold Medal of Conservation from the San Diego Zoological Society, the J. Paul Getty Wildlife Conservation Prize, the Schweitzer Medal of the Animal Welfare Institute, and the National Geographic Society Centennial Award. Much of Goodall's current work is carried on by the Jane Goodall Institute for Wildlife Research, Education, and Conservation, in Ridgefield, Connecticut. Her advocacy of the ethical treatment of animals continues to the current day, and she has even written a children's book, *The Chimpanzee Family Book,* on the subject.

Further Reading

Goodall wrote a number of books about her experiences with the chimpanzees, including *Through a Window* (1990); *My Life with the Wild Chimpanzees* (1988); *The Chimpanzees of Gombe: Patterns of Behavior* (1986); *In the Shadow of Man* (1971); and *Visions of Caliban: On Chimpanzees and People* (1993). For books that show her work in relation to that of other primatologists, see: Donna Haraway, *Primate Visions* (1989); Bettyann Kevles' *Watching the Great Apes* (1976); and Sy Montgomery, *Walking with the Great Apes* (1991).
National Geographic (no. 5, 1979).
American Scientist (Volume 75, number 6, 1987).
Montgomery, Sy, *Walking with the Great Apes: Jane Goodall, Dian Fossey, Biruté* (1991). □

John Inkster Goodlad

Researcher and prophet John Inkster Goodlad (born 1917) was one of the chief movers in American education during the last half of the 20th century.

John Goodlad, one of two boys born to William James and Mary (Inkster) Goodlad, spent the first nine years of his life on the hillsides of North Vancouver, British Columbia. Attendance at the six-room school required a long walk down the hill at the beginning of the day and another back up the hill in the afternoon. The three boys who lived on the hillside had to get along with one another because there were no alternatives.

That isolation, accompanied by periods of isolation from school because of the usual measles, chicken pox, and the like, "probably was a blessing," he noted. "It pushed me into a great deal of reading—a novel a day during times of illness and a great deal of continued reading into my adolescent years." Goodlad recalled the period after the age of nine and during the Great Depression when remarking, "The only thing good about those years was that everyone was poor." With the exception of a handful of families in each of the two elementary schools that he attended, everyone belonged to the same low economic class.

University Out of His Reach

He recalls some fleeting thoughts of becoming a physician or a lawyer, but both meant going to the university and there was no prospect of him doing that. A fifth year of high

school, called senior matriculation, made it possible for him to secure an education equivalent to the first year at the university, and from that he went on to the provincial normal school (1938) in Vancouver to qualify for an elementary school teaching certificate. He began teaching in 1939 in a one-room school in a district which at that time did not employ superintendents. The school board employed each teacher; after that, books, materials, and administrative decisions were made by a paid secretary/treasurer of the board. Goodlad's salary for that first year was $780 for the 10-month period. From this he had to save enough money to go to summer school for two successive summers in order to qualify for a permanent teaching certificate.

In subsequent years while working as a teacher and principal he attended the University of British Columbia during the summer sessions and took correspondence courses during the year but did not attend at any time as a full-time student. Both Bachelor's (1945) and Master's (1946) degrees were completed in this fashion, and then he broke loose from British Columbia and went to the University of Chicago for his doctorate (1949). At long last he was a full-time resident college student for the first and only year of his life. In 1945 he married Evalene M. Pearson and was later to have two children, Stephen John and Mary Paula.

Teacher of Teachers

Goodlad's professional work can be divided into two periods, namely, an early period (1947-1960) consisting of a variety of positions in teacher education, including Atlanta Teacher Education Service, Emory University, Agnes Scott College, and the University of Chicago; and a second period (1960-1983) at the University of California, Los Angeles (UCLA), where he served as director of the Laboratory School and as dean of the Graduate School of Education (ranked first in America the last seven years of his tenure). After his retirement from UCLA he assumed the positions of professor (1985) and director of the Center for Educational Renewal (1986) at the University of Washington. He currently is professor emeritus of education and co-director of the Center. Goodlad also is president of the independent Institute for Educational Inquiry. The educator has authored or co-authored more than 30 books; has written chapters and papers in more than 100 other books and yearbooks; and has more than 200 articles in professional journals and encyclopedias. His writings have been translated into Japanese, French, Italian, Spanish, and Hebrew. He also has received numerous awards, including seven honorary degrees.

Prolific Writer

Among Goodlad's more recent books are *Teachers for Our Nation's Schools* (1990), for which he received the Outstanding Writing Award from the American Association of Colleges for Teacher Education; *Educational Renewal: Better Teachers. Better Schools;* and *In Praise of Education,* in which he argues education is an inalienable right in a democratic society.

Since the time of the Great Depression, the effectiveness of American schools has come under increasing criticism. During this period John Goodlad rose in prominence as an effective prophet and mover in educational reform. His research is not regarded as an experiment, but grows out of action, out of his own field experiences as he seeks to close the gap between existing conditions in schools and what policy research models have postulated. The values learned from his parents, teaching in a one-room school, and working in Atlanta during racial unrest were a few of the more meaningful experiences that affected his research.

One idea, "the non-graded school," grew out of his experiences of teaching in a one-room school. Here a student named Ernie, who had a learning disability, did not progress to new grade levels as did the others. As a result he left school as an unhappy child and as a failure. As an alternative to school policies that degrade children and limit learning, Goodlad proposed schools without grade levels. Later he made several suggestions for improving schools in his book *A Place Called School* (1984). In this comprehensive study, one of the more extensive on-the-scene investigations ever undertaken, he began with the premise that our schools need to be redesigned piece by piece. Throughout the entire field of education he called for sweeping changes that "must be guided first and foremost by moral principles." He wanted to create a human school. He said, "When we speak of our pet we refer to it as a dog, then second we may speak of it being different from other dogs. But, when speaking of human beings, we speak of the differences first, then note that they are people later. However, I want to speak of people as human beings first; I want to develop a human school, for we are all one."

Goodlad's engaging style of writing about school reform is illustrated in his discussion of the Roman god Janus. He states, " . . . Janus has been represented as having two faces, one looking forward and the other backward. I look from the present into the recent past and from the present into the imminent future. Second, Janus was the animistic spirit of doorways and archways. I speak to the problems of cutting doorways between buildings and archways over different levels of curriculum decision making. Third, Janus, in Roman mythology, was guardian of the gate of heaven (the 'opener' and the 'shutter') and god of all beginnings. Those of us who work in curriculum might be expected, then, to invoke Janus in making our beginnings and to reckon with Janus at the ending believed by some to be still another beginning." (*Teachers College Record,* November 1968).

More likely due to his love for education than in spite of it, Goodlad has been a critic of the U.S. education system, particularly for the way it trains teachers for the classroom. In a two-part article for *Education Week,* Feb. 5; 12 1997, Goodlad said the gates to admission to teaching in U.S. public schools "always are loosely latched." And he bemoaned the way reform theories come and go, yielding little if any improvement. "The overwhelming majority of those hired each year to teach in our schools are the product of a misbegotten set of conditions that defy accurate pinpointing of accountability. With accountability dispersed, blame and villain theories run rampant: It's the students, it's the teachers, it's the state, it's the schools of education."

Further Reading

Biographical information about John I. Goodlad can be found in the following: *The Canadian Who's Who, The Blue Book* (London), *Who's Who in the World, The Writers Directory* (London), *The International Directory of Distinguished Leadership,* and *The International Who's Who* (London).
A selected list of books that the reader may find useful in tracing the growth of Goodlad's ideas and proposals for changes in schools include: *The Nongraded Elementary School,* in part (revised edition 1963); *School, Curriculum, and the Individual* (1966); *Facing the Future: Issues in Education and Schooling* (1976); *A Place Called School: Some Prospects for the Future* (1984).

Additional Sources

Goodlad, John I., *Teachers for Our Nation's Schools,* Jossey-Bass Publishers (1990).
Goodlad, John I., *Educational Renewal: Better Teachers. Better Schools,* Jossey-Bass Publishers (1994).
Goodlad, John, I., *What Schools Are For,* Phi Delta Kappa Educational Foundation (1994).
Goodlad, John I., *In Praise of Education,* Teachers College Press (1997).
Goodlad, John I., "Producing Teachers Who Understand, Believe,and Care," *Education Week* (February 1997).
Goodlad, John I., "Sustaining and Extending Educational Renewal," *Phi Delta Kappan* (November 1996).
Goodlad, John I., "The National Network for Educational Renewal," *Phi Delta Kappan* (April 1994).
Goodlad, John I., "On Taking School Reform Seriously," *"Phi Delta Kappan/PDKAA* (November 1992).

Goodlad, John I., "Better Teachers for Our Nation's Schools" (summary of a five-year study and recommendations for improvement) *Phi Delta Kappan* (November 1990). □

Benny Goodman

Benny Goodman (1909-1986) was a great jazz clarinetist and leader of one of the most popular big bands of the Swing Era (1935-1945).

Benjamin David Goodman was born in Chicago, Illinois, on May 30, 1909, of a large, poor Jewish family. (A brother, Harry, was later a bassist in Benny's band.) Benny studied music at Hull House and at the age of 10 was already a proficient clarinetist. At age 12, appearing on stage in a talent contest, he did an imitation of the prevailing clarinet favorite, Ted Lewis; so impressed was popular bandleader Ben Pollack that five years later he sent for Goodman to join the band at the Venice ballroom in Los Angeles. After a three-year stint with Pollack, Goodman left in 1929 to free-lance in New York City in pit bands and on radio and recordings. In 1934 he led his first band on an NBC radio series called "Let's Dance" (which became the title of Goodman's theme song). The band also played at Billy Rose's Music Hall and at the Roosevelt Hotel and made a handful of records for the Columbia and Victor labels.

In 1935, armed with a repertory developed by some great African American arrangers (Benny Carter, Edgar Sampson, Horace Henderson, and ex-bandleader and Swing Era genius Fletcher Henderson), the band embarked on a most significant road trip. Not especially successful in most of its cross-country engagements, the band arrived at the Palomar Ballroom in Los Angeles in a discouraged mood. The evening of August 21, 1935, began inauspiciously, the audience lukewarm to the band's mostly restrained dance music. In desperation Goodman called for the band to launch into a couple of "flagwavers" (up-tempo crowd-pleasers)—"Sometimes I'm Happy" and "King Porter Stomp"—and the crowd reaction was ultimately to send shock waves through the entire pop music world. Hundreds of people stopped dancing and massed around the bandstand, responding enthusiastically and knowledgably to arrangements and solos that they recognized from the just recently released records. (Apparently Goodman had been too conservative both early in his tour and earlier that night and had underestimated his audience.)

The Palomar engagement turned out to be not only a personal triumph for the band but for swing music in general, serving notice to the music business that "sweet" dance music would have to move over and make room for the upstart (and more jazz-based) sound. Goodman's popularity soared: the band topped almost all the magazine and theater polls, their record sales were astronomical, they were given a weekly cigarette-sponsored radio show, and they were featured in two big-budget movies, "Hollywood Hotel" and "The Big Broadcast of 1937." But an even

greater triumph awaited. Impresario John Hammond rented that bastion of classical music, Carnegie Hall, for a concert that was to win respectability for the music. The night of January 16, 1938, is now legendary; responding to the electric expectancy of the overflow audience, the band outdid itself, improving on recorded favorites like "King Porter Stomp," "Bugle Call Rag," "Down South Camp Meeting," and "Don't Be That Way." It capped off the evening with a lengthy, classic version of "Sing, Sing, Sing" which featured some brilliant solo work by trumpeter Harry James, pianist Jess Stacy, and Benny himself.

Two of the finest musicians ever to work with Goodman were pianist Teddy Wilson and vibraphonist-drummer Lionel Hampton. Both were with the band from the mid-1930s and both were present at Carnegie Hall, but they were used only in trio and quartet contexts because of the unwritten rule forbidding racially integrated bands. Goodman has the distinction of being the first white leader (Artie Shaw and Charlie Barnet followed suit) to challenge segregation in the music business, and as the restrictions eased he hired other African American greats such as guitarist Charlie Christian, trumpeter Cootie Williams, bassist Slam Stewart, and tenor saxophonist Wardell Gray.

Goodman's band had a greater personnel turnover than most bands, and an endless array of top-notch musicians moved through the band, among them trumpeters Bunny Berigan, Harry James, and Ziggy Elman; trombonist Lou McGarity; tenor saxophonists Bud Freeman, Georgie Auld, Zoot Sims, and Stan Getz; pianists Mel Powell and Joe Bushkin; vibists Red Norvo and Terry Gibbs; and drummers

Dave Tough and Louis Bellson. Most defected to other bands and a few to start their own bands (Krupa, James, and Hampton). Overwhelmingly, musicians found Goodman an uncongenial employer: he was reputed to be stern and tight-fisted. A taciturn, scholarly-looking man, Goodman was unflattering referred to in music circles as "The Ray" because of his habit of glaring at any player guilty of a "clam" or "clinker" (a wrong note), even in rehearsal. A virtuoso clarinetist equally at home performing Mozart (which he did in concerts and on records), Goodman was less than patient with technical imperfection.

After World War II the clarinet, which, along with the tenor saxophone, had been the Swing Era's glamour instrument, was relegated to a minor role in bebop's scheme of things. Even the peerless Buddy DeFranco, the definitive bebop clarinetist, was unluckily marginal in an alto saxophone-and-trumpet-dominated idiom. Goodman struggled for a while to reconcile himself to the new music, but in 1950 he decided to disband, and from that time forward his public appearances were rare and were chiefly with small groups (usually sextets or septets) and almost exclusively for television specials or recordings or European tours. In 1950 he toured Europe with a septet that included two other jazz greats, trumpeter Roy Eldridge and tenor saxophonist Zoot Sims. His most celebrated tour, however, was part of the first-ever cultural exchange with the Soviet Union. In 1962, at the behest of the State Department, he went to Russia with a septet that included Sims and alto saxophonist Phil Woods. The trip was a smashing success and contributed greatly to the popularization of American jazz in Eastern Europe.

After his marriage in 1941, Goodman's home was New York City; his wife Alice (John Hammond's sister) died in 1978; they had two daughters, and she had three by a previous marriage. Goodman maintained his habit of spot-performing and in 1985 made a surprise and, by all accounts, spectacular appearance at the Kool Jazz Festival in New York. He died the following year of an apparent heart attack.

With his withdrawal from the limelight, most observers felt that he became a deeper, less flashy player than he was in the glory years when he was fronting the country's most popular swing band. His ultimate contribution to jazz, however, is still being debated: much post-1940s jazz criticism retrospectively judged him to have been overrated relative to the era's other great clarinetist-leader, Artie Shaw, and to the great early Black players of the instrument (Jimmy Noone, Johnny Dodds, Edmond Hall, and Lester Young, a tenor saxophonist who "doubled" on clarinet) and the great white traditionalist Pee Wee Russell. Esthetic evaluations are problematical at best and tend to fluctuate from era to era, but Goodman's technical mastery, burnished tone, highly individual (and influential) solo style, and undeniable *swing* certainly earned him a permanent place in the jazz pantheon.

Further Reading

There is no serious biography of Goodman. There was a promotional autobiography, written with the help of Irving Kolodin, in 1939 called *The Kingdom of Swing*. A film biography produced in 1955 titled "The Benny Goodman Story" is more Hollywood than Goodman. Probably the best source is a biography-discography by D. Russell O'Connor and Warren W. Hicks, *Benny Goodman—On the Record* (1969). □

Ellen Holtz Goodman

An American journalist, Ellen Holtz Goodman (born 1941) won a Pulitzer Prize for commentary. She wrote about issues that spanned the range from personal to political.

Ellen Goodman was born in Newton, Massachusetts, on April 11, 1941, the daughter of a Boston lawyer/politician of some social standing, Jackson Jacob Holtz, and Edith Weinstein Holtz. Her father died in 1966, when she was 25 years old. He twice had been a Democratic candidate for Congress from Brookline, an affluent suburb, in the Eisenhower years (the 1950s). In her youth Ellen lived a conventional upper-middle-class life. She later wrote in the introduction to one of her books, *Turning Points* (1979), that she wanted everything to stay the same: "I wanted to live in the same house, go to the same school, keep the same friends . . . forever."

Goodman attended Radcliffe College, graduating in 1963 with a degree in modern European history (*cum laude*), and married Anthony Goodman, a medical student, within a week of graduation. They had a daughter, Katherine Anne, then were divorced in 1971. Before that, the couple went to New York, where she got her first job, at *Newsweek* (1963-1965) as a researcher/reporter. Looking back, Goodman said that in the early 1960s women were researcher and men were writers, and even in the mid 1970s men reported on hard news and women covered soft news. "When I first became a columnist," she recalled in 1996, "one of the things I was most interested in doing was breaking down those lines. I always had the sense that life spilled over the retaining walls."

Her husband's career brought the pair to Detroit, where she landed a job as a feature writer at the *Detroit Free Press* (1965-1967), but again her husband's profession called him, this time to Boston, where they returned in 1967. She was hired as a feature writer by the *Boston Globe,* then became an associate editor in 1984.

In 1970, when the *Boston Globe* opened the editorial page to women's issues, Goodman began writing Op-Ed columns. Then came a year-long Nieman Fellowship at Harvard (1973-1974), her *At Large* column in the *Globe* (beginning in 1974), and her successful syndication with the *Washington Post* Writers Group (1976). By the mid 1990s, her column reached more than 440 newspapers around the country. Television appearances, public speaking engagements, and the Pulitzer Prize for Distinguished Commentary (1980) attested to the popularity of her writing.

Goodman's columns covered a wide range of topics, including parenting, divorce, alternative life-styles, feminism, male-female employment roles, and even gardening. In the late 1960s and early 1970s her work also addressed the antiwar and civil rights movements, plus the emerging feminist movement. She wrote about lesbianism in the U.S. Army, feminine hygiene sprays, and whether American women should shave their legs. The sharp change in the U.S. national frame of mind from the reformist 1970s to the more conservative 1980s, coupled with her 1982 marriage to Robert Levey (a colleague and national reporter with the *Boston Globe*), provided some clues to the changed tone of Goodman's newspaper columns. Her writing style remained incisive but became less confrontational.

Her basic audience was American women, many of them college-educated, white-collar, with two-careers, and made to feel that they were individuals in an increasingly uniform society. For some readers Goodman's commentary was meaningful and penetrating; others found it to be predictable. Goodman was not a creator of public policy, instead describing herself as an "observer." She thought that she spoke for the homemaker. "Try to find the obituary of a homemaker someday. . . . There's almost no voice for private lives in the newspapers." She rejected the notion that her topics were trivial. In a 1996 speech in Oakland, California she referred to a slogan from the feminist movement, "The personal is political," and applied the phrase to the focus of her work: "It meant that the things that people cared about and were involved in in their private lives, things like child care or abortion or the food you ate, also had a political context."

Five collections of Ellen Goodman's newspaper columns have been published: *Close to Home* (1979), *At Large* (1981), *Keeping in Touch* (1985), *Making Sense* (1989), and *Value Judgments* (1993). She also authored a book, *Turning Points* (1979), which explored how Americans coped with changes brought about by the feminist movement. Critics missed Goodman's sense of humor in this book, believing that she was a livelier writer doing editorial columns than in producing an extended volume.

Goodman received numerous awards for her reporting and writing. She was honored with the American Society of Newspaper Editors Distinguished Writing Award in 1980; the Hubert H. Humphrey Civil Rights Award by the Leadership Conference on Civil Rights in 1988; the President's Award from the National Women's Political Caucus in 1993; and the American Woman Award by the Women's Research and Education Institute in 1994.

Further Reading

Neil Grauer's *Wits and Sages* (1984) and Barbara Belford's *Brilliant Bylines* (1986), both contain chapters on Ellen Goodman. She is also the focus of a brief piece in *American Women Writers, Volume 5* (1994). *Colorado Business* (April 1981) contains a report on Ellen Goodman's ideas. *Ms.* (July 1983) includes an article by Ellen Goodman: "The Turmoil of Teenage Sexuality." Additional information can be found in David Astor's article in *Editor and Publisher* (June 16, 1984); *Washington Journalism Review* (January/February 1980; (September 1980); *National Review* (February 14, 1986). ☐

Charles Goodnight

The American cattleman Charles Goodnight (1836-1929) opened a series of cattle trails from Texas to New Mexico, Colorado, Wyoming, and Kansas.

Charles Goodnight was born in Macoupin County, Ill. His father soon died, his mother remarried, and the family moved to Milam County, Tex. At the age of 16 Goodnight was hauling freight with oxteams; at 20 he entered the cattle business with a partner and moved to the frontier in northwestern Texas. In an attempt to protect the range from Indian raids, he joined a group known as the Minute Men of Texas. When the Civil War broke out, this body became the Frontier Regiment of the Texas Rangers. Goodnight participated in many Indian fights and earned a distinctive reputation as a guide and scout.

In 1866 Goodnight located a ranch in New Mexico and with a partner, Oliver Loving, established the Goodnight-Loving Trail, driving a cattle herd from Texas to New Mexico. In subsequent years Goodnight blazed other trails into Wyoming and Colorado. In 1868 he established the Apishapa Ranch in Colorado and in 1870 moved to a property north of Pueblo.

Goodnight went to Kentucky and married Mary Ann Dyer, and they developed their Colorado land. With others Goodnight established the Stock Growers Bank in Pueblo. During the panic of 1873, in an attempt to market cattle for needed funds, he opened the New Goodnight Trail to Granada, Colo.

In 1876 Goodnight drove 1,600 head from the overstocked New Mexico ranges to the Texas Panhandle. To obtain capital, he formed a partnership with John George Adair, establishing the JA Ranch, which eventually included nearly 1 million acres of land and 100,000 head of cattle. In 1877 Goodnight opened a trail from this ranch to the railhead at Dodge City, Kans. He also developed a fine herd by introducing Shorthorn and Hereford stock for breeding. He preserved the buffalo of the range and produced a new breed of stock, the cattalo, by crossing buffalo with Polled Angus cattle.

Goodnight stood for law and order and regulating Native American activities. Between 1868 and 1871 he organized Colorado stockraisers into an association, and in 1880 he prompted the establishment of the Panhandle Stock Association to check organized lawlessness. He provided beeves for the hungry Kiowas and Comanches and mediated between these tribes and the U.S. Army.

Goodnight was interested in education and, with his wife, founded Goodnight College in Texas. At his death he was considered "an almost perfect illustration of the cattleman."

Further Reading

J. Evetts Haley, *Charles Goodnight, Cowman and Plainsman* (1949), is a sympathetic biography. Harley True Burton wrote a useful *History of the JA Ranch* (1928). Goodnight's career is discussed in most histories of the cattle industry; Lewis E. Atherton, *The Cattle Kings* (1961), contains a penetrating analysis. See also Mari Sandoz, *The Cattlemen* (1958). ☐

Andrew Jackson Goodpaster

Andrew Jackson Goodpaster (born 1915) was a career Army officer who played a major role in organizing NATO forces in Europe; served as adviser to presidents Eisenhower, Johnson, and Nixon; and served brief terms as commander of the National War College and of West Point.

Andrew Jackson Goodpaster was born in Granite City, Illinois, on February 12, 1915. He graduated second in his class from West Point in 1939 and served with Army Corps of Engineer outfits in Panama and Louisiana. In World War II he saw action as commanding officer of an engineer battalion in North Africa and Italy. In the years after World War II, Goodpaster established ties that would significantly influence his career. In August 1944 he went to the Operations Division of the General Staff in Washington, D.C. Remaining there after V-J Day, he became closely associated with Army Chief of Staff Dwight D. Eisenhower.

Goodpaster was a pioneer among the new breed of postwar "army intellectuals," officers with extensive postgraduate training in civilian universities. He took a Masters degree in engineering from Princeton University in 1948 and a Ph.D. in international relations in 1950.

When General Eisenhower assumed command of the North Atlantic Treaty Organization (NATO) forces in Europe, Goodpaster joined him, serving as assistant to the chief of staff, Gen. Alfred Gruenther. In that capacity Goodpaster played a major role in helping to organize NATO forces and define the political and military aims of the fledgling alliance.

In 1954 Goodpaster joined President Eisenhower as staff secretary in the White House. Eisenhower had organized his presidency along the lines of a military chain of command, and Goodpaster was a key figure. He maintained liaison with all departments engaged in national security issues and coordinated cabinet operations. Working closely with presidential "chief of staff" Sherman Adams, Goodpaster helped to determine which issues would be brought to the president, briefed Eisenhower daily on foreign and defense policy matters, and attended all cabinet and National Security Council meetings. He made sure that key figures were not left out of policy discussions, and he saw that Eisenhower's decisions were executed. He came to know his boss so intimately and was able to anticipate his wishes so well that he became known as the president's

alter ego. Following the end of the Eisenhower administration, Goodpaster returned briefly to Europe, serving as commander of the 8th Infantry Division.

He came back to Washington in November 1962 and remained there for the next seven years, holding a number of different staff positions. He served as a special assistant to the chairman of the Joint Chiefs of Staff, Gen. Maxwell D. Taylor. In August 1966 he became director of the joint staff of the Joint Chiefs of Staff, and in May 1967 he was chosen to be the Army representative on the United Nations Military Staff Command. From July 1967 to June 1968 he was commandant of the National War College.

During these same years Goodpaster carried out important tasks related to the Vietnam War. President Lyndon B. Johnson described him as "one of the ablest officers I knew" and used him to maintain liaison with former President Eisenhower. At Johnson's direction Goodpaster regularly briefed Eisenhower on the course of the war and carried back to Johnson the former president's personal advice and recommendations. Goodpaster also made several trips to Vietnam with groups sent to survey developments there, and while with the Joint Chiefs and the National War College he supervised major study projects relating to various aspects of the war. From May to July 1968 Goodpaster was the U.S. military representative at the Paris peace talks. He then went to Vietnam as deputy to Commanding General Creighton Abrams.

Goodpaster served as chief military adviser to President-elect Nixon during the transition period and continued to play important political and military roles in the Nixon years. In July 1969 he assumed the position of supreme allied commander in Europe, which he held until October 1974.

Following his retirement from the Army in December 1974 Goodpaster became a senior fellow at the Woodrow Wilson International Center for Scholars. He subsequently held the John C. West Chair of Government and International Studies at The Citadel.

In a move that was without precedent, he was called out of retirement in April 1977 to become superintendent of West Point in the wake of a cheating scandal that had severely tarnished the reputation of that venerable institution. He remained at West Point until 1981.

Goodpaster was described by former Secretary of State Henry Kissinger as a "man of vast experience, great honor, and considerable ability." A tireless worker, Goodpaster was utterly devoted to the Army he served for so many years. After his second retirement he was president of the Institute for Defense Analysis, a private think tank in the Washington area. In 1996, Goodpaster with other generals and world-wide political figures helped to determine what steps, both practical and political, needed to be taken to abolish nuclear weapons.

Further Reading

The Eisenhower staff system is capably and sympathetically analyzed in Fred I. Greenstein, *The Hidden-Hand Presidency* (1982). The handling of the Vietnam War during the Johnson years is covered in Maxwell D. Taylor, *Swords and*

Ploughshares (1972) and in Lyndon B. Johnson, *The Vantage Point* (1971). Recent articles referencing Goodpaster include Bill Gertz, "U.S. still needs nukes, official says," *The Washington Times* (February 23, 1997) and Alan Cranston, "Even the generals disagree," *Bulletin of the Atomic Scientists* (November 21, 1996). ☐

Charles Goodyear

Charles Goodyear (1800-1860), American inventor, experimented with, perfected, and promoted the use of vulcanized rubber. He was instrumental in establishing the rubber industry in the United States.

Charles Goodyear was born on Dec. 29, 1800, in New Haven, Conn. He attended the local public schools. His father was an inventor, manufacturer, and merchant of hardware, especially of farm tools. When Charles was 17, his father sent him to Philadelphia to learn the business, and at 21 he returned to become his father's partner. He married at the age of 24 and 2 years later opened a store in Philadelphia. In 1830 a lifetime of financial distress began for the Goodyears when both father and son went bankrupt.

On a trip to New York City that year, Goodyear visited a store that sold goods made of india rubber, a product only recently manufactured in America. Inspired by the possibilities of the material, he determined to improve its usefulness. His first experiments were carried out in jail, where he had been sent for failure to pay his debts.

In 1837 Goodyear settled his family on the charity of friends near New Haven and went to New York to continue his work. He received a patent for an improved type of rubber and was able to find a modest amount of financial backing. After moving to Massachusetts, he met Nathaniel M. Hayward, an inventor, whose patent on a process for mixing sulfur with rubber he bought. Goodyear intended to combine the new patented process with his old one, which involved coating rubber with an acid and metal.

During an argument one day in his shop, Goodyear accidentally dropped a piece of the sulfur-impregnated rubber on a hot stove. Instead of melting, it merely charred slightly. Realizing the importance of this (two major drawbacks to using rubber were that it melted at high temperatures and tended to harden at low temperatures), he began experiments to discover the proper proportions and method of baking the new type of rubber, which he called "vulcanized." His critical patent was issued on June 15, 1844, after he had borrowed $50,000 for experiments, little of which was ever repaid. He claimed to have found more than 500 uses for rubber and received patents in all countries except England, where Thomas Hancock had invented vulcanization in 1843. When Goodyear died in 1860, he left his wife and six children $200,000 in debt.

Further Reading

Biographies of Goodyear include Ralph Frank Wolf, *India Rubber Man: The Story of Charles Goodyear* (1939), and Adolph C. Regli, *Rubber's Goodyear: The Story of a Man's Perseverance* (1941). A shorter study is in John C. Patterson, *America's Greatest Inventors* (1943). ☐

Mikhail Sergeevich Gorbachev

Mikhail Sergeevich Gorbachev (born 1931) was a member of the Communist Party who rose through a series of local and regional positions to national prominence. In March 1985 the Politburo of the Soviet Communist Party elected him general secretary of the party and leader of the U.S.S.R. He resigned in 1991.

Mikhail Gorbachev was born into a peasant family in the village of Privolnoe, near Stavropol, on March 2, 1931, and grew up in the countryside. As a teenager, he worked driving farm machinery at a local machine-tractor station. These stations served regional state and collective farms, but were also centers of police control in the countryside. Gorbachev's experience here undoubtedly educated him well about the serious problems of food production and political administration in the countryside, as well as the practices of the KGB (the Soviet secret police) control, knowledge which would serve him well in his future career.

In 1952 Gorbachev joined the Communist Party and began studies at the Moscow State University, where he graduated from the law division in 1955. Student acquaintances from these years describe him as bright, hard working, and careful to establish good contacts with people of importance. He also met and married fellow student Raisa Titorenko, in 1953.

With Stalin's death in 1953 the Soviet Union began a period of political and intellectual ferment. In 1956 Nikita Khrushchev denounced Stalin and paved the way for a major restructuring of the Soviet Union's political system and economic administration. For young party activists like Gorbachev this was a period of exciting innovations and challenges.

Gorbachev returned after his graduation to Stavropol as an organizer for the Komsomol (Young Communist League) and began a successful career as a party administrator and regional leader. In 1962 he was promoted to the post of party organizer for collective and state farms in the Stavropol region and soon took on major responsibilities for the Stavropol city committee as well. Leonid Brezhnev rewarded his ability by appointing him Stavropol first secretary in 1966, roughly equivalent to mayor.

Climbing the Party Ladder

Soon afterwards, as part of the party's new campaign to assure that its best career administrators were thoroughly trained in economic administration, Gorbachev completed an advanced program at the Stavropol Agricultural Institute and received a degree in agrarian economics. With this additional training he moved quickly to assume direction of the party in the entire Stavropol region, assuming in 1970 the important post of first secretary for the Stavropol Territorial Party Committee. This position, roughly equivalent to a governor in the United States, proved a stepping stone to Central Committee membership and national prominence.

Gorbachev was assisted in his rise to national power by close associations with Yuri Andropov, who was also from the Stavropol region, and Mikhail Suslov, the party's principal ideologist and a confidant of Leonid Brezhnev, who had once worked in the Stavropol area as well. Gorbachev also proved himself a shrewd and intelligent administrator, however, with an extensive knowledge of agricultural affairs, and it was largely on this basis that Brezhnev brought him to Moscow in 1978 as a party secretary responsible for agricultural administration. His performance in this capacity was not particularly distinguished. The Soviet Union suffered several poor harvests in the late 1970s and early 1980s, and its dependency on foreign grain imports increased. Yet Gorbachev gained a solid reputation, despite these problems, as an energetic and informed politician, with an activist style contrasting rather sharply with that of most aging Kremlin leaders.

The ascension of Yuri Andropov to power after the death of Leonid Brezhnev in January 1980 greatly strengthened the position of his protegé Gorbachev. Both men showed impatience with outmoded administrative practices and with the inefficiences of the Soviet Union's economy. Andropov's death returned the U.S.S.R. briefly to a period of drift under the weak and ailing Konstantin Chernenko, but Gorbachev continued to impress his colleagues with his loyal and energetic party service. Beginning in October 1980 he was a member of the ruling Politburo.

A New Type of Russian Leader?

As he took power in March 1985, Gorbachev brought a fresh new spirit to the Kremlin. Young, vigorous, married to an attractive and stylish woman with a Ph.D., he represented a new generation of Soviet leaders, educated and trained in the post-Stalin era and free from the direct experiences of Stalin's terror which so hardened and corrupted many of his elders. His first steps as head of the party were designed to improve economic productivity. He began an energetic campaign against inefficiency and waste and indicated his intention to "shake up" lazy and ineffective workers in every area of Soviet life, including the party. He also revealed an unusual affability. Britons found him and his wife Raisa "charming" when he visited England in December 1984, and he showed a ready wit, "blaming" the British Museum, where Karl Marx studied and wrote, for Communism's success. Shortly after taking power Gorbachev also moved to develop greater rapport with ordinary citizens, taking to the streets on several occasions to discuss his views and making a number of well-publicized appearances at factories and other industrial institutions. In addition, he began strengthening his position within the party with a number of new appointments at the important regional level.

A charismatic personality, Gorbachev also had the youthfulness, training, intelligence, and political strength to become one of the Soviet Union's most popular leaders. Upon assuming power in 1985, he was faced with the need to make significant improvements in the Soviet Union's troubled economy—an extremely difficult task—and to establish better relations with the United States, which might allow some reduction in Soviet defense expenditures in favor of consumer goods. In November 1985 he met with President Reagan in Geneva to discuss national and international problems. Little progress was made but both leaders agreed to hold another "summit" meeting in the United States in 1986.

When new tensions developed between the two superpowers, the leaders agreed to hold a preliminary meeting at Reykjavik, Iceland, October 11-12, 1986. But the clearest signs of improving Soviet-American relations came in 1988. Gorbachev made a positive impression when he entered a crowd of spectators in New York City to shake hands with people. In May and June of the same year, President Reagan visited Moscow.

Within the Soviet Union, Gorbachev promoted spectacular political changes. His most important measure came in 1989 when he set up elections in which members of the Communist Party had to compete against opponents who were not Party members. Later that same year, he called for an end to the special status of the Communist party guaranteed by the Soviet Constitution and ended the Soviet military occupation of Afghanistan.

Two issues, however, caused growing difficulty for Gorbachev. First, there was the problem of nationalities, as the Soviet Union consisted of nearly 100 different ethnic groups. As the political dictatorship began to disappear, many of these groups began to engage in open warfare against each other. Such bloodshed came from longstanding local quarrels that had been suppressed under Moscow's earlier control. Even more serious, some ethnic groups, like the Lithuanians and the Ukrainians began to call for outright independence. Second, the country's economy was sinking deeper into crisis. Both industrial and agricultural production were declining, and the old system, in which the economy ran under centralized control of the government, no longer seemed to work.

Yet, Gorbachev was apparently more willing to make changes in government and international affairs than to focus on the problems associated with ethnic diversity and the economy. Perhaps influenced by more conservative rivals, he cracked down on the Lithuanians when they declared their independence in the summer of 1990. Also, he gradually tried to move toward a private system of farming and privately-owned industry.

At the same time, a powerful rival began to emerge: once considered an ally, Boris Yeltsin became the country's leading advocate of radical economic reform. Although

forced from the Politburo, the small group at the top of the Communist Party, in 1987, Yeltsin soon established his own political base. He formally left the Communist Party in 1990, something Gorbachev refused to do, and was elected president of the Russian Republic in June 1991. Gorbachev, on the other hand, had been made president of the Soviet Union without having to win a national election. Thus, Yeltsin could claim a greater degree of popular support.

Fall From Power

In August 1991, a group of Communist Party conservatives captured Gorbachev while he was on vacation in the Crimea and moved to seize power. Some of these men, like Prime Minister Valentin Pavlov, were individuals Gorbachev had put in power to balance the liberal and conservative political forces. But Yeltsin, not Gorbachev, led the successful resistance to the coup, which collapsed within a few days. When Gorbachev returned to Moscow, he was overshadowed by Yeltsin, and there were rumors that Gorbachev himself had been involved in the coup.

By the end of 1991, the Soviet Union had fallen apart. When most of its major components like the Ukraine and the Baltic states declared themselves as independent, real power began to rest with the leaders of those components, among them Yeltsin, hero of the attempted coup and president of the Russian Republic. Gorbachev formally resigned his remaining political office on Christmas Day 1991.

Private Citizen

As a private citizen, Gorbachev faded from public view, but continued to write and travel. On one occasion, his travels struck an important symbolic note. On May 6, 1992, he spoke at Westminster College in Fulton, Missouri. There, in 1946, Winston Churchill had given his classic speech coining the term "the Cold War." Gorbachev's appearance was a vivid reminder of the changes he had helped bring about during his seven years in power.

In the spring of 1995, Gorbachev began touring factories in Russia, spoke to university students, and denounced President Yeltsin. He stopped just short of formally announcing his candidacy for the presidency in 1996. He wrote an autobiography, which was released in 1995 in Germany and 1997 in the United States.

Like many historical figures, Gorbachev's role will be interpreted in varying ways. While a Russian factory worker stated in *Newsweek*, "He destroyed a great state . . . the collapse of the Soviet Union started with Gorbachev . . . ," some critics in the West saw the fall of Communism as "altogether a victory for common sense, reason, democracy and common human values."

Further Reading

The political tasks Gorbachev faced are well documented in several studies of the Soviet system. These include Seweryn Bialer, *Stalin's Successors: Leadership, Stability, and Change in the Soviet Union* (1980), George Breslauer, *Khrushchev and Brezhnev as Leaders: Building Authority in Soviet Politics* (1982), and Dusko Doder, *Shadows and Whispers: Power Politics Inside the Kremlin From Brezhnev to Gorbachev*

(1986). The first book-length study of the Soviet leader was Thomas G. Butson, *Gorbachev: A Biography* (1985). The second full-life account was Zhores A. Medveder, *Gorbachev* (1986). Articles on Contemporary Soviet affairs can also be found every other month in the journal *Problems of Communism,* which tracks Gorbachev's performance in a number of areas. Helpful magazine articles can be found in *U.S. News & World Report* (November 25, 1996); *National Review* (November 25, 1996); and *Newsweek* (March 13, 1995). Gorbachev's autobiography *Memoirs* was released in the United States in 1997. A summary of Gorbachev's political career can be accessed online at the A&E Biography website at http://www.biography.com (August 5, 1997). □

Raisa Maximovna Titorenko Gorbachev

Raisa Maximovna Gorbacheva (Gorbachev) (née Titorenko; born 1932) set a new style and tradition as first lady of the Soviet Union.

When Raisa Gorbacheva traveled she kept a busy schedule, often independent of her husband Mikhail Gorbachev. Unlike the wives of most former Soviet leaders, Raisa Gorbacheva accompanied her husband on official visits and often traveled with him on trips within the U.S.S.R. The grandmotherly Nina Khrushcheva sometimes accompanied her husband on trips abroad, but Raisa Gorbacheva was of a different generation and possessed her own unique style and demeanor, which captured the attention and interest of the world. She continued to travel with her husband following his ouster as head of the Soviet Union in 1991.

Raisa Gorbacheva was a trendsetter in Soviet society. Beautiful and youthful in appearance, she dressed distinctively and fashionably. She had a petite, attractive figure and a youthful face with short red hair and luminous brown eyes. She was articulate and well-educated. Her husband, Mikhail Gorbachev, once indicated in an interview with a Western journalist that he discussed all issues with her. Following official protocol, she always walked behind her husband on official visits but nonetheless was almost as well-known and admired abroad as he was. In the Soviet Union, her visibility was less appreciated. In Soviet custom it had been considered inappropriate for the wives of political leaders to play a prominent role. There was little or no tradition of "first lady," which was perhaps seen as a Western affectation. At a time of hardship in the U.S.S.R., her clothes and glamour sometimes occasioned negative sentiment at home.

Raisa Maximovna Gorbacheva, née Titorenko, was born on January 5, 1932, in Rubtsovsk, a town in Siberia. Her father was a railroad engineer who, when she was only three, was imprisoned for four years for criticizing collectivized agriculture. A grandfather had been executed under Stalin. She professed to be Russian by nationality, although her father's surname is Ukrainian. Within the U.S.S.R. at the time there were unsubstantiated, even conflicting, rumors about her nationality and family connections. The U.S.S.R. had well over 100 nationalities, and intermarriage among people of different ethnic backgrounds was fairly common. The child could choose to adopt the nationality of either parent. Family connections to powerful political figures were hard to trace, but rumors persisted that Raisa was connected through family ties to former political leaders who gave a boost to her husband's career.

She and Mikhail Gorbachev met at a dance at Moscow State University (MGU) where both were students. He was studying law, and she was studying Marxist-Leninist philosophy. It was love at first sight for him, but she, a beautiful, sophisticated, gold medal student, had numerous admirers. Eventually Gorbachev prevailed over the others, and they married in 1954. He was a country lad from a village in the south of Russia, and she was a sophisticated city girl. She was one of two women credited with teaching the brilliant young student Mikhail Sergeevich about art, culture, and the ballet during his university years in Moscow. In 1955, after graduation, Gorbacheva and her husband settled in Stavropol, the medium-sized city near his hometown. She taught and worked on her graduate degree. She was a lecturer in Marxist-Leninist philosophy at the Stavropol Agricultural Institute, from which Gorbachev himself later received a degree in agricultural science, in addition to his earlier law degree. Pictures of the young wife and mother at work in Stavropol reveal one who even then stood out from the crowd. She was helpful to her husband and credited with assisting him in the arduous climb up the Soviet ladder of political success.

In 1967 Gorbacheva completed her Candidate's degree (equivalent to a Ph.D.) at Moscow State Pedagogical Institute. Her dissertation dealt with the peasants and conditions on collective farms. Her thesis used sociological research methods, one of the first Soviet studies to do so. She sent questionnaires to thousands of collective farmers and then conducted follow-up interviews at five farms. Informed by the results of her research, Mikhail Gorbachev, as secretary of the Stavropol Kraikom (territory party committee), initiated successful agricultural reforms to solve some of the local problems of the area, thereby attracting the attention of national leaders to his work.

The Gorbachevs lived in Stavropol until 1978, when Mikhail Gorbachev was brought to Moscow to work in the Central Committee as secretary for agriculture. The Stavropol region contains several mineral spas and the Gorbachevs frequently met high-level Soviet leaders who visited the spas. These contacts, Gorbachev's record of achievement in Stavropol, and the good impression the young Gorbachevs made on the leadership led eventually to his appointment in the capital. In Moscow Raisa Gorbacheva worked as a lecturer in Marxist-Leninist philosophy at Moscow State University until her husband became first secretary of the Communist Party of the Soviet Union (CPSU). She was an officer of the Soviet Culture Foundation, dedicated to the arts and national preservation, performing numerous ceremonial functions in this capacity.

Raisa and Mikhail Gorbachev had a daughter, Irina, who strongly resembled her mother. They were proud and devoted grandparents, and a number of public pictures show the Gorbachevs with their two grandchildren, daughter, and son-in-law.

On her numerous trips abroad, Gorbacheva impressed foreigners with the breadth of her knowledge and interests. At the same time, she was known for expressing her own strongly held views. It has been said that she sometimes gave little speeches instead of engaging in dialogue with foreign officials. Within the U.S.S.R. her role was more subdued and she was less likely to express her views publicly, but she was often present in the background or presiding at official ceremonies. Gorbachev has been quoted as saying: "My wife is a very independent lady." Whether that was husbandly rhetoric or reality is hard to say. On trips abroad, most of her wardrobe came from Soviet designers, although it is believed that she also patronized some of the Parisian designers. She favored classic styles such as well-tailored dark suits or slim, well-cut dresses and high heels which created an illusion that she was taller than her five feet three inches. She enjoyed visiting art galleries and historic sites, as well as child-oriented social projects.

In the first few Gorbachev-Reagan summits that Raisa Gorbacheva attended, rumors circulated of ill feelings between her and Nancy Reagan. The media followed them with careful attention, noting every gesture and expression of either woman when they met. Whatever de facto rivalry might have existed during the Reagan-Gorbachev summit conferences, Nancy Reagan and Raisa Gorbacheva met cordially and privately, together with their husbands, in San Francisco during Gorbachev's 1990 visit to the United States. The next American first lady, Barbara Bush, a stylish grandmother with little aspiration to be the center of attention, seemed comfortable with Gorbacheva, who accompanied Bush to the latter's controversial, but successful, commencement address at Wellesley College.

Raisa Gorbacheva received flattering attention in the West. From the cover of *TIME* to being named one of the "world's ten most important women" in 1987 in a survey of international newspaper editors conducted by the *Ladies' Home Journal*, Raisa Gorbacheva became a popular figure in the West. In the U.S.S.R. she was admired, envied, and even resented as she sought to carve out the position of "first lady" in Soviet society. She was sometimes compared with Nadezhda Krupskaya, V.I. Lenin's wife, a revolutionary and political leader in the field of education during the early Soviet period. But Krupskaya was never stylish and, although a political activist, was shy and retiring. Gorbacheva changed the world's image of the wives of Soviet and, subsequently, Russian political leaders and broke new ground in Soviet society itself.

A Tumultuous 1991

Life for Raisa Gorbacheva, her husband, and all of Soviet society in 1991 was chaotic. The nation had begun to disintegrate and questions were raised about her health. Coincidentally two books were published about her life that year. *Raisa: The 1st First Lady of the Soviet Union,* authored by Urda Jurgens but reportedly without the participation of the subject herself, was complimented by *Kirkus Reviews* for its "admirable legwork," but criticized as including only "a minimum of anecdotes that might shed color or psychological insight." In September 1991, Gorbecheva's autobiography, *I Hope: Reminiscences and Reflections* went on sale. The book was characterized by *TIME* as "an extended interview with Soviet writer Georgi Pryakhin." In its preface, the work was described by Gorbecheva herself as "probably . . . inconsistent, emotional and patchy," but it was her personal response to the events that were happening around her. It was also the first autobiographical publication by the wife of a Soviet leader since 1957 when Krupskaya's *Reminiscences of Lenin* was released.

I Hope was completed four months prior to the abortive coup that sought to unseat Mikhail Gorbachev and had held his wife and family captive at its Crimea villa for three days in August. However, Raisa Gorbacheva foreshadowed in her book the turmoil that was rampant in the country when she referred to the "fierce struggle now going on between loyalty and treachery." It was in *I Hope* that Gorbacheva first revealed that her grandfather had been executed during the Stalin era, which *TIME* wrote had left her "both fearful and contemptuous of apparatchiks who act one way 'when it is to their advantage' and another when it is not." News reports of the family's ordeal at the Crimea portrayed Raisa Gorbacheva as a stroke or heart attack victim, though she later explained that she "had developed an acute hypertensive crisis that was accompanied by a speech disorder."

Mikhail Gorbachev acknowledged that the attempt to overthrow him was "very hard" on his wife.

Following 1991 Raisa Gorbacheva maintained a relatively low profile. She accompanied her husband on visits to the United States, Britain, Germany, Italy, Japan and South Korea, often in relation to activities of his think-tank, the Gorbachev Foundation, or the ecology lobbying organization, the International Green Cross Society. Speculation surfaced about her health again in 1993 after she checked into a hospital in Richmond, Virginia, during one of the couple's visits to the U.S.

In 1995 Raisa Gorbacheva campaigned alongside her husband during his ill-fated effort to seek the Russian presidency. When asked about his return to politics, however, she pulled no punches. "I'm against it," she said on Russian television.

Further Reading

The personal history as well as an account of the political scene is told by Raisa Gorbacheva in *I Hope: Reminiscences and Reflections* (1991), a series of conversations with the Soviet writer Georgi Pryakhin. A biography, *Raisa: The 1st First Lady of the Soviet Union,* by Urda Jurgens also is available. A number of interesting articles have appeared on Raisa Gorbacheva and on her marriage to Mikhail Gorbachev. *Soviet Life* featured an article, "Raisa Gorbacheva: the first Soviet First Lady," by Swedish journalist Kerstin Gustafsson (June 1990). Gail Sheehy has written an in-depth analysis of Gorbachev, including discussion of his marriage to Raisa, in *Vanity Fair* (February 1990). *TIME* featured Raisa Gorbacheva in a story on Soviet women (June 6, 1988). The editors of *TIME* put together a portrait of Raisa in their *MS. Gorbachev: An Intimate Biography* (1988). □

Nadine Gordimer

Nadine Gordimer (born 1923) was the Nobel Prize winning author of short stories and novels reflecting the disintegration of South African society. While her early works were in the tradition of liberal South African whites opposed to apartheid, her later works reflect a move toward more radical political and literary formulations.

Nadine Gordimer was born on November 20, 1923, in Springs, a mining town on the Eastern Witwatersrand, South Africa. Of Jewish heritage, her mother was from England and her father, from Russia. He worked in the gold mines, first as a mining engineer and later as secretary. Most of Nadine's life, apart from a brief period in Zambia in the middle 1960s, was spent in South Africa and the Witwatersrand, and it was here that she received her education, first as a day scholar at a convent and later as a student at the University of the Witwatersrand.

From the time her first short story, entitled "Come Again Tomorrow," was published in the Johannesburg magazine *The Forum* in November 1939, Gordimer became a prolific author of short stories and nearly a dozen novels. Firmly opposed to notions of racial segregation and apartheid, she wrote in an increasingly polarized and isolated society. This resulted in innovative attempts at developing the South African English novel beyond its conventional tradition of realist literary depiction by exploring the isolated consciousness and experience in what she perceived as a progressively disintegrating society.

In 1953 Gordimer wrote her first novel, *The Lying Days,* which depicts the adolescent awakening of a white South African girl, Helen Shaw. This was followed in 1958 by the more complex portrait of the Johannesburg world of the middle 1950s seen from the standpoint of a young English newspaperman, Toby Hood, called *A World of Strangers*. The novel is an important historical portrayal of the short-lived era of multi-racial parties and social contact before the government clampdown on opposition politics after the Sharpeville shooting in 1960 and the resulting banning of Black nationalist movements.

In the early 1960s Gordimer felt increasingly isolated as a white writer in South Africa, and this was especially reflected in *The Late Bourgeois World* in 1966 in which her central character, Elizabeth Van Den Sandt, sought to forge a new identity for herself after the suicide of her husband, who had been an unsuccessful political activist. The controlled use of time in this novel also indicated a search for an alternative to the conventional novel form as "the bourgeois world" that lay behind this novel tradition appeared to be coming apart.

A short period spent in Zambia with her husband formed the backdrop to her next novel, *A Guest of Honour,* which was distinctive in being set in a fictitious African country outside South Africa. Her central character, Jeremy Bray, was also a former British colonial official, and the novel embraced a wider set of themes involving the counterpoising of the dead and static society of post-imperial Britain with the vital landscape of Africa in the era after independence.

In *The Conservationist* (1974), however, Gordimer returned to more conventional South African themes, though the technical virtuosity of its writing led some critics to see this as the finest of her novels. Dealing with the estrangement of an industrialist turned part-time farmer, the novel focuses on the estrangement of South African whites from the African landscape and so takes up a theme that can be traced back to Olive Schreiner's *The Story of an African Farm.*

By the 1970s Gordimer had moved out of the mainstream liberalism of most South African whites opposed to apartheid and had begun moving toward more radical political and literary formulations. The wide scope of her next novel, *Burger's Daughter* (1979), set in France and England as well as South Africa, reflected a desire to internationalize many of the political issues in South Africa, which were seen as less ones simply of "race" but also of "class" and class conflict. This central character is a jailed white South African communist whose name evokes the memory of Rosa Luxemburg. The novel was for a period banned in South Africa, as had been the case previously with *Occasion for Loving* (1965), banned for its depiction of a sexual relationship between white women and black men, and *The Late Bourgeois World.*

In *July's People* (1981) Gordimer departed from the question of anchoring the white identity in the South African past and confronted the question of the future as a white couple flee Johannesburg after a rocket attack and hide in the African bush where they become increasingly beholden to their former servant, July. As a penetrating study of the element of power that underpins Black-White relations in South Africa the novel links the private realm of the personal with the wider dimension of political institutions and structures.

A collection of her short stories, *Something Out There,* was published in 1984, another insightful novel of South Africa's people, *A Sport of Nature* was published in 1987 and Gordimer's look at post-apartheid South Africa, *None to Accompany Me* in 1994. Nadine Gordimer received the Alfred B. Nobel Prize for literature in 1991.

Further Reading

A bibliography of Nadine Gordimer's work up to 1964 was complied by Racilia Jillian Nell and can be obtained from the Department of Bibliography, Librarianship and Typography, University of the Witwatersrand, Johannesburg. For a study of Nadine Gordimer's work see Michael Wade, *Nadine Gordimer* (1978). Further discussion can be found in Kenneth Parker (editor), *The South African Novel in English* (1978); Stephen Gray, *Southern African Literature: An Introduction* (1979); and Landeg White and Tim Couzens (editors), *Literature and Society in South Africa* (1984). See also Richard Peck's, "Nadine Gordimer: A Bibliography of Primary and Secondary Sources 1938-1992," *Research in African Literatures* (March 1, 1995). □

Aaron David Gordon

The Russian-born Zionist Aaron David Gordon (1856-1922) was the spiritual leader of the Palestinian Jewish labor movement. He taught that work is the basis of human civilization.

Aaron Gordon was born in the village of Troyano, Podolia (region in present-day Ukraine). Because of Gordon's poor health, he was taught the traditional Jewish subjects by a private tutor. Later he studied at the towns of Golovnievsk and Obodovka, where he lived at the house of his relatives and met his cousin and future wife, Feigel Tartakov. For a year he studied in Vilna, after which he went back to his parents. Again Gordon had a private teacher for Jewish studies, but at the same time he devoted himself to the study of modern languages (Russian, German, French, and Hebrew), which gave him the equivalent of a high school education.

After Gordon was rejected because of his health by the Russian army, he married and for 23 years, almost until his emigration to Palestine, he lived in the village of Mohilna. Despite the fact that he was employed at the office of his wealthy relative Baron Ginzburg, he found it distasteful to support his family by the favors of his cousin, especially since no creative work was involved in his position.

At the age of 48, after Gordon's parents had died and his son and daughter were independent, he arrived as a pioneer to Palestine. He sought work as a laborer but the farmers would not employ him, and he refused to consider an office position which was offered to him by the Jewish national authorities. Finally he started to work in the citrus orchards at Petach Tikvah, and as a result of the poor conditions under which he lived he took sick. Friends took care of him. Because he did not like to accept favors, he repaid all expenses to his benefactors after his recovery.

At the end of 1907 Gordon's wife and daughter joined him in Palestine. His son remained in Russia, where he died during World War I. A few months after her arrival in Palestine, Gordon's wife died. Gordon did not like to attach himself permanently to one place or group. He moved from place to place and, finally, in 1912, settled as an agriculture worker in Degania, where he died 10 years later.

In his doctrine of love for, and return to, nature, Gordon was a follower of Jean Jacques Rousseau and Leo Tolstoy. But he disagreed with Tolstoy's belief that to give up the urban life was a sacrifice. Gordon considered that the Jew who left the Jewish Pale in Russia was not sacrificing anything but was taking part in building his individual freedom and that of his national community—the Jewish people.

Gordon also claimed, because of the many roads to Jewish redemption, that there was a need for an integration of ideas. As a result of this, he found a synthesis between the two major spiritual opponents of his generation, Ahad Haam's spiritual nationalism and M. Y. Berdichevsky's material individualism. The result was Gordon's doctrine of the "religion of work," which dictated the return of the Jew to nature and manual labor in order to renew his source of life. These ideas formed the basis of his Labor Zionism and became a cornerstone of the Palestinian non-Marxist labor movement.

Further Reading

A full-length study of Gordon is Herbert H. Rose, *The Life and Thought of A. D. Gordon: Pioneer, Philosopher, and Prophet of Modern Israel* (1964). See also Joseph Aaronovitch and Samuel Dayan, *A. D. Gordon* (1930). □

Charles George Gordon

The English soldier, adventurer, and popular hero Charles George Gordon (1833-1885) was known as "Chinese" Gordon. He was killed at the fall of Khartoum.

Born at Woolwich on Jan. 28, 1833, Charles George Gordon was the son of a lieutenant general. He attended Taunton School and entered the Royal Military Academy at Woolwich in 1848, gaining his commission in the Royal Engineers in 1852.

At the end of 1855, during the Crimean War, Gordon was ordered to the Crimea. He was wounded there and then worked on the demolition of Sevastopol harbor. From May 1856 he was engaged in quasi-political work helping to delimit the frontiers of Bessarabia and Armenia. In 1860 Gordon joined the British forces operating with the French against China and was at the capture of Peking, spending the next 2 years fighting in southern China.

In 1863 Gordon took command of the small Chinese army in Sinkiang, which was officered by Europeans and which had been raised to suppress the Taiping Rebellion. At first Gordon quarreled with the Chinese authorities over the execution of rebels, but he returned to his post at the end of 1863, and by April 1864 the Taiping Rebellion was crushed. Gordon's exploits and his refusal to accept money presents offered by the Chinese emperor made him a popular hero in England from this time forward.

This heroic impression was reinforced during the years from 1865 to 1871, when Gordon served quietly in home army duties as commander of the Royal Engineers at Gravesend, supervising the Thames forts, for he spent much of his free time in social work, interesting himself in hospitals and schools for poor children and even taking destitute boys into his home.

Activities in Africa

In 1871 and 1872 Gordon was sent to Turkey to work on the International Danube Commission. In Constantinople he met Nubar Pasha, the Egyptian politician, and this led to his acceptance of an offer to succeed Sir Samuel Baker as governor of the Equatorial Provinces of the Sudan. Characteristically Gordon requested the salary of £10,000 be cut and accepted £2,000. Gordon's vigorous opposition to slave trading led to a quarrel with the Egyptian governor general of the Sudan, and Gordon resigned in 1876, but in January 1877 Gordon returned as governor general of the Sudan and Darfur and Equatoria, the other Egyptian provinces on the Red Sea. For the next 2 years he spent his time fighting in Darfur, suppressing rebellions elsewhere, and failing to secure agreement with Ethiopia on frontiers. When the British and French deposed Khedive Ismail, Gordon resigned at the end of 1879.

In April 1880 Gordon accompanied Lord Ripon, the new viceroy of India, as his private secretary but quickly resigned and spent the remainder of the year in China. During 1881 and 1882 he worked with the Royal Engineers in Mauritius and was in command of the British troops there from January 1882. In May he assumed command of the forces in Cape Colony but quarreled with the Cape government over its handling of the Basuto and left in October 1882, visiting Palestine the next year.

At the end of 1883 Gordon was approached by King Leopold II of the Belgians, who wished to employ him to take charge of plans to create the Congo Free State, from what was at that time ostensibly a philanthropic organization for "civilizing" the Congo Basin. In January 1884 Gordon accepted the offer, but the British War Office refused to sanction the appointment, and Leopold eventually chose H. M. Stanley for the post.

Gordon had intended to defy the War Office and resign his commission in the army. He was actually enroute for Brussels and the Congo when he was recalled by telegram to meet the British Cabinet, which persuaded him to accept the task of returning to the Sudan to withdraw the British and Egyptian troops there who were threatened by the successful revolt of the Mahdi. At the same time he was told to leave behind an organized government, so that his instructions were unclear.

Fall of Khartoum

By temperament Gordon was hardly the man to preside over the Sudan's abandonment (which the British government wanted so as to cut Egyptian expenditures). Arriving in Khartoum in February 1884, Gordon proceeded to proclaim the Sudan's independence, open communications with the Red Sea, demand Turkish troops to assist him, and request the presence of Zobeir Pasha, a notorious slave dealer, to form an alternative leadership to the Mahdi. Meanwhile Gordon made little move to withdraw, and the British and Egyptian governments did nothing to reinforce him. In March 1884 the Mahdists began their attack on Khartoum, and Gordon sent telegrams bitterly denouncing the government for neglect, until communications were cut off in April.

There followed a 10-month siege of Khartoum, during which William Gladstone's Liberal government resisted a growing popular clamor for Gordon's relief. In August 1884 money was voted for relief "should it become necessary," and Lord Wolseley was put in command of a force which left, after many delays, in September. But the expedition was too late; Khartoum fell to the Mahdi's army on Jan. 26, 1885, and Gordon was killed. The news reached England in February, and Friday, March 13, was officially declared a national day of mourning in Britain.

Gordon's death stirred a popular movement of indignation against Gladstone's Liberal government, which has been seen as one of the first stirring of popular "imperialism" in Britain and contributed to the collapse of the Liberals in 1885.

Further Reading

Gordon's own *Journal,* which he kept at Khartoum during the Mahdist siege, was edited by Lord Elton (1961), who also wrote a biography, *Gordon of Khartoum: The Life of General Charles George Gordon* (1954). Bernard M. Allen, *Gordon and the Sudan* (1931), is useful. The most recent treatment of Gordon's last months is John Marlowe, *Mission to Khartoum: The Apotheosis of General Gordon* (1969).

Additional Sources

Chenevix Trench, Charles, *The road to Khartoum: a life of General Charles Gordon,* New York: Norton, 1979, 1978.

Chenevix Trench, Charles Pocklington, *Charley Gordon: an eminent Victorian reassesed,* London: Allen Lane, 1978.

Hake, A. Egmont (Alfred Egmont), *Gordon in China and the Soudan,* London: Darf Publishers, 1987.

MacGregor-Hastie, Roy, *Never to be taken alive: a biography of General Gordon,* New York: St. Martin's Press, 1985.

Pollock, John Charles, *Gordon: the man behind the legend,* London: Constable, 1993.

Strachey, Lytton, *Eminent Victorians: the illustrated edition,* New York: Weidenfeld & Nicolson, 1989, 1988.

Waller, John H., *Gordon of Khartoum: the saga of a Victorian hero,* New York: Atheneum, 1988. □

John Brown Gordon

American businessman and politician John Brown Gordon (1832-1904), a distinguished Confederate officer, was one of the politicians who dominated Georgia after the Reconstruction period.

John B. Gordon was born on Feb. 6, 1832, in Upson County, Ga. He attended the University of Georgia and was developing coal mines in north-western Georgia when the Civil War began. He went on to an outstanding career as a Confederate Army officer. He rose to the rank of lieutenant general and took part in the last military operations near Appomattox. In the minds of fellow Georgians he shared with Robert E. Lee the tragic glory of the surrender.

After the war Gordon became active in a number of business enterprises, including railroads and life insurance. He also opposed the Republican party, and his name has been linked with Ku Klux Klan terrorism in his state. After the Democrats regained control of Georgia, he was elected to the U.S. Senate in 1873 as a "New Departure Democrat." In the Senate his name was associated in an unfavorable way with congressmen who were attempting to obtain government subsidies for certain railroad builders. In 1880, about halfway through his second term, he suddenly resigned. Charges of "bargain" were made when Georgia governor Alfred H. Colquitt immediately appointed Joseph E. Brown in Gordon's place. These three men dominated Georgia politics until 1890 by controlling the positions of senators and governor.

Upon his return to Georgia, Gordon again engaged in business activity, especially transactions dealing with railroads and real estate. A distinguished-looking man with a fine figure and manner, he gained popularity as a Confederate war hero and speaker on the "Lost Cause" of the South. In 1886 he was elected governor.

During Gordon's administration the small farmers, increasingly unhappy because the New Departure Democrats were ignoring their needs in favor of business interests, formed the Farmers' Alliance; in the election of 1890 they won the governorship and control of the legislature. Gordon, who wanted to become senator again, now endorsed most of the proposals of the alliance. The legislature sent him to the Senate in 1891, where, contrary to the expecta-

tions of his new constituency, he continued to support business interests. At the end of his term he retired from politics and traveled around the country lecturing on the last days of the Confederacy, stressing the view that both sides had been "right." He died in Miami, Fla., on Jan. 9, 1904.

Further Reading

A full and laudatory account of Gordon's life is Allan P. Tankersley, *John B. Gordon: A Study in Gallantry* (1955). A brief but more critical sketch of him can be found in C. Vann Woodward, *Tom Watson, Agrarian Rebel* (1938). See also Douglas Southall Freeman, *Lee's Lieutenants: A Study in Command* (3 vols., 1942-1944).

Additional Sources

Eckert, Ralph Lowell, *John Brown Gordon: soldier, southerner, American,* Baton Rouge: Louisiana State University Press, 1989. □

Berry Gordy Jr.

Berry Gordy, Jr. (born 1929), founded Motown, the fledgling record company of 1959 that grew into the most successful African American enterprise in the United States and was responsible for a new sound that transformed popular music.

B erry Gordy, Jr., was born in 1929 and reared in Detroit. He was not the first businessman in the family; both parents were self-employed, his father as a plastering contractor, his mother as an insurance agent. Gordy dropped out of Northeastern High School in his junior year to pursue a career as a Featherweight boxer. Between 1948 and 1951 he fought 15 Golden Gloves matches, 12 of which he won, but his fighting career was clipped short when he was drafted to serve in the Korean War.

Upon his discharge from the Army in 1953, Berry Gordy returned to Detroit and used his service pay to open the Three-D Record Mart. His love for the jazz of Stan Kenton, Charlie Parker, and Thelonius Monk influenced his inventory more than his customers' requests for "things like Fats Domino," and his business soon failed.

Gordy worked for his father for a short period and then as a chrome trimmer on the assembly line at the Ford Motor Company. The monotony was formidable, and Gordy's way of overcoming it was to write songs in his head, some of which were recorded by local singers. Decca Records bought several of his compositions, including "Reet Petite" and "Lonely Teardrops" (both recorded by Jackie Wilson), and when Gordy compared his royalty checks to what Decca made from the modest hits, he realized that writing the hits wasn't enough. He needed to own them.

At the suggestion of a friend, teenaged singer William "Smokey" Robinson, Gordy borrowed $700 from his father and formed his own company to manufacture and market

records. Motown Records was headquartered in a row house on Detroit's West Grand Boulevard, where Gordy slept on the second floor and made records on the first. In time the company expanded, with nine buildings on the same street housing its branches: Jobete, music publishers; Hitsville USA, a recording studio; musical accompanists; International Talent Management Inc; the Motown Artist's Development Department (the embodiment of Gordy's personal interest in his performers, where they were taught to eat, dress, and act like polished professionals); and the Motown Record Corporation, an umbrella for several labels of Motown, including Gordy, Tamla, VIP, and Soul (the last being reserved for the hit song-writing machine of Brian Holland, Lamont Dozier, and Eddie Holland).

In 1960 Motown released "Shop Around," written by Smokey Robinson and performed by him and the Miracles. The song sold more than a million copies, and with that gold record, Berry Gordy's company launched the most successful and influential era in the history of popular music.

The Motown Sound was a musical genre that combined classic African American gospel singing with the new rock-and-roll sound that was being shaped by Elvis Presley and the Beatles. In a sense, this reflected the old "R & B" (for rhythm and blues), but it defined a new generation.

Motown produced over 110 number one hit songs and countless top-ten records, including "Please Mr. Postman," "Reach Out, I'll Be There," "My Girl," "Stop! In the Name of Love," "For Once in My Life," "How Sweet It Is To Be Loved by You," "Heard It Through the Grapevine," "My Guy," "Dancing in the Streets," "Your Precious Love," "Where Did Our Love Go," "Baby Love," "I Hear a Symphony," "I Want You Back," and "I'll Be There." Equally impressive is a list of artists that Gordy brought into the spotlight: Diana Ross and the Supremes, the Jackson Five, Stevie Wonder, Smokey Robinson and the Miracles, the Four Tops, the Temptations, Gladys Knight and the Pips, Tammi Terrell and Marvin Gaye, the Marvelettes, Mary Wells, and Martha Reeves and the Vandellas.

By the mid 1970s, some of the Motown artists had begun to resist Gordy's tight control. Defectors began to break up Gordy's "family" of stars. The first to leave was Gladys Knight and the Pips, and in 1975 the Jackson Five announced that they would be moving to Epic Records when their Motown contract expired.

Although Gordy kept Stevie Wonder at Motown by promising him $13 million over seven years in the famous "Wonderdeal" of 1975, Gordy's public statements usually expressed disappointment that his superstars came to value money over loyalty. This sentiment was heard often from Gordy when, in 1981, Diana Ross announced her move to RCA Records.

Ross's move was particularly surprising and bitter for Gordy in view of the fact that in 1972 he moved his headquarters to Los Angeles to begin a career in film, not only for himself, but so he could turn Diana Ross into a movie star. His first production was the 1972 Paramount release "Lady Sings the Blues," the story of Billie Holiday starring Ross. The picture was nominated for five Academy Awards and grossed more than $8.5 million. In 1975 Gordy directed Ross in "Mahogany," the story of a African American fashion model's rise to fame. Although the film did well at the box office, it was not nearly the critical success of "Lady."

Other Gordy films were "The Bingo Long Traveling All Stars and Motor Kings" (1976), "Almost Summer" (1978), "The Wiz" (1978) starring Michael Jackson and Diana Ross, and "The Last Dragon" (1985).

In June 1988 Gordy sold his company to MCA, Inc. He retained control of Jobete, the music publishing operation, and Motown's film division, but sold the record label to the entertainment conglomerate for $61 million. He told the newspaper *Daily Variety* that he wanted to "ensure the perpetuation of Motown and its heritage."

Esther Edwards, Berry Gordy's sister, was also interested in preserving Motown's heritage. The brick house at 2648 West Grand Boulevard, once modestly and unknowingly named "Hitsville USA," is now the site of the Motown Museum, thanks to the pack-rat tendency of Edwards. She saved hundreds of boxes of memorabilia, including original music scores, posters, and photographs, and until 1988 most of the mementos were stuck to the walls with thumbtacks. In an effort to have the collection professionally preserved, Michael Jackson, whose ties to Berry were still strong in 1990, donated the proceeds of the Detroit stop of his "Bad" tour—$125,000—to the Motown Museum.

Berry Gordy married Thelma Coleman in 1953. They had two sons, Berry IV and Terry, and one daughter, Hazel, who married Jermaine Jackson in 1973. Gordy's second marriage was to Raynoma Liles in 1959; they had one son, Kerry. Gordy also had a son with Margaret Norton in 1964 whom they named Kennedy, after John F. Kennedy, and who changed his name to Rockwell and recorded for Motown in 1984. In the Los Angeles area Gordy lived in a Bel Air estate and highly valued his privacy, rarely dealing with the press. In late 1994 a plan was announced to make a tribute album to Gordy. Even though Gordy was often times hailed as an entrepreneur, he was first and foremost a songwriter. Singers who have signed on to sing some of Gordy's songs on the tribute album include Diana Ross, the Four Tops, the Temptations and Smokey Robinson.

Further Reading

Numerous books recount the rise of Motown as a major contributor to popular music, all of which feature Berry Gordy as the man who started it all. Two books which tell the story particularly well, with outstanding photographs, are *Motown: Hot Wax, City Cool and Solid Gold* (1986) by J. Randy Taraborrelli and *The Motown Story* (1985) by Don Waller. Two more worthy accounts of Gordy and his empire are *Motown: This History* (1988) by Sharon Davis and *Where Did Our Love Go? The Rise and Fall of the Motown Sound* (1985) by Nelson George, with a foreword by Quincy Jones. Two of Gordy's family members have written telling tales of the man: *Berry, Me and Motown* (1990) by Raynoma Gordy Singleton, Gordy's second wife; and *Movin' Up: Pop Gordy Tells His Story* (1979) by Berry Gordy Senior. Gordy was interviewed by the popular media numerous times over the years, especially in 1983 during the celebration of Motown's 25th anniversary. *Newsweek* (May 23, 1983) featured an interview and well-told background story. □

Albert Gore Jr.

U.S. representative, senator, and 45th vice president of the United States, Albert Gore, Jr. (born 1948), was the son of a long-time Democratic congressman from Tennessee.

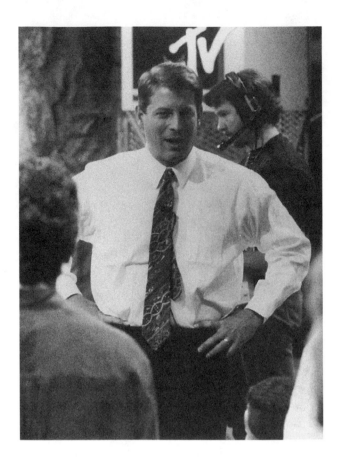

Albert Gore, Jr., was born in Washington, D.C., on March 31, 1948. His father, Albert Gore, Sr., was serving as a Democratic member of the U.S. House of Representatives from Tennessee. The senior Gore was to serve in the House and the Senate for nearly three decades. His mother was Pauline (LaFon) Gore. She had the distinction of being one of the first women to graduate from the law school at Vanderbilt University.

Since his father's occupation kept the family mainly in the nation's capital, young Gore grew up in Washington, D.C. He attended St. Alban's Episcopal School for Boys, where he was an honor student and captain of the football team. Gore went to Harvard University. In 1969 he received a B.A. degree, with honors, in government. He was interested in becoming a writer, rather than entering his father's "business" as a politician. After graduation he enlisted in the army, although he opposed the United States' intervention in the Vietnam War.

While stationed in Vietnam, Gore served as an army reporter. He sent some of his stories to a newspaper in Nashville, Tennessee, which published them. After Gore left the military service in 1971, the Nashville *Tennessean* hired him as an investigative reporter and, later, as an editorial writer. In addition to his journalism career, Gore was a home builder, a land developer, and a livestock and tobacco farmer.

Interested in religion and philosophy, Gore enrolled in the Graduate School of Religion at Vanderbilt University during the 1971-1972 academic year. In 1974 he entered Vanderbilt's law school but left to enter elective office two years later.

In 1976 Gore decided to run for a seat in the U.S. House of Representatives. Having a famous name, running in the district that sent his father to the Congress for many terms, he won the primary election against eight other candidates and went on to win in the general election. He ran successfully in the three following elections. Gore claimed some early attention in 1980 when he was assigned to the House Intelligence Committee studying nuclear arms. Gore researched and eventually published a comprehensive manifesto on arms restructuring for future security, which was published in the February 1982 issue of *Congressional Quarterly*. In 1984 Gore campaigned for a seat in the U.S. Senate that had just become vacant. He won that office with a large margin of votes.

While in Congress Gore was interested in several issues. He focused attention on health-related matters and on cleaning up the environment. He worked for nuclear arms control and disarmament, as well as other strategic defense issues. He stressed the potential of new technologies, such as biotechnology and computer development.

The race for the 1988 presidential election attracted Gore. He was only 39 years old at the time. He ran on traditional domestic Democratic views and was tough on foreign policy issues. He failed, however, to develop a national theme for his campaign and was criticized for changing positions and issues. He was successful in gaining public support in the primaries during the early spring and won more votes than any other candidate in southern states. However, he obtained only small percentages of votes in other states and withdrew from the presidential nomination campaigns in mid-April. Two years later he won election to a second term in the U.S. Senate. He chose not to seek the presidency in 1992, citing family concerns (young Albert had been hit by an automobile and was seriously injured). It was during this time that Gore wrote the book *Earth in the Balance: Ecology and the Human Spirit,* which expressed his concern, ideas, and recommendations on conservation and the global environment. In the book he wrote about his own personal and political experiences and legislative actions on the environmental issue. One of Gore's statements in the book that sums up his philosophy regarding the environment and human interaction is, "We must make the rescue of the environment the central organizing principle for civilization."

Events took a surprising turn in the summer of 1992. Bill Clinton selected Gore as his vice-presidential nominee. The choice startled many people because it ended a long-standing pattern of a candidate choosing a vice presidential nominee to "balance the ticket." Both men were of the same age, region, and reputation and moderate in political outlook. Clinton's idea was to project a new generation of leadership as a campaign theme. Gore did balance Clinton's strength by bringing to the ticket his experience in foreign and defense policy, expertise in environmental and new technology matters, and an image as an unwavering family man.

The highlight for many who followed the campaigns of 1992 was a series of debates, one of which involved Gore and his opponents, Republican Dan Quayle and Independent James Stockdale. The proceedings were marked by moments of high comedy—Quayle and Gore arguing over the wording of *Earth in the Balance*; Stockdale admitting his hearing aid was off—and clear party positioning. Qualye attacked Gore's record of environmental concern, claiming Gore was placing endangered species over people's jobs. Gore countered that a well-run environmental program would create jobs while preserving nature. Stockdale pointed out that such bickering was exactly why Congress was engulfed in gridlock.

Clinton and Gore won the election in 1992. Gore was inaugurated as the 45th vice president on January 20, 1993. At the age of 44 years, he became one of the youngest people to hold the position. Clinton and Gore were re-elected in 1996, running against Republicans Bob Dole and Jack Kemp.

During his time as vice-president, Gore continued to stress environmental concerns. In 1997 the White House launched an effort to start producing a report card on the health of the nation's ecosystems. This project was carried out by an environmental think tank and initiated by Gore.

Also in 1997, Gore's crystal clear reputation was somewhat tarnished when he was accused of—and admitted to—making fund-raising telephone calls from the White House during the 1996 presidential campaign. Gore held a press conference on March 3, 1997, to defend his actions, saying there was nothing illegal about what he had done, although he admitted it may not have been a wise choice. Gore was also criticized for toasting Li Peng, initiator of the Tiananmen Square Massacre, during a trip to China. In September 1997, Buddhist nuns testified before the Senate panel investigating the abuses of campaign fund-raising. The nuns admitted that donors were illegally reimbursed by their temple after a fund-raiser attended by Gore, and that they had destroyed and/or altered records to avoid embarrassing their temple. Some believe these incidents have further damaged Gore's reputation.

Gore is a devoted family man. He married his college sweetheart, Mary Elizabeth "Tipper" Aitcheson, on May 19, 1970. Tipper was born on August 19, 1948, in Washington, D.C. She held a B.A. degree from Boston University and a master of arts in psychology from George Peabody College. She was an active mother and politician's spouse, as well as working to forward her own issues. She gained attention through her efforts to influence the record industry to rate and label obscene and violent lyrics. She was co-founder of the Parents Music Resource Center, which monitors musical and video presentations that glorify casual sex and violence.

The Gores had four children: Karenna (born August 6, 1973), Kristin (born June 5, 1977), Sarah (born January 7, 1979), and Albert III (born October 19, 1982). When not in Washington, D.C., the Gores returned to the family livestock farm in Carthage, Tennessee.

Further Reading

Albert Gore, Jr., wrote *Earth in the Balance: Ecology and the Human Spirit* (1992). Gore also wrote a book with Bill Clinton outlining their 1992 campaign issues and policies, *Putting People First* (1992). The book includes a brief biography of Gore's public service. His political career can be followed in issues of *The Almanac of American Politics* by Michael Barone and Grant Ujifusa, which appeared during the years Gore was in Congress. His activity as Congressman and vice president can be followed in the *Congressional Quarterly's Weekly Reports*. Gore is listed in *Who's Who in America* (1996) and *Who's Who in the World* (1996). Peter Goldman and Tom Mathews, *Quest for the Presidency: The 1988 Campaign*, is one of many books recording the politics of that year. For information on his bid for the presidential nomination in 2000, see *National Journal* (March 29, 1997; May 31, 1997), *Time* (April 28, 1997), and *Chicago Defender* (April 5, 1997). For a report on Gore's encounter in China, see *New Republic* (April 14, 1997). *Science* (May 9, 1997) discusses some of Gore's environmental efforts. □

Josiah Gorgas

Josiah Gorgas (1818-1883), American soldier and educator, served as chief of ordnance of the Confederate Army.

J osiah Gorgas was born in Running Pumps, Pa., on July 1, 1818. The 10 Gorgas children had to work to help the family, and Josiah eventually became an apprentice on a newspaper in Lyons, N.Y. While there he won appointment to the U.S. Military Academy, from which he graduated in 1841.

Commissioned a second lieutenant in the ordnance (military supplies) service, Gorgas went abroad to survey European arsenals. He was assigned to the Watervliet, N.Y., arsenal when the war with Mexico began, and in January 1847 he joined Gen. Winfield Scott's Veracruz expedition. Gorgas participated in the siege of Veracruz and commanded the ordnance depot established there. After the Mexican War, Gorgas had routine assignments to various arsenals around the country. In 1855 he was promoted to captain.

When the Civil War began, Gorgas accepted a commission in the Confederate Army. This decision—which long estranged him from his family—undoubtedly was brought about by lengthy service in the South and by his marriage, in 1853, to Amelia Gayle, daughter of a former governor of Alabama.

Assuming his duties as chief of ordnance in the Confederacy, Gorgas found that the resources of his bureau were alarmingly small. Since manufacturing facilities were virtu-

Further Reading

Frank E. Vandiver edited *The Civil War Diary of General Josiah Gorgas* (1947) and wrote *Ploughshare into Swords: Josiah Gorgas and Confederate Ordnance* (1952).

Additional Sources

Vandiver, Frank Everson, *Ploughshares into swords: Josiah Gorgas and Confederate ordnance,* College Station: Texas A & M University Press, 1994. □

William Crawford Gorgas

William Crawford Gorgas (1854-1920), surgeon general of the U.S. Army, conquered yellow fever in the Panama Canal Zone, thus making the building of the canal possible.

W illiam C. Gorgas was born Oct. 3, 1854, near Mobile, Ala., the son of Josiah Gorgas, later a Confederate general and vice-chancellor of the University of the South at Sewanee, Tenn. Young Gorgas's early education was irregular because of the Civil War, but in 1875 he took a bachelor of arts degree from the University of the South.

Desiring a military career, Gorgas exhausted every possible means of getting an appointment to West Point, then decided to enter the Army by way of a medical degree. After graduating from the Bellevue Medical College in New York City and serving an internship at the Bellevue Hospital, he was appointed to the Medical Corps of the U.S. Army in June 1880. Then followed tours of duty at various Texas posts, in North Dakota, and nearly 10 years at Ft. Barrancas, Fla., a notorious yellow fever area to which Gorgas was assigned because he had previously had the disease and was therefore immune. In 1883 he married Marie Cook Doughty.

After the occupation of Havana, Cuba, by American troops in 1898, Gorgas took charge of a yellow fever camp at Siboney. Later that year he became chief sanitary officer of Havana. Acting on information furnished by the Yellow Fever Commission of U.S. Army physician Walter Reed that a particular strain of mosquito was the carrier of yellow fever, Gorgas deprived the mosquito of breeding places, quickly destroying the carrier and ridding the city of yellow fever. This work brought him an international reputation.

In 1904, when work commenced on the Panama Canal, Gorgas went to the Canal Zone to take charge of sanitation. Although it was known that yellow fever had been largely responsible for the French failure to build the canal, Gorgas encountered continuing opposition to his antimosquito measures from an economy-minded administration. He persevered, however, and, with the support of President Theodore Roosevelt, finally succeeded in making the cities of Panama and Colón models of sanitation.

ally nonexistent in the South, Gorgas sent an agent to purchase munitions in foreign markets and organized a program of battlefield scavenging to augment Southern supplies of guns, ammunition, and powder.

Gorgas's success with the Ordnance Bureau was phenomenal. He expanded arsenals, built new ones, established one of the most effective powder works in the world at Augusta, Ga., built a Central Laboratory at Macon, and expanded foreign trading with bureau-owned blockade-runners. Through his efforts the Niter and Mining Bureau was established to find and exploit mineral resources; he helped organize the Bureau of Foreign Supplies to increase the efficiency of blockade-running. A colonel through most of the war, he was promoted to brigadier general on Nov. 19, 1864.

After the war Gorgas tried unsuccessfully to run an ironworks at Brierfield, Ala. In July 1869 he assumed the post of headmaster of the junior department of the University of the South at Sewanee, Tenn. In 1872 he was appointed vice-chancellor of the university. His stormy tenure ended in 1878, when he was appointed president of the University of Alabama. He held this position for a year until illness compelled him to accept the less demanding post of university librarian. Gorgas died on May 15, 1883, in Tuscaloosa, Ala.

As a result of his work in the Canal Zone, Gorgas came to be generally regarded as the world's foremost sanitary expert. A number of foreign governments and international commissions sought his aid, and his book *Sanitation in Panama* (1915) quickly became a classic in the public health field. In 1914 he was appointed surgeon general of the Army, and he served in that capacity until his retirement 4 years later. He died in London on July 3, 1920, and is buried in the Arlington National Cemetery.

Further Reading

Marie D. Gorgas and Burton J. Hendrick, *William Crawford Gorgas: His Life and Work* (1924), is an intimate biography from material furnished by Gorgas's wife. See also John M. Gibson, *Physician to the World: The Life of General William C. Gorgas* (1950). □

Sir Ferdinando Gorges

The English colonizer and soldier Sir Ferdinando Gorges (1568-1647) was an important promoter of New England colonization.

Ferdinando Gorges's career covered the years from the defeat of the Spanish Armada (1588) to the surrender of Charles I (1645) during the English civil war. This was the era when English efforts at North American coloni-

zation became successful, and Gorges was a significant figure in that drama. While he never established a permanent settlement or profited financially from his endeavors, he founded Maine and kept the idea of colonization in New England alive.

Gorges was born into a prosperous landowning family in Dorset. Although he was an infant when his father died, Gorges received a good education and entered into a military career. He served in Holland against the Spanish and in France in support of Henry IV's struggle for the French throne. While in France he was knighted by the Earl of Essex. Queen Elizabeth later rewarded Gorges by appointing him commander of the fort at Plymouth, responsible for organizing the defense of the western counties against possible Spanish invasion. Gorges's fortunes collapsed, however, when he was drawn into a rebellion being plotted by the Earl of Essex. The revolt fizzled, and Gorges testified against Essex at his former commander's trial. This experience convinced Gorges to support the monarchy ever after. As punishment for his complicity in the plot, he lost his position at Plymouth.

Gorges regained his command on the accession to the throne of James I in 1603, and it was after returning to Plymouth that he developed his interest in colonization. In 1605 Gorges met George Weymouth, who had returned from New England with five Native Americans. Gorges kept three of them in his household in order to learn about the New World. When peace was established with Spain, Gorges became active in colonization, promoting the Virginia Company of 1606 and participating in outfitting and supplying an ill-fated colony at the mouth of the Kennebec River in Maine.

Council for New England

Attempting to forestall permanent failure in English colonization, Gorges led in reorganizing the Plymouth branch of the Virginia Company. The new charter created the Council for New England, a group of 40 distinguished citizens who controlled all land in North America between the 40th and 48th parallels. The council was not interested in establishing colonies of its own but in encouraging others to do so. One of its first grants was to the Pilgrims on Cape Cod.

Members of the council were also given land, and in 1622 Gorges received a large grant jointly with John Mason. Gorges attempted one settlement on the New England coast when he had the council grant his son Robert a proprietary colony northeast of Massachusetts Bay. Robert Gorges sailed in 1623 but returned to England the following spring, and the enterprise was abandoned.

Struggles with Massachusetts Bay Colony

Gorges was forced to forsake his interest in the Council for New England when war broke out with France in 1627, and he was therefore unable to supervise the council's 1628 grant to the New England Company. When that company received a royal charter as the Massachusetts Bay Company, antagonism between Gorges and Massachusetts was certain. Not only did the Massachusetts land claim overlap

Gorges's own, but Massachusetts' Puritan emphasis and company organization conflicted with Gorges's Anglicanism and dedication to proprietorship.

At war's end, Gorges, finding his interests had been preempted, set out either to get the Massachusetts charter annulled or to bring the colony under control of the Council for New England. For 3 years Gorges petitioned the English government regarding the threat to religious and political uniformity posed by Puritan Massachusetts. After investigation it was decided that Massachusetts must defend its charter. Gorges was appointed governor general of New England and instructed to present the order to Massachusetts. However, when his ship broke apart upon launching and, just as they were preparing to leave, his second in command, John Mason, died, Gorges abandoned the mission.

Meanwhile Gorges had decided to abolish the Council for New England, and after effecting a general division of the council's territory among its members, he engineered the surrender of its charter. It had been an interesting phase of English colonization, even though the council had accomplished little of permanent worth. In the last analysis it was Gorges's concept of colonization that defeated his goals. He viewed colonies as vast proprietary holdings into which the social, economic, and political institutions of England would simply be transferred. He never understood that the New World would not support such an unmodified transplantation.

Royal Grant for Maine

Gorges made one last attempt to salvage something from his efforts. In 1639 he received a royal confirmation of his earlier grant for the "Province of Maine." Since he was a royalist during the English civil war, however, his fortunes diminished with those of the King, and his plans for a vast proprietary colony were never fulfilled. He died in 1647, and his claims passed to his heirs, who eventually lost out to land-hungry Massachusetts.

Further Reading

The only recent biography of Gorges is Richard A. Preston, *Gorges of Plymouth Fort* (1953). Information about Gorges's colonial plans can also be found in Henry S. Burrage, *Gorges and the Grant of the Province of Maine, 1622* (1923) and *The Beginnings of Colonial Maine, 1602-1658* (1914). More general information is available in Herbert L. Osgood, *The American Colonies in the Seventeenth Century* (3 vols., 1904-1907), and Charles M. Andrews, *The Colonial Period of American History* (4 vols., 1934-1938). □

Gorgias

Gorgias (ca. 480-ca. 376 B.C.) was a Greek sophist and rhetorician. He believed that prose should rival poetry as a vehicle of persuasive and lofty expression and made important contributions to the development of epideictic, or ceremonial, oratory.

Gorgias was born in Leontini on the island of Sicily and is said to have lived more than 100 years. He went to Athens in 427 B.C. at the head of a delegation from his native city and caused a great stir with his new rhetorical style. His fame became immense throughout the Greek world, and according to Isocrates, his pupil, he was able to make a handsome fortune through the fees he charged. Noteworthy among the honors he received were invitations to deliver a funeral oration at Athens and to speak on Hellenic unity at Olympia. He was permitted to have a golden statue of himself erected at Delphi. Although he was popular, he was not without enemies, among whom was Aristophanes, the Athenian comic poet, who lampooned him and his extravagant rhetorical style in at least three comedies. Gorgias never married and left no direct descendants.

Writings and Ideas

Gorgias's writings include a single philosophical essay, listed by Sextus Empiricus as either *On Being or On Nature*, and Gorgias also wrote a *Handbook of Rhetoric* (now lost) and several speeches of which extensive fragments remain. The main points of the philosophical essay as preserved by Sextus are: nothing exists; if anything does exist, it is unknowable; if anything can be known, knowledge of it is incommunicable. In the tradition of Parmenides and Zeno of Elea, who developed certain types of rigorous logical arguments, Gorgias pursues an indirect kind of argumentation to arrive at an extreme conclusion.

More important than his contributions to philosophy are Gorgias's rhetorical works. His lost rhetorical treatise probably contained extensive examples of various types of arguments and rhetorical devices with little or no theoretical discussion (a fault of all of the handbooks before Aristotle). But if Gorgias published no elaborate theory, it is nevertheless evident from the extant *Encomium of Helen* that he had strong theoretical arguments for the power of the *logos,* and the importance and effect of his innovations could be readily seen in his successes as a speaker and teacher.

Gorgias's influence was immediate and widespread. His prose, which made lavish use of poetic diction, symmetrical clauses, various rhythms, and musical effects, revealed new possibilities to writers and speakers.

Further Reading

The surviving fragments of Gorgias's works are collected in Hermann Diels, ed., *Die Fragmente der Vorsokratiker,* translated by Kathleen Freeman in *Ancilla to the Pre-Socratic Philosophers* (1946; 3d ed. 1953) and discussed by her in *The Pre-Socratic Philosophers* (1946; 3d ed. 1953). Assessments of Gorgias's importance are given in George Kennedy, *The Art of Persuasion in Greece* (1963); C. S. Baldwin, *Ancient Rhetoric and Poetic* (1965); and Albin Lesky, *A History of Greek Literature* (trans. 1966). □

Hermann Wilhelm Göring

The German politician and air force commander Hermann Wilhelm Göring (1893-1946) was second in command to Adolf Hitler in Nazi Germany.

Hermann Göring was born in Rosenheim, Bavaria, on Jan. 12, 1893, son of the consul general of the German Empire in Haiti. He was educated in the Kadettenkorps (military school), where he performed outstandingly and earned a commission in the army in 1912.

After the outbreak of World War I, Göring moved to the newly created air force and in October 1915 became a fighter pilot. The daring young flier quickly distinguished himself and by 1918 had been shot down once and had won all the important military distinctions, including the highest award of the German army. After the famous Manfred von Richthofen ("Red Baron") was killed in the spring of 1918, Göring was chosen to succeed him in his former command.

After the German defeat the young captain left the Republican Army in disgust and went to Denmark to fly as a private pilot. In 1922 he returned to Germany, where he met Hitler. He immediately offered his services to the Nazi party and in short order became commander of the Nazi storm troopers (SA) in Munich. In the unsuccessful Beer Hall Putsch by the Nazis in November 1923, he received a painful injury which brought on his first drug addiction. He

had to flee Germany and once again took up work abroad as a pilot and airplane demonstrator.

In 1927 Göring returned to Germany and in 1928 successfully ran for the Reichstag (lower house of the legislature) as a National Socialist. He was reelected in July 1932 and became president of the Reichstag. With the election of Hitler to the chancellorship in January 1933, Göring joined the Cabinet as minister without portfolio and, more importantly, became minister of interior in Prussia. In the latter position he quickly brought the Prussian police under his control by co-opting SA troops and created the Nazi secret police, which he later turned over to the command of Heinrich Himmler for use in the Roehm purge of 1934.

In the fall of 1933 Göring became prime minister of Prussia and minister of air travel in the central government—an office he used for the illicit creation of a new air force whose commander in chief he officially became in 1935. From 1936 on he also directed the economic Four-Year Plan, which was above all a plan for stepped-up rearmament. In this position he acquired considerable power in the economic life of Germany, especially in the steel industry. He ordered extensive economic reprisals against Jews from 1938 on and engaged in considerable plunder for personal profit in occupied areas during the war years.

As commander in chief of the air force and, after the outbreak of World War II, as chairman of the War Cabinet, Göring played a vital role in promoting the policy of senseless aggression and destruction pursued by Hitler. After the initial victories in Poland and on the western front, he received the additional title of marshal of the Reich. As the war wore on, however, he proved increasingly wasteful in the use of the air force and incapable of maintaining its strength in spite of the massive and ruthless use of foreign slave workers in the air industry. His exaggerated promises of air strength caused frequent miscalculations which had serious consequences for the German war effort.

In the critical days at the end of the war Göring made several attempts to negotiate with the Allies and on April 23, 1945—as officially designated successor to the Führer—suggested to Hitler that he (Göring) assume the leadership of the Nazi state immediately. Hitler reacted with Göring's dismissal from all of his offices and expulsion from the party. Arrested on May 21, 1945, by the Americans, he was tried and sentenced to death at the Nuremberg Trials but committed suicide on Oct. 15, 1946, the night before his scheduled execution.

Further Reading

The best, most carefully balanced biography of Göring in English is Roger Manvell and Heinrich Fraenkel, *Goering* (1962). The other recent biography, by Charles H. Bewley, the fiercely anti-Communist former Irish minister in Berlin, is a favorable account based on family records, *Hermann Göring and the Third Reich* (1962). Other studies are H. W. Blood-Ryan, *Göring: The Iron Man of Germany* (1938), portraying Göring as a formidable yet thoroughly sincere and personally loyal German nationalist; Erich Gritzbach, *Hermann Göring: The Man and His Work* (trans. 1939); Kurt Singer, *Goering: Germany's Most Dangerous Man* (1940), a bitterly accusing wartime biography; Ewan Butler and Gordon Young, *Marshall without Glory* (1951), a more popularized, somewhat sensational account; and Willi Frischauer's interesting *The Rise and Fall of Hermann Goering* (1951).

Additional Sources

Butler, Ewan, *The life and death of Hermann Göring,* Newton Abbot, Devon: David & Charles Publishers; New York, NY: Distributed in the United States by Sterling Pub. Co., 1989.

Irving, David John Cawdell, *Göring: a biography,* New York: Morrow, 1989.

Overy, R. J., *Göring, the "iron man",* London; Boston: Routledge & Kegan Paul, 1984. □

Arshile Gorky

The American painter Arshile Gorky (1905-1948) created a personal language of form dealing with the iconography of the unconscious that enabled him to extend surrealism in the 20th century.

B orn in Turkish Armenia, Vosdanig Manoog Adoian changed his name in 1925 to Arshile Gorky, meaning the "bitter one." He emigrated to the United States with his sister at the age of 15. After studying briefly at the Rhode Island School of Design, he moved to Boston in 1923, where he secured part-time work. He continued his studies at the New School of Design, where he was engaged as instructor in 1924. The following year Gorky moved to New York City, where for the next 6 years he was on the faculty of the Grand Central School of Design. In this period Gorky's work drew on a variety of sources, including Camille Corot, J. A. D. Ingres, and Pablo Picasso.

The key work of Gorky's early period is the *Artist and His Mother* (ca. 1926-1929), a double portrait composed of cool flowing shapes which evokes a mood of stillness. Although this portrait is reserved in terms of its painterly qualities, relying heavily on the fine flowing line of Ingres, Gorky was simultaneously exploring the colorspace synthesis of Paul Cézanne (*Staten Island,* 1927/1928) and the surrealist-inspired figurative phase of Picasso (*Still Life,* 1929). This latter interest, in surrealist biomorphic shape, Gorky mastered and extended during the next 2 decades.

Gorky's work during the 1930s was divided between drawing and painting. The rather geometrical *Organization Series* (1933-1936) was probably a result of the artist's awareness of the work of Josef Albers. Gorky's *Aviation* mural (a Federal Art Project commission now lost), the theme of which was repeated in the *Aviation* murals for the 1939 New York World's Fair, broke away from the more enclosed forms of the *Organization Series* and exploited photomontage and cubist pictorial space. As public art, Gorky's murals make no attempt to create an easy visual experience for the layman.

Toward the end of the 1930s, as Gorky came under the influence of the work of André Masson, his work seemed to depend less on explicit references verifiable to the spectator

and more on a felt memory expressed in his developing, vibrant palette. The *Image of Xhorkhom* (ca. 1936) exists in four versions and, like the numerous versions of his *Garden in Sochi* (1938-1940), ostensibly refers by its title to the remembrance of things past. The latter series is a development from the former, with the images grown more delicate and cleaner in shape, the surfaces less densely painted, and the legibility of the artist's forms increasingly ambiguous as Gorky achieved a complete metamorphosis of floral and anatomical imagery.

Gorky's last years witnessed a further extension of surrealist devices, stimulated by the presence in America of Roberto Matta Echaurren and later by the arrival of the remaining coterie of surrealists headed by André Breton. Gorky's application of paint achieved a greater freedom, the resulting images shining through the thin pigment, as in the *Pirate I* (1942). His palette increased in intensity, and great puffs of florescent color seemed to vibrate from *The Liver Is the Cock's Comb* (1944). But during the same period Gorky could turn to the arabesque line of Ingres and the delicate hues found in his *Good Afternoon, Mrs. Lincoln* (1944). In the works of the last 2 years of his life, of which *Agony* (1947) and *Betrothal II* (1947) are exemplary, Gorky successfully achieved the visual metaphors of felt new experience. He committed suicide on July 21, 1948.

Further Reading

Harold Rosenberg, *Arshile Gorky: The Man, the Time, the Idea* (1962), is a valuable critical interpretation of Gorky and his paintings but the illustrations are poor. One of the most important critical studies of Gorky is Ethel K. Schwabacher, *Arshile Gorky* (1957), which contains biographical and bibliographical information. For a study of Gorky's work with excellent illustrations see Julien Levy, *Arshile Gorky* (1966), which includes a study of the artist's last years by a close friend. □

Maxim Gorky

The cultural and political activities of the Russian author Maxim Gorky (1868-1936) made him known in the Soviet Union as the greatest Russian literary figure of the 20th century.

M axim Gorky whose real name was Aleksei Maximovich Peshkov, was born on March 16, 1868, in the Volga River city of Nizhny Novgorod, which in 1932 was renamed Gorky in his honor. His father, a cabinetmaker, died when Gorky was 4 years old, and the boy was raised in harsh circumstances by his maternal grandparents, the proprietors of a dye works. From the age of 10 Gorky was virtually on his own, and he worked at a great variety of occupations, among them shopkeeper's errand boy, dishwasher on a Volga steamer, and apprentice to an icon maker. At a very tender age he saw a great deal of the brutal, seamy side of life and stored up impressions and details for the earthy and starkly realistic stories, novels, plays, and memoirs which he later wrote.

Almost completely self-educated, at the age of 16 Gorky tried without success to enter the University of Kazan. For the next 6 years he wandered widely about Russia, the Ukraine, and the Caucasus. In 1888 he worked in fisheries on the Caspian Sea. Gradually he developed revolutionary sympathies; he was arrested for antigovernmental activities for the first time in 1889 and from then on was closely watched by the police. In 1891-1892 he spent a year in Tiflis, where he worked in railroad workshops, and where his first published short story, "Makar Chudra," appeared in a newspaper in 1892.

First Works

From then on Gorky devoted himself mainly to literature, and in the next 5 years his stories appeared chiefly in newspapers along the Volga. His first collection of stories, published in 1898, made him famous throughout Russia, and his fame spread rapidly to the outside world. These early stories featured tramps, vagabonds, derelicts, and social outcasts. Gorky portrayed the bitterness of the oppressed and exploited people of Russia and demonstrated a proud defiance against organized, respectable society. He often found strong elements of humanity and individual dignity in even the most brutalized and demoralized of these "down-and-outers." His sympathy for the underdog made him known as a powerful spokesman for the illiterate masses—their sufferings and their dreams of a better life.

Foma Gordeyev (1899) established Gorky as a major novelist. It is the story of a well-intentioned but weak man who feels disgust, boredom, and guilt as the inheritor of a profitable family business. He rebels against his family and his class, but he is lacking in moral fiber, and in the end the forces of tradition defeat and destroy him. In this novel and all his later works, Gorky identified himself as being a bitter enemy of capitalism and depicted the society of prerevolutionary Russia as drab and dreary.

During this same period Gorky began writing plays and formed close connections with the Moscow Art Theater, which in 1902 produced his most famous play, *The Lower Depths*. It shows the misery and utter hopelessness of the lives of people at the bottom of Russian society and at the same time examines the illusions by means of which many of the unfortunate people of this earth sustain themselves.

Tall and rawboned, Gorky affected coarse dress and often crude manners at this stage of his life, but his personality was colorful and attractive. Even as a young man, he made many influential friends, including the two most famous writers of the day, Leo Tolstoy and Anton Chekhov. His memoirs of these two men, written many years later, are among his finest works.

Revolutionary Activities

Gorky became increasingly active in the revolutionary movement. He was arrested briefly in 1898, and in 1901 he was exiled to the provinces for having helped organize an underground press. When he was elected to the Russian Academy of Sciences in 1902, the Czar vetoed the appointment because of the author's subversive activities. During the 1905 Revolution, Gorky was again imprisoned for writing proclamations calling for the overthrow of the Czar's government.

In 1906 Gorky left Russia illegally and went to America to raise funds for his fellow revolutionists and spent most of the year there, where he wrote the novel *Mother*. This is a propaganda novel which tells of how a simple working-class woman, inspired by the example of her son, who is a militant revolutionist, herself becomes an activist in the class struggle. *Mother* was regarded in the Soviet Union as a classic of "socialist realism."

From 1906 to 1913 Gorky lived in Italy on the island of Capri, where his home became a center of literary and political activity among Russians abroad. In 1913 he received an amnesty from the Czar's government and returned to Russia. In the next 3 years he completed the first two volumes of his autobiography, *Childhood* (1913) and *My Apprenticeship* (1915). (The third volume, *My Universities,* was published in 1922.) Gorky's autobiography is his finest work, describing dramatically and colorfully the people he knew and the adventures he had from boyhood to young manhood. It paints a fascinating picture of the Russia of his times. In many respects Gorky's nonfiction works are superior to his fiction.

Later Career

In the years immediately following the October Revolution of 1917, Gorky worked tirelessly to help preserve the

Russian cultural heritage. He organized homes for writers and artists, founded publishing houses and theaters, and used his influence with the new Soviet regime to encourage the development of the arts. He spent most of the period from 1921 to 1933, however, in Germany and Italy, partly for treatment of a lung ailment and partly because of disagreement with policies of the Soviet government. During this period he wrote the large novels *The Artamonov Business* (1925) and *The Life of Klim Samgin* (an epic novel translated into English as four separate novels—*The Bystander, The Magnet, Other Fires,* and *The Specter*), all of them severely critical of life in prerevolutionary Russia. These novels are long and slow-moving, and many readers find them dull and ponderous.

In the late 1920s and early 1930s Gorky made several trips to the Soviet Union, and he returned to stay in 1933. Once again he was very active on the cultural scene, chiefly in book and magazine publishing and literary criticism.

Gorky died near Moscow in 1936. Even in his lifetime he had been enormously celebrated in his native land. Since his death he has been officially hallowed as the greatest Russian writer of the 20th century, and numerous theaters, museums, streets, universities, and even factories and collective farms were named after him.

Further Reading

The best study of Gorky's works and of his place in Russian literature is Irwin Weil, *Gorky: His Literary Development and Influence on Soviet Intellectual Life* (1966). An interesting account of Gorky's life and works up to 1930 is Alexander Kaun, *Maxim Gorky and His Russia* (1931). Helen Muchnic, *From Gorky to Pasternak: Six Writers in Soviet Russia* (1961), contains a stimulating critical analysis of his works.

Additional Sources

Troyat, Henri, *Gorki,* Paris: Flammarion, 1986; New York: Crown, 1989. ☐

Samuell Gorton

Samuell Gorton (ca. 1592-1677), an English colonizer, held religious views that made him a misfit in early New England and led him to establish his own settlement in Rhode Island.

Samuell Gorton was born near Manchester. Little is known of him before he left his work as a clothier in London to emigrate to Massachusetts. He expected to find toleration for his unique religious views in the New World but instead met with antagonism. He advocated a personal religious belief which denied governmental intervention, and he also challenged New England's political autonomy by asserting the supremacy of English governmental institutions.

Gorton arrived in Massachusetts at the height of the crisis surrounding heretic Anne Hutchinson and soon was

forced to leave. He went to Plymouth briefly, then moved to Portsmouth. He left both communities chiefly because of his conviction for "contempt of court" in defending an accused servant. He settled in Providence, R.I., then journeyed to Pawtuxet and to Shawomet near Providence. There he bought land from the Native Americans and appeared to have found peace. But Massachusetts would not leave him alone. Gorton and his followers were ordered to appear in Boston to defend their land claims. When they refused, Massachusetts sent three commissioners and forty militiamen to Shawomet. After negotiations failed, the militia attacked, captured Gorton and eight others, and confiscated their cattle. The men were taken to Boston, where the proceedings against them resembled an inquisition. After political and religious examinations, they were convicted of blasphemy and of being enemies of the true religion. Placed in irons, they were dispersed among the communities of Massachusetts with orders not to continue their "errors." The men from Shawomet could not be silenced, however, and eventually they were banished.

Gorton took his case to England and applied for Parliament's protection against the encroachments of Massachusetts. He won his case and was granted the right to live unmolested at Shawomet, which he renamed Warwick in honor of the English earl who had been its protector. Once safe politically and religiously, Gorton became a respectable and useful, if less exciting, individual. The leading citizen of Warwick, he was active in the government of Rhode Island, serving in both houses of the Assembly and acting as its president in 1651. He died in 1677.

Further Reading

There is no recent biography of Gorton. Information about him, as well as general background material, can be found in Irving B. Richman, *Rhode Island: Its Making and Its Meaning* (2 vols., 1902); Herbert L. Osgood, *The American Colonies in the Seventeenth Century* (3 vols., 1904-1907); James T. Adams, *The Founding of New England* (1921); Perry Miller, *Orthodoxy in Massachusetts, 1630-1650* (1933); and Charles M. Andrews, *The Colonial Period of American History* (4 vols., 1934-1938). ☐

Goshirakawa

Though emperor of Japan for only 3 years, Goshirakawa (1127-1192) continued to attend to affairs of state for over 30 years from the safety of a monastery. His reign was beset by civil wars.

Born Masahito, Goshirakawa was the fourth son of Emperor Toba and Fujiwara Akiko (Shoshi). He ascended the throne as Japan's seventy-seventh emperor in 1155, toward the end of what is often called the period of "cloister government," or the *Insei* system. Under this system the titular sovereign would abdicate at his own pleasure, placing a suitable and docile heir upon the throne, and he would continue to direct affairs of state from the retreat, or cloister. Most of the "cloistered emperors" then "entered religion" and were given the appellation of *Hō-ō,* or Sacred Ruler, which gave them some protection against secular dangers.

The effectiveness of the *Insei* system lasted for about 70 years, from 1086 to 1156, although the system survived in form for a little longer. After 1156 it lost much of its political significance, because almost the last shred of power had been torn from both titular and cloistered emperors by the rising military clans.

After Goshirakawa became a cloistered emperor, these military clans and even armed monks of various monasteries made use of him in their struggle for supremacy. Each clan claimed to be the protector of the throne, and Goshirakawa stood as the symbol of a sovereign power that he was unable to wield. During the last half of the 12th century a transfer of power took place, from the imperial court and nobility to the land-owning classes. New power centers formed in the provinces which based their claims upon the possession of manors and the control of armed forces. At that time the most powerful clans were the Fujiwaras, the Minamotos, and the Tairas.

Soon after Goshirakawa's enthronement, the civil war of the Hogen era broke out in 1156. Following his abdication, warrior families rapidly gained power, and Kyoto, the imperial capital, was thrown into confusion, often as a result of armed clashes among military clans. First the fighting took place between different factions of the Fujiwara clan, each supporting a different emperor. But in the Heiji Rising of 1159-1160 warriors of the Fujiwaras, the Tairas, and the Minamotos were engaged in plots and counterplots. Both former emperor Goshirakawa and Emperor Nijo were seized and detained under strict guard by different groups of warriors during the disturbances.

Goshirakawa attempted to play one military clan against another, hoping to maintain the prestige and power of the imperial court. The military families were, however, too powerful for the cloistered former emperor to control, and the imperial court had to grant Minamoto Yoritomo's request entrusting him with the administration of territories conquered by him and his followers during the civil wars.

Goshirakawa died of illness in the spring of 1192. During his lifetime Minamoto Yoritomo was unable to obtain the imperial commission as *sei-i tai shogun* (barbarianquelling generalissimo), a position which carried practically dictatorial powers and which he ardently desired both for its prestige and for its practical advantage. But after Goshirakawa's death youthful Gotoba (reigned 1184-1198) was readily persuaded to make the appointment. Thus began the shogunate that was to control Japan for most of the next 7 centuries.

Further Reading

A detailed discussion and cogent analysis of Goshirakawa and the *Insei* system is in Sir George B. Sansom, *A History of Japan,* vol. 1 (1958). For general background on the development of the early feudal system and of the shogunate see Edwin O. Reischauer and John K. Fairbank, *East Asia: The Great Tradition* (1960). □

Gottfried von Strassburg

The German poet and romancer Gottfried von Strassburg (ca. 1165-ca. 1215) wrote "Tristan und Isolt," the best-known version of that famous love story.

There is little information about the life of Gottfried von Strassburg. He was not of noble lineage but a freeman, had a good education, moved in higher society, and was well versed in literature, German and French, and theology. He was municipal secretary in his native Strassburg. Except for *Tristan und Isolt,* some lost minnesongs, and a few gnomic poems (*Sprüche*), no other works are known. He completed about 20,000 lines of *Tristan.* Fortunately the later portion of his source, the French romance of Thomas of Brittany, is extant.

The tale that Gottfried tells only for "noble hearts," a select spiritual community in the courtly world, recounts the mission of Tristan to win a bride, the fair Isolt of Ireland, for his aging uncle Mark, King of Cornwall. He succeeds, but on the return he and Isolt by mistake drink a love potion intended by Isolt's mother for the King. Unwittingly they fall madly in love. So spontaneous, overwhelming, and supernal is this love that even after Isolt and Mark are married, the reader does not think of the lovers as adulterers but as living in a world of their own, that of the "courts of love." Sordidness is ruled out. Indeed, Gottfried creates the impression that this love may even partake of the nature of a transcendent emotion. And so one follows their secret, ingeniously planned trysts almost as a well-wisher. Just as the Grail assumes a deeper meaning in the works of Wolfram von Eschenbach, representing the acme of human striving on earth and toward heaven, so the love potion here connotes the means for the perfect expression of that courtly spirit of love which does not debase but ennobles man, yet not without a strong suggestion of heresy. In Gottfried as in Wolfram, however, human suffering must precede attainment.

Mark's suspicions are often aroused; finally the lovers are detected. Tristan flees to Brittany. He weds another Isolt—of the White Hand—but only in name. Secretly he still yearns for the other Isolt. Here Gottfried's poem breaks off. Had he continued, he would doubtless have followed the plot of Thomas, who tells how Tristan is wounded by a poisoned spear and can be healed only by the arts the first Isolt had learned from her sorceress mother. Against his wife's will, Isolt is sent for—to arrive in a ship with a white sail, a black one denoting that she is not aboard. She approaches, but his wife lies to the invalid that the ship has a black sail. He dies of grief, and when his beloved arrives, she too dies, of a broken heart.

Thomas found the originally crude story as a courtly romance, which he refined. Gottfried gave it a more spiri-

Gottfried von Strassburg (3rd from left)

tual, mystical quality. Two other poets before Gottfried, the German Eilhart (ca. 1185) and the Frenchman Béroul (ca. 1192), both deviating from the Thomas school, are inferior in many respects. Two major German continuators of Gottfried, depending upon Eilhart, were Ulrich von Türheim (ca. 1240) and Heinrich von Freiberg (ca. 1290), a more gifted poet than Ulrich, but neither measuring up to Gottfried.

Numerous more recent writers in England, America, Germany, France, Italy, Spain, and Russia have been attracted to the theme. Richard Wagner's opera *Tristan und Isolde* (1859) neither deals with the legend as a whole nor follows Gottfried closely; it does, however, represent a magnificent distillation of the supernal love inherent in Gottfried's masterpiece.

Further Reading

Recent English translations of Gottfried's *Tristan* are by Edwin H. Zeydel (1948) and A. T. Hatto (1960). Zeydel summarizes less important parts but translates the rest in the original meter. Hatto, in prose, misses Gottfried's poetic spirit and elegance. Michael S. Batts, *Gottfried von Strassburg* (1969), is a general introduction to the poet and his work. Recommended for historical background is Roger S. Loomis, *Celtic Myth and Arthurian Romance* (1927). □

Adolph Gottlieb

The American painter Adolph Gottlieb (1903-1974) was a pioneer in the movement of Abstract Expressionism, working closely with other artists seeking new ways of self-expression.

Adolph Gottlieb was born in New York City on March 14, 1903. He left high school when he was 16 and enrolled in the Art Students League in New York where he studied painting under Robert Henri and John Sloan. In 1921 Gottlieb worked on a steamer for his passage to Europe. He took classes at the Académie de la Chaumière in Paris and later traveled to Munich and Berlin. Returning to New York in 1923, he finished high school and for the next six years studied at art schools in the city.

Gottlieb was awarded a joint prize in the Dudensing National Competition in 1929 and in the following year shared a two-man exhibition with Konrad Cramer at Dudensing Galleries in New York. In the early 1930s he met Mark Rothko and Milton Avery, painters at the Art Students League, who represented the expressionist movement in America at the time. Works by these artists dealt primarily with the depiction of contemporary life through emotions, along with mythological themes from African and Northwest Native American legends. Also incorporated into this expressionist vocabulary were Freudian and Jungian interpretations of dreams and literature. Thus, in the 1930s Gottlieb turned inward to representations of his own character and philosophy rather than explicit social themes, even though during this period he was an easel painter for the Work Projects Administration Federal Art Project. As his interest in primitive art forms emerged, anticipating his "pictographic" paintings of the 1940s, Gottlieb won a U.S. Treasury competition for a post office mural in Yerrington, Nevada.

In 1937 Gottlieb moved to the desert near Tucson, Arizona, an environment whose flora and relics contributed to a transformation in his subject matter and in his approach to painting. These abstract forms required an abstract environment in which to exist, and Gottlieb supplied this by tipping the table on which the still-life objects were placed. This moved the surface sharply toward the picture plane, flattening and reducing the space. He also compartmentalized objects as if by a personal mental discipline of sorting and regrouping. His palette then was rather limited, employing the soft earth colors of his environment. He returned to New York in 1939.

Pictographs

Gottlieb began to paint what he called "pictographs" in 1941. Again, it was the change in subject matter that provided some resolution for his problems with form. As he reported in 1955, "It was necessary for me to repudiate so-called 'good painting' in order to be free to express what was visually true for me."

The word "pictograph," a hybrid derived from Latin and Greek (pingere, to paint; graphien, to write), refers to the representation of an idea by a pictorial symbol. The term's reference to an archaic art form was a spiritual link that Gottlieb wished to stress. In the early pictographs, symbols or images remained recognizable and close to figuration—bits of nature or man-made objects, for example. These shapes, juxtaposed or overlapped in the composition, gradually became more abstract. The flattened images were applied to canvas with thick impasto and loose brush strokes and were organized into regular or irregular grid systems. The horizontal tiers and vertical rows seem to lend meaning to the otherwise static images. Contrarily, such compartmentalization, as in *The Sea Chest* (1942), may also reflect the already intrinsic meaning of the forms. In a statement to the *New York Times* in 1943, Gottlieb and Mark Rothko summarized their aesthetic beliefs: "We want to reassert the picture plane. We are for flat forms, because they destroy illusion and reveal truth."

Imaginary Landscapes

By the end of the 1940s Gottlieb's images transcended narrative or illustrative connections. The particular identities of the shapes became obscure, but while they denied reference to a specific image, they acquired meaning as pure form. Gottlieb's reason for breaking with the pictographs was essentially his wish to leave the "all over" aspect of composition. In this new process the pictograph evolved into "bursts" of paired monumental shapes, sometimes placed on bare canvas.

Archer (1951), a work which shows the transition from the pictographs to the imaginary landscapes, keeps residual regulations of the formerly divisive lines, but these are now placed randomly on the canvas. This looser linear arrangement is combined with two motifs, focused in the upper and lower zones, which are then more subtly repeated, in different colors, over the surface of the picture. The imaginary landscapes release the grid structure completely and become increasingly non-representational. They abandon recourse to mythical symbols and show Gottlieb's exploration of pure form and color.

Bursts

Gottlieb's most effective works were his oppositions of both colors and shapes in canvases called bursts. In these paintings the picture plane is divided into two arbitrary horizontal zones; in one of these zones is placed a bright geometric form or an irregular aggregation of brushstrokes (*Glow,* 1966). These works reveal what Gottlieb felt were the contradictions in human life: the order and chaos, possession and loss, etc. For him, such intangible and illusive images were representations of his deepest inner feelings. His desire for pure expression was fulfilled with color and form arranged with apparent disregard for both subject and object, the simple depiction of a complex thought.

In the 1960s Gottlieb's work received increasing acclaim. Among other honors, he was awarded the Grand Premio at the VII Bienal de São Paolo, Brazil. In 1968 a major retrospective exhibition was organized jointly by the Whitney Museum of American Art and the Guggenheim Museum in New York. Both exhibitions opened simultaneously on February 14 of that year.

Gottlieb suffered a stroke in 1971, but continued to paint from a wheelchair. The following year he was elected to the National Institute of Arts and Letters, a tribute to his teaching and to his artistic innovation and production. He died in Easthampton, New York on March 4, 1974.

Further Reading

Robert Doty and Diane Waldman, *Adolph Gottlieb* (1968) is the catalogue of the exhibition at the Whitney and Guggenheim Museums and presents an essay on the evolution of Gottlieb's style and a chronology of his exhibitions. Many illustrations are in color. *Adolph Gottlieb: Paintings* (1980), catalogue from the exhibition held at the Joslyn Art Museum in Omaha, Nebraska, also includes an informative essay on the artist's life and work. For the artist's lesser known three-dimensional pieces, see *Gottlieb: Sculpture* (1970). Another overview is *Adolph Gottlieb: A Retrospective* (1981), with text by Lawrence Alloway and Mary Davis MacNaughton. Brief summaries of Gottlieb and his work appear in numerous resource publications such as *Contemporary Artists* (1989) and the *Encyclopedia of American Biography* (1996). □

Louis Moreau Gottschalk

Louis Moreau Gottschalk (1829-1869), probably the most important American composer of the 19th century, infused European romanticism with indigenous North and South American elements.

Louis Moreau Gottschalk was born on May 8, 1829, in New Orleans, the son of a Jewish Englishman and a Creole woman. He exhibited extraordinary talent at the age of 3. At 13, after experience as a church organist and a concert pianist, he went to Paris to study, absorbing the romantic ideas and attitudes of the time and acquiring an elegant, polished manner.

Gottschalk took Paris by storm when he made his 1845 concert debut. Frédéric Chopin predicted a brilliant future for him, and Hector Berlioz spoke of his "exquisite grace . . . brilliant originality . . . charming simplicity . . . thundering energy."

When Gottschalk returned to America, P. T. Barnum offered him a contract for $20,000 yearly plus expenses; Gottschalk refused scornfully. Compared favorably to Beethoven in the reviews of his New York debut, he launched his American career.

But Gottschalk's world soon collapsed. His father died, and he was forced to assume a considerable debt and to support his mother and six brothers and sisters. The stress caused the quality of his compositions to deteriorate. He wrote shameless potboilers. His fresh, original impulses were eroded as he became more adept at composing vapid salon music. He gave concerts almost daily—80 concerts in New York alone within a 2-year period.

Then Gottschalk retreated for almost 6 years to a life of splendid dissipation in Cuba and the Caribbean islands. Yet there he wrote some of his best compositions.

Gottschalk resumed his hectic activity during the Civil War period. His concerts inspired phenomenal enthusiasm. Moreover, he organized mammoth festivals involving hundreds and even thousands of musicians, receiving thunderous ovations from the public. During his largest festival, in Rio de Janeiro in 1869, Gottschalk's *Marche triomphale* aroused tremendous enthusiasm. Exhausted by his feverish way of life and weakened by yellow fever, he died 2 weeks later.

Gottschalk's music infuses European structures with American folk and popular music as well as Latin American elements. He wrote two operas and several orchestral works. His piano works show his wide range, romantic sweep, rhythmic freshness, and varieties of mood and color.

Bamboula and *Le Bananier*, early works, contain infectious rhythms and Creole tunes. *Souvenirs d'Andalousie* and *Manchega* use Spanish color and rhythms. *El cocoyé* and *La gallina* are musical essays on Cuban music. *Suis-moi* and *O! Ma charmante, epargnez-moi!* are forays into the music of the Antilles. *L'Union* and *America* utilize patriotic airs. *Chant du soldat* suggests the romantic sweep of Berlioz or Chopin. *Impromptu* and *Danza* are sparkling salon pieces. However, Gottschalk's best-known works, *The Dying Poet* and *The Last Hope,* are both considered potboilers.

Further Reading

In addition to his musical accomplishments, Gottschalk produced imaginative writings; his *Notes of a Pianist* (1881; repr. 1964) provides a fascinating chronicle of 19th-century American musical life. See also Vernon Loggins, *Where the Word Ends: The Life of Louis Moreau Gottschalk* (1958). There are illuminating chapters on him in Gilbert Chase, *America's Music: From the Pilgrims to the Present* (1955), and Harold C. Schonberg, *The Great Pianists* (1963).

Additional Sources

Gottschalk, Louis Moreau, *Notes of a pianist,* New York: Da Capo Press, 1979, 1964.
Starr, S. Frederick, *Bamboula!: the life and times of Louis Moreau Gottschalk,* New York: Oxford University Press, 1995. □

Klement Gottwald

Klement Gottwald (1896-1953) was one of the founders of the Czechoslovak Communist Party. He masterminded the coup d'état by which the Communists seized power in Czechoslovakia in February 1948 and served as the country's first Communist president from June 1948 until his death in 1953.

Gottwald was born on November 23, 1896, the son of a small farmer in the village of Dedice in Moravia, then part of the Austro-Hungarian Empire. At the age of 12 he was sent to Vienna to become an apprentice to a woodworker. Four years later he joined the Social Democratic (Marxist) youth movement. When World War I broke out he was drafted into the imperial army. As an artilleryman he saw action on both the Russian and Italian fronts, was wounded, and rose to the rank of sergeant major. Before the war ended, however, he deserted (as did many Czechs) and organized sabotage activities against the Austro-Hungarian forces.

In the new state of Czechoslovakia after 1918 Gottwald was a member of the left wing of the Czechoslovak Social Democratic Party, leaving with it to form the new Czechoslovak Communist Party in 1921. Thereafter, he gained prominence as a Communist speaker, writer, and general organizer. He became editor of the party's Czech (*Pravda*) and Slovak (*Hlas ludu*) publications, was elected to its executive committee in 1925, and in 1927, at the age of 31, was elected its secretary general. In 1935 he led a group of 30 elected Communist deputies to the Czechoslovak parliament, promising in his inaugural speech to "break the necks" of his bourgeois political opponents.

After Hitler came to power in Germany Gottwald was among those who warned of the fascist threat to Czechoslovakia and demanded that the country prepare a strong military defense against it. After the infamous Munich Pact of September 1938 had crippled Czechoslovakia, Gottwald, who had vehemently opposed compliance with it, was sent by his party to safety in the Soviet Union. He remained there

throughout World War II, organizing underground resistance and making propaganda broadcasts to the Czech and Slovak lands. In 1943 Eduard Beneš, the Czechoslovak president-in-exile, came to Moscow, and Gottwald worked out with him a new compromise political-economic structure for the freed and reunited country after the war. This program was put into effect in April 1945 at Košice in Slovakia, the first Czechoslovak city to be liberated.

On his return home, Gottwald became a vice-premier in the National Front, a provisional government composed of a coalition of parties that administered Czechoslovakia in the immediately postwar period. In the spring of 1946 he was also elected chairman of the Czechoslovak Communist Party (his best friend, Rudolf Slánský, assumed the more workaday executive position of secretary general). In the national elections of June 1946 the Communists—drawing upon enormous popular goodwill for the liberating Soviet Army and much resentment of the perfidious behavior of the Western powers at Munich-received 38 percent of the votes cast, becoming the largest single party in the Czechoslovak parliament. On July 3, 1946, Gottwald became prime minister, heading a cabinet of Communist and non-Communist representatives. He was viewed at home and abroad as a "moderate" Communist who would respect the established Czechoslovak traditions of democracy and pluralism, and his early actions seemed reassuring. The new constitution guaranteed free elections; a free press; freedom of religion and assembly; the right to work and receive disability compensation, to education, and to recreation; equal rights for women; and an independent judiciary. Financial institu-

tions, mines and other natural resources, and basic industries were to be socialized, but private property and private enterprises of moderate size were protected. There were some worrisome moments, to be sure. In 1947 Gottwald's government first accepted, then—at Soviet insistence—rejected an invitation to take part in deliberations on the U.S.'s Marshall Plan, asserting that Czechoslovakia's ties were totally and irrevocably with the Soviet Union. At the same time, a "millionaire's tax" on more affluent citizens was levied to help support the peasantry, which had suffered severe crop losses.

Covertly, Gottwald and his party were executing a detailed, progressive plan for a Communist seizure of power, aware that waning popular support for them meant a coming defeat at the polls. This plan was publicly exposed in February 1948 when the non-Communist ministers of the government charged the Communists with planning assassinations, dismissing non-Communist police chiefs, and other illegal actions. A majority of the cabinet resigned in an effort to topple Gottwald's government. In response, Gottwald mobilized his party and its followers in a show of force. "Action Committees" seized control of local governmental bodies, factories, schools, and large popular organizations. The army and police arrested alleged "conspirators." Factory workers paraded with arms through the streets and threatened a general strike. On February 25 President Beneš yielded to Gottwald's demand that he be permitted to form a new government of Communists and sympathizers. Three months later, in May, Beneš resigned, and Gottwald replaced him as president a few days later, in June. A new constitution of April 1948 sanctioned a one-party (Communist) dictatorship and completed the nationalization and collectivization process.

Gottwald was still seen by many as a leader who would avoid the excesses of other new Communist regimes. However, the "Soviet viceroy" promptly set about in dogmatic Marxist fashion to reshape the Czechoslovak "people's democracy" into a one-party workers' state, totally reoriented toward the Soviet Union (following the slogan "With the Soviet Union Forever"), Sovietized in its institutions, and heavily Russianized in its culture.

When the Soviet dictator Stalin ordered all of the new "satellites" to purge themselves of "national Communists" and "potential Titoists," Gottwald dutifully sent more than a dozen of his oldest Czech and Slovak Communist comrades (including Slánský) to death or life imprisonment. Although himself unwell, Gottwald attended Stalin's funeral in Moscow on March 9, 1953, occupying the most prominent place of all the satellite leaders on the tribune. While there he contracted pneumonia. On March 14, 1953, nine days after the death of Stalin, Gottwald himself was dead in Prague.

Further Reading

There is no biography of Klement Gottwald in English, but there are some good books on the historical background of his life and career. *A History of the Czechoslovak Republic, 1918-1948*, edited by Victor S. Mamatey and Radomír Luža (1973), provides a detailed account by many authors of Czech and Slovak history from the founding of Czechoslovakia to the

Communist coup. There are also two authoritative treatments of the rise of Communism in Czechoslovakia from the foundation of the Czechoslovak Communist Party in 1921 to its triumph in 1948: Joseph Korbel, *The Communist Subversion of Czechoslovakia, 1938-1948: The Failure of Coexistence* (1959) and Paul E. Zinner, *Communist Strategy and Tactics in Czechoslovakia, 1918-1948* (1963). ☐

Claude Goudimel

The French composer Claude Goudimel (ca. 1514-1572) is best known for his various settings of the French Psalter. He also wrote Roman Catholic church music and French chansons.

C laude Goudimel was born in Besançon; little is known of his early training. He was living in the French capital when his first chansons were issued (1549) by the Parisian music printer Nicolas du Chemin. Additional volumes under Du Chemin's imprint followed, but the composer's conversion to Protestantism probably forced his relocation to Metz about 1557. Ten years later, because of an administration unfriendly to Huguenots, Goudimel once again had to flee, first to his native town and then to Lyons. The massacres that began in Paris on St. Bartholomew's Day reached Lyons on Aug. 28, 1572, when Goudimel fell at the hands of religious fanatics.

Goudimel's devotion to the secular song is attested by numerous French publications, beginning in 1549. The many chansons printed during and after his lifetime suggest that he composed them throughout his career. Most of his extant music for Roman Catholic worship, however, was probably written before his conversion: five Masses, five motets, and three Magnificats.

Goudimel composed 66 psalms in the form of motets for three to six voices between 1551 and 1566. These imitative works constitute the first and most elaborate of the three settings he made of the French Psalter, translated by Clément Marot and Théodore de Bèze. Even though Goudimel elaborated in these psalms the Huguenot tunes of Louis Bourgeois, most of Goudimel's pieces were probably still acceptable to Catholics, who only later were forbidden to traffic with heretic texts and tunes.

Goudimel's second (1564 at Paris, 1565 at Geneva) and third (1568) settings of the French Psalter were probably intended for the Huguenots from the outset. A simple chordal style sufficed for the second version of 1564, but the third setting of 1568 saw the reappearance of the elaborate imitative style of the first setting. Unlike the early psalm settings, each of which Goudimel treated as a series of through-composed motets, the psalms of the third version were strophic songs with the music of the first standing for later stanzas.

Of all Goudimel's works the note-against-note pieces of the second version proved most successful and were sung (in translation) throughout Protestant Europe. Designed for home rather than choir singing, they are the least complex of his works. By meeting the need of the new faith for simple choral music, they became the most enduring creations of the master.

Further Reading

A useful discussion of Goudimel's music is in Gustave Reese, *Music in the Renaissance* (1954; rev. ed. 1959). For background see Donald Jay Grout, *A History of Western Music* (1960). ☐

Jean Goujon

The French sculptor Jean Goujon (ca. 1510-ca. 1568) designed sculpture for architectural settings. His work in low relief is comparable to some of the finest examples of ancient architectural sculpture.

N othing is known of the birth or early years of Jean Goujon. He is presumed to have been born about 1510 on the basis of the competence and maturity shown in the tomb of Louis Brézé in Rouen Cathedral (after 1531), much of which is believed to be his work, and from a documented reference (1540) to a column he made for the organ loft of St-Maclou, Rouen.

By 1544 Goujon was in Paris, working on the rood screen for St-Germain-l'Auxerrois, and he may have executed prior to this date reliefs of the Four Evangelists for the Écouen Chapel (now in Chantilly). The *Deposition*, the most impressive of the reliefs from St-Germain (now in the Louvre, Paris), presents the dead Christ surrounded by a group of mourning figures as a classic tragedy interpreted by an artist of the French Renaissance. The relief reveals the terms of such an artist: trained by sculptors working in the lingering late Gothic tradition, Goujon and his generation swiftly adopted the attenuated figures, complex linear patterns, and extreme technical sophistication of their Italian contemporaries, expressing ideas in the late Renaissance or mannerist style. Goujon's personal translation of this idiom is distinguished by the incisiveness and assurance of his sharply defined figures tightly pressed into a shallow layer of space; the smooth surfaces of their forms are relieved and balanced by the curvilinear patterns indicating drapery and landscape. A crisply carved, rich ornamental border enframes the relief.

The sharp edges, flat planes, and hard carving of the *Deposition* are softened, relaxed, and varied in the programs of sculpture Goujon completed in mid-century: the Fountain of the Innocents (1547-1549) and the relief sculpture executed in collaboration with the architect Pierre Lescot for the courtyard facade of the west wing of the Louvre (ca. 1549-1553).

Originally a corner rectangular structure, the Fountain of the Innocents was reconstructed in the late 18th century as a freestanding block. Most of its sculpture is now in the Louvre: six tall, narrow reliefs of nymphs and six long reliefs with nymphs, tritons, putti, and victory figures. In the reliefs

of the nymphs each of the slim, fashionable figures stands with an effortless grace; complex positions seem easy and natural as infinitely subtle gradations of carving suggest forms revealed, concealed, and unified by gossamer-thin drapery dextrously manipulated and skillfully arranged.

Despite 19th-century restorations, the Louvre facade still reveals the fine balance achieved by the coordination of Goujon's controlled and disciplined sculpture with Lescot's architecture. In one instance their roles were reversed: Goujon is known to have carved the caryatid figures supporting a gallery in the interior of the Louvre from a plaster model by Lescot. Goujon's concern with architecture and with the problems of optical effects of reliefs is found in an appendix he wrote for a French edition of Vitruvius (1547), which he illustrated with woodcuts.

The one freestanding group traditionally attributed to Goujon, *Diana and the Stag* from the château of Anet (Louvre, Paris; first mentioned in 1554), is now rejected by most scholars and believed the work of a still-unidentified French sculptor.

Goujon's later life is as mysterious as his birth. There are no references to him in the royal accounts after 1562. One theory that he left France as a Protestant in this period of religious conflict is interesting but not proved. The evidence for Goujon's life is, in brief, sparse and his remaining works few in number, but they demonstrate his ability to master the essentials of a new vocabulary of formal ideas imported from Italy and then produce work sufficiently original and accomplished to exert a lasting influence.

Further Reading

Most of the literature on Goujon is in French. In English, a clear, able summary is in Anthony Blunt, *Art and Architecture in France, 1500-1700* (1953). □

João Goulart

João Goulart (1918-1976) was a highly popular president of Brazil for a brief but turbulent two-and-a-half years. He was removed from office by the military in 1964; civilians did not rule the country again until 1985.

João Goulart was born in São Borja, Rio Grande do Sul, in March 1918. In 1939 he graduated from the law school of Pôrto Alegre. After practicing law for several years, he was elected president of the municipal committee of the Brazilian Labor party (PTB), which had been created by Getulio Vargas in 1945. Two years later, Goulart became a PTB member of the state legislature.

Goulart was a wealthy landowner in São Borja, with his *fazenda* ("farm") near that of President Getulio Vargas, and during the 5 years that Vargas spent in self-imposed exile (1945-1950) on his own *fazenda,* the two men became close friends. Vargas is credited with having urged Goulart to be candidate in his successful contest for federal deputy in 1950, when Vargas himself returned to the presidency. Soon afterward Goulart became state president of the PTB.

In 1953 Goulart was appointed minister of labor by President Vargas in order to get control of the ministry away from anti-Vargas factions. Goulart's appointment aroused immediate, extensive, and vocal opposition among the right-wing press and alarm among officers in the military. In early 1954, Goulart offered his proposals for a 100 percent increase in the minimum wage and at the same time offered his resignation because of the political embarrassment his proposals would be for Vargas. Vargas accepted Goulart's resignation, and Goulart returned to the Chamber of Deputies. With the suicide of Vargas in August 1954, Goulart succeeded to leadership of the Labor party. In the national election of 1955 he was the successful PTB candidate for vice president on a ticket headed by Juscelino Kubitschek of the Social Democratic party.

During the Kubitschek administration, Goulart was given extensive patronage, particularly in the social security system, and he continued as head of the Labor party. In the 1960 election Goulart was again candidate for vice president, only this time the electoral system had been changed to separate the election of president and vice president; as it happened, Goulart was chosen vice president in spite of the fact that his running mate, Gen. Henrique Teixeira Lott, was defeated by the conservative National Democratic Union's (UDN) Janio Quadros. During the brief Quadros presidency, Goulart, widely seen as Vargas's protege, was under constant attack.

The Presidency

President Quadros resigned his presidency after only seven months with the hope (given Goulart as the alternative) that he would be invited back and given more power; at the time, Goulart was on a state visit to Communist China at Quadros's request. Rather than take Quadros back, a Congressional committee proposed a constitutional change creating a parliamentary system with reduced presidential powers; when the change was adopted in September, 1961 Goulart was inaugurated as president.

During the first 15 months of his administration Goulart concentrated on trying to regain full presidential powers by establishing himself as a moderate, credible and reliable politician. His cabinet was relatively well balanced and moderate. In this period, Goulart nominated four persons to be Prime Minister, but for a variety of reasons they either resigned quickly or were not approved by Congress. At the Punta del Este meeting of Foreign Ministers in January 1962, Goulart's government stood against the United States by refusing to exclude Castro's Cuba from the community of Latin American nations, a move supported by the Brazilian Congress but negatively noted by Washington. Later that year, opinion had shifted even amongst Goulart's enemies in favor of returning to the presidential system (they thought that "only full executive power would reveal the president in his 'true colors'"). In January 1963 a national referendum restored the full power of the presidency by a margin of nine to one.

During the first months after his full powers were restored, Goulart committed himself to a three-year plan of economic development and restraint of inflation, as worked out by the minister of economy, Celso Furtado. Goulart often spoke of the need for "structural reforms"(especially agrarian reform) as being necessary for development, but he remained loyal to the ideas of economic emancipation and social justice bequeathed by Vargas. He wanted the existing system to work more smoothly and effectively. Stabilization of the economy was vigorously opposed by bankers and big industrialists who benefited most from inflation and by the press, but the biggest blow to stabilization came from the government's having to give in to the inflationary 70 percent wage hikes demanded first by civil servants and the armed forces, and then by trade union leaders and workers. People inside and outside Congress saw Goulart's agrarian reform bill as "an outrageous assault" on the ownership of land and rural property interests very strongly represented in Congress, which rejected the bill. Goulart abandoned the stabilization program and, trying to improvise solutions to meet mounting criticisms, in June 1963 dismissed his entire cabinet.

From that point on, politics in Brazil became increasingly polarized. Rhetoric overran reality; outside government, the left's over-inflated claims of growing support and successes provoked and alarmed their enemies on the right. Rumor fed on rumor, and all across the political spectrum confidence in Goulart's ability to hold the system together diminished.

Goulart was by early 1964 more the servant of opposing forces than their leader. Events were running ahead of him. Too many people believed either the system could no longer work or were unwilling to make it work. Goulart's Congressional base was gone, and his request of special powers from Congress failed. Goulart decided on a direct appeal to the mass of Brazilian people, articulating a program of basic reforms. His appeals grew more emotional, his rhetoric more heated and in the process, his enemies (especially in the military) more alarmed and more organized. The final blow for the military was a nationally televised speech Goulart made on March 30 to an association of enlisted personnel; in supporting the troops, Goulart incited the officers.

The coup was bloodless. It consisted of troop movements towards Goulart in Rio de Janeiro, and generals throughout the country withdrawing their support from him. Goulart flew to Brasilia, the capital, where there was no good news, then to Pôrto Alegre, and finally into exile in Montevideo, Uruguay.

Those who planned the coup knew the move would have the approval of the U.S. embassy. The American Ambassador to Brazil, Lincoln Gordon, characterized the coup as "the greatest victory of the West against Communism, greater than Cuba's nuclear disarmament, greater than the crisis of the Berlin Wall." Just after, the U.S. moved "with almost embarrassing speed" to recognize and welcome the new regime, and the U.S. was influential in the choice of Castello Branco as the new president.

Goulart died in December 1976 at the age of 59, still in exile. The regime in power in Brazil ordered that only a simple note of his death could appear in the press, with no extensive comment on his life or career. Nevertheless, more than 20,000 mourners filled the town of Sao Borja after the news came, and in the center of Rio de Janeiro shops and businesses were quietly closed by their owners "because the president has died."

Further Reading

Detailed accounts of Goulart's life and recent Brazilian history are in Thomas E. Skidmore, *Politics in Brazil 1930-1964: An Experiment in Democracy* (1967), and in John F.W. Dulles, *Unrest in Brazil: Political-Military Crises, 1955-1964* (1970). See also José Maria Bello, *A History of Modern Brazil, 1889-1964* (1940; 4th ed. 1959; trans. 1966), and Vladimir Reisky de Dubnic, *Political Trends in Brazil* (1968) For a recent account, see Peter Flynn, *Brazil: A Political Analysis* (1978). □

Glenn Gould

Canadian musician Glenn Gould (1932-1982) provoked much controversy with his piano interpretations, his writings on music, and his preference for recording to playing live concerts. Unlike most renowned pianists, he avoided much music of the 19th century, concentrating instead on that of the Renaissance, Baroque, and early 20th century.

Glenn Herbert Gould was born in Toronto September 25, 1932, and died in the same city October 4, 1982. He was the only child of musical parents, his father being an amateur violinist, and his mother a pianist and organist who had aspired to a musical career earlier in life and who taught him until age ten. Gould was musically precocious, though he denied having been a prodigy. He began reading music at the age of three, discovered that he had perfect pitch at around the same time, and was composing small pieces when he was five. At ten he could play the entire first book of Bach's *Well Tempered Clavier*.

In that year, 1942, he began studies at the Toronto Conservatory of Music (since 1947 called the Royal Conservatory of Music of Toronto). His teachers there included Frederick C. Silvester, organ; Leo Smith, theory; and Alberto Guerrero, piano. Guerrero, with whom he studied for ten years, was to be his only piano teacher. Gould, himself, minimized the importance of his piano lessons, but fellow pupil John Beckwith attributed Gould's position at the piano, the angle of his fingers to the keyboard, and his pure finger technique to Guerrero's teaching. To Gould, the greatest influences of his youth were the playing of Artur Schnabel, which showed a greater respect for the music than for its medium, the piano; Rosalyn Tureck, for her approach to Bach; and the organ, which he credited as the basis of both his piano technique and his interpretations of

Bach. Gould composed throughout his student years, in both tonal and twelve-tone idioms. He passed his associateship exam, by which he established a professional rank, and his music theory exam in 1945 and 1946 respectively.

Years on the Concert Stage

His career as a concert performer also had its beginnings in his student years. In a Toronto Conservatory concert of June 1946 he appeared as soloist in the first movement of Beethoven's fourth piano concerto, and in January of the following year he performed the entire concerto with the Toronto Symphony under Bernard Heinze. By 1952 he had given several performances with orchestras in Toronto, Hamilton, and Vancouver; had toured the western provinces; and had given network radio performances for the Canadian Broadcasting Corporation (CBC). That same year he stopped his lessons with Guerrero and partially withdrew from the public eye in order to examine music more carefully and to assess his musical possibilities.

Re-emerging onto the concert stage, Gould made his American debut, playing recitals at the Phillips Gallery in Washington, D.C., on January 1, 1955, and at Town Hall in New York City ten days later. The program chosen for these recitals represented the affinity for introspective and contrapuntal writing that Gould maintained throughout his career. It consisted of music by Beethoven, Bach, Webern, Berg, Sweelinck, and Gibbons.

A contract with Columbia Records the day after his New York debut attested to the success of that performance.

The first product of what would be a life-long affiliation with Columbia was a recording of Bach's *Goldberg Variations* in June 1955. This best-selling, highly acclaimed record catapulted Gould into the front rank of concert artists. His *String Quartet No. 1*, a post-Romantic work owing much to Richard Strauss, received its premier by the Montreal String Quartet in February 1956 and was subsequently recorded and published. In May 1957 he began his first tour outside of North America with several concerts in both Moscow and Leningrad. No Canadian musician had performed in the Soviet Union prior to Gould's appearance. After hearing the pianist's Berlin debut in the same month, the noted German critic H. H. Stuckenschmidt hailed him as "an absolute genius, the greatest pianist since Busoni."

End of His Concert Career

Gould continued to play concerts for the next seven years, to perform on television, and to lecture both in Canada and the United States. He also began to contribute frequently to periodicals, including *High Fidelity, Saturday Review,* and *Piano Quarterly.* Throughout these years, however, he became increasingly attracted to the recording medium, and in 1964, after an appearance in Chicago, chose to abandon the concert stage altogether in its favor. He offered several reasons for doing so: a dislike of applause and of "being demeaned like a vaudevillian;" a dislike of music suited for a large hall, especially the bravura concertos of Chopin, Liszt, Schumann, and Rachmaninoff; a reluctance to use those devices, such as rubato and exaggerated dynamics, necessary to project music in a large hall; and what he called "the none-take-twoness of public performances."

Throughout the remainder of his life Gould explored the prospects of recording. The editing process became a vital and integral part of his musical expression, and he felt that even the splicing of two distinct interpretations showed neither a lack of integrity nor necessarily interrupted the continuity of a performance. Eventually he produced his own recordings. Apart from the sound recordings, Gould became involved in film. The series *Conversations with Glenn Gould,* produced by the BBC in 1966, featured the pianist on four occasions discussing the music of Bach, Beethoven, Schoenberg, and Richard Strauss. For the 1972 film of Kurt Vonnegut's *Slaughterhouse Five,* Gould performed and arranged the music, some of which he also composed. He also wrote two radio plays, *The Idea of North* and *The Latecomers,* which employ a carefully controlled overlapping of spoken voices that Gould calls "contrapuntal radio," and which he regarded as a distinct musical genre.

Gould was certainly among the most remarkable and interesting pianists of the century. His interpretations intentionally confronted the listener with the thoroughness and originality of their conception, often achieved through such means as extreme tempos and novel articulations. Among the most convincing are those of Bach and Schoenberg, both of whom were well-served by his complete finger independence and his attention to overall design. He also championed unusual repertory, including English Renais-sance composers and the little-known piano music of Sibelius and Richard Strauss. His renderings of Mozart, for whom he admitted a lack of sympathy, were often less successful.

The possessor of an astounding technique, Gould eschewed music that drew attention to technical feats of the performer or to the instrument, rather than to the piece itself. Throughout his career Gould displayed several unconventional mannerisms, among them humming audibly while playing and conducting himself whenever he had a free hand. Most agree that these were part of his musical personality and not conscious attempts to attract attention to himself.

Further Reading

Gould wrote voluminously during his career, usually in the form of record jacket notes or magazine articles, and on every subject that appealed to him. Excepting autobiographical information, which he dismissed as uninteresting, he remains the best source for his ideas. His writing is usually cogent and always spiced with wit. Three volumes of his selected writings provide perhaps the most accessible basis for study. *The Glenn Gould Reader* (1984), edited and with an introduction by Tim Page, contains the largest and most broadly chosen selection. *Conversations with Glenn Gould* (1984) contains interviews by Jonathan Colt, originally published in *Rolling Stone* magazine, with updated and added material. *Glenn Gould Variations, By Himself and His Friends* (1983), edited by John McGreevy, contains some of Gould's writings interspersed with tributes from other musical luminaries, including Herbert von Karajan, Leonard Bernstein, and Yehudi Menuhin. Geoffrey Payzant's *Glenn Gould, Music and Mind* (Toronto, 1978) provides the most comprehensive biographical information and attempts to interpret Gould's writings and his often unorthodox opinions. Two interviews with Gould have also been recorded: *At Home with Glenn Gould,* by Vincent Tovell (CBC, 1959); and *Glenn Gould: Concert Dropout,* by John McClure (Columbia BS 15, 1968). □

Jay Gould

American financier and railroad builder Jay Gould (1836-1892) began as an unprincipled stock manipulator and became one of the most acute businessmen in America's age of industrial capitalism. He operated in an era when speculative capital could play a constructive role.

Jay Gould, christened Jayson, was born in Roxbury, N.Y., on May 27, 1836, a farmer's son. He obtained some education in a local academy and also learned surveying. Between the ages of 18 and 21 he helped prepare maps of New York's southern counties. By 21, with a stake of $5,000, he and a partner opened a leather tannery in northern Pennsylvania.

Gould then moved to New York City, where he set up as a leather merchant in 1860. Before long, however, he found his forte in Wall Street, ostensibly as a stockbroker but really as a speculator. In that period of unregulated finance Gould quickly mastered the intricacies of corporate management and of security trading and manipulation. He traded in the securities of his own companies, manipulating banks he was associated with to finance his speculations and corrupting legislators and judges. From 1867 to 1872 he was a power and a terror in Wall Street.

Erie War

In 1867 Gould was already on the board of directors of the Erie Railroad, which was in financial difficulties. He set out to control it, push its expansion westward as far as Chicago, and defeat Cornelius Vanderbilt's efforts to acquire this potential competitor. Gould was the behind-the-scenes strategist (using Daniel Drew and James Fisk as his fronts) in the "Erie war" with Vanderbilt in 1868. To check Vanderbilt, Gould issued 100,000 shares of new Erie stock by illegally converting debentures and then went to Albany, where, with the Erie's money, he bribed legislators to legalize the conversion. Vanderbilt discovered he had met his match and settled with Gould, receiving $1 million as a sweetener and leaving the Erie to Gould.

Gould launched the Erie on an expansion campaign that vastly increased its capital debt. Meanwhile, he traded in Erie stock, sold it short, and made a killing before the road went bankrupt in 1875.

Buying Gold to Sell Wheat

As part of the Erie's move westward, Gould obtained control of the Wabash, a wheat-carrying railroad. To improve the fortunes of the Wabash, Gould hit on the scheme of pushing up the price of gold, thus weakening the dollar, and thereby encouraging foreign merchants to buy more wheat.

Using Fisk's brokerage house as a cover, in the summer of 1869 Gould began buying gold secretly in the free market—hoping the U.S. Treasury would not sell—and ran the price up from 135 to 160, where it was on the "Black Friday" of Sept. 24, 1869. By that time Gould had created a short interest in gold of $200 million with only a fraction of that amount available to the short sellers. Then the U.S. Treasury, realizing it had been duped by Gould, sold gold, and the price dropped to 140 and then to 133. A panic hit Wall Street, depressing all stocks. Gould had speculated not only in gold but in stocks and lost a fortune. However, in 1871-1872 he made another.

Well-heeled again, Gould moved his operations westward into the Wabash, the Texas and Pacific, the Missouri Pacific, and the Union Pacific railroads. His operations in the last two exemplify his methods. He bought their securities when they were low during the depression of 1873, obtaining control of both; he also acquired securities of independent lines and feeder lines he wished to add the two trunk systems. Then he forced up the prices of the two amplified major companies. When the stock market recovered during 1879-1884, he sold, making a large fortune out of capital gains.

Manipulator Turned Businessman

Gould was pushed out of the Wabash and the Union Pacific in the early 1880s. He then turned his complete attention to the Missouri Pacific (of which he had gained control in 1879) and built it into a great power. He acquired feeder lines and independent companies; he used stock market profits and capital gains for financing; and he waged a relentless war on competitors, breaking up traffic pools and forcing rates down sharply. His biographer Julius Grodinsky wrote that Gould was "transformed from a trader into a business leader of national proportions." From 1879 to 1882 Gould added 2,500 miles to the road, making a capital addition of about $50 million. And between 1885 and 1889 he reentered the Wabash and the Texas and Pacific railroads, reorganized them, and tied them into his Missouri Pacific system.

At the same time Gould strengthened the other two elements in the triad that constituted his estate. One was the Manhattan Elevated Railroad of New York, which he created as a monopoly of Manhattan's rapid transit system. The second was the Western Union Telegraph Company. Gould had bought the unimportant American Union Telegraph in 1879, consolidated it with the Western Union in 1881, and 7 years later added the influential telegraph network of the Baltimore and Ohio Railroad. By the end of the 1880s Western Union, now the parent company, had no real competitor in the two important businesses of railroad telegraphy and the transmission of Associated Press stories to member newspapers. It was one of the most profitable companies in the country. Gould died in New York on Dec. 2, 1892, leaving the management of his properties to his son George Jay Gould.

Further Reading

An excellent biography and railroad history of the period is Julius Grodinsky, *Jay Gould: His Business Career, 1867-1892* (1957). A lively study of the family is Edwin P. Hoyt, *The Goulds: A Social History* (1969). The story of the "Erie war" is in Charles F. Adams, Jr., and Henry Adams, *Chapters of Erie* (1871). For a broad understanding of the era that made the emergence of industrial capitalists like Gould possible, see Louis M. Hacker, *The World of Andrew Carnegie, 1865-1901* (1968). Gustavus Meyers, *History of the Great American Fortunes* (1907), portrays Gould as the "robber baron" par excellence. □

Stephen Jay Gould

The American paleontologist Stephen Jay Gould (born 1941) was awarded the Schuchert Award for 1975 by the Paleontological Society for his work in evolutionary theory. He was also the author of several books popularizing current scientific issues.

Stephen Jay Gould was born on September 10, 1941, in New York City, the son of Leonard and Eleanor (Rosenberg) Gould. His father was a court reporter and amateur naturalist. Leonard Gould was a self taught man and a Marxist who took his son to the American Museum of Natural History when the boy was five years old. It was here that the young Gould saw his first dinosaur, a Tyrannosaurus Rex, and decided that he was going to devote his life to the study of geologic periods. Gould's his mother was an artist. After a summer at the University of Colorado, Gould received his education at Antioch College in Yellow Springs, Ohio, graduating with an A.B. in 1963. He then moved on to graduate school in evolutionary biology and paleontology at Columbia University, where he remained for two years. He married Deborah Lee, an artist, on October 3, 1965, then left to take a job in 1966 at Antioch College as professor of geology. The following year he moved on to Harvard to take an assistant professorship, and in that same year he finished his doctoral work, completing his degree program from Columbia. In 1971 he was promoted to associate professor, and in 1973 to full professor of geology. He also became curator of invertebrate paleontology at Harvard's Museum of Comparative Zoology. At Harvard he expanded his study of land snails to the West Indies and other parts of the world.

Gould was one of the founders of the punctuated equilibrium school of evolution. The gradualism promoted by Charles Darwin and propounded in the neo-Darwinian synthesis of the 1930s stressed gradual modification of organic structures over long periods of geologic time. Gould argued that evolution proceeds quite rapidly at crucial points, with

speciation occurring almost instantaneously. This could be due to quite sudden genetic mutations—his favorite example is the panda's "thumb," a modification of the wrist bone allowing the panda to strip leaves from bamboo shoots. Such a transformation must have occurred all at once, he reasoned, or it would not have been preserved by natural selection, having no useful function in a rudimentary stage. This process would account for the lack of transitional forms throughout the fossil record, a problem Darwin lamented but expected to be resolved by future paleontologists.

In addition to his work as a serious professional paleontologist, Gould spent much time trying to make science accessible to lay readers as well as scholars As a popular writer and amateur historian of science, Gould concentrated upon the cultural "embeddedness" of science, seeing it as a creative human endeavor neither abstracted from society nor objectively pursuing un-interpreted data. Such embeddedness means that the science of a particular period shares the assumptions and prejudices of that period. This is as characteristic of modern science as it was of the science of antiquity—Arthur Jensen, who argued for the genetic inferiority of Blacks, for instance, is probably not more, and possibly much less, objective than Aristotle. Both tend to biologize human nature and intelligence. In his book *The Mismeasure of Man,* for which he won the National Book Critics Circle Award for Essays and Criticism in 1982, Gould features an explanation of the misuse of intelligence testing to assign value to human beings and to promote cultural prejudice. Although he concedes that human intelligence has a specific location in the brain and that it can be measured by a standard number score, he argues that any efforts to label groups as possessing inherently inferior or superior intelligence based upon these measurements represent a misuse of scientific data and a violation of the scientific process.

In 1981 Gould served as an expert witness at a trial in Little Rock Arkansas that challenged a state law mandating the teaching of creation science in tandem with evolution. Gould's testimony argued that the theories of creationism are belied by all available scientific evidence and therefore do not deserve scientific status. Due to this testimony, Creationism was recognized as a religion and not a science. During that same year, Gould was awarded a prose fellows award from the MacArthur Foundation.

In July of 1982 Gould was diagnosed with mesothelioma, a particularly deadly form of cancer. He recovered from his illness and the treatment, but found that he had to continue his work with a new sense of urgency. He further explored the misuse of standardized testing to label social groups rather than study the effects of social factors on intelligence.

Both of Gould's careers gave evidence of a firm commitment to the liberatory elements in science. He borrowed legitimately upon his earned prestige in biology to argue against one of its central paradigms—biological determinism—and he used his literary skills to popularize the debate, exposing the dangers inherent in all biologizations of human abilities. Gould received critical recognition for his work in both areas. In 1975 he was given the Schuchert Award by the Paleontological Society for his original work in evolutionary theory. For his book *The Panda's Thumb,* he received two awards: the Notable Book citation from the American Library Association in 1980 and the American Book Award in Science for 1981. Likewise, he received two awards for his other major work, *The Mismeasure of Man:* the National Book Critics Circle Award for general nonfiction in 1981 and the American Book Award nomination in science for 1982. Gould was also a National Science Foundation grantee. He was a member of several scientific societies—American Association for the Advancement of Science, American Society of Naturalists, Paleontological Society, Society for the Study of Evolution, Society of Systematic Zoology, and Sigma Xi. As the author of more than 200 evolutionary essays collect in eight volumes Gould was a publishing phenomenon, with topics ranging from evolution, to his successful battle with cancer, Edgar Allan Poe, shells, and why there are no .400 hitters in baseball to name a few. Eminently readable, Gould explains complex ideas in simple understandable language that bridges the gap between scholars and lay persons alike. It is this that gives his work durability and credibility.

Gould resided in Cambridge, Massachusetts, with his wife and two children, Jesse and Ethan. He was an accomplished baritone with an undying love for Gilbert and Sullivan operettas, sang in the Boston Cecilia Society. In *The Flaming's Smile* he wrote "I could not dent the richness in a hundred lifetimes, but I simply must have a look at a few more of those pretty pebbles."

Further Reading

There is little biographical information on Stephen Jay Gould, though *Contemporary Authors, New Revision Series,* vol. 10, provides a brief but intelligent sketch.
All of his popular works are worth reading. These are, chronologically: *Even Since Darwin* (1977); *Ontogeny and Phylogeny* (1977); *The Panda's Thumb* (1980); contributor, Ernst Mayr, editor, *The Evolutionary Synthesis* (1980); *A View of Life* (1981); *The Mismeasure of Man* (1981); and *Hen's Teeth and Horse's Toes* (1983). □

Charles François Gounod

The French composer Charles François Gounod (1818-1893) is best known for his operas. His music tends to be more lyric than dramatic, his melodic writing at its best revealing a considerable warmth of feeling.

Charles Gounod was born on June 17, 1818, in Paris. His father was a prominent painter; his mother was a pianist, and Charles received his first musical education from her. In 1836 he entered the Paris Conservatory, where he studied counterpoint with Jacques Fromentin Halévy and composition with Jean François Lesueur.

In 1837 Gounod won second place in the coveted Prix de Rome award and in 1839 the Grand Prix. This enabled him to study in Italy, where he was exposed to the choral music of Giovanni Pierluigi da Palestrina. This remained an important influence throughout his life, perhaps even to the detriment of his own choral writing. Returning from Rome through Austria, he also had the chance to hear some of the more romantic compositions of Robert Schumann and Felix Mendelssohn.

For a time Gounod studied theology and even considered becoming a priest. His theological interests ultimately earned him the title "Abbé." Eventually he returned to music, and he attempted to gain success through the composition of operas, the surest road to fame for any French composer. His first opera, *Sapho* (1851), achieved only a moderate success. With his fourth opera, *Faust* (1859), he achieved international renown. Although both the libretto and the music have been criticized for their sentimental oversimplification of Goethe's great drama, *Faust* maintained its position as the most popular French opera in the repertoire for almost a century. Gounod completed 12 operas, but only one other, *Roméo et Juliette* (composed 1864, first performed 1867), has remained in the repertoire. Its fame rests on Juliette's waltz song and the numerous love duets.

From 1870 to 1875 Gounod lived in London, where, in addition to presenting concerts and composing a number of religious works, he organized the Gounod Choir, later to become the Royal Choral Society. In his last years he concentrated almost exclusively on composing large choral

of land ownership in early-19th-century Upper Canada.

Robert Gourlay was born on March 24, 1778, in Ceres, Fifeshire, Scotland. He was educated at St. Andrews University, and in the summer of 1817 Gourlay arrived in Upper Canada. He immediately began to interest himself in the system of land ownership. In the official *Upper Canada Gazette,* Gourlay published an address and a series of questions and had them distributed throughout the province. The answers to his questionnaire strengthened his belief that the methods of granting land tended to stifle immigration into the colony.

In February 1818 Gourlay published a second address, demanding an inquiry into the abuses he had uncovered, but the legislature failed to act. He now saw not only the system of landholding as corrupt but the whole system of government as unresponsive to the needs of the settlers. In yet another pamphlet he urged the people to petition collectively for needed reforms.

The ruling oligarchy in Upper Canada now began to move against Gourlay. Arrested twice in June 1818 on charges of criminal libel, he was tried in August but acquitted of both charges by juries sympathetic to his aims.

Gourlay now unsuccessfully turned to the newly arrived governor, Sir Peregrine Maitland. Frustrated, Gourlay became more radical in his pronouncements. In December 1818 he was arrested once more and given 10 days to leave the province. When he refused, he was jailed, and in August 1819 he was ordered to leave the province, with the threat of death if he returned. He went to the United States and returned to England before the end of the year.

In 1822 Gourlay published a *Statistical Account of Upper Canada,* detailing the conditions in the province. In 1842 the government of Canada erased the 1819 sentence against Gourlay. He returned to Canada in 1856 and in 1860 ran for a seat in the Legislative Assembly. He lost and shortly afterward returned to Scotland, where he died, in Edinburgh, on Aug. 1, 1863.

Many of Gourlay's charges, though exaggerated, were not without substance, and he was instrumental in focusing attention upon some of the real grievances of the common people in the colony and in encouraging the reform impulse there.

Further Reading

There is no definitive biography of Gourlay. His own works are helpful: *Chronicles of Canada: Being a Record, of Robert Gourlay, Esq., Now Robert Fleming Gourlay, "The Banished Briton"* (1842) and *Statistical Account of Upper Canada* (2 vols., 1822), which reveals much concerning conditions in the province. William S. Wallace, *The Family Compact: A Chronicle of the Rebellion in Upper Canada* (1915), and Gerald M. Craig, *Upper Canada: The Formative Years, 1784-1841* (1963), discuss Gourlay's Canadian career within the political and social milieus of the time. □

works, but none of these added to his stature as a composer. He died at Saint-Cloud on Oct. 18, 1893.

Two short compositions by Gounod have attained sufficient popularity to merit mention. One is the orchestral *Funeral March for a Marionette* (1873), which captures perfectly the peculiar humor suggested in the title. The other is the *Ave Maria* (1859) based on Johann Sebastian Bach's first prelude from *The Well-tempered Clavier.* This has been criticized as a sentimentalization of the work of a great master, but it is in actuality an ingenious display of compositional craft in which Gounod kept Bach's prelude unchanged but used it as an accompaniment for his own expressive melody.

Further Reading

Gounod wrote his *Autobiographical Reminiscences* (trans. 1896; repr. 1970). There are no major biographies of Gounod in English. Norman Demuth, *Introduction to the Music of Gounod* (1950), is a study of his work. Brief material on Gounod is in Edward J. Dent, *Opera* (1940; rev. ed. 1949), and Donald Jay Grout, *A Short History of Opera* (1947; 2d ed. 1965). □

Robert Gourlay

Robert Gourlay (1778-1863) was a British reformer who attempted to bring about reforms in the system

Remy de Gourmont

The French author Remy de Gourmont (1858-1915) was the most brilliant French critic and essayist of the period from 1900 to the outbreak of World War I.

R emy de Gourmont was born on April 4, 1858, at the Château de La Motte in Normandy, the son of an old Norman family of minor nobility. He went to school at Coutances and studied law at the University of Caen before moving to Paris to take a post at the National Library at the age of 25. Once in Paris he came under the influence of the Decadent writers the Comte de Villiers de l'Isle-Adam and J. K. Huysmans, and his early work is marked by a similar decadentism, extreme preciosity of style, and interest in the occult. In his mid-20s Gourmont fell victim to lupus, a skin disease which disfigured his face so badly that for some years he scarcely dared go out; his natural bent toward solitude was powerfully reinforced by this cruel experience and by his dismissal from his post as a librarian in 1891 for having published an attack on what he considered the excessively patriotic and nationalistic sentiment of the time.

In the meantime Gourmont's literary career had already begun, with a novel, *Merlette,* in 1886 and his collaboration as one of the founding members of the literary review *Mercure de France* in 1889. This review rapidly became a keen supporter of the symbolist movement in literature, largely through Gourmont's influence, and he remained one of its most important contributors for the rest of his life. In the next few years he published, in elegant, limited editions, several volumes of stories, poetry, and a play, all in the symbolist manner and dealing with the fantastic or supernatural; the best-known of these is the novel *Sixtine* (1890).

Gourmont as a writer of fiction is largely known for his cerebral qualities, combining mysticism, sensuality, and a highly artificial style. But he is better remembered today as critic and essayist: his *Livre des masques* (1896; *The Book of Masks*), criticism of the symbolist poets, various works on language and style, and above all the collected essays in *Promenades littéraires* (7 vols., 1904-1927) and in *Promenades philosophiques* (3 vols., 1905-1909). During his lifetime he published over 60 books of various kinds.

As a critic, Gourmont was distinguished by an inquiring mind and extremely wide tastes, claiming that "a work of art exists only through the emotion it gives us." The result is impressionistic criticism with keen insight. His interest in language and style also produced ideas of lasting influence, in particular on the poets Ezra Pound and T. S. Eliot. Gourmont was saddened and impoverished by the outbreak of war in 1914, and his remaining time was unhappy; he died of a stroke on Sept. 27, 1915.

Further Reading

The best of the English translations of Gourmont's works is Richard Aldington, *Remy de Gourmont: Selections from All His Works* (1928). Aldington also wrote *Remy de Gourmont: A Modern Man of Letters* (1928). Other studies include Paul Emile Jacob, *Remy de Gourmont* (1931), and Glenn S. Burne, *Remy de Gourmont: His Ideas and Influence in England and America* (1963). □

John Gower

The English author John Gower (ca. 1330-1408) was one of the major court poets of the 14th century. His poems are not so vigorous as Chaucer's, but his criticism of his contemporaries is more direct.

V ery little is known about John Gower's early life. He probably held a legal office of some kind, perhaps in Westminster. His first major work, probably begun about 1376, was in French. It is called *Miroir de l'Omme,* or *Speculum meditantis.* In it Gower describes the development of sin, the vices and virtues, and the remedy available to man, with a special appeal to the Blessed Virgin Mary.

Some time about 1377 Gower retired to the priory of St. Mary Overy in Southwark. He soon began work on his long Latin poem *Vox clamantis.* Book I, written after 1381, contains a vivid description of the Peasants' Revolt, used to set the theme for a moral analysis of social decay in England. At this time Gower was acquainted with Geoffrey Chaucer, who gave him power of attorney while Chaucer was away on the Continent in 1378. Chaucer later dedicated *Troilus and Criseyde* to Gower and to Ralph Strode.

In 1390 Gower completed the first version of his most famous poem, written in English but given the Latin title *Confessio amantis.* He says that he wrote it at the request of King Richard II, who had asked him for "som newe thing" to read. The first version of the poem was dedicated to Richard. In a later version Gower dedicated his poem to Henry of Derby, the son of John of Gaunt and the future King Henry IV.

Confessio amantis means "the lover's confession," but it is not an autobiography of the poet and it does not concern itself with Gower's amorous adventures. After a prologue in which Gower points out that division in the soul introduced by sin creates division and strife in the world, he introduces the lover, a man overcome by lust and the desire for selfish pleasure. In the remainder of the poem, which occupies 8 books and some 34,000 lines, the lover confesses to Genius, the priest of Venus, gradually recovering his reason and overcoming the division within himself. The poem ends with a prayer for good government and the rule of reason in the commonwealth. Gower's masterpiece contains an enormous amount of standard medieval moral philosophy and is illustrated by a great variety of exemplary tales. Some of the tales are very well told.

Between 1394 and the end of his life Gower wrote some Latin poems and, probably, some of his French ballades. He married late in life in 1398.

Further Reading

For a careful account of Gower's life and works see John H. Fisher, *John Gower* (1964). □

Francisco de Paula José de Goya y Lucientes

Francisco de Paula José de Goya y Lucientes (1746-1828) was Spain's greatest painter and printmaker during the late 18th and early 19th centuries, a wayward genius who prefigured in his art the romantic, impressionist, and expressionist movements.

orn in Fuendetodos near Saragossa on March 30, 1746, Francisco Goya died a voluntary expatriate in Bordeaux, France. Tradition has it that a priest discovered talent in the boy upon seeing him draw a hog on a wall. Oddly enough, a testament submitted for the process of beatification of Father José Pignatelli disclosed (not detected until 1962) that he taught Goya, who "instead of paying attention, kept his head down so that his teacher couldn't see him and occupied himself in sketching...." Pignatelli ordered him to the front of the class but recognized an artistic gift in the sketches. The priest called upon José Goya, the boy's father, and advised him to dedicate his son to painting. Perhaps owing to this same priest's influence, Goya at 12 years of age painted three works (destroyed 1936) for the church in Fuendetodos.

Two years later, Goya was apprenticed to José Luzán y Martínez, a mediocre, Neapolitan-trained painter who set his pupil to copying the best prints he possessed. After 4 years of this training, Goya left. He went to Madrid in 1763 to compete unsuccessfully for a scholarship to San Fernando Academy. The tests ended on Jan. 15, 1764, and nothing is known of the artist until 2 years later, when he entered another academic competition calling for a painting of the following subject: Empress Martha presents herself to King Alphonse the Wise in Burgos to petition a third of the ransom required by the sultan of Egypt for the rescue of her husband, Emperor Valduin; the Spanish king orders the full sum to be given her. The competitors were granted 6 months to execute this theme; Goya failed again. On July 22 he entered a competition to sketch another complicated historical scene and lost for the third time.

Early Works

Little is known of Goya's subsequent activities until April 1771, when he was in Rome. Two small paintings, both dated 1771 and one signed "Goya," were recently discovered: *Sacrifice to Pan* and *Sacrifice to Vesta*. The monumental figures are classical but executed with sketchy brushstrokes and bathed in theatrical lighting. From Rome he sent to the Academy of Parma for an open competition another painting, *Hannibal in the Alps Contemplating the Italian Lands,* and signed himself as a pupil of Francisco Bayeu in his accompanying letter. Although he was not the winner, he did receive six of the votes and laudatory mention. Immediately after he had received this news, Goya departed for Saragossa.

The aforementioned works, and a handful more, are all that is known of Goya's art between 1766 and 1771. Sánchez Cantón (1964) pointed out that there are no concrete incidents to document the usual explanation, adduced from his known temperament, that he was otherwise occupied in womanizing, bullfighting, and brawling.

In Saragossa, Goya received important commissions, which he executed with success. On July 25, 1775, he married Josefa Bayeu, Francisco's sister. Bayeu, who was a director of the San Fernando Academy, used his influence to help his brother-in-law. Goya was commissioned to paint cartoons of contemporary customs and holiday activities for the Royal Tapestry Factory of Santa Barbara. This work, well suited to his nature, lasted from 1774 to 1792. He completed 54 cartoons in a rococo style that mingled influences from Michel Ange Houasse, Louis Michel Van Loo, Giovanni Battista Tiepolo, and Anton Raphael Mengs.

Following an illness in 1778, Goya passed his convalescence executing his first series of engravings from 16 paintings by Diego Velázquez. Goya began to enjoy signs of recognition: he was praised by Mengs, named as a court painter by Charles III in 1779, and elected to membership in San Fernando Academy after he presented a small, classical painting, the *Crucified Christ,* in 1780. On the crest of this wave of approval, a quarrel with his important brother-in-law had serious consequences upon his career: in 1780 he was commissioned to paint a dome and its pendentives for the Cathedral of El Pilar in Saragossa. Bayeu suggested certain corrections in the domical composition, which Goya rejected. Then the council of the Cathedral took objection to certain nudities in his preparatory sketches for the pendentives and ordered him to submit his designs to Bayeu for correction and final approval. Goya accepted this condition, but afterward he declared he would "take it to court first." Later he wrote to a friend that, just to think about the incident, "I burn alive." This affair seems to have caused a hiatus (1780-1786) in his cartoons for the royal factory.

The Portraits

The King commissioned Goya in 1780 to paint an altarpiece for the church of S. Francisco el Grande, Madrid; this work, the *Preaching of St. Bernardino,* was completed in 1784. No works by Goya are known for the year 1782 and only portraits for 1783, among which is one of the Count of Floridablanca, First Secretary of State. Other portraits of this period include those of the members of the family of the infante Don Luis (1783-1784) and the brilliant portrait of the Duke of Osuna (1785).

The artist was back in favor sometime before May 11, 1785, when he was appointed lieutenant director of painting (under Bayeu) in the Academy of San Fernando. The following year he was again working on the tapestry cartoons, and in June he was named painter to the king. Bayeu, clearly reconciled, sat for his portrait in 1786. Goya also executed many portraits of the royal family and members of the nobility, including the very appealing picture of the little Manuel Osorio de Zuñiga (1788).

In 1792 a committee was appointed to reform the academic methods of teaching at the Academy, and the minutes read in part: "Señor Goya openly declared himself in favor of freedom in the mode of teaching and in stylistic practices, saying that all servile submission of a children's school should be excluded, as well as mechanical precepts, monthly awards, tuition aids, and other trivialities that feminize and vilify painting. Nor should time be predetermined to study geometry or perspective to conquer difficulties in sketching."

Goya fell gravely ill in Seville at the end of 1792. He was left totally deaf and underwent a personality change from extrovert to introvert with an intense interest in evil spirits, a temporary avoidance of large canvases, and a preference for sketches in preparation for prints. He was back at work in Madrid by July 1793, and that year he produced a series of panels which he presented to the Academy of San Fernando. They include a scene in a madhouse, a bullfight, and an Inquisition scene.

Duchess of Alba

Goya received a commission from the noble house of Alba in 1795. Since he moved in aristocratic circles, it is clear that he must have known the duchess for some time before this. At any rate, after the duke's death in July 1796, she retired to her villa in Sanlucar, and Goya was one of her guests. Upon his return to Madrid in 1797, he painted the duchess in black but with a wide colored belt (therefore not a mourning garment), wearing two rings, one imprinted "Alba" and the other "Goya." He signed the work "Goya, always."

Whatever their relationship was, it is clear that Goya had high hopes. It is also true that in the spring following the duke's death the duchess's servants were gossiping in correspondence about her possible remarriage. Nevertheless, Señora Goya was still living, and Goya could not be the unnamed swain. In any event, the duchess never did remarry. At best, Goya's painting was a brazen flaunting of illicit hopes; at worst, a vulgar display of kiss-and-tell.

Goya's first great series of etchings, *Los caprichos* (1796-1798), were based on drawings from his *Madrid Sketchbook.* They include scenes of witchcraft, popular traditions, bullfights, and society balls. In the *Caprichos* Goya mercilessly and vindictively lampooned the duchess, depicting her in immodest postures; representing her as "a stylish fool" and adding, "There are heads so swollen with inflammable gas that they can fly without being helped by a balloon or by witches;" and likening her to a two-headed, butterfly brain of a "lie and inconstancy." The duchess died in 1802, following a long illness. Goya painted the *Nude Maja* and the *Clothed Maja* later (usually dated between 1805 and 1807). The heads in both appear to float, neckless, above the shoulders.

Inquisition and the Peninsular War

By the first years of the 19th century Goya was a wealthy man able to purchase an impressive home in 1803 and marry his son to an heiress in 1805. Simultaneously he was attracting the attention of the Holy Office of the Inquisition owing to the anticlerical satire in the *Caprichos* as well as his salacious subject matter. He donated all the *Caprichos* plates and the 240 unsold sets of the edition to the King under the pretext of seeking a pension for his son to travel; once the donation was accepted, the Holy Office perforce withdrew. The inquisitors did not forget, however; they investigated him again in 1814 concerning the nude and dressed *Majas.* Incomplete documentation leaves this incident obscure.

During the Napoleonic usurpation of the Spanish throne and the consequent War of Independence (1808-1813) Goya had an enigmatic record. With 3,000 other heads of families in Madrid on Dec. 10, 1808, he swore "love and fidelity" to the invader. In 1810 he attended the Academy to greet its new protector appointed by Joseph Bonaparte, but that same year he began work on his series of 80 etchings, *Los desastres de la guerra* (*The Disasters of War*), which, in many cases, is a specific condemnation of the Napoleonic war, although the expressionistic rendering makes the series a universal protest against the horrors of war. He finished the *Desastres* in 1814, the same year he painted the *Executions of May 3, 1808,* a grim depiction of a brutal massacre.

Goya applauded, understandably, the French suppression of the Inquisition and the secularization of religious orders. Yet in the joint will he made with his wife in 1811, he requested that he be buried in the Franciscan habit and have Masses offered and prayers said for his soul, and he made grants to holy places. His wife died in 1812, the year in which Goya painted the *Assumption of the Virgin* for the parish church of Chinchón, where his brother, Camilo, was the priest.

Goya executed two more series of etchings. *Los proverbios* (1813-1815; 1817-1818), or *Disparates,* as he himself called the series, are monstrous in mood and subject. The *Tauromachia* (1815-1816) is a series devoted to the art of bullfighting.

Last Years

In 1819 Goya purchased a villa, La Quinta del Sordo (Villa of the Deaf Man), at a time when his son and daughter-in-law were estranged from him, perhaps owing to another affair. His housekeeper was Leocadia Zorrilla de Weiss, a distant relative who was separated from her German husband, by whom she had had a son and daughter. Goya was so fond of the latter, Rosario, born in 1814, that some believe he was her father. Goya frescoed two rooms of the villa with his "black paintings." These profoundly moving works are a strange mixture of the horrendous (*Saturn Devouring His Son*), the diabolic (*Witches' Sabbath*), the salacious (*The Jesters*), the devout (*Pilgrimage of San Isidro*), and the ordinary (*Portrait of Leocadia Zorrilla,* previously called *Una manola*). These subjects and the others in the series make an ensemble that is as puzzling to interpret psychologically as it is emotionally overpowering.

In 1823 political events greatly affected Goya's life: Fernando VII, discontented with the constitution that had been forced upon him, left his palace in Madrid and went to Seville. Two months later the Duke of Angoulême with "one hundred thousand sons of St. Louis" invaded Spain to help Fernando VII. Goya, a liberal, immediately turned over the title to his villa to his grandson Mariano and took refuge in a friend's house. The following year Goya sought permission to spend 6 months enjoying the waters of Plombières "to mitigate the sickness and attacks that molested him in his advanced age." All this time Goya was receiving his royal salaries (and continued to do so up to his death) even though he had ceased to create works as First Court Painter or to teach in the Academy of San Fernando.

When the King granted his request, Goya immediately went to Bordeaux with Leocadia and her children. A friend described Goya's arrival: "deaf, sluggish and weak, without one word of French yet so happy and so desirous to see the world." He went back to Spain in 1825 to ask to be retired and was granted permission to return to France "with all the salary." His paintings in Bordeaux, especially the *Milkmaid of Bordeaux,* indicate a release from his dark emotions. He died of a stroke on April 15, 1828, in Bordeaux.

Further Reading

There are many good books on Goya and his art. In English, José López-Rey, *Goya's Caprichos* (2 vols., 1953), provides an excellent understanding of Goya's tormented genius. A sensitive insight is given by André Malraux, *Saturn: An Essay on Goya* (1950; trans. 1957). See also Charles Poore, *Goya* (1938); Francis Donald Klingender, *Goya in the Democratic Tradition* (1948); Pierre Gassier, *Goya: A Biographical and Critical Study* (trans. 1955); Royal Academy of Arts, London, *Goya and His Times* (1963); Francisco Javier Sánchez Cantón, *The Life and Works of Goya* (trans. 1964); and Tomás Harris, *Goya: Engravings and Lithographs* (2 vols., 1964). □

Jan van Goyen

The Dutch painter Jan van Goyen (1596-1656) was a leader in the progressive landscape style of the 1630s and 1640s, which achieved a new freedom from traditional formulas.

Jan van Goyen was born in Leiden on Jan. 13, 1596. Apprenticed from the age of 10, he had several masters. About 1617 he went to Haarlem to study with Esaias van de Velde, an important innovator in the Haarlem movement of realistic landscape painting. Van Goyen's works between 1621 and 1625 are sometimes hard to distinguish from those of his teacher. They are colorful, detailed views of villages and roads, usually busy with people, as in *Winter* (1621).

It was Van Goyen's usual practice to sign or monogram and date his paintings. He traveled extensively through the Netherlands and beyond, recording his impressions in sketchbooks, occasionally with dates and often depicting recognizable scenes. Thus the chronology of his development is clear. His paintings of the late 1620s show a steady advance from the strong colors and scattered organization of his early works toward tonality and greater simplicity and unity of composition. By 1630 he was painting monochromes in golden brown or pale green; he played a leading part in the tonal phase of Dutch landscape painting.

In 1631 Van Goyen settled in The Hague, where he became a citizen in 1634. The simplicity, airiness, and unification of his compositions continued to increase in his abundant production of dune landscapes, river views, seascapes, town views, and winter landscapes. The *River View* (1636) displays a river so open and extensive as to suggest the sea, with reflections that prolong the vast and luminous sky. In its monumentalization of humble structures and its composition built on a firm scaffolding of horizontal and vertical forces, it forecast at this early date developments that dominated landscape painting in the 1650s and later.

In the *Village and Dunes* (1647) the traditional double-diagonal composition still exists, but it is dominated by horizontal and vertical accents. Stronger contrasts of light and dark replace the earlier tonality. In the last year of his life Van Goyen produced an eloquent new style, in which powerful forms stand out against the radiant sky and water in an exquisitely balanced composition (*Evening Calm;* 1656).

The commission in 1651 to paint a panoramic view of The Hague for the Burgomaster's Room shows the high regard in which Van Goyen was held. He was enormously productive; well over 1,000 of his paintings still exist, and almost as many drawings. Yet he died insolvent, perhaps because of losses in his various business ventures, and soon after his death on April 27, 1656, in The Hague, he was virtually forgotten. Interest revived in 1875, and from then on his popularity continued to increase, for the freedom and directness of his style and the liveliness of his brushstroke appeal to the modern eye, as do the intimacy and spontaneity of his drawings.

Further Reading

Hans-Ulrich Beck, *Jan van Goyen* (2 vols., 1970), is a *catalogue raisonné* in German of nearly 1,300 paintings and more than 1,000 drawings. Van Goyen is discussed in Wolfgang Stechow, *Dutch Landscape Painting of the Seventeenth Century* (1966). ☐

Tiberius and Gaius Sempronius Gracchus

Tiberius Sempronius (ca. 163-133 B.C.) and Gaius Sempronius (ca. 154-121 B.C.) Gracchus, commonly known as the Gracchi, were Roman political reformers who, through their use of the plebeian tribunate, set Roman politics on a course that ended in the collapse of the republic.

Sons of Tiberius Sempronius Gracchus, twice consul and censor, and Cornelia, daughter of Scipio Africanus, the conqueror of Hannibal, the Gracchus brothers belonged to one of the most distinguished families in Rome with wide connections among the nobility. But their liberalism and overzealous desire to correct existing abuses brought them into collision with senatorial conservatives who killed them.

Tiberius Sempronius Gracchus

Tiberius began his political career in 147/146 B.C. on the staff of his brother-in-law Scipio Aemilianus at Carthage, where he was the first Roman soldier over the wall. In Spain, as quaestor to the consul C. Hostilius Mancinus in 137 B.C., Tiberius saved a Roman army of 20,000 men from destruction at the hands of the Celtiberi because of the trust of the Spaniards in his good offices.

Tiberius ran for the tribunate of 133 B.C. as the representative of a large liberal faction in the Senate which included Q. Mucius Scaevola, consul in 133 B.C.; Appius Claudius Pulcher, the father-in-law of Tiberius and ranking senator; and P. Licinius Crassus, father-in-law of Gaius and one of the leading lawyers of the day. This group helped Tiberius draw up his land reform bill, the purpose of which was to distribute land held by the state to city and rural poor while recognizing the rights of existing renters.

Tiberius's general aim was to increase the number of small farmers in Italy, who alone were liable for conscription into the legions. While the measure was eminently fair, Tiberius angered traditionalists by taking his bill directly to the people without consulting the Senate. He then violated constitutional practice by impeaching Marcus Octavius, a conservative tribune who had vetoed the bill, on the grounds that a tribune who thwarted the will of the people was no true tribune. After passage of the bill he further outraged the Senate by threatening to appropriate for the purpose of land settlement revenues from the province of Asia. He thus tread on senatorial prerogatives in provincial affairs. When, again contrary to accepted practices, he ran for a second term as tribune, his opponents took direct action against him. Led by his cousin Scipio Nasica, they killed Tiberius and some 300 followers in bloody riots over the election.

Gaius Sempronius Gracchus

Plutarch says that while Tiberius had a mild and temperate disposition Gaius was impulsive and volatile. Gaius was also an electrifying orator and a more astute politician than his brother.

Gaius served with Scipio Aemilianus at Numantia in Spain. He returned from there in 133 B.C. to become, along with his brother and Appius Claudius, one of the land commissioners under Tiberius's bill. In 126 B.C., while still commissioner, he went to Sardinia as quaestor to the consul L. Aurelius Orestes. There, because of his influence with the

Sardinians, Gaius persuaded them to help relieve the plight of the Roman soldiers stationed on the island.

Gaius left Sardinia in 124 B.C. to run for the tribunate of 123 B.C. with a full program of reform in mind and broad support among the people and liberal senators. But so strong was conservative opposition to him that he came in only fourth at the polls. As tribune, he introduced some 15 reform measures.

Gaius benefited the people and tied them to him politically by passing a stronger land bill, regulating the grain supply to the city of Rome, undertaking ambitious road-building and other public-works projects, and establishing colonies in Italy and abroad. He drove a wedge between the *equites* (equestrians) and the Senate by transferring the juries in extortion cases to the *equites* and auctioning off the tax contract for Asia in Rome. As a result, he stood at the head of the polls when he ran for a second tribunate for 122 B.C.

When Gaius went to Africa at the beginning of 122 B.C. to organize his new colony on the site of Carthage, the opposition rallied against him. A conservative tribune, M. Livius Drusus, outbid Gaius among the city poor by proposing 12 new colonies in Italy rather than abroad and split Gaius's Italian and Latin supporters by offering special benefits to the Latins. Returning from Africa, Gaius rashly insisted on introducing his citizenship bill. But the Senate had his Italian supporters expelled from the city, and the mounting opposition of the plebeians led to its defeat. In consequence Gaius also failed in his bid for a third tribunate.

Opposition continued even after Gaius left public office. When riots broke out in 121 B.C. over repeal of the bill to found the colony at Carthage, the Senate gave emergency powers to the consul Lucius Opimius to deal with the situation. In the armed action which followed, Gaius committed suicide rather than fight, but Marcus Fulvius Flaccus, his colleague in the tribunate and violent proponent of Italian citizenship, together with 3,000 of his followers, was killed.

Gaius Gracchus showed how a tribune with the backing of the city poor and the equestrians could maneuver successfully against the senatorial leadership. But, in defending its position, the Senate taught popular leaders a lesson in violence which eventually undid the republic.

Further Reading

The principal ancient sources for the Gracchus brothers are Appian and Plutarch. D. C. Earl, *Tiberius Gracchus: A Study in Politics* (1963), is a penetrating analysis of the political issues at stake in Tiberius's tribunate. There is no separate study of Gaius in English. Scholarly and detailed, although an inadequate portrayal of the brothers' character, is Henry Charles Boren, *The Gracchi* (1969). See also J. B. Bury and others, eds., *The Cambridge Ancient History* (12 vols., 1923-1939), and Howard H. Scullard, *From the Gracchi to Nero: A History of Rome from 133 B.C. to A.D. 68* (1959; 2d ed. 1963). □

William Russell Grace

William Russell Grace (1832-1904), Irish-born American entrepreneur and politician, dominated commerce between Peru and the United States and promoted industrial and agricultural development in South America.

William R. Grace was born in Queenstown, Ireland, on May 10, 1832. Desiring adventure and travel, he went to sea at the age of 16 but returned 2 years later to work in his father's ship chandlery business. In 1846, at the height of the potato famine in Ireland, he joined a group emigrating to Peru. Shortly after arriving there, the group disbanded, and Grace went to work as a clerk in a ship chandlery firm in the port city of Callao. At that time guano, a natural fertilizer, was Peru's principal export to the United States and Europe. Aware of the opportunities for trade in this, Grace provided supplies for the guano fleets. By 1852, as a partner in a trading firm, he was traveling extensively in Peru, exploring opportunities for commercial and industrial development and becoming the principal agent for Peru's commercial relations with Europe and the United States.

Forced to leave Peru for reasons of health, Grace settled in New York in 1865. A wealthy man by now, he founded the trading firm of W. R. Grace and Company, designed primarily to act as commercial correspondent for his Peruvian company. He also established other trading partnerships in London and San Francisco.

Slowly acquiring a fleet of their own, the Grace companies built up a triangular trade between Europe, the United States, and Peru and became the principal importers of Peruvian goods in the Northern Hemisphere. Grace also secured developmental capital for Peru and was responsible for building that nation's railroads and equipping its army. So extensive did his interests become that in 1890 a Grace firm assumed the interest payments on Peru's defaulted foreign debt in return for control over much of the nation's transportation and industrial enterprises.

Although he had no experience in politics, Grace was elected mayor of New York in 1880, largely because of a widely publicized gift of $40,000 worth of supplies for famine-struck Ireland. Reelected in 1884, he headed reform administrations which cleaned up much of the city's chronic political corruption.

Constantly expanding his business interests, Grace played prominent roles in scores of commercial, industrial, and financial enterprises in the United States and South America. A devout Catholic, and the first Catholic to be elected mayor of New York City, Grace gave much time, energy, and money to Catholic philanthropies. He died in New York City on March 21, 1904.

Further Reading

Grace's grandson, Joseph P. Grace, presents the history of the Grace enterprises as well as a biographical sketch in *W. R. Grace and the Enterprises He Created* (1953).

Additional Sources

James, Marquis, *Merchant adventurer: the story of W.R. Grace,* Wilmington, Del.: SR Books, 1993. □

Baltasar Jerónimo Gracián y Morales

Baltasar Jerónimo Gracián y Morales (1601-1658), Spanish humorist, satirist, baroque stylist, and philosophical novelist, is classed with the greatest prose masters of Spain's Golden Age.

Born into a religious family in Calatayud, Aragon, son of a doctor, Baltasar Gracián was sent at 12 to study in the medieval atmosphere of Toledo. At 18 he entered the Society of Jesus and was sent to Saragossa and later to Valencia to study theology. Soon after his ordination as a Jesuit in 1635, he met Juan de Lastanosa, who provided Gracián and several of his creative contemporaries a home and financial support affording unlimited leisure for peripatetic conversation and meditation, as well as a means to publication.

After holding several pastorates, Gracián served as field chaplain to the Spanish army under Gen. Pablo Parada.

Later, while professor of religion at Saragossa, he published without the permission of his order a philosophical novel, *El criticón,* for whose cynical and pessimistic tone he received a reprimand from Goswin Nickel, the superior of the Jesuits. When Gracián published two other books under pseudonyms, Nickel ordered an official investigation of his defiance of Jesuit authority. As a result, Gracián was watched, his quarters were searched regularly, and no ink, pen, or paper was permitted him. Under this humiliation, Gracián petitioned for permission to resign from the order, a petition not only denied but punished by denying him his pulpit. Silenced, disgraced, and embittered, Gracián withdrew in poor health to Tarazona, where he died on Dec. 6, 1658.

Gracián wrote five works important in the history of Spanish thought, of which *El héroe* (1637; *The Hero*), *El discreto* (1646; *The Discreet Person*), and *El criticón* (1651-1657; *The Critic*) stand out. In *The Hero* Gracián characterized qualities essential to leadership: wit, charm, discretion, and especial vigilance against fools. A leader, he says, must close his ears to the common people or lose them, for they respect not the leader whose ways they believe they fathom. "Let no one say *Vox populi, vox dei;* rather it is the voice of ignorance." "Use a little mystery in everything," counsels Gracián. Elsewhere he says, "Every success is due three-quarters to luck, one-fifth to sweat, only one-twentieth to ability." Gracián's hero is a unique person who succeeds by integrity, discretion, linguistic gifts, and above all by shrewd political achievements. He is the product of a mind steeped in the classic Italian publications on political philosophy. In *The Discreet Person* Gracián presents his friend and patron, Lastanosa, as a model leader of men.

Gracián's most ambitious book, *The Critic,* is a kind of Spanish *Pilgrim's Progress* in that both are allegorical stories with a moral purpose. The work's lengthy and complex plot provides a broad and pessimistic allegorical vision of human life. The story revolves around two characters, Andrenio and Critilo, symbols of nature and civilization. They meet when the learned Critilo is shipwrecked on Saint Elena, where he finds Andrenio, a man untouched by civilization, living in a cave, ignorant of his parentage and of any language. Critilo adopts Andrenio and teaches him to talk. After they are rescued from the island and taken to Spain, they remain friends and share many adventures. When Andrenio is victimized by the deceitful Falsirena in Madrid, Critilo looses a diatribe against all mankind, concluding that "Men are bad, women worse."

As Gracián mixes reality with allegory, the two travel in Spain, France, Germany, and Italy. In the principal square of an imaginary city, they find not men but lions, tigers, dragons, wolves, bulls, and panthers. In this land the rich are regaled with presents while the poor are neglected and the wise held in contempt. The two pilgrims see a judge sentence a mosquito to be hanged and quartered, while exonerating a criminal elephant. They go from the spring of youth, through the middle age of maturity, into old age, traveling via fanciful courts and palaces, plazas of illusion, squares of hypocrisy, and mansions of integrity, until finally they glimpse the wheel of time and death and the island of immortality, where they hope to find rest from their journeying. Rather than a novel in the 20th-century sense, *The Critic* is a vehicle employed by one of the most brilliant minds of 17th-century Spain to interpret the universe as he observed it. This canny and pessimistic Jesuit interpreted life in the light of one of his maxims, "Things pass for what they seem, not for what they are."

Gracián's reputation as a baroque writer arises mainly from his *Agudeza y arte de ingenio* (*Mental Alertness and Ingenuity as an Art*), in which he characteristically followed such baroque form patterns as use of neologisms, antitheses, parallelisms, inversions, epithets, obscure metaphors, and ellipses. In order to collect and anthologize his innermost thoughts, Gracián thoroughly combed his own works published before 1647 to compile *Oráculo manual y arte de prudencia* (*The Art of Worldly Wisdom*). This book is one of the great modern collections of maxims.

Further Reading

The lengthiest recent study in English of Gracián is L. B. Walton's introduction to his translation of Gracian's *The Oracle: A Manual of the Art of Discretion* (1953). An older study in English is the introduction of Joseph Jacobs in his translation of the same work, entitled *The Art of Worldly Wisdom* (1892; repr. 1943). Recommended for detailed analyses in English of Gracián's works is Aubrey F. G. Bell, *Baltasar Gracián* (1921). A more recent work is Monroe Z. Hafter, *Gracián and Perfection: Spanish Moralists of the Seventeenth Century* (1966). General historical background is in John Crow, *Spain: The Root and the Flower* (1963). □

Henry Woodfin Grady

Henry Woodfin Grady (1850-1889) was the foremost American journalist of the "New South"—a term he invented—and a renowned orator.

A descendant of old native stock, Henry W. Grady was born May 24, 1850, in Athens, Ga. His father was killed during the Civil War. In 1868 Grady received a bachelor's degree from the University of Georgia. Pursuing postgraduate studies at the University of Virginia, he became interested in journalism. His first venture into newspaper work was a series of articles for the *Atlanta Constitution* on the resources and future possibilities of his war-ravaged state.

In the early 1870s, having married into a cotton goods-manufacturing family, Grady settled in Rome, Ga. Three attempts to establish his own newspaper failed within 5 months. In 1876 the dejected young man went to New York City in quest of work. A piece he wrote for the *New York Herald* was so well received that he returned to Georgia as the paper's special correspondent. Four years later, with a $20,000 loan from Cyrus W. Field, Grady purchased a quarter interest in the *Atlanta Constitution* and became its editor.

Grady's reputation soared, as did the circulation of the *Constitution,* which in 8 years became the most popular weekly in the nation. Grady did not hesitate to attack graft

and corruption in Georgia. Yet he became more famous for his economic and political crusades. In brilliant oratory he preached the virtues of a "New South" and continually urged embittered Southerners to seek reconciliation with the North.

Grady launched a one-man drive for new industry in his region. A contemporary wrote that he did not "tamely promote enterprise and encourage industry; he vehemently fomented enterprise and provoked industry until they stalked through the land like armed conquerors." The South's slow but steady recovery from the destruction of the Civil War is a tribute in no small part to Grady's efforts.

Grady also launched a misguided political dream: to unite all Southern whites into one party and then amalgamate it with the financial and industrial combine of the East—with Atlanta as the base of operations. Though he was frequently mentioned as a prospect for the U.S. Senate, Grady avoided political office.

On Dec. 23, 1889, Grady died of pneumonia. A number of buildings and monuments in Atlanta commemorate his service to his city, his state, and the South he loved. In his own day Grady was considered "a genius born for an era."

Further Reading

A number of good studies of Grady are available. The largest collection of his own utterances is Joel Chandler Harris, ed., *Life of Henry W. Grady: Including His Writings and Speeches* (1890). The first full-scale biography is F. H. Richardson's eulogistic work, *A Fruitful Life: The Career, Character and Services of Henry Woodfin Grady* (1890). A later study is

Raymond B. Nixon, *Henry W. Grady, Spokesman of the New South* (1943).

Additional Sources

Davis, Harold E., *Henry Grady's New South: Atlanta, a brave and beautiful city,* Tuscaloosa: University of Alabama Press, 1990. □

Heinrich Hirsch Graetz

The German historian and biblical exegete Heinrich Hirsch Graetz (1817-1891) wrote one of the great monuments of the Jewish Enlightenment, "History of the Jews."

Heinrich Graetz was born in the village of Xions in the Prussian province of Posen on Oct. 31, 1817. The Jewish communities of Germany at this time were seething with cultural conflicts and religious disputes. The emancipation of the Jews at the end of the 18th century, the influence of the Enlightenment on such figures as Moses Mendelssohn, and the establishment of public schools had begun to crack the ghetto walls. For some these movements were the forces of progress, for others they were a fearful threat to religious practice and traditional custom. These conflicts left their mark on Graetz's education and his career.

At Wollstein, where he was sent to study after his confirmation, Graetz followed the traditional Talmudic training. At the same time he taught himself Latin and French and read Euclid, the French and Latin classics, Gotthold Ephraim Lessing, Mendelssohn, J. C. F. von Schiller, and Heinrich Heine. His religious faith was soon shaken. Then one day he read a small book entitled *Nineteen Letters,* by Rabbi Hirsch of Oldenburg, an eloquent and scholarly defense of orthodoxy. In 1837 he resolved to go to Oldenburg to study with the author. Here he completed his Talmudic education.

In 1842 Graetz entered the University of Breslau, from which he received a doctoral degree in 1845. It was no help, however, in finding a position. Graetz was temperamentally ill-fitted for the rabbinate, and his theological position by now pleased neither the traditionalists nor the innovators. Finally, in 1853, he was named to the faculty of a newly founded rabbinical seminary at Breslau.

In the same year appeared the first volume of Graetz's *History of the Jews.* Though not the first attempt to write such a work, it was, as he said, the first "Jewish history of the Jews." When completed in 1876, it ran to 11 volumes. The theme of the work was "how the family of a petty sheik became the nucleus of a people; how this people was humiliated to the condition of a horde; how this horde was trained to become a nation of God through the law of self-sanctification and self-control; and how these teachings became breathed into it as its soul." Opposing the Christian view that Judaism completed its historic mission with the coming of Christ, Graetz insisted on the continuing vitality of the Jewish tradition through its many declines and revivals. Graetz wrote without the aid of detailed monographic studies and therefore often called upon his fantasy to fill in gaps of ignorance. He did not hesitate to voice his strong and sometimes unfavorable opinions of men and ideas. The work remains a vivid narrative and a classic in its field.

After completing the *History,* Graetz turned to biblical exegesis, publishing works on the Psalms, Jeremiah, and Proverbs. He projected a critical edition of the Bible but died before he could complete it, on Sept. 7, 1891.

Further Reading

A sympathetic "Memoir" by his student Philip Bloch appears in the translation of Graetz's *History of the Jews* (6 vols., 1891-1898). Graetz is discussed in Salo W. Baron, *History and Jewish Historians: Essays and Addresses* (1964). □

Katharine Meyer Graham

The renown publisher Katharine Meyer Graham (born 1917) took over management of *The Washington Post* after the death of her husband. She guided it to national prominence and acclaim while expanding her publishing empire.

Katharine Meyer Graham was born in New York City on June 16, 1917, the fourth of five children born to Eugene Meyer, a banker, and Agnes Elizabeth (Ernst) Meyer, an author and philanthropist. In 1933, when Katharine was still a student at the Madeira School in Greenway, Virginia, her father bought the moribund *Washington Post* for $875,000. Already retired, Meyer purchased the paper because he had grown restless and wanted a voice in the nation's affairs. His hobby became the capital's most influential paper.

From an early age Katharine Meyer showed an interest in publishing. At the Madeira School she worked on the student newspaper. In 1935 she entered Vassar College, but the following year transferred to the University of Chicago, which she regarded as a more stimulating campus. During her summer vacations she worked on *The Washington Post.* After her graduation with a B.A. degree in 1938 she went to California to take a job as a waterfront reporter for the *San Francisco News.* She returned to Washington a year later and joined the editorial staff of the *Post,* where she also worked in the circulation department.

On June 5, 1940, she married Philip L. Graham, a Harvard Law School graduate and clerk for Supreme Court Justice Felix Frankfurter. Her husband entered the Army in World War II, and she gave up reporting to move with him from base to base. When he was sent overseas to the Pacific Theater, Katharine returned to her job at the *Post.* After his discharge in 1945, Eugene Meyer persuaded Philip Graham to join *The Washington Post* as associate publisher. Meyer, who had a warm relationship with his son-in-law, eventu-

ally turned the business over to him, selling all the voting stock in the company to the Grahams for $1 in 1948. Philip Graham helped his father-in-law to build the business, acquiring the *Post's* competitor, the *Washington Times Herald,* in 1954 and in 1961 purchasing *Newsweek* magazine for a sum estimated to be between eight and 15 million dollars. He also expanded the radio and television operations of the company and in 1962 helped to establish an international news service.

In 1963 Philip Graham shot himself to death. Katharine Graham took over the presidency of the company. A prominent Washington matron who had devoted her time to the raising of her daughter and three sons, she had never lost her interest in the affairs of the family business. She studied the operations, asked questions, consulted with such old friends as James Reston and Walter Lippmann, and made the key decisions which helped to bring in skilled journalists to improve the quality of the paper. She selected Benjamin C. Bradlee, the Washington bureau chief for *Newsweek,* as managing editor in 1965.

Graham gave Bradlee, who later became executive editor, a free hand and backed him during the 1970s when the Post began making news as well as reporting it. In June of 1971 the *Post,* along with the *New York Times,* became embroiled with the government over their right to publish excerpts from a classified Pentagon study of U.S. military involvement in Vietnam compiled during President Lyndon Johnson's administration. A court order to restrain the publication of the documents led to an appeal to the U.S. Supreme Court and, in a decision judged a major victory for

freedom of the press, the Court upheld the papers' right to publish the "Pentagon Papers."

Further controversy erupted when the investigative reporting team of Bob Woodward and Carl Bernstein began to probe the break-in at the Democratic National Headquarters at the Watergate apartment complex in June of 1972. Woodward's and Bernstein's articles in the *Post* linked the break-in to the larger pattern of illegal activities that ultimately led to the indictment of over 40 members of the Nixon administration and to the resignation of President Richard Nixon in August of 1974.

Graham, generally conceded to be the most powerful woman in publishing, held the title of publisher at *The Washington Post* starting in 1969. As chairman and principal owner of the Washington Post Company, she controlled the fifth largest publishing empire in the nation. In the period 1975 to 1985 profits grew better than 20 percent annually.

In 1979 Graham turned the title of publisher over to her son Donald (born 1945). But she remained active in all areas of the business, from advising on editorial policy to devising strategies for diversifying the company's holdings, which included, in addition to the *Post* and *Newsweek,* the Trenton *Times,* four television stations, and 49 percent interest in a paper company. In Washington she was a formidible presence. Heads of state, politicians, and leaders in journalism and the arts gathered at her Georgetown home and weekends at her farm in northern Virginia.

Under Graham's leadership, *The Washington Post* grew in influence and stature until by common consent it was judged one of the two best newspapers in the country. It was read and consulted by presidents and prime ministers in this country and abroad and exerted a powerful influence on political life. At the same time, the *Post,* which boasts a circulation of 725,000, served as a hometown paper for a general audience who enjoyed the features, cartoons, and advice columns.

Katharine Graham was described as a "working publisher." Determined to preserve the family character of the business, she took up the reins after the death of her husband and worked hard not only to build but to improve her publishing empire. A forceful and courageous publisher, she knew when to rely on the expertise of professionals and allowed her editors maximum responsibility, at the same time strengthening her publications by her willingness to spend to attract top talent in journalism and management.

Further Reading

Arthur Schlesinger Jr.'s article in *Vogue* (January 1, 1967) provides interesting insights into Katharine Meyer Graham's background and career. Martin Mayer in "Lady as Publisher," *Harper's* (December 1968), interviewed Graham. For articles dealing with her business empire, see *Time* (February 7, 1977) and *Forbes* (April 19, 1984). She was listed in *Who's Who in America* (43rd edition, 1984-1985) and *The World Who's Who of Women* (4th edition). Carl Bernstein and Bob Woodward in *All the President's Men* (1974) deal with *The Washington Post's* investigation of Watergate. For an unauthorized biography, see Deborah Davis, *Katharine the Great: Katharine Graham and the Washington Post* (1979) or Carol

Felsenthal, *Power, Privilege, and the Post: The Katherine Graham Story* (1993). In 1997, Katherine Meyer Graham published her memoirs *Personal History* □

Martha Graham

Martha Graham (1894-1991), American dancer, choreographer, and teacher, was the world's leading exponent of modern dance.

Martha Graham was born in a suburb of Pittsburgh, PA, in May 1894. Her family moved to California when she was 10. Graham became interested in dance when she saw Ruth St. Denis perform in 1914. Overcoming parental restraint, Graham enrolled in the Denishawn Studio. This small, quiet, shy, thin, but perceptive and hardworking girl impressed the leader of the studio, Ted Shawn, and toured with his troupe in a production of *Xochitl,* based on an Aztec Indian legend. In 1923 she left this company to do 2 years of solo dancing for the Greenwich Village Follies.

In 1925 Graham became dance instructor at the Eastman School of Music and Theater in Rochester, N.Y. She began experimenting with modern dance forms. "I wanted to begin," she said, "not with characters or ideas but with movement. . . . I wanted significant movement. I did not want it to be beautiful or fluid. I wanted it to be fraught with inner meaning, with excitement and surge." She rejected the traditional steps and techniques of classical ballet, for she wanted the dancing body to be related to natural motion and to the music. She experimented with what the body could do based on its own structure, developing what was known as "percussive movements."

Graham's first dances were abstract and angular, almost "cubist" in execution. "Like the modern painters," she said, "we have stripped our medium of decorative unessentials." The dances were performed on a bare stage with only costumes and lights. The dancers' faces were taut, their hands stiff, and their costumes scanty. Later she added scenery and costumes for effect. The music was contemporary and usually composed especially for the dance. Whereas Isadora Duncan, the first modern dancer, had used music to inspire her works, Graham used music to help dramatize hers.

Martha Graham's process of creation usually began with what she called a "certain stirring." Inspiration might come from classical mythology, the American past, biblical stories, historical figures, primitive rituals, contemporary social problems, Zen Buddhism, the writings of psychoanalyst Carl Jung, the poems of Emily Dickinson the flower paintings of Georgia O'Keeffe, or the puberty rites of Native Americans. After the initial inspiration she developed a dramatic situation or character to embody the emotion or idea. She then found music, or commissioned new music from her longtime collaborator Louis Horst, to sustain the inspiration while she created movements to express it.

The purpose of Graham's dance was to evoke a heightened awareness of life, to develop psychological insights about the nature of man. Dance was to her an "inner emotional experience." Her themes were often overtly psychological. Characters in her dance plays were divided into two complementary parts, each representing an aspect of the psyche. Her stage sets were filled with huge phallic symbols, as in *Phaedra,* a rite of sexual obsession.

Martha Graham introduced a number of other innovations to modern dance. She established the use of mobile scenery, symbolic props, and speech with dancing and was the first to integrate her group racially, using blacks and Asians in her regular company. She replaced the traditional ballet tunic or folk dress with either a straight, dark, long shirt or the common leotard. Using the stage, the floor, and props as part of the dance itself, in all she produced a whole new language of dance.

In 1926 Graham introduced this new language of dance in her first solo recital in New York. Her first large group piece, *Vision of the Apocalypse,* was performed in 1929. The most important early work was a revolutionary piece called *Heretic.*

Graham toured the United States for 4 years (1931-1935) in the production *Electra.* During this trip she became interested in the American Indians of the Southwest. One of the first products of this interest was *Primitive Mysteries.* Her increasing interest in the American past was seen in her dance on the American pioneer women, *Frontier* (1935), and culminated in her famous *Appalachian Spring* (1944), in which she recreated in dance what composer Aaron Copland had done in his music. Among her other accomplishments during the 1930s was her performance of the principal role in Igor Stravinsky's American premiere of *Rite of Spring* (1930). She was the first dancer to receive a Guggenheim fellowship (1932), and she danced for President Franklin Roosevelt at the White House in 1937.

Graham founded the Dance Repertory Theater in New York in 1930. She helped establish the Bennington School of Arts at Bennington College in Vermont, where her teaching made Bennington the mecca for avantgarde dance in America. With the later establishment of the Martha Graham School of Contemporary Dance in New York, she taught a large number of modern dancers who have spread her ideas, techniques, and style to the rest of the world.

Graham danced her last role in 1969, but she continued to choreograph. In 1976 she received the Presidential Medal of Freedom. A year before her death, in 1990, she choreographed *Maple Leaf Rag,* a show that featured music by Scott Joplin and costumes by Calvin Klein. Today, her name is synonymous with modern dance. She died April 1, 1991, known as one of the 20th century's revolutionary artists.

Further Reading

One biography is Agnes DeMille, *Martha: The Life and Work of Martha Graham* (1991). A biographical study is LeRoy Leatherman, *Martha Graham: Portrait of the Lady as an Artist* (1966). Merle Armitage, ed., *Martha Graham* (1966), is an anthology of articles discussing Miss Graham's contributions and significance to modern dance. See also Barbara Morgan, *Martha Graham: Sixteen Dances in Photographs* (1941). □

Sylvester Graham

Sylvester Graham (1794-1851), American reformer, was a temperance minister and an advocate of healthful living.

Sylvester Graham was born on July 5, 1794, in West Suffield, Conn. His father, a 72-year-old clergyman, died 2 years later. Graham was raised by relatives who gave little attention to his development, and he worked at scattered tasks until he was 19 years old, when he began to cultivate his mind. He became a teacher, but poor health forced him to reconsider his future. He determined to become a minister and entered Amherst College in 1823. There his histrionic manner was scorned by fellow students, and he withdrew from college.

In 1826 Graham married and 3 years later became a Presbyterian minister. He had joined the crusade against drink and in 1830 became an agent of the Pennsylvania Temperance Society. His ardor for the cause led him to study anatomy and to consider the effects of liquor and other substances on the human body. He branched out in his lectures, dealing not only with the evils of drink and gluttony but also with the need for hygienic care of the body. To Graham and his followers the issue was not only health but moral living. His *Lecture on Epidemic Diseases Generally and Particularly the Spasmodic Cholera* (1833) brought together some of his findings, which eventually led him to prescribe physical exercise, sensible clothing, continence, good sleeping habits, and vegetarianism.

Graham's lectures drew concerned audiences and created both friends and foes. His talks on chastity, though moral in tone and intention, shocked the delicate. His emphasis on a discriminatory diet offended traditions of heavy eating and meat consumption. His advocacy of homemade bread from unbolted wheat, with which his name was ultimately identified (Graham crackers), roused the ire of bakers. Graham's partisans kept Graham boardinghouses and issued *Graham's Journal of Health and Longevity* (1837-1839). They circulated such works as his *Treatise on Bread and Breadmaking* (1837) and *Lectures on the Science of Human Life* (1839).

Graham's vogue faded as suddenly as it had flourished, partly because his disciples divided into parts what he had seen as a grand design. His own increasing emphasis on scriptural authority for personal hygiene failed to attract wide interest. He planned four volumes on the subject but wrote only one before his death on Sept. 11, 1851. Friends completed *The Philosophy of Sacred History* in 1855.

Further Reading

A memoir of his life was included in Graham's *Lectures on the Science of Human Life* (repr. 1858). Information on him is in

Franklin B. Dexter, *Biographical Sketches of the Graduates of Yale College with Annals of the College History* (1885), and James H. Trumbull, ed., *The Memorial History of Hartford County, Connecticut, 1633-1884* (2 vols., 1886).

Additional Sources

Nissenbaum, Stephen, *Sex, diet, and debility in Jacksonian America: Sylvester Graham and health reform,* Chicago, Ill.: Dorsey Press, 1988, 1980. □

William Franklin Graham Jr.

The American evangelist and charismatic preacher Billy Graham (born 1918) became a leading spokesman for Fundamentalism when he initiated a series of tours of the United States and Europe that led to large-scale evangelism.

William Franklin Graham, Jr. was born November 7, 1918, on a dairy farm near Charlotte, N.C. which his paternal grandfather Crook Graham bought after serving in the Confederate army. Young Billy would read from his collection of history books. He also practiced baseball when finished with his chores, because and his ambition was to become a professional baseball player. It was changed into a commitment to an evangelical career by a religious conversion experience when he was 16. Graham was ordained a Southern Baptist minister in 1939. He was educated in conservative Christian colleges: Bob Jones University in Greenville, S.C., the Florida Bible Institute (now called Trinity College) near Tampa, and Wheaton College in Illinois where receiving a bachelor of arts degree in anthropology in 1943. On August 13 of that year he married Ruth McCue Bell, a fellow student and daughter of a medical missionary. Their first daughter, Virginia, was born two years later, followed by Anne in 1948, Ruth in 1950, and sons William in 1952 and Nelson in 1958. For many years the Graham family made its home in Montreat, N.C.

After a period as minister of the First Baptist Church in Western Springs, IL, Graham became a traveling "tent evangelist," the calling which in a few years brought him to national prominence.

Graham was first vice president of Youth for Christ International from 1945 to 1948. He served as president of Northwestern College in Minneapolis from 1947 to 1952. He met singer George Beverly Shea and song leader Cliff Barrows and the three formed a lasting partnership. The three began offering revival meetings in small churches and started developing a following. In 1949, Graham, Shea, and Barrows had a meeting in Los Angeles and rather than the usual crowd of 3,000 or so, more than 10,000 turned out to hear the backwoods preacher and his team. He was the founder and president of the Billy Graham Evangelistic Association and editor in chief of *Decision* magazine. The organization is run by a board of directors that pays Graham an annual salary equivalent to that of a community pastor.

The first year it amounted to $15,000. Today, the institute has a cash flow of more than $50 million a year. His radio program, "Hour of Decision," began in 1950, and he wrote a daily newspaper column. Graham's published writings include *Calling Youth to Christ* (1947), *Revival in Our Times* (1950), *America's Hour of Decision* (1951), *Korean Diary* (1953), *My Answer* (1960), and *World Aflame* (1965). Graham turns over all the royalties from his books and all his speaking fees.

Graham launched his worldwide ministry with his first overseas tour in 1954 to Great Britain. Crowds of more than two million people attended his rallies. He even met with Queen Elizabeth II. At a 16-week rally in New York City three years later, more than two million packed Madison Square Gardens to hear the young preacher. Graham has preached the Gospel to more people in live audiences than anyone else in history totaling more than 210 million people in more than 185 countries and territories. Since his crusades began his work has propelled him to more than 400 rallies in nearly every corner of the world. He conducts an average of six crusades a year in the United States and abroad. In the mid-1950s Graham took his crusade to India, Hong Kong, Japan, Korea, and the Philippines. He has also been to Rio de Janeiro, Nairobi, Seoul, Poland, Romania, and Slovakia, filling jam-packed churches and meeting with government and religious leaders wherever he travels.

Graham's Message

Graham's message has remained the same and is based on traditional Biblical study. It is simply this: "Choose Christ as I did. Mankind is sinful, but through Christ those sins are forgiven and people can live in peace." In other words, this is a message of love and hope. Graham has been friends with many world figures, especially the presidents starting with Harry Truman who sought advice from Graham and Richard Nixon was a frequent golf partner. On April 9, 1996, together with President William Clinton, he led 12,000 mourners in Oklahoma City to grieve for victims of the Federal Building bombing. Graham has been the chaplain at many Inaugural Ceremonies; in fact his eighth Inauguration invocation in January 1997 was inspired by our Founding Fathers, noting that "technology and social engineering had yet to solve the ancient problems of human greed and selfishness." Graham has maintained an untouchable integrity, unlike Jimmy Swaggart and Jim Bakker who were involved in sex and money scandals that ruined their careers.

Prodigal Son To Take Over

Graham has decided that when he retires or dies his son Franklin will take over his $88 million-a- year ministry. The younger Graham, who continually rebelled against his father as a teenager and was expelled from college, was a "heck-raiser" as a boy, has long since gone straight. He now runs two world relief organizations, and has done some preaching. It has been said that Franklin does not have the presence of his father and will not be able to replicate the senior Graham's impact on American Protestantism. Graham, in his seventies, shows no sign of slowing down regardless of his advancing illness, Parkinson's disease. It will eventually take away his ability to feed himself or even button his clothes. He walks with difficulty now and can write only his name, but he still has enough energy to work on his memoirs. Ruth, Graham's wife, "never slows down." Her presence and vitality have helped ease the frustration brought on by his illness. Together, Ruth and Billy have three daughters, two sons, 19 grandchildren and eight great grandchildren. Graham states that "I don't see anybody in Scripture retiring from preaching," and along with Pope John Paul II, who also has Parkinson's Disease, keeps chugging along.

The Cove

One of Graham's dreams was to build a training center to serve as a retreat for religious evangelists. It is located in Asheville, NC. In 1997, 30 seminars will be taught, featuring biblically grounded speakers. Cove seminars help those attend to Grow in God's Word, gain a deeper understanding of God, take time for personal renewal, and acquire tools for stronger Christian walk.

Graham Archives

The Archives of the Billy Graham Center are located at Wheaton College in Wheaton, IL. They contain many collections with documents relating to African Christianity. Most of these contain the work of North American missionaries or evangelists in Africa, though there is a substantial amount of material documenting the activities and beliefs of African churches, leaders, and quasi-ecclesiastical organi-

zations. Most of the records are twentieth century and about seventy-five percent are concerned with east or central Africa.

Graham has received numerous awards from various institutions and organizations, including honorary doctorates from Baylor University, the Citadel, and William Jewell College. He received the Barnard Baruch Award in 1955; Humane Order of African Redemption, 1960; gold award of the George Washington Carver Memorial Institute, 1963; Horatio Alger Award, 1965; Franciscans International Award, 1972; Man of the South Award, 1974; Liberty Bell Award, 1975; Templeton Prize for Progress in Religion, 1982; and the William Booth Award of the Salvation Army, 1989.

Graham's crusades have taken him to all the major cities of the United States and Europe and to such far-off areas as North Africa, India, and Australia. Although basically a fundamentalist in his theology, individualistic in his religious and ethical approach, and traditional in his appeal, he always sought and obtained a broad base of ecumenical support for his evangelistic campaigns. Graham brought evangelism to a new level of sophistication in organization, techniques, support, and prestige. Graham once stated that "It seems to me that the whole world, regardless of culture and religious tradition, is searching for something spiritual." The most important thing that counts (for Graham) is what happens in the hearts of men." Graham is the most respectable symbol of American evangelicalism.

Further Reading

The official biography of Graham is John C. Pollock, *Billy Graham: The Authorized Biography* (1966). Other helpful biographical studies include William G. McLoughlin, *Billy Graham: Revivalist in a Secular Age* (1960), Curtis Mitchell, *Billy Graham: The Making of a Crusader* (1966), *The Reader's Companion to American History* (1997), Gospel Communications Network (GCN), *Time Daily* (Nov. 95), and *People* (1997). □

Antonio Gramsci

The Italian Communist leader Antonio Gramsci (1891-1937) was a highly original Marxist who, working from Leninist principles, developed a new and controversial conception of hegemony in Marxist theory.

Antonio Gramsci was born in Ales in Sardinia on January 22, 1891. As the fourth son of Francesco Gramsci, a clerk in the registrar's office at Ghilarza, Gramsci was brought up in poverty and hardship, particularly during the five years his father was in prison for alleged embezzlement. As a child Antonio was constantly ill and withdrawn, and his anguish was compounded by physical deformity.

He was compelled to leave school at the age of 12 but following his father's release he was able to resume his education at Santa Lussurgia and Cagliari. On winning a scholarship to the University of Turin in 1911 he came into contact with future Communist leader and fellow Sardinian Palmiro Togliatti. During the elections of 1913—the first to be held in Sardinia with universal male suffrage—Gramsci became convinced that Sardinia's acute problems of under-development could only be solved in the context of socialist policies for Italy as a whole. (Gramsci retained a lively interest in his native Sardinia throughout his life and wrote a major essay on *The Southern Question* in 1926.)

Like many of his generation at the university in Turin, Gramsci was deeply influenced by the liberal idealism of Benedetto Croce. Gramsci's hostility to positivism made him a fierce critic of all fatalistic versions of Marxism. By 1915 he was writing regularly for the socialist *Il Grido del Populo* (The Cry of the People) and *Avanti* (Forward), often on cultural questions in which he stressed the importance of educating the workers for revolution.

Following a four day insurrection in August 1917 Gramsci became a leading figure in the Turin workers' movement. He welcomed the Russian Revolution (although in Crocean style he presented it as a "Revolution against *Das Kapital*") and in May 1919 he collaborated with Togliatti, Angelo Tasca, and Umberto Terracini to found *L'Ordine Nuovo* (The New Order) as an organ of "proletarian culture." The paper saw the factory committees in Turin as Soviets in embryo and the nuclei of a future socialist state. Thousands responded to the call to establish workers' councils in the Turin area, and during the "red years" of 1919 and 1920 there was a general strike and factories were occupied. *L'Ordine Nuovo's* critique of the passivity and reformism of the Italian Socialist Party won the approval of Soviet leader Lenin, and although Gramsci would have preferred to continue working within the Socialist Party at a time of rising fascist reaction, a separate Communist Party of Italy was formed at Livorno in 1921.

Gramsci was on the Communist Party's central committee, but the newly formed party was dominated by Amadeo Bordiga, a powerful figure whose purist elitism brought him into increasing conflict with the Third Communist International (Comintern). Gramsci became his party's representative on the Comintern, and it was while recovering from acute depression in a clinic in Moscow that Gramsci met his future wife Julia in 1922. They had two children, Delio and a younger boy—Giuliano—whom Gramsci never actually saw. Despite some happy moments, particularly when the two were together in Rome in 1925 and 1926, the relationship between Gramsci and Julia was a fraught one. Julia was in poor mental health, and later with Gramsci's imprisonment all communication between them more or less ceased. It was with Julia's sister, Tatiana, who was devoted to Gramsci's well-being during the torturing years of incarceration, that he found real companionship.

In October 1922 Mussolini seized power. The head of the Communist Party was arrested, and Gramsci found himself party leader. He was elected parliamentary deputy in 1924 and by 1926, when the party held its third congress in Lyons, Gramsci had won wide membership support for a Leninist strategy of an alliance with the peasants under proletarian hegemony. In his one and only speech to the Chamber of Deputies Gramsci brilliantly analyzed the distinctive and lethal character of fascism and in 1926 he was arrested. Two years later he was brought to trial—"we must prevent this brain from functioning for twenty years," declared the prosecutor—and Gramsci spent the first five years of his sentence in the harsh penal prison at Turi. He was able to start work on his famous *Prison Notebooks* early in 1929, but by the middle of 1932 his health was beginning to deteriorate rapidly. Suffering from (among other ailments) Potts disease and arterio-sclerosis, he was eventually moved as a result of pressure from an international campaign for his release to a prison hospital in Formia, but by August 1935 he was too ill to work. Transferred to a clinic in Rome, he died on April 27, 1937, after a cerebral hemorrhage.

Tatiana had his 33 notebooks smuggled out of Italy and taken to Moscow via the diplomatic bag. These notebooks, despite the often rudimentary state of their drafts, are undeniably Gramsci's masterpiece. They contain sharply perceptive analyses of Italian history, Marxist philosophy, political strategy, literature, linguistics, and the theater. At their core stands Gramsci's over-riding preoccupation with the need to develop critical ideas rooted in the everyday life of the people so that the Communist cause acquires irresistible momentum. Opposed both to Bordiga's elitism and the sectarian policies of the Comintern between 1929 and 1934, Gramsci's stress on the moral and intellectual element in political movements offers a challenge not only to Marxists but to all seeking to change the world radically.

Further Reading

An entry on Gramsci appears in *A Dictionary of Marxist Thought* edited by Bottomore (1983). Giuseppe Fiori's *Antonio Gramsci: Life of a Revolutionary* (1970) is particularly useful, as is Paolo Spriano's *The Prison Years* (1979). A select bibliography of the now enormous literature on Gramsci can be found in Roger Simon's *Gramsci's Political Thought* (1982), and John Hoffman seeks to place Gramsci's ideas within a classical Marxist framework in *The Gramscian Challenge* (1984). □

Enrique Granados

The Spanish composer and pianist Enrique Granados (1867-1916) contributed significantly to the creation of a national Spanish music. His best-known work is the piano suite Goyescas.

Enrique Granados (y Campiña) was born in Lérida, Spain, on July 27, 1867. After his family moved to Barcelona he took piano lessons from Francisco Jurnet and Joan Baptista Pujol. In 1883 he began to study composition with Felipe Pedrell, composer, musicologist, and passionate champion of Spanish folk music, who introduced Granados to the principles of musical nationalism. In

1887 he went to Paris, where he studied piano privately with Charles de Bériot, one of the leading professors at the Conservatoire. He returned to Barcelona in 1889 and gave his first recital there the following year. This successful debut launched the concert career that eventually earned him an international reputation.

Despite the demands of performance, he also composed and taught piano. Among his most distinguished early works for piano are the *Danzas españolas,* 12 pieces gathered into four sets written in the 1890s. In these pieces—much admired by Massenet, Cui, Saint-Saëns, and Grieg—Granados incorporated elements of Spanish folk dances in a most distinctive and personal way. Of these deservedly popular dances, the fifth in E minor is the best known. Granados' first major success as a composer came in 1898 with the production of his opera *Maria del Carmen* in Madrid, for which he was honored by the king. He wrote four other operas which were produced in Barcelona, but they met with little success. In 1901 he established his own piano school, the Academia Granados.

Granados' most celebrated work, the piano suite *Goyescas,* received its first performance in Barcelona on March 9, 1911. It was a great success. When Granados played it in Paris on April 4, 1914, it was given an equally enthusiastic reception. Soon after, he was elected a member of the Legion of Honor and was asked by the Paris Opéra to turn *Goyescas* into an opera. The operatic version, with a libretto by Fernando Periquet, was accepted by the Opéra, but the outbreak of World War I put an end to plans for its production. The Metropolitan Opera took it over, and it had its world premiere in January 1916 in New York. Granados came to the United States to supervise the production and to attend the premiere.

Despite the favorable response of the audience and critics, the opera did not sustain interest and never found a place in the operatic repertory. Granados' trip to the United States ended in tragedy. Invited by President Wilson to play at the White House, Granados delayed his return home. Instead of taking a boat directly to Spain as he had planned, he went first to England and there boarded the Sussex for Dieppe. On March 24, 1916, the *Sussex* was torpedoed by a German submarine in the English Channel. A survivor reported that Granados was safe in a lifeboat when he saw his wife struggling in the water. He jumped in to help her, and they both drowned. Shortly before he died Granados had written to a friend, "I have a whole world of ideas. I am only now starting my work." These ideas were never to be realized. Despite his early death, Granados left a sizable body of works. But he is remembered today chiefly for *Goyescas, Danzas españolas,* and his *Tonadillas,* songs for voice and piano.

Goyescas, subtitled "Los majos enamorados" ("The majos, or gallants, in love") consists of six pieces in two books. The title *Goyescas* means "in the manner of Goya" or "after Goya." Each of the six pieces is a musical evocation of a painting or etching by Francisco Goya, the famous 18th-century Spanish painter. Granados was totally captivated by the painter and his works, especially by his paintings of the "majas," those beautiful, mysterious aristo-

cratic Spanish women with their mantillas and fans. In these pieces Granados brilliantly blended the stylistic and technical elements inherited from Chopin, Schumann, and Liszt with Spanish melodies, rhythms, and colors to achieve a highly individual, poetic musical expression.

Frank Marshall, a pupil of Granados and the teacher of Alicia de Larrocha, wrote: "Granados manages to capture all the elegance, subtlety and aristocracy of eighteenth-century Spain. He stylized, formalized and polished the folklore of his music." Technically the pieces are fraught with difficulties—rich, quasi-orchestral textures, wide stretches, numerous countermelodies, and much ornamentation. Of the six pieces the most famous is the fourth, *Quejas, ó la maja y el ruiseñor* (*The Complaint, or The Maja and the Nightingale*). It is followed by the first piece of Book II, *El amor y la muerte* (*Love and Death*), the most brilliant and dramatic of the set, in which Granados recalls themes previously heard in Book I. *El pelele* (The Strawman), although not published as part of the *Goyescas,* is usually appended to it. In performance it is played as the seventh and last piece. It is based on the music of the opening scene of the opera *Goyescas,* in which a "strawman" is being tossed in the air by the "majas."

Ernest Newman, the English critic who in 1917 called *Goyescas* "the finest piano music of our day," summarized the work's special quality and appeal: "The music, for all the fervor of its passion, is of classical beauty and composure. The harmony is rich but never experimental. The melodies have new curves, the rhythms new articulations. Informing it all is a new grace, a new pathos, a new melancholy . . . but, above all, the music is a gorgeous treat for the fingers, as all music that is the perfection of writing for its particular instrument is. It is difficult, but so beautifully laid out that it is always playable: one has the voluptuous sense of passing the fingers through masses of richly colored jewels. . . . It is pianoforte music of the purest kind."

Further Reading

The following books have sections on Granados: Gilbert Chase, *The Music of Spain* (1941, 1959); Ann Livermore, *A Short History of Spanish Music* (1972); Harold C. Schonberg, *The Lives of the Great Composers* (1970); and David Ewen, *The World of Twentieth-Century Music* (1968). □

Cary Grant

Hollywood legend Cary Grant (1904-1986) won audiences the world over with his charm and sophistication. With a career that spanned over 72 films in forty years, Grant established himself as an icon of American film.

One of the most charming, elegant, and likeable of Hollywood leading men, Cary Grant created a light, comic style that many have tried to imitate but none have surpassed. In 72 films made over four decades, Grant served as both a romantic ideal for women and a dashing role model for men.

Grant was born Archibald Alexander Leach on January 18, 1904, in Bristol, England. His parents were poor, and they quarreled often as they struggled to raise their children. Grant's father pressed trousers in a factory. When war broke out between Italy and Turkey in 1911 and England increased its production of armaments (though they weren't involved directly in the war), he temporarily moved to another town to make uniforms at higher pay.

With his father gone and an increase in the family's income, Grant and his mother enjoyed their time together. After six months, however, his father lost his job and returned to Bristol. Family life was again tense. Grant's father came home from work late, if at all, and spent his time avoiding confrontations with his wife. Although it was unknown to Grant at the time, his father had fallen in love with another woman.

Through all this, Grant found escape in the newly emerging "picture palaces." There he would lose himself in the exciting adventures of movie heroes and heroines and laugh at the comic antics of silent-screen stars.

Mother Sent to Mental Institution

At the age of ten, Grant received news that would forever change his life and influence his future relationships with women. Arriving home from school one day, Grant was told his mother had left for a seaside resort. In reality, she had been locked away in a nearby mental institution

where she remained for 20 years. Grant was an adult before he learned of his mother's true whereabouts. Until then she was a topic never discussed, and Grant was left to wonder why she had abandoned him. "There was a void in my life," Grant reflected on this time, "a sadness of spirit that affected each daily activity with which I occupied myself in order to overcome it."

In later years, Grant surmised that his mother had had a nervous breakdown, having never recovered from his elder brother's death. Aged only two months, this child died as a result of convulsions brought on by gangrene. Others have speculated, however, that Grant's father locked her away because at that time divorce was costly and socially unacceptable, and he wanted to provide a home for his pregnant mistress.

In 1915 Grant won a scholarship to Fairfield Academy. There he received good grades with the exception of those in Latin and mathematics, which he disliked. He also received a reputation for playing jokes and getting in trouble. During the summer of 1916 Grant volunteered to use his Boy Scout training to help with the war effort. World War I was well under way and England needed the help of all volunteers. Grant became a messenger and errand boy at the military docks of Southampton. Here, Grant was filled with wanderlust as he watched the ships depart for new and exciting destinations. At summer's end, Grant roamed the Bristol waterfront and fantasized about a life far away.

Decides to Become an Actor

It was at the Hippodrome, Bristol's premier vaudeville theater, that Grant realized just how he would escape his working-class environment and have some adventures. After being allowed backstage during a Saturday matinee, Grant decided to become an actor. "I suddenly found my inarticulate self in a land of smiling, jostling people wearing all sorts of costumes and doing all sorts of clever things," Grant remembered. "And that's when I knew! What other life could there be but that of an actor? They happily traveled and toured. They were classless, cheerful and carefree. They gaily laughed, lived and loved."

In 1919 Grant ran away from home and joined the Bob Pender Troupe of comedians and acrobats. He was soon forced to return home when they discovered that he had lied about his age and about having his father's permission to work. At 13, Grant was a year too young to obtain a work permit and work legally. Undeterred, Grant waited until he turned 14 and then tried to get expelled from school so that his father might let him rejoin the group. Grant's plan worked.

Grant learned comedy, gymnastics, and pantomime from Pender's group. His later skill at physical comedy and timing owed much to this very early training. Grant traveled with the troupe throughout Europe and in July 1920 arrived in New York to tour the United States. When the rest of the troupe returned to England, Grant decided to stay and seek success in America. He worked as a barker on Coney Island, a stilt walker at Steeplechase Park, and in vaudeville as a straight man (the "unfunny" half of a comedy duo). He also won roles in light musicals and in plays. In 1932 Grant took the advice of actress Fay Wray and went to Hollywood to find work. After a screen test, Paramount offered Grant a contract but insisted he change his name from Archie Leach. So the more glamorous Cary Grant was chosen— and a great film career began.

Trademark Sophistication Surfaces Early

Even in his earliest film roles, Grant demonstrates the elegant sophistication that is the very opposite of his working-class background. His credentials as a traditional leading man were established with his appearances opposite Marlene Dietrich in *Blond Venus* (1932) and Mae West in *She Done Him Wrong* (1933) and *I'm No Angel* (1933). The full range of Grant's talent was used most successfully with the directors George Cukor, Howard Hawks, and Leo Mc-Carey.

The perfect format for displaying Grant's verbal and physical agility was in the screwball comedies of the 1930s. These films are marked by their fast pace, unconventional characters, and absurd situations. Grant's romantic sparring with Irene Dunn in McCarey's *The Awful Truth,* Rosalind Russell in Hawks's *His Girl Friday,* and Katharine Hepburn in Cukor's *Holiday* and Hawks's *Bringing Up Baby* displayed Grant's deft comic touch. His role as the daredevil flyer in *Only Angels Have Wings* and his Oscar-nominated performances in *Penny Serenade* and *None But the Lonely Heart* show that Grant was a capable dramatic actor as well, but it was in sophisticated comedy that his real strength lay. Throughout his career, Grant continued to successfully play the charming leading man, even as late as 1964, with the film *Charade.*

Works with Hitchcock

Although Grant's comedies represent the majority of his best-remembered roles, his work with the director Alfred Hitchcock in several classic films offers a departure from his usual image. Hitchcock deliberately played against Grant's familiar persona by introducing psychological twists that are in startling contrast to the actor's smooth surface elegance. *To Catch a Thief* (1955) is probably the Hitchcock film in which Grant plays a character closest to his trademark style—that of a glamorous and well-known jewel thief. In *Suspicion* (1941) Grant plays a seemingly loving husband who may or may not be trying to kill his wife. While Grant's wise-cracking character in *North by Northwest* (1959) has a surface charm, the audience gradually discovers that underneath lies a man with a basically selfish nature whose only lasting relationship is his amusing but obsessive bond with his mother.

It is in *Notorious* (1946), however, that Hitchcock fully uses the conflict between Grant's image and his character's personality. As Devlin, an emotionally repressed American agent, Grant sends the woman he has unwillingly come to love into the arms of a Nazi collaborator. Devlin's struggle against his attraction to this woman nearly causes her death when he blindly ignores signs that she might be in danger. The bizarre love triangle in this film hinges on the woman's attraction to Grant despite his unfeeling behavior, and his performance is both fascinating and disturbing.

Troubled Marriages

Although Grant achieved tremendous success as an actor, his personal life had some disappointments. His first four marriages ended in divorce and Grant speculated that this poor record was tied to the disappearance of his mother. "I was making the mistake of thinking that each of my wives was my mother, that there would never be a replacement after she left," he said. "I had even found myself being attracted to people who looked like my mother—she had olive skin for instance. Of course, at the same time I was getting a person with her emotional makeup, too, and I didn't need that." In 1981 Grant married Barbara Harris. This marriage was reported to be happy, and with her he was said to have found contentment. Harris was at his side when he died of a massive stroke in 1986.

Until his retirement from the screen in 1966, Grant continued to play romantic leads while other actors of his generation often found themselves cast in supporting roles and character parts. Today Grant's name remains a symbol of the stylish sophistication that was his trademark, and repeated viewings of his films reveal an actor whose ability to delight an audience is timeless.

Further Reading

Interview, January 1987.
Newsweek, December 8, 1986.
New York Times, July 3, 1977; December 1, 1986.
People, December 15, 1986.
Time, December 15, 1986. □

Ulysses Simpson Grant

Ulysses Simpson Grant (1822-1885), having led the Northern armies to victory in the Civil War, was elected eighteenth president of the United States.

As a general in the Civil War, Ulysses S. Grant possessed the right qualities for prosecuting offensive warfare against the brilliant tactics of his Southern adversary Robert E. Lee. Bold and indefatigable, Grant believed in destroying enemy armies rather than merely occupying enemy territory. His strategic genius and tenacity overcame the Confederates' advantage of fighting a defensive war on their own territory. However, Grant lacked the political experience and subtlety to cope with the nation's postwar problems, and his presidency was marred by scandals and an economic depression.

Ulysses S. Grant was born on April 27, 1822, in a cabin at Point Pleasant, Ohio. He attended district schools and worked at his father's tannery and farm. In 1839 Grant's father secured an appointment to West Point for his unenthusiastic son. Grant excelled as a horseman but was an indifferent student. When he graduated in 1843, he accepted an infantry commission. Although not in sympathy with American objectives in the war with Mexico in 1846, he fought courageously under Zachary Taylor and Winfield Scott, emerging from the conflict as a captain.

In subsequent years Capt. "Sam" Grant served at a variety of bleak army posts. Lonely for his wife and son (he had married Julia Dent in 1848), the taciturn, unhappy captain began drinking. Warned by his commanding officer, Grant resigned from the Army in July 1854. He borrowed money for transportation to St. Louis, Mo., where he joined his family and tried a series of occupations without much success: farmer, realtor, candidate for county engineer, and customshouse clerk. He was working as a store clerk at the beginning of the Civil War in 1861.

Rise to Fame

This was a war Grant did believe in, and he offered his services. The governor of Illinois appointed him colonel of the 21st Illinois Volunteers in June 1861. Grant took his regiment to Missouri, where, to his surprise, he was promoted to brigadier general.

Grant persuaded his superiors to authorize an attack on Ft. Henry on the Tennessee River and Ft. Donelson on the Cumberland in order to gain Union control of these two important rivers. Preceded by gunboats, Grant's 17,000 troops marched out of Cairo, Ill., on Feb. 2, 1862. After Ft. Henry surrendered, the soldiers took Ft. Donelson. Here Confederate general Simon B. Buckner, one of Grant's West Point classmates (and the man who, much earlier, had loaned the impecunious captain the money to rejoin his family), requested an armistice. Grant's reply became famous: "No terms except an unconditional and immediate surrender can be accepted. I propose to move immediately upon your works." Buckner surrendered. One of the first important Northern victories of the war, the capture of Ft. Donelson won Grant promotion to major general.

Grant next concentrated 38,000 men at Pittsburgh Landing (Shiloh) on the Tennessee River, preparing for an offensive. He unwisely neglected to prepare for a possible Confederate counteroffensive. At dawn on April 6, 1862, the Confederate attack surprised the sleeping Union soldiers. Grant did his best to prevent a rout, and at the end of the day Union lines still held, but the Confederates were in command of most of the field. The next day the Union Army counterattacked with 25,000 fresh troops, who had arrived during the night, and drove the Southerners into full retreat. The North had triumphed in one of the bloodiest battles of the war, but Grant was criticized for his carelessness. Urged to replace Grant, President Abraham Lincoln refused, saying, "I can't spare this man—he fights."

Grant set out to recoup his reputation and secure Union control of the Mississippi River by taking the rebel stronghold at Vicksburg, Miss. Several attempts were frustrated; in the North criticism of Grant was growing and there were reports that he had begun drinking heavily. But in April 1863 Grant embarked on a bold scheme to take Vicksburg. While he marched his 20,000 men past the fortress on the opposite (west) bank, an ironclad fleet sailed by the batteries. The flotilla rendezvoused with Grant below the fort and transported the troops across the river. In one of the most brilliant gambles of the war, Grant cut himself off from his base in the midst of enemy territory with numerically inferior forces. The gamble paid off. Grant drove one Confederate Army from the city of Jackson, then turned and defeated a second force at Champion's Hill, forcing the rebels to withdraw to Vicksburg on May 20. Union troops laid siege to Vicksburg, and on July 4 the garrison surrendered. Ten days later the last Confederate outpost on the Mississippi fell. Thus, the Confederacy was cut in two. Coming at the same time as the Northern victory at Gettysburg, this was the turning point of the war.

Grant was given command of the Western Department, and in the fall of 1863 he took command of the Union Army pinned down at Chattanooga after its defeat in the Battle of Chickamauga. In a series of battles on November 23, 24, and 25, the rejuvenated Northern troops dislodged the besieging Confederates, the most spirited infantry charge of the war climaxing the encounter. It was a great victory; Congress created the rank of lieutenant general for Grant, who was placed in command of all the armies of the Union.

Architect of Victory

Grant was at the summit of his career. A reticent man, unimpressive in physical appearance, he gave few clues to the reasons for his success. He rarely communicated his thinking; he was the epitome of the strong, silent type. But Grant had deep resources of character, a quietly forceful personality that won the respect and confidence of subordinates, and a decisiveness and bulldog tenacity that served him well in planning and carrying out military operations.

In the spring of 1864 the Union armies launched a coordinated offensive designed to bring the war to an end. However, Lee brilliantly staved off Grant's stronger Army of the Potomac in a series of battles in Virginia. Union forces suffered fearful losses, especially at Cold Harbor, while war weariness and criticism of Grant as a "butcher" mounted in the North.

Lee moved into entrenchments at Petersburg, Va., and Grant settled down there for a long siege. Meanwhile, Gen. William T. Sherman captured Atlanta and began his march through Georgia, South Carolina, and North Carolina, cutting what remained of the Confederacy into pieces. In the spring of 1865 Lee fell back to Appomattox, where on April 9 he met Grant in the courthouse to receive the generous terms of surrender.

Postwar Political Career

After Lincoln's death Grant was the North's foremost war hero. Both sides in the Reconstruction controversy, between President Andrew Johnson and congressional Republicans, jockeyed for his support. A tour of the South in 1865 convinced Grant that the "mass of thinking men" there accepted defeat and were willing to return to the Union without rancor. But the increasing defiance of former Confederates in 1866, their persecution of those who were freed (200,000 African Americans had fought for the Union, and Grant believed they had contributed heavily to Northern victory), and harassment of Unionist officials and occupation troops gradually pushed Grant toward support of the punitive Reconstruction policy of the Republicans. He accepted the Republican presidential nomination in 1868, won the election, and took office on March 4, 1869.

Grant was, to put it mildly, an undistinguished president. His personal loyalty to subordinates, especially old army comrades, prevented him from taking action against associates implicated in dishonest dealings. Government departments were riddled with corruption, and Grant did little to correct this. Turmoil and violence in the South created the necessity for constant Federal intervention, which inevitably alienated large segments of opinion, North and South. In 1872 a sizable number of Republicans bolted the party, formed the Liberal Republican party, and combined with the Democrats to nominate Horace Greeley for the presidency on a platform of civil service reform and home rule in the South. Grant won reelection, but as more scandals came to light during his second term and his Southern policy proved increasingly unpopular, his reputation plunged. The economic panic of 1873 ushered in a major depression; in 1874 the Democrats won control of the House of Representatives for the first time in 16 years.

Yet Grant's two terms were not devoid of positive achievements. In foreign policy the steady hand of Secretary of State Hamilton Fish kept the United States out of a potential war with Spain. The greenback dollar moved toward stabilization, and the war debt was funded on a sound basis. Still, on balance, Grant's presidency was an unhappy aftermath to his military success. Nevertheless, in 1877 he was still a hero, and on a trip abroad after his presidency he was feted in European capitals.

In 1880 Grant again allowed himself to be a candidate for the Republican presidential nomination but fell barely short of success in the convention. Retiring to private life, he made ill-advised investments that led to bankruptcy in 1884. While slowly dying of cancer of the throat, he set to work on his military memoirs to provide an income for his wife and relatives after his death. Through months of terrible pain his courage and determination sustained him as he wrote in longhand the story of his army career. The reticent, uncommunicative general revealed a genius for this kind of writing, and his two-volume *Personal Memoirs* is one of the great classics of military literature. The memoirs earned $450,000 for his heirs, but the hero of Appomattox died on July 23, 1885, at Mount McGregor before he knew of his literary triumph.

Further Reading

The *Personal Memoirs of U.S. Grant* (2 vols., 1885-1886; rep. 1962) is a starting point for a view of Grant's generalship. Important primary sources are the accounts by Grant's military aide, Adam Badeau, *Military History of Ulysses S. Grant: From April, 1861 to April, 1865* (3 vols., 1868-1881) and *Grant in Peace: From Appomattox to Mount McGregor* (1887). The best one-volume study of Grant's military leadership is J. F. C. Fuller, *The Generalship of Ulysses S. Grant* (1958). Lloyd Lewis, *Captain Sam Grant* (1950), carries Grant's career to the outbreak of the Civil War. Bruce Catton's *Grant Moves South* (1960) and *Grant Takes Command* (1969) provide the best account of Grant's military career. Still the fullest study of Grant's presidency is William B. Hesseltine, *Ulysses S. Grant, Politician* (1935). □

Evelyn Boyd Granville

Evelyn Boyd Granville (born 1924) was the first African American to receive her doctoral degree in mathematics.

Evelyn Boyd Granville earned her doctorate from Yale University in 1949; in that year she and Marjorie Lee Browne (at the University of Michigan) became the first African American women to receive doctoral degrees in mathematics; it would be more than a dozen years before another black woman would earn a Ph.D. in the field. Granville's career has included stints as an educator and involvement with the American space program during its formative years.

Granville was born in Washington, D.C., on May 1, 1924. Her father, William Boyd, worked as a custodian in their apartment building; he did not stay with the family, however, and Granville was raised by her mother, Julia Walker Boyd, and her mother's twin sister, Louise Walker, both of whom worked as examiners for the U.S. Bureau of Engraving and Printing. Granville and her sister Doris, who was a year and a half older, often spent portions of their summers at the farm of a family friend in Linden, Virginia.

The public schools of Washington, D.C., were racially segregated when Granville attended them. Dunbar High

School (from which she graduated as valedictorian) maintained high academic standards. Several of its faculty held degrees from top colleges, and they encouraged the students to pursue ambitious goals. Granville's mathematics teachers included Ulysses Basset, a Yale graduate, and Mary Cromwell, a University of Pennsylvania graduate; Cromwell's sister, who held a doctorate from Yale, taught in Dunbar's English department.

With the encouragement of her family and teachers, Granville entered Smith College with a small partial scholarship from Phi Delta Kappa, a national sorority for black women. After her freshman year, she lived in a cooperative house at Smith, sharing chores rather than paying more expensive dormitory rates. During the summers, she returned to Washington to work at the National Bureau of Standards.

Granville majored in mathematics and physics, but was also fascinated by astronomy after taking a class from Marjorie Williams. She considered becoming an astronomer, but chose not to commit herself to living in the isolation of a major observatory, which was necessary for astronomers of that time. Though she had entered college intending to become a teacher, she began to consider industrial work in physics or mathematics. She graduated summa cum laude in 1945 and was elected to Phi Beta Kappa.

With help from a Smith College fellowship, Granville began graduate studies at Yale University, for which she also received financial assistance. She earned an M.A. in mathematics and physics in one year, and began working toward a doctorate at Yale. For the next two years she received a Julius Rosenwald Fellowship, which was awarded to help promising black Americans develop their research potential. The following year she received an Atomic Energy Commission Predoctoral Fellowship. Granville's doctoral work concentrated on functional analysis, and her dissertation was titled *On Laguerre Series in the Complex Domain*. Her advisor, Einar Hille, was a former president of the American Mathematical Society. Upon receiving her Ph.D. in mathematics in 1949, Granville was elected to the scientific honorary society Sigma Xi.

Granville then undertook a year of postdoctoral research at New York University's Institute of Mathematics and Science. Apparently because of housing discrimination, she was unable to find an apartment in New York, so she moved in with a friend of her mother. Despite attending segregated schools, Granville had not encountered discrimination based on race or gender in her professional preparation. Only years later would she learn that her 1950 application for a teaching position at a college in New York City was turned down for such a reason. A female adjunct faculty member eventually told biographer Patricia Kenschaft that the application was rejected because of Granville's race; however, a male mathematician reported that despite the faculty's support of the application, the dean rejected it because Granville was a woman.

In 1950, Granville accepted the position of associate professor at Fisk University, a noted black college in Nashville, Tennessee. She was a popular teacher, and at least two of her female students credited her with inspiring them to earn doctorates in mathematics in later years.

After two years of teaching, Granville went to work for the Diamond Ordnance Fuze Laboratories as an applied mathematician, a position she held for four years. From 1956 to 1960, she worked for IBM on the Project Vanguard and Project Mercury space programs, analyzing orbits and developing computer procedures. Her job included making "real-time" calculations during satellite launchings. "That was exciting, as I look back, to be a part of the space programs—a very small part—at the very beginning of U.S. involvement," Granville told Loretta Hall in a 1994 interview.

On a summer vacation to southern California, Granville met the Reverend Gamaliel Mansfield Collins, a minister in the community church. They were married in 1960, and made their home in Los Angeles. They had no children, although Collins's three children occasionally lived with them. In 1967, the marriage ended in divorce.

Upon moving to Los Angeles, Granville had taken a job at the Computation and Data Reduction Center of the U.S. Space Technology Laboratories, studying rocket trajectories and methods of orbit computation. In 1962, she became a research specialist at the North American Aviation Space and Information Systems Division, working on celestial mechanics, trajectory and orbit computation, numerical analysis, and digital computer techniques for the Apollo program. The following year she returned to IBM as a senior mathematician.

Because of restructuring at IBM, numerous employees were transferred out of the Los Angeles area in 1967; Granville wanted to stay, however, so she applied for a teaching position at California State University in Los Angeles. She happily reentered the teaching profession, which she found enjoyable and rewarding. She was disappointed in the mathematics preparedness of her students, however, and she began working to improve mathematics education at all levels. She taught an elementary school supplemental mathematics program in 1968 and 1969 through the State of California Miller Mathematics Improvement Program. The following year she directed a mathematics enrichment program that provided after-school classes for kindergarten through fifth grade students, and she taught grades two through five herself. She was an educator at a National Science Foundation Institute for Secondary Teachers of Mathematics summer program at the University of Southern California in 1972. Along with colleague Jason Frand, Granville wrote *Theory and Application of Mathematics for Teachers* in 1975; a second edition was published in 1978, and the textbook was used at over fifty colleges.

In 1970, Granville married Edward V. Granville, a real estate broker. After her 1984 retirement from California State University in Los Angeles, they moved to a sixteen-acre farm in Texas, where they sold eggs produced by their eight hundred chickens.

From 1985 to 1988, Granville taught mathematics and computer science at Texas College in Tyler. In 1990, she accepted an appointment to the Sam A. Lindsey Chair at the University of Texas at Tyler, and in subsequent years continued teaching there as a visiting professor. Smith College awarded Granville an honorary doctorate in 1989, making her the first black woman mathematician to receive such an honor from an American institution.

Throughout her career Granville shared her energy with a variety of professional and service organizations and boards. Many of them, including the National Council of Teachers of Mathematics and the American Association of University Women, focused on education and mathematics. Others, such as the U.S. Civil Service Panel of Examiners of the Department of Commerce and the Psychology Examining Committee of the Board of Medical Examiners of the State of California, reflected broader civic interests.

When asked to summarize her major accomplishments, Granville told Hall, "First of all, showing that women can do mathematics." Then she added, "Being an African American woman, letting people know that we have brains too."

Further Reading

Grinstein, Louise S., and Paul J. Campbell, editors, *Women of Mathematics,* Greenwood Press, 1987, pp. 57–61.
Hine, Darlene Clark, editor, *Black Women in America,* Volume 1, Carlson, 1993, pp. 498–499.
Women, Numbers and Dreams, U.S. Department of Education, 1982, pp. 99–106.
Kenschaft, Patricia C., "Black Women in Mathematics in the United States," in *The American Mathematical Monthly,* October, 1981, pp. 592–604. □

Günter Grass

The German novelist, playwright, and poet Günter Grass (born 1927) is internationally known as one of the most important literary figures of postwar Germany; he is also known as an exemplar of his own saying, "The job of a citizen is to keep his mouth open."

Born in the free city of Danzig (Now Gdansk, Poland) on Oct. 16, 1927, Günter Grass was strongly influenced by the political climate of Germany in the era following the disasters of World War I. A Hitler "cub" at 10 and member of the "youth movement" at 14, the boy was infused with Nazi ideology. At 15 he served as an air force auxiliary; he was called to the front and was wounded in 1945. Confined to a hospital bed and then a prisoner of war, Grass later was forced to view the liberated Dachau concentration camp. He left the army at the age of 18, angry about the loss of his childhood, about the fierce and ugly German nationalism which had robbed him of it, and about the almost total destruction of the city of his youth.

Rather than pursue a school-room education, Grass wandered about, working as a farmhand, then miner, then stonemason's apprentice. He became aware of class differences and antagonisms; he developed a dislike for idealists with abstract theories and ideologies and a preference for pluralist skeptics of the non-ideological Left. Everafter, for Grass, in art or in politics, experience was always more significant than theory.

In 1949 he began to study painting at the Düsseldorf Academy of Art, at nights supporting himself as the drummer in a jazz band. He also started to write, poems at first, beginning slowly, experimenting with forms, working out his relationship with the past. When he moved to the Academy of Art in Berlin in 1953, he later said, "I came as a writer."

Grass married a ballet student named Anna Schwarz, and (the story has it) it was she who sent some of his poems to a radio station competition; he won third prize, and was then published in the magazine of the "Gruppe 47," a group of writers working to develop a postwar renaissance of German literature. In 1958, Grass again turned to Gruppe 47, this time to read two chapters of his new novel. He won first prize. The novel was published a year later, and brought Grass immediate worldwide attention. It was *The Tin Drum*.

The Tin Drum's narrator, a complex and self-contradictory drummer named Oskar, a dwarf, leads readers through the events of the war and postwar years through a distorted and exaggerated perspective. The second novel in what came to be known as the Danzig Trilogy, *Cat and Mouse* (1961), features a hero deformed by his times, playing the cat to the world's mouse, rendered impotent by time's unalterable concern with the trivial. The basic idea of the

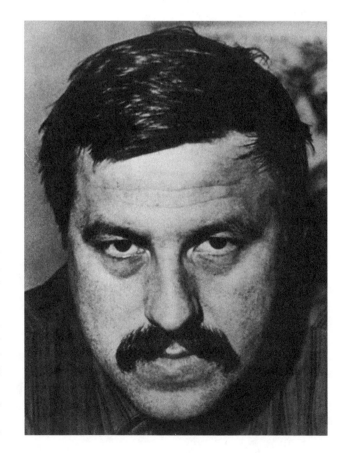

story is that no single perspective can do justice to a plural reality. The last of the trilogy, *Dog Years* (1963), deals with the ways in which the past (and its myths) help shape and determine the present. Like *The Tin Drum*, its structure is circular, ending as it begins, suggestive of Grass's sense of despair. In the Danzig Trilogy and in later novels, the characters are often mythic or folkloric or grotesque (very small and/or very different), in order to make the ordinary and the usual appear in a different perspective.

Grass's work as a poet and playwright would not have established his reputation as a significant contemporary writer. There are foreshadowings of images and themes that appear in later prose works. His poetry has been translated in *Selected Poems* (1966), *In the Egg and Other Poems* (1977) and *Novemberland: Selected Poems, 1956-93*. His most popular and controversial play *The Plebians Rehearse the Uprising: A German Tragedy* (1965, English translation, 1977) deals with the role of the committed artist in society, one of Grass's constant concerns and one that led in the mid-1960s to his direct involvement in politics as a supporter of Willy Brandt and the Social Democratic Party

An ardent socialist, Grass campaigned actively in German politics and denounced the re-emergence of reactionary groups, and his contemporary political concerns formed the core of his later novels. *Local Anesthetic* (1969) is an attack on linguistic confusions Grass saw in the slogans of the radical Left, and *From the Diary of a Snail* (1972), his fictionalized account of his involvement with Brandt's 1969 campaign, he supports gradualism. *The Flounder* (1977), perhaps Grass's funniest novel, deals with the history of women's emancipation and does not find, in the attitudes of radical feminists, a convincing alternative to the male-dominated past. In *Headbirths: or, The Germans are Dying Out* (1980), *The Meeting at Telgte* (1979), and *The Rat* (1986), Grass shows a world that is going to be worse because it is not getting better.

For a long time, Grass was considered the conscience of Germany's postwar generation, but that time has passed. In the 1990s, Grass still believed in "the literature of engagement" and that "to be engaged is to act," but his readers have changed. When his novel on German-Polish reconciliation *The Call of the Toad* came out in 1992, it was savagely reviewed in Germany as having nothing new to say. And on the subject of German re-unification, Grass had often said that the experience of Auschwitz was enough to prove that Germans should never again be allowed to live together in one nation; his 1995 novel based on that theme, *A Broad Field*, provoked harsh literary and political attacks. Nevertheless, at the end of the year more than 175,000 copies were in print and the book was at the top of Germany's best-seller lists.

Further Reading

An early book in English on Günter Grass is W. Gordon Cunliffe, *Günter Grass* (1969). Other works on Glass include Ray Lewis White, *Günter Grass in American: The Early Years* (1981); Richard H. Lawson, *Günter Grass* (1985); Patrick O'Neil, *Critical Essays on Günter Grass* (1987); Michael Hollington, *Günter Grass: The Writer in a Pluralist Society* (1987); Alan Frank Keele, *Understanding Günter Grass* (1988). □

Caesar Augustin Grasselli

Caesar Augustin Grasselli (1850-1927) was the third generation to head the Grasselli Chemical Company. Following his death, one of America's oldest chemical businesses was merged into the E.I. du Pont Company.

Caesar Grasselli, son of Eugene Ramiro Grasselli, was born in Cincinnati, Ohio. He inherited his father's interest in and aptitude for chemistry and the family enterprise. Starting at age 15 he received on-the-job training, including stints as bricklayer and pipefitter, from his father. In addition, a chemistry professor from Karlsruhe University (in Germany) tutored him and he attended Mount St. Mary's College in Emmitsburg, Maryland. "C.A.," as he was known, married in 1871 and went on an extended honeymoon, in part a business holiday, visiting chemical plants in France, Germany, and Britain as well as the ancestral home at Torno, Italy; he made a similar chemical tour in 1899. He became a partner in Eugene Grasselli & Son in 1873, senior partner in 1882 after his father's death, and followed closely in his father's footsteps. Credited with a broad array of product and process innovations, he had a lifetime of entrepreneurial achievement.

President of the Grasselli Chemical Company (1885-1916) and chairman of the board of directors (1916-1927), C.A. led his company through decades of rapid growth; by 1916 it operated 14 factories. His notable friends included Mark Hanna, William McKinley, and John D. Rockefeller. He was honored in 1910 by King Victor Emmanuel III for his humanitarian philanthropy after natural disasters in Italy and in 1923 by both King Victor Emmanuel III and Pope Pius XI for helping Italy's World War I victims.

Under C.A. the Grasselli Chemical Company had been incorporated in 1885 with capital of $600,000; by 1913 its worth had risen to $15 million. Three years later Grasselli Chemical was operating 14 factories and had property worth over $30 million. Its capital jumped to $35 million in 1918, undoubtedly a consequence of World War I, giving it a rank of 192 among the 500 largest American industrials.

Developments in Grasselli Chemical

Having first specialized in heavy chemicals such as sulfuric acid, in 1904 Grasselli Chemical had introduced the production of zinc as spelter. By 1928 Grasselli Chemical, a vertically integrated enterprise, manufactured heavy chemicals, fertilizer, black scrap, zinc, and explosives with plants in 22 cities; owned zinc ore and pyrite deposits as well as coal deposits; and employed between 3,700 and 4,500 workers. Despite its size, Grasselli remained a family enterprise with the Grassellis and their in-laws serving as officers and dominating the board of directors.

Chemical manufacturers shared certain patterns in the decades before World War I. Owing to limited economies of scale, Grasselli Chemical expanded by adding more plants rather than by increasing the size of plants. Also, it integrated forward, replacing its sales agents with direct selling, and grew more by internal expansion than by merger.

Grasselli Chemical had gradually drifted into manufacturing explosives. It sold mixed acids for the production of nitroglycerine in the late 1860s and early 1870s. Since Grasselli supplied superior acids for the manufacture of dynamite, an explosives firm built a dynamite factory in Cleveland to take advantage of Grasselli Chemical as a supplier. The Grassellis improved the product by suggesting the substitution of nitrate of soda for the saltpeter. In 1900 E.I. du Pont de Nemours & Co. and the Grasselli Chemical Company jointly organized a company to supply nitroglycerine. Finally, in 1917 a Grasselli subsidiary acquired and consolidated three explosives companies.

World War I affected Grasselli Chemical in an unanticipated way; the United States Government confiscated German patents, selling them to American interests through the Alien Property Custodian. This gave Grasselli Chemical the chance to become a producer of drugs and intermediates, broadening its product line. The Alien Property Custodian sold Bayer dye and drug patents to Grasselli Chemical, which transferred the medicinals to Sterling Products, and sold patents to Sterling Products, which resold them to Grasselli Chemical. However, Grasselli Chemical later sold out its coal-tar chemicals facility.

History of the Business

From the 15th century onward the Grassellis were chemists, druggists, perfumers, and the like at Torno on Lake Como in northern Italy. When Napoleon Bonaparte made this Po valley region a part of France, Giovanni Angelo Grasselli saw an opportunity. With another Italian emigrant he became a manufacturing chemist in Strasbourg in northeastern France. He built his first chemical plant there about 1800 and a second in 1810 at Mannheim in western Germany.

His son, Eugene Ramiro Grasselli (1810-1882), was born in Strasbourg, studied chemistry at the Universities of Strasbourg and Heidelberg, and worked with his father. Emigrating in 1836, he apprenticed in Philadelphia, Pennsylvania. In 1839 he started a chemical business, selling sulfuric acid, a good proxy for economic development, and other mineral acids to the meatpacking industry in Cincinnati, Ohio, known then as "Porkopolis." In response to his competitors, and to be nearer oil refining customers who wanted to integrate backwards by producing their own sulfuric acid, he opened a second factory in Cleveland, Ohio, in 1867 and also relocated the main office as well as his family there.

The new chemical works, on the Cuyahoga River, virtually adjoined the Rockefeller refinery; as Standard Oil prospered, so did the Grasselli firm. In that year Caesar Grasselli participated in Cleveland sulfur price-fixing; in 1872 the Cleveland oil refiners tried to depress the sulfuric acid price but the parties compromised. His partnership, doing business as Eugene Grasselli & Son (1873-1883), diversified in the late 1870s, manufacturing higher value-added products.

Under C.A.'s leadership the company continued to prosper as a private concern. In the year following his death, Grasselli Chemical embarked on a new direction; it obtained a listing on the New York Stock Exchange, becoming a publicly held corporation. Then came a bigger change. Later that year (1929) Grasselli Chemical was acquired by du Pont in the largest merger in which one of the top 200 nonfinancial companies acquired a company not on the list. Du Pont exchanged stock valued at $73 million for the Grasselli stock, 26 plants, and assets of $56 million. Thus the third-generation heirs of an Italian immigrant entrepreneur ended the independent family enterprise; such family enterprises typically do not endure beyond the third generation.

Further Reading

For additional information on Caesar and other Grassellis see William Haynes, *Chemical Pioneers* (1970 reprint of 1939), and David Van Tassel and John J. Grabowski, eds., *Encyclopedia of Cleveland History* (1987). □

Gratian

Gratian (died ca. 1155) is known as the father of canon law. His book on the laws of the Catholic Church revolutionized the study of canon law and was the single greatest authority on the subject until the 20th century.

Gratian was a monk in the Camaldolese congregation of the Order of St. Benedict. Hardly anything is known about his life. He was one of those historical figures whose works completely hide their persons. He was a lecturer at the monastery of Saints Felix and Nabor in Bologna in Italy at the time when that city was beginning to be widely known as a center for the study of law. The Catholic Church then had no uniform law. Over the centuries popes had made legal decisions, councils had issued decrees, and Church officials throughout Europe had used their authority in various ways. Doctrine and theology were also considered as guides for conduct.

For a century before Gratian, scholars had attempted to collect all this material and put it in some kind of order, but no one had been really successful. Sometime in the 1140s, after years of study, Gratian completed a work in this field that was outstanding. It was easily the best handling of this difficult subject that the world had seen, and it quickly became the most important textbook on Church law for all of Europe.

Gratian called his work *Concordia discordantium canonum* (Harmony of Conflicting Canons). In its almost 3,800 chapters he collected decrees from the councils and the popes, extracts from Roman laws, statements from the Church Fathers, and theological opinions—material which had been used to regulate the life of the Church for 10 centuries. He arranged the material systematically, according to subject matter. But his greatest contribution was the way in which he applied the newly emerging techniques of logic and dialectics to resolve conflicting decrees. The texts Gratian collected often were in contradiction to each other. He was able to show that the conflicts were frequently caused by different ways of using the same terms and so were usually more apparent than real.

This was not just another collection of laws but a new kind of book altogether. It taught a way of interpreting the law and a way of making practical sense of it according to the needs of different situations. Although it was never officially adopted by the Church, "Gratian's Decrees," as his work was known, became the most important legal guide for popes, bishops, and ecclesiastical courts until it was finally replaced by a completely new code of canon law in 1917.

Further Reading

A good discussion of Gratian is in Brian Tierney, *Foundations of the Conciliar Theory: The Contribution of the Medieval Canonists from Gratian to the Great Schism* (1955). A detailed discussion of Gratian and his place in the history of canon law is in Robert W. and Alexander J. Carlyle, *A History of Mediaeval Political Theory in the West* (6 vols., 1909-1936). Short histories of canon law and information on Gratian can also be found in Amleto G. Cicognani, *Canon Law* (1925; trans. 1934), and in T. Lincoln Bouscaren and others, *Canon Law: A Text and Commentary* (1946; 4th ed. 1963). □

Henry Grattan

The Irish statesman and orator Henry Grattan (1746-1820) led the nationalist fight for Ireland's legislative independence from England, for parliamentary reform, and for Catholic emancipation.

Henry Grattan distinguished himself at Trinity College, Dublin, where he acquired his passion for the classics and for eloquent oratory. He left the university in 1767 and was called to the Irish bar in 1772. With another Irish patriot, Henry Flood, Grattan contributed articles to the nationalist *Freeman's Journal*. They were at first great friends and united in the Irish cause. Grattan entered Parliament in 1775, the same year in which Flood lost his position as parliamentary leader by accepting the office of vice-treasurer of Ireland. Grattan's eloquence quickly allowed him to move into the leadership that Flood had vacated.

The American Revolution helped bring Irish matters to a head, and in 1778-1779 Britain finally granted some of the concessions to Irish trade for which Grattan and Flood had worked. Grattan's greatest efforts then went toward securing Ireland's legislative independence. He made speech after speech in Parliament, declaring that Ireland had as much right to its freedom as the English king had to his crown. Hard-pressed by defeat in America and alarmed by the convention of the Volunteers, an Irish nationalist organiza-

tion at Dungannon, in 1782 England granted legislative independence and ended penal laws against Catholics. The Irish Parliament recognized Grattan's primary role in securing its liberty and granted him £50,000, a sum which made him financially independent. The free Irish legislature, which lasted only 18 years, was called Grattan's Parliament.

With their chief object thus achieved, the Irish patriots fell into disagreement over some of their other goals. Grattan and Flood were themselves both Protestants, but they differed on Catholic emancipation. Grattan believed in the future of a unified nationalist Ireland and wished to grant Catholics full civil liberties; Flood, however, wanted to guarantee Protestant ascendancy by withholding from Catholics the rights to vote and hold office. Both wanted to reform the corrupt Irish legislature, but they differed on methods. They also disagreed over disbanding the Volunteers, which Grattan desired and Flood opposed.

In Parliament, Grattan at first generally supported the administration but moved into opposition as he saw governmental intransigence against the reforms he wanted, especially tithe commutation. He steadily refused office, lest it appear that he had sold out to government. He continued to attack parliamentary corruption and to support Catholic emancipation. The latter was moving closer under the guidance of William Pitt the Younger, but the rashness of Lord Fitzwilliam in 1795 made it impossible. In the face of growing disorders, Grattan made a final appeal for reforms and emancipation. His efforts failing, he seceded from the legislature (1797) but returned to Parliament to speak against the Union (1800).

For the last 15 years of his life Grattan sat in the Union House of Commons, frequently urging Catholic emancipation and once (1813) coming near success. He died in 1820 and was buried in Westminster Abbey.

Further Reading

Roger J. McHugh, *Henry Grattan* (1936), and Stephen Gwynn, *Henry Grattan and His Times* (1939), are the best modern biographies. William Edward Hartpole Lecky's biographical essay on Grattan occupies more than 200 pages of his *Leaders of Public Opinion in Ireland*, vol. 1 (3d ed. 1903). General histories for background include Edmund Curtis, *A History of Ireland* (6th ed. rev. 1950), and J. C. Beckett, *A Short History of Ireland* (1952; rev. ed. 1958). □

Ramón Grau San Martin

Ramón Grau San Martin (1887-1969) was a Cuban physician. Appointed provisional president of Cuba in 1933, he was elected to the presidency in 1944.

Ramón Grau San Martin was born in Pinar del Río Province on Sept. 13, 1887. Although his father, a prosperous tobacco grower, wanted him to continue in the business, Grau dreamed of becoming a doctor. Despite family opposition he entered the University of Havana, receiving his degree of doctor of medicine in 1908.

He then traveled to France, Italy, and Spain to round out his medical training. He returned to Cuba and in 1921 became professor of physiology at the University of Havana. He wrote extensively on medical subjects, including a university textbook on physiology.

Political Career

Grau's reputation, however, rests not on his medical achievement but on his political involvement. In the late 1920s he supported student protests against dictator Gerardo Machado and in 1931 was imprisoned. After his release he went into exile in the United States.

With the overthrow of the Machado regime, Grau was catapulted into national prominence. When, on Sept. 4, 1933, students and the military led by Sgt. Fulgencio Batista deposed the provisional government of President Carlos Manuel de Céspedes and appointed a five-man junta to rule Cuba, Grau was selected as one of its members. The junta, however, was short-lived, and the students soon chose their old professor as provisional president.

First Presidency

Grau's regime (Sept. 10, 1933-Jan. 14, 1934) was the high-water mark of a revolutionary process that had begun with Machado's overthrow. In a unique alliance, students and the military ruled. The government was prolabor and nationalistic, opposing the dominance of foreign capital. Grau denounced the Platt Amendment and advocated its abrogation.

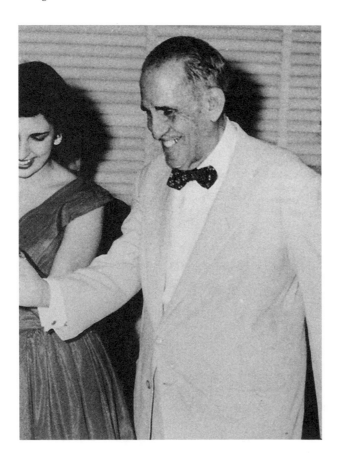

These measures aroused American hostility, and the United States government refused to recognize Grau. Since recognition was considered by Cuban political leaders as a key factor for the existence of any Cuban government, United States policy in effect condemned the Grau regime and encouraged opposition. On Jan. 14, 1934, Batista, now army chief, forced Grau to resign.

Grau went into exile, where he was soon appointed president of a newly created Nationalist party, the Partido Revolucionario Cubano (Auténtico). He returned to Cuba in time to be elected to the convention that drafted the 1940 Constitution. In the presidential election held that same year, he was defeated by his old rival, Batista. In 1944 he tried again, this time successfully.

Second Presidency

Grau's administration coincided with the end of World War II, and he inherited an economic boom as sugar production and prices rose. He inaugurated a program of public works and school construction. Social security benefits were increased, and economic development and agricultural production were encouraged.

But increased prosperity brought increased corruption. Nepotism and favoritism flourished, and urban violence, a legacy of the early 1930s, reappeared now with tragic proportions. The reformist zeal evident during Grau's first administration had diminished considerably in the intervening decade. He faced, furthermore, determined opposition in Congress and from conservative elements in his own party. For many Cubans, Grau failed to fulfill the aspirations of the anti-Machado revolution.

After turning over the presidency to his protégé, Carlos Prío, in 1948, Grau virtually withdrew from public life. He emerged again in 1952 to oppose Batista's coup d'etat. Grau ran for president in the 1954 and 1958 Batista-sponsored elections but withdrew just prior to each election day, claiming government fraud. After Castro came to power in 1959, Grau retired to his home in Havana, where he died on July 28, 1969.

Further Reading

For valuable information on Grau's first administration see Commission on Cuban Affairs, *Problems of the New Cuba* (1935). Grau's political career is discussed in detail in William S. Stokes, *Latin American Politics* (1959), and in Ramon Eduardo Ruiz, *Cuba: The Making of a Revolution* (1968). See also Hubert Clinton Herring, *A History of Latin America* (1955; 3d ed. 1968). □

Michael Graves

Michael Graves (born 1934) was a leading American architect and designer, instrumental in the emergence of Post-Modernism in the mid-1970s. His classicizing and colorful buildings are intended to make contemporary architecture more meaningful and ac-

cessible, referring to past tradition while also responding to contemporary surroundings.

Born in Indianapolis, Indiana, on July 9, 1934, Michael Graves studied architecture at the University of Cincinnati (B. Arch., 1958), at Harvard University (M. Arch., 1959), and, as winner of the Prix de Rome, at the American Academy in Rome (1960-1962). Beginning in 1962, he taught architecture at Princeton University and also maintained a private practice. From here his importance as both teacher and practicing architect steadily increased.

Early in his career Graves was identified as a member of the New York Five, a group of young architects whose largely residential designs were reminiscent of the Swiss architect Le Corbusier in their geometric abstraction. A 1972 book on this group first brought Graves exposure and drew attention to the distinctive characteristics of his work. In his Hanselmann House (Fort Wayne, Indiana, 1967) a complexity of form and yet a transitory quality were created by his layering of exterior spaces. These qualities became more pronounced in his Benacerraf House addition (Princeton, New Jersey, 1969) and in his Snyderman House (Fort Wayne, 1972), as did his organization of interiors into distinct rooms, an approach at odds with the Modern movement's traditional emphasis on openness of plan.

Graves also showed an interest in metaphor which would eventually separate him further from established Modernism. This metaphor was expressed variously in the classical sense of processional entry at the Hanselmann House or the color coding of the Benacerraf addition, suggesting analogies with the natural environment. While still abstract, Graves' Snyderman House has surfaces that are eroded by porches, balconies, and open framing, liberally splashed with soft, bright colors that break emphatically with the whiteness of Modernism. The color, collage-like murals, and almost Cubist spatial effects of his early projects reveal Graves' activity as a painter, as well as an architect.

Modifying the Modern Tradition

By the mid-1970s Michael Graves was moving vigorously away from the Modern tradition and toward an architecture he characterized as "figurative"—that is, related in visual and symbolic ways to human beings. Graves' architecture increasingly used anthropomorphic metaphors, such as the classical three-part division of a wall to suggest the feet, body, and head of a human figure. He distinguished between traditional elements such as wall and window, rejecting the Modern movement's blending of these into "window-wall." Graves began to mix pragmatic aspects of building with a more poetic sensibility, seeking to re-humanize architecture so users could identify with and relate to it both physically and symbolically. In all of these ways, Graves was part of the emergence of a new style dubbed Post-Modernism.

Although variously defined, Post-Modern architecture is, at its most basic, architecture that is rooted in the Modern movement, yet reacts against basic tenets established by such masters as Walter Gropius and Ludwig Mies van der Rohe. Graves' Post-Modernism is decidedly classicizing. His architecture utilizes forms and concepts that derive from the classical architectural tradition. To his love of the classical, however, Graves added his training in Modernist structure and his awareness of American traditions, developing a personal form of Post-Modern classicism.

More three-dimensional and expressive, Graves' architecture of the mid-1970s included more direct symbolic references, alluding to tradition to re-establish meaning. His design for the Fargo-Moorhead Cultural Center Bridge (North Dakota-Minnesota, 1977) was denser, more massive than his earlier buildings, less brightly colored, and more clearly related to particular sources, like the work of French architect Claude Ledoux. Graves' motifs (columns, pediments, arches, keystones) were fragmented, suggesting a classical past but never recalling any particular monument directly, as in the Plocek House (Warren, New Jersey, 1977).

Post-Modernism Becomes Controversial

Michael Graves' works after 1980 brought him international recognition as a leading figure in Post-Modernism, but not without engendering controversy. With other Post-Modernists, he was accused of extremism for radically departing from Modernism's pragmatic expression of function and materials. Graves, however, found Modernism alienating and created architecture intended to communicate with its surroundings and with the public by referring to architectural tradition. Especially important to him was ornament, rejected by Modernism but seen by Post-Modernists as essential to giving a building meaning. Despite this serious concern with meaning, Graves' Post-Modern buildings are colorful, paradoxical, even witty hybrids of references. A good example of all these qualities is his Portland (Oregon) Public Services Building (1980), the first substantial public project to use the Post-Modern style.

The Portland Building also represents well the controversy surrounding Post-Modernism. Graves' competition-winning project was attacked by local architects of the Modernist camp. The uproar forced a second competition, but Graves' design won again, both for its style and its cost-effectiveness. Differentiated by form, color, and material into three sections, his building suggests a classical organization of base, body, and crown. Graves' design was also highly contextual in complementing in style and scale the adjacent older city buildings and public park. Yet it is distinctive and celebratory; accented with stylized columns and a huge keystone, billowing garlands, and an allegorical statue, the building seeks to symbolize and inspire the city through multiple figurative references.

Other buildings of the 1980s show that Michael Graves took on diverse large and small public and private projects from the Spanish mission style San Juan Capistrano (California) Public Library (1980) to the environmentally sympathetic Liberty State Park Environmental Education Center (Jersey City, New Jersey, 1980). In his 27-story Humana Medical Corporation Headquarters (Louisville, Kentucky, 1982), Graves' fragmented, metaphorical references continued, as did his use of color to enliven surfaces, distinguish components, and relate building, nature, and people. Asserting its own personality, Graves' design was also contextual, healing the breach between small-scale downtown buildings and a tall glass-box skyscraper adjacent. Graves' first major building in New York City was the expansion of the Whitney Museum of American Art. His proposed design continued his vocabulary of distantly classical forms, blocky proportions, and varied colors and stirred up controversy.

Resistance to Specialization

Beginning in the late 1970s, but particularly by the mid-1980s, Graves expanded his range of influence to the design of furniture (initiated when he was hired by Sunar Hauserman furniture to design a furniture showroom), rugs, kitchen products, dinnerware, jewelry, clocks, and watches. Quoted in the *The Indianapolis Star* in 1994, Graves said, "It's only in recent times that we've drawn the lines, that (we think) an architect only designs buildings."

Graves' most famous small-scale creation was the chirping birdie teakettle produced by Alessi in 1985. He followed that with two different tea kettle designs for Moller International, one that featured the cartoon character, Mickey Mouse. It and a gourmet collection of housewares illustrated the many ties that developed between Graves and The Walt Disney Company. Graves also designed the company's corporate headquarters in Burbank, California, its Swan and Dolphin hotels at Walt Disney World in Orlando, Florida, EuroDisney's Hotel New York in Marne-La-Vallee, France, and a post office for Disney's planned Community of Celebration, Florida.

A multifaceted and innovative artist and architect, Graves won numerous prizes and awards from such organizations as the American Institute of Architects and such professional journals as *Progressive Architecture* and *Interiors*. He also exhibited his drawings and designs nationwide.

Further Reading

A discussion of Graves' early work in relation to that of some of his contemporaries may be found in *Five Architects: Eisenman, Graves, Gwathmey, Hejduk, Meier* (1972 and 1975). The monograph *Michael Graves*, edited by David Dunster (1979), surveys Graves' work to that date and incorporates interpretive essays by Alan Colquhoun and Peter Carl. One overview of Graves' work is his own *Michael Graves, Buildings and Projects 1966-1981* (1982), which begins with Graves' essay "A Case for Figurative Architecture," presents his work chronologically with numerous drawings and photographs, and includes an interpretive essay by Vincent Scully, "Michael Graves' Allusive Architecture." Two subsequent editions covering Graves' work from 1982-1989 and 1990-1994 have been published. Graves' relationship with Post-Modernism in general is considered in Charles Jencks' *Post-Modern Classicism* (1980) and *The Language of Post-Modern Architecture* (4th edition, 1984). □

Nancy Stevenson Graves

The American sculptor Nancy Stevenson Graves (1940-1995) established herself with the life-sized, realistic camel constructions she developed between 1965 and 1969. Using a multiplicity of materials and a wide range of sources, she focused her talents on filmmaking, painting, printmaking, stage designing, and watercolor as well as sculpture.

Nancy Stevenson Graves was born on December 23, 1940, in Pittsfield, Massachusetts, where her father worked as assistant to the director of the Berkshire Museum. Her early exposure to this institution where art, history, and science were presented under the same roof profoundly influenced her later work. She attended Vassar College, majoring in English literature and studying painting and drawing (B.A. 1961), but it was not until she entered the Yale School of Art and Architecture that the intense, competitive world of a fine arts education became available to her. She earned B.F.A. and M.F.A. degrees at Yale.

After graduation in 1964 she received a Fulbright-Hayes grant in painting to study in Paris for a year. She and fellow classmate Richard Serra were married there in the summer of 1965, and in 1966 they moved to Florence, Italy. It was in this city's natural-history museum that Graves found the work of Clemente Susina, an 18th-century anatomist. His life-sized wax models of human and animal bodies and their organs provided an impetus for Graves' first experiments with sculpture.

Beginning with small-scale animals, she soon turned to life-sized models and selected the camel for its scale and shape as well as its lack of Western art historical references. She thoroughly studied the camel: from the desert to the slaughterhouse to the natural-history museum. Between 1965 and 1969 she constructed 25 camels, no more than five of which are extant, and first exhibited some at the Graham Gallery in New York in 1968. The following year she had a solo exhibition of three new Bactrian camels (*Camel VI, Camel VII* and *Camel VIII*) at the Whitney Museum of American Art. Her increasing skill at creating these strange desert beasts was evident, and even more importantly, their striking contrast to the clean cool Minimalist art of the 1960s caused a stir in the art world. Critics and viewers were befuddled by the use of nontraditional materials and techniques, nonartistic sources, and an image alien to the traditional world of sculpture.

Having worked from the internal supports to the exterior covering in constructing her camels, Graves selected structure in the forms of bones and fossils made of inorganic materials for her next sculptural explorations. *Variability of Similar Forms* (1970), a work of 36 unique front and back Pleistocene camel legs made of wax over a steel armature, reflects not only her concern with the techniques of sculpture, but with the illusion of motion. Influenced by Eadweard Muybridge's photographs of animals and humans

in sequential motion, she created a work in which the illusion of motion is attained by the viewer walking around the sculpture.

In 1970 Graves made the first of five films. Each one was preceded by travel and research, and though the images are "representational" the films are fundamentally abstract in their exploration of color, light, form, and surface. She considered *200 Stills at 60 Frames* (8 minutes, silent) and *Goulimine* (8 minutes, color, sound), her earliest films about the camel, as study projects. *Izy Boukir* (1971, 20 minutes, color, camel sounds) also uses camels and their motion as its subject, but Graves had refined her style and produced a mature work. Her next film, *Aves* (1973, 23 minutes, color, sound), contrasts the dissimilar profiles and flight patterns of the graceful black frigate bird with the great pink flamingo against a blue sky. *Reflections on the Moon* (1974, 23 minutes, black and white, electronically synthesized sound) was filmed from a series of 200 stills (as was her first film) chosen from NASA's Lunar Orbiter collection. Graves' intent was "to overwhelm the viewer with the presence of the moon."

Just as Graves challenged the traditional materials and techniques of sculpture, she also challenged the viewer's position in observing a work. In *Variability and Repetition of Variable Forms* (1971) she created a work with no single viewpoint, but rather a series of informed views to be experienced in time. The viewer's experience is one of cumulative comprehension. The 38 units, each between nine feet four inches and ten feet in height, are spaced approximately three feet apart on the floor to create a complex whole from

single totem-like forms. South Pacific island cultures provided the inspiration for this imagery, which Graves created by fabricating artificial replicas of beetles, berries, bones, butterflies, twigs, vines, cowerie shells, and feathers and welding them to steel shafts. These objects from nature would be used again by Graves in the 1980s as the basis for direct casting in bronze.

In 1972, because of the demands of working with assistants and time in creating her sculptures, Graves stopped and returned to painting. Like her sculptures, the paintings have multiple viewing points (from a few inches to 20 feet in a 180 degree range) which create an experience in time for the viewer. She used an array of media including oil, acrylic, encaustic, and ink and applied them in a variety of ways. A sense of depth was retained through the use of the Cubist figure-ground relationship rather than the Renaissance system of perspective. Satellite photo sources provided black and white data for her colored paintings whose pictorial themes, as indicated by their titles, covered a broad spectrum. The earliest group (1971-1973) included renderings of the surfaces of the Earth, moon, and Mars as well as undersea topography and the morphology of sea animals. The use of a pointillist technique of close-set dots on a pale ground provided a methodical basis for her imaginative reconstructions of visual information.

In 1973 and 1974 Graves experimented with shaped canvases in order to physically shift the perimeters of painting. She used irregular, segmental panels either set together or separated. Satellite-relayed weather photographs of nimbus cloud formations provided the data for this group of paintings. Graves expanded her methods of paint application from the pointillist stippling to include fluid washes, hatched areas, and twisting brush strokes. Each member of this segmental series has a dominant color tonality as indicated by its title (*Untitled #1, Green*). Graves' experimentation next led to the Antarctic paintings of 1974. They were paler in tonality, smaller in size, and more heavily encrusted with paint.

In general, her painting became more expressionistic, more abstract, and carried fewer—and more general— references to the satellite photographs she had originally used as sources. Throughout the development of her ideas in painting, the critics did not favor her with the same praise they reserved for her sculpture.

She returned to sculpture in 1976 when she was commissioned by Peter Ludwig to create a bronze version of some of her earlier bone sculptures for the Ludwig Museum in Cologne, Germany. This led Graves to the Tallix Foundry in New York where she learned the lost-wax process and a method of patinating bronze by painting it with chemicals and sealing this coating with a gas torch. The resultant sculpture was entitled *Ceridwen, Out of Fossils,* referring to the medieval Welsh name for the goddess of death and immortality and to Graves' prototype sculpture, *Fossils, 1969-70.*

Graves' practice of making preliminary drawings or diagrams for her sculptures gradually disappeared as her collaboration with Tallix developed in the late 1970s. By 1979 foundry artisans were directly casting natural objects for her and she was able to build an inventory of cast bronze forms from which she could assemble her works. This freedom to juxtapose objects at random allowed her to abandon the thematic focus of her earlier work. Graves spoke of her asymmetrical, open sculptures as "balanced by imbalance." By directly casting forms, their original shape and surface texture are retained, and with the addition of color by means of patination, fired enamel, or polyurethane paint "a second composition is imposed." Through an art of assemblage and construction, Graves was able to combine permanent forms of real, perishable objects with the found-objects and ready-mades of her culture.

The American sculptor David Smith prefigured Graves in his construction of welded, open-form sculptures and additionally influenced her with his reliance on nature for inspiration. She paid tribute to his Zig series (1961-1963) with her 1983 sculptures *Zag, Zaga,* and *Zeeg.* With her Pendula series she recognized her debt to Alexander Calder for lessons in balance, structure, and the use of moving parts.

After returning to sculpture, Graves continued to paint and worked to bring the two together based on the strengths of each medium. Her use of color on her sculptures drew from her painter's eye, while forms and lines in her paintings derived from her sculpture. She physically joined the two in works such as *Raukken* (1985) where painted aluminum sculptures were attached to a canvas of oil and acrylic. Suggestions of forms from nature appear in the colorful canvas and the colors of the sculptures reflect those of the painting. In addition, Graves added shadow on the painting and a three-dimensional element to what was basically two-dimensional. She continued to challenge the traditional, accepted norms of the media in which she worked.

Collaboration with the choreographer and dancer Trisha Brown in 1985 gave Graves a different experience. In designing the set and costumes for *Lateral Pass* she learned about the artistic and practical aspects of dance and discovered areas of similarity and dissimilarity with sculpture and painting. Later, a critic noted the incorporation of human references previously not found in her sculptures. Graves brought continuity to her work with references to her previous work, yet allowed herself great freedom by employing a multiplicity of materials in a variety of techniques from a diversity of sources. By conjoining the worlds of natural history, archaeology, geology, meteorology, nature, topography, and art history, she presented reconstructions from her imagination that inform the viewer.

"Nancy was one of the first artists of her era to break away from the rigid formulas of minimalism and look at other aspects of contemporary culture," said Debra Balken, a Boston-based independent curator. Quoted in *The Boston Globe,* Balken added that Graves' introduction of decorative elements distinguished her work from that of a whole generation of artists. Even toward the end of her life, Graves had begun to experiment with poly-optics, a synthetic glass-like material, and was incorporating handblown glass into her sculptures.

M. Knoedler & Co. represented her in New York and mounted yearly exhibitions of her work beginning in 1980.

She was represented by the Janie C. Lee Gallery in Houston as well. In 1985 she received the Yale Arts Award and in 1986 Vassar acknowledged her accomplishments with an exhibition and the Vassar College Distinguished Visitor Award. Solo exhibitions of her work appeared in Philadelphia, Pennsylvania; Buffalo, New York; Cleveland, Ohio; Fort Worth, Texas; and Aachen, Germany. Her works have also been included in numerous groups shows.

Graves died in New York on October 21, 1995, a victim of cancer. At the time of her death, she was married to Avery L. Smith.

Further Reading

The most comprehensive book on the sculpture of Nancy Graves is *The Sculpture of Nancy Graves: A Catalogue Raisonné,* edited by the Fort Worth Art Museum (1987) in conjunction with their exhibition of her work. Two additional exhibition catalogues of interest are *Nancy Graves: A Survey 1969/1980* by Linda Cathcart (1980) and *Nancy Graves: Painting, Sculpture, Drawing, 1980-85* by Debra Bricker Balken (1986). Information related to Graves' work in the years immediately preceding her death was drawn from news articles in *The Boston Globe* and *The New York Times.*
Two articles of particular significance are Avis Berman, "Nancy Graves' New Age in Bronze," *Artnews* (February 1986) and Lucy Lippard, "Distancing: The Films of Nancy Graves," *Art in America* (November/December 1975). □

Robert Ranke Graves

The English poet Robert Graves (1895-1985) was also a very productive novelist, mythographer, critic and historian, with over 130 books to his credit. He was once nominated for the Nobel Prize.

R obert Ranke Graves was the son of a minor poet and celebrated Irish balladeer. His stepmother, a grandniece of German historian Leopold von Ranke, imposed a rigid morality on her husband and children which made young Robert poorly prepared for the rigor of English public school. He left school at the onset of the First World War, and enlisted promptly. He was wounded by shrapnel, not yet 21, and went home shell-shocked and suffering from severe neurosis because of the daily horrors of his year in France. Graves was treated by Dr. W.H.R. Rivers, an anthropologist turned neurologist, and it was Rivers who convinced Graves that his cure lay in writing. Rivers also was responsible for Graves's interest in matriarchal societies and women in power; this interest was later manifested in his controversial work *The White Goddess.* From then on, Graves wrote whenever he could, and constantly, convinced by Rivers that his life and his art were the same.

While still in the Army, Graves proposed to Nancy Nicholson—an 18-year-old feminist. He enrolled at Oxford to read for a degree in literature and occupied himself with domestic chores such as shopping, cooking, washing

went through many printings, and provided a measure of financial stability for Graves and his family on Majorca. But Laura Riding disparaged these works, and he begged his friends to not mention any of his work in her company. The couple spent endless hours discussing his interest in goddess worship; she later claimed that she was the source of all his ideas about poetry as goddess worship. Her dominance of Graves was such that she became the incarnation of those ideas, particularly in *The White Goddess*.

In 1936, with the Spanish Civil War clearly looming, Graves and Riding returned to England on a British destroyer. Riding became attracted to an American writer, Schuyler Jackson (a friend of Graves), and all moved to Pennsylvania, near Jackson's farm. With Riding in charge of everyone's lives, Jackson's wife was declared to be a witch and driven to breakdown, and Graves was dismissed as Riding's collaborator and lover. Graves's spirit was broken (but nevertheless mesmerized by Riding for years to come), and he found solace in the calmness, sanity, and devotion of Alan Hodge's young wife Beryl. The Hodge's had followed Graves to America, and with Alan's eventual approval, Beryl joined Graves in England and stayed with him for the rest of his life despite all the women with whom he would become involved during that period. Settled in England in the early 1940s, Graves produced poems, historical novels for which he read voluminously, and a collaborative study with Alan Hodge on English rose style, *The Reader Over Your Shoulder,* which he later thought was the most useful of all his books.

Driven by a moment of insight from seeds long since planted by Rivers and Riding, in 1944 Graves began writing *The White Goddess,* a book which later became sacred to a number of poets and enjoyed great popularity in the 1960s (it became a source book for readers of *The Whole Earth Catalogue*). Subtitled "A Historical Grammar of Poetic Myth," *The White Goddess* was at first dismissed by anthropologists and philologists as "irresponsible scholarship;" it is now recognized as an important work which demonstrates that mythic perception is a valid form of knowledge.

For Graves, it was much more than that; he became the Goddess's acolyte and devotee, her high priest. In the poet Alistair Reid's words, "only he could interpret her wishes, her commands." Writing *The White Goddess* gave order to Graves's deepest convictions and restored a sanctity to poetry he felt had been lost by neglecting myth for reason. She was also his muse, and his devotion to her was such that much of his last work from the 1960s on was given over to love poetry, inspired at the moment by whichever young woman had stepped into the muse-role (there were at least four).

After the Spanish Civil War, Graves and family moved back to Majorca. Though he had no strict schedule, he continued his habit of writing every single day, always in longhand. A classicist of the first order, he worked on translations alone (Lucius Apuleius' *The Golden Ass,* Homer's *Iliad,* which he entitled *The Anger of Achilles*) or with a collaborator *(The Rubaiyat of Omar Khayam)*; and wrote novels (*Homer's Daughter, The Greek Myths, The Hebrew Myths*), critical essays (*The Crowning Privilege* and *Food for*

clothes, raising the children (of which there were eventually four), and writing "manically" all the time.

After correspondence with an American poet whose work he liked, Graves invited her to work with Nancy and him. Laura Riding arrived in England in 1926; for the following 13 years, she dominated Grave's life and his work. In the beginning, Graves and his wife and his new companion declared themselves to be The Trinity and lived together in Cairo (briefly) and England. The Trinity broke apart; in 1929, Graves and Laura left England for the Spanish island of Majorca, a departure punctuated by the publication of *Goodbye to All That,* an autobiography which became regarded as "one of the most outstanding first-hand accounts" of World War I in English. The work's financial success showed Graves that he could support his poetic ambitions by writing prose; Graves eventually wrote 20 volumes of fiction to support his 55 volumes of poetry, to say nothing of edited works, translations, adaptations, and other works.

In 1927, Graves's early poems were published in a volume called *Collected Poems,* beginning what turned out to be a series of such volumes published roughly every 10 years. In each of the successive volumes, Graves replaced earlier poems with later ones; consequently, none of them displays the full range of his poetic accomplishments. Nevertheless, they established Graves as the most important British poet of his age, and in the 1960s and 1970s, he became the chosen mentor of the next generation of poets. But it was Graves's novels and nonfiction works that created his international reputation. Among these, the 1933 novels *I, Claudius* and *Claudius the God* met with great acclaim,

Centaurs), and muse poetry. In 1959, Graves's prostate operation in London produced serious complications and trauma from the massive blood transfusions he required. Friends and family thought this had much to do with his increasingly irrational behavior throughout the 1960s and his increasing insistence that he was a spokesman for his times whose long-held views were becoming generally accepted as the truth. In the early 1970s, Graves's productivity declined, and his last years, from 1975-1985, were given over to silence and senility.

Further Reading

For a critical account of Graves's life by a friend and fellow-poet, see Alastair Reid, "Remembering Robert Graves," *The New Yorker* (Sept. 4, 1995). For excellent biographies, see Miranda Seymour, *Robert Graves: Life on the Edge* (1995); William Graves, *Wild Olives: Life in Majorca with Robert Graves* (1995); Richard Percival Graves, *Robert Graves and the White Goddess,* vol. III (1995); Martin Seymour-Smith, *Robert Graves: His Life and Work,* second edition (1995). For the Robert Graves Society Information Center, see www.nene.ac.uk/graves/graves.html. □

Asa Gray

Asa Gray (1810-1888), American botanist, pioneered in the study of plant geography and made early attempts to reconcile Darwinian concepts of evolution with traditional religious beliefs.

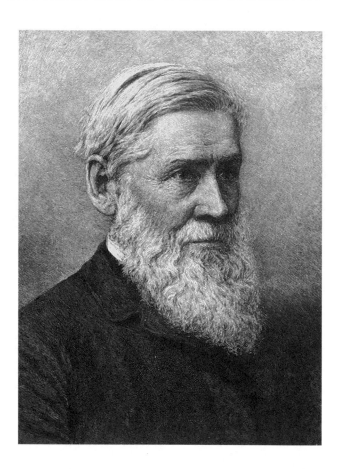

During the 19th century botany in America emerged as a highly professional vocation involving collaboration among collectors and herbarium specialists. A new method of classification was coming into use early in Asa Gray's career—the so-called natural system, which aimed at classification on the basis of general similarities instead of by the old, Linnaean method of counting the male and female parts of a flower. The new system forced botanists to look more closely at the forms and structures of plants. They began to study the interrelations between plants and their environment and to inquire into their meaning. Gray's professional lifetime bridged these important developments, and he played a part in all of them.

Asa Gray was born at Sauquoit, N.Y., on Nov. 18, 1810. After attending medical courses he received his degree in 1831 and began practice as a country physician. But he had already developed an interest in botany and began to drift away from medicine. From 1832 to 1835 he taught science at a high school in Utica, N.Y., utilizing the summers to improve his botanical knowledge. In 1835 he moved to New York City to begin collaborating with John Torrey on *Flora of North America* (2 vols., 1838-1843), which firmly established the new natural system of classification in American botany. Publication of the first volume made Torrey and Gray the leading botanists of North America and brought them international attention.

Academic Career

After accepting the professorship of botany at the newly founded University of Michigan, Gray sailed for Europe in 1838 to purchase books for the university and to study the type specimens of American plants in various herbaria. The year-long trip not only prepared Gray for his later task of coordinating North American botany but also laid the foundation of his lifelong friendship with leading European botanists. However, because the opening of the university was delayed, Gray never assumed the professorship.

In 1842 Gray became professor of natural history at Harvard, a post he held until retiring in 1873. The first edition of his *Botanical Text-Book* (1843) was long a standard work that did much to unify the interpretation and application of technical terms in America. Gray never lost his early interest in popular instruction; he produced five other textbooks, all important in lower-school education.

While at Harvard, Gray became the unofficial but widely recognized coordinator of American botany, maintaining regular correspondence with prominent European botanists and receiving a constant supply of specimens from U.S. government exploring expeditions and correspondents in the West. He created the Harvard department of botany and made its herbarium and botanical garden the finest in America.

Distribution of Plants

Gray was a pioneer in the field of plant geography. In 1859 he published his most famous contribution to this field, a monograph on the botany of Japan and its relations to that of North America. He demonstrated that the similar flora in the two regions had originated in one center and had been dispersed as conditions permitted. (This material was used by Charles Darwin to support his theory of evolution.) To explain the migration of flora in this case, Gray suggested that past geological changes would have made it possible; he thus joined a dynamic theory of the earth with a theory of plant distribution. Relying greatly upon information supplied by James Dwight Dana, a Yale geologist, Gray showed that, on at least two occasions in the past, conditions existed that could have allowed continuity between the flora of the two regions.

Advocate and Critic of Darwin

On Sept. 5, 1857, Darwin wrote Gray the famous letter in which he first outlined his theory of the evolution of species by natural selection. Gray became Darwin's first American advocate and also one of his most searching critics. Although Gray accepted the main outlines of Darwin's theory, his insistence that evolution must be *directed* by some external force allowed him to preserve his own Presbyterian beliefs. After Gray's initial review of Darwin's *Origin of Species* in the *American Journal of Science,* of which he was a coeditor, Gray spent much of his life arguing on both a popular and a scientific level for the compatibility of evolutionary theory and religion. He also arranged for the first American edition of *Origin of Species.*

One of the original members of the National Academy of Sciences, Gray was president of both the American Academy of Arts and Sciences and the American Association for the Advancement of Science and was a regent of the Smithsonian Institution. He died at home in Cambridge, Mass., on Jan. 30, 1888. His wife, Jane Loring Gray, whom he had married in 1848, edited his autobiography and letters.

Further Reading

Gray's correspondence was edited by Jane Loring Gray, *Letters of Asa Gray* (2 vols., 1893). An excellent biography which includes an analysis of Gray's contributions to botany is A. Hunter Dupree, *Asa Gray, 1810-1888* (1959). See also Andrew D. Rodgers, *American Botany, 1873-1892: Decades of Transition* (1914; repr. 1944), and Edward Lurie, *Louis Agassiz: A Life in Science* (1960). For the general scientific background see George H. Daniels, *American Science in the Age of Jackson* (1968).

Additional Sources

Dupree, A. Hunter, *Asa Gray, American botanist, friend of Darwin,* Baltimore: Johns Hopkins University Press, 1988. ☐

Hannah Holborn Gray

Hannah Holborn Gray (born 1930) was an education administrator who served as the first woman provost at Yale and as the first woman president of the University of Chicago. She thus became the first **woman to serve as the chief executive of a major coeducational university.**

Hannah Holborn Gray was born on October 25, 1930, in Heidelberg, Germany, the second child and only daughter of an academic couple, Hajo Holborn, a renowned professor of history, and Annemarie Bettman, who held a Ph.D. in classical philology. When the Hitler regime dismissed the liberal-thinking Hajo Holborn from his post at the Institute of Politics in Berlin, he emigrated with his family to New Haven, Connecticut, joining the History Department at Yale University where he remained for 35 years. Hannah Holborn grew up within Yale's ivy-covered walls. It was at Yale, too, that she later achieved national prominence when she became its first woman provost in 1974 and, in 1977, its acting president during a year of turmoil.

Emigre friends of the Holborn family influenced the choice of Bryn Mawr as a college for the young Hannah, from which she graduated in 1950 summa cum laude. She went to Oxford on a Fulbright scholarship and then continued her studies in intellectual history at Harvard University, from which she received her Ph.D. in 1957. Gray noted that as a female graduate student in the 1950s she was not immune from the climate of the "feminine mystique" which dictated dating and early marriage. However, in marrying Charles Gray, a legal historian, she remained wedded as well to the academic world. She was a teaching fellow at Harvard University from 1955 to 1957, an instructor from 1957 to 1959, and an assistant professor in 1959-1960.

In the early 1960s the academic marketplace offered few opportunities for women historians. Hence it was Charles Gray's career that flourished. He joined and gained tenure in the History Department at the University of Chicago. Hannah Holborn Gray followed her husband to Chicago, spending a year as a fellow in the Newberry Library, but on the margins of the university that was ultimately to offer her its presidency. She considered going to law school. Finally, the History Department made Hannah Gray an offer, abolishing its nepotism rules to secure its first academic couple. She was granted tenure in 1964.

Asked to redesign the history program, Hannah Gray got her first taste of administration. But it was her service on a faculty committee to review the non-reappointment of a controversial woman faculty member whose dismissal had provoked a major student sit-in that catapulted Hannah Gray into the limelight at Chicago. Demonstrating the powerful combination of rational discourse and steel nerves that was her trademark, Hannah Gray helped to resolve the explosive conflict. In 1972 she became the dean of the College of Arts and Sciences at Northwestern University. There she contributed to planning and to the strengthening of academic programs.

In 1974 the president of Yale, Kingman Brewster, who knew of Gray from her service on the Yale board, named her Yale's first woman provost. Those were dark days for Yale, including a decline in finances and a debate over coeducation. In 1977, when Kingman Brewster became U.S.

ambassador to Great Britain, he chose Gray to succeed him as acting president. She never winced at making tough decisions, particularly in paring down a large deficit and taking a hard line on contract negotiations with Yale's striking cafeteria and maintenance workers. Whether it was the effects of the protracted strike which alienated many, or simply her gender, Gray did not receive the offer of the Yale presidency, which went instead to Bartlett Giamotti, with whom she had taught a course in Renaissance history. Almost overnight she was invited to become president of the University of Chicago.

According to Gray, the offer came as a "great surprise." While she considered Yale her "second home," she was helped in her decision to return to Chicago by the fact that Charles Gray felt like a "well-connected anamoly" at Yale. The Grays returned to the University of Chicago, where he held an appointment in history and she presided over a research university of 7,900 students, a faculty of over 1,000, and an endowment of $350 million. She was the first woman to serve as the chief executive of a major coeducational university.

Her presidency spanned a time of economic decline in academe, especially a contraction in the numbers of graduate students, the hallmark of the intellectual life at Chicago. A major achievement of her administration was the formation of a faculty committee to study the future of graduate education in the United States. Gray espoused a concern for limits, but without thinking that "limitations are necessarily negative." Facing a deficit budget, she continued via a successful fundraising campaign to spend money to maintain quality in academic programs and to attract faculty. Once again confronted with a student protest, this one precipitated by the granting of a controversial award to former Secretary of Defense Robert McNamara, Gray held her ground and delivered the award, but then appointed a faculty committee to consider abolishing the prize entirely.

There were sometimes contradictory impressions of Gray—to some she seemed cold and ruthless; to others warm, witty, and effusive—but even her critics recognized her longstanding commitment to academic values. "She has spent her life steeped in them," said one observer.

Gray was a fellow of the American Academy of Arts and Sciences, a member of the American Philosophical Society, and a trustee of Bryn Mawr College. She was a member of the Pulitzer Prize board, the Council on Financial Aid to Education, and the Council on Foreign Relations in Chicago and New York. She served on the board of directors of J.P. Morgan & Company/Morgan Guaranty, Atlantic Richfield Company, and Ameritech. She held honorary degrees from 42 colleges and universities, received the Medal of Liberty in 1986 and the Medal of Freedom in 1991.

Further Reading

Additional information can be found in Carol Felsenthal, "Gray Among the Gargoyles," in *Chicago* (November 1984); *Who's Who of American Women,* 1985-1986; Gene I. Maeroff, "University of Chicago Accommodates Easily to a Woman President," in *New York Times* (March 16, 1980); and "Hannah Gray" (Interview), in *Educational Record* (Fall 1980). □

Robert Gray

Robert Gray (1755-1806) was the first American to circumnavigate the globe. He discovered the Columbia River while exploring the coastline of the Oregon country.

Robert Gray was born in Tiverton, R.I., on May 10, 1755. He served in a privateer during the American Revolution, and in 1787 he sailed with Capt. John Kendrick on the first Yankee trading voyage to China. The project was to tie the new fur trade of the Pacific Northwest into the ancient commerce of Cathay. Gray commanded the little sloop *Lady Washington,* and Kendrick sailed the full-rigged ship *Columbia Rediviva* (usually called the *Columbia*). Transferred from the little consort to the command of the larger vessel, Gray returned to New England in August 1790, after selling his cargo of sea otter skins in Macao for $21,000 and buying tea in Canton.

From a strictly monetary point of view, the voyage just about broke even, but it was immensely profitable in terms of American prestige, for Gray had sailed 42,000 miles to become the first circumnavigator of the globe from the United States. Also, he had flown the "Stars and Stripes" for the first time in some of the most out-of-the-way corners of the world.

Gray's greatest service to his country came after he sailed the *Columbia* from Boston in 1790 to Vancouver Island with a cargo of Indian trade goods—copper, iron, and blue cloth. After wintering on the coast and building a second boat there, he explored southward, discovering Gray's Harbor, on which Washington's modern ports Hoquiam and Aberdeen are located. On May 11, 1792, guided by the crew of the little pinnace he had sent ahead, Gray brought the *Columbia* through the breakers of the bar and into the mouth of the legendary "River of the West," which he renamed the Columbia for his ship.

By July 1793 Gray was back in Boston. He married Martha Atkins and settled down to raise a family. Henceforth, the navigator confined his voyaging to the coastal trade. En route to Charleston, S.C., in the summer of 1806, he died on shipboard and was buried at sea.

Gray was largely unaware of the import of his discovery of the Columbia River. He did not know that his discovery, when reinforced by the expedition of Meriwether Lewis and William Clark in 1805-1806, would establish a firm American claim to the Washington and Oregon area of the Pacific Northwest.

Further Reading

There is no biography of Gray. Details of his voyages and assessments of their results are available in such histories of the Northwest as Charles M. Gates and Oscar O. Winther, *The*

Great Northwest (1947), and Dorothy O. Johansen, *Empire on the Columbia* (1957; 2d ed. 1967). □

Thomas Gray

The English poet Thomas Gray (1716-1771) expressed deep and universal human feelings in forms derived from Greek and Roman literature. Although his output was small, he introduced new subject matter for poetry.

Thomas Gray was born on Dec. 26, 1716, of middle-class parents. He was the only one of 12 children to survive infancy. In 1727 Thomas became a pupil at Eton, where he met several bookish friends, who included Richard West (his death, in 1742, was to reinforce the melancholy that Gray often felt and expressed in his poems) and Horace Walpole, son of England's first modern-style prime minister and later an important man of letters.

Gray attended Cambridge University from 1734 to 1738 and after leaving the university without a degree undertook the grand tour of Europe with Walpole from 1739 to 1741. During this tour the two friends quarreled, but the quarrel was made up in 1745, and Walpole was to be a significant influence in the promulgation of Gray's poems in later years. In 1742 Gray returned to Cambridge and took a law degree the next year, although he was in fact much

more interested in Greek literature than in law. For the most part, the rest of Gray's life, except for an occasional sojourn in London or trip to picturesque rural spots, was centered in Cambridge, where he was a man of letters and a scholar.

Gray's poetry, almost all of which he wrote in the years after he returned to Cambridge, is proof that personal reserve in poetry and careful imitation of ancient modes do not rule out depth of feeling. (He was one of the great English letter writers; in his letters his emotions appear more unreservedly.) The charge of artificiality brought against him later by men as different in their poetic principles as Samuel Johnson and William Wordsworth is true, but there is room in poetry for artifice, and while spontaneity has its merits so also does the Virgilian craftsmanship that Gray generally practiced.

The "Ode on a Distant Prospect of Eton College" (1747) certainly inflates its subject when it describes schoolboy swimmers as those who "delight to cleave/With pliant art [the Thames's] glassy wave," but it concludes with a memorably classic sentiment that deserves its lapidary expression: "where ignorance is bliss,/ 'Tis folly to be wise." Even so playful a poem as the "Ode on the Death of a Favourite Cat, Drowned in a Tub of Gold Fishes" (1748) concludes with the chiseled wisdom, "Not all that tempts your wand'ring eyes . . . is lawful prize;/Nor all that glisters, gold."

In his greatest poem (and one of the most popular in English), the "Elegy Written in a Country Churchyard" (1751), Gray achieves a perfect fusion of the dignity of his

subject and the habitual elevatedness of his poetics. His style and his melancholy attitude toward life are perfectly adapted to the expression of the somber, time-honored verities of human experience. In the two famous Pindaric odes "The Progress of Poetry" and "The Bard" (published with Walpole's help in 1757) Gray seems to anticipate the rhapsodies of the romantic poets. Some readers in Gray's time found the odes obscure, but they are not so by modern standards. Much of Gray's energy in his later years was devoted to the study of old English and Norse poetry, a preoccupation that reveals itself in his odes.

Gray declined the poet laureateship in 1757. After a somewhat hypochondriacal middle age he died on July 30, 1771.

Further Reading

The standard biography of Gray is Robert W. Ketton-Cremer, *Thomas Gray* (1955; rev. ed. 1958). For critical comment on the "Elegy" see Cleanth Brooks's essay in his *The Well-Wrought Urn: Studies in the Structure of Poetry* (1947) and the essays by Frank Brady, Bertrand Bronson, and Ian Jack in Frederick W. Hilles and Harold Bloom, eds., *From Sensibility to Romanticism* (1965). Broader studies of Gray include Patricia Spacks, *The Insistence of Horror: Aspects of the Supernatural in Eighteenth-Century Poetry* (1962), and Arthur Johnston, *Thomas Gray and "The Bard"* (1966).

Additional Sources

Hudson, William Henry, *Gray & his poetry*, Norwood, Pa.: Norwood Editions, 1977.

Roberts, S. C. (Sydney Castle), *Thomas Gray of Pembroke*, Norwood, Pa.: Norwood Editions, 1978.

Thomas Gray, his life and works, London; Boston: G. Allen & Unwin, 1980. □

William H. Gray III

Democratic congressman from Philadelphia from 1979 to 1991, William H. Gray III (born 1941) became the highest-ranking African American leader in the history of the U.S. House of Representatives when colleagues elected him the House Whip on June 14, 1989.

William H. Gray III was born in Baton Rouge, Louisiana, on August 20, 1941. He was the only son of Dr. William H. Gray, Jr., clergyman and educator, and Hazel Yates Gray, a high school teacher. Shortly after his birth Gray moved with his parents and an older sister, Marion, to St. Augustine, Florida, where his father served as president of Florida Normal and Industrial College. After a move to Tallahassee so his father could become the president of Florida A&M College, the Gray family moved to Philadelphia, where Dr. Gray became pastor of the Bright Hope Baptist Church.

During this time William, who lived with his family on the city's north side, attended public schools. He graduated

from Simon Gratz High School in 1959 and enrolled in Franklin and Marshall College in Lancaster, Pennsylvania, majoring in sociology. Gray served as an intern for Pennsylvania Representative Robert N. C. Nix during his senior year in 1963. He also decided to become a minister at this time. In 1966, he secured a Master of Divinity degree from Drew Theological Seminary. While at Drew, Gray served as assistant pastor of the Union Baptist Church in Montclair, New Jersey. The same year he received his degree from Drew, Gray became senior minister of the Union Baptist Church and was installed by The Reverend Dr. Martin Luther King, Jr., a close friend of the family.

During his pastorate at Union Baptist, Gray emerged as a leading community activist. He founded several nonprofit corporations, including the Union Housing Corporation, which developed housing for low- and middle-income African Americans. In 1970 Gray sued a Montclair landlord who, Gray contended, had refused him an apartment because of his race. In a landmark decision, the New Jersey Superior Court ruled in favor of Gray and awarded him financial damages as a victim of discrimination. He also pursued educational goals during this time and received a Master of Theology degree from Princeton Theological Seminary in 1970. That same year St. Peter's College in Jersey City, New Jersey, named him assistant professor. Previously he had taught at Jersey City College, Montclair State College, and Rutgers University.

After his father died in 1972, Gray was named pastor of the Bright Hope Baptist Church in Philadelphia, succeeding not only his father but also his grandfather, who had

founded the 4,000-member church. A concern that the incumbent congressman from the Second Congressional District, the same Robert N.C. Nix with whom Gray interned years earlier, ignored the needs of African Americans in the congregation and the community helped persuade Gray to enter secular politics and run for that office as a Democrat in 1976. Though he lost to his old boss in the primary by 339 votes, he tried again in 1978 and defeated Nix, a ten-term incumbent, receiving 58 percent of the vote. In the general election in November he overwhelmed the Republican candidate, capturing 84 percent of the vote.

Early on, Gray established an impressive record as a congressman. During his first term in office colleagues elected Gray to the prestigious Steering and Policy Committee, charged with making committee assignments. He also landed a seat on the powerful Budget Committee, where he opposed President Ronald Reagan's budget cuts and worked with other members of the Black Caucus to expand social programs. In another committee assignment, Foreign Affairs, Gray successfully sponsored a bill that established the African Development Foundation, which provided American aid directly to African villages. This was the first time in the 20th century that a freshman congressman had secured congressional approval for a new program. Gray also pushed hard for sanctions against the apartheid government then in control of the nation of South Africa.

In 1981 Gray resigned from the Budget Committee and took a place on the House Appropriations Committee. But in 1983 he returned to the Budget Committee and a year later campaigned for the committee's chairmanship. By putting together a diverse regional and ideological coalition, Gray won and became chairman of the committee on February 4, 1985. Although some feared that the urban liberal would be unable to work with conservative Democrats, he proved them wrong. During his four years as budget chair Gray was successful as a coalition builder and in returning unity to the Democratic Party. To gain support from conservatives for a middle-of-the-road budget, Gray cut programs he personally favored. As a result of his willingness to compromise, Gray received the support of southern conservatives such as Texans Marvin Leath and Charles W. Stenholm, men who had earlier abandoned the Democratic budget and sided with Reagan Republicans. A tribute to Gray's abilities, the four budgets written under his leadership received a cumulative total of 919 Democratic votes in support with only 77 in opposition.

Forced to abandon the Budget chairmanship in the 101st Congress by a two-term rule, Gray next campaigned for the chairmanship of the House Democratic Caucus. On December 5, 1988, he trounced two opponents to become the first African American to win a top House leadership post. His meteoric rise to power did not end with this achievement, however. When the House Majority Whip, Representative Tony Coelho of California, resigned from office on June 15, 1989, Gray launched a campaign for that post. He withstood challenges from David E. Bonior of Michigan, who won this post following Gray's later resignation, and Beryl Anthony, Jr., of Arkansas, winning the number three leadership post in the House of Representatives on June 14, 1989. As the House Whip, Gray was the highest-ranking African American leader in the history of the House. Even before this success *U.S. News and World Report* had called him "one of the most successful Democrats of the 1980s."

Despite a heavy workload, Gray kept in close touch with his constituents. He continued to preach at least twice a month at the Bright Hope Baptist Church in Philadelphia, where his wife, Andrea Dash, and three sons, William H. 4th, Justin Yates, and Andrew Dash, lived in an integrated Mount Airy neighborhood. Articulate and well-informed, Gray continually won reelection to Congress by huge margins, gaining more than 90 percent of the vote in his 1988 and 1990 reelections. Based on his performance and his formidable political intuition, many thought Gray might become the first African American on a major party presidential ticket.

A New Direction

Gray continued to represent his district in Congress until the summer of 1991, when he gave up his seat to become president and chief executive officer of the United Negro College Fund (UNCF). Though he described his new post as "a higher calling" as well as "a step up in public service," his move from the political arena was lamented by people such as Kitty Dumas of *Black Enterprise* who said "his departure dashed the hopes of many in the Black community that one of their own might control the House by the turn of the century." A glimpse of Gray's rationale was evident during a 1996 speech at Harvard University in which he said, "I believe that education is the key. And I believe that those institutions that have been bridges in my community . . . like the historically Black colleges, are going to be needed more in the future than they ever have been."

During Gray's tenure as head of the UNCF, he made a brief return to politics, but as a short-term special advisor to the president, not an elected official. In May, 1994, he began service as an unpaid advisor to President Bill Clinton in the administration's effort to restore democracy to Haiti.

Further Reading

A biography of Gray's life appears in *Contemporary Black Biography, Volume Three* (1993). An analysis of Gray's role as Budget Committee chairman can be found in *Congressional Quarterly Weekly Report* (August 2, 1986). Additional information on his voting record can be found in the semi-annual edition of Barone, Ujifusa, and Matthews, *The Almanac of American Politics.* □

El Greco

El Greco (1541-1614), a Greek painter who settled in Spain, evolved a highly personal style with mannerist traits. He was a great religious painter of a visionary nature and a master portraitist.

El Greco is regarded as one of the greatest painters of all time. He was rescued from critical and popular neglect by the French impressionists in the late 19th century, but his rise to fame came with the reevaluations of the first decade of the 20th century. El Greco's mature art, which is notable for its emotional expressionism rather than realism or idealism in the neoclassic sense, fulfilled the concepts of the new cult of expressionism at the beginning of the 20th century.

El Greco, whose real name was Domenikos Theotokopoulos, was born in Candia, Crete, in 1541, according to his own statement. The artist must have had some preparation as a painter before he went to the great artistic center of Venice. Since Crete was a Venetian possession during that period, he logically chose to go to Venice rather than to Florence or Rome. The precise date of his arrival in Italy is unknown; it may have been as early as 1560. The fact that he witnessed a document in Candia in 1566 has caused some writers to insist that his first voyage to Venice came later, yet he may have returned to Crete for a visit the year of his father's death (1566). During his stay in Italy he became known as Il Greco ("the Greek") because his name was too difficult to pronounce. Later, in Spain, he was called El Greco.

El Greco was said to be a pupil of Titian in a letter the miniaturist Giulio Clovio wrote to Cardinal Alessandro Farnese on Nov. 16, 1570, asking that the young man be given lodging in the Palazzo Farnese in Rome. El Greco's trip to Rome in 1570 is thus proved, and he was still there on Oct. 18, 1572, when he paid his dues to the painters' guild

of St. Luke. It is speculated that he subsequently returned from Rome to Venice and that he departed for Spain in 1576, possibly because of a plague in Venice.

The story has often been repeated that Giulio Clovio visited the young painter in Rome and found that he had closed his blinds on a sunny day because the light of day would destroy his inner light. That tale was invented by a Yugoslavian student studying in Munich in 1922-1923. A much earlier fabrication given circulation by Giulio Mancini (ca. 1614-1621) holds that El Greco had to flee from Rome to Spain because he had criticized Michelangelo's *Last Judgment* in the Sistine Chapel and said that he could do better.

Various reasons for El Greco's migration to Spain have been advanced, among them that he hoped for commissions to work at the great monastery of the Escorial, which King Philip II had begun in 1536. El Greco knew that Philip had been a great patron of Titian, who provided several religious compositions for the Escorial as well as mythological pictures and portraits for Philip's art collection. Another probable enticement was the advance promise of a commission for the altars for the church of S. Domingo el Antiguo in Toledo.

In 1577 El Greco arrived in Madrid and soon visited Toledo. There he executed his first great commission, the high altar and the two lateral altars of S. Domingo el Antiguo, and the *Espolio,* or *Disrobing of Christ,* in the Cathedral (both 1577-1579). A controversy over payment for the latter work led to a litigation, the preserved document for which provides valuable information about El Greco at the beginning of his Spanish years, when he still understood little Castilian.

At this time El Greco formed a liaison with a young woman, Doña Jerónima de las Cuevas, by whom he had a son, Jorge Manuel Theotocopuli (1578-1631). El Greco's failure to marry her despite the respectful reference to her in his last testament has given rise to considerable speculation. The possibility that he left an estranged wife in Italy is by no means unreasonable.

El Greco's only connection with Philip II and the Spanish court occurred in the early Spanish years, when he painted the *Allegory of the Holy League* (1578-1579) and the *Martyrdom of St. Maurice* (1580-1582; both Escorial). That Philip did not like the latter picture is reported by the contemporary historian of the Escorial, Padre Sigüenza.

El Greco settled in Toledo between 1577 and 1579, and there he remained until his death on April 6 or 7, 1614. His fame spread to other parts of Spain, but most of his commissions were in Toledo and the vicinity.

Personality of the Artist

El Greco was a Renaissance man of great culture, familiar with Greek and Latin literature as well as Italian and Spanish. His remarkable library, the inventory of which is known, demonstrates his broad humanistic interests. He owned copies of the architectural treatises of Leon Battista Alberti, Giacomo da Vignola, Andrea Palladio, and Sebastiano Serlio. El Greco prepared an edition of the Roman architectural treatise of Vitruvius, which has been lost.

El Greco numbered among his intimate friends the leading humanists and intellectuals of Toledo, men such as the scholar Antonio de Covarrubias, Pedro Salazar de Mendoza, Fray Hortensio Paravicino, and the poet Luis de Góngora y Argote. The last two men wrote poems about El Greco's works.

Earliest Works

Two works signed by Master Domenikos, an icon (Athens) and a small portable triptych (Modena), have frequently been attributed to El Greco, but, as the patronym is lacking, his authorship cannot be established with certainty. After World War II a vast number of mediocre panels by so-called Madonna painters (*Madonneri*) were attributed to the youthful El Greco, but they have now been discredited.

Italian Period (ca. 1560-1576)

Signed works of this period by El Greco include the *Purification of the Temple* (Washington and Minneapolis), *Christ Healing the Blind* (Parma), *St. Francis Receiving the Stigmata* (Geneva and Naples), *Pietà* (Philadelphia), *Boy Lighting a Candle* (Manhasset), and the portraits *Giulio Clovio* (Naples) and *Vincenzo Anastagi* (New York). At this time he signed his paintings in Greek capital letters. His style is notably Venetian in richness of color and illusionistic application of the paint. His interest in the composition of deep space reveals his knowledge of Raphael's murals in the Vatican, Serlio's books on architecture, and contemporary developments in Venice.

Early Spanish Period (1577-1588)

El Greco's first masterpiece of this period is the *Assumption of the Virgin* (signed and dated 1577; Chicago) from the high altar of S. Domingo el Antiguo, Toledo. Based on Titian's *Assumption* in the church of S. Maria dei Frari in Venice, it nevertheless shows independence in spatial organization and technical brilliance in the colors. The powerful physical types and certain poses in the *Trinity* (Madrid) from the same altar reveal El Greco's admiration of the heroic concepts of Michelangelo, whose art he had obviously studied in Rome. At the same time El Greco's color and technical procedures remain Venetian. The *Espolio* (1577-1579; sacristy of Toledo Cathedral) shows even greater originality in the composition: the figures are brought into the foreground, largely excluding depth, in a way that constitutes El Greco's interpretation of mannerism. But the medieval Byzantine tradition is reflected in the way the heads of the tormentors are placed in superimposed rows.

Masterpieces followed with such rapidity and in such great quantity that only a few can be mentioned. The *Martyrdom of St. Maurice* (1580-1582; Escorial) is astonishing in the brilliance of color, with the yellow against the blue producing a dazzling effect. The pale tonalities have antecedents in late Roman mannerism, but El Greco achieved expressionistic results using them. Other important paintings are the *Crucifixion with Two Donors* (Paris) and the *Holy Family* (New York).

This period culminated in the large canvas *Burial of the Conde de Orgaz* (1586-1588; church of S. Tomé, Toledo), a work that, combining all aspects of the artist's genius, is generally regarded as his greatest masterpiece and one of the outstanding paintings of all time. The figures are brought into a wall-like composition in the foreground, eliminating space in depth, a method that characterizes mannerism as distinguished from the deep space of High Renaissance composition. Some portraits of El Greco's Toledan contemporaries in the burial scene are identifiable. They are presented in normal human proportions, but the extreme elongation and distortion of the figures in heaven combined with the glacial clouds create a vision of a supernatural world.

Late Style (1588-1614)

El Greco maintained a sense of idealism in his late pictures when the subject demanded it, as in his lovely conception of the Madonna in the *Holy Family with St. Anne* (Hospital of St. John Extra Muros, Toledo) and the *Holy Family with the Magdalen* (Cleveland; both ca. 1590-1595). In these compositions the figures are brought into the foreground with only the sky as background, a method of organization that is distinctly mannerist.

El Greco received a number of important commissions at this time. The high altar (1597-1599) of the chapel of S. José, Toledo, is dedicated to *St. Joseph with the Christ Child,* tenderly interpreted with the tall otherworldly Joseph crowned from above by the wildly distorted and foreshortened angels; the city of Toledo is seen in the background. *St. Martin Dividing His Cloak with the Beggar* and the *Madonna with Saints Agnes and Martina* (both Washington) originally occupied the lateral altars of the same chapel. *St. Martin* impresses the spectator because of the extreme elongation of the partly nude body of the pathetic young beggar. Here El Greco's personal interpretation is fully in evidence in his use of mannerist elongation, a trait widely characteristic of Italian art as early as 1520. The technical brilliance of both pictures is memorable, most especially in the landscape glimpse of Toledo behind St. Martin.

Between 1596 and 1600 El Greco was busily engaged in preparing three large canvases for the high altar of the now-destroyed church of the Colegio de Doña María de Aragón in Madrid. The center of the altarpiece contained the *Annunciation* (Villanueva y Geltrú), the *Adoration of the Shepherds* (Bucharest), and the *Baptism of Christ* (Madrid). Here the supernatural atmosphere is maintained throughout, especially in the *Annunciation,* where the Madonna and Gabriel are enveloped in swirling clouds removed in time and place from all earthly experience.

El Greco's next major commission involved the altars (1603-1605) of the Hospital of Charity at Illescas in the province of Toledo, where litigation ensued and the trustees of the organization threatened to discharge him and engage a "good painter in the city of Madrid" at a time when El Greco was by far the greatest master in Spain. He finally agreed to accept a miserably inadequate payment, and there remains in the church today the celebrated picture *St.*

Ildefonso, one of the artist's finest interpretations of an austere and ascetic saint.

El Greco's last major commission was for the high altar and lateral altars of the Hospital of St. John Extra Muros, unfinished at his death. The architectural design of the high altar was modified by the artist's son (1625-1628). In one fragment, the *Fifth Seal of the Apocalypse* (New York), El Greco reached the ultimate in the expression of the fantastic vision as described in the Book of Revelations.

El Greco produced numerous religious works dedicated to the Passion of Christ, such as *Christ Carrying the Cross* and the *Crucifixion,* as well as two series of the 12 Apostles (all Toledo). His votive pictures include *St. Francis, St. Jerome,* the *Magdalen in Penitence,* and *St. Peter in Tears.* Two famous landscapes survive: the stormy, romantic, and highly subjective *View of Toledo* (ca. 1595; New York) and the later topographic *View and Plan of Toledo* (ca. 1610; Toledo), so beautifully painted in thin grayish tones. In the center the artist placed the Hospital of St. John Extra Muros on a cloud so that it could be seen better, as he explains in the legend on the canvas. To these last years too belong his fantastic interpretation of *Laocoön and His Sons,* with the subjects being strangled by the serpents sent by Neptune—against another mirage of the city of Toledo.

In addition to the portraits in the *Burial of the Conde de Orgaz,* El Greco executed throughout his career a considerable number of single figures, such as *Antonio de Covarrubias* (Paris), *Fray Hortensio Paravicino* (Boston), and *Cardinal Fernando Niño de Guevara* (New York), depicting the fiery inquisitor. Equally unforgettable are those in half length in a restricted palette of grays and blacks, thinly painted, such as *Jerónimo de Cevallos* (Madrid).

Further Reading

The most complete study of El Greco, which includes biography, stylistic development, and a *catalogue raisonné* with full bibliography and 405 illustrations, is Harold E. Wethey, *El Greco and His School* (2 vols., 1962). Pál Kelemen, *El Greco Revisited: Candia, Venice, Toledo* (1961), is largely devoted to a defense of the thesis that El Greco was a Byzantine master. Antonina Vallentin, *El Greco* (1954; trans. 1955), is an intelligently conceived biography. Paul Guinard, *El Greco: Biographical and Critical Study* (1956), is a small volume that contains a useful account of the major aspects of the artist's career. □

Andrew M. Greeley

An American Catholic priest, Andrew M. Greeley (born 1928) wrote sociological studies of American religion and of ethnicity, popular presentations of the Catholic faith, and a number of novels.

Andrew M. Greeley was born in Oak Park, Illinois, February 5, 1928. From an early age he determined to become a priest, attending a seminary high school and college. He received an A.B. from St. Mary of the

Lake Seminary in Chicago in 1950, an S.T.B. in 1952, and an S.T.L. in 1954, when he was ordained. From 1954 to 1964 he served as an assistant pastor at Christ the King parish in Chicago, during which time he studied sociology at the University of Chicago, receiving a Ph.D. in 1962. His dissertation dealt with the influence of religion on the career plans of 1961 college graduates.

Combined Sociology and Faith

Sociology, an interest in Catholic education, and a ministry to Catholic youth dominated Greeley's early career and writings. From 1961 to 1968 he was a program director at the National Opinion Research Center in Chicago, and in 1973 he became the director of the Center for the Study of American Pluralism. He taught sociology at the University of Chicago from 1963 to 1972, and beginning in 1978 he taught intermittently at the University of Arizona.

Greeley's first writings included such titles as *The Church and the Suburbs* (1959) and *Religion and Career* (1963), works in which he put empirical sociology to use. At the same time, he was drawing on his ministerial work with young Catholics in books such as *Strangers in the House* (1961), which described the problems of Catholic teenagers. In the late 1960s he did several studies of Catholic education, concluding that the religious impact of parochial schooling seemed negligible. He was also intent on explaining the Christian faith to lay people, producing readable books such as *The Jesus Myth* (1971) and *The Moses Myth* (1971). In 1972 he published the results of a two-year study of American priests, reporting widespread dissatisfaction.

Although this work had been underwritten by the American Catholic bishops, they repudiated its findings, leading Greeley to comment: "Honesty compels me to say that I believe the present leadership in the church to be morally, intellectually, and religiously bankrupt." A significant aspect of Greeley's profile after 1972 was alienation from the American Catholic bishops.

Joining his interest in sociology to a strong sense of his Irish-Catholic heritage, Greeley ventured into the area of ethnicity in 1974, studying the impact of ethnic background and lamenting the assimilation of Irish-Catholics to American Protestant models. In his assessments of American Catholic faith after the Second Vatican Council (1962-1965), he focused on the 1968 encyclical of Pope Paul IV that reaffirmed the ban on artificial birth control. In Greeley's view, this encyclical greatly lowered the credibility of church leaders in the eyes of American Catholics and accounted for a significant drop in church attendance. Another reason for the drop was Vatican II's shift from a God of law to a God of love, who might be presumed to look more to the heart than such externals as attendance at Sunday Mass.

Became a Popular Novelist

Greeley had always written for newspapers and magazines, as well as giving radio and television interviews, but he advanced the popular thrust of his work in 1979 with reports on the elections of Popes John Paul I and John Paul II, for which he traveled to Rome. In 1981 he launched what proved to be a hugely successful career as a novelist with *The Cardinal Sins,* a potboiler depicting the sordid, all-too-human inside of clerical and upper-class Chicago Catholic culture. After that beginning he poured forth a stream of best-sellers (*Thy Brother's Wife* [1982], *Ascent into Hell* [1984], *Virgin and Martyr* [1985], *The Final Planet* [1987], and *Angel Fire* [1988]). From the handsome royalties these novels earned, Greeley endowed a chair at the University of Chicago Divinity School in memory of his parents.

Few literary critics spoke well of Greeley's novels, but obviously they struck a chord in the lay population. Readers of newspapers, secular and Catholic, were familiar with Greeley's syndicated columns and occasional pieces, which were remarkable for their cantankerous ability to spotlight troubling issues (for example, homosexuality among the Catholic clergy). Greeley had a great gift for clear prose and a courageous desire to speak frankly about the actual experience of faith, both personal and social. He continued to draw on data of the National Opinion Research Institute to illuminate religious, ethnic, educational, and other trends in American culture. His own theological positions were moderate to slightly conservative, but he championed a reworking of the Church's attitudes toward sexuality and made a strong case for the importance of the religious imagination (so as to express theology through stories). Steadily he urged the Church to attend to the findings of empirical social science, so as to make its ministry more realistic and credible. His feuds with the late Cardinal Cody, and with many other personages with whom he disagreed, enlivened church life in Chicago and intrigued readers of his columns.

Living independently, and wealthy because of his royalties, Andrew Greeley went his own way, making a unique contribution to American church life. His books number over 100, and he was one of the most quoted American Catholic priests, appearing in *TV Guide* and on numerous talk shows. In fact, few American Catholics have had a greater popular impact. Slowly, serious students of current American Catholic culture are beginning to account Greeley an influence worthy of scholarly investigation.

Further Reading

So prolific is author Andrew Greeley that the best policy would be to sample the several different genres in which he wrote: sociological studies of American religion, popular presentations of Catholic faith, studies of ethnicity, and novels. A good specimen of the first genre might be *Communal Catholics* (1976), *Religion: A Secular Theory* (1982), or *The Catholic Myth* (1990). Among his popular presentations of Catholic faith, *The Jesus Myth* (1971) remains a high point. His works on ethnicity are illumined by his 1974 book *Ethnicity.* His novels have improved from the 1981 *The Cardinal Sins,* so the more recent works are more impressive. As an example of the critical attention that Greeley is beginning to receive, see Ingrid Shaefer, editor *Andrew Greeley's World* (1989). □

Horace Greeley

Editor and reformer Horace Greeley (1811-1872) changed the direction of American journalism and played an important role in the social and political movements surrounding the Civil War.

Horace Greeley was born on Feb. 3, 1811, in Amherst, N.H. At the age of 14 he became an apprentice on a newspaper in Vermont, where he learned the journalist's and printer's arts. He followed his trade in New York and Pennsylvania before moving to New York City in 1831. He worked on miscellaneous publications before founding a weekly literary and news magazine, the *New Yorker,* in 1834. Though not a lucrative undertaking, this established Greeley as one of the able young editors of popular journalism.

Greeley's political emergence as both a Whig and equalitarian caused him to seek out practical political solutions, while also encouraging debate and radical experimentation. In 1838 he edited a partisan publication, the *Jeffersonian,* for the New York Whigs. He also began an association with Whig leaders William H. Seward and Thurlow Weed that continued for 20 years.

Birth of the "New York Tribune"

In the election of 1840 Greeley edited the memorable *Log Cabin* for the Whigs. Meanwhile he was working on an organ of social and political news and discussion for the general reader: in 1841 he launched the *New York Tribune.*

The key to Greeley's editorial policy was his belief that progress demanded a serious effort to better society. He

abhorred revolution or turbulence among the masses. Though one of his major interests was free land for settlers in the West and he approved of individual initiative, he also welcomed cooperative efforts and social planning. The *Tribune* published the theories of Albert Brisbane, who wanted society organized into cooperative communities. To the *Tribune* as literary editor came George Ripley, a founder of the radical commune Brook Farm. Charles A. Dana, who became Greeley's second-in-command, wrote articles in praise of French Socialist Pierre Proudhon, who believed that "property is theft." Greeley later published the foreign comment of Karl Marx.

Greeley's radicalism was qualified by his more general orthodoxy. He held rigid temperance principles and scorned woman suffragists and divorce reformers. He adhered to conventional political patterns. Moreover, his receptivity to social experiment enabled him for many years to avoid the slavery problem as being remote from immediate issues. As his paper's most influential commentator, Greeley produced a flow of articles and editorials, and the *Tribune* rapidly gained national importance.

Multifaceted Man

Greeley was often caricatured as absentminded, half bald, carelessly dressed, and with childish features fringed by whiskers. He was impetuous and impressionable, committing himself rashly to numerous, disparate ventures and fads. These included the Red Bank (N.J.) Phalanx, spiritualism, vegetarianism, phrenology, and a formidable list of investments and loans, of which almost none were profit-

able. Generous and improvident, he dissipated the fortune the *Tribune* 's success had brought him.

Greeley's lecturing began as an adjunct of his political and social interests, but this took increasing portions of his time. He traveled throughout the East and in 1859 to San Francisco. He also lectured in Europe. Though his speaking engagements became lucrative, they did no more for his financial state than had his journalism. *Hints toward Reforms* (1853) includes some of his lectures.

Greeley's commitments interfered with his home life. He had married Mary Youngs Cheney in 1836. In youth his wife had been talented and enthusiastically reformminded, but she deteriorated into a hypochondriac. Though Greeley's Westchester County farm was known for its modern agricultural techniques, the house itself was randomly administered. The unhappy household was further upset by the fact that of their nine children only two survived to adulthood.

Equally unfortunate was Greeley's political career. He wanted to influence state and national politics and gain power for himself, but he was no match for adroit associates who used the *Tribune* 's columns. Greeley's ambitions for Henry Clay were frustrated. He had to accept Zachary Taylor's Whig candidacy in 1848, though Taylor was a slaveholder and a hero of the Mexican War, which Greeley did not endorse. Greeley's own dreams of office brought him no more than a 90-day election to Congress in 1848.

Civil War and After

Nevertheless, Greeley's editorial voice grew with the increasing strength of the Free Soil party and abolitionism. He opposed the Compromise of 1850, with its notorious Fugitive Slave Law provision. In 1856 he became one of the founders of the Republican party and spoke out clearly against the extension of slavery.

Greeley's editorial policies during the Civil War swung erratically from appeals for peaceful separation to the all but fatal slogan "On to Richmond!" His most famous editorial, "The Prayer of Twenty Millions," in 1862, symbolized Northern determination to make the war sacrifices meaningful by abolishing slavery. In 1864 Greeley, with President Abraham Lincoln's sanction, probed peace possibilities in a meeting with Confederate agents. His efforts, though futile, helped make clear that Southern plans did not include preservation of the Union.

In the postwar era Greeley cooperated with the Radical Republicans, opposing President Andrew Johnson and appealing for African American rights. A meeting of disillusioned party members in 1872 sought alternatives to the era's corruption and political incompetence. As a result, the Republican Liberal party was formed, and Greeley became its presidential candidate.

His qualities of reason and compassion expressed themselves during Greeley's campaign. But the Radical Republican attack was fierce and effective, and he was overwhelmingly rejected at the polls. The strain of the election and his sense of personal humiliation, together with his wife's death a week before the election, unbalanced Greeley's mind. He died in a private mental hospital on Nov. 29, 1872.

Further Reading

Greeley's own writings, including *Recollections of a Busy Life* (1868), provide important information. There are many biographies about him. An account by Greeley's contemporary James Parton, *The Life of Horace Greeley, Editor of the New York Tribune* (1855), is still useful. A recent study is G. G. Van Deusen, *Horace Greeley: Nineteenth-Century Crusader* (1953). William Harlan Hale, *Horace Greeley: Voice of the People* (1950), successfully captures the tone of the man and his times. See also Jeter A. Isely, *Horace Greeley and the Republican Party, 1853-61: A Study of the New York Tribune* (1947); Harlan H. Horner, *Lincoln and Greeley* (1953); and Ralph Ray Fahrney, *Horace Greeley and the Tribune in the Civil War* (1936).

Additional Sources

Linn, William Alexander, *Horace Greeley, founder of the New York tribun,* New York, Beekman Publishers, 1974.
Schulze, Suzanne, *Horace Greeley: a bio-bibliography,* New York: Greenwood Press, 1992. □

Adolphus Washington Greely

Adolphus Washington Greely (1844-1935), American soldier, Arctic explorer, and writer, is remembered for his ill-fated expedition to the Arctic in 1881-1884.

B orn in Newburyport, Mass., on March 24, 1844, Adolphus Greely enlisted in the Civil War in 1861, serving valorously. Afterward he joined the U.S. Army Signal Corps, and he directed the erection of military telegraph lines from Texas to California and from the Dakotas to Washington Territory.

A serious student of meteorology, and influenced by a fellow officer's promotion of polar exploration, Greely devoured the literature of the Arctic and determined to lead an expedition there. When Congress, in 1881, authorized American participation in the International Polar Year project to establish numerous circumpolar observation stations, Greely, by virtue of his experience, scientific background, and interest, was chosen to command the U.S. mission.

Greely's party of 25 landed in northern Grinnell Land in August 1881 and established Ft. Conger, sending their ship home. In the next months the expedition's major scientific and exploration objectives were achieved. The outlines of Grinnell Land were fixed; invaluable meteorological, magnetic, biological, and oceanographic records were obtained; and on May 13, 1882, three men from the party reached 83°24′N, a new northing record.

When relief ships failed to return in 1882 and 1883, Greely followed his original orders. He left Ft. Conger, hazardously moving south 200 miles to Cape Sabine, where the party spent the winter of 1883/1884 in unimaginable deprivation. By the time a rescue squadron arrived in June 1884, 18 of the 25 men had perished, one man was dying, and the remaining 6 were near death.

The survivors were at first hailed as heroic explorers. But reckless charges of cannibalism soon leveled against them tainted their lives, even though all evidence strongly suggests their innocence. After Greely recovered his health, he resumed his career in the Signal Corps, advancing to chief signal officer in 1887. He published regional climatology studies between 1881 and 1891 and later built communication lines in Puerto Rico, Cuba, the Philippines, and Alaska.

Retiring in 1908, Gen. Greely devoted himself to study and writing. The story of his expedition had appeared as *Three Years of Arctic Service* (1886); later works included *True Tales of Arctic Heroism* (1912), *Handbook of Alaska* (1925), and *The Polar Regions in the 20th Century* (1928). A founder of the National Geographic Society, Greely contributed to its magazine and donated his collection of Arctic books and scrapbooks to the society. Honored belatedly by his government, Greely received the Congressional Medal of Honor in 1935, a few months before his death.

Further Reading

Gen. William Mitchell wrote an adulatory biography, *General Greely: The Story of a Great American* (1936). A thorough and objective account of the Greely expedition is A. L. Todd, *Abandoned: The Story of the Greely Arctic Expedition, 1881-1884* (1961). Jeannette Mirsky, *To the Arctic!* (1948; originally published as *To the North,* 1934), contains a brief account. □

Constance McLaughlin Green

An expert in urban history, Constance McLaughlin Green (1897-1975) won the 1963 Pulitzer Prize for history at a time when there were few published women historians.

Constance McLaughlin Green was born into an academic family August 21, 1897, at Ann Arbor, Michigan. Her father, Andrew Cunningham McLaughlin, was a professor of constitutional history at the University of Michigan and then at the University of Chicago. He won the Pulitzer Prize for history in 1936, an accomplishment his daughter repeated in 1963 for the first volume of her study of Washington, D.C.

Green was a pioneer in the field of urban history, and her work provides an example of the early narrative approach to the subject. She began to write on the subject prior to its becoming popular in America's colleges and universities during the 1960s. Moreover, she was a successful published female historian at a time when the discipline of history did not include many women.

She spent most of her childhood in Chicago in the neighborhood surrounding the University of Chicago where her neighbors included an aggregation of the nation's leading scholars, scientists, and intellectuals. Her mother, who was the daughter of a university president, served as hostess to many of these academic neighbors. The Green home bubbled with stimulating conversation and ideas. Green's mother, however, never attended college herself because the historian's grandmother thought it unsuitable for women. As a consequence, Constance's mother compensated for her own lack of higher education by asserting that no daughter of hers would ever grow up without professional training to ensure the ability to earn her own living.

Green attended the University of Chicago's famous laboratory school for elementary and secondary education and then in the fall of 1917 went east to Smith College, a woman's school in Northampton, Massachusetts. In contrast to the University of Chicago she found Smith intellectually tepid. After graduation she taught briefly at Chicago and then was married in 1921 to Donald Green, a textile executive who took her back to Holyoke, Massachusetts, a New England mill town which she found provincial. Ironically, her first book was a history of that city, *Holyoke,*

Massachusetts: A Case History of the Industrial Revolution in America.

The genesis of the book rests in Green's enrollment in Yale's graduate school at the height of the Great Depression, after having been discouraged from studying at Harvard by two eminent historians; they believed it would be too difficult for a woman to commute from Holyoke to Cambridge. At her Yale interview the historian Ralph Gabriel inquired about what she would like to investigate for her dissertation. When she mentioned a topic in intellectual history for which he considered her ill prepared, he asked, "Well, what kind of a city, what kind of a town, do you live in?" She replied that it was a dreary prefabricated industrial city feeling the impact of immigration and ethnocultural and religious conflict. Gabriel then said, "Good, that sounds like just the thing." As a consequence, a distinguished career of writing urban and local history began, although Green denied credit for being a founding mother of the field. She modestly pointed out that she simply wrote about something that was convenient—the city in which she lived.

Green, by then the mother of three children, received her doctoral degree two months before her 40th birthday. The Holyoke history was published two years later in 1939. While scholars still find the book useful, at the time Holyoke locals resented it. At a next door neighbor's bridge party Green heard a woman saying, "How did she have the gall to think that she could write a history when we know so much better than she does." This highlighted some of the dangers facing a scholar who writes local history.

During World War II she worked as a historian for the Army ordnance department, which led to the publication of a volume on the role of women as production workers in war plants in the Connecticut Valley. Green, acknowledging that contemporary feminists might think her attitude nonsense, admitted enjoying the fact that she was often the only woman working in a male setting with military historians. Green also researched her *History of Naugatuck, Connecticut,* which was commissioned by the town's Chamber of Commerce because of her Holyoke study, during this period.

In 1946 her husband died, and she moved to Washington, D.C. the following year. Six years later the Rockefeller Foundation requested that she write a pilot study of American urban history. Again, she chose the city in which she resided for her subject—to the good fortune of her readers. Her work, which first appeared in 1963, earned her the coveted Pulitzer Prize, which she thought she had "not a chance" to win. Her two volume history of Washington was followed by a third on race relations in that city. Just before she died on December 5, 1975, she seemed pessimistic about the racial situation in that city and the general urban condition of the nation's capital. This, however, had not dulled her optimism for young historians to study the city. She urged them to maintain their enthusiasm and to continue in their scholarship.

Further Reading

For an oral history interview in which Green talks about her life and work, see Bruce M. Stave, *The Making of Urban History* (1977). Green's special brand of urban history can be found in her two early works, *Holyoke, Massachusetts: A Case History of the Industrial Revolution in America* (1939) and *History of Naugatuck, Connecticut* (1948), and in *American Cities in the Growth of the Nation* (1957 and 1965), which contains individual chapters devoted to a number of U.S. cities. Her three volumes on Washington, D.C., including the award winning book which covers the city's early development, are: *Washington: Village and Capital, 1800-1878* (1962); *Washington: Capital City, 1879-1950* (1963); and *The Secret City: A History of Race Relations in the Nation's Capital* (1967). In *The Rise of Urban America* (1965) Green attempted a synthesis of U.S. urban history which some critics thought too broad and sweeping. Her interest in industrial development and technology, which was demonstrated in her writing on urban history, appeared more expressly in: *The Role of Women as Production Workers in War Plants in the Connecticut Valley* (1946); *The Ordnance Department: Planning Munitions for War* (1955); and *Eli Whitney and the Birth of American Technology* (1956), which was a volume in a series of biographies on famous Americans. □

Edith Starrett Green

A U.S. congresswoman from Oregon from 1954 to 1974, Edith Starrett Green (1910-1987) worked vigorously for improved education and educational opportunity and for women's rights.

dith Starrett Green was born January 17, 1910, in Trent, South Dakota, to James and Julia Starrett, who soon moved to Oregon. By 1930 she began a teaching career which was interrupted when she married businessman Arthur N. Green and had a family.

Although a daughter of two school teachers, Edith Starrett had preferred to be a lawyer or engineer. However, others persuaded her to pursue a more conventional woman's profession. She earned a Bachelor's degree from the University of Oregon in 1939 and did graduate work at Stanford University. In the 1940s she was a free-lance writer and radio commentator, but her interest in education continued and she served as a state lobbyist for education groups.

A life-long Democrat, she first ran for political office in 1952 and, although she lost, it provided valuable exposure for her next race. In 1954 she won Oregon's Third Congressional House seat in the closest race of her career. Thereafter, she captured at least 63 percent of all general election votes in nine subsequent elections.

As the second woman to represent Oregon in its history, Green became one of only 17 women then in the U.S. House of Representatives. Acting on her 1954 slogan that "Education should be the number one business in this country," Green became known as "Mrs. Education" and "Mother of Affirmative Action" for her role in legislation which vitally affected federal aid to education and women's rights.

In her first congressional term Green introduced the Library Service Bill which provided access to libraries for millions of persons in rural areas. Her imprint was on the National Defense Education Act of 1958, America's effort to "catch up" after Russia orbited Sputnik. She was largely responsible for the Higher Education Facilities Act of 1963, which President Lyndon Johnson called "the greatest step forward in the field since the passage of the Land-Grant Act of 1862." Perhaps recalling her own experience of being forced to leave college because of inadequate funds, she pushed through work study and grant programs. She worked for the 1965 Vocational Rehabilitation Act which gave urban youths training opportunities and was largely responsible for the 1965 and 1967 Higher Education Acts.

One of her few legislative defeats came when riots swept American campuses in the late 1960s. Fearing that the full House might cut off all federal aid to colleges and universities, she wrote what she believed was a moderate bill to deny government financial support to educational institutions unless their administrators filed a students' code of conduct and a plan for handling student rioting. Many committee members thought her proposal too punitive and too repressive and her measure was defeated 18 to 17.

Green also struggled for equal rights for women. She believed one of her most significant accomplishments was the Equal Pay Act of 1963, although she was astonished that it took eight years to persuade Congress that men and women doing identical work should be paid the same salary. More women have entered the fields of health and education as a result of her amendments to House bills. Especially significant was her 1972 Omnibus Higher Education Act, which prohibited sexual discrimination in institutions receiving federal funds.

Several presidential aspirants noted her political clout. In 1956 Adlai Stevenson asked her to second his nomination at their party's convention. She later headed Oregon primary campaigns for John Kennedy, Robert Kennedy, and Henry M. Jackson.

Although Green probably could have won a Senate seat, she declined three offers to run for senator. She reasoned that she could have more influence in the House since fellow Oregonian Wayne Morse was already on the Senate Education Committee. Also, she did not want to be obligated to the large donors needed to finance a state-wide campaign. Further, she said that the party should choose a person young enough to serve many years.

Critics argue that Green's congressional career was flawed by too many contradictions: She supported a Supreme Court decision to abolish segregation, but refused to support bussing. She supported the Equal Pay Act in 1963, but never supported the Equal Rights Amendment. Some even perceived a contradiction in her support of various educational programs while deploring the federal government's role in administering them. Yet Green was always against a too-powerful federal government, noting that Oregonians best knew their education problems.

Green retired to her Oregon home in 1975, having served in the House for 20 years and through four different presidential administrations. She continued her interest in education, serving as a member of several boards of directors and continuing to speak out against officials who gave politics a bad name.

Further Reading

Biographical material for Edith Green may be found in Hope Chamberlain's *A Minority of Members, Women in the U.S. Congress* (1973) and in Esther Stineman's *American Political Women* (1980). Additional analysis of her career and voting record are in *Ralph Nader Citizens Look at Congress Project* (1972). □

Thomas Hill Green

The British philosopher Thomas Hill Green (1836-1882) founded the school of more or less Hegelian idealists that dominated British philosophy in the late 19th century.

The son of a clergyman, Thomas Hill Green was born on April 7, 1836, in Birkin, Yorkshire. Distantly related to Oliver Cromwell, he resembled him in being sober, conscientious, and practical. In 1855 Green entered Balliol College, Oxford, where he studied under Benjamin Jowett, obtained a first-class honors degree in 1859, and was elected a fellow the following year. He soon concentrated his teaching work on philosophy and, after Jowett became master of the college in 1870, took on much of the responsibility for running the college. In 1865 and 1866 he served on a commission of inquiry into the outdated grammar schools of England. In 1878 he became professor of moral philosophy.

Green expressed himself plainly and often cumbrously and was not a superficially attractive teacher. But his originality, moral seriousness, and reforming zeal had a profound influence. He firmly rejected the native philosophical tradition: its empiricist theory of knowledge, in the massive introduction to his edition of David Hume's *Treatise of Human Nature;* its hedonistic ethics, in his posthumously published *Prolegomena to Ethics* (1883). Against empiricism he argued that the mind is active in knowledge; against hedonism, that human action is free, not the causal outcome of natural desires, and that its end should be self-fulfillment, not pleasure. This conception of man's moral agency led him in *Principles of Political Obligation* (1883) to assign to the state the task of creating the conditions for individuals to pursue their moral perfection freely.

Green was an ardent advocate of temperance and an effective member of the Oxford town council. He was a partisan of the North in the American Civil War and was extremely hostile to the patriotic, imperialist mood inspired by Benjamin Disraeli. Green's disciples dedicated themselves to the education of a responsible, socially reforming elite and were soon active in all spheres of public life.

Further Reading

Memoir of Thomas Hill Green (1906), written by Green's pupil R. L. Nettleship, is an admirable, rather solemn work which concentrates on Green's thought. For details on his life a better source is Melvin Richter, *The Politics of Conscience: T. H. Green and His Age* (1964), which is also through and discerning on the question of Green's influence. There is a useful essay on Green in James Bryce, *Studies in Contemporary Biography* (1903). See also Y. L. Chin, *The Political Theory of Thomas Hill Green* (1920), and J. Charles McKirachan, *The Temporal and the Eternal in the Philosophy of Thomas Hill Green* (1941). □

William R. Green

William R. Green (1872-1952) was president of the American Federation of Labor during the stormiest period in United States labor history.

William Green was born on March 3, 1872, in Coshocton, Ohio, the son of English immigrants. He wanted to become a Baptist minister, but economic circumstances compelled him to enter the local mines. Soon the labor movement became his ministry.

Green rose gradually through the hierarchy of the United Mine Workers of America (UMWA). He passed from president of subdistrict 6 to president of the Ohio district union in 1906 and 5 years later to UMWA statistician. In 1913 Green was elected UMWA secretary-treasurer and later that year a vice president of the American Federation of Labor (AFL). He served two terms (1911-1915) in the Ohio Senate, where he sponsored the Workmen's Compensation Act.

Green maintained excellent relations with the barons of the American labor movement but could not command the respect of more obdurate labor leaders. Basically accommodating, he proved unable to discipline quarrelsome union officials or to negotiate with strong antilabor employers.

When Samuel Gompers, the tough and resourceful president of the AFL, died in 1924, Green replaced him. Taking over the AFL at a time when it was declining, Green watched it sink even lower during the late 1920s and the Great Depression.

Although President Franklin Roosevelt's New Deal promised labor great organizing opportunities, Green failed to command enough support within the AFL to launch a vigorous membership campaign. Devoted to the concept of the AFL as a harmonious family that could amicably settle its internal conflicts, he allowed the craft unionists, who dominated the executive council, to drive the industrial unionists out of the organization. Green thus became a party to the civil war between the AFL and the Congress of Industrial Organizations (CIO) that raged unabated from 1936 to 1941. Always loyal to his original union, the UMWA, in 1937 he was suspended from it because John L. Lewis, UMWA president, was leader of the CIO.

President of the AFL for 28 years, Green continually backed down under pressure from powerful craft union leaders. On Nov. 21, 1952, he died of a heart attack.

Further Reading

No adequate biography of Green exists. However, Irving Bernstein's *The Lean Years: A History of the American Worker, 1920-1933* (1960) and *Turbulent Years: A History of the American Worker, 1933-1941* (1970) contain sympathetic and critical information about Green. Philip Taft, *The A.F. of L. from the Death of Gompers to the Merger* (1959), gives a dry, detailed history of the organization during Green's presidency. For the conflict with the CIO see Walter Galenson, *The CIO Challenge to the AFL: A History of the American Labor Movement, 1935-1941* (1960).

Additional Sources

Phelan, Craig, *William Green: biography of a labor leader*, Albany, NY: State University of New York Press, 1989. □

Clement Greenberg

Clement Greenberg (1909-1994) was an influential art critic whose writings helped define "Modernism."

Clement Greenberg was born on January 16, 1909, in the Bronx in New York City. He was the oldest of three sons born to Joseph and Dora (Brodwin) Greenberg. In 1914 the family moved to Norfolk, Virginia, where his father was a storekeeper. Six years later the Greenbergs moved again, this time to Brooklyn, New York, where Joseph Greenberg became a manufacturer.

Clement Greenberg was educated in public high schools and graduated from Syracuse University with a Bachelor's degree in literature in 1930. When he graduated Greenberg was unable to find a job, but during this time he studied German, Italian, French, and Latin. In 1933 he and his father began a wholesale dry goods business from which Clement resigned in 1935. A turning point for Greenberg came the following year, when he went to work for the federal government, first in the office of the Civil Service Commission and in 1937 in the Appraiser's Division of the Customs Service in the Port of New York. This latter position gave him time to begin his career as an essayist. In winter 1939 Greenberg published his first review—a commentary on Bertolt Brecht's *A Penny for the Poor*. This began a period of critical writing about art and culture that would span five decades.

The 1940s marked Greenberg's greatest activity as a critic. From 1940 to 1942 he was an editor of *Partisan Review*, and from 1942 to 1949 he published regularly as the art critic for the *Nation*. In August 1944 he accepted the position of managing editor of the *Contemporary Jewish Record*. When this bimonthly magazine was replaced by *Commentary*, Greenberg was named associate editor, a position he held until 1957.

Until 1941 Greenberg's criticism was largely confined to literary subjects. In May of that year, however, he published an appreciation of the artist Paul Klee in the *Nation*. This initiated the art criticism for which he became most widely known. The intellectual justification for his approach had been articulated a few years earlier in two essays published in *Partisan Review*. "The Avant Garde and Kitsch" (1939) was a manifesto in which Greenberg made a sharp distinction between "true culture" and "popular art." He asserted that quality in a work of art had nothing to do with contemporary social and political values. "Retiring from the public altogether," he wrote, "the avant-garde poet or artist sought to maintain the high level of his art by both narrowing it and raising it to the expression of an absolute. . . ." This was necessary, he argued, because of the ways in which modern society had debased high art into kitsch. In "Towards a Newer Laocoon" (published in *Partisan Review* in 1940) Greenberg explained the necessity for avant-garde artists to break away from the traditional dominance of subject matter and place a new emphasis on form.

Greenberg's early thinking was influenced by the theories of Karl Marx and Hans Hofmann. Greenberg's study of Marxist theory made the avant garde of interest to him, and it suggested that abstract art was a revolutionary move away from the popular appeal of narrative painting in America. More important, however, was the influence of Hans Hofmann, the German artist and educator. In 1938 and 1939 Greenberg attended Hofmann's classes in which he stressed the importance of the formal qualities of painting—color, line, plane, and the "push" and "pull" of shapes on the flat canvas. In his criticism of the 1940s and the 1950s Greenberg developed these ideas into a unique critical tool.

In the mid-1940s Greenberg was the first to champion the work of the New York School of abstract artists such as Jackson Pollock, Willem de Kooning, Robert Motherwell, and David Smith. When, in the 1950s, the New York School of painters gained recognition, the quality of Greenberg's criticism brought him a great deal of attention. He was asked to organize exhibitions and was invited to teach and lecture at Black Mountain College, Yale University, Bennington College, and Princeton University, among others. Greenberg continued to refine his ideas about art and to write art criticism. In concise prose, Greenberg mixed references to the history of modern art and his analysis of the formal properties of painting in such a way as to make the abstract work of these artists accessible to critics and students of art. His criticism was characterized by a personal and passionate articulation of his artistic enthusiasms. In 1961 Greenberg published a collection of his essays in *Art and Culture*, a book that would influence the next generation of critics.

In the early 1960s Greenberg also published one of his most influential essays. "Modernist Painting" outlined a formalist history in which the preoccupation of painters with the formal elements of painting, particularly the flatness of the picture plane, was the common thread of his reading of the history of modern art. From Edouard Manet to the contemporary paintings of the New York School of the 1940s and the 1950s, Greenberg traced a continuous stripping away of subject matter, illusion, and pictorial space. Caught within the internal logic of their medium, painters rejected narrative in favor of painting's unique, formal qualities.

With the emergence of Pop Art in the 1960s Greenberg's formalist approach was no longer relevant. Pop Art, with its reliance on conceptual wit and its sources in "low," popular art, was the antithesis of Greenberg's formalist theories. As an answer to the success of Pop Art, in 1964 Greenberg organized the exhibition "Post Painterly Abstraction." In the accompanying exhibition catalogue he extended his critical principles to argue that paintings exhibiting openness, linear clarity of design, and high-keyed, even-valued color were the natural progression of the formal history of art that he had outlined earlier in "Modernist Painting." Despite his arguments, Greenberg's emphasis on a formalist interpretation came under increasing criticism during the 1970s and the 1980s.

Even to his challengers, however, Greenberg remains one of the most important critics of his time. All recognize that he articulated clearly and concisely an approach to art that has remained prevalent for almost half a century. Greenberg's influence is so significant that for contemporary critics his articulation of art criticism has come to define the Modernist movement.

Further Reading

The most important publications of Clement Greenberg's criticism are *Clement Greenberg: The Collected Essays and Criticism,* John O'Brian, editor (1986 and 1993). This four-volume work provides a short introduction and gives the reader the first published version of Greenberg's essays. The question of the edition of the essays is important because when Greenberg himself published a collection of his essays, *Art and Culture: Critical Essays* (1961), he re-edited his writing to more closely reflect his thinking at that time. Monographs of important artists of the 20th century written by Greenberg include *Joan Miró* (1948), *Matisse* (1953), and *Hans Hofmann* (1961). A complex and thorough consideration of Greenberg's criticism can be found in Donald Kuspit's *Clement Greenberg: Art and Critic* (1979). □

Graham Greene

The works of the English novelist and dramatist Graham Greene (1904-1991) explore different permutations of morality and amorality in modern society, and often feature exotic settings in different parts of the world. A storyteller with a spare and elegant style, he divided his literary output into two categories. The first identified his long, serious works as "novels", while the second, which he called "entertainments", were shorter, taut-paced political thrillers with boldly-defined characters designed to satisfy the reader whose main concern is plot rather than theme. He also wrote screenplays and dramas, but they have not stood the test of time as steadfastly as his fiction, which has been translated into 27 languages.

Graham Greene was born on October 2, 1904, in Berkhamsted, Hertfordshire, in England. He was one of six children born to Charles Henry Greene, headmaster of Berkhamsted School, and Marion R. Greene. He did not enjoy his childhood, often preferring to skip classes rather than endure the baiting of his fellow students. When Greene suffered a mental collapse, his parents sent him to London for psychotherapy administered by a student of the famous Sigmund Freud. While he was living there, he became a voracious reader and began to write poetry. Ezra Pound and Gertrude Stein became lifelong mentors to him before he returned to high school.

After graduating in 1922, Greene went on to Oxford University's Balliol College. When he was a junior in 1924, he contacted the German embassy and offered to write some pro-German articles for an Oxford paper. Intrigued, an embassy official accepted his offer, and sent him on an all-expenses-paid trip to the Rhineland, where Germany and France were vying for superiority in the creation of a separatist republic. As promised, Greene returned from Germany and wrote an article favoring Germany in the *Oxford Chronicle* of May 9, 1924.

His next attempt to enliven his studies brought him to a flirtation with the Communist party, which he abandoned after a mere six weeks, though he later wrote sympathetic profiles of Fidel Castro and Ho Chi Minh. Otherwise, Greene spent his vacations at Oxford roaming the English countryside. Despite all these efforts to distract himself from his studies, he graduated from Oxford in 1925 with a second-class pass in history, and a slender, badly-received volume of poetry with the effusive title *Babbling April.*

The following year Greene decided to convert from Anglicanism to Roman Catholicism, the religion of his fiancee. The shift brought him a new perspective in his search for the origins of human morality and amorality.

The same year he began his professional writing career as an unpaid apprentice for the *Nottingham Journal,* moving on later to become a subeditor for the *London Times.* The experience was a positive one for him, and he held this position until the publication of his first novel, *The Man Within* (1929). Here he began to develop the characteristic themes he later pursued so effectively: betrayal, pursuit, and the yearning for death.

His next works, *Name of Action* (1931) and *Rumour at Nightfall* (1931), were not well-received by critics, but Greene regained their respect with the first book he classed as an entertainment. Called *Stamboul Train* in England, it was published in 1932 in the United States as *Orient Express.* The story revolves around a group of travelers on the Orient Express, a setting mysterious enough to permit a large helping of melodrama and grotesque character-building. *Journey without Maps,* published in 1936, was a travel-ogue, detailing Greene's fascination with the lush and decadent outposts of colonization.

Major Themes

Twelve years after his conversion, Greene published *Brighton Rock* (1938), a novel with a highly melodramatic plot full of sexual and violent imagery that explored the interplay between abnormal behavior and morality.

The entertainment *The Confidential Agent* was published in 1939, as was the work *The Lawless Roads,* a journal of Greene's travels in Mexico in 1938. Here he had seen widespread persecution of Catholic priests, which he documented in his journal along with a description of a drunken priest's execution. The incident made such an impression upon him that this victim became the hero of *The Power and the Glory,* the novel considered by Greene to be his best.

Later Life

During the years of World War II Greene slipped out of England and went to West Africa to do some clandestine intelligence work for the British Government. The result, a novel called *The Heart of the Matter* appeared in 1948, and greatly appealed to American readers.

Steadily, Greene produced a succession of works that received both praise and crtiticism. He was considered for the Nobel Prize but failed to become a candidate. Still, many other honors were bestowed upon him, including a 1966 accolade from Queen Elizabeth as a Companion of Honor, and the Order of Merit, a much higher honor, in 1986.

In 1979 Greene underwent surgery for intestinal cancer, but had no lasting ill-effects. However, in 1990, he was stricken with an unspecified blood disease so debilitating that he decided to move from his home in Antibes, the South of France, to Vevey, Switzerland, so that he could be closer to his daughter. He lingered until the beginning of spring, then died on April 3rd, 1991, in La Povidence Hospital.

Further Reading

Full-length studies of Greene include John A. Atkins, *Graham Greene* (1957; rev. ed. 1966); Francis L. Kunkel, *The Labyrinthine Ways of Graham Greene* (1959); Lynette Kohn, *Graham Greene, The Major Novels* (1961); A. A. De Vitis, *Graham Greene* (1964); and David Lodge, *Graham Greene* (1966). For a variety of opinions on Greene's work see Robert O. Evans, ed., *Graham Greene: Some Critical Considerations* (1963). François Mauriac, *Men I Hold Great* (1951), discusses Greene.

Additional Sources

Shelden, Michael, *Graham Greene: The Enemy Within,* Random House, 1994.
New York Times, (April 4, 1991). □

Graham Greene

A film actor who has found success in both Canada and the United States, Graham Greene (born 1952) is a full-blood Oneida, born on the Six Nations Reserve in southwestern Ontario in the early 1950s.

Graham Greene, one of the most visible Native American actors working on the stage and in film today, is probably best known for his roles in the popular films *Dances with Wolves* and *Thunderheart.* Greene was the second of six children born on the Six Nations reserve near Brantford, Ontario, to John, an ambulance driver and maintenance man, and Lillian Greene. At the age of 16, Greene dropped out of school and went to Rochester, New York, where he worked at a carpet warehouse. Two years later he studied welding at George Brown College in Toronto, then worked at a Hamilton factory, building railway cars. In the 1970s Greene worked as a roadie and sound man for Toronto rock bands and ran a recording studio in Ancaster, Ontario. He has also worked as a high-steelworker, landscape gardener, factory laborer, carpenter, and bartender.

Greene took his first acting role (a Native American) in 1974 as part of the now-defunct Toronto theater company, Ne'er-Do-Well Thespians. In 1980 he played a Native American alcoholic in *The Crackwalker* by Judith Thompson, and in the 1982 theater production of *Jessica,* co-authored by Linda Griffiths, he played the role of The Crow. In the 1980s Greene worked with the Theatre Passe Muraille, acting in an "irreverent set of plays, The History of the Village of the Small Huts." When not acting, he welded sets and worked lights.

The first film role Greene took came in 1982 in the movie *Running Brave;* he played a friend of Native American track star Billy Mills. Two years later, in 1984, Greene played a Huron extra in *Revolution,* a movie about the U.S. War of Independence which was shot in England and starred Al Pacino. In the meantime, Greene had a daughter by Toronto actress Carol Lazare in 1981. The death of his father in 1984, however, started what Greene described in a *Maclean's* interview with Brian D. Johnson as a "period of fast cars and guns." Moving to the country around the same time, Greene found himself out of work and selling hand-painted t-shirts in Toronto by 1988.

Events took another upward turn in 1989 when Greene played a cameo role as Jimmy, an emotionally disturbed Lakota Vietnam veteran, in *PowWow Highway.* That same year he received the Dora Mavor Moore Award of Toronto for Best Actor in his role as Pierre St. Pierre in Cree author Tomson Highway's play *Dry Lips Oughta Move to Kapuskasing.*

Lands Key Role in *Dances with Wolves*

Greene's largest film success came with the 1990 production of *Dances with Wolves;* the role of Kicking Bird, a Lakota holy man who befriends Kevin Costner, brought Greene an Academy Award nomination for Best Supporting Actor in 1991. And Greene's personal life moved forward at the same time. While shooting *Dances with Wolves,* he married Hilary Blackmore, a Toronto stage manager. As his film career took off, Greene continued his theater work, playing "a toothless, beer-guzzling Indian buffoon" in an all-native cast of *Dry Lips Oughta Move to Kapuskasing.* Television also came into the picture in 1990 when Greene played a Navajo lawyer in "L.A. Law," and Leonard, a Native American shaman, on the series "Northern Exposure."

Apart from his supporting role in *Dances with Wolves,* and his brief cameo appearance in *PowWow Highway,* Greene is probably most popular for his role as the mystical, murderous, Native activist Arthur in the 1991 Canadian movie *Clearcut,* based on Toronto writer M. T. Kelly's novel *A Dream Like Mine.* Two other movie roles that display Greene's acting talents were undertaken by the actor in 1992: the role of Ishi, the last Native American in California to live completely apart from U.S.-Anglo culture, in the made-for-television movie *The Last of His Tribe;* and the role of Lakota tribal policeman Walter Crow Horse in *Thunderheart,* a drama loosely based on events in Oglala, South Dakota, in which two FBI agents were shot and killed.

Also among Greene's more recent works is the 1991 adventure movie *Lost in the Barrens;* the role of a baseball catcher in the 1992 TNT movie *Cooperstown* with Alan Arkin; the role of an Anishinabe/Ojibway grandfather living on the reservation in the made-for- television children's movie *WonderWorks Spirit Rider;* the Native mentor in

Huck and the King of Hearts - a loose and modern adaptation of the adventures of Mark Twain's Huckleberry Finn; a local sheriff in the movie *Benefit of the Doubt* with Donald Sutherland; and a role in the film *Maverick* with Mel Gibson, Jody Foster, and James Garner.

Greene's future is also full. He appears in the movie of Thomas King's *Green Grass, Running Water,* and in the television movie *The Broken Chain* with other Native actors Wes Studi, Eric Schweig, and Floyd Red Crow Westerman. Overall, Greene has had roles in over 13 stage performances and more than 30 movie and television productions. □

Nathanael Greene

American Revolutionary War general Nathanael Greene (1742-1786) was considered "the greatest military genius of the war." His chief contribution to the American victory lay in his brilliant southern campaign.

Nathanael Greene was born in Potowomut, R.I., on Aug. 7, 1742. Although he had only a slight formal education, he read voraciously on his own in a large variety of subjects, including military science, history, and mathematics. To satisfy his interest in learning, he amassed a private library of some 200 volumes.

As a young man, Greene went to work in the family iron foundry but moved in 1770 to nearby Coventry to operate a new forge established by his father. In the same year he was elected a deputy to the Rhode Island General Assembly and was returned to office in 1771, 1772, and 1775. On July 20, 1774, he married Catherine Littlefield.

In the growing conflict between England and its American colonies, there was no question where Greene's sympathies lay. He was on the side of the Colonies, and when, in 1775, Rhode Island raised three regiments to join the fight against England, he was named commander with the rank of brigadier general. At once he marched his troops to Cambridge, Mass., to take part in the siege of Boston under Gen. George Washington. When the British evacuated that city in the spring of 1776, Greene moved with Washington's army to New York, where a campaign was under way to save that strategic area from the enemy.

Taken with a sudden illness, Greene missed the Battle of Long Island but fought in the later, autumn engagements in and around New York. Retreating with Washington to New Jersey, at Trenton he commanded the left wing in the surprise attack on the Hessian mercenaries on the British side. In January 1777 Greene was in the Battle of Princeton. For the remainder of the year he was at Washington's side in every encounter. At Brandywine and at Germantown his superb generalship helped keep small defeats from becoming total routs.

In February 1778, when Washington was seeking to replace the quartermaster general with an officer who would bring greater efficiency to the task of supplying the army, he chose Greene. Despite his reluctance to give up commanding troops, Greene accepted the assignment and for slightly more than 2 years held that post. His performance, according to Theodore Thayer (1960), was "little less than miraculous."

Although he disliked the job, considering it derogatory, Greene was able to realize a financial profit from the 3 percent commission allowed him on all purchases made by his department. He was finally rescued from the office in October 1780, when Congress, on Washington's recommendation, appointed him to take command of the army in the south, which had been led by Gen. Horatio Gates. Three months earlier Gates had been defeated by the British at Camden, S.C., in a battle that shattered the American army and put the English in control of the Carolinas and Georgia.

Washington's choice was entirely logical, for in the 5 years since Greene had served under him, he had come to depend on the Rhode Islander more and more for advice and had repeatedly sent him on important missions. Once when he had to be away from the army, Washington had designated Greene to act as commander in chief in his place, and on one occasion he let it be known that should he be killed or captured Greene would be his best successor.

Greene lost no time in journeying south to assume command of the army and reorganize it. He arrived in

Charlotte, N.C., in December 1780. By the end of the next year he had cleared the British completely from the Carolinas and Georgia (except for Charleston) and sent them scurrying into Virginia and into the trap at Yorktown which led to England's surrender. Greene's brilliant strategy, characterized as "dazzling shiftiness," consisted of dividing the enemy, eluding him, and tiring him. Greene lost battles— Guilford Court House in March 1781, Hobkirk's Hill in April, and Eutaw Springs in September—but in every instance, it was the British who suffered the heaviest losses and who found it necessary to withdraw, regroup, and await reinforcement. Meanwhile, Greene sent small units to destroy isolated British garrisons. By the time of the British surrender at Yorktown on October 1781, which brought the war to an end, only Charleston remained under British occupation; it fell in December 1782.

Greene spent the few years left to him after the war on the plantation Mulberry Grove, near Savannah, which the grateful state of Georgia had given him. There he died of sunstroke on June 19, 1786.

Further Reading

The best biography of Greene is Theodore Thayer, *Nathanael Greene: Strategist of the American Revolution* (1960). A good description of his military career is Francis Vinton Greene, *General Greene* (1893). For Greene's southern campaigns see John Richard Alden, *The South in the Revolution, 1763-1789* (1957). Information on the part he played in the north is in volumes 3 and 4 of Douglas Southall Freeman, *George Washington: A Biography* (6 vols., 1948-1954).

Additional Sources

Abbazia, Patrick, *Nathanael Greene, Commander of the American Continental Army in the South,* Charlotteville, N.Y.: SamHar Press, 1976. □

Alan Greenspan

Appointed chairman of the nation's central bank just two months before the stock market crash of 1987, American economist Alan Greenspan (born 1926) acted quickly to avert a general financial collapse.

Alan Greenspan was born in New York City on March 6, 1926, to Herman H. and Rose G. Greenspan. His Bachelor's (1948), Master's (1950), and Ph.D. (1977) degrees in economics were all earned at New York University. For three decades, 1954-1974 and 1977-1987, he was chairman and president of an economic consulting firm in New York City, Townsend-Greenspan & Co., Inc. His distinguished record during this time is reflected by his elections as chairman of the Conference of Business Economists, president of the National Association of Business Economists, and director of the National Economists Club.

His career in the private sector was interrupted by calls to public service, first as chairman of President Ford's Council of Economic Advisors (1974-1977), then as chairman of President Reagan's Commission on Social Security Reform (1981-1983), as well as several other presidential boards and commissions. These included President Reagan's Economic Policy Advisory Board, and a consultant to the Congressional Budget Office.

Career With the Federal Reserve System

Greenspan assumed his most important public position on August 11, 1987, replacing Paul A. Volcker as chairman of the Board of Governors of the Federal Reserve System (the Fed). The Fed seeks to control the creation of money and to influence key interest rates, thereby controlling fluctuations in prices of financial market assets, such as stocks and bonds. Perhaps most important among the Fed's responsibilities is to provide temporary loans (through the so-called "discount window") to banks and other financial institutions in times of need. This "lender of last resort" function was the primary reason the Fed was created by Congress in 1913, since individual bank failure had often spread to other banks, leading to a general financial market collapse.

Less than two months after assuming office, Greenspan was faced with such a financial market crisis. After peaking at 2,722 in August of 1987, the Dow Jones industrial average (an index of 30 major industrial stock prices) floated downward by 17 percent over the next month and a half. Suddenly, on "Black Monday," October 19, the market collapsed by more than 500 points as terrified sellers dumped millions of shares. Falling stock prices automatically triggered millions of additional sale orders owing to

computerized program trading. Buyers that had previously bought stocks "on margin"—borrowing some portion of the purchase price using the stock as collateral—were then subject to margin calls and forced to provide additional collateral when these stock prices fell. Many of these stock holders were thus also forced to sell.

What consequently resulted was the largest one-day drop in stock prices in U.S. history, with over 20 percent of the New York Stock Exchange wealth evaporating overnight. The securities firms (brokerage firms and dealer-brokers) that as middlemen provide for orderly trading in stocks on the New York Exchange were hard-pressed to find operating capital as Black Monday wore on, particularly when major domestic and foreign banks withdrew their loans as the alarm spread. The financial system neared collapse from a lack of ready cash (a "liquidity" crisis). Many other financial institutions would have faced insolvency had the market continued to drop the following day.

Acting quickly, Greenspan met with top Fed officials and mapped a strategy for easing the cash crunch, using the Fed's virtually unlimited reserves to bolster the troubled financial institutions. Before the market opened on Tuesday, October 20, Greenspan announced the Fed's "readiness to serve as a source of liquidity to support the economic and financial systems." With the full force and power of the Fed backing these institutions, fear of a general collapse receded and the Dow-Jones industrial average rebounded with a rally of over 100 points on that day.

Incidentally, the bull market of the "Roaring Twenties" had collapsed on October 29, 1929, with again the Fed, acting through the New York Regional Federal Reserve Bank, providing needed short-term liquidity to stop the financial panic from spreading to other sectors of the economy. In contrast to 1987, however, the Crash of 1929 foretold and contributed to a long-term economy-wide collapse. This was partially due to infighting over monetary policy at the Fed, which allowed the money supply to fall by a third over the period from 1929-1933 and which contributed to banking panics that led more than a fifth of the nation's banks to suspend operation.

Yet Greenspan's worries were far from over. On the inflation front, he found cause for considerable alarm. The federal budget deficit had swollen to $221 billion by 1986 and was exerting a powerful inflationary effect on the macroeconomy. While the deficit stabilized at around $150 billion for the remainder of the decade, the collapse of many federally-insured savings and loan institutions was obligating the government to pay out many hundreds of billions of dollars more in the future. The overall effect was to raise interest rates, thereby supplanting spending for capital investment in the private sector. Thus future supply productivity might be hampered at the very time demand was increasing.

Reappointed Despite Differences

Having weathered the financial market panic of 1987, Greenspan sought to send a clear signal that the fight against inflation was now his top priority. This meant slowing the growth of financial reserves that add to the money supply, which, when spent, put upward pressure on prices. Thus the Fed is faced with the dubious task of fighting unemployment (by expanding reserves) and simultaneously fighting inflation. His four-year term as chairman expired in 1991. However, President Bush announced that he would reappoint Greenspan to another term, although the recession caused tension between them.

In 1996, Clinton also reappointed him, despite different financial policies. Greenspan has been criticized for raising interest rates at the first sign of inflation even when the economy has been slow and unemployment high, whereas Clinton believed in strong economic growth, even if it meant a small rise in inflation. Since interest rate hikes mean fewer businesses take out loans to expand, and therefore fewer jobs, the 1996 reappointment surprised many. On April 6, 1997 Greenspan married NBC reporter Andrea Mitchell.

He had also served previously as a member of *TIME* magazine's Board of Economists and senior advisor to the Brookings Institution Panel on Economic Activity. In addition, Greenspan served as corporate director to numerous banks and manufacturing companies, including J. P. Morgan (the nation's fourth-largest commercial bank) and Alcoa (the nation's largest aluminum company). His honorary degrees were numerous, including those from Wake Forest, Colgate, Hofstra, and Pace, and he was the joint recipient with Arthur Burns (a Fed chairman in the 1970s) and William Simon (a former treasury secretary) of the Thomas Jefferson Award for the Greatest Public Service Performed by an appointed official, presented by the American Institute for Public Service (1976).

Further Reading

General discussion of the Fed's operating procedures are outlined in U.S. Board of Governors, *The Federal Reserve System: Purposes and Functions.* For an inside look at the workings of the Fed, see William Greider, *Secrets of the Temple: How the Federal Reserve Runs the Country* (1987). Greenspan's views on inflation are given in *Weapons Against Inflation* (1979). As Greenspan is always making new decisions regarding interest rates, there are numerous articles to be found in periodicals such as *Business Week* and *Money.* For a good comprehensive work on his career, see Robert Sherrill "The Inflation of Alan Greenspan", *The Nation* (March 11, 1996). For a brief look at the differences in the philosophies of Greenspan and Clinton, see Owen Ullmann "Clinton and Greenspan: Is an Explosion Coming?", *Business Week* (June 6, 1994).

Fascinating discussions of the Crash of 1987 are found in "Terrible Tuesday: How the Stock Market Almost Disintegrated a Day After the Crash," *Wall Street Journal* (November 20, 1987) and Frederic S. Mishkin, *Money, Banking, and Financial Markets* (1989). The most famous monetary scholars of the Great Depression are Milton Friedman and Anna J. Schwartz, *A Monetary History of the United States, 1867-1960* (1963), but for a more readable classic account, see John Kenneth Galbraith, *The Great Crash, 1929* (1955). □

Germaine Greer

The author Germaine Greer (born 1939) was born in Australia and lived in England. The publication of her book *The Female Eunuch* in 1970 established her as a writer and as an authoritative commentator on women's liberation and sexuality.

Germaine Greer was born on January 29, 1939, in Melbourne, Victoria, and was educated at the Star of the Sea Convent, Gardenvale. Her father was a newspaper executive and she came from a middle class background. She completed an honors arts degree at Melbourne University in 1959 and a Masters degree with first class honors at Sydney University in 1962 before going as a Commonwealth Scholar to Newnham College, Cambridge, where in 1967 she wrote her doctorate on Shakespeare's early comedies.

In 1970 the publication of *The Female Eunuch* made her a public figure in the United States, Australia, Britain, and Europe (where it was widely translated) and identified her with the new women's liberation movement which was then emerging in the West. While the media saw Germaine Greer as the high priestess of "women's lib" and her book as its bible, Greer herself was quick to repudiate these descriptions, although it was apparent that *The Female Eunuch* was a significant catalyst in the popularization of ideas about women's liberation. Greer saw her book as part of a second wave of feminism.

The Female Eunuch

The Female Eunuch is witty, polemical, and erudite, especially in Greer's excursions into the literature of romance and the language of abuse. In it she attacked the social conditioning of women in which the roles and rules taught from childhood to "feminize" girls also deform and subjugate them.

While feminists since Mary Wollstonecraft have explored the limitations placed by society on women's knowledge, behavior, and education, Greer looked at the mystery and shame surrounding knowledge of women's bodies and the constrictions placed on their sexuality. Women, she argued, are conditioned under pressure from the "feminizers" to abandon their autonomy and embrace a stereotyped version of femininity. The result is helplessness, resentment, a lack of sexual pleasure, an absence of joy.

The Female Eunuch also examines the women's movement in the United States and in Britain. Greer was critical both of the idea that emancipation can be achieved by women adopting male roles or merely by economic change. Nor did she believe in the possibility of women's self-determination within the nuclear family. Two themes here point toward Greer's later book *Sex and Destiny:* her belief that the suburban, isolated, and consumer-oriented nuclear family is both constraining for women and an undesirable environment in which to bring up children, and her dislike of the way Western industrialized society "manufactured" and therefore confined sexuality.

A Controversial Life Style

In developing these ideas and in writing about sexuality in a way that was both intellectual and explicit Greer took advantage of and helped to create a new permissiveness in publishing and in public discussion about sex. While increasingly involved in mainstream journalism as a freelance writer and in television, Greer also had a background in underground magazines and in struggles against censorship. She was an original contributor to the Australian magazine *OZ* (and later as "Rose Blight" wrote a regular gardening column for *Private Eye*). While promoting *The Female Eunuch* in Australia and New Zealand in 1972 she was a witness for the defense in two obscenity trials in which the offending publications included counter-culture magazines and the novel *Portnoy's Complaint*. In New Zealand she was charged with using indecent language at a public meeting in the Auckland Town Hall. Censorship was one of the reasons she gave at that time for her decision not to live and work in Australia.

Greer's intellectual background was molded by the libertarian and anarchist ideas of the group in Sydney known as The Push, who drank, at that time, at the Royal George Hotel and who were influenced by the ideas of Sydney University professor of philosophy John Anderson. Greer described it this way: "When I first came to Sydney what I fell in love with was not the harbour or the gardens or anything else but a pub called The Royal George, or, more

particularly with a group of people who used to go there every night . . . and sit there and talk. . . .'' Richard Neville, editor of *OZ*, saw her not as part of an Oxbridge liberal-intellectual tradition but as "a militant anti-authoritarian, trained in Australia. . . . The regular diet of reasoned anarchy, sexual precosity and Toohey's Bitter helped mould her unique shock style.''

Germaine Greer's three-month visit to Australia in 1971-1972 was the first since her departure to study at Cambridge. She continued to live for the most part in Britain, becoming a well-known Australian expatriate, whose comments on her place of birth (its men, its "stupifying dullness") were anxiously awaited by the local press on each of her intermittent visits. In 1968 in London she married Australian journalist Paul du Feu, a union which ended in divorce in 1973.

Between 1967 and 1972 she lectured in English literature at the University of Warwick. After the publication of *The Female Eunuch* she lectured on the American circuit, wrote a column in the London *Sunday Times,* and between 1972 and 1979 worked as a free-lance journalist, reviewer, and broadcaster. Part of her time she spent at her house in Italy. In 1979 Greer became a professor in the Graduate Faculty of Modern Letters at the University of Tulsa in Oklahoma, and she later became director of that university's Center for the Study of Women's Literature, positions she relinquished to return to full-time writing and broadcasting. In 1984 she described herself as having given up teaching except for lecture tours and visiting fellowships.

The Obstacle Race

Germaine Greer's second major book was a work of feminist scholarship which attracted less public attention than her earlier work but which explored a kindred theme. In *The Obstacle Race* (1979) she looked at the work and fortunes of women painters. She did not begin with what she called the false question based on the prejudices of the layman: "Why were there no great women painters?" Instead, she asked, "What has women's contribution been to the visual arts; why if there were some women artists were there not more; how good were those women who did succeed in earning a living by painting?" Greer's intention was to discuss women painters not as individuals but as a group sharing common difficulties.

In an encyclopedic study of European and American artists she allowed only one woman the status equivalent to that of "Old Master," the 17th-century Italian painter Artemisia Gentileschi, whose achievements and struggles she described in a chapter entitled "The Magnificent Exception."

Women artists, she found, were not always ignored, but excessive praise could be even more damaging if it served to confine women to a separate sphere of womanly art in which qualities despised in the work of men were encouraged. Rosa Bonheur was described as "the best female painter who ever lived," but her reputation failed to survive changes in taste. *The Obstacle Race* reasserts the argument of Greer's earlier book: to express themselves fully, to be "truly excellent," women had to struggle against the confines of the conventional female role.

Sex and Destiny

Germaine Greer's next book, *Sex and Destiny: The Politics of Human Fertility* (1984), is a detailed and polemical assault on Western attitudes toward sexuality, fertility, family, and children. Her antagonism to the nuclear family, to government intervention in sexual behavior and fertility, and to the commercialization of sexuality and her endorsement of traditional communities were all apparent in *The Female Eunuch.* In 1972 Greer went to Bangladesh to investigate the situation of women raped during the conflict with Pakistan. In 1972 the Australian government gave—and subsequently withdrew—a grant to enable her to make a series of films on human reproduction. After that she spent considerable time in India.

Greer's approval of Third World life styles, of traditional values and customs in preference to those of the West, and of poverty in preference to materialism led her, in *Sex and Destiny,* to endorse practices which are frequently in conflict with the beliefs of Western feminists. As its author stated, *Sex and Destiny* does not attempt to resolve all the problems it raises, but it does seek "to gore the reader slightly with its horns."

More Recent Publications

In 1989 Greer authored *Daddy, We Hardly Knew You,* a combination biography, diary and travelogue that traced her efforts to discover her father's true identity. Two years later came the release of *The Change: Women, Ageing, and the Menopause* (1991), in which she explored medical theories and treatments that she contended were often contradictory, excessive and potentially dangerous.

Greer also assembled a collection of her essays and wrote two books providing literary criticism. *The Madwoman's Underclothes: Essays and Occasional Writings* (1986) was a compilation of newspaper and magazine essays authored between 1968 and 1985, some of which were originally rejected by publishers. In *Slip-Shod Sibyls: Recognition, Rejection and the Woman Poet* (1995) she advanced the theory that not only have women poets been exploited by men, but they have been a party to their own downfall. She also authored *Shakespeare* (1986), another work of literary criticism.

In 1989 Greer became a special lecturer and unofficial fellow of Newnham College, Cambridge. Though her idiosyncratic lifestyle remained unchanged, she acknowledged one adjustment in a 1995 interview published in *Elle* magazine: "The great liberation of my past ten years is that I've stopped thinking about men."

Further Reading

Most of the biographical information about Germaine Greer, as well as critical discussions of her work, can be found in newspaper and magazine articles and interviews; David Plante, *Difficult Women* (1983) contains a memoir; *Feminist Writers* (1996) provides a capsule summary of her life and work; *Who's Who of Australian Women* (1982) contains

biographical information and details of Germaine Greer's minor publications; Julie Rigg and Julie Copland (editors), *Coming out! Women's Voices, Women's Lives* (1985) includes an interview recorded in Australia in January 1979; a brief interview appears in *Elle* magazine (November 1995). □

William Gregg

American manufacturer William Gregg (1800-1867) was known as the father of the textile industry of the South.

William Gregg was born in Monongalia County, Va., on Feb. 2, 1800. His mother died when he was 4. After several years with a neighbor he joined the household of his uncle, a successful watch-maker and textile machinery manufacturer in Virginia. Gregg's apprenticeship in watchmaking was interrupted when his uncle moved to Georgia and established a small cotton factory. Nor did Gregg's career in textiles last, for at the end of the War of 1812 a flood of goods from England swamped many American manufacturing enterprises.

In 1824 Gregg established a jewelry and watchmaking business in Columbia, S.C. He prospered until ill health interrupted his career. In 1829 he married Marina Jones of Edgefield District, where he made his home. Although retired, he acquired an interest in a cotton factory, which he reorganized and put on a paying basis.

In 1838 Gregg became a partner in a jewelry business in Charleston, S.C. Convinced that the salvation of the South lay in a diversified economy which combined manufacturing with agriculture, Gregg began to study the problems involved. Following a tour of Northern textile centers he wrote essays criticizing the South's emphasis on agriculture.

Gregg also began organizing a cotton factory, which was chartered subsequently by South Carolina. He was involved in every step of the enterprise, from corporate organization to design, construction, and administration. The Graniteville Manufacturing Company became the prototype of the Southern textile mill: it used native materials and labor for its buildings and consumed Southern raw materials which were fabricated by Southern operatives for the Southern market. Its first years were difficult because of an economic depression, but the company survived and then prospered.

As a representative in the state legislature and a member of the South Carolina Institute for the Encouragement of the Mechanical Arts, Gregg made strenuous efforts to industrialize the South. As the Civil War approached, he stressed that the South must place itself in a defensive posture. In 1860 he was a member of the convention that took South Carolina out of the Union. During the war he kept his mill operating despite commercial problems and the loss of a son in battle. Shortly after Appomattox he contracted a fatal illness. A benevolent despot, he had organized many social services for his employees, including housing, credit cooperatives, and education.

Further Reading

Gregg's views are presented in his *Essays on Domestic Industry* (1845). Broadus Mitchell deals with Gregg and the economic background in *William Gregg, Factory Master of the Old South* (1928) and *The Rise of Cotton Mills in the South* (1921; with a new introduction by the author, 1968). ☐

Gregory I

Gregory I (ca. 540-604), commonly called St. Gregory the Great, was pope from 590 to 604. He was truly a founder of the Middle Ages, both through his decisive policies as pope and through his widely read writings.

Born at Rome about 540, Gregory was the son of a prominent senatorial family and the great-great-grandson of Pope Felix III. He began his adult life on a path that would doubtless have led him to the highest offices in the government of the Roman Empire. In 573 he was prefect of Rome, a post which made him the highest civil official of the city. Like many leading spirits of the age, however, he renounced this career and retired into the monastic life of contemplation. His vast property holdings he either sold for the relief of the poor or used for the endowment of monasteries, seven of which he personally founded, six in Sicily and one in Rome. The Roman one, which he himself entered about 574 as one of the brothers, was established in his own family house on a street which may still be visited, the Clivus Scauri.

Papal Envoy

Pelagius II became pope in 579, a year in which the city of Rome was under siege by the invading Lombards from the north. The new pope quickly summoned Gregory from his monastery, ordained him deacon, and dispatched him as his personal envoy to the imperial court at Constantinople. There his chief business was to represent to the Emperor the urgent need of Italy for defense against the barbarian invaders. Though Gregory stayed at the capital for almost 6 years, he was without success in this particular task, the Emperor being too preoccupied with the defense of the eastern frontier to take seriously the situation in the West.

A newly found friend in the person of Leander, bishop of the Spanish city of Seville, who was at the capital on a mission from his native land, pressed Gregory to undertake a literary project which was to become the longest work from his pen, extending to 35 books: the *Moralia,* a commentary on the biblical book of Job. About 585 Gregory returned home, probably again taking up the life of ascetic discipline, study, and contemplation at his monastery on the Clivus Scauri.

On the death of Pelagius II in 590, the people of Rome demanded that Gregory be made pope. Though he attempted to escape from the city in his efforts to avoid the exalted office in favor of the contemplative life, he finally accepted the voice of his Church as the voice of God and ascended the papal throne in the year of Pelagius's death.

Pope and Patriot

Among the most pressing of Gregory I's concerns from the moment of his becoming pope were the physical well-being of his people and the political situation in Italy. The effects of the overflowing of the river Tiber, plague, and famine made the organization of resources and the alleviation of suffering matters of urgent necessity. On receiving news that the Lombard duke Ariulf was marching on Rome, Gregory stepped into the power vacuum; he directed the defense of the city and appointed military governors to other Italian cities as well. What was left of imperial authority in Italy was vested in an official called the exarch, residing in Ravenna. Gregory was driven to distraction by the unwillingness of the exarch to take steps either toward the defense of the country or toward a truce with the Lombards. In 593, with his city under siege, Gregory himself negotiated a truce between Ariulf and the city of Rome. A change of exarchs in 598 saw the fulfillment of one of Gregory's cherished goals, a formal peace between the Lombards and all of Italy.

The Pope did not allow his administrative duties to extinguish his activity as a writer. Soon after his taking office appeared the *Book of Pastoral Rule,* written ostensibly in explanation of his initial unwillingness to become pope. It is an extended discussion of the awesome responsibilities of the office of bishop in the Church, in which much that is repetitious and common-place is interwoven with remarks of acute psychological insight into the delicate relations between a ruler of souls and his people.

The *Moralia,* begun in Constantinople, both exemplifies at length Gregory's allegorical method of interpreting Scripture and portrays his deep sense, nurtured by the uncertainties and crises of the times, of the Church as participating in the sufferings of Christ: Job in his agonies is a figure representing both Christ and the Church united to Christ in his suffering. In the *Dialogues* Gregory with more than a little credulity records for popular edification the lives and miracles of holy men of Italy; one entire book of this work is in fact the first biography of Benedict of Nursia, known as the father of Western Christian monasticism. In addition to these works there are extant over 60 sermons preached at various times, plus 854 letters, which reveal his engaging personal manner as well as his wide-ranging concerns.

Servant of the Servants of God

Gregory entertained no mean estimate of the significance of the papal office. To the successor of the apostle Peter as bishop of Rome is entrusted a primacy over the whole Church. Gregory interpreted this primacy as a primacy of service and was the first to style himself "servant of the servants of God." His service was one of upholding the canonical procedures of the Church and of admonishing bishops and secular rulers when such procedures were ignored. It was a service of eradicating corruption and vice among the clergy and of mobilizing the resources of the Church for the benefit of the poor.

The vast and far-flung estates of the papacy, the Patrimony of Peter, played an important role in the achievement of these ends. Just as Pope Pelagius had called the monk Gregory to active service in the Church, so did Gregory summon trusted monks from their cells to be overseers of the Patrimony and in this capacity both to be local protectors and benefactors of the poor and to act as agents of the Pope, reporting ecclesiastical irregularities to him and acting as his local representatives.

Gregory, the first monk-pope, did not as pope forsake the outlook of a monk; he regarded the lust for power as one of the severest threats to the health of the Church. Thus, from his point of view, he could do nothing but offer the most stringent opposition against the claim of the bishop of Constantinople to the title "universal bishop," asserting that such a vainglorious title did not belong even to himself.

Though Gregory on the one hand saw himself as a loyal citizen of the Roman Republic and thus a subject of the Roman emperor at Constantinople, he on the other hand saw clearly that the "barbarian" kingdoms of western Europe had seriously to be reckoned with as a permanent political fact. Thus, for example, did he enter into direct relations with the Merovingian rulers of Gaul in regard to the regulation of Church affairs there.

Probably Gregory's single most significant act as pope was the sending in 596 of 40 monks under the leadership of Augustine, monks from his own monastery on the Clivus Scauri, to accomplish the conversion of the heathen English. In England his monks were to establish the two archbishoprics of Canterbury and York, directly under papal control, and it was from England in the 8th century that monks thoroughly loyal to the papacy were to set out as missionaries to the Germans. Through his employment of monks as papal agents and missionaries he translated the inherited theory of papal supremacy over the Church into a program for actual papal governance of the Catholic Church in the West. Thus the pattern of medieval Catholicism was laid.

After some years of contending with prolonged attacks of gout and gastritis, Gregory died on March 12, 604.

Further Reading

The classic biography of Gregory I is F. Homes Dudden, *Gregory the Great: His place in History and Thought* (2 vols., 1905), which provides a detailed account of his life and teachings and valuable information on the period. A shorter and quite valuable biography, with important excerpts from Gregory's writings, is Pierre Batiffol, *Saint Gregory the Great* (trans. 1929). For general historical background the following are recommended: *The Cambridge Medieval History,* vol. 2: *The Rise of the Saracens and the Foundations of the Western Empire,* edited by H. M. Gwatkin (1913); Margaret Deanesly, *A History of Early Medieval Europe,* 476 to 911 (1956); and R. H. C. Davis, *A History of Medieval Europe* (1957). □

Gregory VII

Gregory VII (ca. 1020-1085) was pope from 1073 to 1085. One of the greatest medieval popes, later canonized, he was a man of intense conviction and will. He vigorously initiated reforms and asserted the papal claim to primacy of jurisdiction in the Church.

Although Gregory VII did not create the grandiose structure of the medieval papacy, he was certainly one of its chief architects. He became pope at a time when powerful forces were striving to rid the Latin Church of moral corruption and organizational confusion, when the papacy had already begun to assume the role of reforming leadership previously filled by emperors, kings, and lesser churchmen, and when imperial control over the Church in Italy (and, therefore, the papacy) had already weakened. Gregory continued the policies he had previously advocated as a prominent member of the papal court. He intensified papal involvement in the reforming movement and directed that movement along the road that was to lead to the first major clash between pope and Western emperor and ultimately to the papal theocratic claims of the High Middle Ages.

Fully reliable evidence about Gregory VII's origins and early career is scanty. His name was Hildebrand, and he was born in Tuscany, probably in the early 1020s. He spent his early years at Rome, where he received his education and first came into contact with the papal court, then still wracked with corruption. About 1046 he became associated in Lorraine with the most vigorous of the reforming groups of the day. Probably at this time, too, he became a monk, though probably not, as once was assumed, at the great reforming monastery of Cluny.

Early Career

Returning to Rome in 1049 as a follower of the newly elected pope, Leo IX, Hildebrand spent the next 24 years in the service of that pope and his four successors. During this vital period in the history of both the reforming movement and its papal leaders, he was involved in every aspect of the reform and in every phase of the process by which the papacy liberated itself from lay control, German as well as Italian, and sought to establish its rights of jurisdiction over the local churches of Latin Christendom. He was sent on legatine missions in Italy, France, and Germany, and his influence over both the formulation and implementation of papal policy grew steadily, so that by the 1060s he had become preeminent among papal advisers.

Though physically small and weak of voice, Hildebrand possessed a commanding personality, and his contemporaries were impressed by the keenness of his glance, the vigor of his enthusiasm, and the persistence and prophetic ardor with which he denounced what he conceived to be wrongdoing and pursued his lifelong aim of vindicating righteousness in a sinful world.

When Alexander II died in April 1073, Hildebrand was so obvious a choice as successor that, despite the 1059 election decree placing the choice of popes in the hands of the cardinals, he was acclaimed pope by a tumultuous crowd, the cardinals later acceding to the popular choice. His enemies were later to make much of these irregular proceedings; the cardinals, however, acceded willingly at the time, and Hildebrand, taking the name of Gregory VII, was able to embark upon his pontificate without the embarrassment of a contested election.

Character of His Pontificate

Gregory's interests and activities as pope were extremely varied, ranging from the introduction of the Roman liturgical rite into Spain to the promotion of the crusading ideal, soon after his death to be transformed into a reality. In pursuit of the complex diplomatic initiatives which his policies necessitated, he was in contact with most of the rulers of Latin Christendom, to whom, as with William the Conqueror of England, he did not always show the inflexibility that was increasingly to mar his relations with the German emperor-elect, Henry IV.

Three related objectives dominated Gregory's pontificate: Church reform, assertion of his jurisdictional primacy in the Church, and vindication of reform and of his primacy against Henry IV's spirited defense of the religiopolitical status quo.

Gregorian Reform

The dominant concern of the reforming movement had long been with the twin corruptions of simony (the buying and selling of ecclesiastical office) and clerical marriage, which was common despite its prohibition by ancient disciplinary regulations in the Latin Church. Both of these corruptions were symptomatic of the degree to which, during centuries of invasion and turmoil, the spiritual goals of the Church had been subordinated to family, proprietary, and political interests.

Intimately connected with these developments was the gradual extension of lay control, royal or aristocratic, over ecclesiastical appointments, a control symbolized by the ceremony of investiture, by which the lay ruler conferred Church office on the chosen nominee. Only in the latter half of the 11th century did the more radical reformers begin to challenge this principle of lay control. Gregory was not the most radical among these, but unlike the more moderate reformers, he was convinced that the traditional goal of moral reform was unattainable without the elimination or regulation of lay control. To this Gregory added the further conviction that the papal primacy of jurisdiction in the universal church—involving also for him an inexactly defined superiority to all temporal rulers—was no longer to be minimized or gainsaid. These convictions were not the outcome of the pressure of events during Gregory's pontificate: they were deeply held even at the very outset and are reflected in the clauses of the peculiar document known as the *Dictatus papae,* which was inserted in his register and which included the unprecedented claim "that he [the Pope] may depose emperors."

Investiture Contest

Gregory's attempts to realize his reforming objectives led, by a process which in retrospect seems inevitable, given the dependence of Henry IV's government upon the loyalty and resources of his bishops, to a clash between Pope and Emperor and to the onset of the "Investiture Contest." This conflict, which outlasted both of the initial protagonists, involved the tragedy of civil war and set Germany on the course that was ultimately to lead it to political disintegration. During its long and tortuous course, Gregory excommunicated Henry IV on two occasions, throwing his support finally to a rival claimant, Rudolf; while Henry twice sought Gregory's dismissal and sponsored the election of an antipope, Clement II.

Two dramatic events may be singled out for mention. The first is Gregory's absolution of Henry IV in January 1077. Henry had appeared before the Pope at Canossa as an abject penitent—for Henry, a personal humiliation but a diplomatic victory; for Gregory, a diplomatic disaster but a triumph of priestly conscience. The second is Gregory's death at Salerno on May 25, 1085. Undaunted by what must have seemed a disastrous defeat, he is reputed to have said, "I have loved righteousness and hated iniquity; therefore I die in exile." Since 1606 he has been venerated as a saint in the Roman Catholic Church.

Further Reading

Ephraim Emerton translated and edited *The Correspondence of Pope Gregory VII* (1932). The most significant Gregorian studies are in French and Italian. In English see A. J. Macdonald, *Hildebrand: A Life of Gregory VII* (1932), and J. P. Whitney, *Hildebrandine Essays* (1932). For a succinct account with an extensive bibliography see Z. N. Brooke in *The Cambridge Medieval History,* vol. 5, edited by J. R. Tanner and others (1929). Studies on the general background include Margaret

Deanesly, *A History of the Medieval Church, 590-1500* (1925; 8th ed. 1954); Gerd Tellenbach, *Church, State and Christian Society at the Time of the Investiture Contest* (1940); Brian Tierney, *The Crisis of Church and State, 1050-1300* (1964); and Geoffrey Barraclough, *The Medieval Papacy* (1968). □

Gregory XIII

Gregory XIII (1502-1585) was pope from 1572 to 1585. He was one of the more original and constructive popes of the 16th century, and his influence on religious life Europe and missionary activity overseas was impressive.

Ugo Boncompagni was born on Jan. 1, 1502, in Bologna. At the university there he acquired his doctorate in canon and civil law and then taught between 1531 and 1539. In 1539 he went to Rome. For 33 years before his election as pope he had wide experience in the papal service. Pope Paul al used his legal expertise widely. When about 40 years old, Boncompagni was ordained priest. Pope Paul IV employed him on several diplomatic missions and in 1558 appointed him bishop of Viesti. Pope Pius IV sent him to the last and most tumultuous period of the Council of Trent (1562-1563) and in 1565 created him a cardinal. Charles Borromeo, a paragon of the Tridentine reform, deeply influenced his religious attitudes. On May 14, 1572, he was elected pope and took the name Gregory XIII.

Simple in his style of life and sincerely pious, Gregory energetically advanced the Catholic Reformation. He insisted that bishops reside in their sees and fulfill their episcopal obligations. Convinced of the value of education, he founded at Rome several national colleges for the training of priests, the English, the Greek, the Maronite, the Armenian, and the Hungarian, joining the last to the already established German College. For the Roman College, which eventually became known as the Gregorian University in his honor, Gregory had a special predilection. He approved the Oratory of Philip Neri and the reform of the Carmelites by Theresa of Ávila. He charged Palestrina to revise the books of liturgical chant, and he supported the historical work of Baronius.

Gregory was most active in the fields of science and art. In 1582 he promulgated the revision of the calendar, supplanting the Julian with the Gregorian. He constructed the Quirinal Palace and the chapel named after him in St. Peter's Basilica. In diplomacy he took the initiative, giving permanent establishment to the system of resident papal nuncios. He tried, unsuccessfully, to bring about church union with Russia and Sweden. With the Maronites he renewed the old medieval ties.

In the fluid political life of Europe, Gregory supported the League in France, championed the cause of Mary Stuart in England, and recognized Stephen Báthory as king of Poland. The greatest weakness of his pontificate was his failure to eradicate the rash of brigandage in the Papal States. As a consequence, commerce and finance suffered seriously. Gregory died on April 10, 1585.

Further Reading

Even though recent research calls for some modifications, the best modern comprehensive study of Gregory XIII is Ludwig Pastor, *History of the Popes,* vols. 19 and 20, translated by Ralph F. Kerr (1930). It includes a full bibliography and list of sources. □

St. Gregory of Tours

The Frankish bishop and historian St. Gregory of Tours (538-594) was a Christian leader who wrote a valuable history of the Franks.

The son of a prominent family in the territory of the Arverni in south-central France, Gregory was born on Nov. 30, 538. His father had been a Roman senator, and relatives of his mother had held high offices in the Church. As a boy, he studied not only the Bible and the lives of the Christian martyrs but also the secular literature of his time. At 25 he became a deacon in the Church. In 573, while he was in Tours to seek a cure at the tomb of St. Martin for a mysterious sickness he had contracted, Gregory was asked by the people to stay and become their bishop.

Two years later the city of Tours came under the control of Chilperic, a cruel and callous king of the Franks, a man who enforced his orders by blinding those who disobeyed him. For 9 years Gregory matched wits with Chilperic, trying to protect his people from the King's brutality. Chilperic did not dare attack the bishop openly because Gregory had too much support among the people. Over the years the two leaders learned to live together in an uneasy peace. When a visiting bishop, appalled at the stories of Chilperic's atrocities, asked Gregory what he saw on top of the King's palace, Gregory wearily replied, "A roof." The other bishop said, with some fervor, "I see the naked sword of the wrath of God."

In his last 10 years as bishop after Chilperic had died in 584, Gregory was involved in a great deal of political and diplomatic activity. He kept peace and order in the church of Tours, reacting with a quiet firmness to those monks and nuns who occasionally proved troublesome.

Gregory also found time to write. He produced a history of the Frankish people which, despite its being overly long and crudely written, has become the principal source of knowledge about the history, language, religion, and social customs of that people. Gregory wrote from a partisan, Christian point of view, excusing the crimes of those kings who favored the Church and pointing out the defects in the others.

Gregory also wrote on miracles and on the lives of the saints, frequently revealing a personal belief which was close to superstition. His liturgical manual, in which he described how the hours for the various prayers can be figured from the arrangement of the stars, is another valuable relic of his age. Gregory died on Nov. 17, 594, and was quickly accepted by the people of Tours as a saint.

Further Reading

Gregory's *The History of the Franks,* translated by O. M. Dalton (2 vols., 1927), contains a lengthy introduction on his life and importance. Ernest Brehaut's translation (no date) of Gregory's *History* has some of Gregory's writings on miracles as well and attempts to analyze Gregory's religious ideas in the context of the 5th century. A useful chapter on Gregory is in Sir Samuel Dill, *Roman Society in Gaul in the Merovingian Age* (1926). □

Lady Augusta Gregory

The Irish dramatist Lady Augusta Gregory (1852-1932) is best known for her collaboration with Yeats and Synge in the formation of the Irish National Theatre and the Abbey Theatre Company.

Isabella Augusta Persse was born on March 15, 1852, to Dudley Persse and his second wife, Frances Barry, near Gort, County Galway, in the west of Ireland, where Gaelic is still the language spoken by the people. In 1881 she married Sir William Gregory of Coole Park (an estate

near Gort), member of Parliament, former governor of Ceylon, and a friend of the English novelist Anthony Trollope. Their only son, the artist Robert Gregory, was shot down over Italy in World War I; he was memorialized in several poems by William Butler Yeats ("An Irish Airman Foresees His Death," among others).

After her husband's death in 1892, Gregory began collecting legends and history concerning the west of Ireland; these she translated into the dialect she called "Kiltartanese" (from the Kiltartan region of Galway). Her meeting with Yeats in 1896 marked the beginning of a fruitful collaboration in "mythmaking" and supplied Yeats with financial support, a summer home, and needed translations. Of her contribution to his art Yeats wrote, "Lady Gregory helped me . . . in every play of mine where there is dialect, and sometimes where there is not."

Gregory's best plays were comedies. The one-act farce *Spreading the News* (1904) has been popularized through study in high schools in America, and two longer comedies, *The Rising of the Moon* (1907) and *The Workhouse Ward* (1908), were perennial favorites in the Abbey repertoire. Her *Cuchulain of Muirthemne* (1902) became the major source of information concerning the heroes of the Red Branch line of Ulster kings, used by Yeats, AE, and others in their poetry and plays. Her longer history plays, *Colman and Guaire* (1901) and *Grania* (1911), have been less successful.

Among Gregory's other works were *The Kiltartan History Book* (1909), intended for use in Irish schools, and *Our Irish Theatre* (1913), still a basic source of information on

the Irish literary renaissance. Her prose translation of Gaelic poems, *The Kiltartan Poetry Book,* appeared in 1919 and was followed by *Visions and Beliefs in the West of Ireland* (1920), containing valuable material for anthropologists and poets. Because of her tireless activities on behalf of the Irish theater, she has been called the "godmother of the Abbey Theatre," and George Bernard Shaw referred to her as its "charwoman." Gregory died on May 22, 1932.

Further Reading

Although there is no full-length biography of Lady Gregory, much biographical information is contained in her *Journals 1916-1930,* edited by Lennox Robinson (1947). A posthumous tribute, Mario M. Rossi, *Pilgrimage in the West* (1933), contains some valuable information on her life. The best critical studies are Elizabeth Coxhead, *Lady Gregory: A Literary Portrait* (1961), and Ann Saddlemyer, *In Defence of Lady Gregory, Playwright* (1966), both of which contain biographical material.

Additional Sources

Lady Gregory: interviews and recollections, Totowa, N.J.: Rowman and Littlefield, 1977. □

Dick Gregory

A renown comedian, Dick Gregory (born 1932) used his wit and humor to advance his deep interest in civil rights and world peace.

D ick Gregory was born Richard Claxton Gregory on October 12, 1932, into poverty and deprivation in St. Louis, Missouri. In some ways his humble beginnings fueled the topical racial comedy which catapulted him into fame in the 1960s. He attended Southern Illinois University in Carbondale from 1951 to 1956. In 1953 he received the school's Outstanding Athlete Award.

By 1958 Gregory was making his debut in show business by appearing at the Esquire and Roberts show clubs in Chicago and at the Club Apex in nearby Robbins, Illinois. His regular appearances on television included the Jack Paar and Mike Douglas shows which made him one of the best known Blacks in America. The radicalization which transformed many Americans during the 1960s led Gregory to see things in a global perspective. Many of his public appearances started to combine comedy with political commentary. He became an outspoken opponent of American involvement in Vietnam and of racial as well as ethnic discrimination in America and elsewhere.

In the United States Gregory was one of the first modern spokespersons to suggest that the Census Bureau undercounts minorities, particularly in large cities. In 1966, through a series of fund-raisers, he shipped 10,000 pounds of navy beans to Marks, Mississippi, to feed hungry people. In addition, he advocated large families as a way to both counter and protest racism.

Internationally, Gregory was a major leader of the antiwar movement. He traveled to France to protest French involvement in Indo-China and to Northern Ireland to advise Irish Republican Army (IRA) political protesters on techniques for fasting. In his campaign against hunger he traveled to Ethiopia more than ten times. In 1968 the Peace and Freedom Party nominated him as its presidential candidate in recognition of his efforts to make the world a better place.

In 1981 Gregory—who formerly weighed 350 pounds, smoked four packs of cigarettes and drank a fifth of Scotch a day—put his dietary knowledge to the test. In the planning stages for more than six years, he conducted "the longest medically supervised scientific fast in the history of the planet." During this "Dick Gregory's Zero Nutrition Fasting Experiment" he lived on a gallon of water and prayer for 70 days at Dillard University's Flint-Goodridge Hospital. Upon its completion, he demonstrated his good health by walking and jogging the 100 miles between New Orleans and Baton Rouge, Louisiana. From this experiment he created his "4-X Fasting Formula," which included a "Life-Centric Monitor" and an emphasis on colonetics. The fast also indicated that the body can prolong the time it can go without food.

Gregory announced a vow of celibacy in 1981. As the father of ten children and a former performer of a risqué night club act, this news was somewhat surprising. It was a part of a philosophy of life which sought to switch from the animal to the divine nature of man.

In his concern for health and nutrition, he came to believe that agricultural resources exist to assure each man, woman, and child a chemically safe, nutritionally sound, and physiologically efficient diet. Multi-level distribution rights to his nutrition formula—Dick Gregory's Slim-safe Bahamian Diet—were sold for a reported $100 million when the special formulation became commercially available in August of 1984. Articles in *People* and *USA Today* made the diet a favorite among the general public. Gregory lamented the lack of health food stores in Black communities and sought to promote an awareness of the importance of natural foods and the dangers of the traditional soul food diet. He believes because their diets and lifestyles tend to include higher than average amounts of salt, sugar, cholesterol, alcohol and drugs that Blacks have a shorter life expectancy.

A large percentage of the profits from the sales of products developed by the Dick Gregory Health Enterprise in Chicago was earmarked for the poor and for Black civil rights groups such as the National Association for the Advancement of Colored People (NAACP), the Southern Christian Leadership Conference (SCLC), the United Negro College Fund, and the Rosa Parks Foundation. In addition, Gregory acquired a major interest in the Frankie Jennings Cosmetics Company to fulfill his dream of marketing products such as vitamins, shampoo, juices, and cookies. Howard and Xavier universities were researching and testing sites for his products. Another campaign was to inform the public about the ills of alcohol, caffeine, and drug consumption.

Dick Gregory was a deeply spiritual man but was not limited to any traditional religion or formulized dogma. Instead, he advocated the attainment of oneness with a "Godself," which he believed was the most complete state of being. He advocated a holistic approach to life through diet, fitness, and spiritual awareness.

Even at 64 Gregory was still doing his one-man stand up comedy show, *Dick Gregory, LIVE!* As late as 1996 he was opening in Chicago. In March of 1997 he was the fifth annual Dr. Martin Luther King, Jr., Guestship speaker at Elmhurst College. He credited much of his success to the support and trust of his wife Lillian (Lil), whom he married in 1959.

Further Reading

There is no published biography of Dick Gregory. He has, however, written extensively of himself and his beliefs in *Nigger: An Autobiography* (1964). Two magazine articles of interest are "My Answer to Genocide," *Ebony* (October 1981) and a discussion of his 4-X Formula in *Black Enterprise* (May 1985). Gregory has published the following books: *From the Back of the Bus* (1962); *What's Happening* (1965); *The Shadow That Scares Me* (1968); *Write Me In* (1968); *No More Lies* (1971); *Dick Gregory's Political Primer* (1972); *Dick Gregory's Natural Diet . . . Nature* (1973); *Up From Nigger* (1976); and *Dick Gregory's Bible Tales* (1978).

Additional Sources

Newsmakers 1990, issue 3.

Chicago Tribune, "Comedian-activist set to speak at college," 2/16/97; "Long Comedy Club Absence Hasn't Dulled Dick Gregory," 08/24/96.
Village Voice, 1/16/96, Vol. 41 Issue 3, p64.
Amsterdam News, 11/23/96, Vol. 87 Issue 47, p30. □

Wayne Gretzky

Wayne Gretzky (born 1961), known by hockey fans simply as "The Great One," showed great talent even in the junior leagues in Canada. He went on to become the first player to win the Hart Trophy for eight consecutive years and beat hockey legend Gordie Howe's all-time point record of 1,850.

Wayne Gretzky was born on January 26, 1961, in Brantford, Ontario, Canada, of Russian and Polish descent. His father, Walter, had hoped himself to become a hockey player but was discouraged because of his size. Wayne displayed an early interest in skating and received his first pair of skates when he was three years old. He learned to skate on the Ninth River near his grandfather's farm in Canning, Ontario, and at public rinks on weekends. But it was the rink built for him by his father behind the little house on Varadi Avenue in Brantford that received the acclaim of being the birthplace of his skating skills.

Showed Early Talent

He was only six years old when he saw his first year in organized hockey, scoring one goal, the lowest yearly total of his career. As a nine-year-old in 1970-1971 he scored 196 goals in 76 games, with 120 assists. The next year he scored 378 goals in 82 games. In 1972-1973 he scored 105 goals in the major pee wee league, and in 1974-1975 he scored 90 goals in the major bantam league. As a 16-year-old in the Junior "A" league he continued his high scoring and packed the arenas with fans eager to witness his skills. He wore number 99, because number 9 was still being worn by his idol, Gordie Howe. In 1975 he moved to Toronto to play for the Young Nats, where he won the league's rookie of the year award. Two years later he was drafted by the Sault Ste. Marie Greyhounds, where he again won rookie of the year honors.

In 1978 he turned pro with the Indianapolis Racers of the World Hockey Association (WHA). Less than two months later Peter Pockington, owner of the Edmonton Oilers of the same league, purchased his contract from the financially troubled Racers and signed Gretzky to a 21-year contract. In 1979-1980, the Edmonton Oilers, along with the New England (Hartford) Whalers, the Quebec Nordiques, and the Winnipeg Jets, were admitted to the National Hockey League (NHL). In his first year in the NHL Gretzky scored 51 goals, 8 more than he had scored in the WHA, and he made the second All-Star team. He won his first Hart Trophy, for being the most valuable player in the league, and the Lady Byng Trophy for his sportsmanship,

gentlemanly conduct, and skating ability. He went on to become the first player to win the Hart Trophy for eight consecutive years, from the 1979-1980 season through the 1986-1987 season.

Turnaround for the Oilers

Despite Gretzky's talents, the struggling Oilers remained at the bottom of the league. In his second year he led the league in assists and points, made the first All-Star team, and won his second most valuable player trophy award, but the Oilers lost in the quarter-finals to the New York Islanders. During the 1981-1982 season he continued to break records, including some of his own. He scored 50 goals in 38 games, breaking Maurice Richard's record. And on February 24, 1982, he broke Phil Esposito's single season scoring record with a goal against the Buffalo Sabres. But the Oilers had not yet made it past the first round of the playoffs. Although Gretzky had won the most valuable player award for each year that he had been in the NHL, fans began to wonder who really was the best player. While Gretzky had all the records, Brian Trottier of the New York Islanders owned four Stanley Cup rings. In 1983-1984, however, the Oilers won their first Stanley Cup. They won their second in 1984-1985, and repeated in 1986-1987.

In the summer of 1988 what was to have been a 21-year contract with the Oilers came to an end when Gretzky was traded to the Los Angeles Kings. He quickly turned that team from a weak one into one of the best. A knee injury kept him out of several games, and his consecutive league's most valuable trophy string came to an end. However, he

did win the Conn Smyth trophy for being the most valuable player in the playoffs. He also won the Hart trophy again.

Broke Howe's Record

During his career Gretzky, a left-handed shooting center, developed a style that was as distinctive as it was exciting to watch. Listed in the program as 6 feet and 170 pounds, he always stayed away from fights, preferring to drift and glide around the ice. He combined mental and physical skills to transform himself into a scoring machine. Some fans believed that he viewed the rink as a chess board and that he had the ability to sense where the puck was going to end up and skated to that position. Others believed that his greatest asset was his ability to move laterally across the ice at full speed. But it was his assists that made him especially valuable to his team. In becoming the leading scorer in NHL history he set a new record for assists (more than 1,300) in just 12 seasons. In 1989, he passed his idol Gordie Howe's all-time point record of 1,850. Howe supported Gretzky, according to *Maclean's* and called Gretzky "a great kid," and "great for hockey."

Such accolades brought Gretzky numerous commercial endorsements for companies as diverse as General Mills and Nike. Consumers found his personality appealing, and he only endorsed products he used. *Advertising Age Magazine* called him "an ideal athlete to endorse products."

Traded To the Blues

Gretzky continued breaking records and winning awards in the 1990s and in the late 1993-1994 season broke another Howe record of 801 career goals, accomplishing this in 650 fewer games than Howe played. Then Gretzky began to get frustrated with the unsuccessful attempts of the Kings. Although in 1995 he said his "life is in L.A." and he intended to "end my career as an L.A. King," he now wanted to be traded. Richard Hoffer of *Sports Illustrated* said Gretzky demanded that the Kings "either acquire top-notch talent to make a run at the cup immediately or trade him."

Gretzky was traded to the St. Louis Blues in the 1995-1996 season. He received some criticism for what seemed to be his selfishness and lack of loyalty to the Kings, because of his desire for another Stanley Cup. Gretzky defended his actions. He told *Sports Illustrated,* "I want to win . . . for people to accept losing in life, that's not right."

Gretzky's career with the Blues was brief. He had not yet officially signed with the team when they lost the first two games in the play-off series with the Detroit Red Wings. Mike Keenan, the coach and general manager of the Blues, blamed Gretzky for the losses. Keenan later apologized and the Blues won the next three out of four games with Detroit, but Gretzky had already decided not to sign with St. Louis. Instead, he signed with the New York Rangers for the 1996-1997 season. Gretzky fully intended to sign with St. Louis, but, as he told *Sports Illustrated,* "you want to play for people who believe in you."

Further Reading

Gretzky (1984) by Walter Gretzky, Wayne's father, and Jim Taylor, is an affectionate look at the entire Gretzky family, written before the trade to Los Angeles.

Hockey: Twenty Years (1987), an official publication of the National Hockey League, covers the years 1967 to 1987. A heavily illustrated volume, it traces Gretzky's career and his effect on the success of the Edmonton Oilers.

Younger readers will enjoy: *Wayne Gretzky: The Great Gretzky* (1982) by Bert Rosenthal; *Sports Star: Wayne Gretzky* (1982) by S. H. Burchard. A good pictorial history of Gretzky's life is Jim Taylor's *Wayne Gretzky* (Opus Productions, 1994).

Articles about Gretzky's trade to the Blues: Michael Farber, "Less Than Great," *Sports Illustrated*, (March 6, 1995); Richard Hoffman, "King No More," *Sports Illustrated*, (March 11, 1996).

A look at Gordy Howe when Gretzky neared his record: Joe Chidley, "Still Mr. Hockey," *Maclean's* (March 21, 1994).

Gretzky's trade to the New York Rangers: E.M. Swift, "The Good Old Days," *Sports Illustrated* (October 7, 1996). □

Jean Baptiste Greuze

The French painter Jean Baptiste Greuze (1725-1805) was most famous for his sentimental genre scenes of peasant life.

Jean Baptiste Greuze was born at Tournus on Aug. 21, 1725. His early life is obscure, but he studied painting in Lyons and appeared in Paris about 1750. He entered the Royal Academy as a student and worked with Charles Joseph Natoire, a prominent decorative painter. During the 1760s Greuze achieved a significant reputation with his sentimental paintings of peasants or lower-class people seen in humble surroundings and in the midst of theatrically emotional family situations; examples are *The Village Bride* (1761), *The Father's Curse* (1765), and *The Prodigal Son* (1765).

In 1769 Greuze was admitted to the academy as a genre painter. Ambitious to become a member of the academy as a history painter, which was a higher rank, he was so angered by his admission as only a genre painter that he refused to show his paintings at the academy's exhibitions (the Salons). But by that time he was already famous and could afford to ignore the Salons.

French painting during the 18th century was dominated by the rococo style. Rococo painting was aristocratic in nature, elegant, and sensuous; stylistically it depended upon soft colors, complex surfaces, refined textures, free brushwork, and asymmetrical compositions based upon the interplay of curved lines and masses. Produced for highly sophisticated patrons, rococo painting concentrated on aristocratic diversions, decorative portraits, mythological and allegorical themes frequently treated in a playful or erotic manner, and idyllic pastoral scenes.

Greuze's pretentiously moralizing rustic dramas constituted a reaction against rococo frivolity in art; by appealing to emotion they were also a revolt against the emphasis placed upon reason and science by the philosophers of the Enlightenment, the intellectual movement that pervaded the first half of the 18th century. A strong undercurrent of emotionalism appeared early in the artistic and intellectual history of the century, but it manifested itself with genuine vigor only after about 1760. In this context, Greuze's work is but one facet of a general cultural phenomenon that emphasized "sentiment" and appeared in novels, plays, poetry, and the protoromantic philosophy of Jean Jacques Rousseau.

The rising importance of the middle class, and of middle-class morality, also played a part in the success of Greuze's cottage genre. His work seemed to preach the homely virtues of the simple life, a "return to nature," and the honesty of unaffected emotion. The blatant melodrama of his preaching was not found offensive, and visitors to the Salons wept in front of his paintings. The intellectuals of the day were generally opposed to the rococo as a decadent style; rather paradoxically, Greuze's most influential champion was Denis Diderot, one of the leading philosophers of the Enlightenment, who hailed Greuze as "the painter of virtue, the rescuer of corrupted morality." The fashion for simplicity and the "natural man" penetrated the highest circles, and engravings of Greuze's work were popular with all classes of society.

In terms of style, Greuze has been linked to neoclassicism. The complexity of his compositions, however, and his interest in surface textures place him within the general stylistic pattern of his period. In his sensual paintings of girls (such as *The Morning Prayer* and *The Milkmaid*), with their veiled eroticism, pale colors, and soft tonality, his connection with the rococo is most evident. Some of Greuze's best work is to be seen in his portraits (for example, *Étienne Jeaurat*), which are often sensitive and direct.

Greuze survived the French Revolution but his fame did not. He died in Paris on March 21, 1805, in poverty and obscurity.

Further Reading

The most important work on Greuze is in French. References to Greuze in English are in François Fosca, *The Eighteenth Century: Watteau to Tiepolo* (trans. 1952), and Arno Schönberger and Halldor Söehner, *The Rococo Age* (1960), a handsomely illustrated work dealing with many facets of 18th-century culture. For an extremely interesting view of Greuze within the context of 18th-century painting in general see Michael Levy, *Rococo to Revolution* (1966). □

Charles Grey

The English statesman Charles Grey, 2d Earl Grey (1764-1845), served as prime minister from 1830 to 1834. He is best known for securing the passage of the Reform Bill of 1832.

Charles Grey was born at Fallodon, Northumberland, on March 13, 1764, the son of Col. Charles Grey (later, 1st Earl Grey) and heir to his father's elder brother, Sir Henry Grey of Howick. The Greys were an ancient Northumberland family, and the young Charles received an aristocratic education at Eton and Trinity College, Cambridge. In 1786, at the age of 22, he became a member of Parliament for the county, joining the followers of Charles James Fox.

Tall, slim, and aristocratic, with great debating talent, Grey early won a leading place among the exclusive Foxite Whigs. The most prominent among those who founded the Society of the Friends of the People in 1792, Grey deserves most of the credit for attaching his party to the cause of parliamentary reform. In 1793 and 1797 he moved reform motions in the Commons.

The Whig support of reform and opposition to British participation in the wars of the French Revolution condemned them to long years in opposition. It was not until 1806 that they finally achieved office in the coalition ministry of "All the Talents." Grey served as first lord of the Admiralty and, on Fox's death in September 1806, succeeded him as foreign secretary and leader of the party. He played a leading part in the abolition of the slave trade and was a firm supporter of extended civil rights for Catholics, which caused the downfall of the government early in 1807.

Grey's support for Catholic emancipation kept him out of office until 1830. He had, however, never abandoned his belief in the necessity for parliamentary reform, and when the Duke of Wellington opposed it and the Tory ministry collapsed, Grey got his opportunity. He became the head of a coalition of Whigs, Canningites, and one or two High Tories, who eventually carried the Reform Bill of 1832. Grey's role was crucial. He insisted on a bill broad enough to satisfy public opinion and resisted all efforts to water it down. He also handled King William IV with a happy combination of tact and firmness. The result was a measure which largely eliminated the rotten boroughs and enfranchised a large section of the middle classes. Grey believed that by carrying timely reform he had saved the country from revolution, and he may well have been right. Though he remained in office until 1834, Grey did not play a major role in the great reform measures which followed parliamentary reform.

Upon leaving office Grey retired to his beloved Northumberland and spent his last years in the country pursuits he loved and in the bosom of his large and happy family. He died in 1845, at the age of 81.

Further Reading

George Macaulay Trevelyan, *Lord Grey of the Reform Bill* (1920), remains an excellent biography. Asa Briggs, *The Making of Modern England, 1783-1867: The Age of Improvement* (1959), contains a more recent commentary on Grey's political career and achievements.

Additional Sources

Derry, John W. (John Wesley), *Charles, Earl Grey: aristocratic reformer,* Oxford, UK; Cambridge, Mass.: B. Blackwell, 1992. □

Sir George Grey

Sir George Grey (1812-1898) was a controversial British explorer and colonial governor. A troubleshooter in South Australia, in New Zealand, and in the Cape Colony, he was a liberal opportunist who expected more egalitarian societies to evolve in new colonial environments.

George Grey was born on April 14, 1812, in Lisbon, educated at Sandhurst, and after 1830 served in Ireland. Following Charles Sturt's exploration of the Murray River system, he obtained support from the Royal Geographical Society for an expedition to Western Australia to find a river leading into the interior. He landed at Hanover Bay in 1837 and explored the Kimberley district. In 1839 he entered Shark Bay and discovered the Gascoyne River. After losing its stores, the party made an arduous trip south to Perth. The expedition discovered little apart from aboriginal cave paintings.

In 1841 Grey was appointed governor of South Australia when the new colony suffered from economic depression. By a vigorous policy of retrenchment he forced settlers onto the land and recovery followed. By 1844 the colony no longer depended on annual grants from the British government, and the Colonial Office was so impressed that Grey was sent to New Zealand, another new colony on the brink of ruin.

After defeating rebellious Maori chiefs, Grey embarked on a policy of assimilation and controlled land sales. Land-hungry settlers objected, and when Grey persuaded the Colonial Office to defer the introduction of representative self-government, he was accused of despotism. In 1852 Grey introduced a federal constitution in which the governor retained responsibility for native policy and land sales.

From 1854 to 1861 Grey, who had been knighted in 1848, was governor of the Cape Colony and high commissioner for South Africa. In addition to preventing a Kaffir rebellion, he acted as arbitrator between the Free State Boers, who wanted more land, and their Basuto neighbors. For advocating confederation as the best way to secure peace and cheap government in South Africa, Grey was recalled. Later reinstated, he was sent back to New Zealand in 1861, following a Maori uprising.

This time Maori nationalism undermined Grey's efforts at conciliation, and he failed to pacify the natives. During a period of open warfare from 1863 to 1866, Grey assumed personal command at Weroroa. Because of their land policies Grey could not work harmoniously with local politicians, and he was dismissed in 1868 for insisting that British troops remain in the colony.

Grey returned to New Zealand as a private citizen in 1870. From 1874 to 1894 he was a member of the House of Representatives, and as premier in 1877-1879, he introduced a radical program which failed to gain sufficient party support. Some of Grey's objectives—manhood suffrage, triennial parliaments, and government purchase of large estates—were later realized. In 1891, as a New Zealand delegate to the Australian Federal Convention in Sydney, he advocated a "one man, one vote" policy. He returned to England in 1894 and became a privy councilor. His works on Maori language and customs brought him repute as a scholar. He died on Sept. 19, 1898.

Further Reading

The biography by George C. Henderson, *Sir George Grey: Pioneer of Empire in Southern Lands* (1907), portrays Grey as a successful colonial governor motivated by radical ideals. In a more comprehensive and critical assessment of this enigmatic character, James Rutherford, *Sir George Grey, K. C. B., 1812-1898: A Study in Colonial Government* (1961), shows how Grey's belief in human perfectibility and his inflexibility prevented him from moving with the times and achieving worthwhile results. See also James Collier, *Sir George Grey, Governor, High Commissioner, and Premier: An Historical Biography* (1909). □

Edvard Hagerup Grieg

Edvard Hagerup Grieg (1843-1907) is Norway's greatest composer. Although his style was shaped by the Norwegian folk spirit, it assimilated German romanticism and even anticipated features of French impressionism.

Edvard Grieg was born in Bergen on June 15, 1843. His father was a merchant; his mother, a talented musician, gave Grieg his first music lessons. At 15 he was sent to the Leipzig Conservatory, where he studied under the leading German academicians of the day. An attack of pleurisy in 1860 destroyed one of his lungs and undermined his studies, and in 1862 he quit Leipzig for good. Though Grieg looked back with loathing upon this phase of his life, his music often showed the influence of the Leipzig tradition of German romanticism.

In 1863 Grieg went to Copenhagen to seek advice from Niels Gade, the leading Scandinavian composer. Gade commanded the young Norwegian to compose a symphony—an uncongenial task over which Grieg toiled for a year, producing a stilted work he soon repudiated.

In Denmark, Grieg met the two most influential people in his life. One was his first cousin, Nina Hagerup, whom he married in 1867. A gifted singer, she became an important influence on his vocal composition, as well as the beloved companion of his life. The other was Rikard Nordraak, another blossoming composer, who had developed a passionate enthusiasm for Norwegian folk culture.

This was the period when cultural leaders were attempting to throw off the bonds of the Danish-oriented language and thought dominating Norwegian life, and in

which Grieg had been raised. In its place they hoped to create a new national language and literature based upon Norwegian peasant traditions. In 1865 Nordraak and Grieg were among the founders of the Euterpe Society to promote the performance of new Scandinavian music. Nordraak died the following year, and Grieg dedicated his orchestral overture *In Autumn* to him. Nordraak roused Grieg from his essentially Germanic orientation and awakened him to the possibilities of developing a new, distinctly Norwegian musical style.

This new direction was more clearly displayed in the next few years, during which Grieg became musical director in Christiana (later Oslo), where he established his residence. The first of his 10 books of *Lyric Pieces* for piano appeared in 1867; in them Grieg achieved his first fusion of Felix Mendelssohn's keyboard-miniature style with a Norwegian character. In 1869 Grieg was soloist in the original version of his Piano Concerto. Stage music for Bjørnstjerne Bjørnson's *Sigurd Jorsalfar* (1872) was followed by an abortive attempt at an opera. But collaboration with the dramatist Henrik Ibsen produced his famous music for the play *Peer Gynt* in 1876.

During the late 1870s Grieg became subject to ill health and to the fits of depression and inactivity that plagued him chronically thereafter. Though rapidly acquiring an international reputation and becoming his nation's leading musician, he was troubled with doubts about his "national" music and began to seek more "respectable" expression with such works as his String Quartet in G Minor (1877-1878). Nevertheless, his love of the Norwegian countryside and his commitment to Norwegian art persistently reasserted themselves.

Grieg built a house at Troldhaugen in 1885 and there passed his later years almost entirely in composition. From this last period came such works as his *Norwegian Dances* (piano duet 1881, later orchestrated), his *Holberg Suite* (piano version 1884, orchestrated 1885), the *Haugtussa* song cycle (1896-1898), the *Symphonic Dances* (1898), and numerous songs and piano pieces. Yet, with his urge for formal achievement unsatisfied still, he continued to compose chamber works, such as the last of his Sonatas for Violin and Piano, in C Minor (1886-1887), and another String Quartet (begun 1892; unfinished). His nerves badly strained and his health ravaged in his closing years, Grieg died on Sept. 4, 1907, and was paid final homage in national mourning throughout Norway, which had achieved its independence only 2 years before.

While remembered outside Norway mainly for his orchestral works, Grieg was highly esteemed in his day for his piano music. But his most unique and perfect achievements were probably his songs, especially those set to Norwegian verse.

Further Reading

The authoritative study of Grieg will be the four-volume one in English by Dag Schjelderup-Ebbe, *Edvard Grieg,* of which the first volume, covering 1858-1867, has appeared (1964). A somewhat sentimentalized and not always fully accurate account is by the composer David Monrad-Johansen, *Edvard Grieg: His Life, Music, and Influence,* translated by Madge Robertson (1938); briefer but useful is John Horton, *Grieg* (1950). Excellent discussions of aspects of his work are in Gerald Abraham, ed., *Grieg: A Symposium* (1948).

Additional Sources

Benestad, Finn, *Edvard Grieg: the man and the artist,* Lincoln: University of Nebraska Press, 1988. ☐

John Grierson

Canadian and British filmmaker John Grierson (1898-1972) used documentaries to build the National Film Board of Canada into one of the world's largest studios.

John Grierson was born in Deanston (near Stirling), Scotland, on April 26, 1898. His ancestors were lighthouse keepers and his father was a school teacher. He was one of eight children in a family that valued curiosity and delighted in argument. Grierson served as a seaman in World War I and completed a brilliant academic career after the war, graduating with distinction in moral philosophy.

On a Rockefeller scholarship to the University of Chicago, Grierson began his lifelong study of the influence of media on public opinion. He worked with editorial writers on several newspapers and went to Hollywood to study film. There he befriended the American filmmaker Robert Flaherty, whose haunting film *Nanook of the North* celebrated the daily survival of an Inuit hunter. Grierson was one of the first intellectuals to take film seriously, and in a 1926 review of one of Flaherty's films he coined the term "documentary" to describe the dramatization of the everyday life of ordinary people.

Grierson returned to England in 1927, intrigued with the idea of applying Flaherty's technique to the common people of Scotland. He first sold his idea of documentary film to the Empire Marketing Board, playing on a bureaucrat's love of the sea to pry money for his first film, *Drifters,* in 1929. This silent depiction of the harsh life and dangerous work of herring fishermen in the North Sea revolutionized the portrayal of working people in the cinema. The film had a profound impact on all who saw it, but Grierson directed only one more film. He decided to devote his energies to building a movement dedicated to using film to see into ordinary things with such perception as to make them as dramatic as the pasteboard excitements of Hollywood.

In 1938 the Canadian government invited Grierson to come to Canada to counsel on the use of film. The Canadian prime minister, William Lyon Mackenzie King, a "fellow Scot" to Grierson, was concerned with the pervasive influence of American magazines, radio, and movies in Canada. Grierson prepared a report, and on his recommendation King created the National Film Board of Canada (NFB) in May 1939 and appointed Grierson its first commissioner in October 1939.

With the outbreak of World War II, Grierson would use film to instill confidence and pride in Canadians. He was general manager of Canada's Wartime Information Board at the same time and thus had extraordinary control over how Canadians perceived the war. Grierson created the NFB from almost nothing. He imported talented filmmakers such as Norman McLaren. In film series such as *Canada Carries On* and *The World in Action* he reached an audience of millions in Canadian and American cinemas. By 1945 the NFB had grown into one of the world's largest film studios and was a model for similar institutions around the world.

Grierson's emphasis on realism—he was intolerant of artistic pretension—had a profound long-term influence on Canadian film. "Art is not a mirror," he said, "but a hammer. It is a weapon in our hands to see and say what is good and right and beautiful." Nevertheless, Grierson did not believe that documentary film is a mere public report of the activities of daily life. "For me," he said, "it is something more magical. It is a visual art which can convey a sense of beauty about the ordinary world."

As the war came to a close, Grierson grew weary of Canadian bureaucrats and resigned. In the panic of suspicion surrounding the infamous Gouzenko spy case in Canada, Grierson was brought before a secret tribunal and questioned about his one-time secretary, who was connected to the spy ring. The investigators then threw doubt on Grierson himself for his alleged "communist" sympathies. The shadow of mistrust followed him to the United States where the Federal Bureau of Investigation (FBI) ensured that the State Department lifted his work permit. He moved to the United Nations Educational, Scientific, and Cultural Organization (UNESCO) in Paris where Europe's documentary filmmakers flocked to his door and rising directors such as Roberto Rosellini paid him homage. He was soon almost forgotten in Canada. He returned to his native Scotland in the mid-1950s. He persuaded Roy Thomson, the Canadian millionaire who owned the independent television network in Scotland, to create a public affairs program, *This Wonderful World,* which Grierson hosted for ten years. But Grierson had great misgivings about television. Referring to Marshall McLuhan's famous dictum, he described television as "a massage that puts you to sleep . . . an instrument of domestic ease," the very antithesis of documentary film.

Grierson was nearly broke when McGill University in Montreal invited him to lecture in 1968. He began as a curiosity but soon was attracting up to 800 students to his lectures. Indira Gandhi called him to India to find ways to spread the principles of birth control to the villages. Sick with cancer, he returned home to England where he died at Bath on February 19, 1972.

Grierson was a firebrand whose single-minded devotion to the principle that "all things are beautiful, as long as you have them in the right order" had a profound influence on the history of film, and on the cultural life of Canada in particular.

Further Reading

Grierson's friend H. Forsyth Harding wrote the official biography, *John Grierson: A Documentary Biography* (1979). There are several books on Grierson's career at the National Film Board of Canada, for example, Gary Evans, *John Grierson and the National Film Board* (1984), and many others on Grierson's British career, for example, Ian Aitken, *Film and Reform: John Grierson and the Documentary Film Movement* (1990). Grierson's own thoughts can be read in H. Forsyth Hardy, ed., *Grierson on Documentary* (1946). The NFB produced an appreciative film on its founder, *John Grierson,* which is now available on video cassette.

Additional Sources

John Grierson, film master, New York: Macmillan, 1978. □

Charles Tomlinson Griffes

Charles Tomlinson Griffes (1884-1920) was one of the most important American composers at the beginning of the 20th century.

Charles Griffes was born in Elmira, New York, on September 17, 1884. He began his musical studies with his sister Katharine, who gave him his first piano lessons. In about 1899 he completed his piano education under Mary Selena Broughton, a professor at Elmira College. In 1903 she financed Griffes' musical stay in Berlin, where he studied piano with Ernst Jedliczka and Gottfried Gaston, composition with Engelbert Humperdinck and Philipp Rufer, and counterpoint with Wilhelm Klatte and Max Lowengard, all at the Stern Conservatory. A brilliant piano student, Charles Griffes nevertheless felt more attracted to composition. Thus he decided to leave the Stern Conservatory in September 1905 to study privately with Humperdinck.

When he returned to the United States in September 1907 he had already composed several songs and a *Symphonische Phantasie* for orchestra. At that time, Griffes became director of the music department of Hackley School in Tarrytown, New York. He kept this post until he died in 1920. An excellent teacher, Griffes was held in high esteem by his colleagues. He spent most of his free time composing and promoting his work each summer in New York City. He died at the age of 35 while he was working on a drama, *Salut au Monde,* based on texts of Walt Whitman. In November 1964 Elmira College held a Griffes festival to commemorate his 80th birthday.

Griffes' music reflected his eclecticism, as it revealed first German, then French and Oriental, influences before becoming more abstract. His works parallel the musical eclecticism of the Polish composer Karol Szymanowski. It is probably fair to describe Griffes' work as pre-eminent American compositions of the 20th century. Throughout his life he kept in touch with famous composers such as Feruccio Busoni and Sergei Prokofiev. He also maintained relations with American composers as revealed in his diary. Writing in this journal, he says: "At 4 [o'clock], Varèse and I came up to Laura's [Mrs. Elliot] where I played the Pantomine [*The Kairn of Koridwen*], [Charles] Cooper, [Henry] Cowell were there. Varèse turned [pages] for me and was much interested."

Griffes first began to write music in Berlin, where he was in contact with several German composers. He wrote at that time the songs for voice and piano based on German texts and utilizing a musical language profoundly influenced by Brahms and Richard Strauss. After 1911 Griffes' music included more elements borrowed from the French impressionists; their timbre, their free structures, and their composers' preference for descriptive pieces (see *Three Tone Pictures* and *Roman Sketches*). *The Three Poems* (1916) reveal a more experimental language, incorporating a lot of dissonances within the framework of a free tonality.

In 1916 Griffes became involved with Orientalism, preceding a similar interest on the part of such American composers as Harry Partch, Lou Harrison, Henry Cowell, and John Cage. After *Five Poems of Ancient China and Japan* (1916-1917), Charles Griffes wrote *Sho-Jo* (1917-1919) for *Le Ballet Intime* and the Japanese dancer Michio Ito. (*Le Ballet Intime* was directed by Adolf Bolm, ex-dancer at *Les Ballets Russes.*) This piece achieved several Oriental effects through delicate orchestration. In 1917 Griffes wrote a colorful orchestral version of his most successful Oriental work, *The Pleasure Dome of Kubla Khan.* It was probably through French music (for example, Debussy, St-Saëns) that Charles Griffes became attracted to Orientalism.

In his last works, Charles Griffes tended to use a more abstract and structured musical style whose language became deeply complex. His *Sonata* for piano in three movements (1917-1918) and his *Three Preludes* for piano, Griffes' last completed work, clearly revealed this new turn in his music. The *Three Preludes* showed several similarities to Schoenberg's *Sechs Kleine Klavierstücke.*

Further Reading

E. M. Maisel, *Charles T. Griffes: The Life of an American Composer* (1943, 1984); D. K. Anderson, *The Works of Charles T. Griffes: A Descriptive Catalogue* (1966); and D. Boda, *The Music of Charles Griffes* (Dissertation, Florida State University, 1962) are major sources of information on Charles Griffes and his work.

Additional Sources

Anderson, Donna K., *Charles T. Griffes: a life in music,* Washington: Smithsonian Institution Press, 1993.
Maisel, Edward, *Charles T. Griffes, the life of an American composer,* New York: Knopf: Distributed by Random House, 1984. □

David Wark Griffith

David Wark Griffith (1875-1948), American film maker, was a pioneer director-producer who invented much of the basic technical grammar of modern cinema.

On Jan. 22, 1875, D. W. Griffith was born at Crestwood, Oldham County, Ky., the descendant of a distinguished (but impoverished) Southern family. Scantily educated but convinced of his "aristocracy," he became an actor at 18 in Louisville. For 10 years he was a supporting player in provincial companies, using the stage name Lawrence Griffith to protect his family's honor but his real name for the plays and poetry he was trying to publish. In 1906 he secretly married actress Linda Arvidson Johnson, who viewed his literary and directorial aspirations unsympathetically and, after 5 years, left him.

Early Films

In 1907 Griffith sold a poem to *Frank Leslie's Weekly* and a play, *A Fool and a Girl,* to actor James K. Hackett. The play promptly failed, and Griffith was driven to try the then unsavory movie business. E. S. Porter, whose *Great Train Robbery* was the first "story" film, gave him the lead in a primitive one-reeler called *Rescued from an Eagle's Nest* and unwittingly started Griffith toward greatness.

In 1908 Griffith sold several stories to the Biograph Company and also acted in them. Within a few months he had a chance to direct. The success of his first effort, *The Adventures of Dollie,* led to regular employment, a series of rapidly improving contracts, and pride enough in his work to use his real name.

During 5 years with Biograph, Griffith made hundreds of short pictures and gradually won consent to increase their length beyond one reel, thus enabling him to expand narra-

tive content. With the help of his famed cameraman, G. W. "Billy" Bitzer, he made revolutionary technical innovations in film making. He also started the cinema careers of Mary Pickford, Mack Sennett, the Gish sisters, Lionel Barrymore, and many others.

Griffith Classics

In 1913 Griffith formed an independent company. Within 2 years he completed his epic masterpiece *The Birth of a Nation* (1915), often considered the most important film ever made. Dealing with the Civil War and its aftermath in the South, it was, for its day, incredibly long (12 reels) and expensive ($100,000). However, it grossed $18 million within a few years of release and established once and for all the astonishing power and potentiality of cinema as a serious art form. The film also aroused storms of controversy because of its treatment of African Americans and Ku Klux Klansmen.

Determined to clear himself of charges of prejudice, Griffith next made one of the most enormous, complex, and ambitious pictures in history. *Intolerance* (1916) attempted to interweave four parallel stories—modern, biblical, 16th-century French, and Babylonian—into a monumental sermon on the evils of inhumanity. His financial backers were appalled; audiences found it chaotic and exhausting; but for all its faults, *Intolerance* established techniques and conventions which permanently affected film making. Individual fragments of this huge, disjointed picture became the basis for entire schools of cinematic development. The overpowering Babylonian sequences with immense crowds and sumptuous spectacle provided Cecil B. DeMille and others with the substance of their whole careers.

Formation of United Artists

In 1917 Griffith made a propaganda film for the British government, *Hearts of the World,* which served mainly to display the director's ultimately fatal tendency toward melodrama and sentimentality.

Returning to the United States, Griffith joined Mary Pickford, Douglas Fairbanks, and Charlie Chaplin in forming United Artists, through which he released such famous pictures as *Broken Blossoms* (1919), *Way Down East* (1920), and *Orphans of the Storm* (1921); their varying success temporarily relieved his steadily mounting financial difficulties.

After his important film *Isn't Life Wonderful* (1924), Griffith was increasingly out of tune with popular taste and with the growing film industry. He was obliged to work as an employee in the new Hollywood studio system. After 1927 the transition to "talkies" posed further problems, and although he managed one more independent production in 1930 (*Abraham Lincoln*), his career was finished by 1931. He received one small directing assignment, for which he was not paid, in 1936.

Griffith had led the new medium of film into unexplored areas of spectacle, realism, intimacy, and social content. His contributions to the technique of film art include the invention of the close-up, the long shot, the fade-out, night shots, high and low photographic angles, cross-cutting, backlighting, the moving camera, and many other devices that are now taken for granted. Despite his genius, he was, except for 39 weeks on radio, unemployed and unemployable for the last 17 years of his life. A second marriage ended in divorce in 1947, and a year later, at age 73, he died, alone and almost forgotten, in a shabby side-street Hollywood hotel.

Further Reading

The literature on Griffith and his achievements is extensive. Useful introductory works are Iris Barry, *D. W. Griffith, American Film Master* (1940); a popular biography by Homer Croy, *Star Maker: The Story of D. W. Griffith* (1959); and Lillian Gish, *Lillian Gish: The Movies, Mr. Griffith and Me* (1969).

Additional Sources

Schickel, Richard, *D.W. Griffith: an American life,* New York: Limelight Editions, 1996.
Williams, Martin T., *Griffith, first artist of the movies,* New York: Oxford University Press, 1980. □

Sir Samuel Walker Griffith

Sir Samuel Walker Griffith (1845-1920), premier of queensland and chief justice of Australia, was one of the ablest advocates of the federation of the Australian colonies and one of the greatest jurists produced by Australia in the 19th century.

S amuel Griffith was born at Merthyr Tydfil, South Wales, on June 21, 1845, the son of Edward Griffith and his wife, Mary Walker Griffith. Edward Griffith was a Congregational minister who migrated with his family to Queensland in 1854. The family finally settled in Brisbane in 1860.

Samuel Griffith was educated at the University of Sydney, where he received a baccalaureate in 1863 with first-class honors in classics, mathematics, and natural science. In 1865 he was awarded the T. S. Mort traveling fellowship and visited Europe, where he became fascinated with Italy and developed the interest and skill in the Italian language which flowered in his widely acclaimed translations of *The Inferno of Dante Alighieri* (1908) and *The Divina Commedia of Dante Alighieri* (1912).

Griffith was admitted to the Queensland bar in 1867 and soon proved successful. Attracted to politics, he won the seat of East Moreton in 1871. Three years later he became attorney general under Arthur Macalister and embarked on an active legislation program, including an important bill in 1875 to establish free, compulsory, and secular education. In 1876-1878 he was attorney general and secretary for public instruction.

An ardent opponent of the use of Kanaka labor, Griffith was premier of Queensland from 1883 to 1888. He was premier again in 1890-1893. Griffith represented Queensland at the Colonial Conference in London in 1887 and was vitally interested in the annexation of part of New Guinea by Britain. At the Intercolonial Conference of 1883 in Sydney he successfully moved for the establishment of the Federal Australasian Council and presided over its discussions in 1888, 1891, and 1893. He took an active interest in the federation movement and welcomed Henry Parkes's decisive moves in 1888-1890. He was the chief draftsman of the constitution adopted at the 1891 convention in Sydney, and it was the basis of the final Australian Commonwealth constitution.

In 1893 Griffith became chief justice of Queensland and proved a valuable reformer of the criminal law. In 1903 he became first chief justice of the High Court of Australia. In the pioneering stages of the High Court his great political and legal experience was invaluable. He emphasized the role of the court in interpreting the constitution. His natural stress on states' rights was not continued after his retirement in 1919, but he had set a high standard of meticulous analysis, objectivity, and great dignity.

Knighted in 1886, Griffith died at Brisbane on June 9, 1920. In 1870 he had married Julia Janet Thomson, who survived him with one son and four daughters.

Further Reading

There is no up-to-date biography of Griffith. Austin Douglas Graham, *The Life of the Right Hon. Sir Samuel Walker Griffith* (1939), is useful. There are references to him in various legal reminiscences, including Philip A. Jacobs, *Judges of Yesterday* (1924), and Albert B. Piddington, *Worshipful Masters* (1929). Much of his federation work is covered in John Quick and Robert R. Garran, *The Annotated Constitution of the Australian Commonwealth* (1901), and his colonial political work in Charles A. Bernays, *Queensland Politics during Sixty Years* (1919).

Additional Sources

Joyce, R. B., *Samuel Walker Griffith,* St. Lucia, Queenlands; New York: University of Queensland Press, 1984. □

Franz Grillparzer

Franz Grillparzer (1791-1872) is generally considered to be Austria's greatest playwright. His plays are well-written dramas of sentiment and psychological conflict, which often express a resigned attitude toward the problems of life.

At the beginning of the 19th century Austrian literature was not very far advanced in comparison with the literature of northern and western Germany. This may be attributed in part to the strictness of state censorship and a reluctance to support or encourage talented writers. Whatever the reasons, Austrian literature had remained largely unaffected by such developments as the Enlightenment or philosophical romanticism. The Austrian stage tended toward popular farces or old-fashioned bombastic tragedies. Although Franz Grillparzer was not without some talented predecessors in the Austrian drama, he was the first Austrian playwright fully to assimilate contemporaneous developments in German literature and to write plays equal to those being written in Germany itself.

Grillparzer was born in Vienna on Jan. 15, 1791. His father was an unsuccessful lawyer whose fortunes were ruined by Napoleon's invasion, and his mother came from the Viennese upper bourgeoisie. Franz studied law at the University of Vienna from 1807 to 1811. He became a government official in 1813 and eventually became imperial librarian. He was to remain in the state employment throughout his literary career, a fact which complicated his relationship to the government censors.

Grillparzer is said to have been generally unimpressive in personality and appearance. His quiet manner, however, served to conceal a number of inner conflicts, some of which were thought to originate in a disinclination to assert his will. His customary response to serious problems in life was generally an attitude of submission or resignation, rather than any decision to challenge the situation.

Career as a Dramatist

The theme of moral helplessness and the necessity for submission to fate can be noted in Grillparzer's first successful drama, *Die Ahnfrau* (1817; *The Ancestress*). He had earlier written a derivative tragedy, *Blanka von Kastilien,* which had never been staged, but the first performance of his *Ahnfrau* produced an immediate success. The "Ancestress" is a castle ghost who represents a curse on the

Borotin family. Jaromir (who, unknown even to himself, is the son of old Count Borotin) returns to the family castle as an outlaw, kills his father, commits incest with his sister, and brings about her death and his own. In the end the curse is thus fulfilled, but it is also terminated with the extinction of the family, and the spirit of the Ancestress is permitted to rest at last. The dominant theme of the play is the helplessness of individuals before the evil forces of destiny. Although it was strongly influenced by the German *Schicksalstragödie* (fate-tragedy) of Zacharias Werner and his followers, the general effect of Grillparzer's play is one of freshness and originality.

Following his initial success, Grillparzer wrote Sappho (1818), which concerns the Greek poetess's renunciation of human love, and the ambitious trilogy, *Das goldne Vliess* (1820; *The Golden Fleece*). This trilogy retells the Greek story of Jason, who voyages to Colchis and returns with both the magical golden fleece and the barbarian queen, Medea. Medea proves socially unacceptable in Greece, however, and Jason is finally estranged from her. But Medea avenges herself by burning down the palace where she is staying and killing her children to spite their father. In the concluding scene she lectures Jason on the futility of human life. Like many of Grillparzer's works, this trilogy reflects the author's attitude of helplessness toward fate.

Grillparzer's success led to his appointment as court dramatist. His next play, however, which dealt with sensitive matters of Austrian history, created difficulties with the censors. *König Ottokars Glück und Ende* (*King Ottokar's Fortune and End*) was finally performed in 1825. Ottokar, the medieval king of Bohemia, had dreams of great conquests but was finally undone by destiny and Rudolf von Hapsburg, founder of the Austrian imperial dynasty. Ottokar is shown as a Napoleonic character whose pride is the ultimate cause of his fall.

In 1826 Grillparzer traveled to Germany, where he met the poet J. W. von Goethe in Weimar. On returning to Vienna he continued to write plays, of which the most important are *Des Meeres und der Liebe Wellen* (1831; *The Waves of Love and the Sea*), a retelling of the classical love story of Hero and Leander, and *Der Traum ein Leben* (1834, *The Dream as a Life*), inspired by the Spanish dramatist Pedro Calderón. An ambitious young man has a dream in which hollow success is followed by disaster, and this persuades him to stay at home. In the conclusion he declares: "There is only one happiness in this life, calm inner peace and a heart free of guilt. Greatness is dangerous, and fame is an empty play."

Later Years

Grillparzer's last play to be performed was the comedy *Weh dem, der lügt* (1838; *Woe to Him Who Lies*). Although now recognized as a good play, it was then a complete failure. Embittered, the author withdrew from the scene as an active playwright. In his remaining years he wrote only three plays, which were not published until after his death. One of these, *Libussa,* was a mythical drama about the founding of Prague. Other literary works of his later life are two short stories and essays in dramatic theory and criticism, especially on the Spanish theater. Throughout his life Grillparzer also composed several volumes of lyric poetry.

The final years of Grillparzer's life remained outwardly uneventful. Although long engaged, he never married. He traveled to Greece in 1843 and revisited Germany in 1847. He remained a librarian until 1856, when he was retired on a pension. Toward the end of his life he gained some measure of recognition as a major dramatist. He died in Vienna on Jan. 21, 1872.

Further Reading

The best general study of Grillparzer is Douglas Yates, *Franz Grillparzer: A Critical Biography* (1946). Edward John Williamson, *Grillparzer's Attitude towards Romanticism* (1910), places him in the context of intellectual history, while Gustav Pollak, *Franz Grillparzer and the Austrian Drama* (1907), views him against the background of his national literary traditions. A more specialized study, concentrating on *Libussa,* is Gisela Stein, *The Inspiration Motif in the Works of Franz Grillparzer* (1955). An interesting experiment in comparative literature is Norbert Fuerst, *The Victorian Age of German Literature: Eight Essays* (1966), which compares Grillparzer's period with the English literature of his time.

Additional Sources

Fink, Humbert, *Franz Grillparzer,* Innsbruck: Pinguin, 1990. □